ORACLE®   *Oracle Press*™

Oracle Certified Professional Financial Applications Consultant Exam Guide

Christopher Allen
& Vivian Chow

Osborne **McGraw-Hill**

Berkeley New York St. Louis San Francisco
Auckland Bogotá Hamburg London Madrid
Mexico City Milan Montreal New Delhi Panama City
Paris São Paulo Singapore Sydney Tokyo Toronto

Osborne/**McGraw-Hill**
2600 Tenth Street
Berkeley, California 94710
U.S.A.

For information on translations or book distributors outside the U.S.A., or to arrange bulk purchase discounts for sales promotions, premiums, or fund-raisers, please contact Osborne/**McGraw-Hill** at the above address.

Oracle Certified Professional Financial Applications Consultant Exam Guide

1234567890 DOC DOC 019876543210

Book P/N 0-07-212356-7   and   CD P/N 0-07-212357-5
parts of
ISBN 0-07-212358-3

Publisher
  Brandon A. Nordin

Associate Publisher & Editor-In-Chief
  Scott Rogers

Acqusition Editor
  Jeremy Judson

Project Editor
  Jody McKenzie

Acquisitions Editor
  Monika Faltiss

Technical Editors
  Shankaran Iyer
  Kevin Fox
  Lynne Rougeau
  Graham Seibert

Copy Editor
  Dennis Weaver

Proofreader
  Doug Robert

Indexer
  Jack Lewis

Computer Designers
  Gary Corrigan
  Lucia Ericksen
  Jim Kussow
  Roberta Steele

Illustrators
  Michael Mueller
  Beth Young

Series Design
  Jani Beckwith

Cover Design
  Lisa Schultz

This book was composed with Corel VENTURA™ Publisher.

For Grace
—Christopher Allen

To my family for their continued support
—Vivian Chow

About the Authors

Christopher Allen has been a professional in the computer industry since 1981. He is an Oracle Certified Professional (OCP) DBA and an OCP Application Developer, as well as the author of numerous computer books, including *OCP Application Developer Exam Guide* (Oracle Press, 1999). His clients have included IBM, Microsoft, MCI, Xerox, Arco, California Institute of Technology, U.S. Army, and the Departments of Labor, Transportation, Justice, Customs, and Treasury.

Vivian Chow is one of the founders of Métier, an Oracle Partner company that provides consulting services in Southern California and Arizona. She has more than nine years of experience in implementing Oracle Applications and has managed several large-scale projects. Her writing includes the Métier Oracle Applications Quick Reference Guide. Ms. Chow was recently awarded the Ernst & Young Technological Entrepreneur of the Year award for the Greater Los Angeles area. She can be contacted at vivian.chow@metier.com.

ORACLE®
Certified Professional

About the Oracle Certification Exams

Oracle Corporation is very committed to helping professionals learn how to use the inherently complicated products they sell. Oracle's Education division produces a wide variety of quality courses, along with a growing battery of exams designed to recognize those who have both "book learning" about Oracle products and plenty of hands-on experience with those products. While these exams do not guarantee that someone is an expert, they do guarantee that someone is not an amateur.

The response to the Oracle Certified Professional (OCP) programs has been impressive. In a study performed by International Data Corporation, companies that advocated certification had 49 percent less downtime than companies that did not. For most of the companies surveyed, the increased effectiveness of OCP-certified professionals resulted in savings that paid for the certification in less than nine months! Not surprisingly, when OCP professionals were surveyed, 97 percent said they benefited from becoming certified. These benefits include increased knowledge, of course, but there can be other, less tangible benefits: getting in the door for a more fulfilling job, being given more complicated (and more visible) projects at the job you are at, and gaining concrete leverage for increased pay. OCP-certified professionals also receive the right to use the OCP logo.

Requirements for Certification

You must answer approximately 70 percent of the questions correctly in order to pass an exam. We say "approximately" because Oracle Education changes the exams on a regular basis, and reserves the right to change the passing scores without notice. We recommend that you schedule your exam when you are consistently scoring at least 85 percent on the practice exams in this book.

If you take an exam and do not pass, you have to wait 30 days before you can take it again. You may repeat an exam three times in a 12-month period.

Recertification

As Oracle products are upgraded, so too must be the exams. When a new version of an exam track is released, candidates are given notice that their certification will remain valid for six more months. During that time, you can become certified in the new version of the product by taking a New Features exam that covers the features added in the new release of the software.

Exam Format

The OCP exams are administered by Sylvan Prometric, an independent professional testing company with over 800 locations worldwide. Because the exams are computer based, they can be scheduled at your convenience—you don't have to go at a specific predetermined time. You only need to call Sylvan, identify what exam you want to take, select the location you want, and identify when you want to go. Generally, you will take the exam in a room with a few computers in it; you will be assigned a computer, and you will take your exam individually. There may or may not be anyone else in the room at the same time, and if there is, the chances are good they will be taking some other exam. The exams consist of 60 to 90 questions; you have 90 minutes to answer them. The questions are either multiple choice, or "scenario based," in which you are presented with a problem, shown an image of an Oracle product, and asked to click on the areas of the product that you would use to solve the problem. While taking the exam, you can mark questions to come back to later for further review. Once you have finished, your exam will be graded on the spot.

Special 10 Percent Exam Discount Offer

Because you have purchased this Oracle Press Exam Guide, you can receive a special 10 percent discount when you register for the OCP exam. To do so, you must request the discount and mention this book. This offer is valid through April 15, 2001.

To register for an Oracle test, call Sylvan Prometric at (800) 891-EXAM (3926), extension FAC10. Outside of the United States, call 1 (612) 820-5000.

You can contact a local Oracle Education representative for exam preparation courses and materials by calling (800) 529-0165. You can also download this certification track's *Candidate Guide* at http://education.oracle.com/certification to learn more about exam objectives and preparation methods.

Contents

UNIT I
Preparing for OCP Exam 1: Financial Management

UNIT II
Preparing for OCP Exam 2: Applied Technology

UNIT III
Preparing for OCP Exam 3: Procurement

UNIT IV
Preparing for OCP Exam 4: Order Fulfillment

Preface

There are two tracks you can take to become an Oracle Certified Applications Consultant. For both tracks, the first two exams are the same. The content of your third exam depends on which track you select. An overview of the tracks is shown in Figure i-1.

This book is comprised of four units, each covering one of the exams that make up the Oracle Certified Applications Consultant tracks.

The exams are:

- Financial Management

- Applied Technology

- For the Procurement track: Procurement

- For the Order Fulfillment track: Order Fulfillment

Within each unit, you will find a number of chapters that teach the information you need to know to achieve a successful score on the related exam.

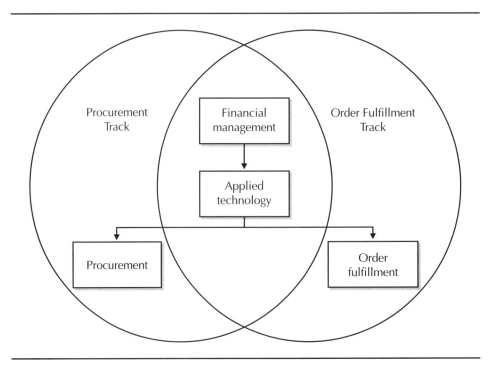

FIGURE i-1. *Oracle Certified Applications Consultant: Overview of tracks and exams*

How Chapters Are Organized

The chapters in this book observe the following format.

Discussion Sections

Each subject covered in an exam will be addressed with a discussion section in this book. Each discussion section will be immediately followed by a brief set of questions that review the material just presented. The answers to these questions are not printed elsewhere in the book; the idea is that if you read the questions and don't know the answers, you have not absorbed the information just presented, and you should go back and reread it before you continue forward.

Chapter Summaries

On the included CD-ROM you will find a summary of the chapter's main points. In addition to helping drive home the important points after you have read the discussion sections, this compressed review is a powerful, efficient review tool to use before you take the exam. We recommend that you reread the chapter summaries once a day for several days just before taking the exam.

Two-Minute Drills

Following the chapter summary, the same information is presented in an even briefer format: as a series of bullet points called Two-Minute Drills. These are great to read over just before you go in to take your exam.

Chapter Questions and Answers

The final part of each chapter is a series of multiple-choice questions, on the CD-ROM, that emulate the questions you will encounter in the actual exam. After the questions, you will find the answers, along with an explanation of why the correct answer is correct … and why the others are not. Answer these questions after reading the chapter. If you get 85 percent or more correct, proceed to the next chapter. If you don't, go back and read the chapter sections related to the questions you missed, then wait a couple of days and answer the sample questions again.

Conventions Used in This Book

Bold text indicates text that you will type as shown. *Italics* are used to identify new terms the first time they are presented, as well as to emphasize key facts. Items that deserve special notice are set apart as Notes or Tips. They look like this:

NOTE
Remember to do all the right things, and to not do the things that aren't.

TIP
Never tie your shoelaces together before a hike.

How to Get the Most Out of This Book

There are three things you must do to get the most out of this book:

1. Do.

2. The.

3. Exercises.

The exercises will take the "book learning"—which is quickly forgotten—and put it into your hands, where it can be retained for a long, long time. Through the course of this book, you will go through the steps to set up a new company. If you want to *really* maximize your learning and retention, do the exercises—and then do them *again* with a company of your own. Your company can be real or fanciful—it doesn't matter. The magical retention phenomenon called "transferring the knowledge" will happen either way.

The only exception to doing the exercises is if you are a seasoned Oracle Financials professional who has set up numerous companies already. If this is the case, you can "test out" of chapters by going directly to the questions at the end, answering them, and checking your score. If you get 85 percent or more of the answers right, and you are pressed for time, it's worthwhile to consider skipping that chapter and proceeding to the next one … which you might test out of as well.

Acknowledgments

Once again I find myself privileged to be part of the distinguished Oracle Press collection. A tip of the hat to Brandon Nordin and Scott Rogers for guiding the Oracle Press line to become the quality series that it is. I'm honored to be in such company.

Putting together a book covering as much material as this one requires the coordinated efforts of many talented people. Monika Faltiss got things where they needed to be in an organized and timely manner. Deborah Brown, GinaMaria Jerome, Lynda Lotman, Bridget McCrea, and Gael O'Keefe provided invaluable editorial assistance. Amber Allen-Sauer lent her considerable knowledge of Oracle Financials and made major contributions to the breadth and depth of this book. Kevin Fox, Shankaran Iyer, Lynne Rougeau, and Graham Seibert ensured that technical accuracy was held to the highest standards. When it was time for the book's contents to go to layout, Jody McKenzie demonstrated a remarkable ability to juggle numerous processes simultaneously and still pay admirable attention to detail. Dennis Weaver once again divinely annoyed me with detailed questions that really needed to be answered. Managing this book from beginning to end was Jeremy Judson. Besides being absolutely dedicated to his job and easy to work with, he never *ever* lets me pick up the tab. It's a character flaw, but his other qualities make up for it.

Finally, I want to thank my wife Grace, whose innate goodness drives me to do things like this.

Christopher Allen

It has been a fulfilling experience for me to write this book, it is something I have always wanted to accomplish. But it would not have happened without the help and support from the following people. First of all, I would like to thank Dave, Greg, Holly, Ken, Mehrina, Rick, Ron, and Teresa for all their great work, ideas, and contributions to this book. In addition, I would like to thank my business partners at Métier—Arabella, Ron, and Yayoi for holding down the fort while I buried myself in writing this book. I would also like to thank my parents, Anthony and Ida Chow, as well as my other family and friends, Patricia, James, Gladys, Ron, Sheri, and Peter, for all their patience, care and support during this seemingly endless project. Finally, I would like to thank Teresa for being there to keep me company and to keep me motivated throughout the writing of the entire book.

Vivian Chow

Introduction

The market for professionals who understand how to install, modify, and manage Oracle Financials is exploding. As competitive products sputter and fall, Oracle Financials keeps getting better and better, and companies are switching to it at a breakneck pace. For those of us who are tired of learning a new programming language every 18 months or so, the beauty of learning Oracle Financials is that once it is installed at a company, it would take a Herculean effort for a competitive product to replace it. As a result, this is a skill set that has "legs"—it can provide years of income for those who are good at it. Companies are clamoring for Oracle Financials consultants. As of this writing, the job-oriented Internet newsgroups contained 3,700 messages from people looking to hire Oracle Financials experts. This is approximately the same number of job postings found for Oracle database administrators (DBAs), which are considered one of the hottest commodities in the computer field. So, the market for Financials experts is extremely strong.

But how does a company know who is good? Well, there's always word of mouth … if you trust the mouth you're listening to. Getting in the door can be a challenge. It helps to have something that makes you stand out. Putting the Oracle Certified Professional logo in your resume can certainly help. And once you are on the job, you have an advantage too. On-the-job training is great, but it tends to be spotty—you learn the things that particular job calls for, filtered by whatever the people around you happen to already know. In contrast, studying for the OCP exams takes you into every area of Oracle Financials Procurement and Order Fulfillment.

It is extremely likely that you will learn things you can apply in your work—things you didn't even know were available. That helps make you an expert, and experts are noticed and rewarded in the workplace.

How Should You Prepare for the OCP Exams?

With dedication. You will get the most out of this process if you can set aside a certain amount of time each day (or, perhaps, each *work* day … let's be realistic) for study and practice. This enables you to build on recently acquired knowledge while it is still fresh. At the end of each chapter, take the sample exam. If you answer 85 percent or more of the questions correctly, proceed to the next chapter. If not, go back and reread the chapter, taking special care to answer the small collection of exercises that follow each subject point. If you follow this approach, you should do quite well on the sample exam at the end of the chapter. Continue this process, as regularly as possible, until you have completed one of the book's four units.

Then, take the Oracle Assessment Test for the Financial Applications Consultant, which is available online at http://education.oracle.com/certification. You can also take the practice tests on the CD provided with this book. Taking these tests will benefit you in two ways. First, they will identify the areas where your knowledge of the required material is strong or weak, which will help you focus your study and practice. Second, they will give you a sense of how the actual exams work, which can help you feel more comfortable with the process.

After you have successfully gone through the Assessment Test for the unit you covered, schedule your OCP exam with Sylvan. Then read through the Chapter Summaries and the Two-Minute Drills (included on the CD-ROM with this book) until the day you take the exam. On that day, wear comfortable clothing (nobody cares how you look there) and plan to arrive early so that unforeseen delays don't ruffle your feathers. When it is time to take the exam, you will be seated in front of a PC at the testing center you've selected. The Sylvan personnel will not let you take any books or note paper in with you—they even ask that you turn off your pager so an accomplice can't page you with answers! (Remember, they're just doing their job.) They do provide some note paper of their own, which you have to turn in after the exam (to be thrown away, not graded).

The computer-based exam starts by asking you to identify yourself. Then it offers to give you an introduction to how the testing software works. It's a good idea to go through this introduction, and it will not count against your time. When you do decide to start the actual test, you will be presented with the first question and the timer will start. Each screen contains a question, several potential answers (or a screen shot on which you will click), buttons to go to the next or prior question, and an option to mark that question for later review. If you read a question and are reasonably sure of the correct answer, select the answer and move on to the next question. If you are not sure, ponder the question for a bit of time—you have an average of a minute and a half per question—and if you don't know the answer after several moments, mark it to be reviewed later and move on. After you have answered all the questions you know, you can return to the questions that stumped you earlier and spend more time thinking about the answer to each. If you really don't know the answer to a question, then guess. A question left blank is considered incorrect, so you have nothing to lose by guessing an answer to a question you don't know.

After you are done with the exam, you will be shown an onscreen analysis of how you did. This is where you hoot and holler, congratulate yourself, and tell the Sylvan administrator that he or she is your best friend. Or maybe it's where you introspectively ponder how you can study more effectively, and think about scheduling an improved performance in 30 days. The onscreen analysis will include both an overall score and a subject-by-subject summary. This screen will also be printed for you to take home with you.

Remember, you have taken two important steps already. First, you have decided what you want: OCP certification. Knowing what you want allows you to focus your attention and schedule your time accordingly. Second, you have acquired a big honkin' study guide to help you prepare. These steps reflect a level of commitment that will serve you well as you study. Keep that level of commitment high and do the work ... and you will get the rewards.

Go for it!

UNIT
I

Preparing for OCP
Exam 1: Financial
Management

CHAPTER
1

Introduction

his unit focuses on the first Oracle Certified Professional (OCP) Applications Consultant exam, which is titled Financial Management. In this first chapter, you will cover the following areas of the Financials package:

- Essential setup and implementation steps

- Oracle General Ledger and Assets functionality

- Overview of information flow between Oracle integrated applications

The chapter begins with an overview of the steps necessary to set up and implement the Oracle financial management applications, including special considerations you must take into account along the way. The second section of this chapter provides an introduction to the Oracle Financials Applications, describing the purpose and functionality of each application. The chapter wraps up with a section discussing how the Financials Applications integrate with other Oracle Applications modules, and how information is shared between these applications.

Essential Setup and Implementation Steps

To set up and implement Oracle financial management applications, you must follow a proven methodology. Methodology serves as a road map for the implementation process. It consists of defined steps, and within each step there is a concrete list of tasks and deliverables. The following are essential steps in setting up and implementing Financial Management Applications:

    1. Planning   During the planning step, you will complete the following tasks:

- Determine project goals, milestones, and critical success factors

- Define the implementation team staffing, roles, and responsibilities

- Develop the implementation timeline

- Design the technical architecture

- Plan initial training

    2. System configuration   During the system configuration step, you will complete these tasks:

- Install hardware and software

- Establish the network infrastructure to allow connectivity

3. **Requirements gathering**   During the requirements gathering step, as the name indicates, you gather requirements. This is not an easy process, but it is an essential one. The more detailed your requirements are, the more successful your implementation will be.

   When you gather requirements, your deliverables will include:

   - Narrative documents, which provide text descriptions of each requirement

   - Process flow diagrams, which graphically depict how work flows from one stage to the next

   Be sure to include your reporting requirements in this documentation. This is a step that is often forgotten, to the regret of the project manager!

4. **Fit analysis**   During fit analysis, you map your requirements to the functional components of the Oracle Applications. If you discover that certain requirements do not fit the default functionality inherent in Oracle Applications, you have three choices:

   - Customize the Oracle Applications

   - Modify the requirements

   - Create workarounds

5. **Setup**   During the setup step, you perform two types of setup: business and technical. For the business setup step, you configure the Oracle Applications according to the requirements. For the technical setup step, you must build conversion programs, interfaces, and customizations. This will be covered in greater detail in later chapters.

6. **Testing**   During the testing step, you test your installation of the Oracle Applications. You will create test scripts to automate the process and then compare the results produced with the results you expected. Inevitably, issues will come to light at this stage, so be sure to allow time in your schedule at this stage to resolve those issues.

7. **Transition**   During the transition step, you will complete the following tasks:

   - Prepare end-user procedures and training

   - Set up help desk infrastructure

- Perform data conversion for production cutover
- Evaluate system readiness

In your own methodology, you might assign different names to the above steps, but all of the steps must be included. You might also add other steps, depending on the requirements of your workplace.

Review Question

1. What are the seven main steps that are necessary in any Oracle Financial Management Applications implementation?

Oracle General Ledger and Assets Functionality

The first step to using Oracle's General Ledger and Assets packages successfully is understanding what they can do for you. This section provides an overview of the functionality provided by each package.

Oracle General Ledger

Oracle General Ledger is the central repository of all accounting information in the Oracle Applications. It provides the following functionality:

- General accounting
- Budgeting
- Multiple currencies
- Intercompany accounting
- Cost accounting
- Consolidation
- Financial reporting

General Accounting

In general accounting, you set up charts of accounts and fiscal calendars that fit your company's needs. You can have multiple chart-of-accounts structures, as well as multiple fiscal calendars. You can also set up suspense accounts, statistical accounts, and summary accounts. You can enter and post journal entries for budget, encumbrance, or actual transactions, and the entries can be single or recurring. Oracle General Ledger supports both cash-basis and accrual-basis double-entry accounting.

The setups tied to this functionality include Chart of Accounts, Set of Books, Period Type, Accounting Periods, Automatic Posting, Journal Sources, Journal Categories, Suspense Accounts, Statistical Units of Measure, and Summary Accounts.

Budgeting

In Oracle Financials Applications, you can implement budgetary control in either *mandatory* mode or *advisory* mode.

In mandatory mode, you can only create purchase orders and invoices if sufficient budget is currently available. *Available budget* is a value derived by taking a budget number and reducing it by known encumbrances and actual expenditures. An encumbrance is a dollar figure resulting from an approved purchase order, and an actual expenditure comes from a payable invoice.

In advisory mode, you will be warned if budget is not available, but you can override the warning and still create purchase orders or invoices.

Budget amounts can be entered manually, uploaded automatically, or calculated using standard rules or budget formulas.

The setups tied to this functionality include Budgetary Control Group and Encumbrance Types.

Multiple Currencies

Oracle General Ledger performs automatic currency conversion, storing daily, period-end, historical, and weighted-average exchange rates. Realized and unrealized gains and losses are also automatically calculated. The Oracle General Ledger module can generate financial reports for balances for any currencies. However, if you want to report and maintain accounting transactions in multiple currencies—as opposed to just maintaining balances in multiple currencies—you will need to set up multiple reporting Sets of Books. You can set up as many reporting Sets of Books as you want, in addition to your one primary Set of Books.

As you enter transactions, the transactions are translated into the functional currency of your primary Set of Books, and also translated into the functional currencies of your reporting Sets of Books. Using multiple reporting Sets of Books, Oracle General Ledger can be used for companies that are part of the European Monetary Union (EMU) and that would like to create reports with transaction-level detail in both the Euro and their original functional currency.

The setups tied to this functionality include Currencies, Exchange Rate Types, Exchanges Rate, and Multiple Reporting Currencies.

Intercompany Accounting

You can use Oracle General Ledger to manage intercompany journals. Your parent company and your subsidiaries can review and approve intercompany transactions manually originated in Oracle General Ledger. You can also generate recurring intercompany journals in Oracle General Ledger, as well as specify intercompany clearing accounts. When you set up different journal sources and journal categories, you can specify different intercompany accounts for each combination of journal source and journal category.

The setups tied to this functionality include Intercompany Accounts and Centralized Transaction Approval (CENTRA).

Cost Accounting

Cost accounting in Oracle General Ledger can be manual or automatic. If you elect to use automatic cost accounting, you can set it up to be based on either formulas or statistics such as headcount or square footage.

You can also perform iterations of automatic allocations based on a particular grouping of accounts. For example, let's say you want to distribute the corporate rent account into every cost center's rent account based on the square footage occupied by each cost center. You can specify a formula such as this:

corporate rent account balance

*

(cost center square footages / total corporate square footage)

=

rent balance to be allocated to each cost center rent account

Oracle General Ledger also handles step-down allocation by running the automatic allocation process multiple times. Using the cost center rent example, step-down allocation means that the cost center rent *center balance* is further allocated to *another, lower level*. For example, each cost center's rent balance can be further allocated among projects belonging to that cost center.

The setups tied to this functionality include Mass Allocations, Mass Budgeting, and Recurring Journals.

Consolidation

Oracle General Ledger allows you to consolidate between different charts of accounts. You can define, map, transfer, and combine consolidation data. You can also create eliminating entries automatically. If you wish, a report-only consolidation can be performed so that the underlying data remains unchanged until you verify the proposed results. The consolidation process creates consolidation journals, providing either summaries or details, at your discretion.

The setup tied to this functionality is the Global Consolidation System (GCS).

Financial Reporting

You can produce all kinds of financial reports in every currency defined in Oracle General Ledger. Each report is defined using rows and columns; typically, each row reflects a set of accounts to be shown in the financial reports, and each column defines an amount type. An amount type determines what balances to show in the financial reports.

If you wish, you can reverse the typical role of rows and columns to suit your reporting needs. You can also define what order the rows in the report should be displayed in, along with other display attributes that will be discussed in detail later. If you need multidimensional reporting with drill-down capability, you can get it by integrating Oracle General Ledger with Oracle Financial Analyzer (a separate module).

The setups tied to this functionality include Define Financial Statement Generator (FSG) components, Integrating with Financial Analyzer, and General Ledger Desktop Integrator (GLDI) Report Wizard.

Oracle Assets

Oracle Assets is the asset management subledger. It provides the following functionality:

- Assets tracking

- Assets transactions

- Depreciation

- Tax accounting

- Construction-in-Process

- Capital budgets

Assets Tracking

Oracle Assets tracks attributes such as:

- Asset number, serial number, and tag number

- Asset description, purchase order, invoice, and components

- The date the asset was placed in service, the location to which the asset is assigned, and to which employee

- Other financial and lease information

The setups tied to this functionality include Asset Category flexfield, Location flexfield, and Asset Key flexfield.

Assets Transactions

Oracle Assets tracks all transactions that affect an asset during its lifetime. These transactions include additions, cost adjustments, transfers, reclassifications, retirements, reinstatements, and revaluations. Transactions that led to adjustments— such as cost adjustments and reclassifications—can be defined to either expense the adjustment amounts in the current period or amortize the adjustment amounts over the remaining life.

Depreciation

Oracle Assets accommodates three different categories of depreciation:

- **Flat-rate depreciation** Depreciates assets using a fixed rate.

- **Life-based depreciation** Depreciates assets over a fixed time using specified rates. Oracle Assets supports two types of life-based depreciation:

Calculated or *straight-line* depreciation is based on an asset's useful life. The depreciation rate per period is calculated by prorating the asset's value evenly over all of the periods in the asset's useful life.

Table depreciation is based on rate tables. Oracle Assets includes seeded rate tables for numerous table-based depreciation types, including declining balance, bonus depreciation, diminishing value, sum of year's digits, Accelerated Cost Recovery System (ACRS), and Modified Accelerated Cost Recovery System (MACRS).

- **Units of production method** Depreciates the asset based on units used during the depreciation period. Time is not taken into consideration, and only recoverable cost can be used as the basis. In contrast, the flat-rate and life-based methods can be based on either recoverable cost or recoverable net book value of the assets (except for calculated/straight-line depreciation, which can only use recoverable cost as the depreciable basis).

Oracle Assets can automatically perform year-end processing. It also enables you to perform what-if analyses and project all asset depreciation entries.

Tax Accounting

Assets can only be tracked in one corporate book. However, for tax accounting purposes, assets can be copied into multiple tax books. This enables users to maintain depreciation data separately on the corporate book vs. tax books. Assets on different books can have different lives, recoverable costs, depreciation methods, and depreciation ceilings. You can maintain separate books for state, federal, and alternative minimum tax (AMT) purposes. Oracle Assets also supports special tax accounting options such as adjusted current earnings (ACE) and investment tax credit (ITC).

The setups tied to this functionality include Book Controls and Mass Copy.

Construction-in-Process

Oracle Assets supports construction-in-process (CIP) assets, which do not start depreciating until the assets are capitalized. The Assets module allows you to capture raw materials and labor and tie them to CIP assets. Together, these form the cost basis of CIP assets when those assets start to depreciate. If you use Oracle Projects to track raw materials and labor costs, you can transfer that information into Oracle Assets.

Capital Budgets

Capital budgets can be entered manually or uploaded automatically. Oracle Assets handles an unlimited number of capital budgets. Within the module, you can compare any one of numerous different predefined capital budgets to actual spending.

Review Questions

1. What are the key functions provided by Oracle General Ledger?

2. What are the key functions provided by Oracle Assets?

3. What is the difference between flat-rate depreciation and units of production depreciation?

4. What is the difference between table depreciation and straight-line depreciation?

Overview of Information Flow Between Oracle Integrated Applications

Oracle Applications is an integrated enterprise management system, so processes flow between Financial modules and non-Financial modules. All accounting entries generated in Oracle Inventory, Work in Process, Payroll, and Projects interface to Oracle General Ledger. All inventory transactions affect Oracle Inventory on-hand balances. Oracle Master Scheduling/MRP recommends and generates work orders and purchase orders. Work orders flow into Oracle Work in Process. Purchase orders flow into Oracle Purchasing. Purchase orders can include raw materials acquisition or outside processing labor. Oracle Project Costing accumulates commitments for projects from Oracle Purchasing purchase orders and actual costs for projects from Oracle Payables invoices. If projects are billing, Oracle Project Billing generates invoices automatically based on data in Oracle Project Costing. Oracle Quality collects quality-related data from various user-defined collection points in all Oracle Applications. Figure 1-1 illustrates how some of these different modules work together.

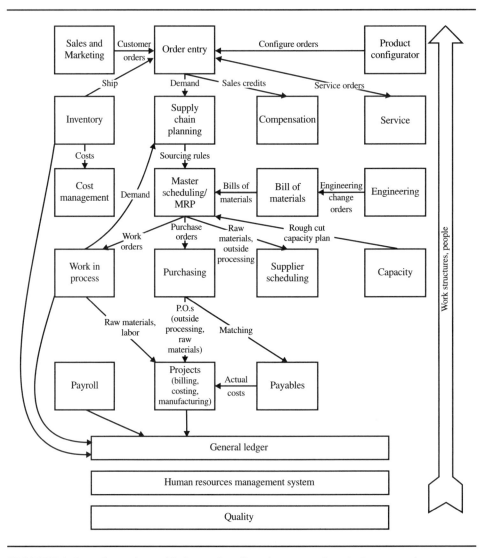

FIGURE 1-1. *Overview of information flow between Oracle integrated applications*

Review Questions

1. What modules send data to Oracle General Ledger?

2. What information does the Master Scheduling/MRP module send to other modules?

Introducing Financials Applications Implementation

In this section, you will cover the following points about Oracle Financials Applications:

■ High-level process flows of Oracle Applications

■ Integration among Oracle Applications

High-Level Process Flows of Oracle Applications

In Oracle Financials Applications, the General Ledger module is the destination for all accounting entries. Many of these entries are produced by the Oracle Assets system, which generates additions, capitalization, depreciation, retirements, reinstatements, revaluations, tax-accumulated depreciation adjustments, and CIP-related entries during every depreciation period.

In addition to the core Financials applications, there are two major tracks in Oracle Financials Applications: procurement and order fulfillment. Figure 1-2 provides a high-level diagram of how processes flow between these modules.

Procurement

In the procurement track, you create suppliers and then create purchase requisitions and purchase orders. You can create purchase orders manually, or you can use the Autocreate feature to automatically generate purchase orders from purchase requisitions. When the products you have ordered arrive, you enter the receiving information into Oracle Purchasing.

You can create invoices automatically upon receiving the products by using Oracle Payables' Pay-on-Receipt option, or you can enter the payables invoices manually. Checks or other forms of payment will then be generated when the payment is due, based on the payment terms defined in the Payables system. When a bank statement arrives, the checks can be cleared automatically or manually through Oracle Cash Management. Receipt accruals, invoice distributions (expense,

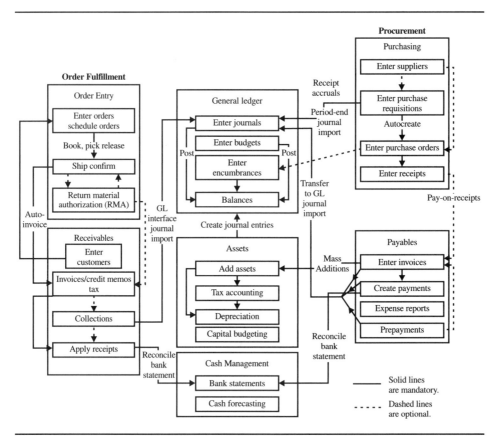

FIGURE 1-2. *High-level process flow diagram*

inventory, and work in process), payables liability, and payment accounting entries are posted to Oracle General Ledger through the Journal Import batch interfaces.

Order Fulfillment

When performing order fulfillment tasks, you create customers, followed by orders and, finally, invoices. When you create new orders, they are assigned a schedule date in either of two ways:

- Manually

- Based on Available to Promise (ATP), which checks the quantities on hand and adjusts them based on scheduled purchase orders and scheduled work orders.

Once orders are booked and are ready to be shipped, batches of pick slips are generated by the **Pick Release** function. Once the products have been picked and packed for shipments, you can employ the **Ship Confirm** function to generate the necessary documents and ship the products to customers. Next, Oracle Receivables automatically generates the appropriate invoices via its **Autoinvoice** function. When the receipts arrive at the remittance address, whether it is in-house or through lockboxes, they are manually or automatically applied to invoices or customer accounts. When a bank statement arrives, the receipts can be cleared automatically or manually through Oracle Cash Management. Finally, the receivables, receipts accounting entries, and invoice distributions (revenue, unbilled receivables, unearned revenue, tax, and freight) are posted to Oracle General Ledger through batch interfaces.

Review Questions

1. What accounting entries are posted to Oracle General Ledger from assets management?

2. What accounting entries are posted to Oracle General Ledger from procurement?

3. What accounting entries posted are to Oracle General Ledger from order fulfillment?

Integration Among Oracle Applications

As you are probably aware, Oracle Financials Applications depends on the Oracle database to store its data. That data is shared within the Applications modules by way of *share tables*. There are three types of tables in each Oracle Financials Applications module: master tables, setup tables, and transaction tables.

Master tables store static data. (Interestingly, in this case the "static" data is not completely static—it just changes more slowly than the transactional data.) The master tables usually store data that is shared within each module, as well as across all of the Oracle Financials Application modules. Examples of this type of data include information about accounts, suppliers, customers, items, and assets. Oracle stores this so-called static data in master tables, using unique values in each record (known as *primary-key* values) to identify each record uniquely within each master table. These primary-key values serve as *foreign keys* in the setup tables and transaction tables that reference records in master tables. This relationship between parent tables (the master tables) and child tables (the setup tables) is how information is shared among the modules.

To be more specific, every master table in Oracle Applications designates one or more of its columns as a primary key. Data in a table's primary-key column(s) must be different from record to record—that is how each individual record is identified when referred to by other tables. When other tables want to identify a record in another table, they do so by storing the primary-key value of that other table's record in a column of their own.

For instance, in Oracle General Ledger, the master table that stores all information about accounts is called GL_CODE_COMBINATIONS. Its primary-key column is named code_combination_id. When a record in Oracle Assets wants to relate an Assets record to a GL account, it does so by storing the GL account's primary-key value in the Assets record. Oracle Payables works the same way. In fact, all of the modules use this approach to refer to tables in other modules.

Figure 1-3 gives a graphic representation of how this works. (Note that the figure does not show all of the columns for the Assets and Payables tables but only those that relate to this discussion).

Setup tables store setup data that is seldom shared between applications, such as application parameters and lookup tables. They are shared within an Oracle

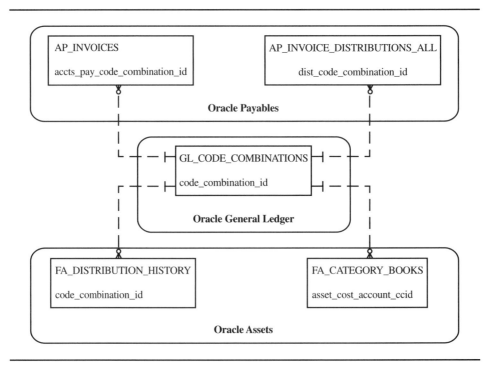

FIGURE 1-3. *How tables are linked in Oracle Applications*

Applications package, but are seldom shared across Oracle Applications packages. One exception to this guideline is *lookup tables*, which store your accounting department's standard codes, their meanings, and supertype information defining groups within the codes. For instance, a lookup table might contain the codes available to denote the posting status of asset additions. Lookup tables give you a chance to add codes to an accounting system, or to customize the meanings of existing codes so they more closely match your specific business.

Transaction tables are tables that store day-to-day transaction data, such as payable invoices, receivable invoices, and journal entries. Transaction tables, just like setup tables, are usually not shared across applications, since the content is application-specific. An exception to this rule is the transaction table that stores demand data. Since demand can come from several different applications—for example, Oracle Order Entry and Oracle Work in Process—the demand table in Oracle Inventory stores the transaction ID of *all* source transactions, together with each transaction's type.

Table 1-1 shows some information that is shared among Oracle Financials Applications modules. The top row of the table lists the application module that owns the data being shared, and the left column of the table lists the modules that utilize, or receive, the shared data.

Review Questions

1. What are the three types of tables in Oracle Applications? What are the differences between them?

2. What is the purpose of a master table's Code_combination_id column?

3. How are relationships enforced between master tables and setup tables?

High-Level Setup and Implementation Issues for the Enterprise Management Applications

Chapter 2 covers implementation considerations that commonly need to be taken into account when you set up a Chart of Accounts and a Set of Books. What follows is a high-level summary of these considerations, to introduce you to the concepts. If the concepts seem a bit deep at this point, don't worry … you will learn about them in more detail later.

When setting up a Set of Books, you must consider how many functional currencies you need; how many accounting calendars your company will use; and how many Charts of Accounts structures your business has. If you are dealing with multiple organizations, your setup will vary depending on whether all your

Recipients	Owner						
	GL	**FA**	**AP**	**PO**	**AR**	**OE**	**CM**
GL	N/A						
FA	Assets accounts	N/A	Invoices	Suppliers			
AP	Liability accounts Distribution accounts Invoice price variance accounts Cash accounts		N/A	Suppliers Purchase orders			
PO	Purchase price variance accounts Accrual accounts Budgets Encumbrances			N/A			
AR	Receivables accounts Revenue accounts Unbilled receivable accounts Unearned revenue accounts Tax accounts Freight accounts				N/A	Orders	
OE				Internal requisitions	Customers Sales reps	N/A	
CM	Reconciliation clearing accounts		Payments		Receipts		N/A

TABLE I-I.   *Owners and Recipients of Data Shared by Applications Modules*

organizations practice the same general accounting processes for handling suspense accounting, intercompany accounting, budget journals, manual journal entries approval, and taxation for journals; whether all your organizations allow the same time frame for entering journals into future periods; and whether you will use average balance processing as well as standard balance processing.

When setting up a Chart of Accounts, your considerations fall into the following categories: reporting, growth, budgeting, security, validation, datatypes, and ordering. *Reporting* concerns center around capturing and partitioning data in such a way that later reporting needs can be satisfied. *Growth* is a consideration because the system will run more efficiently if its tables are sized accurately from the start, rather than expanded after the system is operational. In the area of *budgeting*, you must decide the level at which you will be budgeting and encumbering, because while you can budget and encumber at a summary level of your Chart of Accounts, you cannot budget or encumber at a level *lower* than your Chart of Accounts. *Security* comes into play as you decide what job role will be allowed to execute which tasks, and what data each person will be allowed to see, change, add, and delete. *Validation* in a Chart of Accounts comes from the ability to cross-validate information in one data segment with information in other data segments; this powerful tool can help ensure that your system is populated with "clean" data that satisfies the criteria you specify. The *datatypes* these segments can contain are assigned at setup and cannot be changed later, so they deserve some thought: the lowest levels of the segments are always numeric, but higher-level segments can be defined as alphanumeric datatypes to store rollup values such as "CASH". The term *ordering* refers in this case to the order of data in the tables, and this can be impacted by cross-validation rules and dependent value sets.

Review Question

1. What six areas must be considered when implementing Enterprise Management applications?

Financials Applications Integration

In this section, you will cover the following points about Financials Applications integration:

- How information is shared and integrated with other Oracle Applications

- Implementation considerations for Enterprise Management Applications

- Features of the Application Desktop

How Information Is Shared with Other Oracle Applications

Information is shared with other Oracle Applications modules in a relational database format. Data is stored in a single database table, and, whenever necessary, the data is referred to by other tables that record the unique identifiers of the records they want to reference.

For example, information for items is owned by Oracle Inventory, which stores a unique identifier combination of INVENTORY_ITEM_ID and ORGANIZATION_ID for each item. This pair of columns is the means by which other tables refer to items. Using this technique, Oracle Bill of Materials can get information about items without having to store that information itself; instead, it stores the INVENTORY_ITEM_ID and ORGANIZATION_ID for each item it refers to. The same technique is used by assembly items in Oracle Work in Process.

This technique has a number of advantages. It eliminates double data entry and maintenance. Also, since an object's information is only stored in one place, rather than several, you avoid the problems inherent in trying to keep two parallel, independent data sources synchronized. The bottom-line result is that the implementation is completed more quickly and with higher-quality data.

Table 1-2 shows some additional Oracle Applications modules that share information in this way. As with the last table, the top row of this table lists the Applications module that owns the data being shared, and the left column of the table lists the modules that utilize, or receive, the shared data.

OPEN INTERFACES   Oracle Applications provides *open interfaces* to help integration among Oracle Applications modules, as well as with non-Oracle applications. These open interfaces consist of *interface tables*—which store data that must be imported into Oracle Applications—and *import programs*, which validate the data in the interface tables and then import that data into Oracle Applications' production tables.

There are numerous benefits to using open interfaces. They include:

- **Easy to use**   Understanding the design of Oracle Applications' production tables, and then writing an import program to match them, can be a complicated process. When you use one of Oracle Applications' preexisting open interfaces, most of the work is done for you. All you need to do is to load the interface tables.

- **Standard inputs and outputs**   Using the preexisting interface tables provides common standards, which makes it easy for third-party programs (those not supplied by Oracle Corporation) to feed legacy data into the interface tables.

Recipients	Owner							
	INV	MS/MRP	OE	GL	BOM	HR	WIP	FA
INV	N/A		Orders Reservations	Cost of sales accounts Inventory accounts		Organizations	Work orders	Asset category can be used on an item (purchasing attribute). This comment may apply best to inventory - item
MS/MRP	Items Manufacturing calendar	N/A	Orders		Bills of material Bills of resources	Organizations	Work orders	
OE	Items Warehouses Locations Serial numbers Lot numbers On-hand quantity	Supply	N/A		Bills of material	Organizations		
GL	Unit of measure			N/A				
BOM	Items				N/A	Organizations Employees		
HR				Cost allocation accounts	N/A	N/A		
FA	Unit of measure							
WIP	Items Manufacturing calendar	Recom- mendation	Orders	Work in process accounts	Bills of material Bills of resources	Organizations Employees	N/A	

TABLE 1-2. *Owners and Recipients of Data Shared by Additional Applications Modules*

■ **Data validation**   The provided import programs will automatically validate legacy data in the interface table. This ensures that the imported data is "clean" and satisfies data-integrity requirements.

■ **Error reporting**   The provided import programs generate error reports if any data in an interface table is invalid. You can use the error report to clean the interface data so that it is acceptable to Oracle Applications.

The open interfaces included in Oracle Financials modules are listed in Table 1-3.

Review Questions

1. Can a unique identifier consist of more than one database column?

2. What is the benefit of sharing data with other Oracle Applications modules?

3. How is information shared with other Oracle Applications modules?

4. How is information shared with non-Applications modules?

5. What are four advantages of using the Oracle Applications open interface to import data into tables?

Oracle Financials Module	Open Interfaces Provided
Oracle Assets	Mass Additions, Budget, Production, ACE
Oracle Cash Management	Bank Statement, Reconciliation
Oracle General Ledger	Journal Import, Budget Upload
Oracle Order Entry	Ship Confirm, Order Import
Oracle Payables	Expense Express
Oracle Purchasing	Requisitions
Oracle Receivables	AutoInvoice, AutoLockbox, Customer, Sales Tax Rate

TABLE 1-3.   *Oracle Open Interfaces*

Implementation Considerations for Enterprise Management Applications

Every installation of Enterprise Management Applications will entail a different set of considerations. In the following section, you will learn about the most common considerations and what to do about them. These implementation considerations include:

- Organization structure
- Centralization vs. decentralization
- Rollout strategy
- Multiple currencies
- Data conversion strategy
- Naming conventions
- ISO certification or other audit requirements
- Identifying critical success factors and areas of improvement
- Technical architecture
- Security
- Master files
- Language support
- Reporting needs

The implementation considerations for your particular installation will define the scope of the project. Therefore, the earlier you identify the implementation considerations that are relevant to your project, the more focused your project will be—and the more likely it will be to succeed. The biggest enemy of a successful implementation is *scope creep*, a phrase that refers to expansions in a project's scope that occur after the project is underway. Working in a situation that has scope creep is a lot like trying to hit a moving target. The best defense is to define the scope of the project in writing, before work starts, and get the scope document signed by the same people who will sign off on the project once it is finished.

Organization Structure

Organization structure is the first thing you must consider. Within a given legal entity (an organization with its own employer identification number (EIN)), there are two types of groups: companies and operating units. These groups may or may not overlap. Companies represent the business requirements, ensuring that debits equal credits. Operating units reflect security requirements, segregating data into discrete groups.

With that in mind, ask yourself the following questions:

1. How many legal entities will this implementation involve? Remember that a *legal entity* is defined as having its own separate EIN.

2. Within each legal entity, how many companies are there? A *company* is defined as the lowest level where total debits equal total credits.

3. Within each legal entity, how many operating units are there? An *operating unit* is defined as unit that needs their payables, receivables, cash management, order entry, and purchasing transactions data separated. Sometimes a legal entity can also be the operating unit if the relationship between operating unit and legal entity is one to one.

4. Which operating units must be inventory organizations or have inventory organizations? An *inventory organization* is an operating unit that needs its own separate data for bill of materials, work in process, engineering, master scheduling, material requirement planning, capacity, and inventory. An operating unit may consist of just a single inventory organization, or it may have numerous inventory organizations. Each inventory organization can have its own item master table, manufacturing calendar, costing method, and inventory control.

5. How many business groups do you have? A *business group* is defined as having its own employee master table.

With answers to the above questions, you will start to have an idea of how your organization is structured. You will probably find it very useful to capture your organization's structure on paper.

The organization structure of the VISION demo database supplied with Oracle Financials is shown in Figure 1-4. Since the Sales organization and the Finance Administration organization are big organizations, they are shown in greater detail in Figures 1-5 and 1-6. Looking at those figures, you will see that the mythical Vision Corporation is a business group, legal entity, and operating unit. The Singapore and Miami distribution centers are legal entities and operating units, as are Vision ADB, Vision Operations, Vision Project Manufacturing, and Vision Services. The inventory organizations include all of the distribution centers, all of the manufacturing facilities, Vision Project Manufacturing, Chicago Subassembly Plant, Vision Operations, Vision ADB, and Vision Services.

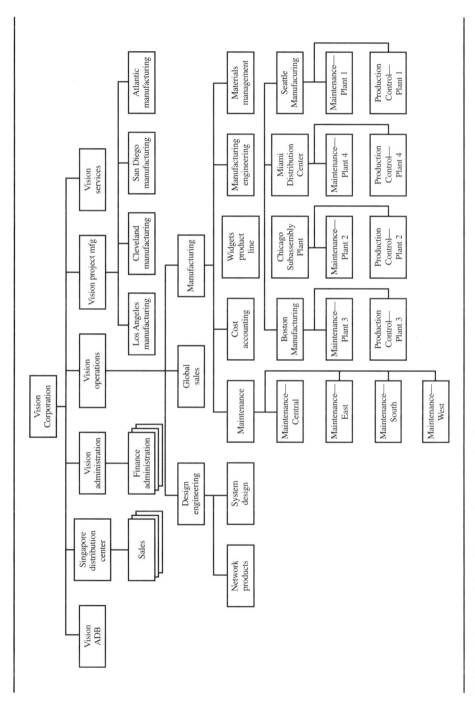

FIGURE 1-4. *Vision Corporation organization*

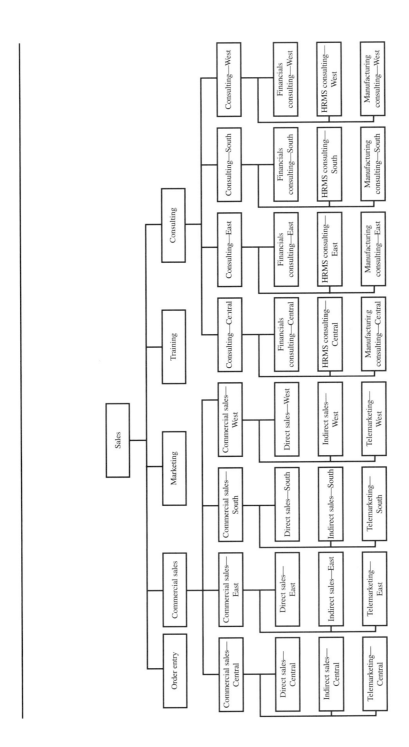

FIGURE 1-5. *Sales organization detail*

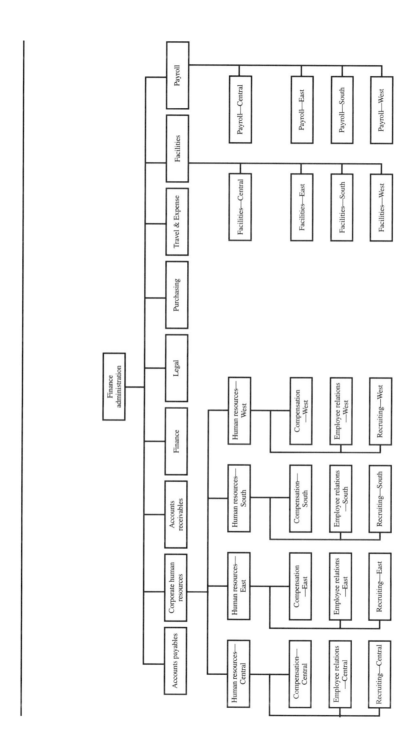

FIGURE 1-6.   *Finance administration organization detail*

Figure 1-7 shows the scenario that you will use in the exercises in this book. Note the addition of the new distribution center, which represents a new legal entity, operating unit, and inventory organization.

Centralization vs. Decentralization

Once you have identified the organization structure, you must determine what types of users will be tied to each organization, and where those users will be located. First, determine which Oracle Applications packages will be needed by each organization. Then, within each application package, determine what functionality each organization needs. Create an organization chart on paper, and next to each box on the chart write the business functions that each box (organization) will provide. Now, you should decide whether you are going to centralize or decentralize (distribute) certain functions to gain efficiency. For example, you might be able to increase the efficiency of your asset management and payable payment processes by centralizing or decentralizing them. Ultimately, the decision to centralize or decentralize is driven by your company's specific resources situation and physical locations.

For instance, assume you want to centralize the asset management and payable payment processes. In that scenario, the central organization tracks assets and cuts the checks to pay for assets. The company's other organizations only need the purchasing function to submit purchase requisitions and receive assets. In the new distribution center, every function is decentralized so that you can get experience setting up every module.

Rollout Strategy

There are two basic rollout strategies:

- Big bang approach
- Phased approach

BIG BANG APPROACH   In the big bang approach, all application modules are placed into production simultaneously. For this approach to work, the implementation phases of the modules must be kept synchronized. Since all of the work is happening at one time, this approach requires more people than the phased approach. For this reason, it is more often chosen by large organizations than by small ones. However, it is more efficient, because you do not have to create temporary interfaces as described in the next paragraph.

PHASED APPROACH   In the phased approach, the application modules are implemented in groups, and each group goes into production at a different time.

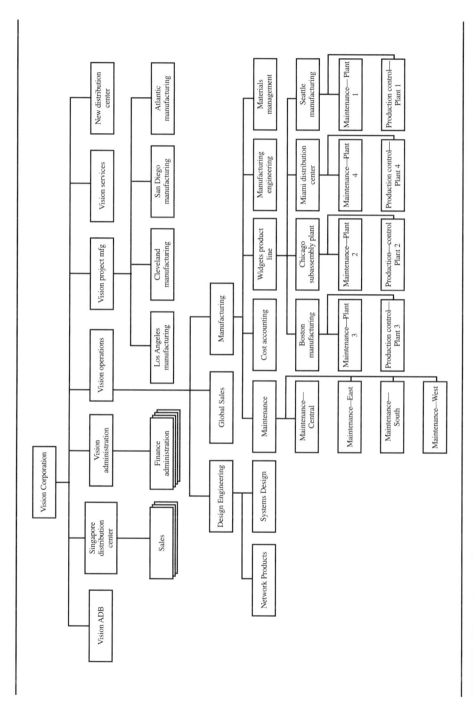

FIGURE 1-7. *Vision demo organization with your addition*

This approach requires the use of temporary automatic or manual interfaces to act as bridges between the Oracle applications and your existing legacy systems before all the modules are in production.

For example, let's say your complete Applications installation will include the following components:

- General Ledger

- Assets

- Payables

- Purchasing

- Cash Management

In this example, assume that the first phase of your installation will include Oracle General Ledger and Oracle Assets, with the other three modules due in phase 2. You would need an interface to post journals for reconciliations, receipts accrual, encumbrances, payables distributions, and payables liability from your existing legacy system to Oracle General Ledger. As an option, you could also create an interface to bring legacy payable invoices into Oracle Assets through the Oracle Assets interface, in order to have assets created automatically in the new installation.

The exercises you do later in this book will employ the big bang approach.

Multiple Currencies

There are two basic types of multiple-currency implementations:

- Transactions and balances are maintained in a single currency (called the *functional currency*). Journals showing other currencies translate their values to the functional currency before posting.

- Transactions and balances are maintained in multiple functional currencies. This may be necessary if the company has organizations in different parts of the world, or if it must report in both its functional currency and the Euro.

Utilizing a single functional currency and translating the journals is easy to implement in Oracle Applications, as long as you maintain the exchange rates for the currencies you need. On the other hand, utilizing multiple functional currencies requires the creation of multiple Sets of Books. (Sets of Books will be described in the next chapter.) The exercises you do later in this book will utilize two functional currencies: the Euro and the deutsche mark (DEM).

Data Conversion Strategy

The first step you must take when considering your data conversion strategy is deciding what data is important to your business, and how many years of data must be transferred from the old implementation to the new one. For instance, if you would like to take advantage of such features as volume discounting, supplier performance analysis, and creating financial reports spanning multiple fiscal years, you will need to convert some historical data from the existing *legacy* accounting system. The data may or may not be easy to obtain from the legacy system, and it may or may not be "clean" enough (complete, free from errors) to import into the new implementation without requiring some data cleansing first.

The following is a list of data elements that are typically considered for data conversion when Oracle Applications is replacing an existing implementation:

Oracle Applications Module	Data Elements
Oracle General Ledger	Chart of Accounts
	Journal entries
	Actual balances
	Budgets
Oracle Assets	Assets
Oracle Order Entry	Sales orders
	Agreements
Oracle Receivables	Customers
	Invoices
	Receipts
	On account
	Salesperson
	Territory
Oracle Purchasing	Purchasing items
	Suppliers
	Purchase requisitions
	Purchase orders
	Receipts
Oracle Payables	Invoices
	Payments

Naming Conventions

Because Oracle provides seed data when you install Applications, the potential exists for that data to become confused with real business data. It makes sense to adopt a company naming convention to be used as the prefix for any setups. Doing this will also allow you to easily identify and preserve your company's custom setups during an application upgrade.

The earlier you decide on this, the better. When you do, let everyone in the project know about it, and then check the data that is being entered to ensure that everyone is adhering to the naming convention.

An abbreviation of your company's name is a common and effective choice. For example, to avoid having multiple AT&T entries in your list of suppliers, you can adopt a naming convention stipulating that all abbreviations should be capitalized and free of spaces. This way, AT&T will be the only way you can name that supplier. Note that in order for this to work, you needed to specify two restrictions: case (uppercase only) and whether spaces are allowed. Specifying one without the other can result in entries like AT&T, A T & T, and A T&T all being accepted as unique.

For the exercises in this book, you will utilize a setup prefix of NEW.

ISO Certification or Other Audit Requirements

Hundreds of books have been written about ISO certification, and if that is a major part of your requirements, you should investigate and read some of those dedicated texts. Having said that, there is still some high-level guidance that is within the scope of this book. The first step you will want to take is making a written list of all your certification and audit requirements. Next, correlate those requirements with relevant stages of your implementation. Then define checkpoints at those implementation stages, designed to ensure that the requirements related to each stage are met. If some requirements will be fulfilled procedurally—that is, by how people use the system, rather than by the system itself—document the actions the users must take for specific tasks, and create training materials that explain and emphasize those actions.

Identifying Critical Success Factors and Areas of Improvement

The key steps to take when identifying your project's critical success factors and areas of improvement are as follows:

- Do it early. The first written documentation of a project should include a statement of what the project will be doing for your business when it is working ideally.

- Be extremely specific. Make statements that will be measurable later.

- Map the critical success factors and areas of improvement to the Oracle Applications functionality and processes that will help realize the improvements.

These steps require time at the beginning of a project, and they are easy to dismiss. However, they are an important time investment that will pay for itself many times over. The information you gather during these steps will help you maintain focus as the project progresses, by providing concrete issues to discuss in meetings and helping to clarify what is important and what is not.

Technical Architecture

The area of technical architecture consists of two components:

- Hardware selection and configuration

- Oracle database configuration

To make the best decisions about these issues, be sure that all meetings and decisions in these areas include staff members responsible for network architecture and database administration.

Your hardware configuration will depend on your organization's structure, how centralized or decentralized your data will be, and your company's network architecture.

The Oracle database configuration that is important at this stage is the number of *database instances* the implementation will require. A database instance is a complete, functioning Oracle database with its own files, configuration, and application codes. It is possible for a single Oracle server to run more than one database instance, and when it does, the instances appear completely independent to the applications using them.

It is very common to have separate instances representing how "finished" a particular part of an implementation is. For example, a common arrangement is to have three instances:

- **Development**   This is where software is first created and installed. This stage of the implementation process deserves its own instance because all sorts of things happen to programs and data while they are in development— not all of them good. This provides a safe place for those things to occur. The data in the development instance is often in much smaller quantities than it will be in real life—a couple of departments, a handful of employees, etc.

■ **Test**   Once software has been created, installed, configured, tweaked, and determined to be running properly within the narrow confines of the development environment, it gets copied into a test instance. Here, a group of knowledgeable users use the software and try to break it. This process almost always brings to light problems that were not apparent in the development environment. The solutions to these problems are created in the development instance and then copied to the test instance for further testing. The data in the test instance should be as similar to real data as possible, both in content and in quantity.

■ **Production**   This is the instance where the software that runs your business resides. Ideally, the software installed in this instance is completely reliable. This is the instance that stores your company's real, business-critical data.

In some environments, there is also a need for a DEMO instance. Additionally, you may need extra instances if you are implementing Oracle Applications in a phased approach, because different modules might be in a different stage of the project.

TIP
If you decide to use a single server for multiple organizations in different parts of the world, remember that the timestamp that is placed into Oracle tables will reflect the time at the server, not the time where the data originated. In other words, if your server is in the United States, records inserted by an application running in another country will still have a timestamp reflecting the United States transaction time.

Security
Data security is a complicated issue that, like ISO certification, has deservedly spawned its own library of books. Unit II contains a more complete treatment of data security. For the time being, consider the following factors:

■ What data must be secured?

■ Should users of a particular application be able to see all records that application has? For instance, should a General Ledger user in the Legal department be able to see all GL records, or only those that belong to the Legal department?

■ What type of access should each user role have? In general, the lowest-level access is the ability to view records. A higher level of access is the ability to insert new records, and update those that already exist. The highest level of access is the ability to delete existing records.

Answers to the above questions will form the foundation for an implementation's security matrix.

Master Files

As you recall, master files are shared across Oracle Applications modules. Because of the central role they play, it is very important that the data in your master files be clean—free of duplicate records, and with all of the important data elements populated—before the data is converted into Oracle Applications.

If your implementation requires that portions of the master files be spread among multiple systems, or that complete copies of the master files be kept on more than one system, you will need to establish a procedure to synchronize the files in a reliable and timely fashion.

Language Support

If your implementation will need to support more than one language, Oracle Applications provides three sets of features that will help:

■ Forms can display their prompts in different languages. For example, forms in the German region of your application can display their prompts in German, while forms in the Japanese region can display their prompts in Japanese.

■ Multiple-language support is built into some of the data. For example, flexfield values have multiple-language support. (Flexfields store values in your Chart of Accounts, among other places.) You can create a set of flexfield descriptions for each language you must support. For example, assume you have "natural account" as part of your Chart of Accounts, and your cash account is represented by flexfield value 10100. You can enter **Cash** as the description of that flexfield in English, and **Kasse** as the description in German.

Not all data can be defined in more than one language. For instance, customer name can be stored in only one language.

■ Specific features can be correlated to geographic regions as *localizations*. For example, the Mexican localization includes a check format that is necessary for the Mexican government.

TIP
*The **Translations** button on the toolbar and the menu bar switches descriptions between multiple languages as described above.*

Reporting Needs

Among the first things you must define before an implementation commences are the reports that the business needs the implementation to produce. Once you have defined these reporting requirements, determine what data elements the reports will require and correlate them to the data in Oracle Applications. This will impact your implementation decisions because, for example, if you must see financial reports by funds, then funds must be part of your Chart of Accounts—so information can be captured into the correct fund "bucket" to allow reporting by fund.

Review Questions

1. What is the definition of a legal entity? An operating unit? An inventory organization? How do they correlate with each other?

2. Under what circumstances do you need to set up multiple Sets of Books?

3. What data elements are common for data conversion for Oracle General Ledger and Oracle Assets?

4. What features do Oracle Applications provide to support multiple languages?

Features of the Application Desktop

The Application Desktop of Oracle Financials Applications contains two components: the application toolbar and the Navigator window. Figure 1-8 shows the Application Desktop and identifies each component.

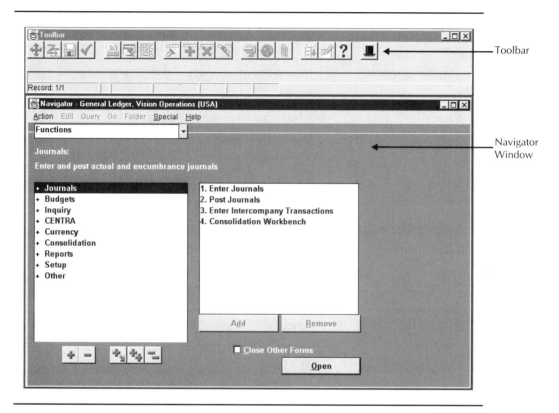

FIGURE 1-8.   *Application Desktop*

Toolbar

The application toolbar contains a subset of functions selected from the Applications menu. Buttons on the toolbar will be grayed out if that particular function is not available in a particular form. When appropriate, the toolbar also displays informational messages. The toolbar also displays the total number of records available within a given form, as well as the number of the record you are on. The toolbar buttons include:

Button	Function
Navigate To	Return to Navigator
Zoom	Invoke defined zoom

Button	Function
Save	Save pending changes
Save and Proceed	Save pending changes and start new record
Print	Print the current form
Clear All	Clear all data in current window
Summary/Detail	Toggle between Summary and Detail view (if available)
Find	Invoke Query Find window
New Record	Start new record
Delete Record	Delete the current record from the database
Clear Record	Clear record from the form (not from the database—the record still exists in the database)
Folder Tools	Invoke the Folder Tools palette
Translations	Invoke Translation window to translate between languages (if available)
Attachments	Invoke the Attachments window
List of Values	Invoke List of Values window
Edit Field	Invoke field editor
Window Help	Invoke context-sensitive help
Responsibilities	Switch to a different responsibility

Navigator Window

The top of the Navigator window displays the responsibility selected when you logged into Oracle Applications. Inside the Navigator window you will see a menu bar, a function/document alternative region, a Function window, a collection of function buttons, and a Top Ten List window. There is also a Close Other Forms checkbox that is available in the Navigator window. If you enable the Close Other Forms checkbox, any forms you have open will automatically close when you elect to navigate to another function. Figure 1-9 shows the Navigator window.

MENU BAR   There are seven menus in the Oracle Applications menu bar:

■ Action

■ Edit

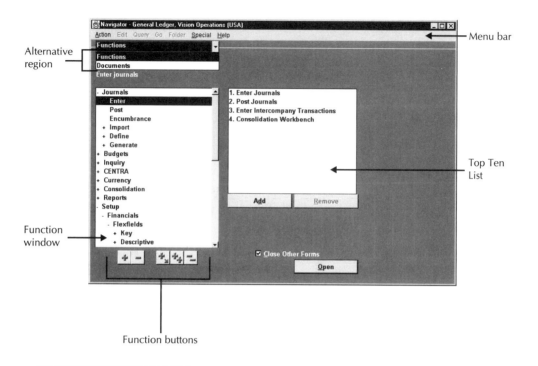

FIGURE 1-9. *Navigator window*

- Query
- Go
- Folder
- Special
- Help

Functions that are not available will be grayed out in the menus.

ACTION MENU   The Action menu contains commands that control the display of a form and the records within it. The following table details these commands.

Menu Item	Function
Navigate To	Display the Navigator.
Zoom	Invoke another form to view or change information, and then return to the original form and pick up from where it was left off.
Save	Save pending changes.
Save and Proceed	Save pending changes and insert new record.
Print	Print current window.
Export	Export data to spreadsheet format.
Place on Navigator	Place document of interest onto the Navigator for easier access.
Refresh	Refresh display.
Close Window	Close open window.
Close Form	Close form and all its related windows.
Exit Oracle Applications	Close the Oracle Applications software on this computer.

EDIT MENU   The Edit menu contains commands that affect the data displayed in a form. The following table details these commands.

Menu Item	Function
Clear Field	Clear entire entry in the field where the cursor is.
Duplicate Field Above	Duplicate value of current field from same field in the previous record.
List of Values	Invoke List of Values window.
Edit Field	Invoke field editor for the current field. Field editor is a wider, scrollable window that makes editing or viewing long text easier. The Edit Field button will also invoke the Shorthand Alias window or the Flexfield window if the cursor is placed on a flexfield. See Chapter 9 for more information on flexfields.

Menu Item	Function
New Record	Insert new record before current record.
Delete Record	Delete current record from the database.
Clear Record	Clear current record from the form (but not from the database).
Duplicate Record Above	Create new record based on contents of the previous record. All primary-key information and other application information such as the WHO information unique to a record will be blanked out automatically. (WHO information in Oracle Applications includes the user login that creates or updates the record and the time that the record is created or last updated.)
Translations	Invoke Translation window to translate between languages if available. Foreign language must be separately installed.
Attachments	Invoke attachment table.
Select All	Select all data.
Deselect All	Deselect all data.
Clear Block	Clear the entry in the block where the cursor is from the form.
Clear Form	Clear the entry in the entire form from the form.

TIP
You must be careful with the Clear Record and Delete Record functions. Both functions appear to perform the same thing since both functions clear the record from the form. However, only the Delete Record function will delete the record from the database. If you requery the database after clearing the record, you will see that the record still exists.

QUERY MENU   The Query menu contains commands that allow you to easily locate records. The following table details these commands.

Menu Item	Function
Find	Invoke Query Find window to enter search criteria.
Find All	Find all records (same as the Run function below, but with no query criteria).
Enter	Enter query mode where query criteria can be entered.
Run	Execute a query while in query mode with the entered criteria. (Doing this without first entering query criteria produces a *blind query* that will return all records, just like the Find All function above.)
Cancel	Leave query mode.
Show Last Criteria	Repeat last entered query criteria while in query mode.
Count Matching Records	Count the number of records that matched the specified query criteria.
Get More Records	Get the next batch of matching records.

GO MENU   The Go menu contains commands for navigating around a form. The following table details these commands.

Menu Item	Function
Next Field	Go to next field
Previous Field	Go to previous field
Next Record	Go to next record
Previous Record	Go to previous record
First Record	Go to first record
Last Record	Go to last record
Next Block	Go to next block
Previous Block	Go to previous block
Summary/Detail	Toggle between Summary and Detail view (if available)

TIP
The scroll bar that appears alongside records in Oracle Applications shows your current position relative to the retrieved data. Since Oracle Applications retrieves data by batches for performance reason, the scroll bar position is not always accurate relative to all potential records that match the query criteria. In order to make the scroll bar accurate relative to all records, you must explicitly go to the last record. This may take a long time if the number of matching records is high.

FOLDER MENU   Using folders, the user can predefine query criteria for a form, and customize the look and feel of a form. Each folder definition can be stored as a file. Once you have entered query criteria, if the folder feature is allowed in the form you are on, you can save the query as part of the folder definition. If the folder feature is available in the form, you can also choose to show more fields or hide an existing field, so that different data will be displayed on the form. In addition, you can rearrange the order in which the fields appear, alter the display width of the fields, and change the sort order in which the data is presented.

Menu Item	Function
New	Create new folder
Open	Open existing folder
Save	Save folder definition with its existing filename
Save As	Save folder definition with a new filename
Delete	Delete folder file
Show Field	Show selected field as additional field on the form
Hide Field	Hide selected field from form
Move Right	Move selected field to the right of the next field
Move Left	Move selected field to the left of the previous field
Move Up	Move selected field on top of the previous field if data is displayed in a tabular format
Move Down	Move selected field below the next field if data is displayed in a tabular format
Widen Field	Increase field width

Menu Item	Function
Shrink Field	Shrink field width
Change Prompt	Change field prompt
Autosize All	Autosize field based on the values it contains
Show Order By	Show which fields determine the order by criteria for the query
View Query	View the query attached to the folder definition
Reset Query	Reset the query attached to the folder definition
Folder Tools	Invoke the Folder Tools palette

SPECIAL MENU   The contents of the Special menu vary depending on which form you are in. If there are no specific functions available for the form, the Special menu is disabled. As an example, the Special menu for the Navigator window includes:

Menu Item	Function
Switch Responsibility	Change to another responsibility level
Change Password	Change user password
Sign On Again	Sign on to the Oracle Applications as another user
Expand	Expand menu into next lower level
Collapse	Collapse functions back into menu
Expand Branch	Expand selected menu (branch) into functions
Expand all	Expand all menus included in Navigator into functions
Collapse all	Collapse all functions included in Navigator back up to the highest level

HELP MENU   The Help menu contains not only commands to display help screens, but also commands to help you determine the status of jobs you have run. The following table details these commands.

Menu Item	Function
Window Help	Shows context-sensitive help. A **Glossary** button is available to take users to the glossary for the particular Oracle Applications module they are in. A **Navigation** button is available to display navigation help. Navigation help lists the navigation paths that will take you to forms within the Oracle Applications module they are in.

Menu Item	Function
Oracle Applications Library	Invokes Oracle Applications Documentation Library
Keyboard Help	Shows "hot-key" shortcuts for different functions
Display Database Error	Displays the most recent database error
Tools	Available if the profile option *Utilities : Diagnostics* is set. This function has a menu enabling you to perform different diagnostic functions. These diagnostic tools include: **Examine:** User can examine the value for any field in the form, including nondisplayed fields. **Trace**: Provides a trace file with all of the SQL statements executed during the trace session. The trace file contains performance statistics and other useful information about each SQL statement **Debug:** Invokes the Oracle Forms V4.5 debugger if Oracle Applications is started in debug mode. The property sub-function can display item property or folder property. **Custom Code:** Toggles custom code on or off.
View My Requests	Invokes concurrent requests viewing form.
About This Record	Shows information about current record, including the base table/view of the record, and the login IDs and timestamps that created and last updated the record.
About Oracle Applications	Shows information specific to Oracle Applications, including the version number, name of current form, and the database instance that Oracle Applications is running on.

FUNCTIONS/DOCUMENT ALTERNATIVE REGION   The Navigator has two different regions: Functions or Documents. The Functions region is the default region; it displays all menus and functions available to the responsibility you logged on with. Menus can contain further submenus, or a list of functions. To expand or collapse menus, you can double-click on the item of interest or use the function buttons as described below. When you place the cursor on a function, a description of that function appears above the Function window. Beneath the Function window is the Functions region, where you will find the following buttons:

- ■ **Expand**   Expand menu into next lower level

- ■ **Collapse**   Collapse functions back into menu

- ■ **Expand Branch**   Expand selected menu (branch) into functions

- ■ **Expand All**   Expand all menus included in Navigator into functions

- ■ **Collapse All**   Collapse all functions included in Navigator back to the highest level

In contrast, the Document region lists all documents or screen dumps that have been placed on the Navigator by the user. In this window, the user can choose to see documents in either an Icon view or a List view, as well as rename, remove, or open documents. Figure 1-10 shows the Document window.

TOP TEN LIST   To simplify navigation between functions, you can keep a list of ten often-used functions in the Top Ten list. To add a function to the list, select

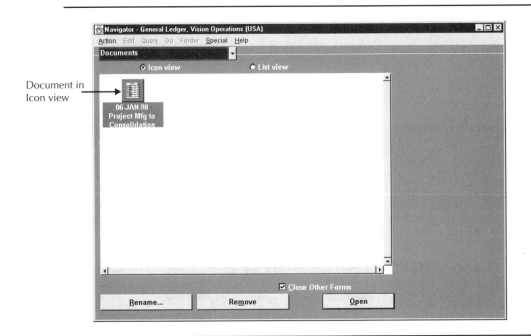

FIGURE I-10.   *Document window*

the function in the Function window and click on the **Add** button below the Top
Ten list. To remove a function from the list, select the function and click on the
Remove button. To invoke a function from the Top Ten list, just type the number
(from 0 to 9) that represents the desired function.

TIP
*The Function window lists menu prompts, while the
Top Ten list lists the function description.*

Review Questions

1. How is information shared in Oracle Applications?

2. What is the difference between master tables, setup tables, and transaction tables?

3. What does the Close Other Forms checkbox do?

4. What is the purpose of the Top Ten list?

For the Chapter Summary, Two-Minute Drill, and Chapter Questions and
Answers, open the summary.htm file contained in the Summary_files directory
on the book's CD-ROM.

CHAPTER
2

Financial
Management Setup

n this chapter, you will learn how to set up Oracle General Ledger and Oracle Assets. You will learn about the following factors in Financial Management setup:

- Implementation process steps for Oracle GL and Assets

- Creating a Chart of Accounts

- Creating a Set of Books

- Implementation considerations

You will be introduced to the functionality of Multiple-Organization Support and get a detailed description of the Vision database structure. Then you will create a new Chart of Accounts and a Set of Books. In the final section, you will be presented with implementation considerations you must take into account when setting up a Chart of Accounts and a Set of Books.

Implementation Process Steps for General Ledger and Assets

In this section, you will cover the following subjects regarding implementing Oracle General Ledger and Assets:

- Major aspects of implementing General Ledger and Fixed Assets

- Functionality of Multiple-Organization Support

- Vision demonstration database structure

Major Aspects of Implementing General Ledger and Fixed Assets

This section describes all of the steps necessary to set up Oracle General Ledger and Assets. If you use the Vision database provided with the product, you can follow the steps described in this section by comparing the figures provided in the book with the screens you see on your computer.

To log on to the Oracle Applications, obtain a user name and password from your system administrator. If the default user names and passwords are still in place, you can use the user name **OPERATIONS** and the password **WELCOME** to log on. This user has all responsibilities related to the Vision Operations organization in Vision Corporation.

Once you are logged in and looking at the Responsibilities window, select the responsibility named *General Ledger, Vision Operations (USA)* and click on the **OK** button. This will open the Navigator window. Double-click on the Setup function in the Function window, and your screen should look similar to the one shown here:

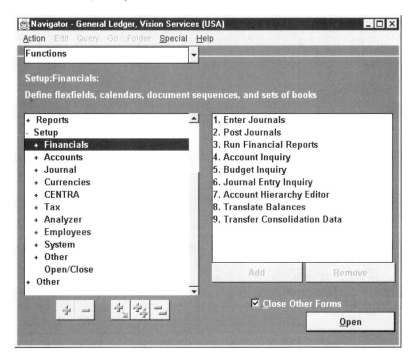

Oracle General Ledger Setups

The flow of Oracle General Ledger setup steps is shown in Figure 2-1. What follows is an overview of each of the steps identified in that figure.

I. **Chart of Accounts**   This setup step is discussed in detail later in this chapter in the section "Creating a Chart of Account."

2. **Account Combinations**   If account combinations have been set up so that new account combinations cannot be created dynamically, you must set up a few account combinations before you set up your Set of Books. These accounts include the Retained Earnings account and the Suspense account. This will be discussed in more detail later in this chapter.

3. **Period Types**   Period types are used to create the accounting calendar. Seeded period types include Month, Quarter, and Year. You can specify a

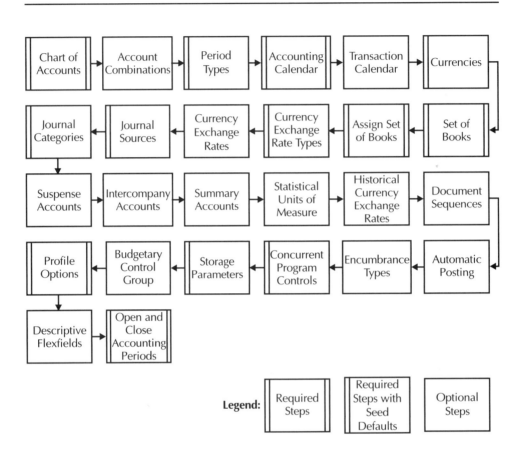

FIGURE 2-1. *Oracle General Ledger setup steps*

year type of Fiscal or Calendar for each period type. You can get to the Period Types form by following the navigation path *Setup : Financials : Calendar : Types.*

4. **Accounting Calendar** By following the navigation path *Setup : Financials : Calendar : Accounting,* you can get to the Accounting Calendar form. In the exercises to come, you will use the predefined Fiscal accounting calendar, which you can see within the Accounting Calendar window by following these steps:

■ Open the Accounting Calendar form, if you haven't already.

■ Execute the menu command Query | Enter.

■ Type **Fiscal** in the Name field of the Accounting Calendar form.

■ Execute the menu command Query | Run.

You screen should now look similar to Figure 2-2. Because this accounting calendar is based on a fiscal year, the years shown in each period's name (in the far-right column of the form) may not necessarily match the actual calendar year in which the period happens.

5. **Transaction Calendar**   You can get to the Transaction Calendar form by following the navigation path *Setup : Financials : Calendar : Transaction.* If you plan to use average balance processing, you must define a transaction calendar with valid business days to control transaction posting. Average balance processing allows you to track both average and end-of-day balances instead of accounting period-end amounts. This is usually a requirement for regulated financial institutions. You can use the **Defaults** button to change the business day defaults before your transaction calendar is generated.

6. **Currencies**   Oracle Applications comes with hundreds of International Organization for Standardization (ISO) currencies predefined. To see this list, follow the navigation path *Setup : Currencies : Define.* Considering that the list runs the gamut from the Andorran Peseta to the Vanuatu Vatu, the

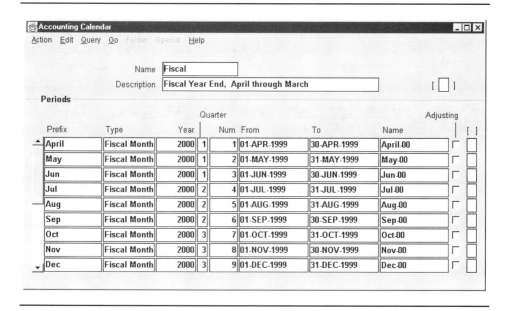

FIGURE 2-2.   *Accounting calendar*

chances are high that the currency you need is already defined and just needs to be enabled. The Currencies form also lets you define additional currencies, which would be handy if you needed to establish a new currency, perhaps for an island you just purchased.

7. **Set of Books**   This setup step is discussed in detail in the section "Creating a Set of Books."

8. **Assign Set of Books**   This setup step is discussed in detail in the section "Setting Up Financial Controls."

9. **Currency Exchange Rate Types**   Conversion rate types are used to label conversion rates. They do not add functionality, but rather are meant to facilitate selecting correct conversion rates. Oracle GL comes seeded with the following conversion rate types: User, Spot, Corporate, and EMU Fixed. You can define additional conversion rate types to suit your business requirements, if necessary. To get to the appropriate form, shown in Figure 2-3, follow the navigation path *Setup : Currencies : Rates : Types.*

10. **Currency Exchange Rates**   GL allows you to set up two different types of currency conversion rates: *daily* conversion rates and *period-end* conversion rates. Daily conversion rates are used to convert foreign currency journal entries into the functional currency of the Applications implementation. In contrast, period-end conversion rates are used to revalue or translate foreign currency denominated balances. Figure 2-4 shows both exchange-rate setup screens, which are accessible by following the navigation paths *Setup : Currencies : Rates : Daily* and *Setup : Currencies : Rates : Period.* Oracle General Ledger also accommodates other conversion rate types that are derived, such as period average.

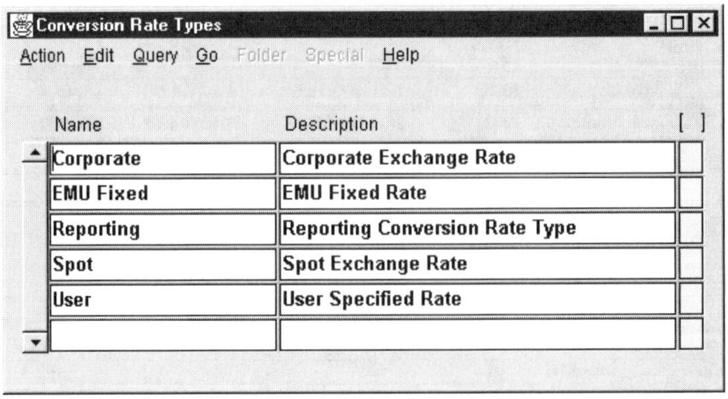

FIGURE 2-3.   *Conversion rate types*

11. **Journal Sources** Oracle General Ledger comes seeded with many predefined journal sources. You can see these by following the navigation path *Setup : Journal : Sources.* You can define additional journal sources to use for manual journal entries, or for automatic interfaces you plan to build. When creating a new journal entry, you can specify whether references for the new entry should be imported, as well as whether approval is required before posting to that journal source. More importantly, you can freeze any journal source. If a journal source is frozen, no changes can be made to the journals. For average balance processing, you can choose from three Effective Date rules for the journal source: *Fail* rejects transactions when the effective date is not a valid business day; *Roll Date* accepts transactions on nonbusiness days and rolls them back to the last business day; and *Leave Alone* accepts all transactions regardless of their date.

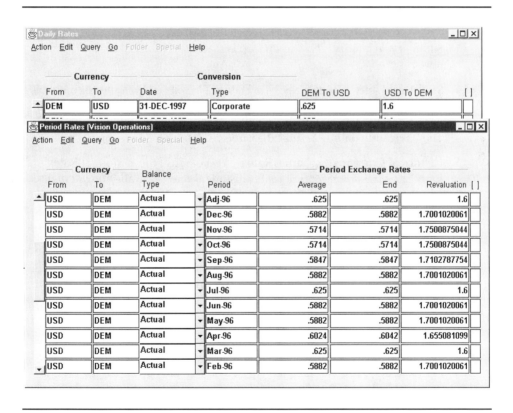

FIGURE 2-4. *Daily and period-end conversion rates*

12. **Journal Categories**   Oracle General Ledger comes seeded with numerous predefined journal categories. You can define additional ones, specifying how reverse journals should be created for each journal category. *Switch Db/Cr* causes reverse journals to be created by switching debit amounts with credit amounts and vice versa, and *Change Sign* causes reverse journals to be created by changing the sign of the amounts. The navigation path to this form is *Setup : Journal : Categories.*

13. **Suspense Accounts**   The Suspense Accounts form appears when you follow the navigation path *Setup : Accounts : Suspense.* You can use this form to define Suspense accounts that override what you have in your Set of Books.

14. **Intercompany Accounts**   Similar to Suspense accounts, you can define additional intercompany accounts to override what you have in your Set of Books. For each combination of Journal Source and Journal Category, you can set up accounts to receive debit balances or credit balances. This form is available via the navigation path *Setup : Accounts : Intercompany.*

15. **Summary Accounts**   This setup step is discussed in detail in the next chapter.

16. **Statistical Units of Measure**   The Statistical Units of Measure form enables you to set up accounts to store statistical balances. This allows you to, for instance, tie a statistical balance call Headcounts to your payroll account. The navigation path is *Setup : Accounts : Units.*

17. **Historical Currency Exchange Rates**   You can use the Historical Rates form, shown in Figure 2-5, to enter historical rates for translating actual and budget balances in your ownership/stockholder's equity accounts to remeasure balances. This is particularly useful in highly inflationary economies. Historical rates can be defined for a single account, as well as for a range of accounts. The navigation path for this form is *Setup : Currencies : Rates : Historical.*

18. **Document Sequences**   This setup step is discussed in detail in Chapter 8 in Unit II.

19. **Automatic Posting**   The Oracle General Ledger offers a feature named AutoPost that enables you to set up automatic posting based on criteria of your choosing. Your criteria can include date ranges, journal sources, journal categories, and balance types. You can also prioritize the criteria you established. AutoPost activities can be submitted immediately or scheduled to run periodically. Figure 2-6 shows the AutoPost form, which is available via the navigation path *Setup : Journal : AutoPost.*

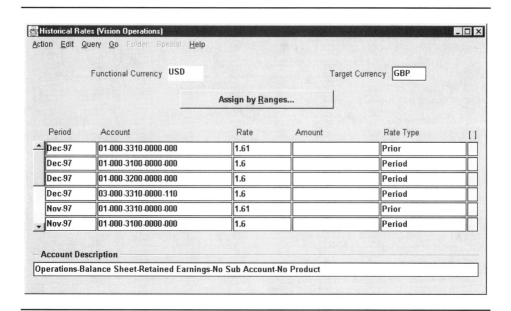

FIGURE 2-5.   *Historical rates*

20. **Encumbrance Types**   Oracle General Ledger has two predefined encumbrance types with Oracle Purchasing: Commitment and Obligation. Commitment is an encumbrance you record when you complete a purchase requisition, while Obligation is an encumbrance you record when you turn a requisition into a purchase order. The Encumbrance Types form (*Setup : Journal : Encumbrances*) is where you can create new encumbrance types for classifying encumbrance journals. The additional encumbrance types are only informational; no functionality is associated with specific encumbrance types. They are just for identifying and grouping journal entries. This form also lets you rename encumbrance types to something more descriptive, if you wish.

21. **Concurrent Program Controls**   The Concurrent Program Controls form (*Setup : System : Control*) allows you to specify parameters to optimize the performance of specific concurrent programs. You can select which segment in your Chart of Account structure the Mass Allocations and Mass Budgeting programs use to perform searching. You can also define how many accounts those programs should store in memory while doing their work, which rollback segment to use when the Open Period program is run, whether the system archives journal import data during a journal import, and how many journal lines should be processed at a time by Mass Allocations, Mass Budgeting, and Journal Import.

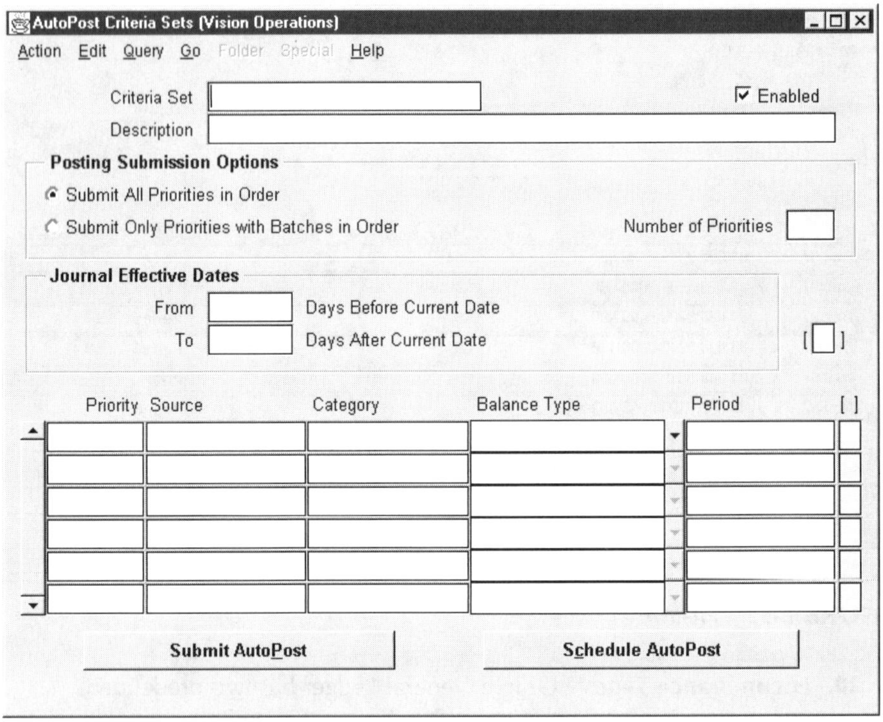

FIGURE 2-6. *Automatic Posting*

22. **Storage Parameters** By following the navigation path *Setup : System : Storage*, you can control the storage parameters used by GL's temporary tables. These settings are available because the temporary tables are re-created every time they are needed.

TIP
Before changing anything in the Storage Parameters screen, you should talk to your system's database administrator (DBA) to get valid information about tablespaces and storage parameters. These items are very familiar to the DBA, and she or he can suggest settings that will optimize the performance of your system. Always be nice to your DBA; they are essential contributors to the success of your implementation.

23. **Budgetary Control Group**   This form allows you to define rules controlling how strongly a budget controls spending. For each combination of journal source and journal category, you can define whether expenditures beyond a budget are accepted without comment, accepted with an advisory, or rejected. The form enables you to define a percentage or amount above budget that each rule will tolerate, as well as an override amount that can serve as a reserve fund when the rule is enforcing an absolute limit on spending. The form appears when you follow the navigation path *Budgets : Define : Controls.*

24. **Profile Options**   Profile options are updatable configuration parameters enabling you to modify the behavior of Oracle Applications. You can see your own profile option settings if you follow the navigation path *Other : Profile.* Table 2-1 lists the profile options available in Oracle General Ledger. Of these, the only required profile option is *GL Set of Books Name,* which defines which Set of Books is assigned to Oracle Applications. Profile options are described in more detail in Chapter 8.

Profile Options	Functions
Budgetary Control Group	Assigned Budgetary Control Group
Daily Rates Window: Enforce Inverse Relationship During Entry	Should inverse rate be calculated automatically in the Daily Rates form
Dual Currency	Second currency to use if *Dual Currency* is on. (It is now preferable to use the *Multiple Reporting Currencies* option instead of this option.)
Dual Currency Default Rate Type	Default rate type for the assigned *Dual Currency*
FSG: Accounting flexfield	Accounting flexfield structure to use for the Financial Statement Generator (FSG), which will be discussed in the section "Considerations for Setting up a Chart of Accounts"
FSG: Allow Portrait Print Style	Specifies whether FSG reports will be printed in portrait orientation when less than 80 characters wide
FSG: Enforce Segment Value Security	Specifies whether segment value security should be enforced in FSG

TABLE 2-1.   *Oracle General Ledger Profile Options*

Profile Options	Functions
FSG: Expand Parent Value	Specifies whether parent value should be expanded into child values when summary balance is reported in FSG
FSG: Message Detail	Log file message level
GL AHE: Saving Allowed	Specifies whether changes can be saved in Account Hierarchy Editor (AHE)
GL: Owners Equity Translation Rule	If no historical rates are specified, use either period-to-date (PTD) or year-to-date (YTD) period-end rates as specified in this profile option
GL Set of Books ID	Display the Set of Books ID specified by *GL Set of Books Name* profile option
GL Set of Books Name	Assigned Set of Books
GLDI: AutoCopy Enforcement Level	Specifies whether *AutoCopy* in General Ledger Desktop Integrator (GLDI) should copy report objects or work form the original objects
GLDI: Budget Wizard Enforce Segment Value Security	Specifies whether segment value security should be enforced in GLDI Budget Wizard
GLDI: Budget Wizard Privileges	Specifies what privileges are allowed in GLDI Budget Wizard
GLDI: Journal Wizard Privileges	Specifies what privileges are allowed in GLDI Journal Wizard
GLDI: Report Wizard Privileges	Specifies what privileges are allowed in GLDI Report Wizard
Intercompany Subsidiary	Assigned subsidiary used in intercompany transactions
Intercompany: Use Automatic Transaction Numbering	Specifies whether intercompany transactions should be automatically numbered
Journals: Allow Multiple Conversion rates	Specifies whether multiple conversion rates should be allowed in journals
Journals: Allow Non-Business Day Transactions	Specifies whether posting will be allowed on nonbusiness day when average balance processing is used

TABLE 2-1.   *Oracle General Ledger Profile Options* (continued)

Profile Options	**Functions**
Journals: Allow Preparer Approval	Specifies whether preparer can approve own journal
Journals: Default Category	Default journal category used in manual journals
Journals: Display Inverse Rate	Specifies whether conversion rates should be displayed in the functional-to-foreign format or foreign-to-functional format
Journals: Enable Prior Period Notification	Specifies whether you should be notified when journals are entered for a prior period
Journals: Find Approver Method	Defines what approval method to use for approving journals
Journals: Mix Statistical and Monetary	Specifies whether both statistical and monetary amounts can be entered into journals at the same time
Journals: Override Reversal Method	Specifies whether reversal method defined in setting up journal categories can be overridden
MRC: Reporting Set of Books	Set of books the reporting Set of Books points to
Use Performance Module	Specifies whether Posting, Summarization, Mass Allocations, Consolidation, Year End Carry Forward, Budget Range Assignments, and Historical Rates Assignment concurrent programs should use statistical data collected by the Optimizer. (The Optimizer program creates or drops indexes for those segments in your Chart of Accounts that you have marked for indexing. The Optimizer program also updates statistical information, such as the size of your balances and combinations tables. This information helps improve the performance of your journal entry posting and financial reporting process.)

TABLE 2-1. *Oracle General Ledger Profile Options* (continued)

25. **Descriptive Flexfields**   This setup step is described in detail in Chapter 9.

26. **Open and Close Accounting Periods**   Once you have completed the preceding setup steps, you are ready to conduct General Ledger business. In order to enter transactions, you must open the current accounting period. This is done through the Open and Close Periods form, available by following the navigation path *Setup : Open/Close*, and shown in Figure 2-7. You will learn more about this form, and use it in your own exercises, later in the book.

Review Questions

1. What is the very first step in setting up Oracle General Ledger? The very last step?

2. What is the purpose of a transaction calendar?

3. What setup form enables you to enforce budgetary control?

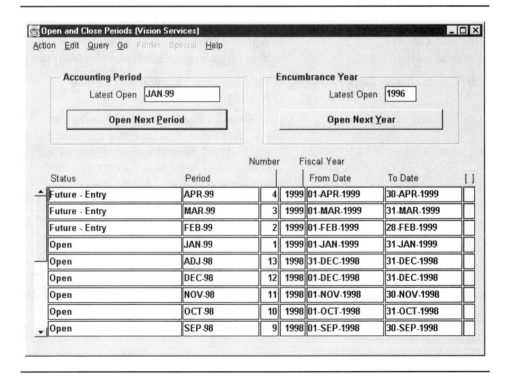

FIGURE 2-7.   *Open and Close Periods form*

Oracle Assets Setup Steps

The flow of Oracle Assets setup steps is shown in Figure 2-8. Each step shown in that figure is described briefly in the overview that follows. To see the forms described in the overview, switch your responsibility to *Assets, Vision Operations (USA)*.

I. **Asset Category Flexfield**   The Asset Category flexfield is used to group assets by financial information such as depreciation rules and depreciation ceilings. You can have up to seven segments in the Asset Category flexfield. (A *segment* is a single field within a key flexfield. Each account combination consists of multiple segments, or multiple fields. Common segments include company, cost center, and natural account. Segments are separated by a *segment separator*, which is a single character you select.) The maximum combined length of all segments together with the segment separator is 30 characters. Setting up the Asset Category flexfield is discussed in more detail in Chapter 9.

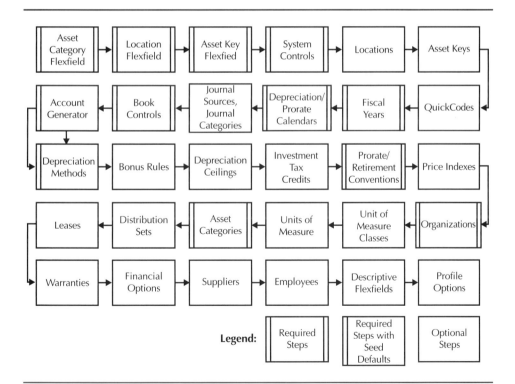

FIGURE 2-8.   *Oracle Assets setup steps*

2. **Location Flexfield** The Location flexfield is used to group assets by physical location. It has the same capacity and limitations as the Asset Category flexfield, and is also discussed in more detail in Chapter 9.
3. **Asset Key Flexfield** The Asset Key flexfield is used to group assets by nonfinancial information, such as the project number to which the asset is assigned. While this flexfield can contain up to 10 segments, its combined length is still limited to 30 characters. This flexfield is discussed in more detail in Chapter 9.
4. **System Controls** Using the form at the end of the navigation path *Setup : Asset System : System Controls*, you can specify a variety of system-wide parameters. These include the enterprise name you want to show on Oracle Assets reports, the oldest date placed in service for all assets, the starting and next asset numbers (if automatic asset numbering is turned on), and the name of the flexfield structures used for category, location, and asset key.
5. **Locations** You can use this form to enter location combinations based on the Location flexfield you defined. (You only need to predefine location combinations if the *Allow Dynamic Inserts* option was not enabled when the Accounting flexfield structure was defined.) Shown in Figure 2-9, the form's navigation path is *Setup : Asset System : Locations*.
6. **Asset Keys** You can use this form to enter asset key combinations based on the Asset Key flexfield you defined. (You only need to predefine asset

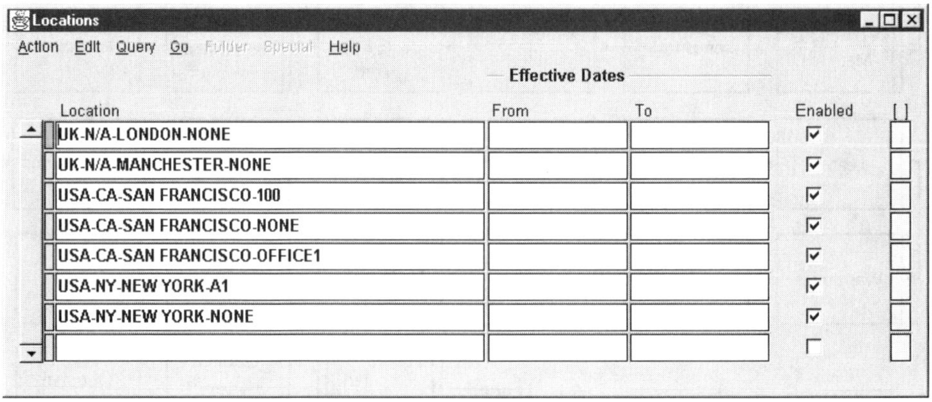
Locations

Action Edit Query Go Folder Special Help

Location	Effective Dates From	To	Enabled	[ ]
UK-N/A-LONDON-NONE			☑	
UK-N/A-MANCHESTER-NONE			☑	
USA-CA-SAN FRANCISCO-100			☑	
USA-CA-SAN FRANCISCO-NONE			☑	
USA-CA-SAN FRANCISCO-OFFICE1			☑	
USA-NY-NEW YORK-A1			☑	
USA-NY-NEW YORK-NONE			☑	
			☐	

FIGURE 2-9. *Locations form*

key combinations if *Allow Dynamic Inserts* is not enabled.) The Assets Keys form is available via the navigation path *Setup : Asset System : Asset Keys.*

7. **QuickCodes** QuickCodes are values that populate Lists of Values (LOVs) elsewhere in Assets. The QuickCodes form is at *Setup : Asset System : QuickCodes.* This form allows you to define the short name for the value (keeping this to 12 or fewer characters is a good idea, because that is the maximum display width of an LOV), the description, and a date on which the value will no longer be enabled. QuickCodes are stored in the client computer's memory, not in the database, which allows them to be accessed much more quickly. QuickCode types in Oracle Assets include Asset Category, Asset Subcategory, Asset Description, Journal Entries, Lease Frequency, Lease Payment Type, Property Type, Queue Name, Retirement, and Unplanned Depreciation Type.

TIP
Since QuickCodes are stored in memory, if you make changes to any QuickCodes, you must switch responsibility or sign on as another user for the changes to take effect.

8. **Fiscal Years** The Asset Fiscal Years form is where you define the start and end dates for fiscal years. In an implementation, you must set up fiscal years back to the oldest date placed in service that you defined in System Controls. Then, when this current fiscal year ends, the Depreciation program automatically generates the following fiscal year. Different fiscal years can be assigned to different corporate books, but fiscal years must be the same for the tax books and their corresponding corporate books. The form is available via navigation path *Setup : Asset System : Fiscal Years.*

9. **Depreciation/Prorate Calendars** This form enables you to set up your depreciation calendars and prorate calendars. (These can be the same, if you wish.) Each corporate book and tax book can have its own depreciation calendars and prorate calendars. The depreciation calendar defines the number of accounting periods in a fiscal year, while the prorate calendar defines the number of prorate periods in a fiscal year. Figure 2-10 shows this form, which is available by following the navigation path *Setup : Asset System : Calendars.*

10. **Journal Sources and Journal Categories** Journal sources and journal categories are next in an Oracle Assets setup *if* General Ledger is not installed. If you would like more details, you can refer to the earlier section "Oracle General Ledger Setup."

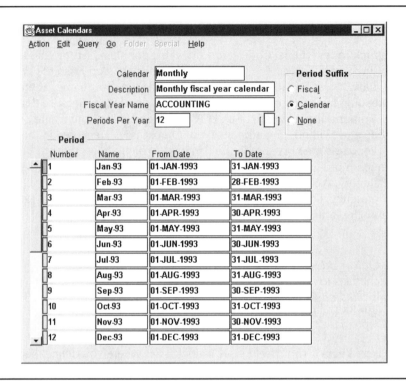

FIGURE 2-10. *Calendars form*

11. **Book Controls** You can set up corporate, tax, and budget depreciation books. The corporate book generates asset-related journals for Oracle General Ledger. Multiple tax books and budget books can tie to a corporate depreciation book. You will set up your own corporate and tax books in Chapter 5.

12. **Account Generator** The Account Generator creates account combinations for asset-related journals. Oracle Assets also comes with default account combinations that you can modify using Oracle Workflow.

13. **Depreciation Methods** Depreciation methods determine how each asset should be depreciated. Via the navigation path *Setup : Depreciation Methods*, Oracle Assets allows you to specify flat-rate, life-based, and units-of-production depreciation methods. For life-based depreciation, Oracle Assets supports Calculated and Table method types. The Calculated life-based depreciation method uses a straight-line approach in which the depreciation amount is calculated as (recoverable cost/number of

depreciation periods of the asset). Figure 2-11 shows the Depreciation Methods form set to this type of depreciation. The Table life-based depreciation method, shown in Figure 2-12, can use either recoverable cost or recoverable Net Book Value (NBV) as its basis. This form's **Rates** button enables you to enter annual depreciation rates. For the cost-basis method, rates for all years must add up to 1. For the NBV basis, all rates in years other than last year can be <= 1 and the last year rate must be 1 so the NBV will be 0 after the asset is retired. If you wish, you can enter the number of prorate periods per year for the Table method you defined. For flat-rate depreciation, shown in Figure 2-13, you specify the Flat method type, selecting either cost or NBV as the basis. If you choose NBV, you can exclude the salvage value from the depreciable basis. Use the **Rates** button to enter basic % and adjusting %. For both flat-rate and life-based depreciation, you can determine whether an asset is depreciable in the year the asset retired. For units-of-production depreciation, shown in Figure 2-14, you select the Production method type.

14. **Bonus Rules** If you are using the flat depreciation method type, you can create a bonus rate for each year or range of years of the asset's life. The form for doing this can be found by following the navigation path *Setup : Depreciation : Bonus Rules.*

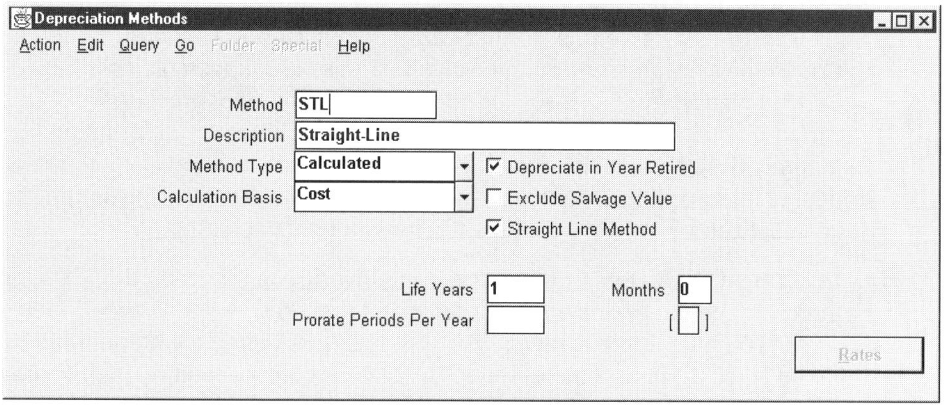

FIGURE 2-11. *Calculated depreciation method*

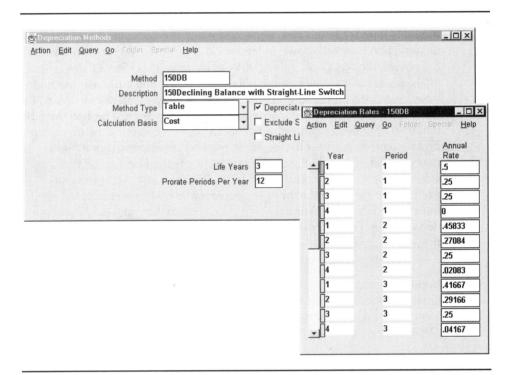

FIGURE 2-12. *Table depreciation method*

15. **Depreciation Ceilings** There are three types of depreciation ceilings: cost, expense, and investment tax credit. You can set each of these types up using the Asset Ceilings form (*Setup : Depreciation : Ceilings*). A Cost ceiling sets the maximum cost you can use as recoverable cost in depreciation. An Expense ceiling sets the maximum depreciation expense you can take each depreciation period. This is useful for luxury automobiles, for instance, which in the United States will need an expense depreciation ceiling. An investment tax credit ceiling sets the maximum cost that can be used to calculate the investment tax credit.

16. **Investment Tax Credits** If you are using investment tax credit (ITC), setting the ceiling in the prior step is just the beginning. You will also need to set up the ITC rates and ITC recapture rates. ITC rates define the amount of ITC for an asset, and they can be set up by following the navigation path *Setup : Depreciation : ITC Rates*. ITC recapture rates define the amount of ITC that needs to be recaptured if the asset with ITC retires before its life is up, and they can be set up via the navigation path *Setup : Depreciation : ITC Recapture Rates*.

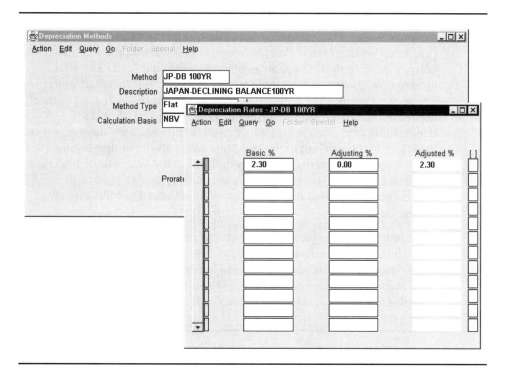

FIGURE 2-13. *Flat depreciation method*

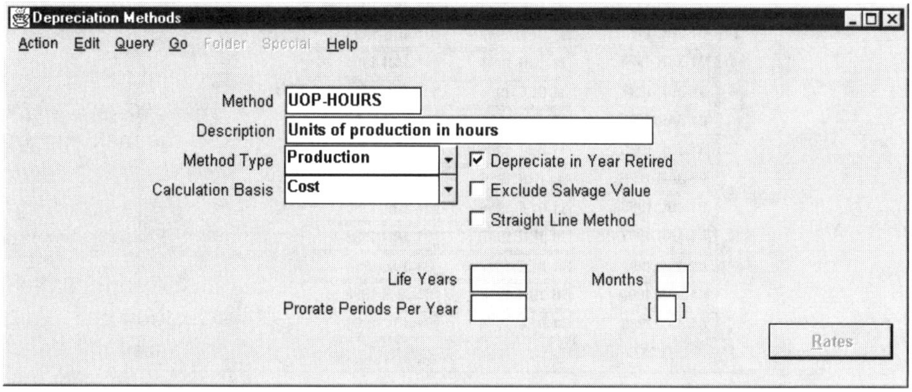

FIGURE 2-14. *Production depreciation method*

17. **Prorate/Retirement Conventions**   Using the Prorate Conventions form shown in Figure 2-15 (*Setup : Asset System : Prorate Conventions*), you can set up prorate conventions and retirement conventions. A prorate convention determines how an asset depreciates in its first year, while a retirement convention determines how it depreciates in its last year. The form's Prorate Date column lets you specify when each asset starts depreciation. For the Half-Year prorate convention, an asset starts depreciating in the first accounting period of the year if the asset is placed in service in the *first* half of the year; otherwise, the asset depreciates in the first accounting period of the *second* half of the year. For depreciation methods other than straight-line, you can specify that an asset will start depreciating when it is placed in service, instead of following the prorate convention.

18. **Price Indexes**   Price indexes allow you to calculate retirement gains or losses based on current value instead of historical cost. This is useful in countries with high inflation. The price index defined is used to adjust the recoverable cost before calculating retirement gains or losses. This form is available via the navigation path *Setup : Asset System : Price Indexes.*

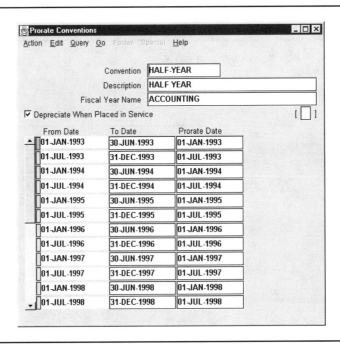

FIGURE 2-15.   *Prorate/Retirement Conventions screen*

19. Organizations   Creating an organization—which you will do later in this book—is a prerequisite to entering Unit of Measure classes. Later on, after you create your Set of Books, you will set up an organization.

20. Unit of Measure Classes   Unit of Measure classes group together Units of Measure based on an attribute. Common Unit of Measure classes include length, quantity, time, and weight. The navigation path for this form is *Setup : Financials : Units of Measure : Classes.*

21. Units of Measure   Units of Measure are used in Oracle Assets if you use the production depreciation method. For each Unit of Measure class, you define one unit of measure as the *base unit*; for additional units of measure, you define conversion rules to relate them to the base unit. There are three conversion types: Standard, Intraclass, and Interclass. *Standard* conversion is conversion to the base unit applicable for all items; for instance, standard conversion in the Length class might include "1 foot = 12 inches". *Intraclass* conversion translates values into the base unit for a specific item. *Interclass* conversion changes values into the base unit of *another* Unit of Measure class. The forms that allow you to create these rules are available by following the navigation path *Setup : Financials : Units of Measure : Units of Measure.*

22. Asset Categories   You must specify asset categories and their default financial data. This step will be covered in more detail in Chapter 5.

23. Distribution Sets   You can establish sets of employees to whom assets can be distributed in predefined portions, for predefined accounts and locations. Figure 2-16 shows the form that provides this functionality (*Setup : Asset System : Distribution Sets*). Using distribution sets facilitates faster and more accurate data entry by reducing manual entry of repetitive data. This will also reduce chances of human error.

24. Leases   You can enter leases to be assigned to assets. You can also analyze alternate leasing schedules and options to compare. You enter lease details in the Lease Details form (*Setup : Asset System : Leases : Lease Details*) shown in Figure 2-17. This form is where you enter the lease number, lease description, lessor, lease term, asset life, and whether ownership is transferred to lessee. To enter a payment schedule for the lease, you can use the Lease Payments form (*Setup : Asset System : Leases : Lease Payments*) shown in Figure 2-18. The Lease Payments form is the same as the form invoked by the **Payment Schedule** button of the Lease Details form. In addition, you can view the amortization schedule through the Car Lease Schedule form, which analyzes leases from the Lease Payment form. The Car Lease Schedule form is available from the Lease Payments form by clicking on the **View Amortization** button.

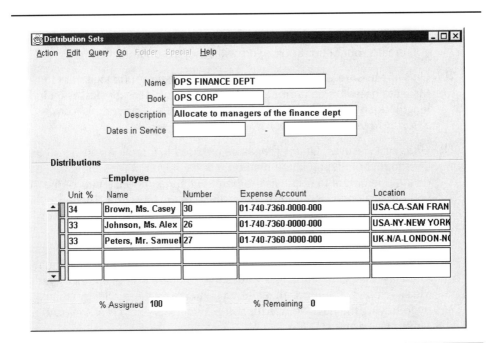

FIGURE 2-16. *Distribution Sets form*

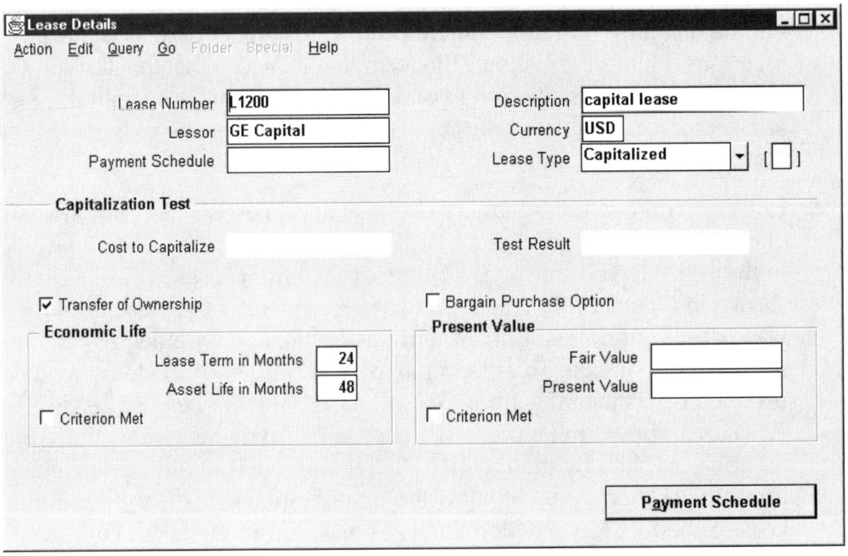

FIGURE 2-17. *Lease Details form*

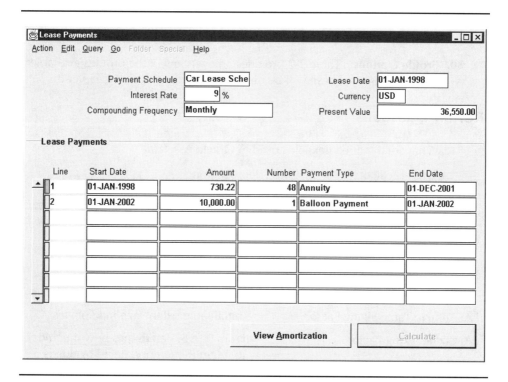

FIGURE 2-18.   *Lease Payments form*

25. **Warranties**   You can define warranties in Oracle Assets and then assign them to assets. Warranty information includes description, start date, end date, cost, assigned employee, and supplier. This form is available by following the navigation path *Setup : Asset System : Warranties.*

26. **Financial Options**   Financial options are set during an Oracle Purchasing or Oracle Payables setup, which is covered in Chapter 3.

27. **Suppliers**   Entering supplier information is another step related to the setup of Oracle Purchasing and Oracle Payables.

28. **Employees**   You can enter employees to be assigned to use assets. For a full-blown HR implementation, you can provide a lot of details for an employee. For other purposes such as Assets, you can enter the minimum required fields, such as name and national identifier.

29. **Descriptive Flexfields** See Chapter 9 for implementing Descriptive flexfields.

30. **Profile Options** Table 2-2 provides an overview of the profiles available in Oracle Assets. These will be discussed in more detail in Chapter 8.

Review Questions

1. What are the three flexfields used in Oracle Assets?

2. What is calculated/straight-line depreciation?

Profile Option	Functions
Account Generator: Purge Runtime Data	Specifies whether the Account Generator should purge runtime data generated after completion
FA: Archive Table Sizing Factor	Initial table extent size in kilobytes
FA: Cache Sizing Factor	From 0 to 5, determines how much data to retain in memory; default value is 5
FA: Large Rollback Segment	Rollback segment to be used by a long-running concurrent program, such as Depreciation
FA: Number of Parallel Requests	From 1 to 20, determines how many requests can be run in parallel to allow concurrency
FA: Print Debug	Specifies whether debug messages should be saved to log file
FA: Print Timing Diagnostics	Specifies whether timing diagnostics should be saved to log file
GL Set of Books Name	Assigned Set of Books

TABLE 2-2. *Oracle Assets Profile Options*

3. How many depreciation ceilings are there? What are they?

4. How do you set up an Investment Tax Credit (ITC)?

5. How are price indexes used?

Functionality of Multiple-Organization Support

In this section, you will learn the following about Multiple-Organization Support:

■ Organization classifications

■ Technical architecture

■ How to set up Multiple-Organization Support

Multiple-Organization Support allows you to set up multiple legal entities within a single installation of Oracle Applications. Multiple-Organization Support employs operating units to segregate data, allowing each operating unit to have its own setup parameters in the Applications subsidiary modules. Prior to Multiple-Organization Support, if you needed to segregate data from two different entities in Oracle Payables, you had to implement two separate installations of Oracle Payables.

Organization Classifications and Roles

The following organization classifications play a role in Multiple-Organization Support:

■ Government Reporting Entity (GRE)/legal entity

■ Operating unit

■ Inventory organization

■ Intercompany accounting

The following illustration depicts the relationships between legal entity, operating unit, and inventory organization:

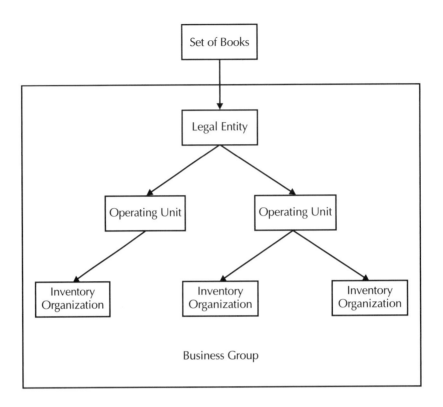

GOVERNMENT REPORTING ENTITY (GRE)/LEGAL ENTITY   A legal entity has its own employer tax identification number and prepares its own tax forms. Each legal entity has its own set of federal tax rules, state tax rules, and local tax rules, and each legal entity must point to a single Set of Books, which defines a Chart of Accounts structure, an accounting calendar, and a functional currency for that legal entity. The Set of Books segregates General Ledger and Assets data.

Later in this chapter, in the section "Setting Up Financial Controls," you will go through the steps to create a legal entity in Oracle Financials.

OPERATING UNIT   Operating units are what segregate the payables, receivables, cash management, order entry, and purchasing data. Each operating unit must point to a legal entity that has its own set of setup data and transaction tables. This means that while master table data such as supplier name, supplier type, and taxpayer ID is shared across all operating units, site-level data such as address is unique to each operating unit. If you happen to use the same supplier across two operating units, you must enter the supplier twice, once in each operating unit. When viewing data, you can only see the records for your own operating unit. Your operating unit is defined by the profile option *MO: Operating Unit* value.

INVENTORY ORGANIZATION Inventory organizations are the segregating units for bills of materials, work in process, engineering, master scheduling, material requirement planning, capacity, and inventory data. Each inventory organization must point to an operating unit. Unlike an operating unit, an inventory organization has its own set of data, including master files such as items masters. You must select an inventory organization before performing any functions related to bills of materials, work in process, engineering, master scheduling, material requirement planning, capacity, or inventory.

Another organization classification that is related to Multiple Support Organization is business group. Business groups segregate human-resources data such as employees. Business group is assigned with the profile option *HR: Business Group.* When viewing records, you can only see those assigned to your business group.

Technical Architecture

The preceding text explained how Multiple-Organization Support works from a functional perspective. How about the technical viewpoint? With Multiple-Organization Support, all Oracle Applications objects are accessed from a user schema called APPS. Figure 2-19 illustrates how the APPS schema works, using suppliers as an example.

You may recall that data about suppliers is shared across all operating units. The supplier data is stored in the PO schema, within a table named PO_VENDORS (this would be addressed as PO.PO_VENDORS in a query). This table is referred to by a synonym in the APPS schema, and the synonym has been given the same name as the table. Because a synonym has no filtering capability, the APPS.PO_VENDORS synonym provides full access to the PO.PO_VENDORS table.

The situation is a little different for supplier sites, because that data is segregated by operating units. Therefore some filtering must be put into place so that only the supplier sites related to the user's operating unit are shown to that user. This can be accomplished by using an Oracle *view*. A view is basically a SQL query statement that is stored in the database. A view can be referenced in SELECT statements like a table. Because a view can contain a SQL WHERE clause, it can filter the supplier-site data. By writing a view that selects records from PO.PO_VENDOR_SITES_ALL (the table that stores data about supplier sites) and including a WHERE clause in the view, only the appropriate records are returned to the user. The WHERE clause in the view compares the operating unit assigned to a vendor site with the operating unit ID assigned to the user through profile option *MO: Operating Unit.*

It is useful to note how the underlying table is called PO_VENDOR_SITES_ALL and the view is call PO_VENDOR_SITES. The table name and the view name give you an idea of what is going on in the background: every table whose name ends with _ALL stores data that is segregated by operating unit. As a rule of thumb, tables that contain transactional data and operating-unit partitioned module setup are always segregated by operating unit.

This example showed how the APPS schema contains synonyms and views giving the user access to records in other schemas. That is the APPS schema's job. It provides access to all of the tables in Oracle Applications, but does not itself contain any tables.

Setting Up Multiple-Organization Support

To set up Multiple-Organization Support, follow these steps:

1. Define Set of Books.

2. Define organizations.

3. Enable Multiple-Organization Support.

4. Assign or define responsibility to operating unit.

5. Assign responsibility to inventory organizations.

6. Set up the operating unit partitioned modules for each operating unit.

7. Secure companies by legal entity.

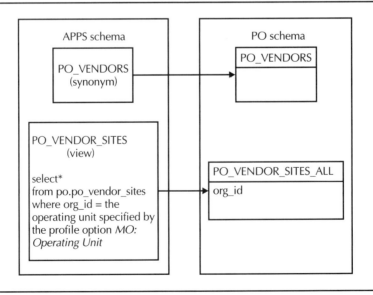

FIGURE 2-19. *Multiple-Organization schemas*

What follows is an overview of these steps.

DEFINE SET OF BOOKS   This subject is addressed in detail in the "Creating a Set of Books" section later in this chapter. We recognize that having to jump around the chapter can be somewhat inconvenient, and we apologize for that. The organization of the chapter is designed to match that of the certification Candidate Guide.

DEFINE ORGANIZATIONS   When setting up the organizations, you will need to select the correct organization classifications, and create the correct organization relationships. In order to establish a hierarchy, you must perform this step from the top down—meaning that you must define all your legal entities first, followed by the operating units that refer to the legal entities.

ENABLE MULTIPLE-ORGANIZATION SUPPORT   This step must be performed by your database administrator (DBA). It can be performed during or after the initial installation. The DBA runs the Oracle Applications AutoInstall installation process. From the AutoInstall menu, the DBA selects the option to enable multiorganization support.

ASSIGN RESPONSIBILITY TO OPERATING UNIT   Once you have set up the organization structure, it is time to assign operating units to responsibilities. This is done through the profile option *MO: Operating Unit.* If you only have one operating unit, you can set this at the site level—that is, for each inventory organization.

ASSIGN RESPONSIBILITY TO INVENTORY ORGANIZATIONS   This step only applies if you are using the Oracle Manufacturing or Supply Chain modules. Those are outside the scope of this book, so we will move on.

SET UP THE OPERATING UNIT PARTITIONED MODULES FOR EACH OPERATING UNIT   The "operating unit partitioned modules" are the applications: Oracle Payables, Receivables, Cash Management, Order Entry, and Purchasing. These must be set up separately within each operating unit that will be using them. For example, if you have two operating units and both plan to use Oracle Payables, you must set up Oracle Payables twice: once while logged on under a responsibility for operating unit 1, and again while logged on under a responsibility for operating unit 2. Logging on as a different responsibility gives you different profile option values—one set for each operating unit.

SECURE COMPANIES BY LEGAL ENTITY   A single legal entity can have multiple companies, and each company only needs to have its own balance sheet—it does not need to segregate data from other companies within the legal entity. (In other words, a company does not need to be an operating unit.) That being said, you do have the option of providing security by balancing company within a legal entity. (Remember that companies are defined as the lowest level where total debits equal total credits.) To accomplish this, you can establish accounting flexfield security rules and tie them to responsibilities that belong to the legal entity. This will be discussed in more detail in Chapter 9.

Intercompany Accounting

With Multiple-Organization Support, you can sell from one operating unit, ship from another operating unit, and have Oracle Financials generate the necessary intercompany accounting transactions. This feature of Multiple-Organization Support is in Oracle Inventory and will be covered briefly here.

To set up intercompany relations, you must log on using the responsibility *Inventory, Vision Operations (USA)* and follow the navigation path *Setup : Organizations : Intercompany Relations* to reach the Intercompany Relations form (shown in Figure 2-20). You start by identifying the shipping operating unit and the selling operating unit. Then, you specify the customer in the shipping operating unit that represents the selling operating unit. Next, you identify the supplier in the selling operating unit that represents the shipping operating unit, and then save the setup.

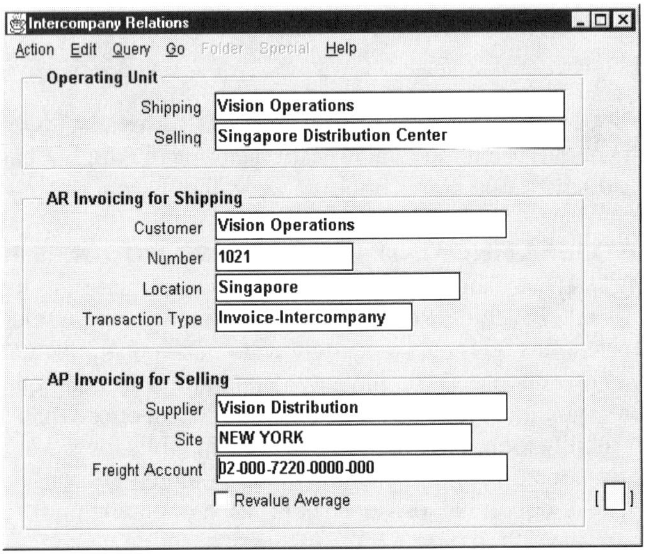

FIGURE 2-20. *Intercompany Relations form*

Once you have set up intercompany relations, there are two processes in Oracle Inventory that facilitate the creation of intercompany payable and receivable invoices. The first process is *Create Intercompany AP Invoices*, which generates intercompany payables invoices in the shipping operating unit. These invoices show the selling operating unit as the supplier, and they contain accounting entries in the following format:

Accounts	Debit	Credit
Selling Cost of Sales	Transfer Price	
Selling Freight		Freight amount
Selling Intercompany Payables		Transfer Price + Freight amount

The second process is *Create Intercompany AR Invoices*, which generates intercompany receivable invoices in the selling operating unit. These invoices show the shipping operating unit as the customer, along with accounting entries like this:

Accounts	Debit	Credit
Shipping Receivables	Transfer Price + Freight amount	
Shipping Intercompany Revenue		Transfer Price
Shipping Freight		Freight amount

Review Questions

1. What are operating units, Sets of Books, legal entities, and inventory organizations? How are they related?

2. What Oracle Applications modules are partitioned by operating units?

3. Which profile option enables you to assign an operating unit to a responsibility?

4. Which database schema provides access to all Oracle Applications tables?

Vision Demonstration Database Structure

In this section, you will find out how the Vision demonstration database provided with Financials is structured, how the Sets of Books are set up, and what applications can be used by the main seeded users.

Table 2-3 shows how the Vision database is structured.

Legal Entities	Operating Units	Inventory Organizations	Sets of Books
Singapore Distribution Center	Singapore Distribution Center	Singapore Distribution Center	Vision Distribution
Vision ADB	Vision ADB	Vision ADB	Vision ADB
Vision Operations	Vision Operations	Boston Manufacturing	Vision Operations
Vision Operations	Vision Operations	Chicago Subassembly Plant	Vision Operations
Vision Operations	Vision Operations	Dallas Manufacturing	Vision Operations
Vision Operations	Vision Operations	Maintenance-Plant 2	Vision Operations
Vision Operations	Vision Operations	Miami Distribution Center	Vision Operations
Vision Operations	Vision Operations	Seattle Manufacturing	Vision Operations
Vision Operations	Vision Operations	Vision Operations	Vision Operations
Vision Project Mfg.	Vision Project Mfg.	Atlanta Manufacturing	Project Mfg.
Vision Project Mfg.	Vision Project Mfg.	Cleveland Manufacturing	Project Mfg.
Vision Project Mfg.	Vision Project Mfg.	Los Angeles Manufacturing	Project Mfg.
Vision Project Mfg.	Vision Project Mfg	San Diego Manufacturing	Project Mfg.
Vision Project Mfg.	Vision Project Mfg.	Vision Project Mfg.	Project Mfg.
Vision Services	Vision Services	Vision Services	Vision Services

TABLE 2-3. *Vision Database Structures*

Table 2-4 shows how the Sets of Books are set up.

Table 2-5 shows some of the predefined users, along with the application modules they can access.

Review Questions

1. How many legal entities are in the Vision database? How many operating units? How many inventory organizations?

2. What are the differences between the Sets of Books in the Vision database?

Short Name	Name	Accounting Flexfield	Currency	Calendar
Project Mfg.	Vision Project Mfg. (MRC)	Project Mfg. Accounting Flex	ANY	4-4-5 Calendar
Project Mfg. (EURO)	Vision Project Mfg (EURO Rpt)	Project Mfg Accounting Flex	EUR	4-4-5 Calendar
Project Mfg. (USA)	Vision Project Mfg. (USA Rpt.)	Project Mfg. Accounting Flex	USD	4-4-5 Calendar
Vision ADB	Vision ADB (USA)	ADB Accounting Flex	USD	Accounting
Vision Corporation	Vision Corporation (UK)	Corporate Accounting Flex	GBP	Fiscal
Vision Distribution	Vision Distribution (SNG)	Distribution Accounting Flex	SGD	Accounting
Vision Operations	Vision Operations (USA)	Operations Accounting Flex	USD	Accounting
Vision Services	Vision Services (USA)	Service Accounting Flex	USD	Weekly

TABLE 2-4. *Vision Sets of Books*

User	Assigned Modules
ADB	General Ledger, Assets, Payables, Purchasing, System Administration
CORPORATE	General Ledger
DISTRIBUTION	General Ledger, Receivables, Inventory, System Administration
MFG	Alert, Service, EDI, Purchasing, Supplier Scheduling, Receivables, Quality, Order Entry, Manufacturing, Project Manufacturing, Inventory, System Administration
OPERATIONS	Alert, EDI, General Ledger, Assets, Payables, Purchasing, Receivables, Quality, Cash Management, Sales and Marketing, Sales Compensation, Order Entry, Inventory, Manufacturing, Project Manufacturing, Human Resources, System Administration
PROJMFG	General Ledger, Assets, Alert, Payables, Purchasing, Receivables, Cash Management, Projects, Order Entry, Inventory, Human Resources, System Administration
SERVICES	General Ledger, Assets, Alert, Payables, Purchasing, Receivables, Cash Management, Projects, Inventory, Human Resources, System Administration

TABLE 2-5.   *Users and Their Assigned Modules*

Creating a Chart of Accounts

In this section, you will learn more about:

■ Value sets

■ Accounting flexfield structure

■ Entering and controlling accounting flexfield segment values

■ Entering and maintaining accounting flexfield combinations for posting and budgeting

■ Creating flexfield security and cross-validation rules

Now you are ready to create your Chart of Accounts. A Chart of Accounts is the account structure you use to record accounting transactions and maintain accounting balances. In Oracle General Ledger, the Chart of Accounts is a key flexfield. (Key flexfields are discussed in more detail in Unit II.) Briefly, a flexfield is a combination of one or more data segments defined by the user. For an Oracle Chart of Accounts, you can configure up to 30 segments in a flexfield. At a minimum, you must define two segments: one for the balancing segment, and one to record the natural account. In the following exercise, you will create a Chart of Accounts with three segments: company, cost center, and account.

Value Sets

Value sets govern the valid values for each segment of your Chart of Accounts. There are six validation types: Dependent, Independent, None, Pair, Special, and Table. The most common of these are Independent, in which case you predefine the valid values, and None, where there is no validation—you can enter whatever you want as long as the data fits the field's format.

For your Chart of Accounts, you will create three Independent value sets. To do this, make sure you are logged in under the responsibility *General Ledger – Vision Operations (USA)*. Then, follow the navigation path *Setup : Financials : Flexfields : Validation : Sets*. This will take you to the Value Sets form, shown in Figure 2-21. For the first value set, enter a Value Set Name of **NEW-Company**, enter a Maximum Size of **2**, and enable the option labeled *Right-justify and Zero-fill Numbers (0001)*. Then, use the menu command Action | Save to save the data. For the second value set, enter a Value Set Name of **NEW-Cost Centers**, enter a Maximum Size of **4**, and enable the option labeled *Right-justify and Zero-fill Numbers (0001)*. Save that value set, and then for the third value set, enter a Value Set Name of **NEW-Accounts**, enter a Maximum Size of **6**, and enable the option labeled *Right-justify and Zero-fill Numbers (0001)*.

The other options in the Value Sets form will be described in Unit II.

Review Questions

1. What is the business purpose of value sets?

2. What are the six validation types? What are the differences between them?

Accounting Flexfield Structure

Once you have set up your three value sets, you are ready to create the accounting flexfield structure for your Chart of Accounts. You do this through the Key Flexfield Segments form, which appears when you follow the navigation path *Setup :*

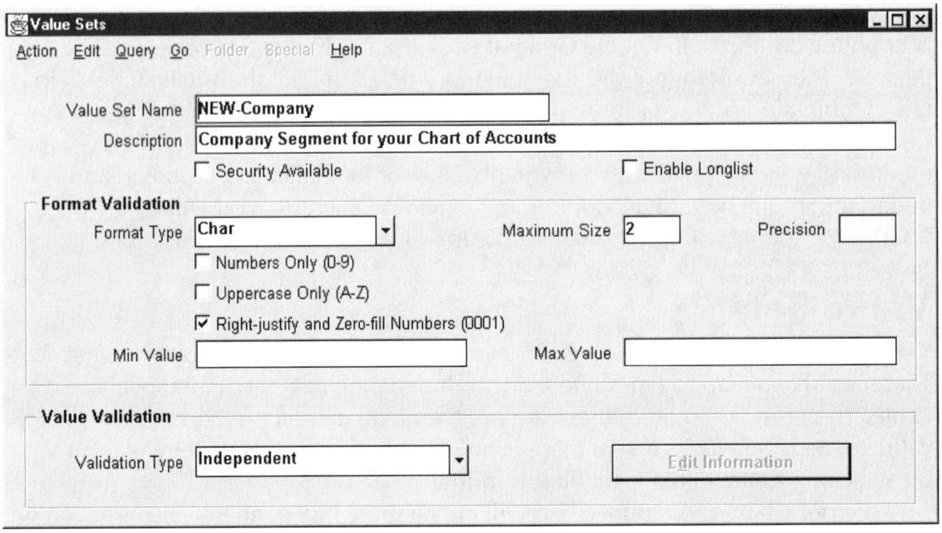

FIGURE 2-21. *Value Sets form*

Financials : Flexfields : Key : Segments. To create a new accounting flexfield structure, execute the menu command Query | Find…, select the title Oracle General Ledger in the Find Key Flexfield window, and click on the **OK** button. This will produce a form that looks like Figure 2-22, displaying the existing flexfield structures for that application. Using your mouse, click on any of the structure lines shown in the middle of the form, in order to move the focus to that portion of the form. Now click on the **New** button in the toolbar to add your own accounting flexfield structure (you can also execute the menu command Edit | New Record). Enter a title of **NEW Accounting Flex**, and check the *Cross-Validate Segments* checkbox and the *Allow Dynamic Inserts* checkbox. Then click on the **Segments** button. When the Segments Summary form appears, enter the values shown in Table 2-6.

You may get a warning message complaining that your list of values prompt is longer than your segment size. If so, dispatch it by clicking on its **OK** button. Once you have entered the segment structure of the accounting flexfield, you must identify the three segments you just entered as the flexfield's *qualifiers*. A key flexfield requires the following three types of qualifiers:

- The Balancing Segment qualifier is used to denote the segment used to balance the account. Oracle General Ledger will ensure that all debits equal all credits for each unique value in the balancing segment.

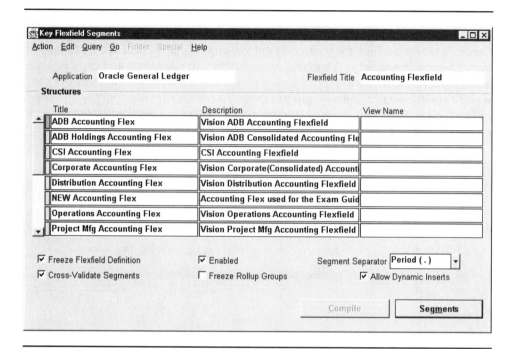

FIGURE 2-22.   *Key Flexfield Segments*

■   The Cost Center Segment qualifier identifies the cost center segment for this
    flexfield. This is only used in the Oracle Assets module.

■   The Natural Account Segment qualifier specifies which segment contains
    the account type for an account combination. (Account types can be Assets,
    Liability, Expense, Revenue, or Ownership/Stockholder's Equity.)

Number	Name	Window Prompt	Column	Value Set	Displayed	Enabled
1	Company	Company	SEGMENT1	NEW-Company	√	√
2	Cost Center	Cost Center	SEGMENT2	NEW-Cost Center	√	√
3	Account	Account	SEGMENT3	NEW-Accounts	√	√

TABLE 2-6.   *Segment Values for a New Key Flexfield*

Click on the button labeled **Flexfield Qualifiers**. Check the appropriate qualifier checkboxes to mark Balancing Segment qualifier for your company segment, Cost Center Segment qualifier for your cost center segment, and natural account segment for your account segment. When you are finished, you can freeze and compile your accounting flexfield. To do this, you must go back to the first form in either of two ways: close the second form, or just put the focus back to the first form by clicking on it. Once you are back in the first form, check the *Freeze Flexfield Definition* checkbox and save the record. Figure 2-23 shows the Key Flexfield Segments form.

Review Questions

1. What are the six types of validation sets?

2. How do you create a new flexfield structure?

3. What are the three types of qualifiers an accounting flexfield needs?

4. What are the five account types for a natural account?

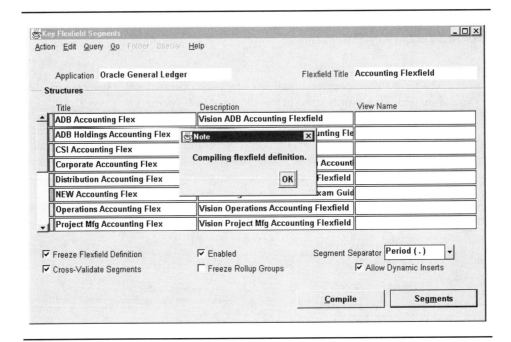

FIGURE 2-23. *Key accounting segments*

Entering and Controlling Accounting Flexfield Segment Values

Now that you have set up your Chart of Accounts, it is time to enter some valid values for each of the Chart of Accounts' segments. Follow the navigation path *Setup : Financials : Flexfields : Key : Values* and you will see that two forms open: the Segment Values form stays in the background, waiting for you to choose your segment structure in the Find Key Flexfield Segment form. To do this, make sure the *Find Values By* option group in the form is set to Key Flexfield, and then click on the Structure field and execute the Edit | List of Values menu command. Choose your structure from the list, click on the **OK** button and then click on the **Find** button. This will return you to the Segment Values form. If the drop-down list in the middle of the form says *Effective*, change it to *Hierarchy, Qualifiers*. Then create segment values using Table 2-7 as your guide. Figure 2-24 will help you correlate values from the table with their appropriate locations on the Segment Values form.

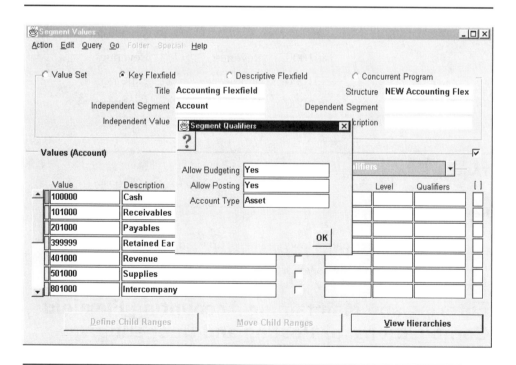

FIGURE 2-24.   *Segment Values form*

Independent Segment	Value	Description	Account Type
Company	01	Wing Company	
	02	Golden Company	
Cost Center	0000	Corporate	
	1000	Administration	
	2010	East	
	2020	West	
	2030	North	
	2040	South	
Account	100000	Cash	Asset
	101000	Receivables	Asset
	201000	Payables	Liability
	399999	Retained Earnings	Ownership/ Stockholder's Equity
	401000	Revenue	Revenue
	501000	Supplies	Expense
	801000	Intercompany	Expense
	999999	Suspense	Expense

TABLE 2-7. *Accounting Flexfield Segment Values*

Review Questions

1. What navigation path allows you to set up valid segment values?

2. What segment requires you to enter account types?

Entering and Maintaining Accounting Flexfield Combinations for Posting and Budgeting

You can use the GL Accounts form (navigation path *Setup : Accounts : Combinations*) to enter accounting flexfield combinations. When you set up an account combination, the *Allow Posting* and *Allow Budgeting* checkboxes take their default values from the *Allow Posting* and *Allow Budgeting* settings at the segment values level. Figure 2-25 shows these options.

Since you enabled the *Allow Dynamic Inserts* option earlier in this chapter, you do not have to define account combinations before you can use them.

Review Questions

1. What does the *Allow Budgeting* option control? The *Allow Posting* option? At what level can you set these options?

2. Where does the *Allow Budgeting* option on the GL Accounts form get its value by default?

3. What does the *Allow Dynamic Inserts* option do?

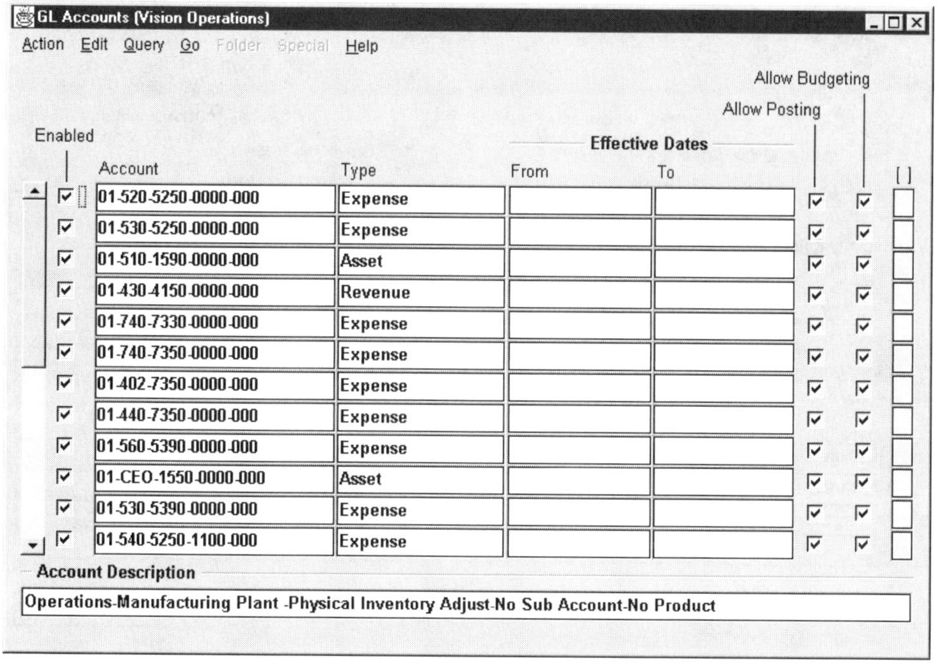

FIGURE 2-25. *GL Accounts screen*

Creating Flexfield Security and Cross-Validation Rules

This section provides an overview of security rules and cross-validation rules. These topics will be covered in more detail in Chapter 9.

Security Rules

Security rules are used to limit access to certain segment values for a particular segment. They are commonly used to limit access to specific companies within a legal entity, as well as to define which responsibilities can access a secured cost center. Figure 2-26 shows a sample form (*Setup : Financials : Flexfields : Key : Security : Define*) in which security rules are defined, and Figure 2-27 shows the form (*Setup : Financials : Flexfields : Key : Security : Assign*) in which a rule is assigned to an application and a responsibility.

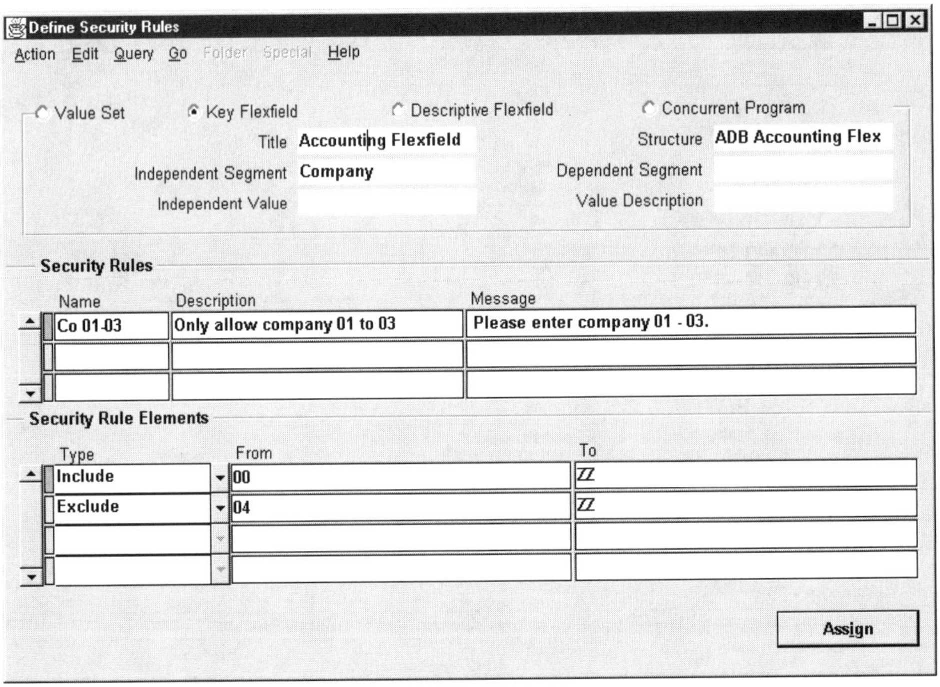

FIGURE 2-26. *Define Security Rules form*

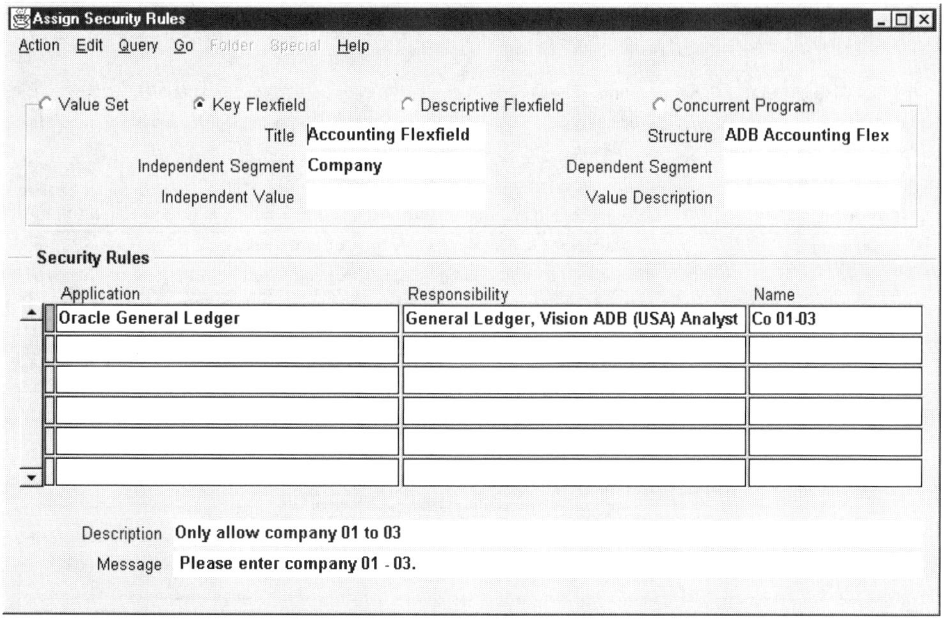

FIGURE 2-27. *Assign Security Rules form*

Cross-Validation Rules

Cross-validation rules validate data across segments of a flexfield. For example, if cost center 2010 is valid for company 01 but not for company 02, you can set up cross-validation rules that exclude account combinations between 02.2010.000000 and 02.2010.ZZZZZZ. The values 0 to Z span all valid characters and are used to exclude or include all possible segment values. If a segment is numeric only, you can use 0 to 9 instead. Figure 2-28 shows a sample Cross-Validation Rules form, which is available via the navigation path *Setup : Financials : Flexfields : Key : Rules.*

Review Questions

1. What is the purpose of a security rule?

2. What do cross-validation rules do?

3. What is the difference between a value of 9 in a cross-validation rule and a value of Z?

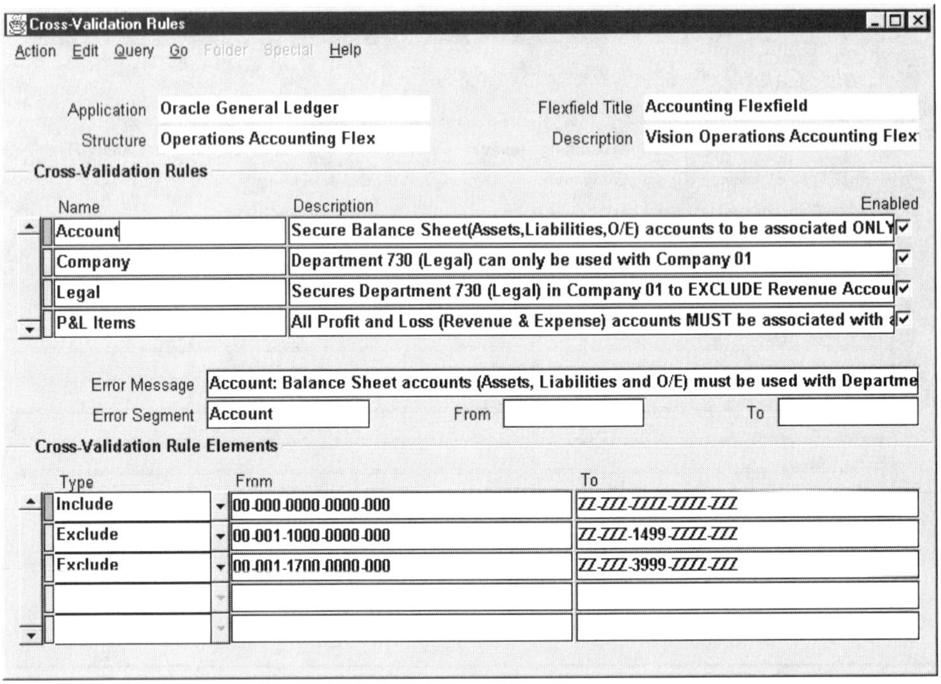

FIGURE 2-28. *Cross-Validation Rules form*

Creating a Set of Books

Now that your Chart of Accounts has been set up, you are almost ready to establish a Set of Books. There are a few prerequisites that must be taken care of first. The following list identifies tasks that must be completed before you can establish a Set of Books.

1. Define the Chart of Accounts (you have already done this).

2. Define the accounting calendar.

3. Define your implementation's functional currency.

This section will cover all of these items. It will then step you through the process of defining a Set of Books and setting up financial controls.

Defining an Accounting Calendar

To set up an accounting calendar, go to the Accounting Calendar form (*Setup : Financials : Calendar : Accounting*). After entering a calendar name and description, you define the periods that make up the calendar. Each period's name starts with its prefix, which is combined with the last two digits of the calendar's year to create the complete accounting period name. In a standard calendar, prefixes are usually month names or abbreviations. Next, you specify the period type, the year, the quarter and period number within that year, and the date range for the period. The calendar you set up here serves as a master to most of the other application modules. (Oracle Assets has depreciation and prorate calendars of its own, and Oracle Inventory has its own manufacturing calendar.) If a period is an adjustment period, you can specify so by checking the *Adjusting* checkbox. Only an adjusting period can have dates overlapping those of another accounting period in the same calendar.

TIP
In some versions of the Vision database, there is a gap in the fiscal calendar where the February 2000 period's end date is 28-FEB-00 instead of 29-FEB-00. Check yours and fix it if it manifests this problem.

Review Questions

1. How are accounting period names derived?

2. If you are setting up a calendar fiscal year, what will you enter as September's period number? How about for its quarter number?

3. How will Oracle subledgers use the accounting calendar?

4. How is an adjustment period different than an accounting period?

Defining Currencies

Because of the number of currencies already defined in Oracle Financials, it is unlikely you will need to actually define a new one. If you ever do need to define a new currency, however, you can do so by using the Currencies form (*Setup : Currencies : Define*).

Defining a Set of Books

Now you can set up your Set of Books. Follow the navigation path *Setup : Financials : Books : Define* to go to the Set of Books form. Enter a Set of Books name of **Vision NEW (DEM)**, and then a short name of **Vision NEW**. In the other fields, select the Chart of Accounts you defined, the functional currency DEM, and an accounting calendar setting of Fiscal. Then, enter your Retained Earnings, Suspense and Intercompany accounts. You can do this by placing your cursor in the Retained Earnings field and typing in the Retained Earnings account combination, and then following similar procedures for the Suspense and Intercompany accounts.

There are four options tied to a Set of Books:

1. *Standard options* let you enable or disable the following features:

   - Suspense posting

   - Automatic balance intercompany journals during posting

   - Average balance processing

   - Journal approval feature for manual journals

   - Automatic generation of tax journal lines based on tax amounts

2. *Average Balance options* apply only if you enabled average balance processing in the standard options. Average Balance options are where you specify the following parameters:

   - Whether the Set of Books is the consolidation Set of Books

   - Transaction calendar used to verify business days if the Set of Books is not the consolidation Set of Books

   - Conversion rate type to be used to translate average balance

   - Any additional amount types to translate besides period-to-date balances

3. *Budgetary Control options* let you enable budgetary control. If you turn on the *Require Budget Journal* option, the user can only enter budget amounts through journals or other programs that generate budget journals; they cannot enter budget amounts directly, use budget upload, or use a budget formula. You may want to implement this option if you always want an audit trail for entering or modifying budgets.

4. *Reporting Currency options* are used only when you want to use Multiple Reporting Currencies (MRC). If you use MRC, this is where you identify the Set of Books as the primary Set of Books or reporting Set of Books.

You will go through these options step by step in Chapter 3.

Review Questions

1. What three prerequisites must be in place before you can define a Set of Books?

2. What four options are tied to defining a Set of Books?

3. What control can you exercise through the Average Balancing options?

Setting Up Financial Controls

Once you set up your Set of Books, you can assign it to a responsibility by opening the Profile Values form (navigation path *Other : Profile*) and modifying the profile option *GL: Set of Books Name*. This will limit user access to financial data within the assigned Set of Books. (In Unit II you will create a responsibility and then assign your Set of Books to it.)

Now you are ready to set up your organization structure. Change your login responsibility to *Assets, Vision Operations (USA)* and then follow the navigation path *Setup : Financials : Organizations* to the form titled Organization. Enter an organization name of **New Distribution Center**, specify that the location is **Bristol**, and save your work by executing the menu command Action | Save. Your form should now look similar to Figure 2-29.

The organization you just created, New Distribution Center, is a division that will tie to your Set of Books. New Distribution Center will also serve as a legal entity, an operating unit, and an inventory organization.

Now you will set up the organization's classifications. Move to the Organization Classifications area of the form and click on the first blank field in the Name column. Type **GRE / Legal Entity** (or you can select it using the Edit | List of Values command). Check that row's *Enabled* checkbox, and save your work using the Action | Save menu command. Then click on the **Others** button. From the list of values that appears, choose Legal Entity Accounting. This will cause a dialog box titled Additional Organization Information to appear, and when you click on the large open field in that dialog box, a second dialog box titled Legal Entity Accounting appears. Enter your Set of Books in this dialog box's Set of Books field and compare the results with the illustration shown here.

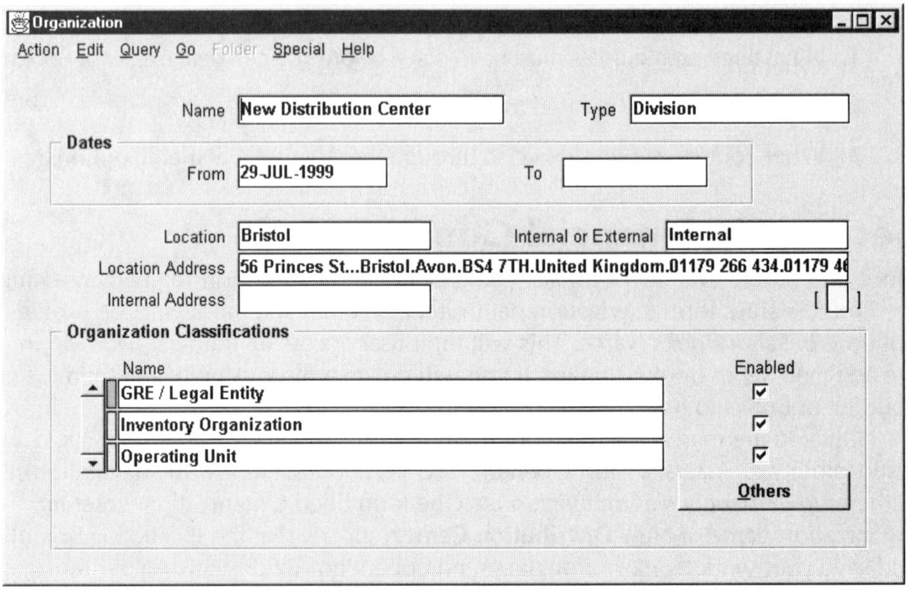

FIGURE 2-29. *Organization form*

Click on the **OK** button to close this dialog box; then click on the Additional Organization Information dialog box's **OK** button, and then on the **Yes** button on the Confirmation dialog box that appears.

For the next Organization Classification entry, enter **Operating Unit**, check its row's *Enabled* checkbox, and save your work. Then click on the **Others** button and enter **New Distribution Center** as the legal entity to which this operating unit is assigned. (Yes, you are pointing New Distribution Center to New Distribution Center itself.) Save this information, and then for the third Organization Classification enter **Inventory Organization**, check the *Enabled* checkbox and save your work. Click on the **Others** button while your cursor is on the Inventory Organization entry and select Accounting Information from the list of values that appears. When the Accounting Information dialog box appears, enter your Set of Books name in the Set of Books field, and enter **New Distribution Center** as the legal entity and the operating unit. Then click on **OK** buttons until you are back to the Organization form, and save your work.

Review Questions

1. What prerequisites must be taken care of before you can enter a Set of Books?

2. What four options are included in the definition of a Set of Books?

3. What does the *Suspense Account* checkbox do?

4. What does the *Intercompany Account* checkbox do?

Implementation Considerations

In this final section of Chapter 2, you will learn about the common implementation considerations that arise when you set up a Chart of Accounts and a Set of Books.

Considerations for Setting Up a Set of Books

Before you create a Set of Books, ask yourself the following questions:

- How many functional currencies do you need?

- How many accounting calendars do you use?

- How many Chart of Accounts structures do you have?

- Do all of your organizations practice the same general accounting processes for handling suspense accounting, intercompany accounting, budget journals, manual journal entries approval, and taxation for journals?

- Do all of your organizations allow the same timeframe for entering journals into future periods?

- Do your organizations use average balance processing as well as standard balance processing?

- Can you consolidate your business processes and setups so you can answer more of the preceding questions with a Yes? Besides the three major areas—Chart of Accounts, functional currency, and accounting calendar—the general accounting practices can often benefit from being consolidated.

Create a matrix with your organizations and the way each organization handles the preceding questions. Each unique combination of how your organization handles those questions will become one Set of Books. The matrix might look like this:

	Chart of Accounts	Calendar	Currency	Suspense	Inter-company	Future Periods ...
Org 1, Org 2	Comp.Acct.CC	Fiscal	USD	N	N	1
Org 3	Comp.CC.Acct.Sub	Account	GEM	N	Y	1
Org n	Comp.Prod.Acct	Fiscal	GBP	Y	Y	2

TIP
If the only difference between organizations is functional currencies, you still need two Sets of Books. However, with Multiple Reporting Currencies you can set one Set of Books as the primary Set of Books and the other as the reporting Set of Books. The advantages and disadvantages will be discussed in Chapter 4.

Review Questions

1. Name at least five factors to consider before setting up Sets of Books.

2. Under what conditions would it make sense to use multiple Sets of Books?

3. In what situation would you consider using Multiple Reporting Currencies instead of multiple Sets of Books?

Considerations for Setting Up a Chart of Accounts

The elements to consider before setting up a Chart of Accounts fall into the following categories:

- Reporting
- Growth
- Budgeting
- Security
- Validation
- Datatypes
- Ordering

Reporting

One of the most important functions of a Chart of Accounts is satisfying reporting needs. The Chart of Accounts is used everywhere in the Oracle Applications system, and it serves as an easy, effective way to capture and partition data. For example, all payables distributions have account combinations, and all purchasing distributions have account combinations. If data is captured and partitioned correctly, you can develop reports showing the correct data— regardless of what reporting tool you use.

With financial reports, it is even easier. In General Ledger, you can use the *Financial Statement Generator* (FSG) to create user-defined financial reports based on the Chart of Accounts. In other words, without any third-party reporting tools, you can still create essential financial reports in General Ledger…*if* your Chart of Accounts is designed correctly.

However, not all reports should be produced using the Chart of Accounts. There is a trade-off for everything. If you create too many segments, trying to capture data at too detailed a level, you will have two problems. First, data entry will be very cumbersome; a Chart of Accounts with 15 segments will be difficult to use. Second, because balances are stored by Chart of Accounts, a Chart of Accounts with many segments creates a large volume of balances, and performance could suffer as a result. Consider using other means—such as Oracle Projects—to capture detailed data. Payables and purchasing data are also partitioned by projects and tasks in Oracle Projects.

Growth

Consider growth when designing the Chart of Accounts. You will encounter two types of growth:

- The need for more segments
- The need for more room within each segment

SEGMENTS   Your business may only need a three-segmented Chart of Accounts today. However, tomorrow you could need another segment to support new reporting requirements, or to reflect mergers and acquisitions, or any of numerous other business possibilities. It is a good idea to include a "to be determined" (TBD) segment in your Chart of Accounts to accommodate future growth. Since you will not be using the segment right away, you can set up a default value for it to speed data entry.

ROOM WITHIN EACH SEGMENT   Be reasonably generous when deciding the number of bytes for each segment in the Chart of Accounts. For example, if you only have 25 cost centers, a 2-byte segment would seem to be plenty, since it can identify a total of 100 companies (including company "00"). However, you may find in the future that you want to add a cost center whose number is *between* two existing cost centers. You cannot do that if the segment's limited size forced you to number cost centers sequentially. With this in mind, you might prefer to number your existing cost centers in intervals of 10—so your first cost center would be number 10, and your second cost center would be number 20. In addition, rollup groups are based on phantom values in the segments, so if you want rollup functionality, you must provide sufficient segment space to include rollup values in the segment numbering.

If you choose to make a numeric segment larger than its current values require, you can simplify data entry by enabling the segment's *Right-Justification* and *Zero-Fill* options. This way the user can, for instance, enter **10** in a two-digit field and have it automatically become 0010.

Budgeting
At what level will you be budgeting and encumbering? This will affect your Chart of Accounts design, since you budget and encumber by the Chart of Accounts. You can budget and encumber at a summary level of your Chart of Accounts, but you cannot budget and encumber at a level lower than your Chart of Accounts.

Security
Financial reports and financial data can be filtered based on security rules, and security rules can be based on combinations of segment values. How do you want to take advantage of these security rules? If cost center is a segment of your Chart of Accounts, you can achieve cost-center-level security.

Validation
You may recall from earlier sections about cross-validation rules that you can use these to validate data across segments. It pays to think about this before setting up the Chart of Accounts and determine whether you can utilize this feature to your benefit.

Datatypes
It is important to select the datatypes of your Chart of Accounts carefully, because you cannot change them later on. Remember that rollup values are also valid segment values, so if you want to have character-based rollup values such as CASH, you will need to set the rollup segment up as alphanumeric, even if the lowest levels of the segment are always numeric.

Ordering
The order of the sequence of segments in the Chart of Accounts is important for logical and easy data entry. You can rearrange the order easier in FSGs, because

you can use row order to place the segments in any order you want...or even hide some of the segments. In addition, the use of cross-validation rules and dependent value sets may dictate the order: if you want to have a cross-validation rule or dependent value be based on another segment, that segment must be earlier in the segment sequence than the cross-validation rule or the dependent value.

Review Questions

1. Name the three major things that lead to a separate Set of Books besides general accounting practices.

2. Name three general accounting practices that will lead to a separate Set of Books.

3. What are the trade-offs for having a detailed Chart of Accounts?

4. What are the two kinds of growth you can build into your Chart of Accounts?

For the Chapter summary, Two-Minute Drill, and Chapter Questions and Answers, open the summary.htm file contained in the Summary_files directory on the book's CD-ROM.

CHAPTER
3

Basic Journal Entries
and Reporting

n this chapter, you will learn about basic journal entries and reporting. The chapter is divided into two major sections, which will cover the following topics:

- Creating basic journal entries
- Reporting and analysis tools

Creating basic journal entries involves a variety of different facets. You will learn how to enter, post, review, and reverse journal entries; how to import journals from the Application Desktop Integrator (ADI) (formerly referred to as General Ledger Desktop Integrator (GLDI)) and import journal entries from subledgers; and how to create formula journals, recurring journals, allocation journals, and summary accounts. Then you will progress to the reporting and analysis tools. You will start by learning how to use Financial Statement Generators (FSGs) and the ADI to generate financial reports. You will also learn how to integrate Oracle General Ledger with Oracle Financial Analyzer. To wrap the chapter up, you will run simple consolidations.

Creating Basic Journal Entries

In this section, you will learn how to perform the following functions:

- Enter, post, review journal entries
- Reverse journal entries
- Import journal entries
- Enter journal entries through GLDI
- Create recurring and formula journal entries
- Approve manual journal entries
- Use balancing accounts
- Create summary accounts
- Transfer balances between accounts

Journal entries are accounting transactions. They can be manually entered; or they can come from subledgers such as Payables, Purchasing, and Receivables; or they can be automatically generated as formula journals and recurring journals. Journal entries have no effect on account balances until they are posted. For manually entered journals, you can even require approval before posting. Once journal entries are posted, the account balances are updated and you cannot "undo" them—you can only reverse them.

You can also use journal entries to transfer balances between accounts. Summary accounts come into play here, because summary accounts are frequently used as source accounts in allocations.

Entering, Posting, and Reviewing Journal Entries

In this section, you will:

- Enter journal entries

- Review journal entries

- Post journal entries

- Review posting results

Entering Journal Entries

To enter journal entries, log in to Oracle Financials using the *General Ledger, Vision Operations (USA)* responsibility and follow the navigation path *Journals : Enter.* You will be presented with a window titled Find Journals. This window is presented so you can identify the batch in which the journals should be entered. Batches contain journals, and journals contain journal entries. When you want to add journals to an existing batch, or add journal lines to existing journals, you use this form to find the batch or journal first.

Since you have not entered any data yet, choose the **New Batch** button now to create a new batch for storing journals. This opens the Batch form, which is shown in Figure 3-1. Enter a batch name and description of your choosing. Notice that the accounting period is already filled in with the value of the latest period. You can enter a different accounting period if you wish, or clear the field and not enter one at all. If you do enter an accounting period at the batch level, all journals belonging to that batch must be in that accounting period.

For the purposes of this exercise, accept the default accounting period.

Note that the value in the Posting Status field defaults to Unposted. In the Control Total field, you can enter a value that will be matched with the total debits of all journal lines. This is to ensure accuracy and completeness when the journal lines are entered. (You can also leave this field blank.)

Click on the **Journals** button now to open the Journals form. Once it has opened, enter whatever values you like for the journal name, category, description (optional),

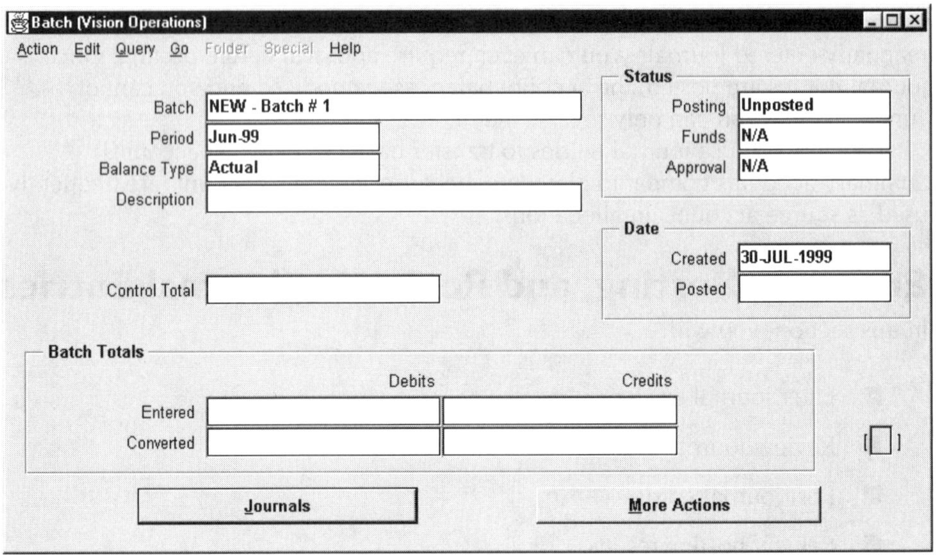

FIGURE 3-1. *Journal Batch form*

and control total (also optional). The journal source is set to Manual and cannot be updated—this is how the system identifies manual journal entries.

Now you are ready to enter journal lines. Enter a line number of **1** and then enter an account of your choosing, the debit amount or credit amount, and an optional description. After the first line, the line numbers will fill in automatically. Figure 3-2 shows a pair of journal lines that transfer $100 to pay property tax.

Posting Journal Entries

You have completed a journal and now you are ready to post. There are two ways of posting journal entries. One approach—which you should *not* complete right now, because this exercise will take you through the other approach—is to click on the **More Actions** button, and then click on the **Post** button. However, the approach you will take is more interesting from a learning perspective. This second approach is to post through the Post Journals form available via the navigation path *Journals : Post*. (Be sure to save your work before returning to the Navigator window to follow this navigation path.) Go to the Post Journals form and query/find the journal batch you just created. Verify the information and, assuming it is satisfactory, check the checkbox on the left side of its line to indicate it should be included in posting. Then click on the

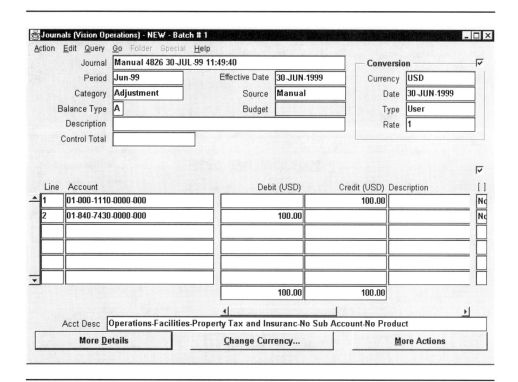

FIGURE 3-2. *Journals and journal lines*

Post button. A dialog box will appear showing the "concurrent request ID" for your posting (shown in Figure 3-3). As the posting process is run via a concurrent process, click on the dialog's **OK** button to continue.

Reviewing Posting Results

To check the status of your posting, open the Help menu and select View My Requests. Enter your concurrent request ID and then click on the **Find** button. The View My Requests form includes a button labeled **View Output**. This takes you to a posting execution report, which should show that all batches have completed status check with no errors. Then, you can review the results using the Account Inquiry form (navigation path *Inquiry : Account*, shown in Figure 3-4). Enter criteria that fit the journal you entered, then click on the **Show Balances** button. The Detail Balances form that appears lists the balances that hit the account(s) you identified during the specified accounting period(s).

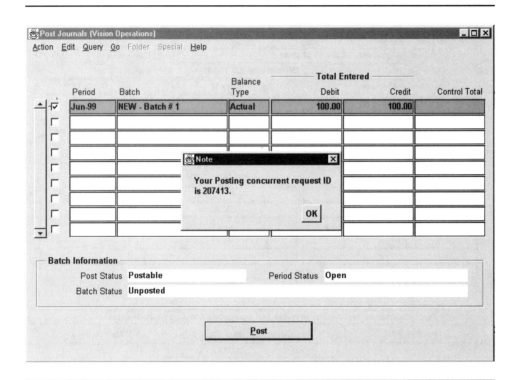

FIGURE 3-3. *Post Journals form*

Now click on the **Journal Details** button to see what journal entries make up the account balances. You should find your journal in the list.

Review Questions

   1. How are journal entries organized?

   2. What effect do journal entries have on account balances?

   3. Name two things you can do using the **More Actions** button in the Enter Journals form.

Reversing Journal Entries

As mentioned earlier in this chapter, once the posting program in Oracle Financials has updated account balances, you cannot alter the posted journals—you can only

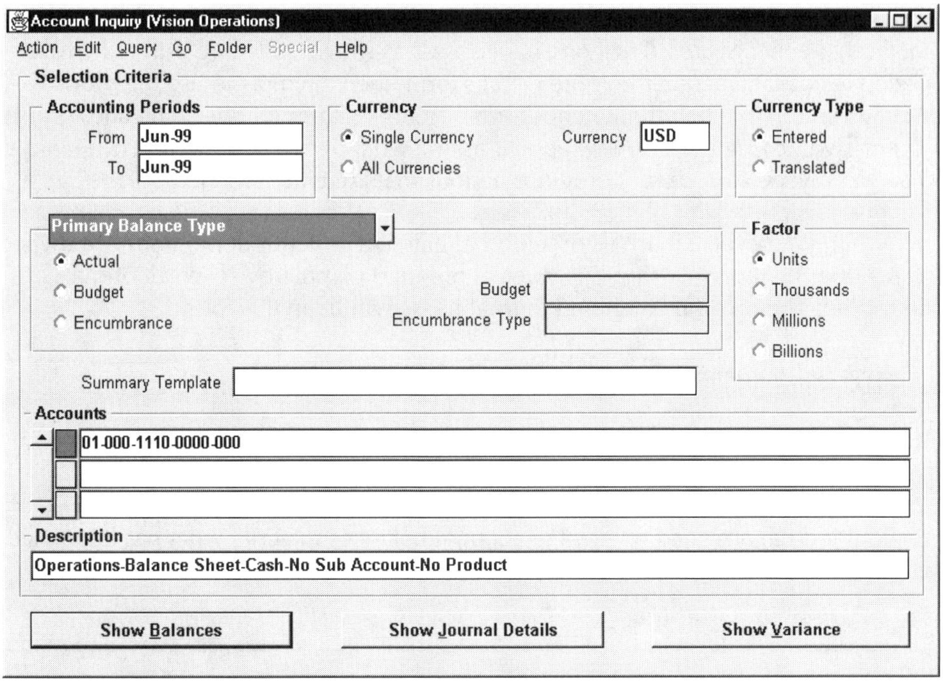

FIGURE 3-4. *Account Inquiry form*

post additional entries that negate the original values. These entries contain either the negative values of the original posted amounts, or the original values but with the debit amounts and credit amounts reversed. This second approach, called the *reversal method*, is generally the default but can be overridden in the Enter Journals form by clicking on the **More Details** button.

To see this in action, go to the Enter Journals form and locate your journal batch. You then have three choices:

- You can reverse the entire journal batch in the Batches form by selecting the **More Actions** button and then choosing Reverse Batch.

- You can click on the **Review Journal** button to go to the Journals form, click on the **More Actions** button in that form, and then click on Reverse Journal.

- You can click on the Review Journal button to go to the Journals form, click on the **More Details** button, enter the reverse period, and then click on the **Reverse Journal** button.

In the More Details zone, you also can override the reversal method set in the journal source and journal category level. Remember that you can set the reversal method to either *Switch Dr/Cr* or *Change Sign*, as shown in Figure 3-5. If the reverse period is not specified in the More Details form, then attempts to use the **More Actions** button in either the Batches form or Journals form to reverse batches or journals will cause a window to appear asking what period you are reversing into. You can reverse into current or future periods that are either opened or future-enterable.

When you reverse journals or a journal batch, a concurrent program is spawned to perform the reversal. After this reversal program completes, reversal journals are generated. The reversal batch and journal name will be in this form:

Reverse-*Journal Name-reversal system date-reversal system time*

In order for the reversal to update account balances, you must post the reversal journals, just as you would regular journals. You can either post the reversed journals from the Enter Journals form or from the Post Journals form. Post the reversal journal now and review the account balances to verify what has happened is what you are expecting.

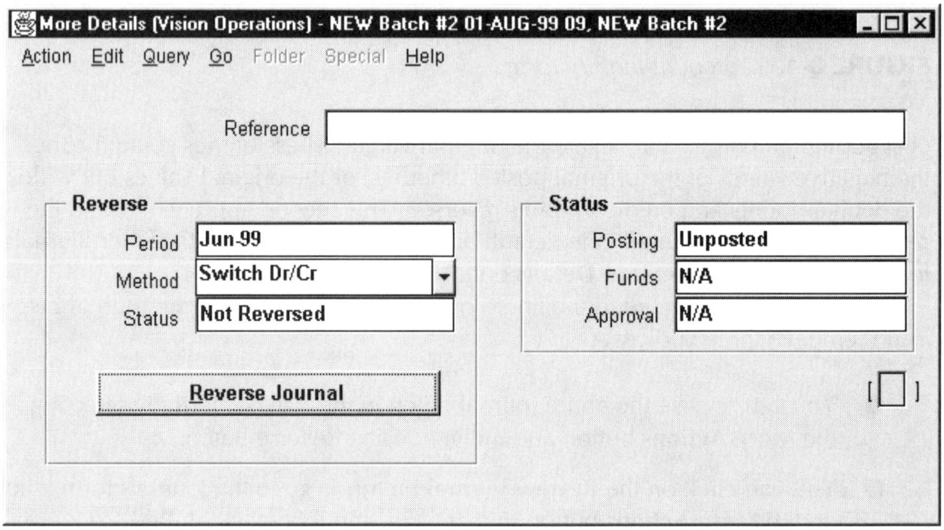

FIGURE 3-5. *More Details zone*

Review Questions

1. What are the two reversal methods?

2. If you have posted journals and cannot find them in the Reverse Journals form, what may be wrong?

Importing Journal Entries

In this section, you will learn how to import, correct, and delete journals from subledgers and systems outside of Oracle General Ledger.

Importing Journals

In addition to manually entering, posting, reviewing, and reversing journals using the techniques you just learned, you can also import journal entries from subledgers such as Oracle Receivables and Oracle Payables. Importing journal entries is a function performed by the *Journal Import* program.

Most Oracle Financials subledgers post their accounting journals into an interface table called GL_INTERFACE. The Journal Import program reads the records in this interface table and processes them into GL's production tables, creating journal entries with batches, journals, and journal lines. There are two exceptions to this:

- Oracle Assets posts its accounting journals directly into GL's production tables, bypassing the interface table.

- Oracle Purchasing encumbrance journals also post directly into GL's production tables, bypassing the interface table.

The other subledgers all go through the interface table, and they generally provide an option to run the Journal Import program automatically after posting the accounting entries to Oracle General Ledger. If Journal Import is *not* set to run automatically after the subledgers transfer, you must run Journal Import manually. You can do this by following the navigation path *Journals : Import : Run*. This will call up the Import Journals form, which is shown in Figure 3-6. In this form, you start by selecting the journal source you want to import. One easy way to do this is to execute the Edit | List of Values menu command, which will produce a list of valid journal sources. You can select a source and then click on the **OK** button to have it placed into the Source column in the Import Journals form. Do this now.

Some journal sources, such as Oracle Receivables, send journals to Oracle GL in groups. When importing journals from such sources, you must select the group ID. (Group IDs are assigned automatically by subledger and are used to subdivide the interface journals into separate batches. Different subledgers have different rules in deriving group IDs—some subledgers do not even use a group, and just send the

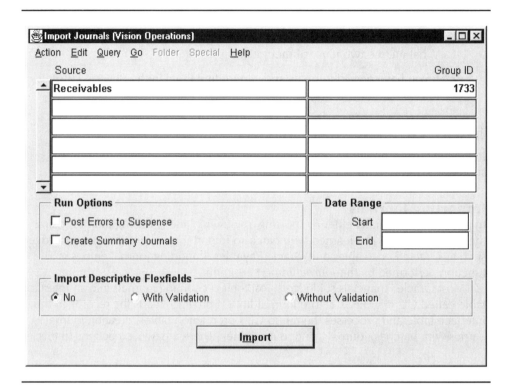

FIGURE 3-6. *Import Journals form*

journals as a single large batch.) The Import Journals form includes checkboxes offering two different run options:

■ **Post Errors to Suspense** causes the Journal Import program to balance journals by posting the difference between debit and credit amounts to a suspense account. You can only select the *Post Errors to Suspense* option if suspense accounting is allowed at the Set of Books level. Suspense accounts can be defined at the Set of Books level or overridden by the journal source and journal category combinations. If *Post Errors to Suspense* is not enabled, then Journal Import will reject any unbalanced journals.

■ **Create Summary Journals** causes the Journal Import program to add journal lines together (summarize them) by account combination, currency, and accounting period. The detailed journal lines are retained in your journal source if it has been configured to keep import journal references. Selecting the *Create Summary Journal* option disables the import of descriptive flexfield information.

The Import Journals form also provides two Date Range fields allowing you to filter the accounting dates to be imported. It also allows you to determine whether descriptive flexfields should be ignored, imported and validated against the value sets specified, or imported without such validation.

Once you have chosen the import settings you desire, clicking on the **Import** button initiates the Journal Import program. (You do not need to actually initiate Journal Import now, although you can *if* you know that doing so will not interfere with your company's accounting.) In addition to performing the import, Journal Import also produces an execution report that you can use to verify whether the import completed successfully. You can use this report to track down import errors and eliminate their causes. You can view or reprint the report using the View My Requests form; the report is associated with the Journal Import concurrent request.

Correcting Journals

If the Journal Import program reports import errors, you can correct data in the interface table and rerun Journal Import. This will require one of two different approaches, depending on where the erroneous data came from:

- If the problem data came from Oracle subledgers, you must fix the problem in two places: their source and the interface table. This is because Oracle subledgers will not retransfer journals to the interface table. So after you fix the source—an essential step because the problem is likely to occur again next accounting period if the subledger is not fixed—you must still correct data in the interface table and rerun Journal Import.

- If the problem is related to how Oracle GL is set up—for instance, a segment value being disabled or an accounting period not opened—you can simply fix the GL setup and rerun Journal Import. You don't need to correct the interface table in this situation.

If you do need to correct records in the interface table directly, you can do so by following the navigation path *Journals : Import : Correct*. This causes two forms to appear: the Correct Journal Import Data form is in the background, while the Find Journal Import Data form opens in the foreground. Using the Find Journal Import Data window, you can specify a wide variety of search criteria: the desired status (the error code *Error* or *Corrected*), journal source application, transaction category, accounting date range, journal type (actual, budget, encumbrance), currency, and group IDs range.

Once you have specified the Journal Import data you wish to find, you are returned to the Correct Journal Import Data form. The bottom portion of this form is capable of displaying five different sets, or regions, of data: batches/journals, accounts, journal lines, descriptive flexfields, and references. You select the region you want by choosing it from a drop-down list. Select the appropriate region from the list, correct the problems, save your corrections, and rerun Journal Import (which you can invoke from this form using the Special I Import Journals menu command).

Deleting Journals

You can delete journals using the Delete Journal Import Data form, which is available via the navigation path *Journals : Import : Delete.* You can specify the journal source application, the concurrent request that corresponds to a Journal Import run, or a group ID.

NOTE
This procedure must be used with extreme caution: remember that Oracle subledgers will not retransfer! You should use this step only if the data is from a source that can be requeried, such as a data conversion or another interface that can regenerate and reinterface the accounting entries.

Review Questions

1. What does Journal Import do?

2. What data can *not* be part of a summary journal?

3. What is the purpose of the Correct Journal Import Data form?

4. For what is the Delete Journal Import Data form used?

Entering Journal Entries Through ADI

In this section, you will learn how to enter journal entries through the Application Desktop Integrator (ADI). You will learn how to:

■ Create journal worksheets

■ Create journal entries

■ Upload journal entries

ADI is client-side software that allows you to perform several General Ledger and Fixed Asset functions from outside of Oracle Applications. Prior to the Applications Desktop Integrator (ADI), Oracle Applications provided the GLDI, which offered spreadsheet-based integration with Oracle General Ledger. Now ADI exists, providing GLDI functions and more. GLDI/ADI is a separate program—you cannot access it from the Oracle Applications. Your system administrator installs GLDI/ADI in much the same way they install Oracle Financials, generally providing a desktop icon for you to use to start the program. (If you don't see such an icon, talk to your system administrator.) Using the GLDI/ADI icon, start the GLDI/ADI program and sign on. You will then see the GLDI/ADI toolbar (Figure 3-7 shows an ADI toolbar).

Use the **Sign On** button to sign on to the Vision demonstration database. Use the same user name and password as you use for logging on to the Oracle Applications. The **Database** button allows you to add or delete databases that you can sign on to. Check the *Use Last Responsibility* checkbox to use the last responsibility automatically; otherwise, you will have to select a responsibility. In your case, select the responsibility *General Ledger, Vision Operations (USA)*. Click on the **Checkmark** button and you will see the ADI going through the following processes: connecting to the database, starting the Request Center, gathering Set of Books data, and checking security rules. After the ADI login is complete, your ADI toolbar will have two additional buttons: **Change Responsibility** and **Assets Poplist**. Also, you will have the Request Center window. The Request Center window is similar to the View My Requests form.

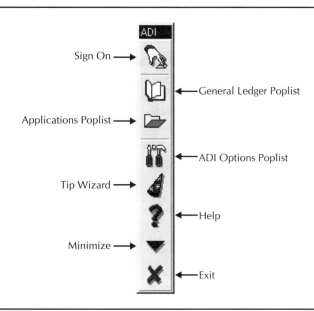

FIGURE 3-7. *ADI toolbar*

Creating Journal Worksheets

You now are going to create journal worksheets. Journal worksheets are spreadsheet templates where you enter your journal entries. To create journal worksheets, click on the **General Ledger Poplist** button from the toolbar and choose Enter Journals. A Create Journal Worksheet window appears. See Figure 3-8.

You can choose the journal type from *Functional Actuals, Foreign Actuals, Budgets,* or *Encumbrances.* For budgets, you must also select a budget organization. Choose Functional Actuals for this exercise. Next, choose whether you want *Single* or *Multiple* number of journals. Single number of journals means that only one journal is created, whereas multiple number of journals means that multiple journals are created in one batch. For a single number of journals, you only type in journal source, journal category, currency, and accounting date once at the journal worksheet header. For a multiple number of journals, you type in journal source, journal category, currency, and accounting date for every journal lines. During upload, the journal lines with common journal source, journal category, currency, and accounting date will be combined into a single journal. In your exercise, choose single number of journals. As a last step, you must decide whether you want to create the journal worksheet as a new Excel workbook, or whether you want to create the journal worksheet as a new worksheet in the opened Excel workbook, by choosing *New Workbook* or *Current Workbook.* Choose New Workbook.

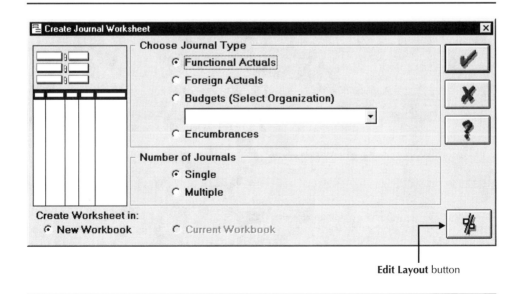

Edit Layout button

FIGURE 3-8. *Create Journal Worksheet window*

If you wish, you can customize the journal worksheet layout by clicking on the **Edit Layout** button. See Figure 3-9 for the Define Worksheet Layout window.

You see three layout option tabs: Worksheet, Header, and Lines. The first tab is the Worksheet tab, where you see the same options you went through just now. Why do you have to select again? The Worksheet tab is for setting up your default options for future journal worksheets. Check the *Sample* checkbox to see a preview of the journal worksheet.

The next tab is the Header tab. The Header tab is only available if you choose Single Number of Journals. In the Header tab, you can add the optional fields Group ID, Batch Name, Batch Description, Journal Name, Journal Description, Journal Reference, Reverse Journal, and Reversal Period to required fields, which include Category, Source, Currency, and Accounting Date by checking the checkbox next to the optional fields. You can use the directional buttons to change the order of the required fields and, independently, the order of the optional fields. There are four buttons. See Figure 3-10. If you check the *Database Columns* checkbox, the field names will change to the column names in the database. If you check the *Sample* checkbox, you can see a sample of the journal worksheet as it is currently defined.

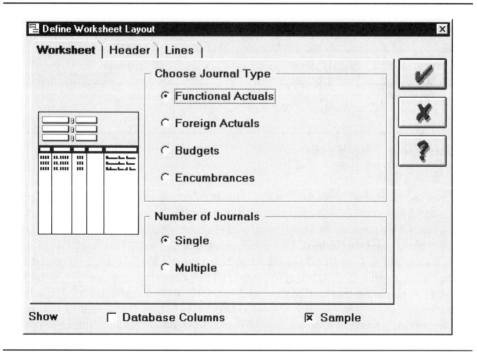

FIGURE 3-9. *Define Worksheet Layout window*

Up one row   Top of header

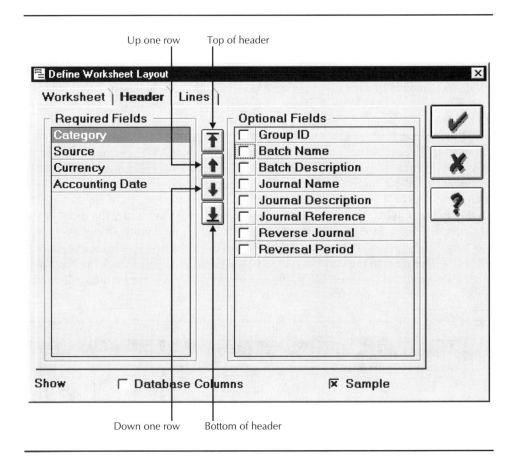

FIGURE 3-10. *Header tab*

The last tab is the Lines tab. This tab is identical to the Header tab excepts that the fields are different and the layout governs the journal lines, not the journals. Required fields in the Line tab are Account, Debit, and Credit. Optional fields are Description, Stat Amount, Line DFF Context, Line DFF 1, Line DFF 2, Line DFF 3, Line DFF 4, Line DFF 5, Line DFF 6, Line DFF 7, Line DFF 8, Line DFF 9, Line DFF 10, Captured Info Context, Captured Info DFF 1, Captured Info DFF 2, Captured Info DFF 3, Captured Info DFF 4, Captured Info DFF 5, Captured Info DFF 6, Captured Info DFF 7, Captured Info DFF 8, Captured Info DFF 9, Captured Info DFF 10, Line Detail Report, Source Detail Report, Additional Line Info 1, Additional Line Info 2, Additional Line Info 3, Additional Line Info 4, Additional Line Info 5, Additional Line Info 6, Additional Line

Info 7, and Additional Line Info 8. For Foreign Actuals, Converted Debit and Converted Credit are included as optional fields. If Multiple Number of Journals is selected, the required fields and optional fields from the Header tab are included in the Lines tab. Click on the **OK** button to exit the Worksheet Layout window, and then click **OK** again to invoke the journal worksheet.

NOTE
DFF stands for Descriptive flexfield.

Creating Journal Entries

ADI will invoke Microsoft Excel and communicate to Excel, and the journal worksheet you defined will be displayed as a template. First, you enter the journal (header) information if Single Number of Journal is selected. If the profile option *GLDI: Journal Source* is set, then the journal source specified in the profile option will be used in the journal. You cannot change the defaulted journal source. Next, you enter the journal lines. You can use the list of values for accounts or other list of values enabled fields by double-clicking the left mouse button or using the List of Values entry from the General Ledger Poplist from the toolbar. As you enter journal lines, a flag will appear in the Upload column to indicate that the journal lines have not been uploaded. If you copy and paste journal lines, the flag will not appear, and you can make it appear by placing the cursor in the Upload column and typing in any characters. The **View Context** and **View Header** buttons on the top of the journal worksheet are used to toggle between viewing and not viewing context and header information. Context information includes template type, template style, set of books, and database. See Figure 3-11. After you create the journal entries, you can upload to Oracle General Ledger.

Uploading Journal Entries

The Upload Journal Entries feature in ADI creates the journal entries you entered in the journal worksheet to the Oracle General Ledger interface table (GL_INTERFACE). Invoke the Update Journal Entries Program from the Update to Interface entry in the General Ledger Poplist. See Figure 3-12.

Select what rows you want to upload. You have the choices of *Flagged Rows* or *All Rows.* Flagged rows means all rows that have a flag in the Upload column. As mentioned before, if you copy and paste rows, they will need to be manually flagged for update. You can also choose whether you want to prevalidate journal entries. Your choices are *Full, Partial*, and *None*. Full means that the journal entries are all validated before uploading to the interface tables. Cross-validation rules will only be enforced if the profile option *Flexfields: Validate On Server* is set to Yes.

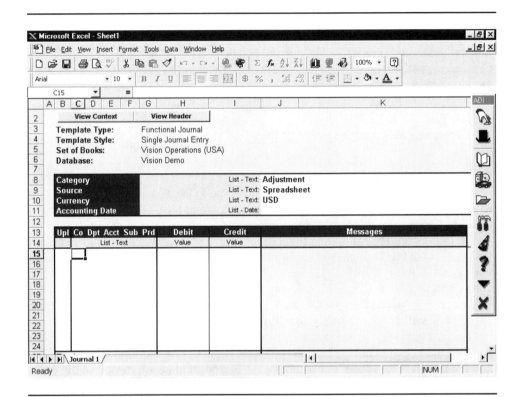

FIGURE 3-11. *Journal worksheet*

Partial means that the accounts are not validated. None means no validation. However, security rules will still be enforced even for Partial or None options. As a last step, you can optionally initiate the Journal Import program automatically after the Upload Journals program. If you choose to invoke Journal Import automatically, you can select Journal Import options, which include *Post Account Errors to Suspense, Create Summary Journal*, and *Descriptive Flex*. These options are the same as if you invoke Journal Import from Oracle Applications.

TIP
You can upload the same journal lines as many times as you want, creating duplicate journals, so be careful.

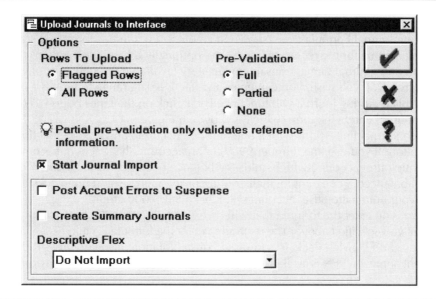

FIGURE 3-12. *Upload Journals to Interface screen*

Review Questions

1. What are the three options in creating journal worksheets?

2. When will the flag appear in the Upload column? How about for copy-and-paste journal lines?

3. What will the **View Context** and **View Header** buttons do?

4. What does the Upload Journal program do?

Creating Recurring and Formula Journal Entries

Recurring journals, as the name suggests, are journals that recur at some predefined interval of time. In this section, you will learn how to

■ Create recurring journal entries

■ Generate recurring journal entries

■ Use recurring journal entries as skeleton journal entries

Creating Recurring Journal Entries

Use the navigation path *Journals : Define : Recurring* to navigate to the Define Recurring Journal Formula form (shown in Figure 3-13). On this form, you start by entering a name for the recurring batch, and optionally a batch description. Next, you enter the journal name, transaction category (available through a list of values), and currency. If you wish, you can enter an effective date range to limit the dates for which this recurring journal will function. Then click on the **Lines** button to proceed to the Journal Entry Line form, which is shown in Figure 3-14.

Each journal line begins with a line number, account, and an optional line description. If you use line number 9999 for an account, that account becomes the automatic offset account, which holds the balance necessary to make this recurring journal balanced. For example, if all your recurring journals add up to a $100,000 debit, your automatic offset account will have a $100,000 credit.

Next, you enter the formula that will be used to calculate the balance for the account you specified above. The method to enter the formula is called *EasyCalc*, and its is based on Hewlett Packard's Reverse Polish Notation, also known as RPN (an excellent primer on RPN is available on the Web at http://www.hpmuseum.org/rpn.htm).

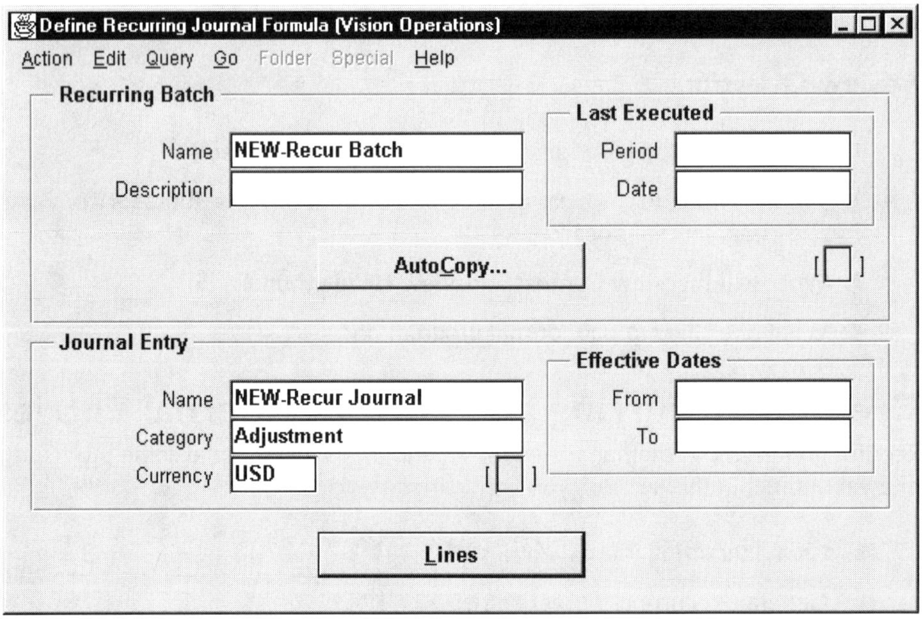

FIGURE 3-13. *Define Recurring Journal Formula form*

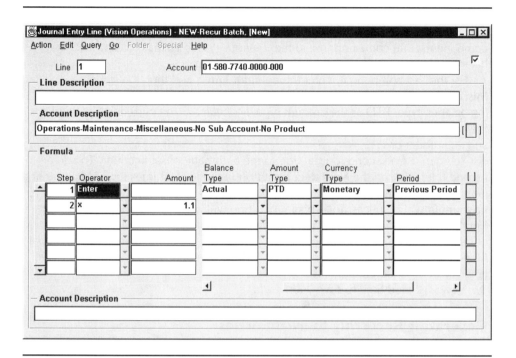

FIGURE 3-14.   *Recurring Journal Line form*

When applied to this form, the process involves specifying a step number in the first column, selecting a mathematical operator from the drop-down list in the second column, and so on.

TIP
*The first step of a formula always starts with the operator **Enter**. From the second step on, you can choose to use any other operator—+, -, x, or /—but not **Enter**.*

For this exercise, you are going to give a 10 percent increase to the Miscellaneous account balance from the last period balance; the offsetting account will be Cash. To accomplish the exercise, you must enter two journal lines. For the first journal line, enter a step value of **1** and then select the operator **Enter** from the drop-down list. Move to the Account field, click on the **List of Values** button, and select the Miscellaneous account from the shorthand alias field. Next, you will enter the formula, which in logical terms will be (Previous Period Actual Monetary PTD balance * 1.1). To create this formula using EasyCalc, you must enter two formula components: one corresponding to the Previous Period Actual Monetary PTD balance, and the other corresponding to the constant 1.1.

For the first component, enter the operator **Enter**, and then the same Miscellaneous account you entered in the journal line. Next, choose Actual as the balance type, PTD as the amount type, Monetary as the currency type, and Previous Period as the period. For the second component, enter the operator * and an amount of **1.1**.

You can use a second journal line as the automatic offset account. To add a second line, click on the **New Record** button in the journal lines region. Enter a line number of **9999** and use the account Cash. Since this is an automatic offset account, no formula will be necessary. This journal line will cause the amount calculated from the (Previous Period Actual Monetary PTD balance * 1.1) calculation to be offset by the Cash account automatically. For example, if the (Previous Period Actual Monetary PTD balance * 1.1) is a $95,000 debit, then the Cash account will have an entry of $95,000 credit.

Now is a good time to save your work.

Generating Recurring Journal Entries

To generate the recurring journals you just created, follow the navigation path *Journals : Generate : Recurring*. Within this form, select your recurring batch by checking the checkbox on the left end of its row. Then, enter the accounting period in which you wish to generate recurring journals. For journal formulas that include budget amount type, you must enter the budget you want to use. Then click on the **Generate** button to generate the recurring journal. Execute the menu command Help | View My Requests to open the View My Requests window. A Find Requests window will appear first; click on the **Find** button to see all of your requests. From this list, you can verify completion of the recurring journal entry by selecting the appropriate request and clicking on the **View Output** button. When you are done, return to the Enter Journals form to see the generated recurring journal batch you created.

Using Recurring Journal Entries as Skeleton Journal Entries

You can use recurring journals to generate skeleton journal entries. These skeleton journal entries can be with or without amounts. To create skeleton journal entries without amounts, you enter multiple journal lines with accounts only and no formula; this causes the recurring journal to contain journal lines and accounts but no amounts. To create skeleton journal entries with a fixed amount, you enter multiple journal lines with accounts, formulas, and amounts with the **Enter** operator.

Review Questions

1. What is a recurring journal?

2. What is line number 9999 used for in recurring journals?

3. Which operator is used as the first step in defining recurring journals?

4. What are the steps for creating skeleton journals?

Approving Manual Journal Entries

If your Set of Books has been configured to require journal approval and the journal source you are using needs journal approval, then you will need to approve manual journal entries before posting. There are three steps to approving manual journal entries:

- Set up employee authorization limits

- Submit journal batches for approval

- Approve journal batches

Setting Up Employee Authorization Limits

To set up employee authorization limits, follow the navigation path *Setup : Employees : Limits*. Once the Journal Authorization Limits form is open, you can use the menu command Query | Find All to get a list of employees who are already configured to approve journal batches. To add another employee, click on a blank row in the form, execute the Menu | List of Values command, choose an employee from the list, and define the maximum amount that the person can approve for each journal batch.

Submitting Journal Batches for Approval

Click on the **More Actions** button from the Enter Journals form. When the More Actions dialog box appears, click on the **Approve Batch** button. This will submit the journal batch for approval. A message will be displayed to show you the approval status, which can be any of the following:

- Journal batch has been sent to an approver

- Journal batch is invalid

- Journal batch is self-approved if you are authorized to approve your own journal batches (profile option *Allow Preparer Approval* is set to Yes), and the batch is within your employee-specific limit

Approving Journal Batches

The appropriate approver will receive a notification to approve the submitted journal batch. (Who this person is depends on which approval method you set up.) All journal batches waiting for your approval will be in a Notifications Summary form. To act on a notification in this form, select the notification and click on the **Respond** button, and then choose either Approve or Reject. (Notifications that do not need a response will not show the button.) You can also optionally enter a comment. Your Notifications Summary form can be invoked through the navigation path *Other : Notifications*. In return, all approved or rejected batches will become notification lines in the submitter's Notification Summary form, shown in Figure 3-15.

Review Questions

1. What profile option governs whether a preparer can approve his/her own batches?

2. At what level is journal authorization set?

3. What is the process for approving journal batches?

4. How do you find out whether submitted batches are approved or rejected?

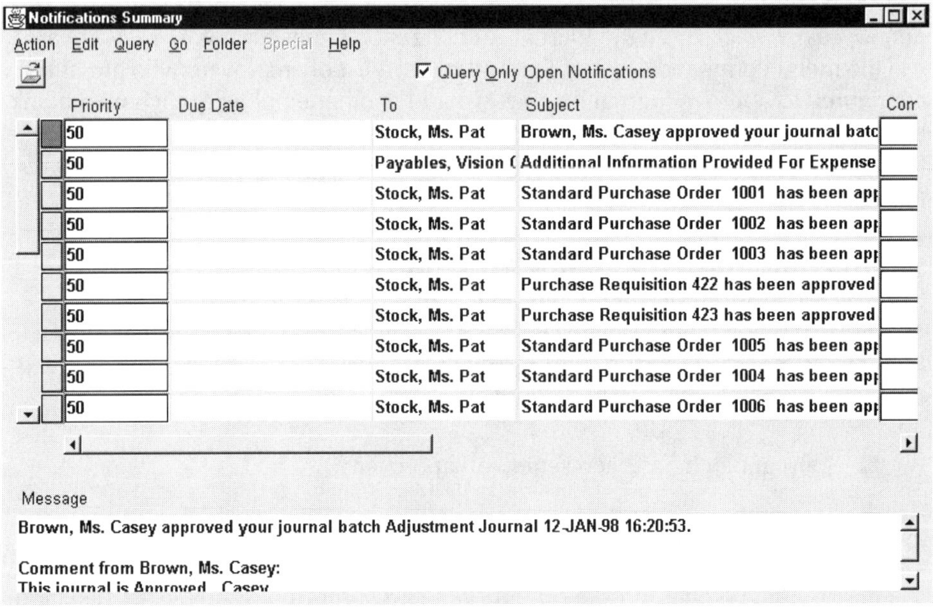

FIGURE 3-15. *Notification Summary form*

Using Balancing Accounts

Balancing accounts are used to balance the journals created during journal import, recurring journals generation, and posting. In journal import, the balancing account can be the suspense account. In the Recurring Journals Generation program, the balancing account can be any user-defined account identified with a line number of 9999. In the Posting program, the balancing account can either be the suspense account or the intercompany account. The suspense account and intercompany account are enabled when you define the Set of Books.

Suspense Account

During the execution of Journal Import or Posting, if posting to suspense accounts is allowed, out-of-balance journals are automatically balanced to the summary (suspense) accounts defined at one of two levels: the journal source and category combination level, or the Set of Books level. The suspense accounts generated by this process will balance the journal within the scope of a balancing entity (an entity in which total debits must equal total credits). You don't need to worry about setting up suspense accounts for each balancing entity, because GL uses the suspense accounts assigned as templates and automatically substitutes the balancing entities of the assigned suspense accounts with the balancing entities from the journal.

For example, say you have set up a suspense account at the Set of Books level and identified it as 01-0000-SUSPENSE (balancing entity-cost center-account). If you try to post a journal like the one shown in Table 3-1, suspense accounts will be generated during the Posting program, and the updated journal will look like Table 3-2.

Intercompany Account

If journal lines belong to more than one balancing entity, and the journal is not out of balance, the Posting program will balance the overall journal to the intercompany account you defined for the specific journal source, journal category, and debit/credit type. This process generates intercompany accounts that balance the journal by balancing entity. As was the case with suspense accounts, you need not set up intercompany accounts for each balancing entity, because Oracle General

	Debit	Credit
01-0000-CASH	100	
02-1000-PAYABLES		90

TABLE 3-1. *Journal Before Posting*

	Debit	Credit
01-0000-CASH	100	
02-1000-PAYABLES		90
01-0000-SUSPENSE		100
02-0000-SUSPENSE	90	

TABLE 3-2. *Journal After Posting*

Ledger uses the intercompany accounts assigned as templates. It will automatically substitute the balancing entities of the assigned intercompany accounts with the balancing entities from the journal.

For instance, if you set up the intercompany account at the Set of Books level with the identifier 01-0000-INTER (balancing entity-cost center-account), posting a journal like the one shown in Table 3-3 would produce an updated journal like the one shown in Table 3-4.

Review Questions

1. What are the different kinds of balancing accounts? What are the differences between them?

2. When are suspense accounts used? How about intercompany accounts?

3. Do you need to set up suspense and intercompany accounts by each company? Explain why or why not.

	Debit	Credit
01-0000-CASH	100	
02-1000-PAYABLES		100

TABLE 3-3. *Journal Before Posting*

	Debit	**Credit**
01-0000-CASH	100	
02-1000-PAYABLES		100
01-0000-INTER		100
02-0000-INTER	100	

TABLE 3-4.   *Journal After Posting*

Creating Summary Accounts

In this section, you will learn to:

- Define parent segment values (parent values)

- Define rollup groups

- Assign rollup groups

- Define summary accounts

- Maintain summary accounts

Summary accounts store balances of multiple accounts. To define how balances roll up into a summary account, you must set up summary templates. Summary templates can be defined by regular flexfield values, parent values, and rollup groups.

Defining Parent Segment Values

Parent segment values (also called *parent values*) are values that reference other segment values typically known as *child segment values* (also called *child values*). You can set up parent values for any segment of the Chart of Accounts. Parent values are used to group logical segment values together, and they are utilized in reporting and/or assigned to rollup groups. Child values can be defined in ranges or individually.

Using the Chart of Accounts you defined earlier, you are going to add a parent value called ASSETS to include balances from the Cash and Receivables asset accounts you created earlier. You define parent values in the same form you define your segment values. Find your accounting flexfield structure and the account segment. To do this, enter your accounting flexfield structure and the segment name corresponding to the account segment in the Find window, then click on the **Find** button. You will see the values that are valid for the account segment. Go to the Values (Account) region, add a new record, and enter the value **ASSETS** and a description. Navigate to the *Hierarchy, Qualifiers* alternative region and check the *Parent* checkbox to make this a parent value. Your form should now look similar to the one shown in Figure 3-16.

Next, you must define child values for the ASSETS parent value. Save your work first, and then click on the **Define Child Ranges** button to enter the child values. Enter child values for the Cash account and the Receivables account, and in the Include column select *Child Values Only*.

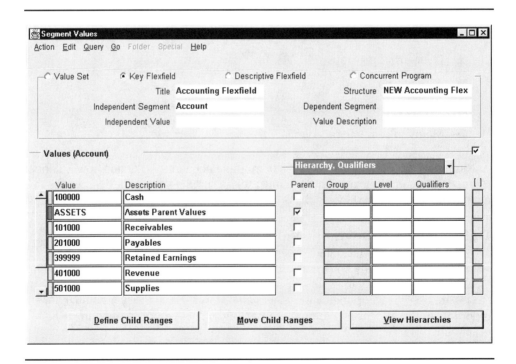

FIGURE 3-16. *Parent Values form*

TIP
Defining child values in ranges will minimize maintenance if your Chart of Accounts segment values are designed in a logical order. For example, you might reserve cost center values 101 through 199 for all your consulting cost centers, even though you only have cost center 101, 111, and 121 now. Then you can set up a parent value called Consulting to extend from child value 101 to child value 199. Later on, if you set up another cost center and number it 131, it will be included automatically in the consulting parent value without redefining the parent value. In contrast, if you enter the cost centers individually (e.g., 101), you will have to explicitly add cost center 131 when it becomes a valid center.

Defining Rollup Groups

Rollup groups are one level higher than parent values. You use rollup groups in summary account templates. You assign parent values to rollup groups. In order to use parent values in summary account templates, you must first assign the parent values to rollup groups.

You can define rollup groups via the navigation path *Setup : Financials : Flexfields : Key : Groups.* You will be presented with a Find Key Flexfield Segment window; enter the name of your accounting flexfield structure in the Structure field and then click on the **Find** button. Go to the Rollup Groups region and enter your rollup group names and descriptions. Create a rollup group called **ASSETS** now so you can assign the parent values you defined in the Define Segment Values form. Compare the contents of your form to Figure 3-17, then save your work.

Assigning Rollup Groups

Rollup Groups are assigned to parent values in the Segment Values form (navigation path *Setup : Financials : Flexfields : Validation : Values*). In this form, the Group field is in the *Hierarchy, Qualifiers* group, just to the right of the *Parent* checkbox.

Defining Summary Accounts

Now you can create summary accounts. Summary accounts will be described in detail in a later chapter, but an overview is provided here. After following the

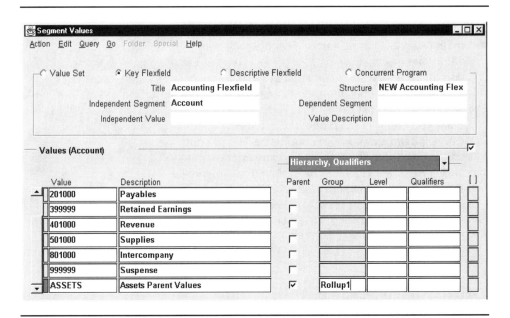

FIGURE 3-17. *Rollup Groups form*

navigation path *Setup : Accounts: Summary*, you enter a name, a template, and a description for the summary account template. You must also enter the earliest period for which Oracle General Ledger should generate summarized balances.

Summary accounts are generated based on the defined summary account templates. To set up summary account templates, you define a template option for each segment of the Chart of Accounts. Options include:

- D
- T
- Rollup Groups

D *D* means to create a summary account for each segment value of the segment. The system will not allow you to set up a summary account template with all Ds, because doing so would cause each segment to expand to include every possible segment value.

T *T* means to create one summary account that summarizes all segment values. T must be a defined parent value with the entire segment's possible values as child values. No rollup group must be assigned to T. When using this option, the *Detailed Posting Allowed* and *Detailed Budgeting Allowed* parameters are set to No. You do not need to set up a summary account with Ts in every segment because doing so would create one account that totals the system—and this account combination would always have a balance of 0.

ROLLUP GROUPS A rollup group is used to create one summary account for each parent value assigned to it. For instance, assume you have three companies, five departments, ten accounts, and a Rollup Group R1 in the account segment with two parent values. A summary account template of D-T-D will create 3*1*10=30 summary accounts. A summary account template of D-T-R1 will create 3*1*2=6 summary accounts.

Maintain Summary Accounts

You do not need to maintain summary accounts if you only add child values to parent values. The new child values will automatically be included when the Maintain Summary Templates program is executed. The Maintain Summary Templates program can be invoked manually; it is also called automatically by the Posting program. You may want to run the Maintain Summary Templates program prior to posting if you add a lot of child values for performance reasons. However, if you add parent values to rollup groups and the rollup groups are used in summary account templates, you will need to delete the related summary accounts and re-create them. Adding or deleting summary accounts will initiate the Add/Delete Summary Accounts program automatically.

TIP
If you have a lot of summary accounts, the Posting program will take longer to run because each time a child value balance is updated, the corresponding summary accounts balance must be updated as well.

Review Questions

1. What are parent values?

2. What are rollup groups?

3. How should a summary account template with the option T be defined?

Transferring Balances Between Accounts

To transfer balances between accounts, you create journal entries. You can create them manually, or as recurring journal entries, or as allocation journal entries. The allocation journal entries are generated by a process known as *MassAllocation/MassBudgeting* in Oracle General Ledger. This section covers the MassAllocation function. MassBudgeting works the same way, but applies to budget balances. In this section, you will learn to:

■ Define MassAllocations

■ Generate MassAllocations

Defining MassAllocations

You can navigate to the Define MassAllocations form (shown in Figure 3-18) by following the navigation path *Journals : Define : Allocation*. For each MassAllocation, you must set up two parts:

■ MassAllocation batch

■ MassAllocation formulas

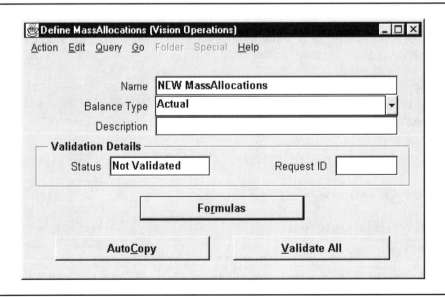

FIGURE 3-18. *Define MassAllocations form*

MASSALLOCATIONS BATCH   To define a MassAllocations batch, you enter
a MassAllocation name, the balance type that this MassAllocation uses (Actual or
Encumbrance), and an optional description. If you have prior MassAllocation batches,
you can use the **AutoCopy** button to copy settings from existing MassAllocation
batches. Once you have created allocation formulas, you can validate them using the
Validate All button, which changes their status to Validated if they pass validation.

MASSALLOCATION FORMULAS   To enter MassAllocation formulas, click on
the **Formulas** button. This takes you to the Formula form shown in Figure 3-19. When
entering a MassAllocation formula, you enter a journal name, a journal category,
and an optional journal description. Then you choose whether to include the *Full
Balance* from the allocation account, or just the balance of a *Single Entered Currency*.
For example, if you only want balances entered as USD, you can choose *Single
Entered Currency* and enter **USD** as the currency. The generated MassAllocations
journals will be the same as the currency of the allocation account's original
entered currency. If the MassAllocation's balance type is Encumbrance, you can
only allocate balances from a full balance.

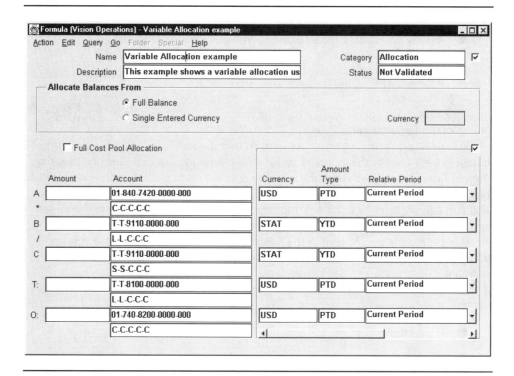

FIGURE 3-19.   *Variable allocation example*

You can also choose to perform *Full Cost Pool Allocation*. This option will put any rounding differences into the allocation cost pool with the largest relative balance. If you do not elect to use this option, rounding differences stay with the allocation accounts.

After you set up the general MassAllocation journal information and options, you are ready to enter a formula line. A formula line uses the following format:

```
Target Account (T)=
Allocation Cost Pool    *    Rate or Usage Factor    /    1 or Total Usage
A                       *    B                       /    C
```

Allocation Cost Pool can be a fixed amount, or a balance from an allocation account. Rate or Usage Factor can be either a fixed rate or a statistical account balance. If using a statistical account, Total Usage will be the sum of all balances of the involved statistical accounts.

Balances used for allocation accounts are defined as follows:

- **Currency**   The functional currency or STAT for statistical balance

- **Amount type**   PTD, QTD, YTD, or Project-to-date (PJTD)

- **Relative period**   Current Period, Previous Period, or Year Ago - Same Period

- **Balance type**   Actual, Budget, or Encumbrance

For Budget and Encumbrance balance types, you must also enter the Budget Name of the Encumbrance Type.

You must also enter an offset account so that the journals created will be in balance. Let's refer to this account as "0". If the amount calculated is positive, the journal lines created will debit the target account(s) and credit the offset account(s). Usually, the offset account(s) are the same as the allocation cost account(s), since you will usually transfer balances from the allocation cost account(s) to the target account(s).

When entering an account in the MassAllocation formula—whether it is an allocation, target, or offset account—you have the following options for each segment value:

- C   Constant

- L   Looping

- S   Summing

C   CONSTANT   Entered segment value will be used as a constant in the allocation account(s). You can use the *Constant* type if you want to refer to a specific child value or rollup group in summary accounts.

L   LOOPING   The entered segment value will be looped to create one allocation account for each child value. This option should only be used with parent values.

S   SUMMING   The entered segment value will be used as a sum of the assigned child values. Like Looping, this option should only be used with parent values.

To learn more about MassAllocation formulas, let's take a look at the MassAllocation example that comes with the Vision database. It is named "Variable Allocation example," shown in Figure 3-19, and you can see it by following the navigation path *Journals : Define : Allocation* to reach the Define MassAllocations form, executing the Query | Enter menu command, entering **Variable Allocation example** as the criteria, and executing the Query | Run menu command. When the variable allocation example record appears, click on the **Formulas** button to see the formulas it contains.

In this example, balances are transferred from the Operations-Facilities-Rent Expense account, based proportionally on the YTD Headcount statistical account balance by company and department, to the MassAllocation In account of each company and department. The account information is as follows:

A = Operations-Facilities-Rent Expense account
B = Headcount statistical account performs balancing by each company and each department, since it loops through the first and the second segments (company and department). This means that if you have three companies and five departments, you will have 3*5 = 15 Headcount statistical account balances. Notice that the currency is STAT instead of USD and the amount type is YTD.
C = Total YTD Headcount statistical account balance
T = MassAllocation In performs accounting by each company and each department, since it loops through the first and the second segments
O = Operations-Facilities-Rent Expense account

TIP
Target accounts must loop in the same frequency as the B account.

Generating MassAllocations

You can now validate the Variable Allocation example if it is not already validated. You do not need to explicitly validate the batch, because the Generation program will initiate the Validation program automatically. You generate MassAllocation batches using the navigation path *Journals : Generate : Allocation*, which opens the Generate MassAllocation Journals form shown in Figure 3-20. Enter **Variable Allocation example** as the MassAllocation batch name, and then enter the accounting period ranges. You can select either the *Full* or *Incremental* allocation method; Full will allocate the full amount, whereas Incremental will allocate based on your already allocated target balances. To ensure that Incremental works properly, do not modify the target balances between incremental runs. If you use the Full method and the MassAllocation batch has run before, you will need to reverse the original allocation manually to avoid double posting.

After you have made your choices, click on the **Generate** button to complete the process. The MassAllocation batch generated will be in the format of *MB : <the concurrent request ID used in generating MassAllocations journals> <MassAllocation Batch name> <the Accounting Period used>*.

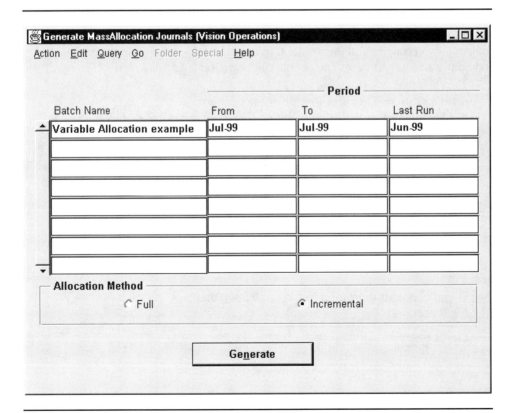

FIGURE 3-20. *Generate MassAllocation Journals form*

Review Questions

1. What are the three ways to transfer balances?

2. What is the format of a MassAllocations formula?

3. What are the C, L, and S options used for when defining accounts?

4. How is offset account used in MassAllocations?

Reporting and Analysis Tools

In this section, you will cover basic reporting and analysis tools available in Oracle General Ledger. These tools include:

- Standard reports
- Basic FSG reports
- ADI Report Wizard
- ADI Request Center
- ADI Analysis Wizard
- Integration with Oracle Financial Analyzer

Running Standard Reports

Standard reports are reports that come seeded with Oracle General Ledger and are usually written with Oracle Reports 2.5. They are classified into the following categories:

Program	Account Analysis
Analyzer	Budget
Chart of Accounts	Consolidation
Currency	FSG
General Ledger	Intercompany
Journals	Other
Trial Balance	

After a brief discussion and example of each report category, you will learn how to run Standard reports.

Program

The Program reports perform functions that are necessary in the Oracle General Ledger system. These functions include deleting ad hoc FSG reports, transferring FSGs between Oracle instances, setting up automatic posting, maintaining summary account templates, and optimizing Chart of Accounts indexes.

Account Analysis

Account Analysis reports show account balances, along with details of your own choosing. Options include average balance audit, functional/foreign currency payables detail, and subledger detail. Usually, Account Analysis reports come in two formats: 132 char (landscape) or 180 char (landwide).

Analyzer

The Analyzer programs assist in the process of integrating with Oracle Financial Analyzer. They detail extracting balances, calendars, currency, hierarchy, period rates, and segment values.

Budget

Budget reports show budget-related information. This information includes budget accounts listings, hierarchy listings, budget journals, budget organization listings, and summary/detail budget data.

Chart of Accounts

Chart of Accounts reports show information such as account hierarchy, rollup groups, segment values, and suspense accounts.

Consolidation

Consolidation reports provide information such as disabled parent accounts, consolidation journals, consolidation rules, and unmapped subsidiary accounts.

Currency

Currency reports are listing reports for daily exchange rates, period-end exchange rates, and historical rates.

FSG

FSG reports provide listings showing column set, content set, report, report set, row order, and row set. Most of these listings are available in either summary or detail format. There is also a Where Used report that shows where FSG components are used.

General Ledger

General Ledger reports show beginning and period-end account balances, as well as journal lines.

Intercompany

Intercompany reports list such data as transaction details, transaction trial balances, and unapproved transactions.

Journals

Journal reports show journal entries matching criteria you specify. These criteria can include subledger, level of details, day entered, foreign currency, tax, journal status, and document numbering.

Other

This classification provides such reports as MassAllocation formula listing, recurring formula listing, Units of Measure listing, and Value Added Tax (VAT) listing.

Trial Balance

Trial Balance reports show account balances and all their related activities. These reports show different types of account balances including Average, Budget, Detail, Encumbrance, Summary, Foreign Currency, and Translation.

Run Standard Reports

To initiate Standard reports, follow the navigation path *Reports : Request : Standard*. GL will ask you whether you want to submit a *Single Request* or a *Request Set*. Select the *Single Request* option and click on the **OK** button. This will take you to the Submit Request form. Use the Edit | List of Values menu command to see a list of available reports; select the Program - Optimizer report and click on the LOV's **OK** button. When the Parameters dialog box appears, click on the **OK** button to accept the default values. This will take you to the Submit Request form, at which time you can click on the **Submit Request** button to run the selected report. A dialog box will appear with the concurrent request ID and ask the question whether you want to submit another request. Click on the **No** button for this exercise. Back in the Navigator window, execute the Help | View My Requests menu command, select the *Specific Requests* option, type your request ID into the appropriate field, and click on the **Find** button to verify the completion and content of your report.

Review Questions

1. What is the process for submitting Standard reports?

2. What does an Account Analysis report show?

Creating Basic FSG Reports

In addition to Standard reports, you can create custom financial reports called Financial Statement Generator (FSG) reports. The Financial Statement Generator reports are the most important reports in Oracle General Ledger—they enable you to create your balance sheet, income statement, and cash flow. In this section, you will learn how to create FSG reports using the five required components:

- Row set
- Column set
- Row order
- Display set
- Content set

Then you will learn how to:

- Create FSG reports
- Create FSG report sets
- Submit FSG reports/report sets

Row Set

To begin, look at Figure 3-21 to see how the five components fit together. The rows of the FSGs are defined by their Row Set, which you can control using the Row Set form (*Reports : Define : RowSet*). To see how this works, enter a name of your choosing, and a description if you wish, for a new Row Set. Then click on the **Define Rows** button to define rows. This takes you to the Rows form, which is shown in Figure 3-22.

When defining rows, you must enter a line number for each row. You can use the line number to refer to this particular row definition during row calculation. You

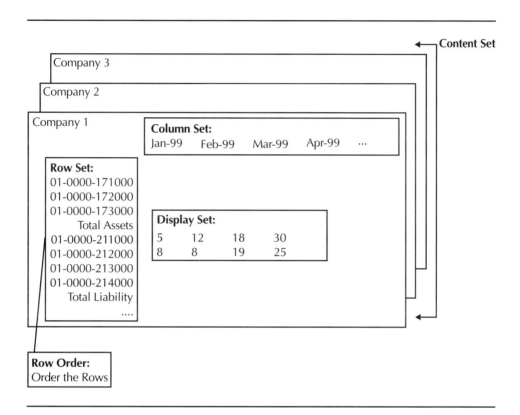

FIGURE 3-21. *FSG report components*

can also optionally enter a line item, which appears as a label on each row. It is useful to use the Line Item field to enter headings that will make a report look tidier. Next, you select format options. You can indent the row a certain number of characters, skip lines before or after this row, place a full line of underline characters before or after this row to improve visual separation, and specify a page break before or after the row.

You can also specify a number of advanced options. These include:

- **Row Name** Provides a way to refer to this row by name, rather than by number, in calculations. The row name will not appear on the FSG report; that is what the Line Item field is for. Row names are useful if a row is used a lot in row calculations. Even if it is used in only a few, giving a row a name helps make calculation formulas more readable.

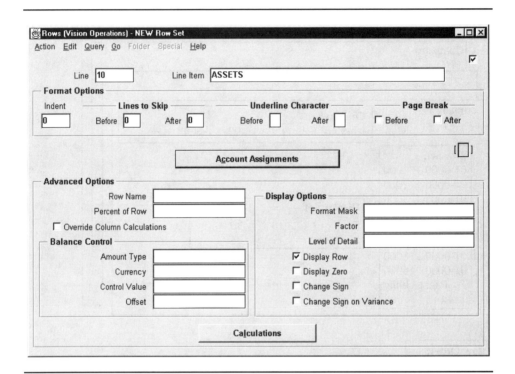

FIGURE 3-22. *Rows form*

- **Percent of Row** Stores the line number of a row that will be used as the denominator in calculating percentages. This allows you to use the **%** operator when defining a calculation column, causing GL to perform a percentage calculation based on the value in another row.

- **Override Column Calculations** Instructs GL to override column calculations with this row's calculations. This is useful when a column-based calculation will not produce an accurate answer. For instance, suppose you have designed a row that calculates the ratio between two line-item rows. Each row has three columns: Period 1 amount, Period 2 amount, and a total for the two periods. In your ratio row, you do not want the Total column to add the ratios of Period 1 and Period 2; the answer would be meaningless. Instead, you want the ratio row's formula to take precedence, calculating the total ratio by dividing the total for the first row by the total for the second row. Table 3-5 depicts this situation.

	Prd 1	**Prd 2**	**Total**
Line item 1			= Line item 1 Prd 1 + Line item 1 Prd 2
Line item 2			= Line item 2 Prd 1 + Line item 2 Prd 2
Ratio	= Line item 1 Prd 1 / Line item 2 Prd 1	= Line item 1 Prd 2 / Line item 2 Prd 2	= Line item 1 Total / Line item 2 Total

TABLE 3-5. *Example of "Override Column Calculations" Use*

- **Balance Control**   Contains options that are usually set at the column set level. If you decide to reverse the traditional role of row set and column set, then you will define Balance Control. Otherwise leave this blank. In the Balance Control region, you can specify the amount type to use. Amount types include BAL-Actual (FY Start), PTD/Project/QTD/YTD-Actual, PTD/Project/QTD/YTD-Budget, PTD/Project/QTD/YTD-Encumbrance, PTD/Project/QTD/YTD-Variance, PTD/Project/QTD/YTD-Variance%, YTD-Budget (FY End), and YTD-Encumbrance (FY End). You can also specify a currency to use for translated account balances. If you want to create FSG reports in a currency that is not functional, reporting, or translated, then use the *Control Value* option, which defines runtime parameters for budget names, encumbrance types, or foreign currencies. If you specify an amount type, you must also enter an offset, which is the accounting period offset to be used for this row. For example, if the FSG with this row is submitted for Jun-99, the offset for this row is –1, and the amount type is PTD-Actual, then this row will display the May-99 PTD-Actual values.

- **Display Options**   Set at the row level, will override column display options. They include:

  - **Format Mask**, which affects how numbers are formatted in the report. The character "9" denotes a digit in format mask, and you can specify whether to include a thousands separator, decimal indicator, currency symbol, and other characters of your choosing.

- **Factor** controls whether the numbers shown represent billions, millions, thousands, units, or percentiles. If you use the *Factor* option, note it in your row or column headings.

- **Level of Detail** has three predefined choices: Controller, Supervisor (a superset above Controller), and Financial Analyst (a superset above Supervisor). You can associate each row in a row set to a level, and then specify at runtime the level for which the report is being run. Each row is checked while the report is run, and displayed if its level is the same as, or below, the level of detail specified for the report.

You can also choose whether the row is displayed, whether zero values are displayed, whether you want to change the sign (explained in a moment), and whether you want to change sign on variance amount types. Why would you want to switch a number's sign? The system treats positive amounts as debits and negative amounts as credits regardless of account type. So for a liability account, you may want to show a negative balance as positive number—in which case you will need to change its sign. This can apply to Variance amount types as well.

Once you have defined all of the advanced options, the row is suitable for use as a heading. If you intend to use it only as a heading, click on the **New Record** button to proceed. If this row is *not* a heading, then you will instead assign accounts to the row, or define calculations for it.

ACCOUNT ASSIGNMENTS   To assign accounts to each row, click on the **Account Assignments** button. When the Account Assignments form (shown in Figure 3-23) appears, select the +/- sign to indicate whether the balance of the defined account range should be added or subtracted from the total. When you click on an Account field, a new dialog box named Operations Accounting Flex will appear. This dialog box allows you to enter low and high flexfield values at the company, department, account, subaccount, and product level. For each level, you can specify a *Display* option that determines how many account lines will be included in that level. The choices are as follows:

- **E (Expand)**   If you enter an account range, E will include all segment values defined within that range.

- **T (Total)**   T will sum up the amount types of all segment values defined within the account range, and return one total balance.

- **B (Both)**   Displays both categories.

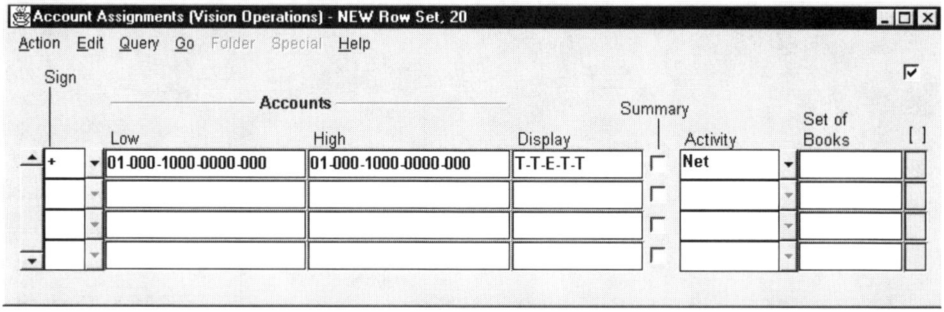

FIGURE 3-23. *Account Assignments form*

If you use a parent value that consists of three child values and you specify a display mode of E, then you will have three account lines for that row: one for each child value. If the display mode is T, a single line will display the sum of the three child values. If you set the display to B, you will have four accounting lines: the three child values, along with a line showing the their combined value.

Back in the Account Assignments form, checking the *Summary* checkbox causes only summary balances to be reported. This means that the parent value will not be expanded to include child values. (However, if the profile option *FSG: Expand Parent Value* is set to Yes, and the *Summary* checkbox is checked, parent values that belong to a rollup group will not be expanded to include child values, and parent values that do not belong to a rollup group will be expanded.) In the account's Activity field, you can specify whether you want to display Net activity, or just the debit/credit activity. As a last step, you can specify another Set of Books to use if the Chart of Accounts structure and accounting calendar of the specified Set of Books is the same as the assigned Set of Books.

CALCULATIONS   Return to the Rows form now, and click on the **Calculations** button to define calculations. The Calculations form employs the same Reverse Polish Notation as MassAllocation. The first calculation step uses the operator **Enter**; the subsequent steps can use all of the valid operators (+, -, x, /, %, Average, Median, and StdDev). You can enter a constant to be used as a fixed number, or you can enter a sequence of row line numbers, or you can enter the row name you defined. See Figure 3-24.

To practice using the forms you have just learned about, set up a row set that matches the specifications in Table 3-6. Name it **NEW Row Set**.

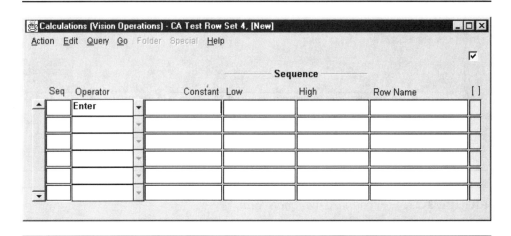

FIGURE 3-24. *Calculations form*

Review Questions

    1. What form and field control a row's heading in a report?

    2. How can you make a blank line be inserted before a total row in a report?

    3. What is the difference between the E, T, and B display options when assigning accounts?

    4. Why is the ability to change a number's sign important in Oracle General Ledger?

Row Number	Row Definition	Description
Row 10	Line item: Assets	Assets
	No account assignments/calculations	
Row 20	Account assignment :01-000-10000-0000-000, T-T-E-T-T	All of the asset accounts
	Where 10000 is the all assets parent value	
Row 30	Calculations: Summation of Row 20, add underline character before row	Total assets

TABLE 3-6. *Row Set Exercise*

Column Set

Oracle comes with a number of predefined column sets, providing output for common requirements such as monthly, PTD, QTD, and YTD Actuals. You can also create your own column sets. Using the Column Set form (navigation path *Reports : Define : ColumnSet*), the process of defining a column set is very similar to that for defining a row set. You start by entering a name for the set, along with an optional description. Then you encounter a new option: an override segment. The override segment—together with column override values—allows you to create a report in which each column can be a specific segment value of the override segment. For example, if you have companies 101, 102, and 103, and you want to create a report with a column for each company, you can do so by entering **company** as the override segment and **101**, **102**, and **103** as the override values for the three columns.

The Column Set form contains three buttons not found on the Row Set form:

■   **Define Columns**

■   **Create Heading**

■   **Build Column Set**

DEFINE COLUMNS   As you can see from Figure 3-25, the Define Columns form is very similar to the Define Rows form. One new item is Position, which indicates the starting position of the column. There is also a new button labeled **Exceptions**. Exceptions are user-defined flags that appear next to a row when it meets conditions you specify. Click on the **Exceptions** button now, and you should see a form similar to Figure 3-26. Enter a character you want to use as an exception flag (the flag is limited to a single character), along with a description. Then specify the condition that will make that flag appear. If you define multiple exceptions, only rows that meet all the exceptions will be flagged.

TIP
To flag rows when just one of multiple conditions is met, rather than when all are met, you can use nondisplayed columns. Separate the conditions so that one condition is applied to each nondisplayed column. This way, if any one of the conditions is met, the row will be flagged.

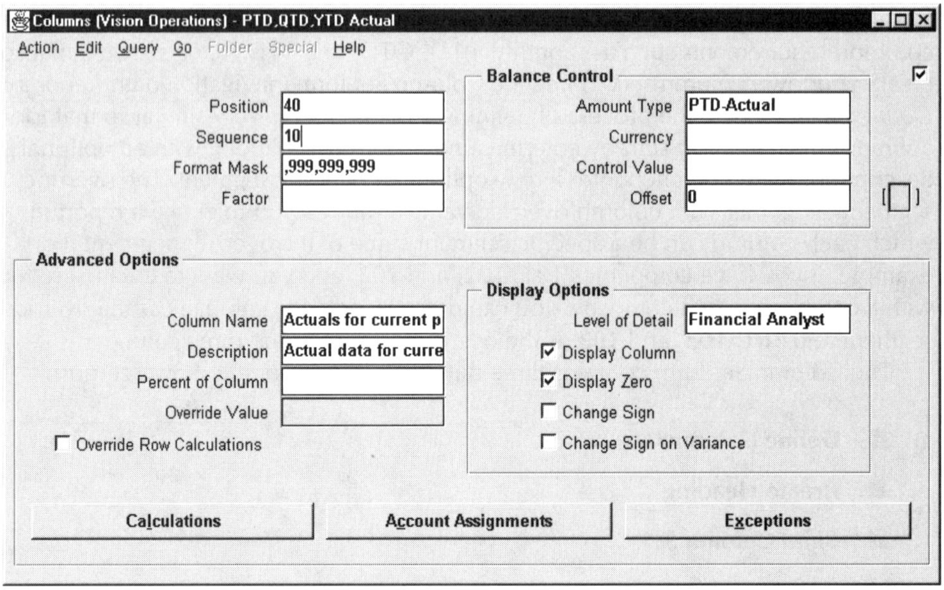

FIGURE 3-25. *Define Columns form*

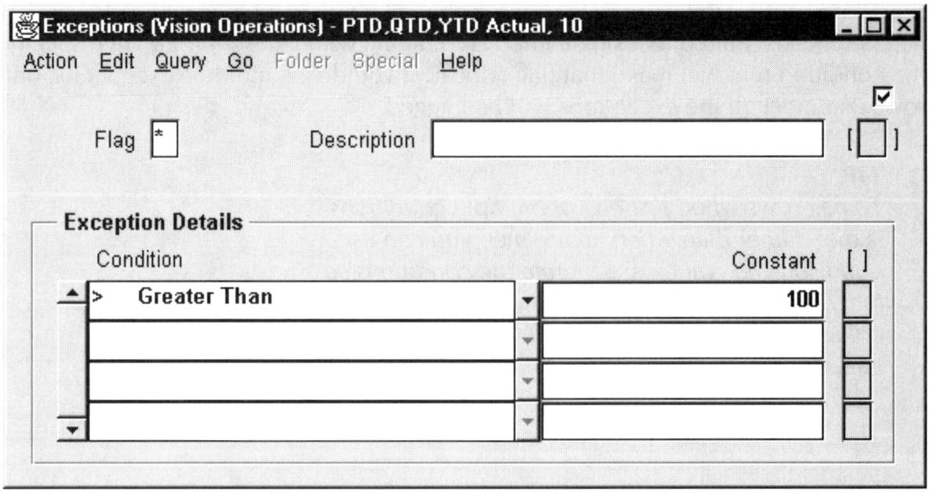

FIGURE 3-26. *Exceptions form*

If there are conflicts between row definitions and column definitions, row definitions take precedence for the following options:

- Amount Type
- Offset
- Format
- Factor
- Display Zero
- Level of Detail

Column definitions take precedence for these options:

- Activity in Account Assignments
- Override Row Calculations

In these options, a setting of Yes always overrides a setting of No:

- Change Sign
- Change Sign on Variance

There are a few options that must be the same in both row and column definitions. They are:

- Control Value
- *Summary* checkbox in Account Assignments
- Currency

If account assignments are assigned to row definitions and column definitions, only the intersecting account assignments will be shown in the FSG reports.

CREATE HEADING   Back in the Column Set form, the **Create Heading** button displays how the column heading you defined will look in an FSG report. You can use the **Create Default Heading** button to generate default column headings after you have defined your columns. Default column headings are generated using the amount types and period offsets you have defined in your columns. Period offset is used to generate relative Period-of-Interest (POI) as the column heading. Placing **&POI0** in a column heading specifies the current period-of-interest, which will be the accounting period provided as a parameter when the FSG report is submitted. Relative to Period-of-Interest, &POI-1 means one accounting period before the Period-of-Interest, and &POI+1 means one accounting period after the Period-of-Interest.

BUILD COLUMN SET   Returning once again to the Column Set form, the **Build Column Set** button takes you to a graphic interface where you can lay out columns. Figure 3-27 shows the Column Set Builder for the seeded Column Set *PTD, QTD, YTD Actual.*

In the top-left corner of the Column Set Builder form are six buttons that can change column widths, add and delete columns, and move a column left or right. In the Column Set Builder, you can define sequence numbers, names, amount types, and period offsets for columns.

The Left Margin field in the form is especially important: if the left margin is not wide enough, the first column may overlap with the account lines of the rows. In addition, you can enter the widths, headings, and format masks for columns. For the headings, you can add more lines by clicking on the **New Record** button in the toolbar. You can use any free text in the heading, as well as system-defined tokens such as Period-of-Interest (&POI), &BUDGET, &ENCUMBRANCE, and &CURRENCY. When using the last three of these, you append to the end of the token the control value they are assigned to; that is, the runtime parameters you set when FSG reports are submitted. For example, you can assign Control Value 1 to a

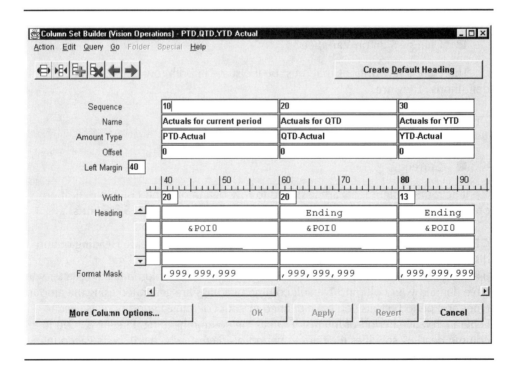

FIGURE 3-27.   *Column Set Builder form*

budget amount type; at runtime, you choose what budget to tie to Control Value 1 to generate the report. *&BUDGET1*, in this case, will be replaced by the chosen budget name in the generated report.

This form contains two buttons related to Column Sets. The **Create Default Heading** button generates a default column heading based on amount types and period offsets you have defined in your columns. The **More Column Options** button enables you to set up additional column options.

In the Column Set Builder form, you can apply your changes by clicking on the **Apply** or **OK** buttons. If you are not satisfied with your changes and want to revert to the last saved column heading, use the **Revert** button. The **Cancel** button will abandon the changes and close the Column Set Builder form.

Take some time now and create your own column set. Play with its various options until you feel comfortable with each one.

Review Questions

   1. What is the function of an override segment?

   2. What does &POI-12 represent?

   3. What does the Column Set Builder do?

   4. What is an exception?

Row Order

Row Order determines how the rows are sorted in the FSG reports. You can order rows by column rank or Chart of Account segment values. To define Row Order, follow the navigation path *Reports : Define : Order* to open the Row Order form.

If you want to sort the report by values in a particular column, enter the column's name or order number in the Rank by Column section of the form. The column's order is the number of columns from the starting column, with the first column identified as 1. That means that if you have three columns, you will have column 1, column 2, and column 3. Then you select a ranking method of either Ascending or Descending. Finally, you move to the Account Display portion of the form, select a Chart of Accounts Segment, and assign ranking in its Order By column.

To order by a Chart of Account segment value, enter the sequence of segments that you want your Chart of Accounts to display and order by. Start by entering the first sequence number (1), then the segment assigned to that sequence. Specify that the segment should be ordered by Value and should display its Value. Finally, set the segment's width in the report (or set it to zero to suppress the segment from displaying in the FSG reports). The example in Figure 3-28 shows row order in which only the Account segment values and descriptions will display, ordered by Account segment values.

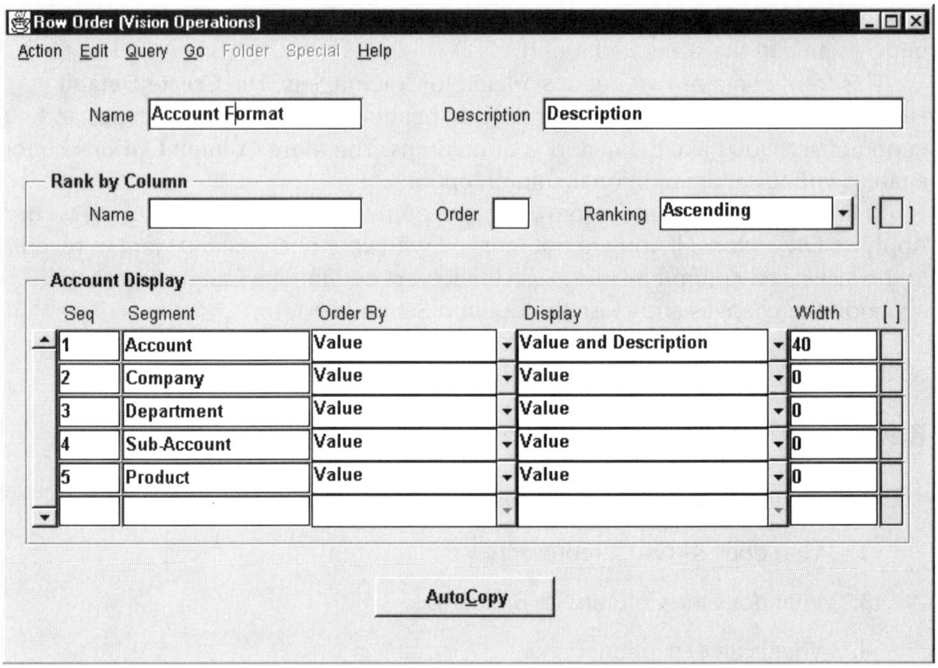

FIGURE 3-28. *Row Order form*

Display Sets and Display Groups

Display sets and display groups give you a way to display selected portions of the FSG reports. A Display Group is a range of rows or columns. To define a Display Group, follow the navigation path *Reports : Define : Display : Group*. Enter the name of the Display Group and an optional description. Select the row set or column set on which the Display Group should be based. Then choose the sequence range. As an exercise, create a Display Group called **New Display Group** with your Row Set, and configure it to include only the second row.

A Display Set groups Display Groups and assigns them to a row set or column set. You create them using the Display Set form (*Reports : Define : Display : Set*). Once you have entered the name of the display set and an optional description, you select the row set or column set to which the display set should be assigned. In the Display Group Assignments region, you enter the sequence number, check the *Display* checkbox if you want to display the Display Group, and enter the Row

Group and/or Column Group you want to assign to the selected row set or column set. You can also enter an optional description. If the row sequences or column sequences are not included in any Display Groups assigned to the row set or column set, those rows and columns will be displayed.

Create a display set now. Use your row set and your display group, and uncheck the *Display* checkbox.

Review Questions

1. How does the Rank by Column feature affect the output of a report?

2. How do you omit a segment and its heading from a row set?

3. What options do you have for ordering and displaying Chart of Accounts segments?

4. What is a display set? A display group?

Content Set

A content set is used to override row set account assignments to generate different variations of the same report without defining separate reports. Most of the time, content sets are used to generate a given report for every value in a segment of the Chart of Accounts—for example, a Standard report that repeats for each company in the Chart of Accounts. To enter content sets, follow the navigation path *Reports : Define : ContentSet*. Enter the name of the content set, an optional description, and the type. The type determines whether the run order of the reports will be *sequential* or *parallel*.

Next, you define the Account Assignments for the content set. This is very similar to the Account Assignments form you saw in the Define Rows/Columns form. However, since content set overrides the row set, you do not need to fill in all segments. The segments without any value will fall back to the row set account assignments. You do need to define what display types to use to override the row set. Valid display types are listed in Table 3-7. As a last step, you can override whether the account is a summary. Your form should now look like Figure 3-29.

Review Questions

1. What is the purpose of a content set?

2. What is the difference between display types PE and RE?

3. What is the difference between display types PT and RT?

Display Type	Description
N	No override
CT	Summation of balances of all segment values within the account range.
PE	Expand the account range or parent value into detail segment values. In addition, it will page break after each segment value creating a different report.
PT	Override the account range but maintain the row set display types (E, T, B).
RE	Expand the account range or parent value into detail segment values. Same as E in defining rows.
RT	Total the segment values for the segment. Same as T in defining rows.
RB	Show both detail and total for the account range or the parent value. Same as B in defining rows.

TABLE 3-7. *Content Set Display Types*

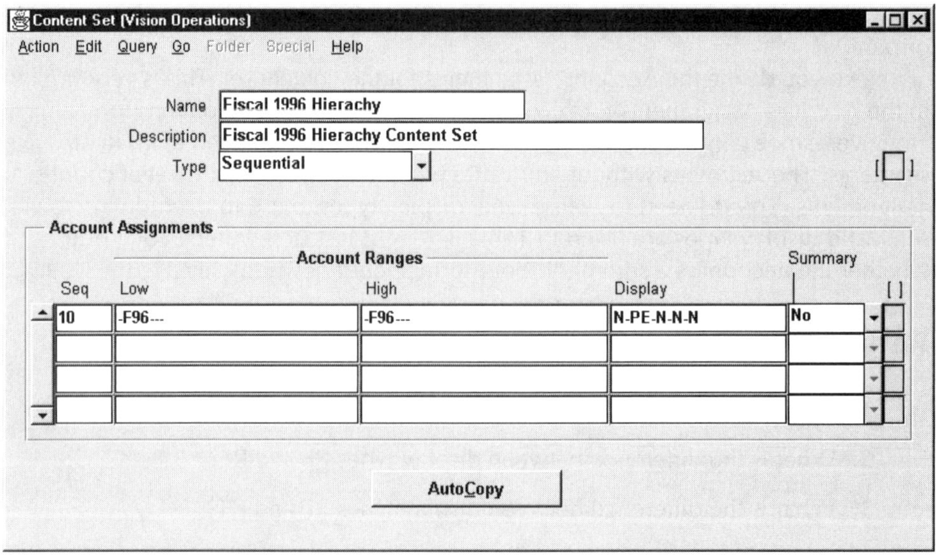

FIGURE 3-29. *Content set form*

Create FSG Reports

Now that you have learned the five required and optional components of an FSG reports, you can combine them into a single report. To define an FSG report, follow the navigation path *Reports : Define : Report.* Enter the name, the title, and an optional description of the report. The title you enter will be displayed on the top of the report. Next, enter the two required components: row set and column set. Select the row set you have created, and for the column set select PTD, QTD, YTD Actual. Then enter the three optional components: content set, row order, and display set. In the Other Options region, you can select a runtime Segment Override, a default Currency for rows and columns with no defined currency, a Rounding Option (*Calculate Then Round* or *Round Then Calculate*), a Level of Detail (*Financial Analyst, Supervisor* or *Controller*), and an Output Option (*Spreadsheet: Tab Delimited* or *Text*). Figure 3-30 shows how your form should look when you are done.

If your row set or column set has a control value assigned, the **Control Value** button will be active and you will need to enter the corresponding control value for currency, budgets, and/or encumbrance types. When you are done, save your report.

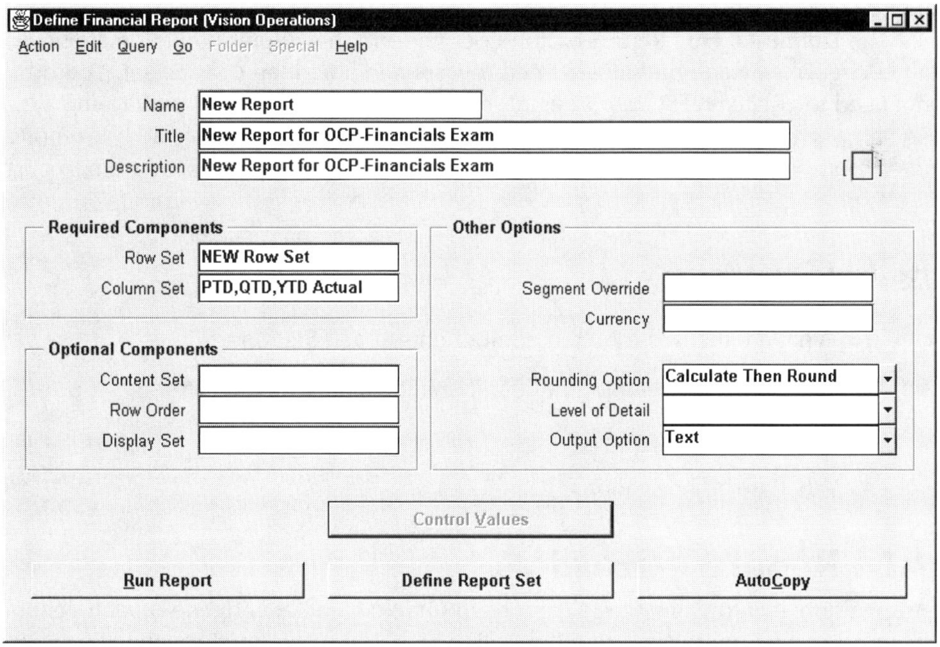

FIGURE 3-30. *Define Financial Report form*

Create FSG Report Sets

To create an FSG report set, you can follow the navigation path *Reports : Define ReportSet* or click on the **Define Report Set** button from the Define Reports form. Report sets are essentially sequences of individual FSG reports submitted together to save time. For example, you may run the same report each time at month-ends. Including this group of reports in a report set is a convenient way to reduce your month-end close time. To create your own report set, enter a name and an optional description. Then, enter the sequence and the FSG reports you would like to include in the report set.

Submit FSG Reports/Report Sets

To submit a report or a report set, you can follow the navigation path *Reports : Request : Financial* or click on the **Run Report** button from the Define Report/Report Sets forms. You can choose to run individual reports, a single report set, or multiple report sets. Start by selecting the reports or report sets you want to run. Then enter the accounting period of interest and determine whether you want to override the currency, segment override, content set, row order, display set, rounding option, *Exception* checkbox, or output option. (If the *Exception* checkbox is checked, the report will only display rows that are exceptions.) Click on the **Submit** button to run the selected reports.

The **Define Ad Hoc Report** button opens a form that allows you to create new ad hoc reports by combining a defined row set and a defined column set. You do not need to create an FSG report first. This is helpful if you are just performing a one-time what-if analysis, or are testing potential reports. If you create ad hoc reports often, you will periodically need to run the Delete Ad Hoc Reports program to clean them up.

Review Questions

1. What are the two required components of an FSG report?

2. What are the three optional components of an FSG report?

3. What are report sets?

4. What are ad hoc reports?

ADI Report Wizard

As an alternative to defining FSG reports in Oracle General Ledger, you can define them using the Report Wizard in the ADI, which will walk you through the process of creating an FSG. To create an FSG report in the ADI, you choose the General

Ledger Poplist from the ADI toolbar and select the *Define Report* option from the list of values. This will initiate the Report Wizard. Then take these steps:

1. Select *Define Report* in the Definitions group, as shown in Figure 3-31. Then, click on the **Next** button.

2. Select *Blank Report* in the Define New Report Using group. Then, click on the **Next** button.

3. Enter a name for the report, the number of rows, the number of columns, the default column width, and the line item width for the FSG report.

4. Select *New Workbook* or *Current Workbook* in the Destinations group. Then, click on the **Next** button.

5. In the next dialog box, select a Format Mask and Factor.

6. If you want to create a trend report, select the *Yes* option for Trend Report and click on the **Next** button.

7. In Step 5, select the balance type you want the report to reflect. Then choose whether you want the report's trend to roll forward or backward, and whether the reporting increment should be days, months, or quarters. Then, click on the **Finish** button to generate the Report Worksheet.

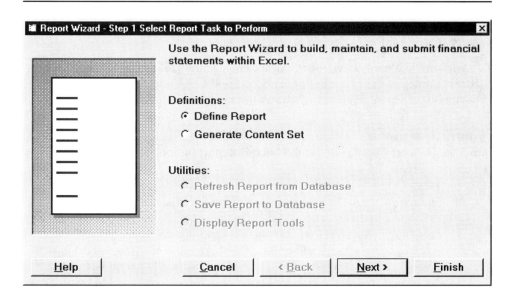

FIGURE 3-31. *Select Report Task to Perform*

The ADI will communicate with the database, prepare the report components, and then create the report in Microsoft Excel. Once the report worksheet is invoked, you can use Report Wizard tools to define report objects, row properties, and column properties; to insert or delete row and column objects; to move columns; and to save the report to the database or refresh it from database.

Review Questions

1. How do you invoke the Report Wizard from the ADI?

2. What options can be defined for a trend report?

ADI Request Center

You can use the Request Center from the ADI to submit reports (standard and financial), show request details, and view output and logs. You can also format and publish output, print output, and print logs. In addition, you can monitor requests, add requests to the Hotlist (a user-defined list of requests you want to watch in the Request Center), and stop monitoring one or all requests, among other things. In this section, you will learn how to:

■ Submit a report

■ Set report publishing options

■ Set report submission options

You should already have the Request Center running. If not, you can invoke the Request Center by going to the Applications Poplist and selecting *Request Center* from the list of values. Figure 3-32 shows the Request Center display.

Submit Report

From the Request Center, choose the **Submit Report** button. You can submit two types of reports:

■ **Standard** reports come in two flavors: fixed format and variable format. With the variable format, you can create and apply an attribute set to change the delivered format of the standard reports. Using an attribute set, you can move, group, and order attributes to customize the report format. If you want the reports to be published automatically after the reports are completed, check the *Publish Report* checkbox. If you want to be prompted before publishing, check the *Prompt* checkbox.

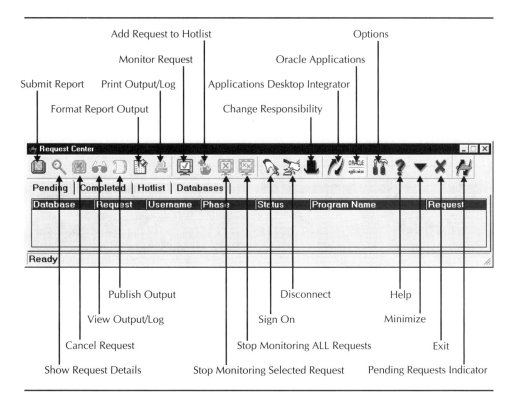

FIGURE 3-32. *Request Center screen*

As an exercise, click on the **Submission** button, select the Standard report, and enter the necessary parameters. Then, save your work.

■ **Financial Statement** reports are available by selecting that option in the Report Type group and then clicking on the **Submission** button. The bottom portion of the dialog box changes to show related options. You can either selecting an existing report or create an ad hoc report. If you choose the latter approach, leave the report name blank and enter the required and optional report components. Enter the FSG parameters, including accounting period, currency, segment override, and rounding options. Be sure to save your work when you are done.

Publishing options determine how your report will be presented once it has completed. Click on the **Publishing** button, and a new array of options will appear.

You can modify the appearance of the output by applying a theme to it. You can also determine whether the output should be sent to a text file, an HTML file, Microsoft Excel, or Oracle Discoverer. If your report format is standard (variable format), you can select an attribute set to apply to the output. Finally, if you selected an output type of Web or Spreadsheet, you can set a variety of options specific to that output type. The Web options are shown in Figure 3-33 and detailed in Table 3-8, and the Spreadsheet options are shown in Figure 3-34 and detailed in Table 3-9.

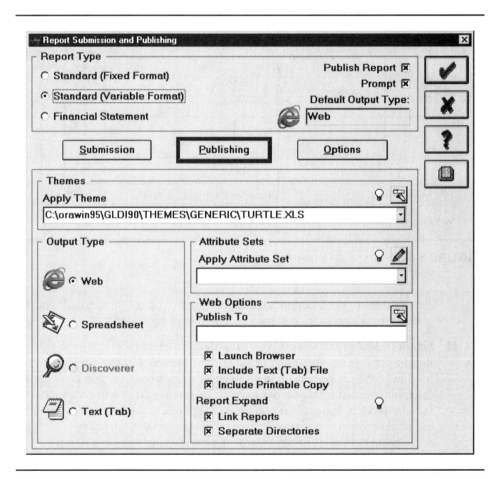

FIGURE 3-33. *Web Report Publishing Options screen*

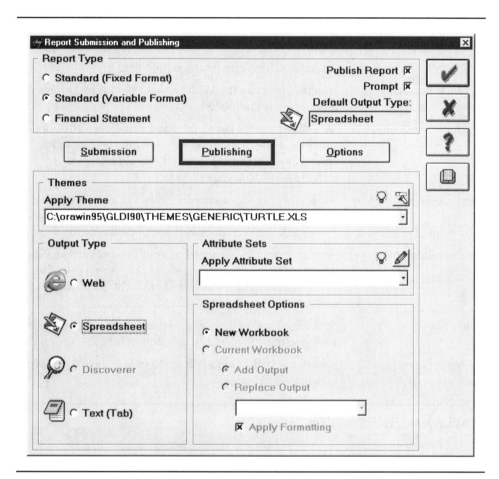

FIGURE 3-34.   *Spreadsheet Report Publishing Options screen*

Report Submission Options

To set submission options for the report, click on the **Options** button. This causes the bottom portion of the dialog box to display the contents shown in Figure 3-35. You can set the date and time the report will be submitted, the printer to which it will be sent, and how many copies will be printed.

Option	Description
Publish To	A path and filename for the output file.
Launch Browser	Specifies whether the Web browser should be launched after report is completed.
Include Spreadsheet	Available only for Financial Statement reports, this option specifies whether the report should also be output in spreadsheet format—if selected, the Web page will include a link to the spreadsheet.
Include Text (Tab) File	Available only for standard reports, this option specifies whether the report should also be output in text format—if selected, the Web page will contain a link to the text file.
Include Printable Copy	Available only for standard reports, this option specifies whether the report should also be output in a printable Web-based format—if selected, the Web page will contain a link to the printable file.
Link Reports	Specifies whether links to other reports should be included in the Web page for content sets.
Separate Directories	Specifies whether reports in content sets should be saved in separate directories.

TABLE 3-8.   *Web Publishing Options*

Option	Description
New Workbook	Specifies whether report should be published to a new workbook in Excel
Current Workbook	Within the current workbook, specifies whether output should go to an existing worksheet or a new worksheet
Apply Formatting	Specifies whether a theme's formatting should be applied to the spreadsheet

TABLE 3-9.   *Spreadsheet Publishing Options*

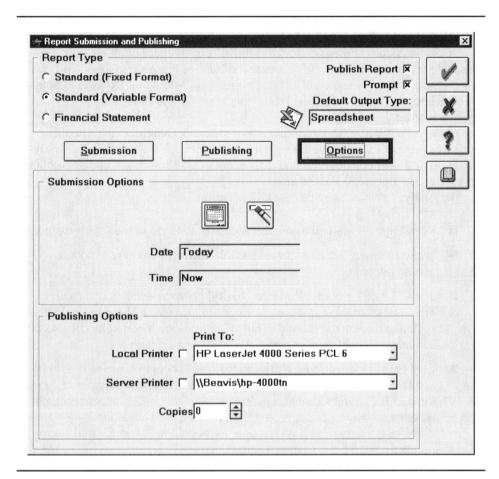

FIGURE 3-35. *Submission options*

Once these options are set, click on the **Submission** button. You will be presented with a concurrent request ID for the request, and you will see the request in the Request Center window.

Review Questions

1. What are the steps for publishing a report to the Web? What options let you control the content and appearance of the report?

2. How do you exercise control over report submission?

ADI Analysis Wizard

The Analysis Wizard allows you to "drill-down" on summary numbers, to see greater levels of detail about the figures that produced those summaries. You can select amounts from the spreadsheet and perform drill-down to details in Oracle General Ledger. You can also pivot different dimensions and perform multidimensional analysis.

You invoke Analyze Report from the ADI toolbar's **General Ledger Poplist** button when your cursor is on the amount you want to drill-down on. The Analysis Wizard will show the amount, amount type, detail on what makes up the amount, and the accounting period and currency.

The Analysis Wizard provides the following functions:

- View/Filter allows you to see the accounts assigned to the selected amount.

- Show Summary Accounts provides drill-down to summary accounts and amounts.

- Show Detail Accounts allows you to drill down to detail accounts and amounts. From there, the Analysis Wizard provides a **Show Journal Details** button to display the journal details. The drill-down hierarchy consists of summary accounts, detail accounts, and journal details.

- Drill Options let you to specify whether the account segments should be displayed separately or together; whether descriptions should be included for your balancing segment, cost center segment, and/or account segment; whether to show account type, zero balances, expand/collapse indicators, and totals; the minimum width for amount columns; and the maximum number of active drills, among other things.

- Data Source shows information about the database, application, workbook name, worksheet name, and worksheet cell.

Review Questions

1. What is the purpose of the Analysis Wizard?

2. What is the drill-down hierarchy in the Analysis Wizard?

Understanding the Integration with Oracle Financial Analyzer

This section provides an overview of Oracle Financial Analyzer and how it integrates with Oracle General Ledger. The details of how to integrate these two products will be covered in Chapter 7.

Oracle Financial Analyzer (OFA) is a tool that facilitates multidimensional analysis of financial data. In order to integrate OFA with GL, you must map GL segments and segment values to dimensions and dimension values in OFA. OFA also maps a time dimension based on the accounting calendars defined in GL. Further, OFA uses GL account hierarchies to create a structure for online drill-down analysis.

When using OFA, you map the dimensions and drill-down hierarchy, and then define a *financial data set* specifying what data to load. The data set can include all of the GL balance types, including Actual, Budget, Encumbrance, and Statistical. The loaded financial data sets, partitioned by the dimension, are the foundation of OFA's data model.

Review Questions

1. What is the basis of OFA dimensions?

2. What is a financial data set?

For the Chapter Summary, Two-Minute Drill, and Chapter Questions and Answers, open the summary.htm file contained in the Summary_files directory on the book's CD-ROM.

CHAPTER

4

Multiple-Currencies
Accounting

racle General Ledger supports multiple-currencies accounting in compliance with FAS52—the Financial Accounting Standards Board guidelines dictating how American companies reporting in U.S. dollars must account for business activities initially carried out in foreign currencies. In this chapter, you will learn about:

■ Multiple-currencies accounting

■ Implementation considerations

Oracle GL offers full multiple-currency capabilities, including daily, period-end, and historical exchange rates; revaluation for unrealized gain/loss; translation; and reporting in any defined currency. GL also supports European Monetary Union (EMU) currency, along with the currency derivations to the official Euro (EUR). At the end of the chapter, you will learn about implementation considerations surrounding multiple-currencies accounting.

Accounting for Foreign and Multiple Currencies

This section explains how to perform multiple-currencies accounting in Oracle General Ledger. Topics include:

■ Defining foreign currencies

■ Entering foreign-currency journals

■ Revaluing foreign-currency balances

■ Translating foreign-currency balances

■ Multiple Reporting Currencies

You will see how to define foreign currencies (including derivations between EUR and EMU currencies), how to enter foreign-currency journals, and how to revalue and translate foreign-currency journals in compliance with FAS52. Next, you will learn about Multiple Reporting Currencies (MRC), including how and when you should set up an MRC implementation. Finally, you will read about the many considerations involved in implementing multiple-currencies accounting.

Defining Foreign Currencies

Figure 4-1 shows an overview of the steps involved in multiple-currency accounting in Oracle General Ledger. The program comes with all ISO currencies already defined, so if you are going to use ISO currencies, all you need to do is make sure those currencies are enabled. A currency is defined with a currency code, name, and description. When creating a new currency record in GL, you have the option of entering the issuing territory, currency symbol, precision and extended precision, minimum accountable unit, and effective date range. Once a currency is enabled, you cannot change its currency code, even if you disable it later.

FIGURE 4-1. *Multiple-currencies accounting*

The Euro—the Pan-European currency—is defined in GL with the currency code EUR and a currency derivation type of *Euro currency*. If you are defining a new currency that is a national currency from one of the member states of the EMU, you must also define the currency's derivations to EUR. To do this, go to the Currencies form shown in Figure 4-2 (navigation path *Setup : Currencies : Define*). Select a derivation type of *Euro Derived* and enter the derivation's factor and effective date. Be sure you have an effective currency derivation for the EMU currency before entering any period-end rates for it.

Entering Foreign-Currency Journals

Once you have defined or enabled one or more currencies, you can enter foreign-currency journals. This is done through the same form as functional-currency journals. First, create a new journal. Next, enter the conversion information, since this is a foreign journal. Choose DEM as the foreign currency—the conversion date will be defaulted from the effective date. The conversion date is used for selecting a daily conversion rate based on the conversion type you select. If you select User as the conversion type, you can enter any exchange rate. Otherwise, using the conversion date and the conversion type, the conversion rate will be automatically

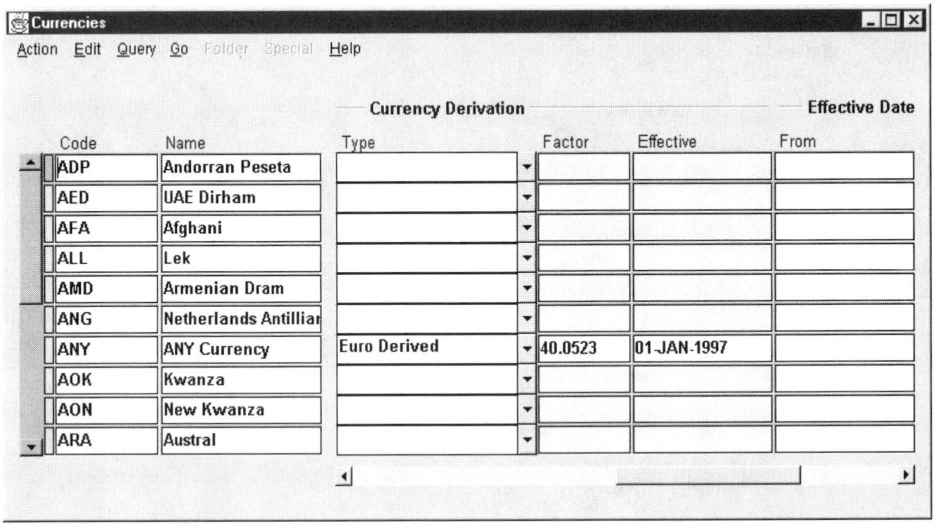

FIGURE 4-2. *Currency derivation*

retrieved. If no conversion rate is defined for that date and type, you will receive an error message.

For EMU currency, conversion rates are not retrieved directly from the daily exchange-rate table. In other words, in our example there is no DEM-to-USD daily exchange rate. EMU currency uses a currency derivation factor to convert to EUR first, then uses a daily conversion rate from EUR to the functional currency based on the conversion date and the conversion type.

Referring to Figure 4-3, you are now ready to enter journal lines. Notice how the Entered Debit and Entered Credit categories now show the foreign currency. As you enter the journal lines, the amount in foreign currency will be automatically translated to the functional currency based on the conversion rate. You can override the Converted Debit and Converted Credit if the profile option *Allow Multiple Exchange Rates* is enabled.

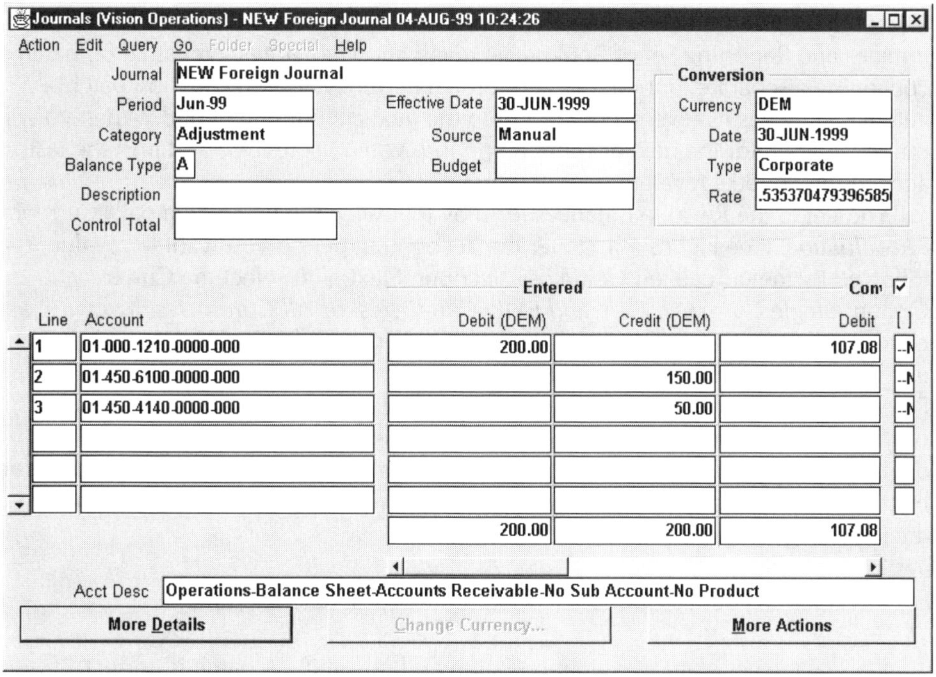

FIGURE 4-3. *Foreign journals*

Review Questions

1. What is the currency code and derivation type for Pan-European currency?

2. How are conversion rates derived in the Enter Journals form for EMU currency?

3. For what are user conversion types used?

4. When can you override the converted debit and converted credit amounts?

Revaluing Foreign Currency Balances

Asset and liability accounts that are entered in foreign currencies must be revalued every period in accordance with FAS52. The Revaluation program adjusts the value of the balance sheet accounts based on current-period exchange rates. It then generates revaluation journals with adjustments to the defined unrealized gain/loss account. The Revaluation program generates adjustments in the functional currency. If you have a Reporting Set of Books, you must run revaluation once for each Primary and Reporting Set of Books. The revaluation generates a revaluation batch containing a separate journal for each foreign currency. The revaluation batch automatically has its reversal period set to the next accounting period. When you run revaluation for the next accounting period, you must reverse and post the last accounting period's revaluation batch first.

You get to the Revalue Balances form by following the navigation path *Currency : Revaluation*. (See Figure 4-4.) Enter the accounting period you want to revalue, followed by the unrealized Gain/Loss Account. Next, you select the Currency Option: *Single Currency, Euro and EMU Currencies*, or *All Currencies*. If you choose *Single Currency*, you must enter the currency code. The period-end exchange rate will be automatically retrieved. If the currency you choose is not Euro-derived, then you can update the revalue rate. If you choose *All Currencies*, only those currencies with the appropriate period-end exchange rates will be defined. Enter the account range you want to revalue, and then click on the **Revalue** button. The Revaluation program will generate a revaluation batch with a name in the following format:

Revalues (accounting period) (concurrent request date and time)

Review the generated revaluation batch and post it if the batch is correct.

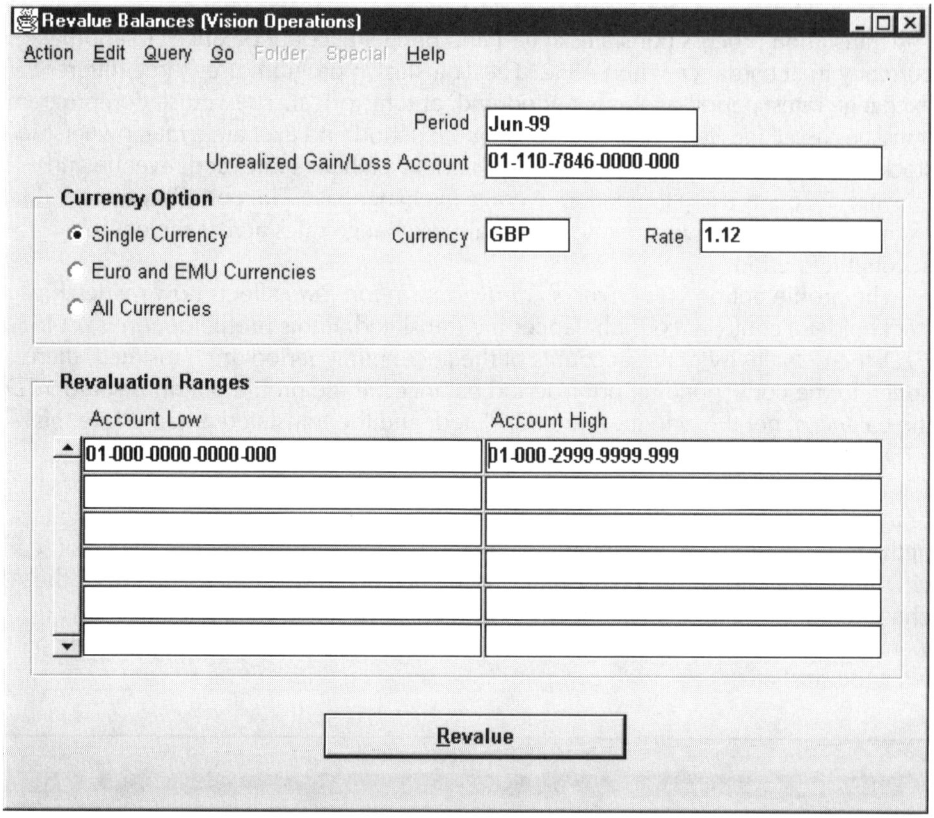

FIGURE 4-4. *Revalue Balances form*

Review Questions

1. What does revaluation do?

2. What accounts should you revalue?

3. How often should you revalue?

4. What is the prerequisite for revaluation if you have revalued before?

Translating Foreign Currency Balances

The translation process translates actual and budget account balances to another currency in accordance with FAS52. The Translation program uses three different exchange rates: period-average, period-end, and historical. The Translation program translates asset and liability accounts using the period-end exchange rate, ownership/stockholder's equity accounts using the historical exchange rate, and revenue and expense accounts using the period-average exchange rate. The period-average exchange rate is the average rate of all daily exchange rates across the entire accounting period.

The profile option *GL: Owners Equity Translation Rule* affects how ownership/stockholder's equity account balances are translated. If this profile option is set to *PTD*, the net activity of the accounts of the accounting period are translated, then added to the corresponding prior-period balances. If the profile option is set to *YTD*, the balances, not the activities, are translated, and the translated amounts are the YTD balances. There is no need to add the balances to previous balances.

You can reach the Translate Balances form via the navigation path *Currency : Translation.* As shown in Figure 4-5, the functional currency is displayed at the top of the form. Enter the balance type you want to translate: *Actual* or *Budget.* You can choose to translate all segment values for the balancing segment if you check the *All* checkbox. If not, skip the *All* checkbox and enter the specific segment value you want to translate. Next, enter the Target Currency, then the accounting period you want to translate.

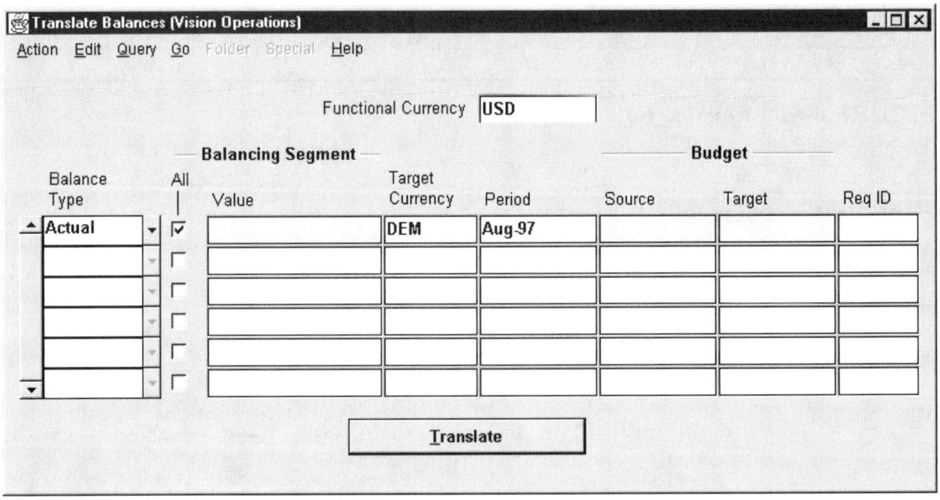

FIGURE 4-5. *Translate Balances form*

NOTE
You can never go back and translate a prior accounting period.

If you want to translate the Budget balances, you must enter the Source Budget and the Target Budget. Click on the **Translate** button to initiate the Translation program. It will automatically post the net translation adjustments to the cumulative translation adjustment accounts specified in the Set of Books. The Translation program does not generate journal batches.

After translation, you can perform online account inquiries and run FSG reports in the currency to which you translated. You can run the translation program as many times as you wish, but for performance reasons, it is best to run the program once after all of the journal entries are posted.

Review Questions

1. What rates are used to translate revenue and expenses accounts? Assets and liability accounts? Ownership/stockholders' equity accounts?

2. For the profile option *GL: Owners Equity Translation Rule*, what are the differences between the PTD and YTD settings?

Multiple Reporting Currencies

In this section, you will address the following points regarding Multiple Reporting Currencies (MRC):

- Do you need MRC?

- How does MRC work?

- Setting up MRC Sets of Books

- Assigning Reporting Set of Books

- Setting up Reporting Set of Books

- Currency conversions

Multiple Reporting Currencies allows you to maintain accounting transactions in more than one functional currency. MRC is set up by creating one or more Reporting Sets of Books and associating these Reporting Sets of Books to the Primary Set of Books. The Primary Set of Books uses the primary functional currency and the Reporting Set of Books uses reporting functional currencies. You can only have one

Primary Set of Books. As you enter accounting transactions, they are translated into the reporting functional currencies as necessary. You can look at the translated transactions of the Reporting Set of Books through responsibilities assigned to the Reporting Set of Books.

Do You Need MRC?

After learning how translation works, you might wonder: why would you need MRC? The Translation program translates account balances only—not accounting transactions. If you only want the inquiry ability and reporting ability on account balances, you do not need MRC. However, you will need MRC if:

■ Your company is located in a member state of the EMU and would like to report financial data, including transaction-level data, in both your functional currency and the Euro.

■ You must regularly report financial data—including transaction-level data—in more than one currency because your company is multinational.

■ You are in a country with high inflation and, because your functional currency is unstable, you must report financial data in a more stable currency. However, you still want to maintain financial data, including transaction-level data, in the less-stable functional currency.

How Does MRC Work?

The following Oracle Applications modules support MRC:

■ Assets

■ Cash Management

■ Cost Management

■ General Ledger

■ Payables

■ Projects

■ Purchasing

■ Receivables

MRC works differently depending on whether you enter the transactions in Oracle subledgers or Oracle GL. When you enter transactions in subledgers, the accounting transactions are translated into the Reporting Set of Books as you enter the transactions. When you transfer to Oracle GL, you must transfer to both the Primary Set of Books and the Reporting Sets of Books. You should post the transferred subledgers' accounting transactions to the Primary Set of Books, as well as to all of the Reporting Sets of Books.

When you enter transactions in GL, the journal entries entered in the Primary Set of Books are not translated immediately into any reporting functional currencies. They are translated and transferred to the Reporting Set of Books when the journal entries are posted in the Primary Set of Books. This also applies to reversed journals in the Primary Set of Books. You must post these transferred journal entries from the Primary Set of Books in all your Reporting Sets of Books. In the Reporting Sets of Books, you can post, revalue, translate, and consolidate. In fact, you must post and revalue in the Reporting Sets of Books to keep in synchronization with the Primary Set of Books. You can also perform online inquiries and run FSG reports in all Reporting Sets of Books.

Review Questions

1. What is the functional difference between the Translation program and MRC?

2. Which Oracle Applications modules support MRC?

3. How are accounting transactions transferred from Oracle subledgers?

4. How are accounting transactions transferred from Oracle GL?

Setting Up MRC Sets of Books

You must set up at least two MRC Sets of Books—one for the Primary Set of Books, the other for the Reporting Set of Books. (See Figure 4-6.) You set up MRC Sets of Books the same way you set up your regular Set of Books, with the exception that you must specify the reporting currency options for your Primary Set of Books and Reporting Set of Books.

Assigning Reporting Set of Books

After setting up the MRC Sets of Books, you must assign the Reporting Sets of Books to the Primary Set of Books. To assign a Reporting Set of Books, follow the navigation path *Setup : Financials : Books : Assign*. The Primary Set of Books data is

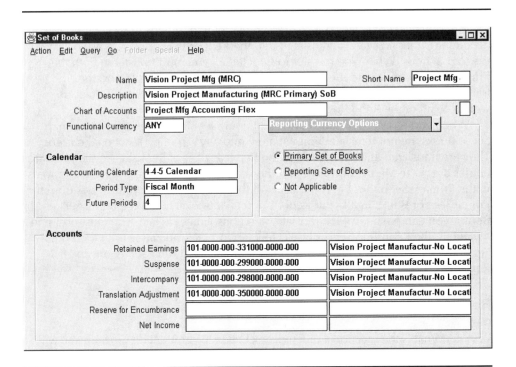

FIGURE 4-6. *MRC Sets of Books form*

filled in automatically—all you need to do is to select your Reporting Set of Books. Figure 4-7 shows an example in which the *Vision Project Mfg (EURO Rpt)* and *Vision Project Mfg (USA Rpt)* Reporting Sets of Books are assigned to the *Vision Project Mfg (MRC)* Primary Set of Books.

Your next step is to assign conversion options and GL conversion rules.

CONVERSION OPTIONS   Click on the **Conversion Options** button and you can set up conversion options for the following modules (see Figure 4-8):

- Assets

- General Ledger

- Payables

- Projects

- Purchasing

- Receivables

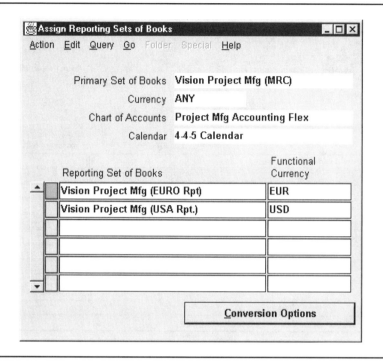

FIGURE 4-7.   *Assigning Reporting Sets of Books form*

For the Assets, Payables, Projects, Purchasing, and Receivables modules, you must specify what to place in the Reporting Conversion Type and No Rate Action fields when accounting transactions are being translated to this Reporting Set of Books. If you are implementing multiple-organization support, you must specify a Reporting Conversion Type and a No Rate Action for each operating unit for the Payables, Projects, Purchasing, and Receivables modules. For Assets, you must specify a Reporting Conversion Type and a No Rate Action to take for each corporate book when accounting transactions are being translated to this Reporting Set of Books. If you are using combined-basis accounting in Oracle Payables, you may also want to define the AP Reporting Secondary Book, which determines the corresponding Reporting Set of Books the secondary Set of Books will convert to during posting.

The Reporting Conversion Type is used during translations into a Reporting Set of Books. It can be different from the conversion type defined for transactions, which is used to translate foreign currency to the primary functional currency. Note that the user conversion type cannot be used as a Reporting Conversion Type.

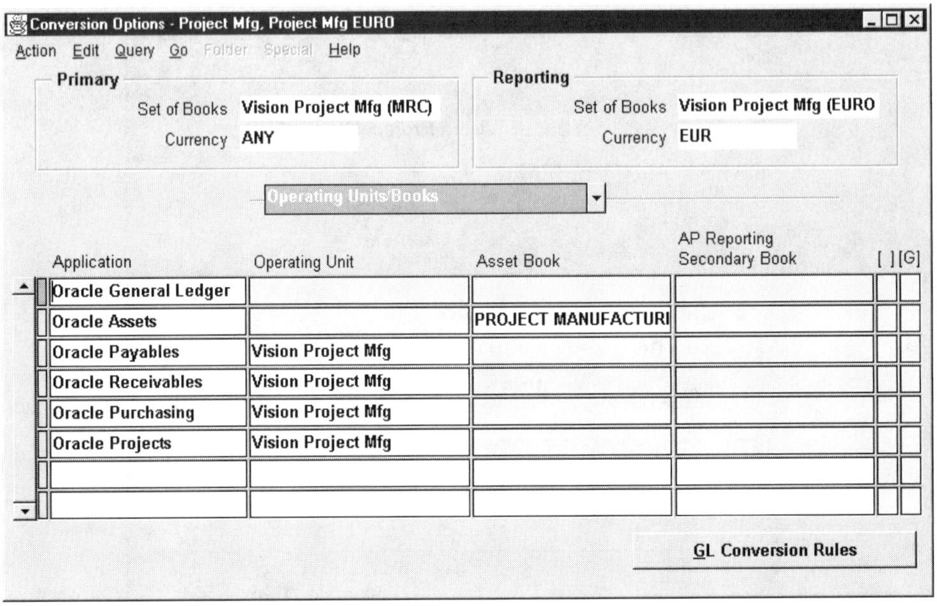

FIGURE 4-8. *Conversion Options form*

The No Rate Action determines what Oracle Applications does if no rate is found when translating into the Reporting Set of Books. Choices are *Report Error* or *Use Last Rate*. *Report Error* will give you an error message when you try to save your transactions and no conversion rate is found. *Use Last Rate* will utilize the most recent rate, without prompting, if no conversion rate is found. You can set the profile option *MRC: Maximum Days to Roll Forward Conversion Rate* to prevent the system from using a conversion rate too far back in the system.

You have the choice of entering an effective date range for these conversion options.

GL CONVERSION RULES   Click on the **GL Conversion Rules** button when you are on the General Ledger row to enter General Ledger Conversion Rules. GL Conversion Rules are set up by journal sources and journal categories. The *Convert* checkbox determines whether a particular combination of journal source and journal category should be converted.

There are a few activities that must be performed explicitly in the Reporting Set of Books, and therefore cannot be simply translated from the Primary Set of Books. As a result, the following journal sources cannot have conversion options:

- Move/Merge
- Move/Merge Reversal
- Revaluation

There are also journal sources that cannot have conversion options because they are transferred separately to the Primary Set of Books and the Reporting Set of Books. They are:

- Assets
- AX Payables
- AX Receivables
- Projects
- Receivables

You can set up Payables and Purchasing journal sources to have conversion options. Payables and Purchasing transfer journal entries separately to the Primary Set of Books and the Reporting Sets of Books. However, for encumbrance journals, they must be translated. Oracle GL will automatically filter out the actual balances from the Payables and Purchasing journal sources during translation to a Reporting Set of Books.

As shown in Figure 4-9, the Reporting Conversion Type and No Rate Action choices are also available for GL Conversion Rules. The journal source *Other* and journal category *Other* are treated as a "catchall" source and category. This means that when journal entries come in, if there are no exact matches with the combinations of the specific journal sources and the specific journal categories, it will then search for the combination of the specific journal source and journal category *Other*. If no conversion rules are found, it will then search for the journal source *Other* and the specific journal category. Finally, it will default to conversion rules for the journal source-and-category combination *Other-Other*. If you do not have *Other-Other* defined, the journal entries will not be converted.

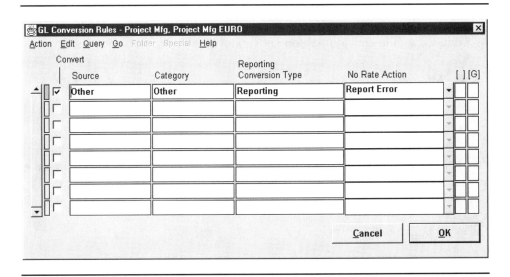

FIGURE 4-9. *GL Conversion Rules form*

Review Questions

1. What option or options must you set up when defining a Primary or Reporting Set of Books for MRC?

2. At which level are conversion rules assigned to Oracle Assets?

3. At which level are conversion rules assigned to Oracle General Ledger?

4. Name three situations in which journal entries are not translated from the Primary Set of Books to the Reporting Set of Books.

Reporting Set of Books Setup

Once you have set up and assigned your Reporting Set of Books, you must perform the following steps to finish establishing your Reporting Set of Books:

- Open accounting periods

- Initialize Reporting Set of Books balances

- Enter budgets

OPENING ACCOUNTING PERIODS   Since the Primary Set of Books and Reporting Set of Books are two different Sets of Books, you must separately maintain the accounting period status for each. In order for the following step to work, you must open your Reporting Set of Books one accounting period before the accounting period in which you want to start recording transactions. In addition, in order for the translated transactions to hit your Reporting Set of Books, you must have the accounting period either open or future-enterable. Ideally, you should maintain the same status for both sets of accounting periods.

INITIALIZING REPORTING SET OF BOOKS BALANCES   Once you set up and assign your Reporting Set of Books, you must initialize Reporting Set of Books balances. You can do this by first performing a translation in your Primary Set of Books, followed by a consolidation in the Reporting Set of Books.

You start by posting all accounting transactions in the Primary Set of Books. Then you translate the Primary Set of Books balances from the primary functional currency to the reporting currency of your Reporting Set of Books. Next, in the Reporting Set of Books, create a consolidation mapping between the Reporting Set of Books and the Primary Set of Books. You can then generate the consolidated journal entries and post them to an accounting period prior to when you want to start recording transactions in your Reporting Set of Books.

ENTERING BUDGETS   Budgets are not automatically transferred from the Primary Set of Books to the Reporting Set of Books, so if you need a Reporting Set of Books, you must enter budget figures into it separately. You can also translate and consolidate budget amounts the same way you initialized the Reporting Set of Books balances. In this situation, make sure you set up the budget organization in your Reporting Set of Books as well.

TIP
You can produce a budget vs. actual report in the Reporting Set of Books without the budget amounts actually being in the Reporting Set of Books. To do this, translate budget amounts from your Primary Set of Books to your reporting functional currency. Then use the account assignments Set of Books option when defining an FSG Column Set in your Reporting Set of Books to point to the Primary Set of Books for budget amount type.

Currency Conversion

Currency conversion behaves differently depending on whether your company is located in a member state of the EMU. If it is in a member state of the EMU and you set up a Primary Set of Books with Euro and a Reporting Set of Books with your EMU currency, then the currency conversion between the Primary and Reporting Sets of Books is fixed, based on the currency derivation factor. If it is not in a member state of the EMU, the currency conversion is variable, based on the Reporting Conversion Type you specified.

Review Questions

1. Why do you have to open accounting calendars in both the Primary Set of Books and the Reporting Set of Books?

2. How do you initialize a Reporting Set of Books' balances?

3. What must you do if you want budget amounts in both the Primary Set of Books and the Reporting Set of Books?

4. On what criteria are the currency conversions between an EMU currency and a Euro based?

Implementation Considerations

For multiple-currencies implementation, you must consider the following:

- Inquiry/reporting requirements
- Security
- Effective date for conversion options
- When to initialize balances for Reporting Sets of Books
- Special accounting steps

Inquiry/Reporting Requirements

There are a number of factors to consider when you are identifying your online inquiry and reporting requirements. Do you need the Translation program or MRC (or both)? How often will you need to produce multiple-currency reports? Do you need reports once a quarter—or once a year—or will you always have online inquiry requirements? MRC allows you to query transactions in reporting functional currencies online within most supporting subledgers. If you do need MRC, determine how many Reporting Sets of Books you need by considering the number of currencies and the different conversion options needed.

Security

Journal entries are transferable; they translate from the Primary Set of Books to the Reporting Sets of Books. If you enter journal entries in the Reporting Sets of Books, they will not be transferred to the Primary Set of Books, so you should consider whether users should be allowed to create manual journal entries in the Reporting Sets of Books. One approach to this is to enable manual journal entries approval in the Reporting Set of Books only.

You should determine how many different responsibilities you will need for your Primary Set of Books and Reporting Sets of Books, and what activities each responsibility should be able to perform.

Effective Date for Conversion Options

To determine when to have the system perform MRC translation into your Reporting Set of Books, fill in the Effective From field in the Conversion Options form. Leave the Effective To field blank to continue conversion indefinitely. Accounting transactions entered before this effective date will not be translated. You should set this date far back in the system in case you have backdated transactions. For Assets, the effective from date is automatically the oldest date placed in service in the corporate book. For Projects, on the other hand, the effective from date is the system date on which conversion options for the Projects module were entered.

When to Initialize Balances for Reporting Sets of Books

Pick the accounting period that is immediately prior to the one in which you want account transactions to start translating into your Reporting Set of Books. Ideally, for cleaner initialization, the period you converted should be the first period of a quarter. In addition, the journal data should start on the first day of the month to ensure correct PTD, QTD, and YTD balances.

Special Accounting Steps

If you want to implement MRC, you must take the following special accounting steps:

- You must maintain separate accounting statuses in both your Primary Set of Books and Reporting Sets of Books, yet keep them synchronized most of the time (at least weekly is recommended).

■ Unposted journal entries are created in your Reporting Sets of Books when you post the manual or imported journal entries in the Primary Set of Books. You must wait and post these generated journal entries in your Reporting Sets of Books to keep account balances in sync with the Primary Set of Books.

■ When you reverse journal entries in your Primary Set of Books, you must post these reversed journal entries so they can be transferred and translated to your Reporting Sets of Books. Then, you will need to post the generated reversed journal entries in your Reporting Sets of Books to keep account balances up-to-date with the Primary Set of Books.

■ You must transfer subledger accounting transactions once to your Primary Set of Books and once to every single Reporting Set of Books.

■ Oracle subledgers behave different when MRC is enabled. For example, in Oracle Payables and Oracle Projects, you must only open the accounting period for the Primary Set of Books. MRC will automatically open the accounting periods for all associated Reporting Sets of Books, whereas in Oracle Receivables, you must open an accounting period for every Reporting Set of Books. Further, MRC will automatically open the accounting period of the associated Primary Set of Books.

Review Questions

1. What should you do to prevent users from entering journal entries in the Reporting Set of Books?

2. What controls the setting of Oracle Assets' effective from date?

3. When will the Reporting Sets of Books see reversed journal entries from the Primary Set of Books?

For the Chapter Summary, Two-Minute Drill, and Chapter Questions and Answers, open the summary.htm file contained in the Summary_files directory on the book's CD-ROM.

CHAPTER
5

Oracle Assets
Fundamentals

racle Assets is the asset-management component of Oracle Applications. In this chapter, you will learn how to begin using Oracle Assets. The basic topics covered in this chapter are as follows:

- Creating fixed asset books and parameters
- Managing assets
- Adding assets from external sources
- Implementation considerations

The chapter starts by presenting essential setups, including Key flexfields, locations, and asset categories. Next, you will learn how to manage basic asset transactions: additions and depreciation. After that you will see how to add assets from external sources. Finally, you will learn about a variety of factors to consider when implementing Oracle Assets.

Creating Fixed Asset Books and Parameters

In this section, you will see how to:

- Define Key flexfields
- Set up system controls
- Create locations
- Enter asset accounting information
- Create asset categories
- Set up depreciation

All the above are required steps for using Oracle Assets. These steps were discussed briefly in Chapter 2, and they will now be covered in greater detail.

Defining Key Flexfields

Just like Oracle General Ledger, the first setup step for Oracle Assets is defining its Key flexfields. The three Key flexfields in Oracle Assets are as follows:

- Asset Category

- Asset Key

- Location

(Flexfield setup is covered in greater detail in Chapter 9.)

Asset Category Flexfield

The Asset Category flexfield is used to group assets based on financial characteristics. It can contain up to seven segments, and it must have a total length (including segment separator) of 30 or fewer characters. The Asset Category flexfield is typically made up of a major category and a subcategory, although only the major category is required.

You can design an Asset Category flexfield to include financial information such as depreciation method, depreciation life, prorate conventions, and retirement conventions. You can also tie it to capital budgeting. Understanding how you need to group your assets' financial information and how to do capital budgeting helps determine how many segments the flexfield needs, as well as each segment's data type and length.

After you determine the number of segments, segment datatypes, and segment lengths, you must define value sets governing the valid values of each segment. In the Asset Category flexfield, it is not uncommon to use dependent value sets instead of independent value sets. Both are sets of user-defined valid values, but with dependent value sets only a subset of the entire value set is valid for each independent value of a prior segment. For example, in the Vision database, the Asset Category flexfield has two segments: major category and minor category. The dependencies set up between major category and minor category are shown in Table 5-1. There is a qualifier tied to the Asset Category flexfield to identify which segment is the major category. Capital budgeting uses this qualifier to identify the major category segment.

Asset Key Flexfield

The Asset Key flexfield is used to group assets based on *nonfinancial* characteristics, such as the project number to which the asset is assigned. The Asset Key flexfield allows you to capture important information that is otherwise not stored in asset attributes or categories. It can have up to 10 segments, with a total combined length (including the segment separator) of up to 30 characters. Even if you do not currently need an Asset Key flexfield, you must set up at least one segment; if necessary, it can be a dummy segment with a default value of NONE or N/A. (In the

Major Category	Minor Category
Land	Occupied
	Unassigned
Vehicle	Leased standard
	Owned heavy
	Owned luxury
	Owned standard
	Unassigned
Computer	NC
	PC
	Software
	Unassigned
Machine	Fabricate
	Unassigned
Tenant Improvement	Removable
	Unassigned
Building	Manufacturing
	Office
	Unassigned
Expense	Expense
	Unassigned
Furniture	Desks
	Unassigned

TABLE 5-1. *Asset Category Values in Vision Database*

Vision database, the Asset Key flexfield contains only one segment.) When setting up your Asset Key flexfield, enable the *Allow Dynamic Inserts* checkbox if you do not want to have to create asset key combinations explicitly before using them.

Location Flexfield

The Location flexfield groups assets by physical location. It can have up to seven segments in the Location flexfield, and the usual 30-character length limit applies. To accommodate property tax reporting, the Location flexfield must include a state segment that is marked by the state segment qualifier. Understanding the level of detail at which you want to track your assets will help determine the number of segments, segment lengths, and segment datatypes your implementation requires. Consider including a segment to store a location's country, even if your business is currently limited to just one country—with the Internet, it is easy for a business to become global very quickly. Enable the *Allow Dynamic Inserts* checkbox if you do not want to create Location combinations explicitly before using them.

In the Vision database, the Location flexfield has four segments: country, state, city, and building.

Review Questions

1. What information is grouped by asset category?

2. What segment is a required segment in the Asset Category flexfield?

3. What segment is a required segment in the Location flexfield?

Setting Up System Controls

The System Controls form (navigation path *Setup : Asset Systems : System Control*) lets you identify the enterprise name that will be printed on asset reports, the oldest date placed in service, and the starting asset number for automatic asset numbering. More importantly, System Controls lets you define which Asset Category, Asset Key, and Location flexfields to use. Even though Oracle Assets supports multiple Sets of Books, they must all share the three Key flexfield structures.

Review Questions

1. What is the enterprise name in System Controls used for?

2. Can multiple Sets of Books use different Key flexfields in Oracle Assets?

Creating Locations

If *Allow Dynamic Inserts* is not enabled, you must create location combinations before they can be assigned. You can do by logging in under the *Assets, Vision Operations (USA)* responsibility, and then following the navigation path *Setup : Asset System : Locations*. You enter the location combination and an optional effective date range, and then check the *Enabled* checkbox. See Figure 5-1.

Review Question

1. When do you need to create locations? What other parameter affects the answer to this question?

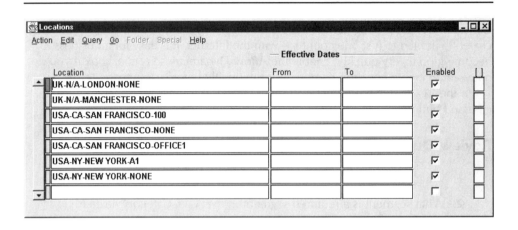

FIGURE 5-1. *Locations form*

Entering Asset Accounting Information

Entering asset accounting information is a big part of the Oracle Assets setup. It includes:

■ Fiscal year

■ Calendars

■ Book Controls

■ Account Generator

Fiscal Year

You use the Fiscal Year form (navigation path *Setup : Asset Systems : Fiscal Years*) to define the start date and end date of a fiscal year. A set of fiscal years is grouped under a fiscal year name and description. You must set up fiscal years starting from the *oldest date placed in service* you defined in System Controls. When the current fiscal year ends, the Depreciation program automatically generates the following fiscal year. Different fiscal years can be assigned to different corporate books. However, fiscal years must be the same for the tax books and their corresponding corporate books.

Calendars

Calendars define how a fiscal year breaks down into accounting periods. Use the Calendars form (navigation path *Setup : Asset Systems : Calendars*) to set up your depreciation and prorate calendars. You must set up calendars to go back to the oldest date placed in service, such as fiscal year. Each calendar has a name, description, associated fiscal year Name, and quantity of periods. You can also choose to use fiscal or calendar as a prefix, or no prefix at all. You then enter the accounting period names, along with their corresponding From and To dates. Each corporate book and tax book can have the same or different depreciation and prorate calendars. However, the tax book's fiscal year must be the same in its associated corporate book. At the end of a fiscal year, the Depreciation program automatically generates the following fiscal year's accounting periods.

The depreciation calendar is used as the reference for calculating depreciation amounts based on the *Divide Depreciation* option. It must have the same accounting period name as Oracle General Ledger in order for Assets to post to GL. The prorate calendar is used as the reference for deriving the prorated period based on an asset's date placed in service.

Review Questions

1. Can your corporate book and tax book have different depreciation calendars?

2. Can your corporate book and tax book have different prorate calendars?

3. Can your corporate book and tax book have different fiscal years?

Book Controls

An asset can be assigned to one, and only one, corporate book. To go to the Book Controls form (shown in Figure 5-2), use navigation path *Setup : Asset System : Book Controls.* Book Controls determine the accounting behavior of corporate, budget, and tax books. For each book, you enter a name, description, and class. The class can be either *Corporate, Budget,* or *Tax.* If you are defining a budget or tax book, you must associate it with a corporate book. After defining the basic information of a book, you define its calendar, accounting rules, natural accounts, and journal categories. These choices are available in subforms selectable using the drop-down list on the Book Controls form.

CALENDAR   The depreciation calendar you select must contain at least one period prior to the book's current open period. After entering the current open period, you have two options for dividing depreciation: *Evenly* or *By Days.* The *Divide Depreciation Evenly* option causes the depreciation amount to be divided evenly by the number of accounting periods in the fiscal year. In contrast, the *Divide Depreciation By Days* option causes the depreciation amount to be divided proportionally by the number of days of each accounting period in the fiscal year. Thus, an accounting period of 30 days will have a bigger depreciation amount than a period of 28 days.

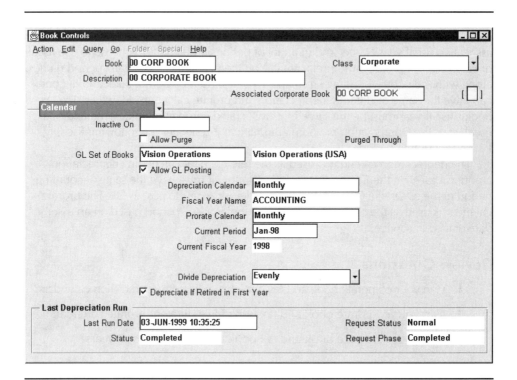

FIGURE 5-2.   *Book Controls – Calendar form*

If you want to depreciate assets in this book even if they retire during their first year, enable the *Depreciate If Retired in First Year* checkbox. You can also enter the last run date to identify when depreciation was last run for this book. You can only enter this date once during setup; after you run the Depreciation program from Oracle Assets, the program automatically updates the Last Run Date field.

Your prorate calendar can be the same as, or different from, the depreciation calendar.

Review Questions

1. What are the three classes for asset books?

2. What are the two criteria for posting to the General Ledger from Oracle Assets?

3. Describe the two *Divide Depreciation* options.

4. How should you select the current period?

ACCOUNTING RULES   In the Accounting Rules alternate region (shown
in Figure 5-3), you can check the *Allow Amortized Changes* checkbox to allow
amortization of changes, and the *Allow Mass Changes* checkbox to allow mass
changes. Mass changes is a function in Oracle Assets enabling you to change
information in an entire group of assets. You can also enter a capital gain threshold
in years and months. If you enter a capital gain threshold, any gain from retiring
an asset before the threshold is considered ordinary income, instead of capital gain.

   You can check the *Allow Revaluation* checkbox to allow revaluation of assets
in this book. If you allow revaluation, you can then decide whether the system
will revalue accumulated depreciation, retire revaluation reserve, and amortize
revaluation reserve. If you choose to revalue fully reserved assets, you can also
specify a life extension factor, the maximum number of revaluations you want to
allow for an asset, and the life extension ceiling for the maximum depreciation
adjustment allowed.

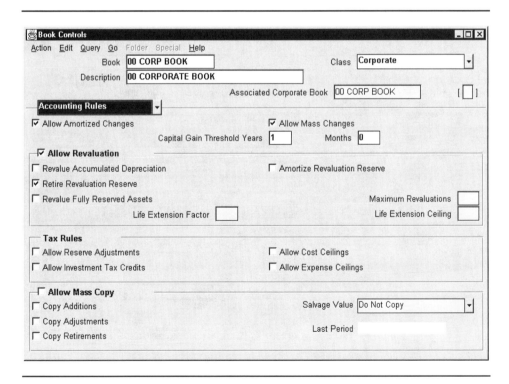

FIGURE 5-3.   *Book Controls – Accounting Rules form*

In the area of tax rules, you can enable special tax rules to allow adjustments to depreciation reserve, investment tax credits, and cost and expense ceilings within this book.

You can also enable the *Allow Mass Copy* option to copy assets from a corporate book to a tax book. If you enable mass copying, you can specify whether the process will include additions, adjustments, and retirements. You can also specify whether the salvage value should be copied.

NATURAL ACCOUNTS   In the Natural Accounts alternate region (shown in Figure 5-4), you specify the natural account segment to be used in proceeds of sale gain, loss, and clearing; cost of removal gain, loss, and clearing; net book value retired gain and loss; and revaluation reserve retired gain and loss. You can also define natural account segments for intercompany receivables and payables, deferred depreciation reserve and expense, and depreciation adjustment. Also in this region, you enter the account combination to be used as a default by the Account Generator for segments other than the balancing segment, cost center segment, and natural account segment.

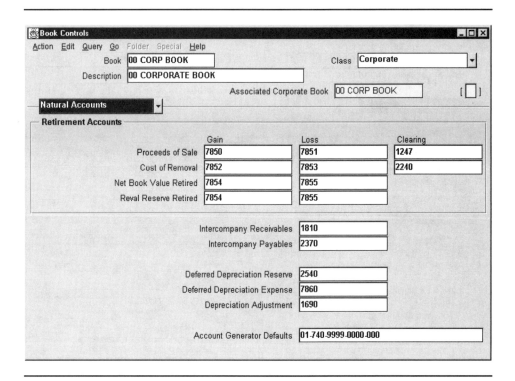

FIGURE 5-4.   *Book Controls – Natural Accounts form*

JOURNAL CATEGORIES   In the Journal Categories alternate region (shown in Figure 5-5), you start by defining which journal source to use for all journal entries. The default is *Assets*. You can then elect to group the journal entries within the following categories: Additions, Adjustments, Retirements, Reclass, Transfers, Revaluation, Depreciation, CIP Additions, CIP Adjustments, CIP Retirements, CIP Reclass, CIP Transfers, Deferred Depreciation, and Depreciation Adjustment.

Account Generator

The Account Generator generates full account combinations for journal entries to post to Oracle General Ledger. You can modify the default processes for Oracle Assets in Oracle Workflow, which is covered in detailed in Chapter 11.

   By default, the Account Generator gets the balancing segment value from the distribution line of the asset assignment for all account combinations. For depreciation-expense account combinations, it also gets the cost center segment value from the distribution line. All the other asset-related account combinations get

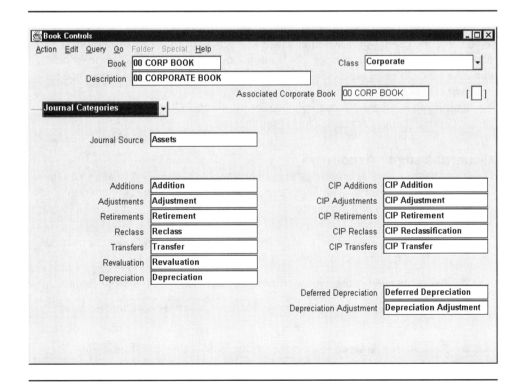

FIGURE 5-5.   *Book Controls – Journal Categories form*

the cost center segment value from the Account Generator Default in the Book Controls (except the natural account segment, which comes from either the Book Controls or asset categories).

Review Questions

1. How can changes be amortized in Oracle Assets?

2. What is the Account Generator Default used for?

3. What module do you need to modify the default Account Generator processes?

4. When will the default Account Generator process use the cost center segment value?

Creating Asset Categories

Asset categories define a set of accounts to use, along with a set of depreciation rules. You can set up asset categories by following the navigation path *Setup : Asset System : Asset Categories* (shown in Figure 5-6). This form allows you to enable asset categories, determine whether assets in each asset category should be capitalized, and control whether assets are included in physical inventory. You can also set each category's description, category type, ownership, property type, and property class.

In addition to an asset category's header information, this form allows you to define General Ledger accounts and default rules.

General Ledger Accounts

For this step, you start by entering the book with which you want to associate the asset category. Then for each asset category and book, you can enter account numbers for the following accounts:

■ **Asset Cost** is used for regular asset additions, capitalization, cost changes, reclassifications, revaluations, retirements, and transfers.

■ **Asset Clearing** is used for regular asset additions and cost adjustments.

■ **Accumulated Depreciation** is used as the contra-account for the asset cost account.

■ **Revaluation Reserve** is used for the net book value gain/loss during revaluation (only applicable if the *Revalue Accumulated Depreciation* option is selected in this book).

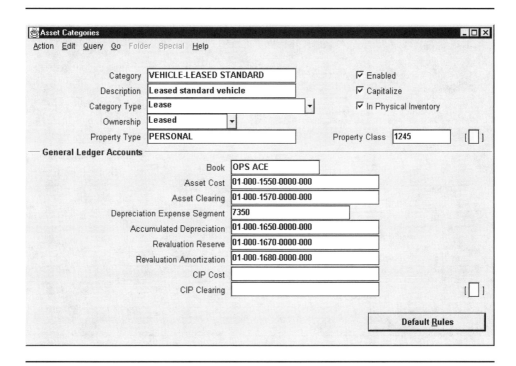

FIGURE 5-6.   *Asset Categories – General Ledger Accounts form*

- **Revaluation Amortization** is used for the amortized revaluation reserve (only applicable if the *Amortize Revaluation Reserve* option is selected in this book).

- **CIP Cost** is used for CIP asset additions, capitalization, cost changes, reclassifications, revaluations, retirements, and transfers.

- **CIP Clearing** is used for CIP asset additions and cost adjustments.

Default Rules

Click on the **Default Rules** button to display the default depreciation rules for the asset category and book combination (shown in Figure 5-7). You can have multiple sets of depreciation rules for a single asset category/book combination, with different date ranges for the Placed in Service fields. If this is the case, the asset's depreciation rules will be based on the date placed in service.

Depreciation rules can be used to determine whether assets should be depreciated, what depreciation method to use, and length of life. For each

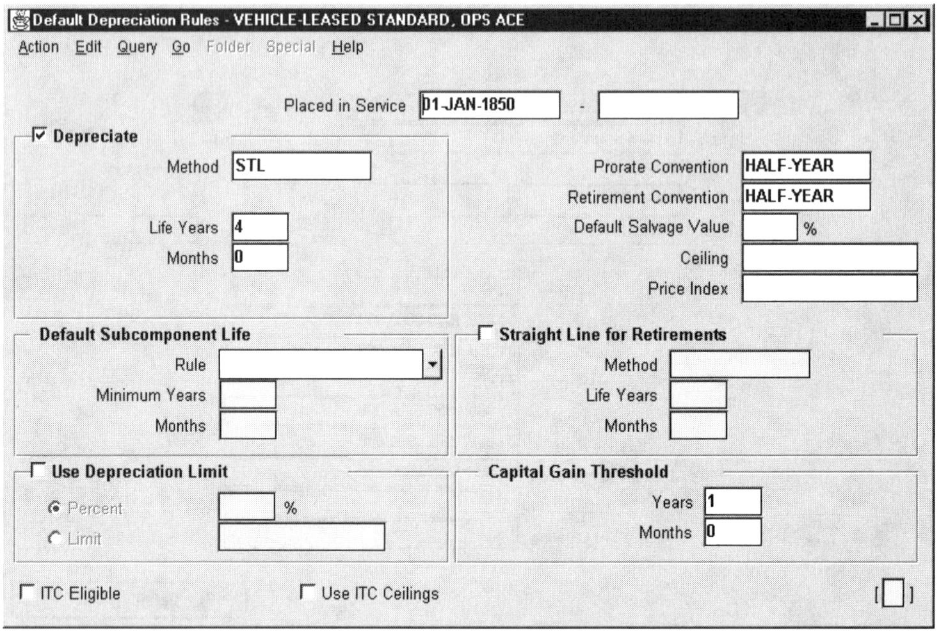

FIGURE 5-7. *Asset Categories – Default Depreciation Rules form*

subcomponent, you can select the rule to determine the subcomponent life. The rule can be *Same Life* or *Same End Date*. *Same Life* means the subcomponent will have the same life as its parent asset. *Same End Date* means the subcomponent's life will *end* on the same date as the parent asset. Two factors play into this latter option. First, you can set a minimum subcomponent life in years and months; if the parent asset's life ends before the subcomponent reaches its minimum life, the subcomponent will continue to depreciate until its minimum life is reached. Second, if the subcomponent's default life ends before its parent asset's life ends, the subcomponent's default date will take precedence.

If you want to set a depreciation limit, you can do so using either a percentage of the asset's cost or a hard limit. The depreciation limit allows assets to depreciate beyond the recoverable cost within the default life and the limit defined on this form.

You can also specify which prorate and retirement conventions to use, and you can set the default asset-cost percentage to use when calculating its salvage value. If the book is of class *Tax*, you can use a cost ceiling or an expense ceiling. You can also specify a price index to use for revaluing assets before calculating retirement gains or losses.

If the asset category is associated with the 1250 property class—which in the United States is the class for real property, and the book is a tax book, you have the option to select a straight-line depreciation method for retirement. If you enable the *Straight Line for Retirements* option, you can enter the straight-line depreciation method and default life to be used in calculating retirement gains/losses for 1250 property class assets. Finally, you can enter the capital gain threshold. Most depreciation rules are default and can be overridden when the assets are entered manually. For assets from external sources, you can change these defaults after the assets are created.

Review Questions

1. What is the Asset Cost account used for?

2. How will the subcomponent life be calculated if the rule of *Same End Date* is selected?

3. What is a capital gain threshold?

4. When can you select the *Straight Line for Retirements* checkbox option?

Setting Up Depreciation

To set up depreciation, you must define the following characteristics:

- Depreciation methods

- Prorate/retirement conventions

- Bonus rules

- Depreciation ceilings

- Investment tax credits

Depreciation Methods

By following the navigation path *Setup : Depreciation : Methods*, you can select from four different depreciation methods. They are as follows:

- **Calculated** is a straight-line method. It calculates an asset's annual depreciation rate by spreading its recoverable cost evenly across its useful life. The calculation basis has to be Cost. You can elect to depreciate the asset in the year it retires. You can also select the asset's useful life.

■ **Table depreciation** method determines the depreciation rate based on a user- or system-defined table. The calculation basis can be *Cost* or *NBV*. You can also enter the number of prorate periods per year this depreciation method uses. Clicking on the **Rate** button allows you to enter annual depreciation rates. Since assets must be fully depreciated when they are retired, for the Cost calculation basis, all annual rates must add up to exactly 1. For the NBV calculation basis, the annual rate for the asset's last year has to be 1, and the rates prior to the last year must be between 0 and 1.

■ **Production** is used for units-of-production depreciation, in which the depreciation rate is based on consumption. You cannot modify any parameter for this depreciation method, and no life needs to be defined.

■ **Flat** uses a flat rate as the depreciation rate. The calculation basis can be *Cost* or *NBV*. You can elect to depreciate the asset in the year the asset retires, and you can specify whether to exclude salvage value if the cost basis is NBV. No life needs to be defined for this depreciation method.

Prorate/Retirement Conventions

The prorate convention is used to determine how much depreciation to take in the first year of an asset's life, while the retirement convention is only used when an asset is retired before it is fully reserved. In this case, the retirement convention is used to determine how much depreciation to take in the last year of the asset's life. For depreciation methods other than straight line, you can enable the *Depreciate When Placed in Service* option to force use of the date placed in service instead of the prorate date. Common prorate conventions include:

■ Following month starts depreciating in the period following the asset's date placed in service. For example:

From Date	To Date	Prorate Date
01-JAN-99	31-JAN-99	01-FEB-99
01-FEB-99	28-FEB-99	01-MAR-99

■ Half year starts depreciating at the beginning of the fiscal year or at the half-year point of the fiscal year, depending on whether the asset is placed in service in the first half of the fiscal year or the second half of the fiscal year. For example:

From Date	To Date	Prorate Date
01-JAN-99	30-JUN-99	01-JAN-99
01-JUL-99	31-DEC-99	01-JUL-99

■ Mid-month applies when an asset is placed in service after mid-month: take the half-month depreciation in the period the asset is placed in service, and half-month depreciation in the month the asset is retired. Otherwise, take a full month in the period the asset is placed in service and nothing in the month the asset is retired. For example:

From Date	To Date	Prorate Date
01-JAN-99	15-JAN-99	01-JAN-99
16-JAN-99	31-JAN-99	16-JAN-99

■ Mid-quarter is similar to mid-month, but instead of month, use the quarter as the date range. For example:

From Date	To Date	Prorate Date
01-JAN-99	15-FEB-99	01-JAN-99
16-FEB-99	31-MAR-99	16-FEB-99

Bonus Rules

For the flat depreciation method, you can create a bonus rate for each year, or range of years, of the asset's life.

Depreciation Ceilings

There are three types of depreciation ceilings:

■ A *cost ceiling* sets the maximum value you can use as recoverable cost in depreciation.

■ An *expense ceiling* sets the maximum value you can take as a depreciation expense each depreciation period. You can set either a cost ceiling or an expense ceiling for assets in the tax book—but not both. For luxury automobiles in the United States, you must set an expense depreciation ceiling.

■ An *investment tax credit ceiling* sets the maximum amount that can be used to—not surprisingly—calculate an investment tax credit.

Investment Tax Credits

In order for investment tax credits (ITC) to work, you must also set up the ITC rates and ITC recapture rates. ITC rates define the amount of ITC for an asset, while ITC recapture rates define the amount of ITC that needs to be recaptured if the asset retires before its useful life is complete.

Review Questions

1. How is the depreciation rate derived for the calculated depreciation method? For the table depreciation method? The production depreciation method? The flat depreciation method?

2. What is the result of enabling the *Depreciate When Placed in Service* checkbox?

3. Which date in Oracle Assets is compared with the prorate convention's From and To date range to determine the prorate date?

4. How does the following month prorate convention work?

5. When can you use a bonus rule?

6. What is a cost ceiling? An expense ceiling?

7. What are the three components for setting up ITC?

Managing Assets

In this section, you will learn about:

- Adding assets manually
- Depreciating assets

Once Oracle Assets is set up, you are ready to begin its two fundamental processes: adding and depreciating assets. In this section, you will learn how to add assets manually through the Asset Workbench, and then perform depreciation on them. (You will see how to get asset data from external sources in the next section.)

Adding Assets Manually

Oracle Assets provides two ways to enter assets manually: QuickAdditions and DetailAdditions.

QuickAdditions

QuickAdditions allows you to add assets quickly by accepting the defaults from the asset categories. To perform QuickAdditions, you go to the Asset Workbench through navigation path *Assets : Asset Workbench* (shown in Figure 5-8) and then click on the **QuickAdditions** button.

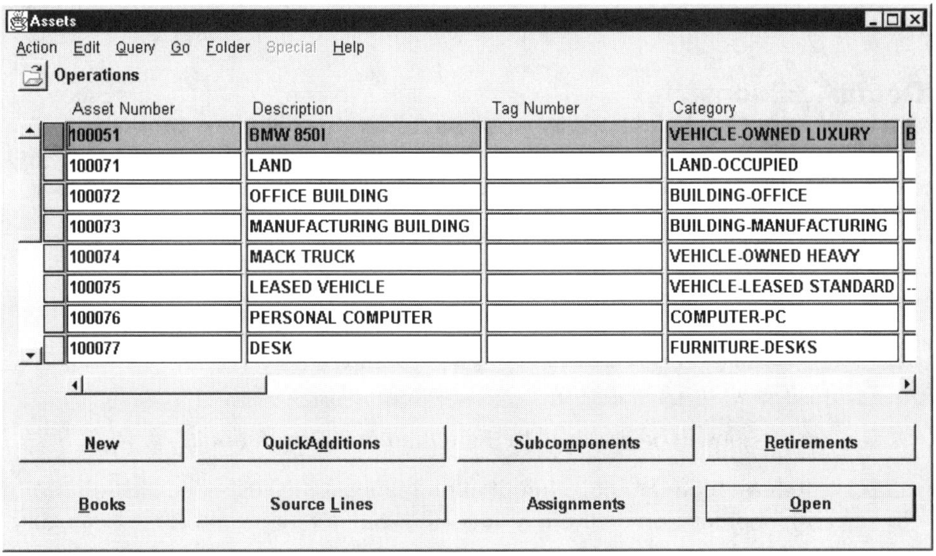

FIGURE 5-8. *Asset Workbench form*

If your system has not been set up to generate asset numbers automatically, you must first enter an asset number. Next, enter a description for the asset. For the asset description, there is a QuickCodes type that allows you to select a standard description from the list of values. You can either select a standard asset description (by executing the menu command Edit | List of Values) or enter a unique description. Then enter a tag number, which must be unique across all assets in Oracle Assets. Unlike an asset number, which is a system identifier, a tag number is manually entered and is usually physically placed on an asset.

Next you enter an asset category. By default, the asset category depreciation rules effective for the date placed in service will be used. Then you can enter a serial number, asset key, and asset type of either *Capitalized*, *CIP*, or *Expensed*. You can change units from 1 to the number of units that are included in your asset. Next, you can optionally enter a supplier name, supplier number, invoice number, and PO number.

After you enter all the asset information, you can assign the asset to a corporate book and enter the asset's cost. The date in service will be populated with the last day of the latest open period if that day is prior to system date; otherwise, the system date will be used. You must associate a depreciation expense account combination and location to the asset; you can also assign it to an employee.

When you are finished entering all these attributes, your form should look similar to Figure 5-9. Click on the **Done** button to save your asset.

DetailAdditions

You cannot use QuickAdditions if any of the following conditions are true:

- Your asset has more than one assignment

- Your asset has more than one source line

- Your asset has subcomponents

- Your asset is leased

- Your asset has a warranty

- Your asset will be assigned to more than one distribution

- You have more financial information than just the cost—such as salvage cost, depreciation method, or life—that is different from the asset category default or prorate convention

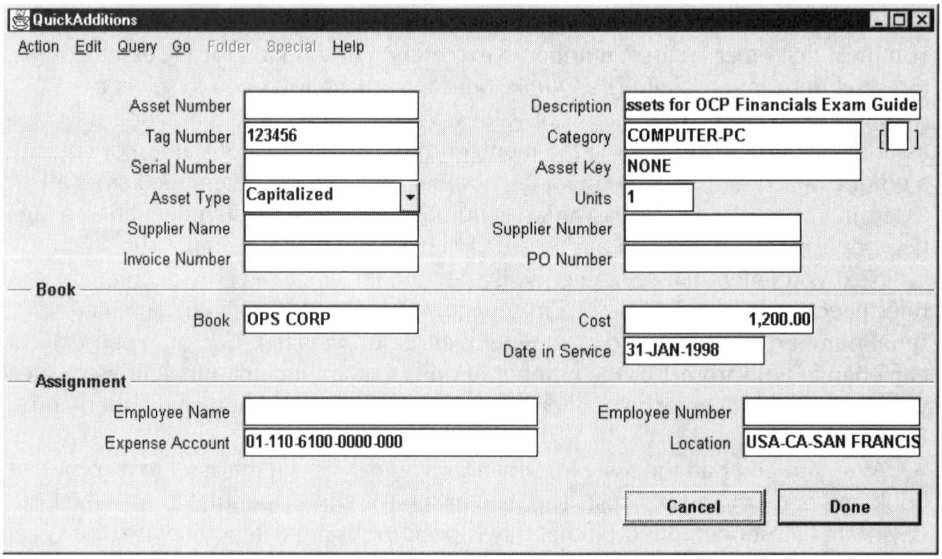

FIGURE 5-9. *QuickAdditions form*

If any of these conditions are true, you must use DetailAdditions.

To use DetailAdditions from the Workbench, follow the navigation path *Assets : Asset Workbench* and click on the **New** button. DetailAdditions consists of a series of forms that guide you through the process of adding detailed assets. After you finish filling out the data in a form, the **Continue** button takes you to the next form; at the end, a **Done** button completes the process.

The first form is the Asset Details form (shown in Figure 5-10). At this Asset Details form, you can enter the same fields as QuickAdditions: Asset Number, Description, Tag Number, Category, Serial Number, Asset Key, Asset Type, and Units. When you enter the Asset Category, the In Physical Inventory, Property Type, Property Class, and Ownership fields are populated with default values, which you can override later.

In addition to the fields just mentioned, you can enter the Parent Asset number if the new asset is a subcomponent. You can also enter the asset's Manufacturer, Model, Warranty Number, Lease Number, Lease Description, Lessor, Property Type, and Property Class. You can only define whether the asset is in use, whether it is in physical inventory, whether it is owned or leased, and whether it is new or used.

At this point, you have the option to add source line information to the asset. If you wish to do so, click on the **Source Lines** button to get to the Source lines form

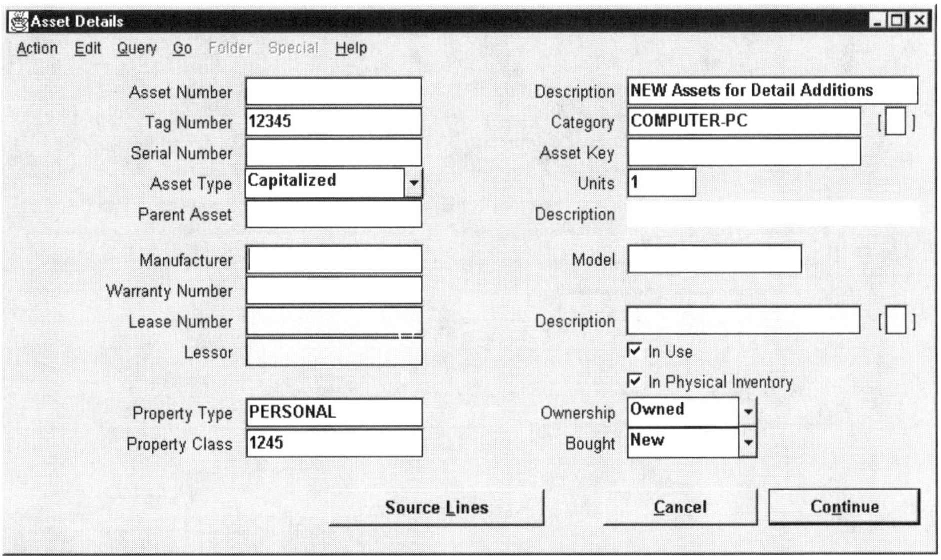

FIGURE 5-10. *Asset Details form*

(shown in Figure 5-11). Source line information includes invoice information such as invoice number, invoice line number, and invoice description, as well as supplier information such as supplier name, supplier number, and PO number. By using DetailAdditions, you have the ability to enter more than one source line for each asset.

Click on the **Continue** button to proceed to the Books form (Figure 5-12). This is where you enter financial information. Start by assigning the new asset to a corporate book; after you do, depreciation rules will take on default values based on the asset category and book combination. Default information includes the depreciation method, depreciate flag, date in service, and prorate convention. Based on the date in service and the prorate convention, the prorate date is displayed. Of course, you can override these depreciation defaults later.

Next, you enter the cost information of the new asset. Cost information includes the current cost of the asset, YTD depreciation amount, accumulated depreciation reserve, applicable revaluation ceiling, revaluation reserve,

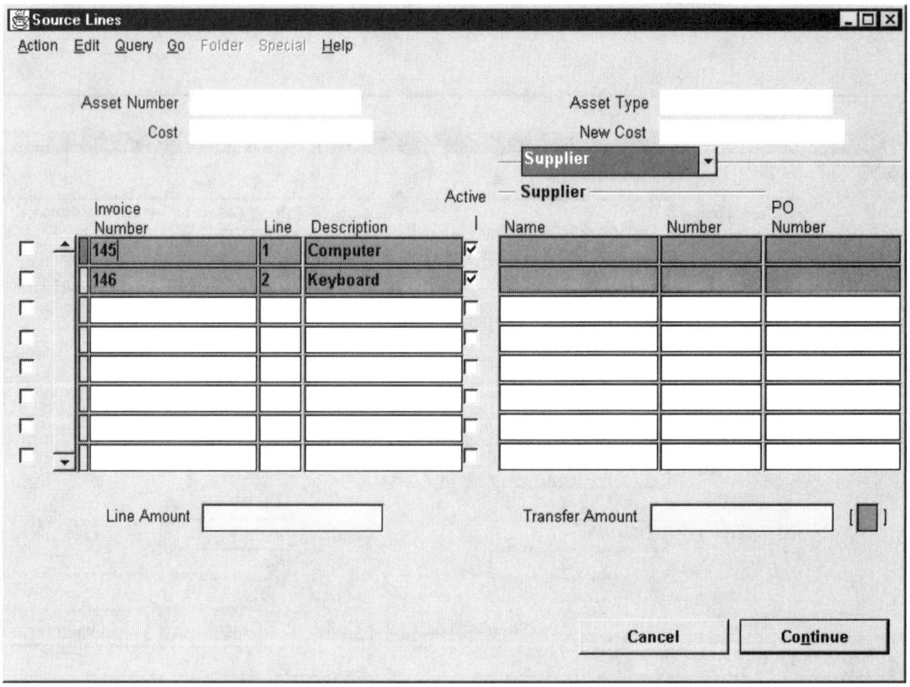

FIGURE 5-11. *Source Lines form*

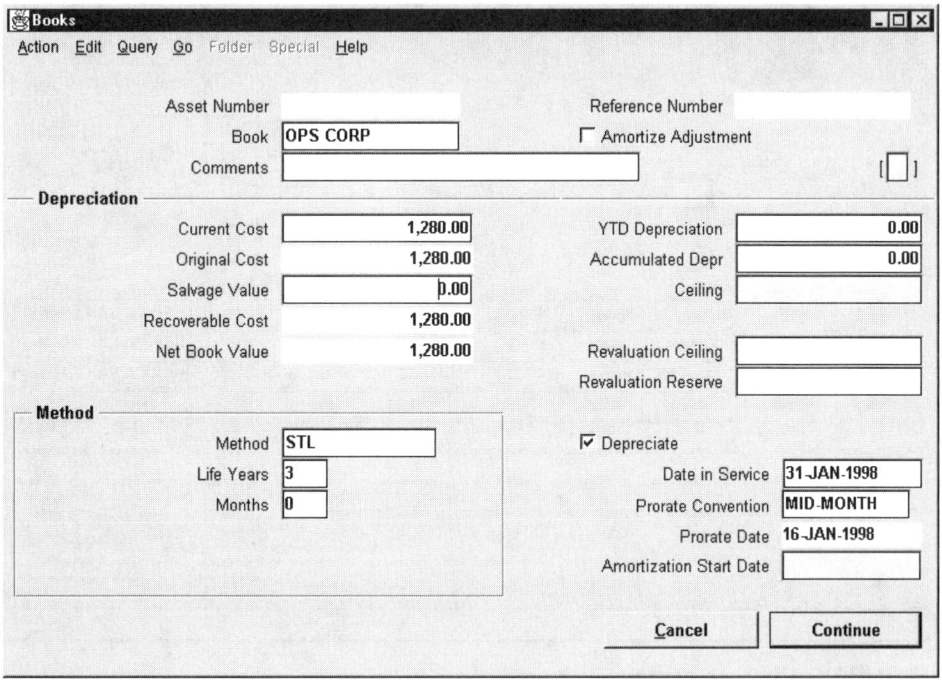

FIGURE 5-12. *Books form*

depreciation method, date placed in service, prorate convention, and whether the
asset should be depreciated.

Now click on the **Continue** button to go to the Assignments form (Figure 5-13).
This is where you assign one or more distributions to the new asset. You can use
a predefined distribution set containing such data as the depreciation expense
account and location. Optionally, the distribution can include specific employees
to whom the asset or part of the asset is distributed. You can distribute the number
of units to multiple locations/employees even if the number of units is 1, as long as
the distributed unit adds up to the number of units. Click on the **Done** button to
complete the process, and your new asset is created.

Using the Asset Workbench buttons **Subcomponents**, **Books**, **Source Lines**, and
Assignments, you can return to this information and modify it as necessary. After the
initial depreciation run, some of the fields will no longer be updatable, including
the YTD depreciation amount and accumulated depreciation reserve.

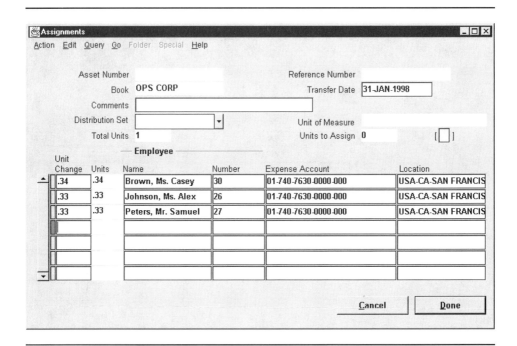

FIGURE 5-13. *Assignments form*

Review Questions

1. When do you have to use DetailAdditions vs. QuickAdditions?

2. What is the Source Lines form used for?

3. What information does the Books form contain?

4. What are distribution sets used for?

Depreciating Assets

The depreciation process in Oracle Assets calculates retirement gains/losses, depreciation expenses, and adjustments for all assets associated with the selected book. It also updates the YTD depreciation, accumulated depreciation, and depreciation reserve amounts. At the end of the depreciation process, you transfer the generated journal entries to GL and then close the current period in Oracle Assets. If the current period is the final period of the year, the depreciation process resets the YTD depreciation amount and, if necessary, creates the new fiscal year and calendar.

Once a period is closed and its journal entries are transferred to GL at the end of the depreciation process, you cannot reopen a period in Oracle Assets as you can in the other modules. An Assets close is considered a "hard close." Thus, you must make sure that all the necessary transactions are performed before running the depreciation process. These actions may include:

- **Entering production units**   For units-of-production depreciation, you must enter or upload the production units used. Use the navigation path *Production : Enter* to enter the production units manually. Enter the book, period range, asset number, and unit of measures (UOM) consumed.

- **Running listing reports**   There are two listing reports that can help you ensure that all assets will depreciate: *Assets Not Assigned to Any Books Listing*, and *Assets Not Assigned to Any Cost Center Listing*. These two reports will identify any assets not assigned to a corporate book or cost center.

- **Running projections**   Use the navigation path *Depreciation : Projections* to project depreciation expense. You can select the calendar to use, the number of periods to project, and the starting period. You can run the Depreciation Projections program for any books either in summary or with cost center and/or asset details. See Figure 5-14.

- **Calculating gains and losses**   The Calculating Gains and Losses program is used to calculate retirement gains and losses. This program is automatically initiated by the depreciation process. However, you can explicitly invoke this program throughout the period—after processing retirements—to save some time during the depreciation process.

- **What-if analysis**   Depreciation expenses can be projected based on the asset depreciation rules. (Meaning that if you want different projection results, you must change the asset setup.) What-if analysis allows you to analyze changes in depreciation rules without saving them as setups. To initiate a what-if analysis, use the navigation path *Depreciation : What-If Analysis*. Enter the book you want to use, the starting period, the number of periods, and the range of assets on which the what-if analysis should be performed. These criteria can include an asset number range, date-in-service range, and/or asset category. In addition, you can enter a description for this what-if analysis, and select whether to analyze fully reserved assets. You can also enter overriding depreciation rules: a depreciation method, prorate convention, salvage-value percentage, and whether to amortize adjustments. When you are satisfied with your settings, click on the **Run** button to initiate the what-if analysis. See Figure 5-15.

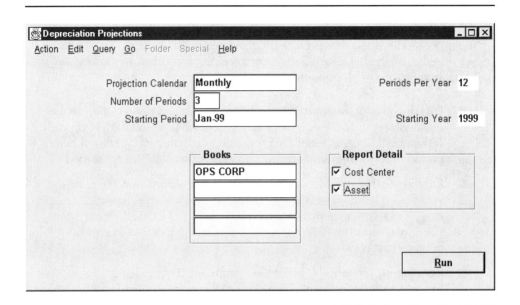

FIGURE 5-14. *Depreciation Projections form*

Run Depreciation

Once the preparatory steps just described are completed to your satisfaction, you can run the depreciation process. To run depreciation, use the navigation path *Depreciation : Run Depreciation*. Enter the book for which you want to run depreciation and click on the **Run** button. See Figure 5-16. Be careful, since you cannot reverse depreciation. Three programs will be initiated: Calculate Gains and Losses; Depreciation Run; and Journal Entry Reserve Ledger report/Tax Reserve Ledger report.

TIP

For MRC, you must run the depreciation process for each asset book associated with MRC before you run the depreciation process for the primary Set of Books.

The Depreciation Run program calculates assets' depreciation for a period based on their depreciation method, date in service, prorate convention, salvage value, ITC, and ceilings. The depreciation amounts go to the depreciation expense account, and the accumulated depreciation and YTD depreciation amounts are

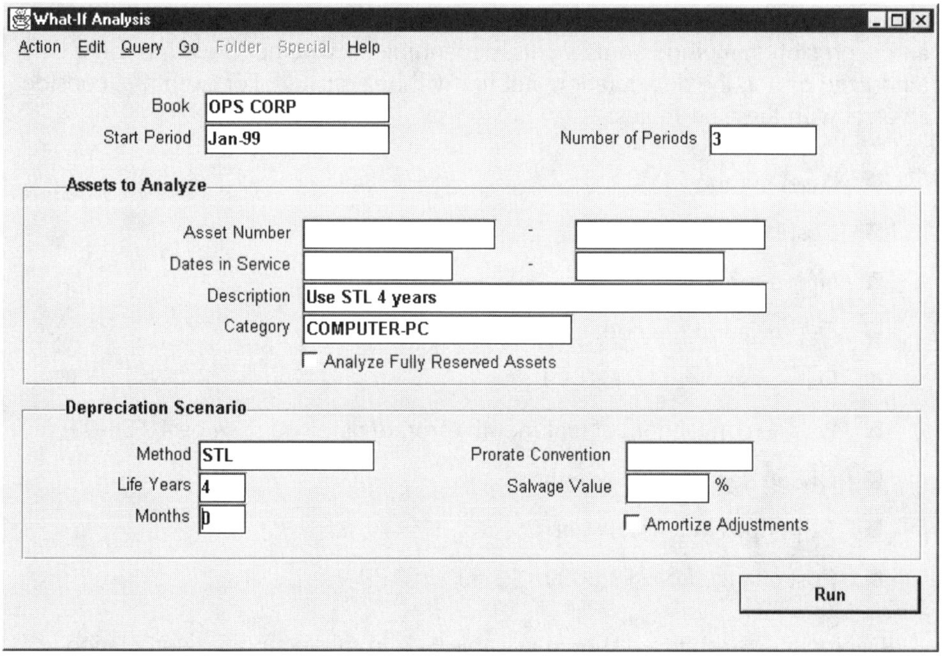

FIGURE 5-15. *What-If Analysis form*

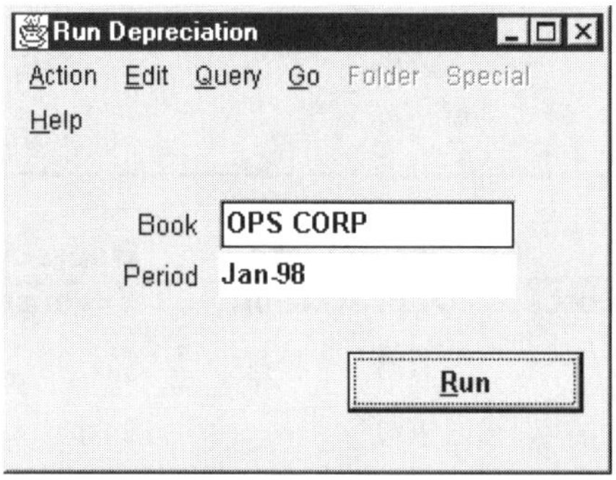

FIGURE 5-16. *Run Depreciation form*

increased by the calculated depreciation figures. If there are adjustments such as cost adjustments, life adjustments, rate adjustments, salvage value adjustments, and depreciation method adjustments, depending on whether the adjustment is amortized or not, the depreciation amount will be adjusted. For example, consider an asset with these attributes:

- Asset number: 111

- Cost: $3,600

- Life: 3 years

- Depreciation method: straight line

- Date in service: 16-FEB-99

- Prorate convention: actual month (prorate date will then be 1-FEB-99)

- Divide depreciation evenly

- 12 periods in a fiscal year

- Cost change from $3,600 to $3,960 in APR-99

Depreciation results are shown in Table 5-2. In this example, depreciation expense = 3,600/12/3 = 100)

Depreciation results with the cost change expensed are shown in Table 5-3. There, depreciation expense = 3,960/12/3 = 110. Expensing the cost change, instead of amortizing, means catching up with the changes in the current period. That means in APR-99, accumulated depreciation needs to be at the new accumulated depreciation rate, with the new cost. New accumulated depreciation = 110*3 = 330, so you need an extra $20 in depreciation expense to expense the change.

Period	Asset Cost	Accumulated Depreciation	Depreciation Expense
FEB-99	$3,600	$100	$100
MAR-99	$3,600	$200	$100

TABLE 5-2. *Initial Depreciation*

Period	Asset Cost	Accumulated Depreciation	Depreciation Expense
MAR-99	$3,600	$200	$100
APR-99	$3,960	$320.59	$130
MAY-99	$3,960	$441.18	$110

TABLE 5-3. *Depreciation After Cost Change with the Expense Option*

Depreciation results with the cost change amortized are shown in Table 5-4. In this instance, depreciation expense = 3,960/12/3 = 110. Amortizing the cost change means distributing the change from the current period on until the end of asset useful life; in this case, that means that the change needs to start in APR-99 and spread out for 34 periods. The change is 3,960 – 3,600 = 360, so each period, there is an extra depreciation expense amount of 360/34 = $10.59. The new depreciation expense is 110 + 10.59 = $120.59.

Review Questions

1. What does the depreciation process do?

2. What is a hard close?

3. What is the difference between a projection and a what-if analysis?

4. What programs are initiated by the Run Depreciation form?

Period	Asset Cost	Accumulated Depreciation	Depreciation Expense
MAR-99	$3,600	$200	$100
APR-99	$3,960	$330	$120.59
MAY-99	$3,960	$440	$120.59

TABLE 5-4. *Depreciation After Cost Change with the Amortize Option*

Adding Assets from External Sources

In this section, you will learn how to add assets automatically through an interface: a program called Mass Additions. Similar to Journal Import, Mass Additions imports assets from an external source through an interface table into Oracle Assets production tables. The Oracle Assets interface table is called FA_MASS_ADDITIONS. You can populate the interface table from Oracle Payables, from Oracle Projects, or with a third-party program. In the scope of this exam, you will assume that the interface table is populated and you will see how to do the following:

- Prepare mass additions

- Post mass additions

- Delete mass additions

TIP
Create Mass Additions is the process that populates the interface table from Oracle Payables and Oracle Projects. If you are importing assets from third-party systems, you will need to write a custom program that populates the interface table.

Preparing Mass Additions

The Prepare Mass Additions process allows you to review and add additional information to assets in the interface table before importing them into the Oracle Assets production tables. A row in the interface table corresponds to an invoice line and may or may not correspond to an asset, so you can refer to each row as a mass additions line. To invoke the Prepare Mass Additions process, use navigation path *Mass Additions : Prepare Mass Additions*. A Find window appears, and you can employ criteria such as book, queue name, and invoice number to locate the desired mass additions lines. See Figure 5-17. Queue name is a special field that you can use to determine whether a particular mass additions line should or should not be included in a Mass Additions Post run. Queue name can be user-defined; Mass Additions Post will only pick Mass Additions lines with a queue name of POST.

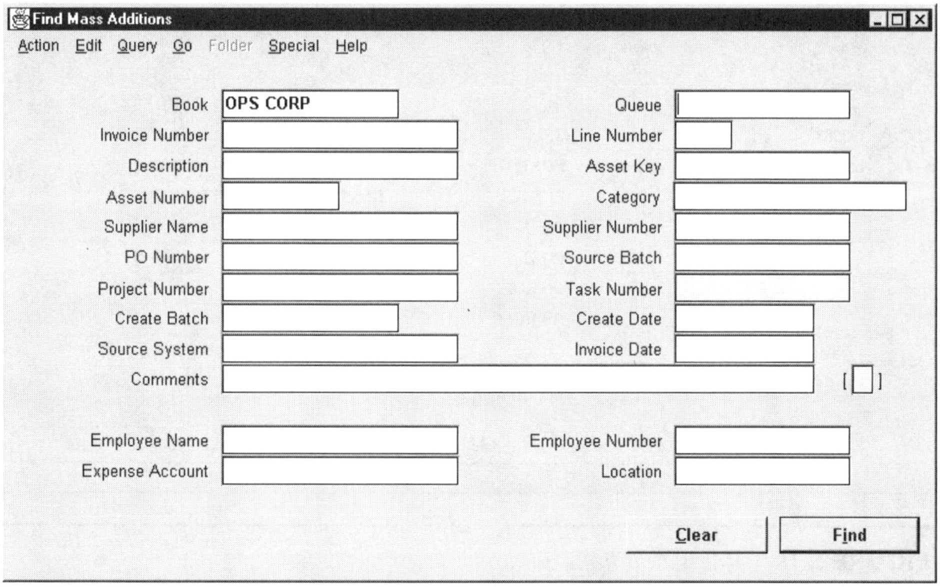

FIGURE 5-17.   *Find Mass Additions form*

Click on the **Find** button and a Mass Additions Summary window appears showing you mass additions lines that fit your find criteria. See Figure 5-18. For each mass additions line, you can:

■   Split mass additions lines

■   Add mass additions lines to existing assets as cost adjustments

■   Merge mass additions lines

■   Open mass additions lines to add information and change queue name

Split Mass Additions Lines

You can split mass additions lines containing multiple units into several single-unit lines. The cost of the asset will be divided proportionally. The original mass

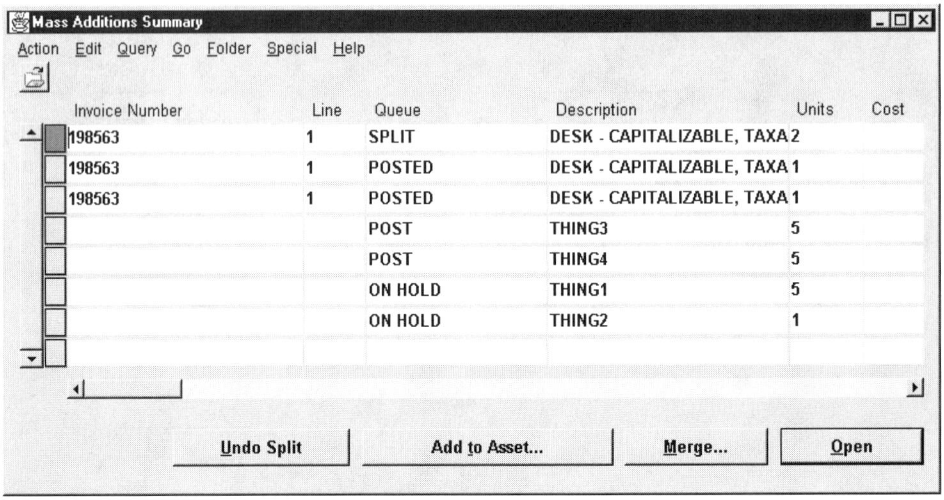

FIGURE 5-18. *Mass Additions Summary form*

additions line will be assigned to queue SPLIT and will not be posted. The single-unit mass additions lines will be assigned to queue ON HOLD. Upon review, you must change them to queue POST to be picked up by the Mass Additions Post program and become assets.

You can undo a split using the **Undo Split** button, which will appear if your cursor is on a split mass additions line.

Add Mass Additions Lines

You can add mass additions lines to existing assets as cost adjustments by selecting the **Add to Assets** button. A Find window appears. You can use asset detail, assignment, source line, or lease information as criteria. Click on the **Find** button to retrieve the selected assets. Then highlight the asset you want to use and indicate whether you want to amortize the cost adjustment by checking the *Amortize Adjustment* checkbox. You can also choose to override the existing asset information with the mass additions lines information to perform a reclass by checking the *New Category and Description* checkbox. Click on the **Done** button to add the mass additions line to the selected asset. See Figure 5-19.

When you change the queue name of such mass additions lines to POST, the form automatically changes them to queue COST ADJUSTMENT. To undo the cost adjustment, change the queue from COST ADJUSTMENT back to ON HOLD.

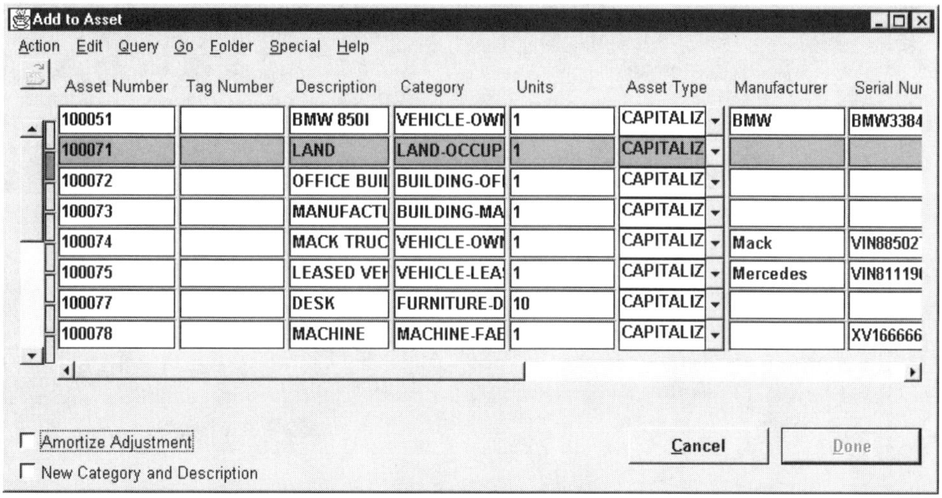

FIGURE 5-19.   *Add to Asset form*

Merge Mass Additions Lines

You can merge multiple mass additions lines into a single mass additions line to be picked up by the Mass Additions Post program and become a single asset. Select the parent mass additions line and click on the **Merge** button. In the Merge Mass Additions form, select the mass additions lines to be child lines. To select all mass additions lines in the form, use *Merge All* from the Special menu. The cost of the selected mass additions lines will be added to the cost of the parent mass additions. You have the option to sum the number of units of all involved mass additions lines or keep the number of units of the parent mass additions line. To keep the number of units in the parent mass additions line, do not check the *Sum Units* checkbox. Click on the **Done** button to merge the mass additions lines. See Figure 5-20.

The parent mass additions line queue name will be changed to ON HOLD, and the merged child mass additions lines queue will become MERGED. MERGED mass additions lines will not be picked up by the Mass Additions Post program.

A common merge scenario is when you want to merge discount and/or tax lines into the associated invoice lines to form single assets. You do not want to ignore discounts or taxes as the cost basis just because they are on an invoice as separate line items. You can undo a split using the **Undo Merge** button, which will appear if your cursor is on a merged mass additions line.

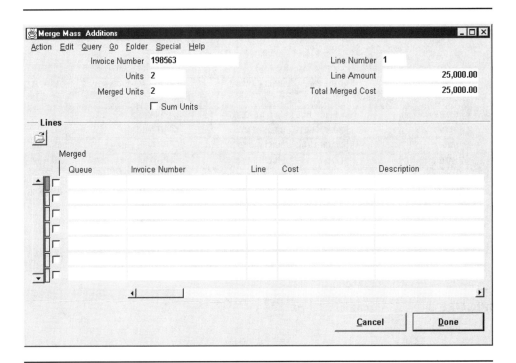

FIGURE 5-20. *Merge Mass Additions form*

Open Mass Additions Lines

You can open mass additions lines to add additional information such as depreciation expense account, source information, and tag number before posting. You can change the queue name to POST for the reviewed assets or you can mass change the queue name by using the Special menu from the menu bar. You can choose Post All, Hold All, or Delete All. See Figure 5-21.

You can also add assignments to each mass additions line. If the mass additions line you are on is MERGED, then checking the *Show Merged Distributions* checkbox will show you all distributions tied to the merged mass additions lines. See Figure 5-22.

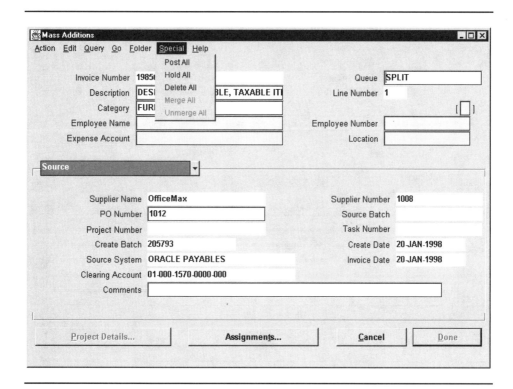

FIGURE 5-21. *Mass Additions form*

Review Questions

    1. What does a row in the mass additions interface table correspond to?

    2. Why will you merge mass additions lines?

    3. How do you perform cost adjustments in the Prepare Mass Additions process?

    4. What does queue POST do?

Posting Mass Additions

After reviewing the mass additions lines and changing the appropriate ones to POST, you can kick off the Mass Additions Post process through navigation path *Mass Additions : Post Mass Additions*. The Mass Additions Post process is a

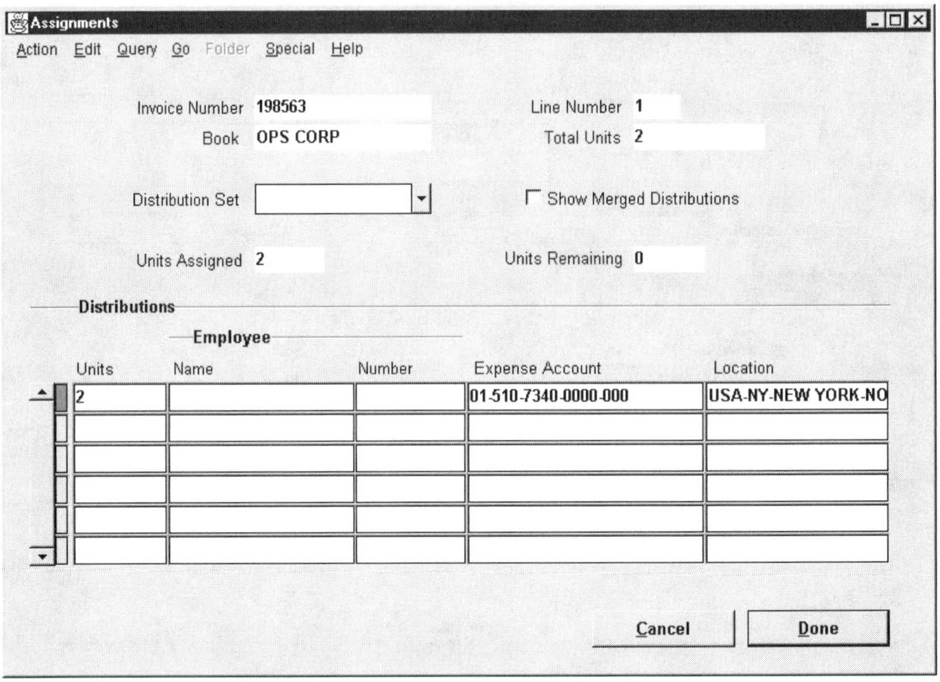

FIGURE 5-22. *Assignments form*

predefined report set that consists of the Mass Additions Post program and the Mass Additions Posting report. Select the book for which you want to run the Mass Additions Post process and submit the request. See Figure 5-23.

The Mass Additions Post program will gather all the mass additions lines with queue names of POST and COST ADJUSTMENT and turn them into assets. Once the assets are created, the corresponding mass additions line queue name will be changed to POSTED. Use the Delete Mass Additions program to mass delete all POSTED mass additions lines if you wish.

Review Questions

1. What does the Mass Additions Post program do?

2. What queues will the Mass Additions Post program select as mass additions lines to be processed?

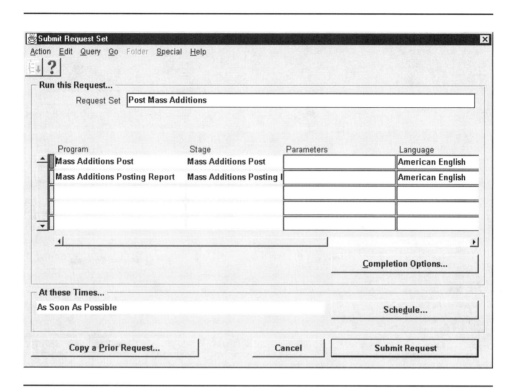

FIGURE 5-23. *Post Mass Additions form*

Deleting Mass Additions

You can use the Mass Additions Delete program to delete all mass additions lines
with the queue name of DELETE. You can kick off the Mass Additions Delete
process through navigation path *Mass Additions : Delete Mass Additions*. The
Mass Additions Delete process is a predefined report set that consists of the Mass
Additions Delete report (which lists the records that are about to be deleted), and
the Mass Additions Delete program. Select the book that you want to run the Mass
Additions Delete process for and submit the request. See Figure 5-24.

Review Questions

1. What does the Mass Additions Delete program do?

2. What queue will the Mass Additions Delete program select as mass
   additions lines to be processed?

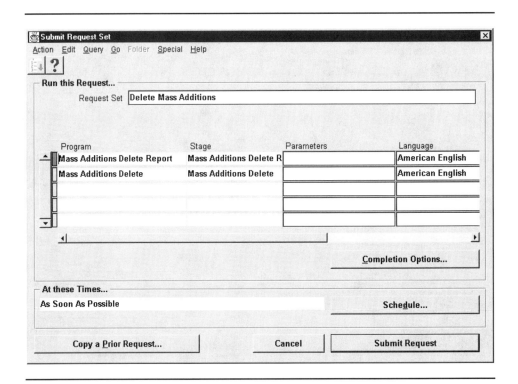

FIGURE 5-24. *Delete Mass Additions form*

Implementation Considerations

When implementing Oracle Assets, you must consider the following:

- Key flexfields
- Initial assets conversion
- Depreciation requirements
- Tax requirements
- Importing assets from external systems and other modules
- Multiple-currencies requirements
- Setting up oldest date in service
- Asset accounting
- Capital budgeting
- Security

Taking all of the previous factors into consideration will ensure a more successful implementation. Pay special attention to the Key flexfields and depreciation requirements, because they are fundamental to setting up Oracle Assets.

Key Flexfields

You can categorize your assets information into three groups: financial, physical location, and others.

The financial group should include account defaults, depreciation methods, ceilings, and default life. Match these financial attributes to the fields in asset categories. The matched attributes should indicate how to structure your Asset Category flexfield. If you can establish standardized financial information to use as defaults for each asset category, it will eliminate the need to have any human overrides during manual or automated assets additions. You must have one segment identified as the major category segment, because capital budgeting uses the major category segment.

The physical location groups allow you to identify where assets are assigned. Physical location groups can include country, state, region, office, building, and others. Create a Location flexfield that satisfies your requirements in these areas. As mentioned earlier, you must have one segment identified as the state segment for property tax reporting.

The other asset attributes should be matched to the asset fields in the Asset Workbench. If you can match them all, that is very convenient—all you need to add is one dummy segment for your Asset Key flexfield. If you cannot, then group the unmatched attributes that you want into the Asset Key flexfield.

Once you have determined the structure of the three Key flexfields, you can decide on the validation criteria.

Review Questions

1. Which Key flexfield in Oracle Assets is used to group financial information?

2. Which Key flexfield in Oracle Assets is used to group nonfinancial information?

3. Which Key flexfield in Oracle Assets is used to group physical locations?

Initial Assets Conversion

The initial conversion of data into assets will consist of legacy asset data containing accumulated depreciation and YTD amounts, belonging to the period just prior to the one in which Oracle Assets will start capturing asset transactions. This is because you must run depreciation once and reconcile the accumulated depreciation amounts and YTD amounts to the current period of your legacy system.

A lot of the depreciation rules established as defaults by asset category are not in the interface table. When you convert assets and run Mass Additions Post, the depreciation rules are based on the asset categories assigned. Most likely, your legacy system does not have standardized depreciation rules from the beginning of its accounts, so there will be quite a bit of cleanup needed after the assets are created before you can reconcile. Because depreciation does a "hard close" on the period, you will find yourself in a situation where you cannot easily roll back the conversion and reconvert. You must either restore the system or create new corporate books. To avoid this complication, use depreciation projections first.

Review Questions

1. What period should you choose for initial assets conversion?

2. What is meant by hard closing a period?

Depreciation Requirements

Gather all your depreciation methods, prorate conventions, price indexes, depreciation ceilings, bonus rates, and ITCs. Match all the depreciation methods to seeded Oracle depreciation methods. Remember that Oracle Assets considers *straight line with 4 years life* and *straight line with 4 years and 1 month life* to be two different depreciation methods. You can also create new depreciation methods that are not included in Oracle Assets. After you have set up all the prorate conventions and other depreciation requirements you need, you can run depreciation projections on a selection of complicated assets and check whether all the depreciation requirements are met.

Review Question

1. What factors should you consider when defining your depreciation requirements?

Tax Requirements

Tax requirements in Oracle Assets include investment tax credit (ITC), alternative minimum tax (AMT), adjusted current earnings (ACE), and tax ceilings. Many factors affect your implementation's tax requirements. The differences in how you report taxes will determine how many tax books you need, as well as the depreciation rules default for asset categories assigned to tax books.

You may have to create different depreciation calendars if you report taxes quarterly instead of monthly. You may also want to set up different prorate conventions. For example, you may want to depreciate quarterly for tax purposes, but depreciate monthly for your books. To do this, you need to have a quarterly prorate calendar, along with a separate monthly prorate calendar to allow for more detailed granularity and flexibility in selecting a prorate date.

Review Question

 1. Name three asset tax requirements.

Importing Assets from External Systems and Other Modules

If you wish to import assets from other Oracle Applications modules, it is relatively simple: you need only ensure that the Mass Additions Create process is run from those Oracle Applications modules. However, if you will be importing assets from external sources, you must ensure that the interface table is populated correctly, that the assets are assigned to the right asset categories, and that the asset categories can be recognized by the Mass Additions Post process. You will need to validate the data before the Mass Additions Post process, or you could get an error message caused by data integrity problems. One common problem is that the mass additions lines do not even show up in Mass Additions Prepare because Oracle Assets is expecting data to have a certain value or to be presented in a certain way. For example, having a wrong queue name and a nonexisting supplier will prevent the mass additions lines from showing up in the Prepare Mass Additions process.

Review Question

 1. What steps do you need to perform when importing assets from an external source?

Multiple-Currencies Requirements

If you are implementing MRC, you will need multiple corporate books. You must run depreciation in each separate MRC corporate book before running the general Oracle Assets depreciation process. Be sure that the Reporting Sets of Books are pointing to the correct Oracle Assets corporate book when you assign the Reporting Sets of Books to the Primary Set of Books.

Review Question

 1. What requirements must be satisfied if you want to implement multiple reporting currencies?

Setting Up Oldest Date in Service

The implementation-wide oldest date in service parameter affects whether assets can be placed in service: assets with a date in service before the oldest date in service cannot be added. In addition, you must ensure that your depreciation calendar and prorate calendar go back to this oldest date in service. Once you have set up the oldest date in service and assigned calendars to books, you cannot change the oldest date in service.

Review Question

1. When can you change the oldest date in service?

Asset Accounting

It is important to verify that the Account Generator is generating account combinations in the way you wish. By default, the Account Generator gets the balancing segment value from the distribution line of the asset assignment for *all* types of accounts, and it gets the cost center segment value from the distribution line of the asset assignment *only for depreciation expense* accounts. All other asset-related account combinations will get their cost center segment values from the Account Generator Default in the Book Controls. For the natural account segment, the Account Generator uses either the book's controls or asset categories. For all other segments, the Account Generator gets the segment values from the Account Generator Default in the Book Controls. If you want the Account Generator to operate in a different way, you must modify it through the Oracle Workflow tool. This program lets you "flow out" the source of each segment value in your Chart of Accounts, modifying the Account Generator accordingly. (Oracle Workflow will be covered in detail in Chapter 11.)

Review Question

1. How does the default Account Generator work?

Capital Budgeting

You must use the Major Category flexfield to perform capital budgeting in Oracle Assets. How do you perform capital budgeting? You need to consider what your capital budget is based on, and you need to set up the Category Flexfield appropriately for this purpose. You need to use the major category to perform capital budgeting in Oracle Assets. Another consideration is how you plan to upload or enter capital budget amounts. You can enter the amount manually, or you may want to upload the capital budget amounts automatically. This decision is usually based on volume and frequency of your capital budgeting process. Furthermore, you should determine what kind of capital budgeting reports you need: for example, how you want data in the report to be grouped and sorted. It is best to decide ahead of time what your reporting needs will be, and match them with the Oracle Assets reports.

Review Question

1. Which Key flexfield in Oracle Assets do you need in order to perform capital budgeting?

Security

Having two corporate books will help enforce security, because each responsibility can have a different corporate book; this enables two users with two responsibilities to look at two different sets of assets. However, you cannot transfer assets from one corporate book to another, so you will need to weigh the benefits of this approach. If you do set up two corporate books and need to transfer assets, you must retire the assets from the original corporate book and then add them to the destination corporate book. However, you still will have an issue, because an asset transferred from one book to another will need to have different asset and tag numbers in each book.

It is important to decide whether your security constraints require certain assets to be visible to some users but not to others, and to allow the Mass Additions Post process to be run by some users but not by all. This applies to reports as well. You will find it to your advantage to identify all your implementation's security requirements up front, and then to determine which of those requirements can be supported by Oracle Assets.

Review Question

1. What limitations are imposed by having two corporate books?

For the Chapter Summary, Two-Minute Drill, and Chapter Questions and Answers, open the summary.htm file contained in the Summary_files directory on the book's CD-ROM.

CHAPTER
6

Oracle Applications
Integration

n this chapter, you will see how the various Oracle Applications modules integrate with one another. Chapters 1 and 3 provided high-level overviews of Oracle Applications integration. In this chapter you will learn about the detailed setups necessary to make that integration happen. This discussion covers the following subjects:

■ Integration

■ Managing budgets

■ Reporting and analysis tools

First, you will see how Oracle Assets integrates with other Oracle Financials modules, and learn what setups are necessary to facilitate this integration. This section focuses especially on how to set up Oracle Assets to work with the Multiple Reporting Currencies (MRC) feature in Oracle General Ledger. Next, you will see how Oracle Payables integrates with Oracle Assets, and cover the corresponding setups that facilitate this integration. Next, you will learn how to create, enter, and maintain budgets. The last section in the chapter addresses how Oracle General Ledger integrates with Oracle Financial Analyzer.

Integration

In this section, you will cover:

■ How Oracle Assets integrates with Oracle Financials modules

■ How Oracle Payables integrates with Oracle Assets

■ Implementation considerations

How Oracle Assets Integrates with Oracle Financials Modules

To be fully integrated, Oracle Financials modules share a lot of common setups. In this section, you will see what setups you must perform to integrate Oracle Assets with GL and other Financials modules. In particular, you will study how to create MRC reporting responsibilities in Oracle Assets so the program points to GL's Reporting Sets of Books. This section covers the Oracle Assets common setups with Oracle General Ledger, Human Resources, and Purchasing.

Oracle General Ledger

The Oracle Assets depreciation process generates journal entries that are transferred directly to General Ledger production tables. To accomplish this, the following setups are shared between the two modules:

- Accounting calendars
- Chart of Accounts
- Sets of Books
- Journal sources
- Journal categories
- Depreciation books
- MRC reporting responsibilities
- Reporting Sets of Books

ACCOUNTING CALENDARS   Oracle Assets has its own depreciation and prorate calendars, while GL has its own accounting calendars. If your Assets depreciation book wants to post to GL, the period names in Assets must be identical to those in GL's accounting calendar. This is how the depreciation process makes a match and determines the accounting period to which generated journal entries should be applied.

CHART OF ACCOUNTS   Oracle Assets and Oracle General Ledger must share the same Chart of Accounts structure. The Chart of Accounts structure shared is dictated by the GL Sets of Books defined in the Assets depreciation books. Assets uses the three segment qualifiers to identify the balancing segment, cost center segment, and natural account segment within the Chart of Accounts structure. In particular, the cost center segment qualifier is set up only for Assets, so the program can derive the appropriate depreciation expense account based on the cost center used in the asset's distribution.

SETS OF BOOKS   In addition to defining the Chart of Accounts structure, the Sets of Books also defines which set of balances should be updated by Assets-generated journal entries. In an environment with multiple Sets of Books, you will need to set up one depreciation book per Sets of Books. Depreciation books can post to GL if the period names are identical and the *Allow GL Posting* option is enabled in the depreciation book.

JOURNAL SOURCES   You need one or more journal sources in GL to identify journal entries transferred from Assets. You select the journal source to use in the Book Controls form, within the Journal Categories alternative region.

JOURNAL CATEGORIES   You need journal categories in GL to identify journal entries transferred from Assets. Using the Journal Categories alternative region of the Book Controls form, you select the journal categories to use for each category, such as additions or transfers.

DEPRECIATION BOOKS   When assigning Reporting Sets of Books in GL to the Primary Set of Books for MRC, you must associate a depreciation book with each Reporting Sets of Books through the Conversion Options form.

MRC REPORTING RESPONSIBILITIES   In addition to the regular Oracle Assets responsibility, you must set up an Assets MRC Reporting responsibility for each Reporting Sets of Books. (MRC Reporting responsibilities are used primarily for reporting purposes for Reporting Sets of Books—they should not be used for transactional activities.) Oracle Applications come with predefined product-specific MRC menus and request groups that you should use to create MRC Reporting responsibilities. The MRC menus are in the format of (*Module*)_MRC_ NAVIGATOR_GUI, and the MRC request groups are in the format of MRC Programs (*Module*). Remember, in order for depreciation to work, you must run it for each MRC Reporting responsibility, and then run it for the regular Oracle Assets responsibility last.

REPORTING SETS OF BOOKS   To enable MRC, you must set the profile option *MRC: Reporting Sets of Books* value to point to the Reporting Sets of Books for each MRC Reporting responsibility in Oracle Assets. For the regular Assets responsibility, there is no need to set up this profile option.

Oracle Human Resources

Assets refers to the Oracle Human Resources module's Employees setup when assigning assets to employees. Because of this, you must set up employees before assigning or distributing assets to them, even if you are not otherwise using the Human Resources module.

Oracle Purchasing

Assets in Oracle Assets have source line information where you can specify supplier data from Oracle Purchasing. Also, in order to use units of production depreciation, you must complete the units of measure setup for the production units of measure. To accomplish this, the following setups are shared between the two modules:

- **Financial options** Before you can create suppliers and employees, you must set up financial options in Oracle Purchasing. Financial options define whether suppliers and employees numbers are manually entered or automatically generated. If automatically generated, you must specify the starting number.

- **Suppliers** To enter suppliers as source line information for assets, you must first define the suppliers. Suppliers belong to Oracle Purchasing; Oracle Assets refers to Oracle Purchasing to retrieve supplier names and numbers.

- **Units of measure** To use the units of production depreciation method, you must record production unit consumption in a defined unit of measure class and a defined unit of measure. The unit of measure class—and the units of measure setup—are shared between Oracle Purchasing and Oracle Assets, as well as with several other modules.

Review Questions

1. How does a Reporting Sets of Books in GL point to a depreciation book in Assets?

2. How does an MRC Reporting responsibility know which Reporting Sets of Books it is pointing to?

3. What are units of measure used for in Oracle Assets?

How Oracle Payables Integrates with Oracle Assets

You can use the Mass Additions Create Program to create mass additions lines from Payables invoice lines. If the invoice lines are in foreign currencies, the Mass Additions Create program converts them to the functional currency. To initiate the Mass Additions Create Program, you must specify the corporate book for which you want the program to run, as well as a date. Oracle Payables and the selected corporate book must use the same GL Sets of Books.

The Mass Additions Create Program can process two types of invoice lines:

- Invoice lines for asset items
- Invoice lines for expense items

Invoice Lines for Asset Items

For asset items, the invoice lines will be processed if they satisfy the following criteria:

- Posted to General Ledger
- Distribution accounts match either the asset clearing account or CIP clearing account
- Distribution accounts are of account type assets
- The General Ledger date is prior to or equal to the date you specified for the Mass Additions Create Program

Invoice Lines for Expense Items

For expense items, the invoice lines will be processed if they satisfy the following criteria:

- Posted to General Ledger
- Tracked as an asset (you can control this option by logging on with the *Payables, Vision Operations (USA)* responsibility and following the *Invoices : Enter* navigation path to reach the Enter Invoice form)
- Distribution accounts are of account type *Expense*
- The General Ledger date is prior to or equal to the date you specified for the Mass Additions Create Program

Review Question

1. What are the differences in the selection criteria for asset items and expense items?

Implementation Considerations

The following are integration implementation considerations that should be considered:

- Sets of Books
- MRC
- Postprocessing after Mass Additions Create

Sets of Books

Perhaps you have noticed by now that in order for Oracle Financials modules to operate in an integrated fashion, they must share the same GL Sets of Books. This is true for integration between Payables and Assets, between Assets and General Ledger, and between all other Financials modules. The Sets of Books represents the backbone of Oracle Financials modules.

MRC

MRC creates another level of complexity within Oracle Financials. You must draw diagrams and process flows on how MRC works within your organization. Decide how many Reporting Sets of Books you need, and how many MRC Reporting responsibilities you need. Then, take the following steps:

1. Set up the Primary Set of Books.

2. Set up the Reporting Sets of Books.

3. Assign Reporting Sets of Books to the Primary Set of Books.

4. Assign operating units and depreciation books to Reporting Sets of Books through conversion options.

5. Set up MRC Reporting responsibilities.

6. Set up the *MRC: Reporting Sets of Books* profile option value to point to the appropriate Reporting Sets of Books for each MRC Reporting responsibility.

Postprocessing After Mass Additions Create

The Mass Additions Create program generates mass additions lines, but the lines generated only contain basic information. You can have asset category defaults if you create an item with a default asset category, then create a purchase order for that particular item, and finally match an invoice to the purchase order. However, this still may not be enough information, because data such as employee, location, and project are not transferred. To solve this, consider creating a postprocessing program or database trigger that transfers the necessary information from Purchasing and Payables to Assets automatically after the Mass Additions Create program runs. Your implementation's database administrator can help you in this area.

Review Questions

1. What are the common criteria for Oracle Financials modules integration?

2. Why should you consider postprocessing after Mass Additions Create?

Features of the Application Desktop

There are features within the Application Desktop that facilitate integration between Oracle Applications modules. These features fall into two categories: Folders and Navigators.

Using the Folder tools, you can customize the query or layout to help you reconcile, as well as to facilitate integration. For example, you can set up a customized folder that calls Assets mass additions lines. In this folder, you can set up a customized query to select all invoice lines (invoice distributions) in Oracle Payables that will be picked up by the Mass Additions Create program. You can alter the layout in many forms, adding, removing, and resizing fields. With the folder tools you can further change the screen to suit the unique way your company tracks assets, by moving the most important fields to the far left. In addition, you can change field prompts to fit more information in the form. This way you can easily reconcile with Oracle Assets or projects and correct mistakes before integrating data with Assets.

You can create custom Navigators (menus) to facilitate integration. For example, you can have a Navigator that will call the Oracle Payables and Assets functions to facilitate the whole Mass Additions process. You can also have a Navigator setup that mixes GL and Assets setup functions. Opportunities to facilitate integration are endless with different combinations of Navigators and responsibilities.

Review Question

1. Which Application Desktop features can you use to facilitate integration between Oracle Applications modules?

Managing Budgets

This section covers the following information about budgets:

- Creating budgets

- Entering budget amounts

- Using the Budget Wizard

- Reviewing and updating budgets

Budgets are part of Oracle General Ledger functionality, but budget amounts are accessed by subledgers such as Oracle Purchasing and Payables. Because budget balances are stored by budgets, account combinations, and accounting period names, you can have multiple budgets. You can use FSG to create budget variance reports with the budget balances and actual balances, and use ADI to upload budget amounts from Microsoft Excel.

Creating Budgets

Before you can use a budget, you must create it. This involves two steps: defining the budget, and then specifying budget organizations. The next few pages will show you how to accomplish both steps. After you see how to create budgets, you will review how to create master/detail budgets. A master/detail budget is a budget hierarchy. A master budget can be a corporate budget. An intermediate budget—a budget that is both a detail budget of a master budget and a master budget of a detail budget—can be by region. A detail budget can be by department.

Defining Budgets

Before you can enter budget amounts to create budget balances, you must first create budgets that can hold the budget amounts. To enter budgets, follow the navigation path *Budgets : Define : Budget* to open the Define Budget form. (For the purposes of this chapter, log in using the responsibility *General Ledger, Vision Operations (USA)* to make the proper navigation paths appear.) You must enter a name and a description when defining a budget. Next, you must enter a budget status, which can be either *Open, Current*, or *Frozen. Open* means that budget amounts can be entered or modified in this budget. *Current* has the same features as *Open*, but each Set of Books can have only one *Current* budget, which will be used as the default in most budget-related forms. *Frozen* means that budget amounts cannot be entered or modified in this budget.

If you wish, you can define whether this budget requires budget journals. Budget journals allow you to maintain an audit trail. However, if you choose to enable the *Require Budget Journals* option, you cannot enter budget amounts directly, and you cannot use the Budget Upload program, which uploads budget data from the open interface table. Next, you enter the first and last periods for the new budget. If you want to specify a control budget, you can choose a master budget to which you assign the new budget. A master budget must have the same range of budget periods.

Now you are ready to generate the budget. To do so, click on the **Open Next Year** button. You will be asked to confirm that you want to open the next budget year for your new budget. Click on the **Yes** button to invoke a concurrent program called Open Budget Year. See Figure 6-1. Use the Help | View My Requests menu command to verify completion of the concurrent program.

The **AutoCopy** button on the Define Budget form does not copy entire budgets; it copies budget amounts. You can copy budget amounts from an existing budget if:

- ■ The source budget has the same first and last budget periods as the destination budget

- ■ The destination budget does not have any open budget years

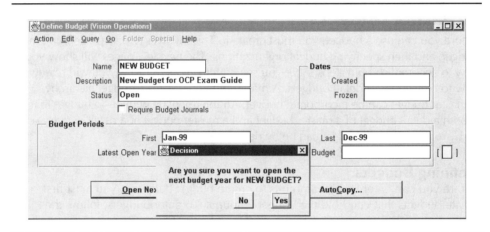

FIGURE 6-1. *Define Budget form*

Review Questions

1. What are the valid statuses of a budget?

2. What does the *Require Budget Journals* option do?

3. What are the criteria for selecting a master budget for a detail budget?

4. What does the **AutoCopy** button in the Define Budget form do?

Define Budget Organizations

After you have defined the budget, you can define what account combinations belong to the new budget. To define sets of valid account combinations, you must define budget organizations. You can find the Define Budget Organization form (shown in Figure 6-2) by following the navigation path *Budgets : Define : Organization.* If you define a budget organization named ALL, General Ledger will automatically include all account combinations assigned to other budget organizations. Otherwise, you must use ranges or assignments to explicitly assign account combinations to the budget organization.

Create your own budget organization now by first entering a name and description for the budget organization. Next, enter the ordering segment for the budget organization. The ordering segment is used to order the account assignments for the budget organization. Next, you can enter a display sequence. The display sequence defines the orders in which the Chart of Accounts segments are displayed. You can also enter an effective date range to specify when the budget organization

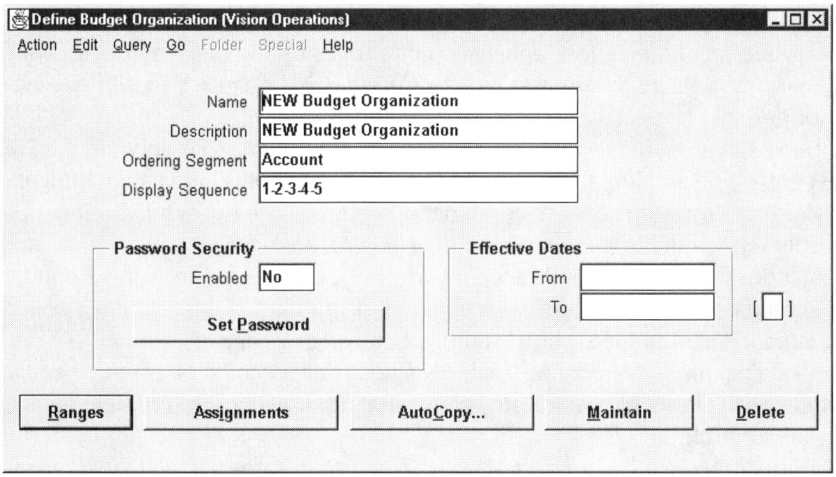

FIGURE 6-2. *Define Budget Organization form*

is valid. For enhanced security, you can password-protect the budget organization so that only authorized personnel can enter, review, or modify budget amounts.

Up to five buttons can appear in the Define Budget Organization form:

■ Ranges

■ Assignments

■ AutoCopy

■ Maintain

■ Delete

RANGES   For ranges, enter line numbers and account combination ranges. You cannot have overlapping ranges with the same currency across the same Sets of Books. Next, enter a budget entry type for the account combinations range. There are two types: *Entered* or *Calculated. Entered* is the required budget entry type if you want to allow budgetary controls. It allows manual entry of data such as budget amounts, budget journals, and budget upload. *Calculated* only allows calculated forms of data entry, meaning only budget formulas and mass budgets. The last step is to define the valid currency for data entry for this account range. For statistical budgets, use currency STAT. For the *Calculated* budget entry method, you can only use STAT or the functional currency of the Sets of Books. The budget currency can only be the functional currency if you are enforcing budgetary controls. For your budget organization, enter account ranges of all company 02 account combinations. Specify an amount type of *Calculated*, because you will need it later for defining budget formulas.

If budgetary control is enabled in your Sets of Books, you can only use the *Entered* budget entry type and functional currency. You have the option to assign budgetary control options for each account combination range. These budgetary control options all exist in the scrollable section on the right side of the Account Ranges form, and they include Automatic Encumbrance, Fund Check Level, Amount Type, Boundary, and Funding Budget. Automatic encumbrance means that all Oracle subledgers will generate encumbrance journals automatically. For budgetary control to work, Automatic Encumbrance must be on. Fund Check Level can be None, Advisory, or Absolute. As the last step, you must specify what funding budget is used in the budgetary control.

Amount Type can be Period-to-date (PTD), Quarter-to-date (QTD), Year-to-date (YTD), or Project-to-date (PJTD). Boundary can be Period, Quarter, Year, or Project. Amount Type specifies which budget amount you can use in budgetary control, while Boundary specifies the boundary period of the budget amount you can use. For example, if Amount Type is QTD, that means you can use the QTD budget amount. Assuming you are in the second period of your first quarter, and you did not use up the budget amount that belongs to the first period of the first quarter, you can use the leftover budget as well as the current period budget. However, depending on the boundary type, you may or may not be able to use the third-period budget amount, which is in the future. A boundary type of Period will not allow you to use the third-period budget amount, while a boundary type of Quarter will. A boundary type of Period means that you cannot go past the current period to obtain additional budget amounts. See Figure 6-3.

After you enter the account ranges, you can save your work. If you do not have any overlapping account ranges, a concurrent program called Assign Budget Account Ranges will be initiated. Use the Help | View My Requests menu command to verify completion of the concurrent program. The concurrent program will assign the existing account combinations to the budget organization. However, if you add or inactivate new account combinations later, you must either run the concurrent program Maintain Budget Organization to maintain the budget organization with the defined account combination ranges, or manually add or delete the account combinations from the Account Ranges form using the **Range Assignments** button. The **Assignments** button on the Define Budget Organization form can only be used to view or delete specific assignments. If you enforce budgetary control, you do not need to run the Maintain Budget Organization program to add new accounts. The budgetary control process always checks the account ranges explicitly.

When you delete an account from the budget organization account assignments, the account is not included in the budget organization immediately. However, if

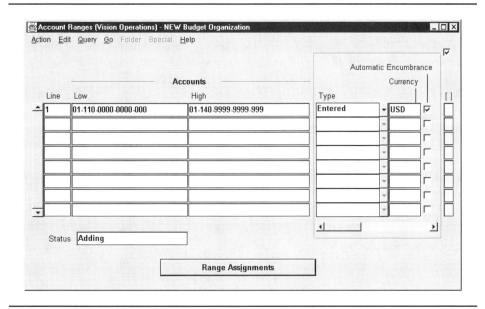

FIGURE 6-3.   *Account Ranges form*

you do not modify the account range defined within the budget organization, when you run the Maintain Budget Organization program the account will be included again, because the account is within the defined account range. To permanently disable an account combination, besides deleting the accounting combination from the account assignments, you also must modify the account ranges defined for the budget organization, or you can inactivate the account combination in the Define Account Combination form.

ASSIGNMENTS   The **Assignments** button can be used to view and delete specific account combinations from the budget organization. Remember, deleting only the specific account combination from the budget organization shows an immediate effect, but it is not a permanent one. When the Maintain Budget Organization concurrent program runs, the account combination will be added back to the budget organization if it is still active, or if the defined account ranges have not been modified to exclude it.

AUTOCOPY   If you have not already defined account ranges for your destination budget, the **AutoCopy** button can be used to copy account ranges from an existing budget organization. To perform the AutoCopy function, you must enter a source budget and the segment overrides. The segment overrides allow you to enter one or more segment values that you want to override in your destination budget. You must specify at least one segment value, because you cannot create duplicate accounts across budget organizations within the same Sets of Books. Click on the **OK** button to initiate the concurrent program AutoCopy Budget Organization. See Figure 6-4.

MAINTAIN   The **Maintain** button initiates the Maintain Budget Organization concurrent program. You initiate this concurrent program to maintain account assignments within the budget organization. You can also invoke the Maintain Budget Organization concurrent program from the Standard Report Submission form.

DELETE   The **Delete** button allows you to delete the budget organization. It initiates the Delete Budget Organization concurrent program. You can use the Help | View My Requests menu command to verify completion of successful completion.

Review Questions

   1. How should the ALL budget organization be defined?

   2. What are the differences between *Entered* and *Calculated* budget entry types?

   3. What does the concurrent program Maintain Budget Organization do?

   4. What are Amount Type and Boundary used for in budgetary control?

   5. What is the purpose of the **Assignments** button? The **Maintain** button? The **Delete** button?

   6. When defining a budget organization, what does the **AutoCopy** button copy?

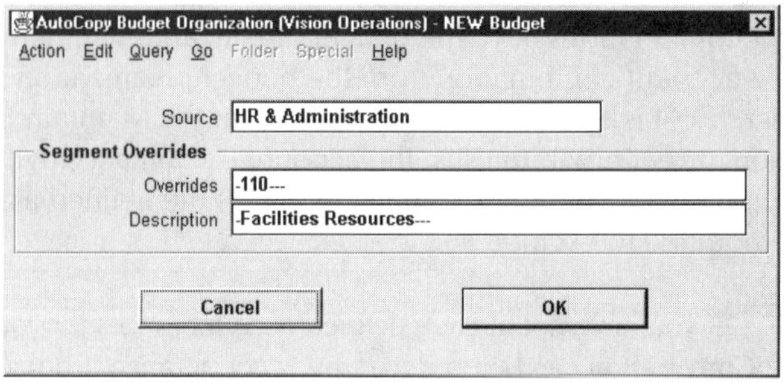

FIGURE 6-4.   *AutoCopy Budget Organization form*

Define Master/Detail Budgets

To create master/detail budgets, you create the master budgets first, followed by the detail budgets. If you have intermediate master budgets, define them before the detail budgets. In other words, you must define the budget hierarchy from the top down. When you define an intermediate budget or a detail budget, select the immediate master budget to which the intermediate budget or the detail budget is tied. One master budget can be assigned to multiple intermediate or detail budgets.

For each budget, you must define a budget organization. Use the Define Budget Organization form to create budget organizations. Use rollup and parent values for your nondetail budgets. Do not overlap accounts assigned to a master budget with accounts assigned to a detail budget, because overlapping the accounts will cause an error in the budget balances. For example, if your master budget organization includes detail accounts, the budget balance of the master budget will be overstated, and if your detail budget organization includes master accounts, the budget balance of the detail budget will be overstated.

After you finish creating budget organizations, you must define summary accounts to store summarized balances. These summary accounts should correspond to the budget organizations at the nondetail level. Oracle General Ledger uses these summary account balances to create master/detail reports and variance reports. Use the following reports to help with master budget control:

- **Budget – Hierarchy Listing** lists one or more master budgets with their associated detail budgets.

- **Budget – Master/Detail** lists one or more master budgets with the available funds for their associated detail budgets. Detail budgets with total budget amounts that are more than the master budget will be marked as exceptions.

- **Budget – Organization Listing** lists budget organizations with their associated account assignments and budgetary control parameters.

- **Budget – Organization Range Listing** lists budget organizations with their associated account ranges and budgetary control parameters.

- **Budget – Summary/Detail** lists one or more summary accounts with the budget amounts for their associated detail budgets.

- **Budget – Unbudgeted Master/Detail Accounts** lists budget amounts for the detail budgets that do not roll up to their associated master budget amounts.

Review Questions

1. What is the sequence in establishing master/detail budgets?

2. What is the difference between the Budget – Master/Detail report and the Budget – Summary/Detail report?

3. For what purpose can you use the Budget – Unbudgeted Master/Detail Accounts report?

Entering Budget Amounts

After you create budgets—whether master or detail—you must enter budget amounts. There are a variety of ways to enter budget amounts:

- Entering budget amounts manually

- Using budget journals

- Using budget formulas

- Mass budgeting

- Budget uploads

- Transferring budgets

Entering Budget Amounts Manually

You can use the Enter Budget Amounts form (*Budgets : Enter : Amounts*) to enter budget amounts directly if the budget entry type is *Entered*, as long as the status is not *Frozen*. You must enter the budget organization, a budget and the desired accounting period. You can enter a currency of STAT to enter statistical budget amounts. To experiment with this, try to use the *Operations* budget organization, budget PRELIM 1999, and accounting periods from Jan-99 to Dec-99. Place your cursor in the Account field and a Find window will appear. Click on the **Find** button to retrieve all account assignments or accounts within a specified range. In your exercise, just retrieve all account assignments. The budget balances for the accounts will be displayed.

You can enter budget amounts in worksheet mode or single-row mode. In worksheet mode, shown in Figure 6-5, you will see multiple accounts and a scrollable region with the accounting periods you chose and a total. You can use the **Show Total** button to shrink the scrollable window and display the total as a separate column. Click on the **Hide** button to hide the Total column.

In single-row mode you are shown a single account and the accounting periods as individual fields. In either mode, you can directly enter the amount. Click on the **Post** button after you are done, and the Budget Posting concurrent program will be initiated. When the Budget Posting program completes, the budget amounts you entered become the budget balances. Use the Help | View My Requests menu

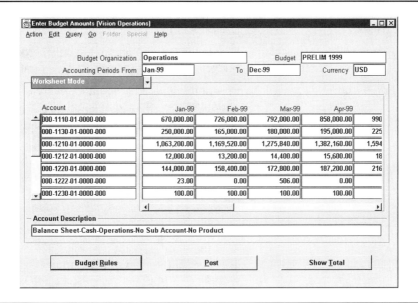

FIGURE 6-5. *Worksheet mode*

command to verify completion of the Budget Posting program. You can also click on the **Budget Rules** button and apply budget rules, as shown in Figure 6-6. Table 6-1 lists the available budget rules.

Select the budget rule, the amount, and the optional budget you want. Then, either click on the **Apply** button to apply the budget rule and stay within the Budget Rules window or click on the **OK** button to apply the budget rule and close the

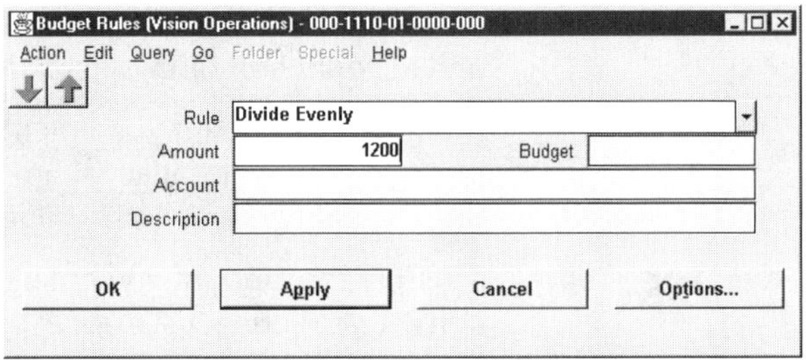

FIGURE 6-6. *Budget Rules form*

Budget Rules	Description
Divide Evenly	Divide the entered amount evenly across the budget periods for the selected account.
Repeat Per Period	Repeat the entered amount for every budget period for the selected account.
4/4/5	Distribute 4/52 to period 1, 4/52 to period 2, 5/52 to period 3, and then repeat the pattern. This budget rule can only be applied to a year with 12 or 13 budget periods. If there is a period 13, the distributed amount will be 0 for period 13.
4/5/4	Distribute 4/52 to period 1, 5/52 to period 2, 4/52 to period 3, and then repeat the pattern. This budget rule can only be applied to a year with 12 or 13 budget periods. If there is a period 13, the distributed amount will be 0 for period 13.
5/4/4	Distribute 5/52 to period 1, 4/52 to period 2, 4/52 to period 3, and then repeat the pattern. This budget rule can only be applied to a year with 12 or 13 budget periods. If there is a period 13, the distributed amount will be 0 for period 13.
Prior Year Budget Monetary	Multiply the amount you entered by the prior-year budget amount of the budget and account combination you entered.
Current Year Budget Monetary	Multiply the amount you entered by the current-year budget amount of the budget and account combination you entered.
Prior Year Budget Stat	Multiply the amount you entered by the prior-year budget statistical amount of the budget and account combination you entered.
Current Year Budget Stat	Multiply the amount you entered by the current-year budget statistical amount of the budget and account combination you entered.

TABLE 6-1. *Budget Rules*

Budget Rules	Description
Prior Year Actual Monetary	Multiply the amount you entered by the prior-year actual amount of the account combination you entered.
Current Year Actual Monetary	Multiply the amount you entered by the current-year actual amount of the account combination you entered.
Prior Year Actual Stat	Multiply the amount you entered by the prior-year actual statistical amount of the account combination you entered.
Current Year Actual Stat	Multiply the amount you entered by the current-year actual statistical amount of the account combination you entered.

TABLE 6-1.   *Budget Rules* (continued)

Budget Rules window. Click on the **Options** button to determine whether the rule applies the amount to the adjusting periods, and whether rounding errors should be ignored or distributed to a selected period.

Review Questions

 1. When can you use the Enter Budget Amount form?

 2. What is the difference between worksheet mode and single-row mode?

 3. If you want to apply $100 to each budget period for a selected account, which budget rules can you use?

 4. If you want to apply a .5 percent increase from last year's budget to a selected account, which budget rule can you use?

Using Budget Journals

Budget journals offer an alternative way to enter budget amounts, and they assist in maintaining an audit trail. As is the case with actuals journals, you must post budget journals in order to update the budget balances. To enter budget journals, you can use the Enter Budget Journals form (navigation path *Budgets : Enter : Journals*). The only difference between this form and the Enter Budget Amounts form is that this one has a **Create Journals** button instead of a **Post** button. You must enter the budget organization, a budget, and the desired accounting period. You will not be able to enter budget amounts for budgets with a status of *Frozen*. You can enter a currency of STAT to enter statistical budget amounts. Positive numbers will appear as the debit amounts on the budget journals.

In the Enter Budget Journals form, the worksheet mode and the single-row mode are supplemented by a journal mode. The journal mode allows you to enter a budget amount in a journal format just as if you were entering an actual amount. You can enter both monetary and statistical amounts in the journal mode if the profile option *Journals: Mix Statistics and Monetary* is enabled. If the accounts have statistical units tied to them, you can enter the quantity as the budget statistical amount.

For exercise purposes, once again try to use the Operations budget organization, budget PRELIM 1999, and accounting periods from Jan-99 to Dec-99. Place your cursor in the Account field and a Find window will appear. Click on the **Find** button to retrieve all account assignments and the budget balances of the selected account will be displayed. Using account 000-1222-01-0000-000, enter a direct budget amount of your choosing. Then use budget rules to divide $1,200 evenly for account 000-1230-01-0000-000. Next, modify some of the existing budget amounts. Your form should now look similar to Figure 6-7.

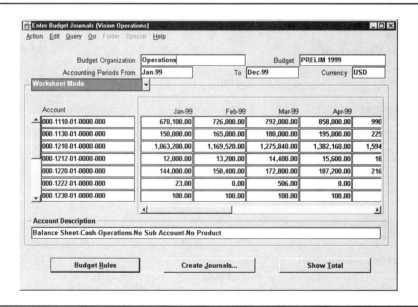

FIGURE 6-7. *Enter Budget Journals form*

When you are finished, click on the **Create Journals** button. Once the Create Journals window appears, enter your journal batch name and a defined journal category. After you choose the journal category, the funds status becomes required if budgetary control is enabled. If budgetary control is not enabled, you can select the **Run Journal Import** button to create the unposted budget journal batch right away. You will receive the journal import group number as reference.

If budgetary control is enabled, you can use the **Check Funds** button to check whether there are available funds for your budget journals. You can also use the **Reserve Funds** button to reserve the available funds for your budget journals. You cannot change budget journals after you reserve funds. After you check or reserve funds, you can select the **View Results** button to view the fund-checking results. You can use the **Print All** button to print all budget transactions applying to the selected budget. You can also use the **Print Errors and Warnings** button to print only budget transactions that violate available funding.

If budgetary control is enabled, you must reserve funds before creating budget journals. When you select the **Done** button, a concurrent program named Create Journals will be initiated. This program creates the unposted budget journal batch. Use the Help | View My Requests menu command to verify completion of your concurrent program. The batch name is automatically created using the following format:

CJE: (Your batch name) Budget Journal (Your Request ID): B

The generated budget journal batch will have one journal per budget period.

To see this in action, you will post the budget journal. From the Post Journals form, find all batches that start with the letter CJE. Select your generated batch and post it. Notice that budget journals do not have to be balanced.

Review Questions

1. What is the difference between entering budgets through the Enter Budget Amounts form vs. Define Budget Journals?

2. After the unposted budget journal batch is created, what must you do to update budget balances?

3. What is the default format for the generated unposted journal budget batch name?

4. What is the purpose of journal mode?

Using Budget Formulas

You can also enter budget amounts by using budget formulas. Budget formulas are very similar to recurring formulas for actual amounts. To use budget formulas, you must first define the budget formula and then generate it.

DEFINING A BUDGET FORMULA   To enter budget formulas, use the navigation path *Budgets : Define : Formula*. You first enter the recurring batch name and an optional batch description. Then enter the journal name, journal category, and currency. You can choose to enter an effective date range to limit the timeframe for which this recurring budget journal is generated. Leaving the effective date range blank means it is valid at any time. See Figure 6-8.

You are now ready to enter journal lines. You can enter any number of journal lines. A journal line consists of line number, account, and an optional line description. Then, you enter the formula that will calculate the balance for the account you specified. Entering the formula requires using EasyCalc, the formula-definition method based on Hewlett Packard's Reverse Polish Notation. The first step of the formula must begin with the operator Enter. You can then enter either an amount or an account. You can use a summary account since balances are kept for summary accounts. If you specified an account, you must further specify the balance type, amount type, currency type, and period. From the second step on, you can no longer use the Enter operator, but must instead use +, -, x, or /. You can repeat the exercise for recurring journals, only this time you are going to give a 10 percent increase to the Distribution Organization freight account budget balance from the last period budget balance. In order to perform this step, the Distribution Organization freight account must belong to company 02. This is because when you define your budget organization, only

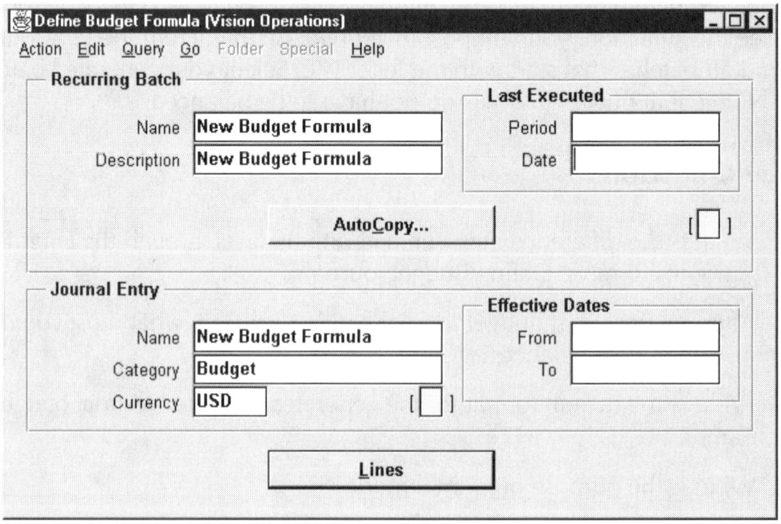

FIGURE 6-8.   *Define Budget Formula form*

company 02 account combinations have a budget entry type of *Calculated*, which you need in order to enter budget formulas.

GENERATING A BUDGET FORMULA   Once you have defined the budget formula, you can generate budget journals using the Generate Budget Formula form. Go to this form now using navigation path *Budgets : Generate : Formula.* Enter your budget name and you will see your budget formula batch appear as a recurring batch. Check the leftmost checkbox next to your recurring batch, enter the budget period's range, and click on the **Calculate** button. A concurrent program called Budget Formulas will be initiated. The Budget Formulas program will calculate the budget amounts and update the budget balances accordingly. Use the Help | View My Requests menu command to verify completion of the program.

Mass Budget

Just as Budget Formulas is similar to Recurring Journals, Mass Budget is similar to Mass Allocations. You can use the Mass Budget process to allocate a higher-level budget to a lower-level budget. You can navigate to the Define MassBudget form using the navigation path *Budgets : Define : MassBudget.* For each mass budget, you must establish a batch and its formulas, and then generate the mass budget.

MASS BUDGET BATCH   To define a mass budget batch, you enter a mass budget name, the balance type used by this mass budget (*Actual* or *Encumbrance*), and an optional description. If you have prior mass budget batches, you can use the **AutoCopy** button to copy from them. The **Validate All** button will validate your allocation formulas and change the status to *Validated* if your formulas are valid.

MASS BUDGET FORMULAS   Now you can enter mass budget formulas. Click on the **Formulas** button. When entering a mass budget formula, you enter a journal name, a journal category, and an optional journal description. Then you have the option to include the full balance from the allocation account or the balance of a single entered currency. For example, if you only want balances entered as USD, you can choose *Single Entered Currency* and enter USD as the currency. The generated mass budget journals will use the same currency as the allocation account's original entered currency. You can also choose to perform full cost pool allocation. This option will put any rounding differences into the allocation cost pool with the largest relative balance; otherwise, any rounding differences will stay with allocation accounts. After you set up the general mass budget journal information, you are ready to enter a formula line. The formula line is in the following format:

$$\text{target account (T)} =$$
$$\text{allocation cost pool * rate or usage factor/1 or total usage}$$
$$A \qquad * \qquad B \qquad / \qquad C$$

Allocation cost pool can be a fixed amount or a balance from an allocation account. Rate or usage factor can be a fixed rate or a statistical account balance. If using a statistical account, total usage will be the summation of all balances of the involved statistical accounts. Balances used for allocation accounts have the following parameters:

- **Currency**   Functional currency or STAT for statistical balance

- **Amount Type**   PTD, QTD, YTD, or Project-to-date (PJTD)

- **Relative Period**   Current Period, Previous Period, or Year Ago, Same Period

- **Balance Type**   Actual, Budget, or Encumbrance

For budget and encumbrance balance types, you must also enter the budget name of the encumbrance type. You must also enter one or more offset accounts, referred to as O, so that the allocation accounts balances will be reduced when higher-level budgets are allocated to the more detailed budgets. If the amount calculated is positive, the journal lines created will debit the target accounts and credit the offset accounts. Usually, the offset accounts are the same as the allocation cost accounts, because you are likely to transfer budget balances from the allocation cost accounts to the target accounts.

When entering allocation, target, or offset accounts for each segment value, you have the following options:

- **C: Constant**   Entered segment value will be used as a constant in the allocation account(s). You can use this constant on child values or parent values/rollup groups referred to in summary accounts.

- **L: Looping**   Entered segment value will be looped to create one allocation account for each child value. This option should only be used with parent values. If not, when you validate the mass budget formulas, the validation will fail.

- **S: Summing**   Entered segment value will be used as a summation of the assigned child values. Similar to looping, this option should only be used with parent values. If not, when you validate the mass budget formulas, the validation will fail.

Let's look at the mass budget example that comes with the *Vision* database. Shown in Figure 6-9, it is named **Variable Allocation example for Budgets**. In this example, budget balances from the CORPORATE 1997 budget are transferred from

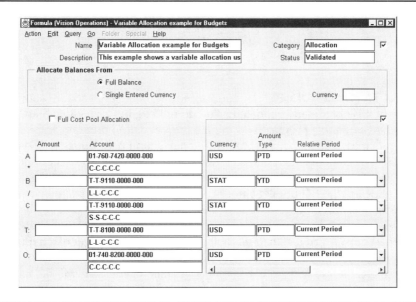

FIGURE 6-9. *Variable Allocation example*

the Operations-Payroll-Rent expense account to the Mass Allocation In account of each company and department. The transfer is performed proportionally, based on the YTD Headcount statistical account balance by company and department. When you use budget balances, be sure to select balance type Budget and a budget. The mass budget formula allocates budget based on the following formula:

$$T= A*B/C$$
$$O+T = 0$$

- **T** = The Mass Allocation In accounts by each company and each department since it loops through the first and the second segments

- **A** = The Operations-Payroll-Rent expense account

- **B** = The Headcount statistical account balances by each company and each department since it loops through the first and the second segments (company and department). Thus, if you have three companies and five departments, you will have 3*5 = 15 Headcount statistical account balances. Notice how the currency is STAT instead of USD and the amount type is YTD.

- **C** = The total YTD Headcount statistical account balance

- **O** = The Operations-Corporate Finance-MassAllocation Out

TIP
*Target accounts cannot loop in a different frequency
as B; otherwise the validation will fail. The Validation
program does not validate cross-validation rules.*

GENERATE MASS BUDGET   You can now validate the variable allocation
example (if it is not already validated). You do not need to explicitly validate the
batch—the Generation program will initiate the Validation program automatically.
To generate mass budget batches, follow the navigation path *Budgets : Generate :
MassBudgets.* Select the mass budget batch name, along with the accounting period
ranges. You can select an allocation method of either *Full* or *Incremental.* The *Full*
method allocates the full budget amount, whereas the *Incremental* method allocates
budget amounts based on your already allocated target budget balances. To ensure
that *Incremental* works right, do not modify the target budget balances between
incremental runs. If you use the *Full* method and the mass budget batch has run
before, you must reverse the original allocation manually to avoid double posting.
Click on the **Generate** button. The mass budget batch generated will be named
using the following format:

MB : (concurrent Request ID) (Mass Budget Batch name) (Accounting Period used)

Review Questions

1. What type of formula is similar to the budget formula?

2. What process is similar to the mass budget process?

3. If you want to use budget balance, what additional information must
   you enter?

Budget Upload
Besides using Oracle General Ledger to enter budget amounts, you can also upload
budget amounts through budget upload. You can populate the budget interface
table (GL_BUDGET_INTERFACE) with budget amounts (via ADI or a custom
program) and run the Budget Upload program. The Budget Upload program imports
budget amounts from the interface table to the production table. (You can refer to
the Open Interface manual for more details on the interface table.) The Budget
Upload program validates the data in the interface table before importing it. The
program validates that the budget is not frozen; the budget year is open; the budget
entry type for the account combination is *Entered*; and the account combinations

are assigned to the selected budget organization. The Budget Upload program then uses the validated amounts to update the budget balances directly.

You can initiate the Budget Upload program using the navigation path *Budgets : Enter : Upload.* From the form, you enter the budget and the budget organization you want to upload, and then click on the **Upload** button. See Figure 6-10. A concurrent program called Budget Spreadsheet Upload will be initiated. Use the Help | View My Requests menu command to verify completion of this program.

Transfer Budget

The last way to modify budget balances in GL is to transfer budget amounts between account combinations within the same budget. You can even transfer budget amounts between two budget organizations if the two budget organizations are within the same budget. To transfer budgets, use the navigation path *Budgets : Enter : Transfer.* Start by entering the budget within which you want to transfer budget amounts. (As with the other approaches, the budget cannot be frozen.) For the purposes of this exercise, use the PRELIM 1999 budget. Then enter a batch name, and select a currency (or use STAT currency to transfer statistical budget amounts). Enter the source budget organization and source account, followed by the destination budget organization and destination account. Select two account combinations that have budget amounts.

Select the budget period in which you want the transfer to take place. Use any budget period in the open budget year (1999 to match the figures in this book). The old (existing) balances of both the From and To accounts will be automatically displayed. You can either enter a percentage or an amount to be transferred. If you enter an amount, the amount must be less than or equal to the old balance of the From account. The new balances of From and To accounts will be automatically calculated. Use the **Show PTD Balances** or **Show YTD Balances** buttons to toggle between displaying PTD or YTD balances. See Figure 6-11.

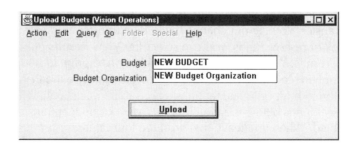

FIGURE 6-10. *Upload Budgets form*

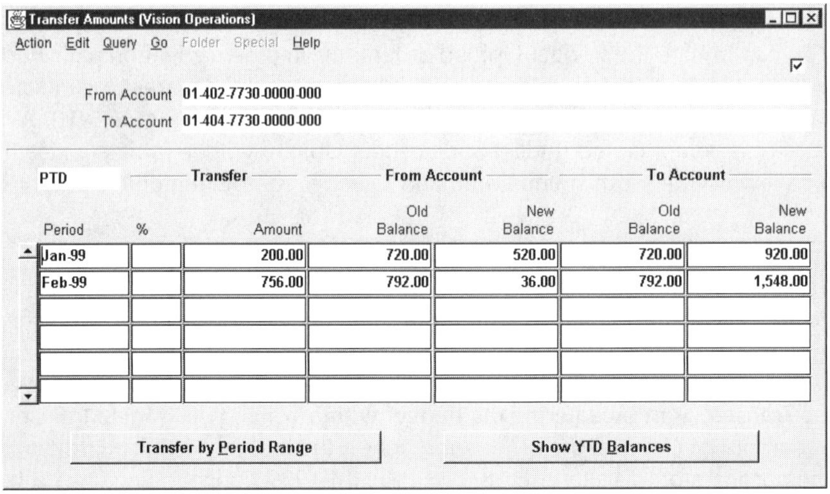

FIGURE 6-11. *Transfer Amounts form*

To transfer budget amounts for an entire period range, click on the **Transfer by Period Range** button. Enter the From and To periods, along with the percentage or amount you want to transfer. The **Apply** button creates the lines corresponding to your selection and keeps the Transfer Period Range window open. The **OK** button creates the lines corresponding to your selection and closes the Transfer Period Range window. For this example, use several budget periods in 1999 and enter either the Percentage or Amount field. Click on the **OK** button.

Notice the additional lines in the Transfer Amounts form. Then save your work and close the Transfer Amounts window. If budgetary control is enabled, you can use the **Check Funds** button to check if there are available funds for your budget transfer, or you can use the **Reserve Funds** button to reserve the available funds for your budget transfer. You cannot change the budget transfer after you reserve funds. After you check or reserve funds, you can select the **View Results** button to view the fund-checking results. You can use the **Print All** button to print all budget transactions applying to the selected budget. You can also use the **Print Errors and Warnings** button to print only budget transactions that violate available funding. You must reserve funds before creating journals for your budget transfer if budgetary control is enabled. When you leave the form, the Journal Import program creates an unposted journal. Post the journal to update the budget balances.

Review Questions

1. What is the budget interface table name?

2. What will the Budget Upload program do?

3. Can you use the Transfer Budget form to transfer between budgets?

4. How are the budget balances updated by the Transfer Budget process?

Using the Budget Wizard

The Applications Desktop interface provides a tool for entering budgets: the Budget Wizard. To invoke the Budget Wizard, you first must invoke ADI. After ADI is up, sign on to it using the same user name and password you used for Applications. Select *Enter Budgets* from the General Ledger Poplist. This will invoke the Create Budget Worksheet. Select the Operations budget organization. Next, you can use the **Limit Accounts** button to limit the worksheet to certain account ranges. See Figure 6-12. After you specify an account range, the number of accounts in the specified budget organization is automatically calculated in the Number of Accounts field. Click on the **Checkmark** button to return to the Create Budget Worksheet form.

Next you can use the **Set Characteristics** button to set the display characteristics of the Chart of Accounts. You can select the display order, the sort order and direction, and whether you want to show the segment description. Display order is the order in which the segments are displayed; the sort order and sort direction

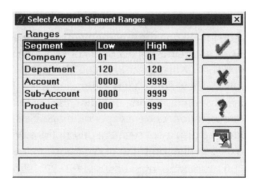

FIGURE 6-12. *Select Account Segment Ranges form*

govern how the account combinations are ordered. For example, you can display company before department, but sort department before company. To experiment with this, change your display characteristics now to display Chart of Accounts fields in the order Company-Department-Account-SubAccount-Product. Specify that the description for the account should be displayed, and sort the Chart of Accounts records by department first, then account, then company, followed by subaccount and product. When you are through looking at this screen, click on the **Checkmark** button to return to the Create Budget Worksheet form.

NOTE

While it is an interesting experiment to have the output sorted in an order different from the order of the columns, it is rarely a good idea in real life. In general, people looking at a report expect it to be sorted in the order of the columns, from left to right.

When selecting the budget and currency, remember to specify STAT as the currency for statistical budget amounts. Next, you can select a period range. Use budget PRELIM 1999 and the period range from JAN-99 to DEC-99. In the Worksheet Options area, you can select whether to insert the budget worksheet into a current or new Excel workbook, as well as whether to include actuals figures with the budget figures. If you choose both budgets and actuals, you will have two worksheets in Excel: one for budget and one for actuals. After you have changed the account range of the budget worksheet, you can use the **Question Mark** button next to the number of accounts to recalculate the number of accounts within the budget organization that fit the changed criteria.

The budget worksheet will go through a series of budget refreshes, which include creating the criteria sheet, initializing the environment, finding a list of periods, retrieving period balances, and retrieving account codes. Once the budget refresh process finishes, the worksheet will appear in Excel. The top of the worksheet includes four buttons: **View Context, View Desc, View Filter,** and **Reset Filter**. You can use **View Context** to toggle between displaying or hiding the context information such as budget name, budget organization, currency, period range, Sets of Books, and database name. **View Desc** toggles the display of segment descriptions. **View Filter** displays all of the possible filters. You can filter on Chart of Accounts segment, Chart of Accounts description, amount, and messages. These filter options are the same as those on Excel, including custom filtering and a Top 10 list. **Reset Filter** resets all filters to their default values. See Figure 6-13.

There are several functions you can use within the budget worksheet. You can insert budget accounts, apply budget rules, add budget notes, create graphs, and upload data to the Oracle General Ledger interface table.

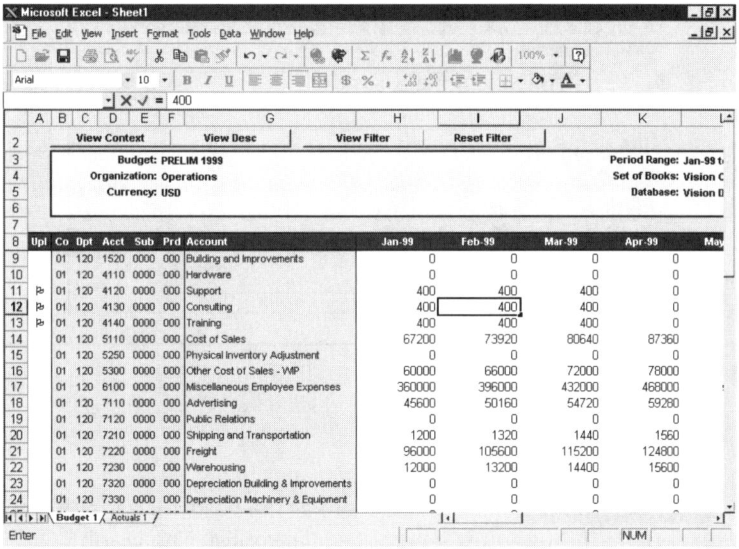

FIGURE 6-13. *Budget worksheet*

Insert Budget Accounts

You can insert budget accounts through the General Ledger Poplist. You can select an account alias to enter the account combination directly. Use the **Find Accounts** button to select an existing account combination.

Apply Budget Rules

You can select a section of cells and apply budget rules. Select a section of six or more cells and select *Apply Budget Rule* through the General Ledger Poplist. You can choose from the following budget rules: *Divide Evenly by Row, Divide Evenly by Cells, Repeat per Cell,* or *Multiply Each Cell by a Factor.* After choosing a budget rule, you enter an amount, and the cells you selected will each get an amount based on the rule you selected. You will see a sample of the result of the budget rules as you select the budget rules and the amount. When you are satisfied with the results, click on the **Checkmark** button to apply the budget rules. See Figure 6-14.

Add Budget Notes

You can put justification notes on the budget, account, or amount. Select *Add Budget Note* through the General Ledger Poplist.

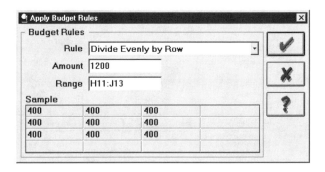

FIGURE 6-14. *Apply Budget Rules form*

Create Graph

You can select a section of cells and use them as the basis for a graph. Select the *Create Graph* option through the General Ledger Poplist. The graph will be created as a separate worksheet.

As you modify the budget amounts or add the budget amounts, you can see flags appearing in the Upload column. (As is the case with the Journal Wizard, cells produced by a cut/copy/paste operation will *not* cause the Upload Column to be flagged automatically.) If you initiate the Budget Wizard now through the *Enter Budgets* option of the General Ledger Poplist, you will have three choices: create a new budget worksheet, refresh the current budget worksheet with budget values from the database, or enter different criteria for the budget worksheet.

Upload to Interface

You can upload the budget amounts in the worksheet to Oracle General Ledger through the *Upload to Interface* option from the General Ledger Poplist. The Upload to Interface program populates the budget interface table, and the Budget Import program updates budget balances using the budget interface table's data.

You can set up options to govern the behavior of the Upload to Interface program. You can choose whether to upload *All Rows* or *Flagged Rows*. You can select whether the Upload Mode will be *Replace*, in which budget worksheet amounts replace existing budget balances, or *Increment*, in which budget worksheet amounts are added to existing budget balances. You can also choose whether to perform prevalidation (security rules will still be enforced regardless of this option's setting). You can also control how duplicate rows in the interface table will be handled. As a last step, you can choose whether to initiate the Budget Import program automatically after the Upload to Interface program. The Budget Import program will import the budget balances from the interface table to the production table to update budget balances. See Figure 6-15.

Review Questions

1. How do you invoke the Budget Wizard?

2. Where do you define how the Chart of Accounts should be displayed and ordered in the budget worksheet?

3. What does the *Apply Budget Rules* option let you control?

4. What will the Upload to Interface program do?

Reviewing and Updating Budgets

Now that you have seen how to enter budget amounts, you are ready to learn how to review and update them. This section also covers how to create budget reports and freeze budgets.

Reviewing Budgets

You can review budgets using the Budget Inquiry form (navigation path *Inquiry : Budget*, shown in Figure 6-16). When entering your selection criteria, start with the budget name, which can be for either a master budget or a detail budget. If you enter a detail budget, the only inquiry type you can select is *Drilldown this Budget*, whereas entering a summary budget will also offer inquiry type options of *Query Detail Budgets* and *Query Budget Violations Only*. *Drilldown this Budget* allows

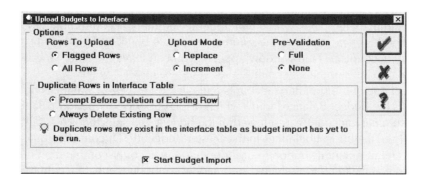

FIGURE 6-15. *Upload Budgets to Interface form*

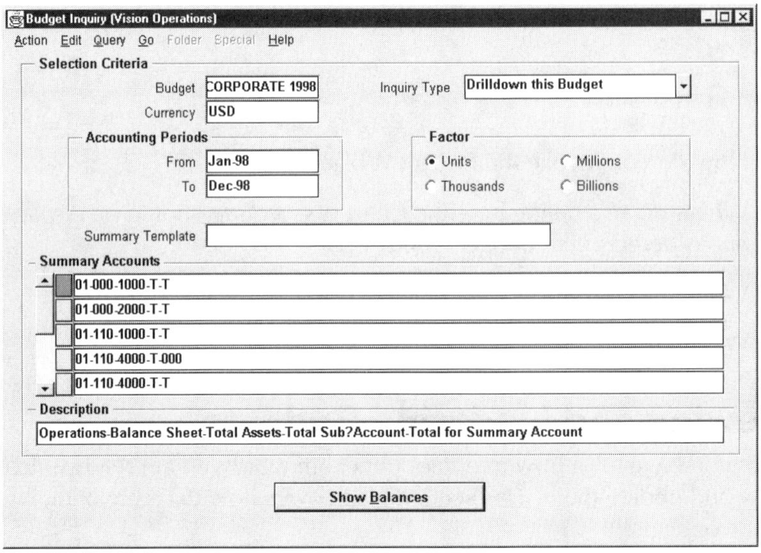

FIGURE 6-16. *Budget Inquiry form*

you to review master budget balances with a drill-down to detail accounts. *Query Detail Budgets* allows you to review both master budget and detail budget balances with a drill-down to detail accounts. *Query Budget Violations Only* allows you to review violations where detail budget balances are greater than the master balances.

Next, enter the currency you want to review, followed by the budget period range you want to review. If your budget will be showing large values, you may want to select a review factor of thousands, millions, or billions. You can optionally enter a summary template, which will limit the summary accounts you can inquire about. For this exercise, leave the summary template blank and go directly to the summary accounts. A Find window appears; you can leave the Find window blank and bring up the summary accounts.

Select one of the summary accounts and click on the **Show Balances** button. This calls the Budget Balances form, which displays period-by-period balances for the summary account you selected. If the budget you selected is a detail budget, you will see the budget balances in the Master Budget (PTD) column. You can then use the **Detail Accounts** button to drill down to the account-combination budget balances that make up the selected summary account budget balance. In this detailed Budget Balances form you will see the PTD, QTD, and YTD budget balances. You can use the folder tools to add the PJTD budget balances, the beginning budget balances, and the account combination description.

You can use the **Budget Journals** button to review the budget journals that are tied to the account budget balances (if such budget journals exist). One thing to remember: if your Sets of Books does not require budget journals, you can use other methods to update the budget amounts without creating budget journals. From the Budget Journals form, you can click on the **Detail Accounts** button to get back to the Detail Accounts form. The Budget Journals form displays the journal batch name, journal name, journal line number, entered debits, and entered credits. You can also use the folder tools to include journal source, journal category, description, statistical amounts, and other fields. If the budget you selected is a master budget, then depending on the inquiry option you selected, you will see different results. There are three options:

- ■ *Drilldown this Budget* works the same way as if the selected budget were not a master budget: only the master budget balances are shown, and you have the option to see detail accounts and budget journals.

- ■ *Query Detail Budgets* works slightly differently: when you click on the **Show Balances** button, this option shows the budget balances of the master budget, the total budget balances of the detail budgets associated with the master budget, and the available budget balances. The available budget balances are the master budget balances minus the total detail budget balances. To see the budget balances of the detail budgets, you can use the additional button **Show Budgets** to display the details. All the other options available for the *Drilldown this Budget* option still exist for the *Query Detail Budgets* option.

- ■ *Query Budget Violations Only* is the same as *Query Detail Budgets*, except that only account combinations whose master budget balance is less than the total detail budget balances are shown. In other words, the available budget balances column contains only negative amounts.

Creating Budget Reports

You can also review budget information using reports. Standard reports related to budgets include Frozen Budgets Accounts Listing, Hierarchy Listing, Journals by Flexfield, Master/Detail, Organization Listing, Organization Range Listing, Summary/ Detail, and Unbudgeted Master/Detail Accounts. If you wish, you can also utilize FSG reports to see budget figures.

Updating Budgets

When the time comes to update budgets, you have the same options as when you originally entered budget amounts. In fact, your exercises up to this point have been a mixture of inserts and updates. You can update budget information using the Enter Budget Amounts form, budget formulas, budget journals, Mass Budget, Budget Upload, Transfer Budgets, and ADI Budget Wizard. Be careful when you update budget balances in the Enter Budget Amounts form, Define Budget Journals form, or using budget formulas, because the values you enter replace prior values. When transferring budget amounts, the generated journals update the budget balances. Budget Upload, ADI Budget Wizard, and Mass Budget actually give you a choice between replacing the budget balances or adding to the existing budget balances. Budget Upload offers the choice with a column in the interface table.

Freezing Budget

After you enter the budget amounts and are satisfied with your budget, you can freeze the budget to prevent further modifications. The Freeze Budget form is available via the navigation path *Budgets : Freeze*. To use the form, select the budget you want to freeze. The form that appears, shown in Figure 6-17, allows you to change the status of the entire budget to *Frozen*. For a finer degree of control, you can use the alternative region in the lower portion of the form—the Batches alternative region to freeze budget formula batches, or the Organizations alternative

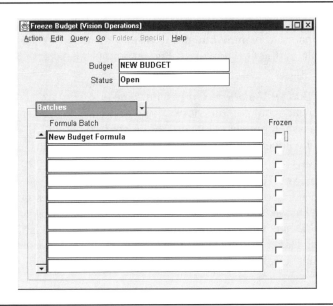

FIGURE 6-17. *Freeze Budget form*

region to freeze the budget by organizational group. You can click on the **Account Ranges** button to freeze only certain ranges of accounts.

Review Questions

1. What does the optional Summary Template field do in the Budget Inquiry form?

2. What are the budget inquiry options for a master budget?

3. How are the budget inquiry options different for a detail budget?

4. Which of the methods for entering budgets create unposted journals?

Reporting and Analysis Tools

In this section, you will learn how to integrate Oracle General Ledger with Oracle Financial Analyzer. There are two aspects to this integration:

- Setting up the interface
- Running data extraction jobs

Before reading about these aspects, you will first review some fundamental concepts regarding Oracle Financial Analyzer and integrating it with General Ledger.

Integration Fundamentals

In Financial Analyzer, there are two fundamental concepts: dimensions and financial data items. Financial data items can be thought of as "buckets" in which financial data is stored, while dimensions are the different ways you can "slice and dice" the data to organize it. When integrating Financial Analyzer with GL, financial data items in Financial Analyzer correspond to balances in Oracle GL, and a dimension in Financial Analyzer corresponds to one or more segments in the GL Chart of Accounts. In other words, GL balances are represented as financial data items, and the Chart of Accounts segments are used as dimensions to break down and analyze this data. In addition, time is always a dimension in Financial Analyzer, and it is derived from the accounting calendar for your Sets of Books.

Another important concept in Financial Analyzer is that of dimension hierarchies. A dimension hierarchy specifies parent-child relationships among the various values in a dimension. For instance, suppose that the Account segment contains summary segment values that you defined in GL's Key Segment Values form. In this case, Financial Analyzer will automatically create a dimension hierarchy in the Account dimensions according to the segment value hierarchy that you already defined.

When loading GL balances into Financial Analyzer financial data items, different types of balances are supported. You can load actual balances, budget balances, encumbrance balances, or average balances if your GL Sets of Books is configured with average balance processing enabled. In addition, you can choose to either load detail balances into Financial Analyzer detail financial data items, or load summary balances into summary financial data items. If you choose to load detail balances, summary balances will need to be calculated in Financial Analyzer. If you choose to load summary balances already calculated in GL, you must properly set up rollup groups and summary templates to precalculate the summary balances. You can still choose to further roll up the financial data in Financial Analyzer.

Consider a simple example: Suppose your GL Chart of Accounts consists of four segments: Company, Department, Product, and Account. Each of these segments can be simply mapped to a single dimension in Financial Analyzer. In this case, your financial data items will have a total of five dimensions, including the time dimension.

However, suppose that the Company segment has only one value, and all financial activity is posted to GL using that one value. In this case, there is no need to map this segment to a dimension. The Company segment is required by GL, but is not required by Financial Analyzer. In this case, your financial data items will have a total of four dimensions, including the time dimension.

In addition, suppose that departments are mostly unique to individual companies, or, for any other reason, you do not need to compare departments across companies. In this case, there is a parent-child relationship between the Company and Department segments. You can map both the Company segment and the Department segment to a single Organization dimension in Financial Analyzer, and define a hierarchy based upon the parent-child relationship that exists between these two segments. This will produce financial data items with fewer dimensions, as well as richer drill-down analysis capabilities. This arrangement allows you to very easily create a report in Financial Analyzer showing financial data by companies, and allows the user to expand on each company, as well as drill down to see the financial data broken down by the departments that make up each company. However, this arrangement will not allow comparison of departments among the various companies.

In the following sections, the scenario just described will be used as an example for discussion purposes. This scenario is summarized in the Table 6-2.

Review Questions

1. What is a dimension?

2. What are financial data items?

3. What are dimension hierarchies?

GL Segment	OFA Dimension
Company	Organization
Department	Organization
Product	Product
Account	Account

TABLE 6-2. *Exercise Scenario*

Setting Up the Interface

Setting up the interface between GL and Financial Analyzer requires performing the following steps:

- Defining filters
- Defining dimensions
- Defining hierarchies
- Defining financial data items
- Defining financial data sets

Defining Filters

Filters are used to specify a subset of a segment's possible values. Filters can be used when defining dimensions and financial data items to limit segment values. Filters are created by specifying ranges of segment values you wish to include or exclude. Filters are defined in the Filters form using navigation path *Setup : Analyzer : Filter.*

The top portion of the form allows you to specify general information regarding the filter. The Name field is required and specifies the name of the filter you are creating. This filter will then be referred to by the name that you specify in this field when used in the Dimension form. The Segment field is also required; it specifies the segment to which this filter applies. Use the List of Values feature to bring up a list of segments to choose from. The Description field is optional.

The bottom portion of the form specifies the ranges of segment values to include and exclude. A common practice is to first include the entire range of values for the segment, and then selectively exclude those segment value ranges that should not be included. To experiment with this, create a filter named Products that includes product segment values from 000 to 250. Then, filter out product segment values from 120 to 130 and 220 to 230. See Figure 6-18. Next, create a department segment filter that filters out all resources departments from 100 to 140.

Defining Dimensions

This step specifies the dimensions that will be created in Financial Analyzer, as well as the segments in GL from which the dimensions will be created. In addition, any filters that were created in the prior step can be used in this step to limit the segment values that will be extracted and loaded into Financial Analyzer. All of this is performed in the Dimension form. You can go to the Dimension form using the navigation path *Setup : Analyzer : Dimension.*

The Name field of this form specifies the name of the dimension. The Level field specifies whether detail segment values or summary segment values are extracted. You can map multiple segments to detail dimensions, but you can only map a single segment to summary dimensions. On the other hand, summary dimensions allow you to load summary balances that are already calculated in GL to Financial Analyzer, without having to solve hierarchy models to calculate them. The Description field is optional, and allows for text describing the dimension's perspective.

The Labels group of fields specifies how the dimension values of this dimension are displayed in Financial Analyzer reports and worksheets. The Row field specifies how dimension values are displayed when the dimension is used on the row edge in a tabular report. The Column field specifies how dimension values are displayed when the dimension is used on the column edge in a tabular report. The Selector field specifies how dimension values are displayed when using the Financial

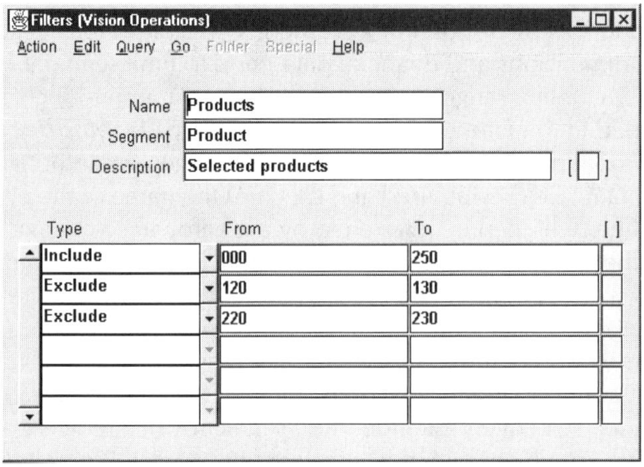

FIGURE 6-18.   *Filters form*

Analyzer Selector to select dimension values to include in a report or worksheet. The possible values for all three of these fields are as follows:

- **Value** When displaying dimension values for this dimension, only the dimension value should be shown.

- **Description** When displaying dimension values for this dimension, the description of the dimension value should be shown.

- **Both** When displaying dimension values for this dimension, both the dimension value and its description should be shown.

The Object group of fields specifies various internal identifiers for Financial Analyzer. The Name field specifies the internal name of the dimension. It can be up to 16 characters long, and the allowable characters for it are alphanumeric characters (A–Z, 0–9), underline (_), and period (.). Also, the first character must be alphabetic (A–Z). The Prefix field specifies an object prefix to use when naming other internal objects associated with the dimension. It can be up to six characters long, and the allowable characters for it are the same as the allowable characters for the internal name of the dimension. The first character also must be alphabetic. The Value Prefix field specifies a prefix to use for all dimension values of the dimension. It must be a single character, and it must be alphabetic (A–Z).

The Segment Mappings group of fields specifies the mapping of GL segments to the dimension. Each row in this group specifies a segment to map to the dimension. The Seq column specifies a sequence number that determines the order for combining segment values when creating dimension values. The Segment column specifies the GL segment for the row. The Max Desc Size column specifies the maximum number of characters to use when displaying the description of a dimension value. This is used only if either *Description* or *Both* are selected for the Row, Column, or Selector fields in the Labels group. The Filter column specifies the filter to use to limit the segment values to extract. If no filter is specified, all segment values are extracted. The Account Type column is used only if the segment is the natural account segment. It allows you to specify that only segment values of a particular account type are to be extracted. See Figure 6-19.

You can create three dimensions: Organization, Product and Account. Use the filters that you built on the Product and Account dimensions. For the Organization dimension, you must include both the Company segment and Department segment since they will form a hierarchy later on.

Define Hierarchies

This step specifies the hierarchies to create for the dimensions established in the prior step. Multiple hierarchies can be created for each dimension. In Financial Analyzer, if a dimension has multiple hierarchies, the user is allowed to select the hierarchy to

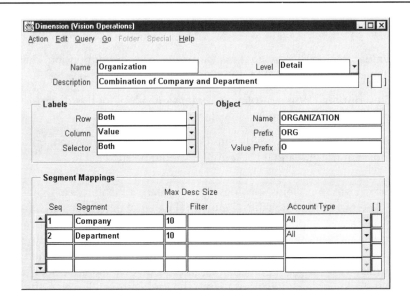

FIGURE 6-19. *Dimensions form*

utilize when rolling up data and when drilling down during analysis. Hierarchies are created via the Hierarchy form using navigation path *Setup : Analyzer : Hierarchy*.

The Name field is the name of a hierarchy. If creating multiple hierarchies, each hierarchy must have a different name. The Base Dimension field specifies the dimension to which the hierarchy belongs. The Description field is optional, and allows for descriptive text associated with the hierarchy.

In the bottom portion of the form, a separate row must exist for each segment that maps to the base dimension. The Seq column specifies the sequence number for the segment. Higher-level segments—that is, those with lower sequence numbers—should be listed first. The Segment column specifies the GL segment. The Root Node column specifies the highest-level summary segment value where the hierarchy begins. All descendants (children and children of the children, etc.) of the root node will be included in the hierarchy. Create a hierarchy between Company and Department in the Organization dimension. See Figure 6-20.

Defining Financial Data Items

This step specifies the financial data items to create in Financial Analyzer, as well as what GL balances map to financial data items, and how. This is all done in the Financial Data form using navigation path *Setup : Analyzer : Financial Data*.

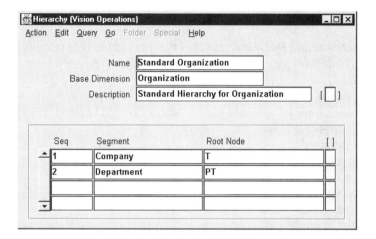

FIGURE 6-20. *Hierarchy form*

The top half of the form specifies some general information regarding the financial data item. The Name field specifies a unique name for the financial data item. The Sets of Books field specifies the GL Sets of Books to use. The Description field is optional, and allows the specification of descriptive text for the financial data item.

The Balances group of fields specifies the type of GL balances to extract. The Balance Type field can be one of the following possible values: Actual, Budget, and Encumbrance. If you select the budget balance type, you must specify the name of the budget version to use in the Budget/Encumbrance field. If you select the encumbrance balance type, the Budget/Encumbrance field specifies the name of the encumbrance type to load. Alternatively, you can specify Total to load the total of all encumbrance types.

The Currency Type field specifies the type of currency to use when extracting GL balances. The possible values are as follows:

■ **Functional Only** specifies that financial data in the functional currency, or converted to the functional currency, will be extracted. Since GL requires that the encumbrance balances be kept in the functional currency, this is the only setting allowed if the balance type is set to encumbrance.

■ **Statistical Only** specifies that only data entered in STAT will be extracted.

■ **Foreign Entered** specifies that only data entered in a specified foreign currency will be extracted.

- **Foreign Translated** specifies that data entered in a specified foreign currency will be extracted.

- **Functional and Statistical** specifies that data entered in or converted to the functional currency, as well as data entered in STAT, will be extracted.

The Currency field specifies the currency to extract. This field can only be changed if the Currency Type field is set to either Foreign Entered or Foreign Translated. In these two cases, this field specifies the foreign currency for which data will be extracted.

The Object group of fields specifies various settings related to the internal financial data item object. The Level field specifies whether detail balances or precalculated GL summary balances will be loaded into the financial data item. If detail balances are to be loaded into Financial Analyzer, then all dimensions assigned to the financial data item must be detail dimensions. If summary balances are to be loaded, then at least one dimension assigned to the financial data item must be a summary dimension. In addition, in order to load precalculated summary balances, summary templates must be defined in GL and assigned to the financial data in the Summary Templates alternative region, as discussed below.

The Status field must show Validated to complete the form. This field is set to Validated by default, but becomes Not Validated when the Level field is set to Summary. Upon completion of the Summary Templates specification, click on the **Validate** button in the Summary Templates alternative region to perform a validation check. If the summary specifications are correct, this field will be set to Validated.

The Label field specifies an internal identifier used to identify the financial data item. The Object Name field is the internal name of the financial data item object. This internal identifier can be up to 16 characters long, and the allowable characters are alphanumeric characters (A–Z, 0–9), underline (_), and period (.). The first character must be alphabetic (A–Z).

The bottom portion of the form initially shows the Dimensions region, which allows the assignment of dimensions to the financial data item. Each row assigns a different dimension to the financial data item. The Seq column specifies the sequence number for the assigned dimensions, delineating the ordering of the dimensions. The Dimension column specifies the dimension for the row. The Level column is automatically populated. The order in which the dimensions are listed is significant in that it affects the performance of loading data into Financial Analyzer and solving models in Financial Analyzer. Dense dimensions should always be placed before sparse dimensions. If the dimension mapped to the natural account segment (usually named Account or Line) is among the dense dimensions, then it should usually be placed as the very first dimension. The time dimension is always a dense dimension, and it should generally be situated as the last of the dense dimensions. All other dimensions should be sorted in descending order according to the number of dimension values that the dimension contains. Dimensions with more values should be placed before dimensions with fewer values. These simple guidelines will help ensure that Financial Analyzer performs reasonably well. See Figure 6-21.

If, after assigning the necessary dimensions, there are GL segments that have not been assigned to the financial data item (through a dimension), then the balances will be rolled up over all segment values for the unassigned segments. If, however, you do not want to roll up over all segment values, you can use filters created in the first step to limit the segment values to roll up. To assign filters in this way, switch to the Filters alternative region in the bottom portion of the form by clicking on the drop-down list. The Segment column specifies the unassigned segments to filter, and the Filter column specifies the filter to use to limit the segment values to roll up. Create a financial data item called Actual to capture actual functional only balances with the dimensions: Organization, Product, Account, and Time.

If the financial data item is to be loaded with GL precalculated summary balances, then GL summary templates must be assigned to the financial data item. This is done in the Summary Templates alternative region on the bottom portion of the form, shown in Figure 6-22. The Structure to Match field shows the structure of the financial data item, represented as a combination of the allowable segment values for each segment of the Chart of Accounts. The Name column specifies the name of the GL summary template. The Structure column is automatically populated

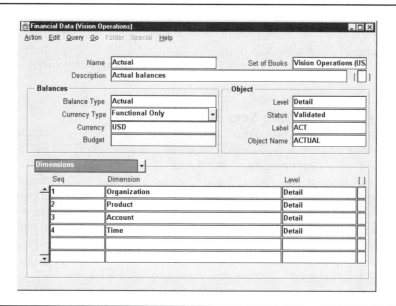

FIGURE 6-21. *Financial Data form*

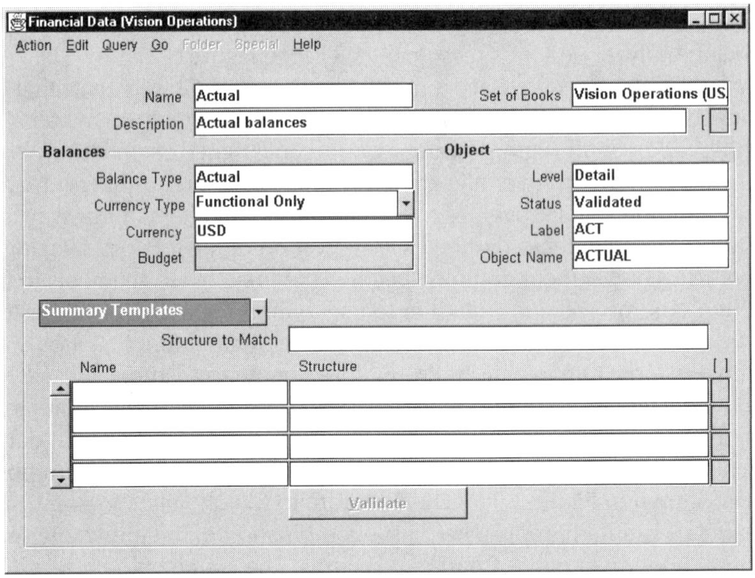

FIGURE 6-22. *Financial Data form—Summary Templates*

and shows the structure of the chosen summary template. Upon completion of this form, clicking on the **Validate** button will cause the financial data item specification to be checked. If the specifications are valid, then the Status field will be set to Validated.

Defining Financial Data Sets

A financial data set is a group of financial data items that are to be extracted from GL and loaded into Financial Analyzer together. The Financial Data Set form can be navigated to through navigation path *Setup : Analyzer : Financial Data Set.*

The Name field specifies the name for the financial data set. This name is used to identify the financial data set to Financial Analyzer when configuring it to interface with GL. The *Freeze* checkbox specifies that the specification of the financial data set, the financial data items that belong to it, and the dimensions that are assigned to the financial data items are all complete, and are to be frozen. Only frozen financial data sets can be loaded into Financial Analyzer. By default, the form shows the Financial Data Items region, which allows the specification of the list of financial data items to include in the financial data set. See Figure 6-23. The form's other alternative region, named Segment Sort Order, allows you to specify the order in which segments should be used for sorting.

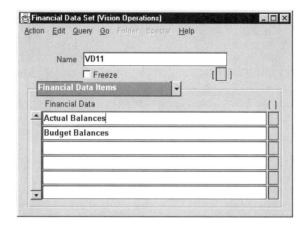

FIGURE 6-23.   *Financial Data Set form—Financial Data Items*

The table in this alternative region is a list of the segments in the GL Chart of Accounts, ordered according to the sequence order. The Seq column is the segment sequence number, and the Segment column specifies the GL Chart of Accounts segment. The segment sort order is significant for ensuring optimal performance when loading data into Financial Analyzer. The segment sort order should correspond to the dimension sort order for the financial data items in the financial data set. Segments that are not mapped to dimensions should be sorted after all segments that are mapped to dimensions (i.e., segments that are not mapped to dimensions should be assigned higher sequence numbers than segments that are mapped to dimensions). See Figure 6-24. You do not have to create a financial data set.

Review Questions

1. How are filters used?

2. What are the purposes of the row, column, and selector labels?

3. How do you define a hierarchy?

4. What balance types can you specify for a financial data item?

Running Data Extract Jobs

Once the interface is set up, GL data can be extracted to be loaded into Financial Analyzer. Data is extracted by executing various GL data extraction programs that extract various types of data from GL into temporary files to be loaded into Financial

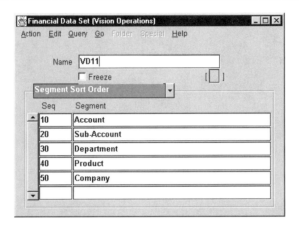

FIGURE 6-24. *Financial Data Set (Segment Sort Order) form*

Analyzer. Since Financial Analyzer is not part of the OCP exam, you are only going to learn about the various programs and how to check the status, but you do not have to submit the data extract jobs. The various extraction programs are listed below:

- Analyzer – Extract Balances

- Analyzer – Extract Calendar

- Analyzer – Extract Currency

- Analyzer – Extract Hierarchy

- Analyzer – Extract Period Rates

- Analyzer – Extract Segment Values

- Analyzer – Load Extracts

These programs are run through the Standard Report Submission form under the navigation path *Reports : Request : Standard.* Standard report submissions will be covered in Chapter 8.

Analyzer – Extract Balances
This program extracts the GL account balances. Only balances for segment values that have been extracted by the Extract Segment Values program will be loaded. Therefore, this program should be run in conjunction with the Extract Segment Values program to ensure that the balances get loaded properly.

Analyzer – Extract Calendar

This program extracts information regarding a fiscal year based on the GL accounting calendar for creating the Financial Analyzer GL time dimension. To extract multiple fiscal years, submit multiple requests, one fiscal year each.

Analyzer – Extract Currency

This program extracts the currencies that are used in GL to be used with the conversion rates data extracted by the Extract Period Rates program.

Analyzer – Extract Hierarchy

This program extracts the parent-child relationships defined in the GL segment hierarchies. Only parent-child relationships for segment values that have been extracted by the Extract Segment Values program will be loaded. Therefore, this program should be run in conjunction with the Extract Segment Values program to ensure that the hierarchy gets loaded properly.

Analyzer – Extract Period Rates

This program extracts the currency conversion rates for the current period.

Analyzer – Extract Segment Values

This program extracts the segment values of your GL Chart of Accounts. These segment values are loaded into Financial Analyzer dimensions as dimension values if there are balances associated with the segment values.

Analyzer – Load Extracts

This program automatically invokes the programs to load the extracted information into Financial Analyzer. It does not extract any data from GL.

Checking Extract Programs Status

At any point in time, you can view the status of your extraction requests through the Transfer Requests form. You can use the navigation path *Reports : Request : Analyzer.* See Figure 6-25.

The Program column specifies the data extraction program that was requested. The ID column is the unique identifier for the program execution. The Status column can have one of the following values:

- **Extracting** indicates that the data extraction program is executing.

- **New** indicates that the data extraction program is complete and there is new data ready to be loaded into Financial Analyzer.

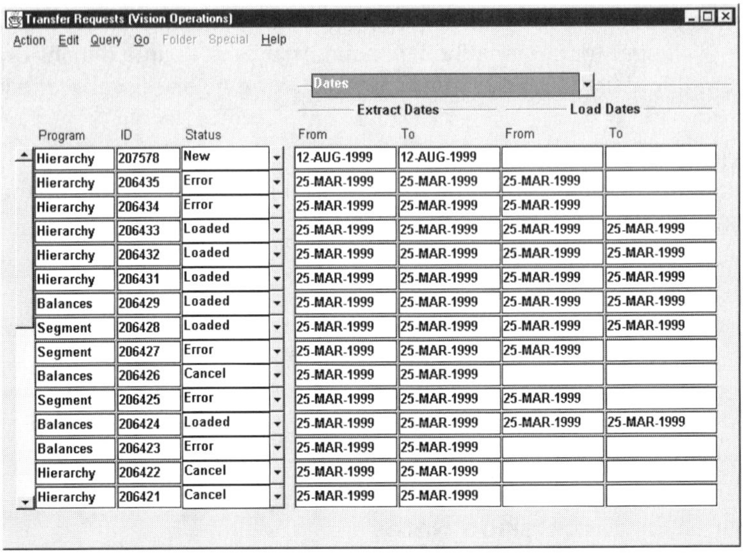

Transfer Requests (Vision Operations)

Action Edit Query Go Folder Special Help

Dates

Program	ID	Status	Extract Dates From	Extract Dates To	Load Dates From	Load Dates To
Hierarchy	207578	New	12-AUG-1999	12-AUG-1999		
Hierarchy	206435	Error	25-MAR-1999	25-MAR-1999	25-MAR-1999	
Hierarchy	206434	Error	25-MAR-1999	25-MAR-1999	25-MAR-1999	
Hierarchy	206433	Loaded	25-MAR-1999	25-MAR-1999	25-MAR-1999	25-MAR-1999
Hierarchy	206432	Loaded	25-MAR-1999	25-MAR-1999	25-MAR-1999	25-MAR-1999
Hierarchy	206431	Loaded	25-MAR-1999	25-MAR-1999	25-MAR-1999	25-MAR-1999
Balances	206429	Loaded	25-MAR-1999	25-MAR-1999	25-MAR-1999	25-MAR-1999
Segment	206428	Loaded	25-MAR-1999	25-MAR-1999	25-MAR-1999	25-MAR-1999
Segment	206427	Error	25-MAR-1999	25-MAR-1999	25-MAR-1999	
Balances	206426	Cancel	25-MAR-1999	25-MAR-1999		
Segment	206425	Error	25-MAR-1999	25-MAR-1999	25-MAR-1999	
Balances	206424	Loaded	25-MAR-1999	25-MAR-1999	25-MAR-1999	25-MAR-1999
Balances	206423	Error	25-MAR-1999	25-MAR-1999		
Hierarchy	206422	Cancel	25-MAR-1999	25-MAR-1999		
Hierarchy	206421	Cancel	25-MAR-1999	25-MAR-1999		

FIGURE 6-25. *Transfer Requests form*

- **Loading** indicates that the extracted data is being loaded into Financial Analyzer.
- **Loaded** indicates that the data has been successfully loaded into Financial Analyzer.
- **Launched** indicates that the Load Extracts program was executed, and the process for loading the extracted data into Financial Analyzer has been launched.
- **Cancel** indicates that the extraction request was canceled.
- **Error** indicates that the extraction request was terminated due to an error.

The rest of the columns on this form show the beginning and ending dates for the data extraction program execution and the loading of the extracted data into Financial Analyzer.

This form has alternative regions to show the program parameters for the various data extraction programs as they were specified for each execution. These parameter alternative regions include Balance Parameters, Hierarchy Parameters, Calendar/Rates Parameters, and Segment/Load Parameters. In addition, the File

Specification alternative region of this form shows the path and filename for the extracted data for the particular data extraction program execution, if applicable.

Review Questions

1. Where are the extraction programs initiated?

2. What does the Transfer Requests form do?

3. What does the Analyzer – Extract Segment Values program do?

4. What does the Analyzer – Load Extracts program do?

For the Chapter Summary, Two-Minute Drill, and Chapter Questions and Answers, open the summary.htm file contained in the Summary_files directory on the book's CD-ROM.

CHAPTER
7

Consolidation and Advanced Assets Functionality

his chapter covers two major topics: multicompany accounting and consolidations in Oracle General Ledger; and advanced Assets functionality, which includes managing tax books and capital budgets. The chapter is broken down into the following sections:

- Multicompany accounting and consolidations

- Managing assets

- Adding assets from external sources

- Managing budgets

- Maintaining tax books

- Reporting, reconciling and year-end processing

Multicompany accounting in Oracle General Ledger allows you to maintain balances by company, enforces security rules by company, and performs consolidated reports of multiple companies. Consolidation in General Ledger allows you to consolidate similar or different Charts of Accounts. This chapter will review how to set up, use, and report on the consolidation functionality in General Ledger.

You have been introduced to the basic setups and functionality of Oracle Assets in previous chapters. Now you will be presented with more advanced functionality. This begins with a study of additional options you can establish, along with instructions for cleaning up and purging historical data. You will also see how to adjust, transfer, and retire assets; how to manage CIP assets; and how to integrate with Oracle Projects. The final part of the chapter shows how to maintain capital budgets and tax books, as well as how to perform year-end processing. Once you have completed this chapter, you will have concluded the preparation for the OCP Financial Management exam.

Multicompany Accounting and Consolidations

The first section in this chapter addresses multicompany accounting and consolidations. Topics include:

- Controlling intercompany transactions using Centralized Transaction Approval (CENTRA)

- Performing multicompany accounting within one Set of Books

- Setting up the Global Consolidation System (GCS)

- Running consolidations

Controlling Intercompany Transactions with Centralized Transaction Approval (CENTRA)

Oracle General Ledger's Centralized Transaction Approval (CENTRA) allows you to use a central repository for intercompany transactions. Subsidiaries and parent companies can send intercompany transactions to each other for review and approval *before* posting to the corresponding Sets of Books. The subsidiaries and parent companies can also share the same Set of Books.

In this section, you will learn about:

- Setting up CENTRA

- Entering intercompany transactions in CENTRA

- Defining recurring intercompany transactions in CENTRA

- Reviewing and approving intercompany transactions in CENTRA

- Transferring intercompany transactions in CENTRA

- CENTRA reconciliation

There are two sides to every intercompany transaction: the sender and the receiver. The sender begins by entering intercompany transactions, and then submits them to the receiver. If the sender's associated subsidiary and the transaction type allow AutoApproval, the intercompany transactions are automatically approved when they are submitted. If AutoApproval is not allowed, the receiver must approve the intercompany transactions. If the receiver rejects the intercompany transactions, they must be edited by the sender and resubmitted to the receiver for approval. Once the intercompany transactions are approved, they are ready to be picked up by the Run Intercompany Transfer program. Both the sender and the receiver must run the Run Intercompany Transfer program to generate journal entries. Both sides must then post these journal entries.

Setting up CENTRA

Setting up CENTRA consists of the following steps:

- Set up subsidiaries

- Assign profile option *Intercompany: Subsidiary* to responsibility

- Set up intercompany clearing accounts

- Set up intercompany transaction types

In the Vision database, Operations is a subsidiary of the Corporate organization. For the exercises in this chapter, you will use Operations as the subsidiary and

Corporate as the parent, because they are seeded data. However, you will configure your own subsidiary for setups.

SETTING UP SUBSIDIARIES The first step in configuring CENTRA is setting up the subsidiaries. In General Ledger, you must set up any parent company as a subsidiary as well. The only difference is that the parent company has parent privileges. To define subsidiaries, log in using the *General Ledger, Vision Operations (USA)* responsibility, and then follow the navigation path *Setup : CENTRA : Subsidiaries.* Enter your subsidiary name, an optional description, and the name of your Set of Books. The Default Currency field will be populated automatically; if you override it, the currency you select will become the default when intercompany transactions are entered into CENTRA. (You do not need to override the currency code for this exercise.)

Enter the company that is tied to this subsidiary. Because the Set of Books you set up in Chapter 2 contains two companies—Wing Company and Golden Company—you must set up two subsidiaries. Specify that each subsidiary is not a parent subsidiary, and select the conversion rates to be used during CENTRA transfers when converting intercompany transactions. Your screen should now look similar to Figure 7-1.

ASSIGNING PROFILE OPTION INTERCOMPANY: SUBSIDIARY TO RESPONSIBILITY Once you have defined all your subsidiaries (including the parent companies), you can assign them to responsibilities. This is accomplished by having the profile option *Intercompany: Subsidiary* set at the responsibility level.

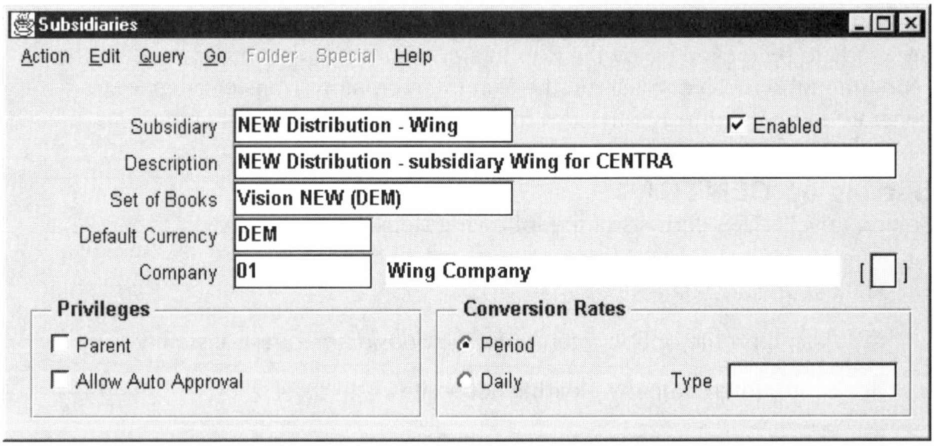

FIGURE 7-1. *Subsidiaries form*

Once you have assigned a subsidiary to a responsibility, the responsibility can only access intercompany transactions in CENTRA belonging to the associated subsidiary. Assigning profile options is a system administrator function. In the Vision database, the *Intercompany: Subsidiary* profile option is set appropriately.

SETTING UP INTERCOMPANY CLEARING ACCOUNTS   Intercompany clearing accounts are used to balance out-of-balance intercompany transactions. You can specify an intercompany clearing account for each intercompany transaction. To set up intercompany clearing accounts, follow the navigation path *Setup : CENTRA : Clearing Accounts.* Enter the natural account-segment values corresponding to your intercompany accounts.

SETTING UP INTERCOMPANY TRANSACTION TYPES   The next step is defining intercompany transaction types, which group similar intercompany transactions together for reviewing and reporting purposes. Follow the navigation path *Setup : CENTRA : Transaction Types.* After entering a name and optional description, you can specify whether the intercompany transaction type allows AutoApproval. If both the intercompany transaction type and the subsidiary allow AutoApproval, then intercompany transactions entered with these parameters will be approved automatically after submission. See Figure 7-2. (In Release 11, the options labeled Allow Interest Accrual, Allow Invoicing, and VAT Taxable do not yet have any functionality. Stay tuned for future versions!)

Review Questions

1. Should the parent company for CENTRA be defined as a subsidiary? Why or why not?

2. What does AutoApproval do?

3. What profile option is used to assign a subsidiary to a responsibility?

4. What is the purpose of intercompany clearing accounts?

Enter Intercompany Transactions in CENTRA

Now that you have set up CENTRA, you can enter intercompany transactions. To do this, you use the Enter Intercompany Transaction form found via the navigation path *CENTRA : Enter.* (Despite its name, this form can also be used to update, submit, delete, approve, or reject intercompany transactions.) When the Find Transactions window appears, you click on the **New** button to enter new intercompany transactions. If automatic transaction numbering is not enabled on your system, you must enter a transaction number manually, and it must be unique across all subsidiaries in the entire CENTRA system. The transaction will automatically be given a status of New, and the sender is automatically identified as the sender

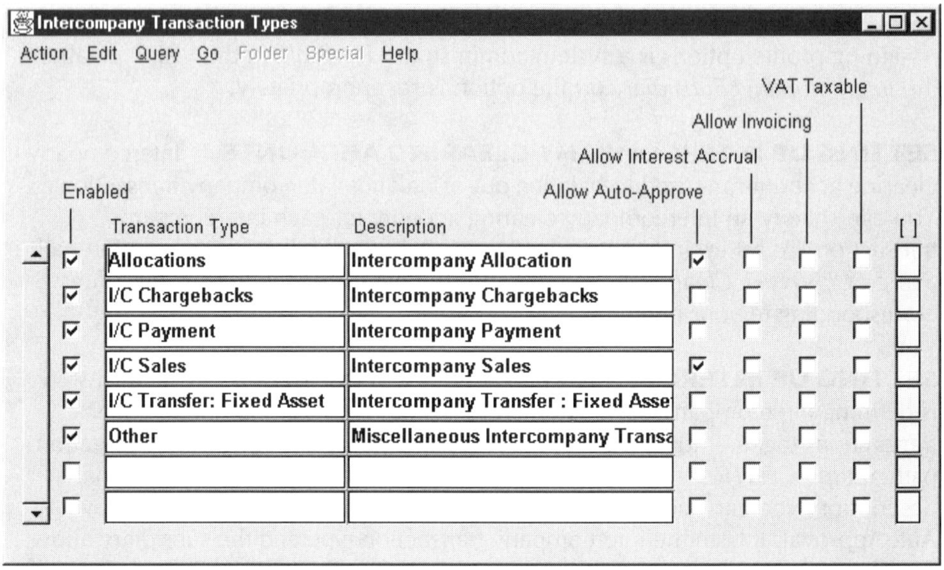

FIGURE 7-2. *Intercompany Transaction Types form*

associated with the subsidiary. You enter the receiver subsidiary in the Receiver field; for the purposes of this exercise, enter **Operations** for the sender and **Corporate** for the receiver. Then enter a GL date for the transaction, and it will serve as the basis for the sender's and receiver's accounting period. (The accounting periods are in two separate fields because the sender and receiver can belong to different Sets of Books, which may have different accounting calendars with different accounting period names.) You now can select an intercompany transaction type, a currency, a description, a control total, and a note. If you enter a control total, it must be the same as the intercompany clearing account total before submission or approval.

Now you are ready to enter journal lines for the intercompany transaction. There are two alternative regions for journal lines: one for the sender, and the other for the receiver. You must enter both if Auto Approval is enabled. These journal lines work just like regular ones: you must enter a line number, an account combination, a debit or credit amount, and the intercompany clearing account. When you have finished, click on the **Submit** button to submit the intercompany transactions for approval, or click on the **Approve** button to approve the intercompany transactions. You can only use the **Approve** button if AutoApproval is allowed or if the sender-associated subsidiary is a parent subsidiary. The transaction's status will change to Review after submission, or to Approve after approval. See Figure 7-3.

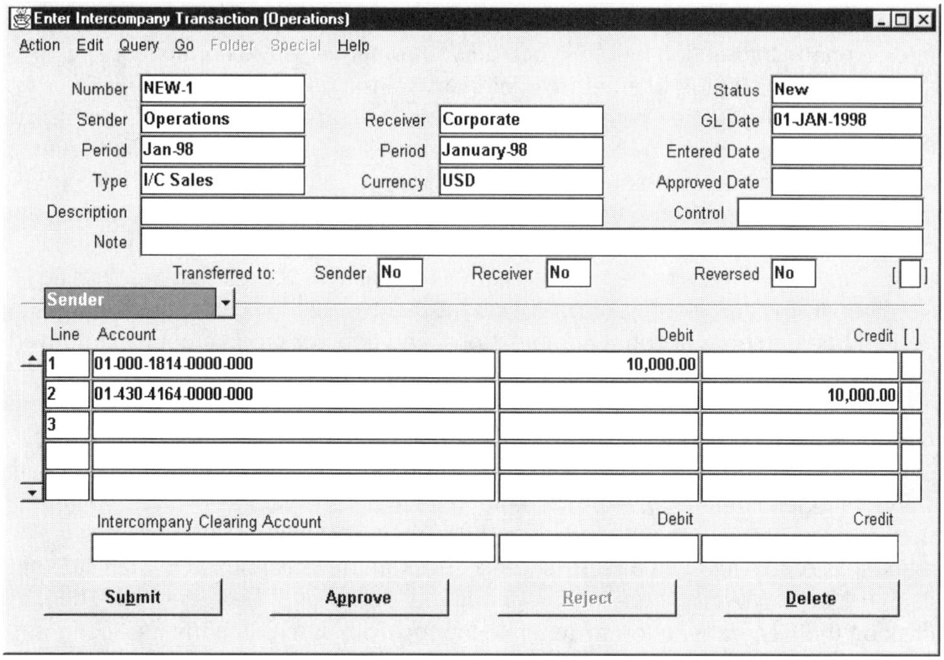

FIGURE 7-3. *Enter Intercompany Transaction form*

Defining Recurring Intercompany Transactions in CENTRA
In addition to entering intercompany transactions manually, you can define recurring intercompany transactions. As in the case of regular recurring journals, these require you to define the recurring intercompany transactions first, and then generate them.

DEFINE RECURRING INTERCOMPANY TRANSACTIONS Follow the navigation path *CENTRA : Define Recurring*, which will take you to the form shown in Figure 7-4. Enter the batch name and, if you wish, a description. The Sender field will automatically be populated with the sender-associated subsidiary. Enter an effective date range, which determines when this recurring intercompany transaction batch can be selected by the generation program. As a last step, you can choose to check the *AutoSelect* checkbox, which causes the recurring intercompany batch to be automatically selected by the generation program if the effective date range fits. Otherwise, you must explicitly specify the batch name in the Generate Recurring

Transactions form. While creating your recurring intercompany transaction batch, you can use the **AutoCopy** button to copy parameters from an existing recurring intercompany transaction batch. When all your parameters are populated, click on the **Transactions** button to enter intercompany transactions.

Follow the navigation path *CENTRA : Define Recurring* to open the Define Recurring Intercompany Transactions form, which is shown in Figure 7-5. As with a standard Enter Intercompany Transactions form, you enter a transaction name, transaction type, receiver, currency, and, optionally, a control total, description, and note. Then you are ready to enter the recurring intercompany transaction journal lines. This form has the same two alternative regions you saw earlier: Sender and Receiver. If AutoApproval is allowed, you must enter data in both regions. Enter the desired line numbers, account combinations, and debit or credit amounts, followed by the intercompany clearing account.

GENERATE RECURRING INTERCOMPANY TRANSACTIONS   To generate the recurring intercompany transaction batches, follow the navigation path *CENTRA : Generate Recurring*. First, enter the GL date; as soon as you leave this field, the rest of the form will update to show eligible batches. Any batch that was marked as AutoSelect will already show a check in the checkbox at the left side of its row. You can override the default or add more batches to be generated. Then, click on the **Generate** button to generate the recurring intercompany transactions.

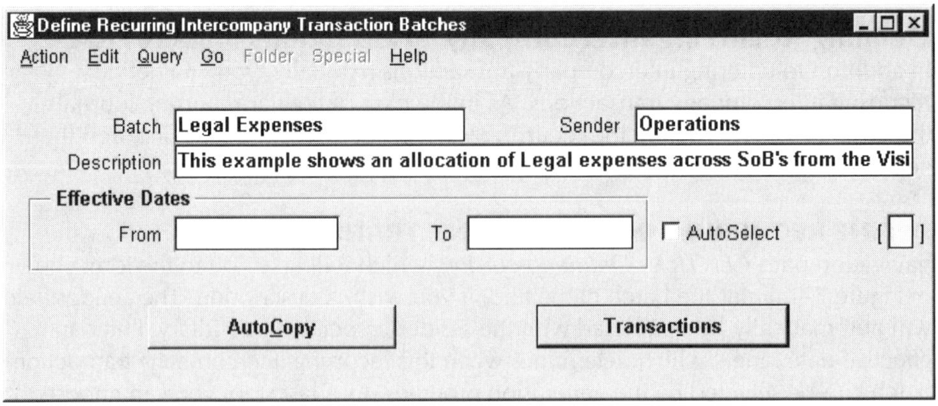

FIGURE 7-4.   *Define Recurring Intercompany Transaction Batches form*

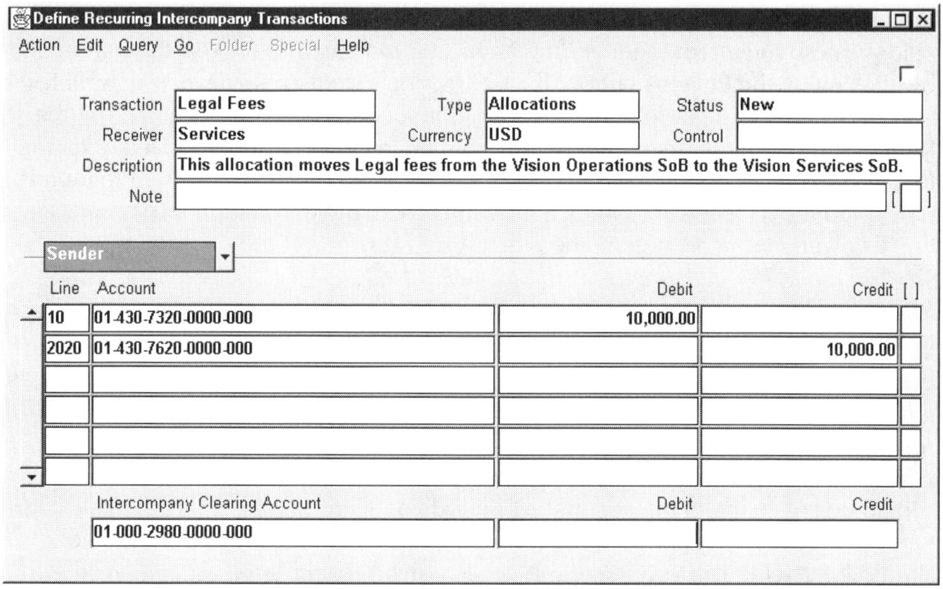

FIGURE 7-5.   *Define Recurring Intercompany Transactions form*

Review Questions

1. What is the control total compared against?

2. Why are there two separate accounting periods, one for the sender and one for the receiver?

3. When must you set up intercompany transaction journal lines for both the sender and the receiver?

4. What are the two steps for defining recurring intercompany transactions?

Review and Approve Intercompany Transactions in CENTRA
Once you have entered manual or recurring intercompany transactions, you can review and approve them. To do this, use the Enter Intercompany Transaction form again. When the Find Transactions window appears, enter appropriate criteria to locate the transactions you desire. If you are a parent subsidiary, receiving

subsidiary, or sending subsidiary, you will be able to see the intercompany transactions. If a transaction's status is Approve, you can only update its Note field—unless you are the sender, in which case you can also reverse the transaction by clicking on the **Reverse** button. If a transaction's status is Review, your abilities vary depending on your relationship with it. If you are its sender, you can use the **Recall** button to retrieve the transaction from the receiver, or use the **Delete** button to have the transaction deleted the next time the Intercompany Transfer Program is run. If you are its receiver, you can enter intercompany transaction journal lines in the Receiver alternative region and either approve or reject the transaction.

Transfer Intercompany Transactions in CENTRA

Before you can post intercompany transactions, those that were approved must become journal entries. To accomplish this, run the Intercompany Transfer program through standard report submission (navigation path *Reports : Request : Standard*—select the report named *Program - Intercompany Transfer*). You can then specify whether the journal import should be run automatically, whether summary journals should be created, and the accounting period you want to transfer. The subsidiary name and accounting period specify which approved intercompany transactions should be selected; if you leave the accounting period blank, all approved intercompany transactions with the specified subsidiary name as the sender or receiver will be generated. If the journal import is not initiated automatically, you must run the journal import manually. If you choose to create a summary journal as an option of Journal Import, the journal import will summarize journals by accounting period and account combinations.

CENTRA Reconciliation

CENTRA makes it easy to reconcile intercompany transactions. First, General Ledger provides three intercompany transaction reports: Intercompany Transactions Detail, Intercompany Transactions Trial Balance, and Unapproved Intercompany Transactions Listing. The parent subsidiary can match its own Intercompany Transactions Detail report to those from all its subsidiaries. In addition, all intercompany transactions have been assigned unique transaction numbers. Furthermore, you can specify different intercompany clearing accounts for various subsidiaries and intercompany transaction types.

Review Questions

1. What will the **Recall** button do in the Enter Intercompany Transactions form?

2. What will the **Delete** button do in the Enter Intercompany Transactions form?

3. What will the Intercompany Transfer program do?

4. What three factors help with CENTRA reconciliation?

Multicompany Accounting Within One Set of Books

If all your companies are in the same Set of Books, you can set up a separate balancing segment value to store just eliminating journal entries. You can then create and generate recurring journals to perform the elimination from the regular companies to this eliminating company each accounting period. The consolidated balances will include account balances from all your regular companies and the eliminating company. You can use FSG to run the consolidation reports. If all your companies are not in the same Set of Books, consider setting up the Global Consolidation System (GCS).

Review Question

1. When can you set up multiple companies within one Set of Books?

Setting Up the Global Consolidation System (GCS)

You can use the Global Consolidation System (GCS) to consolidate accounting information from multiple companies with multiple Sets of Books. If you have average balance processing, you will also need the GCS, since the average balances are maintained in a separate Set of Books. *If you only have one Set of Books, you do not need the GCS.* Oracle General Ledger provides a Consolidation Workbench to help set up the GCS and run consolidations. Let's take a look at this Consolidation Workbench.

Consolidation Workbench

To get to the Consolidation Workbench, follow the navigation path *Consolidation : Workbench.* The Consolidation Workbench shows the parent Set of Books and its accounting period, the subsidiary Sets of Books, their consolidation mappings, and their corresponding statuses. See Figure 7-6.

State Controller

You can invoke the State Controller from the Consolidation Workbench. The State Controller is a navigation tool guiding you through the consolidation states, which are Mapping, Mapping Set, Translation Status, Transfer, Transfer Set, Review Journal, Post, Eliminate, Report. These states display in one of three colors: blue indicates recommended next steps, gray identifies states that are not applicable, and red reflects a warning status.

The Consolidation Workbench works together with the State Controller to simplify setting up the GCS. (You can also use the Navigator and navigate to the

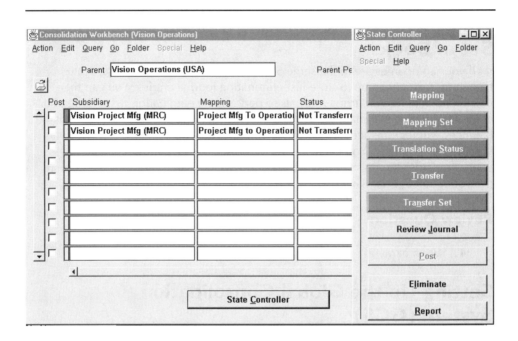

FIGURE 7-6. *Consolidation Workbench screen*

appropriate forms.) To set up the GCS, you will start by mapping consolidation data, and then you prepare the consolidation data.

Mapping Consolidation data

There are two steps in mapping consolidation data: defining consolidation mappings, and then defining consolidation mapping sets.

DEFINING CONSOLIDATION MAPPINGS   Consolidation mapping consists of a set of rules that map accounts from the subsidiary to the parent. You must define one consolidation mapping for each subsidiary. To define consolidation mappings, you can use the **Mapping** button from the State Controller or the navigation path *Consolidation : Define : Mapping.*

You first enter the mapping name and a mapping method. The two valid mapping methods are Balances and Transactions. The Balances method consolidates using balances without journal details, while the Transactions method consolidates using journal details. You can only select the Transactions mapping method if both the subsidiary and the parent share the same functional currency.

Enter the subsidiary Set of Books and the parent Set of Books. You can also enter the currency. There are limitations; you can only enter the STAT currency or the functional currency of the parent Set of Books if you choose the Balances mapping method. For practice, set up a consolidation mapping between your Set of Books and the Vision Operations Set of Books. (Since they have different functional currencies, you can only consolidate by balances.) You can enter an effective date range identifying when the consolidation mapping is valid. Next, you can select a usage if you are using average balance processing; choices include Standard, Average, or Standard & Average. (For the Transactions mapping method, you can only specify a usage option of Standard.) As a last step, you can specify Run Options for this consolidation mapping. These include whether you want to run the journal import automatically after the consolidation journals are generated; whether summary journals should be created; and whether the consolidation should be run in audit mode. Your form should now look similar to Figure 7-7.

Once you have configured the consolidation mapping definition, you must set up segment rules and/or account rules as mapping rules from the subsidiary Chart of Accounts to the parent Chart of Accounts. If you have a combination of segment rules and account rules, the account rules override the segment rules. Segment rules map subsidiary account segment(s) to parent account segment(s). Usually, you should use segment rules as the primary mappings and account rules as exceptions.

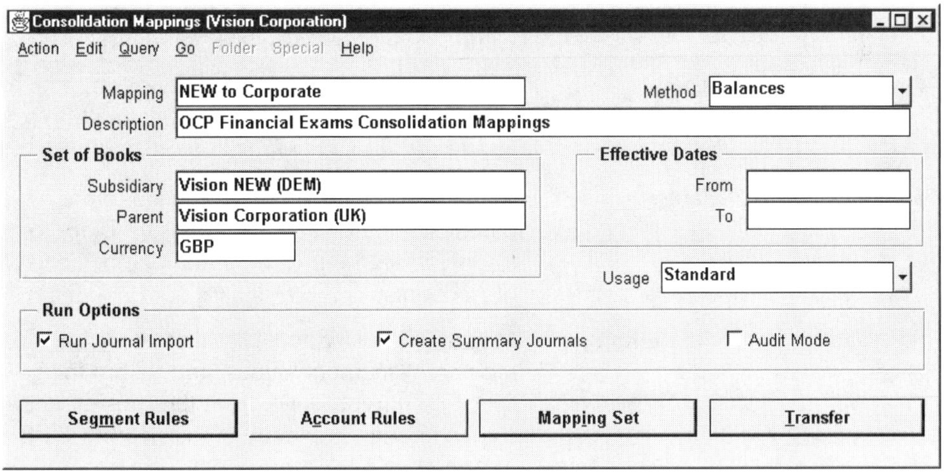

FIGURE 7-7.   *Consolidation Mappings form*

Click on the **Segment Rules** button now to go to the Segment Rules form. You will see the segments of your Charts of Accounts for the parent and the subsidiary. You must map each segment of your parent's Chart of Accounts. Each segment is mapped with one action. The action choices are as follows:

- **Copy Value From**   Copies the segment value of the subsidiary Set of Books directly into the segment value of the parent Set of Books. The two Sets of Books do not need to share the same value set, but must have the same valid segment values.

- **Assign Single Value**   Uses a constant as the segment value for the parent Set of Books.

- **Use Rollup Rules From**   Maps segment values from the subsidiary Set of Books to the parent Set of Books using rollup rules specified in the Rollup Rules region. A rollup rule consist of two fields: Transfer Level and Using. Table 7-1 identifies the valid values for each field and describes the results each combination produces.

Transfer Level	Using	Description
Detail	Detail ranges	Map segment values in the specified range from the subsidiary to a specific segment value in the parent Chart of Accounts.
Detail	Parent	Map a parent segment value from the subsidiary to a specific segment value in the parent Chart of Accounts.
Summary	Parent	Map all summary accounts related to the parent segment value from the subsidiary to a specific segment value in the parent Chart of Accounts.
Summary	Parent Ranges	Map all summary accounts that are related to the parent segment values, and within the specified parent range, from the subsidiary to a specific segment value in the parent Chart of Accounts.

TABLE 7-1.   *Rollup Rules*

For the purposes of this exercise, choose Assign Single Value as the action and put **05** for the balancing segment in the Subsidiary: Vision NEW column. This causes your subsidiary to always be represented by 05 in your parent Chart of Accounts. Next, create a line for Department and specify the Copy Value From action, with Cost Center in the Subsidiary column. Then create a line for Account and specify the Copy Value From action, with Account in the Subsidiary column.

Account rules map an account range from the subsidiary to an account combination in the parent Chart of Accounts. See Figure 7-8. For your exercise, you do not need to include any account rules.

DEFINE CONSOLIDATION MAPPING SETS   A consolidation mapping set consists of consolidation mappings that point to the same parent Set of Books with the same mapping method. To define consolidation mapping sets, you can use the **Mapping Set** button from the State Controller or follow the navigation path *Consolidation : Define : Mapping Set.* See Figure 7-9. You enter a mapping set name, the parent Set of Books, an optional description, and a mapping method. Next, you specify the Run Options for the mapping set, which will match the Run Options for the consolidation mapping. These include Run Journal Import, Create Summary Journals, and Audit Mode. As a last step, you enter the mappings that you want to include for the mapping set. If the subsidiary is also a parent Set of Books, the mapping set with the subsidiary as the parent Set of Books will be displayed automatically.

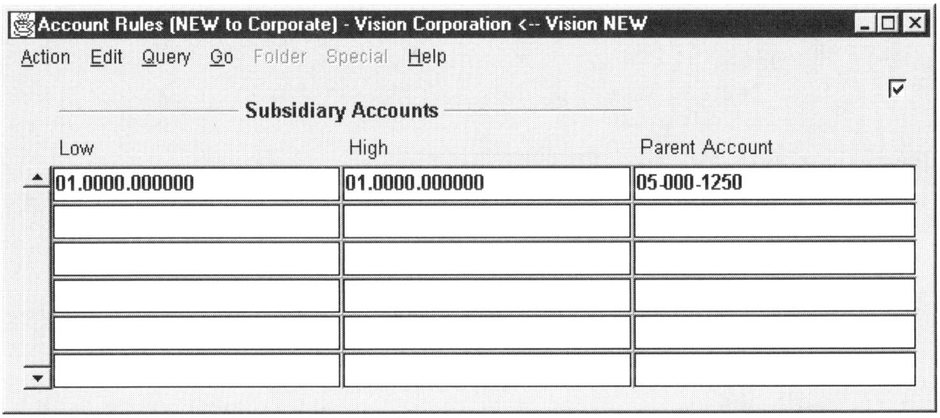

FIGURE 7-8.   *Account Rules form*

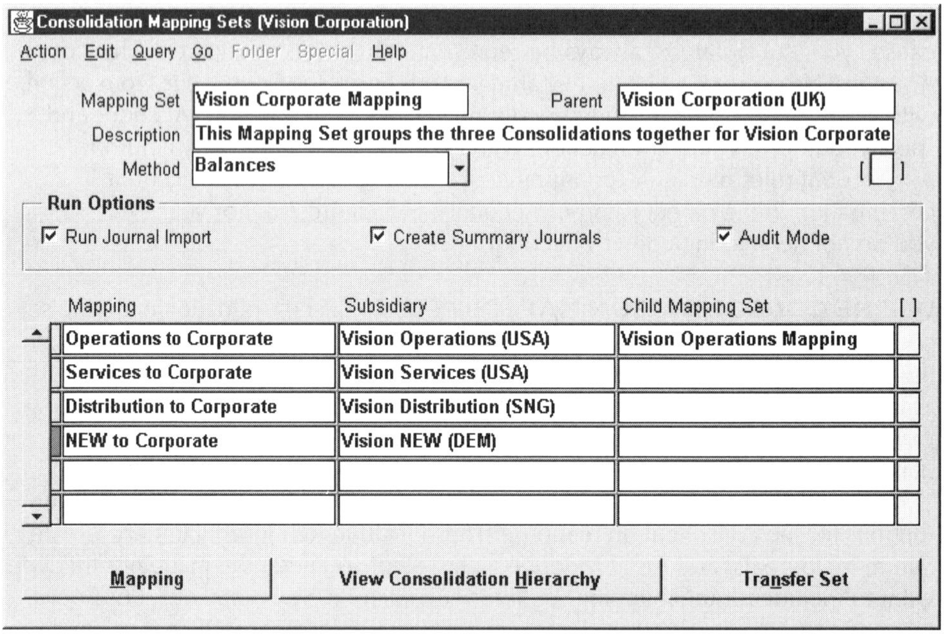

FIGURE 7-9. *Consolidation Mapping Sets form*

You can also click on the **View Consolidation Hierarchy** button to display the consolidation hierarchy in a graphical format. You have three display options: Set of Books Only, Sets and Mappings Only, or Both. Choose Both for now.

Prepare Consolidation Data

To prepare your consolidation data in your subsidiary Set of Books, you need to take three steps:

1. **Revalue balances**   If any of your subsidiary Sets of Books have balance sheet accounts entered in foreign currency, you must revalue the balances and post the revaluation journals before consolidation.

2. **Translate balances**   If any of your subsidiary Sets of Books have currencies differing from the parent Set of Books' functional currency, translate the balances first before consolidation. You can use the **Translation Status** button from the State Controller to see the status of any subsidiary translations. In addition, you can rerun translations for any subsidiary. If you are using

MRC, you may not need to perform this step. Instead of consolidating from the Primary Set of Books that has a different functional currency than the parent Set of Books, use the Reporting Set of Books that has the same functional currency.

3. **Run trial balances**   Each of your subsidiaries should run a trial balance before consolidation in the functional currency of the parent Set of Books. This facilitates reconciliation after consolidations.

Review Questions

1. What is the State Controller and how is it used?

2. What is the difference between account rules mapping and segment rules mapping?

3. What are the four different combinations of Transfer Level and Using for rollup rules?

4. What are the two steps that must be performed when preparing consolidation data?

Consolidating Your Subsidiaries' Sets of Books

Once you have set up the GCS—which includes setting up consolidation mappings and consolidation mapping sets, and preparing consolidation data—you are ready to run consolidations. Doing so involves the following steps:

- Transferring consolidation data

- Posting consolidation data

- Creating eliminating entries

- Reporting on consolidated balances

- Analyzing consolidated results

Transferring Consolidation Data

To transfer consolidation data from subsidiaries to the parent, General Ledger gathers balances or transactions from the subsidiaries based on the consolidation mappings and transfers them into the appropriate segment values of the parent Chart of Accounts. To transfer consolidation data, use the **Transfer** button from the State Controller with the cursor on the selected consolidation mapping in the Consolidation Workbench. The Transfer Consolidation Data form automatically displays the mapping name and method, the functional currency, and the subsidiary and parent Sets of Books. Start by selecting the balance type: either Actual or Budget. For the Budget Balance Type, specify the budget names for the subsidiary and parent. (Note that both budgets must share the same number of budget periods per year.) If you are using average balance processing, you can select Standard, Average, or Standard & Average Usage. Next, select the amount type to consolidate: PTD, QTD, YTD, or PJTD. Then select the accounting periods for the subsidiary and the parent.

When using the Balances mapping method, click on the **Select Accounts** button to select the account ranges you want to consolidate, as shown in Figure 7-10. When using the Transactions mapping method, click on the **Select Batches** button to select the journal batches you want to consolidate, as shown in Figure 7-11. You can choose to see consolidated journal batches, unconsolidated journal batches, or all journal batches.

Click on the **Transfer** button to begin the transfer. The transfer program creates journals in the GL interface table. If you have set the journal import to run

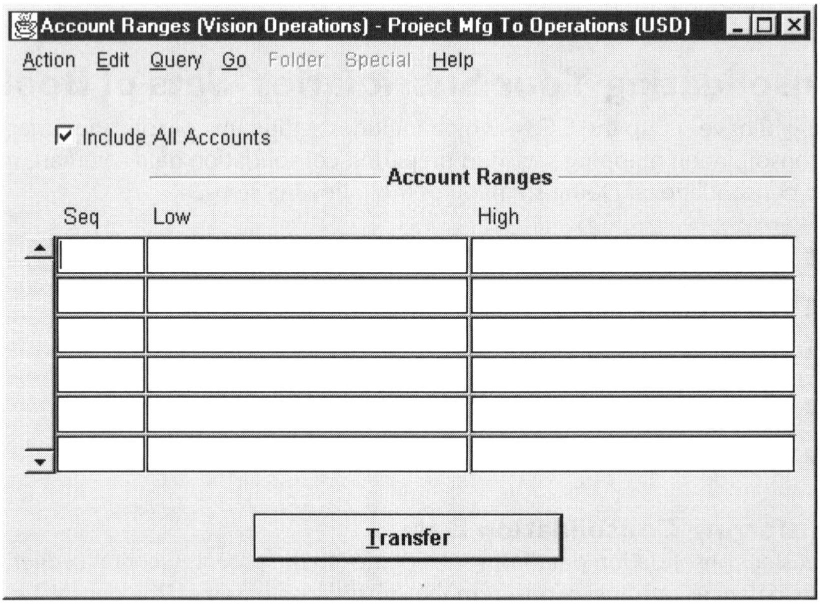

FIGURE 7-10. *Account Ranges form*

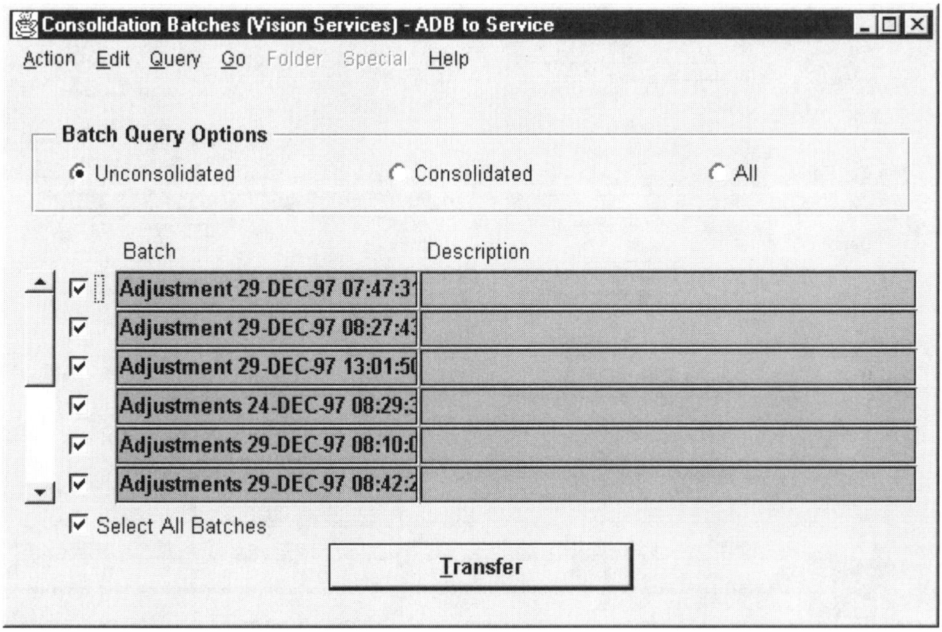

FIGURE 7-11. *Consolidation Batches form*

automatically after the Transfer program, an unposted consolidation batch will be created in the parent Set of Books. Otherwise, you must manually run the journal import to create the unposted consolidation batch in the parent Set of Books.

You can also transfer a mapping *set* instead of a mapping. To do this, click on the **Transfer Set** button from the State Controller. Once you select the consolidation mapping set and mapping method, the form will automatically fill in the functional currency and the subsidiary and parent Sets of Books. Then you fill in the rest of the form as just described for a standard mapping transfer. When you are done, your screen should look similar to Figure 7-12. Click on the **Mappings** button in the State Controller to select all mappings belonging to the mapping set. You can click on the **Options** button to optionally override the run options for the transfer. Click on the **Transfer** button to transfer the consolidation data set.

Posting Consolidation Data

Once the consolidation data is transferred, you can use the State Controller or the Navigator to review and post the unposted consolidation batches. From the State

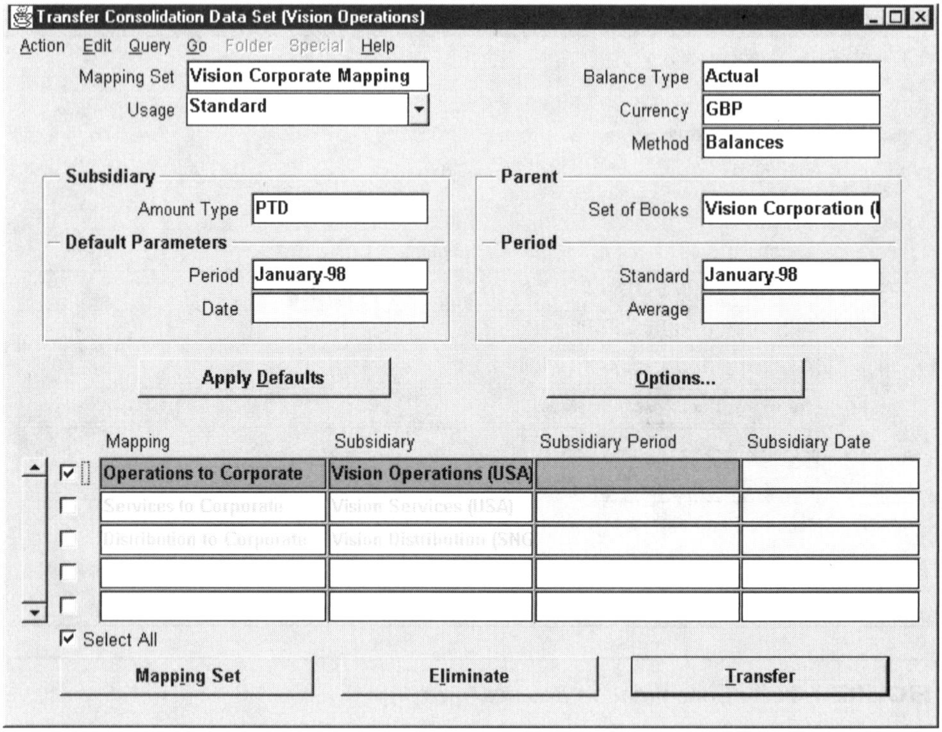

FIGURE 7-12.   *Transfer Consolidation Data Set form*

Controller, click on the **Review Journal** button to display unposted consolidation journal batches. Click on the **Post** button to post unposted consolidation journal batches. You post unposted consolidation journal batches in the parent Set of Books to update the account balances. Now your parent Set of Books has the consolidated balances.

Creating Eliminating Entries

Now that you have the consolidated balances, you must create eliminating entries in the parent Set of Books to eliminate intercompany sales and investments. For example, you must eliminate intercompany payables and receivables. You can create manual or recurring regular journals, or use the GCS to create elimination sets. Practically speaking, these are also recurring journals that run the elimination set every accounting period. You create elimination sets using the **Eliminate** button from the State Controller. The first form that comes up is the Generate Eliminations form, shown in Figure 7-13. You have two buttons on this form: **Elimination Set** and **Generate**. To create an elimination set, click on the **Elimination Set** button. You enter a name for the elimination set and an optional description; you can also use the **AutoCopy** button to copy from an existing elimination set. Next, you enter the name, journal category, and optional effective-date range for the elimination entry. The effective date governs when this elimination entry can be generated.

You are now ready to enter journal lines. Click on the **Lines** button to open the Elimination Line form (Figure 7-14). You enter elimination journal lines just like you enter recurring journal lines. You can enter any number of journal lines. A journal line consists of line number, account, and an optional line description. If you use line number 9999, the account you entered becomes the automatic offset account. The formula you enter to calculate the account's balance will employ the same Reverse Polish Notation described in earlier chapters. Remember that the formula's first step must use the operator Enter. From the second step on, you can choose to use operator +, -, x, or /, but not Enter.

Once you have set up the elimination set, you can generate it by returning to the Generate Eliminations form. Select the elimination set you want to generate by checking the leftmost checkbox and entering the accounting period. If budget balances are used in the elimination lines, you must enter a budget. Click on the **Generate** button to generate the unposted elimination journals. The generated

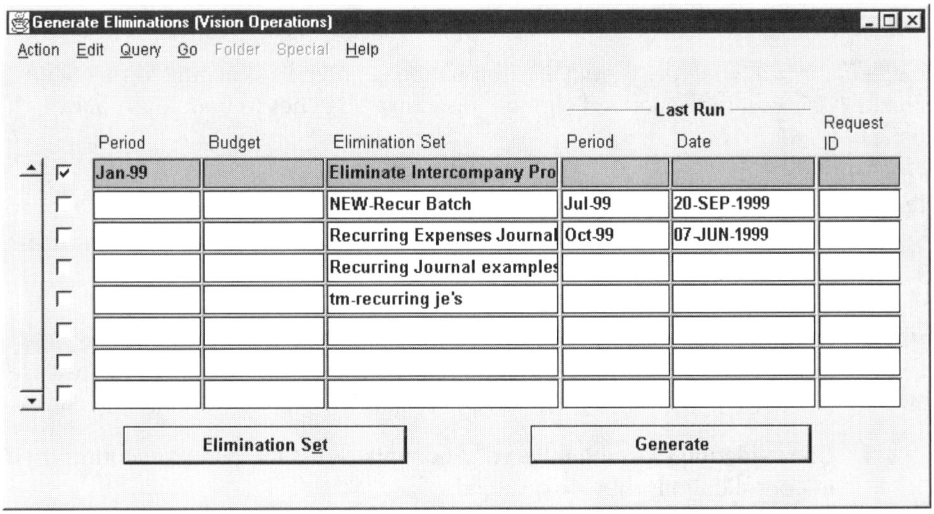

	Period	Budget	Elimination Set	Last Run Period	Last Run Date	Request ID
☑	Jan-99		Eliminate Intercompany Pro			
☐			NEW-Recur Batch	Jul-99	20-SEP-1999	
☐			Recurring Expenses Journal	Oct-99	07-JUN-1999	
☐			Recurring Journal examples			
☐			tm-recurring je's			
☐						
☐						
☐						

Generate Eliminations (Vision Operations)

Action   Edit   Query   Go   Folder   Special   Help

Elimination Set   Generate

FIGURE 7-13. *Generate Eliminations form*

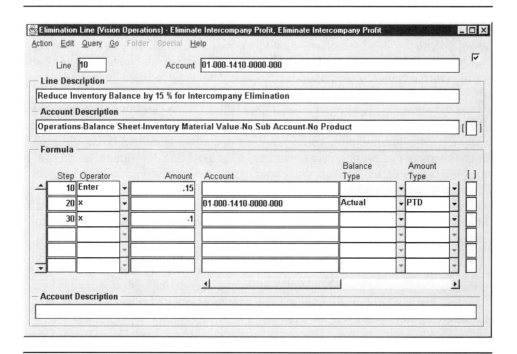

FIGURE 7-14. *Elimination Line form*

batch name will be in the format of (elimination set name) (Date and Time). See Figure 7-15. Post the generated elimination journal batches to update account balances.

Reporting on Consolidated Balances
Standard consolidation reports are available to help with the consolidation process. These reports include:

- **Consolidation - Audit**   If your consolidations are run in audit mode, this report lists how subsidiary account balances map to parent company balances. It also shows any subsidiary accounts being excluded by choice.

- **Consolidation - Disabled Parent Accounts**   Lists the parent accounts used in consolidations that are disabled.

- **Consolidation - Journal**   Shows generated consolidation journals.

- **Consolidation - Rules**   Lists the defined consolidation mapping rules.

- **Consolidation - Unmapped Subsidiary Accounts**   Identifies subsidiary accounts that have not been mapped to parent accounts.

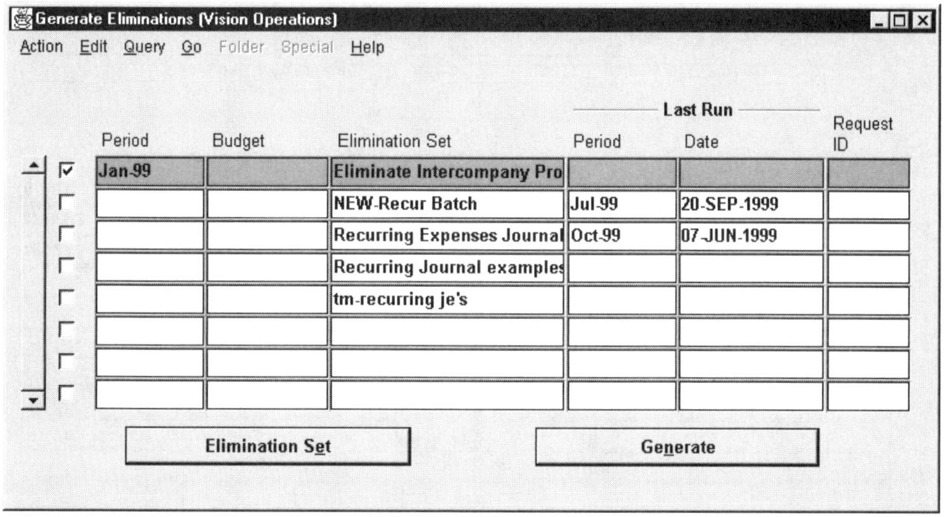

FIGURE 7-15. *Generating Eliminations form*

You can run these reports through standard report submission or by clicking on the **Report** button on the State Controller. Besides these standard reports, you will need FSG reports in the parent Sets of Books to report consolidated balances.

Analyzing Consolidated Results

You can use Financial Analyzer to evaluate consolidated balances, or you can perform the inquiry online. To perform consolidated balance inquiries online, go to the parent Sets of Books and follow the navigation path *Inquiry : Account*. Find the accounts of interest and then click on the **Show Journal Details** button. For consolidated balances, you will see buttons that do not appear during a regular account balance inquiry. You will have the option to drill down to the subsidiary Set of Books, or to show full journals behind the consolidation. See Figure 7-16.

Click on the **Drilldown to Project Mfg** button to see the account balances of the subsidiary that make up the consolidated balance. This form shows the mapping name, the amount type, and the mapping method, along with the account combination and the consolidated amount. From this form, if the Balances mapping method is used, you can click on the **Switch Amount Type** button to see other amount types. See Figure 7-17.

To drill down further on an account balance, place your cursor on it and click on the **Entered Balances** button. From the Enter Balances inquiry form, you will see the journal details in the subsidiary that make up the selected account balance.

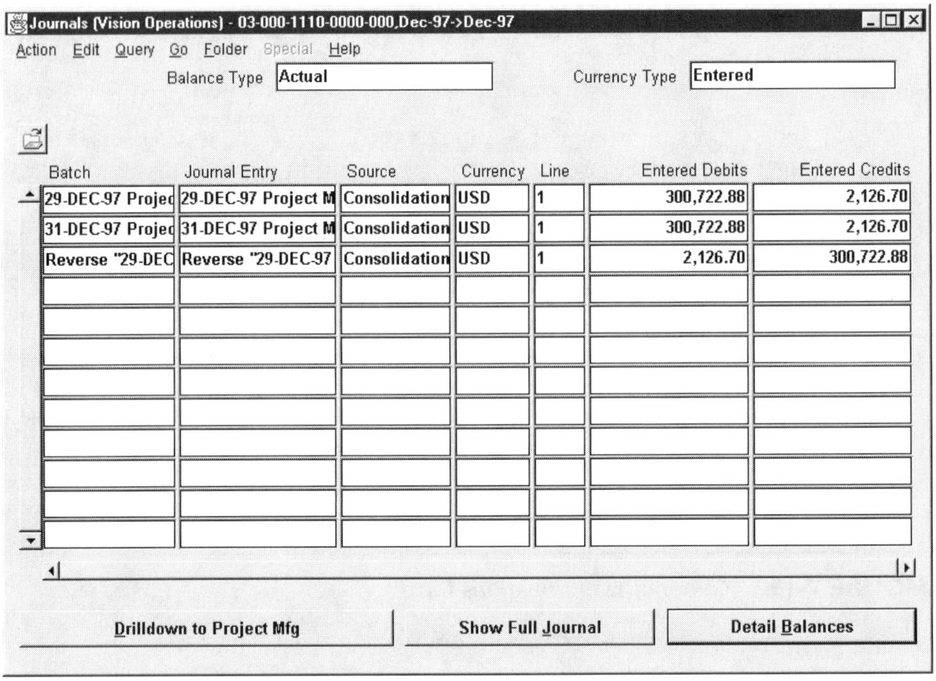

FIGURE 7-16. *Consolidation journals*

These journal details include batch name, journal name, journal source, journal category, line number, and debit amount or credit amount. You can also use the folder tools to customize.

Review Questions

1. What happens when you transfer consolidation data?

2. In which Set of Books will generated unposted consolidation journals be placed?

3. When must you create eliminating entries?

4. What is the purpose of the report *Consolidation – Unmapped Subsidiary Accounts*?

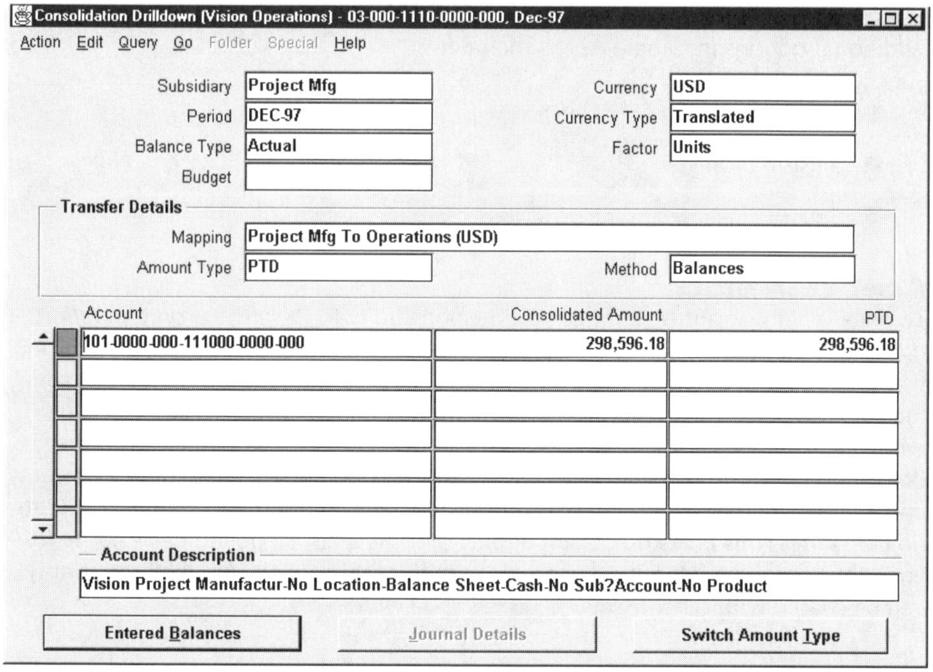

FIGURE 7-17.   *Consolidation Drilldown form*

Managing Assets

Chapter 5 presented the fundamentals of asset management. This section begins your exploration into advanced Assets functionality. In this section, you will learn to:

- ■ Set up additional options

- ■ Clean up and purge historical data

- ■ Adjust assets

- ■ Adjust assets using unplanned depreciation and revaluation

- ■ Retire assets

- ■ View asset information

Setting Up Additional Options

Additional options in Oracle Assets include:

- Asset warranties
- Distribution sets
- Leases

Asset Warranties

To enter asset warranties, change your responsibility to *Assets, Vision Operations (USA)*, then follow the navigation path *Setup : Asset System : Warranties*. Enter the warranty number and a description. The warranty number must be unique across the entire system. You can optionally enter a date range for the warranty. Assets with date in service within this specified date range can be associated with the defined asset warranty. Next, enter the currency code and the cost for the warranty, and decide whether the warranty is renewable. (For an open-ended warranty with no date range, this checkbox is not applicable.) As a last step, you can choose to enter the employee information and the supplier information. An asset's warranty can be shared with other assets.

Distribution Sets

You can set up distribution sets with commonly used distribution lines. Distribution sets are useful when assigning assets to employees or locations. You set up distribution sets using navigation path *Setup : Asset System : Distribution Sets*. (See Figure 7-18) To create a distribution set, you must enter a name, a description, and a corporate book to which it will be assigned. You can also enter an optional date range for the distribution set. Next, you enter the distribution lines, and for each line, you enter the units percent, the depreciation expense account, the location, and an optional employee name or employee number. The units percent of all distribution lines for any given distribution set must add up to exactly 100 percent.

Leases

To set up a lease, follow the navigation path *Setup: Asset System: Leases : Lease Details*. In the Lease Details form, which is shown in Figure 7-19, you enter the lease number, description, lessor, and lease type. Next, you either attach the lease to a predefined payment schedule or create your own. As a last step, enter the currency and an optional present value if the present value is precalculated.

You can perform the capitalization test in the Capitalization Test region. To perform a capitalization test, you must specify whether there is a transfer of ownership at the end of the lease or whether there is a bargain purchase option.

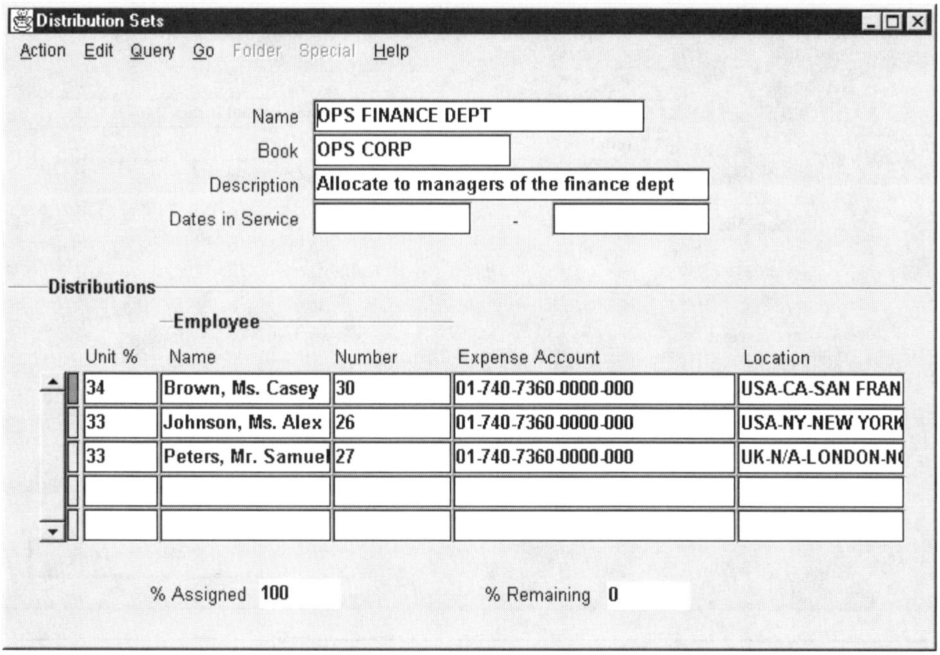

FIGURE 7-18. *Distribution Sets form*

You must also enter the lease term, asset life, and fair value of the asset. A lease can be capitalized if any of the following conditions is true: a bargain purchase option exists, the lessee owns the asset at the end of the lease, the lease term is longer than ¾ of the leased asset's life, or the present value of the minimum lease payment is greater than 90 percent of the initial asset fair value. The Test Result field will show whether the lease can be capitalized. If the leased asset can be capitalized, the Cost to Capitalize field will contain either the fair value or the present value of the minimum lease payment—whichever is less.

To create a payment schedule, click on the **Payment schedule** button from the Enter Lease form or follow the navigation path *Setup : Asset System : Leases : Lease Payments*. To create a payment schedule, enter the payment schedule name, lease date, interest rate, currency, and compounding frequency. Then enter the payment lines for the payment schedule. For each payment line, enter the start date, amount, payment number, and payment type. The end date will be calculated. You can leave the Amount field blank if you have entered a present value for the lease, because the Amount field value will automatically be calculated based on the

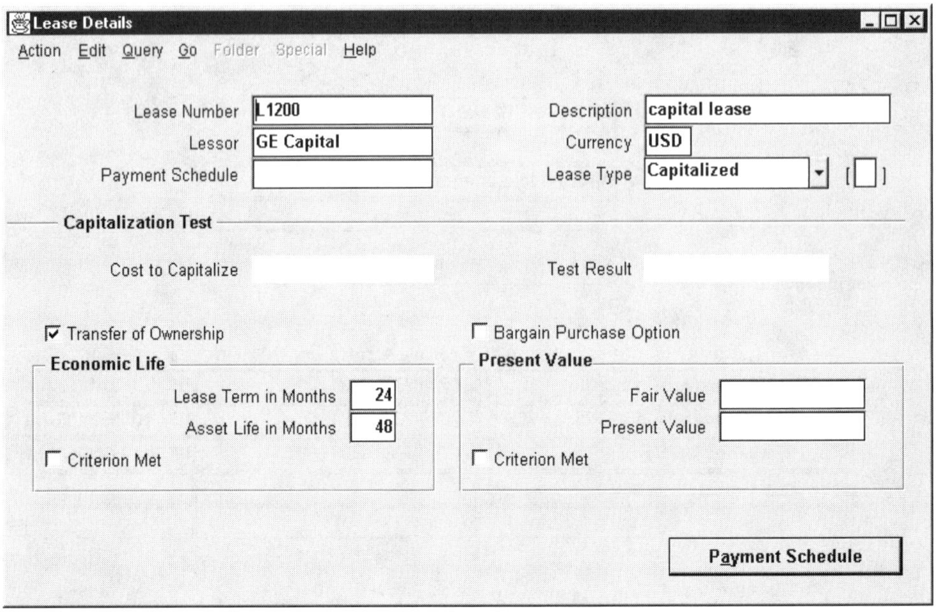

FIGURE 7-19. *Lease Details form*

lease's present value. Otherwise, based on the amount you entered, the present value will be calculated when you click on the **Calculate** button. The payment type can be Annuity, Balloon Payment, Bargain Purchase Option, or Bargain Renewal Option. You can click on the **View Amortization** button to create an amortization schedule for the lease. This represents the amortized interest expense of the lease.

Review Questions

1. What is the purpose of an asset warranty?

2. What is the purpose of a distribution set?

3. How does Oracle Assets determine whether a leased asset can be capitalized?

4. What payment types are included as valid options for lease payment lines?

Cleaning Up and Purging Historical Data

Next, you are going to learn how to purge some historical data from Oracle Assets. The three types of data that you can purge are:

- Mass additions
- Physical inventory
- Depreciation

Mass Additions

Once mass additions lines are posted, the status of each line is changed to POSTED. They are kept as audit trails. To purge them, you can run the Delete Mass Additions program.

Physical Inventory

After you close your physical inventory, you can purge the historical physical inventory data by using the **Purge** button in the Physical Inventory form.

Depreciation

You can purge depreciation expenses and adjustment transactions for fiscal years prior to the current fiscal year. If you have multiple fiscal years before the current fiscal year, you must purge the fiscal years in chronological order. In other words, if you have three fiscal years—1996, 1997, and 1998—prior to the current fiscal year, you must first purge 1996, then 1997, and then 1998. Before you can purge, two things must happen. First, the book you specified must allow purging; and secondly, the data you are purging must be archived to a temporary table. This is to allow restoration of data, if necessary. If you need to restore data after purging, you must restore it in reverse chronological order. Once you have archived to a temporary table, export the temporary table and drop the temporary table to free up space. You can perform the archive and the purge functions using the *Fixed Assets Administrator* responsibility.

Review Questions

1. How is mass additions data purged?

2. How is physical inventory purged?

3. How is depreciation purged?

Adjusting Assets

During the entire life of an asset, you may need to make some adjustments. The adjustments discussed in this section include:

- Units adjustment
- Asset reclass
- Asset transfer
- Financial information
- Invoice information

Units Adjustment

You can adjust the number of units to an asset through Asset Workbench. Find the asset of interest and choose Open to see the asset details. Change the Units field and click on the **Done** button. The Assignments form will appear. The Units to Assign field indicates how many units you must assign. Assign the additional unit(s) to a location, to a depreciation expense account, and, optionally, to an employee. Click on the **Done** button when finished.

Asset Reclass

You can reclass an asset from one category to another using Asset Workbench. Again, find the asset of interest and choose Open to see the asset details. Change the Category field and click on the **Done** button.

Asset Transfer

You can transfer an asset from one distribution line to another. Remember, distribution lines include location, depreciation expense account, and an optional employee. There are two ways to do transfers: regular transfer and mass transfer.

REGULAR TRANSFER   You can transfer an asset through Asset Workbench. Find the asset of interest and choose the **Assignments** button. Use a negative unit change to transfer out of a distribution line and use a positive unit change to transfer into a new distribution line. The total units of the asset remain unchanged. Click on the **Done** button when you are finished transferring.

MASS TRANSFERS   You can follow the navigation path *Mass Transactions : Transfers* to transfer a group of assets. To perform mass transfers, enter the corporate book, the transfer date, and an optional comment. Next, input the Transfer From and the Transfer To data. If you enter multiple Transfer From criteria, only assets matching all of the criteria will be selected. Click on the **Preview** button to generate a Mass Transfers Preview Report. Otherwise, click on the **Run** button to perform mass transfers. See Figure 7-20.

Financial Information

There are two ways to change financial information of assets: through the Asset Workbench, or by performing mass changes. Before depreciation, you can change any of an asset's financial fields. After depreciation, you can only change current cost, salvage value, prorate convention, depreciation method, and depreciation ceilings. When modifying financial information, you must decide whether you want to expense or amortize the changes. You can only choose to amortize adjustments if the depreciation book allows adjustments to be amortized.

CHANGE FINANCIAL INFORMATION THROUGH ASSET WORKBENCH

You can change the financial information of an asset through Asset Workbench. Find the asset of interest and choose the **Books** button. Select the depreciation book for which you want to adjust the financial information and choose whether to amortize the adjustment. Change the financial information and save your work.

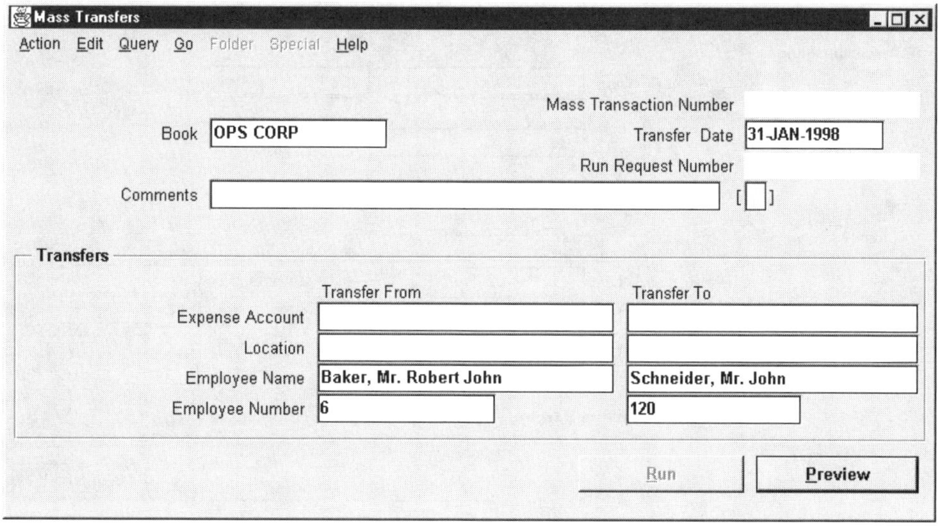

FIGURE 7-20. *Mass Transfers form*

MASS CHANGES   You can perform mass changes through the navigation path *Mass Transactions : Changes.* Select the depreciation book on which you want to perform the mass changes and enter the change date. Next, enter the selection criteria for the assets to change. The selection criteria can be a range of asset numbers, a range of dates placed in service, and an asset category. You can also make changes to include fully reserved assets. If you have more than one selection criterion, only assets that satisfy all specified criteria will be selected. As a last step, you can enter the financial data to find before changes are made (which function as additional selection criteria), followed by the new data to insert as replacements. You can mass change financial data such as prorate convention, depreciation method, and life in years and months. You can also determine whether you want to amortize the adjustments resulting from the mass changes. See Figure 7-21. Then, you can use the **Preview** button to generate the Mass Change Review Report to see a completed mass change, or you can just click on the **Run** button to initiate the mass changes.

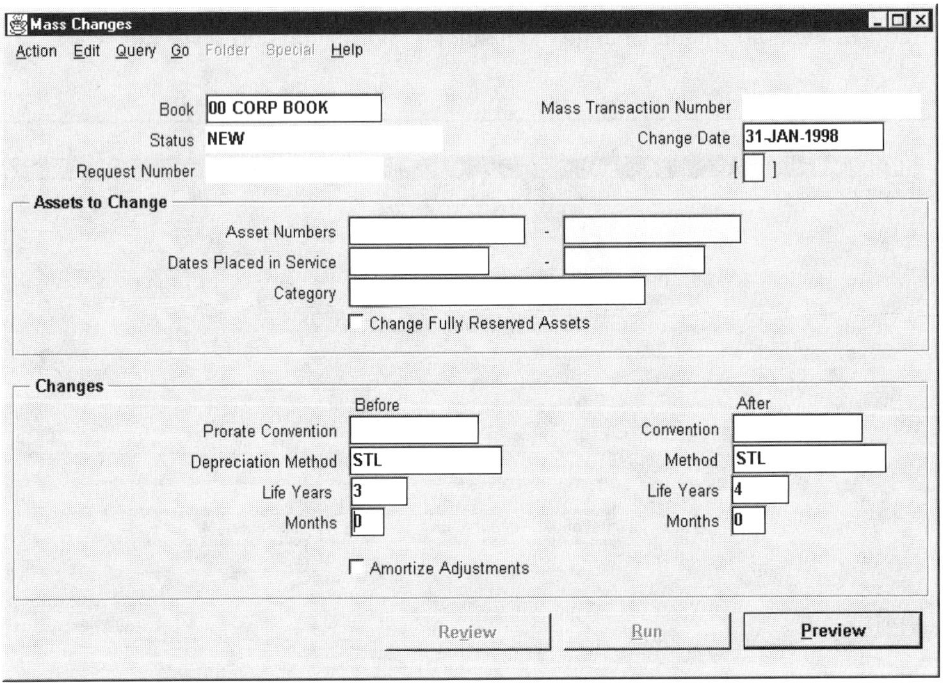

FIGURE 7-21.   *Mass Changes form*

Invoice Information

You can change or transfer invoice information through Asset Workbench. To change invoice information, find the asset of interest and click on the **Source Lines** button. You can then add or delete invoice line(s) or change the amount for a CIP asset. In addition, you can transfer the invoice line from one asset to another. To perform a transfer, click on the **Transfer to** button. Select the destination asset number and click on the **Done** button to perform the transfer. See Figure 7-22.

All of the asset adjustments just detailed will result in the creation of accounting journals. The adjustments may either be amortized throughout the assets' remaining useful lives or be expensed in the current depreciation period.

Review Questions

1. What is an asset reclass?

2. What makes up a distribution line?

3. What selection criteria can you use for mass changes?

4. What can you do with an asset's invoice lines?

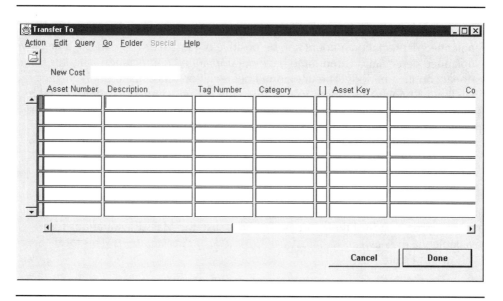

FIGURE 7-22. *Transfer To form*

Adjusting Assets Using Unplanned Depreciation and Revaluation

As you may have surmised from the heading of this portion of the text, there are two special ways to adjust assets: (1) unplanned depreciation and (2) revaluation.

Unplanned Depreciation

The unplanned depreciation feature is used primarily to accommodate special accounting practices in Germany. However, you can also employ it to handle unusual depreciation/accounting situations where you must adjust an asset's accumulated depreciation, YTD depreciation, and net book value without changing its current cost.

To enter unplanned depreciation, start at the Asset Workbench and click on the **Books** button. Select the depreciation book and go to the Depreciation region. The button **Unplanned Depreciation** will appear; click on it to go to the Unplanned Depreciation form, which is shown in Figure 7-23. Enter the unplanned depreciation type, which is defined through QuickCodes. Then enter the unplanned depreciation amount, followed by the expense account to which you want to charge the unplanned depreciation amount, and finally whether you want to amortize the net book value from the current depreciation period. If you do not amortize the net book value, the asset may be fully reserved before its useful life ends. Regular depreciation amounts are added to the unplanned depreciation you entered to form the total depreciation amount when the depreciation program is run. The unplanned depreciation amount can be positive or negative. You can use a negative unplanned depreciation amount to back out unplanned depreciation amounts from prior accounting periods. The unplanned depreciation amount cannot be higher than the net book value, and it cannot be in the period when the asset is placed in service. When you want to amortize the net book value, enter 0 for the unplanned depreciation amount and select the *Amortize From Current Period* checkbox. To amortize net book value in a future depreciation period, leave the *Amortize From Current Period* option unselected.

Revaluation

If your company operates in a highly inflationary economy, you will need to revalue assets to adjust their values. To do so, use the Mass Revaluations form available via the navigation path *Mass Transactions : Revaluations*. This form is shown in Figure 7-24.

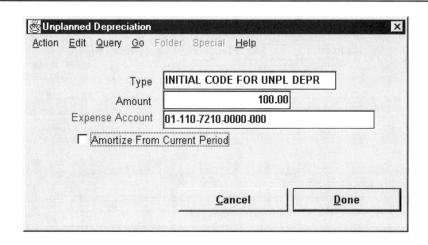

FIGURE 7-23.   *Unplanned Depreciation form*

Once the Mass Revaluations form opens, enter the depreciation book you want to revalue, along with a comment. For revaluation rules, you have four choices:

- **Revalue Fully Reserved Assets**   You can revalue fully reserved assets if they are depreciated under a life-based method and you have specified a life extension factor.

- **Life Extension Factor**   If you choose to revalue fully reserved assets, this value extends the asset's useful life to accommodate extended depreciation based on the revalued asset cost.

- **Maximum Revaluations**   Specifies the number of times a fully reserved asset can be revalued.

- **Life Extension Ceiling**   Specifies the maximum depreciation amount that can be backed out as a result of the revalued asset cost.

Once you have entered the revaluation rules, enter an asset category or asset number to revalue, followed by a revaluation rate, which can be positive or negative. Then you can either click on the **Preview** button to generate the Mass Revaluation Preview report, click on the **Review** button to generate the Mass

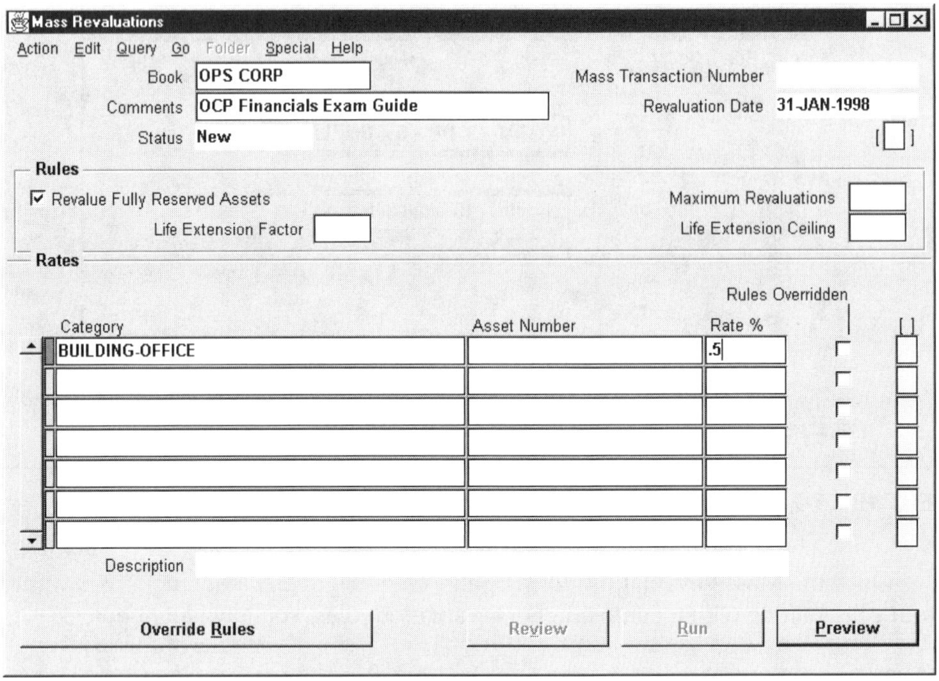

FIGURE 7-24. *Mass Revaluations form*

Revaluation Review report, or click on the **Run** button to initiate Mass Revaluations. Mass Revaluations will not revalue CIP assets, nor will it revalue assets added in the current period.

Review Questions

1. For what reason is unplanned depreciation used?

2. What should you do if you want to take unplanned depreciation but amortize the net book value in a future period?

3. When will you need to revalue assets?

4. What are the revaluation rules in Oracle Assets?

Retiring Assets

In this section, you will explore how to retire assets. Assets can be retired partially, fully, or in mass quantities.

Partial/Full Retirement

You perform partial or full retirements through Asset Workbench. Find the asset of interest and click on the **Retirements** button, which will take you to a form similar to the one shown in Figure 7-25. Enter the depreciation book from which you want to retire the asset. If you want to retire the same asset from the corporate book and the tax book, you must either retire the asset once from each depreciation book or retire it from the corporate book and mass copy the retirement into the associated tax books. (Mass copy will be discussed in more detail later.) Enter the retirement date and an optional comment. The retirement date cannot be earlier than any entered transactions for the asset and must be in the current fiscal year. Next, enter the number of units you are retiring; for partial retirements, the quantity will be less than the current units shown on the form. Then enter the retirement type, any proceeds of sale, and cost of removal. Retirement types are set up as QuickCodes. If the asset is not fully reserved, you must enter the retirement convention to govern how this asset should be depreciated in this last year. If the asset belongs to a property class 1250 in a tax book, you must select a straight line method and a life span to be used in the property report.

You can optionally enter additional information such as check/invoice number, who it was sold to, and trade-in data. If the asset you are retiring is a parent asset, you can click on the **Subcomponents** button to view its subcomponent information. When you finish entering the retirement information, click on the **Done** button to change the status of the asset to PENDING. This status will change to PROCESSED after either the Depreciation program or the Calculating Gains and Losses program is run.

Mass Retirements

You can perform mass retirements to retire a group of assets. To do this, follow the navigation path *Mass Transactions : Retirements* to open the Mass Retirements form, as shown in Figure 7-26. The fields in this form are similar to those for an individual asset's retirement: depreciation book, retirement date and type, proceeds from sale, cost of removal, etc. After entering this data, you enter the criteria to be used when selecting assets to retire. These criteria can include employee name and number, depreciation expense account range, whether assets are fully reserved, and asset type, location, category, key, cost range, number range, and date-in-service range. If more than one selection criterion is specified, only assets that fit all criteria will be selected.

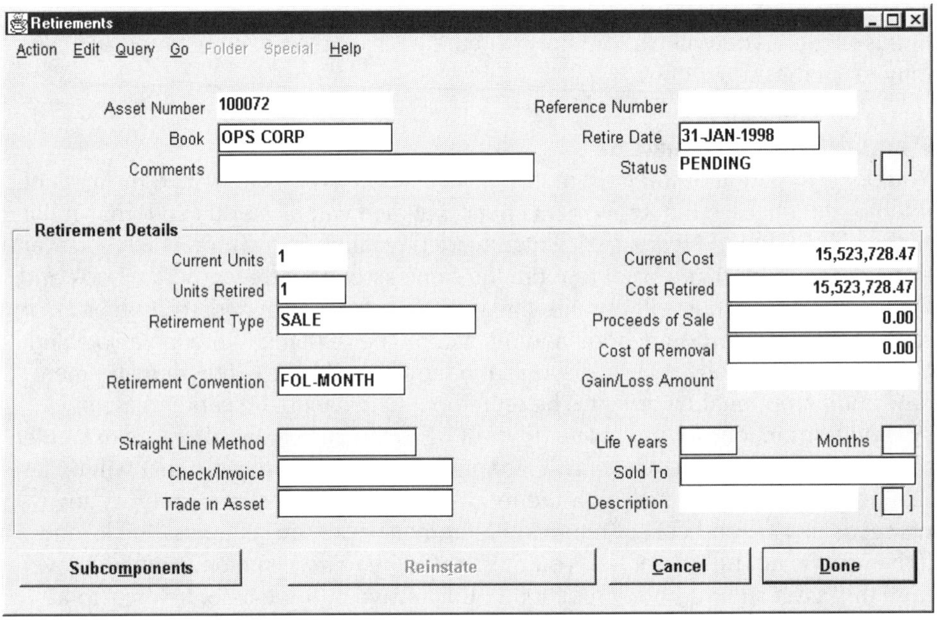

FIGURE 7-25. *Retirements form*

To initiate the mass retirement process, click on the **Retire** button. The selected assets will be given a status of PENDING, and an exception report will be generated. As with individual retirements, the assets' status changes to PROCESSED after either the depreciation program or the Calculating Gains and Losses program is run.

Reinstatements

There are several ways to reinstate assets after you have retired them, depending upon the status of your assets. You can simply undo retirements through the Asset Workbench if the retirements are in the status of PENDING, not PROCESSED. This will delete the retirement transactions as if they were never entered. If the retired assets have statuses of PROCESSED, you must reinstate them. You can reinstate individual retirements through the Asset Workbench, or reinstate mass retirements through the Mass Retirements form. Once you have reinstated assets, you must run the Calculate Gains and Losses program to put the reinstatements into effect.

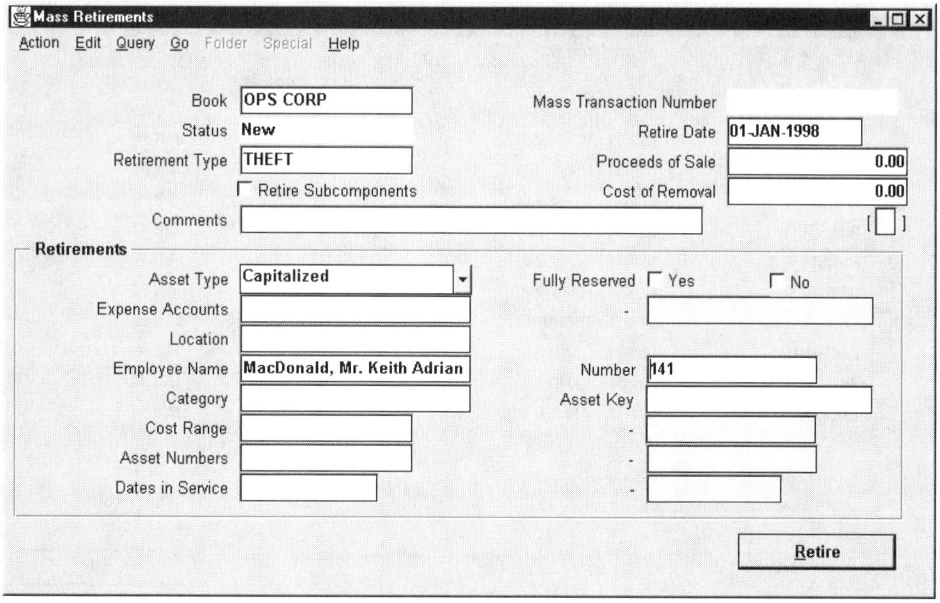

FIGURE 7-26. *Mass Retirements form*

Review Questions

1. What will retiring an asset do before the Calculate Gains and Losses program is run?

2. How can you reinstate retired assets?

Viewing Asset Information

The Asset Workbench provides two inquiry forms for viewing asset information. The first is the Financial Information form, which is available via the navigation path *Inquiry : Financial Information*. In this form, you can view the assignments, source lines, and Books of Assets. Use the Find window to locate assets by asset detail, assignment, source line, and lease. The second is the Transaction History form (*Inquiry : Transaction History*, shown in Figure 7-27), which displays all transactions

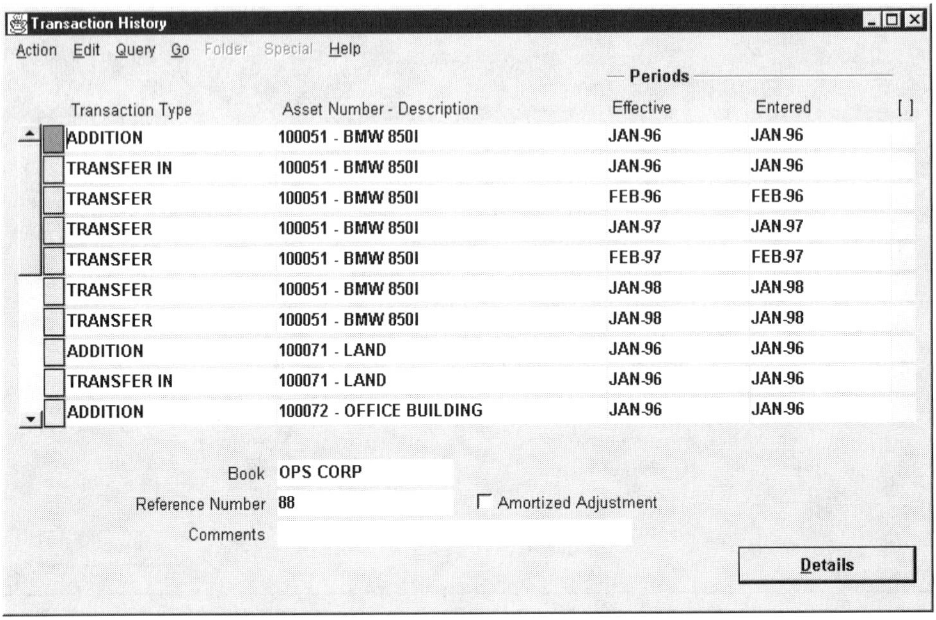

FIGURE 7-27. *Transaction History form*

pertaining to selected assets. You can find assets by depreciation book and reference number, asset number range, transaction period range, transaction type, or asset category. The information displayed includes transaction type, asset number – description, transaction effective date, and transaction entered date. To view transaction details, click on the **Details** button to open the Transaction Details form. Depending upon the transaction type, the Detail form shows different information. For example, for the ADDITION transaction type, financial information such as cost and salvage value is shown.

Review Questions

   1. What is the purpose of the Financial Information inquiry form?

   2. What does the Transaction History inquiry form display?

Adding Assets from External Sources

You have already seen how to add assets from Oracle Payables. This section takes you into new territory: adding construction-in-process (CIP) assets from Oracle Projects. This is a short section, containing just two bullet points:

- Adding CIP assets
- Integrating Oracle Projects to build CIP assets

Adding CIP Assets

You can collect costs related to CIP assets in Oracle Projects. To do so, you must first create the CIP asset and associate it with a capital project in Projects. When defining a CIP asset in Projects, you enter a variety of attributes: asset name, number, category, and description; estimated date in service; depreciation book; number of units; and the depreciation expense account, among other things. A complete treatment of Projects is outside the scope of this book, but it will suffice to say that if you do not enter all of the asset information here—and your capital project does not require it—you can add the asset information in the Prepare Mass Additions form. However, you must at least enter the asset name and the description. See Figure 7-28.

Review Question

1. In which module do you create CIP assets? (If you cannot answer this question after reading the preceding paragraph, this would be a good time to take a break!)

Integrating Oracle Projects to Build CIP Assets

Once you have established CIP assets, you can assign projects or tasks to them. When you are ready to capitalize CIP asset costs and create capitalized assets, you can generate summary asset lines grouped by the grouping levels you specified in the capital project. Asset lines can be summarized by projects, top-level tasks, or tasks. (You initiate the generation process from the Capital Project form in Oracle Projects.) Find the capital project of interest and enter the actual date in service for all of the associated assets. Then click on the **Generate** button. You can specify the date up to which incurred expenditures should be included, as well as whether to include common tasks not tied to any specific asset. Then click on the **OK** button to

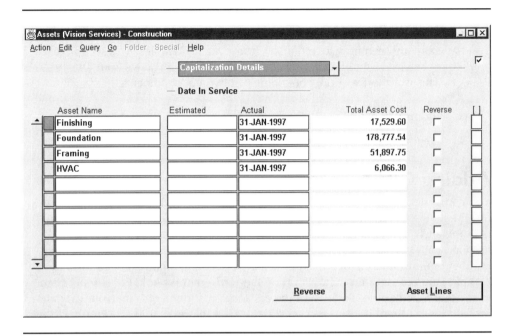

FIGURE 7-28. *Assets in Oracle Projects*

generate summary asset lines. Once the summary asset lines are generated, click on the **Lines** button to see the generated lines. These include transferred, rejected, and new asset lines associated with the capital project. You must use this form to associate unassigned asset lines to assets. Unassigned asset lines can be caused by common costs, or they can be due to expenditures being associated with more than one asset. You can split the asset line and only associate part of the asset line to an asset.

When you finish adjusting and reviewing the asset lines, you are ready to run the Interface Assets process, which mass-creates asset lines as mass additions lines. This process selects asset lines that meet the following criteria: they are posted to the General Ledger, associated with specific assets, and have an actual date in service in the current depreciation period. Run the PRC : Interface Assets process through standard report submission to initiate the process. Once this process is completed, prepare and post the mass additions lines in Assets, using the same technique as for mass additions lines brought in from Payables.

Review Questions

1. What does the Generate Summary Lines process do?

2. What is the purpose of the Interface Assets process?

3. What must you do to create capitalized assets after the Interface Asset process?

Managing Budgets

Capital budgets are estimates of how much money you will spend on capital acquisition. In Oracle Assets, they can be entered manually or uploaded automatically. Capital budgets are captured by depreciation expense account, asset category, and budget book. Once you have assigned assets to the budget book, you can project their depreciation and create a Budget-to-Actual report. This section covers both topics:

- Preparing capital budgets
- Projecting depreciation for budget assets

Preparing Capital Budgets

The steps to preparing capital budgets are as follows:

- Defining budget books
- Entering capital budgets
- Creating budget assets

Defining Budget Books

You use the Book Controls form to define budget books in the same way you define corporate and tax books. Choose the class budget for your budget book, and associate the budget book to a corporate book. Next, enter the same information you would for a corporate book: calendar information, accounting rules, natural accounts, and (optionally) journal categories.

Entering Capital Budgets

You can enter capital budgets manually, or automatically via uploads. To do it manually, follow the navigation path *Budget : Enter* to open the Capital Budgets form. Enter the name of your budget book, the asset category, and the depreciation expense account. Next, enter the budget amount for each budget period in the current fiscal year.

To upload capital budgets, you must first populate the capital budget interface table FA_BUDGET_INTERFACE. Initiate the process using the Upload Capital Budget form (navigation path *Budget : Upload*, shown in Figure 7-29). Select the budget book and choose the option you want. The *Delete Existing Budget* option allows you to delete the existing capital budget tied to the selected budget book, and upload the new capital budget from the interface table. The *Upload Capital Budget* option allows you to upload a new capital budget tied to the selected budget book.

Creating Budget Assets

You must create budget assets before you can project depreciation for them. Use the Upload Capital Budget form to create budget assets. Choose the budget book and select the option *Create Budget Assets*. When you save your work, a concurrent request named Create Capital Budget Assets will be generated. Upon completion, budget assets are created by asset category, and depreciation expense accounts are specified for the capital budget.

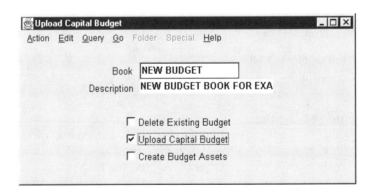

FIGURE 7-29. *Upload Capital Budget form*

Review Questions

1. What are the three steps in preparing capital budgets?

2. What three functions does the Upload Capital Budget form initiate?

3. What is the capital budget interface table called?

Projecting Depreciation for Budget Assets

Once you have defined the budget books, defined the capital budgets, and created the budget assets, you can project depreciation amounts and run a variety of reports for budget assets.

Depreciation Projection

Follow the navigation path *Depreciation : Projections* to project depreciation expenses. You can select the calendar to use, the number of periods to project, and the starting period. You can run depreciation projections for any Set of Books, displaying results either as a summary or with details based on cost center and/or asset. To project depreciation for budget assets, select your budget book.

Budget-to-Actual Report

This report is submitted through the standard report submission. The Budget-to-Actual report shows the capital budget amounts, actual acquisition amounts, and budget-to-actual variances.

Capital Spending Report

The Capital Spending report is also submitted through the standard report submission. This report compares acquisition costs before a specified cutoff date with the acquisition costs for the whole year. It also shows the percentage of the capital budget you have used thus far.

Review Questions

1. What will depreciation projection do?

2. What budget reports can you run?

3. What does the Capital Spending report show?

Maintaining Tax Books

In this section, you will learn how to apply tax accounting concepts within Oracle Assets. Topics include:

- Creating a tax book
- Entering information in a tax book
- Adjusting a tax book depreciation reserve

Creating a Tax Book

Use the Book Controls form to define tax books. Choose the class Tax for your tax book and associate it with a corporate book. Enter the same information you would for a corporate book: calendar, accounting rules, natural accounts, and (optionally) journal categories. You can create multiple tax books for one corporate book; common tax books are state, federal, ACE, and AMT. Assets on the tax book share the same asset categories and assignments as the associated corporate book. The defaults based on the asset categories and the asset financial information can be different.

Review Questions

1. How do you create a tax book?
2. What are some of the common tax books?

Entering Information In a Tax Book

To enter information in a tax book, you can either do it manually or utilize a process called mass copy. Manual entry occurs much like it does for a corporate book, via the Asset Workbench; you just select a tax book instead of a corporate book. However, if the associated corporate book allows it, you can use mass copy instead. The corporate book can also dictate whether the mass copy function will include additions, cost adjustments, retirements, and salvage value. There are two kinds of mass copy:

- Initial Mass Copy
- Periodic Mass Copy

Initial Mass Copy

Use Initial Mass Copy to populate the tax book with the corporate book data. This data includes cost, date in service, units, unit of production, and salvage value.

Other asset information such as depreciation method and prorate convention come from the asset category tax book default. The tax book's fiscal year determines which corporate book fiscal year will serve as the source of the copy. For Initial Mass Copy to work, the fiscal year of the corporate book must be closed. The Initial Mass Copy program copies asset information at the end of the corporate book's fiscal year to the tax book's current accounting period. Use Initial Mass Copy only for the very first period in the tax book.

The Initial Mass Copy program will ignore CIP assets, expensed assets, assets retired in the corporate book before the fiscal year of the tax book, and assets added in the corporate book after the fiscal year of the tax book. To launch Initial Mass Copy, follow the navigation path *Tax : Initial Mass Copy*. Enter the tax book name and click on the **OK** button, followed by the **Submit Request** button.

Periodic Mass Copy

Once you have used Initial Mass Copy in the first depreciation period in the tax book, you should never use Initial Mass Copy again—that is why it is called *Initial*. After the first time, use Periodic Mass Copy instead. Periodic Mass Copy replicates additions, cost adjustments, retirements, and reinstatements from the corporate book. It does not copy revaluations, and it only copies transactions that are allowed in the associated corporate book. For transfers and reclasses, because tax books share the same asset categories and assignments as the corporate books, there is no need for Periodic Mass Copy to copy those transactions. The tax book's current accounting period determines which accounting period Periodic Mass Copy will duplicate from the corporate book. The accounting period or the corporate book must be closed in order for Periodic Mass Copy to work.

Since a tax book accounting period may not line up exactly with corporate book periods—in fact, it could span multiple corporate book periods—corporate book transactions spanning multiple periods could end up in a single accounting period in the tax book. One particular problem is that assets that are added and retired in different accounting periods in the corporate book may translate to an addition and retirement in the same accounting period in the tax book. Since this is not a valid condition in Oracle Assets, the retirement will be deferred until the next accounting period in the tax books as a retroactive retirement. Another problem is cost adjustments. Even if the corporate book allows cost adjustments to be mass copied, Periodic Mass Copy will only work if the tax book and associated corporate book contain the same costs.

Periodic Mass Copy will ignore CIP assets, expensed assets, assets retired in the corporate book before the start date of the current accounting period of the tax book, and assets added in the corporate book after the end date of the current accounting period of the tax book. To initiate a periodic mass copy, follow the navigation path *Tax : Periodic Mass Copy*. Enter the tax book name and the corporate period from which you want to perform a periodic mass copy. Click on the **OK** button, followed by the **Submit Request** button.

Review Questions

1. How can you enter asset information in tax books?

2. What is the difference between Initial Mass Copy and Periodic Mass Copy?

Adjusting a Tax Book Depreciation Reserve

If your tax book allows reserve adjustments, you can adjust its depreciation reserve for a closed fiscal year. The changes you make will affect the closed fiscal year and all subsequent fiscal years up to the current fiscal year. In this section, you will study:

- Adjusting the tax book depreciation reserve for a single asset

- Mass depreciation adjustments

- Depreciation reserve adjustments reports

Adjusting the Tax Book Depreciation Reserve for a Single Asset

To adjust the depreciation reserve for a single asset, follow the navigation path *Tax : Tax Workbench* to open the Tax Reserve Adjustments form (shown in Figure 7-30). Find the asset of interest and click on the **Reserve Adjustments** button. (If you cannot perform this step in the Vision database, change one of the Operation tax books to allow for reserve adjustments.) Enter the tax book and an optional comment. Then key in the fiscal year in which you want to make depreciation adjustments. As a last step, enter the new fiscal year depreciation expense. Click on the **Done** button to update.

NOTE
You cannot change the depreciation reserve if you have amortized any cost adjustment beyond the fiscal year you are adjusting, or if the asset in question uses the units of production depreciation method.

Mass Depreciation Adjustments

Four key factors control how the Mass Depreciation Adjustments program calculates adjusted depreciation expense amounts: minimum accumulated depreciation

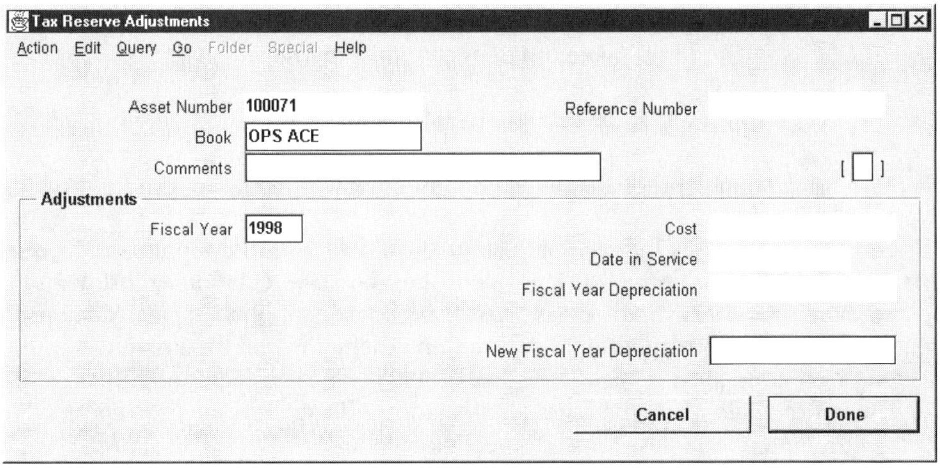

FIGURE 7-30. *Tax Reserve Adjustments form*

reserve, maximum accumulated depreciation reserve, minimum depreciation expense, and maximum depreciation expense.

The minimum and maximum accumulated depreciation reserves are based on the smallest and largest amounts among four different values. The first two values are the depreciation reserve of the adjusting tax book at the beginning and the end of the year. The third value is the depreciation reserve of the control tax book at the end of the year, and the last value is the depreciation reserve of the corporate book at the end of the year. The control book you used must be associated with the same corporate book as the tax book. Calculations are performed as follows:

Minimum depreciation expense

=

minimum accumulated depreciation reserve

-

adjusting tax book's depreciation reserve at the beginning of the year

Maximum depreciation expense

=

maximum accumulated depreciation reserve

-

the adjusting tax book's depreciation reserve at the beginning of the year

$$
\text{Adjusted depreciation expense}
$$
$$
=
$$
$$
\text{minimum depreciation expense}
$$
$$
+
$$
$$
\text{(depreciation adjustment factor}
$$
$$
\times
$$
$$
\text{(maximum depreciation expense} - \text{minimum depreciation expense))}
$$

To perform mass depreciation adjustments, follow the navigation path *Tax : Mass Depreciation Adjustments.* This opens the Mass Depreciation Adjustments form shown in Figure 7-31. Enter the adjusted tax book, control book, depreciation adjustment factor, and an optional description. Then, click on the **Preview** button to generate the Mass Depreciation Adjustments Preview report, the **Review** button to generate the Mass Depreciation Adjustments Review report, or the **Run** button to initiate Mass Depreciation Adjustments.

Depreciation Reserve Adjustments Reports

There are several reports you can use to review tax book depreciation reserve adjustments. These reports can be submitted through the Standard Report Submission form:

- **Adjusted Form 4562 - Depreciation and Amortization report**   Shows the depreciation taken for the fiscal year specified, including depreciation reserve adjustments.

- **Adjusted Form 4626 - AMT Detail report**   Shows the difference in depreciation between an AMT tax book and its corporate book, including the depreciation reserve adjustments in detail format.

- **Adjusted Form 4626 - AMT Summary report**   Shows the difference in depreciation between an AMT tax book and its corporate book, including the depreciation reserve adjustments in summary format.

- **Reserve Adjustments report**   Shows the reserve adjustments you make for the selected tax book and the selected accounting period range.

Review Questions

1. Under what conditions can you not perform depreciation reserve adjustments?

2. How do you calculate the minimum and maximum accumulated depreciation reserves in mass depreciation adjustments?

3. How is the depreciation adjustment factor used?

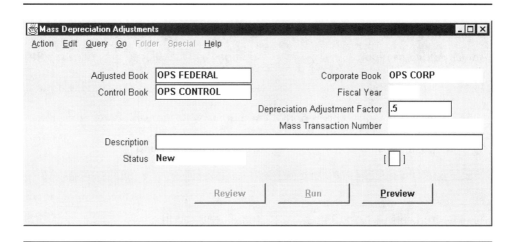

FIGURE 7-31. *Mass Depreciation Adjustments form*

Reporting, Reconciling, and Year-End Processing

The last section in this chapter addresses the following items:

- Submitting reports for printing or viewing online

- Reconciling asset data

- Performing physical inventory on assets

Submitting Reports for Printing or Viewing Online

Most Assets reports are submitted through the standard report submission process, which can be run by following the navigation path *Other : Requests : Run*. (Standard report submissions are covered in detail in Unit 2 of this book.) Other reports run from the Report eXchange, which allows you to customize the reports at run time, download them to applications such as Excel, and publish them on the Web. Table 7-2 shows the relationship between some standard reports and Report eXchange reports.

Standard Reports	Report eXchange reports
Annual Additions report	Additions by Date Placed in Service report
Asset Additions report	Additions by Date Placed in Service report
Asset Additions Responsibility report	Additions by Responsibility reports
Asset Reclassification report	Reclassifications report
Asset Reclassification Reconciliation report	
Asset Retirements by Cost Center report	Retirements reports
Asset Retirements report	
Reinstated Assets report	
Asset Transfers report	Transfer report
Asset Transfer Reconciliation report	
Asset Disposals Responsibility report	
CIP Capitalization report	Capitalizations report
CIP Detail report	CIP Cost Balance report
CIP Summary report	
Cost Adjustments by Source report	Cost Adjustments report
Cost Adjustments report	
Financial Adjustments report	
Parent Asset Transactions reports	
Cost Clearing Reconciliation report	Cost Clearing Reconciliation report
Cost Detail report	Asset Cost Balance report
Cost Summary report	

TABLE 7-2. *Relationship Between Standard Reports and Report eXchange Reports*

Standard Reports	Report eXchange reports
Delete Mass Additions Preview report	Mass Additions report
Mass Additions Create Report	
Mass Additions Delete report	
Mass Additions Invoice Merge report	
Mass Additions Invoice Split report	
Mass Additions Posting report	
Mass Additions Purge report	
Mass Additions Status report	
Unposted Mass Additions report	
Journal Entry Reserve Ledger report	Reserve Ledger report
Property Tax report	Property Tax report
Reserve Detail report	Accumulated Depreciation Balance report
Reserve Summary report	
Revaluation Reserve Detail report	Revaluation Reserve Balance report
Revaluation Reserve Summary report	

TABLE 7-2. *Relationship Between Standard Reports and Report eXchange Reports* (continued)

Review Question

1. How are Report eXchange reports different from standard reports?

Reconciling Asset Data

You can use the Reserve Summary report in Assets to reconcile with the Account Analysis report in GL. If there are any discrepancies, you can use the Reserve Detail report to investigate them. The Reserve Summary report shows beginning balances, asset transactions (additions, depreciations, adjustments, retirements, reclassifications, and transfers), and ending balances by balancing segment value and depreciation reserve account. The Reserve Summary report's ending balances should match the balances in the Account Analysis report.

Review Question

1. How should you reconcile Oracle Assets with General Ledger?

Performing Physical Inventory on Assets

The purpose of performing physical inventory is to ensure that the assets you have in your system match what is actually in inventory. The following topics will be outlined in regard to physical inventory in Oracle Assets:

- Entering physical inventory data

- Running physical inventory comparisons

- Viewing physical inventory comparisons

Only assets whose *In Physical Inventory* checkboxes are checked will be included in physical inventory comparisons.

Entering Physical Inventory Data

To enter items into inventory, you first must define the inventory itself. Follow the navigation path *Physical Inventory : Enter* to bring up the Physical Inventory form shown in Figure 7-32. Enter a physical inventory name, start date, and end date for the physical inventory. You can then click on the **Open** button to start entering items in the Inventory Entries form. If you have a batch of existing physical inventory data that you would like to load, you can transfer it into FA_INV_INTERFACE interface table. This table's structure is as follows:

```
INVENTORY_ID          NUMBER          NOT NULL
INVENTORY_NAME        VARCHAR2(80)    NULL
ASSET_ID              NUMBER(15)      NULL
ASSET_NUMBER          VARCHAR2(15)    NULL
ASSET_KEY_CCID        NUMBER(15)      NULL
TAG_NUMBER            VARCHAR2(15)    NULL
DESCRIPTION           VARCHAR2(80)    NULL
MODEL_NUMBER          VARCHAR2(40)    NULL
SERIAL_NUMBER         VARCHAR2(35)    NULL
MANUFACTURER_NAME     VARCHAR2(30)    NULL
ASSET_CATEGORY_ID     NUMBER(15)      NULL
UNITS                 NUMBER          NULL
```

```
LOCATION_ID          NUMBER(15)      NULL
STATUS               VARCHAR2(30)    NULL
UNIT_ADJ             VARCHAR2(30)    NULL
UNIT_RECONCILE_MTH   VARCHAR2(30)    NULL
LOCATION_ADJ         VARCHAR2(30)    NULL
LOC_RECONCILE_MTH    VARCHAR2(30)    NULL
DISTRIBUTION_ID      NUMBER(15)      NULL
RECONCILIATION_ID    NUMBER          NULL
LAST_UPDATE_DATE     DATE            NULL
LAST_UPDATED_BY      NUMBER(15)      NULL
LAST_UPDATE_LOGIN    NUMBER(15)      NULL
CREATED_BY           NUMBER(15)      NULL
CREATION_DATE        DATE            NULL
```

Running Physical Inventory Comparisons

Once you have entered or loaded the physical inventory data, you can run the physical inventory comparison program to match physical inventory data with asset data in the system. Follow the navigation path *Physical Inventory : Comparison : Run Comparison* to open the Run Comparison dialog box shown in Figure 7-33. After entering the physical inventory name, you have the option of reducing the comparison by entering an asset category and location. Then click on the **Run** button, which initiates the concurrent program named PI Comparison. You can use View My Requests to verify completion of this program.

All physical inventory data starts with a status of NEW. The comparison program uses a methodical approach to matching rows in the interface table with asset data already in the system. For each interface table row, the program tries to find an

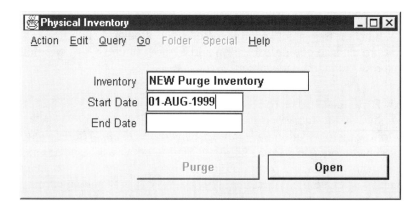

FIGURE 7-32. *Physical Inventory form*

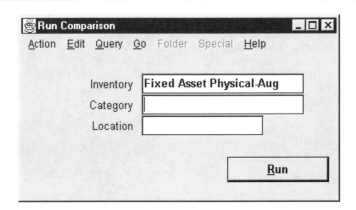

FIGURE 7-33. *Run Comparison form*

existing asset with the same asset number. If an asset with the same asset number exists in the system already, the program compares its location and number of units with the physical inventory data in the interface table. If they match, the physical inventory data's status is changed to RECONCILED; if they do not, the status is changed to DIFFERENCE.

In a perfect world, that would be the end of the description of how inventory comparison works. But sometimes things don't match up. For instance, the interface table could contain a row whose asset number is not already in the system. When the comparison program encounters such a row, it skips that row and proceeds to the next one. The interface table could also contain a row that lacks an asset number altogether. When the comparison program encounters a row with no asset number, it attempts to find a matching asset using the row's tag number, then serial number, then asset key, then asset description and other fields. If it finds a match, it proceeds to compare location and number of units; if it does not, it skips to the next row in the interface table.

Viewing Physical Inventory Comparisons

Once the physical inventory comparison program finishes, you can view its report or follow the navigation path *Physical Inventory: Comparison : View* to view the physical inventory comparison online. A Find window will appear; enter the physical inventory name and other criteria to bring up data you desire. Investigate the differences, and if the physical inventory data is correct, change the asset data in the system to match the physical inventory data. See Figure 7-34.

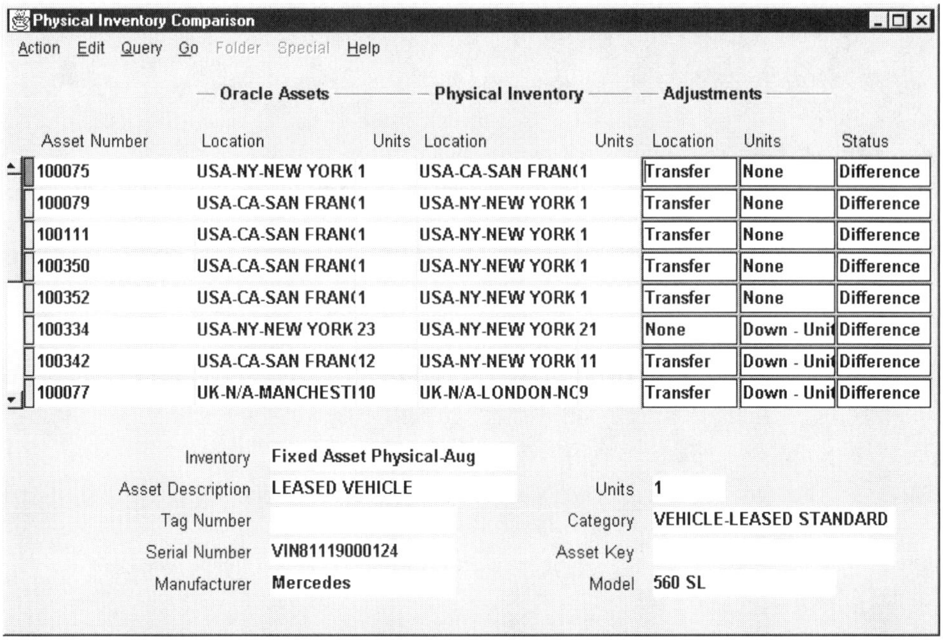

FIGURE 7-34. *Physical Inventory Comparison form*

Once you have reconciled the physical inventory data, you can run the Physical Inventory Missing Assets report to see if there are any assets in the system with the *In Physical Inventory* checkbox selected that do not appear during physical inventory.

Review Questions

   1. What are the steps involved in physical inventory?

   2. How does the Physical Inventory Comparisons program work?

For the Chapter Summary, Two-Minute Drill, and Chapter Questions and Answers, open the summary.htm file contained in the Summary_files directory on the book's CD-ROM.

UNIT
II

Preparing for OCP Exam 2: Applied Technology

CHAPTER

8

System Administration

his unit covers the material tested in OCP Exam 2: Applied Technology. This first chapter in Unit II covers numerous system administration facets within Oracle Applications. In it, you will learn the fundamentals of:

- Managing application security

- Managing concurrent programs and reports

- Administering concurrent managers

- Managing profile options

- Auditing system resources

- Document sequencing

- Incorporating custom programs

- Managing printers

First, you will learn how to manage application security, including creating users, responsibilities, and custom menus. Next, you will explore Oracle's Concurrent Processing environment, and learn how to set up request groups and request sets, as well as how to submit concurrent requests or concurrent request sets through the Standard Request Submission (SRS) form. You will also learn how to configure and schedule concurrent managers.

In addition, you will review how to manage profile options at various predefined levels: system, application, responsibility, and user levels. You will also learn how to audit system resources and data changes, and produce reports from the audit data. Then you'll explore how to enforce document sequencing. Finally, you will cover how to implement custom concurrent programs, and as a last step, how to define printer types, register printers, and create custom print styles for Oracle Applications.

All of these functions are set up in Oracle Applications using the *System Administrator* responsibility. Follow along by logging on to the Vision demonstration database and choosing the *System Administrator* responsibility.

Managing Application Security

First, let's discuss application security. When a user logs on to Oracle Applications, a user name and a password must be supplied. If the user name/password combination is correct, and the user has only one assigned responsibility, they will immediately be taken to the top-level menu for that responsibility and can begin using Oracle Applications. If the user has more than one assigned responsibility, then the list of responsibilities assigned to them will appear. From there, the user selects the desired responsibility and begins using Oracle Applications. In this section, you will review:

■ Defining application users

■ Customizing application privileges

■ Defining responsibilities

■ Defining custom menus

Defining Application Users

An application user is defined through the navigation path *Security : User : Define.* The User Name, Password and From Date fields on this form are required. The user name that you enter will be displayed in capital letters and must be unique across all Oracle Applications modules. After you type a user name, you may optionally enter a description, then the initial password for the application user. Passwords in Oracle Applications must be at least five characters long. Note that the password you enter is only a temporary password; when the application user first logs on, the application user will be asked to change their password. Once you have entered the password, you may specify how often the user-entered password will expire. (Remember that the password you entered expires when the user first logs on, so the password expiration rules only apply to the user-entered password.) You have the choice to expire the password in a selected number of days or after a selected number of accesses. You can also specify that the user-entered password never expire, which means that the password stays the same until the user explicitly chooses to change it.

Next, you can enter a person, a customer, or a supplier to associate with the application user name. A person must be an employee already defined in the system, a customer must be a customer contact defined in the system, and a supplier must be a supplier contact defined in the system. You can also optionally enter the fax number of the application user. The effective date range defines when the application user is valid. You cannot delete an application user, but you can enter an effective end date that falls before or on the system date, in order to inactivate an application user.

There are two alternative regions available when defining an application user: Responsibilities and Securing Attributes. The Responsibilities alternative region allows you to select valid responsibilities for the application user. Enter an effective date range to govern when the responsibility assignment is valid; each user must have at least one responsibility. You can also enter a description for the responsibility assignment. The Securing Attributes alternative region allows you to specify values for attributes that the application user can access when using Self-Service Web Applications. If you enter a person, contact, or supplier to associate with the application user name, certain other attributes are automatically populated. If you enter a person, the ICX_HR_PERSON_ID and TO_PERSON_ID attributes are automatically filled in with the selected employer ID as the value. If you enter a customer, the ICX_CUSTOMER_CONTACT_ID attribute is automatically filled in with the ID of the selected customer contact. If you enter a supplier, the ICX_SUPPLIER_CONTACT_ID attribute is automatically filled in with the ID of the selected supplier contact. The application user can then access his or her own data through Self-Service Web Applications. You may enter one person and/or one customer and/or one supplier; this will control the data the application user may access.

The effective dates define when the application user name is valid. The From date (or start date) is required, and the To date (or end date) is optional. However, since you cannot delete an application user, you must enter an effective end date in order to inactivate an application user. The end date must be on or after the From date, and may be in the past, present, or future.

There are two alternative regions available when defining an application user: Responsibilities and Securing Attributes.

The Responsibilities region allows you to assign one or more valid responsibilities to the application user. Each user must have at least one active responsibility in order to log on. Enter an effective date range to govern when the responsibility assignment is valid. You can optionally enter a description for the responsibility assignment.

The Securing Attributes region allows you to specify values for attributes, in order to restrict the rows of data that the application user can access when using Self-Service Web Applications. For example, if you set up a city attribute to a value of "Los Angeles", then the user could only see data for that city and not for other cities.

Including additional values will allow the application user to access data belonging to the additional values. See Figure 8-1.

When a user logs on to Oracle Applications, Oracle actually connects to the database using a generic gateway user ID, APPLSYSPUB. Once connected, Oracle Applications can look up the user name to obtain and display the list of responsibilities available to the application user. When the application user selects a responsibility, Oracle Applications will log off from APPLSYSPUB, and then log back on to the database using the Oracle database user ID identified for that responsibility. Then the Navigator menu associated with the responsibility will be displayed to the user.

Review Questions

1. Which fields are required when defining a user?

2. For what purpose is the password entered into the Password field?

3. What are the two alternative regions in defining an application user?

4. What is the sequence of events when an application user logs on?

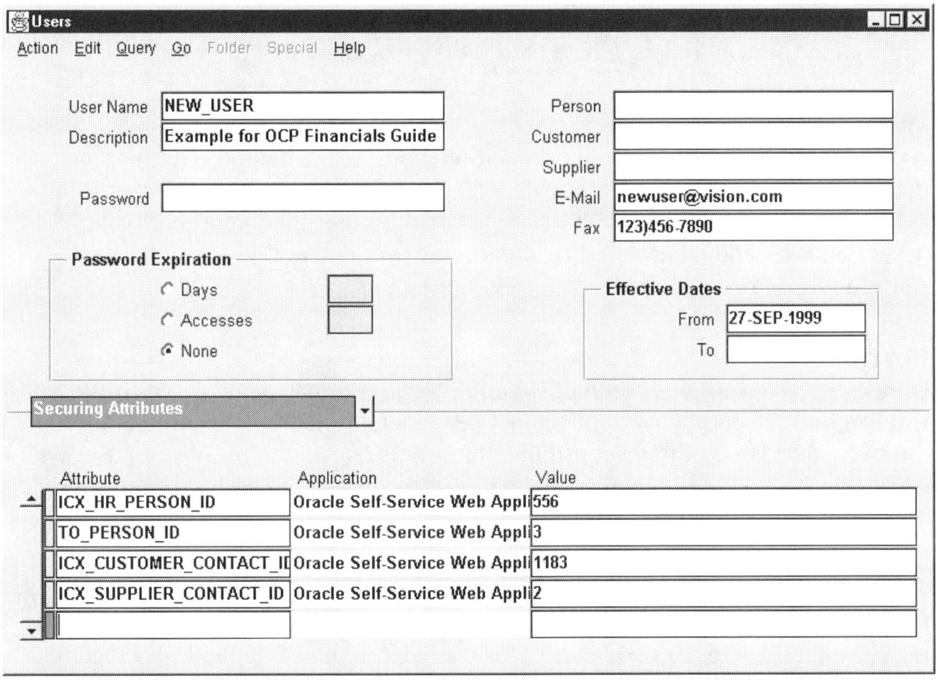

FIGURE 8-1.   *Users form*

Customizing Application Privileges

Application privileges, which govern which aspect of the application can be accessed, can be defined to restrict or allow access at many different levels. There are several kinds of application privileges:

- Set of Books
- Data groups
- Forms
- Functions
- Securing attributes
- Reports/programs

Set of Books

This governs which Set of Books is associated with the application user. The application user can only see data within the associated Set of Books.

Data Groups

A data group maps each Oracle Application module to a database ID. This determines which Oracle database user ID connects to the database when using a certain application module. The Oracle database user ID determines which database tables and other database objects the user can access through Oracle Applications forms, reports, or concurrent programs.

Forms

Forms are the forms/windows that the application user can access. The list of forms that can be accessed by an application user is determined by the configuration of the menu attached to the responsibility the user is connected to. A given user will see a different menu (and can access different forms) each time they connect to a different responsibility.

Functions

Function security governs what functionality can be performed from a given responsibility. There are two kinds of functions: form functions and subfunctions. Form functions are functions that will call a form; subfunctions are those within a form, usually associated with a button. Application users restricted from performing certain functions on a form will still be able to navigate to the form, but will not be able to navigate to the section of the form representing a restricted form function, or to see the buttons or graphics on a form that are associated with a restricted subfunction.

Securing Attributes

Securing attributes governs what set of data values an application user can access through the Self-Service Web Applications.

Reports/Programs

The list of available reports and programs varies, depending on the responsibility the user is connected to. A request group is defined as a list of reports and programs. A request group can then be attached to a responsibility, and this controls the programs and reports that can be accessed by users of that responsibility.

Review Question

1. What are the application privileges that can be customized?

Defining Responsibilities

A responsibility is the bridge between an application user and their application privileges. When an application user chooses a responsibility, they assume all of the application privileges and options defined by that responsibility. Different application users that are assigned the same responsibility will have the same application privileges.

To define a responsibility, follow the navigation path *Security : Responsibility : Define.* Enter the responsibility name, then the application (module name). The responsibility name and the application are required, and the combination must be unique across Oracle Applications. Each responsibility must be associated with an application module, but this is for information purposes only. It does not restrict users of that responsibility from accessing forms, reports, and programs across application modules. In other words, the application module name you enter does not restrict anything. Simply select the application module that owns most of the new responsibility's forms, reports, and programs.

Next enter the responsibility key, which must be unique and is used by programs that load information such as user profile values and messages. Oracle suggests you use the application short name as the prefix of the responsibility key.

You can also enter an effective date range to specify when this responsibility is valid. The From date is required. Since you cannot delete a responsibility, the only way to inactivate a responsibility is to enter an effective end date that falls before or on the system date.

A responsibility can either be tied to a regular Oracle Application module or to a Self-Service Web Application module. Select the desired choice in the Available From region, then select Oracle Applications for your responsibility. Next, enter the data group to which the responsibility should point. The data group defines a mapping between Oracle Application modules and the Oracle database user IDs. Each application module listed in a data group points to one database ID. The name of the data group is a required field. Next, select the Oracle application to designate which Oracle database user ID that responsibility should log on as. Requests are only processed by transaction managers if the responsibility and the transaction manager share the same data group. Oracle comes seeded with the Standard Data Group, which should be sufficient for most Oracle Applications installations. If you're following online, choose the Standard Data Group as your data group name, and Oracle General Ledger as the data group application for your responsibility.

Now enter the menu to which the responsibility is tied. This is the known as the top-level menu, main menu, or the Navigator. Choose GL_SUPERUSER as the menu for your responsibility.

If you want the responsibility to use a Web host and Web agent different from those that the *System Administrator* responsibility uses, then enter them here. Next, enter the name of the request group, which identifies which reports and programs that users of the responsibility can access. If you do not enter a request group, the user will not be able to run any reports or other programs through a Standard Request Submission (SRS) window. The request group selected for the responsibility becomes the request security group. If you're creating a new responsibility online now, you can use the GL Concurrent Program Group as the request group for your responsibility.

NOTE
Some menus are set up to run a specific report or program, and do not refer to the Responsibilities Request Security Group.

You can also exclude menus or functions from a responsibility. In doing so, the excluded menus or functions will not be accessible to users of the responsibility, even if they are contained within the top menu or forms associated with the responsibility. This gives you flexibility in configuring application privileges: you can define one menu to be shared by multiple responsibilities and use this region to exclude only the one function not used by one of the responsibilities.

To enter a function or menu exclusion, go to the Function and Menu Exclusions region. You must first select the type (Function or Menu). Then select the name of the function or menu that you want to exclude from users of this responsibility. If you exclude a menu, all of its entries, submenus, and functions are excluded. If you exclude a function, then any and all occurrences of this function throughout the responsibility's menu structure are disabled.

There are two kinds of functions: form functions and subfunctions. Form functions are functions that will call a form; subfunctions are those within a form, usually associated with a button or drop-down list. If you exclude subfunctions that are related to buttons, users with this responsibility will not see the buttons on the form.

If the responsibility is available for Self-Service Web Applications, you can identify excluded items and securing attributes. Excluded items determine what columns of data the application user using this responsibility cannot see. Securing attributes can be used together with the application user definition to limit the rows of data that an application user can access. See Figure 8-2 for the Responsibilities form.

Oracle has predefined many seeded responsibilities. You can use some of them, but do not customize the seeded responsibilities. Instead, create your own customized version of the report, because during an upgrade, the seeded responsibilities will be replaced by the Oracle Applications upgrade program.

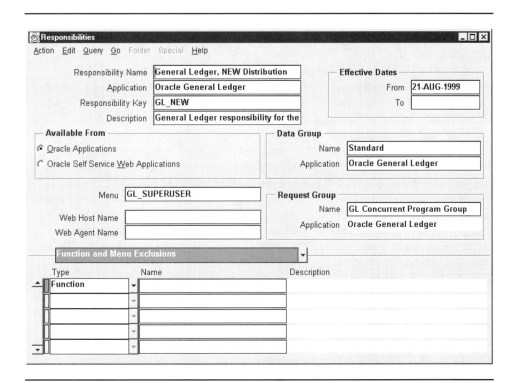

FIGURE 8-2.   *Responsibilities form*

Review Questions

1. What is a responsibility?

2. What is the sequence of events when an application user logs on?

3. What will a request group become after associating with a responsibility?

4. Which components are required for a custom responsibility?

5. What can you set up if a responsibility is available for Self-Service Web Applications?

Defining Custom Menus

The top menu for a responsibility determines which online functionality (i.e., forms) can be accessed by users of that responsibility. A menu may be composed of multiple levels of menus. Each menu may be made up of submenus or forms. When you define a menu composed of submenus, those submenus must be predefined in order to be valid.

You must define menus from the bottom up by defining submenus at the lowest level first, and the top menu last. You must use the List of Values to select the lower-level menu as a submenu. To define menus, follow the navigation path *Application : Menu.* If you want to follow online, query up the GL_SUPERUSER menu to take a look at an example of an existing Oracle menu.

To create a custom menu, you would first fill in the Menu Name and the User Menu Name fields (both are required). The menu name is the name used to store the menu in the system. It must be unique across Oracle Applications. If you change the menu name later, all references to the old menu name will be changed automatically. (You do not need to change all of the references separately.) The user menu name is the name the user will see when selecting menus as submenus or main menus for responsibilities. It too must be unique across Oracle Applications. You can optionally enter a description for your custom menu. Query up the GL_SUPERUSER menu to take a look.

Next, enter the menu entries, which are the choices that will appear in the menu. For each menu entry, you must enter the sequence number and the Navigator prompt that the user will see, then select either the name of a submenu or function (one is required), and an optional description. The description will appear as help text when the application user places the cursor on this menu entry. The sequence number determines the sequence in which menu entries appear inside the Navigator. You can resequence the entries in an existing menu if you wish. However, doing so is a little clumsy since each sequence number must be unique even during the renumbering. So, if you have menu entries numbered 10, 20, 30, and 40, and you want to exchange 10 with 20, you cannot simply change the 10 sequence number to 20 and vice versa because when the form attempts to save your changes, it will find that entries already exist for those numbers. Instead, you need an interim step employing temporary numbers: for instance, change 10 to 21 and 20 to 11, save your work, and then change 11 to 10 and 21 to 20. See Figure 8-3 for the Menus form.

Once you have saved your menu, the changes you made will be seen by users the next time they log on or change responsibilities.

Review Questions

1. How are multiple-level custom menus set up?

2. How do you resequence menu sequence numbers?

3. Do you need to change all references to old menu names when the menu name changes?

4. Which component of the menu entry will appear in the Navigator?

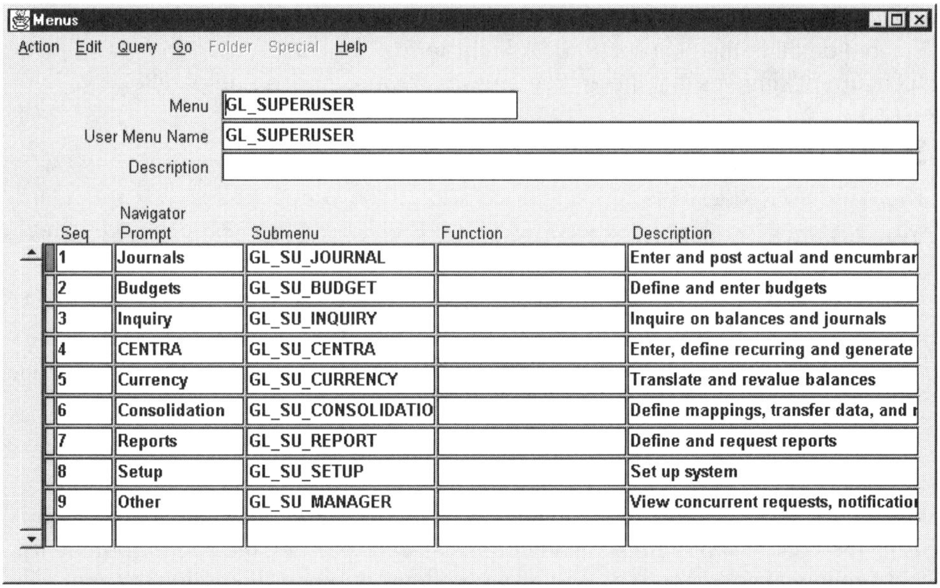

FIGURE 8-3.   *Menus form*

Managing Concurrent Programs and Reports

Now that you have learned how to set up the various aspects of Oracle Applications security, you will learn to manage concurrent programs and reports. This section shows you how to:

- Submit requests through standard request submission (SRS)
- Monitor request processing
- Define request groups
- Customize the SRS processing of reports
- Define request sets
- Control report behaviors
- Control user access to reports and programs

Concurrent programs and reports are submitted for background processing, which is handled by concurrent managers. (Concurrent managers will be discussed in more detail in the next section, "Administering Concurrent Managers".) The word "concurrent" implies that these programs and reports may run in parallel.

Submitting Requests Through SRS

The Standard Request Submission (SRS) window provides all users with a standard way to submit concurrent requests (i.e., reports or programs). You can access the Submit a New Request form through the navigation path *Requests : Run*; the form is shown in Figure 8-4. This standard form gives you the option to submit a request or a request set. (Request sets will be defined later in this section.) An application user can only submit single requests or request sets within the request security group associated with the logged-on responsibility or through menu functions that were specifically programmed to run a report.

First, you will be asked whether you want to run a single request or a request set. Select single request for now, and the Submit Request form will open. You can identify the request either by typing a valid name in the Request Name field or by using the Edit | List of Values menu command and selecting the name from the list that appears. If you choose a concurrent program or report that requires parameters, you will be presented with a dialog box requesting values for those parameters.

Once you have returned to the Submit Request form, you have the option of defining a submission schedule and a variety of completion options.

To see the scheduling parameters, click on the **Schedule** button. When the Schedule form opens, click on the **Apply a Saved Schedule** button to apply a

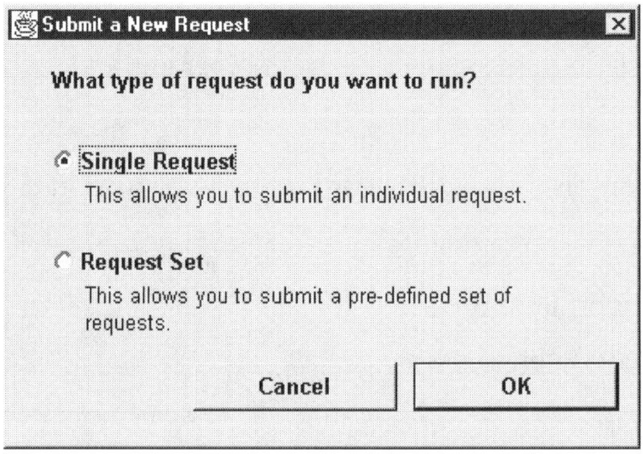

FIGURE 8-4. *Submit a New Request screen*

previously saved schedule. See Figure 8-5. If you're not applying a saved schedule, you can specify your own schedule stating that the job should be run as soon as possible, once, periodically, or on specific days. Each of these choices causes appropriate fields to appear on the form. Once you have specified the parameters for the schedule, you can save it for reuse by checking the *Save this schedule for use again later* checkbox. Click on the **OK** button to apply the schedule information to your submission request.

Once you have returned to the Submit Request form, you may click on the **Completion Options** button to specify actions you want the system to take after the request has been completed. These options include notifying one or more people through Workflow, and printing one or more copies of the output. See Figure 8-6. Click on the **OK** button after you define the completion options you want, and then click on the **Submit Request** button to submit the program or report for processing.

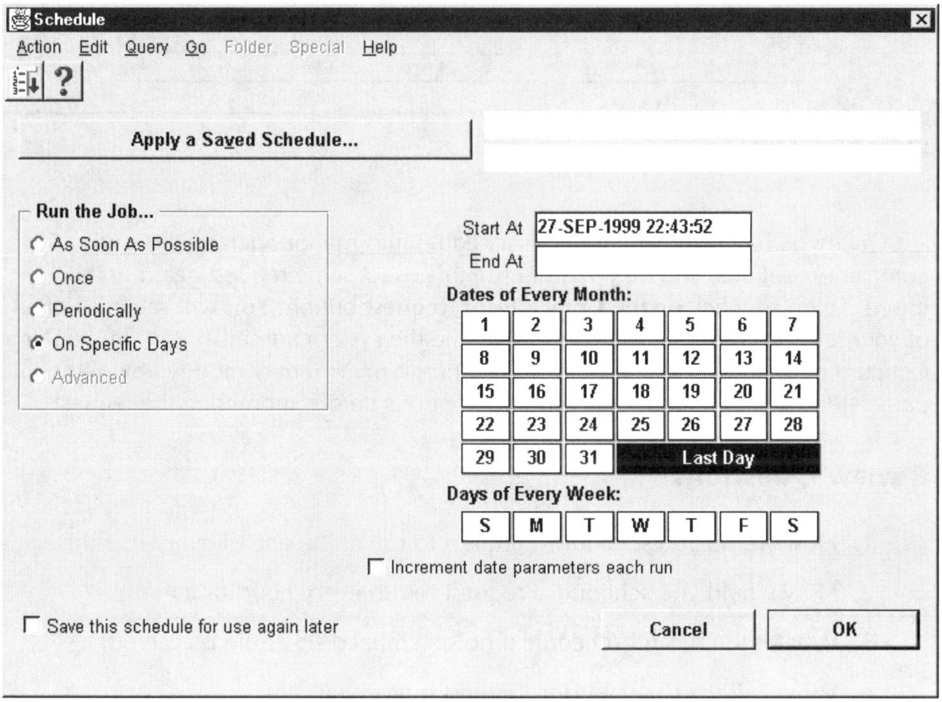

FIGURE 8-5. *Schedule form*

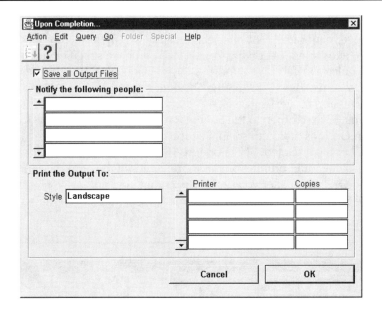

FIGURE 8-6. *Completion options*

Once you have entered all of the schedule information, parameters and completion options, you may wish to run this exact same request again in the future. To do so, click on the **Copy a Prior Request** button. You will see a list of all of your requests submitted since the last time the system administrator ran the Purge Concurrent Request and/or Manager Data program. You may modify any of the parameters, schedule info, or completion options before submitting the request.

Review Questions

1. How would you schedule a request to run at the end of every month?

2. How would you schedule a request to run every hour for a month?

3. What is the default schedule if no specialized schedule is entered?

4. What will the **Copy a Prior Request** button do?

Monitoring Request Processing

You can monitor request processing through the View My Requests form (available from the Help menu). A Find Requests window will appear, and you will have the option of viewing all of your completed requests, all requests in process, all your requests regardless of processing status, or specific requests. Specific requests can be identified by request ID, name, date submitted, date completed, status, phase, and/or requestor. As a last step, you can define what column should be used to sort the list. The list can be ordered by request ID, name, and requested start time. See Figure 8-7. Click on the **Find** button to go to the Requests form, and you will see all of the requests that satisfy your find criteria.

In the Requests form, you can click on the **Refresh Data** button to retrieve the latest list of requests that satisfy your find criteria. (This has the same effect as the Query Run function.) The **Find Requests** button allows you to enter new search criteria, while the **Submit a New Request** button enables you to initiate a new concurrent request through the SRS form. The selected concurrent request will be

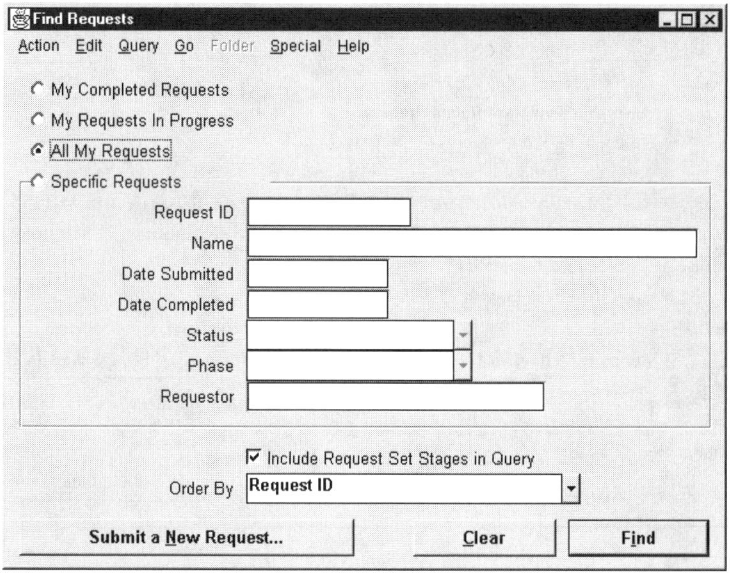

FIGURE 8-7. *Find Requests form*

shown with the request ID, name, any parent requests, phase, status, and the submitted parameters. The phase of a request can be Inactive, Pending, Running, or Completed. Inactive means that the request has been placed on hold, or the concurrent manager that would run this request is inactive/locked/not defined. Pending means the requests are waiting for the concurrent managers to select them. Running and Completed are what the names suggest, while Status shows the status of the request. The valid statuses are Cancelled, Disabled, Error, No Manager, Normal, On Hold, Paused, Resuming, Scheduled, Standby, Suspended, Terminated, Terminating, Waiting, and Warning. The combination of the Phase and Status information will tell you exactly what's happening with a particular request.

The **Hold Request** button delays a request that has yet to run (i.e., its phase is pending). The **Cancel Request** button kills requests that are running, but have not been completed. The **View Details** button opens a form showing more details on the request, as shown in Figure 8-8. These details include the date submitted, date started, requestor, date completed, completion text, the language, the schedule, and the completion options.

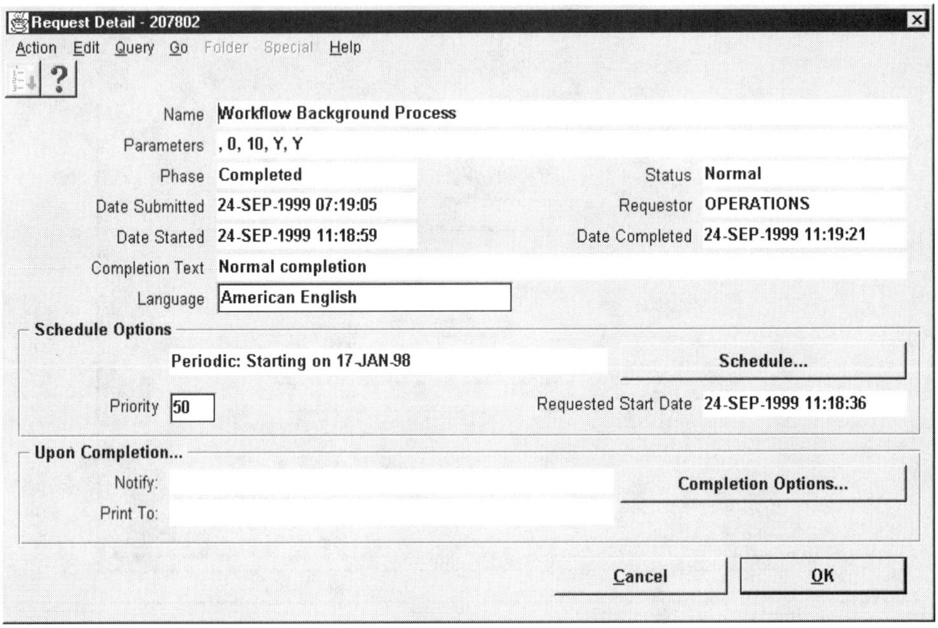

FIGURE 8-8. *Request Detail form*

In the Requests form, the **Diagnostics** button takes you to the Request Diagnostics form, which gives you a brief diagnosis of the request, including its phase and status, as well as when it began and ended. Back on the Requests form, use the **View Output** and the **View Log** buttons to view output files and log files associated with the request online. The output file becomes available after a request has either completed or ended with an error. See Figure 8-9 for the Requests form.

You can also use the menu bar's Special | Managers command to view the concurrent managers, or the Special | Reprint command to reprint an output file. When you reprint, you must specify the number of copies and the printer, and, optionally, override the print style.

If you logged on as a system administrator, you can follow the navigation path *Concurrent : Requests* to view concurrent requests in system administrator mode. The same Find Requests window appears as before. However, if you use specific requests and do not restrict the requests by the requestor, you will be able to view all requests across all requestors. You can also view log files that belong to other application users. You cannot view the output files of other users, but you can always view output files that belong to your requests. If the profile option

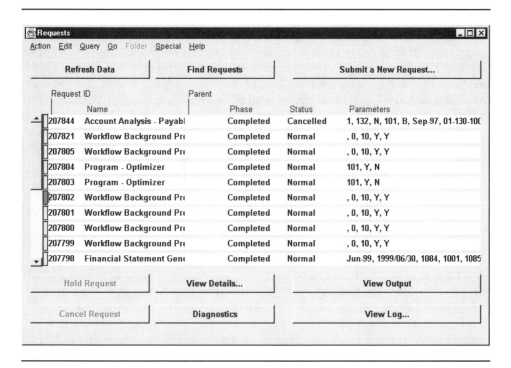

FIGURE 8-9. *Requests form*

Concurrent: Report Access Level is set to Responsibility, then you can see output files that belong to your requests as well as requests submitted by other users of any of your responsibilities. You can never see output files belonging to a user of a responsibility you do not have access to, even if you are in system administrator mode.

Review Questions

1. When you use the Concurrent | Requests navigation path to view requests, what impact can your responsibility have on the requests that are displayed?

2. What are the phases of concurrent requests?

3. What are the statuses of concurrent requests?

4. How can you reprint output files of a completed request?

Defining Request Groups

You should recall that request security groups are used to restrict and group the concurrent reports and programs that you can run. To create a request security group, you attach a request group to a responsibility. (You can also use the request groups to customize the SRS processing or reports, which you will learn about in the next section.) In this section, you will explore defining request groups. You define request groups through the navigation path *Security : Responsibility : Request.* This will take you to the Request Groups form.

To create a request group, you would first enter the group (request group name) and the application. You may include requests from any application in your request group, regardless of the application attached to your request group. The application name is for informational purposes only. The group and application are both required, and must be unique across Oracle Applications. Next, you can optionally assign a code to the request group. This code is used for a custom SRS form so that only programs or reports in this request group could be processed by the custom SRS form. The code—together with the application module—also must be unique. As a last step, you can enter an optional description.

Enter requests that are included in the request groups by selecting the type and the request name. The type can be Application, Program, Set or Stage Function. Application means include all concurrent programs and reports within the application. Program and Set mean a particular concurrent request or a particular request set. Function means a particular request set stage function, which will be covered later when defining a request set. Query up the GL Concurrent Program Group to see the definition of the request group you utilized for your responsibility. See Figure 8-10.

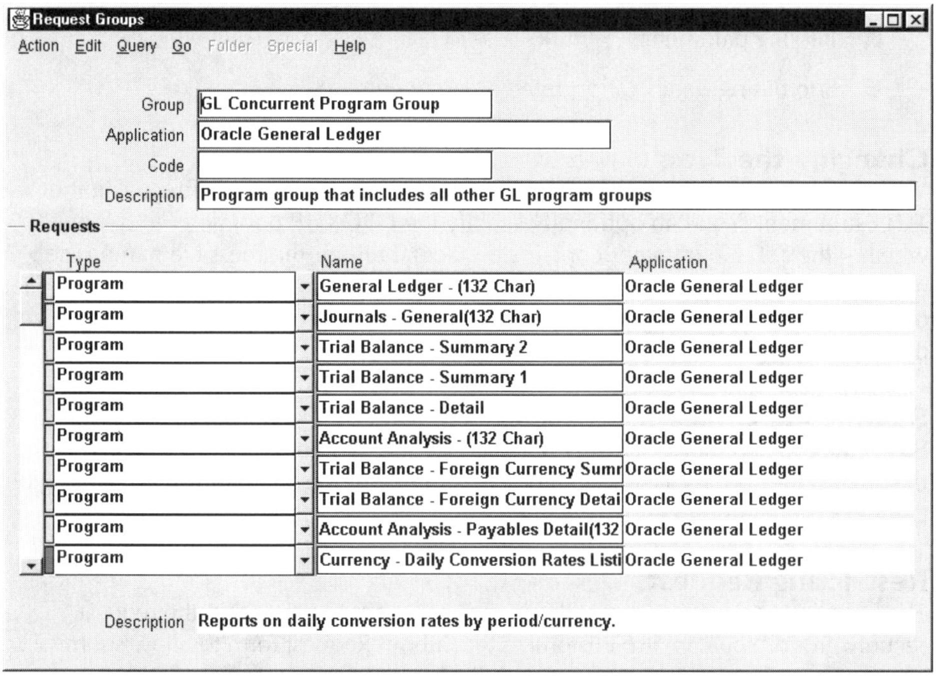

FIGURE 8-10. *Request Groups form*

Review Questions

    1. What types are available to be included in a request group?

    2. What is the purpose of request groups?

Customizing SRS Report Processing

You can define a form function to be a custom version of the Standard Request Submission form, with additional parameters or arguments to customize the SRS processing of reports. To do this, you would have your menu call a predefined form function that references the Submit Requests Window and passes it the appropriate arguments. You have the option of:

■ Changing the title

■ Submitting once

- Restricting requests
- Passing parameters
- Submitting organization-related parameters

Changing the Title

You can change the Submit Request form title to whatever you define using the TITLE argument. You can optionally specify the LOOKUP parameter to denote whether the TITLE parameter contains the actual title or the message name. The message name must be translated to get the title. You can either use LOOKUP="Y" or LOOKUP="N". The default is "Y". This means that the title contains the message name.

Submitting Once

By setting the parameter SUBMIT_ONCE="Y" (the default is "N"), you can change the Submit Request form so that after submitting a request, it will not ask you if you want to submit another.

Restricting Requests

The Submit Request form allows the user to submit requests within the request security group. You can also customize the Submit Request form to allow submissions of concurrent programs and reports with the request group associated with some custom parameters.

You can restrict requests submitted through the customized Submit Request form to those in a request group, to a single request, or to a request set. To restrict the requests to only those in a certain request group, use the REQUEST_GROUP_CODE parameter and the REQUEST_GROUP_APPL_SHORT_NAME parameter. REQUEST_GROUP_CODE refers to the code you associated with the request group and REQUEST_GROUP_APPL_SHORT_NAME refers to the application short name. Remember, the code and the application module name form a unique combination across Oracle Applications.

To allow submission of only a certain request, you would use the arguments CONCURRENT_PROGRAM_NAME and PROGRAM_APPL_SHORT_NAME. CONCURRENT_PROGRAM_NAME refers to the concurrent program name, while PROGRAM_APPL_SHORT_NAME refers to the application module name.

To restrict requests submitted through the Submit Request form, use REQUEST_SET_NAME and SET_APPL_SHORT_NAME. REQUEST_SET_NAME refers to the request set and SET_APPL_SHORT_NAME refers to the application module name.

Submitting Organization-Related Parameters

If you have implemented Multiple-Organization functionality, you can submit organization-related parameters to be used in value sets. Use the parameters shown in Table 8-1.

Parameter	Purpose
USE_ORG	Determines whether the organization ID must be set up before the request is run. If this is set to "Y", then the other four ORG parameters will be used.
ORG_ID	Specifies a particular organization ID.
ORG_NAME	Specifies a particular organization name.
ORG_CODE	Specifies a particular organization code.
CHART_OF_ACCOUNTS_ID	Specifies a particular Chart of Accounts ID.

TABLE 8-1.   *Organization-Related Parameters*

Review Questions

   1. How can you change the title of the SRS Submit Request form?

   2. How can you restrict the SRS Submit Request form to a particular request group?

   3. What are the five organization-related parameters you can use in customizing SRS report submissions?

Defining Request Sets

You can define request sets to run multiple concurrent programs and reports at once. There are two types of request sets: private and public. Private request sets are created by application users that are not logged on as system administrators. These users may include any programs from their responsibility's request security group in their private request set. The application user who creates the request set will become its owner. The private request set will always be available to the owner from the SRS form, regardless of whether the private request set is within the request security group. The only exception is when you use the Submit Request form customized with restrictions. This customized Submit Request form will not include any private request sets.

System administrators can create public request sets that include any concurrent programs and reports, and that assign any application user as the owner, or choose to have no owner. System administrators can also update any request set, regardless of who the owner is. Only the system administrator can update a request set that has no assigned owner. Otherwise, both the system administrator and the owner can update the request set. System administrators can also define request set incompatibilities.

Request sets can be assigned to request groups, just like concurrent programs and reports. When a request set is assigned to a request group, the request set's concurrent programs and reports are automatically assigned to the request group. If the request set contains concurrent programs and reports that do not exist explicitly in the request group, then that group's application user can only run the entire request set, and not the individual program. In addition, the application user cannot edit the request set unless they are the owner of the request set, or are connected with the *System Administrator* responsibility.

As a system administrator, you define request sets using the navigation path *Requests : Set.* (If connected to a responsibility other than *System Administrator*, you would use the navigation path *Other: Requests : Set.*) When creating a new request set, you can use the Request Set Wizard, or simply enter the request set name and code and the application module. Again, the request set name, the request set code, and both application modules must be unique across Oracle Applications. You can also enter the description, and, if you are a system administrator, you can assign an application user as the owner. If you are creating a request set, and you are not a system administrator, you will become the owner. Next, you can enter an active date range to limit when the request set is valid. Then, you can choose whether you want to print all of the concurrent programs and reports in the request set together (or have each one print as it completes). Finally, choose whether to allow incompatibility between other concurrent programs/reports and the request set. See Figure 8-11. For the purposes of this exercise, create a request set called NEW Month End. Enter the necessary information related to the request set and click on the **Define Stages** button.

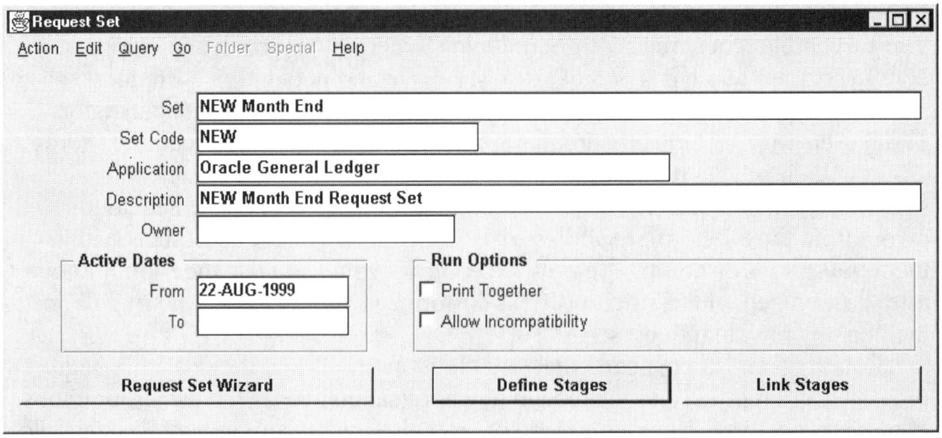

FIGURE 8-11. *Request Set form*

A request set is composed of one or more stages, and each stage is composed of one or more requests. Stages give you the ability to run groups of requests sequentially. All requests within the stage must be completed before the next stage starts. If you do not need the capability to run groups of requests sequentially, you can define only one stage for the request set. To define a request set, you must first define its stages. Do this by creating a request set that consists of two stages: programs and reports. For each stage, you must enter a display sequence, a stage name and optionally a stage description. Also required are a stage code and a function/application. The display sequence determines the order of the stages, and the stage code is used to identify the stage internally. You must also define a function to be used for evaluating the completion status of the stage. Oracle Applications comes seeded with the Standard Evaluation function. As a last step, choose whether you want this stage outcome to define the request set outcome, and whether you allow incompatibility. If you have multiple stages that can impact the outcome of the request set, then the completion status of the last stage that completes will become the completion status of the entire request set. See Figure 8-12.

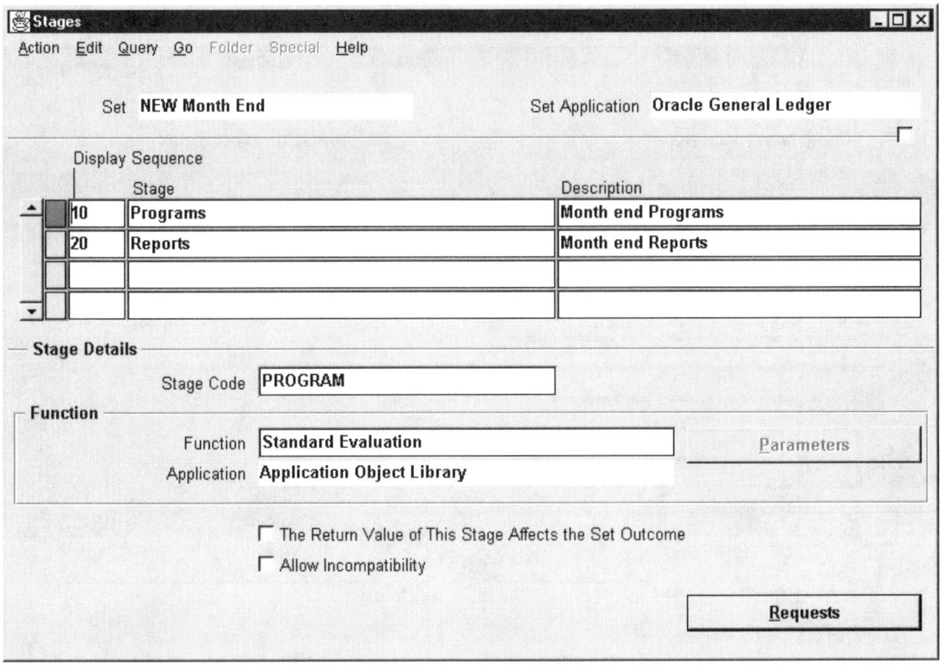

FIGURE 8-12. *Stages form*

Click on the **Requests** button to enter the concurrent reports and/or programs you want to include for the particular stage. Unless you are a system administrator, the concurrent reports and/or programs you may select from are limited to those in your responsibility's request security group. For each program you include, you must enter a sequence number and the program name. You can uncheck the *Allow Stage Function to Use This Program's Result* checkbox if you do not want the status of a specific program to be included in calculation of the status of the stage. You can also specify print options to decide how many copies to print, the print style, the printer, and whether you want to save the output files. In your online exercise, for the Programs stage, select several month-end programs, such as "Program – Automatic Posting" and "Program - Create Journals". For the Reports stage, select a few General Ledger month-end reports, such as one of the "Account Analysis…" reports, and one of the "Trial Balance…%" reports. See Figure 8-13.

Click on the **Parameters** button to see and update parameters for each request. All of the parameters related to the request will be displayed, and the Sequence field shows the order of the parameters. You can choose whether to display or allow the user to modify the parameters, and you can enter a shared parameter in the applicable field. If you enter the same shared parameter label for multiple

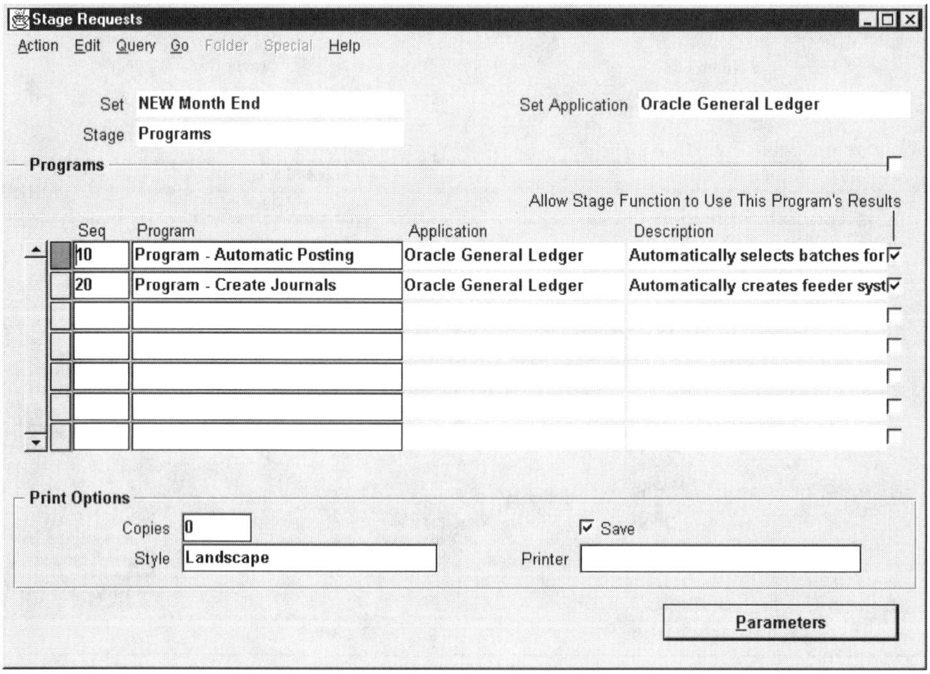

FIGURE 8-13. *Stage Requests form*

parameters within the request set, then at run time the user only needs to enter the value for the first occurrence of the shared parameter, and the rest of the occurrences within the entire request set will default to this value. Thus, you avoid typing in the same parameter multiple times. On the Request Parameters form, you can also specify a default type and default value for each parameter. These values will be applied when a user submits the request. The valid default types are listed in Table 8-2. See Figure 8-14 for the Request Parameters form.

Type	Description
Constant	Use a constant value (literal) as the default value.
Current date	The current system date will be used as the default. The format of the date depends on the length of the parameter. The length of 9 will have the current date in the 'DD-MON-YY' format while the length of 11 will have the current date in the 'DD-MON-YYYY' format.
Current time	The current system time will be used as the default. The format of the time depends on the length of the parameter. A length of 5 will have the current time in the 'HH24:MI' format, a length of 8 will have the current time in the 'HH24:MI:SS' format, while a length of 15 will have the current time in the 'DD-MON-YY HH24:MI' format. A length of 17 will have the current time in the 'DD-MON-YYYY HH24:MI' format, a length of 18 will have the current time in the 'DD-MON-YY HH24:MI:SS', while a length of 20 will have the current time in the 'DD-MON-YYYY HH24:MI:SS' format.
Field	Use the field name as the default value; the value of the field will be used when submitting the request.
Profile	Enter the profile option name as the default value; at the time of submitting the request, the value of the specified profile option will be used.
SQL statement	Enter the SQL statement as the default value; at the time of submitting the request, the SQL statement will be executed.
Segment	Enter the prior segment name as the default value; at the time of submitting the request, the current segment will use the prior segment value.

TABLE 8-2. *Default Types*

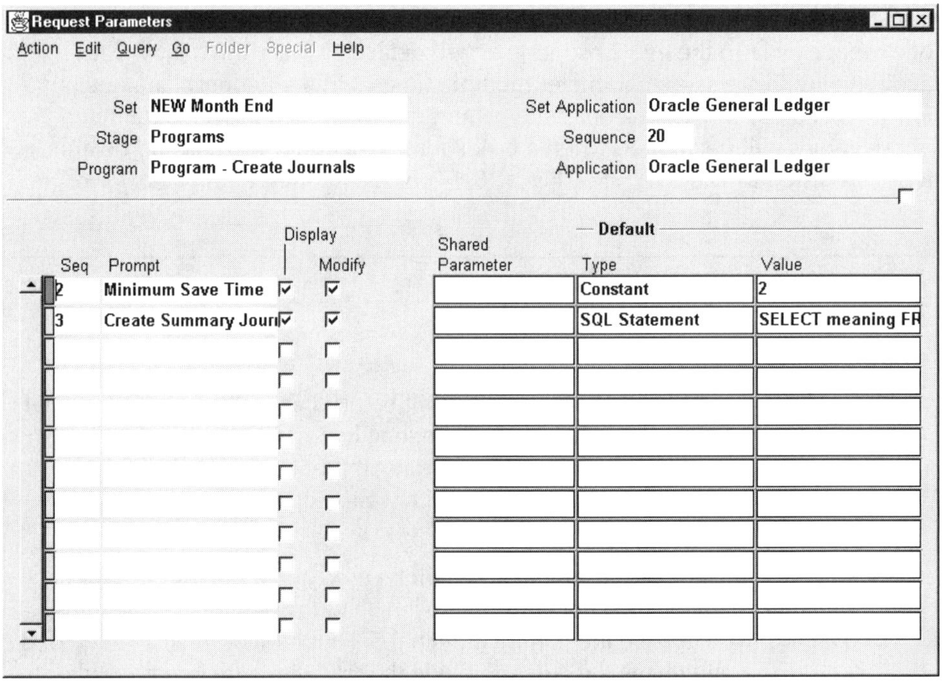

FIGURE 8-14.   *Request Parameters form*

Once the stages, requests, and parameters have been defined, you must link the stages to let the system know how to proceed when each stage is completed—either successfully, with a warning, or in error. In your exercise, from the Request Set form, click on the **Link Stages** button. Link the success and warning completion of the Programs stage to the Reports stage. Click on **Done** when finished. See Figure 8-15.

Request Set Wizard

Alternatively, you can create request sets using the Request Set Wizard, which allows you to follow step-by-step instructions to create a basic request set. To define a new request set using the Request Set Wizard, go to the Request Set form and click on the **Request Set Wizard** button. The first form will appear, so follow the text and decide whether you want the requests in the new set to be run sequentially or in parallel. For your online exercise, select Sequentially and then click on **Next**. Secondly, select whether you want to abort processing or continue processing if one of the requests in the request set completes with an error status. For your online

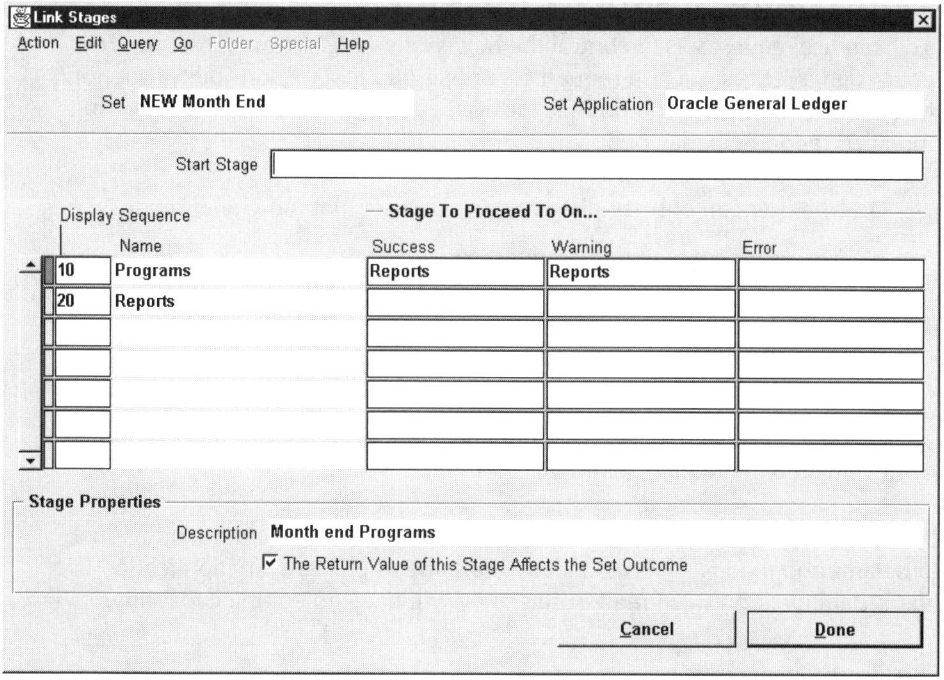

FIGURE 8-15. *Link Stages form*

exercise, select Abort Processing and click on **Next**. Thirdly, enter the request set name, application module, and an optional description. Decide whether the output files of the requests within the request set should be printed after the entire request set has completed processing or as each request in the request set completes. Choose As Each Request in the Set Completes and then click on **Next**. Finally, on the next form, select the concurrent programs that should be included in the request set.

Review Questions

1. What is the difference between a private request set and a public request set?

2. What makes up a request set?

3. What is a Request Set Wizard?

Controlling Report Behavior

You can use request sets to control the behavior and updating of reports. You can assign a request set as a request security group to a responsibility, but not to individual reports. If you do this, the application user exhibits the following modified reporting behaviors:

- The user can only run the entire request set, not individual reports.

- The user cannot edit the request set.

- The user can delete reports from the request set.

- The user can only add reports within the request security group to the request set.

- The user can update report parameters or print options if the report is within the request security group.

If you only use request sets in request security groups—and not individual programs and reports—it is essentially the same as giving every application user the capability to only run request sets; they will have no editing capability.

Review Question

I. How can you use request sets, ownership, request groups, and request security groups to control report behaviors?

Controlling User Access Via Request Sets

One way to control user access to reports and programs is by specifying an owner for a request set. If a request set has an owner, then only the owner or a system administrator can edit the request set. The owner can always run the request sets they own, regardless of the responsibility with which they are logged on. For this reason, a request set does not need to be in the user's request security group in order for the user to run the request set, if the user owns the request set.

If a request set has no owner, the request set cannot be updated by any end user. Only system administrators can update request sets without owners. This way, all of the parameters and print options you specified will be locked (i.e., cannot be updated by users at run time) for the request set.

By employing request sets, request set owners, request groups, and request security groups, you can grant access and modification privileges to concurrent reports and programs on a user-by-user basis.

Review Question

I. How can you use request sets, ownership, request groups, and request security groups to control user access to programs?

Administering Concurrent Managers

In this section, you will learn how to administer Oracle's concurrent manager environment. When an application user submits a concurrent request (i.e., a request to run a program), the request is stored in a database table containing the queue of eligible concurrent requests. Concurrent managers are programs that run in the background, and whose job is to request and initiate the concurrent requests in order. The order that the requests are processed is determined by the scheduled start time, the request priority, and whether there are other, incompatible requests running. Run-alone requests and requests-on-hold also affect the ability of requests in the queue to be initiated by the concurrent managers. In this section, you will explore the following:

■ Defining managers and their work shifts

■ Specializing managers

■ Classifying a program as a request type

■ Controlling concurrent managers

■ Managing parallel concurrent processing

Defining Managers and Their Work Shifts

You can define any number of concurrent managers, but there is always one (and only one) Internal Concurrent Manager predefined by Oracle, whose definition cannot be altered. Its role is to activate, verify, reset, and shut down any other concurrent managers. Oracle Applications provides two other fundamental concurrent managers: Standard Concurrent Manager and Conflict Resolution Manager. The Standard Concurrent Manager is a catchall concurrent manager that is always running and can initiate any concurrent request. The Conflict Resolution Manager resolves program incompatibilities and determines if a request in the queue can be run concurrently with the other running programs. Oracle Applications provides one Conflict Resolution Manager—you cannot add more. You can, however, define additional concurrent managers of the type Concurrent Manager. To define a concurrent manager, follow the navigation path *Concurrent : Manager : Define.* In the form that appears, enter the manager name, a short name, an application module, and an optional description. The application module is for informational purposes only; it does not restrict which concurrent programs and reports cannot be run. Enter a type for the concurrent manager, which falls under the following categories:

- Concurrent Manager
- Internal Monitor
- Transaction Manager

CONCURRENT MANAGER   Concurrent managers are regular managers that initiate concurrent requests. The standard manager is an example of this type of concurrent manager.

INTERNAL MONITOR   Internal monitors are specialized processes that monitor the internal concurrent manager and provide higher fault tolerance in a parallel processing environment. When the internal concurrent manager fails in a parallel processing environment, the internal monitor will spawn a new internal concurrent manager on another node. There can be one and only one internal monitor on each node.

TRANSACTION MANAGER   Transaction managers process synchronous requests on the server from application users. A synchronous request from a client will be processed immediately, while the user waits. Once the transaction has completed, the completion status and data will be returned to the user. Transaction managers in Oracle Applications include demand reservation managers, material cost managers, material transaction managers, move transaction managers, and resource cost transaction managers. Transaction managers are launched through individual Oracle Applications modules such as Oracle Inventory. The requests handled by a transaction manager must originate from a user logged on with a responsibility that shares the same data group as the transaction manager.

Once you have selected the concurrent manager type, you must enter the data group (if the type is a transaction manager), as well as the cache size (if the type is a concurrent manager). Transaction manager–type concurrent managers can only process synchronous requests for the same data group. The cache size determines how many requests a concurrent manager will read into memory at one time. The cache size is very important because the concurrent manager will first process the requests in memory, prior to reading other requests from the database. So, setting the cache size to 5 means you only have to process three out of the five requests.

Even if a new request comes in with a priority higher than the two requests in memory, the new request will not be processed until the two requests in memory are processed. For concurrent managers that are used to run long-running programs and reports, the cache size should be a very small number, like 1, so that all requests will be reevaluated after the concurrent manager finishes processing each request.

If you are running in a parallel processing environment, you must specify the primary and secondary nodes, as well as the primary and secondary system queues, for all concurrent managers. See the "Manage Parallel Concurrent Processing" section for more details. As a last step, you must associate a program library with the concurrent managers. Concurrent managers can only run immediate-type concurrent programs that are included in the specified program library. None of the other concurrent programs are limited by the program library. Transaction manager–type concurrent managers can only run immediate-type concurrent programs. For the purposes of this exercise, examine the three seeded fundamental concurrent managers: the internal concurrent manager, the standard concurrent manager, and the conflict resolution manager. See Figure 8-16.

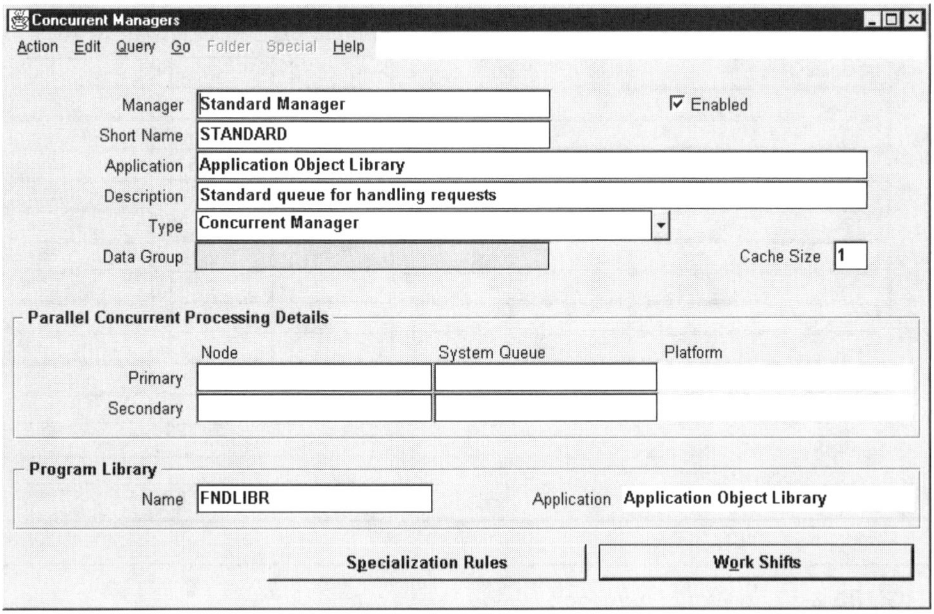

FIGURE 8-16.   *Concurrent Managers form*

Once you have defined the concurrent manager, click on the **Work Shifts** button to associate work shifts with the defined concurrent manager. For the Standard Manager, a Standard work shift is associated. A work shift is defined using the navigation path *Concurrent : Manager : WorkShifts.*

To define a work shift, fill in the fields for the work shift name, the From and To times, and the From and To days of the week. You can also specify a work shift to run on a particular date instead of From and To days of week. See Figure 8-17.

When you assign work shifts to a concurrent manager, you assign the number of target processes and sleep seconds along with it. The number of target processes determines how many concurrent requests the concurrent manager can process simultaneously during that particular work shift. The setting for sleep seconds determines how often the concurrent manager wakes up and reads concurrent requests from the database queue into memory. The number of requests read into memory at one time is based on the cache size.

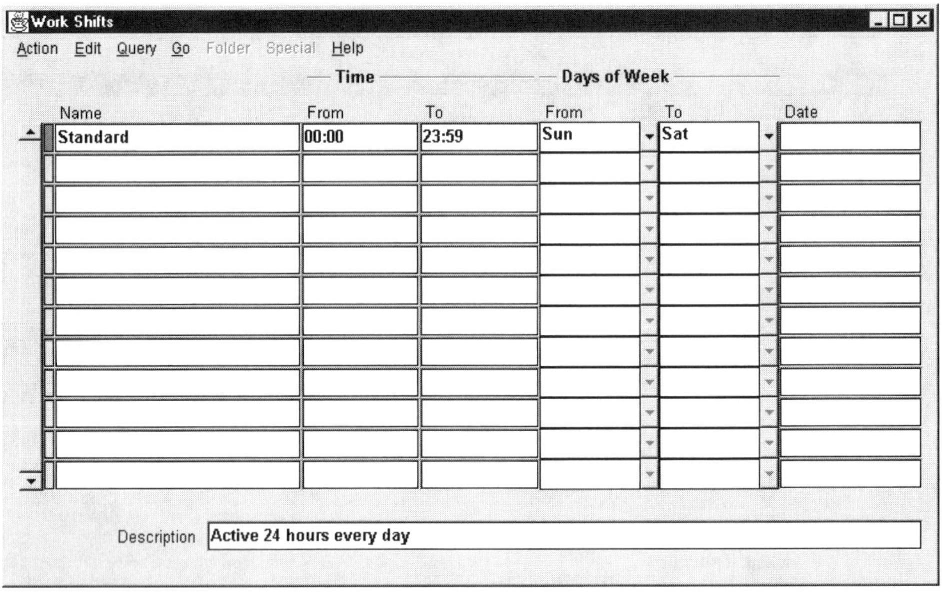

FIGURE 8-17. *Work Shifts form*

You can assign multiple work shifts to a concurrent manager. If the work shifts overlap, the most specific shift will override the next specific shift all the way to the most general shift. The most specific work shift to the most general work shift is defined as follows:

- ■ Specific date with specific From and To times

- ■ Specific date with times From 00:00 and To 23:59

- ■ Specific From and To days of week with specific From and To times

- ■ Specific From and To days of week with From time 00:00 and To time 23:59

- ■ Specific From and To times

- ■ Times From 00:00 and To 23:59; days of week From Sun To Sat

To balance the anticipated workload at specific times of the day, use multiple work shifts to change the number of target processes and sleep seconds throughout the day. See Figure 8-18.

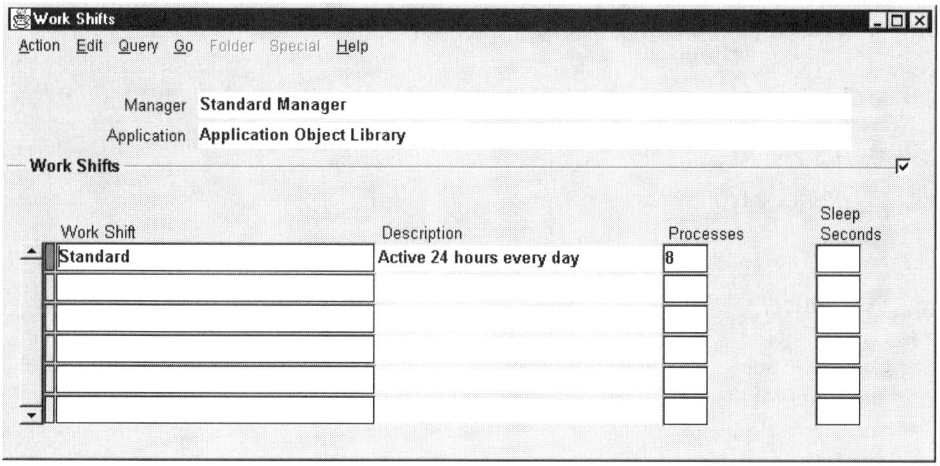

FIGURE 8-18. *Concurrent manager Work Shifts form*

Review Questions

1. What does an internal concurrent manager do?

2. How many internal concurrent managers do you have?

3. What are work shifts and how are overlapping work shifts prioritized in Oracle Applications?

4. What is unique about a transaction manager?

Specializing Managers

You can specialize concurrent managers by entering specialization rules for each concurrent manager. The specialization rules determine which concurrent requests can be processed by the concurrent manager. If a concurrent manager has no specialization rules, the concurrent manager can process all concurrent requests of types other than immediate and the immediate concurrent requests within the specified program library. Remember, transaction manager–type concurrent managers only process immediate-type concurrent requests included in the specified program library. Click on the **Specialization Rules** button to enter specialization rules. There is no need to enter any specialization rules for this exercise.

For each specialization rule, you must specify whether the rule includes or excludes certain types of requests. Valid types can be:

- Oracle ID
- Program
- Request type
- User
- Combined rules

Once you select the type, you may also need to enter the application (module) and the name of the item of the specified type.

Oracle ID

Enter the Oracle ID you want to include or exclude for your concurrent manager. If you choose this type, you do not need to enter the application name.

Program
Enter the program that you want to include or exclude for your concurrent manager. If you only enter an application module and leave the Name field blank, it will include or exclude all programs that belong to the specified application.

Request Type
Enter the request type (which is defined when you register a concurrent program) that you want to include or exclude for this concurrent manager.

User
Enter the application user that you want to include or exclude for this concurrent manager. If you choose this type, you do not need to enter the application name. See Figure 8-19.

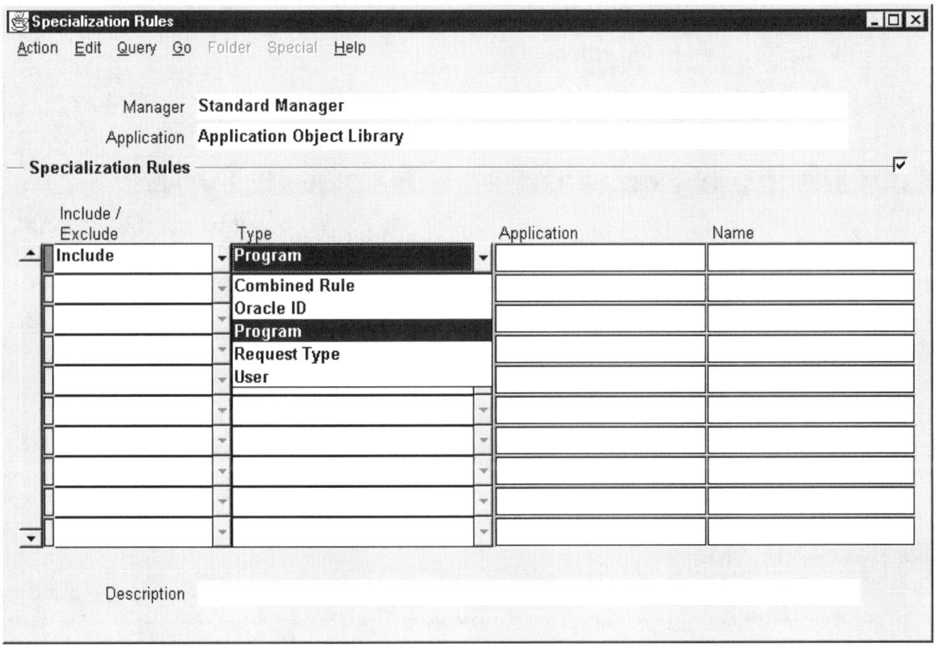

FIGURE 8-19. *Specialization Rules form*

Combined Rules

You can use a combined rule as a specialization rule. Before referencing a combined rule, it must first be defined on the Combined Specialization Rules form, using the navigation path *Concurrent : Manager : Rule.* When defining combined rules, note that the overall rule is the intersection (AND) of all the specialization rules. Note that this is different than defining specialization rules for a concurrent manager, where all of the rules are unioned (OR) together. So when defining a combined rule, it would make no sense to combine two rules that each include a different Oracle ID, because the intersection (AND) of the two rules would be empty. On the Specialization Rules form, select the predefined rule that you want to include or exclude.

Review Questions

1. What are specialization rules?

2. What types of specialization rules are there?

3. What is a combined rule?

4. What happens if the concurrent manager has no specialization rules?

Classifying a Program as a Request Type

You can define a concurrent program to be of a certain request type—this is done on the Concurrent Programs form. On the Concurrent Manager | Specialization Rules form, you can then define a rule to include or exclude a request type. The result would be that all programs registered with that request type would then be included or excluded from being processed by that concurrent manager. Define request types by using the navigation path *Concurrent : Program : Types.* Enter the request-type name, the application name, and an optional description. The application name is for informational purposes only and does not restrict what concurrent programs can be assigned to the request type. See Figure 8-20.

Review Question

1. For what scenarios can you use request type?

Controlling Concurrent Managers

You control the concurrent managers by using the Administer Concurrent Manager form and following the navigation path *Concurrent : Manager : Administer.* The

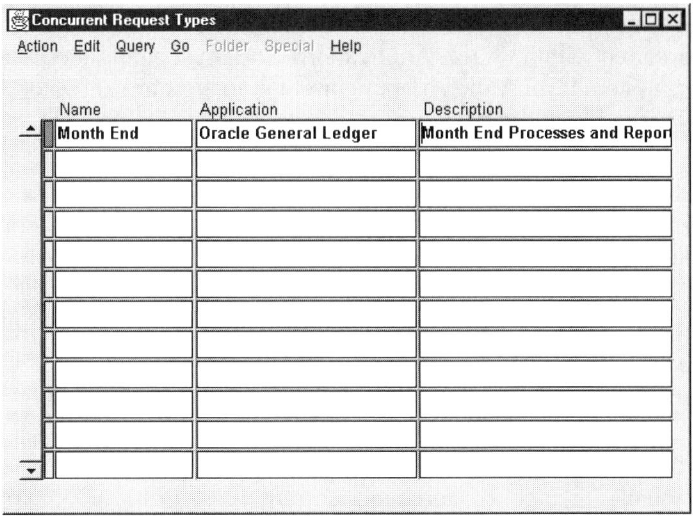

FIGURE 8-20. *Concurrent Request Types form*

Administer Concurrent Manager form displays the name of each concurrent manager, the node the concurrent manager is running on, the actual and target number of processes, and the number of requests running and pending. It also shows the status of all concurrent managers. The actual process is the number of processes actually running, and the target process is the number of target processes you defined for the work shift. If the actual process number is not the same as the target process, then your concurrent manager is probably starting up or coming down, or there are not enough requests in the queue to get the targeted number of processes started. If the number of actual processes is zero, then your concurrent manager is down or there are no requests in the queue. The number of requests running and pending reveals how well your concurrent managers are configured.

For the internal concurrent manager, you can use the Administer Concurrent Manager form to:

- Activate
- Terminate
- Deactivate
- Verify

Activate Internal Concurrent Manager

This activates the internal concurrent manager and all other concurrent managers. It cannot be started within Oracle Applications, and must be initiated from the operating system level. When all concurrent managers are activated, their definitions are read from the database.

Terminate Internal Concurrent Manager

This will terminate all running concurrent requests and deactivate all concurrent managers, as well as the internal concurrent manager.

Deactivate Internal Concurrent Manager

This will deactivate all concurrent managers and the internal concurrent manager. All running requests will be allowed to complete before the deactivation takes place.

Verify Internal Concurrent Manager

This will manually initiate the internal concurrent manager's PMON cycle, which verifies the status of each individual concurrent manager.

For other concurrent managers, you can use the Administer Concurrent Manager form to:

- Activate
- Restart
- Terminate
- Deactivate

Activate Other Concurrent Managers

This activates the selected concurrent manager. When the concurrent manager is activated, its definition is read from the database.

Restart Other Concurrent Managers

This forces the internal concurrent manager to reread the definition of the chosen concurrent manager. Use this if you have modified the concurrent manager's definition—including work shifts or specialization rules—and you want the change to take effect immediately.

Terminate Other Concurrent Managers

This will terminate all running concurrent requests and deactivate the chosen concurrent manager.

Deactivate Other Concurrent Managers

This will deactivate the chosen concurrent manager. All running requests will be allowed to complete before the deactivation takes place.

You can click on the **Requests** button to see pending and running requests associated with the chosen concurrent manager. See Figure 8-21 for the Administer Concurrent Managers form.

Processes

Click on the **Processes** button to view the details of the processes associated with the chosen concurrent manager, including all active, terminating, deactivated, and terminated process. The information displayed about each process includes the status of the process, the concurrent manager ID, the Oracle ID, the operating system ID, the running request concurrent ID, the running request system ID, and the start date of the concurrent manager process. Click on the **Internal Manager Log** button to see the log file associated with the internal concurrent manager and the **Manager Log** button to see the log file associated with the chosen concurrent manager. You can also click on the **Request Log** button to see the log file of the concurrent process. See Figure 8-22.

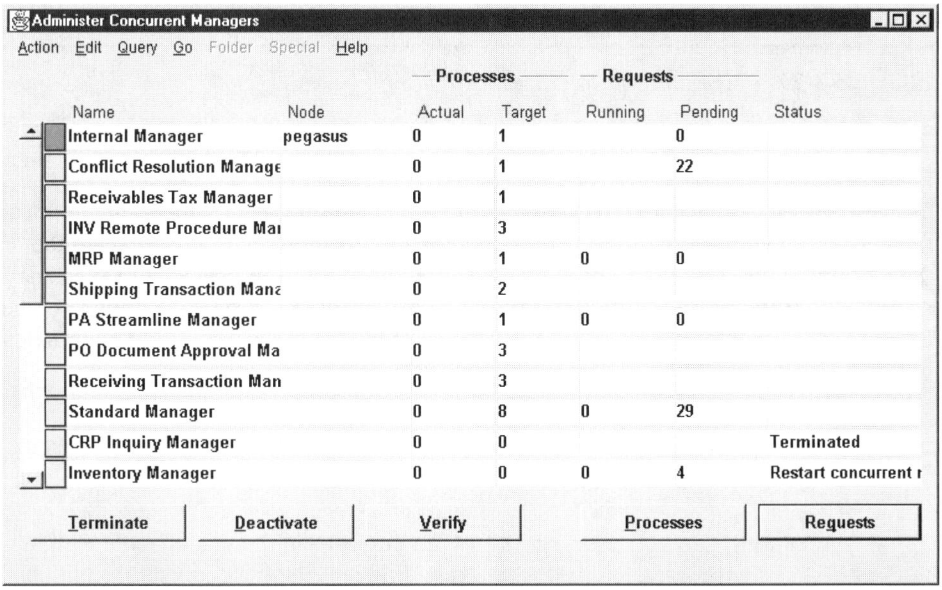

Administer Concurrent Managers

Action Edit Query Go Folder Special Help

| Name | Node | Processes | | Requests | | Status |
		Actual	Target	Running	Pending	
Internal Manager	pegasus	0	1		0	
Conflict Resolution Manage		0	1		22	
Receivables Tax Manager		0	1			
INV Remote Procedure Mar		0	3			
MRP Manager		0	1	0	0	
Shipping Transaction Mana		0	2			
PA Streamline Manager		0	1	0	0	
PO Document Approval Ma		0	3			
Receiving Transaction Man		0	3			
Standard Manager		0	8	0	29	
CRP Inquiry Manager		0	0			Terminated
Inventory Manager		0	0	0	4	Restart concurrent r

Terminate   Deactivate   Verify   Processes   Requests

FIGURE 8-21. *Administer Concurrent Managers form*

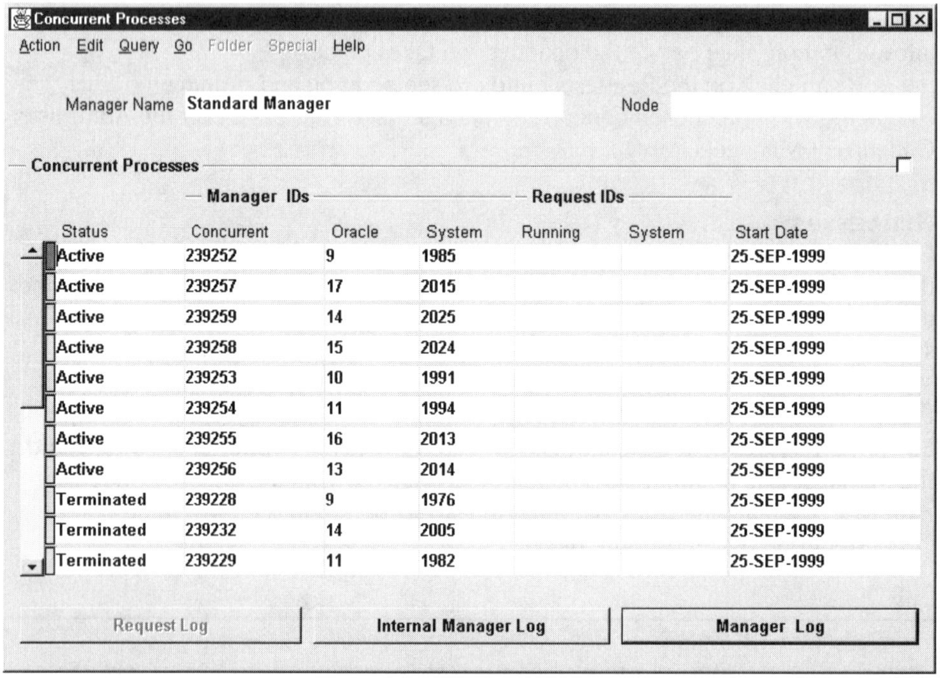

FIGURE 8-22. *Concurrent Processes form*

Requests

Click on the **Requests** button to view pending and running requests associated with the chosen concurrent manager. You can view the positions of the requests in the queue of the chosen concurrent manager, the request IDs, the phases and statuses of each concurrent request, the program names, and the requestors. In addition, you can view the request parameters at the bottom of the form. Click on the **Diagnostics** button to see the diagnostics of any particular running or pending concurrent request. See Figure 8-23.

Review Questions

1. What form can you use to control your concurrent managers?

2. What can you do with the internal concurrent manager that you cannot do with the other concurrent managers?

3. What are the reasons for the actual process number being less than the target process number?

4. What is the difference between deactivating a concurrent manager vs. terminating a concurrent manager?

Managing Parallel Concurrent Processing

In Oracle Applications, you have the option of running parallel concurrent processing in a clustered, massively parallel, or homogeneous networked environment. Parallel concurrent processing lets you distribute concurrent managers across multiple nodes and optionally use different system queues to integrate Oracle concurrent processing with the system-specific load-balancing packages. It works as follows.

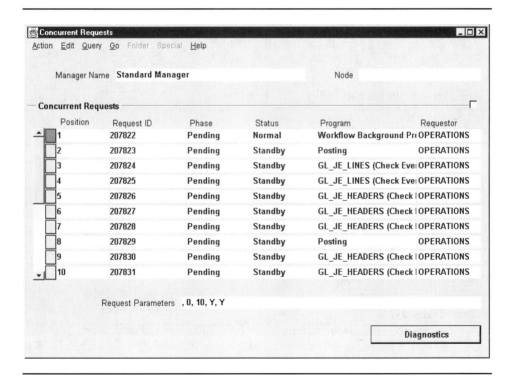

FIGURE 8-23. *Concurrent Requests form*

Concurrent managers can be defined to run on different nodes of your clustered, massively parallel, or homogeneous networked environments. The node either runs an Oracle instance or is configured to use SQL*Net to connect to a node that runs an Oracle instance. You can have a primary node and a secondary node for each concurrent manager. The concurrent manager starts on the primary node, but will switch temporarily to the secondary node in case of failure of the primary node. When the primary node comes back up, the concurrent manager will migrate its active processes back to the primary node.

The internal concurrent manager can run on any node and must be active at all times. To facilitate this, you need internal monitor processes running on different nodes. An internal monitor process will restart the Internal concurrent manager on the internal monitor's node as soon as the internal monitor process detects an internal concurrent manager failure. You can only have one internal monitor process running on a single node.

The benefits of parallel concurrent processing include the following:

- Better performance
- Integration with platform-specific load-balancing systems
- Fault tolerance
- Transparent to application users

Better Performance
You can gain performance improvement by spreading the concurrent managers across multiple nodes of your clustered, massively parallel, or homogeneous network environments because each node can have separate CPUs, memory, and other resources.

Integration with Platform-Specific Load-Balancing Systems
To maximize overall parallel concurrent processing on the operating system, you can integrate the concurrent processing of Oracle Applications with the platform-specific load-balancing packages.

Fault Tolerance
If a node fails, the concurrent manager—including the internal concurrent manager—can start on another node.

Transparency
The concurrent manager administration occurs in one place, and all of the log and output files are automatically shared across nodes. Besides the initial system setup, operation of parallel concurrent processing is transparent to the application

user. Application users manage the concurrent managers the same way, whether or not they are in a parallel processing environment. You can activate, terminate, and deactivate concurrent managers from any node. To manually migrate a concurrent manager from one node to another, change the primary node and the secondary node of the concurrent manager and restart the particular concurrent manager to read in the new definition. The target nodes on which the concurrent managers run are shown in the Administer Concurrent Manager form.

Review Questions

1. What are the uses of the primary node and the secondary node?
2. How does parallel concurrent processing work?
3. What are the benefits of parallel concurrent processing?
4. How will you manually migrate concurrent managers from one node to another?

Managing Profile Options

In this section, you will learn how to manage profile option values, which are updatable options that impact how the Oracle Applications behave. Some options may be set system wide and will impact all Oracle Applications. Also, each application has its own set of profile options. In this section, you will cover:

- Setting profile option values
- Using profile options for concurrent program parameters and flexfield segment defaults
- Typical modified profile options

Setting Profile Option Values

You can typically set profile options at four levels:

- Site
- Application
- Responsibility
- User

The user level overrides the setting at the responsibility level, at the application level, and at the site level. Based on the definition of a profile option, one or more of the levels may not be enterable or updateable.

There are two ways to set profile options:

- In user mode

- In system administrator mode

In User Mode

Application users can set profile option values for themselves by using the Personal Profile Values form. An application user may navigate to this form in different ways, depending on the responsibility they log on with. For example, the navigation path may be *Profile*, or *Other : Profile*, or *Control : Profile Options*, or *Setup : Personal Profile*. You can see all profile options that are viewable by the application user from this form, as well as the corresponding default values. To change the user value, simply enter the desired value in the User Value column. In a later section, we will cover some of the more commonly modified profile options. See Figure 8-24.

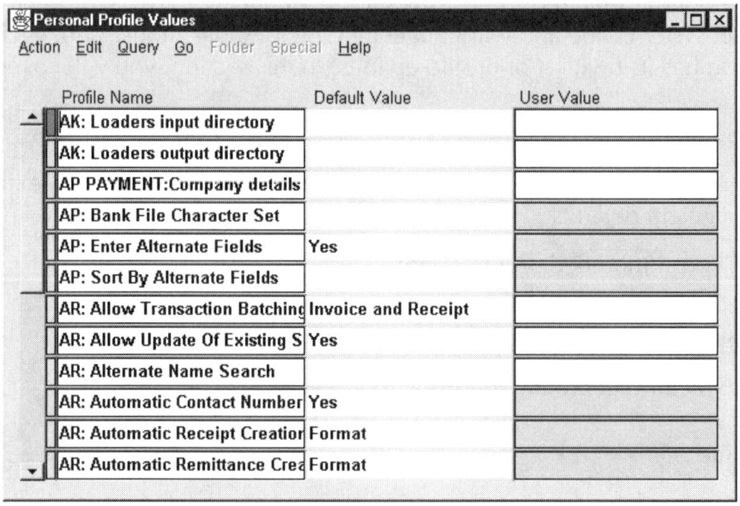

FIGURE 8-24. *Personal Profile Values form*

In System Administrator Mode

You can set up the profile option values in the system administrator mode on four levels: Site, Application, Responsibility, and User. As a system administrator, set up system profile options using the navigation path *Profile : System*. The Find System Profile Values window will appear, and you can select to display particular profile options for any given level. You can also view all profile options—even those with no value set. Unchecking the *Profiles with No Values* checkbox will only show profile options that have their values set. You can use wildcards to find all profile options. For example, to look for the profile options related to concurrent processing, enter **CONC%** in the Profile field. As your online exercise, try to find all concurrent processing–related profile options at the site level. See Figure 8-25.

You can also view all profile options, or those you select, for a specific application, responsibility, or user. For example, to see all profile options that belong to the General Ledger, Vision Operations (USA) responsibility, you can check the *Responsibility* checkbox and enter **General Ledger, Vision Operations (USA)** as the responsibility—or select it from the List of Values, and enter **%** (or nothing) in the Profile field. Then click on the **Find** button.

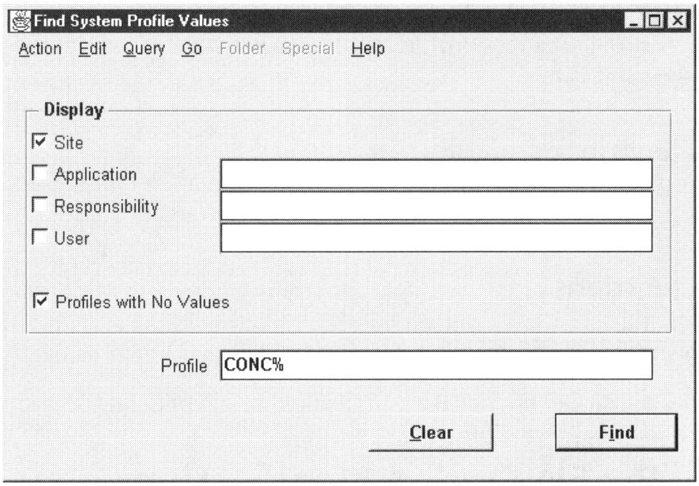

FIGURE 8-25. *System Profile options*

Review Questions

1. For how many levels can you set values in each profile option?

2. How are the levels related to each other?

3. What is the difference between changing profile options in user mode and in the system administrator mode?

Storing User Defaults in Profile Options

In this section, you will see how to use profile options in:

- Concurrent program parameters
- Flexfield segment defaults

Concurrent Program Parameters

You can use profile options as concurrent program parameters and request set parameters. To do this online, navigate to *Concurrent : Program : Define*, find the concurrent program whose parameter you wish to define, and click on the **Parameters** button. This will take you to the Concurrent Program Parameters form. In the validation region, enter **Profile** as the default type and the profile option name as the default value.

Flexfield Segment Defaults

Similarly, you can use profile options as flexfield segment defaults. Enter **Profile** as the default type and the profile option name as the default value.

Review Questions

1. How are profile options used in concurrent report parameters?

2. How are profile options used in flexfield segment defaults?

Typical Profile Option Modifications

There are many profile options in Oracle Applications, with the most commonly modified ones included in Table 8-3. Refer to each application module menu for a complete list of all profile options.

Profile Option	Description
GL Set of Books Name	Points the application user—or, more commonly, the responsibility—to a particular Set of Books.
OE: Set of Books	Points the responsibility—or more commonly, the application—to a particular Set of Books for order entry.
Concurrent: Active Request Limit	Limits the number of requests that can be run simultaneously.
Concurrent: Report Access Level	Can be set to User or Responsibility to determine whether to allow users within the same responsibility to share output files. User means no sharing.
Concurrent: Report Copies	Sets the number of copies that should be printed to the printer. This should be set to zero during development so as not to waste paper.
Currency: Negative Format	Allows you to set the default format for negative currency amounts.
Default Country	Allows you to set the default country to be used through Oracle Applications.
Flexfields: AutoSkip	Allows you to skip to the next segment of the flexfield whenever you enter enough characters to identify a unique value.
Flexfields: Open Descr Window	The Descriptive Flexfield window will be automatically opened when you navigate to it. This applies also to the Parameter window.
MO: Operating Unit	Sets the operating unit to which the user—or, more commonly, the responsibility—points.
Printer	Sets the default printer for the user.

TABLE 8-3. *Commonly Modified Profile Options*

Profile Option	Description
Site Name	Identifies the site name for the Oracle Applications site.
OE: Item Validation Organization	Specifies the inventory organization used to validate order entry.
PO: MFG Organization ID	Specifies the inventory organization used as the manufacturing inventory organization in Oracle Purchasing.
HR: Business Group	Specifies the associated business group.
Budgetary Control Group	Specifies the budgetary control group used in budgetary control.
FSG: Enforce Segment Value Security	Specifies whether security rules are specified in FSG (Financial Statement Generator) reports.
Intercompany: Subsidiary	Specifies the associated subsidiary defined under CENTRA.
MRC: Reporting Set of Books	Specifies the associated Reporting Set of Books for MRC responsibilities.
QuickPick: AutoReduction	Allows you to skip to the next unique character when typing characters in a List of Values window, instead of to the next character.
Utilities: SQL Trace	Allows you to generate SQL trace files from Oracle Applications.

TABLE 8-3. *Commonly Modified Profile Options* (continued)

Review Questions

1. What is the purpose of the profile option *Printer*?

2. For what is the profile option *Flexfields: Open Descr Window* used?

3. What is the purpose of the profile option *MRC: Reporting Set of Books*?

4. For what is the profile option *MO: Operating Unit* used?

Auditing System Resources

In this section, you will study how to audit system resources within Oracle Applications. You will learn:

- Ways to audit Oracle Applications performance and resources
- How to modify auditing-related profile options
- How to use auditing reports
- How to implement auditing to suit your environment

Ways to Audit Oracle Applications Performance and Resources

There are two auditing types in Oracle Applications:

- Users
- Database Changes

Users

You can audit users at four different levels. The level is determined by the profile option *Sign-On: Audit Level*. The four levels are described in Table 8-4.

Audit Level Name	Description
None	No auditing
User	Audit the sign-on application user name, time, and the terminal
Responsibility	Audit the sign-on application user name, time, the terminal, the responsibilities chosen, and the time used for each responsibility
Form	Audit the sign-on application user name, time, the terminal, the responsibilities chosen, the time used for each responsibility, the forms the user utilizes, and the time used for each form

TABLE 8-4. *Audit Levels*

If you set the *Sign-On: Audit Level* option to a level other than None, you can then monitor users online using the Monitor Users form. Follow the navigation path *Security : User : Monitor.* Audit reports will be covered in a later section.

Database Changes
You can set up audit trails to track changes users make in the Oracle database. To enable the audit trail, you must:

- Define audit installations
- Define audit groups
- Define audit tables
- Run the audit trail update tables request

DEFINE AUDIT INSTALLATIONS   During installation, you must enable audit trails for an Oracle database user ID. Follow the navigation path *Security : AuditTrail : Install.* Select the Oracle user name for which you want to enable audit trails and check the *Audit Enabled* checkbox.

DEFINE AUDIT GROUPS   Next, you must define audit groups to identify what tables you wish to audit. For custom tables to appear in the List of Values you select from, you must first register them. To define audit groups, follow the navigation path *Security : AuditTrail : Groups.* On the Audit Groups form, select the application name and enter the audit group name. The combination must be unique across the entire Oracle Applications. Again, the application name is for informational purposes only and will not restrict any table to be audited. The group state displays the state of the audit group. Valid audit group states are Enable Requested, Disable – Interrupt Audit, Disable – Prepare for Archive, Disable – Purge Table, and Enabled.

When you first create an audit group, the state is Enable Requested; after you run the audit trail update tables request, the state becomes Enabled. To disable auditing, you have three choices. You can disable audit by changing the state to Disable – Interrupt Audit. This allows you to interrupt auditing and write one final row into the shadow table whenever the row is being modified (this is a slow disable). Or, you can change the state to Disable – Prepare for Archive. This allows you to copy the existing values of all audited rows to the shadow table immediately and disable auditing right away. You usually use this disable option to perform an archive and enable auditing again. Before you enable auditing again, you must manually purge the shadow table. You can also change the state to Disable – Purge

Table to purge the shadow table and disable auditing immediately. You can also enter an optional description for your audit group.

Next, enter the audit tables to be included in your audit group. Select the user table name. The system table name, and the application, and the description will be automatically filled in. For your online exercise, create an audit group called NEW Audit Group and select a few GL tables such as GL_BALANCES and GL_CODE_COMBINATIONS. See Figure 8-26.

DEFINE AUDIT TABLES   Next, select the columns to be audited for each audited table. Once the columns are selected, they cannot be deleted. Columns can be selected from a List of Values, where the primary-keys column will have the *Primary Key* checkbox checked. All of the primary keys will be automatically audited. You can add the columns using the Define Audit Tables form. To define audit tables, you can follow the navigation path *Security : AuditTrail : Tables.*

Then, query up the user table name and go to the Audit Columns section. Select the columns you wish to audit. See Figure 8-27.

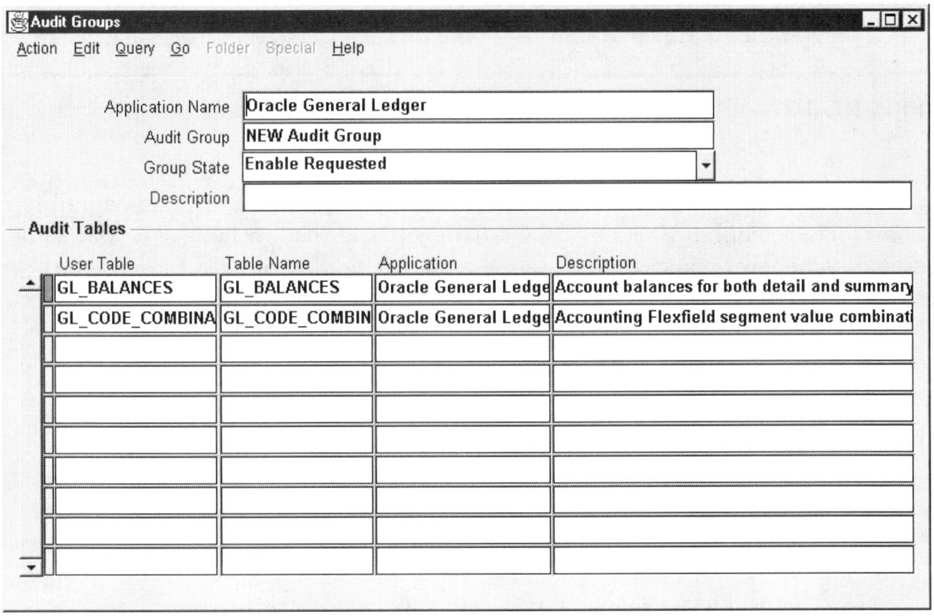

FIGURE 8-26.   *Audit Groups form*

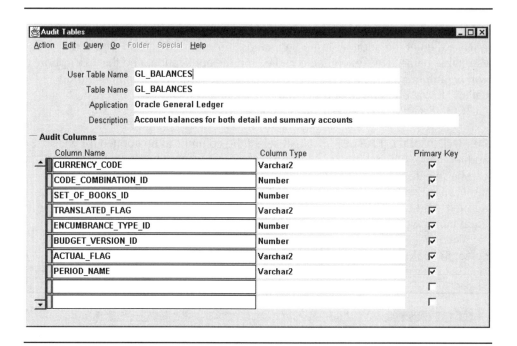

FIGURE 8-27. *Audit Tables form*

RUN THE AUDIT TRAIL UPDATE TABLES REQUEST   The audit trail update tables request generates database triggers and shadow tables for your audit groups. Whenever you change the audit groups or audit tables definitions, you must rerun this request. Run this request through SRS and the audit trail will be enabled. Do not perform this for the purposes of this exercise unless you have enough system resources to perform the auditing you have defined.

Review Questions

   1. At what level can you audit the sign-on information?

   2. What are the four steps in auditing database changes?

   3. What will the Disable – Prepare for Archive state do?

   4. What will the audit trail update tables request do?

How to Modify Auditing-Related Profile Options

Table 8-5 lists all of the audit-related profile options.

Profile Option	Description
AuditTrail: Activate	Specifies whether the audit trail is activated. If activated, each time a record is created or updated, the user's name and the current time will be stored. This is called the WHO information. When you use *Help : About This Record...*, the user that created or updated the row will show up.
Sign-On: Audit Level	Specifies at what level the application user sign-on should be audited. Valid choices are None, User, Responsibility, and Form.
Sign-On: Notification	Specifies whether an application user should be notified during sign-on if there are unsuccessful sign-ons with this user name prior to the current sign-on, if there are failed concurrent requests since the last sign-on, or if the default printer in your *Printer* profile option is invalid.
Sign-On: Password Length	Specifies the minimum password length. If not specified, the minimum is five characters.

TABLE 8-5. *Audit-Related Profile Options*

Review Questions

1. What will the *AuditTrail: Activate* profile option do?

2. What will the *Sign-On: Notification* profile option do?

3. What is the WHO information?

How to Use Auditing Reports

Table 8-6 shows all of the sign-on auditing reports.

You must write your own report for database change audits. The name of the shadow table created for each audited table is the first 26 characters of the audited table name with the suffix _A. The shadow table consists of all the audited columns, plus special auditing columns. Table 8-7 shows the special auditing columns. Oracle does not guarantee that the shadow audit table structure will remain the same from program version to program version, so you will be wise to check this before upgrading a working system to a later version.

Report Name	Description
Sign-on Audit Concurrent Requests	Lists the concurrent requests submitted by the application user
Sign-on Audit Forms	Lists the forms accessed by the application user and the total access time
Sign-on Audit Responsibilities	Lists the responsibilities used by the application user and the total access time
Sign-on Audit Unsuccessful Logins	Lists the unsuccessful logins
Sign-on Audit Users	Lists the users and the total access time

TABLE 8-6.   *Sign-On Audit Reports*

Audit Column	Description
AUDIT_USER_NAME	The application user name or Oracle database user ID
AUDIT_TIMESTAMP	The creation date and time when the audit row is created
AUDIT_TRANSACTION_TYPE	(C)urrent, (D)elete, (I)nsert, (L)ast, or (U)pdate
AUDIT_TRUE_NULLS	Delimited list of column names that have changed from nulls to values
Primary Key	All columns of the audited table that compose the primary key

TABLE 8-7.   *Special Auditing Columns*

Review Questions

   1. What sign-on audit reports are available?

   2. What special auditing columns are added to the shadow tables?

   3. How are the shadow tables named?

How to Implement Auditing to Suit Your Environment

Depending on your auditing needs, you can determine whether you need application users to be able to see the normal or extended "About this Record..." information. This information includes created by, creation date, last updated by, last update date, operating system log-on, and terminal identification. Then, determine whether you want to audit sign-ons and at what level. Finally, decide whether you need to audit database changes. If so, then determine what tables and columns you want to audit and write your own audit reports.

Keep in mind that all auditing requires additional resources—especially when you audit database changes at column levels. The amount of additional resources necessary depends on how much data you are auditing and how many changes you make each day. The archiving mechanism must also be put into place, and archiving and purging of the shadow tables needs to be routine.

Review Question

1. What do you need to consider when implementing auditing?

Document Sequencing

Use document sequencing to assign unique numbers to documents. These sequence numbers are stored in an audit table even when the original transactions are deleted. This will help maintain an audit trail and ensure completeness of your document trail. In this section, you will review:

- Document sequence types
- Sequencing documents in Oracle Applications

Document Sequence Types

There are three types of document sequences:

- Automatic
- Gapless
- Manual

Automatic

Automatic numbering automatically assigns a unique document sequence number when the transaction/document is created. If the transaction is aborted and not saved, the sequence number is not reused.

Gapless

Gapless numbering is nearly identical to automatic numbering except that the unique document sequence number is not assigned until the transaction/document is successfully created. Instead, it waits until the transaction/document is saved. This type may affect system performance and should only be chosen if absolutely necessary.

Manual

Manual numbering allows the user to enter a unique document sequence number when the transaction/document is created.

Review Questions

1. What are the three document sequence types?

2. When should you use the gapless document sequence type?

Sequencing Documents in Oracle Applications

In order to sequence documents, you must do the following things:

- Define document sequence
- Verify document categories
- Assign a document sequence

Define Document Sequence

To define a document sequence, use the navigation path *Application: Document: Define*. First, enter the sequence name and select the document's related application. For example, when creating a sequence for payables invoices, the application will be Oracle Payables. For your online exercise, you can create a sequence for your journal entries by using the name NEW journal entries and the application Oracle General Ledger. You can enter an Effective To date if you want to disable this document sequence in the future; otherwise, leave the Effective To date blank. In selecting the document sequence types—automatic, gapless, or manual—choose automatic as your document sequence type. Next, check the *Message* checkbox if you want to display a message to the user when the document sequence number is generated for their transaction. Finally, enter an initial value—the default is one. The *Message* checkbox and the Initial Value column are not available for manual numbering.

In the Access region of the Document Sequences form, enter the Oracle user name that belongs to the application that will access this document sequence. For Oracle Applications, you almost always select the APPS user, so choose it for your document sequence. Save your work. This will cause a concurrent program named Create Sequences and Access to Sequences to be submitted automatically to create the document sequence. Use View My Requests to verify completion of the concurrent request. See Figure 8-28.

Verify Document Categories

Next, you must verify the document categories to which you want to assign your document sequences. These predefined document categories are used for grouping data in the document tables in a logical manner. For example, you will notice that you have different categories for journal entries. Follow the navigation path

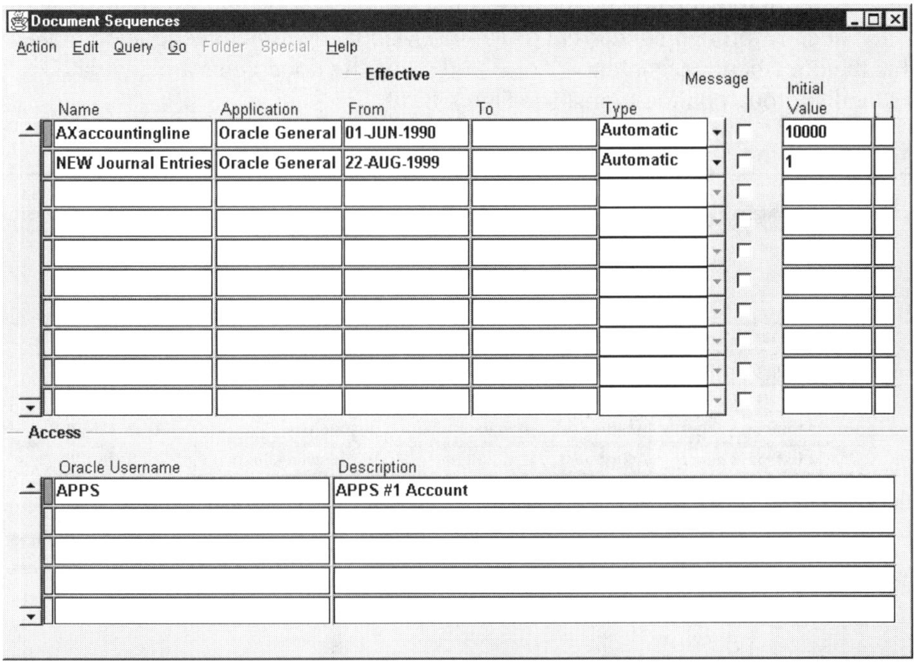

FIGURE 8-28. *Document Sequences form*

Application : Document : Categories. You can use the defined document sequence for all the journal entries categories of the same table, or just one particular category. In your case, use your document sequence only for the Budget journal entries. See Figure 8-29.

Assign a Document Sequence

As a last step, you must assign the document sequence to the document category by entering the application name and document category. Go to the Sequence Assignments form, using the navigation path *Application : Document : Assign.* For your online exercise, select Application = Oracle General Ledger, and Category = Budget. Next, enter a start and an optional end date to determine when the document sequence is in effect. Enter the system date as the start date, leave the end date blank, and select your document sequence name. Use the optional document flexfield to enter a Set of Books and a method to further restrict the document sequence assignment. Set of Books specifies the Set of Books for which the document sequence assignment is valid. Otherwise, the document sequence is valid for all Sets of Books. The method specifies whether the document sequence assignment is only valid for automatic document generation or manual document generation. Automatic document generation means the documents are generated automatically through concurrent programs. Manual document generation means that the document assignment is only valid when the documents are generated manually through online forms. See Figure 8-30.

Application	Code	Name	Description	Table Name
Oracle General Ledger	AP Subledger	AP Subledger Entries	AP Subledger Entries	GL_JE_HEADERS
Oracle General Ledger	AR Subledger	AR Subledger Entries	AR Subledger Entries	GL_JE_HEADERS
Oracle General Ledger	Accrual	Accrual	Month End Accrual En	GL_JE_HEADERS
Oracle General Ledger	Addition	Addition	Addition	GL_JE_HEADERS
Oracle General Ledger	Adjustment	Adjustment	Adjusting Journal Entr	GL_JE_HEADERS
Oracle General Ledger	Allocation	Allocation	Allocation	GL_JE_HEADERS
Oracle General Ledger	Bank Charges	Bank Charges	Bank Collection Charg	GL_JE_HEADERS
Oracle General Ledger	Bank Receipts	Bank Receipts	Bank Collection Recei	GL_JE_HEADERS
Oracle General Ledger	Budget	Budget	Budget	GL_JE_HEADERS
Oracle General Ledger	Burden Cost	Burden Cost	Burden Cost	GL_JE_HEADERS

FIGURE 8-29. *Document Categories form*

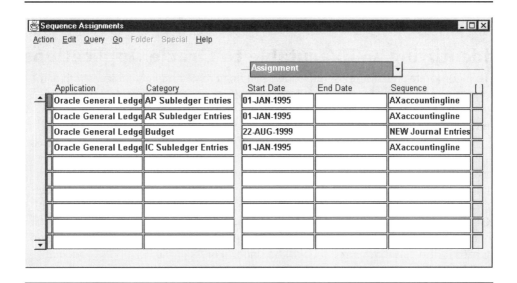

FIGURE 8-30. *Sequence Assignments form*

Review Questions

1. When you define a document sequence, what is the application name used for?

2. What is a document category?

3. By what do you assign document sequences?

Incorporating Custom Programs

In this section, you will learn how to incorporate custom programs, including:

- Identifying an executable to Oracle Applications

- Defining a concurrent program

- Specifying concurrent program parameter information

Oracle Applications comes seeded with many concurrent reports and programs. However, you will most likely need to extend Oracle applications by creating custom reports for any Oracle Applications installation. Oracle suggests you create your own custom application before incorporating custom programs. Since this is out of the scope of the exam, you will not be creating a custom application.

Identifying an Executable to Oracle Applications

To incorporate a custom program, you must first create an executable, which is the operating system file for the concurrent program. For Oracle Reports, for example, the executable is the .RDF executable file. To define an executable, you follow the navigation path *Concurrent : Program : Executable.*

First, enter the required fields, including the executable name, the executable short name, and the application. The executable name is the user name that associates the executable to a concurrent program. The application determines the top directory/base path for the operating system file. For example, if you select Oracle General Ledger as the application, the program file will be found in the GL_TOP directory. You can also enter an optional description. Next, select an execution method, which determines what type of program you are registering and what subdirectory the source file will be under. For example, SQL*Plus executables will be in the subdirectory named **sql** and SQL*Loader or C executables will be in the subdirectory named **bin**. Valid execution methods are included in Table 8-8.

Once you have entered the execution method, enter the required execution filename, which is the operating system filename. If the execution method is Immediate or Spawned, enter the subroutine name in the Subroutine Name field. If the execution method is Request Set Stage Function, click on the **Stage Function Parameters** button to enter parameters. For your online exercise, just query up a few existing program executables to become familiar with the process. See Figure 8-31 for the Concurrent Program Executable form.

Execution Method	Description
Host	Operating system file
Immediate	Concurrent manager program library subroutine
Oracle Reports	Oracle Reports reports
PL/SQL Stored Procedure	Database stored procedure
Request Set Stage Function	Database stored function that calculates the completion statuses of request set stages
Spawned	C or Pro*C program
SQL*Loader	SQL*Loader control file
SQL*Plus	SQL*Plus or PL/SQL program files

TABLE 8-8. *Execution Methods*

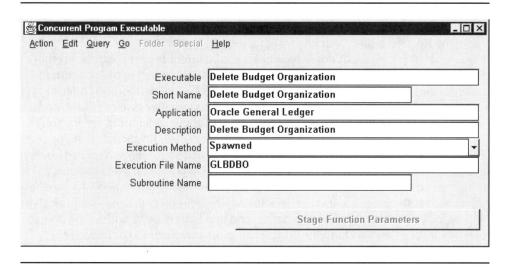

FIGURE 8-31. *Concurrent Program Executable form*

Review Questions

1. For what situation is the application name and the execution method of the executable used?

2. What are the various execution methods?

3. What is the required component of an executable definition?

4. What is the purpose of the Subroutine Name field?

Defining a Concurrent Program

Once you have defined the executable, you can now define a concurrent program. Follow the navigation path *Concurrent : Program : Define*. First, enter the concurrent program name, which will appear to the user in the Submit Request and the View My Requests forms. Check the *Enabled* checkbox to enable the concurrent program. Next, enter a unique short name and the application name. The application name identifies the location of the output and log files, as well as which Oracle database user ID to use at execution time. Enter an optional description.

In the Executable region, select the defined executable. If the execution method is Oracle Reports and the report is in bitmapped mode, you must enter **VERSION=2.0b** in the Options field. You can also pass ORIENTATION and PAGESIZE parameters to bitmapped reports, and assign a priority to the concurrent program. If no priority is defined, the priority will be based on the profile option *Concurrent: Priority* value.

In the Request region, you can assign a request type to the concurrent program. If you wish, you can also identify whether the concurrent program can be used in SRS, whether disabled values are allowed as parameters, whether the concurrent program must be run alone, whether a trace should be enabled for the concurrent program, whether the concurrent program should restart after system failure, and whether the concurrent program is NLS (National Language Support) compliant.

In the Output region, select a valid format type: HTML, PostScript, PDF, or Text. Then, decide whether you want to save and/or print the output file. You can also enter the minimum column and row length for the output file. If you enter the minimum column and row length, some print styles may be eliminated. Key in the print style for the program. If you check the *Style Required* checkbox, the print style will be locked for the concurrent program and application users will not be able to override it. You can also limit the concurrent program to print to a dedicated printer. See Figure 8-32.

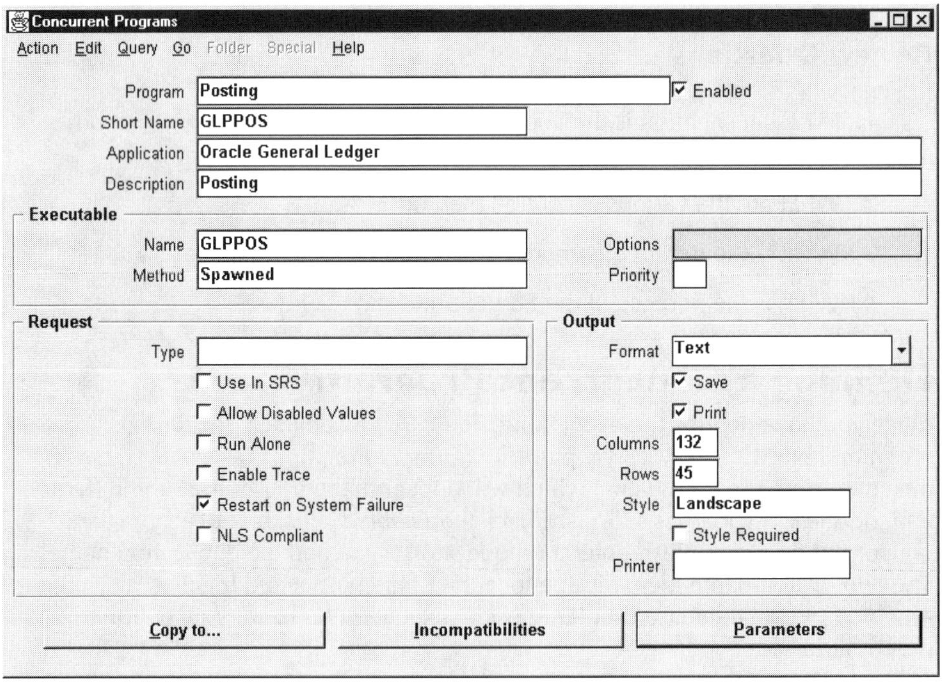

FIGURE 8-32. *Concurrent Programs form*

Click on the **Incompatibilities** button to identify concurrent programs that should not be running along with this particular program. To enter incompatible programs, enter the application and program name. Next, identify whether the scope of incompatibility is a set, or just the individual program alone. A set means that the incompatible program and all its spawned children are incompatible with the concurrent program being defined. One common usage of incompatible programs is to make a program incompatible with itself. For example, when you post using the posting program, you do not want another posting program running since the result may be very unpredictable. See Figure 8-33 for the Incompatible Programs form.

Review Questions

1. What do you need to do for a bitmapped Oracle Reports report?

2. What are the incompatible programs used for?

3. What can you enter for an output format type?

4. What is the purpose of the Priority field?

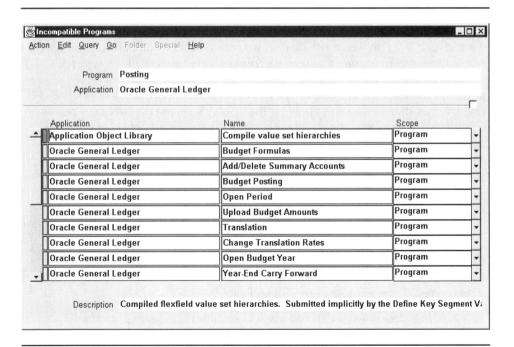

FIGURE 8-33. *Incompatible Programs form*

Specifying Concurrent Program Parameter Information

Click on the **Parameters** button to specify parameters for the concurrent program. For each parameter, enter a sequence number, a parameter name, a description, and whether you want to enable the parameter.

In the Validation region, enter a value set to govern valid values of the parameters. You can also enter a default type and a default value. Default types can be Constant, Current Date, Current Time, Profile, SQL Statement, or Segment. A default value may be defined for a default type of Constant, Profile, SQL Statement, or Segments. For Constant, the default value will be the literal value entered in the Default Value field. For Profile, enter the profile option name in the Default Value field; at execution time, the default value of the parameter will be set to the value of that profile option. For SQL Statement, enter a SQL statement in the Default Value field. For Segments, the default value will be the segment name.

You can determine whether the parameter is required, and you can decide whether you want to enable security for the parameter. If you wish, you can enter Low, High, or Pair as the range. If you enter Low in one parameter, you must enter High for another parameter; otherwise, when the application user submits the program it will produce an error. The low and the high ranges are used to govern two parameters that identify a range. For example, the low can be a start date and the high can be an end date. Oracle Applications will ensure that the end date is after the start date. For Pair, you must identify two parameters as a pair and, again, Oracle Applications will make sure that both parameters identified as Pair are entered.

Check the *Display* checkbox if you want the parameter to be displayed. (If you do not want the application user to change the parameter, uncheck the *Display* checkbox.) As a last step, enter the display size, the description size, the concatenated description size, and the prompt. If the concurrent program is of execution method Oracle Reports, you will need to enter a token—equal to the parameter name defined in Oracle Reports—in the Token field. See Figure 8-34.

Once you have defined the concurrent program and its incompatible programs and parameters, you may click on the **Copy to** button to copy the concurrent program definition to create a new concurrent program. You can also choose (optionally) to copy the incompatibilities and parameters of the concurrent program.

Review Questions

1. What is the purpose of the Token field?

2. What default types can you use for concurrent program parameters?

3. For what is the *Display* checkbox used?

4. What can you use the Range field for?

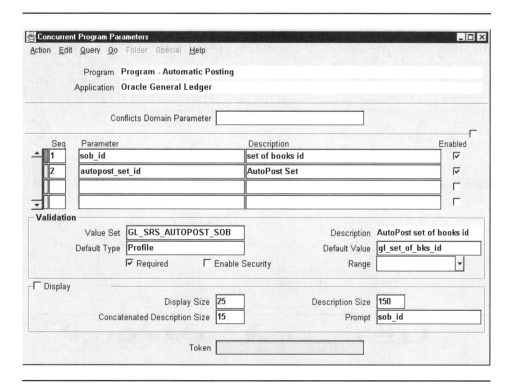

FIGURE 8-34. *Concurrent Program Parameters form*

Managing Printers

In the last section in this chapter, we'll discuss printers. If an output file must be printed, Oracle Applications uses the SRW driver in the Printer Drivers form to determine values for carriage return, page break, and other functions. If a printed output file is unnecessary, then Oracle Applications uses the SRW driver named in the Print Styles form to determine values for carriage return, page break, and other functions. In this section, you will learn to:

- Define printer types
- Register printers
- Associate output files to various printer components
- Create a custom print style and printer driver

Defining Printer Types

To define printer types, follow the navigation path *Install : Printer : Types.* Enter the printer type and a description. Next, using the List of Values, select the print styles and driver names to include in the printer type. Oracle Applications come seeded with many print styles and driver names, and you will learn how to customize your own later in this section. You can click on the **Style** button or the **Driver** button to create new print styles or printer drivers, or to find out details on existing ones. See Figure 8-35.

Review Questions

1. How do you assign a printer driver to a printer type?
2. Which two components are associated with a printer type?

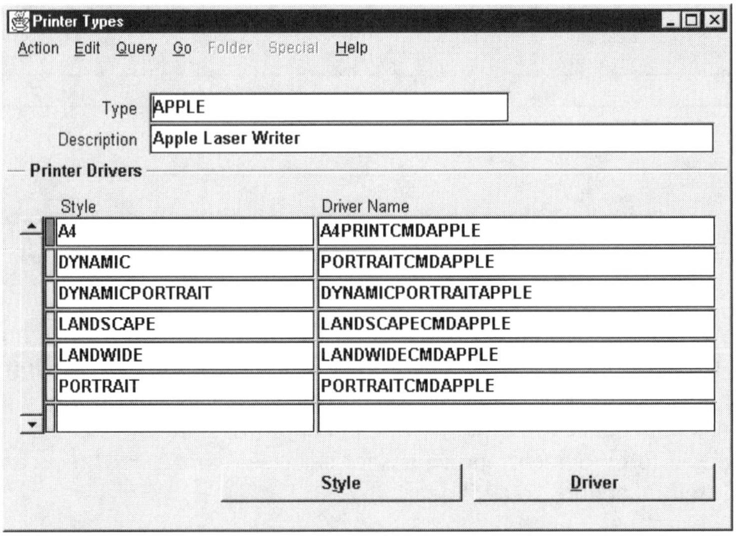
Printer Types

Action Edit Query Go Folder Special Help

Type: APPLE

Description: Apple Laser Writer

Printer Drivers

Style	Driver Name
A4	A4PRINTCMDAPPLE
DYNAMIC	PORTRAITCMDAPPLE
DYNAMICPORTRAIT	DYNAMICPORTRAITAPPLE
LANDSCAPE	LANDSCAPECMDAPPLE
LANDWIDE	LANDWIDECMDAPPLE
PORTRAIT	PORTRAITCMDAPPLE

Style Driver

FIGURE 8-35. *Printer Types form*

Registering Printers

Follow the navigation path *Install : Printer : Register*, then register the printer by providing a printer name, type, and description. The printer name is used to assign the printer to the *Printer* profile option.

Review Question

    1. How do you register a printer?

Associating Output Files to Various Printer Components

Print type is defined by the print style. Because of this, when you select a print style and driver for each printer type, you have also assigned a print type and driver to a printer type. When an output file is printed, it uses the printer driver associated to the combination of printer type and print style.

Review Question

    1. How are the output files linked with the various printer components?

Creating a Custom Print Style and Printer Driver

In this section, you will learn to create a custom:

- Print style
- Printer driver

Print Style

The print style describes how the report should be printed. Define a print style through the navigation path *Install : Printer : Style*, then enter the style name, the sequence number, the user style name, the SRW driver, and an optional description. The sequence number is only used for ordering purposes, and the SRW driver is the operating system driver file that will be used for this print style. You can also specify the number of columns and rows, as well as the orientation of the print style. To suppress the header page whenever this print style is used, check the *Suppress Header* box. See Figure 8-36.

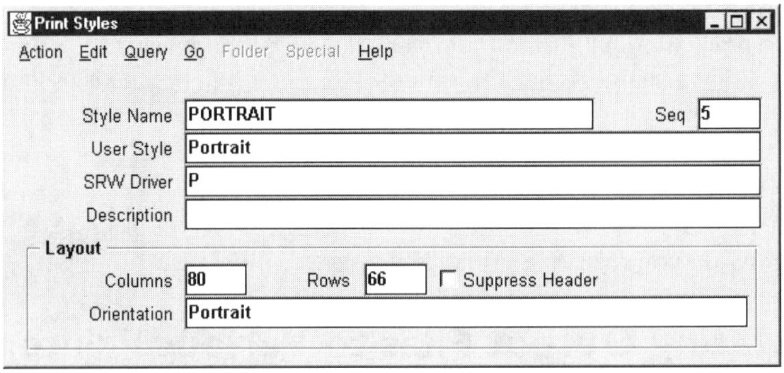

FIGURE 8-36. *Print Styles form*

Printer Driver

The printer driver describes the set of commands to be used for printing. Define a printer driver through the navigation path *Install : Printer : Driver,* then enter the driver name and the user driver name as well as an optional description for the printer driver. Next, enter the SRW driver for the printer driver. The SRW driver is defined both in the printer driver and the print style because, based on whether the output file is printed, a different SRW driver will be used. Enter the platform of the printer driver.

Select Command, Program, or Subroutine from the Driver Method region. The Command driver method uses the operating system command to print; the Program driver method uses a custom print program to print; and the Subroutine driver method uses a predefined Oracle Applications routine. In the Driver Method Parameters region, check *Spool File* to indicate if the printer driver should create its own copy of the output file for printing. You can also check *Standard Input* to indicate whether the printer driver accepts standard input. The Program Name field is used to specify the program name if the driver method is Program, or the subroutine name if the driver method is Subroutine.

As a last step, enter the Arguments, Initialization, and Reset strings. Enter the arguments for the Command driver method, which will be the operating system print command and its arguments. The Initialization field is the command string that will be sent to the printer as the initialization string, and the Reset field is the command string that will be sent to the printer as the reset string. See Figure 8-37.

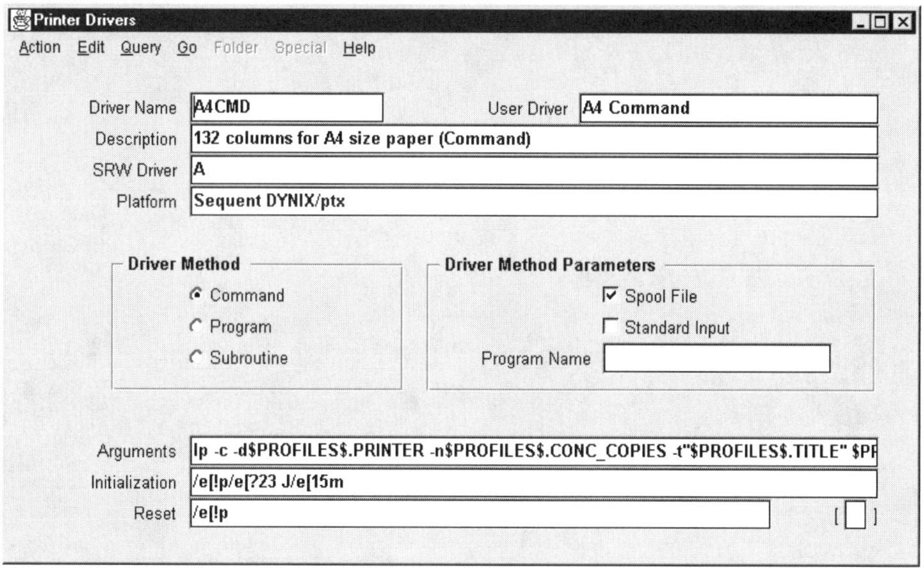

FIGURE 8-37. *Printer Drivers form*

Review Questions

1. What is a print style?

2. What is a printer driver?

3. What are the Command, Program, and Subroutine driver methods?

For the Chapter Summary, Two-Minute Drill, and Chapter Questions and Answers, open the summary.htm file contained in the Summary_files directory on the book's CD-ROM.

CHAPTER
9

Flexfields

n this chapter, you will take a comprehensive look at flexfields and how they are used in Oracle Applications. This study will include the following topics:

- Overview of flexfields

- Implementing value sets

- Planning and defining Key flexfields

- Planning and defining Descriptive flexfields

- Implementing cross-validation rules

- Implementing flexfield value security

- Using advanced validation capabilities

Oracle Applications uses two kinds of flexfields: Key flexfields and Descriptive flexfields. This chapter will present an overview of these two kinds of flexfields in terms of their respective utilization and differences. Next, it will discuss value sets and how they are used for validating both Key flexfields and Descriptive flexfields. In addition, you will be introduced to details involved in planning and defining Key flexfields, as well as Descriptive flexfields. You will also learn about flexfield qualifiers, segment qualifiers, flexfield structures, global descriptive segments, and context-sensitive Descriptive flexfields.

The chapter also covers flexfield security. You will see how to implement flexfield security with cross-validation rules as well as security rules. You will also study how multiple cross-validation rules interact and work together, and explore how multiple security rules interact and work together. At the end of this chapter, you should be able to perform more advanced validation capabilities. These capabilities include cascading flexfields and the use of special and pair value sets.

Flexfield Overview

The first section of this chapter will give you an overview of flexfields in Oracle Applications. This will include the following:

- Explaining flexfields and how they are used by Oracle Applications

- Distinguishing between Key and Descriptive flexfields

■ Identifying Key and Descriptive flexfields used by Oracle Applications

■ Explaining flexfield value security

■ Explaining cross-validation rules used in flexfields

You will be presented with Key flexfields and Descriptive flexfields, as well as the differences between them. Next, you will learn which Key flexfields and Descriptive flexfields are included in Oracle Applications. Additionally, you will receive a brief overview about how both security rules and cross-validation rules work for the Key and Description flexfields. The details on how to set up Key flexfields, Descriptive flexfields, security rules, and cross-validation rules will be discussed in later sections.

How Flexfields Are Used by Oracle Applications

Flexfields in Oracle Applications enable you to have a flexible structure for some of the key information, such as the Chart of Accounts or information specific to your company or industry. They also give you a highly adaptable structure for storing customized information in Oracle Applications. Use flexfields to tailor Oracle Applications for your company's specific needs. Keep in mind that Oracle Applications is a generic package that is used in many diverse fields of business, and thus cannot tailor itself toward any one industry's customized needs. However, to meet specialized needs, Oracle Applications provides flexfields that can accommodate such tailoring.

Flexfields are made up of the following elements:

■ Structure

■ Segment/attribute

■ Segment value

■ Value set

Structure

Structure, as the name implies, defines how the flexfield is constructed. A flexfield's structure determines how many segments it has, as well as how the segments are sequenced. For some flexfields, you can define multiple structures. One such example pertains to the Chart of Accounts. You can have multiple structures for the Chart of Accounts flexfield, and you can use these different structures for various Sets of Books. Each structure is mapped to a Structure ID column in the database table for Key flexfields, along with a context-sensitive column in the database table for Descriptive flexfields.

Segment/Attribute

A flexfield can have multiple fields—a segment is a single field within a flexfield. The definition of the segment gives the field its characteristics, including appearance and meaning. Each segment is mapped to a segment or attribute column in the database table. The segment for the Key flexfield is the same as the attribute for the Descriptive flexfield. The two words are interchangeable, but the word "segment" is more commonly used.

Segment Value

When entering a flexfield, input the value for each segment of the flexfield. The segment value of each segment concatenated together is called a flexfield combination. In the Chart of Accounts, the segment value of each segment concatenated together is called an account combination.

Value Set

The segment value you enter is validated against the value set assigned to the segment. The value set identifies a list of valid values for the segment. Value sets also govern the segment value's length, its datatype, and whether it will be zero filled. You can use the same value set with different segments of the same flexfield or across flexfields. Using the same value set for more than one segment simply means that those segments have the same valid segment values. Sharing value sets can avoid duplicating maintenance efforts.

Defining the flexfield structures and the value sets will help you create the flexible fields you must capture for company-specific data without the need for programming. When you enter a Key or a Descriptive flexfield, a Flexfield window will pop up to capture the flexfield's combination. As mentioned earlier, there are two kinds of flexfields:

- Key flexfield
- Descriptive flexfield

Key Flexfield

A Key flexfield provides you with the ability to customize the structure and appearance of key information. Typically, Key flexfield setup is required, but you are given the flexibility to determine the specifics of its setup. The key information you can tailor in Oracle Applications includes Chart of Accounts, part numbers, and asset categories, among other attributes.

Descriptive Flexfield

A Descriptive flexfield provides you with the ability to capture additional information with a customized structure and appearance. You can view a

Descriptive flexfield as an extension of the standard fields you have in Oracle Applications. When you see a [] field in a form, the [] represents the Descriptive flexfield, and can be expanded to capture additional pieces of information that are otherwise not tracked by Oracle Applications.

Context-sensitive Descriptive flexfields enable you to capture different pieces of additional information, depending on the distinct value of a specified field within the same form.

By utilizing flexfields in Oracle Applications, you receive the following benefits:

- The ability to have a flexible data structure that allows you to customize key information structures and appearances in such a way that will be meaningful to your company, without the need for additional programming.

- The ability to have a flexible structure that enables you to expand forms to capture additional information your company needs—information that is not otherwise tracked by Oracle Applications. This can be done without additional programming.

- Each segment within the flexfield can have a different appearance, datatype, and value set. This will allow each segment to be validated automatically upon data entry.

- You can capture different pieces of additional information, depending on the different value of a specified field.

Review Questions

1. What is a flexfield structure?

2. What is a value set?

3. What is a flexfield combination?

4. What are the benefits of having flexfield capabilities in Oracle Applications?

Differences Between Key and Descriptive Flexfields

In the previous section, you learned the definitions of Key and Descriptive flexfields. Now, you will be presented with how to distinguish their differences. You will study their respective varied capabilities in relation to:

- Business purposes

- Database structures
- Flexfield features

Business Purposes

The business purpose of a Key flexfield is to provide users with the ability to customize key information structures and appearances in a way that will be meaningful to a particular company. The business purpose of a Descriptive flexfield is to expand Oracle Applications to capture additional information, specific to a company need, that would otherwise not be tracked or would have otherwise required a customization.

Database Structures

Key flexfields are stored separately in combination tables. Each segment of the Key flexfield is mapped to a segment column in the combination table. Depending on how many segment columns a combination table has, you can have up to that number of segments for the corresponding Key flexfield. For example, you can have up to 30 segments for Chart of Accounts and up to 20 segments for part number. If you have three segments in your Chart of Accounts Key flexfield, you will map the three segments to three segment columns. Since you can have up to 30 segments, you have the choice of combination table columns from segment1 to segment30. Usually, you use them in numeric order, meaning that if you use three segments, you will utilize segment1, segment2, and segment3. A unique key is assigned to each unique flexfield combination, and the unique key is stored in the key ID column in the combination table. The unique ID is stored in the reference tables to reference to a unique combination. You also have a unique identifier for the Key flexfield structure. This singular identifier is stored in the structure ID column in the combination table.

Descriptive flexfields, on the other hand, are stored as part of most of the Oracle Applications' underlying database tables—they are not stored in separate combination tables, as is the case with Key flexfields. For example, in the CUSTOMER database table, you have columns named attribute1 to attribute10, as well as a column called attribute_category. Columns attribute1 through attribute10 are used to store the Customer Descriptive flexfield. Like Key flexfields, you can have attributes for the Descriptive flexfield up to the maximum number of attribute columns that the Descriptive flexfield fundamental database table has. In the case of the CUSTOMER database table, you can have up to ten attributes. attribute_category is used as the context-sensitive column for the Descriptive flexfield. You will read more about context-sensitive columns in a later section.

Flexfield Features

There are different flexfield features for Key flexfields and Descriptive flexfields. For Key flexfields, there are flexfield qualifiers and segment qualifiers. You can also enable shorthand flexfield entries. In addition, you can enable cross-validation rules for Key flexfields. For Descriptive flexfields, you have context-sensitive flexfields.

Flexfield qualifiers and Segment qualifiers only apply to Key flexfields. Flexfield qualifiers are used to identify a particular segment within the Key flexfield; while segment qualifiers are used to capture values for any particular segment. An example of flexfield qualifiers would be the balancing segment qualifier. You can use this to tag which segment of the Chart of Accounts structure you want to use to identify the balancing segment. An example of segment qualifier capabilities would be the account type qualifier, which you can use to capture the account type for the natural account segment.

Shorthand flexfield entry allows you to enter Key flexfield combinations expeditiously by using a shorthand alias. A shorthand alias can represent a complete flexfield combination and/or a partial combination. If a Shorthand flexfield entry is enabled for a Key flexfield—depending on the profile option *Flexfields: Shorthand Flexfield Entry* value—the Shorthand Alias window will show up on new entries only, query and new entries only, new and updated entries only, or all entries.

Cross-validation rules define whether segment values of a particular segment can be combined with other segment values of another particular segment. Cross-validation will be discussed in more detail later in the section titled "Implementing Cross-Validation Rules." Cross-validation rules can only be enabled for Key flexfields.

The context-sensitive flexfield is a feature of Descriptive flexfields and enables you to control when and which Descriptive flexfield segments are populated based on the value of another field in the same form.

Review Questions

1. What are the different business purposes of Key flexfields vs. Descriptive flexfields?

2. How are Key flexfields stored in the database?

3. How are Descriptive flexfields stored in the database?

4. What are the flexfield features specific to Key flexfields and Descriptive flexfields, respectively?

Key and Descriptive Flexfields Used by Oracle Applications

This section will identify all of the Key flexfields and Descriptive flexfields used by Oracle Applications.

For each Key flexfield, you will see the following:

- The Key flexfield name

■ A brief description of what the Key flexfield is used for

■ The owning application

■ The flexfield code

■ The combination table name

■ The unique identifier column

■ The structure column; the maximum number of segments

■ The maximum width of the columns

Accounting Aliases

The following are used for identifying an account combination used as an alias in another structure:

Application	Oracle Inventory
Flexfield code	MDSP
Combination table	MTL_GENERIC_DISPOSITIONS
Unique identifier column	disposition_id
Structure column	organization_id
Maximum number of segments	20
Maximum width of segments	40

Accounting Flexfield

This is the Chart of Accounts flexfield. It is used for identifying an account combination. It must have a balancing segment, cost center segment, and natural account segment. This is enforced by the flexfield qualifiers.

Application	Oracle General Ledger
Flexfield code	GL#
Combination table	GL_CODE_COMBINATIONS
Unique identifier column	code_combination_id
Structure column	chart_of_accounts_id
Maximum number of segments	30
Maximum width of segments	25

Asset Key Flexfield

This is used for grouping nonfinancial and nonphysical location information. You must have at least one segment for this Key flexfield, even if you have no use for it.

Application	Oracle Assets
Flexfield code	KEY#
Combination table	FA_ASSET_KEYWORDS
Unique identifier column	CODE_COMBINATION_ID
Structure column	Not applicable
Maximum number of segments	10
Maximum width of segments	30

Bank Details KeyFlex Flexfield

This is used to capture bank account information specific to legislation.

Application	Oracle Payroll
Flexfield code	BANK
Combination table	PAY_EXTERNAL_ACCOUNTS
Unique identifier column	EXTERNAL_ACCOUNT_ID
Structure column	ID_FLEX_NUM
Maximum number of segments	30
Maximum width of segments	60

Category Flexfield

This is used to group financial information for assets. Depreciation rules and capital budgets can utilize this Key flexfield. You must have a major category segment. This is also driven by a flexfield qualifier.

Application	Oracle Assets
Flexfield code	CAT#
Combination table	FA_CATEGORIES
Unique identifier column	CATEGORY_ID
Structure column	Not applicable

Maximum number of segments	7
Maximum width of segments	30

Cost Allocation Flexfield

This is used to allocate payroll costs to different general ledger accounts. Each business group can have a Cost Allocation flexfield structure.

Application	Oracle Payroll
Flexfield code	COST
Combination table	PAY_COST_ALLOCATION_KEYFLEX
Unique identifier column	COST_ALLOCATION_KEYFLEX_ID
Structure column	ID_FLEX_NUM
Maximum number of segments	30
Maximum width of segments	60

Grade Flexfield

This flexfield is used to group personnel into different grades according to your company requirements. Each person can be assigned to a grade combination. You can use grades for salary administration and have one grade structure for each business group.

Application	Oracle Human Resources
Flexfield code	GRD
Combination table	PER_GRADE_DEFINITIONS
Unique identifier column	GRADE_DEFINITION_ID
Structure column	ID_FLEX_NUM
Maximum number of segments	30
Maximum width of segments	60

Item Catalogs

These are used to group items into catalog groups:

Application	Oracle Inventory
Flexfield code	MICG

Combination table	MTL_ITEM_CATALOG_GROUPS
Unique identifier column	ITEM_CATALOG_GROUP_ID
Structure column	Not applicable
Maximum number of segments	20
Maximum width of segments	40

Item Categories

These are used to organize items into category groups:

Application	Oracle Inventory
Flexfield code	MCAT
Combination table	MTL_CATEGORIES
Unique identifier column	CATEGORY_ID
Structure column	STRUCTURE_ID
Maximum number of segments	20
Maximum width of segments	40

Job Flexfield

Job flexfields are used to group personnel into different jobs according to your company's requirements. Each person can be assigned to a job combination. You can use job flexfields for career planning, budget information, and other categories. You can establish one job flexfield structure for each business group.

Application	Oracle Human Resources
Flexfield code	JOB
Combination table	PER_JOB_DEFINITIONS
Unique identifier column	JOB_DEFINITION_ID
Structure column	ID_FLEX_NUM
Maximum number of segments	30
Maximum width of segments	60

Location Flexfield

Location Flexfields are used to group the physical location information for assets. You must have a state segment, which is enforced by a flexfield qualifier.

Application	Oracle Assets
Flexfield code	LOC#
Combination table	FA_LOCATIONS
Unique identifier column	LOCATION_ID
Structure column	Not applicable
Maximum number of segments	7
Maximum width of segments	30

People Group Flexfield

This flexfield is used to classify personnel into groups that make sense for your company's needs. People group combinations can be used to determine earnings as well as deduction eligibility. You can have one people group flexfield structure for each business group. It is mandatory to establish at least one segment for this Key flexfield, even if you have no use for it.

Application	Oracle Payroll
Flexfield code	GRP
Combination table	PAY_PEOPLE_GROUPS
Unique identifier column	PEOPLE_GROUP_ID
Structure column	ID_FLEX_NUM
Maximum number of segments	30
Maximum width of segments	60

Personal Analysis Flexfield

This flexfield allows you to track miscellaneous information about people in your organization. For example, it can be used to store information as diverse as training history, performance records, or languages.

Application	Oracle Human Resources
Flexfield code	PEA
Combination table	PER_ANALYSIS_CRITERIA
Unique identifier column	ANALYSIS_CRITERIA_ID
Structure column	ID_FLEX_NUM

| Maximum number of segments | 30 |
| Maximum width of segments | 60 |

Position Flexfield

This is used to classify personnel into different positions according to your company's requirements. Each person can be assigned to a position combination. You can use positions for similar things, such as jobs. In addition, you can utilize Position flexfields in approval and reporting hierarchies. One Position flexfield structure is allowed for each business group.

Application	Oracle Human Resources
Flexfield code	POS
Combination table	PER_POSITION_DEFINITIONS
Unique identifier column	POSITION_DEFINITION_ID
Structure column	ID_FLEX_NUM
Maximum number of segments	30
Maximum width of segments	60

Sales Orders

These are used to identify unique sales orders when placing demands or reservations. This Key flexfield has three default segments: order number, order type, and order source.

Application	Oracle Inventory
Flexfield code	MKTS
Combination table	MTL_SALES_ORDERS
Unique identifier column	SALES_ORDER_ID
Structure column	Not applicable
Maximum number of segments	20
Maximum width of segments	40

Sales Tax Location Flexfield

Utilize this flexfield to group locations in such a way that they can be used to calculate sales tax. In the United States, state, county, and city should be delineated in the Location flexfield. This Key flexfield can also be used to validate address entries.

Application	Oracle Receivables
Flexfield code	RLOC
Combination table	AR_LOCATION_COMBINATIONS
Unique identifier column	location_id
Structure column	location_structure_id
Maximum number of segments	10
Maximum width of segments	15

TIP
The segment columns in the AR_LOCATION_ COMBINATIONS table are location_id_ segment_1 through location_id_segment_10 instead of segment1 through segment10.

Soft-Coded Key Flexfield
This flexfield is used to capture legislation-specific information. You have one soft-coded Key flexfield for each business group. Do not alter these Key flexfield structures that come seeded with Oracle Applications.

Application	Oracle Human Resources
Flexfield code	SCL
Combination table	HR_SOFT_CODING_KEYFLEX
Unique identifier column	soft_coding_keyflex_id
Structure column	id_flex_num
Maximum number of segments	30
Maximum width of segments	60

Stock Locators
These are used to capture unique locators throughout Oracle Applications. You can only have one structure for the entire installation.

Application	Oracle Inventory
Flexfield code	MTLL
Combination table	MTL_ITEM_LOCATIONS
Unique identifier column	inventory_location_id
Structure column	organization_id
Maximum number of segments	20
Maximum width of segments	40

System Items

System items delineate part numbers in the Key flexfield. They are used to identify the part number structure. You can only have one structure for the System Items Key flexfield.

Application	Oracle Inventory
Flexfield code	MSTK
Combination table	MTL_SYSTEM_ITEMS
Unique identifier column	inventory_item_id
Structure column	organization_id
Maximum number of segments	20
Maximum width of segments	40

Territory Flexfield

This is used to group territories according to company needs. Territories can be assigned to salespeople and can be utilized in customer-related transactions.

Application	Oracle Receivables
Flexfield code	CT#
Combination table	RA_TERRITORIES
Unique identifier column	territory_id
Structure column	Not applicable
Maximum number of segments	20
Maximum width of segments	25

Training Resources

This flexfield is used to group training resources information specific to an individual company's needs. You can have one Training Resources flexfield structure for each business group.

Application	Oracle Training Administration
Flexfield code	RES
Combination table	OTA_RESOURCE_DEFINITIONS
Unique identifier column	resource_definition_id
Structure column	id_flex_num
Maximum number of segments	20
Maximum width of segments	60

In contrast to the limited number of Key flexfields in Oracle Applications, there are over 900 Descriptive flexfields. Table 9-1 lists the major ones in the financial modules of Oracle Applications, along with the context-sensitive column name, the maximum number of attributes, and the maximum length of attributes. Notice that some tables have more than one Descriptive flexfield. In this case, the database columns for the context columns and the attribute columns are named differently.

Name	Table	Context column	Max#	MaxLen
Enter Journals: Journals	GL_JE_HEADERS	context	10	150
Enter Journals: Lines	GL_JE_LINES	context	10	150
Enter Journals: Tax Information	GL_JE_LINES	taxable_line_ flag	N/A	N/A
Define Budget Organization: Organization	GL_BUDGET_ ENTITIES	context	10	150
Invoice	AP_INVOICES_ALL	attribute_ category	15	150
Vendors	PO_VENDORS	attribute_ category	15	150

TABLE 9-1. *Sample Descriptive Flexfields in Oracle Applications*

Name	Table	Context column	Max#	MaxLen
Asset Category	FA_ADDITIONS	context	30	150
Customer Information	RA_CUSTOMERS	attribute_ category	15	150
Transaction Information	RA_CUSTOMER_ TRX_ALL	attribute_ category	15	150
Invoice Transaction Flexfield	RA_CUSTOMER_ TRX_ALL	interface_header_ context	15	30
Additional Header Information	SO_HEADERS_ALL	context	15	150
Pricing Attributes	SO_LINES_ALL	pricing_context	15	150
Additional Line Information	SO_LINES_ALL	context	15	15

TABLE 9-1. *Sample Descriptive Flexfields in Oracle Applications* (continued)

Review Questions

1. What is the name of the Key flexfield that delineates part numbers?

2. What is the maximum number of segments for any Key flexfield?

3. What two Descriptive flexfields does the SO_LINES_ALL table have?

4. What are the Descriptive flexfields for the table RA_CUSTOMER_TRX_ALL?

Flexfield Value Security

You can use security rules to restrict segment values that your user can enter during data entry. Data entry includes using the segment value as a concurrent program parameter. The List of Values will only display values that are not restricted by security rules assigned to the responsibility your user logged on as. You can set up security rules by establishing ranges of segment values the user can enter or utilize as report parameters; you can have the security rules include every possible segment value, and then exclude ranges of segment values or specific segment values the user can use during data entry. This is called flexfield value security, which can only be performed on segments that have the *Enabled Security* option turned on, including concurrent program parameters.

Cross-Validation Rules Used in Flexfields

Cross-validation rules define whether segment values of a particular segment can be combined with other segment values of another particular segment when new combinations are created. In other words, cross-validation rules prevent the definition of invalid combinations of segment values. Key flexfields can automatically perform these cross-validations based on the cross-validation rules you define. There may be a business need to define cross-validation rules if dynamic insertion is allowed, since cross-validation rules will govern which newly created combinations are valid combinations. The user will receive an error message if the combination he or she is creating violates any cross-validation rule.

For performance reasons, Oracle Applications checks existing flexfield combinations first, before checking cross-validation rules. In short, when a user enters a flexfield combination, Oracle Applications first checks to see if the flexfield combination already exists. If the flexfield combination exists and the combination is enabled, the flexfield combination will be translated to the existing unique identifier, which in turn will be stored in the table the user utilizes to input data. Even if the flexfield combination currently violates a cross-validation rule, the flexfield combination is treated as a valid combination. If cross-validation rules are changed after some combinations are already created, make sure that you manually disable the flexfield combinations that now violate the cross-validation rules. Changing the cross-validation rules has no effect on existing combinations.

When a user enters a flexfield combination and the flexfield combination does not exist, the flexfield combination will be checked against the enabled cross-validation rules. If the flexfield combination does not violate any cross-validation rules, the flexfield combination will be deemed valid and will therefore be created—if dynamic insertion has been activated. The newly created unique identifier will then be stored in the table the user is accessing to enter data.

Review Questions

1. What will a security rule do in Oracle Applications?

2. Can security rules be applied to both Key flexfields and Descriptive flexfields?

3. What will a cross-validation rule do in Oracle Applications?

4. Can cross-validation rules be applied to both Key flexfields and Descriptive flexfields?

Implementing Value Sets

In this section, you will explore the implementation of value sets via:

- Listing options for validating flexfield segment values and report parameters
- Choosing the appropriate validation option to use with a particular segment
- Identifying issues for consideration when planning a validation strategy
- Defining new value sets
- Defining allowable values for a value set

Defining value sets is the very first step in defining flexfields. Value sets are used to validate segment values. When you define flexfield segments, you must associate a value set for each segment. Use value sets across segments in the same flexfield or different flexfields, including across Key flexfields and Descriptive flexfields.

In this section, you will learn the validation options allowed for each value set. You will next ascertain how to choose the appropriate validation option for each segment. Immediately following, the section will discuss issues for consideration when planning a validation strategy. At the end of the section, you will see how to define new value sets, as well as how to enter allowable values for value sets of particular validation options.

Options for Validating Flexfield Segment Values and Report Parameters

There are several validation options for validating flexfield segment values and report parameters. The validation options are as follows:

- *None*
- *Independent*
- *Dependent*
- *Table*
- *Special*
- *Pair*

None

The *None* validation option means no validation. However, it only means the segment values will not be matched against any predefined entered values or predefined rules. The segment values entered with the *None* validation option will still need to be in the format defined by the value set. These format validations include format types, which can be character, number, date, time, or date and time. Format validation also includes the maximum segment value size, the precision for numeric format type, whether the segment value should be in numbers only, whether the segment value should be uppercase only, and whether the segment value should be right-justified and use zero-fill numbers, as well as a minimum value and/or a maximum value to govern the valid range for any segment value.

Independent

The term independent value set means that the segment values entered are matched against manually entered predefined values. These predefined values are stored in the FND_FLEX_VALUES table by value set. Each predefined value comes with descriptions, which can be entered with any installed language. The descriptions are stored in the FND_FLEX_VALUES_TL table by language. The Oracle Applications Object Library owns these tables.

Dependent

Dependent value sets are very similar to independent value sets except that dependent value sets, as the name implies, depend on an independent value set associated with a prior segment of the same flexfield. The segment values entered are matched against predefined values associated with the independent segment value with a prior segment of the same flexfield. These predefined values are also stored in the FND_FLEX_VALUES table by value set, just as independent values and the associated independent segment values are stored in a column called PARENT_FLEX_VALUE_LOW.

A good example of a dependent value set is the Category flexfield in the Vision demonstration database. The Minor Category segment depends on the Major Category segment. For each Major Category segment value, there is a list of valid segment values for the Minor Category segment. See Table 9-2 for some sample data.

If you are defining dependent value sets, it is important that you heed the following order:

1. Create your dependent value set and specify the associated independent value set, as well as a default value.

2. Define your independent values.

3. Define your dependent values.

Major Category	Minor Category
COMPUTER	NC
	PC
	Software
	Unassigned
VEHICLE	Leased Standard
	Owned Heavy
	Owned Luxury
	Owned Standard
	Unassigned
LAND	Occupied
	Unassigned

TABLE 9-2.   *Sample Category Flexfield Data*

Fail to follow this order and you will start to define your independent values before creating your dependent value set, which specifies the independent value set and default value that the dependent value set relies on. You will find yourself having to enter the default value as a dependent value for every existing independent value. Therefore, if you create your dependent value set first and specify the associated independent value set and default value, the default value will be created automatically in the dependent value set for every independent value you entered. For every independent value, you must have at least one dependent value; therefore, creating the default value automatically is a safeguard feature for users.

Table
The table value set validates segment values entered against a database validation table. You can optionally attach a **where** clause or an **order by** clause to the selected database table. There are advanced validation features you can use for table value sets, such as using multiple prior segment values. These will be covered in the last section of this chapter.

Special

Special value sets provide you with the ability to enter a flexfield for a single segment of a flexfield. This is called a flexfield within a flexfield. You usually use this special value set for a concurrent program parameter segment in the Standard Request Submission form.

Pair

The pair value set is very similar to the special value set, except that instead of providing a flexfield for a single segment, the pair value set provides you with the ability to enter a flexfield range for a segment of a flexfield. You usually use this pair value only in the Standard Request Submission form.

Review Questions

1. What does the *None* validation option do?

2. What is the difference between an independent value set and a dependent value set?

3. What tables store the independent segment values and dependent segment values?

4. What is the difference between a special value set and a pair value set?

Choosing Appropriate Validation Options for a Particular Segment

Now you have been presented with the validation options for value sets. The next step is to determine which validation option is appropriate with a particular segment. You need to evaluate the following factors:

- List of Values

- Dependence on prior segments

- Existing database tables

- Flexfield within a flexfield

- Advanced validation features

List of Values

First, evaluate whether your user must have a List of Values for the segment. A List of Values is a predefined list that determines the valid values for the segment.

If you do not need to validate the segment values entered, and you only need the segment values entered to conform to some format validation, you can use the *None* validation option. If you need a List of Values to validate the segment values entered, use the independent, dependent, or table value sets.

Dependence on Prior Segments

Next, evaluate whether the segment you are viewing must depend on the value(s) of prior segment(s) of the same flexfield. If the segment needs to depend on the value of a single prior segment of the same flexfield, use the dependent value set. If the segment needs to depend on more than one prior segment, utilize the advanced validation feature of a table value set. As a last step, if the segment in question does not depend on any prior segment and you need a List of Values, use either the table value set or the independent value set.

Existing Database Table

If you need to validate the segment value entered against a predefined list that is already captured in a database table, you should create a table value set based on the existing table. Otherwise, if you select an independent value set, you will have to enter the valid values in the existing table again in the Define Segment Values form. This will duplicate your maintenance effort and may introduce human error.

Flexfield Within a Flexfield

If your segment is a concurrent program parameter and must be a flexfield, you will need either the special value set or the pair value set. For example, to enter a Chart of Accounts as a program parameter, use the special value set. To enter a range of Chart of Accounts as a program parameter, utilize the pair value set. The special value set and pair value set will pop up a flexfield or a flexfield range within the segment of the concurrent program parameter flexfield.

Advanced Validation Feature

If you need to include multiple prior segment values, or use profile option values in the **where** clause, use a table value set. The table value set is the most powerful validation option, providing you with additional complicated validation rules.

Review Questions

1. Which validation options provide a List of Values?

2. Which validation options provide dependency on a prior segment or segments?

3. Which validation options provide a flexfield within a flexfield?

4. Which validation options provide advanced validation features?

Considerations When Planning a Validation Strategy

When you plan a validation strategy, you must consider many issues. Some decisions you make will be very hard to change, or changes may compromise data integrity. The following factors should be considered:

- Maximum size
- Validation option
- Naming convention
- Format
- Segment Qualifier
- Common value set

Maximum Size

When you define a value set, specify the maximum size for the value set. The value set can be associated with a segment that has a length that is less than or equal to the maximum size of the value set. Once you set up a maximum size for a value set, you can only increase it: you can never decrease it, because decreasing it will invalidate the existing segment values. For zero-fill number value sets, increasing the maximum size will cause existing zero-filled segment values to be in a different format than the new segment values. Oracle Applications will not allow you to increase the maximum size if the value set is set to right-justify and zero-fill numbers. You must consider the segment(s) to which you are going to apply the value set segment(s) application of the value set and determine the appropriate maximum size—understanding that you can never decrease the maximum size. If the value set is set to right-justified and zero-fill numbers, you can neither increase nor decrease the maximum size.

Validation Option

Determine both the validation option and the value set you need. Once you create a value set with a mandatory validation option, you cannot change the validation option. However, you have the choice of replacing a segment's old value set with a new value set. If the new value set has a different validation option, then you have effectively changed the validation option. This can be very dangerous, and can invalidate existing segment values. The following "rules of thumb" should be used in replacing existing value sets:

- You can always change the validation option to *None* as long as the format validation still fits the existing segment values. The only exception is if you are switching from an independent value set to the *None* validation option and the original independent value set has a corresponding dependent value set. This will cause a data integrity problem.

- You can change from the *None* validation option to an independent set or table value set as long as all the existing segment values are predefined in the independent value set or table value set.

- You can switch table value sets with independent value sets or vice versa if the existing segment values are predefined in the new independent value set or the new table value set.

- You should never switch a validation option from or to a dependent value set unless you are switching from a dependent value set to the *None* validation option. Switching a validation option from or to a dependent value set will invalidate existing segment values.

Naming Convention

You should consider implementing a naming convention for all value sets. Usually, you identify the value sets with your company's unique prefix. Otherwise, if Oracle Applications uses your value set names in a future release, your value set definitions will be overwritten during an upgrade. This may cause a severe data integrity problem, so create your own value sets with a custom prefix to avoid this problem.

Format

Format validations such as format type, numbers only, uppercase only, right-justify, and zero-fill numbers cannot be changed, because changes may invalidate existing segment values. Consider your segment format and create value sets with the appropriate format validations.

Segment Qualifier

If you need to use a segment qualifier, implement the independent value set or dependent value set, because the segment qualifier value is captured in the Define Segment Value form. In seeded Oracle Applications, you only have segment qualifiers for the Accounting flexfield. You can determine whether budgeting or posting is allowed for every segment of the Accounting flexfield. In addition, you can determine the account type for the natural account segment. For example, the account type segment qualifier is used to capture whether the natural account is an asset, liability, ownership/stockholder equity, expense, or revenue account.

Common Value Set

Determine which segments and which flexfields should share value sets. Sharing value sets means that the segments will share the same format validations and value validations. This feature should be used strategically, as you can eliminate double maintenance and ensure that the common segment values are identical.

Review Questions

1. What can you do with the maximum size of a value set?

2. What validation option value set can you use to replace a dependent value set without invalidating existing segment values?

3. What value sets can you use when you need a segment qualifier?

4. What will a naming convention for a value set do?

Defining New Value Sets

After planning the validation strategy and considering all the issues, you are now ready to define your new value sets. To define a new value set, use the navigation path *Application : Validation : Set* if you are using the System Administrator responsibility.

To define a new value set, enter the required value set name. The value set name must be unique across all Oracle Applications. Next, input an optional description. If you want to enable security rules for any segment that uses this value set, you can check the *Security Available* checkbox. *Security Available* does not apply to the validation options *None, Special,* or *Pair.* If your value set provides a List of Values, you can also indicate the *Enable Longlist* checkbox. This will pop up a window to ask for a partial segment value before proceeding to the list of all valid values. The entered partial segment value will be used to reduce the List of Values to be retrieved from the database. This is extremely helpful for value sets that have a long list of valid values. For performance reasons, it is always better to limit the number of valid values retrieved from the database.

Next, fill in the format validation definition. Before you fill in the format validation definition, you must select the mandatory format type. Format types can be:

- Char
- Number

- Standard Date or Standard DateTime

- Time

There are two more format types: *Date* and *DateTime*. These two format types are for backward compatibility only. Do not use Date and DateTime for new value sets.

Char

If you select Char as your format type, you can then enter the required maximum size and optionally select whether the segment value should contain numbers only, be uppercase only, or a right-justify and zero- fill number. You can also enter a minimum value and/or a maximum value to limit the range of segment values you can enter for this value set.

Number

If you select Number as your format type, you can only enter the required maximum size, an optional value for precision, and an optional minimum value and/or maximum value to limit the range of segment values you can enter for this value set. All the other format validation options are defaulted and cannot be updated.

Standard Date or Standard DateTime

If you select Standard Date or Standard DateTime as your format type, the maximum size is defaulted and cannot be updated. You can only enter an optional minimum value and/or maximum value to limit the range of segment values you can enter for this value set. Minimum and maximum values for the Standard Date format type must be in the 'DD-MON-RR' format. Minimum and maximum values for the Standard DateTime format type must be in the 'DD-MON-RR HH24:MI:SS' format. All the other format validation options are defaulted and cannot be updated. DD is the day of the month, MON is the month in a three-letter abbreviation such as SEP, RR is a two-digit year with any number < 50 being interpreted as 20RR, and everything else is 19RR. HH24 stands for military hour, MI is minutes, and SS is seconds.

Time

If you select Time as your format type, the maximum size is not defaulted. However, you only have two choices. You can enter a maximum size of 5 if the Time format is 'HH:MI' or a maximum size of 8 if the Time format is 'HH:MI:SS'. You cannot enter a minimum value or a maximum value. All the other format validation options are defaulted and cannot be updated.

Next, you must select a validation type. The validation type identifies the validation options, which can be *Dependent, Independent, None, Pair, Special*, or *Table*. If you choose the Independent or None validation type, you have completed defining your value set. Save your work. If you choose the Dependent validation type, you must click on the **Edit Information** button to enter the independent value set on which this dependent value depends, as well as the dependent default value. This default value will be created as a dependent value whenever a new independent value is created. After selecting the independent value set and the dependent default value, you have completed defining the dependent value set. Save your work.

If you choose the Pair or Special validation type, click on the **Edit Information** button to enter more information. (You will learn more about Pair and Special in the last section of this chapter.) If you choose the Table validation type, click on the **Edit Information** button to enter the validation table information. See Figure 9-1 for the Define Value Sets form.

Table Validation Type

You will now learn to create a table value set. Create a table value set with the character format type called NEW Asset Number and maximum size of 15. Choose Table as your validation type. You are going to associate this value set with segments that need to select a valid asset number as their segment value. Click on the **Edit Information** button.

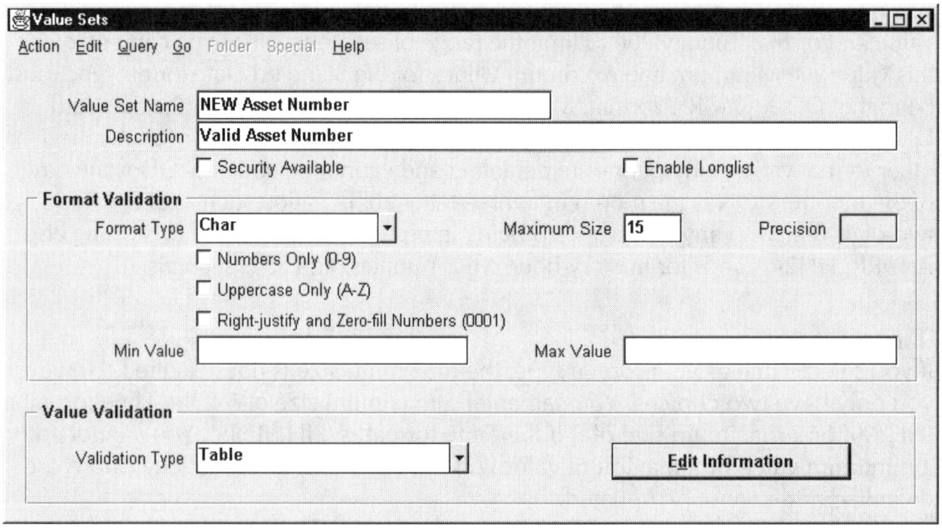

FIGURE 9-1. *Define Value Sets form*

In order to associate a value set with a table, enter the table-owning application name and the table name. If you wish, you can just enter the table name, and the application name will automatically be filled in. Asset numbers are stored in the FA_ADDITIONS table, so you must enter FA_ADDITIONS as the table name. Type **fa_add** and press **Enter**. Usually, the partial data entry will expand to the full name automatically, or, if the partial value is not unique, a List of Values will appear with the table names that start with the letters entered—in this case fa_add. However, a List of Values does not appear in this case. This is because the Table Name field does not perform data validation. Whatever you type is considered valid, and you can use this feature to enter table names that will actually be created in the database later on. If you want to invoke the List of Values, do so by selecting the **List of Values** button. List of Values will show you the tables registered with the Oracle Applications Object Library. Select the FA_ADDITIONS table from the List of Values using the **List of Values** button.

If the table you selected has columns ENABLED_FLAG, START_DATE_ACTIVE, and/or END_DATE_ACTIVE, and the table is registered with the Oracle Applications Object Library, automatic validation will take place when this table is used in a table value set, even without a specific WHERE clause. The rows used for validation must be enabled and the system date must be within the start date and end date active range. If you do not want the automatic validation, change the column names or use column aliases.

You can optionally check the *Allow Parent Values* checkbox if you want the table value set to display parent values entered through the Define Segment Value form. For table value sets, child values come from the database table. Parent values, on the other hand, still need to be entered through the Define Segment Value form to be stored in the FND_FLEX_VALUES table. Checking the *Allow Parent Values* checkbox will allow the List of Values to display both the child values from the database table and the parent values from the FND_FLEX_VALUES table.

Next, enter the table column information. You must enter a value column with the option to enter a meaning column and/or an ID column. If you enter a meaning column, the meaning column will be displayed in the List of Values as the description of the value column you selected. If you enter an ID column, the ID column will not be displayed, but the ID column will become the segment value that will be saved into the database or submitted as parameters to the concurrent request. This is the reason why the ID column is also referred to as the hidden ID column. You should not use the ID column for any Key flexfield. In fact, you cannot use the ID column value set if the Key flexfields do not allow ID value sets. However, the hidden ID is commonly used in concurrent program parameters, as you might want to pass the ID—instead of a value—to the concurrent program. Using the asset number, for example, you can enter the asset ID as the ID column. When a user selects an asset number from your value set as a report parameter, the Asset ID field is passed to the report instead of the Asset Number field.

The column type and size revert to defaults when you use the **List of Values** button to select a registered column. However, similar to the table name, the column name does not perform any data validation and whatever you type is valid. You can type an expression as the column name. For example, you can pad the asset number with '0' up to a fixed length of nine characters as the value column for business reasons. If you decide to do this, enter the appropriate column type and column size manually. Select Asset Number as the value column, Description for the meaning column, and Asset ID as the ID column.

You can also enter a WHERE clause and/or an ORDER BY clause. The WHERE clause can limit the validation table to specific rows that fit the WHERE clause. You can also use the WHERE clause for join conditions if you use more than one table in the Table Name field. You can also refer to segment values of prior segments, profile option values, and field values in the WHERE clause. The ORDER BY clause lets you order the List of Values based on one or more other columns in the database table. You cannot use a group having any set operators (union, minus, or intersect) in a clause for a value set. You can enter additional column(s) to be displayed along with the value column or the meaning column. Additional columns need to be in the following format:

Column1 "column 1 title" (column 1 width), column 2 "column 2 title" (column 2 width)—you can use (*) as the width to specify that the width depends on the value of the column.

See Figure 9-2 for the Validation Table Information form.

Multiple Tables

With the No Validation feature for the table name and the column name, together with the optional WHERE clause, you can create a table value set with multiple tables. Consider this: you want to create a table value set that contains the asset ID as the ID column, the asset number as the value column, and the asset cost in the corporate book as the description. Both asset ID and asset numbers are in the FA_ADDITIONS table, and the asset cost is in the FA_BOOKS table. The two tables are joined by ASSET_ID. You must further limit the FA_BOOKS table by BOOK_TYPE_CODE = 'OPS CORP'. To implement this, you have two options:

- Use a view
- Use multiple tables

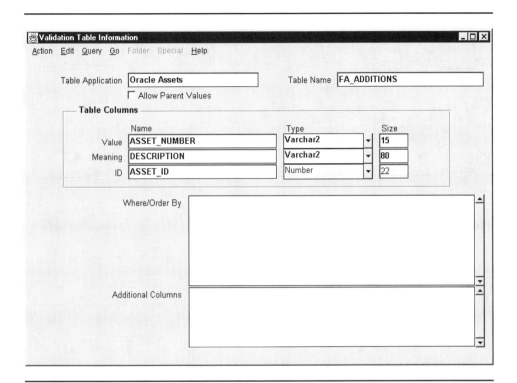

FIGURE 9-2. *Validation Table Information form*

USE A VIEW   You can create a view that joins two tables—FA_ADDITIONS and FA_BOOKS—together with the correct join condition and the correct BOOK_TYPE_CODE. You can then register the view with the Oracle Applications Object Library. When you create a table value set, select the table name view and choose the asset number, asset ID, and asset cost as the value column, and correspondingly, the ID column and description column. No WHERE clause is necessary when using the view in a table validated value set, as the WHERE clause in the view contains all the logic needed.

USE MULTIPLE TABLES   You can also use multiple tables in the validation table information form. Enter **FA_ADDITIONS add, FA_BOOKS book** as the table name. Next, enter **add.ASSET_NUMBER**, **add.ASSET_ID**, and **book.COST** as the value column, ID column, and correspondingly, the description column.

In the WHERE clause, you can add the join condition and the book type code condition. Key in the following:

```
WHERE add.ASSET_ID = book.ASSET_ID
AND book.BOOK_TYPE_CODE = 'OPS CORP'
```

This will accomplish a similar effect as creating a view. Oracle Applications uses the value column, ID column, description column, and the additional column as the select list. It then utilizes the table name in the FROM clause. As a last step, it appends the WHERE clause and ORDER BY clause to form a complete SQL statement. If there is any syntax error in the table value set, you will not know until the value set is utilized.

Review Questions

1. Which validation type allows you to enter additional information?

2. For what purpose is the table name used in the Validation Table Information form?

3. What will happen if you enter the ID column for a value set?

4. What are the two ways to implement multiple tables as a table value set?

Define Allowable Values for a Value Set

Values of a segment should be in logical ranges. Related segment values should be grouped together. This will simplify the definition of parent values, using ranges as concurrent program parameters as well as the implementation of both cross-validation and security rules.

After you define your value sets, delineate allowable values for independent and dependent value sets. In addition, you should also define parent values for table value sets. To enter allowable values, use the navigation path *Application : Validation : Values.*

A Find window appears, and you can identify the allowable segment values through four major find criteria:

- Value set

- Key flexfield

- Descriptive flexfield

- Concurrent program

You have the ability to look up a specific allowable value or all dependent values for a particular independent value. However, for data entry, you should usually use the four major find criteria and enter values into the correct value set. See Figure 9-3.

Value Set

Locate allowable values by value set name. Enter the value set name and all the allowable segment values will be retrieved. Only value sets that allow the entry of values are accessible through this form.

Key Flexfield

You can find allowable values via an application, a Key flexfield title, a Key flexfield structure, or a Key flexfield segment. If you enter an application, you will see all Key flexfield titles within that application, all Key flexfield structures within those Key flexfield titles, and the segments belonging to those Key flexfield structures that have a dependent value set, an independent value set, or a table value set that allows parent values to appear with their own allowable values. They are hierarchical. As you go down the hierarchical chain and use the more detailed find criteria, you will get fewer sets of allowable values. For the most detailed find criteria—segment—you will only see the allowable values for the selected Key flexfield segments.

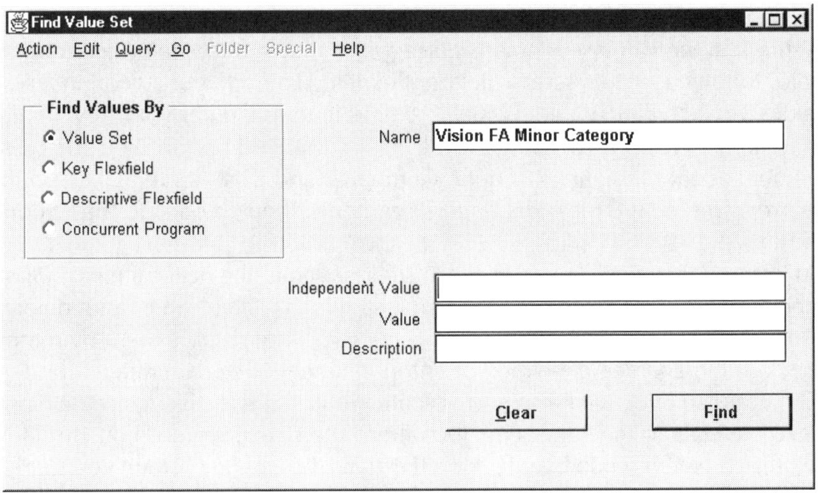

FIGURE 9-3. *Find Value Set form*

Descriptive Flexfield

You can locate allowable values via an application, a Descriptive flexfield title, a Descriptive flexfield context, or a Descriptive flexfield segment. If you enter an application, you will see all Descriptive flexfield titles within that application, all the Descriptive flexfield contexts within those Descriptive flexfield titles, and all the segments belonging to those Descriptive flexfield contexts that have a dependent value set, an independent value set, or a table value set that allows parent values to appear with their own allowable values. They are hierarchical. As you go down the hierarchical chain and use the more detailed find criteria, you will get fewer sets of allowable values. For the most detailed find criteria—segment—you will only see the allowable values for the selected Descriptive flexfield segments.

Concurrent Program

You can locate allowable values via an application, a concurrent program name, or a concurrent program parameter. If you enter an application, you will see the concurrent program names within that application, and the parameters that belong to those concurrent program names that have a dependent value set, an independent value set, or a table value set that allows parent values will appear with their own allowable values. They are hierarchical. As you go down the hierarchical chain and use the more detailed find criteria, you will get fewer sets of allowable values. For the most detailed find criteria—parameter—you will only see the allowable values for the selected concurrent program parameters.

After you have filled in the find criteria, click on the **Find** button. This will retrieve the value sets for which you want to view or enter the allowable values. Make sure that the value set name is correct. Let's look at the first Accounting Flexfield, followed by the Asset Category flexfield. To find your Accounting flexfield, select the Find Value By Key Flexfield item and enter your Key flexfield structure name: **NEW Accounting Flex**. Click on the **Find** button. You should see three independent segments: Account, Company, and Cost Center. Click on the down arrow to see all three independent segments, then go back to the Account segment.

Go to the Values region and you can see the value, the description, an *Enabled* checkbox, an Effective From date, and an Effective To date. You cannot delete segment values once they are saved. However, you can disable them by removing the check in the *Enabled* checkbox or entering an effective date range. The *Enabled* checkbox and an Effective From and To date are in the Effective alternative region.

Next, navigate to the Hierarchy, Qualifiers alternative region. You can identify the value as a parent value by checking the *Parent* checkbox. Once you mark the

Parent checkbox, you can click on the **Define Child Ranges** button to define ranges of child values that belong to the specific parent value. Click on the **Move Child Range** button to move ranges of child values from the source parent value to a specific destination parent value. See Figure 9-4. Next, if the value is a parent value, you can optionally assign the value to a predefined rollup group. Remember, you can use rollup groups to create summary accounts in Oracle General Ledger. If you wish, you can enter a Level field to identify the value level of the hierarchy. The Level field is for informational use only. Click on the **View Hierarchies** button to show you the value hierarchy and use the **Up** and **Down** buttons to navigate up and down the value hierarchy. See Figure 9-5.

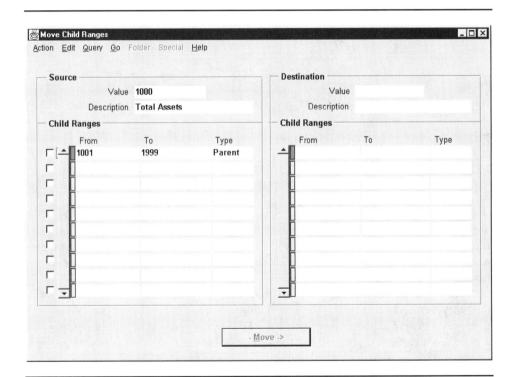

FIGURE 9-4. *Move Child Ranges form*

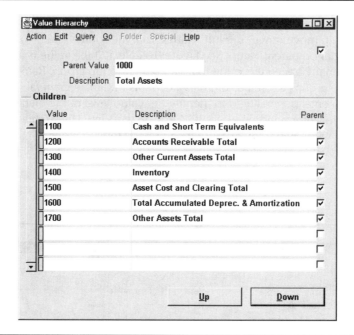

FIGURE 9-5. *Value Hierarchy form*

If there are segment qualifiers associated with those segments for which you are entering values, the Qualifiers field will pop up to capture your specific segment qualifier values. For Accounting flexfields, enter whether you want to allow budgeting and/or posting for each segment. In addition, you can identify the account type for the natural account segment. See Figure 9-6.

Next, let's look at the Category flexfield. You can find the two segments of the Category flexfield by selecting the Find Values By Key Flexfield item and entering **Category flexfield** as the title. Click on the **Find** button. Since the minor category is a dependent value set, you will see the independent value set name as well as the dependent value set name. Also, you will be able to view the independent value that you are entering the dependent values for. The first independent value should be LAND. For LAND, you have dependent values OCCUPIED and UNASSIGNED. Arrow down one record and you will find the independent value VEHICLE.

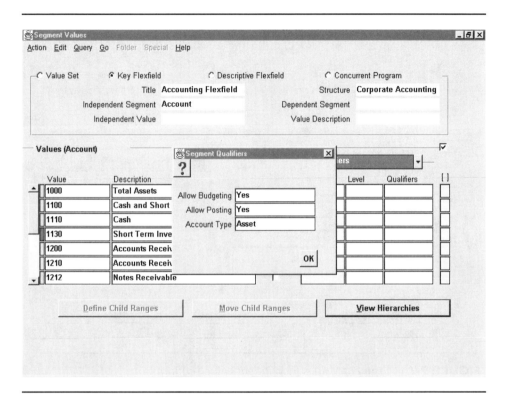

FIGURE 9-6. *Segment Values (independent value set) form*

For the independent value VEHICLE, you have the following dependent values:
LEASED STANDARD, OWNED HEAVY, OWNED LUXURY, OWNED STANDARD,
and UNASSIGNED. See Figure 9-7.

Review Questions

   1. Which validation type allows you to enter allowable values through the
Define Segment Values form?

   2. When will the Qualifiers field pop up?

   3. When can you define or move child ranges?

   4. What additional fields show up when entering allowable values for the
dependent value set as compared to the independent value set?

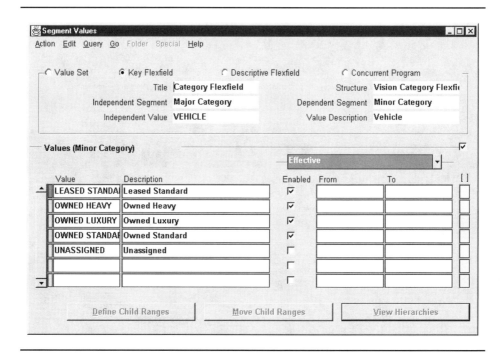

FIGURE 9-7. *Segment Values (dependent value set) form*

Planning and Defining Key Flexfields

Now that you have created all your value sets, you are ready to plan and define Key flexfields and Descriptive flexfields. Initially, you will learn to plan and define Key flexfields, including the following:

- Explaining intelligent keys and providing examples

- Identifying Key flexfields that are required by Oracle Applications

- Explaining the purpose of flexfield qualifiers

- Using optional Key flexfield features where appropriate

- Designing a Key flexfield structure

- Selecting the appropriate Key flexfield to define

- Defining structure information for the Key flexfield

- Defining segment attributes as planned

- Defining flexfield qualifiers

■ Defining segment qualifiers

■ Implementing optional features as needed

Intelligent Keys

Intelligent keys have multiple meaningful codes that combine to form a meaningful key. Each intelligent key is unique, and is used to identify a single entity. For example, you have intelligent keys for accounts and part numbers.

Let's talk about accounts first. You may have an intelligent key that is a combination of company, cost center, and account. You do not want to use a unique identifier to refer to an account, because a unique identifier has no meaning by itself. It is merely a system-assigned unique number. To use a number that has no meaning at all during data entry is very difficult, and can cause many data entry errors. For example, 01-0000-453100 may represent the Wing Company with the corporate cost center and account number 453100 as the benefit account. This is a lot easier to remember than a unique number, such as 1198. Thus, you should use the intelligent key instead during data entry.

Similarly, you should have an intelligent key for your part number. Part numbers should be more meaningful than numbers. For example, if you sell computers and your part number is COMPAQ-366MHz-10GB-2GB, this means a Compaq computer with 266-megahertz CPU, 10GB disk space and 2GB memory. This is a lot easier to remember or relate to than a unique number of, say, 32454. Again, you should use the intelligent key during data entry.

However, even though intelligent keys facilitate data entry, they do not offer easy storage in the database. If every table that refers to these intelligent keys needs to store these multiple part codes, this then becomes a very inefficient way to store data. In order to bridge the gap between what intelligent keys and unique identifiers can offer in terms of data entry and data storage, Oracle Applications created the concept of a Key flexfield. A Key flexfield has segments that store the multiple meaningful codes and have unique system-generated numbers that identify the combinations as a whole. The segments, along with the unique identifiers, are stored in the combination table. The segments are used for data entry, while the unique identifiers are used for storage in the other tables that reference any Key flexfield combination. This is an efficient way to satisfy both the data entry and data storage requirements. A side benefit is that the Key flexfield enables you to create any structure that fits your company's specific intelligent keys.

Key Flexfields Required by Oracle Applications

The first step in planning your Key flexfields is to identify the Key flexfields that are required by the Oracle Applications modules you are implementing. Remember, you have the Key flexfields shown in Table 9-3. Determine which Key flexfields are required.

Flexfield Name	Application
Account Aliases	Oracle Inventory
Accounting flexfield	Oracle General Ledger
Asset Key flexfield	Oracle Assets
Bank Details KeyFlex flexfield	Oracle Payroll
Category flexfield	Oracle Assets
Cost Allocation flexfield	Oracle Payroll
Grade flexfield	Oracle Human Resources
Item Catalogs	Oracle Inventory
Item Categories	Oracle Inventory
Job flexfield	Oracle Human Resources
Location flexfield	Oracle Assets
People Group flexfield	Oracle Payroll
Personal Analysis flexfield	Oracle Human Resources
Position flexfield	Oracle Human Resources
Sales Orders	Oracle Inventory
Sales Tax Location flexfield	Oracle Receivables
Soft Coded Key flexfield	Oracle Human Resources
Stock Locators	Oracle Inventory
System Items	Oracle Inventory
Territory flexfield	Oracle Receivables
Training Resources	Oracle Training Administration

TABLE 9-3. *Key Flexfields in Oracle Applications*

Review Questions

1. What is an intelligent key?

2. How do Key flexfields work with intelligent keys?

3. What Key flexfields are in Oracle General Ledger?

4. What Key flexfields are in Oracle Assets?

Purpose of Flexfield Qualifiers

A flexfield qualifier identifies a particular segment of a Key flexfield. It is used when some Oracle Application modules need a particular segment for some predefined functionality. Since Key flexfield structures are customized to fit your company's needs, flexfield qualifiers provide a mechanism to prevent tagging a segment by segment name or segment order. In other words, the flexfield qualifier is used to tag the particular segment that the Oracle Applications module needs so that the Oracle Applications module can identify it even though the Key flexfield structure is customized.

For example, in Oracle General Ledger, you have flexfield qualifiers to tag the balancing segment, cost center segment, and the natural account segment. In Oracle Assets, you have the flexfield qualifiers to tag the major category segment and the state segment.

There is another kind of flexfield qualifier. It is called a segment qualifier. A flexfield qualifier tags a segment, whereas a segment qualifier tags a value. In Oracle Applications, only Accounting flexfields use segment qualifiers.

In Oracle General Ledger, you have the segment qualifier to tag a natural account segment value for a particular account type, as well as segment qualifiers to tag segment values for any segment to allow budgeting and/or posting.

Optional Key Flexfield Features

Optional Key flexfield features include the following:

- Dynamic Insertion
- Shorthand Flexfield Entry
- Flexfield Value Security
- Cross-Validation Rules

Dynamic Insertion

The Dynamic Insertion feature allows flexfield combinations to be created on the fly the first time it is used as long as the combination does not violate cross-validation rules. If dynamic insertion is allowed, when a user enters a flexfield combination, each segment value is validated against its corresponding value set first; then, the combination is matched against all of the existing combinations. If the combination does not exist, the combination will then be validated against all the enabled cross-validation rules. If the flexfield combination is valid, it will then be inserted into the combination table and the unique identifier will be returned to be stored in the database table the user is currently utilizing. If dynamic insertion is not allowed, after the combination is matched against all the existing combinations—and the combination the user is entering is found not to exist—an error message will be generated and the new combination will not be created on the fly. In other words, without dynamic insertion, all the flexfield combinations must be predefined in the combination table. Not every Key flexfield allows dynamic insertion. If there are attributes that must be associated with each flexfield combination, such as in the case of part numbers and asset categories, dynamic insertion cannot be turned on, because values for all the attributes need to be captured.

Shorthand Flexfield Entry

Shorthand flexfield entry allows you to enter Key flexfield combinations more quickly by using a shorthand alias. A shorthand alias can represent a complete flexfield combination or a partial combination. If the *Shorthand flexfield entry* option is enabled for a Key flexfield, depending on the profile option *Flexfields: Shorthand Flexfield's* entry value, the Shorthand Alias window will show up on new entries only, query and new entries only, new and updated entries only, or all entries.

Flexfield Value Security

Flexfield value security rules restrict ranges of segment values that a user with a certain responsibility can enter. You can either define security rules to include all the valid segment values that a user can enter, or include every possible segment value that the user can enter, and then exclude specific segment values. After you define the security rules and have assigned them to responsibilities, they take effect. You can use flexfield value security to disallow users in one company from entering data for another company. In this scenario, you create a responsibility that only has access to one specific company segment value in the Chart of Accounts by assigning a security rule to include only that one specific company segment value.

Cross-Validation Rules

Cross-validation rules delineate whether segment values of a particular segment can be combined with other segment values of another particular segment. You especially need cross-validation rules if you have dynamic insertion enabled. Cross-validation rules are used to restrict invalid combinations from being entered during data entry. For example, you can rule out any combinations that have the balance sheet accounts associated with specific cost centers.

Review Questions

1. Under what circumstances is dynamic insertion used?

2. What is the Shorthand flexfield entry used for?

3. What is Flexfield Value Security used for?

4. What are cross-validation rules used for?

Designing a Key Flexfield Structure

In this section, you will learn to create worksheets for designing a Key flexfield structure, as well as to ask some fundamental questions regarding Key flexfield structure design. A complete, well-thought-out design is especially important since many options cannot be changed after initial definition.

Design Worksheet

Before defining a Key flexfield in Oracle Applications, it is best to first design a Key flexfield structure on a worksheet. This worksheet should include the following:

- Flexfield structure title

- Flexfield structure description

- Flexfield view name

- Segment separators

- Cross-validation segments

- Freeze rollup groups

- Allowing dynamic inserts

- Numbering of segments

- Ordering of segments

- Segment name

- Segment length

- Flexfield qualifiers

For each Key flexfield structure, you should have a more detailed segment spreadsheet that should include the following:

- Segment name
- Segment number
- Segment description
- Prompts (List of Values, window)
- Column
- Value set
- Default value
- Required
- Security enabled
- Indexed
- Sizes (display, description, concatenated)
- Description size

Design Questions

You should ask yourself the following questions when designing a Key flexfield structure:

- **What is a good segment separator?** Preferably you should choose a character that does not appear in the intelligent key, so that your users will not be confused. If a character is the same as the segment separator, the character will be translated to be displayed as a caret.

- **How do you want to break down inquiries and reporting?** This will determine the number of segments necessary.

- **How fast does your company grow and change?** This will determine the number of segments necessary, as well as the length of the segments. If your company grows quickly, you may want to include to-be-determined segments to allow room for growth. In addition, you may want to reserve more bytes for each individual segment.

- **Do you want flexfield combinations to be created on the fly?** This will determine whether the flexfield structure needs to allow dynamic insertion.

- **Do you want to cross-validate segments?**   If dynamic insertion is on, you probably need to cross-validate segments. If not, you may want to turn them off for performance reasons and enter the flexfield combinations directly into the combination table.

- **What should each segment of the Key flexfield structure include?**   Each segment should include the column name, the sizes, any default value, and whether segments should be required.

Review Questions

1. Name three fields to be included in your Key flexfield structure worksheet.

2. How should you select a segment separator?

3. How do allowing dynamic insertions and cross-validated segments indirectly work hand in hand?

4. What should you consider in determining the number of segments?

Selecting the Appropriate Key Flexfield to Define

After planning the Key flexfield structures and filling in the worksheets, you are ready to define your Key flexfield structures online. To do this, use the navigation path *Application: Flexfield : Key-Segments.* First, you must select the Key flexfield you want to define. Use the **Find** button or the query mode to select the appropriate Key flexfield to define. Not every Key flexfield allows multiple structures. For example, you can only have one structure for Category flexfield, Asset Key flexfield, Location flexfield, Territory flexfield, account aliases, item catalogs, sales orders, system items, and stock locators. You are going to create a new Sales Tax Location flexfield structure. First, select the Sales Tax Location flexfield. In the Structures region, all the existing structures of the Sales Tax Location flexfield are displayed. Create a Sales Tax Location flexfield structure called **NEW Country State County City** with four segments: Country, State, County, and City.

Defining Structure Information for the Key Flexfield

To define a new Key flexfield structure, you must add a new record. You can do so by hitting the **New Record** button on any row in the Structures region. First, enter the required Key flexfield structure title. In your case, use **NEW Country State County City**. You can change the structure title any time you want. The structure title appears as the window title in your Key flexfield. You can then enter an optional description for the structure and an optional database view name. If you enter a view name, the view name can be a combination of letters, numbers, and underscores. However, the view name must begin with a letter. When you freeze and compile the Key flexfield structure, Oracle Applications automatically generates one or two database views.

The first database view is always generated and is called the Key Flexfield Concatenated Segment view. The Key Flexfield Concatenated Segment view name is always the same. It is the combination table name with _KFV added to it as the suffix. For example, the Accounting flexfield concatenated segment view will be GL_CODE_COMBINATIONS_KFV. This view contains all the concatenated segment values across all the Key flexfield structures of the Key flexfield you are compiling. This view contains the unique ID column, the structure ID column, the concatenated segments, the padded concatenated segments (which have all the numeric segment values right-justified and left-padded and all the other datatype segment values left-justified and right-padded), as well as all the segment qualifiers.

The second database view is only generated if you enter a database view name. This view is called the Key Flexfield Structure view. This view is specific to the particular structure for which the entered database view is named. This view uses the segment names as the column names with nonalphanumeric characters replaced by underscores. It also contains the unique ID column, as well as segment qualifiers START_DATE_ACTIVE, END_DATE_ACTIVE, SUMMARY_FLEX, ENABLED_FLAG, and ROW_ID.

The *Enabled* checkbox is checked by default. You can optionally uncheck it. You cannot delete a Key flexfield structure, but you can disable it by unchecking the *Enabled* checkbox. Next, you may select a segment separator other than the default period. Your choices are period, dash, pipe, or any custom character. You must have a segment separator.

Next, you can select whether you want to *Cross-Validate Segments*. Unchecking this checkbox will disable cross-validation for this Key flexfield structure. You can then identify whether you want to *Freeze Rollup Groups*. If you mark this checkbox, you will not be able to change the assigned rollup groups in the Define Segment Values form. As a last step, you can determine whether you want to allow dynamic inserts for Key flexfield structures. If you do not allow dynamic inserts, you must create all flexfield combinations in the combination form. Not all Key flexfields allow dynamic inserts. For example, you cannot allow dynamic inserts for Category flexfields, item catalogs, item categories, and system items.

You can freeze your flexfield structure by checking the *Freeze Flexfield Definition* checkbox. Once frozen, you can only make very limited changes to the flexfield structure definition. If you need to change the flexfield structure definition, first uncheck the *Freeze Flexfield Definition* checkbox and make the changes. Next, reactivate the *Freeze Flexfield Definition* checkbox. You will receive a warning message that tells you that unfreezing this flexfield and making changes to the segment definitions could affect the validity of the data already existing for this flexfield. Changing a Key flexfield structure will not update existing flexfield data. Do not freeze your flexfield structure yet, as you have not entered the segment attributes for your flexfield structure.

You can compile your flexfield structure by hitting the **Compile** button. Compiling a flexfield structure will automatically save the flexfield structure. You must freeze and compile your flexfield structure before your user can utilize the flexfield structure. See Figure 9-8.

Review Questions

1. What do you need to do before a user can access your newly defined flexfield structure?

2. Which two database views can be generated when you freeze and compile a flexfield structure?

3. Which Key flexfields do not allow dynamic insertions?

4. What does the *Freeze Rollup Groups* checkbox do?

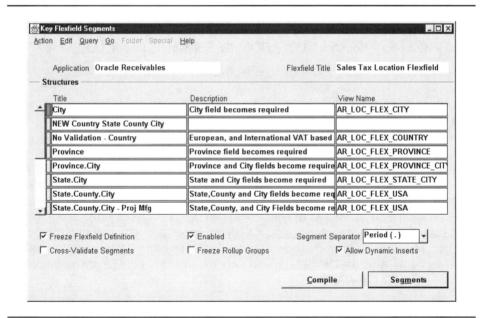

FIGURE 9-8. *Key Flexfield Segments form*

Defining Segments Attributes as Planned

After defining the flexfield structure, you need to enter your four segments. First, key in all the required attributes. These attributes include segment number, segment name, window prompt, and column name. The segment number defines the order of the segments. The segment name can be a combination of letters, numbers, underscores, and spaces. However, the segment name must start with a letter. The window prompt is defaulted with the segment name and can be overridden. The column name defines which column stores the segment value in the combination table. You can optionally enter a value set. With no value set associated, there will be no validation—not even format validation. Next, determine whether this segment needs to be displayed. As a last step, decide whether this segment needs to be enabled. Nondisplayed or disabled segments will not be displayed in a Flexfield window. However, nondisplayed segments with a default segment value will be saved to the database, while disabled segments will not have a default value, and therefore will not be saved to the database. For your four segments, enter the information as follows:

#	Name	Window Prompt	Column	Value Set
1	Country	Country	LOCATION_ID_SEGMENT_1	AR_LOC_COUNTRY
2	State	State	LOCATION_ID_SEGMENT_2	AR_LOC_STATE
3	County	County	LOCATION_ID_SEGMENT_3	AR_LOC_COUNTY
4	City	City	LOCATION_ID_SEGMENT_4	AR_LOC_CITY

All segments should be displayed and enabled. As you scroll between segments, you should receive a warning message that states that you can enter a display size of less than 60, which is the maximum size of your value set. This simply tells you that your users may need to scroll through the flexfield segments to see the entire value. Click on OK to acknowledge the warning. See Figure 9-9.

You can set up the entire Key flexfield structure within the Segments Summary window if you are satisfied with the segment attribute defaults. The only default is that the segment is marked as required. You can save your work at this point, but let's open the Detail Segments window to define more segment attributes for the Country segment. You can do so by clicking the **Open** button. If you want to define new segments using the Detail Segments window instead of the Segments Summary window, use the **New** button.

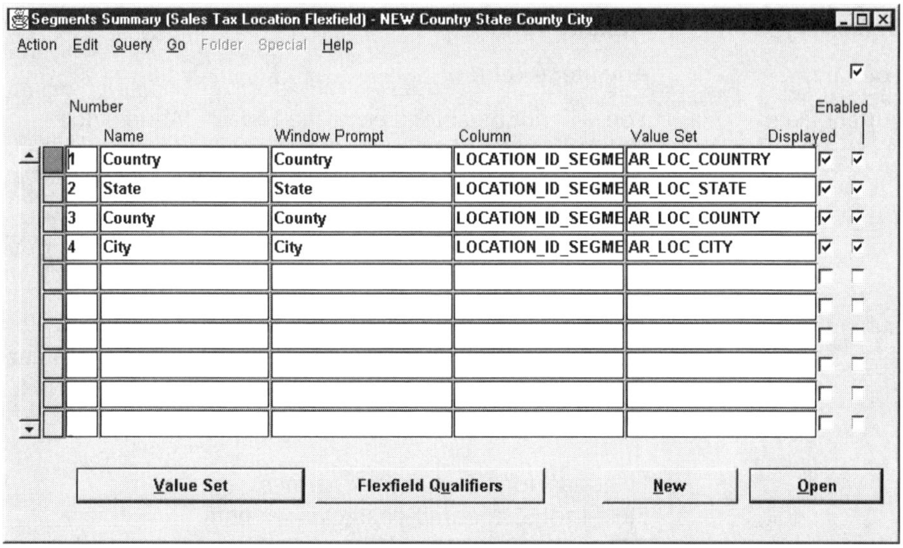

FIGURE 9-9. *Segments Summary form*

Additional segment attributes you can enter include a segment description and whether you want to index the segment. The *Indexed* checkbox is only used for the Accounting flexfield. The optimizer in Oracle General Ledger creates indexes based on the *Indexed* checkbox segments. You can also enter a default type and default value for each segment. Default types can be Constant, Current Date, Current Time, Field, Profile, SQL Statement, or Segment. Specific default values are necessary for each default type. Their relationship is described in Table 9-4.

Additional segment attributes also include whether the segment is required and whether security rules can be applied to the segment. You can optionally identify two segments to represent a low and high range of segment values. For the segment that identifies the low range, select Low in the Range field. For the segment that identifies the high range, select High in the Range field. Oracle Applications will automatically validate that the low range segment is lower than the high range segment based on the segment datatype. The low range segment must come before the high range segment. If the low range segment comes after the high range segment, or if you only have the low range segment or the high range segment, you will receive an error when you compile the flexfield structure. The range will be defaulted to Pair if the value set you select is of type Pair.

Default Type	Default Value
Constant	Any literal value.
Current Date	You will not be able to enter the Default Value field with the Current Date default type. Instead, the current system date will be entered and, depending on the segment size, the value will be in the format of DD-MON-YY for a 9-character segment, or in the format of DD-MON-YYYY for an 11-character segment.
Current Time	You will not be able to enter the Default Value field with the Current Time default type. Instead, the current system time will be entered and, depending on the segment size, the value will be in one of the following formats: HH24:MI for a 5-character segment HH24:MI:SS for an 8-character segment DD-MON-YY HH24:MI for a 15-character segment DD-MON-YYYY HH24:MI for a 17-character segment DD-MON-YY HH24:MI:SS for an 18-character segment DD-MON-YYYY HH24:MI:SS for a 20-character segment
Field	A compound consisting of the field name and the value in the field.
Profile	A compound consisting of the profile option name and the value of the profile option.
SQL Statement	A compound consisting of the SQL statement and the result.
Segment	A compound consisting of the prior segment of the same flexfield and the segment value.

TABLE 9-4.   *Default Types and Default Value Relationships*

As a last step, you can override the default sizes and prompts. You can change the display size, description size, and concatenated description size of the segment, or change the List of Values prompt and/or the window prompt. Click on the **Value Set** button to view or edit the value set associated with the segment. See Figure 9-10.

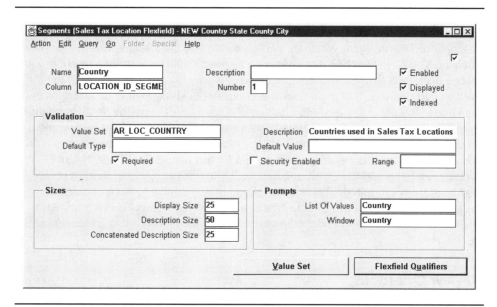

FIGURE 9-10.   *Segments form*

If you need to tag a segment with a flexfield qualifier, click on the **Flexfield Qualifiers** button. Tag your four segments with the Country, State, County, and City flexfield qualifiers accordingly.

Review Questions

1. Which fields are required for defining flexfield segments?

2. What is the Segment Number field used for?

3. What kind of default types are there, and how are default values related?

4. What is the Range field used for?

Defining Flexfield Qualifiers

In order to define flexfield qualifiers, you must change the responsibility to Application Developer and use the navigation path *Flexfield : Key : Register*. For the Key flexfield that you want to define in a flexfield qualifier, click on the **Qualifiers** button. To define a flexfield qualifier, you must enter the name and the prompt. The name must be unique within the Key flexfield. You can also optionally enter a description. The prompt is what you will see when you tag a segment with a flexfield qualifier. You have the choice of defining a flexfield qualifier as unique or not unique. If you check the *Unique* checkbox, then you can only tag, at most, one segment for this flexfield qualifier. If you uncheck the *Unique* checkbox, then you can tag more than one segment for this flexfield qualifier. You can only define the flexfield qualifier as required. If you check the *Required* checkbox, you must tag at least one segment for this flexfield qualifier. Checking both the *Unique* and *Required* checkboxes will ensure that you must tag exactly one segment for this flexfield qualifier. Natural account segments and balancing segments fall into this category, while cost center segments are not required. This is because you may not have to have Oracle Assets installed. If you do not have Oracle Assets, a cost center segment is not required.

The *Global* checkbox and the Segment Qualifiers regions are used for segment qualifiers.

Review Questions

1. Through what navigation path and button do you define flexfield qualifiers?

2. What is the flexfield qualifier prompt used for?

3. What purpose does the *Required* checkbox serve?

4. What is the *Unique* checkbox used for?

Defining Segment Qualifiers

By using the same navigation path and the same **Qualifiers** button you use to define flexfield qualifiers, you can also delineate segment qualifiers. You can define two kinds of segment qualifiers. There can be a segment qualifier for a single segment or a segment qualifier for all segments. A segment qualifier for a single segment is tied to the flexfield qualifier. An example is the Account Type segment qualifier that is tied to the Natural Account segment flexfield qualifier.

A segment qualifier for all segments is called a global segment qualifier. You define a global segment qualifier by tying the segment qualifier to a global flexfield qualifier. You define a global flexfield qualifier by checking the *Global* checkbox in the flexfield qualifier definition. The *Required* checkbox is automatically checked since all global segment qualifiers are required. You use the global flexfield qualifier as a placeholder. It is not shown in the Flexfield Qualifier window when you try to associate a segment with a flexfield qualifier. An example is the GL_GLOBAL flexfield qualifier. It is the placeholder for two global segment qualifiers: Allow Budgeting and Allow Posting.

To define a segment qualifier for either a single segment or a global segment qualifier, you define the flexfield qualifier definition and navigate to the Segment Qualifier region. Enter the required fields for a segment qualifier: name, prompt, derived column, quickcode type, and default value. The name must be unique within the Key flexfield. The segment qualifier captures its value in the Define Segment Value form. You will see Prompt in the Define Segment Value form. The Derived Column field is the database column that will store the segment qualifier value in the combination table. Quickcode type and default values will use a lookup code from an AOL lookup table with the specified quickcode type as the default value. You can also choose to enter a description for the segment qualifier. See Figure 9-11.

Review Questions

   1. What is the *Global* checkbox used for?

   2. What does the Derived Column field define?

   3. What can you use to provide a default value for a segment qualifier?

   4. In what form is the segment qualifier value captured?

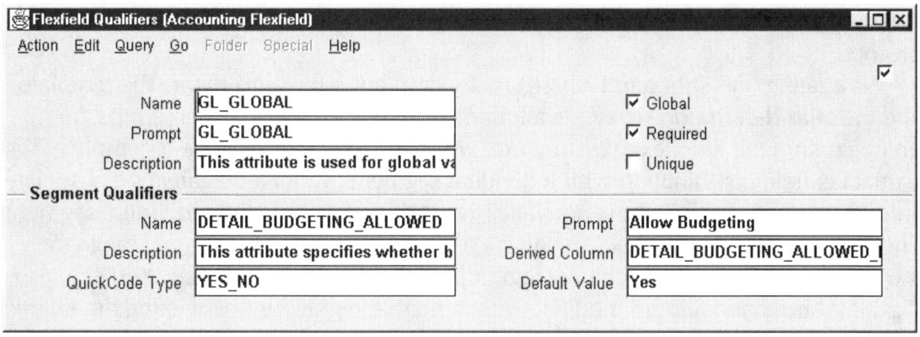

FIGURE 9-11. *Flexfield Qualifiers form*

Implementing Optional Features

The optional features for Key flexfields, excluding flexfield qualifiers and segment qualifiers, are as follows:

- Dynamic Insertion
- Shorthand Flexfield Entry
- Flexfield Value Security
- Cross-Validation Rules

Determine your needs and implement the optional features as needed. All the above optional features are covered in a separate section except the *Shorthand Flexfield Entry* option. In this section, you will see how to enable *Shorthand Flexfield Entry* if you need to create shorthand aliases to speed up data entry for commonly used complete flexfield combinations or partial flexfield combinations.

Shorthand Flexfield Entry

Under the responsibility Application Developer, you can enable *Shorthand Flexfield Entry* using the navigation path *Flexfield : Key : Aliases*. The *Shorthand Flexfield Entry* option is only for Key flexfields. First, select the Key flexfield and the structure that you want to define and enable the shorthand flexfield entry aliases. Choose your accounting flexfield structure to follow along. If you want to enable shorthand flexfield entry, you must check the *Enabled* box and enter the mandatory fields for maximum alias size and prompt. The maximum alias size sets the maximum length of the shorthand alias, while the prompt is what will be displayed in the Shorthand Alias window. You can set the maximum size to 15 and enter **NEW account** as the prompt.

Navigate to the Shorthand Aliases region and enter the alias name, the template, and the alias description. They are all mandatory fields. The alias name must be unique within the Key flexfield structure, while the template must be a complete or partial flexfield combination with individual segments validated against the associated value sets. The combination is not validated at this time, only the individual segments. The alias description describes the alias. You can enter an effective date range for the alias in the Effective alternative region to disable a shorthand alias. You can also disable a shorthand alias in the Effective alternative region by unchecking the *Enabled* checkbox. Create a shorthand alias called **Cash** for the combination 01.0000.100000 and use the alias description, **Wing Company Cash Account**. Save your work. When you save, because you are enabling shorthand flexfield entry, Oracle Applications will ask you to recompile the Key flexfield structure in order to have the changes you made take effect. This is not needed later when you are simply maintaining shorthand aliases. See Figure 9-12.

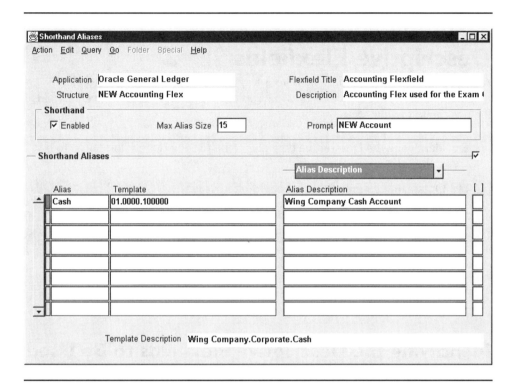

FIGURE 9-12. *Shorthand Aliases form*

You can use the profile option *Flexfields: Shorthand Entry* to allow different types of usage for each responsibility or user. Use shorthand aliases during data entry and for new data entry, updating existing data, and/or querying existing data. The alias template facilitates faster data entry, but validation of the entire flexfield combination still has to take place during data entry, as the most current value sets and cross-validation rules can be applied to individual flexfield segments as well as the entire combination as a whole.

Review Questions

1. What optional features are available for Key flexfields?

2. What are shorthand aliases used for?

3. What are the two ways to disable a shorthand alias?

4. When is the flexfield combination validated and why?

Planning and Defining Descriptive Flexfields

After you have planned and defined your Key flexfields, you will learn to plan and define Descriptive flexfields as well. Topics in relation to Descriptive flexfields include the following:

■ Identifying the Descriptive flexfields to be used and the information to be gathered

■ Organizing the information according to usage

■ Planning the layout of the Descriptive flexfield

■ Planning the behavior of the Descriptive flexfield

■ Defining a Descriptive flexfield structure

■ Defining global segments

■ Defining context-sensitive segments as appropriate

Identifying the Descriptive Flexfields to Be Used

Remember the differences between Key flexfields and Descriptive flexfields? Key flexfields are required by Oracle Applications and are used to store intelligent keys your company may have. Descriptive flexfields are not required by Oracle Applications and are used to expand a form to track additional information specific to your company's needs that would otherwise be not tracked. Oracle Applications' seeded reports do not display Descriptive flexfield values.

In order to identify the Descriptive flexfields you need as well as the additional information that should be gathered, it is important to go through every form. Whenever you see a [] and you have additional information you want to capture, you have identified a need to set up that specific Descriptive flexfield. The [] is the field where the Descriptive flexfield should be invoked.

Keep in mind that a Descriptive flexfield definition is associated with a database table, not with a specific form. This means that once a Descriptive flexfield definition is set up for a specific table, all the forms that used the same database table as a base table will have the same Descriptive flexfield definition. This also applies to the multi-org structure in Oracle Applications. Although all the Descriptive flexfield values are segregated in two operating units, the Descriptive flexfield definitions must be shared across these two operating units since the units share the same database table. Gathering everything you need for Descriptive flexfields is a rather lengthy process, and requirements can keep changing. If you change your Descriptive flexfield definitions after you have some existing data, your existing data may need to be modified to reflect the changes you made.

Review Questions

1. What is the field [] used for?

2. How would you go about gathering what you need for Descriptive flexfields?

3. With what is a Descriptive flexfield definition associated, and how does that affect a multi-org structure implementation?

Organizing the Information According to Usage

Once you have identified the additional information you want to capture in a Descriptive flexfield, you must determine the usage. There are two types of segments for Descriptive flexfields:

- Global segments
- Context-sensitive segments

Global Segments

A global segment is a segment that will always be displayed in a Descriptive flexfield window common to all context values, and it is the most commonly used type of Descriptive flexfield. Each global segment maps one-to-one to a database column. Descriptive flexfield segments are usually stored in columns named ATTRIBUTE1 to ATTRIBUTEn, where n is the maximum number of segments for a given Descriptive flexfield.

Context-Sensitive Segments

A context-sensitive segment is a segment that may or may not be displayed in a Descriptive flexfield window, depending on a context value. A context value can be derived from another field in the same block or from the context field. The field from which a context value derives its value is called a reference field. Remember, a Descriptive flexfield is associated with a database table, not a single form. A context field is a special field appearing in the Descriptive flexfield window. You can use a context field to allow users to enter their own context values or override what is defaulted from the reference field. The context value, whether from a reference field or a context field, determines which context-sensitive segments will be displayed.

Context-sensitive segments from different context values can share a single database column, because the context-sensitive segments will be mutually exclusive and will never overlap. For example, assume that your context value can either be

Yes or No. Yes means that your expense is project-related and the project name must be captured. No means that your expense is not project-related, and you must enter an approval manager name. Since your expense can be either project-related or not, the two context-sensitive segments, project name and approval manager, will never overlap, and therefore can share one single database column.

The maximum number of Descriptive flexfield segments you can have is determined by the number of Descriptive flexfield columns you have in the underlying database table. To calculate how many Descriptive flexfield segments you need, count one for each global segment, because they do not share at all the maximum number of context-sensitive segments across all possible context values.

Organize all your Descriptive flexfield needs and determine the usage. Next, decide which ones should be global segments and which ones should be context-sensitive segments. For the context-sensitive segments, you must delineate the context values, as well as from where they should be derived.

Review Questions

1. What is a global segment?

2. How are global segments stored in the database?

3. What is a context-sensitive segment?

4. How many global segments and context-sensitive segments can you have if you only have 15 Descriptive flexfield columns?

Planning the Layout of the Descriptive Flexfield

The layout of the Descriptive flexfield differs based on what combination of global segments, context-sensitive segments, context fields, and/or default values you will be using. In a Descriptive flexfield window, the global segments come first, then the context field, followed by the context-sensitive segments. Let's explore a few scenarios:

- All global segments

- All context-sensitive segments with a default value

- Global segments and context-sensitive segments with a default value or reference field

- Context-sensitive segments with context fields

- Global segments and context-sensitive segments with context fields

All Global Segments

In this case, all the global segments will be shown in the assigned segment number order of the Descriptive flexfield, with the lowest segment number displayed first.

All Context-Sensitive Segments with a Default Value

In this case, all the context-sensitive segments are displayed in the assigned segment number order of the Descriptive flexfield, with the lowest segment number displayed first.

Global and Context-Sensitive Segments with a Default Value or Reference Field (No Context Field)

In this case, the global segments will be shown in the assigned segment numbers order, followed by the context-sensitive segments in the assigned segment numbers order. The global segments and the context-sensitive segments can share the same segment number. However, the number will be sorted only within the global segments and within the context-sensitive segments, and will never be combined. With a default value or a reference field but no context field, the context field will not appear. The appropriate context-sensitive segments will be displayed automatically, based on the default value or the reference field.

Context-Sensitive Segments with Context Fields

In this case, the context field will come first. Depending on the value in the context field, the appropriate context-sensitive segments will be shown in the assigned segment numbers order with the lowest segment numbers first, following the context field.

Global Segments and Context-Sensitive Segments with Context Fields

In this instance, the global segments will be shown in the order of the assigned segment numbers, with the lowest segment numbers displayed first, followed by the context field. Depending on the values in the context field, the appropriate context-sensitive segments will be shown in the assigned segment numbers order, with the lowest segment numbers first, following the context field.

Review Questions

   I. What is the correct order of display in relation to global segments, context fields, and context-sensitive segments?

2. If you do not have a context field, what can you do to provide a context value?

3. If you have segment numbers 1 and 2 as your global segments, and segment 1 as your context-sensitive segment, in what order should they be displayed?

Planning the Behavior of the Descriptive Flexfield

The behavior of the Descriptive flexfield depends on the arrangement of the Descriptive flexfield. First, let's talk about a Descriptive flexfield containing all global segments, compared to a Descriptive flexfield containing all context-sensitive segments. You may want to have all context-sensitive segments with a default value, even if you have no current needs for a context-sensitive Descriptive flexfield. This is because if you use all global segments and you use up all of the Descriptive flexfield segments, you will have no room for growth. Using context-sensitive segments with a default value gives you room to grow. You can always add another context value later on to reuse the same Descriptive flexfield segments. While the layout of a Descriptive flexfield containing all global segments differs from the layout of one containing all context-sensitive segments, their behavior differs: for the context-sensitive segments Descriptive flexfield, the context-sensitive column will be filled in with the default value.

Next, consider having a reference field. Context-sensitive segments with a reference field but no context field use the values in the reference field as the context values, and will store these values in the reference field in the context-sensitive column in the database table. The user will not have a chance to override the context value without a context field.

On the other hand, if you have both a reference field and a context field, the context field will be defaulted based on the value in the reference field, but the user can override the context value in the context field. In other words, the reference field serves as a default.

If you have a context field and you change the context field value, a set of different context-sensitive segments must be invoked. They will be displayed as soon as the context field value is changed. This is the only time the layout of the Descriptive flexfield window will be altered on the fly.

You can also make a context value required. In this case, Oracle Applications will give you an error if no context value is provided.

Review Questions

1. Why would you have an all context-sensitive segment Descriptive flexfield if there is no current need for a context-sensitive Descriptive flexfield?

2. What is the difference between having and not having a context field with a reference field?

3. Where are the default values, values in the reference field, and the context values stored in the database, respectively?

4. When will the Descriptive flexfield window change on the fly?

Defining a Descriptive Flexfield Structure

If you are logged on with the responsibility *General Ledger, Vision Operations (USA)*, you can define a Descriptive flexfield structure by using the navigation path *Setup: Financials : Flexfield : Descriptive : Segments.* Find the Descriptive flexfield title you want to associate with a Descriptive flexfield structure. You cannot add any Descriptive flexfields in this form. You can change the Descriptive flexfield title by typing over the title in the Title field. To make changes, uncheck the *Freeze Flexfield Definition* checkbox. You must freeze and compile the Descriptive flexfield before the Descriptive flexfield can be used.

NOTE
Descriptive flexfields can be defined from several responsibilities, because their functionality is used throughout Oracle Applications.

Select a segment separator for your Descriptive flexfield. Your choices are dash, period, pipe, and any custom single character. Be careful when you select your segment separator. Choose a character that does not appear in a segment value. If the character appears in a segment value, the character in the segment value will be replaced by a caret to avoid confusion.

Next, define the context information in the Context Field region. You must delineate a context prompt, which is shown in the Descriptive flexfield window next to the context field—if you have a context field. You can optionally select a default value and a reference field, as well as decide whether a context value is required and whether you want a context field to be displayed. If the *Override Allowed* checkbox is checked, the context field will be displayed. When you select a reference field, you need to exercise caution to make sure that all forms with this Descriptive flexfield have the same field—otherwise, you will receive an error message on those forms that do not contain the field.

Every Descriptive flexfield has the Global Data Elements context value code. This code represents the global segment structure that stores all the global segments. Navigate to the Context Field Values region to define additional context value codes, context value names, and context value descriptions for the context-sensitive structures.

Each context value code represents a different Descriptive flexfield structure. The context value code you enter must be identical to the default value or the value in the reference field since the default value or the value in the reference field is matched to the context value code to retrieve the appropriate context-sensitive Descriptive flexfield structure. On the other hand, if you use a context field, you utilize a List of Values and select by context value name and context value description, not context value code. See Figure 9-13 for the Descriptive Flexfield Segments window.

Review Questions

1. Can you change the title of the Descriptive flexfield?

2. What is the reference field used for?

3. What is the *Override Allowed* checkbox used for?

4. What is the context value code used for?

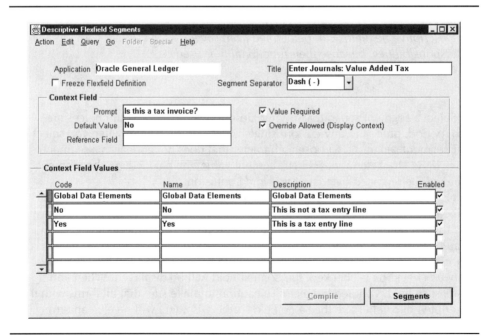

FIGURE 9-13. *Descriptive Flexfield Segments form*

Define Global Segments

Define global segments under the Global Data Elements context value code. You cannot disable Global Data Elements context values, but you can change the name and the description. The Description field is optional. To define global segments, click on the **Segments** button with your cursor on the Global Data Elements context value. Enter the Descriptive flexfield segments in exactly the same way as you enter Key flexfield segments.

You first need to enter all the required attributes. These include the segment number, segment name, window prompt, and column name. The segment number defines the ordering of the segments. The segment name can be a combination of letters, numbers, underscores, and spaces. However, the segment name must start with a letter. The window prompt is defaulted with the segment name and can be overridden. The column name defines in which column the segment value is stored in the combination table. You can optionally enter a value set. With no value set associated, there will be no validation: not even a format validation. Next, determine whether this segment needs to be displayed. As a last step, decide whether this segment needs to be enabled. Nondisplayed or disabled segments will not be displayed in a Flexfield window. However, nondisplayed segments with a default segment value will be saved to the database, while disabled segments will not have a default value and will not be saved to the database. Click on the **Value Set** button to query or edit the associated value set. You can define the summary and required fields in the Segments Summary window if you are satisfied with the segment attribute defaults. You also have the option to open the Detail Segments window to modify the additional segment attributes.

Review Questions

1. What is the context value code for the global segment structure?
2. Can you disable the global segment structure?

Defining Context-Sensitive Segments

To define context-sensitive segments, you first need to define each context-sensitive structure. To define a context-sensitive structure, enter a mandatory unique context value code, a required context value name, and an optional context value description. You cannot delete any context-sensitive structures, but you can disable them by unchecking the *Enabled* checkbox. Click on the **Segments** button while your cursor is on the desired context-sensitive structure to define context-sensitive segments. You define the context-sensitive segments the same way you define Key flexfield segments and global segments. Notice how once the column is selected for a global segment, you cannot select it anymore. However, if the column is only selected for a context-sensitive segment of other context values—as long as the column is not selected for your specific context value—you can still select the column to be used for your specific context value.

Freeze and compile the Descriptive flexfield after all your changes, so that these changes can take effect.

Review Questions

1. What is the difference between disabling the Global Data Elements context value code vs. other context value codes?

2. Which field must be unique in the Context Field Values region?

3. Which fields are optional in the Context Field Values region?

Implementing Cross-Validation Rules

After you have set up your Key flexfield, you can implement cross-validation rules. Remember that cross-validation rules do not apply to Descriptive flexfields. This section will cover the following in relation to cross-validation rules implementation:

■ Explaining the purpose of cross-validation

■ Identifying cross-validation rules

■ Controlling the interaction of multiple cross-validation rules

Purpose of Cross-Validation

Cross-validation rules define whether segment values of a particular segment can be combined with other segment values of another particular segment when new combinations are created. In other words, cross-validation rules prevent the definition of invalid combinations of segment values. Key flexfields can automatically perform these cross-validations based on the cross-validation rules you defined. You have more of a business need to define cross-validation rules if dynamic insertion is allowed, since cross-validation rules will govern which newly created combinations are valid combinations. The user will receive an error message if the combination the user is creating violates any cross-validation rule.

You can use cross-validation rules to perform certain validations in your accounting flexfield. For example, you can use cross-validation rules to secure all balance sheet accounts to be associated only with the balance sheet cost center, or the corporate cost center and profit and loss accounts to be associated with specific cost centers other than the corporate cost center. You can also use cross-validation rules to restrict data entry of cost centers that are not legitimate for a specific company. The Accounting flexfield is being used as an example, but cross-validation rules can be applied to other Key flexfields as well.

The error messages associated with cross-validation rules can be very informative and tell the user exactly what is wrong with the flexfield combination. The invalid segment can also be highlighted accordingly.

Review Questions

1. What will a user see if the flexfield combination violates any cross-validation rule?

2. Describe an example illustrating the appropriate use of cross-validation rules.

Cross-Validation Rules

You identify the need for cross-validation rules by understanding which flexfield combinations should be invalid. Remember that the segment values you design should be grouped in ranges that make sense. This will allow you to identify invalid combinations by range. A cross-validation rule is composed of one or more cross-validation rule elements. There are two types of cross-validation rule elements: include and exclude. Every cross-validation rule must have at least one include rule element, since cross-validation rules exclude all values unless they are specifically included in at least one cross-validation rule element. The exclude elements override include elements. You can always accomplish the same result by either including specific ranges explicitly, or including all possible values and excluding specific ranges. Oracle recommends that you define one, all-encompassing include cross-validation rule element, together with several exclude cross-validation rule elements. For example, to secure a balance sheet account to be associated with a balance sheet cost center or the corporate cost center only, you must include every possible combination, then exclude the balance sheet account ranges for the cost center (other than the corporate cost center). An all-encompassing include for numeric segments is 0 through 9, while for alphanumeric segments it is from 0 through Z. If your flexfield has three segments, the first segment is two numbers and the second and third segments are four characters and six characters, respectively; then, the all-encompassing include is 00-0000-000000 through 99-ZZZZ-ZZZZZZ. If your segment is not required, leaving the segment blank will also include all possible values.

The Operations Accounting Flex serves as an example. All the balance sheet accounts in the Operations Accounting Flex can be identified in two ranges—1000 to 1499; and 1700 to 3999—with the corporate cost center at 000. In order to implement a cross-validation rule that will secure a balance sheet account to be associated only with a corporate cost center, you must have one all-encompassing include cross-validation element rule, as well as two exclude cross-validation element rules. The breakdown would be one for natural account ranges from 1000 through 1499 for all cost centers other than 000, and one for natural account ranges from 1700 through 3999 for all cost centers other than 000. See Figure 9-14. This is accomplished by entering the following values:

Type	From	To
Include	00-000-0000-0000-000	ZZ-ZZZ-ZZZZ-ZZZZ-ZZZ
Exclude	00-001-1000-0000-000	ZZ-ZZZ-1499-ZZZZ-ZZZ
Exclude	00-001-1700-0000-000	ZZ-ZZZ-3999-ZZZZ-ZZZ

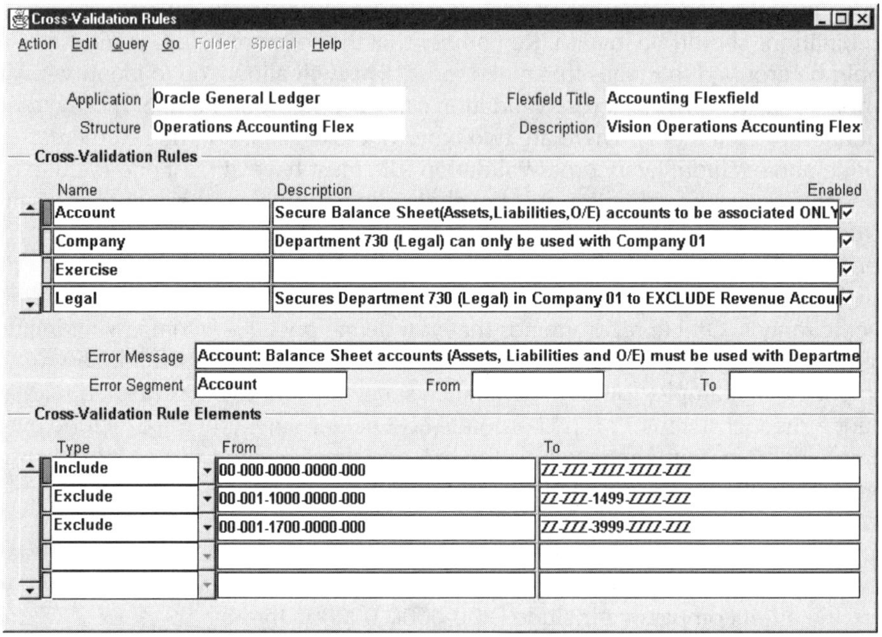

FIGURE 9-14. *Cross-Validation Rules form*

Defining Cross-Validation Rules

To define a cross-validation rule, use the navigation path *Setup : Financials : Flexfield : Key : Rules* under the General Ledger, Vision Operations (USA) responsibility. First, select the Key flexfield and the flexfield structure you want to define in relation to the cross-validation rule. Create an additional cross-validation rule for the Operations Accounting Flex structure that will restrict Department 730 with Company 01.

First, add a new record and enter the cross-validation rule name. The name must be unique. You can enter an optional description and disable the cross-validation rule. You can also delete a cross-validation rule. However, if you have any chance to reuse the cross-validation rule, disabling it will save effort in redefining it in the future. Use the name **Exercise** as the cross-validation rule name. You also need to enter a mandatory error message that will appear if an enabled cross-validation rule is being violated. Next, you can choose to enter an error segment and an effective date range. The error segment will be highlighted if this particular cross-validation is violated. The effective date defines when this cross-validation rule is valid. Choose Account as your error segment.

Next, you must enter the cross-validation rule elements. You should first include all possible combinations, then exclude Department 730 for every company except Company 01. You can accomplish this by using three cross-validation rule elements. They are as follows:

Type	From	To
Include	00-000-0000-0000-000	ZZ-ZZZ-ZZZZ-ZZZZ-ZZZ
Exclude	00-730-0000-0000-000	00-730-ZZZZ-ZZZZ-ZZZ
Exclude	02-730-0000-0000-000	ZZ-730-ZZZZ-ZZZZ-ZZZ

Review Questions

1. How do you define an all-encompassing include cross-validation rule element?

2. What will a blank value do in a cross-validation rule element?

3. What is the error segment used for?

4. What is the difference between disabling a cross-validation rule vs. deleting it?

Controlling the Interaction of Multiple Cross-Validation Rules

You can have multiple cross-validation rules for a single flexfield structure. You should always use multiple cross-validation rules if you need to cross-validate across more than two segments. This allows you to have more direct and meaningful error messages to point the user to specific problems.

For example, using our previous exercise, you exclude Department 730 with every company other than 01. You may also want to exclude an account range from company 01. You can combine the requirements into a single cross-validation rule. However, you only have an error message and one error segment. You must choose between placing the cursor on the department segment or the account segment. In this case, it is better to split the requirements into two cross-validation rules—one for department 730 and one for the account range.

As a rule of thumb, using multiple simple cross-validation rules is better than one single, complex cross-validation rule. If your cross-validation rules overlap, then the oldest enabled cross-validation rule that is being violated will be the rule that displays the error message. Multiple cross-validation rules work together to make the validation more restricted. In other words, combinations are valid if they are in at least one include element and outside of all exclude elements.

Review Questions

1. When should you use multiple cross-validation rules?

2. What will happen if the cross-validation rule has no include element?

3. How many cross-validation rules can you have for a specific Key flexfield structure?

Implementing Flexfield Value Security

Flexfield security can be applied to both Key flexfields and Descriptive flexfields. There are two steps in implementing flexfield value security. You must first define the security rules, then assign the security rules to responsibilities. In this section, the following will be covered regarding flexfield value security implementation:

- Explaining how flexfield security is accomplished

- Identifying which flexfields are candidates for security

- Designing a security plan

- Controlling interactions between security rules

- Defining security rules

- Assigning security rules

- Enabling security

How Flexfield Security Is Accomplished

You can use security rules to restrict segment values that your user can enter during data entry. This can be accomplished by responsibility. Data entry includes using the segment value as a concurrent program parameter. The lists of values will only display values that are not restricted by security rules assigned to the responsibility associated with your logged-on user. If the default value or shorthand alias uses segment values that your responsibility cannot access, the segment value will disappear from the screen and you will need to enter a segment value that you can enter. Flexfield Value Security only applies to the value sets of validation options *Independent, Dependent,* or *Table.*

You can either set up security rules by establishing ranges of segment values that the user can enter or use as a report parameter, or you can have the security rule include every possible segment value and then exclude ranges of segment values or specific segment values that the user can use during data entry. This is called flexfield value security. Flexfield value security can only be performed on segments that have the *Enabled Security* checkbox checked, including concurrent program parameters.

Security rules are associated with value sets and will affect all segments that use the same value set as long as the *Enabled Security* checkbox is checked for the segments and the responsibility your user is using has the appropriate security rules assigned. The same security, therefore, can be applied to Key flexfields, Descriptive flexfields, or the Standard Request Submission form.

In addition to data entry restrictions that will be imposed by flexfield security, inquiry capabilities will be affected too. For example, in queries within the Account Inquiry form, the Funds Available form, or the Summary Account Inquiry form, you cannot query up data with account combinations that you have security restriction rules for. On any other form, the data will be displayed but the account combinations will be blanked out.

Review Questions

1. To which value set validation options can flexfield security rules be applied?

2. Can flexfield value security be applied to Descriptive flexfields?

3. How do Descriptive Flexfields and Key Flexfields share the same security rules?

4. What happens to inquiries if security rules do not allow access to a particular segment value?

Useful Flexfields for Security

All flexfields are candidates for flexfield value security. These include Key flexfields, Descriptive flexfields, and concurrent program parameters. As mentioned in the above section, security rules are associated with value sets and will affect all segments that use the same value set as long as the *Enabled Security* checkbox is checked for the segments and the responsibility your user is using has the appropriate security rules assigned. The same security, therefore, can be applied to Key flexfields, Descriptive flexfields, or the Standard Request Submission form.

Designing a Security Plan

In order to design a security plan, you first need to determine which flexfields require security. Next, you should identify whether there are any common value sets between the flexfields that you need in order to enable security. Identify the levels of security you desire. In other words, by segment value or ranges of segment value, identify the restrictions you want to put into place. As a last step, assign these restrictions to responsibilities. After you design your security plan, you will know how many security rules and how many responsibilities you need. Create a security matrix between the security rules and responsibilities once you are finished.

Review Questions

1. Which flexfields are candidates for security?

2. What steps do you need to take in designing a security plan?

Controlling Interactions Between Security Rules

A single Key flexfield structure can have multiple cross-validation rules. In turn, each rule can have multiple cross-validation rule elements. Security rules are the same way. A value set can have multiple security rules, and each security rule can have multiple security rule elements. If you have multiple security rule elements and they overlap each other, the valid values for the security rule are all the values included in any security rule element, as long as the segment values are not explicitly excluded. In other words, the multiple security rule elements create an OR relationship, forming a union of all included segment values. However, if you have multiple security rules for the same value set and they are assigned to the same responsibility, the following will happen. If the security rule segment ranges overlap, the valid values that users of the responsibility can enter are the values that exist in all the security rules, not in just one security rule. In other words, if the security rules do not overlap, there will be no valid values that users of the responsibility can enter. Multiple security rules create an AND relationship, forming an intersection of all the included segment values. More security rules make the security increasingly restrictive. Segment values must pass all the assigned security rules in order to be valid values.

Review Questions

1. What elements make up a security rule?

2. How are security rule structures similar to those of cross-validation rules?

3. How do multiple security rule elements work together?

4. How do multiple security rules work together?

Defining Security Rules

To define a security rule, use the navigation path *Setup: Financial : Flexfields : Key : Security : Define.* A Find window appears. This is the same Find window as the one used in entering allowable segment values. You can find values by value set, Key flexfield, Descriptive flexfield, or concurrent program.

Define security rules by entering a unique name, an optional description, and a mandatory message. The message will appear if the security rule is violated. After you define the security rule, you should delineate the security rule elements. Similar to cross-validation rule elements, you have two types of security rule elements: include and exclude. It is suggested that you have an all-encompassing include and then several excludes. The range for security rules is not the entire combination, but only for a specific segment.

Find the Operations Accounting Flex and the independent segment department. Create a security rule called **Department Security Group** that includes Departments 110 through 130.

Next, you need to enter security rule elements. Include all possible values and then exclude any values before Department 110 and after 130. Enter the following:

Type	From	To
Include	000	ZZZ
Exclude	000	109
Exclude	131	ZZZ

See Figure 9-15 for the Define Security Rules form.

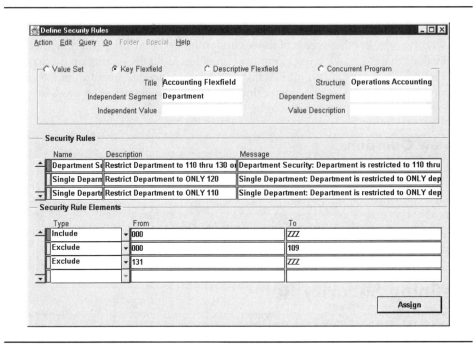

FIGURE 9-15. *Define Security Rules form*

Review Questions

 1. How do you find the desired value set?

 2. How would you set up a security rule to exclude Company 03?

Assigning Security Rules

Once you define the security rules, you must assign these rules to a responsibility. To do this, click on the **Assign** button in the Define Security Rules form. Assign security rules by first selecting the application and responsibility combination, then associating the responsibility by selecting the security rule. See Figure 9-16.

  You can also assign security rules by using the navigation path *Setup : Financials : Flexfields : Key : Security : Assign.* Use the Find window to locate the correct value set and assign security rules in the same way that you would use the **Assign** button in the Define Security Rules form.

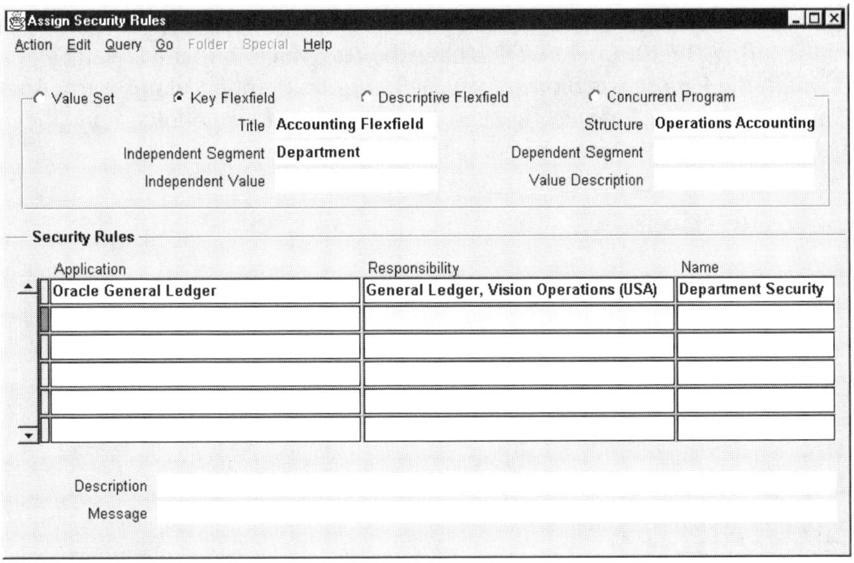

FIGURE 9-16. *Assign Security Rules form*

Review Questions

    1. What are the two routes to assigning security rules?

    2. How do you assign a security rule?

Enabling Security

In order to enable security, you need to enable it at two levels:

- Value set
- Segment

Value Set

Check the *Security Available* checkbox in the value set definition to enable security. This is the first step, because this allows segments that use this value set to enable security.

Segment

Next, check the *Security Enabled* checkbox for the individual segment in order to enable security. The *Security Enabled* checkbox is available in the Detail Segments form and in the Parameters block of the Define Concurrent Programs form. After you mark the *Security Enabled* checkbox, you need to freeze and compile the flexfield structure for the security enabling to take effect.

Review Questions

1. What do you need to do to enable security?

2. What do you need to do after setting *Security Enabled* at the segment level?

3. Where can you find the segment *Security Enabled* checkbox?

Using Advanced Validation Capabilities

In this last section, you will study advanced validation capabilities. These include advanced table validations, cascading flexfields, special value sets, and pair value sets. This section will cover:

■ Explaining the advanced validation capabilities available in Oracle Applications

■ Explaining cascading flexfields

■ Explaining the use of special and pair value sets

Advanced Validation Capabilities in Oracle Applications

With table validation types, you can perform advanced validations using the following:

■ Multiple tables

■ Use of expressions

■ Profile options

- Subquery

- Field value

Multiple Tables

You can use multiple tables in the Table Name field and supply an alias. Recall the asset number example. You can enter **FA_ADDITIONS add, FA_BOOKS book** as the table name. Next, you enter **add.ASSET_NUMBER, add.ASSET_ID**, and **book.COST** as the value column, ID column, and description column, respectively. In order for multiple tables to work, you must specify the join condition. In the Where/Order By field, add the join condition and the book type code condition. You can enter the following:

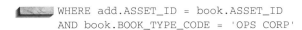

```
WHERE add.ASSET_ID = book.ASSET_ID
AND book.BOOK_TYPE_CODE = 'OPS CORP'
```

Use of Expressions

Use expressions for columns or in the Where/Order By field. A common one would be a DECODE statement. Use a DECODE statement to perform branching logic. For example, DECODE (literal, condition1, result1, condition2, result2, default) functions produce results based on the following logic:

If literal = condition1

then return result1

else if literal = condition2

then return result2

else return default value

Profile Options

Query the value set AP_SRS_ACCOUNTING_PERIOD_MAND and click on the **Edit Information** button. In the Where/Order By field, you can see the use of the profile option *gl_set_of_bks_id*. You refer to a profile option value by *:$PROFILES$.(profile_ option_name you want)*. For example, the value of the profile *gl_set_of_bks_id* is *:$PROFILE$.gl_set_of_bks_id.* This feature allows greater flexibility and helps prevent hard-coding of values that maybe stored as profile options. See Figure 9-17.

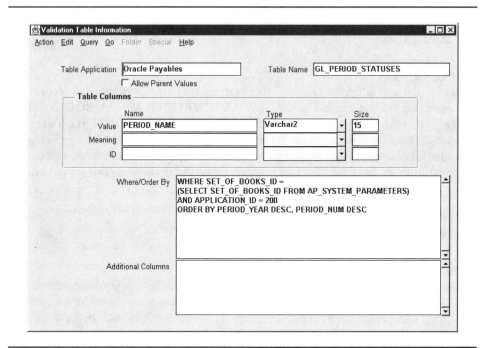

FIGURE 9-17. *Validation Table Information form*

Subquery

You can perform many complex conditions within the value set WHERE clause. The WHERE clause is explicitly added to the value set query with an AND condition and a parenthesis. Query the value set AP_APZACS_PAYMENT_METHOD and click on the **Edit Information** button. In the Where/Order By field, you can see the use of a subquery selecting BANK_ACCOUNT_ID from the AP_BANK_ACCOUNTS table. See Figure 9-18.

Field Value

Use **:block.field** in the Where/Order By field to refer to a value in a specified field in a specified block. You need to make sure that all the forms that use this value set have the same block and the same field. You should not continue to use this type, as it is only being provided for backward compatibility and may not be supported in the future.

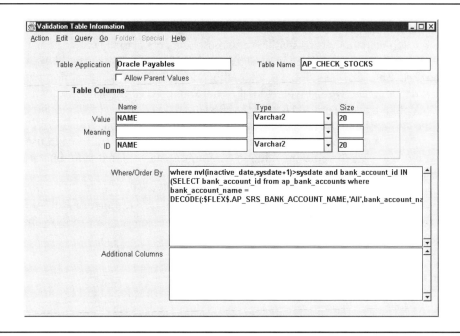

FIGURE 9-18.   *Validation Subquery*

Review Questions

    1. How do you refer to a profile option value?

    2. What do you need to do to use multiple tables in a value set?

    3. How are subqueries included in a value set?

    4. What does **:block.field** do?

Cascading Flexfields

A dependent value set relies on an independent value set, which is a prior segment
of the same flexfield. If you need to depend on more than one prior segment, use
cascading flexfields. In the WHERE clause of a value set, you can refer to a prior
segment value by :$FLEX$.(value set name/name). If more than one of your former
segments uses the same value set, the closest prior segment value will be returned.

If no value set name is matched, Oracle Applications will match the name against the segment name.

The value set name is case-sensitive and must be identical to the value set name or segment name. Since this is used in a WHERE clause, no special character-like quote can be used. The $FLEX$ option will return the hidden ID column of the prior segment if one is defined; otherwise, it will return the value column. To explicitly ask for a different column, add **.ID, .VALUE** or **.MEANING** to the end of the $FLEX$ option.

If the server-side validation of flexfields is not on, you can pass other columns besides the ID, value, or meaning columns. Add an additional column and use an INTO clause to pass the column value into a variable name. Next, add the variable name to the end of the $FLEX$ option as a reference.

Using cascading flexfields, you can derive values based on multiple prior values that can be from the ID column, value column, description column, or even user-defined column if the server-side validation is off. It is a very powerful validation feature.

NULL
You can add :NULL as a suffix to $PROFILE$, $FLEX$, or :block.field to allow null values.

Review Questions

1. How can you return the description column?

2. How do you define additional columns to be used in cascading flexfields, and what is the condition for using them?

3. To what does the value set name after the $FLEX$ option match?

4. What is :NULL used for?

Special and Pair Value Sets
There are two more value sets that have not been discussed:

- Special value set
- Pair value set

Special Value Set
A special value set allows you to invoke a flexfield within a flexfield. A special value set invokes the flexfield by calling some predefined flexfield subroutines.

To define a special value set when delineating a value set, select Special as the validation type and click on the **Edit Information** button.

To define a special value set, select an event and type in a function. The function is invoked when the event happens. Valid events are Edit, Edit/Edit, Insert/Update, ListVal, Load, Query, and Validate. Some of these are for future releases. An Edit event occurs when the user enters into the segment with the special value set. A Load event occurs when the user queries the segment with the special value set. A Validate event takes place when the user leaves the segment with the special value set.

Functions are Oracle Applications Object Library flexfield subroutines. POPID will invoke a Key flexfield window; LOADID will load the Key flexfield information based on the unique identifier; and VALID will validate a Key flexfield. Common parameters for the flexfield subroutines are APPL_SHORT_NAME for the application short name; CODE for the flexfield code, such as "GL#"; NUM for the flexfield structure number; ID for the hidden ID field; SEG for the Concatenated Segments field; REQUIRED to define whether the flexfield is required; DESC for the Description field; DISPLAY for the Flexfield window title; and DINSERT for dynamic insertion. Dynamic insert must be off for special value sets. Use DINSERT="N" to turn dynamic inserts off. The details of these subroutines are documented in the Oracle Applications Object Library Developer's Guide. See Figure 9-19.

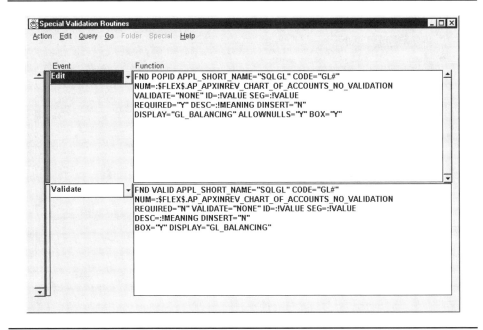

FIGURE 9-19.   *Special Validation Routines form*

Pair Value Set

A pair value set is very similar to a special value set except that it uses the flexfield range subroutines POPIDR, VALIDR, and LOADIDR instead of POPID, VALID, and LOADID to capture a flexfield range. Everything else is the same as a special value set. See Figure 9-20.

Special Arguments

You can have the following special arguments to pass values to and from the flexfield subroutines:

- :!ID

- :!VALUE

- :!MEANING

- :!DIR

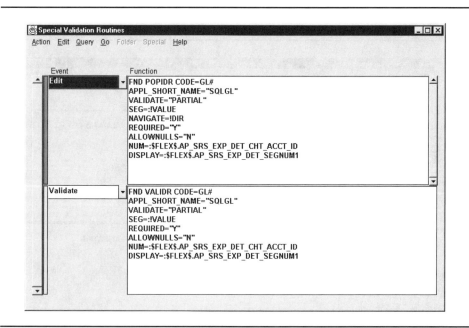

FIGURE 9-20. *Special Validation Routines form using Pair Value Set*

:!ID   This is the combination ID of the flexfield.

:!VALUE   This is the concatenated value of the flexfield and is its displayed value in the Flexfield window.

:!MEANING   This is the concatenated description of the flexfield.

:!DIR   This is the navigation direction of the flexfield.

Review Questions

1. What flexfield subroutines can you use for a special value set?

2. What is an event and a function?

3. What special arguments are available?

For the Chapter Summary, Two-Minute Drill, and Chapter Questions and Answers, open the summary.htm file contained in the Summary_files directory on the book's CD-ROM.

CHAPTER
10

Alerts

n this chapter, you will be presented with a comprehensive overview of Oracle Alert. This chapter explains why Oracle Alert is important, and what business needs it can address. Topics include the following:

- Basics of Oracle Alert

- Implementing periodic alerts

- Alert history

- Response processing

- Implementation considerations

First, you will learn the basics of Oracle Alert. Next, you will be introduced to the different types of alerts you can implement. Alerts trigger actions: the text describes what type of actions can be triggered. The chapter also explains some of the precoded alerts in Oracle Alert, and the functionality these alerts bring to the table.

Next, you will see how to implement alerts by going through exercises to set up alert definitions along with their desired actions. You will establish both an event alert and a periodic alert. Oracle Alert maintains an alert history. This chapter explains the necessity of having an alert history and the features associated with alert histories in Oracle Alert, as well as how to review alert histories.

As a last step, the chapter talks about how response processing works. Response processing allows the user to respond to alerts. Responses can also trigger actions. The last section of this chapter talks about implementation considerations in planning and configuring Oracle Alert.

Oracle Alert

Oracle Alert is an application module that can report exceptions or perform actions based on exceptions or data conditions. This section will:

- Explain the basics of Oracle Alert

- List the business needs satisfied by Oracle Alert

- Explain the types of alerts that can be implemented

- List the business needs that are satisfied by each alert

- Describe alert action types

- Describe alert action levels

- Implement an event alert

■ List and explain the steps involved in implementing alerts

■ Explain the precoded alerts available in Oracle Alert

Basics of Oracle Alert

Oracle Alert is an application module that reports exceptions and performs actions based on the detected exceptions. You can create *alerts* that run when a specific event occurs or that run periodically. Alerts, in turn, can trigger *actions* without user intervention. Actions are transactions that can be simply a notification or a very complex batch program. Based on responses to an alert notification, other actions can be triggered based on user intervention.

In short, Oracle Alert provides a reliable way to monitor activities in Oracle Applications, as well as keeping you informed of unusual conditions. Oracle Alert can also perform routine transactions or transactions that act on unusual conditions. In addition, Oracle Alert keeps both alert histories and action histories for audit trail purposes.

Review Questions

  1. What is an alert?

  2. What is an action?

Business Needs Satisfied by Oracle Alert

Many business needs can be satisfied by Oracle Alert. They are as follows:

■ Integration with email

■ Keeping informed as an event occurs

■ Performing routine transactions

■ Performing actions based on user responses

■ Automatic processing

■ Maintaining information flow without a paper trail

Integration with Email

You may need to associate the Oracle Applications database with your electronic mail system so that you can send information through the associated electronic mail system regarding unusual conditions. Though you need Oracle Office to automatically handle email responses, you do not have to implement it to be able to send messages.

Keeping Informed as an Event Occurs

You may need to be notified when unusual conditions occur. This gives you an immediate view of the important activities happening within Oracle Applications. For example, when the database is getting filled, or when a purchase order total reaches a certain dollar limit, you may want to receive a notification.

Performing Routine Transactions

It is a good idea to schedule routine transactions that generate reports or transactions periodically. You may also want to monitor key information, such as inventory levels and purchase order commitments, periodically, in order to have visibility. For example, you may desire a weekly listing of all requisitions and purchase orders awaiting approval. Exceptions and messages are the key concepts in Oracle Alerts. A standard report would need to be read, whether or not there were any actions to be taken. An alert, on the other hand, is proactive. It produces output only when needed, and sends that output directly to the person who needs to act on it.

Performing Actions Based on User Responses

You may need to send notifications to users when certain specified conditions occur. Based on the user response to the notification, different actions might be triggered.

Automatic Processing

You may desire that the system take care of certain conditions automatically, without any user intervention. For example, concurrent programs and reports can be submitted automatically when a specified data condition is met.

Maintaining Information Flow

It may be necessary to maintain an information flow throughout the system without a paper trail. The user needs to view information online and make decisions that can initiate actions in the background. This initiates a push vs. pull flow of information from Oracle Applications.

Review Questions

1. What are some of the business needs that can be addressed by Oracle Alert?

2. Can Oracle Alert perform actions automatically, as well as based upon user responses?

Types of Alerts

Two types of alerts can be implemented in Oracle Alert. They are:

- **Event alerts**   An event alert is essentially a database trigger that notifies you when a specified database event occurs and a particular condition is met. A database event can be an insert and/or an update to any database table. A specified condition is defined by a SELECT statement. Rows returning from the SELECT statement indicate that the specified condition is met. An event alert can initiate predefined actions. When a database event associated with an event alert happens, a concurrent program called Check Event Alert (ALECTC) is submitted to the concurrent manager. ALECTC executes the SELECT statement and initiates the predefined actions.

- **Periodic alerts**   A periodic alert, on the other hand, is not immediate. It is executed according to a predefined frequency or schedule (for example, weekly or monthly) and checks specified conditions periodically. A specified condition is also defined by a SELECT statement. Rows returning from the SELECT statement indicate that the specified condition is met. Periodic alerts can initiate predefined actions. Similar to an event alert, a concurrent program called Check Periodic Alert (ALECDC) is submitted to the concurrent manager when a periodic alert is initiated. ALECDC executes the SELECT statement and initiates the predefined actions.

Event alerts can keep you informed as specified events occur. They are integrated with your electronic mail system so that event alerts can send a notification to the user when an event occurs. Based on user responses to a notification, specific actions can be initiated. Besides notification, other actions can be initiated to perform automatic processing. With an event alert configured properly, you can maintain an information flow online without a paper trail.

Periodic alerts can perform routine transactions based on specified frequencies or schedules. Routine transactions can be periodic reports or programs. A periodic alert is integrated with your email system so that a notification can be sent to a user when the specified conditions in the periodic alert definition occur. Based on user responses to a notification, a specific action can be initiated.

Other actions can also be initiated to perform automatic processing. With periodic alerts configured properly, you can maintain an information flow online without a paper trail, as in the case of event alerts.

Review Questions

1. What are the two types of alerts?

2. What is an event alert?

3. What is a periodic alert?

4. Which alert types can keep you informed in real time as specified events occur?

5. Which alert type can perform routine transactions based on a specified frequency or schedule?

6. Which business needs do both types of alerts satisfy?

Alert Action Types

There are four types of actions in Oracle Alert:

- **Concurrent program actions** submit a concurrent program registered with Oracle Applications to the concurrent manager as the action.

- **Message actions** send an email message to a user or distribution list you define.

- **Operating system script actions** initiate an operating system script as the operating system user who started the concurrent manager.

- **SQL statement script actions** execute a SQL statement script or PL/SQL script as the action.

Review Questions

1. What is a concurrent program action type?

2. What is a message action type?

3. What is an operating system script action type?

4. What is a SQL statement script action type?

Alert Action Levels

The three alert action levels are as follows:

- **Detail**   An action defined at the detail level is initiated once for each exception found—meaning once for each row returned by the SELECT statement defined in the alert definition.

- **Summary**   An action defined at the summary level is initiated once for all exceptions found or once for each unique output combination, depending on the action type. This means that it is initiated once for all combinations of data returned by the SELECT statement defined in the alert definition, or once for each unique output combination of data returned by the SELECT statement. It is especially useful when the output is in message format: instead of clogging the mailbox, you notify the recipient of all required actions in a single message.

- **No Exception**   An action defined at the no-exception level is initiated once if no data is returned from the SELECT statement.

Review Questions

1. What are the three alert action types?

2. When is an action defined at the detail level initiated? At the summary level? At the no-exception level?

Defining an Event Alert

To use Oracle Alert, you must log on to Oracle Applications with the *Alert Manager* responsibility. To define an event alert, follow the navigation path *Alert : Define.*

First, enter the application name that owned your alert. The application is used to determine what Oracle ID(s) to use to log on to the database when an alert is checked. Next, enter the alert name. The alert name must be unique within the application you specified. Input a meaningful name, then enter an optional description. As a last step, key in the alert type. You can choose either Event or Periodic. To disable an alert, uncheck the *Enabled* checkbox. You are going to create an event alert where you detect a journal entry with an individual line amount greater than $100,000 or a user-defined limit. Select Oracle General Ledger as the application name, and name your alert **NEW journal lines exceeding $100,000**. Select Event as your alert type. Once you have selected the event alert type, the Event Details region appears.

In the Event Details region, specify the table that should be watched for database events. Database events can occur after inserts and/or after updates. To specify an event table, select the application name and the table name. The application name here can be different than the application name that owned the alert, but they must both exist in the same database. You cannot use a view as an event table. The table must be registered with the Oracle Applications Object Library. You can check the *After Insert* checkbox for a database event to happen after any insertion, and you can check the *After Update* checkbox for a database event to happen after any update. An event alert is checked when the specified database event happens in the event table. For example, if you specify a database event as after an insert on table GL_JE_LINES, when a row is inserted into table GL_JE_LINES, the event alert is checked. Check both the *After Insert* and *After Update* checkboxes for your alert, since you want to check the journal line amount after either an insertion or an update.

Next, key in the number of days for which you want to keep an alert history. A history includes exceptions, actions, and responses. Keeping 0 days means no history is kept. You can optionally enter an end date if you want to end this alert on a specified future date. The Last Checked field is a display-only field that shows the date this alert was last marked.

Enter a SELECT statement in the Select Statement field. This SELECT statement is executed when the alert is checked. In other words, when the specified database event happens on the specified event table, the SELECT statement will be executed. Any row returned from the SELECT statement will be an exception. The SELECT statement is in the format:

```
SELECT  COLUMN_NAME
INTO    &OUTPUT1
FROM    TABLE_NAME
WHERE   WHERE_CLAUSE
```

You can have multiple columns in a SELECT statement. If you have multiple columns, you need the same number of output variables in the INTO clause. Output variables are identified by an ampersand. You can format number outputs by applying a SQL*Plus number format mask in the SELECT statement. The SELECT statement must be less than 64KB in length. You cannot use set operators (such as GROUP BY or SUM) in the alert SELECT statement.

You can also have input variables in the SELECT statement. Input variable names are preceded by a colon. You must include the implicit input variable :ROWID, since :ROWID identifies the inserted or updated row of the event table. For your exercise, you are going to select the last updated person name, the last updated date, the journal header name, the period name, the line number, the debit amount, and the credit amount from the GL_JE_LINES table. You are also going to use the input variable :LIMIT to allow users to define a limit for your SELECT statement. After that you will see how Alert prompts you to define the characteristics of the input and output variables that you have implicitly defined in the SELECT statement.

The SELECT statement you can use is:

```
SELECT  u.user_name,
        l.last_update_date,
        h.name,
        h.period_name,
        l.je_line_num,
        l.entered_dr,
        l.entered_cr
INTO    &UPDATE_USER,
        &UPDATE_DATE,
        &HEADER_NAME,
        &PERIOD_NAME,
        &LINE_NUM,
        &DEBIT,
        &CREDIT
FROM    gl_je_lines   l,
        gl_je_headers h,
        fnd_user      u
WHERE   u.user_id = l.last_updated_by
        AND
        h.je_header_id = l.je_header_id
        AND
            (   nvl(l.entered_cr,0) > :LIMIT
                or
                nvl(l.entered_dr,0) > :LIMIT
            )
        AND
        l.rowid = :ROWID
```

TIP
You must include :ROWID in all event alert WHERE clauses; otherwise, Oracle Alert will not be able to identify the particular row that has been inserted or updated into the event table.

Besides :ROWID, there are two more implicit inputs supplied by Oracle Alert: :MAILID and :DATE_LAST_CHECKED. :MAILID is the email address of the application user who inserted or updated the row of the event table. If the email address field is not filled in when the application user is defined, then :MAILID returns either the application user name or the operating system user ID, depending on the default user *Mail Account* option setup. (You establish the default user mail account by following the navigation path *System : Options* and moving to the More Options alternative region.) :DATE_LAST_CHECKED signifies the last date this alert has been marked. You can use :DATE_LAST_CHECKED to create self-referencing alerts. In other words, utilize the date this alert had last been checked as the starting point for selecting new exceptions and avoiding sending duplicate messages. To do this, you can use :DATE_LAST_CHECKED in the WHERE clause of your alert SELECT statement. Compare it against the creation date or the last updated date of the table you are referencing. Only look at the retrieved records that have been created or updated since the last check date.

Review Questions

1. What is an event table?

2. How do you specify an input variable in an Oracle Alert SELECT statement?

3. How do you specify an output variable in an Oracle Alert SELECT statement?

4. What are the three implicit input variables, and what do they represent?

Figure 10-1 shows the Alerts definition form, which provides you with the following choices:

- Import
- Export
- Verify
- Run
- Alert Details
- Actions
- Action Sets
- Response Sets

Import

Instead of typing a SELECT statement, you can import a file containing the SELECT statement using the **Import** button. To import a file, click on the **Import** button and specify the name and location of your file in your operating system. A default INTO clause with three output variables will be inserted if the file contains no INTO clause or an invalid INTO clause with the number of output variables not matching the SELECT list. Modify the output variables according to your needs.

It is usually most practical to debug your SQL statement in SQL*Plus. You can quickly and interactively fix the syntax and determine that the query returns the

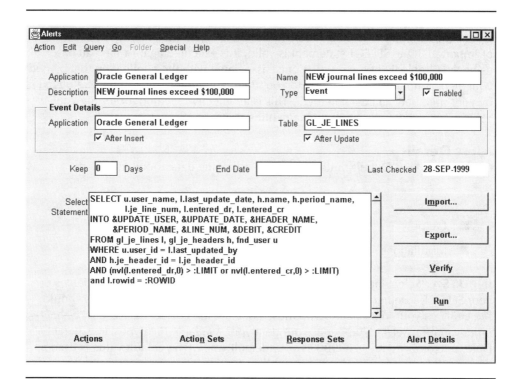

FIGURE 10-1. *Alerts definition form*

expected rows. You can then use the Import function to read the start file and automatically create the variables, or you can cut and paste the statement as if you were typing it.

Export

This works similarly to the Import function. Click on the **Export** button, specify the name and location of the destination file, and your exported SELECT statement will be saved into that file. Export is useful for documenting the SQL in alerts and also for copying them between instances.

Verify

Use the **Verify** button to check the syntax of the SELECT statement you have entered or imported. If the SELECT statement is valid, you will receive a note saying Oracle Alert has successfully parsed your SQL statement. If the SELECT statement is invalid, you will receive a note that displays the SQL error number and a description, together with your invalid SELECT statement. Correct the error and reverify the SELECT statement.

Run

Utilize the **Run** button to parse and execute the SELECT statement you have entered or imported. If the SELECT statement is valid, it is executed against the database using the Oracle ID of the installation(s) associated with the application that owned your alert. A note will be returned to you to tell you how many rows are retrieved by your specified SELECT statement. This is an effective method for testing your SELECT statement before fully implementing it.

Alert Details

Click on the **Alert Details** button to see the following data about your alert:

- Inputs
- Outputs
- Installations

INPUTS   Select Inputs as the alternative region. The explicit input variables of your SELECT statement will be automatically displayed in the region. You should see LIMIT as your input name. You must associate the correct datatype with the input variable. Select Number as your datatype. Available datatypes are Character, Date, or Number. Enter **100000** as your default value. The default value is used as the default for the specified input variable in every action set you defined. Your alert is executed with the default $100,000 limit if the user does not choose to override the default value. Notice that although you used the implicit input :ROWID in your SELECT statement, :ROWID is not shown in the Inputs alternative region. Save your work. See Figure 10-2.

OUTPUTS   Select Outputs as the alternative region. The output variables of your SELECT statement will be automatically displayed in the region. For your alert, you should see the UPDATE_USER, UPDATE_DATE, HEADER_NAME, PERIOD_NAME, LINE_NUM, DEBIT, and CREDIT output variables. You can optionally override the default description (which is the output variable name itself) with a more meaningful description. You can also choose to enter a maximum length when the output variable is being displayed in a detail message or a summary message. Detail messages and summary messages are covered in a later section describing actions. For numeric output variables, enter an optional number format. Key in any valid SQL*Plus number format mask just as you are entering the format mask in the SELECT statement. You can also identify whether the output variables are included when checking against duplicates. To check for duplicates, keep a history of the alert results. The output variables that are marked as Check for Duplicates will be used as a combination to check against the history to see if the same combination already came up. If the combination exists in the alert history, the newly retrieved combination is considered a duplicate. See Figure 10-3.

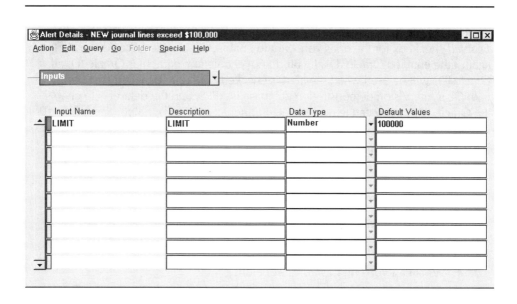

FIGURE 10-2. *Alert Details (Inputs) form*

FIGURE 10-3. *Alert Details (Outputs) form*

INSTALLATIONS   Select Installations as the alternative region. The Oracle IDs associated with the application that owned the alert will be displayed. Check the *Enabled* checkbox for the ones you want to enable. Oracle Alert checks the alert against the enabled Oracle IDs. If you do not enable any particular Oracle ID, all Oracle IDs will be used when the alert is checked. The only Oracle ID associated with GL in the Vision demonstration database is APPS, and the default is to enable the Oracle ID, so you can leave the default unchanged for your alert. See Figure 10-4.

Review Questions

1. What is the difference between verifying and running an Oracle Alert SELECT statement?

2. How long can an Oracle Alert SELECT statement be?

3. What are the two ways of entering an Oracle Alert SELECT statement?

4. What can you enter as an Alert detail?

The previous material described how to define an alert. The following material describes how to define actions related to an alert. Remember the definition of an alert? An alert detects exceptions and—based upon the exceptions—initiates actions.

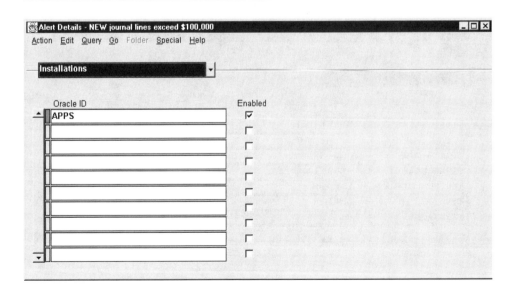

FIGURE 10-4.   *Alert Details (Installations) form*

Actions

To define an action, click on the **Actions** button. Enter an action name and an optional action description. Next, select a level for your action. There are three levels for an action. They are detail, no exception, or summary. Detail-level actions are initiated once for each exception found, meaning once for each row returned by the SELECT statement defined in the alert definition. Summary-level actions are initiated either once for all exceptions found or once for each unique output combination, meaning once for all combinations of data or each unique combination of data returned by the SELECT statement defined in the alert definition. The decision is based on which action type is chosen. No-exception-level actions are initiated once when no data is returned from the SELECT statement, meaning that no row is returned by the SELECT statement defined in the alert definition. First, you are going to create a detail-level action. Call your action **NEW Detail Notification** and select the action level Detail. Click on the **Action Details** button. See Figure 10-5.

There are four action types for each action level:

- Concurrent program

- Message

- Operating system script

- SQL statement script

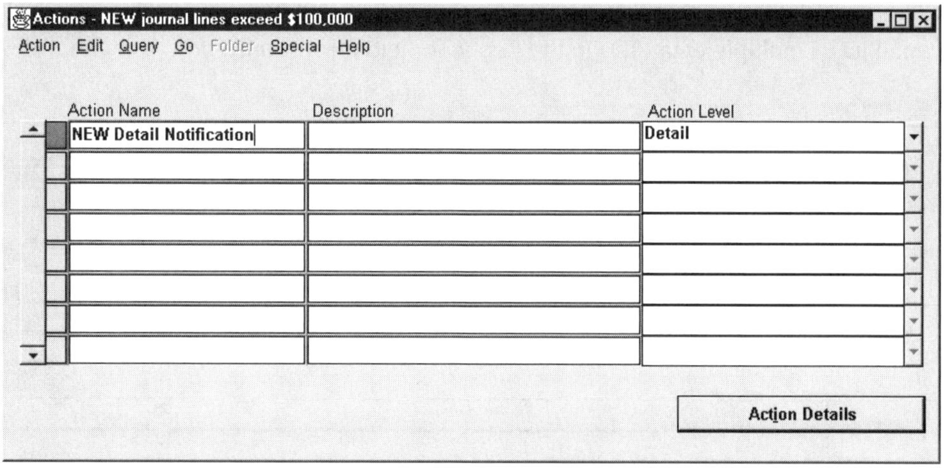

FIGURE 10-5. *Actions form*

CONCURRENT PROGRAM   You are going to select all four action types so that you can see the differences. First, select Concurrent Program as the action type. To specify a concurrent program, enter the application name that owns the program and the program name of the desired concurrent program. The actual program that runs will be determined by the executable associated with the concurrent program and its application and method. The execution method of the executable associated with the concurrent program determines the subdirectory behind the base path. If there are any arguments necessary for the concurrent program, enter the argument values or specify output variables to be the argument values. Put a space between arguments. If an argument is of type Character or Date and you are passing a constant to the argument, put the argument value of type Character or Date inside a pair of single quotes.

Since you are defining a detail-level action, the concurrent program you specified is initiated once for each exception found by the defined alert. See Figure 10-6.

MESSAGE   Once you have selected the Concurrent Program action type, choose Message as the action type. You can enter a distribution list if you have a predefined one for the application that owned the alert. A distribution list allows you to define a commonly used list of email IDs in the To list, Carbon Copy (Cc) list, and Blind Carbon Copy (Bcc) lists. You can also specify the printer to be used for particular email IDs in the To list, Cc list, and Bcc lists. To separate the email IDs, use either a space or a comma. If you choose to use a predefined distribution list, you cannot override the fields defaulted from the distribution list. The To, Cc, Bcc, and Print for User fields will be grayed out.

If Oracle Office is used and a default response mail account is specified for the entire system or for the application that owned your alert, the default response mail account will be defaulted in the Reply To field. You can optionally enter another email ID or multiple email IDs in the Reply To field for response processing in order

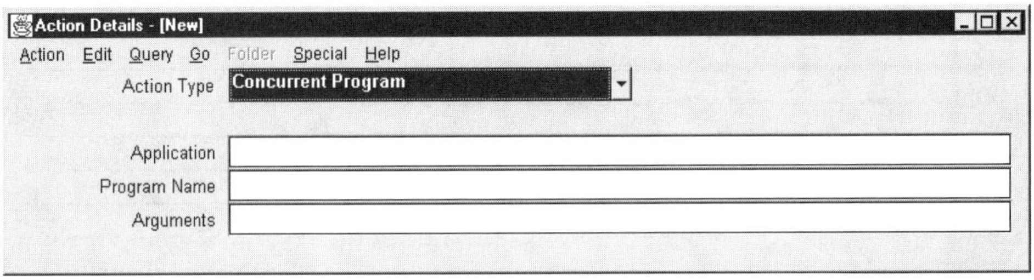

FIGURE 10-6.   *Action Details (Concurrent Program) form*

to override the default value, such as your system administrator or the person responsible for the particular module. If this alert needs response processing, besides the Reply To field, you must also fill in the Response Set field and the Response Days field. Finally, it is important in this example to create a message that solicits a response. In other words, you must ask for a response in your message. For an alert that has a response set attached, two elements are added to the message you provide. First, there will be the response text. The response text instructs the recipients how to respond to the alert message. Second, there will be a list of valid responses the recipient can use. Valid responses are defined by the response sets associated with the alert. Response sets are described in more detail in a later section. The Response Days field is used to determine how many days Oracle Alert waits before classifying the response as a "no response" from the recipient.

If you have not entered a predefined list belonging to the application that owned the alert, you must enter the desired email IDs in the To, Cc, Bcc, and Print for User fields, as applicable. Separate the email IDs by a comma or a space. The Print for User field is used to list the email IDs you want to receive printed messages. If you enter any email ID in the Print for User field, you must select a printer in the Printer field. A header page will be printed with the email IDs you specified in the Print for User field before the actual messages print out. You do not need to enter the Response Set and Response Days fields, since you are not creating an action for a Response action.

If Oracle Alert is integrated with Oracle Office, the entered email IDs are verified before the message is sent. If an email ID is invalid, the message will be sent to the application user initiating the event alert, or to the application user who last updated the periodic alert's definition. To derive the email ID for the application user who initiated the event alert, or the application user who last updated the periodic alert's definition, Oracle Office uses the email IDs from the email fields associated with the application user's definition. If no email ID is provided in the application user's definition, either the operating system login or the application user name is used, depending on the default user *Mail Account* option setup. If Oracle Alert is not integrated, the derived email IDs are not verified and the message is sent anyway.

Between the To field and the Cc field is the Subject field. Enter the subject of your message in the Subject field. The subject you enter cannot be more than 240 characters long.

Once you have entered the email IDs and the subject, you are now ready to enter the message body. You have two choices: you can import a file or you can simply type in the message text. To import a file, select the **File** radio button and enter the full path, together with the filename for the file you want. The file size must be less than 64KB. If you wish, you can use the **Locate File** button to locate a file.

If you want to type in the message text, select the **Text** radio button. Enter the message text you want to use as the message body. The message text cannot exceed 2,000 characters.

Use output variables in alert details fields. Enter the output variables with the ampersand sign. The output variables are replaced by the values retrieved by the SELECT statement at run time. You can use the output variables to create dynamic distribution lists of email IDs, dynamic subjects, dynamic filenames, and dynamic message texts.

Since you are defining a detail-level action, the message you specified will be initiated once for each exception found by the defined alert. You can specify Column Overflow or Max Width fields only if you are entering a summary message. See Figure 10-7.

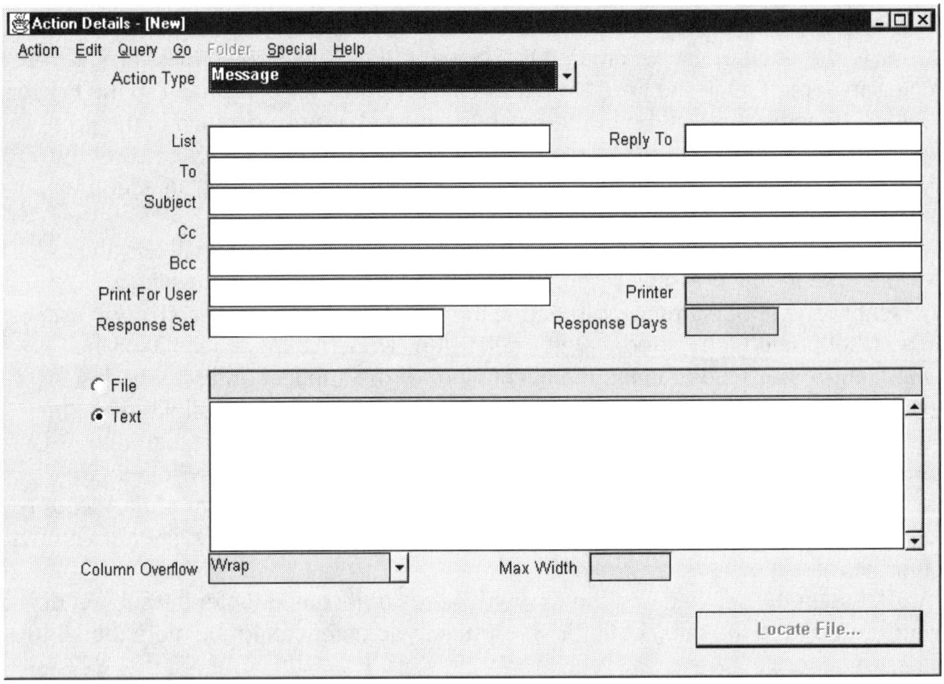

FIGURE 10-7. *Action Details (Message) form*

Create a detail message template that informs your users that there are journal lines that exceed a pre-defined limit. Enter the following message template:

Greetings. Please review the following journal line:

Journal &HEADER_NAME for accounting period &PERIOD_NAME, line number &LINE_NUM, last updated by &UPDATE_USER on &UPDATE_DATE, has a debit amount of &DEBIT and a credit amount of &CREDIT that is over the limit.

Thanks.

Save your work.

OPERATING SYSTEM SCRIPT   Following the selection of Message as the action type, select Operating System Script as the action type. You can optionally choose the application that owns the operating system script. If you specify an application name, the application name defines the base path where the operating system script will be found. All operating system scripts should be located in the **bin** directory underneath the base path. If there are any arguments necessary for the operating system script, enter the argument values or specify output variables to be the argument values. Put a space between arguments. If an argument is of type Character or Date, and you are passing a constant to the argument, put the argument value of type Character or Date inside a pair of single quotes.

Just like the message action type, you can specify an operating system script by a filename, or just type in the operating system script text. Choose the **File** radio button when entering a filename. Utilize the **Locate File** button to find your operating system script file. If you have entered an application name, simply enter the filename that can be found under the **bin** subdirectory from the application base path. If you have not entered the application name, you must enter the filename in the File Name field, including the full directory path leading to the file. Although an operating system script file cannot contain output variables, you can use an output variable in the File Name field to generate dynamic filenames. Maximum size for the file is 64KB.

Choose the **Text** radio button to enter the operating system script text directly. You can use output variables if you type in the text directly. The text cannot be more than 2,000 characters.

Since you are defining a detail-level action, the operating system scripts you specified are initiated once for each exception found by the defined alert. See Figure 10-8.

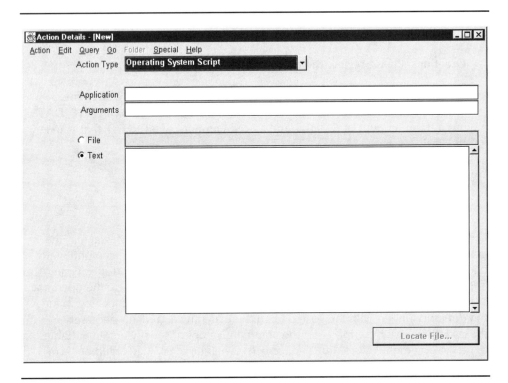

FIGURE 10-8. *Action Details (Operating System Script) form*

SQL STATEMENT SCRIPT   After selecting Operating System Script as the action type, move on to select SQL Statement Script as the action type. You can choose the application that owns the SQL statement script. If you specify an application name, the application name defines the base path where the SQL statement script resides. All SQL statement scripts should be located in the **sql** directory underneath the base path. If there are any arguments necessary for the SQL statement script, enter the argument values or specify output variables to be the argument values. Put a space between arguments. If an argument is of type Character or Date, and you are passing a constant to the argument, put the argument value of type Character or Date inside a pair of single quotes.

As in the case of the message and the operating system script action types, you can specify a SQL statement script by a filename, or just simply type in the SQL statement. Choose the **File** radio button for entering a filename. Use the **Locate File** button to find your operating system script file. If you have entered an application name, simply enter the filename that can be found under the *sql* subdirectory from the application base path. If you have not entered the application name, you must input the filename in the File Name field, including the full path. Use an output variable in the File Name field to generate a dynamic filename. The file cannot be more than 64KB.

Choose the **Text** radio button to enter the SQL statements directly. You must include a semicolon or slash at the end of each SQL statement. The total text cannot exceed 2,000 characters.

Since you are defining a detail-level action, the SQL statement script you specified is initiated once for each exception found by the defined alert. See Figure 10-9.

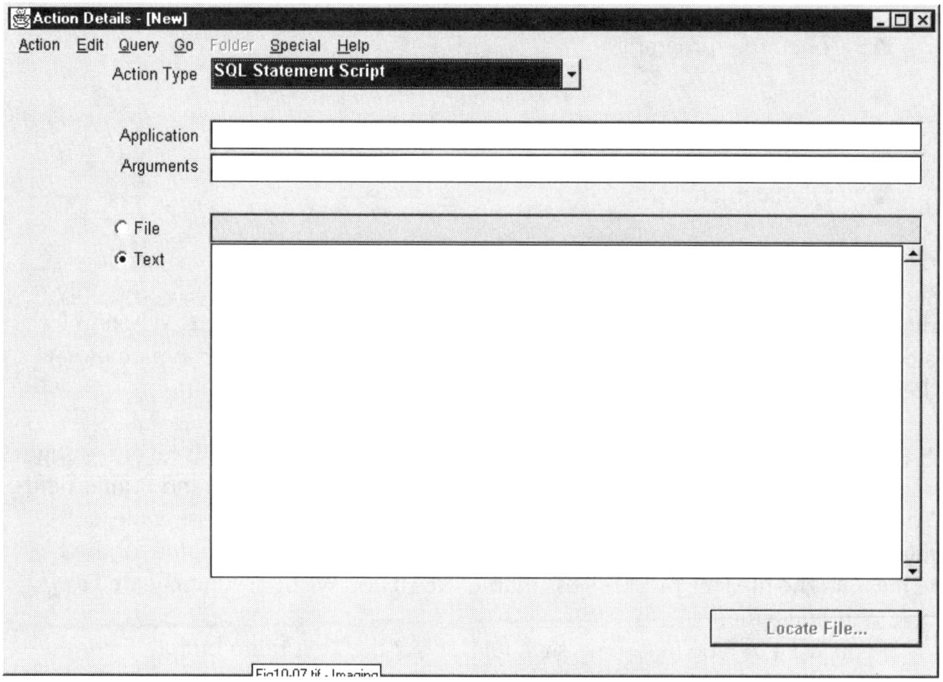

FIGURE 10-9.   *Action Details (SQL Statement Script) form*

Review Questions

1. For what is the application name used when defining an operating system script action, concurrent program action, or SQL statement script action?

2. What is the purpose of a distribution list?

3. For what is the Print for Users field used?

4. What character must you include after each SQL statement in an action's definition?

Once you have entered the action details, you must save your work. Close the Action Details window and you will see the Actions window again. Now, you are going to create a summary-level action. Call your action **NEW Summary Notification**, and select the action level Detail. Click on the **Action Details** button. There are four action types for each action level:

- Concurrent program

- Message

- Operating system script

- SQL statement script

CONCURRENT PROGRAM   You set up concurrent program actions for summary action levels the same way you set them up for detail levels. The only difference is that the concurrent program is executed once for each exception for a detail-level action, while it is executed once for each unique combination of the arguments for a summary-level action.

MESSAGE   A detail-action-level message and a summary-action-level message have the same List, Reply To, To, Subject, Cc, Bcc, Print for User, and Printer fields. You can also include a file for the summary message content. To use a file, select the **File** radio button and enter the full path, together with the filename for the file you want. The file size must be less than 64KB. If you wish, use the **Locate File** button to find a file.

If you want to type in the message text, select the **Text** radio button. Enter the message text you want to use as the summary message body. The message text cannot exceed 2,000 characters.

The difference between a summary message and a detail message lies within the message text. To see the differences, select the **Text** radio button. You will see the following text in the message text field. Compare it to the detail message text previously shown.

=**= Enter summary template below this line =**=

**

=**= Enter summary template above this line =**=

Text entered above the *=**= Enter summary template below this line =**=* is considered the header. Text entered between that and the *=**= Enter summary template above this line =**=* is considered the summary template. Text entered below the *=**= Enter summary template above this line =**=* is considered the footer.

If you have defined a message action header and/or a message action footer as an Oracle Alert system option in the Message Elements alternative region, the message action header will appear before the header you entered in the action details, while the message action footer will appear after the footer you entered in the action details. A separate message is sent for each unique combination of output variable values in the header and footer. For example, if you have a journal name as an output variable in the header, a separate message is sent for each journal. On the other hand, if you have a journal name as an output variable in the summary template—and no output variable in the header or footer—you will have a single message with each journal as a separate row in the message body.

When you enter a summary template, do not use the first two spaces. These two spaces are indicated by two asterisks, and are used for marking duplicates. Enter boilerplate text and output variables in the summary template. The column width extends from the ampersand of the output variable to two characters before the next column. Character and Date fields are left-justified and Number fields are right-justified. When the alert is checked, the summary template is filled once for each unique combination of output variable values, and any text entered here will be repeated for each line.

You can choose to wrap or truncate columns by selecting Wrap or Truncate in the Column Overflow field. However, for Number fields, if the numeric value does not fit the column, ### is displayed and no wrapping or truncating occurs. You can also enter a maximum width for your columns in the Max Width field. See Figure 10-10.

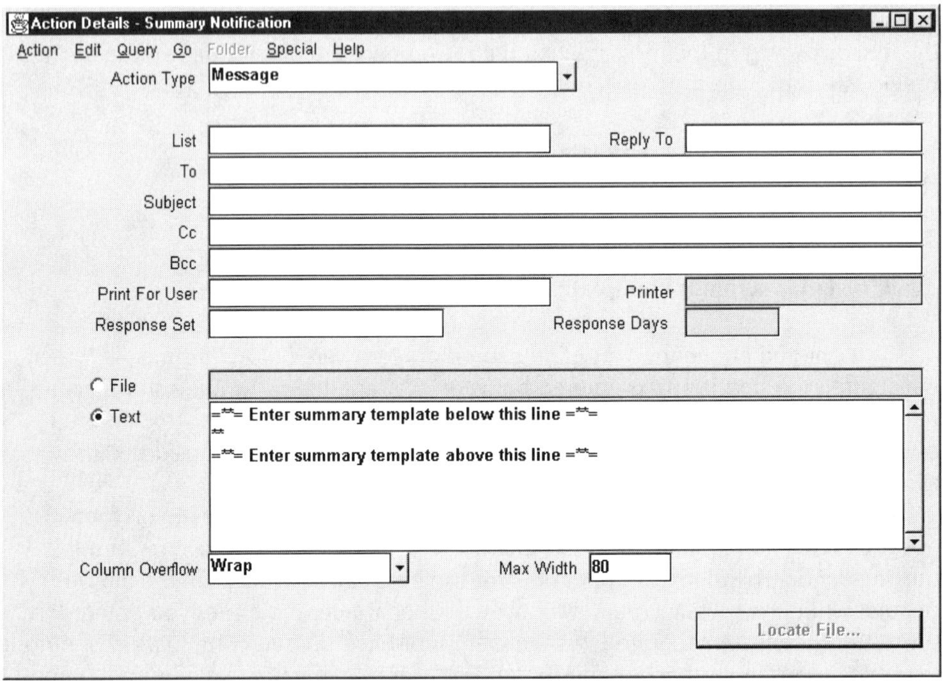

FIGURE 10-10. *Action Details (Summary Message) form*

Create a summary message template that tells your users there are journals exceeding a predefined limit. Ensure that the message displays all offending journal lines displayed. You can enter the following message template:

Please review the following journal:

Journal &HEADER_NAME for accounting period &PERIOD_NAME

Journal Lines:

=**= Enter summary template below this line =**=

**

Line number &LINE_NUM, last updated by &UPDATE_USER on &UPDATE_DATE, has a debit amount of &DEBIT and a credit amount of &CREDIT that is over the limit.

=**= Enter summary template above this line =**=

Thanks.

Save your work.

OPERATING SYSTEM SCRIPT   You set up operating system script actions for summary action levels the same way you set them up for detail levels. The only difference is that at the detail level the operating system script is executed once for each exception, while at the summary level the operating system script is executed once for each unique combination of the output variable values in the operating system script text, or once for each unique combination of dynamic filename and arguments passed to the script.

SQL STATEMENT SCRIPT   You set up SQL statement scripts for summary action levels the same way you set up SQL statement script actions for detail levels. The differences noted previously about when the script is executed apply here as well.

After entering the action details, you must save your work. Close the Action Details window and you will see the Actions window again. Now, you are going to create a no-exception-level action. Call your action **NEW No Exception Notification** and select action level No Exception. Click on the **Action Details** button.

There are four action types for each action level:

- Concurrent program
- Message
- Operating system script
- SQL statement script

A no-exception action is initiated when the alert SELECT statement does not return any rows. Do not use outputs when defining no-exception actions.

Review Questions

1. What is the difference between a detail concurrent program action and a summary concurrent program action?

2. What is a summary message header and footer?

3. What determines how many messages should be sent?

4. What is the limit of a SQL statement script file?

You can also create escalation groups or summary threshold groups in the alert definition form.

ESCALATION GROUP   An escalation group is a group of detail actions with different levels. Whenever an alert selects the exact same data on separate occasions, the next-level detail action is executed. This is an indication to Oracle Alerts that the person notified during previous alerts has not yet acted accordingly. For example, let's say you have three levels of action details. The first time an exception occurs, the first-level detail action is executed. The second time an exception with the same values for output variables that have been marked Check for Duplicates occurs, the second-level detail action is executed. The third time, the third-level detail action is executed. From the third time on, the third-level detail action is executed. To escalate correctly, you must keep a history for the alert. If the history is erased or no history is kept, Oracle Alert will not interpret any exception as a duplicate.

To define an escalation group, use Escalation Groups from the Special menu. You must enter an escalation group name and an optional description. You can then select an action type. Only detail actions with the same action type can be included as an escalation group member. Go to the Escalation Group Members region and select detail actions with an assigned level number to them. The Oracle Alert escalation process escalates from the lower level to the higher level. You can disable an escalation group member by deselecting the *Enabled* checkbox or filling in an end date. You do not have a business need to create an escalation group for this exercise, since you only have one detail action defined. For learning purposes, just create a NEW Escalation Group with your detail action with level 1. Save your work. See Figure 10-11.

SUMMARY THRESHOLD GROUP   A summary threshold group defines a detail action and a summary action of the same action type. When you select a summary threshold group as a member in an action set, you establish a threshold and the number of exceptions found. If the number of exceptions found exceeds the threshold, the summary action is initiated; otherwise, the detail action is initiated. This is an effective way to reduce system load for alerts that may retrieve a large number of records.

To create a summary threshold group, select Threshold Groups from the Special submenu in the Alert Definition form. Enter the summary threshold group name and an optional description. Select the action type for the group. You can only select threshold group members that are of the same action type. Create a summary threshold group called **NEW summary threshold**. Select Message as the Type. Next, select your two messages as the threshold group members. Save your work. See Figure 10-12.

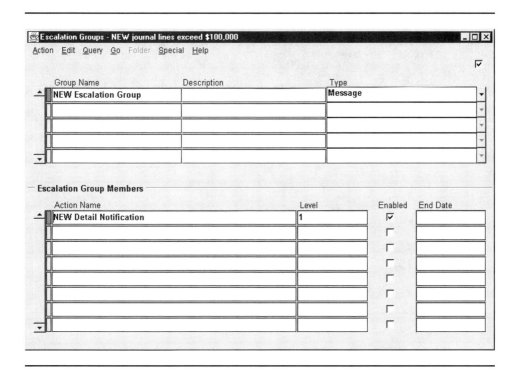

FIGURE 10-11. *Escalation Groups form*

TIP
If you use output variables as distribution lists, it is possible that email IDs on the distribution lists receive a different number of exceptions. The threshold depends on the number of exceptions each email ID receives, not on the total number of exceptions. In other words, different email IDs can receive the summary message or the detail message.

Review Questions

1. What is an escalation group?

2. What must you keep in order to escalate the action correctly?

3. What is a summary threshold group?

4. How can one recipient receive a summary message, while another recipient receives a detail message with the same alert?

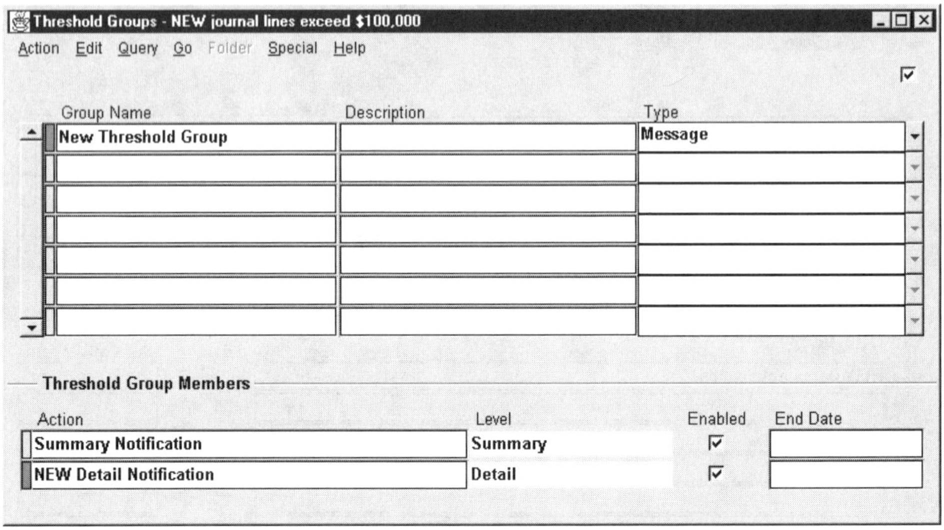

FIGURE 10-12. *Summary Threshold Groups form*

Action Sets

Once you have defined actions, you are ready to define action sets. You must include actions into action sets so that actions can be initiated. You can have as many action sets as you want, and the Oracle Alert SELECT statement will be executed once for each action set. To define action sets, you must save all your actions, close the Action Details window, and click on the **Action Set** button. The top of the form shows the action set definition. First, you must enter a sequence number to sequence the action sets if you have more than one action set. The sequence number determines the order in which action sets are initiated. Next, enter a name for the action set and/or an optional description.

The *Suppress Duplicates* checkbox determines how duplicates are handled. Duplicates are defined by identical combinations of output variable values marked as Check for Duplicates in the Outputs alternative region of the Action Sets form. It only makes sense to enable *Suppress Duplicates* if you choose to keep a history for the alert. Otherwise, there is no history kept to check if the retrieved row from the alert's SELECT statement is a duplicate. If you check the *Suppress Duplicates* checkbox for the action set, you will see different behaviors depending on the action levels and the action types. If the action is at the summary level and the action type is message, the duplicates will display as rows marked with asterisks.

This is why you must leave the first two spaces blank when defining a summary message. If the action is at the detail level, the duplicates will not display. If you use an escalation group, the duplicates drive which escalated action should be initiated. This depends on how many duplicates have occurred in the history of this alert. Oracle Alert escalates the level of the action in the escalation group when a duplicate is found. Check the *Suppress Duplicates* checkbox for your action set.

You must check the *Enabled* checkbox in order to include the action set. You can also enter an end date to define a concrete life span for the action. If you uncheck the *Enabled* checkbox, the end date is automatically populated with today's date. Create an action set called **NEW Notification**, then go to the Members alternative region, where you will use sequence numbers to specify the execution order of the action set's members. You can select actions, escalation groups, and/or summary threshold groups that you would like to include in the action set in the Action field. In your case, select the summary threshold group you have created. The action type of the selected action is automatically displayed. If you select an escalation group as a member, but did not check the *Suppress Duplicates* checkbox, the action with the highest level is executed.

You can use the On Error Action field to define how an error should be handled for the selected action. A setting of Abort ends the action, a setting of Set directs the alert to execute the action set sequence specified in the Seq field, and a setting of Member causes the alert to execute the action set member sequence specified in the Seq field. For your action set member, select Abort. As with the action set, you can disable an action as a member immediately by unchecking the *Enabled* checkbox, or—in the future—enter a future end date. Save your work. See Figure 10-13.

Response Sets

Response sets consist of one or more response actions. Response actions can only be detail-level actions. If an alert message solicits responses, then depending on the response values, some predefined response actions are initiated. This dependency is defined in the response set definition. You define response actions the same way you define regular actions. The only difference is that for response actions, you can use both output variables and response variables. Output variables are from the original message, while response variables get their values from the response message. Response variables are also denoted by the ampersand sign. If the response variables are not included in the response message, the default values for the response variables are used. One common response action is sending a message to inform recipients that there are no responses received, or that the response values are invalid.

Once you define all your response actions, you can create response sets. To define response sets, click on the **Response Sets** button in the Alerts form. Enter a unique response set name and an optional description. Use the *Enabled* checkbox and the End Date field to disable any response set. Disabled response sets will not

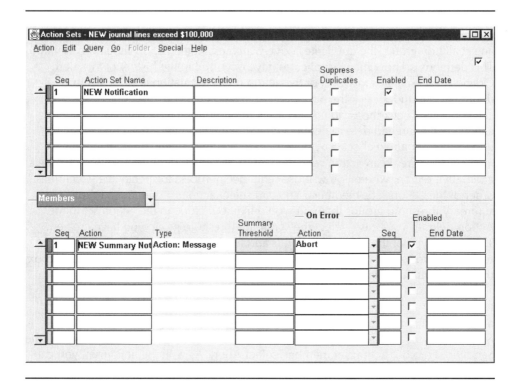

FIGURE 10-13. *Action Sets form*

initiate response processing, even if the response set is already associated with a message action. See Figure 10-14.

Click on the **Response Variables** button to enter response variables. You enter the variable name (without the ampersand), an optional description, the datatype of the response variable (Character, Date, or Number), its maximum length, and a default value. The response variable name must be different than any output variable name. If the response variable value is longer than the maximum length, the response variable value will be truncated if the datatype is either a Character or Date. If the datatype is Number, the response variable value will be all # signs, representing an overflow. See Figure 10-15.

Once you have defined the response variables, you can enter response actions for three response action types: valid, invalid, or none. Valid response action types allow you to list the valid response values. An invalid response action type is initiated if the response values are invalid. A none response action type is initiated if no valid responses are received from the recipients within the timeframe defined by Response Days in the action definition.

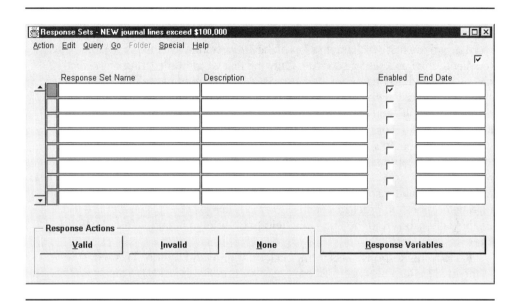

FIGURE 10-14. *Response Sets form*

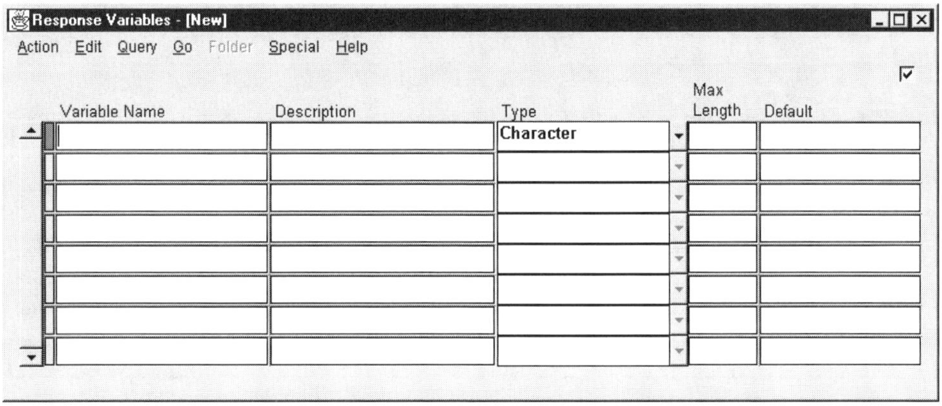

FIGURE 10-15. *Response Variables form*

Click on the **Valid** button to open the Valid Responses form, as shown in Figure 10-16. You must enter a unique response name and text with a unique first word or unique first 30 characters—whichever is shorter. The text is what the recipients enter as a response value. Only the first word or the string of the first 30 characters needs to be unique, because only the first word or the first 30-character string is being compared. If you want the recipients to define a valid value for a response variable, you must include the response variable in the Text field after the first unique word. For example, if your response variable is called AMOUNT and you want the recipient to specify a value for AMOUNT, you must enter AMOUNT="?" after the valid response value. The recipient will replace the ? with the value the recipient wants. You can have as many response variables as you want in the Text field.

For each valid response, enter the list of actions you want to perform. The Seq field determines the order in which the actions are executed. You can use the *Enabled* checkbox and the End Date field to disable an action. Close the window after you are done.

Back in the Response Sets form, click on the **Invalid** button. This will take you to the Invalid Response Actions form, as shown in Figure 10-17. You do not have to

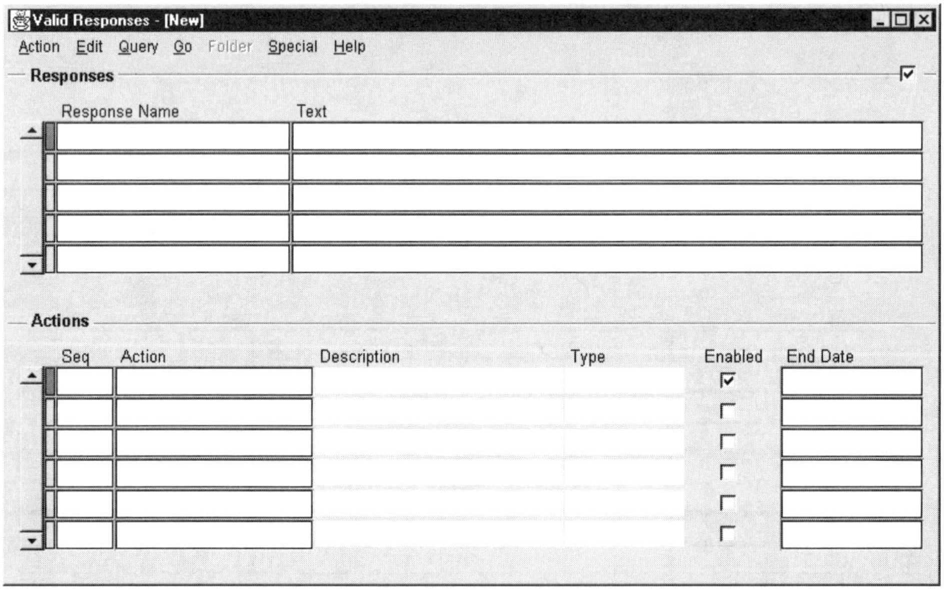

FIGURE 10-16. *Valid Responses form*

enter a response name or text, since all responses outside of the Text field of any valid response is considered an invalid response. You can enter the list of actions that you want to perform in this scenario. The Seq field determines the order in which the actions are executed. You can use the *Enabled* checkbox and the End Date field to disable the action. Close the window after you are done. See Figure 10-17.

Back in the Response Sets form, click on the **None** button. Here, you can enter the actions you want Oracle Alert to perform if you do not receive a valid response within the specified response days. The Seq field determines the order in which the actions are executed. Use the *Enabled* checkbox and the End Date field to disable the action. Close the window after you are done. See Figure 10-18. Again, Oracle Alert response sets can only be implemented with Oracle Office.

Review Questions

1. For what purposes are action sets used?

2. What are the three response action types?

3. How do you ask a recipient to provide a response variable value?

4. When is a response set's No Values action initiated?

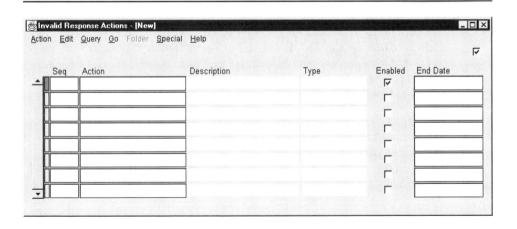

FIGURE 10-17. *Invalid Response Actions form*

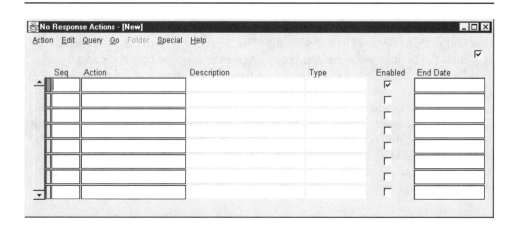

FIGURE 10-18. *No Response Actions form*

Steps Involved in Implementing Alerts

You have now set up an event alert. This section defines the steps involved in implementing alerts. Steps related to response processing are optional. The steps involved in implementing alerts are as follows:

1. **Define the alert** You must define the alert first. Identify whether the alert is a periodic alert or an event alert. You must also provide a SELECT statement that defines the alert. Use the **Verify** button to check the SELECT statement. You can have input variables and output variables for the SELECT statement. Input variables and output variables help create dynamic behaviors within the defined actions.

2. **Create actions** You must create actions that you want to be executed after the alert is checked. There are three levels of action: summary, detail, or no exception. There are four types of action: concurrent program, operating system script, message, or SQL statement script. If you want to perform response processing, one action must be a message type action that solicits a response.

3. **Create response actions** If you wish, you can create response actions if you want to perform response processing. Response actions can use both output variables from the original message or response variables from the response message.

4. **Escalation group/summary threshold group**   After you define the actions, you can optionally include the defined actions in the escalation group or summary threshold group.

5. **Create action sets**   Once you have created the actions, you can create the action set. Attach all actions that you want to be executed with the action set. Only enabled actions associated with enabled action sets are initiated.

6. **Create response sets**   If you perform response processing, you must create response sets and attach response actions to them. Within a response set, you can establish any number of valid response values. For each valid response value, attach the applicable response actions. You can optionally attach response actions to invalid response values or a no-response value.

7. **Associate the response sets to actions**   The last step in performing response processing is to attach the defined response set to the message type action that solicits a response and defines the number of days as the response days. Response days define how many days a lack of response, or a lack of valid responses, are characterized as a no-response value.

Review Questions

1. What is the first step in implementing an alert?

2. What steps must you perform if you want to have response processing?

3. What is the purpose of the Response Days field?

Precoded Alerts Available in Oracle Alert

Oracle Alert comes with a list of precoded alerts. These alerts are divided into two applications:

- Applications DBA
- Oracle Alert

There are other seeded alerts created for specific application modules that are too numerous to detail now. In general, they are functions that are commonly used by many different companies, and you can choose whether to enable them for your site.

Applications DBA

The Applications DBA alerts help you detect potential database storage problems and send you warning messages. Each of these periodic alerts is described in the following text. They reference data about Oracle Applications objects that is stored in the DBA tables and views owned by the SYS and SYSTEM schemas.

INDEXES NEAR MAXIMUM EXTENTS   This alert is defaulted to select all indexes owned by all application users who have used up most of the extents and are within five extents of the maximum extents limit. Extents are storage units allocated to database objects such as indexes and tables. Maximum extents limit the number of extents that can be allocated to database objects. You can change the alert to select specific indexes owned by particular users that are within a specific threshold. Three input variables—available_extents, index_name, and user—allow you to customize the alert in any way. The default values for these three input variables are 5, ALL, and ALL.

INDEXES TOO LARGE OR FRAGMENTED   This alert is defaulted to select all indexes owned by all application users that have over 100,000 blocks or more than 20 extents. A block is another type of storage unit allocated to database objects. You can change the alert to select particular indexes owned by specific users that are within designated thresholds. You can also decide to check the number of blocks only or the number of extents only. Six input variables—check_blocks, check_extents, index_name, maxblocks, maxextents, and user—allow you to configure the alert to your choosing. The default values for these input variables are YES, YES, ALL, 100000, 20, and ALL.

INDEXES UNABLE TO ALLOCATE ANOTHER EXTENT   This alert is defaulted to select all indexes owned by all application users that will be unable to allocate another extent based on the available free space. You can change the alert to select specific indexes owned by particular users. Two input variables allow you to customize the alert: index_name and user. Their default values are ALL and ALL.

TABLES NEAR MAXIMUM EXTENTS   This alert is defaulted to select all tables owned by all application users that have utilized most of the extents and are within five extents of the maximum extents limit. Extents are storage units allocated to database objects such as indexes and tables. Maximum extents limit the number of extents that can be allocated to database objects. You can change the alert to select designated tables owned by particular users that are within a specific threshold. Three input variables—available_extents, table_name, and user—allow you to configure the alert to your needs. Their defaults are 5, ALL, and ALL.

TABLES TOO LARGE OR FRAGMENTED   This alert is defaulted to select all tables owned by all application users that have over 100,000 blocks or more than 20 extents. You can change the alert to select particular tables owned by specific users that are within defined thresholds. You can also decide to check the number of blocks only or the number of extents only. Six input variables—check_blocks, check_extents, table_name, maxblocks, maxextents, and user—allow you to configure the alert in any customized way. Their defaults are YES, YES, ALL, 100000, 20, and ALL.

TABLES UNABLE TO ALLOCATE ANOTHER EXTENT   This alert is defaulted to select all tables owned by all application users that will be unable to allocate another extent based on the available free space. You can change the alert to select specific tables owned by individual users. Two input variables—table_name and user—facilitate configuring the alert. Their defaults are ALL and ALL.

TABLESPACES WITHOUT ADEQUATE FREE SPACE   This alert is defaulted to select tablespaces that satisfy either of two criteria: either their total free space is less than 102,400 bytes, or their contiguous space is less than 10,240 bytes. You can change the alert to select particular tablespaces using specified thresholds for either total free space or contiguous space. You can also decide to check the total free space only or the number of extents only. Five input variables—check_max, check_total, maxsize, mintotal, and tablespace_name—allow you to customize the alert. The defaults are YES, YES, 10240, 102400, and ALL.

USERS NEAR TABLESPACE QUOTA   This alert is defaulted to select all users who have used up to 95 percent of any tablespace assigned to them, or have less than 102,400 free spaces in any tablespace assigned to them. You can change the alert to select specific users for particular tablespaces with a designated percentage used and a delineated minimum of free space. You can also decide to check the percentages used only or the minimum free spaces only. Six input variables—check_free, check_pct, pctused, spacefree, tablespace_name, and user—allow you to configure the alert to your choosing. The defaults are YES, YES, 94, 102400, ALL, and ALL.

Oracle Alert
The alerts produced by Oracle Alert help purge dated objects that are no longer useful in order to free up space. These periodic, precoded alerts include the following.

PURGE ALERT AND ACTION SET CHECKS   This alert is defaulted to purge alert and action set checks for all applications that are older than 30 days. An alert check is a completed concurrent request of a Check Event Alert (ALECTC) or a Check Periodic Alert (ALECDC). These concurrent requests are initiated to run event alerts or on-demand periodic alerts. Action set checks are executions of action sets resulting from running an alert's SELECT statements. If the alert or action set checks are expecting responses because of response processing, the purge program will not purge the checks even if the checks are older than the specified threshold. You can change the alert to purge for specific applications that are over a designated number of days. Two input variables—applications and numdays—give you the opportunity to change the alert in a number of ways. Their defaults are ALL and 30.

PURGE CONCURRENT REQUESTS   This alert is defaulted to purge all concurrent requests of all applications that are older than 30 days. The output files and log files are purged, as well as request information. This information resides at both the operating system level and the database level. You can change the alert to purge for specific concurrent programs for individual applications that are over a designated number of days. Three input variable applications—applications, numdays, and programs—allow you to customize the alert. Their defaults are ALL, 30, and ALL.

PURGE ORACLE OFFICE MESSAGES   This alert is defaulted to purge messages more than 60 days old in the Reviewed and Reviewed_OK folders for all users in Oracle Office. You can change the alert to purge messages for particular folders for specific users that are a certain number of days old. Three input variables—expiration_days, folder, and username—allow you to change the alert to suit your purposes. The defaults are 60, ALL, ALL.

Review Questions

1. What does the alert Tables Near Maximum Extents do?

2. What does the concurrent program ALECTC do?

3. What is an action set check?

4. When are alert and action set checks not purged, even if they are older than the specified limit?

Implementing Periodic Alerts

In this section, you will see how to implement periodic alerts. You have already learned how to implement an event alert. Event alerts are triggered based on an insert/update event on a table. Periodic alerts, as their name suggests, are triggered periodically based on a predefined schedule. In this section, you will learn the following:

- Business requirements satisfied by periodic alerts
- Implementing a periodic alert

Business Requirements Satisfied by Periodic Alerts

Periodic alerts are alerts that are executed on demand or on a predefined schedule. Business requirements satisfied by periodic alerts include:

- Allowing you to be informed of any exceptions within Oracle Applications at a frequency level with which you feel comfortable. For example, you can get a report of all purchase orders over $100,000 every week.

- Helping you monitor the system without printing reams of reports and sorting the information for exceptions. For example, you can get a report of all past-due receivables owed by customers who are also suppliers, and who are owed payable amounts.

- Allowing you to trigger informational actions or preventive actions automatically, without user intervention. For example, if the database is getting full, you can purge old concurrent requests automatically to free up space.

- Allowing you to perform routine tasks. For example, you can send out the monthly company survey.

Periodic alerts offer a better solution than batch processes run as standard reports in situations where you only want to deal with exceptions and in which you need to send messages calling for action.

Review Question

1. What are some of the business requirements that Oracle Alert periodic alerts can satisfy?

How to Implement a Periodic Alert

Setting up a periodic alert is very similar to setting up an event alert. The only difference is the alert type and the periodic details. To set up a periodic alert, enter the application name that owned your alert. The application is used to determine what Oracle ID(s) to use to log on to the database when an alert is checked. Next, enter the alert name. The alert name must be unique within the application you specified. Enter a meaningful name, then key in an optional description. As a last step, input the alert type. Select Periodic as your alert type, since you are implementing a periodic alert. Once you have selected the Periodic alert type, the Periodic Details region appears.

You must first specify the frequency in the Periodic Details region. Your choices are as follows:

- **On Demand**   You can initiate this periodic alert any time by using the Request Periodic Alert Check form. This alert will not ever be scheduled on a regular basis. If you choose On Demand, you do not need to enter any other field.

- **On Day of the Month**   This alert runs on the day of the month you specify in the Day field. You can use 31 to stand for the last day of the month. In other words, if you enter 31, and you are in the month of April, your periodic alert will be run on the last day of April, which is 4/30.

- **On Day of the Week**   This alert runs on the day of the week you specify in the Day field. Your choices are Sunday through Saturday

- **Every *N* Calendar Days**   This alert runs *N* calendar days at specified intervals where *N* is the number you enter in the Days field.

- **Every *N* Business Days**   This alert runs *N* business days where *N* is the number you enter in the Days field. You can specify usage of one of the three business day systems for Oracle Alert. The American system starts with Sunday and delineates Monday through Friday as business days. The European system starts with Monday and considers Monday through Friday as business days. The Middle Eastern system begins with Monday and specifies Monday through Saturday as business days. The default is the American system. Notice that holidays are still counted as business days if they fall on days of the week that are otherwise considered business days.

- **Every Day**   This alert runs every day. This option is no different than selecting the Every *N* Calendar Days frequency with 1 in the Days field.

- **Every Other Day**   This alert runs every other day. This option is no different than selecting the Every *N* Calendar Days frequency with 2 in the Days field.

- **Every Business Day**   This alert runs every business day. This option is no different than selecting the Every *N* Business Days frequency with 1 in the Days field.

- **Every Other Business Day**   This alert runs every other business day. This option is no different than selecting the Every *N* Business Days frequency with 2 in the Days field.

Depending on the frequency you select, you may need to enter the start time and the end time. If you want the periodic alert to be checked only once a day and to be governed by the selected frequency, enter **00:00:00** in the Start Time field and leave the End Time field blank. The request will run every night at midnight. If you want the periodic alert to be checked more than once a day, enter the desired start time in the Start Time field, and the desired end time in the End Time field. Fill in the Check Interval field. For example, you may want the periodic alert to run from 9 A.M. to 5 P.M. on the hour. Enter **09:00:00** in the Start Time field and **17:00:00** in the End Time field. In addition, input **01:00:00** in the Check Interval field. Even though you may have selected a frequency that is not on demand, you still can initiate any such alert with a non-On Demand frequency through the Request Periodic Alert Check form whenever you desire.

Implementing the remaining portion of a periodic alert works the same way as an event alert. You must enter a SELECT statement. Key in input variables and/or output variables, then verify and run the SELECT statement. You must create actions and action sets. If you want to have response processing for your periodic alerts, you must create response actions and response sets. See Figure 10-19.

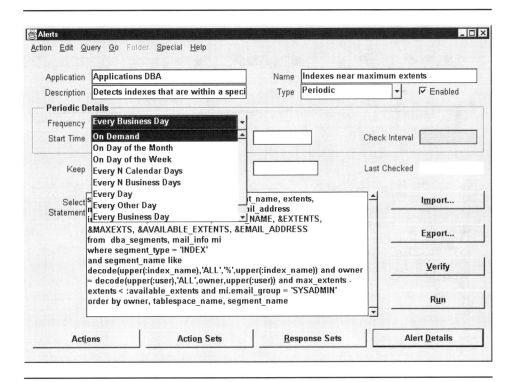

FIGURE 10-19.   *Periodic Alerts form*

Periodic Alert Scheduler

The periodic alert scheduler is a concurrent request that runs every day at midnight. Its job is to schedule the periodic alerts that must be run in the next 24 hours. To initiate the periodic alert scheduler, follow the navigation path *Request : Schedule.* Place your cursor on the periodic alert scheduler and click on the **Activate** button.

Periodic Sets

You can set up periodic sets to group periodic alerts together and submit the periodic set as a single request. To define a periodic set, follow the navigation path *Alert : Periodic Set.* Enter the application that owns the periodic set and give the periodic set a unique name. You can also enter an optional description. Next, enter the periodic set members of the periodic set. Use the Seq field to determine the execution order of the periodic set members. Select the periodic alerts that you want to include as members. You can optionally use the *Enabled* checkbox and the End Date field to enable or disable periodic set members. Create a periodic set called **NEW Database Diagnosis**. Select the Applications DBA periodic alerts as members. Save your work. See Figure 10-20.

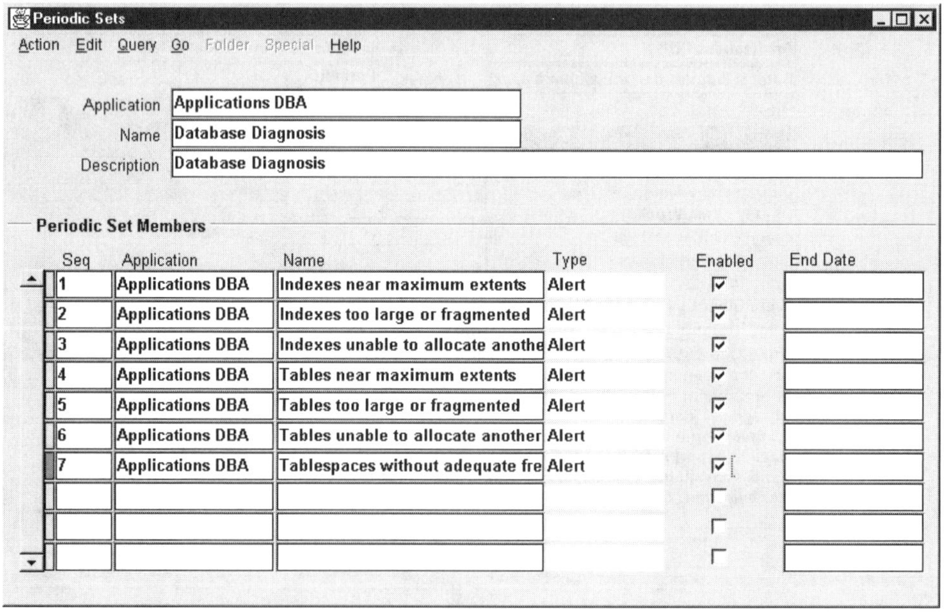

FIGURE 10-20. *Periodic Sets form*

Request Periodic Alert Checks

You can check periodic alerts through the Request Periodic Alert Check form. The navigation path to the Request Periodic Alert form is *Request : Check.* You must enter the application that owns the periodic alert and the periodic alert name. Next, enter the start date and time of the periodic alert. The default is today's date at midnight, which causes the periodic alert to run immediately. Click on the **Submit Request** button. A concurrent program called Check Periodic Alert (ALECDC) is invoked. Select Applications DBA as the application and choose the Indexes near maximum extents alert. Click on the **Submit Request** button. See Figure 10-21. If the periodic alerts you initiated through the Request Periodic Alert Check form are not of the On Demand frequency, the periodic alerts will still continue to run on regular predefined frequencies. This check through the Request Periodic Alert Check will be an additional run.

Review Questions

1. Which days are considered business days in the American system?

2. What fields does a periodic alert have that an event alert does not have?

3. What is the periodic alert scheduler?

4. What happens to an Every Calendar Day periodic alert if you use the Request Periodic Alert Check form to submit it explicitly?

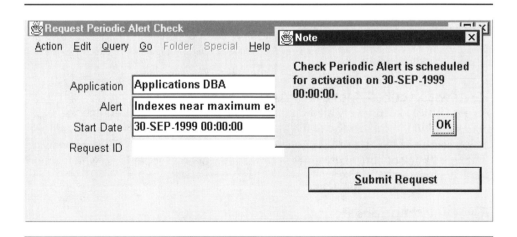

FIGURE 10-21. *Request Periodic Alert Check form*

Alert History

In this section, you will both study and review alert histories in Oracle Alert. You will also find out why Oracle Alert keeps and uses alert histories. An alert history includes historical records of all exceptions found for all alerts. Alert histories are kept for the number of days you specify in each of the alert's definitions. This section will:

■ Explain the need for alert histories

■ List the features of alert histories

■ Review alert histories

■ Document alerts

Why Do You Need Alert Histories?

You need an alert history to:

■ Review executed alert checks

■ Review exceptions found

■ Review executed actions

■ Review received responses

■ Review executed response actions

■ Flag duplicates

■ Escalate action

Review Executed Alert and Action Set Checks

An alert history keeps every alert check that has been executed. Alert checks correspond to the submission of the alerts, while action set checks correspond to action sets executed as a result of one execution of the alert's SELECT statement. This keeps track of how many times your alert has been executed and which action sets have been executed.

Review Exceptions Found

An alert history kept by Oracle Alert includes all of the exceptions found for a specified length of time. This gives you an idea of trends as well as the number of exceptions so you can monitor the system's overall behavior.

Review Executed Actions

Even if the actions have been modified, the alert history keeps a copy of the actions executed at that point in time so that you can go back and find out what happened as well as which actions have been executed.

Review Received Responses

Alert histories also allow you to keep track of the responses received when an action solicits responses. This can give you statistical information that you need in classifying responses.

Review Executed Response Actions

As with executed actions, the alert history keeps a copy of the response actions executed at that point in time so that you can go back and find out what happened and which response actions have been executed.

Flag Duplicates

Keeping alert histories allows Oracle Alert to identify duplicates. Duplicates are defined as the output variables with *Check for Duplicates* checkboxes marked as identical. In summary messages, duplicates can be flagged. In detail messages, duplicates can be suppressed.

Escalate Action

Based on the number of times the duplication has occurred, the action level can be escalated. In other words, Oracle Alert can execute actions of increasing severity every time the same exception occurs.

Review Questions

1. How long does Oracle Alert keep an alert history for each alert?

2. Why is it important to keep executed actions in the alert history?

3. What is action escalation and how does it work?

Features of an Alert History

Various Oracle Alert features are available to support the business needs of keeping alert histories. These features are as follows:

- Review Alert Checks
- Review Alert Actions

- Review Alert Exceptions
- Duplicate Suppression
- Action Escalation

Review Alert Checks

This feature allows you to review all alert checks and action set checks together with the statuses and the number of exceptions found, as well as the number of actions executed for each action set.

Review Alert Actions

This feature allows you to review all alert actions for each action set and displays some important details for each action, such as distribution lists. You can also review the log files associated with each executed action. If the alert has response processing, then a list of the received responses and corresponding executed response sets and response actions is displayed.

Review Alert Exceptions

This feature lists the exceptions found and the corresponding output variable values.

Duplicate Suppression

If the output variable values are identified as duplicates, this feature allows you to suppress the duplicates and just flag the rows that have duplicates in a summary message action.

Action Escalation

If the action is at the detail level and the Suppress Duplicate feature is turned on, the action escalates by the severity level each time a duplicate is found, if your alert's action is associated with an escalation group.

Review Questions

1. Which Oracle Alert feature facilitates seeing the executed action details for each alert?

2. Which Oracle Alert feature facilitates flagging duplicates?

3. What do you need to set up in order for action escalation to work?

How to Review an Alert History

To review alert histories, follow the navigation path *Alert : History*. The Review Alert History form shows up. Use the **List of Values** button to select an application and the alert history you want to review. The alert type, the specified number of days to keep the alert history, and the last checked date of the alert automatically display. You can then select a period range to limit the review to the alert checks within an entered range. Select Oracle General Ledger as the application, and New Code Combination – Vision Operations (USA) as the alert name. See Figure 10-22. Click on the **Find Checks** button.

The Review Alert Checks form displays the alert checks related to the selected alert. It displays the requestor, the request start date and time, the concurrent request ID, and the status of each alert check. It also displays the action sets initiated based on the alert checks and the Oracle ID, status, number of exceptions, and number of actions related to each action set. See Figure 10-23. Close the window. Click on the **Find Actions** button.

The Review Alert Actions form displays the action sets executed for the selected alert, the request start date and time, plus the Oracle ID. For each action set, the executed actions are displayed together with the time finished and the action details. Action details vary based on the action type. Action details can be distribution lists or arguments, depending on the action type. If the alert has response processing, click on the **Response** button to see the received responses and the executed response sets and response actions. If you want to see the exact messages sent or the scripts executed,

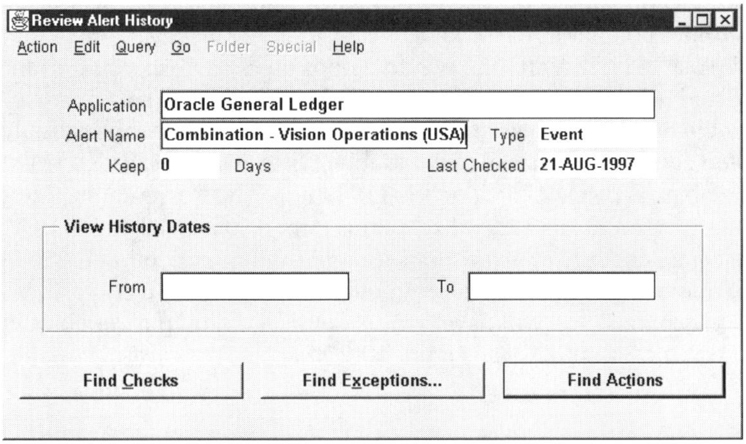

FIGURE 10-22. *Review Alert History form*

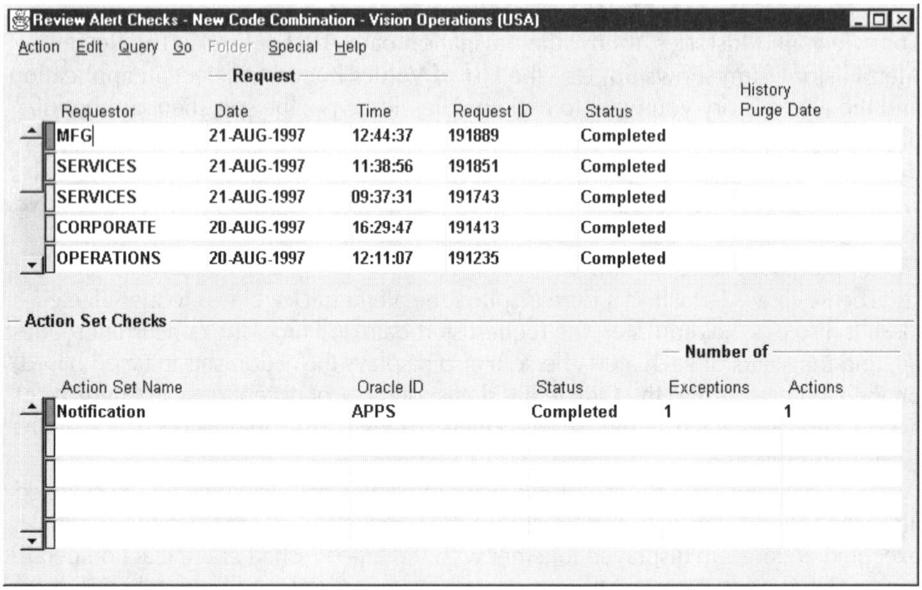

FIGURE 10-23. *Review Alert Checks form*

click on the **Action Log** button. See Figure 10-24. Close the window. Click on the **Find Exceptions** button.

The Display Output Variables window pops up. This gives you a chance to configure and determine which output variables should be displayed. The default is to display the output variables. To hide a particular output variable, simply uncheck the *Enabled* checkbox of that output variable. Once you are satisfied with which output variables to display, click on the **OK** button. The Review Alert Exceptions form shows up. The Review Alert Exceptions form displays the action sets executed for the selected alert and all exceptions found. Any one exception has the same sequence number, and all your selected output variables are displayed. If you have two exceptions, you will have two sets of selected output variables with two different sequence numbers. See Figure 10-25.

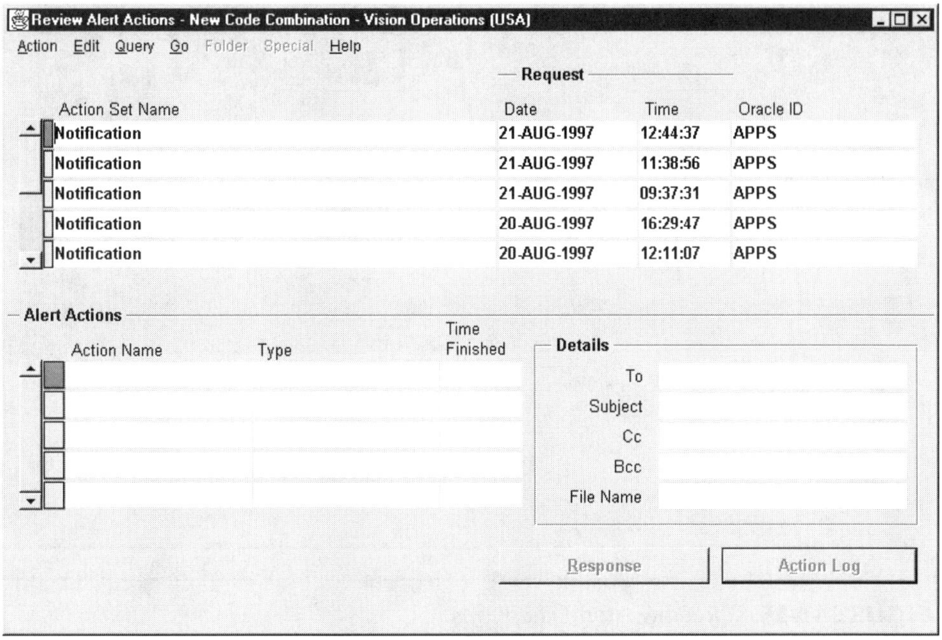

FIGURE 10-24.   *Review Alert Actions form*

Review Questions

1. What is the purpose of the Review Alert Checks form?

2. What is the purpose of the Review Alert Actions form?

3. What is the purpose of the Review Alert Exceptions form?

4. How do you configure which output variables are to be shown for each exception?

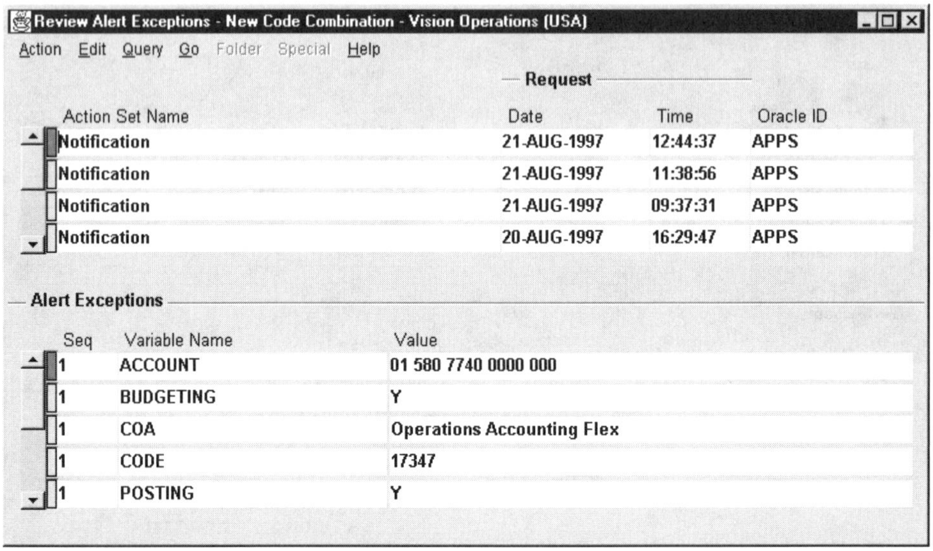

FIGURE 10-25. *Review Alert Exceptions*

Documenting Alerts

With alert histories, the alerts are documented. If the action type is a message, an exact copy of the message is stored. If the action type is a concurrent program, the arguments passed to the concurrent program are stored. If the action type is an operating system script, an exact copy of the script is stored or the filename is stored, depending on whether the action is entered in text mode or file mode. If the action type is a SQL statement script, a copy of the SQL statement is stored. These stored histories serve the business purposes of documenting the alerts that have been executed.

Beside the actions, the exceptions, alert checks, and action sets checked are all stored. If you keep a long enough alert history, the documentation needed will be available to you online.

Review Questions

1. How does an alert history help in documenting alerts?

2. What components of an alert are stored/documented?

Response Processing

From the previous sections, you should already have an idea as to how response processing works. Response processing processes responses received from messages automatically and initiates the appropriate response actions as a result. Response processing can also accept values for response variables from response messages. These response variables can serve as parameters and/or input values for response actions. Oracle Office must be installed in order for response processing to work, as it handles the electronic messaging part of responses. In this section, you will be presented with more details on the business needs and major features of response processing in Oracle Alert, in addition to the details as to how response processing works. This section will:

- Explain the business needs that can be met through response processing

- List the major features of response processing

- Explain how response processing works

Business Needs that Can Be Met Through Response Processing

With response processing, you can satisfy the following business needs:

- Automatically initiate actions based on received valid responses

- Automatically initiate actions based on received invalid responses

- Automatically initiate actions based on not receiving responses

- Be able to accept values from responses to become action parameters and/or input variables

- Have a different set of response actions, valid response values, and response variables for each action that solicits a response

- Keep response processing histories

Automatically Initiate Actions Based on Received Valid Responses

Response actions can be automatically initiated based on received valid responses. A different valid response value can initiate a different action. This can be configured in any way to automate workflow using email messages.

Automatically Initiate Actions Based on Received Invalid Responses

Response actions can be automatically initiated based on received invalid responses. This automates the process of letting the recipient or the responder know immediately after an invalid response is received. You can solicit a new valid response to correct the problem in a timely manner.

Automatically Initiate Actions Based on Not Receiving Responses

Response actions can be automatically initiated based on the lack of responses. This automates the process of letting the recipient know after a predefined period of time that either no response or no valid response has been received. You will notify the recipient and close the responses for the original message in that response set.

Be Able to Accept Values from Responses to Become Action Parameters and/or Input Variables

You may want to have the action behave dynamically based on user inputs from the received responses. For example, you want the recipient or the responder to provide an amount or a quantity to be used in an order.

Have a Different Set of Response Actions, Valid Response Values, and Response Variables for Each Action that Solicits Responses

You may have more than one action that needs to solicit responses in a single action set. You want to have the ability to have a different set of response actions, valid response values, and response variables for each action that solicits responses, because requirements can be very different.

Keep Response Processing History

You may need to keep a response processing history for audit trail purposes and/or for statistical purposes. The response history can give you an audit trail of what responses you have been receiving and what response actions have been initiated. You can also keep statistics on what kind of responses you have been receiving.

Review Questions

1. What are the three different possible outcomes when soliciting responses?

2. Why do you need to keep a response processing history?

Features of Response Processing

A variety of Oracle Alert features are available to support the business needs of maintaining response processing. These features are as follows:

- Response actions associated with user-defined lists of valid responses

- Response actions associated with responses outside of user-defined lists of valid responses

- Response actions associated with no response within a user-defined number of response days

- Response variables

- Linking response sets to action

Response Actions Associated with User-Defined Lists of Valid Responses

Oracle Alert allows you to associate a series of response actions to each valid response value that you defined. The only requirement is that your valid response values must have a unique first word or have a unique string of 30 characters.

Response Actions Associated with Responses Outside of User-Defined Lists of Valid Responses

Oracle Alert allows you to associate one series of actions for all response values outside of the valid response values that you defined.

Response Actions Associated with No Response Within a User-Defined Number of Response Days

Oracle Alert allows you to associate one series of actions when no response or no valid response has been received outside of the response days you defined. You specify the response days by each action that solicits responses. In other words, if you have two actions that solicit responses, one can be considered no response if you have not received a response or a valid response in two days, and the second one can be considered no response if you have not received a response or a valid response in a week.

Response Variables

Oracle Alert allows you to set up as many response variables as you want. Response variables can be used in response actions together with the regular output variables. Response variables can have default values or can accept values from the recipient or the receiver through the response messages.

Linking Response Sets to Actions

Oracle Alert allows you to link a response set to an action that solicits responses. You can link a different response set to different actions. You can also specify a different response day to different actions.

Review Questions

1. How many valid response values can you define?

2. What is the definition of an invalid response in Oracle Alert?

3. What is the definition of no response in Oracle Alert?

4. What are response variables?

How Response Processing Works

Now that you know the business imperatives that can be met through response processing and the Oracle Alert features that support them, let's explore how response processing actually works in Oracle Alert, as in the case of the following:

■ Message handles

■ Oracle Office setup

■ Response processor

Message Handles

Message handles are mechanisms to identify action messages that are linked with response sets. Oracle Alert assigns unique message handles in the format of the Oracle Alert installation number, plus a sequential message number. An Oracle Alert installation number is assigned as a system option for Oracle Alert. To see this system option, follow the navigation path *System : Options* and select the Response Processing alternative region. See Figure 10-26. The message handle appears in the original message that solicits responses. In order to pass the message handle along, and for response processing in Oracle Alert to work correctly, the original message must be included in the reply.

Oracle Office Setup

For response processing to work, you must set up a response mail account in Oracle Office. The response mail account is another system option in Oracle Alert. This system option is in the Oracle Office Options alternative region. See Figure 10-27. Each response mail account must have three mandatory folders in order for response processing to work: Inbox, Reviewed, and Reviewed_OK. Response processing in Oracle Alert uses all three folders.

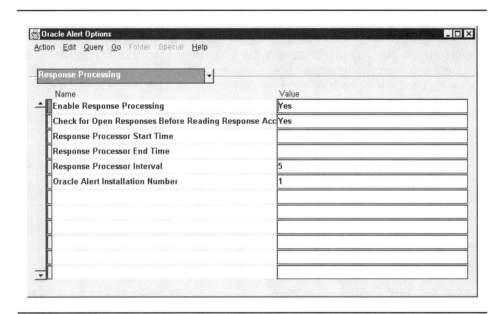

FIGURE 10-26. *Oracle Alert Options (Response Processing) form*

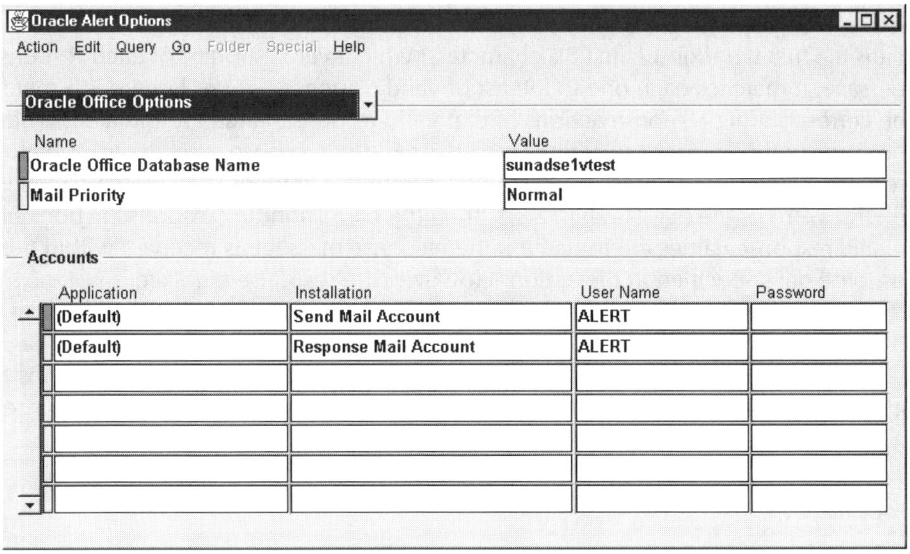

FIGURE 10-27. *Oracle Alert Options (Oracle Office Options) form*

Response Processor

A response processor is a concurrent program that has the job of processing received responses. To implement response processing, you must first enable response processing in the system option under the Response Processing alternative region. In the same region, you have the option of specifying a start and end time for the response processor. You can also define a response processor interval. This interval specifies in minutes how often a response processor can be submitted. If no start time, end time, and interval are defined, but response processing is enabled, the response processor only runs once a day at midnight. After enabling response processing and defining a schedule for the response processor, initiate the response process using navigation path *Request : Schedule*, just as you did for the periodic alert scheduler. Place your cursor on the response processor row and click on the **Activate** button.

When a response processor is submitted to the concurrent manager, the response processor executes. The response processor first moves all response messages from the Inbox folder to the Reviewed folder within the response mail account. Response messages are defined as messages with message handles. Next, the response processor interprets the message handles in the Reviewed folder. If the installation number of a message handle is different than the installation number of the response processor—which can happen if you have more than one installation of Oracle Alert—the response message is moved back from the Reviewed folder to the Inbox folder.

If a message handle is valid—meaning that the installation number matches the installation number of the response processor and the message number is active—the response process interprets the response values. The response processor reads the first word or the first 30 characters, whichever is shorter, of each response message. It matches each one to the list of valid response values. If there is a match, the corresponding response actions of that valid response value are initiated. Once the corresponding response actions are initiated, the response message is moved from the Reviewed folder to the Reviewed_OK folder. If there is no match between the first word or the first 30 characters, then the corresponding response actions of invalid response values are initiated if the response message is received within the response days specified in the action. However, the response message is not moved from the Reviewed folder to the Reviewed_OK folder—it stays in the Reviewed folder. If there is no valid response or no response at all within the response days specified in the action, the response processor initiates the response actions associated with the no-response value and the response processor closes responses of the messages in the response set.

Review Questions

1. What are message handles?

2. Which three folders need to be set up in Oracle Office?

3. How do you schedule a response processor?

4. How does a response processor work?

Implementation Considerations

The last section of this chapter talks about implementation considerations. Discussion focuses on how to plan a successful implementation of Oracle Alert, as well as how to best configure Oracle Alert to fit your needs. This section covers:

■ Planning a successful implementation of Oracle Alert

■ Configuring Oracle Alert for your business

■ Identifying your business needs and mapping them to responsibilities

■ Determining if you can use the predefined Oracle *Alert Manager* responsibility or create a new application *Alert Manager* responsibility

Planning a Successful Implementation of Oracle Alert

In order to plan a successful implementation of Oracle Alert, you must consider the following:

■ Identify all critical exceptions and how you want to handle them.

■ Determine whether you have custom applications that need to be integrated with Oracle Alert.

■ Identify how many alert actions need to be acted upon by Oracle installations.

■ Quantify your alert needs and decide whether you need to streamline Oracle Alert implementation.

Although there is nothing in Oracle Applications to prevent your adding new alerts at any time, you will have more success if you plan them in advance. Alerts, and any documentation describing how your users must act on them, have to be defined in your business processes. Almost any alert you implement will change the way you do business by replacing a manual procedure or a report.

Identify All Critical Exceptions and How You Want to Handle Them

First, identify all of the critical exceptions you want to capture or monitor. Next, determine whether you want to know about the exceptions as soon as they occur, or just periodically. If it is important to know the exceptions as soon as possible, you will need an event alert. Otherwise, you can have a periodic alert. Event alerts, which execute every time a database table is updated, can be very resource intensive. The system can bog down if you have too many of them. Thus, you should be careful in determining the alert type.

Once you have identified all your critical exceptions, determine what actions you need to perform for each exception. Remember, you have four action types: concurrent program, message, operating system script, and SQL statement script. Do you need just a notification, or do you need to perform preventive or corrective actions? Determine which action types are required. For each action, identify the parameters you need and determine how you can obtain the parameter values. Parameter values can be user-entered values or values retrieved from the database.

After identifying the actions, determine the more advanced features, such as summary threshold group and escalation group. Determine when you want to execute a summary-level action vs. a detail-level action. Set up a summary threshold group with the threshold you have in mind to reflect your needs. If the same exception occurs over and over again, do you want to escalate the action along the severity level or do you want the same action to be performed? If you want to escalate the action along the severity level, you must set up escalation groups. Escalation groups can only have detail-level actions as members. If you want to implement action escalation, or simply perform duplicate checking, you still need to keep an alert history. This allows Oracle Alert to check the new exceptions against the past results to determine whether the new exceptions are duplicates. If you do not have a long enough alert history, it will not flag a new exception as a duplicate—that would otherwise be noted if you had a longer history. For example, if you have an exception today and you keep a history only for two days, if the same exception occurs three days from now, it will not be flagged as a duplicate since the history is already gone. If you keep a history for a week, however, and the same exception occurs three days from now, it will be flagged as a duplicate. Be careful in selecting how many days of history to keep if you want to implement either duplicate checking or action escalation.

Next, ask yourself whether you need response processing. In other words, do you need the recipient's input in determining what actions to take? If the answer is yes, determine the list of valid responses and the corresponding actions. In addition, determine what actions you want to perform if the response is invalid, and what actions you want to perform if there is no response or no valid response.

Determine Whether You Have Custom Applications That Need to Be Integrated with Oracle Alert

You need to decide whether you have custom applications that must be integrated with Oracle Alert. A custom application may be a complete and self-contained system, with its own responsibilities, menus, forms, and reports. More often, an installation defines a custom application to serve as the owner of custom tables, forms, and reports developed to enhance one of the standard Oracle Applications. If you have any, identify them and determine what alert requirements you have on these custom applications. Do you need event alerts or periodic alerts, or both? This determines your course of action in terms of additional setups; you need to make sure that Alert has access to the custom tables and views.

Identify How Many Oracle Installations Need Alert Actions

If you have more than one Oracle installation and you want your periodic alert actions to be performed in more than the installation that initiates your periodic alert, you must identify these Oracle installations and which actions need to performed on these additional installations. More setups will be necessary. If you must perform an event alert on another Oracle installation, an additional setup will also be required. However, an event alert cannot work on another Oracle installation that resides in a separate database. If this is the case, you must install Oracle Alert in that separate database.

Quantify Your Alert Needs and Decide Whether to Streamline Oracle Alert Implementation

Taking everything into consideration, you now have an idea as to how many event alerts and periodic alerts you might have. Determine whether these requirements may overload your concurrent manager. For example, if you have a lot of event alerts defined, and the possibility of having an event alert executed every 5 to 10 minutes is pretty high, you will probably overload the concurrent manager. You will then need to reconfigure your concurrent manager to streamline your alert processing by allowing more concurrent processes.

Review Questions

1. When do you need an event alert vs. a periodic alert?

2. Why is it important to determine whether your alerts will use objects that belong to custom applications?

3. Why is determining how many alert actions are needed to perform on Oracle installations important?

4. When should you consider customizing your concurrent manager to streamline your alert processing?

Configuring Oracle Alert for Your Business

Now, you will learn how to configure Oracle Alert to satisfy your business needs. You will see how to:

■ Establish system options

■ Establish custom applications

■ Execute periodic alerts in another installation using a different Oracle ID

■ Customize concurrent managers

System Options

Set up system options using navigation path *System : Options*. You have five alternative regions for system options. The five alternative regions include Mail Systems, Oracle Office Options, Message Elements, Response Processing, and More Options. The Mail Systems alternative region allows you to specify the command used for invoking UNIX sendmail, Oracle Office, or VMS Mail. These three email systems are seeded with Oracle Alert. You can also create new command and email system names used for your specific email system if they are not UNIX, Oracle Office, or VMS Mail. Check the *In Use* checkbox for the mail systems you want to use. See Figure 10-28.

The next region is the Oracle Office Options region. You have seen this screen shot before. In this region, you must specify the Oracle Office database name, the default mail priority, the sendmail account user name, and the response mail account user name for each application. If you want the same sendmail account user name and the response mail account user name for all applications, use (Default) as the application name. You can utilize the same user name across applications and employ the same user name for both the sendmail account user

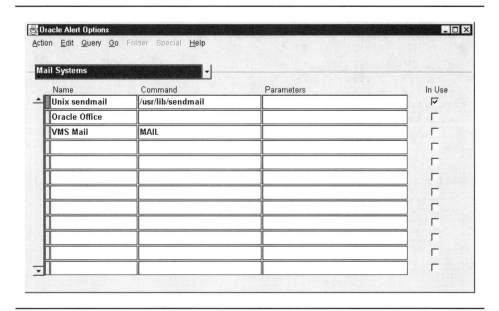

FIGURE 10-28. *Oracle Alert Options (Mail Systems) form*

name and the response mail account user name. You also need to enter the passwords for the mail accounts.

Next is the Message Elements region. You can enter a default message for the message action header, message action footer, response text, and returned message header. The message action header and the message action footer are sent along with whatever message template you have specifically created for your message action. Place your cursor on the response text message element. See Figure 10-29.

The subsequent region is the Response Processing region—you have seen this screen shot before also. In this region, determine whether you want to enable response processing (assuming you are using Oracle Office) and whether you want to check for open responses before reading response accounts. You also need to define a schedule for the response processor, including the start time, end time, and the interval. As a last step, you should assign an installation number for your Oracle Alert installation. If you have multiple installations of Oracle Alert, make sure this number is unique across your company.

The last alternative region is the More Options region. In this region, you can specify a concurrent manager name to which all Oracle Alert concurrent programs submit, the concurrent manager startup command, the default user mail account to use if the Email field of the Oracle application user's definition is null, the location

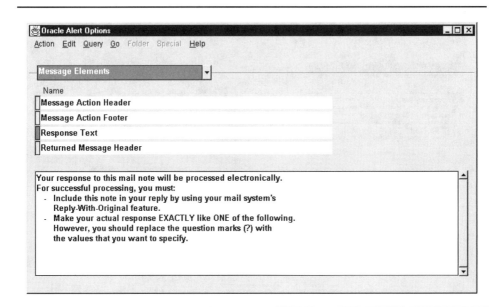

FIGURE 10-29. *Oracle Alert Options (Message Elements) form*

of the diagnostics message file, the operating system command for performing diagnostics, the maximum summary message width, and the sendmail account description when an Oracle Alert message action is sent. See Figure 10-30.

Custom Applications

If you have custom applications and you want the custom applications to integrate with Oracle Alert, you must perform an additional configuration. A custom application is an application that is not installed by the Oracle Autoinstall process. Note that an Oracle Application module that resides on a different database must be considered a custom application as well.

If the custom application is on a different database, you must ask your database administrator to create a database link for you first. The database link establishes connectivity between your two databases. Next, you should register your customer application if it has not already been done in the course of developing the application. To do this, follow the navigation path *System : Applications.* In the Applications form, you can enter your customer application name, an application short name, the base path in the operating system level that corresponds to the custom applications, and an optional description. The application name and the application short name must be unique. See Figure 10-31.

Oracle Alert Options

Action Edit Query Go Folder Special Help

More Options

Name	Value
Business Day System	American System
Concurrent Manager Name	
Concurrent Manager Startup Command	startmgr
Default User Mail Account	Operating System Login ID
Diagnostics: Message File	/appltop/alr/5.0/bin/alrmsg
Diagnostics: Operating System Command	ls
Maximum Summary Message Width	80 Characters
Send Mail Account Description	Oracle Alert

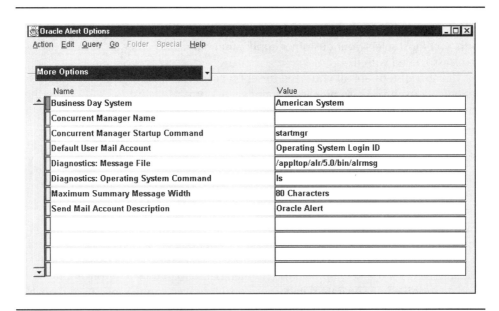

FIGURE 10-30. *Oracle Alert Options (More Options) form*

Applications

Action Edit Query Go Folder Special Help

Application	Short Name	Basepath	Description
Application Implementation	AZ	AZ_TOP	Application Implementation
Application Object Library	FND	FND_TOP	Oracle Application Object Library
Application Report Generator	RG	RG_TOP	Application Report Generator
Application Utilities	AU	AU_TOP	Oracle Application Utilities
Applications DBA	AD	AD_TOP	Applications DBA
Asia/Pacific Localizations	JA	JA_TOP	Oracle Asia/Pacific Localizations
Demo Order Entry (AOL Class)	DEM	DEM_TOP	Demo for AOL class (Develop Extensi
European Localizations	JE	JE_TOP	Oracle European Localizations
Global Accounting Engine	AX	AX_TOP	Global Accounting Engine
Latin America Localizations	JL	JL_TOP	Oracle Latin America Localizations

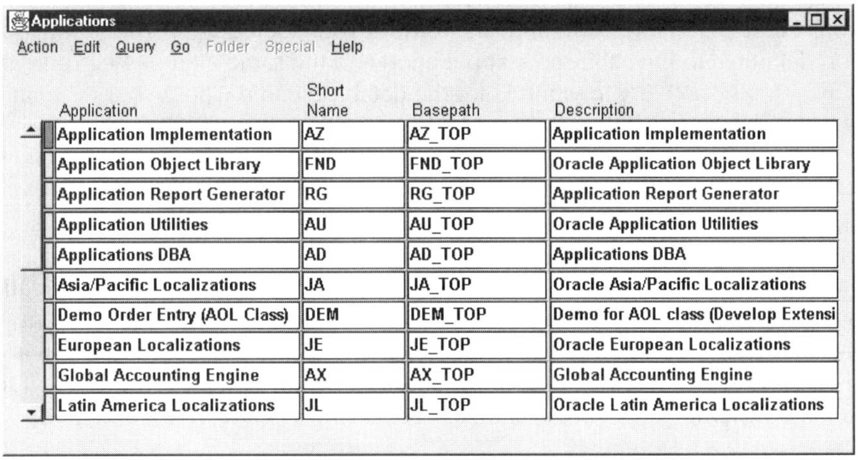

FIGURE 10-31. *Applications form*

Next, register the Oracle ID link with the custom application. To do this, follow the navigation path *System : Installations.* In the Define Application Installations form, you must select your customer application name and enter the Oracle user name associated with it.

The above steps are all you need to set up custom applications that only require periodic alerts. If you also need event alerts, the custom application must be in the same database. If not, install Oracle Alert in the other database in order to make event alerts work. Assuming that the custom application is in the same database, you must finish the steps necessary for periodic alerts and then register the custom tables under your custom applications. Register tables under the *Application Developer* responsibility.

Executing Periodic Alerts in Another Installation Using a Different Oracle ID

You can also configure Oracle Alert to allow periodic alert actions to be executed in another installation of the same application module using a different Oracle ID. You must register the new application. Remember that an Oracle application module residing in a separate database is considered a custom application. The concurrent program associated with the alert action must be connected with this custom application. Next, add the customer application and the corresponding Oracle ID into the Oracle Alert data group. This step must be performed as the system administrator.

Following all of these setups, you must copy the alert definition from your existing application to the custom application. To do this, go to the Alerts Definition form and query up your alert. Select Transfer Alert from the Special menu. The Transfer Alert Definitions form appears, as does your source alert. The destination alert is defaulted to have the same application and the same alert name. You can modify either or both if you want. Enter the database name where your destination alert should reside. Click on the **Transfer** button. See Figure 10-32.

Query up your new alert. Click on the **Alert Details** button and choose the Installations alternative region. Modify the Oracle ID of your source alert to the appropriate Oracle ID of your destination alert. Next, go to the Action Details form by selecting the **Action Details** button and changing the old concurrent program to the new concurrent program you created under the custom application. Save your work. Now you have a periodic alert that will run against a different installation of Oracle Applications under an alternative Oracle ID. If the Oracle ID is the same, you do not need to go through this process. You may find this feature useful in transferring alerts between instances, such as between test and production.

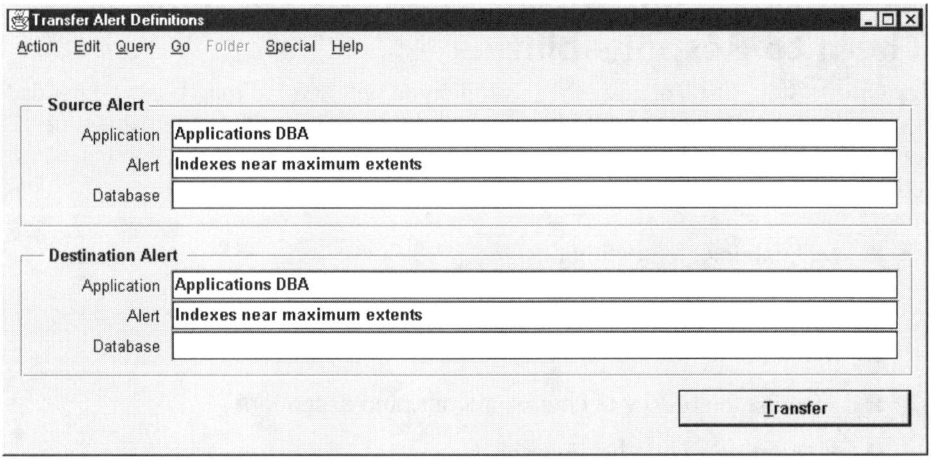

FIGURE 10-32. *Transfer Alert Definitions form*

Customizing Concurrent Managers for Alerts

In order to streamline event alert processing, you can define one specific concurrent manager to run ALECTC only. If you want to do this, you also need to define all of the other concurrent managers to exclude ALECTC. Otherwise, event alert processing will be disturbed and the other concurrent managers will get into a bottleneck if the volume is high.

Review Questions

1. What options do you have in the Message Elements alternative region?

2. For what purpose can you use the transfer alert function?

3. What is considered a custom application?

4. How will you stop event alerts from interfering with regular concurrent request processing?

Identifying Your Business Needs and Mapping Them to Responsibilities

For Oracle Alert, just like any other module, you will need to map business needs to responsibilities and create multiple responsibilities to serve different business needs for various people. In Oracle Alert, you have the following functions you can map to different responsibilities:

- Maintaining alert definitions

- Defining periodic alert sets

- Maintaining distribution lists

- Viewing the history of checks, actions, and exceptions

- Requesting a periodic alert check

- Scheduling Oracle Alert programs

- Maintaining Oracle Alert options

- Registering applications

- Registering application installations

- Running alert reports

Create a matrix and determine how many combinations of different functions you need. Usually, you will have a superuser responsibility that includes all functions. Scale down the functions from that point on. You may have a responsibility that only runs alerts but cannot alter definitions of alerts. Create all of the responsibilities for your business needs.

Review Questions

1. Which function allows you to run periodic alerts?

2. Which functions are considered setup functions?

Predefined vs. Custom Responsibilities and Oracle Alert Manager

You can determine whether you can use the predefined Oracle *Alert Manager* responsibility or whether you should create a new application *Alert Manager* responsibility. You make that determination if you want to keep the person that can create and maintain alerts for the seeded applications separate from the person that can create and maintain alerts for the custom application. Define one custom responsibility for each of your custom applications. Assign the custom responsibility to the person who should create the alerts for the customer application. The custom responsibility connects to the database using an Oracle ID different than the predefined Oracle Alert's Oracle ID.

Review Questions

1. When should you create a new application *Alert Manager* responsibility?

2. How many custom alert responsibilities can you have?

For the Chapter Summary, Two-Minute Drill, and Chapter Questions and Answers, open the summary.htm file contained in the Summary_files directory on the book's CD-ROM.

CHAPTER
11

Workflow

n this chapter, you will learn how to use the Oracle Workflow application. Oracle Workflow allows you to streamline and automate your workflow processes using its components. The topics to be covered include the following:

- Overview of Oracle Workflow

- Overview of the Workflow Engine

- Overview of the Workflow Directory Service

- Planning and monitoring a workflow process

- Diagramming a workflow process

- Fundamentals of the Implementation Wizard

- Using the Implementation Wizard

This chapter takes you through each Oracle Workflow component and explains how each component works. Components include how the Workflow Engine manages workflow processes, how the Workflow Directory Service functions, how Oracle Workflow receives information, and the role of the Workflow Directory Service.

Creating, planning, and monitoring workflow processes are explained. Workflow processes in Oracle Workflow consist of activities and transitions. When you create your workflow processes, Oracle Workflow will ensure that they are executed and enforced.

The last two sections of the chapter deal with the Implementation Wizard. The Implementation Wizard is an Oracle Application module that leads you through the Oracle Application setup modules. The Implementation Wizard maps these setup steps into workflow processes that Oracle Workflow executes and enforces.

Overview of Oracle Workflow

This section will explain the concepts of a workflow and describe the separate components within the Oracle Workflow module.

Concepts of a Workflow

A workflow consists of numerous processes. Workflow processes represent business process flows and information routing. Oracle Workflow defines process rules. Each workflow process contains a set of activities, which can be notifications, PL/SQL stored procedures, or another subprocess. The flow of business processes is less efficient when the information is not routed to the appropriate person(s) or group. The two needs are interdependent. The flow of business processes in Oracle Workflow can have decision points (branches), parallel flows, and loops. A decision point (branch) is where a decision must be made. Various flow options result from choices made at the decision point. Parallel flows are business processes that flow simultaneously. You can decide whether one, some, or all parallel flows must be completed before moving on to the next step. Loops are business processes that flow back to an activity completed earlier.

In the past, information routing was performed primarily on paper. Now, information routing is usually performed through electronic messaging—emails. Electronic messaging is much more efficient, especially if your business process flow includes external organizations or personnel. For example, utilizing email, you can alert relevant parties that a decision needs to be made. You can also notify users when there are current or potential problems, and you can use notifications to solicit responses.

Oracle Workflow drives items or transactions of specific types through workflow processes. If, for example, you use the purchase order approval workflow process, the item type would be the purchase order. Purchase orders of one item type will comprise one specific purchase order. All items that have the same item type share the same set of attributes. Attributes consist of item-type data. Each item will have its own set of attribute values. In this purchase order example, attributes can be the purchase order number and supplier; values can be PO-12345 and ABC Supplier. The workflow process encompasses the entire process, from purchase order creation to completion. A completed purchase order can be approved, rejected, or cancelled. Oracle Workflow makes sure that the created purchase order is routed to the appropriate person(s) for approval and that the correct procedures are followed throughout the entire workflow process.

Review Questions

1. What is a workflow?

2. What can a business process flow contain?

3. Why is Internet communication important in workflow management?

4. What information can be communicated through notifications?

5. What is the difference between a process and an activity?

Oracle Workflow Components

Oracle Workflow contains six major components:

- Workflow Builder
- Workflow Engine
- Workflow Monitor
- Workflow Definitions Loader
- Workflow Directory Services
- Notification System

Workflow Builder

Workflow Builder is the component that provides a graphical user interface for creating, reviewing, and maintaining workflow definitions. A workflow definition includes the workflow processes, attributes, notifications, messages, and functions that make up the workflow. Like Oracle Applications, Workflow Builder has a Navigator to help you find the various components of your workflow definition.

Workflow Engine

Workflow Engine is the component that executes and enforces the defined workflow processes. When a workflow process starts or a step is completed, the Workflow Engine is signaled. The Workflow Engine receives and reads a signal from the defined workflow processes and then determines and executes the appropriate next step. To send a signal or to communicate with the Workflow Engine, Oracle Applications provide several standard Workflow Engine application programming interfaces (APIs).

Workflow Monitor

Workflow Monitor is the component of Oracle Workflow that allows you to review the state or status of an item through any particular workflow process. Workflow Monitor can also be used by application administrators to push through certain items that have errored out. Workflow Monitor provides an overview of a given item in the workflow and helps with tracking.

Workflow Definitions Loader

Workflow Definitions Loader is the component that allows you to download or load workflow definitions to and from the database or text files.

Workflow Directory Services

Workflow Directory Services is the component that identifies the directory repository to be used, tells Oracle Workflow how to find the users, interprets the roles of each user, and sends notifications to those users when necessary.

Notification System

The Notification Mailer is a program that concurrently sends emails and receives responses from the Oracle Workflow Notification System. It will send out notifications and process responses by calling the response functions and completing the notification. Unlike Oracle Alert response processing, you do not need Oracle Office to use this functionality.

Review Questions

1. What does a Workflow Builder do?

2. What does a Workflow Engine do?

3. What does a Workflow Monitor do?

4. What does a Workflow Definitions Loader do?

5. Does Oracle Office need to be configured to run Workflow Notification?

Overview of the Workflow Engine

You now know the function of the Workflow Engine in Oracle Workflow. In this section, you will learn more about how the Workflow Engine executes and enforces each item's defined workflow process. You will also learn how to use Workflow Engine APIs.

The following section explains how the workflow engine manages a process and how to apply Workflow Engine APIs to functional activities.

How the Workflow Engine Manages a Process

The Workflow Engine drives items through workflow processes defined in Oracle Workflow. Each item has a set of attribute values that contains information about the specific item. A workflow process consists of a combination of activities and transitions. An activity can be a function, a notification, or a process. At any point in time, there may be more than one item passing through the workflow process. These items, which can be at found at any activity or at any transition within the workflow process, have their own sets of attribute values. When in the middle of the workflow process, each one of these items with its own set of attribute values is referred to as one instance of the workflow process. Each instance can have a different state. The state of the instance or item is defined by the states of all activities of the workflow process. The Workflow Engine manages all instances of defined workflow processes.

The following describes how the Workflow Engine manages a workflow process. The Workflow Engine is a PL/SQL program residing on the server. It receives APIs from the clients whenever an activity needs to change state. Valid states of an activity are Active, Complete, Deferred, Error, Notified, Suspended, and Waiting. Once the Workflow Engine changes the state of the activity, it evaluates the changed state of the activity. If the activity is changed to a state of Error, the Workflow Engine rolls back the changes made by the erred activity and initiates the defined error-handling routine. The Workflow Engine will first try to run the error-handling routine associated with the erred activity. If no error-handling routine is attached to the erred activity, the Workflow Engine will trace back to the erred activity and determine the parent of the activity. If no error-handling routine is attached to the parent activity, the Workflow Engine traces back to the parent of the parent activity until there is an error-handling routine. Oracle Workflow comes with a default error process, or you can create your own custom error-processing routine that will reset, retry, or ship the erred activity.

If the activity is changed to a state of Active, the activity will be executed, unless the activity has a processing cost higher than the Workflow Engine threshold. Executing an activity means running a function activity in run mode, sending notification for notification activity, or initiating a subprocess in a process activity. In the case where an activity's processing cost is higher than the Workflow Engine threshold, the state of the activity will change to Deferred. Activities are marked as Deferred in order to streamline processing. Deferred activities are run in background batches, not in real time. The Workflow Engine running in the foreground has a defined threshold activity processing cost. If the processing cost of an activity exceeds the defined threshold, the foreground Workflow Engine will not execute the activity and marks it as Deferred. The background Workflow Engine picks up all deferred activities and executes them. You can have more than one background Workflow Engine. To further streamline workflow processing, each Workflow Engine can have different thresholds so that other background Workflow Engines can pick up deferred activities with varying processing costs. Setting up background Workflow Engines is optional, but you need at least one background Workflow Engine to handle timed-out notifications.

If the activity is changed to a state of Complete, the Workflow Engine issues a savepoint and evaluates all of the transitions tied to the completed activity. A savepoint is different than a commit. You can roll back to the savepoint, but you cannot roll back after commit. The Workflow Engine never issues a commit; the calling application is responsible for the commit. If the activities that depend on the completed activity have not been executed before, the Workflow Engine will change the state of the dependent activities to Active. If the activities that depend on the completed activity have been executed before, this will cause a loop. Depending on the setup, the Workflow Engine will then do one of two things. If the executed activities are marked as Run Once, the Workflow Engine will simply skip those transitions. If the executed activities are marked as Loop Reset, the Workflow Engine reverses all of the executed activities in the loop from the loop reset point and reexecutes the activities. Reversing all of the executed activities means running the function activities in cancel mode and marking notification activities as Cancelled. The Workflow Engine reverses all of the executed activities in reverse order back to the loop reset point and reexecutes the activities in the normal order from the loop reset point on. If the completed activity also marks the completion of the workflow process, the Workflow Engine will mark the workflow process as Complete and all outstanding or incomplete activities will be marked Complete with a result code of #FORCE.

In summary, the Workflow Engine can perform the following functions for clients:

- Change the state of an activity
- Function activities
- Notification activities
- Process activities
- Transitions
- Error handling
- Maintain workflow history

Changing the State of an Activity

The Workflow Engine changes the state of the activity. Valid states are:

- **Active**   The activity is ready for execution.
- **Complete**   The activity has been completed and is ready to transition to the next activity.
- **Deferred**   The activity is ready for execution; however, when the processing cost is higher than the foreground Workflow Engine cost threshold, the activity is deferred and eventually executed in the background by the Workflow Engine.
- **Error**   The activity erred and must be rolled back.

- **Notified** The notification activity needs a response and a notification has been sent to solicit a response.

- **Suspended** The activity has been completed, but the transition is on hold until the activity is resumed.

- **Waiting** The completed activity is waiting for other activities in a master detail process to be completed before transitioning.

Function Activity

Function activities are stored in PL/SQL procedures. Each function activity should have two modes: run and cancel. The run mode is for execution of the function activity, while cancel mode is for reversing the function activity. The Workflow Engine can accept parameters from the clients and, depending on processing cost, execute the function activity either in real time or in the background.

Notification Activity

Notification activities are messages. The Workflow Engine can accept parameters from the clients and send messages to users or roles, which are groups of users. A notification activity can also solicit responses.

Process Activity

A process activity is a separate workflow process, which can be a subprocess or a process within a process.

Transitions

When an activity is completed, the Workflow Engine evaluates the transitions and determines whether to mark activities that depend on the completed activity as Active. When the activity marking the completion of the workflow process is finished, the Workflow Engine can mark the process as Complete. If the transition to Active has already been executed, the Workflow Engine may ignore the transition or reverse and reexecute activities.

Error Handling

If an activity erred, the Workflow Engine rolls back the activity and executes the defined error-handling process.

Maintain Workflow History

The Workflow Engine maintains records of all completed or erred activities so that they can be reviewed online or through reports. Workflow Monitor uses this history for reporting the status of an item.

Review Questions

1. When will an activity be deferred?

2. What will the Workflow Engine do if the activity erred?

3. If you have Loop Reset on, and the Workflow Engine comes to an activity that has been executed, what will happen?

4. What can happen when evaluating transitions?

Applying Workflow Engine APIs to Function Activities

Function activities are stored in PL/SQL procedures. There is a standard API format for all stored procedures called by function activities. When the Workflow Engine executes the function activity, the Workflow Engine passes four input variables and, if a result type is set up for the activity, expects one output variable in return. Output variables are:

- **Itemtype**   A category of items that share the same set of attributes (e.g., purchase order).

- **Itemkey**   A unique identifier within the same item type for the specific item passing through the workflow process.

- **Actid**   The unique identifier of the activity that calls this stored procedure.

- **Funcmode**   The execution mode of the function activity. It can be run, cancel, or timeout. The timeout mode is used for an expired notification that was intended to solicit a response. Each notification has a time-out value. If a notification has received no response after the time-out value has been exceeded, the Workflow Engine will execute the dependent activities with an execution mode of TIMEOUT.

- **Result**   The result of the stored procedure. Results can be:

  - **COMPLETE: result_code**   Stored procedure completed. The result code is specified in the type of the function activity.

  - **DEFERRED: date**   The stored procedure is deferred, to be processed in the background or at a specified date (optional).

  - **ERROR: error_code**   The stored procedure erred. You can, if you wish, provide the error code.

- **NOTIFIED: notification_ID: user** The stored procedure sent out a notification to a user. You may return the unique identifier for the notification, the notification ID, and the user who sent the notification.

- **WAITING** The stored procedure has been completed, but there is a waiting period before the function activity is marked as Complete. The background Workflow Engine will mark the function activity Complete after the waiting period has expired.

The stored procedure declaration will be in the following format:

```
PROCEDURE your_procedure_name (
      itemtype in varchar2,
      itemkey in varchar2,
      actid in number,
      funcmode in varchar2,
      result out varchar2) IS
```

Once the procedure declaration is completed, you will then have the stored procedure body. A pair of BEGIN and END markers encloses the stored procedure body. In the procedure body, you must check the Funcmode variable to execute codes that correspond to the RUN, CANCEL, and TIMEOUT modes.

Review Questions

1. What does the input variable Itemkey represent?

2. What does the input variable Actid represent?

3. What three function activity execution modes are in a stored procedure?

4. What are the possible results of a stored procedure in a function activity?

Workflow Engine APIs

Inside the stored procedure, you must use Workflow Engine APIs to communicate with the Workflow Engine. All Workflow Engine APIs are stored in a PL/SQL package called WF_ENGINE. Table 11-1 shows a list of Workflow Engine APIs present inside the WF_ENGINE package.

The last section of the stored procedure body is the EXCEPTION block for exception handling. Any kind of exception handling is allowed in PL/SQL. The only thing you must do is set the context information. This is done by the API calls WF_CORE.CONTEXT('your_package_name', 'your_procedure_name', itemtype, itemkey, to_char(actid), funcmode).

Procedure Name	Description	Variable (I=Input, O=Output)
AddItemAttr	Add a new unvalidated runtime item attribute.	Item type(I)
SetItemAttrText	Set the value of a text item attribute.	Item type(I)
		Item key(I)
		Attribute name(I)
		New value(I)
SetItemAttrNumber	Set the value of a number item attribute.	Item type(I)
		Item key(I)
		Attribute name(I)
		New value(I)
SetItemAttrDate	Set the value of a date item attribute.	Item type(I)
		Item key(I)
		Attribute name(I)
		New value(I)
GetItemAttrInfo	Get type information about an item attribute.	Item type(I)
		Attribute name(I)
		Attribute type(O)
		Subtype(O)
		Format(O)

TABLE 11-1. *WF_ENGINE Procedures*

Procedure Name	Description	Variable (I=Input, O=Output)
GetActivityAttrInfo	Get type information about an activity attribute.	Item type(I)
		Item key(I)
		Activity ID(I)
		Attribute name(I)
		Attribute type(O)
		Sub-type(O)
		Format(O)
SetItemParent	Set the parent/master process for a detail process.	Item type(I)
		Item key(I)
		Parent item type(I)
		Parent item key(I)
		Parent context(I)
SetItemOwner	Set the owner of an item.	Item type(I)
		Item key(I)
		Owner(I)
SetItemUserKey	Set the user-friendly identifier for an item.	Item type(I)
		Item key(I)
		User key(I)

TABLE 11-1. *WF_ENGINE Procedures* (continued)

Procedure Name	Description	Variable (I=Input, O=Output)
CB	Callback function used by the Notification System to get and set process attributes, and mark a process complete.	Action(I)
		Context(I)
		Attribute name(I)
		Attribute type(I)
		Text attribute value(I,O)
		Number attribute value(I,O)
		Date attribute value(I,O)
ProcessDeferred	Process all deferred activities within the threshold limits.	Item type(I)
		Minimum threshold(I)
		Maximum threshold(I)
ProcessTimeOut	Pick up one timed-out activity and execute time-out transition.	Item type(I)
ProcessStuckProcess	Pick up one stuck activity, mark error status, and execute error process.	Item type(I)
Background	Process all current deferred and/or time-out activities within the threshold limits.	Item type(I)
		Minimum threshold(I)
		Maximum threshold(I)
		Process deferred flag(I)
		Process timeout flag(I)

TABLE 11-1. *WF_ENGINE Procedures* (continued)

Procedure Name	Description	Variable (I=Input, O=Output)
BackgroundConcurrent	Send background process for deferred and/or time-out activities to the concurrent manager.	Error buffer(O)
		Return code(O)
		Item type(I)
		Minimum threshold(I)
		Maximum threshold(I)
		Process deferred flag
		Process timeout flag
CreateProcess	Create a new runtime process for an item.	Item type(I)
		Item key(I)
		Root process(I)
StartProcess	Begins execution of the process.	Item type(I)
		Item key(I)
SuspendProcess	Suspends process execution. Outstanding notifications will be allowed to finish, but activity transitions will not occur.	Item type(I)
		Item key(I)
		Process to suspend(I)
AbortProcess	Abort process execution. Outstanding notifications are cancelled. The process is then considered complete, with a status specified by the result variable.	Item type(I)
		Item key(I)
		Process to abort(I)
		Result(O)

TABLE 11-1. *WF_ENGINE Procedures* (continued)

Procedure Name	Description	Variable (I=Input, O=Output)
ResumeProcess	Returns a process to normal execution status. Used after a process is suspended.	Item type(I)
		Item key(I)
		Process to resume(I)
BeginActivity	Determines if the specified activity may currently be performed on the item.	Item type(I)
		Item key(I)
		Activity(I)
CompleteActivity	Notifies the Workflow Engine that an activity for an item has been completed.	Item type(I)
		Item key(I)
		Activity(I)
		Result(I)
AssignActivity	Assigns the user or role (performer) who will perform an activity.	Item type(I)
		Item key(I)
		Activity(I)
		Performer(I)
HandleError	Resets the process thread to the entered activity and begins execution again from that point.	Item type(I)
		Item key(I)
		Activity(I)
		Command(I)
		Result(I)

TABLE 11-1.   *WF_ENGINE Procedures* (continued)

Your stored procedure can be in a PL/SQL package. The package groups store procedures within the same category.

Review Questions

1. Which Work Engine API should you use to begin execution of an activity?

2. Which Work Engine API should you use to get information about an item's attributes?

3. For which functions can you use the Work Engine API Background?

4. How do you notify the Work Engine about a completed activity?

Overview of the Workflow Directory Service

The following sections will:

■ Explain how Oracle Workflow obtains information about a role

■ Map Oracle Workflow to a directory repository

How Oracle Workflow Acquires Information About a Role

In Oracle Workflow a role is a user or a group of users. Oracle Workflow gets information about a role from the following three views:

■ WF_USERS

■ WF_ROLES

■ WF_USER_ROLES

WF_USERS

The WF_USERS view contains information about every user who can receive notifications and responses in Oracle Workflow. Table 11-2 shows all of the columns in the WF_USERS view.

Column	Description
Name	The internal name of the user. This column must be all uppercase and contain no spaces. This is the column that the Workflow Engine will refer to for the user name.
Display_name	The display name of the user.
Description	The description of the user.
Notification_preference	This is the column that identifies the notification preference of the user. Valid values are MAILTEXT, MAILHTML, QUERY, or SUMMARY. When the value is set to MAILTEXT, the user receives notifications and responses by email. When the value is set to MAILHTML, the user receives notifications and responses through HTML email attachments. When the value is set to QUERY, the user receives notifications and responses from the Notifications Web page or Notification Viewer form. The Notification Viewer form is only available to Oracle Applications users. When the value is set to SUMMARY, the user receives emails that contain summaries of all notifications.
Language	The language to use for notification features that are language dependent.
Territory	The territory to determine the date formatting and numeric formatting.
E-mail_address	The email address of the user.
Fax	The fax number of the user.
Orig_system	This column identifies the original system where the user resides.
Orig_system_ID	This column identifies the unique identifier for the user in the original system where the user resides.
Status	The status of the user. Valid statuses are ACTIVE for active users, EXTLEAVE for extended leave, INACTIVE for inactive users, and TMPLEAVE for temporary leave.

TABLE 11-2. *WF_USERS View*

WF_ROLES

The WF_ROLES view contains information about every role in Oracle Workflow that can receive notifications and responses. Each user in WF_USERS must be a role in WF_ROLES. If the attributes of the role are different than the attributes of the users within the role, the attributes of the role will override the attributes of the user. Table 11-3 shows all of the columns in WF_ROLES.

WF_USER_ROLES

In Oracle Workflow, WF_USER_ROLES is the view that resolves the many-to-many relationship between users and roles. One role can contain many users, and one user can belong to many roles. Table 11-4 shows all of the columns in the WF_USER_ROLES view.

Column	Description
Name	The internal name of the role. This column must be all uppercase and contain no spaces. This is the column that the Workflow Engine will refer to for the role name.
Display_name	The display name of the role.
Description	The description of the role.
Notification_preference	This is the column that identifies the notification preference of this role. Valid values are MAILTEXT, MAILHTML, QUERY, or SUMMARY. When the value is set to MAILTEXT, the user receives notifications and responses by email. When the value is set to MAILHTML, the user receives notifications and responses through HTML email attachments. When the value is set to QUERY, the user receives notifications and responses from the Notifications Web page or Notification Viewer form. The Notification Viewer form is only available to Oracle Applications users. When the value is set to SUMMARY, the user receives emails that contain summaries of all notifications.
Language	The language to use for notification features that are language dependent.

TABLE 11-3. *WF_ROLES View*

Column	Description
Territory	The territory determines the formatting of dates and numbers.
E-mail_address	The email address of the role, most likely a mail distribution list. You use the email address of the role if you choose not to expand the role into its users.
Fax	The fax number of the role.
Orig_system	This column identifies the original system where the role resides.
Orig_system_ID	This column identifies the unique identifier for the role in the original system where the role resides.

TABLE 11-3. *WF_ROLES View* (continued)

Column	Description
User_name	The internal name of the user.
User_orig_system	The original system where the user resides. Use this and User_orig_sytem_ID to join to WF_USERS.
User_orig_system_ID	The unique identifier for the user in the original system where the user resides. Use this and the User_orig_system to join to WF_USERS.
Role_name	The internal name of the role.
Role_orig_system	The original system where the role resides. Use this and the ROLE_ORIG_SYSTEM_ID to join to WF_ROLES.
Role_orig_system_ID	The unique identifier for the role in the original system where the role resides. Use this and the ROLE_ORIG_SYSTEM_ID to join to WF_ROLES.

TABLE 11-4. *WF_USER_ROLES View*

Review Questions

   1. When is the WF_USERS view used?

   2. When is the WF_ROLES view used?

   3. When is the WF_USER_ROLES view used?

   4. How many notification preferences do you have and what is the purpose of each one?

Mapping Oracle Workflow to a Directory Repository

To map Oracle Workflow to a directory repository, map the three views—WF_USERS, WF_ROLES, and WF_USER_ROLES—to the database tables in the directory repository selected. If Oracle Workflow is not stand-alone, but is integrated with Oracle Applications, you can map the roles to users and positions defined in the Oracle Human Resources modules. Oracle Workflow provides a seeded script that you can run to map the three views within Oracle Applications.

The three views are mapped in the following way. WF_USERS is mapped to all employees with active primary assignments. WF_ROLES is mapped to all users listed in WF_USERS and to all positions defined as workflow roles. WF_USER_ROLES is mapped to the combination of WF_ROLES and WF_USERS.

In addition, Oracle Workflow provides three local tables that join the three views: WF_LOCAL_USERS, WF_LOCAL_ROLES, and WF_LOCAL_USER_ROLES. You can use these three local views to supplement the database tables in the directory repository.

Review Questions

   1. What does the WF_USERS view map to in Oracle Human Resources?

   2. What does the WF_ROLES view map to in Oracle Human Resources?

   3. What are the names of and uses for the three local tables?

Planning and Monitoring a Workflow Process

This section identifies the workflow process components in Oracle Workflow Builder and explains how to use the Workflow Monitor to monitor workflow processes. Oracle Workflow Builder is initiated from your desktop. Click on **Open File** and select a database. Select apps in the User and Password fields. Type in **vd11** for the Connect field. This will load all seeded workflow into the Vision demonstration database (see Figure 11-1).

Show Item Types is the next form displayed. This form shows all of the available item types in the Hidden list. Select the ones you want and click on the **<<Show**

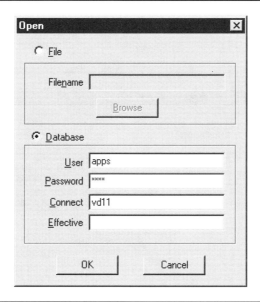

FIGURE 11-1. *Open Workflow File form*

button. The item types will be moved from the Hidden window to the Visible window. Select PO Approval for your review question and click on **OK**. Oracle Workflow Builder will now load the PO Approval workflow and the Navigator will appear on the form (see Figure 11-2). In this section, you will learn to:

■ Identify the components of a workflow process

■ Plan a workflow process

■ Monitor a workflow to view its progress

Components of a Workflow Process

A workflow process consists of several components. Expand the apps@vd11 line by clicking on the plus sign (+) inside the Navigator. You will see three item types: PO Approval, PO Standard, and Standard. You will also see a Hidden Item Types icon. Double-click on the **Hidden Item Types** icon to display the same Show Item Types

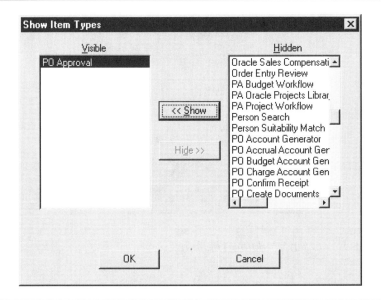

FIGURE 11-2. *Show Item Types form*

window seen when you open a Workflow file. Expand the menu attached to PO Approval and you will see the six components of the PO Approval. They are:

- Attributes
- Processes
- Notifications
- Functions
- Messages
- Lookup types

Item Types

Item types categorize the items. Each activity in a workflow process must be associated with an item type. To create a new item type, right-click on **apps@vd11** and choose New Item Type. In this chapter, the right mouse button is assumed to be the secondary button on your mouse. The Item Type Property window will appear. Enter an internal name for the item type. Type the internal name using uppercase letters. The name can include numeric characters, but cannot contain spaces. You cannot update the internal name once the item type is defined. The internal name must be unique across the entire workflow process. The internal name is used in Workflow Engine APIs. Enter a display name next. The display name is what you use to refer to this item type in any activity. You have the option of entering a description and a selector. A selector is mandatory if your item type is associated with more than one process. The selector returns the process that must be executed in this multiple-process situation. Selector is a PL/SQL stored procedure. Create a new item type called **NEW_PO** with a display name of **NEW PO Item Type** (see Figure 11-3).

The Role tab is designed to let you specify the role that will read, write, and/or execute the item type. (Unfortunately, these security features are not currently active, so you will need to test them in future versions.) Select the Access tab. The red bar, shaded or crossed, represents the access level that can edit objects in the Oracle Workflow Builder. A black vertical bar identifies your access level. You can select combinations of the two options to preserve customizations and lock in at this access level, or to generate different access levels. If both options are checked, you can see that the three levels—Customization, Access, and Protection—are all at 100. This means that only your current access level (100) can update objects. If only the *Preserve Customizations* option is checked, customization and access are both

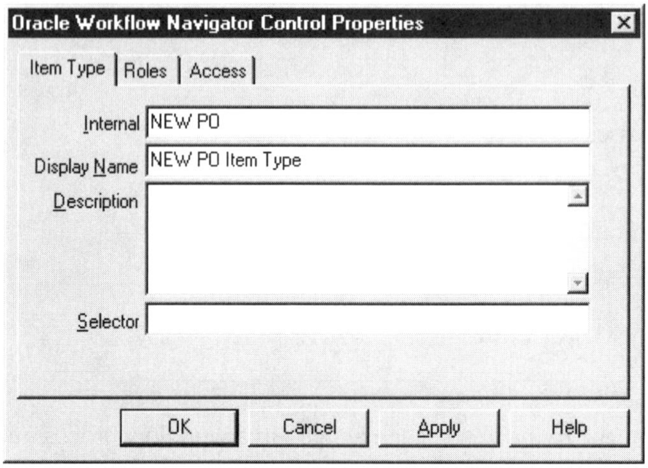

FIGURE 11-3. *Item Type Properties form*

at level 100 while protection is at level 1000. This means access levels 100 to 1000, equal to or higher than your current access level, can update objects. If the *Lock at this Access Level* option is checked, the customization level is at 0 and both access and protection levels are at 100. This means that access levels 0 to 100, equal to or lower than your current access level, can update objects. If neither option is checked, any access level can update objects. Customization is at level 0 and protection is at level 1000.

The red bar will have a crossed pattern if *Allow modifications of customized objects* is checked. To find this option, execute the Help | About Oracle Workflow Builder menu command. If you checked *Allow modifications of customized objects*, you can modify and save objects even if your access level is outside of the customization and protection range. Check *Allow modifications of customized objects*. You must exit the New Item Type properties window to do this. Click **OK** to save your definition. Once you have checked the box under the Help menu, open the Item Type properties window again. Notice that you cannot change the internal name field anymore. Click on the Access tab and check both the *Preserve Customizations* option and the *Lock at this Access Level* option (see Figure 11-4). Click on **OK** to save your changes.

Attributes

All items that have the same item type share the same set of attributes. Attributes are information and properties regarding the item type. Each item will have its own set

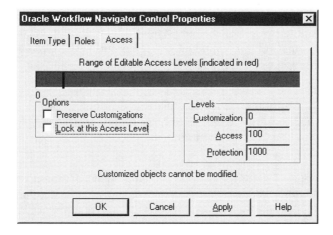

FIGURE 11-4.   *Item Type Properties (Access Tab) form*

of attribute values. Attributes are similar to global variables in that they can be used by any activity in the workflow process. Workflow Engine APIs allow you to get or set attribute values for an item.

Double-click on the attribute to see the properties of the activity. If you want to add a new attribute, right-click when your cursor is on the **Attributes** icon and choose New Attribute. Either way, the Attribute Property window will appear and the item type will be displayed. If you are creating a new item attribute, enter an internal name for the item attribute. The internal name must be uppercase and unique across the same item type; the name cannot contain spaces. Next, enter a display name. The display name will be used in a message or activity. You can then enter an optional description.

Next, select an attribute type. Valid types are:

- **Text**   The attribute value is the text datatype. You can enter an optional length for this attribute type.

- **Number**   The attribute value is the number datatype. You can enter an optional format mask for this attribute type.

- **Date**   The attribute value is the date datatype. You can enter an optional format mask for this attribute type.

- **Lookup**   The attribute value is one of the values specified in a lookup type. You must enter a lookup type for this attribute type.

- **Form**   The attribute value is the internal function name used on an Oracle Application form. You can enter optional function parameters for this attribute type. This attribute type is only useful when using Oracle Applications and the Notifications Viewer form. The Oracle Application form will appear in the Notifications Viewer form. You can bring up the Oracle Applications form from the Notifications Viewer form.

- **URL**   The attribute value is a Universal Resources Locator (URL) to a Web location. This attribute type is only useful if you have the Notifications Web page. The URL will appear in the Notifications Web page. Select it to bring up the Web site.

- **Document**   The attribute value is an attached document. The attribute value is in the format of a document management system and the document name. In the current release, only the PL/SQL document is supported. The PL/SQL document contains data inserted from a database.

- **Role**   The attribute value is a role.

- **Attribute**   The attribute value is the value of another attribute's value at runtime. This is called a reference attribute.

If you enter an optional default value for your attribute, Oracle Workflow Builder provides all of the necessary validation. For example, if you select Attribute as the attribute type, you can only select a defined attribute within the workflow process. If you select Lookup as the attribute type, you can only select a lookup code that is valid for the selected lookup type (see Figure 11-5). Selecting the access level for attributes is the same as selecting the access level for item types. Create a new attribute with an internal name of **NEW_FLAG** and a display name of **NEW Flag**. Choose attribute type Lookup and lookup type Boolean. Choose True as the default value. You are not going to use this attribute in your workflow process, but you are going to build on it later. Click **OK** to save your work.

Review Questions

1. What is the difference between an internal name and a display name?

2. When is the Form attribute type used?

3. What access level can update objects if the option *Allow modifications of customized objects* is checked?

4. When do you need a selector for an item type?

5. What does the *Preserve Customizations* option do?

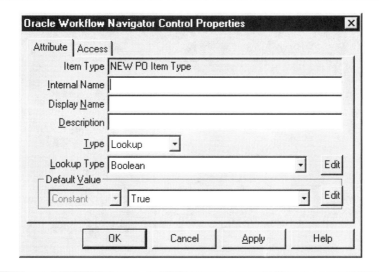

FIGURE 11-5. *Attribute Properties form*

Processes

Process is a workflow progression. Before you can diagram a workflow process, you must define a process activity. To do this, right-click on the **Process** icon and choose New Process. The Process Properties window appears. Enter, in uppercase and with no spaces, a unique internal name for your process. Also, enter a display name. The display name is the one that will appear in your process diagram. You have the option of entering a description. Select the result type for this process. Select None if no specified result codes are necessary for the completion of the process. The result type must be a lookup type. Transitions in the workflow process diagram will differ depending on the result codes of the lookup type. If you have the authority, you can click on **Edit** to view or edit the result type. Check *Runnable* if this process can be called from other workflow processes or from Workflow Engine APIs. Create a process activity called **NEW_PO_PROCESS**. A display name of NEW PO Approval Process appears as an Approval result type. You have the option of checking the *Runnable* box. Last, select an icon to represent this process activity. Click on **Browse** to locate available icons (see Figure 11-6).

Select the Details tab, where you can select the error-handling process. You can also specify the maximum time to wait for notification before a time-out occurs. Since this is a process activity and not a notification activity, the time-out parameters are not applicable. The effective date and version are for display only. If you save your workflow process using the *Save As* option, the effective date and the version number

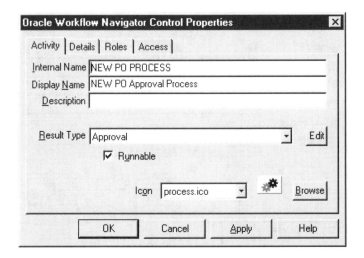

FIGURE 11-6. *Process Activity Properties form*

will be changed. Check *Loop Reset* to identify process activity behavior if a loop condition occurs. A loop condition occurs when the process activity is revisited by the Oracle Workflow Engine. If *Loop Reset* is checked, the process activity will be reexecuted and all of the subsequent processes will be reversed (see Figure 11-7). Click on **OK** to save your work.

The Roles and the Access tabs are the same as the item types and attributes. The next section will demonstrate how to diagram a workflow process.

Notifications

Notifications are messages sent to users. To set up a notification activity, you can either (1) drag and drop a defined message into the notifications arm of the same item type or (2) you can right-click on the **Notification** icon and select New Notification. As in a process activity, you must specify an internal name and a display name for a notification activity. Enter a unique name—in uppercase and without spaces—for your process. The display name is the one that will appear in your process diagram. Entering a description is optional. Select the result type for this process. You can select None if no specified result codes are necessary for the completion of the process. The result type must be a lookup type. Transitions in the workflow process diagram will differ depending on the result codes of the lookup type. Click on **Edit** to view or update the result type.

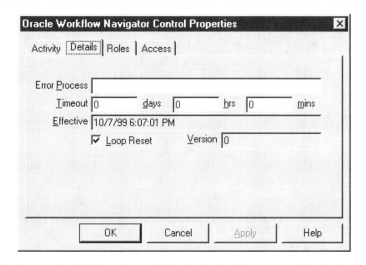

FIGURE 11-7. *Process Activity Properties (Details) form*

Since this is a notification activity, you must select a message. If you use the drag-and-drop message method, the message name will already be filled in. You can click on **Edit** to view or update the message. If the message you selected expects a response, a Function field will appear. This is the response function. Next, you can check *Expand Roles* if you want to expand the role to each individual user's email instead of the role's email. As a last step, you must select an icon to represent this notification activity. Click on **Browse** to locate available icons (see Figure 11-8). Create a notification activity with the internal name of **NEW_PO_APPROVE** and a display name of **NEW PO Approval** by dragging and dropping the Approve PO message. You do not have the Approve PO message yet. You can drag and drop the Approve PO message from the PO Approval item type to your item type. Once you have entered all of the data, click on **OK** to save your work.

Select the Details tab. In the Detail form, you may select the error-handling process. If you wish, you can also specify the allowable wait time for notifications before declaring a time-out. Since this is a notification activity, the time-out parameters are applicable. The effective date and version are display only. If you save your workflow process using the *Save As* option, the effective date and the version number will be changed. Check *Loop Reset* to identify the behavior you want the process activity to perform if a loop condition occurs. Loop conditions occur when the process activity is being revisited by the Oracle Workflow Engine.

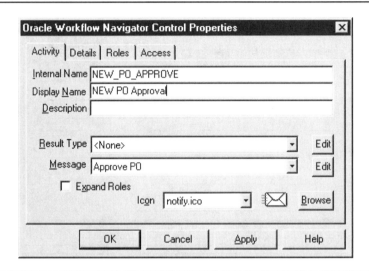

FIGURE 11-8. *Notification Activity Properties form*

If *Loop Reset* is checked, the process activity will be reexecuted and all of the subsequent processes will be reversed. The Roles and the Access tabs correspond to the attributes and process activities item types.

Functions

Functions are PL/SQL stored procedures that can have Workflow Engine APIs. To create a new function, right-click on the **Functions** icon and select New Function. The Function Properties window will appear. Enter a unique internal name in uppercase letters. The name should not contain spaces. Then enter a display name for the function. The display name will appear in the process diagram. You may enter a description. Next, enter the name of the PL/SQL stored procedure in the format of package_name.procedure_name. Select the result type for this process. You can select None if no specified result codes are necessary for the completion of the process. The result type must be a lookup type. Various transitions in the workflow process diagram are possible and will depend on different lookup type result codes. Click on **Edit** to view or update the result type. You can then specify the cost of the activity. Depending on this cost and the threshold of the Workflow Engine, this function activity may be deferred and ultimately processed by the background process. As a last step, you must select an icon to represent this function activity. You can also click on **Browse** to locate icons from your desktop (see Figure 11-9). You do not need to create a function activity for this exercise.

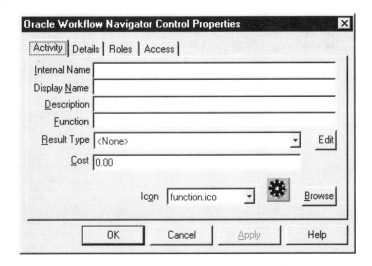

FIGURE 11-9. *Function Activity Properties form*

The Details tab, the Roles tab, and the Access tab are identical to the ones described in the previous sections.

Messages

Messages are templates used by a notification activity. If you want to create new messages, right-click on **New Message**. At this time, you need not create a new message. You have already created a message called Approve PO. Double-click on the Approve PO message to see its properties. There is an internal name, a display name, and a description. The internal name must be unique and typed in all uppercase with no spaces. You may select a default priority for the message. Valid values are from 1 to 99, with 1 designated as highest priority. Priority selection is for informational purposes only; there is no functionality attached to the assigned priority (see Figure 11-10).

Select the Body tab to enter the subject of the message and the body. You can assign message attributes to the subject and body by adding an ampersand sign before the attributes' internal names (see Figure 11-11). The Roles tab and the Access tab are the same as described in the previous sections.

Notice the plus sign (+) next to the Approve PO message in the Navigator. This indicates that the Approve PO message has message attributes. Click on the plus sign next to Approve PO to see all of the message attributes associated with the Approve PO message. A message attribute may have *Send* or *Respond* options. Send attributes

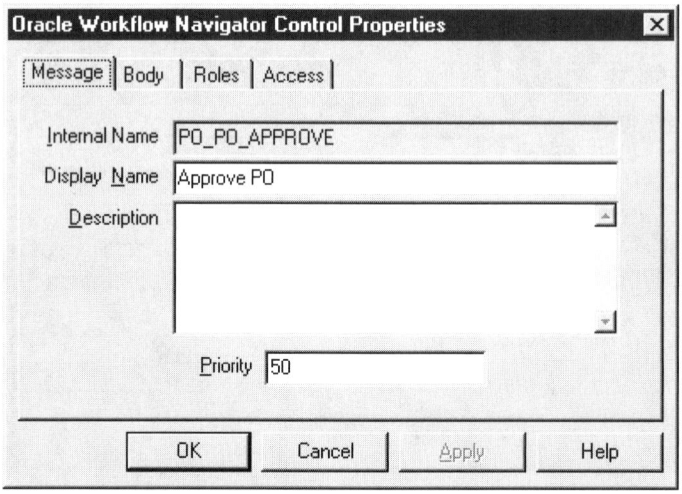

FIGURE 11-10. *Message Properties form*

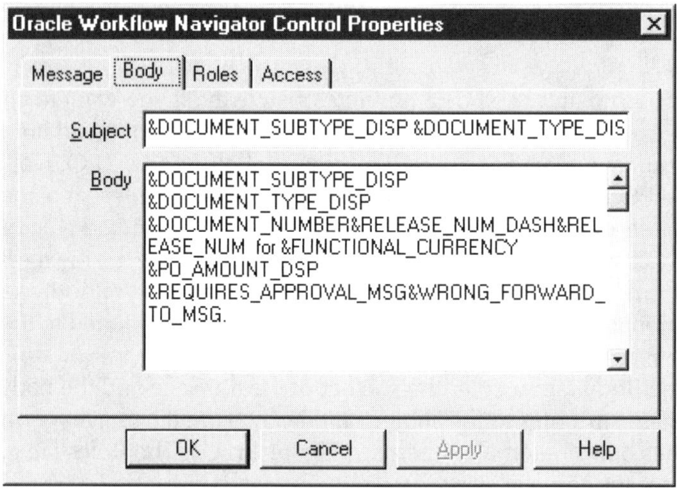

FIGURE 11-11. *Message Properties (Body) form*

are regular attributes. Respond attributes are message attributes that solicit responses in the notification message. Display names of the respond attributes become prompts in the response section of the notification message. Descriptions of the respond attributes are used to describe the expected response. If the respond attribute is a lookup type, the user can respond by selecting from a list of lookup codes. You can specify message attributes to get their values from the item attributes. This is indicated by selecting Item Attribute as the default value for the message attribute and selecting the associated item attribute. To create a new message attribute, right-click on **Attribute**. You must enter a unique internal name typed in all uppercase and without spaces. Next, enter a display name. A description name is optional. Then, select the attribute type. The attribute type of the message attribute is the same as that of the item attribute. Next, specify whether the source is Send or Respond. As a last step, enter a default value, if applicable. You can get the default value from an item attribute. (See Figure 11-12 for the properties of the Approval Action message attribute of the Approve PO message.)

Lookup Types

The last components are the lookup types. Lookup types are lists of lookup codes defined for use by activities. For example, you can find the Approval lookup type in the

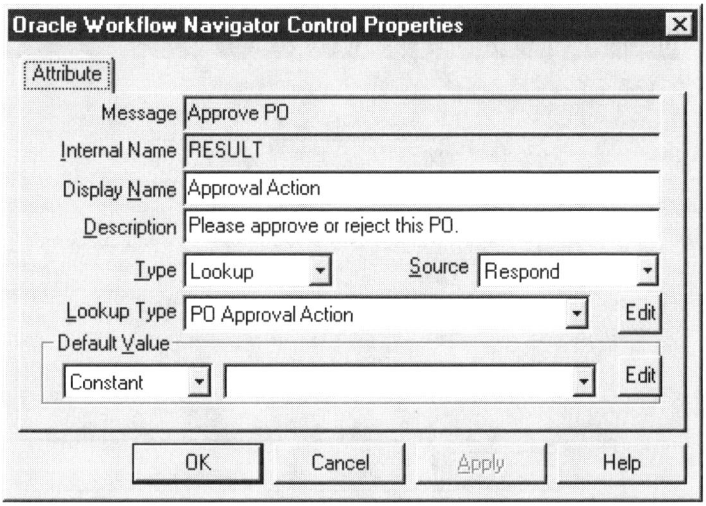

FIGURE 11-12. *Message Attribute Properties form*

Standard item type. If you want to create a new lookup type, right-click on the **Lookup Types** icon and choose New Lookup Type. Double-click to see the properties of the Approval lookup type. You will see the internal name, the display name, and a description for the lookup type. The Access tab is the same as described previously (see Figure 11-13). To add a new lookup code, right-click on the **Lookup Types** icon and choose New Lookup Code. A Lookup Code Properties window appears. Type the internal name and the display name for the lookup code. You can also add an optional description (see Figure 11-14). Once you have defined a lookup code, it will show up as a separate icon under the **Lookup Types** icon.

Review Questions

1. How many types of activities are available?

2. What is a prerequisite for creating a notification activity?

3. When will the time-out parameters apply?

4. How can you find the lookup codes for a specific lookup type?

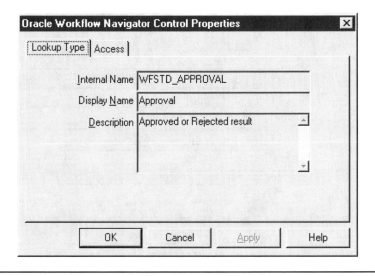

FIGURE 11-13. *Lookup Types Properties form*

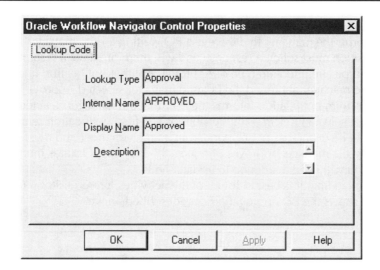

FIGURE 11-14. *Lookup Code Properties form*

Planning a Workflow Process

To plan a workflow process, you must identify all of the activities and transitions for your entire workflow process. You must determine, from the start of the workflow process, how the next activity will be selected and transitioned. You will determine how transitions should branch to other activities based on the result codes of a completed activity, and then establish the order of execution. You will decide who needs to be notified and who needs to respond. You also must identify attributes needed for all of the activities and determine where the values of the attributes will come from.

There are three type of activities: process, notification, and function. Transitions can be based on the specified result code of an activity. For example, once your user has created a PO, you will want Oracle Workflow to send a notification to your user's manager. The notification will include PO information and ask the manager to either approve or reject the PO. The approval or rejection will be sent back to the user as a notification. If the manager does not respond within the time-out period, a time-out notification will be sent to the user.

Every workflow process should have a start and an end function. The start and end functions for the Standard item type are necessary only for visual purposes. In this particular PO approval process, you will need a function activity to find the appropriate manager, and you need four notification activities. One notification activity informs the manager that there is a PO waiting for the manager's approval. This notification must solicit a response and will therefore have a respond attribute of Lookup Type and a lookup type of Approval. Another notification informs the user that the manager approved the PO (the manager selected Approve as the response). A third notification informs the user that the manager rejected the PO (the manager selected Reject as the response). The final notification reminds the manager that he or she has not responded in a timely manner and must respond ASAP. Once the manager approves or rejects the PO, the PO status must be updated. You will need a function to update the PO.

During planning, it is best to list all of the activities, prerequisites, and steps. Table 11-5 shows the PO approval process described above.

Activity	Prerequisite	Steps
Start	Processes initiated with the CreateProcess API with input variables such as PO number, requestor, PO dollar amount, and other attributes.	Set the item attributes with the input variables. Set the item owner and call the StartProcess API.
Find manager		Function activity to find the manager based on the requestor.
Notify manager	Create message to attach to the notification with a respond attribute of lookup type Approval.	Send notification to manager and ask for response. Response can either be Approve or Reject.
Manager responds		Select Approve or Reject.
Manager does not respond		Send reminder to manager and ask for response again.
Update PO	Manager approves or rejects PO.	Update PO.
End	PO update successfully completed.	

TABLE 11-5. *PO Approve Process Plan*

Review Questions

1. What factors should you identify when you plan your workflow process?

2. Which two functions must you have in any workflow process?

Monitoring Workflow to View its Progress

You can use the Workflow Monitor to view the progress of any workflow process. There are two forms of Workflow Monitor. One is the Workflow Status form in Oracle Applications. The other is the Java-based Workflow Monitor tool. There are two modes for both forms of the Workflow Monitor: user mode and admin mode. admin mode will provide more information and allow more functionality. (You must log in to Oracle Applications as a system administrator to see the Workflow Status form.)

The Workflow Status form has the item type and the item key as the title. It lists the activity name, type, status, result, start date, end date, assigned user, error name, error message, error stack, activity internal name, activity description, and user name. You can use the folder tools to change the form to fit your needs (see Figure 11-15).

The Java-based Workflow Monitor tool has four regions:

■ Workflow process title

■ Process diagram

■ Detail tabs

■ Administration buttons

Workflow Process Title

The process title shows the workflow process name, the item type internal name, and the user item key that identifies the item. These are the context values of the workflow instance.

Process Diagram

This shows the process diagram associated with the workflow process. This is for display only. Color is used to represent the state of an activity or transition. Green means active or in progress, yellow means suspended, and red means erred. A thin black transition means that the transition has not been visited. A thick green transition means that the transition has been visited. You may look at the subprocess diagram by double-clicking on any subprocess.

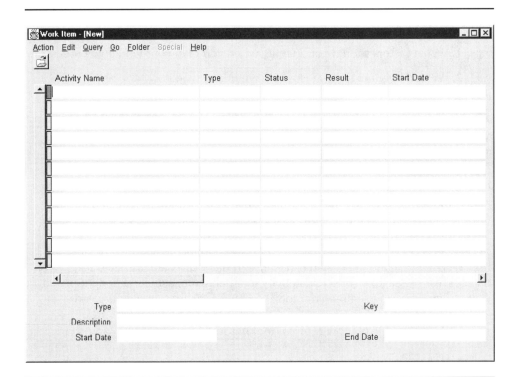

FIGURE 11-15. *Workflow Status form*

Detail Tabs
Select the Detail tab to reveal the definition, usage, status, notification, and item of a node. The Definition tab shows the item type, display name, description, activity type, message, function, result type, any time-out parameters, cost, loop check, and error process. The Usage tab reveals performers and comments. The Status tab shows the status, result, begin date, end date, and any error information. The Notification tab provides recipient, status, begin date, and end date information. The Item tab discloses the item type, item key, item owner, begin date, end date, and item attributes.

Administration Buttons
Administration buttons are only available if you are running in the ADMIN mode. These buttons allow you to abort process, suspend process, resume process, reassign process, or expedite process. Each button corresponds to an API call. You may select Attribute to change the value of an item attribute.

Review Questions

1. What is the difference between the ADMIN mode and the USER mode?

2. What do the colors in the process diagram represent?

3. What two forms monitor workflow processes?

4. For what purposes are the administration buttons used?

Diagramming a Workflow Process

In this section, you will learn to diagram a workflow process using the Oracle Workflow Builder. You have already planned a simple PO approval process; now you will learn how to diagram the process, incorporate standard activities, and review the process definition. This section teaches you how to:

■ Prepare a workflow diagram

■ Incorporate standard activities in a process

■ Review the process definition for the item type

Preparing a Workflow Diagram

To prepare a workflow diagram, double-click on the process activity. In our example, double-click on the NEW PO Approval Process. The Process window will appear. The Process window shows the graphical representation of your workflow process. Initially, the Process window is blank. Drag and drop activities from the Navigator into the Process window. Between activities, define transitions by drawing arrows using the right mouse button. If the result code of the source activity is None, the transitions will not have a label. If the result code of the source activity is not None, label the transition arrow with the result code that will initiate the transition.

To diagram the NEW PO Approval process, create the item attributes for a NEW PO. To do this, copy the item attributes from the PO Approval item type and paste them to your NEW PO item type. Press CTRL-C on the PO Number from the PO Approval item type. Then press CTRL-V to paste the PO Number to your PO item type. Repeat the same copy-and-paste step for the PO Amount, the Requestor Name Line1, and the Approver User Name (see Figure 11-16).

You must then create the function that selects the approver, which is the next manager in H.R. Create a PL/SQL stored procedure that will search out the next manager based on the requestor and tie the stored procedure to a function activity. In this review question, you can assume that the stored procedure will always retrieve a valid manager. In this case, the result type of the function activity can be None and the function activity is NEW Get Next Manager in H.R.

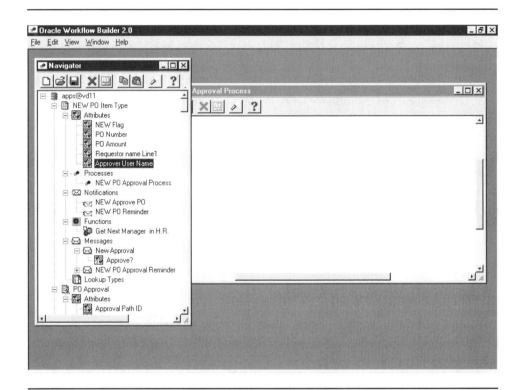

FIGURE 11-16.   *Item Attributes for NEW PO item type form*

Create notifications that allow the manager to approve or reject the PO and that send a reminder if the notification timed out. You do this by creating a message that asks the manager to approve or reject the PO. Use **NEW_APPROVE** as the internal name and **New Approval** as the display name. You can type a message body like the one in Figure 11-17. Your message must have a Respond message attribute. Use **NEW_RESULT** as the internal name. Since the display name becomes the prompt, use **Approve** as the display name. Enter **Please either approve or reject the PO** as the description. Select Lookup as the type and, since you are soliciting a response, select Respond as the source. Select Approval as the lookup type. This will allow the user to respond with either Approve or Reject (see Figure 11-18).

Once you have created the New Approval message, attach the message to a notification activity called **NEW_APPROVE_PO**. Use a display name of **NEW Approve PO**. Select the same result type as your message, which is Approval, and

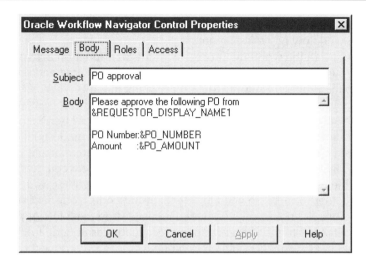

FIGURE 11-17. *Exercise Message Body form*

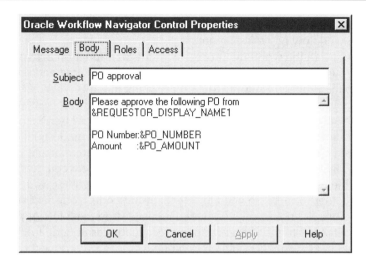

FIGURE 11-18. *Exercise Message Attribute form*

select New Approval as the message. Click on the Details tab to change the Timeout field to 3 days. Create a reminder notification in the same way. Now you are ready to create the workflow process diagram.

You should start the workflow process with the Start function activity. You can find the Start function activity from the Standard item type. Drag and drop the Start function into the Process window. You are assuming that this NEW PO Process is initiated by a CreateProcess API and StartProcess API with the correct attributes: PO Number, PO Amount, Requestor Name Line1, and Approver User Name.

The Start function activity will be your source activity. The destination activity, NEW Get Next Manager in H.R., will retrieve the appropriate manager. Create a transition by right-clicking the mouse and dragging a line between the Start function activity and the NEW Get Next Manager in H.R. function activity. Since the result code is None, there will be no need to select a result code. Your next activity will be NEW Approve PO notification activity. Drag and drop the NEW Approve PO notification activity into the Process window. Since the result code from NEW Get Next Manager in H.R. function activity is None, you can just connect the NEW Get Next Manager in H.R. function activity to the NEW Approve PO notification activity. You must identify the performer for the NEW Approve PO notification activity. The performer is the role receiving the notification. In your case, select the item attribute Approver User Name as the performer. To select a performer, double-click on the notification activity in the Process window and select the performer. You can only do this if you invoked the Notification Activity Property window inside the Process window; you cannot do this if you invoked the Notification Activity Property window in the Navigator (see Figure 11-19). You can use the Attribute Values tab to specify a value for any selected attribute in this tab. You do not need this feature for this review question.

The manager can ignore the notification, approve the PO, or reject the PO. Treat all three conditions with three different transitions. If the manager approves or rejects the PO, the workflow process is considered completed. In this case, it must flow to the End function activity. To show the Or condition, you can use the Or function activity. Both the End and Or function activities can be found under the Standard item type. If the manager chooses to ignore the notification, you must send a reminder to the manager and branch back to resend the NEW Approve PO notification activity. To make sure that the NEW Approve PO notification can be resent, make sure that *Loop Reset* is not checked. When you create a transition between the NEW Approve PO activity and the Or activity, a window appears and asks which result code should be tied to this transition. Your choices are Approved, Rejected, <Default>, or <Timeout> (see Figure 11-20). The <Default> transition is used if result codes other than any selected result codes are returned. Choose Approved for the transition. Repeat the same step and create a transition for Rejected between the NEW Approve PO activity and the Or activity. Create a transition between the NEW Approve PO

Oracle Workflow Navigator Control Properties ☒

Process Activity | Attribute Values |

Item Type |NEW PO Item Type ▾| Edit

|Notification ▾| |NEW Approve PO ▾| Edit

Label |NEW_APPROVE_PO |

Start/End |Normal ▾|

Comment | |

Performer

Type |Item Attribute ▾| |Approver User Name ▾| Edit

OK   Cancel   Apply   Help

FIGURE 11-19. *Notification Activity Property Window (Process Window) form*

activity to the NEW PO Reminder activity and select <Timeout> for the transition. Since you want to route back from the NEW PO Reminder activity to the NEW Approve PO activity, you must create a transition from the NEW Approve PO activity to the NEW PO Reminder activity. To see labels, which are display names in the Process window, you can either execute Designer's View | Show Label | Display Name menu command, or right-click on the Process window and execute the Show Label | Display Name menu command. See Figure 11-21 for the complete process you have created.

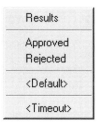

Results

Approved
Rejected

<Default>

<Timeout>

FIGURE 11-20. *Result codes for transition*

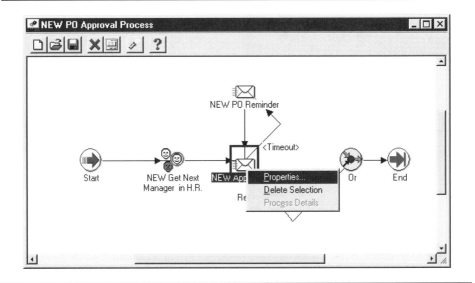

FIGURE 11-21. *Complete PO Workflow Process form*

Other options in the Process window include copying diagrams, printing diagrams, and displaying an Overview window. All of these options are found when you click the right mouse button in the Process window. You can verify your workflow process by executing the File | Verify menu command.

Review Questions

 1. When will you need to select a label for a transition?

 2. What is the purpose of the <Timeout> label?

 3. How will your NEW PO Process be invoked?

 4. What is a performer and how do you specify a performer for a notification activity?

Incorporating Standard Activities in a Process

Oracle Workflow comes seeded with commonly used standard activities that you can use in any workflow process. The standard activities are:

- And
- Assign
- Block
- Compare Date
- Compare Number
- Compare Text
- Continue Flow
- End
- Get Monitor URL

- Loop Counter
- NoOp
- Or
- Role Resolution
- Start
- Default Voting Message Yes/No
- Wait
- Wait For Flow

And

When multiple transitions flow into the And function activity, the And function activity is considered complete when all of the transitions are completed.

Assign

The Assign function activity has four attributes: Item Attribute, Date Value, Numeric Value, and Text Value. Use the Assign function activity to assign an item attribute specified in the Item Attribute value with the Date Value, Numeric Value, or Text Value. Determine whether to use the Date Value, Numeric Value, or Text Value based on the date type of the item attribute.

Block

The Block function activity blocks the activity until a complete activity API call is made.

Compare Date

The Compare Date function activity has two attributes: Test Value and Reference Value. Reference Value contains an item attribute. The Test Value is a constant. The Compare Date function activity compares the value of the item attribute in Reference Value to the constant in Test Value and produces results labeled Equal, Greater Than, Less Than, or Null (if the reference value is null). The Compare Date attributes are both of datatype Date.

Compare Number

The Compare Number function activity has two attributes: Test Value and Reference Value. The Reference Value contains an item attribute. The Test Value is a constant. The Compare Number function activity compares the value of the item attribute in Reference Value to the constant in Test Value and produces results labeled Equal, Greater Than, Less Than, or Null (if the reference value is null). The Compare Number attributes are both of datatype Number.

Compare Text

The Compare Text function activity has two attributes: Test Value and Reference Value. The Reference Value contains an item attribute. The Test value is a constant. The Compare Text function activity compares the value of the item attribute in Reference Value to the constant in Test Value and produces results labeled Equal, Greater Than, Less Than, or Null (if the reference value is null). The Compare Text attributes are both of datatype Text.

Continue Flow

Continue Flow is used for master and detail coordination. The master process can start detail processes, and you can use the Continue Flow and Wait for Flow function activities to coordinate a process flow between master and details. The Continue Flow function activity signals the flow of a waited process to continue. The Continue Flow function activity has two attributes: Waiting Activity Label and Waiting Flow. The Waiting Activity Label identifies the label of the activity that was waiting for the completion of this Continue Flow function activity. Waiting Flow identifies whether the waiting activity is a master process or a detail process.

End

The End function activity marks the end of a process. You can use it to return result codes. The End function activity is not required; it is only for visual purposes.

Get Monitor URL
The Get Monitor URL function activity retrieves the Workflow Monitor and stores the URL in the item attribute specified. You can use the other attribute, administration Mode, to specify whether the Workflow Monitor should be run in admin mode.

Loop Counter
You can use the Loop Counter function activity to limit the number of times the Workflow Engine can transition through any particular activity. Use the Loop Limit attribute to specify the limit. If the loop limit is not reached, the activity completes with a result code of Loop; otherwise, the activity will complete with a result code of Exit.

NoOp
The NoOp function activity has no functionality. Use it as a placeholder in the workflow process.

Or
When multiple transitions flow into the Or function activity, the Or function activity is considered complete when any one of the transitions is completed.

Role Resolution
The Role Resolution function activity selects one user from a role with multiple users. You can use its Method attribute to specify whether you want the user to be selected based on the number of open notifications or just sequentially assigned. The first method is Load Balance and the second method is Sequential.

Start
The Start function activity marks the beginning of a process. The Start function activity is not required; it is only for visual purposes.

Default Voting Message
The Voting Message is a message you can use to create a notification activity that tallies responses from users or roles, depending on whether *Expand Roles* is checked. The message subject and the body make up the message that will be sent to the users or roles. It has a Respond message attribute with the internal name of RESULT. You can specify the list of possible responses for this Respond message attribute using a specific

lookup type. In the notification activity that uses the voting message, you must create a Number Type attribute with each possible response value as the name. These attributes will capture the percentages necessary for the response values to become the result. If the value of the attribute is set to Null, then the value will be treated as the default value. In other words, if you have two response values, Yes and No, and you have the attribute Yes set with a value 50 and the attribute No set as Null, anything less than 50 percent Yes will be a No.

You can specify the voting option using the Voting Option attribute. You can select *Require All Votes* to have the Workflow Engine tally all responses only after all votes have been cast. If not all votes are received before the notification times out, then the timed-out transition is used. *Tally on Every Vote* instructs the Workflow Engine to keep a running tally after each vote is cast. If the notification times out, the response percentage to date is used. *Wait for All Votes* instructs the Workflow Engine to wait until all votes come in before tallying response percentages. The only difference between this option and the *Require All Votes* option is that, if the notification times out before all of the votes came back, the *Wait for All Votes* option will still tally the response percentages before the time-out occurred.

Wait

The Wait function activity defines the specified waiting period for a response. The Wait mode specifies whether the wait is calculated by absolute date, day of month, day of week, relative time, or time of day. If the Wait mode is set to absolute date, enter the final date into the Absolute Date attribute. If the Wait mode is set to day of month, enter the day into the Day of Month attribute. If the Wait mode is set to day of week, enter the day of the week into the Day of Week attribute. If the Wait mode is set to relative time, enter the number of days you want to wait in the Relative Time attribute. If the Wait mode is set to time of day, enter the time of day into the Time of Day attribute.

Wait for Flow

Wait for Flow is used for master and detail coordination. The master process can start detail processes, and you can use the Continue Flow and Wait for Flow function activities to coordinate the process flow between the master and details. The Wait for Flow function activity signals the process flow to wait. The Wait for Flow function activity has two attributes: Continuation Activity Label and Continuation Flow. The Continuation Activity Label identifies the activity label that must be completed before the Wait for Flow function activity continues. The Continuation Flow activity identifies whether the waiting activity is a master process or a detail process.

Review Questions

1. How do the Continue Flow and Wait for Flow function activities work together?

2. How does the Voting activity work?

3. How can you use the Role Resolution function activity?

4. Do you need the Start and End function activities?

Reviewing the Process Definition for the Item Type

The best way to review the process definition for the item type is to use the Navigator. The item types are shown at the top level. Within each item type, you can find the attributes, processes, notifications, functions, messages, and lookup types. You can use the Edit | Find menu command to search for a specific object. You can find objects by display name or internal name. You can also search within a specific component or within all components inside the Workflow Builder (see Figure 11-22).

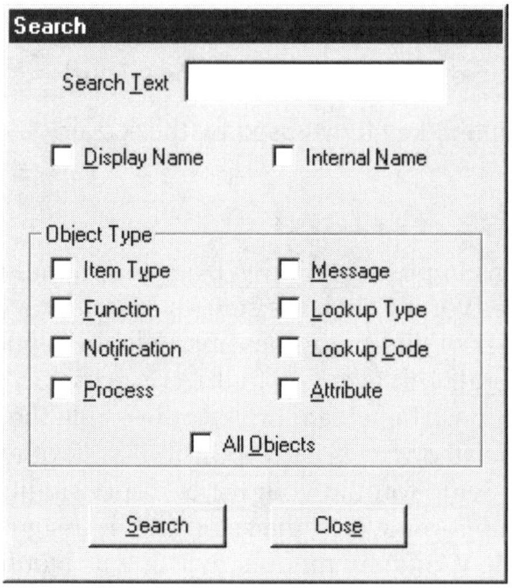

FIGURE 11-22. *Search form*

In the Navigator, you can use the plus sign (+) to expand a component or a minus sign (-) to contract a component. When you want to view properties, double-click on the object of interest.

Review Questions

1. What is the best way to review the process definition?

2. How do you search for a specific message within the Workflow Builder?

3. How do you invoke a function activity's Properties window?

Fundamentals of the Implementation Wizard

This section covers the fundamentals of Oracle Applications Implementation Wizard—the wizard, for short. This section will:

- Describe the features of the wizard

- Explain the importance of the wizard in AIM

- Explain the process grouping used in the Wizard

- Explain the process hierarchy used in the wizard

- List and explain the key terms used by the wizard

Features of the Wizard

The Oracle Applications Implementation Wizard is a module in Oracle Applications that guides you through the setup steps of Oracle Applications. It knows the dependencies of the setup steps and will guide you through the steps in the appropriate order. It will take you to the correct setup forms and find the associated documentation. The wizard does not override the menu/function security you have associated with your responsibility. In other words, if you do not have access to the Setup form in your list of responsibilities, you still cannot have access to the Setup form even if the setup task is assigned to you. It takes advantage of the Oracle Workflow module by using its Notification System and Workflow Monitor. The following describes how the wizard works. Each implementation process is a workflow process in Oracle Workflow. When an implementation process is initiated, Oracle Workflow will start sending notifications to ask users to perform setup steps. A user can use a notification to launch the Setup form or can reassign the setup steps. When the user completes the Setup form, the user sends a response to the wizard to indicate completion of the setup step. The wizard provides guidance for the following modules:

- Oracle General Ledger
- Oracle Payables
- Oracle Receivables
- Oracle Cash Management
- Oracle Assets
- Oracle Purchasing
- Oracle Order Entry
- Oracle Product Configurator
- Oracle Supply Chain Planning
- Oracle Supplier Scheduling
- Oracle Quality
- Oracle Cost Management

- Oracle Work in Process
- Oracle Bills of Material
- Oracle Engineering
- Oracle Forecasting
- Oracle Inventory
- Oracle MRP
- Oracle Projects
- Oracle Human Resources
- Oracle Payroll
- Oracle Sales and Marketing
- Oracle Sales Compensation

The wizard helps increase productivity and reduce the time and effort involved in implementing Oracle Applications. The wizard's documentation contains comments and responses from users who have set up Oracle Applications. You are not required to use the wizard during implementation of Oracle Applications. It is simply a tool to ease the process.

Review Questions

1. On which module does the wizard rely?

2. If you cannot invoke a form embedded in the wizard's notification, what is a possible reason?

3. How can the user notify the wizard of a completed setup step?

Importance of the Wizard in AIM

The wizard automates the setup of Oracle Applications and complements the Oracle Application Implementation Method (AIM). AIM is a methodology that guides you through the entire Oracle Applications implementation process. It identifies tasks and deliverables necessary for every phase of the implementation process. AIM provides templates for documentation. Oracle Applications setup/configuration is one phase of the implementation process. Using the wizard, you can replace some of the standard setup/configuration documentation in AIM. In other words, AIM is the method that guides you through the implementation process, in which setup/configuration is one of the phases in the process, and the wizard automates this setup/configuration phase.

Review Questions

1. What is AIM?
2. How does the wizard complement AIM?

Process Grouping Used in the Wizard

There are three groups of implementation processes within the Oracle Applications Implementation Wizard. They are:

- Primary implementation processes
- Secondary implementation processes
- Final implementation processes

Primary Implementation Processes
Primary implementation processes include setup steps that cross multiple modules across the financial, distribution, and manufacturing product families. These include wizard installation and common applications, including system administration.

Secondary Implementation Processes
Secondary implementation processes are defined as setup steps that cross multiple modules within the financial, distribution, and manufacturing product families. These include common distribution, common financial, and common manufacturing.

Final Implementation Processes
Setup steps for each individual module independent of other modules are considered final implementation processes. This means that each setup process within this final implementation process can be run independently of each other. In other words, you can run the setup steps simultaneously. The processes include

setup within General Ledger, Payable, Receivable, Assets, Cash Management, Projects, Inventory, Purchasing, Order Entry, Product Configurator, Supplier Scheduling, Bill of Material, Cost Management, Engineering, Forecasting, Quality, Supply Chain Processing, Work in Process, Sales and Marketing, Sales Compensation, Service, Human Resources, and Payroll.

Review Questions

1. What are considered primary implementation processes?

2. What are considered secondary implementation processes?

3. What are considered final implementation processes?

4. Which group of processes allows simultaneous setup of individual modules?

Process Hierarchy Used in the Wizard

The process hierarchy used in the wizard consists of primary implementation processes, secondary implementation processes, and final implementation processes. You must finish all of the processes within a group before proceeding to the next group. This assures common setup steps are completed before proceeding to other setup steps. The primary implementation processes are common steps that affect many modules across product families. One example is the System Administration module. Once you have finished the primary implementation processes, you can implement the secondary implementation processes. Secondary implementation processes are setups common to a product family: common distribution, common financial, and common manufacturing. This means that setup steps are common to more than one module within the same product family. You can run each product family simultaneously. The last component in the process hierarchy is the final implementation processes. This component includes setup steps specific to each individual module, with no dependencies across modules. You can complete the remaining setup steps in these modules simultaneously.

Each implementation process is a workflow process in Oracle Workflow. The implementation may also require subprocesses.

Review Questions

1. What makes up a process hierarchy?

2. Why do you have a process hierarchy?

Key Terms Used in the Wizard

The following is a list of key terms used in the wizard:

- **Context**   Organization context. Some setup steps are organization-specific. For example, you must set up a corporate book in Oracle Assets for each Set of Books. Context can be Business Group, Set of Books, Operating Unit, or Inventory Organization.

- **Dependency**   Prerequisites for completing a setup step.

- **Implementation process**   Group of setup steps in the wizard. Each implementation process corresponds to a workflow process in Oracle Workflow.

- **Notification**   A message to notify the user that a setup step is assigned to the user. The user can use the form in the notification to link directly to the Setup form and respond to the notification to signal the completion of a setup step.

- **Notification Summary form**   A form where the user can find assigned notifications. The user can respond to notifications, reassign them, and open them to drill down to the attached form.

- **Oracle Workflow**   An Oracle module that maps business processes and rules into notifications, PL/SQL stored procedures, transitions, and subprocesses.

- **Role**   The role is a user or a group of users. You can assign an implementation process to a role.

Review Questions

1. What is a context?

2. What is an implementation process?

3. What is a Notification Summary form?

4. What is a role?

Using the Wizard

In this last section of the chapter, you will learn to use the wizard to set up applications.

Using the Wizard to Set Up Applications

Log on to the Oracle Applications Vision demonstration database using the application user name **WIZARD** and the password **WELCOME**. The user WIZARD contains the following components: *Implementation Financials, Implementation Human Resources, Implementation Manufacturing, Implementation Sales and Service*, and *Implementation System Administration*. All of these responsibilities utilize the wizard Setup form, the Notification Summary form, and all of the related setup forms. Select the *Implementation System Administration* responsibility.

The first step for initiating any implementation process in the wizard is to submit the process with the Implementation Wizard form. The *Implementation Wizard* navigation path allows you to open the Implementation Wizard form. Choose the implementation process you want to submit. Not all implementation processes will show up in the process List of Values. If an implementation process does not show up, it can be due to one of two reasons. First, only implementation processes related to your installed products will show up. Second, even if the implementation processes are related to the installed products, if the implementation processes are based on organization context, and such organization context has not been set up yet, the implementation processes will not be shown. Valid organization contexts are: None, for no organization context necessary; BG, for business group; IO, for inventory organization; OU, for operating unit; and SOB, for Set of Books. If the implementation processes depend on organization context None, they will only need to be done once across your entire company. If the implementation process depends on, for example, context OU, then such processes must be done once per organization context; in this case, once per operating unit. Since the Vision demonstration database consists of all modules, you will see the implementation processes for all of the supported modules.

Next, if applicable, enter the context. Before you submit the implementation process, you must assign a role to receive the setup notification. The role you specified becomes the owner of the setup step (see Figure 11-23). To verify that the Wizard is installed properly, select the Wizard Installation Process and click on **Submit**.

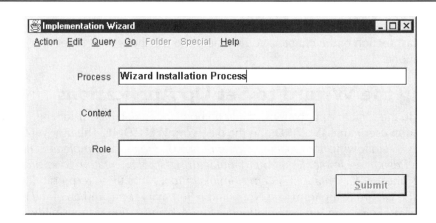

FIGURE 11-23. *Wizard Startup form*

Next, you may start other implementation processes. Once an implementation process starts, and if you are the role that gets the assigned setup steps, you will receive notification(s) from the wizard. You will see the notifications in the Notification Summary form following the *Notifications* navigation path. You may be able to execute one of the following steps in the Notification Summary form:

- **Complete the setup step.**   You can use the Notification form to invoke the corresponding Setup form and complete the setup. The Setup form is found in the References section of the notification. You can record any comments and respond to let the wizard know that you have completed the setup step. Click on **Respond** and select Done as the respond value. You can respond with Done without really completing the setup steps. The wizard will not check, and you may receive errors down the setup path.

- **Reassign the setup step to another role.**   You may click on **Reassign** and select another role to receive the notification.

- **Read the corresponding setup documentation.**   If the URL to the documentation is provided in the Reference section, you can call up the URL and read the corresponding setup documentation.

- **Read the comments that correspond to this setup step.**   You can review the comments in the Comment section.

- **Review the entire implementation process.** If the Workflow Monitor URL is attached as a reference, you can employ the Workflow Monitor to review the entire implementation process.

- **Leave the setup step open.** You can ignore the notification and come back to it later.

- **Skip the setup step.** You can record any comments and respond to let the wizard know that it should skip the setup step. You respond by clicking on **Respond** and selecting Skipped. The wizard will not check the dependencies of this skipped setup step, and you may receive errors down the setup path.

Review Questions

1. How can you verify that the wizard has been installed correctly?

2. How do you reassign a setup step to another role?

3. How do you complete a setup step?

4. Where will you find forms and URLs in the Notifications Summary form?

For the Chapter Summary, Two-Minute Drill, and Chapter Questions and Answers, open the summary.htm file contained in the Summary_files directory on the book's CD-ROM.

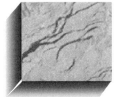

UNIT III

Preparing for OCP Exam 3: Procurement

CHAPTER
12

Basic Purchasing and Receipts

his chapter marks the beginning of Exam 3: Procurement, which includes Oracle Purchasing, Oracle Payables, and the procurement-related portion of Oracle Cash Management. In this chapter, you will learn the basics of purchasing and receipts, including:

- Integration with Oracle Applications

- Setup and implementation

- Creating supplier information

- Creating purchase requisitions

- Creating standard purchase orders

- Entering purchase order receipts

Oracle procurement modules integrate with each other and with other Oracle Applications modules outside of the procurement modules. In particular, Oracle Purchasing tightly integrates with Oracle Payables. First, the chapter covers the integration of Oracle Purchasing, Oracle Payables, and other Oracle Applications modules. Next, it will discuss setup steps and considerations of the three modules in the procurement track: Oracle Purchasing, Oracle Payables, and Oracle Cash Management.

Once you have learned how to set up the procurement modules, you will create supplier information in the Supplier form, which is linked to the procurement modules' master file po_vendors. You first must set up the supplier information necessary for conducting your procurement processes. Then, you will create purchase requisitions and standard purchase orders, which are key documents in Oracle Purchasing. As a last step, you will learn how to receive goods and services against created purchase orders.

Integration with Oracle Applications

This chapter first discusses the integration of Oracle Purchasing, Oracle Payables, and other Oracle Applications modules, particularly the tight integration of Oracle Purchasing with Oracle Payables. Oracle Purchasing manages suppliers and purchasing documents such as purchase requisitions and purchase orders, and Oracle Payables pays suppliers and matches invoices to purchase orders, both of which are stored in Oracle Purchasing. This section discuss the following integration:

- Within the Procurement modules

- Oracle Purchasing with other Oracle Applications modules

- Oracle Payables with other Oracle Applications modules

Within the Procurement Modules

Oracle Purchasing and Oracle Payables integrate tightly in the following areas:

- Suppliers

- Matching and tolerances

- Pay on receipts

- Budgetary control

- Receipt accrual

- Bank statement reconciliation

Suppliers

The Supplier form, which contains all supplier information, is shared between Oracle Purchasing and Oracle Payables. This ensures consistency and avoids double data entry. In Oracle Purchasing, supplier is structured as the highest level; supplier site, which contains the address information, is the second highest level; and supplier contacts is at the lowest level. Suppliers and supplier sites definition provides much of the default information for Oracle Payables, including payments terms and payment methods. Defaults, which serve as a method of information standardization and control, can be overridden on purchasing documents or payables invoices.

Matching

In Oracle Procurement, you can implement two-way, three-way, and four-way matching, which enforces integration between Oracle Purchasing and Oracle Payables. Two-way matching matches purchase orders to invoices. With this method, payables invoices will not be approved if the purchase orders related to the invoices do not match invoices within the defined tolerances, which are defined by quantity or amount. For example, if both the tolerance amount and quantity are set to zero, then the invoice's amount and quantity cannot exceed the matching purchase orders by any quantity or dollar amount. This ensures that suppliers are not overpaid in surplus of the purchase order. With a higher tolerance, you can overpay a supplier, but you cannot go over the defined tolerance quantity or amount.

Three-way matching goes a step further by ensuring that invoices cannot be approved and paid unless the amount and quantity match the purchase order, *and* the purchase order has been physically received. The amount and quantity the invoices compare to are the received amount and received quantity. So, assuming the tolerances are both set to zero, and that an invoice for 10 printers is matched to a purchase order for 10 printers, it cannot be approved and paid until those 10 printers are received against that particular purchase order. This ensures that you pay only for the goods you have received.

Four-way matching goes even further than three-way matching by ensuring that invoices can only be approved and paid if the matching purchase order's amount and quantity within defined tolerances are not only received, but also inspected.

Pay on Receipts
Pay on receipts allows you to create payments based on the transactions you receive, including electronic receipts such as advance shipment notices (ASN) and advanced shipment and billing notices (ASBN).

Budgetary Control
In Oracle Purchasing, budgetary control is tied to Oracle Payables and Oracle General Ledger. Funds available equals budget amounts in Oracle General Ledger, the encumbrance amount in approved purchase orders in Oracle Purchasing, and the actual amount in approved invoices in Oracle Payables. When an invoice is matched to a purchase order, Oracle Applications handles the reversal of the encumbrance amounts automatically.

Receipt Accrual
Receipt accrual occurs automatically in Oracle Purchasing. For inventory items, the accrual usually happens perpetually. For purchasing items, the accrual usually happens at the end of an accounting period. *When to accrue* is a setup option in the Purchasing Options form, and the accrual accounting entry is calculated as goods received but not invoiced for the items that accrue at the end of an accounting period. Invoiced in Oracle Payables means the invoice is approved and posted to Oracle General Ledger.

In addition to Oracle Payables, Oracle Purchasing also integrates with Oracle Cash Management.

Bank Statement Reconciliation
By using Oracle Cash Management, you can reconcile payments to your bank statements in Oracle Cash Management. In doing this, Oracle Cash Management will automatically update the status of the payment records in Oracle Payables.

Review Questions

1. Why do Oracle Purchasing and Oracle Payables share the same supplier master?

2. What is a three-way matching in Oracle Applications?

3. What is pay on receipts?

4. How does Oracle Cash Management integrate with Oracle Payables?

Oracle Purchasing with Other Oracle Applications Modules

Oracle Purchasing integrates with a number of other Oracle Applications modules, including:

- Oracle Order Entry
- Oracle Inventory
- Oracle Workflow
- Oracle MRP
- Oracle Projects
- Oracle Human Resources
- Oracle Alert
- Oracle Quality
- Oracle EDI Gateway
- Oracle General Ledger

Oracle Order Entry

Once the internal requisition has been approved and interfaced to Order Entry, the sales order must proceed through the order cycle. This includes pick release, ship confirm, and inventory interface processing (not Supplier), which can automatically create internal sales orders in Oracle Order Entry. Internal sales orders are those that are ordered from another organization within your own company. The organization that fulfills the order is the selling organization, while the organization with the purchase requisition is the buying organization.

Oracle Inventory

Purchasing increases Inventory's on-hand balance when POs are received and delivered. Internal requisitions, mentioned above, also affect demand once the item has been reserved and depletes the shipping organization's on-hand balance once it has been shipped.

Oracle Workflow

There are two areas where Oracle Purchasing integrates with Oracle Workflow. The first is Account Generator, with a workflow process that defines the business rules in which account combinations are generated. The second area consists of some seeded approval workflow processes. These workflow processes read the approval business rules and hierarchies you set up in Oracle Purchasing, and they drive purchasing documents such as purchase requisitions and purchase orders through defined approval business rules and hierarchies.

Oracle MRP

The material planning process in Oracle MRP automatically generates purchase requisitions for raw materials (goods) or outside processing (services).

Oracle Projects

When you buy goods and/or services for a particular project, Oracle Purchasing, which allows you to capture project information on purchasing documents, integrates with Oracle Projects.

Oracle Human Resources

Oracle Purchasing shares employees and positions information with Oracle Human Resources. The two also share position hierarchies if approvals in Oracle Purchasing and Human Resources are set up to use the same position hierarchies.

Oracle Alert

Oracle Purchasing has some seeded alerts to help monitor exceptions and buyer performances, get notified with releases and expirations against planned and/or blanket purchase orders, and identify potential forecast overconsumption.

Oracle Quality

You can capture quality data, which will be automatically stored in Oracle Quality, during receiving. You can also make the capturing of quality data mandatory in Oracle Purchasing.

Oracle EDI Gateway

Oracle EDI gateways offers EDI capability to Oracle Purchasing. Supported purchasing EDI transactions in Oracle EDI gateways are Inbound Price/Sales Catalog (832), Inbound Response to Request for Quote (843), Inbound Ship Notice/Manifest (856), Inbound Shipping and Billing Notice (857), Outbound Planning Schedule (830), Outbound Shipping Schedule (862), Outbound Purchase Order (850), and Outbound Purchase Order Change request (860).

Oracle General Ledger

Oracle Purchasing posts encumbrance entries and receipt accrual entries to Oracle General Ledger.

Review Questions

1. How does Oracle Purchasing integrate with Oracle Order Entry?

2. How does Oracle Purchasing integrate with Oracle Workflow?

3. How does Oracle Purchasing integrate with Oracle Quality?

4. How does Oracle Purchasing integrate with Oracle General Ledger?

Oracle Payables with Other Oracle Applications Modules

Oracle Payables integrates with a number of other Oracle Applications modules, including:

- Oracle Assets

- Oracle Projects

- Oracle Workflow

- Oracle Web Employees

- Oracle EDI Gateway

- Oracle Inventory

- Oracle General Ledger

Oracle Assets

To start depreciation, invoices for capital acquisition can be interfaced automatically to Oracle Assets, and all assets related to invoices posted to Oracle General Ledger will be sent to Oracle Assets. All expense-related invoices can be sent to Oracle Assets if these invoices are posted to Oracle General Ledger and if they are marked in Oracle Payables to track them as assets.

Oracle Projects

When you receive invoices for goods and/or services for a particular project, Oracle Payables, which allows you to capture project information on payables invoices, integrates with Oracle Projects.

Oracle Workflow

If you installed Oracle Web Employees, then Oracle Payables comes with seeded workflow processes in Oracle Workflow for expense reporting. This workflow process automatically populates the open interfaces in Oracle Payables for expense reports submitted through the Web with Oracle Web Employees.

Oracle Web Employees

In addition to expense reporting, Oracle Web Employees also handles procurement card integration with Oracle Payables, which allows for company procurement card purchases and expense reports that drive invoices to pay the card issuer directly.

Oracle EDI Gateway

Oracle EDI gateways offers EDI capability to Oracle Payables. Supported payables EDI transactions in Oracle EDI gateways are Inbound Invoice (810), Outbound Application Advice (824), and Outbound Payment Order/Remittance Advice (820).

Oracle Inventory

To be in compliance with the European Union's Intrastat requirements, you must record inventory movement statistics between statistics-gathering countries. You can do so when you are entering payables invoices by using the Special menu in Oracle Payables.

Oracle General Ledger

Oracle Payables posts invoice entries and payment entries to Oracle General Ledger.

Review Questions

1. How does Oracle Payables integrate with Oracle Assets?

2. How does Oracle Payables integrate with Oracle Web Employees?

3. How does Oracle Payables integrate with Oracle Projects?

4. How does Oracle Payables integrate with Oracle Inventory?

Setup and Implementation

This section covers the setups and considerations for implementing Oracle Purchasing, Oracle Payables, and Oracle Cash Management. Please refer to Figure 12-1 for Oracle Purchasing setup steps, and Figure 12-2 for Oracle Payables setup steps. You will learn these setup steps in five groups:

- Identification of the setup steps and considerations that are common to Oracle Purchasing and Payables

- Setup steps and considerations that are unique to Oracle Purchasing

- Setup steps and considerations that are unique to Oracle Payables

- Setup steps and considerations that are unique to Oracle Cash Management

- Description of the financial, purchasing, receiving, and payables options

Setup Steps and Considerations Common to Oracle Purchasing and Payables

Some setup steps are common to both Oracle Purchasing and Oracle Payables. First, we will discuss the common setup steps and considerations. The common setup steps are as follows:

- System administrator

- Other modules' flexfields

- Accounting calendars

- Workday calendar

- Currencies

- Conversion rates

- Set of Books

- Opening and closing accounting periods

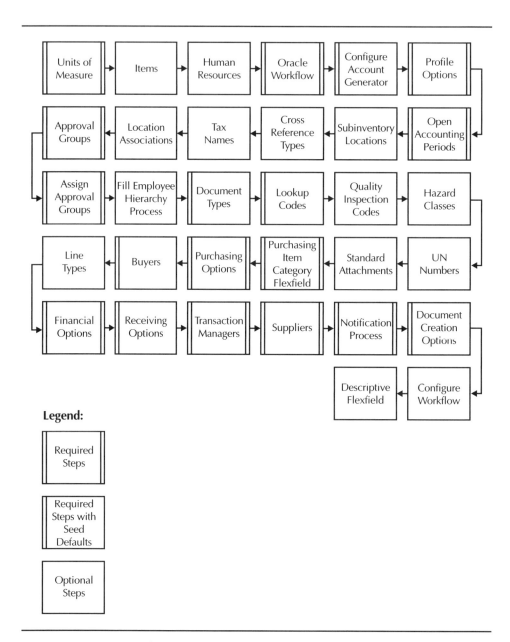

Legend:

Required Steps

Required Steps with Seed Defaults

Optional Steps

FIGURE 12-1. *Oracle Purchasing setup steps*

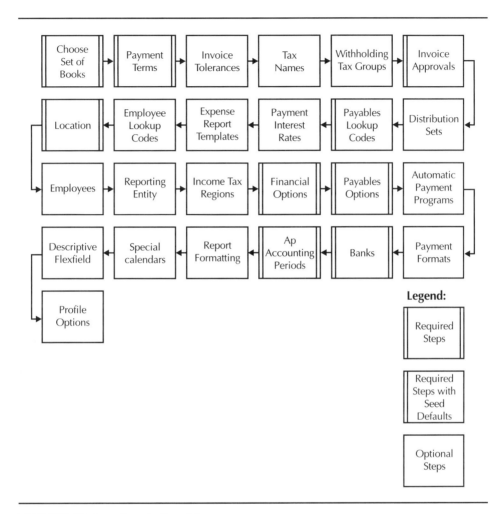

FIGURE 12-2. *Oracle Payables setup steps*

- Organizations
- Human resources
- Tax names
- Locations
- Suppliers

System Administrator

Setting up system administrator functions is a required task, and involves setting up system security, defining user names, and defining system printers. User IDs must be defined for all users, and additional responsibilities may also need to be defined. The Oracle *System Administrator* responsibility will need to be set up to perform this task.

Considerations involved in this step are security and establishing naming conventions to be used throughout Oracle Applications. You must determine which responsibilities should be tied to which users and whether to exclude forms and functions from the standard menu. You must also establish a naming convention for printers and set them up. This lets users know where the printer will be located by simply reading the printer name. You must also determine whether a dedicated printer will be necessary for checks and purchase orders, which usually have special preprinted forms.

Other Modules Key Flexfields

This step involves setting up other modules' Key flexfields related to Oracle Purchasing and Oracle Payables. These Key flexfields include accounting, human resources, and inventory. The accounting Key flexfield must be defined through the General Ledger setup and configuration. Next, set up the four human resources Key flexfields: job, position, grade, and people group. You needn't set up these flexfields if you already have installed Oracle Human Resources, or if you're installing in a common application setup (in which case, it will be done during the HR setup). The following inventory Key flexfields should be defined as part of the inventory setup: item catalog, item category, and system items. Once you have defined the system items flexfield, you must run the Item Flexfield view.

Considerations involved in this step involve constructing Key flexfields that have room to grow, that can be used across modules, and that can be validated according to everyone's need. You must also determine how to maintain valid values, whether to allow dynamic insertions, and how to enforce security.

Accounting Calendars

If you have not defined your accounting calendars in Oracle General Ledger, then you must define them for Oracle Purchasing and Oracle Payables. If you are performing a multi-org implementation of Purchasing and Payables, you may also create more than one calendar.

Whether you need an adjusting period and how to name your accounting period are the two considerations for this setup step. Your accounting calendar is dictated by your business needs, and all Oracle Applications modules share the same accounting calendar, yet they maintain a separate status for each module. For example, an open period in Payables can be a closed period in Receivables.

Workday Calendar

If you have not defined your workday calendars in Oracle Inventory, you must define them for Oracle Purchasing and Oracle Payables. If you are performing a multi-org implementation of Purchasing and Payables, you may also create more than one calendar.

How to name your inventory period and how to create an exception template to filter out nonworking days are the two considerations for this setup step. Your workday calendar is dictated by your business needs, and all Oracle Applications modules share the same workday calendar.

Currencies

If you are planning to use the multicurrency features of Oracle, you must also enable the currencies you need. This step is done in Oracle General Ledger.

Determining which currencies you need is the only consideration for this setup step. Oracle Applications has all ISO currencies, but if you have a currency that is not defined, you must define it in Oracle General Ledger.

Conversion Rates

If you plan to use Oracle's multicurrency features, you must also define conversion rate types, daily rates, period rates, and historical rates in Oracle General Ledger.

Determining what kind of exchange rates to use and who will maintain the exchange rates for your company are the two considerations for this setup step.

Set of Books

At least one Set of Books must be defined in Oracle General Ledger in order to use the other modules. Once you have created the Sets of Books, assign responsibilities of *Oracle Purchasing* and *Oracle Payables* to the defined Sets of Books.

Considerations for this step, which include whether you want to perform suspense accounting, intercompany accounting, and budgetary control, among others, are covered in the first part of this book.

Opening and Closing Accounting Periods

Next, you must open the appropriate accounting period in Oracle General Ledger. Whether you should open and close the accounting periods is the only consideration for this step. If you open the accounting period, accounting entries and transactions can be entered for the opened accounting period. Open the appropriate inventory and purchasing periods, and open purchasing periods for which you have purchasing activity. Oracle Purchasing will only create journal entries for transactions in an open purchasing period, including creating the correct receipt accrual journal entry. Use the Control Purchasing Periods form to open/close purchasing periods.

Organizations

If you use expense reporting in Oracle Payables, you must define one or more organizations before using Oracle Purchasing and Oracle Payables. Organizations describe and define unique entities within your company, such as manufacturing plants, warehouses, distribution centers, and sales offices. Oracle Purchasing fully supports both centralized and decentralized purchasing for multiple receiving organizations. You can change your current receiving organization at any time with the Change Organization form.

There are multiple considerations for this step. You must determine your company structure, and what kind of security precautions to enforce. In other words, define how you want to segregate data and how you want personnel from one organization to interact with data from another organization. You also need to determine whether you want to centralize or decentralize each Oracle Applications module.

Human Resources

You will need to set up personnel, or human resources information if Human Resources is not installed. This step involves defining employee lookup codes, supplier and employee numbering, positions, position hierarchies, and employees. You must define employees when you define buyers, which is a required step for Oracle Purchasing. You must also define positions, position hierarchies, and employees if you will be using hierarchies for approvals and workflow.

How you want to number your employees and approve purchasing documents are the two considerations for this step. Approving purchase orders can be very complicated, and you can use a purchasing hierarchy for this task. A purchasing hierarchy is a position hierarchy that you can use to determine the relationship between employees when Oracle Purchasing tries to get the next level of approval.

Tax Names

Until now, all common setups have been performed in Oracle Applications modules, with the exception of the procurement modules. The remaining common setup steps are specific to Oracle Purchasing and Oracle Payables. To get to the Setup form, you must sign on as the Operation user and select the *Purchasing, Vision Operations (USA)* responsibility. The tax name, which you can use when entering tax amounts in payables invoices, defines a specific tax rate and tax account. You must define tax names for each operating unit. To set up tax names, you follow the navigation path *Setup : Financials : Accounting: Taxes*.

The only consideration for this step is that the tax name you choose be sufficiently descriptive when your users select it within the Payables invoices.

Locations

For purchasing, you must set up locations, which can be defined as ship-to, bill-to, office, internal, or receiving sites. You can follow the navigation path *Setup : Organizations: Locations* to set up locations. See Figure 12-3.

Giving locations descriptive names and determining what functionality you want to allow for each location are the two considerations for this step. If you use the Expense Report open interface, the location name must be less than 30 characters.

Suppliers

Suppliers can be created and maintained in Oracle Purchasing or Oracle Payables. You define the suppliers, the supplier sites, and the supplier contacts. Deciding who should maintain suppliers, since you do not want two departments within your organization to duplicate maintenance of the supplier master, is the primary consideration for this step. You must also establish and maintain a naming convention so that your users know how to select existing suppliers.

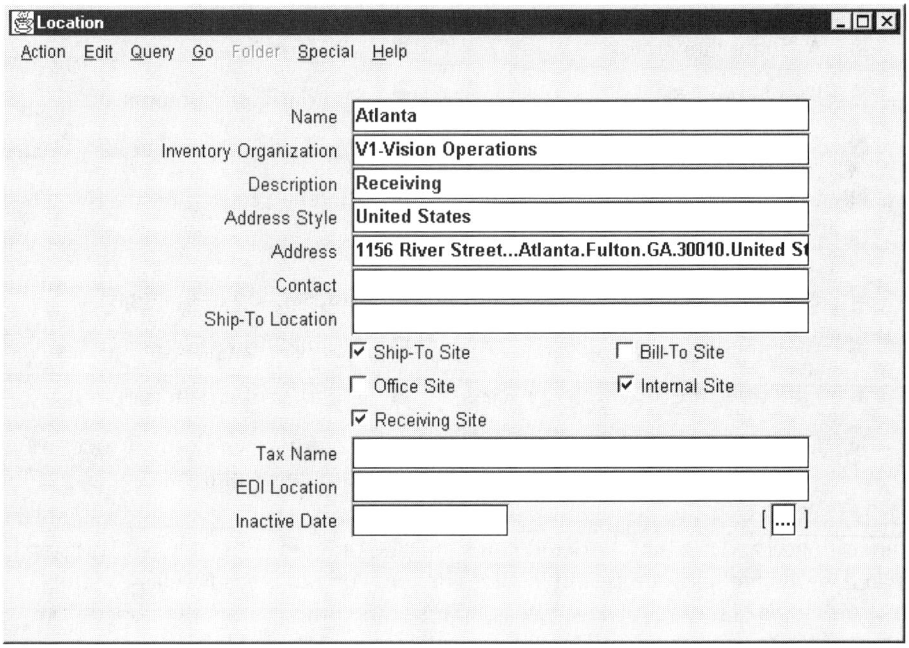

FIGURE 12-3. *Location form*

Review Questions

1. Which Key flexfields in other Oracle Applications modules must be set up for Oracle Purchasing and Oracle Payables?

2. When do you need to set up currencies and conversion rates?

3. What is the purpose of tax names?

4. What do you need to set up in Oracle Human Resources?

Setup Steps and Considerations Unique to Oracle Purchasing

Steps that are unique to Oracle Purchasing are as follows:

- Units of measure
- Items
- Oracle Workflow
- Account Generator
- Profile options
- Subinventory locations
- Cross-reference types
- Location associations
- Approval groups
- Assign approval groups
- Fill Employee Hierarchy process
- Document types
- Lookup codes
- Quality inspection codes
- Hazard classes
- UN Numbers
- Standard attachments
- Purchasing Item Category flexfield
- Buyers
- Line types
- Transaction managers
- Notification process
- Document creation options
- Configure workflow processes in Oracle Workflow

Units of Measure

Requisitioned and purchase ordered items must be ordered with a UOM. This step is shared with Oracle Inventory and involves defining unit of measure classes, units of measure, units of measure conversion, and interclass units of measure conversions. To set up units of measure, follow the navigation path *Setup : Units of Measure : Units of Measure.*

Naming the units of measure code and deciding which of them you want to set up as base units are the two primary considerations for this step. You must also determine how to convert between the units of measure within the same class, and whether you want to have conversion rules cross units of measure classes.

Items

Items used on requisitions and purchase orders are owned by Oracle Inventory. This step includes defining items at the master level, items at the organizational level, item relationships, item attributes, container-type lookup codes, statuses, item-type lookup codes, customer item commodity codes, and item templates. All of these setups can be done under the *Setup : Items* submenu in the Navigator.

To satisfy only Oracle Purchasing, you need only create items that are purchasing items. Consider setting up a purchasing item template that defaults item attributes applicable only to purchasing items, and use the purchasing item template as the basis for setting up purchasing items.

Oracle Workflow

Since Oracle Purchasing uses Oracle Workflow to perform document approvals, automatic document creation, and General Ledger account generation, you must set up Oracle Workflow if it is not already installed and running. This is a required step.

Account Generator

Next, you must decide how to use the Account Generator and define how the Account Generator for purchasing variance and charge accounts should construct the General Ledger accounts. You must review the default process that Oracle Workflow uses to see if it meets your business requirements. If not, then you can customize the Account Generator using the Workflow Builder in Oracle Workflow. To customize the Account Generator, you must repeat this step for each defined operating unit. Oracle Workflow must be installed and running in order to customize the Account Generator.

Determining how your account combinations should be constructed, and what account combinations are needed to make parameters to the Account Generator, are the two considerations for this step.

Profile Options

Profile options direct how Oracle Purchasing controls access to, and how Oracle Purchasing processes, system data. Profile options can be set at one or more of the following levels: site, application, responsibility, and user. Oracle Purchasing users can change option values at the user level only. The system administrator can set profile options at the site, application, responsibility, and/or user levels. You must set up profile options for each defined operating unit. Purchasing profile options are as follows:

- *PO: Allow Buyer Override in AutoCreate Find*
- *PO: Allow Category Override in AutoCreate Find*
- *PO: AutoCreate GL Date Option*
- *PO: Change Supplier Site*
- *PO: Default Supplier Item Catalog Option*
- *PO: Display the AutoCreated Document*
- *PO: Display the AutoCreated Quotation*
- *PO: Item Cross-Reference Warning*
- *PO: Legal Requisition Type*
- *PO: Override Approved Supplier List Status*
- *PO: Release During ReqImport*
- *PO: Set Debug Workflow ON*
- *PO: Supplier Pricing Method*
- *PO: Warn if RFQ Required Before AutoCreate*
- *PO: Workflow Processing Mode*

When setting profile option values, you must determine at what levels the profile option values should be set. Remember that user level overrides responsibility level overrides application level overrides site level.

Subinventory Locations

If subinventories are already set up in Oracle Inventory, you needn't define subinventory locations. Make sure that this step is done once for each operating unit. Subinventory is a physical area or a logical grouping of items, and can be a warehouse or a receiving dock. To set up subinventories, use responsibility *Inventory, Vision Operations (USA)* with the navigation path *Setup : Organizations : Subinventories.*

You must determine your company's subinventories. You can have separate on-hand quantities, different types of locator control, and different picking orders, and you can determine whether to be included in the ATP calculation of each subinventory.

Cross-Reference Types

Cross-reference types, which you can use to define relationships between items and other representations of items, are part of Inventory setup. Such representations can be supplier item numbers and old item numbers. To set up cross-reference types, you must use the *Inventory, Vision Operations (USA)* responsibility and the navigation path *Items : Cross References.*

   You must determine what other representations of item numbers are necessary for conducting business. Use the cross-reference types, which do not drive any functionality, as lookup dictionaries.

Location Associations

Location associations need only be assigned if you are going to use internal requisitions, and they must be performed for each operating unit. Remember that an internal order generates a purchase requisition, so you must associate a location to a customer site so that when an internal order is placed, the purchasing location is retrieved based on the customer site. Associate a location to customer site when you define a customer in Oracle Receivable, which will be covered in Exam 4 (Unit IV of this book).

   Identifying all of your internal customers and associating a purchasing location to every internal customer are the two considerations for this step.

Approval Groups

You must define approval groups, which define approval rules for your organization. These rules set approval limits for your employees for requisitions, purchase orders, and releases. You can define controls for document total, account range, location, item category range, and item range. You cannot delete an approval group that has an active assignment, but you can enable or disable entire groups. To set up approval groups, you must switch back to the Purchasing responsibility *Purchasing, Vision Operations (USA)* with navigation path *Setup : Approvals : Approval Groups.*

   You must determine the number of approval groups your company has, and how each is defined. You only have five standard parameters in Oracle approval groups: document total, account range, location, item category range, and item range. If your implementation requires more parameters, you will need to customize the workflow.

Assign Approval Groups

Once you have defined approval groups, assign them to the various purchasing document types. If you are using approval hierarchies, you must first establish the rules for your approval groups. When not using approval hierarchies, use this window to assign approval groups and functions to jobs within your organization. To assign approval groups, follow the navigation path *Setup : Approvals : Approval Assignments.*

Determine what purchasing document types will use which approval groups, and decide how the defined approval groups will be assigned.

Fill Employee Hierarchy Process

If you are using position hierarchy for approvals or security, you must fill employee hierarchy. Run the Fill Employee Hierarchy program to control document access security and determine the correct employee to forward to for approvals. The program assigns employees to the position hierarchy based on the current primary assignments. You must rerun this program whenever changes are made to your personnel or personnel assignments. To submit the Fill Employee Hierarchy process, you must follow the navigation path *Reports : Run.* Select Single Request and the program Fill Employee Hierarchy. Click on the **Submit Request** button.

Document Types

You must define document types and all of the attributes for each purchasing document type. Document types include purchase agreement, purchase order, quotation, release, request for quotation, and requisition. For each document type, there can be subtypes, and for each document type and subtype, you can assign attributes. These attributes include whether the owner can approve, modify, change the forward-to or forward-from person on the requisition, and whether the approval hierarchy can be changed. For security level, you can select Hierarchy, Private, Public, or Purchasing. With hierarchy, only the document owner and users above the document owner can access the document. With private, only the document owner can access the document. Public means all users can access the document, and purchasing means only the document owner and buyers can access the document. Access level can be defined as View Only, Modify, or Full. You can also select Direct or Hierarchy for forwarding documents. Direct means to forward directly to the next user with the approval authority, and Hierarchy means to forward to the next level regardless of approval authority. To set up document types, follow the navigation path *Setup : Purchasing : Document Types.*

Determine the attributes—which include whether an owner can approve or modify documents, and who can view and modify the purchasing documents—for each document type.

Lookup Codes

You must define purchasing lookup codes, which Oracle Purchasing uses throughout the system. You can add additional codes to meet your requirements in addition to the seeded codes. For example, Purchasing supplies the following vendor-type codes: Employee and Vendor. You might define an additional code called Contractor to use for the purchasing of outside contracting services, but you cannot change or delete them once they have been saved. However, you can change the description. You can find the lookup codes through the navigation path *Setup : Purchasing : Lookup Codes.*

Determine the lookup codes necessary for conducting business by reviewing each lookup type and comparing to what you currently have and what you wish to add.

Quality Inspection Codes

You can also define quality inspection codes, which are used to record the quality of goods received. Define as many codes as you need, and assign each code a ranking. Quality inspection codes are normally defined in Inventory setup; however, you can also follow the navigation path *Setup : Purchasing : Quality Inspection Codes* within the *Purchasing* responsibility. Determine the number of quality inspection codes you need and the relative ranking.

Hazard Classes

You can optionally define hazard codes to classify items as hazardous materials. Purchasing automatically copies this data onto your documents and prints it on your purchase orders, requests for quotes, and receipt travelers. To set up hazard classes, follow the navigation path *Setup : Purchasing : Hazard Classes.* Determine the hazard classes you need and any descriptions associated with each class.

UN Numbers

You can also define United Nations (UN) numbers to identify items you order for international trade, and you can assign a hazard class to UN numbers to identify hazardous materials. To set up UN numbers, follow the navigation path *Setup : Purchasing : UN Numbers.* Determine the UN numbers you need in order to conduct your business.

Standard Attachments

You can also define standard notes and attachments to provide additional information on your requisitions, requests for quotes, and purchase orders. Oracle Purchasing allows for the creation of attachments in any number of standard documents or templates that can be attached at the header and/or line level of purchasing documents. To set up standard attachments, follow the navigation path *Setup : Attachments.* See Figure 12-4.

Determine which standard attachments you need and whether they are word processing documents, spreadsheets, or images.

Purchasing Item Category Flexfield

To set up the Purchasing Item Category flexfield, you must define purchasing category, value sets, flexfield segments, segment values, the Account Aliases flexfield and cross-validation rules. You must also define and assign security rules.

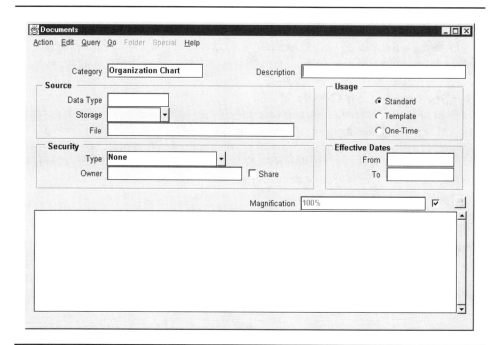

FIGURE 12-4. *Documents form*

Use the same forms to define the Purchasing Item Category flexfield, like any other Key flexfields.

Determine how you want to group your purchasing items, and remember to allow for future expansion.

Buyers

You must define purchasing buyers for your company, because an application user cannot create purchasing documents unless they have been defined as a buyer. To define a buyer, you must first define the employee and associate that employee with the buyer and user name. You can control whether the buyer is active by effective date. To set up a buyer, follow the navigation path *Setup : Personnel : Buyers.* See Figure 12-5.

Determine the number of buyers, and also determine what categories they should be assigned to.

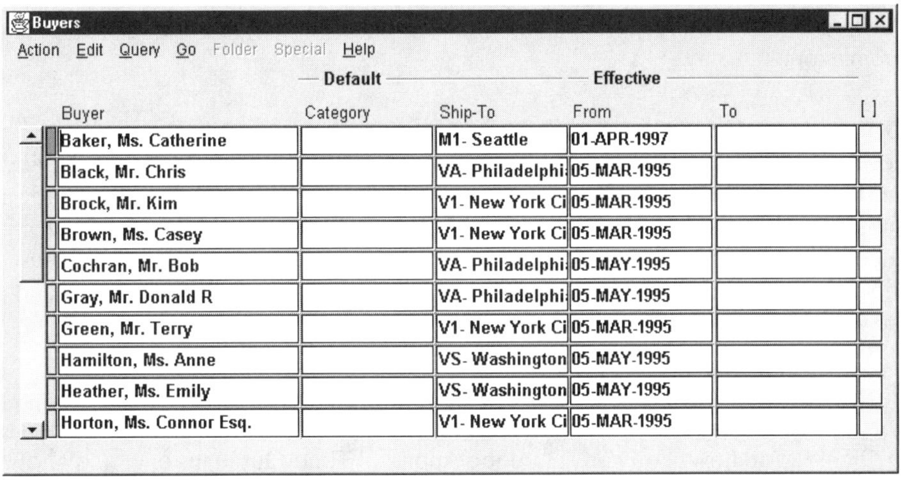
Buyers

Action Edit Query Go Folder Special Help

Buyer	Default Category	Default Ship-To	Effective From	Effective To	[ ]
Baker, Ms. Catherine		M1- Seattle	01-APR-1997		
Black, Mr. Chris		VA- Philadelphi	05-MAR-1995		
Brock, Mr. Kim		V1- New York Ci	05-MAR-1995		
Brown, Ms. Casey		V1- New York Ci	05-MAR-1995		
Cochran, Mr. Bob		VA- Philadelphi	05-MAY-1995		
Gray, Mr. Donald R		VA- Philadelphi	05-MAY-1995		
Green, Mr. Terry		V1- New York Ci	05-MAR-1995		
Hamilton, Ms. Anne		VS- Washington	05-MAY-1995		
Heather, Ms. Emily		VS- Washington	05-MAY-1995		
Horton, Ms. Connor Esq.		V1- New York Ci	05-MAR-1995		

FIGURE 12-5. *Buyers form*

Line Types

Next, you must define the line types that will be used to identify ordered items, and whether you order them by price and quantity or by amount. You can create line types—defined as goods, services, outside processing, or others—to reflect differences in purchased items. Outside processing line types are required if you are using Oracle WIP with outside processing. To set up line types, follow the navigation path *Setup : Purchasing : Line Types*. Determine the necessary line types and whether the seeded line types satisfy your need. If not, create new line types as necessary.

Transaction Managers

To process batch transactions, you must start your transaction manager. The purchasing transaction managers include the receiving transaction manager and document approval manager. You must be the system administrator to start transaction managers.

Notification Process

To conduct the approval workflow processes, you must start the Send Notifications for Purchasing Documents concurrent program setup, which will send notifications of incomplete purchasing documents, rejected purchasing documents, or purchasing documents that need reapproval. Submit this program through standard report submission.

Document Creation Options

Review the seeded document creation options to determine if the standard behavior must be changed. Document creation options include: Is Automatic Creation Allowed, Should Workflow Create the Release, and Is Automatic Approval Allowed. These document creation options govern how the purchasing-related workflow processes should be enforced. Document creation options are found in Oracle Workflow and the workflow process is called PO Create Documents.

Configure Workflow Processes in Oracle Workflow

The final setup step in Oracle Purchasing involves configuring workflow processes in Oracle Workflow. You can set up the Approval Time-Out feature, which allows for the specification of a period of time after which—if no response has come from an approver—to send a reminder. You must also start the Workflow Background process. You can also modify *Change Order Workflow profile* options.

You must review the PO Approval, Requisition Approval, Purchase Order Variance Account Generator, Purchase Order Charge Account Generator, Requisition Variance Account Generator, and the Requisition Charge Account Generator workflow processes to ensure that they satisfy your business needs.

Descriptive Flexfield

You must set up all of the Descriptive flexfields, which are an expansion of the Oracle Applications table, that you will you need. Determine your Descriptive flexfield needs by reviewing all forms and identifying fields that you need, but that are not
a part of the standard fields.

Review Questions

1. What transaction managers are used in Oracle Purchasing?

2. Which workflow processes can you configure in Oracle Workflow for Oracle Purchasing?

3. When must you perform location association?

4. How do you run the Fill Employee Hierarchy process?

Setup Steps and Considerations Unique to Oracle Payables

Steps that are unique to Oracle Payables are as follows:

- Choose Set of Books
- Payment terms
- Invoice tolerances
- Withholding tax groups
- Invoice approvals
- Distribution sets
- Payables lookup codes
- Payment interest rates
- Expense report template
- Employee lookup codes

- Reporting entity
- Income tax regions
- Automatic payment programs
- Payment formats
- Banks
- Report formatting
- Special calendars
- Descriptive flexfield
- Profile options

You must switch to the *Payables* responsibility *Payables, Vision Operations (USA)*.

Choose Set of Books

For each installation of Oracle Payables, you must select one primary Set of Books. This defines the Chart of Accounts structure, the functional currency, and the accounting calendar used by Oracle Payables. Follow the navigation path *Setup : Set of Books – Choose*.

Payment Terms

Payment terms define payment schedules with the corresponding discounts. For example, you can have a payment term that allows the payer to pay an invoice in 30 days. A different payment term could specify that if an invoice is paid within the first 10 days, it is given a 2-percent discount. To set up payment terms, follow the navigation path *Setup : Invoice : Payment Terms*. See Figure 12-6.

Determine what payment terms you need and how each should be defaulted for suppliers and supplier sites.

Invoice Tolerances

Invoice tolerances define the matching and tax tolerances that vary between invoice, tax, purchase order, and receipt. These tolerances can be by percentage or by amount. To set up invoice tolerances, follow the navigation path *Setup : Invoice : Tolerances*.

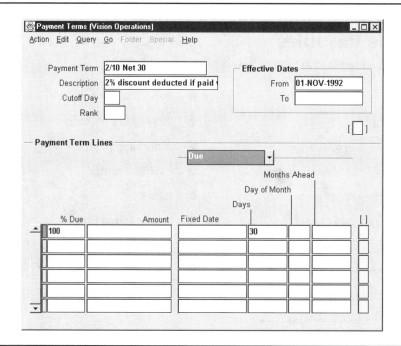

FIGURE 12-6. *Payment Terms form*

Determine the amount of tolerance you can allow for when matching invoice amounts and matching tax amount. For example, zero tolerance means that the invoice amounts or tax amounts cannot exceed the matching invoice amounts or tax amounts.

Withholding Tax Groups

Each withholding tax group can have one or more withholding tax types. When creating invoices with a withholding tax group, the withholding tax amount based on all of the withholding types is calculated automatically. To set up a withholding tax group, follow the navigation path *Setup : Tax : Withholding : Groups.*

Determine how many withholding tax types you have, or whether you have any at all. If you have withholding tax types, determine how to group and rank them, with the withholding tax type with a lower rank getting withheld first. The ranking is important because the withholding tax amount is calculated against the remaining invoice amount after each withholding.

Invoice Approvals

Oracle Payables comes with a list of predefined invoice approval codes, and you can define additional codes as needed. Invoice approval codes are used to apply or release invoice holds. To set up invoice approvals, follow the navigation path *Setup : Invoice : Approval.*

Using descriptive invoice approval codes so users will be able to look at the code and know why the invoice is being put on hold, or why the invoice is released, is an important consideration for this step.

Distribution Sets

A distribution set is a predefined allocation structure—with or without percentages—that you can use on invoices to facilitate faster data entry. You can attach distribution sets to suppliers so every invoice for that supplier will be defaulted with the associated distribution sets. Distribution sets can also be used to default Descriptive flexfields from the distribution sets to invoices. To set up distribution sets, follow the navigation path *Setup : Invoice : Distribution Sets.* See Figure 12-7.

Determine which allocation structures or percentages are used most frequently and define them as distribution sets. Then, determine whether you can assign preassigned percentages, or if you simply want to use the distribution sets as skeletons. If you only need skeletons, use zero as the percentages.

Payables Lookup Codes

Oracle Payables uses the following lookup types for Payables lookup codes: AWT Certificate Type, AWT Rate Type, FOB, Freight Terms, Minority Group, Pay Group, disbursement type, Don't Pay Reason, Source, Tax Type, and Supplier Type. It also comes with predefined lookup codes for each lookup type, and you can add your own user-defined lookup codes. Follow the navigation path *Setup : Quickcodes : Payables* to set up Payables lookup codes. Review the seeded lookup codes to determine if you need to set up your own codes.

Payment Interest Rates

Set up payment interest rates if you want to calculate interest automatically. This will make you compliant with the United States Prompt Payment Act. Enter the interest rate if your company is observing the United States Prompt Payment Act. To enter payment interest rates, follow the navigation path *Setup : Payment : Interest Rates.*

Expense Report Template

You can define expense report templates, which contain commonly used expense items, to be used when your users enter expense reports. Your users can enter expense

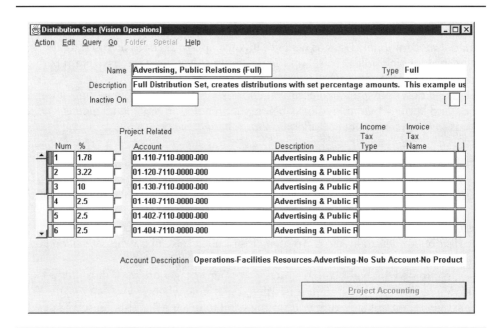

FIGURE 12-7. *Distribution Sets form*

reports through the Oracle Applications Enter Expense Report form or through the Web using Oracle Web Employees. To set up an expense report template, follow the navigation path *Setup : Invoice : Expense Report Templates.* See Figure 12-8.

Employee Lookup Codes

Oracle Payables has the following lookup types for employee lookup codes: GB_COUNTY, SEX, TITLE, and US_STATE. Oracle Payables comes with predefined lookup codes for each lookup type, and you can add your own if necessary. Follow the navigation path *Setup : Quickcodes : Employee* to set up employee lookup codes. Review the seeded lookup codes to determine if you need to set up your own codes.

Reporting Entity

A reporting entity is any individual or organization with a tax identification number (TIN). For each reporting entity, you can have separate 1096 forms, 1099 forms, 1099 tape, 1099 Payments report, and 1099 Exceptions reports. To set up a reporting entity, follow the navigation path *Setup : Tax : Reporting Entities.* Determining the number of TINs you have will drive how many reporting entities you have.

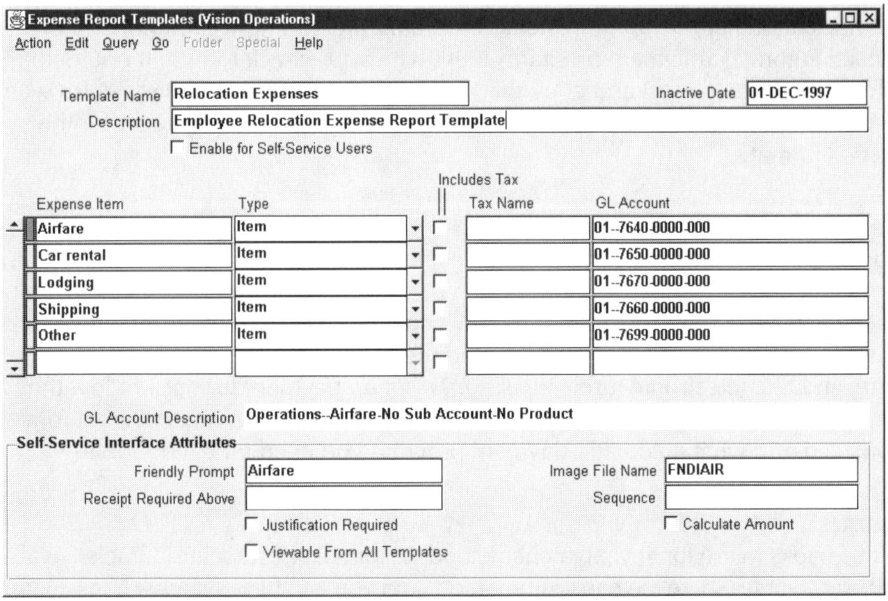

FIGURE 12-8.   *Expense Report Templates form*

Income Tax Regions

If you use the Combined Filing program, you must define your income tax regions. A K record is produced for each income tax region when the 1099 tape is generated, and a B record is generated for suppliers within the income tax regions that have payment amounts greater than or equal to the income tax region's reporting limit. Oracle Payables comes with predefined region codes that participate in the Combined Filing program. You can use these codes for your income tax regions, and you can associate income tax regions to the site level, supplier site level, or at the invoice level. To set up income tax regions, follow the navigation path *Setup : Tax : Regions*.

Determine whether you want to use the Combined Filing program, and if so, how many income tax regions you need. Create the income tax regions and attach them to the 1099 supplier sites as appropriate.

Automatic Payment Programs

Automatic payment programs are programs that build the payment runs, format checks, and create remittance advice. Oracle Payables has one seeded automatic payment program of type Build Payment and several seeded automatic payment programs of type Format Payments. To set up automatic payment programs, follow the navigation path *Setup : Payment : Programs.* Determine whether one of the seeded automatic payment programs work with your check format. If not, determine which one is the closest and copy that program and modify it. You may also want to consider changing your existing check format and order new checks for the seeded format.

Payment Formats

You must set up payment formats by selecting the build program, format program, and remittance advance program. Attach the payment formats to payment documents when you set up your banks. You need one payment format for each payment method in Oracle Payables, and the payment method includes check, wire, and EFT (electronic funds transfer). To set up payment formats, follow the navigation path *Setup : Payment : Formats.* Determine how many payment formats you need and what automatic payment program you need for each format.

Banks

Set up banks to use for any payment method, or for clearing receipts. Oracle Payables and Receivables share the bank information, and you can have external banks with suppliers or customers as account holders. Clearinghouses, which disburse receipts information to your remittance banks, are also considered banks. For each bank, you must enter all of the bank branches, bank accounts, and payment documents that come out of each bank. To set up banks, follow the navigation path *Setup : Payment : Banks.* See Figure 12-9.

   Determine how many banks you have and what kind of payment methods are supported by each. Obtain a list of your bank accounts, the accounts for your suppliers or customers that need to be set up, and the EFT numbers (as necessary).

Report Formatting

There are two kinds of special report formatting you can perform in Oracle Payables (both are optional). The first is for expense reporting, while the second is for aging periods. Use the account segments for expense reporting to determine the format and sorting sequence of your Expense Distribution Detail report. Use aging periods to determine your aging buckets for your Invoice-Aging report. These two features allow for the customization of the two reports in the necessary format and sorting. To set up account segments for expense reporting, follow the navigation path *Setup : Invoice : Distribution Detail Report.* To set up aging periods for the Invoice-Aging report, follow the navigation path *Setup : Calendar : Aging Periods.*

   Considerations for this step include determining how you want the Expense Distribution Detail report and your Invoice-Aging report to look. From there, you simply set up the report formatting accordingly.

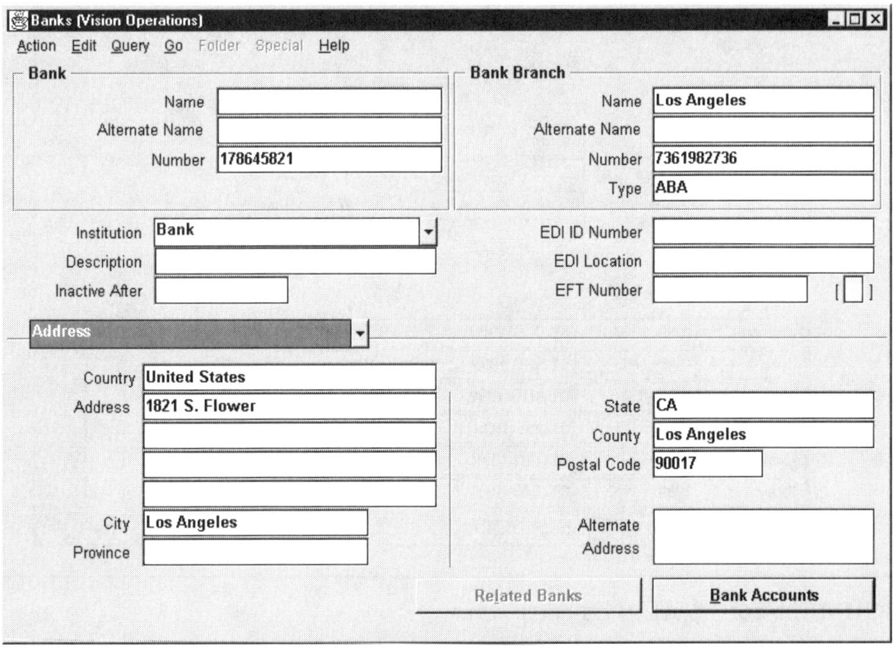

FIGURE 12-9.   *Banks form*

Special Calendars

You can define special calendars for recurring invoices, automatic withholding tax, and the Key Indicators report. The Key Indicators report is used to measure individual performances, and special calendars comprise periods that you define. Periods can be weekly, monthly, or any other format that you customize. To set up special calendars for recurring invoices, automatic withholding tax, and the Key Indicators report, follow the navigation path *Setup : Calendar : Special Calendar*. See Figure 12-10.

Determine how you want your invoices to recur, how often you want to withhold tax, and how you will measure individual performance.

Descriptive Flexfield

Set up all necessary descriptive flexfields, which are expansions of the Oracle Applications table. Determine your descriptive flexfield needs by comparing your implementation's needs with the fields provided on standard Oracle Applications forms. Any item you need to store that is not already part of an existing form is a candidate to be stored in a descriptive flexfield.

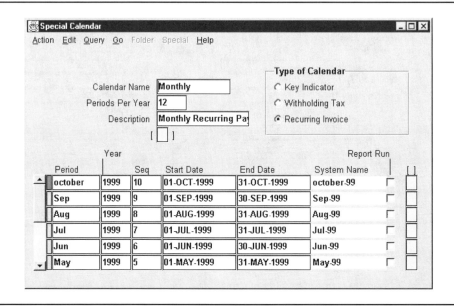

FIGURE 12-10. *Special Calendar form*

Profile Options

Profile options direct how Oracle Payables controls access to, and how Oracle Payables processes, system data. Profile options can be set at one or more of the following levels: site, application, responsibility, and user. Oracle Payables users can change option values at the user level only, and the system administrator can set profile options at the site, application, responsibility, and/or user levels. You must set up profile options for each defined operating unit. Payables profile options are as follows:

- *AP: Bank File Character Set*
- *AP: Enter Alternate Fields*
- *AP: Sort by Alternate Fields*
- *WebExpenses: Allow Non-Base Pay*
- *WebExpenses: Allow Non-Base Pay*
- *WebExpenses: CC Overrider Req*

- *WebExpenses: Enable DescFlex*
- *WebExpenses: Enable Tax*
- *WebExpenses: Overrider Required*
- *WebExpenses: Purpose Required*
- *WebExpenses: Report Number Prefix*
- *Audittrail: Activate*
- *Budgetary Control Group*
- *Journals: Display Inverse Rate*
- *Default Country*
- *Enable Transaction Codes*
- *Folderview: Allow Customization*
- *Language*
- *GL: Create Interfund Entries*
- *Sequential numbering*
- *Printer*
- *Site Language*
- *MO: Operating Unit*

When setting profile option values, determine at what levels to set the profile option values, and remember that user level overrides responsibility level overrides application level overrides site level.

Review Questions

1. What is the purpose of setting up invoice tolerances?
2. What is the purpose of setting up expense report templates?
3. What is the purpose of setting up income tax regions?
4. What is the purpose of setting up special calendars?

Setup Steps and Considerations Unique to Oracle Cash Management

The Cash Management module is designed to run in conjunction with the Receivables and Payables modules, and as interface to the General Ledger module. Therefore, the Cash Management setup is dependent on some of the configurations of those modules. For Oracle Payables, you must have banks set up, and you also must have the following accounts set up in Oracle Payables: accounts for the charges, errors, and clearing. You can also enable Automatic Offsets, which is a feature in Oracle Payables that automatically balances the payable liability accounts to the invoice distribution accounts by balancing entity or by account. For example, in balancing entity, if you are buying stationery for two balancing entities/companies, your invoice for the stationery is charged to two different distribution accounts: one for company 1 and one for company 2. With this scenario, you can only enter one payable liability for each invoice in Oracle Payables. However, with the Automatic Offsets feature enabled—regardless of which company payable liability account you entered for the invoice—the payable liability account will be split proportionally into the two companies of the invoice distributions according to the percentages. As a last step, you must enable the *Allow Reconciliation Accounting* option.

For Oracle Receivables, you must set banks up just like Oracle Payables. You also need the remittance and cash accounts, and you must turn off the Set the Account Requirement feature for the *Payment Methods* option. As a last step, you must define the Receivables activities: at least one for Cash Management functions.

In order to complete the Oracle Cash Management setup, and provided you satisfied the prerequisites, perform the following setup steps:

- Transaction codes
- System parameters

Transaction Codes

To set up transaction, follow the navigation path *Setup : Bank Transaction Codes*. Define the transaction codes for each type of banking transaction that your bank defined. For instance, your bank may assign a number or alpha code to a non-sufficient funds (NSF) transaction, which would appear on your bank statement. Cash Management defines the following possible codes:

- Payment
- Receipt
- Miscellaneous Payment

- Miscellaneous Receipt

- NSF

- Rejected

- Stopped Payment

You may define multiple codes for each of the above, or no code at all for those codes that are unused. First, use the drop-down menu to select the type of code you wish to define. Then, enter the bank code for that type of transaction. Next, enter the Description field and a clarifying description of the code (optional). You can also create effective date ranges that govern when the transaction codes are active. The Float Days field is optional, and allows you to enter the number of float days you wish to add to the bank statement date in order to create an effective date for the transaction.

Next, enter the transaction source. You can leave this field blank if you want to reconcile your statement lines to transactions that were generated in either Oracle Receivables or Oracle Payables. If you want to reconcile the lines to General Ledger journal entries, select Journals. To reconcile lines to items in the open interface, select Interface. If the transaction type is Miscellaneous Receipt or Miscellaneous Payment, select the type of transactions to match, the ordering of matching, and the correction method. Valid choices for matching are Misc, for matching only against miscellaneous transactions; Stmt, for matching only against statement lines; Misc, Stmt, for first matching against miscellaneous transactions, then matching against statement lines; and Stmt, Misc, for matching against statement lines, then matching against miscellaneous transactions. Valid choices for correction method are Reversal, Adjustment or Both. You can check the *Create* checkbox to automatically create a miscellaneous line item—which will be assigned the transaction code—for unanticipated items that appear on the bank statements.

If you choose to create miscellaneous line items, you must select an activity type to be assigned to the item. As a last step, if you choose to create miscellaneous line items, you must select a payment method that will be assigned to the item; then save your work. The transaction codes must be assigned for each bank that is set up in either Receivables or Payables to be reconciled with Cash Management.

System Parameters

To set up system parameters, follow the navigation path *Setup : System Parameters*. See Figure 12-11. Choose a Set of Books from the List of Values, then enter the begin date, which must be backdated far enough to cover any transactions that will appear in the bank statement. It is generally safe to calculate that the opening date of the first statement will not contain entries earlier than its own date. For instance, a check may be issued on January 25, but cashed on February 5. If your system begin date was dated February 1, Cash Management would recognize it. The system only recognizes the transaction date of the bank record, not your Payables or Receivables transaction date. Next, decide whether you want to see cleared transactions that are available for reconciliation by checking the *Show Cleared Transactions* checkbox. If you want to reserve the ability to add lines to a statement that is loaded automatically, and not manually, you must check the *Add Line to Automatic Statements* checkbox. If your bank statements will be loaded through the interface instead of being loaded manually, check the *Use Reconciliation Open Interface* checkbox. Large statements should be loaded through the interface to maximize the functionality of the program.

Go to the General alternative region and select the matching order—either transaction or batch—for both Payables and Receivables. If your system requires reconciliation only at the batch level, select Batch; otherwise, select Transaction. This is how Cash Management will search the statement lines in order to match them up during AutoReconciliation. Next, enter the tax codes that are used when there are

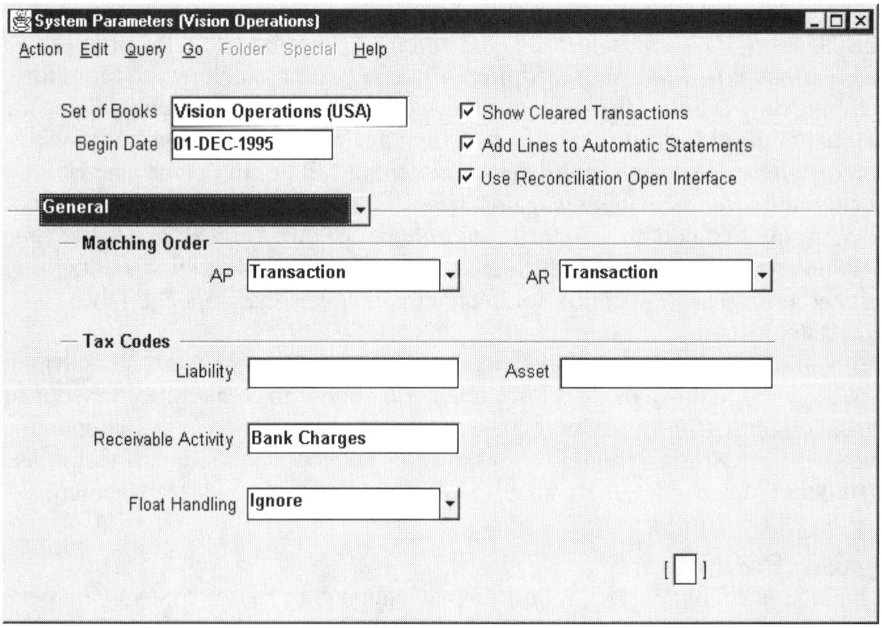

FIGURE 12-11. *System Parameters (General) screen*

differences in the bank statement associated with VAT. If the transactions are in dollars, select Standard. Otherwise, select a VAT code to represent the liability and assets for miscellaneous payments and miscellaneous receipts. When you select an activity, a default General Ledger account is automatically associated with the transaction line. Select an activity to which you will charge the differences. This is usually a clearing account, a bank charges account, or a miscellaneous costs account. The last field in the region is for float handling, where you have two management options. Error: Cash Management will display a warning while reconciling. You can ignore or reconcile the line, and Ignore: Cash Management will allow reconciliation of lines with postdated transaction dates.

Once you have selected the General alternative region, change the alternative region to Automatic Reconciliation—a setting that will not have any effect on manually reconciled statements, only for automatic reconciliation. See Figure 12-12. Choose the amount and percentage of variance you want Cash Management to use in trying to match statement lines to available transactions in the Tolerances fields. The Amount field is a specific dollar amount of either the statement line or the transaction line, and the Percentage field sets the tolerance on either the statement line or the available transactions. Next, enter the Tolerance Differences fields. In the AP field, select Charges or Errors. Charges will send the difference to the General Ledger to the charge account setup in Payables, and Errors will not send the differences to the General Ledger, but will err out. In the Foreign field, you can select Gain/Loss, Charges/Errors, or No Action. Differences will be posted to the General Ledger as a gain/loss or as bank charges or bank errors. No action means that this item will not reconcile and that it will display an error status. Next, check the *Purge* checkbox to purge from the interface once the statement is transferred. You can also select automatic archive of the statements from the interface tables by checking the *Archive* checkbox; you must archive if you purge. The Lines per Commit field determines the number of lines that Oracle Cash Management should process before committing. Setting the Lines per Commit field to a low number of 5 or less prevents the systems from stalling while processing large statements during AutoReconciliation. Finally, save your setup configurations.

Review Questions

    1. For what purpose is the transaction source of a transaction code used?

    2. What is the purpose of the Float Days field in a transaction code?

    3. For what purposes are the *Purge* and *Archive* checkboxes used?

    4. What is the purpose of the Activity field in the System Parameters form?

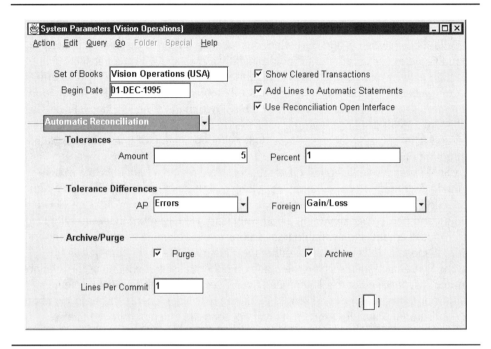

FIGURE 12-12. *System Parameters (Automatic Reconciliation) form*

Financial, Purchasing, Receiving, and Payables Options

You will learn about the following options in Oracle Purchasing and Oracle Payables:

■ Financial options

■ Purchasing options

■ Receiving options

■ Payables options

Financial Options

Financial options combine options from Oracle General Ledger, Oracle Payables, Oracle Human Resource Management Systems, and Oracle Purchasing. Use this form to choose a Set of Books for your Oracle Purchasing application and your Oracle

Payables application. You can also use the Define Financials Options form to choose an inventory organization from Oracle Inventory. During this step, you establish accounting, budgetary control, encumbrance, payment, personnel, purchasing, VAT registration, and vendor options. This step must be completed, even if you do not install Oracle General Ledger or Oracle Payables. This step must be performed for each operating unit. Follow the navigation path *Setup : Organizations : Financial Options* within the *Purchasing* responsibility. There are seven alternative regions in the Financial Options form. They are as follows:

- Accounting
- Encumbrance
- Human Resources
- Supplier – Payables
- Supplier – Purchasing
- Supplier Entry
- Tax

ACCOUNTING   Use this alternative region to enter the future period limit and all of the various General Ledger accounts used in Oracle Purchasing and Oracle Payables. Future period limit determines the number of future periods you can enter invoices in. See Figure 12-13.

ENCUMBRANCE   Use this alternative region to determine whether you want to use requisition encumbrance and/or PO encumbrance. If you decide to use encumbrances, you must also enter the encumbrance types.

HUMAN RESOURCES   Use this alternative region to select which business group to use, whether approval hierarchies should be used, whether an expense check is defaulted to be sent to the home address or the office address, and what the employee numbering option is.

SUPPLIER – PAYABLES   Use this alternative region to select the default payment terms, payment method, receipt acceptance days, whether you want to always take a discount, and whether you want to allow invoices to be marked as "pay alone" (meaning that each invoice generates a separate payment).

SUPPLIER – PURCHASING   Use this alternative region to select the default ship-to location, bill-to location, inventory organization, FOB, ship via, and freight terms.

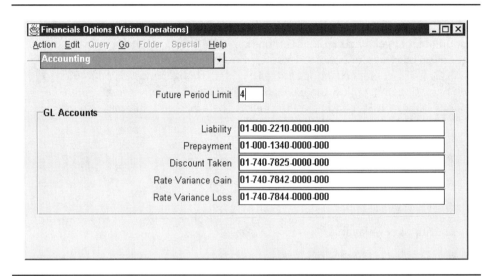

FIGURE 12-13. *Financials Options (Accounting) form*

SUPPLIER ENTRY   Use this alternative region to select whether you want RFQ Only Site and Hold Unmatched Invoices to be defaulted when entering supplier. You can also determine how you want the supplier numbered.

TAX   Use this alternative region to select the default tax name and the VAT information.

Purchasing Options

By using the Purchasing Options window, you can define default values and controls for functions throughout Purchasing. If necessary, you can override many of these options at appropriate entry stages. The Accrual options will determine if you accrue expense items at period end or upon receipt. Control options set default values for price tolerance, full lot quantity, receipt close point, cancelling requisitions, security hierarchy, displaying messages, notification of blanket POs, allowance of item description updates, enforcing of buyer name, and enforcing of vendor holds. Default options are requisition group import, minimum release amount, price break type, quote warning delay, receipt close percent, line type, rate type, taxable, price type, RFQ requested, invoice close percent, and invoice matching. Internal requisition options are order type and order source. Numbering options set manual or automatic and type for RFQs, quotations, purchase orders, and requisitions. Use tax defaults for ranking tax information for shipment lines.

Follow the navigation path *Setup : Organizations : Purchasing Options* within the *Purchasing* responsibility. There are six alternative regions:

- Accrual

- Control

- Default

- Internal Requisition

- Numbering

- Tax Defaults

ACCRUAL Use this alternative region to determine when to accrue expense and inventory items, as well as the default account to use for expense AP accrual. See Figure 12-14.

CONTROL Use this alternative region to enter the price tolerance, which—if *Enforce Price Tolerance* is enabled—is the percentage by which the purchase order line price cannot exceed the requisition line price. You can enable *Enforce Prices Tolerance* in the same region and select whether full lot quantity should be enforced, or whether you should only receive an advisory. This is determined by the *Enforce Full Lot Quantity* option. Select whether you want to show displayed disposition messages,

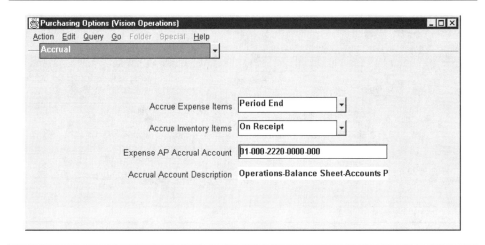

FIGURE 12-14. *Purchasing Options (Accrual) form*

and decide at which point a receipt is considered closed. Valid choices for the Receipt Close Point field are Accepted, Delivered, and Received. You can select whether you want to be notified when entering a requisition line, and that a blanket order exists. You can also select whether you want to cancel requisitions automatically, optionally, or never, when the corresponding purchase orders are cancelled. You can also select whether you can update item description and whether you can select any buyer or only yourself to be the buyer of the purchasing documents you entered. As a last step, you can determine whether to be able to approve purchase orders if the supplier is on hold. See Figure 12-15.

DEFAULT   Use this alternative region to select purchasing option defaults, which include what to import requisitions by, the exchange rate type, the minimum release amount, taxable, the price break type, and the receipt close percentage, among others.

INTERNAL REQUISITION   Use this alternative region to select the internal order type and the internal order source that will be defaulted in Order Entry when a sales order is created from an internal requisition.

NUMBERING   Use this alternative region to determine the numbering options for RFQ, quotation, PO, and requisition. You can choose automatic or manual numbers,

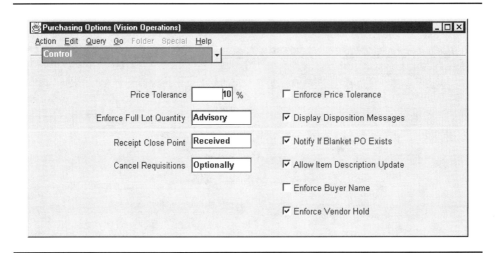

FIGURE 12-15.   *Purchasing Options (Control) form*

and for automatic you can enter the starting number and view the next to be used. For manual, you choose to limit the values to numeric only or alphanumeric.

TAX DEFAULTS   Use this alternative region to determine the order in which the tax name should be defaulted to purchasing documents. The hierarchy field determines the order.

Receiving Options

Receiving options will control receipt of purchase orders in the system. Most of the options established during this setup step can be overridden for specific suppliers, items, and purchase orders. The options consist of receipt days (early, late, and warning), over-receipt control tolerance and warning, receipt numbering, allow substitutions, allow unordered, allow express transactions, allow cascade transactions, allow blind receiving, receipt routing, whether to enforce ship-to, the ASN control code, and receipt accrual account. Follow the navigation path *Setup : Organizations : Receiving Options* within the *Purchasing* responsibility See Figure 12-16.

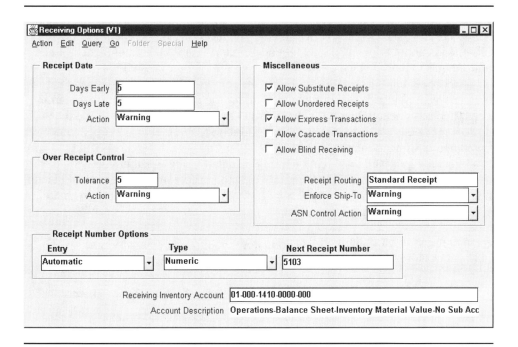

FIGURE 12-16.   *Receiving Options form*

Payables Options

Use the Payables Options form to enter setups and defaults for Oracle Payables. The form can be accessed using navigation path *Setup : Options : Payables*. There are 11 alternative regions. They are as follows:

- Accounting
- Currency
- Expense Report
- Interest
- Invoice
- Invoice Tax

- Matching
- Payment
- Supplier
- Withholding Tax
- Tax Name Defaults

ACCOUNTING   Use this region for accounting options, and enable automatic offsets by account or balancing. By account means that the account segment from the invoice distribution overwrites the account segment of the liability account, while by balancing means that the balancing segment from the invoice distribution overwrites the balancing segment of the liability account. If you enable automatic offset, you cannot allow reconciliation accounting, enable withholding tax, or allow adjustments to paid invoices. After automatic offset, determine whether you want to allow reconciliation accounting and whether you want to allow future payment method. Next, select the accounting method for the primary Set of Books. Enable combined basis accounting by selecting accounting method for the secondary Set of Books. Choose None for Secondary Accounting Method if you do not have combined basis accounting.

Select the Journal Entry Creation mode by determining whether you want the default to have audit entries for your liability, gain or loss, rounding, discount taken, and cash clearing journals. Finally, select whether you want the default to create summarized journals. See Figure 12-17.

CURRENCY   This alternative region allows you to specify a variety of currency-related factors:

- Whether you want to use multiple-currencies accounting when entering and paying the same invoice
- Whether you require an exchange rate when you enter an invoice or payment
- The default exchange rate type
- All the currency-related accounts: realized gain, realized loss, and rounding

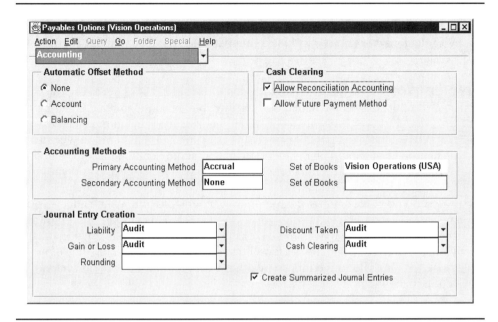

FIGURE 12-17. *Payables Options (Accounting) form*

You cannot set the *Allow Multiple Currencies* option to No if you have one or more multicurrency bank accounts.

EXPENSE REPORT Use this alternative region to enter the terms, pay group, payment priority, settlement days, default value for whether to apply advances, default value for whether to hold unmatched expense report, and whether the employee should be created automatically as supplier.

INTEREST Use this alternative region to enable automatic interest calculation, enter a minimum interest amount, and enter the default interest invoice accounts (expense and liability).

INVOICE Use this alternative region to determine whether you want to do the following: use batch controls, confirm using date as the invoice number, allow online approval, allow adjustments to paid invoices, allow your user to override the default document category for document sequencing, and if a single freight distribution should be automatically generated using the freight account entered in this region. If you want to enter freight distribution(s) manually, or if you want to prorate freight charges, do not enable the *Automatically Create Freight Distribution* option. As a last step, select how the GL date should be defaulted. It can be based on invoice date, system date, receipt date then invoice date, or receipt date then system date.

INVOICE TAX   Use this alternative region to determine whether tax should be excluded from the discount calculation, whether the tax name and tax amount will be required at the invoice header level, and if the tax should be automatically calculated. If you choose to enable automatic tax calculation, determine whether the calculation level should be defaulted to appear at the header level or the line level. You can allow the user to override the calculation level default, and you can determine whether the calculated tax amount should be rounded up, down, or to the nearest number. Next, enter the minimum accountable unit, which affects your tax amount after rounding by ensuring that the calculated tax amount is within the increments of the minimum accountable unit. Finally, decide whether the invoices should be defaulted to calculate tax for all distribution lines. Checking the *Allow Override* checkbox allows the user to override the *Distribution Amounts Include Tax* option in the invoices.

MATCHING   Use this alternative region to determine the matching options, which are Allow Final Matching, Allow Distribution Level Matching, Allow Matching Account Override, Transfer PO Descriptive Flexfield Information, and Recalculate Scheduled Payment. The matching options are shown in Figure 12-18.

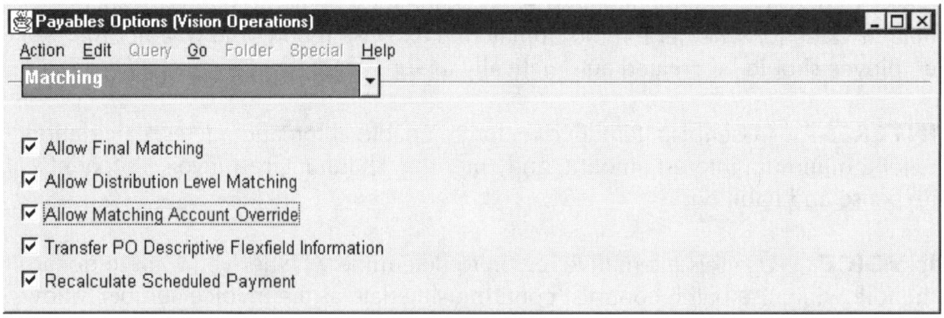

FIGURE 12-18.   *Payables Options (Matching) form*

PAYMENT   Use this alternative region to define the default bank account, the payment batch limit, the EFT user number, the discount distribution method (i.e., *Prorate Expense, Prorate Tax, System Account*), the additional pay through date used to calculate the pay through date for the payment batch, and whether to allow document category override. You can also specify whether you allow printing, predating, voiding and reissuing, and allow address modification of quick payments, which are payments that aren't made through payment batches. Finally, you can use this alternative region to determine whether the Remit To account can be overridden and whether you use bank charges.

SUPPLIER   Use this alternative region to enter the defaults for pay date basis, terms date basis, pay group, the bank charge bearer, and invoice currency for new suppliers. You can also determine whether to enable a combined filing program and ask Oracle Applications to use the Income Tax region from the supplier sites if a combined filing program is adopted. If not, and if a combined filing program is adopted, then you must enter a default income tax for all suppliers.

WITHHOLDING TAX   Use this alternative region to determine whether to enable withholding tax. Additionally, you can determine whether to allow manual withholding, and whether to enter the default withholding tax group. You can select when to apply withholding tax, and apply withholding tax at invoice approval or at invoice payment. You can also decide whether the withholding amount basis includes discount amount and/or tax amount, and you can select when to create the withholding invoice, and whether it should be created at invoice approval or invoice payment.

TAX NAME DEFAULT   Use this alternative region to set the tax name default. Oracle Payables can enforce the tax account used to match that of the tax name, and it can enforce the tax name in an invoice match to the matched PO's tax name. You can also specify the hierarchy in which the tax name defaults, similar to the purchasing options. See Figure 12-19.

Review Questions

1. What is included in the financial options setup?

2. What options do you lose if you enable automatic offsets?

3. How does the hierarchy in tax name works?

4. What is a receipt close point?

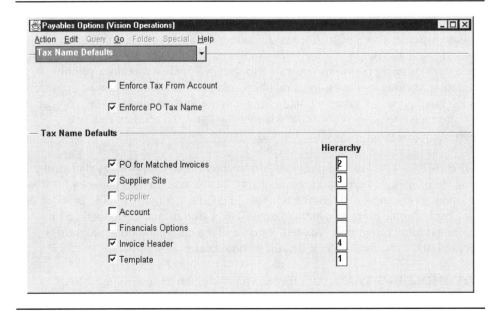

FIGURE 12-19.   *Payables Options (Tax Name Defaults) form*

Creating Supplier Information

In this section, you will learn how to create supplier information. Supplier is the master file of Oracle Purchasing and Oracle Payables, and is defined in a hierarchy. Supplier has supplier sites, and a supplier site has contacts. In this section, you will learn to:

- Create supplier information

- Define supplier site information

- Identify supplier contact information by site

- Merge suppliers

Steps to Create Supplier Information

To enter purchase orders, you must first set up your suppliers. As you do so, the entered information will save time at the transaction level. Oracle Purchasing and Oracle Payables share the same supplier tables, and it is important for ownership and control of the supplier tables to be determined at the start of implementation.

To ensure that only approved suppliers are entered and duplication is avoided, responsibilities and business processes must be in place.

When entering a supplier, you can also record information for your own reference, such as names of contacts or the customer number your supplier has assigned to you. The terms "supplier" and "vendor" are used interchangeably. Before entering a new supplier, you should do a Find first to ensure that the supplier does not already exist in your system. If you do find a duplicate supplier, use the Merge function to combine the two. If you have logged on using the *Purchasing* responsibility, the navigation path to the Suppliers Summary form is *Supply Base : Suppliers*. If you have logged on using the *Payables* responsibility, the navigation path is *Suppliers : Entry*. See Figure 12-20.

The Suppliers Summary form allows for querying and finding of existing suppliers. If you queried/found the supplier you are interested in, click on the **Open** button. To enter the Suppliers form and enter a new supplier, click on the **Open** button on a new line or click on the **New** button and then the **Open** button. See Figure 12-21.

When entering a unique supplier name, you should also develop a document for naming standards and conventions. The supplier number is generated by the

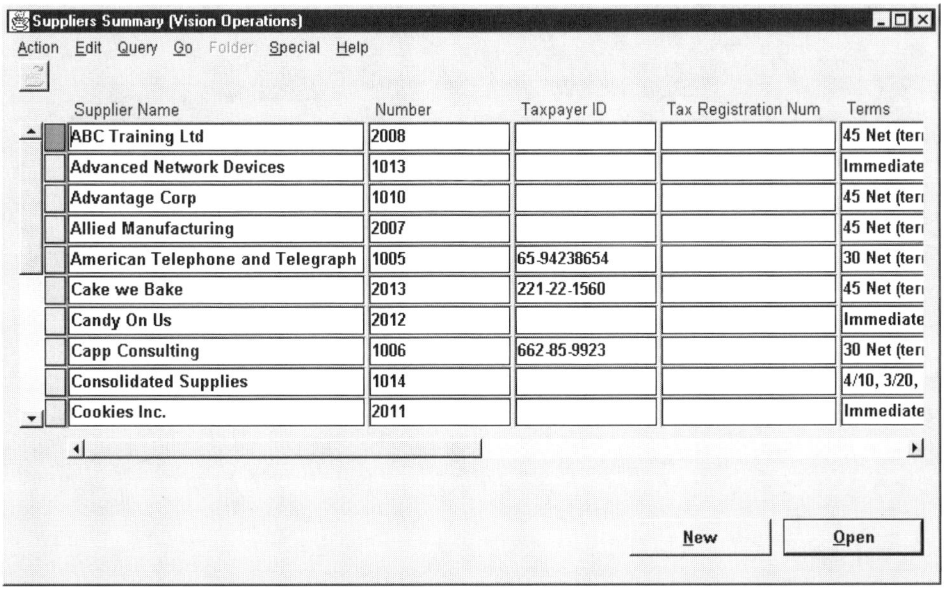
Suppliers Summary (Vision Operations)
Action Edit Query Go Folder Special Help
Supplier Name
Number
Taxpayer ID
Tax Registration Num
Terms
ABC Training Ltd
2008
45 Net (terı
Advanced Network Devices
1013
Immediate
Advantage Corp
1010
45 Net (terı
Allied Manufacturing
2007
45 Net (terı
American Telephone and Telegraph
1005
65-94238654
30 Net (terı
Cake we Bake
2013
221-22-1560
45 Net (terı
Candy On Us
2012
Immediate
Capp Consulting
1006
662-85-9923
30 Net (terı
Consolidated Supplies
1014
4/10, 3/20,
Cookies Inc.
2011
Immediate
New
Open

FIGURE 12-20. *Suppliers Summary form*

system when the *Automatic Supplier Numbering* option in the Financials Options window has been enabled. If this feature has not been enabled, then you must enter the supplier number manually. Or, you can also enter an alternate name, and the taxpayer ID if it is known (this is the federal identification number for corporations and partnerships—for individuals, it is their social security number). If applicable, enter the tax registration number. Note that the tax registration number applies to VAT and does not apply to U.S. supplier sites. If you have a requirement, or if you need to prevent invoices and purchase orders from being assigned to this supplier after a certain date, enter an inactive after date. Create your own supplier, call it **New supplier**, then save your work. Defaults from the financial options and other site-level forms will be filled in.

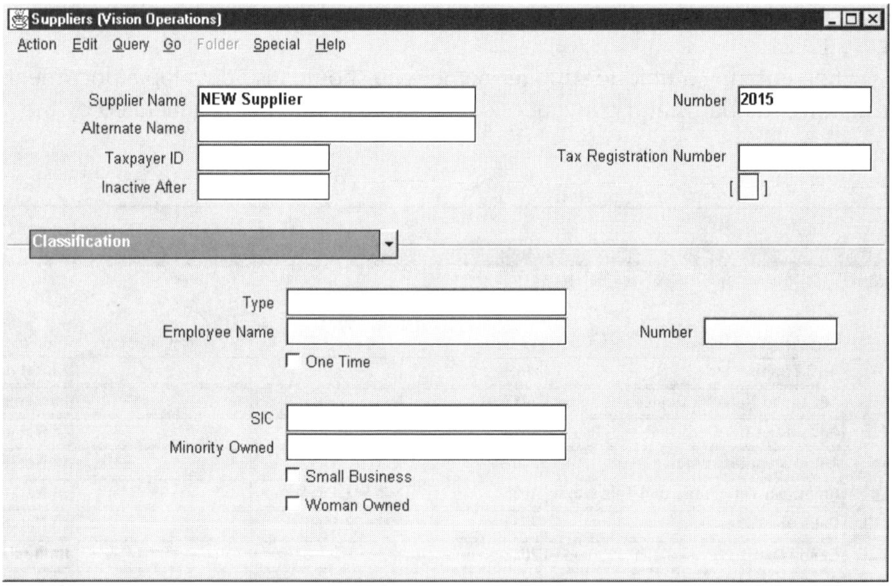

FIGURE 12-21. *Suppliers form*

TIP
If you are operating in a multi-org environment, the supplier header information is shared across all organizations. You should: 1) always use Find before adding a supplier to determine if that supplier may have been already created by another organization, and 2) if that supplier already exists, go directly to the Sites alternative region and set all organization-specific parameters at the site level. Information for the Classification, General, and Receiving regions can only be set at the header level. If you need the options within those regions set differently, then you must create a new supplier with a different name.

Enter any additional supplier information you want to record in the appropriate region of the Suppliers detail window. If the information also appears in the Supplier Sites window, the supplier information will default to the supplier site. There are a total of 13 regions. They are as follows:

- Classification
- General
- Bank Accounts
- Accounting
- Invoice Tax
- Tax Reporting
- Control

- Payment
- Electronic Data Interchange
- Purchasing
- Receiving
- Withholding Tax
- Sites

Classification
With the exception of the type and employee name, classification information is not used by the system and is for your reference only. Select the appropriate supplier type

from the List of Values, which includes: Vendor for trade suppliers, Employee for employees of your company, and Reportable for 1099 reportable suppliers. Enter an employee name by selecting the name of an active employee from the List of Values. You cannot select an employee name unless you enter Employee as the supplier type. Enter the employee number if you know it and the employee name will be populated automatically. Check the *One Time* box to designate a supplier with whom you do not expect to do repeat business. Enter the SIC (standard industry code) if available. Select Minority Owned from the List of Values if the supplier is a minority-owned business. Enter minority group codes for this list of values in the QuickCodes window. Some examples are Native American, Asian, Hispanic, etc. Check the *Small Business* checkbox for tracking business with small companies. Check the *Woman Owned* checkbox for tracking business with companies owned by women.

General

If the supplier is a franchise or subsidiary, enter or select the parent supplier name from the List of Values. Enter the customer number that your supplier uses to identify your company. This number defaults to the supplier site and appears on the Oracle Purchasing standard purchase order. See Figure 12-22.

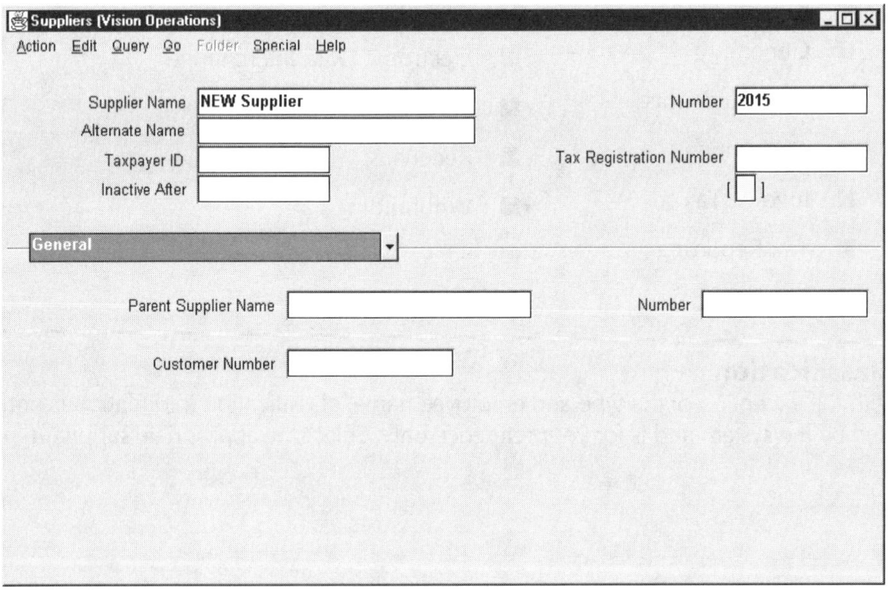

FIGURE 12-22. *Suppliers (General) form*

Bank Accounts

Use this region to view the supplier bank accounts that your suppliers will be using for electronic payment transactions. The actual setup of a supplier's bank account information is done from the Bank Account form (via the path *Setup : Banks*). Once you have entered your supplier and site information, go to the Bank Accounts form to enter the appropriate information. From the Bank Accounts region of the Suppliers form, you can select any existing bank name/bank account number that has been previously defined. You may also check the *Primary* checkbox for the primary bank account. You can also enter an effective date range for when the bank account is effective. See Figure 12-23.

Accounting

Use this region to enter the default distribution set, liability account, and prepayment account for the suppliers.

Invoice Tax

Enter the invoice tax name that represents the tax charges you generally receive on supplier invoices, and enter the offset tax name to record zero-rated taxes on

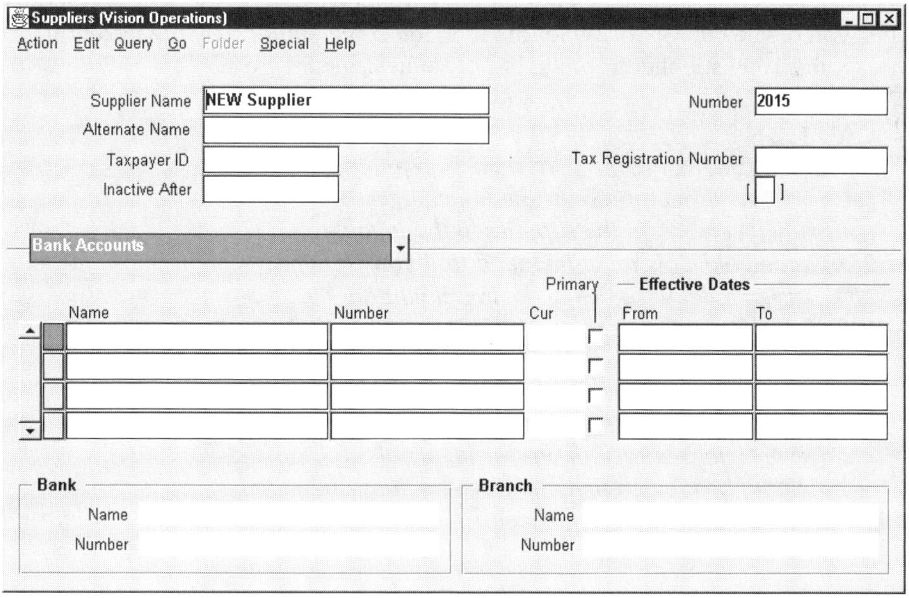

FIGURE 12-23. *Suppliers (Bank Accounts) form*

invoices. Select the calculation level at which you want Payables to automatically calculate tax for this supplier. If you enable this option by checking the *Allow Calculation Level Override* box for a supplier—during invoice entry and after you enter a tax name in the Invoices window—Payables opens a window in which you can change the calculation level. If you use automatic tax calculation, select the rounding rule method you want the system to use to round the automatically calculated tax amount. If you use automatic tax calculation at the line level, and if you want Payables to subtract the calculated tax from distributions when Payables automatically creates tax distributions, then enable the *Distribution Amounts Include Tax* option.

Tax Reporting

The following values need only be set for 1099-reportable suppliers. Check *Federal* if you must report to the IRS certain types of payments you make to the supplier. Enter a default income tax type, which defaults to purchase order lines and invoice distribution lines for 1099 reporting. Enter the reporting name if the 1099 tax reporting name for the supplier is different from the supplier name.

Once you have received and entered a supplier's taxpayer ID, enter a verification date (date received or current date) to prevent the tax information verification letter being generated for the supplier. For name control, enter the first four characters of the supplier's last name. This appears in the supplier's B record when you create the 1099 tape for the IRS. Select the appropriate organization type for the 1099 supplier from the List of Values. See Figure 12-24.

CAUTION
*In the Invoice Tax region, you can assign a default sales tax name that represents the tax charges you generally receive from the supplier in the Invoice Tax Name field. **It is recommended that you DO NOT assign a default sales tax name.** If you do, the system will force you to create a sales tax distribution line as soon as the invoice header detail is entered and it will default the accounting flexfield to the 'dummy' AP sales tax account (which must be changed). Expense distributions for invoice Item lines should be created first, then the tax lines, then either directed to an expense account or prorated over the distribution lines.*

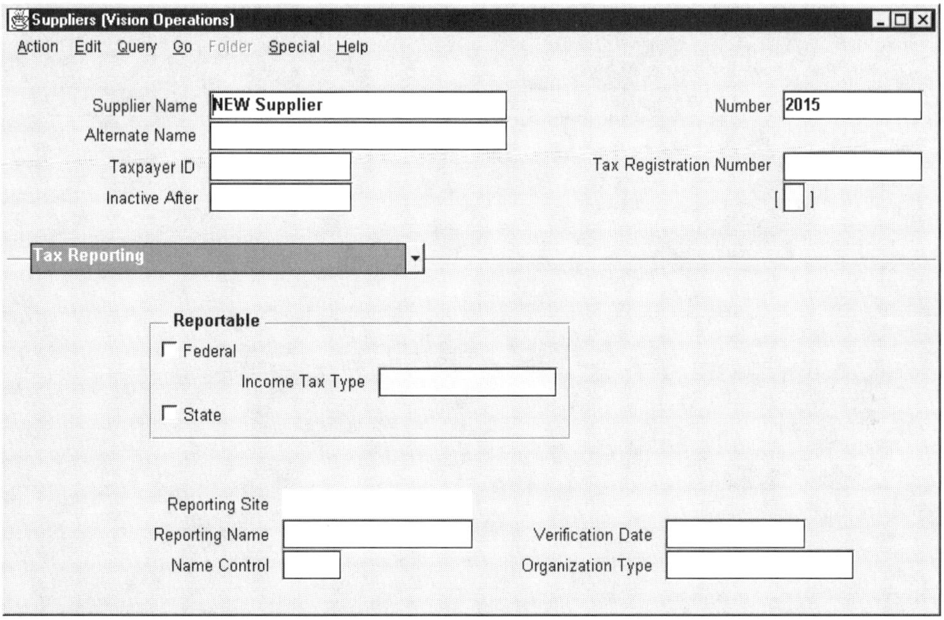
Suppliers (Vision Operations)
Action Edit Query Go Folder Special Help
Supplier Name NEW Supplier
Number 2015
Alternate Name
Taxpayer ID
Tax Registration Number
Inactive After
Tax Reporting
Reportable
Federal
Income Tax Type
State
Reporting Site
Reporting Name
Verification Date
Name Control
Organization Type

FIGURE 12-24. *Suppliers (Tax Reporting) form*

Control

Oracle Payables applies an amount hold to the invoice during invoice approval if a supplier invoice exceeds the invoice amount limit you have specified. If you want to hold future payments for this supplier, check the *Hold All Payments* box. This doesn't place invoices on hold, but does prevent payment until the value is unchecked. This is the most restrictive supplier hold, and it prevents the supplier from being selected for payment. If this is a direct pay supplier for whom you do not match invoices to purchase orders, or if the supplier is an employee, uncheck the *Hold Unmatched Invoices* box. If you enable this feature, a hold is applied to an invoice with distributions that are not matched to a purchase order. If you wish to automatically place all future invoices for the supplier on hold, check the *Hold Future Invoices* box. See Figure 12-25.

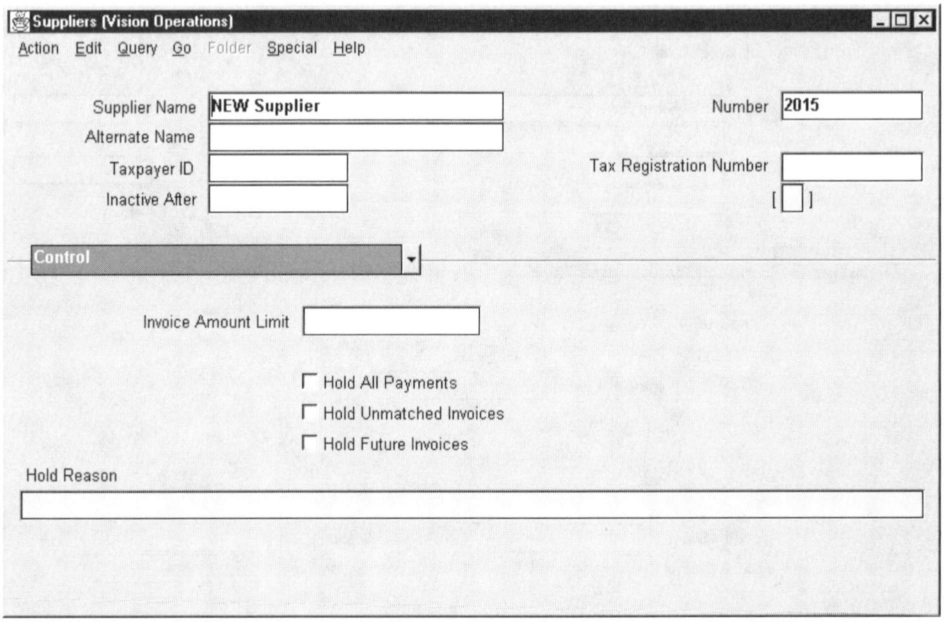

FIGURE 12-25. *Suppliers (Control) form*

Payment

Most of the options displayed are derived from the system defaults defined in the Payables options. These include: Terms, Pay Group, Payment Priority, Invoice Currency, Payment Currency, Terms Date Basis, Pay Date Basis, Payment Method, *Always Take Discount, Exclude Freight From Discount, Allow Interest Invoices*, and *Pay Alone*. Change any of these values if they are not the appropriate defaults for the supplier. For most suppliers, the default should be to *Exclude Freight From Discount* and this option should be checked. See Figure 12-26.

Electronic Data Interchange

Go to the Electronic Data Interchange (EDI) alternative region. Select the payment method from the List of Values, and select the payment format from the List of Values. Enter the remittance method, and enter remittance instructions if necessary. Select one of the standard EDI transactions codes for transaction handling. Valid transaction handling codes are Payment Accompanies Remittance Advice, Make Payment Only, Remittance Information Only, Split Payment and Remittance, or Other Handling.

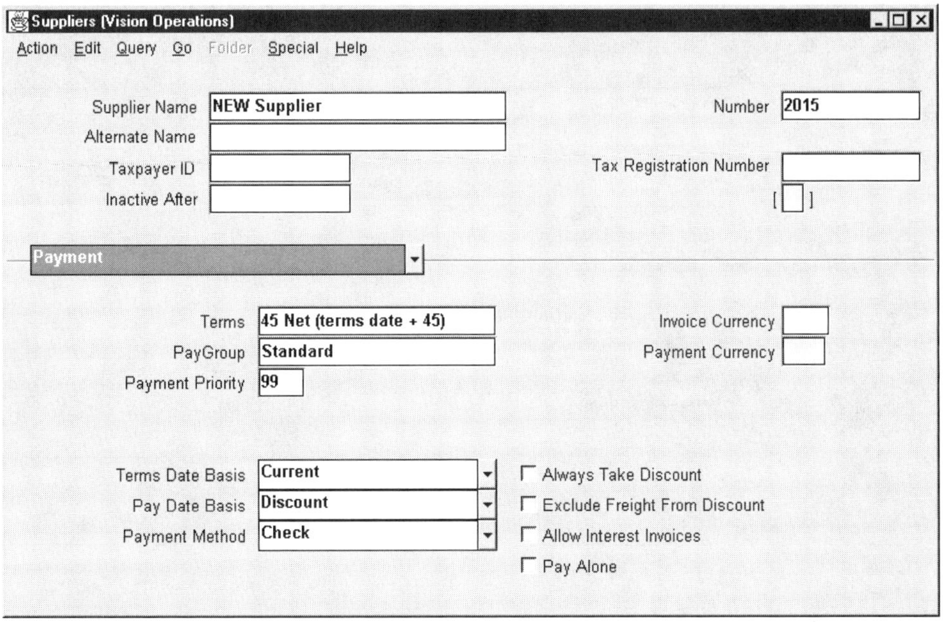

FIGURE 12-26. *Suppliers (Payment) form*

Purchasing

Most of the options displayed are derived from system defaults defined in the Purchasing options and the Payables options. Options in this region are: Ship-To Location, Bill-To Location, Ship Via, FOB, and Freight Terms. Change any of these values if they are not the appropriate defaults for this specific supplier. You can also place all new purchase orders for this supplier on hold and supply a purchasing hold reason. See Figure 12-27.

Receiving

Receiving defaults are set in the receiving options. If you enter defaults at the supplier level, they will override the receiving options when new purchase orders are entered. These options include: Enforce Ship-To Location, Receipt Routing, Invoice Matching, Qty Received Tolerance, Qty Received Exception, Days Early Receipt Allowed, Days Late Receipt Allowed, *Allow Substitute Receipts, Allow Unordered Receipts*, and Receipt Date Exception. The Enforce Ship-To Location field determines when the ship-to location is different in receiving, and whether you will receive no warning, warning, or rejection. Receipt routing can be Standard Receipt, which requires

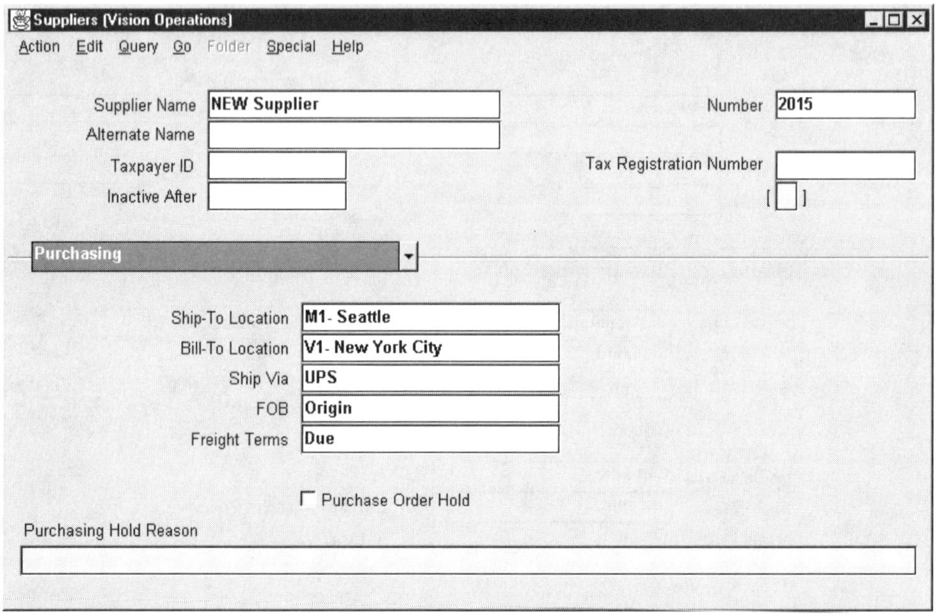

FIGURE 12-27. *Suppliers (Purchasing) form*

standard receipt and delivery; Inspection Required, which requires standard receipt, inspection, and delivery; or Direct Delivery, which requires direct receipt. Invoice matching can be two-way, three-way, four-way, or blank. The quantity received tolerance defines the threshold when the receiving quantity is different than the order quantity. The quantity received exception determines whether to give no warning, warning, or rejection when the received quantity exceeds the threshold. The Days Early and Late Receipt Allowed fields define the window when receiving can take place compared to the promise date. If the receiving is outside of the window, the Receipt Date Exception field determines whether your user will get a warning, no warning, or rejections. The *Allow Substitute Receipts* and *Allow Unordered Receipts* checkboxes determine whether your users can receive substitute items and unordered items. Make all necessary changes for this supplier, if necessary. See Figure 12-28.

Next, select the Sites alternative region, and then fill in a supplier site and supplier contact to complete the process.

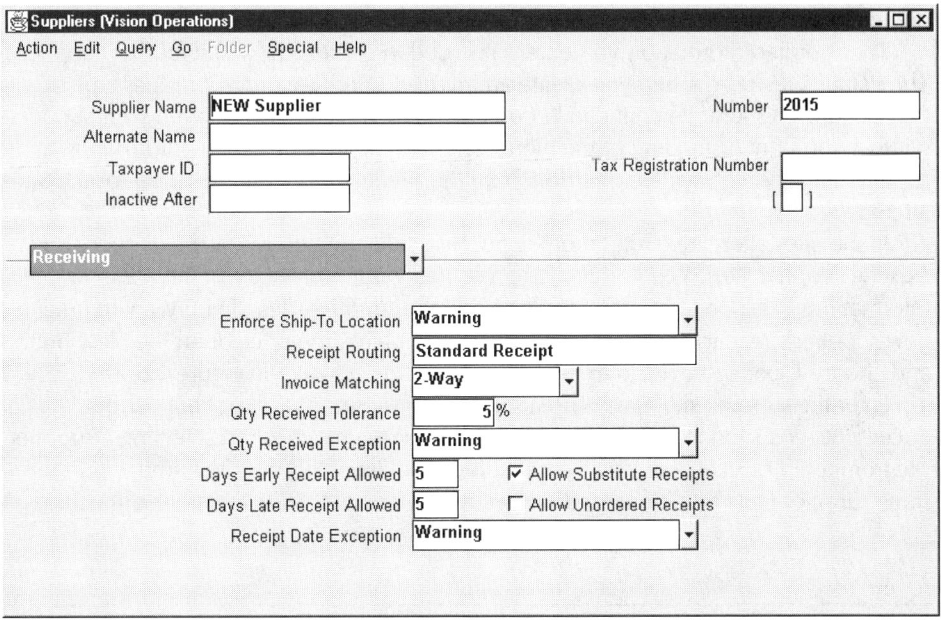

FIGURE 12-28. *Suppliers (Receiving) form*

Review Questions

   1. What is a taxpayer ID?

   2. How do you specify that all invoices for the supplier must be matched to a purchase order and a receipt?

   3. When shouldn't you set default sales tax name in the Invoice Tax region?

   4. What is the hierarchy of a supplier definition?

Defining Supplier Site Information

A supplier site is an address where your supplier conducts all or a portion of their business. Sites are classified in Oracle Purchasing as purchasing sites, RFQ only sites, and/or pay sites. You cannot enter an invoice for a supplier that has not been defined with a pay site.

The supplier information you entered is used to create a new site for that supplier. The defaults are used when you create an invoice, purchase order, or other type of transaction. This arrangement can become confusing when dealing with your suppliers without a full understanding of the hierarchy. You may change some information at the supplier level, which will be overridden by the site level. See Figure 12-29 for the Sites alternative region.

In the Sites alternative region of the Suppliers detail window, you can query/find existing supplier sites. You will first be presented with a summary of the address information. Click on the **Open** button to edit the supplier sites. If you want to enter a new supplier site, click on the **Open** button on a blank line or click on the **New** button and choose Open to navigate to the Supplier Sites window. See Figure 12-30.

Enter the supplier site name and address. The site name will not appear on documents you send to the supplier—it is for your reference when selecting a supplier site from a List of Values during transaction entry. However, the site name within the same supplier must be unique and uppercase. Enter **NEW SITE 1** as your site name,

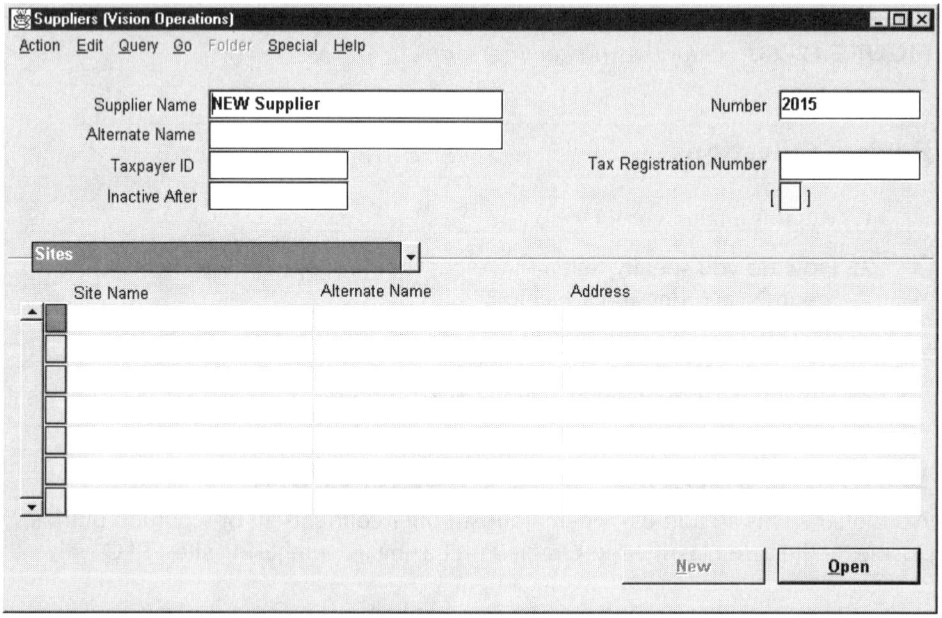

FIGURE 12-29. *Suppliers (Sites) form*

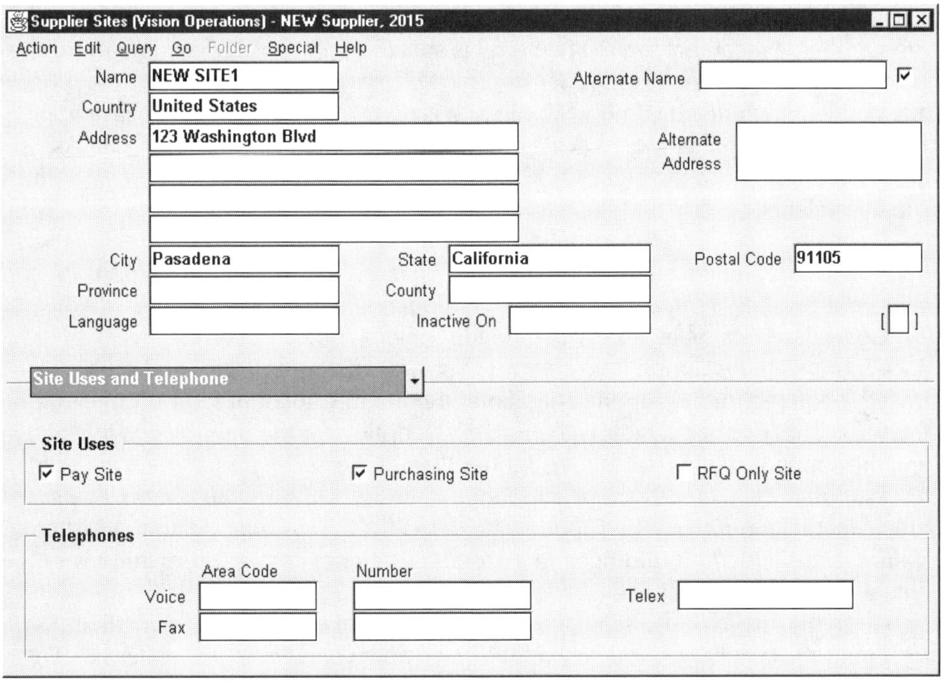

FIGURE 12-30. *Supplier Sites form*

enter an arbitrary address, then save your work. If your address is incomplete, you will get a warning message. An address is considered incomplete if you do not have address line 1, city, state, and postal code. When this step is complete, save your work.

Enter any additional supplier site information you want to record in the appropriate alternative region. Supplier information automatically defaults to the new supplier sites you enter for the supplier. You can override these defaults. You should only enter information in the Sites region if the supplier has multiple sites with different values for the following information. Supplier sites have the following regions:

- Site Uses and Telephone
- Bank Accounts
- Accounting
- Invoice Tax
- Tax Reporting
- Control
- Payment
- Electronic Data Interchange
- Purchasing
- Withholding Tax
- Contacts

The only two alternative regions unique to supplier sites are Site Uses and Telephone and Contacts. The rest of the alternative regions are the same as those of the supplier, except that the data entered is specific only to that site and not for the other supplier's sites or the supplier in general. Go to the Site Uses and Telephone alternative region first. Define what this site is used for—payment, purchasing, or RFQ only. The supplier must have a pay site to enter invoices and issue checks, and a purchasing site to enter POs. Check the appropriate site uses, then enter the supplier telephone, fax, and telex information, if available.

Once again, the Bank Accounts alternative region is used to view the supplier bank accounts that the supplier site uses for electronic payment transactions or to select existing bank/bank account combinations.

Go to the Accounting alternative region, where you can override any accounting defaults during invoice entry. Select the default distribution set for all invoices entered for the supplier site. Enter the liability account for a supplier site's invoices. The supplier default is the *Financials* option for the liability account and the supplier site default is the supplier default. Enter the prepayment account for a supplier site's invoices. The supplier default is the *Financials* option for the prepayment account and the supplier site default is the supplier default. A List of Values is available for building your account numbers, but this information is only entered at the supplier site level.

Go to the Invoice Tax alternative region and enter the invoice tax name that represents the tax charges you generally receive on invoices from a supplier site. Enter the offset tax name to record zero-rated taxes on invoices, then select the calculation level at which you want Payables to automatically calculate tax for this supplier site. If you enable this option by checking the *Allow Calculation Level Override* box for a supplier site—during invoice entry after you enter a tax name in the Invoices window—Payables opens a window where you can change the calculation level. If you use automatic tax calculation, select the rounding rule method you want the system to use to round the automatically calculated tax amount. Enable the *Distribution Amounts Include Tax* option if you use automatic tax calculation at the line level, and if you want Payables to subtract the calculated tax from distributions when Payables automatically creates tax distributions.

Go to the Tax Reporting alternative region and enable *Income Tax Reporting Site* by checking the box to select a site as the reporting site for a supplier. Payables requires one tax reporting site for each 1099 supplier for income tax reporting purposes. Enter the supplier's tax registration number—for example, a supplier's value-added tax (VAT) registration number.

Go to the Control alternative region to enter the invoice amount limit. If you enter an invoice for a supplier site that exceeds the invoice amount limit you have specified, Oracle Payables applies an amount hold to the invoice during invoice approval. If you wish to hold future payments for this supplier site, check the *Hold All Payments* box. Invoices are not placed on hold, but payment is prevented until this value is unchecked. This is the most restrictive supplier site hold, and it prevents the supplier site from being selected for payment. If this is a direct pay supplier site for which you do not match invoices to purchase orders, or if the supplier is an employee, uncheck the *Hold Unmatched Invoices* box. If you enabled this feature, a hold is applied to an invoice if it has distributions that are not matched to a purchase order. Check the *Hold Future Invoices* box if you wish to automatically place all future invoices for the supplier site on hold.

Go to the Payment alternative region, where all of the options displayed are derived from the system defaults defined in the Payables options, or from the supplier. Change any of these values if they are not the appropriate defaults for the supplier site. For most supplier sites, the default that should be checked is *Exclude Freight From Discount.*

Go to the Electronic Data Interchange alternative region and select the payment method from the List of Values. Select the payment format from the List of Values, enter the remittance method, and enter remittance instructions, if applicable. Select one of the standard EDI transactions codes for transaction handling.

Go to the Purchasing alternative region, where all of the options displayed are derived from the system defaults defined in the Purchasing options and Payables options, or from the supplier. Change any of these values if they are not the appropriate defaults for the supplier site.

Go to the Withholding Tax alternative region, where you can allow withholding tax for this supplier site. If you allow withholding tax, enter the default withholding tax group. Next, enter contact information for this supplier site, if applicable. To do this, select the Contacts alternative region.

Review Questions

1. What regions are unique to a supplier site?

2. What are the valid site uses for a supplier site?

3. What comprises a complete address without warning in Oracle Purchasing?

Identifying Supplier Contact Information by Site

Go to the Contacts alternative region, where contact information is for your reference only and is not used by the system. See Figure 12-31. Enter all information available for this contact site, including: last name, first name, middle initial, prefix, title, telephone number, and mail stop. Prefix is whether the contact is Mr., Mrs., or another designation. Title is the title of the contact such as Buyer, President, or other. Enter the inactive date after which this contact will no longer appear on the contact list for this supplier site, if applicable. You can have as many contacts as you need for each supplier site. Save your work after creating contacts.

Review Questions

1. What is a prefix?

2. What is a title?

3. How many contacts can you have for each supplier site?

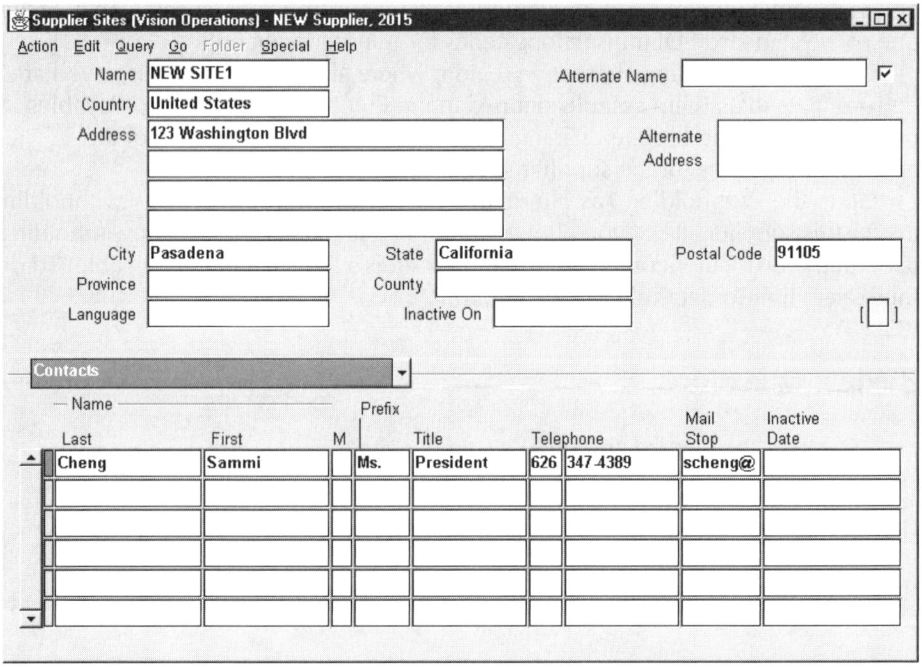

FIGURE 12-31. *Supplier Contacts form*

Merging Suppliers

In case of a merger between two vendors, a data entry error, or company acquisition, you can use the Vendor Merge function to merge the vendors and their existing purchase orders and invoices. The Vendor Merge function can also be used to merge duplicate vendors or vendor sites. Oracle provides the option of merging existing purchase orders alone or only invoices, or both. An old vendor site can be copied to a new vendor, or it can be merged with an existing new vendor site.

The first step is to determine the vendors to be merged. You can submit the Vendors report or Vendor Audit report to identify duplicate vendors. The system identifies vendors with the same name but in different case as different vendors. For example, Oracle Financials considers "Oracle" and "ORACLE" to be two different vendors.

The navigation path to the Supplier Merge window is *Supply Base: Supplier Merge.* The Supplier Merge window will appear. See Figure 12-32. Specify merge criteria for existing invoices (All, Unpaid, or None), and specify whether to merge existing purchase orders by checking the *PO* checkbox. Enter the name of the old supplier and supplier site to be merged or select from the List of Values. Specify whether to copy the old site or merge the old site with an existing new supplier site. Copy means to create another copy of the site and merge with the new supplier. Merge will not keep a copy and will simply repoint to the new supplier. Enter the name of the new supplier and site to be merged into or select from the List of Values. Click on the **Merge** button to initiate the merge process. To avoid excess use of this feature, it is important to establish and maintain a corporate naming standard for your suppliers and customers.

Oracle Applications will display a Caution dialog box warning that the Merge function is irreversible. Click on the **OK** button to continue. The system will submit a concurrent request that automatically prints two reports: the Purchase Order Header Updated report and the Vendor Merge report. You can navigate to Help View My Request to view the status of concurrent requests, and you should also review the reports produced by the processes. The Oracle system will not merge invoices if it creates duplicate invoices. The Vendor Merge report identifies any duplicate invoices. Update the unpaid and unposted invoice numbers and resubmit the merge process. Save the reports for future reference and audit purposes.

Review Questions

1. What is the difference between Copy Site and Merge Site?

2. Which two reports will be automatically generated by the supplier merge process?

3. Which options should you select if you want to merge all invoices and purchase orders?

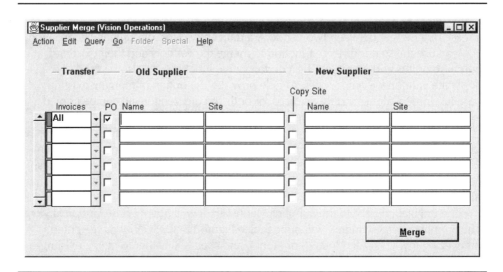

FIGURE 12-32. *Supplier Merge form*

Creating Purchase Requisitions

In this section, you will learn to manually create purchase requisitions, which are internal requests for purchase orders. Manual purchase requisitions are initiated by the requestor, with requisition lines for each requested item. If the preparer—the person who enters the purchase requisition—is different from the requestor, then Oracle Purchasing will record both employees. You can also import requisitions from other Oracle Applications, like Oracle Inventory and Oracle MRP, or other third-party systems by using Requisition Import, which imports purchase requisitions from open interface into the production tables in Oracle Purchasing. In this section, you will learn to:

- Create a purchase requisition
- Set up a requisition template
- Use the Order Pad in the Supplier Item Catalog

Creating a Purchase Requisition

Online requisitions eliminate paper and allow the buyer to minimize data entry by converting online requisitions to purchase orders, with minimal keystrokes.

Purchase requisition has three levels in Oracle Purchasing. It has a requisition header that has the requisition type, description, status, and total. Each requisition header has requisition lines that contain the items, need-by date, price, and quantity. Each requisition line has distributions that have the charge account, budget account, variance account, accrual account, and project-related information. Purchase requisition lines in Oracle Purchasing can automatically create purchase orders with the AutoCreate function once the requisition has been approved. The navigation path to the Requisition window is *Requisitions: Requisitions*. See Figure 12-33.

Enter the header information in the Requisitions window. Enter the requisition number if manual numbering is enabled. If automatic numbering has been enabled, you will bypass this field and the number will be assigned when you save your work. The document type defaults to Purchase Requisition, and you can select from the List of Values to enter either Purchase Requisition (demand satisfied by an outside supplier and purchase order) or Internal (demand satisfied from your own inventory and internal

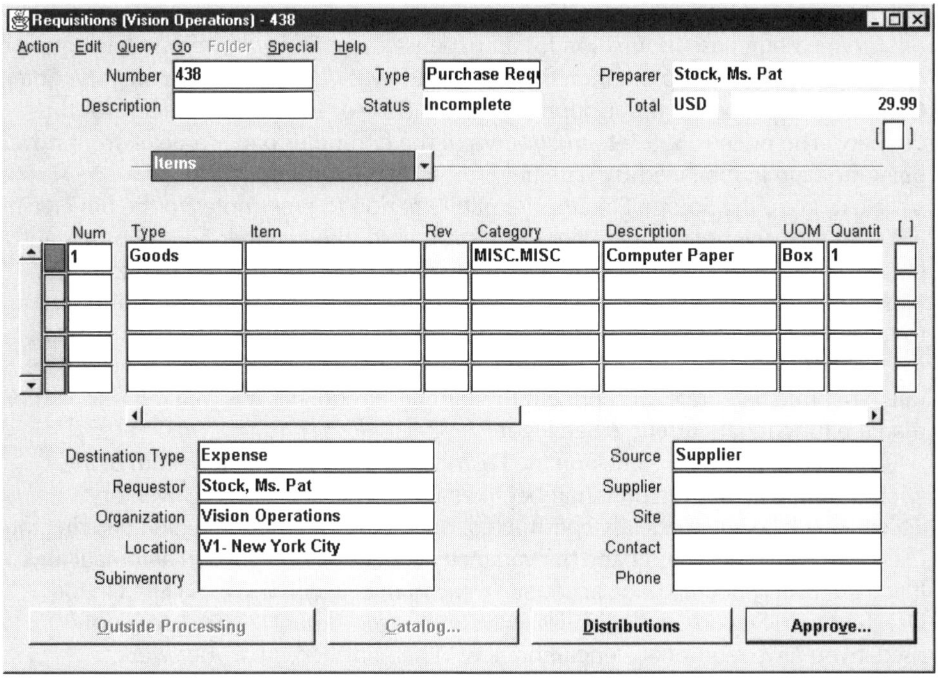

FIGURE 12-33. *Requisitions form*

sales order). When you source detail lines, they can be independent of the document type. You can also mix requisition lines that source from both supplier and inventory, even though the document type is Purchase Requisition or Internal. The preparer name automatically defaults for the user sign-on. Enter a description for your requisition; the currency will automatically default for your setup. The Status and Total fields are populated when the requisition is saved.

Go to the Lines alternative region to enter your line information. The line number and the line type will be automatically assigned by the system; you can override the default line type, which is derived from the Purchasing options. You can use the List of Values to select from the types that have been defined in your system. If you are requesting an inventory item, enter the item number; if it is an expense item, skip the Item field. A List of Values is available to assist in finding item numbers. A List of Values for the category is available, and a description will be defaulted for an inventory item but must be entered for expense items—it is a mandatory field. Enter the unit of measure, but if you entered an item number, unit of measure will default from the item master. Enter the quantity you are requesting. Oracle Purchasing will default the price for the item, if available, or from an established sourcing rule. If not, enter in a unit price greater than or equal to zero. You can also enter the need-by date, which is only required for planned items.

Create a purchase requisition for an expense item. Say you are purchasing a box of computer paper. Skip the Item field and enter **MISC.MISC** for the category. Enter **Computer Paper** as the description and select Box for UOM, and enter 1 for the quantity. The price is $29.99, and you want the computer paper a week from now. Enter the date in the Need-By date field, then save your work.

Next, go to the Source Details alternative region to enter notes to the buyer. This includes the buyer name, whether RFQ is required, the supplier item number, and the document type. Document type can be blanket purchase order or quotation. Next, go to the Details alternative region to enter the urgent flag, justification, note to receiver, transaction nature, reference number, UN number, and hazard class.

Next, go to the Currency alternative region and enter an alternative currency, rate type, rate date, rate, and price if the purchase requisition is in a currency other than the functional currency. See Figure 12-34.

If it is an expense line, click on the **Distributions** button on the bottom of the window and enter the account number to charge. See Figure 12-35. Inventory accounts will be automatically constructed, but can be overridden. Upon entering the charge account, the accrual and the variance account will be filled in automatically. If you are using encumbrance accounting, the budget account will be filled in too. Use the Miscellaneous account alias for your charge account. A GL date is only used if you have requisitions encumbrance. When finished, save your work.

If the purchase requisition is project related, go to the Project alternative region and enter the project, task, expenditure type, expenditure organization, expenditure date, and the project quantity.

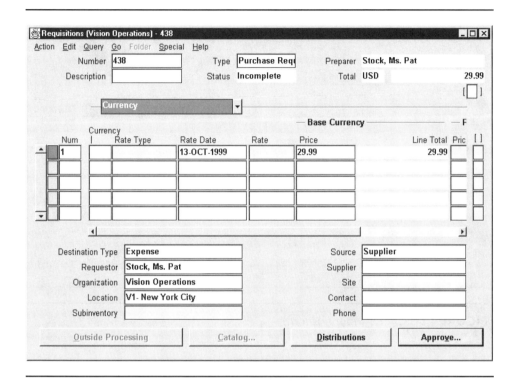

FIGURE 12-34. *Requisitions (Currency) form*

Close the Distributions window and go back to the Requisitions window. Then, go to the lower part of the window below the Alternative Region section to complete the requisition. These are fields where defaults can be set in the Requisition Preferences window. For the destination type, choose Expense if goods are to be delivered to an expense location or Inventory if goods are to be received into inventory. Enter the name of the employee requesting the item(s) (the default is the preparer). Enter the organization and location names. If the destination type is Inventory, enter the subinventory. For supplier, you have three options: select an active supplier from the List of Values, enter in a supplier name if not a current supplier, or leave it blank to have a buyer assigned. If you have a suggested supplier site, enter that site name. Enter the contact name and phone number, if available, for the selected supplier. This information will be used during the AutoCreate step.

To facilitate data entry, you can use the Special | Preferences menu command to enter default information that will be defaulted for the lines in your new requisition. Default information includes the need-by date, GL date, charge account, justification,

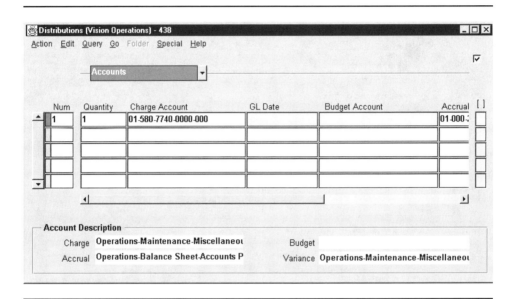

FIGURE 12-35. *Distributions form*

reference number, transaction nature, urgent, requestor, destination type, deliver-to organization, deliver-to location, currency, exchange rates, source type, and project information. If the purchase requisition is an internal requisition, then you can enter a default note to the receiver. If purchase requisition lines are source Inventory, then enter a default subinventory. If purchase requisition lines are source Supplier, enter the default buyer, a note to buyer, that RFQ is required, supplier, supplier site, supplier contact, and phone. Click on the **Apply** button to apply the entered defaults, and you will save a great deal of time and errors when entering large requisitions.

If budgetary control is enabled, you can perform fund checks using the Special | Check Funds menu command. This will check if the funds are available. If they are, then you can encumber the requisitions. This encumbrance will be transferred to the purchase order where these requisition lines went to automatically.

Click on the **Approve** button to approve your requisition and the Approve Document window will open. See Figure 12-36. The completed requisition can be submitted to an approver for approval. If your setup allows, you can forward the requisition to another employee, along with an optional note. If you want to print the purchase requisitions, check the *Print* box. Select Submit for Approval and click on the **OK** button.

The approver can use the Approve Document form to approve, forward, reserve, accept, or reject submitted requisitions. Before requisition approval, the

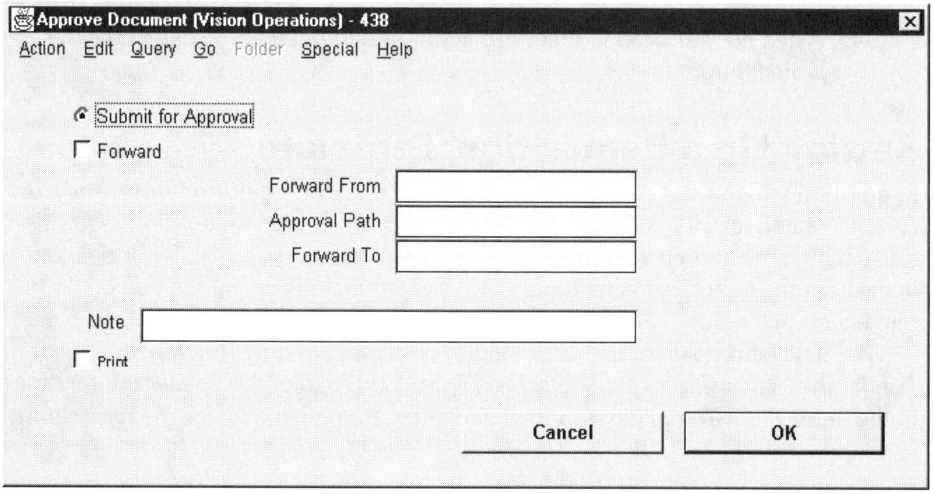

FIGURE 12-36. *Requisition Approval form*

requisition can be viewed or modified by the approver. A rejected request returns to the requestor. Using the Forward Documents form, an approver can forward all or selected documents awaiting approval to a new approver. If you wish, a designated administrator can use the Enter Signature Approvals form to update the approval status of documents when the designated approver does not have access to Oracle Purchasing. Requisitions returned as Not Approved can be modified by the requestor and resubmitted for approval from the Enter Requisitions form. Using the Control Requisitions form, the requestor either modifies or cancels the returned requisition. Optionally, the purchasing manager can review the pool of approved requisitions and assign requisitions to buyers by using the Assign Requisitions form. Buyers view assigned requisitions and can make modifications if required, but they must be reapproved before becoming revalidated for purchase order creation. Buyers use the AutoCreate Purchase Orders program to automatically create purchase orders. The requestor can view the status of a request at any time during the process.

Review Questions

1. Who is a preparer and who is a requestor?

2. When do you enter an item number on a purchase requisition?

3. How can a requisition be approved?

4. When do you need to enter project information and how can you enter project information?

Setting Up a Requisition Template

Requisition templates are used to streamline the entry of requisition lines. They can be created for all frequently ordered items, or even from an existing requisition, thus saving time and preventing possible errors. You can modify, add, or delete items from the template at any time. Once the template is defined, it can be referenced in the Supplier Item Catalog.

The navigation path to the Requisition Templates window is *Setup: Purchasing: Requisition Templates.* See Figure 12-37. Enter the header information in the Requisition Templates window, and enter a unique name for the requisition

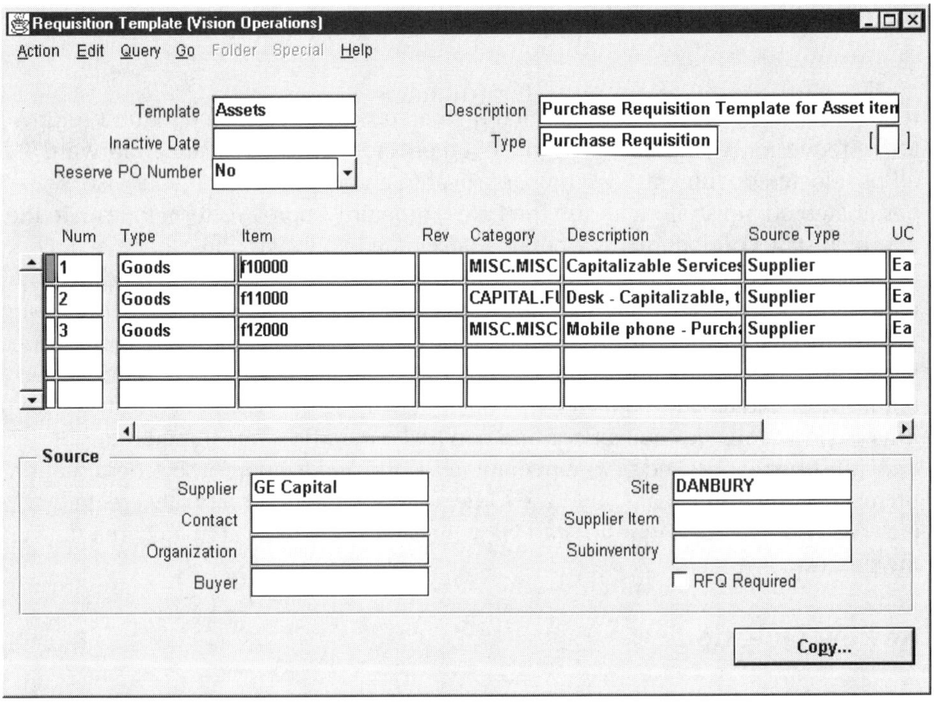

FIGURE 12-37. *Requisition Templates form*

template and a description for the template. If you want to inactivate the template on a certain date, then enter an inactive date. Otherwise, leave the field blank. Then, enter Internal or Purchase for the requisition type. If you selected Yes in the Reserve PO Number field when the requisition was created, then the system will reserve a purchase order number.

Next, manually add lines to a template and enter a number to identify the sequence of the line on your requisition. If you do not manually enter a line number, Oracle Purchasing provides default sequence numbers in increments of 1. Enter the line type and item number, and enter the item revision number (for inventory items only), if applicable. If an item was entered, Oracle Purchasing will display a purchasing category that cannot be changed. If you are buying an expense item, skip the Item field and enter a purchasing category. If it is an inventory item, the system will automatically display the item description from the item master. Otherwise, type in a description for the expense item. Select the source type from the List of Values; available choices are based on profile options. Enter the unit of measure. For supplier-sourced lines, you can enter the unit of measure, but this field is not available for inventory-sourced lines.

Enter sourcing information for the current line in the lower part of the window. For supplier source type lines, enter the name of the buyer for this requisition template. The buyers will be able to query requisition lines assigned to them during AutoCreate. Check the *RFQ Required* checkbox to indicate that you want to require an RFQ before the buyer can create a purchase order for a particular requisition. If you attempt to create the purchase order without a required RFQ, Oracle will display a warning message.

By using the List of Values, you can enter a suggested supplier for your requisition items. You can also suggest a new supplier by entering the name of the new supplier. For supplier source type lines, enter the supplier site. You can only enter this field if you provide a suggested supplier name. Select a supplier site from the List of Values and enter a new site if needed. In supplier type, enter the contact and supplier or manufacturer item number. For inventory source type lines, you can specify the source organization and subinventory source. If you do enter this information, Oracle Order Entry uses the specified subinventory for allocation.

For inventory source type lines, you can also specify the subinventory source. Also, if there is no on-hand quantity at the designated subinventory, the item will be back-ordered even though on-hand quantities may exist in other subinventory locations.

To copy lines to a template, click on the **Copy** button at the bottom of the window to open the Base Document window. See Figure 12-38. You can use the List of Values to select the base document type of Purchase Order or Requisition. Enter the base document number from which you want to copy lines over to the template. Click on the **OK** button to copy all lines of the base document onto the template. Click on the **Cancel** button to return to the Requisition Templates window without copying. You can perform this operation on multiple documents in one template.

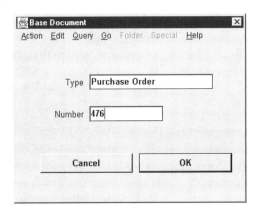

FIGURE 12-38. *Base Document form*

Query up the Assets requisition template in the Vision database and review them.

Review Questions

1. For what is the Reserve PO Number field used?

2. Which setup drives the valid values for source type?

3. When do you have to enter an item category?

4. How do you copy multiple documents into one template?

Using the Order Pad in the Supplier Item Catalog

Using the Order Pad, you can enter requisition lines by clicking on the **Catalog** button to open the Search Supplier Item Catalog window. This allows for a search of catalog items by commodity, requisition template, category set, category, item with revision, item description, supplier, supplier site, supplier item, due date, deliver-to organization, line type, deliver-to locations, UOM, or currency. To use requisition templates, select the desired requisition template and click on the **Find** button. To use other search criteria, enter them and click on the **Find** button. See Figure 12-39.

Now, you will search for items to place on the Order Pad. Use the search criteria in the Item Description field to retrieve prior purchases with the keywords you specified in the field. Use generic words to make your search more effective.

Once the search has retrieved past purchases or requisition templates, select the lines to place on your Order Pad. Click your cursor on the down arrow of the Order

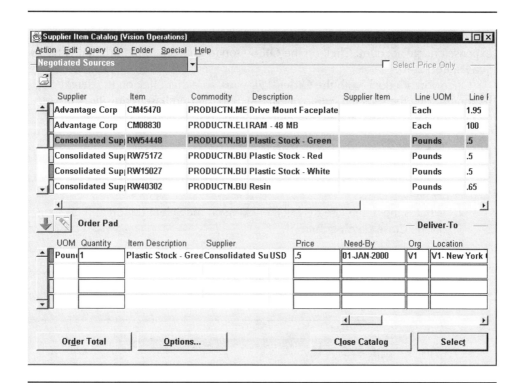

FIGURE 12-39. *Supplier Item Catalog form*

Pad and the lines will be filled into the Order Pad. Alternately, you can double-click on the supplier item you want to purchase to fill in the Order Pad. You can use the Eraser icon on the top toolbar to erase any line from the Order Pad. Then, enter the quantity, price, need-by date, organization, location, destination type, and subinventory on your Order Pad line. You can use the Options form to enter default values, and you can select as many supplier items you want. Click on the **Select** button to add the lines to your requisition—this action will close the Supplier Item Catalog window—then return to completing your requisition. If you want to see the order total, click on the **Order Total** button.

You can check the *Select Price Only* checkbox in order to only select price from the Supplier Item Catalog. In this case, you will not be able to use the Order Pad. Once you have saved the requisition, your only option is to enable *Select Price Only*.

Through the Order Pad Options window, you can control the default values used in the Order Pad. This is done by clicking on the **Options** button when using the Order Pad. In the Options window, you can specify default options: whether to default from options or from the previous line. You can also specify the default need-by date, destination type, organization, location, requestor, subinventory, and expense charge account. Click on the **OK** button to go back to the original window. See Figure 12-40.

Once you are done with the Order Pad, you can either click on the **Select** button to bring the selected catalog items back to the purchase requisition, or you can click on the **Close Catalog** button to cancel the selection.

Review Questions

1. How can you use requisition templates to enter requisition lines?

2. What is the difference between clicking on the **Select** button and clicking on the **Close Catalog** button?

3. What is the purpose of the *Select Price Only* checkbox?

4. For what do you use the Order Pad Options window?

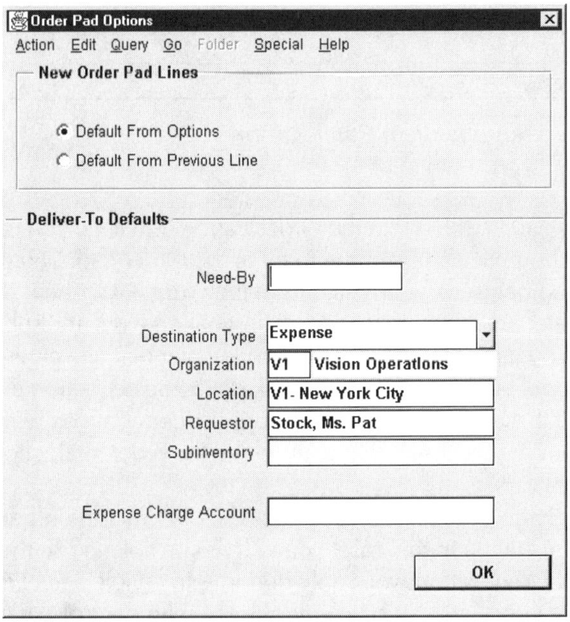

FIGURE 12-40. *Order Pad Options form*

Creating Standard Purchase Orders

In this section, you will learn how to create standard purchase orders. You can enter purchase orders manually or you can AutoCreate purchase orders from purchase requisitions.

Creating a Standard Purchase Order

Standard purchase orders can be created for all types of goods and services. The purchase order has a header that consists of one or more lines. Each line can consist of one or more shipments, and each shipment can consist of one or more distributions. The purchase order header contains supplier, supplier site, and purchase order type information. Lines contain information about the items, shipments define where the purchasing line ships, and distributions define the deliver-to locations. In other words, the purchase order contains one more level than a requisition and includes the header, line, shipment, and distribution level. The requisition contains the header, line, and distribution level. At the start of each session, set the purchase order preferences that will default values to your purchase order, just like you would for requisitions. You must be defined as a buyer to create purchase orders.

To create a standard purchase order and open the Purchase Orders window, follow the navigation path *Purchase Orders: Purchase Orders*. See Figure 12-41.

Enter the header information in the Purchase Orders window. If manual numbering was enabled in the purchase options, then use a unique purchase order number. You needn't enter data in this field if automatic number generation was enabled. The purchase order will be generated when the work is saved, and a revision number is generated when changes are made and the work is saved after a purchase order was approved or printed (depending on your setup), then modified. For the type, select Standard Purchase Order from the List of Values. The system date will be displayed as the creation date and is display only. Enter the name of the supplier or select an active supplier from the List of Values. You cannot change the supplier once the purchase order has been approved. If a change in supplier is required, you must cancel the purchase order and create a new one. Next, enter the supplier site. If the supplier has only one defined site, then the site will automatically default into this field. Once the purchase order is approved, you can change the supplier site only if the *PO: Change Supplier Site* profile option is set to Yes. If you change the supplier site, the revision will be incremented, and will require reapproval. Select the supplier contact from the List of Values or accept the default.

Next, enter the ship-to and bill-to addresses, which will default if they are defined as defaults in Supplier Entry form. You can accept the default or change it, but the currency default in the Set of Books is tied to the purchasing operating unit. This currency will be overwritten by a different supplier setup. The buyer name defaults

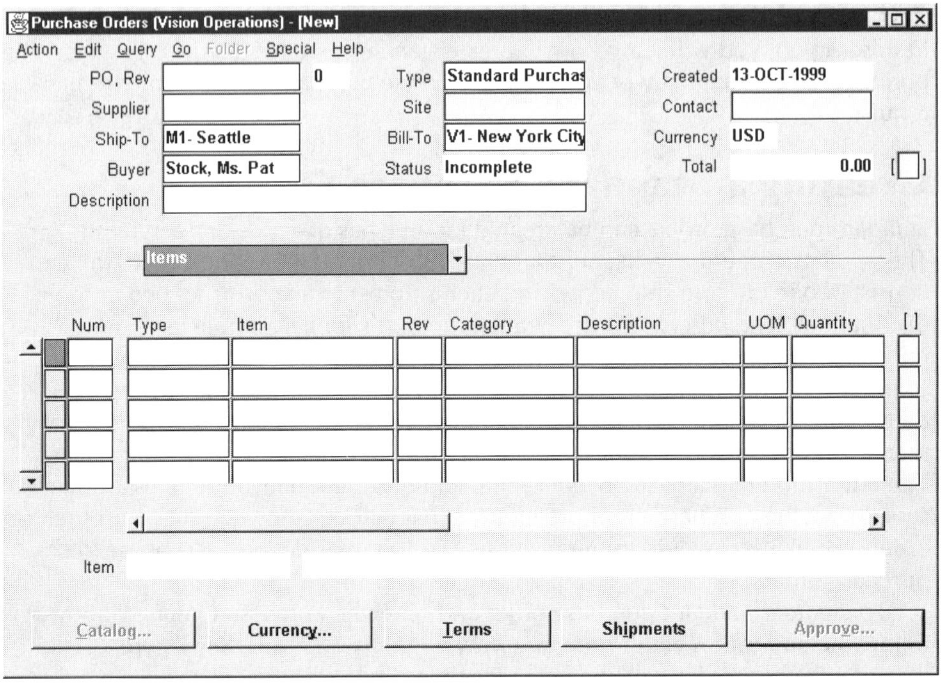

FIGURE 12-41. *Purchase Orders form*

from the user sign-on when the *Enforce Buyer Name* option in the purchasing options is set to Yes. If set to Yes, you cannot change the defaulted value. If not, you can enter a buyer from the List of Values. The Status and Total fields are display only. Statuses are Incomplete (PO being created or modified), Approved, Requires Reapproval (PO was approved but has been modified), and In Process (PO has been forwarded for approval). The Total field will automatically track the sum of the purchase order as lines are added. Enter an optional description—which is for internal use only and does not print on the standard purchase order form—for the purchase order. Use **NEW Supplier** as the supplier of the PO.

Click on the **Currency** button to change any currency information defaults. See Figure 12-42. The defaults are the functional currency information defined in your Set of Books. You can accept or change the values. If you do change currency, pricing on existing line items is not converted to the new currency. You can enter rate data only if the currency is different from your base currency. Click on the **Done** button to apply your changes or after your review, or the **Cancel** button to

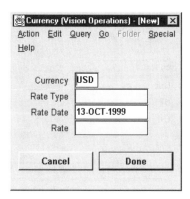

FIGURE 12-42.   *Currency form*

cancel your entries and return to the Purchase Orders window. Since your PO is in USD, you needn't enter any currency information. Click on the **Cancel** button to go back.

Click on the **Terms** button to change any default terms from the supplier information. In the Terms window, you can enter or change payment terms, freight terms, freight carrier, FOB point, mark for confirming order, mark as firm order, require acceptance and acceptance date, supplier note, and receiver note. When you are done reviewing or updating, close the Terms and Conditions window and return to the Purchase Orders window. See Figure 12-43.

Input the basic line item information in the Items alternative region. The Oracle system will automatically generate a line number for each line you create, starting with number one. Select the type from List of Values, and enter an item number if applicable. Enter the item revision number from the List of Values, or accept the default. The description will default from the item master for items. If purchasing expense goods or services, you must manually add the description. You can change the item description if the item attributes were set to allow this type of change. Enter the unit of measure. You can change the unit of measure until the item is received or billed. Enter a quantity greater than zero, and enter the unit price for the item. For service items, the unit price will be the service cost and the quantity will be 1. You can also enter the need-by date noted by the requestor, and the supplier's item number. Reserve, which is used only for encumbrance accounting, indicates whether funds are reserved for the purchase order line. See Figure 12-44. Select MISC.MISC as your item category and use Computer Paper as the item description. Enter **Box** as the UOM, **1** as the quantity, and **$20.00** as the price.

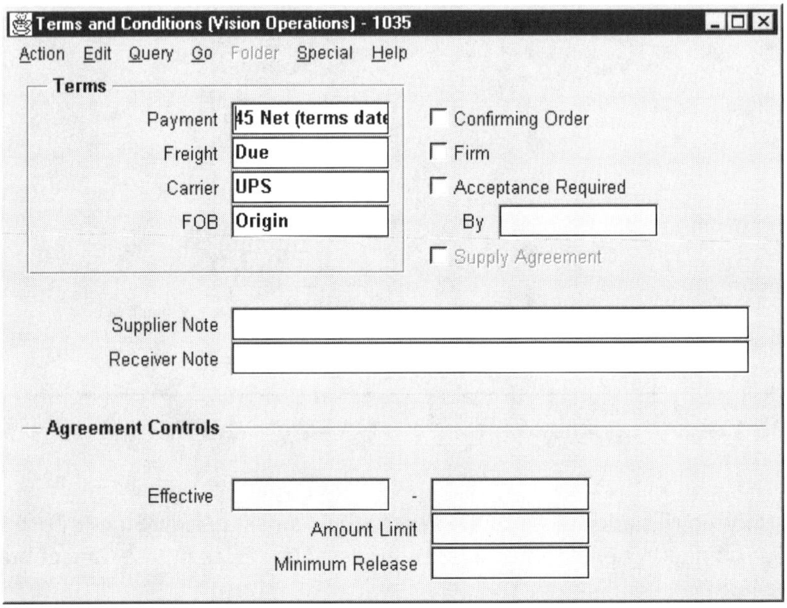

FIGURE 12-43. *Terms and Conditions form*

Enter basic pricing information in the Price Reference alternative region. See Figure 12-45. The number defaults for the item line number. You can also enter the item's list price (used in the Saving Analysis report), and the item's market price (used in the Saving Analysis report if a list price has not been entered). Enter the price type from the List of Values, and check the *Allow Price Override* box for planned purchase orders and blanket purchase agreements only. This allows the release price to be greater than the purchase agreement price. Enter an upper price limit for the price override—this will be the maximum allowable price for an item. Check the *Negotiated* checkbox if the price was negotiated with the supplier.

Enter reference information related to your purchase order lines in the Reference Documents alternative region. See Figure 12-46. The number defaults from the item line number. You can also enter the contract purchase agreement number. The contract must be for the supplier entered in the header. Oracle Purchasing displays

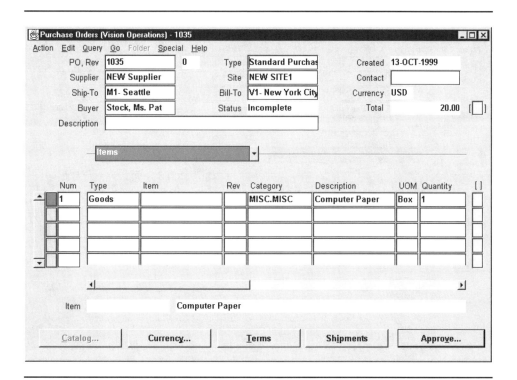

FIGURE 12-44.   *Purchase Orders (Items) form*

quotation, quotation line, quotation type, and supplier quotation number if a quotation was selected from the Supplier Item Catalog or Supplier Item Attributes window.

Enter various miscellaneous information for purchase order lines in the More alternative region. The number defaults from the item line number. You can also enter a note to the supplier, UN identification number, hazard class, and transaction nature, which is a lookup code. Check the *Capital Expense* box if the purchase is for capital expenditures. Use the Attachments feature if you want to enter unlimited notes or other documents.

You can click on the **Shipments** button to enter multiple shipments for each standard purchase order line entered. You can also click on the **Shipments** button to edit the shipment line information that was automatically created when you entered

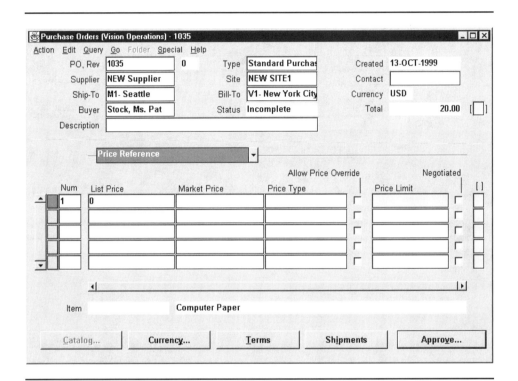

FIGURE 12-45. *Purchase Orders (Price Reference) form*

the line information. The accounting distribution is also accessed through the Shipments window, which you can open by clicking on the **Shipments** button.

Enter or edit your shipment information in the Shipments alternative region window. See Figure 12-47. Enter the line number for the shipment line. If you enter a new shipment line, the system will display the next sequential line number. You can enter any line number that does not already exist. (Pay attention to where you are on this form—it can get confusing very quickly.) Enter the ship-to organization, and keep in mind that this field cannot be updated once the order has been saved, and that you can only select from the List of Values organizations that the item has been assigned to. Enter the ship-to location for the organization. The unit of measure will default from the item line information. If you are splitting the shipments for the purchase order line, enter the quantity for this shipment line and continue adding lines to equal the sum of the item line quantity. The promise date will default from the order line or the Purchase

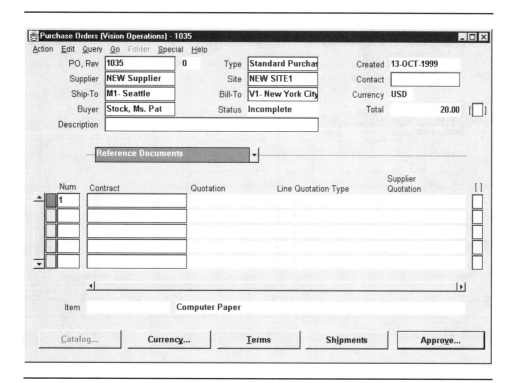

FIGURE 12-46. *Purchase Orders (Reference Documents) form*

Order Preference window; change this date if necessary. The need-by date will default from the order line; change this date if necessary. The need-by date will print on the standard purchase order if you did not enter a promise date. You must provide a need-by date for planned items. The Original Promise field will display the original promise date if the promise date is changed. Checking the *Taxable* checkbox makes the line taxable. Enter the tax name, which defaults from the Purchase Order Preference and Purchasing Options windows, if the shipment is taxable. The charge account will be created based on the account generation setups. The Amount field shows the shipment line total. Check the *Reserved* checkbox if the line was reserved when the requisition was created.

You can review and change receiving information in the More alternative region of the Shipments window. The number defaults from the shipment line number. Enter the receipt close tolerance because Purchasing automatically closes the shipment for

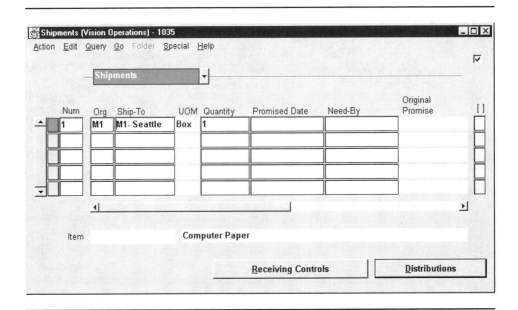

FIGURE 12-47. *Shipments (Shipments) form*

receiving if the shipment is within the receiving close tolerance. Enter the invoice close tolerance percent because Purchasing automatically closes a shipment for invoicing if it is within the invoice closing tolerance at billing. Select an invoice-matching option (two-, three-, or four-way matching). Check the *Accrue on Receipt* checkbox to indicate that shipment line items will accrue upon receipt. Check the *Firm* checkbox if Planning should not reschedule this shipment during the next MRP process.

The Status alternative region of the Shipments window displays the current status of this shipment line, including status, quantity ordered, quantity received, quantity cancelled, and quantity billed. See Figure 12-48.

Use the Receiving Controls form to enter receiving control information for purchase orders. See Figure 12-49. The receiving control options you enter in this form will override the site settings in the receiving controls setup or profile options. Define the receipt window by the Days Early and Days Late fields, and determine if your users are receiving outside of the receipt window, whether your user should receive a warning, no warning, or rejection. You can also enter the maximum acceptable over-receipt tolerance percent. Next, enter whether your user should receive a warning, no warning, or rejection when the quantity is over the over-receipt tolerance percent. You can also determine whether substitute items can be received, what the

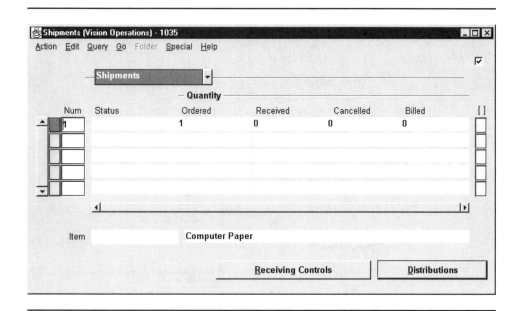

FIGURE 12-48. *Shipments (Status) form*

receipt routing should be, and whether the receiving location must be the same as the ship-to location. If the receiving location is not the same as the ship-to location, then you can choose whether you will receive a warning, no warning, or rejection. Click on the **OK** button to accept the entered receiving controls or click on the **Cancel** button to cancel the entered defaults.

Once you have entered the shipment information, update the account distribution information by clicking on the **Distributions** button. All accounts should default based on the Account Generator rules defined. If you need to modify the accounts generated, click on the **Distributions** button, make the necessary changes, and then return to the Shipments form. Once you have returned, select the Distributions alternative region.

In the Distributions alternative region, the number defaults sequentially starting at 1. Enter the destination type: Expense, Inventory, or Shop Floor. Depending on the item entered, the type will default. The destination determines the final destination of the purchased item. You can also enter the requestor, deliver-to, and subinventory (if the destination type is inventory) information for this shipment. Enter the quantity you wish to charge to this account. The default value comes from the quantity entered in the Shipments window. Enter the charge account from the List of Values. For outside processing items, you will not be able to enter this field. The GL date is only for encumbrance accounting to specify when to reserve the funds.

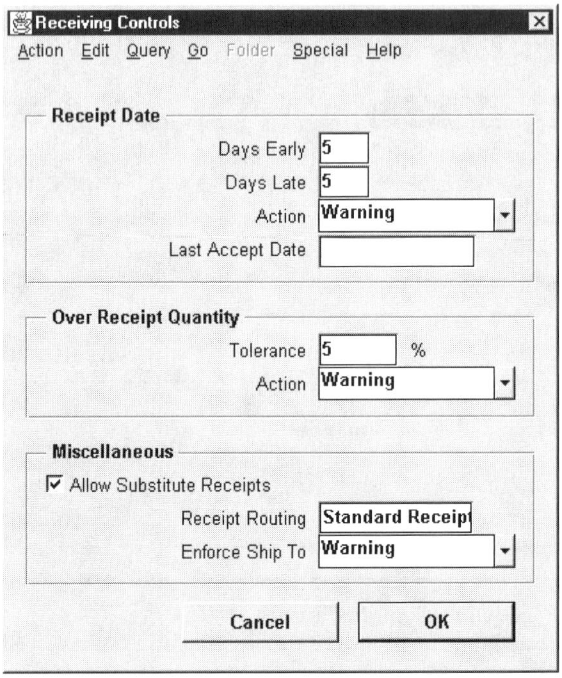

FIGURE 12-49. *Receiving Controls form*

Review requisition information in the More alternative region of the Distributions window. If the distribution is derived from an online requisition, then the requisition number, line, and online requisition will be displayed but cannot be updated. If the distribution does not come from an online requisition, enter the paper requisition information. The default of a paper requisition would be derived from the Purchase Order Preferences window. If the base currency is different than the line currency, enter the rate date and rate. The Account Generator automatically generates the accrual account. Use the Miscellaneous account alias for your charge account. Save your work after validating your account distributions.

In the Project alternative region—if the purchase order is project related—you must enter the project, task, expenditure type, expenditure organization, expenditure date, and the project quantity, similar to what was done for purchase requisition.

Close the Distributions and Shipments windows, return to the Purchase Orders window, and the purchase order is now complete. If you are under budgetary control, use the Special | Check Funds menu command to check fund availability. To approve the purchase order, click on the **Approve** button. See Figure 12-50. You will move to the Approve Document window, where you can check the *Submit for Approval* box and click on the **OK** button. The purchase order will move through Workflow, and the status will change to In-Process and then Approved once the order has been approved. When approved, you can receive against the purchase order. You can also forward the purchase order to another employee, add a note, or print the purchase order. Check the *Submit for Approval* checkbox and click on the **OK** button to approve the document. You will receive a message stating that the document has been submitted for approval.

Review Questions

1. How many levels does a purchase order have and what are they?

2. When do you need to click on the **Currency** button?

3. When will you have a new revision for a purchase order?

4. What is the difference between ship-to locations and deliver-to locations, and what levels are they at in a purchase order?

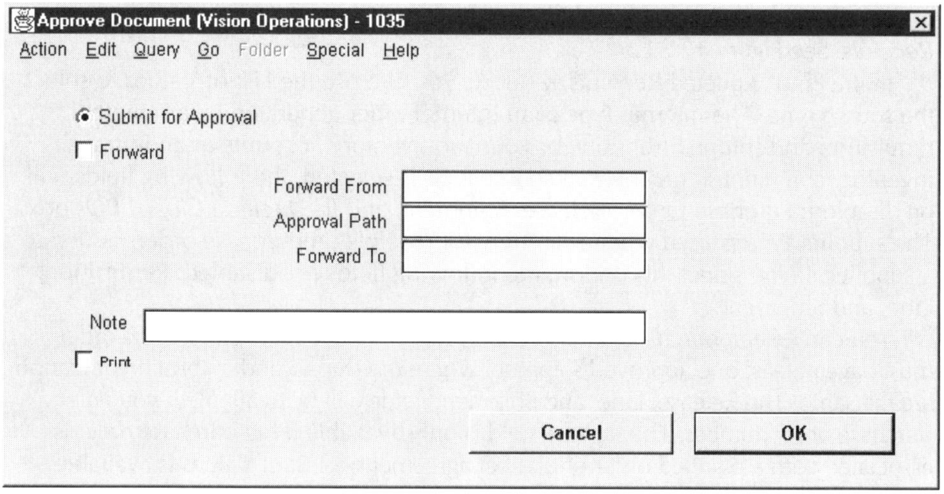

FIGURE 12-50. *Approve Document form*

Entering Purchase Order Receipts

In this section, you will learn how to receive against your purchase order. When the goods arrive, you must alert Oracle Purchasing that the goods have been received against the PO. To do this, you must enter receipts into the system. In this section, you will learn to:

- Find expected receipts

- Receive an item (Manual, Express, Cascade)

- Receive unordered items

- Receive substitute items

- Define payment-on-receipt options

- Define EDI options

Finding Expected Receipts

Use the Find Expected Receipts window to locate source documents for which you can enter receipts. You must enter the appropriate search criteria: the more information you include, the more restrictive the search will be. Expected receipts are those purchase orders that are expected to have goods or services arrive. To go to the Find Expected Receipts window, follow the navigation path *Receiving : Receipts.* See Figure 12-51.

In the Find Expected Receipts window, you can use the List of Values to select the source type. The internal type is an internal order generated by an internal requisition and shipped from one of your subinventory accounts or an in-transit inventory shipment. If the internal source type is selected, the following fields will be disabled: Purchase Order, Release, Shipment, and the *Include Closed POs* box. The supplier type is used when searching for receipts on purchase orders issued to a supplier. If you select this option, the following fields are disabled: Requisition, Line, and Shipment.

You can enter a purchase order number, but for one to be available, the order must have at least one approved shipment where the ship-to and current organization are the same. The Release, Line, and Shipment fields will be available if you enter a purchase order number. The Release field is only available if the purchase order is associated with a planned order or blanket agreement; a List of Values is available. You can enter the shipment number of the advance shipment notice.

You can enter the requisition number, which allows you to enter a shipment and/or line. Again, available shipments must relate to the same organizations.

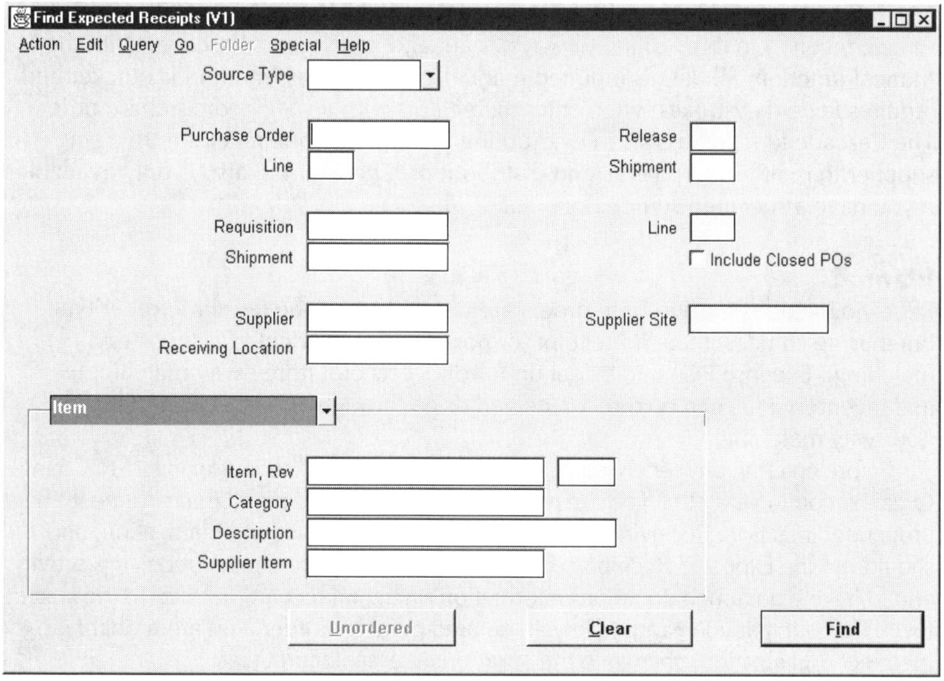

FIGURE 12-51.   *Find Expected Receipts form*

Check the *Include Closed POs* checkbox to include soft-close purchase orders in your search. By not checking this box, you will exclude all purchase orders that have a status of Closed or Closed for Receiving.

You can enter the supplier, which, for the Internal source type, will be the organization. For the Supplier source type, this is the supplier name or the supplier site in the source site. You can also enter the receiving location.

Use the alternative regions—Item and Date Range—to further restrict your search. In the Item region, you can also enter the item, revision, category, description and supplier item. In the Date Range alternative region, you can restrict the search to items that are due today, or enter a to-from date range.

Select the **Find** button to initiate the search to open up the Receipt Header window. Select the **Clear** button to clear your existing search criteria. Select the **Unordered** button to enter unordered receipts. For your exercise, click on the **Find** button to select all outstanding receipts.

Receiving an Item (Manual, Express, Cascade)

Oracle receives in three different ways: Manual, Express, and Cascade. With the Manual function, all data is inputted manually. The Express method is quicker and requires fewer keystrokes when entering receipts with a specified purchase order. The Cascade function assists in distributing the quantity of a receipt from a single supplier to multiple shipments and distributions. This method also is only available if you have a specified source document.

Manual

Receiving actions for purchase orders are dependent on the purchase order type. Purchasing can designate no receipt for nonmaterial (service) POs (two-way matching). Expense POs can be set up for direct receipt (three-way matching), and inventory POs can be direct received or go through an inspection process (four-way matching).

Before entering any receiving or inventory transactions, always navigate to Change Organization to verify that you are not in Global organization and that you are in the proper organization. Receiving must be done in your transaction organization, and should run the Expected Receipts report daily to preview anticipated receiving activity, and to have a document to record information on actual receipts to enter to the system. If you find out that you cannot view an entered purchase order, you are probably in the incorrect organization; change to the appropriate organization first.

Enter your receipt header information, which is the receipt number if automatic receipt numbering is not enabled. If you have automatic receipt numbering, you will not be able to enter a receipt number. The number will be assigned when you save your work. Enter the receipt date, shipment number, shipped date, packing slip number, waybill/airbill number, freight carrier, bill of lading number, number of containers in the shipment, received-by person, source (supplier or organization), dependent on source type, and any comments you may have regarding this receipt. This information will be the default information for your receipt lines. Be sure that the **New Receipt** button is selected if you are entering a new receipt. Otherwise, select the **Add to** radio button to open a List of Values showing the receipts to which you can add lines to existing receipts. Be sure to select New Receipt, then click on the underlying Receipts window.

The alternative region should say Lines. See Figure 12-52. Enter a check in the checkbox next to the line you want received, and enter the quantity or accept the default of the PO line quantity not previously received. Then, enter the unit of measure and the destination type: Receiving, Expense, Inventory, or Shop Floor. This determines the final destination of the receipt. If the item is under revision control, you must enter the revision number. Enter the receiving location, an

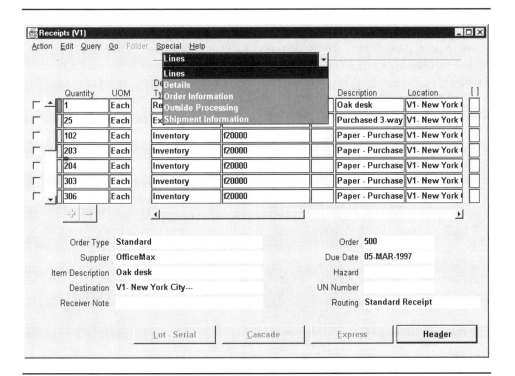

FIGURE 12-52. *Receipts (Lines) form*

optional requestor, and the subinventory into which the goods will be delivered. When the destination type is Inventory and locator control is enabled, enter the stock locator.

Use the Details alternative region to add the packing list, supplier lot number, reason code, and other comments for the line. If you want to enter an exception for this receipt, select Receipt Exception. Use the Order Information alternative region to view the purchase order detail, and the Outside Processing alternative region to view the OSP information.

If the items are under lot number and/or serial number control, click on the **Lot-Serial** button to navigate to the Lot Number and Serial Number windows. Enter the lot number to which the items will be received, and enter the serial numbers assigned to the received items. Save your work and the system will generate a receipt number, which you can view by clicking on the **Header** button.

Express

Once you have located the expected receipts, click on the **Express** button to perform an express receipt. In the Express Details window, select the destination type: Final Destination or Receiving Location. Click on the **OK** button, which changes the **Express** button to **Unexpress** and selects all express receipt lines. Deselect the lines to omit them from the express receipt. Upon saving your work, the system will validate your express receipt.

Cascade

Once you have located the expected receipts, click on the **Cascade** button to perform a cascade receipt. Enter the total quantity expected in the Cascade Details window, and enter the unit of measure. Click on **OK** button and the quantity will cascade line to line until the total quantity is received.

Use the Special | Movement Statistics menu command to capture movement statistics for Oracle Inventory. To view your receiving activity, go to the Receiving Transactions summary window. The navigation path is *Receiving : Receiving Transactions*. Enter your receipt number first, click on the transactions, click on the **Receipt Details** button (in the alternative region), then click on the **Find** button.

Review Questions

1. What is the difference between manual receipts, express receipts, and cascade receipts?

2. In receiving, what is the significance of knowing which organization you are in?

3. What are the different ways items can be received? What are the differences between them?

4. What is the difference between new receipts and add to receipts?

Receiving Unordered Items

With this function, you can receive shipments from your suppliers if a purchase order is missing, or if you are not sure which purchase order to receive the shipment against. This allows for the receipt and tracking of shipments in Oracle while a decision is made as to which purchase order to receive the shipment.

The navigation path to the Find Expected Receipts window is *Receiving : Receipts*. When the Find Expected Receipts window appears, click on the **Unordered** button on the bottom of the form. The Receipts Header window will open, just like it does with regular receipts.

Enter the header information in the Receipts Header window. Select the **New Receipt** radio button if this is a new receipt, or select the **Add To Receipt** button to add it to an existing receipt. If automatic receipt numbering in enabled, the receipt number will be assigned when the receipt lines are saved, and you will not be able to modify or change it. The system will automatically default the receipt date to today's date, but you can override this date. You can also enter the supplier shipment number, supplier shipped date, packing slip number, and waybill/airbill number. For freight carrier, you can select an active carrier from the List of Values. You can also enter a bill of lading number and the number of containers received on this shipment. The received-by name defaults from the user logon, but you can change to another person if required (a List of Values is available for selecting another person). Enter the name of the supplier from whom the receipt was generated (a List of Values is available to assist in selecting an active supplier). The supplier is required, and is used to assist in the matching of unordered receipts. You can also enter in any additional comments you may have about this receipt. When finished, save your work.

The Receipts window is located behind the Receipts Header window. Once you have entered the receipt header information, navigate to the Receipts window by clicking on the underlying Receipts window.

In the Lines alternative region, enter a check in the box next to the line you want to receive by pointing the mouse at the box and left-clicking. Enter the quantity received and the UOM (unit of measure) for this line (use the List of Values for valid options). For the destination type, select Receiving from the List of Values, and enter the item number of the item received. Enter the item revision number if the number of items is greater than one. The revision number will default if there is only one number, and a List of Values is available to assist in your selection; the description will default from the item description. Enter the received-from location for the supplier (a List of Values is available). The Requestor field will be shaded out.
The Subinventory and Locator fields will be shaded out because the destination is Receiving. The category will default from the item category, and the ASN type will be blank.

In the Details alternative region on the Receipts window, you can enter a packing number, supplier lot, reason code, and any comments you may have for this receipt line. Select Receipt Exception if you want to enter a release exception for this receipt line.

Because this is an unordered receipt, the Order Information alternative region will be blanked. After checking your work, save it. Once you have done so, the system will generate the receipt number if this is a new receipt. Click on the **Header** button to return to the Receipts Header window. The new receipt number that was generated will be displayed in the Receipt field.

Review Questions

1. What differentiates a substitute item from a standard item?

2. Which alternative region will be always blank for unordered item receipts?

Receiving Substitute Items

If you allow for the receipt of substitute items, you can enter the substitute item during receiving. These are items that can be replaced or that are interchangeable with other items in the system.

Use the Find Expected Receipts window to find source documents for which you can enter substitute receipts, then enter the appropriate amount of search criteria. The more information you include, the more restrictive the search will be.

The navigation path to the Find Expected Receipts window is *Receiving : Receipts.* Refer to Find Expected Receipts to locate your source document, then use the Find Expected Receipts window to specify your search criteria.

In the Receipts window, select the line on which you wish to receive substitute items. In the Item field, use the List of Values to select the substitute item. If the item does not appear in the List of Values, you will not be able to continue with this receipt. Once you have selected the proper substitute item, click on the **OK** button. The Item field on the Receipts window will change to the substitute item number. Continue your receiving transactions as required.

Review Questions

1. What is a substitute item?

2. How do you receive substitute items in Oracle Purchasing?

Defining Payment-on-Receipt Options

Oracle Purchasing and Oracle Payables work together to streamline the payment to suppliers based on receipt transactions. You can set up your suppliers to be paid on receipt or delivery with the Purchasing alternative region in the Supplier form. If the suppliers are pay on receipt or pay on delivery, you can also select the level of invoice consolidation—packing slip, receipt, or across all for a supplier site—and whether consolidated invoice should be created after receipt or delivery transaction creation. Pay on receipt means that invoices can be generated after receiving, and pay on delivery means that invoices can be generated after receiving and delivering. Consolidation by packing slip means that one invoice is created by the same packing slip number entered. Oracle Purchasing will automatically create an invoice in

Oracle Payables and match it to the corresponding purchase order. The invoices will be paid following the standard payment functionality in Oracle Payables.

You must run the Payment on Receipt program to automatically create the invoices for the payment-on-receipt suppliers as described above. Returns and receipt adjustment transactions debit memos are not automatically created once an invoice has been generated using the Payment on Receipt program.

TIP
Strong internal controls, discipline, and supplier integrity should be in place to enable this function in your system.

Review Questions

1. What is the difference between pay on receipt and pay on delivery?

2. What program creates the invoices for the payment on receipt?

3. What will not be automatically created once an invoice has been generated using the Payment on Receipt program?

Defining EDI Options

If the supplier or the supplier sites are paid via Electronic Data Interchange (EDI), you must specify the appropriate options for the supplier or the supplier site. EDI options include the following:

- Payment method

- Payment format

- Remittance method

- Remittance instruction

- Transaction handling

Payment Method

This is the method by which electronic payments will be made. Valid choices include Automated Clearing House (ACH), Bankers Automated Clearing System (BACS), Financial Institution Option (BOP), Wire transfer via CHIPS (CWT), Wire Transfer using FED wire method 1 (FEW), Wire transfer via FED wire method 2 (FWT), Wire transfer using SWIFT network (SWT), or Other Method (ZZZ).

Payment Format

This is the format that indicates the information type that will be transmitted with the funds if the payment method is ACH. Valid choices include Cash Concentration/Disbursement (CCD), cash concentration/Disbursement plus Addenda (CCP), Corporate Trade Payment (CTP), Corporate Trade Exchange (CTX), Prearranged payment and Deposit (PPD), or Prearranged payment and Deposit plus addenda (PPP).

Remittance Method

This is the method that determines which party is responsibility for sending the remittance advice. Valid choices include EDI to payer's bank, EDI to payee's bank, EDI to payee, EDI to Third Party, or Do not route.

Remittance Instruction

Remittance instruction, as its name implies, is used to capture instructions for an intermediary or recipient bank.

Transaction Handling

This is the ANSI ASC X12 EDI transaction code to classify how the transaction should be handled. Valid choices include Payment Accompanies Remittance Advice(C), Make Payment Only (D), Remittance Information Only (I), Split Payment and Remittance (U), or Other Handling (Z).

Review Questions

1. When must you define EDI options?

2. Where do you define EDI options?

3. What is payment method?

For the Chapter Summary, Two-Minute Drill, and Chapter Questions and Answers, open the summary.htm file contained in the Summary_files directory on the book's CD-ROM.

CHAPTER
13

Document Approval and Invoice Entry

his chapter is divided into two major parts. The first half of the chapter covers document approval and teaches you how to define approval rules and how to assign approval groups to users. The second part of the chapter teaches you how to enter payable invoices in Oracle Payables. This covers both basic and detail invoice information. The following topics will be covered in this chapter:

- Defining approval rules

- Defining document routing

- Entering invoices

- Matching invoices to purchase orders

The first sections discuss to how define document types and how to set up document routing with each document type. The later sections will teach you how to enter freight and other miscellaneous charges. These sections also teach you how to match invoices to PO shipments and PO distributions, and how to enter debit memos and credit memos and match those memos to invoices. You will also be taught how to record price corrections, how to review matching exceptions, and how to adjust PO-matched invoices.

Defining Approval Rules

Oracle Purchasing uses Oracle Workflow for its document approval process. For the document approval process to work accurately, you must define the approval groups and assign them to employees of specific jobs and positions within your organization.

In this section, you will learn how to:

- Define approval groups

- Define approval assignments

Defining Approval Groups

Approval groups define the authorization limits by *objects*. It is a set of approval rules. An object can be Document Total, Account Range, Item Category Range, Item Range, or Location. Object options are discussed in detail later in this section.

Once you have defined your approval groups, you can use the Approval Assignments form to assign approval groups and functions to jobs or positions.

To define approval groups, log in under the *Purchasing, Vision Operations (USA)* responsibility and then follow the navigation path *Setup : Approvals : Approval Groups.* To initiate the form, double-click on Approval Groups or click on the **Open** button. The Approval Groups window appears. This window shows all of the existing approval groups together with their descriptions.

If you want to edit an existing approval group, select that group and click the **OK** button. To begin your exercise of adding a new group, click on the **Cancel** button. This takes you to the Approval Groups form shown in Figure 13-1.

For the name, enter **New Executive** as the approval group. For the description, enter **Approval group for the executives**. You can disable the approval group by unchecking the *Enabled* checkbox located in the upper-right corner of the form.

Next, enter the approval rules corresponding to your approval group. In the Approval Rules section, select an object from the List of Values.

Your options for the objects are as follows:

■ **Document Total** Allows you to define the dollar limit the user can approve on a single document. For this object, the type defaults to Include.

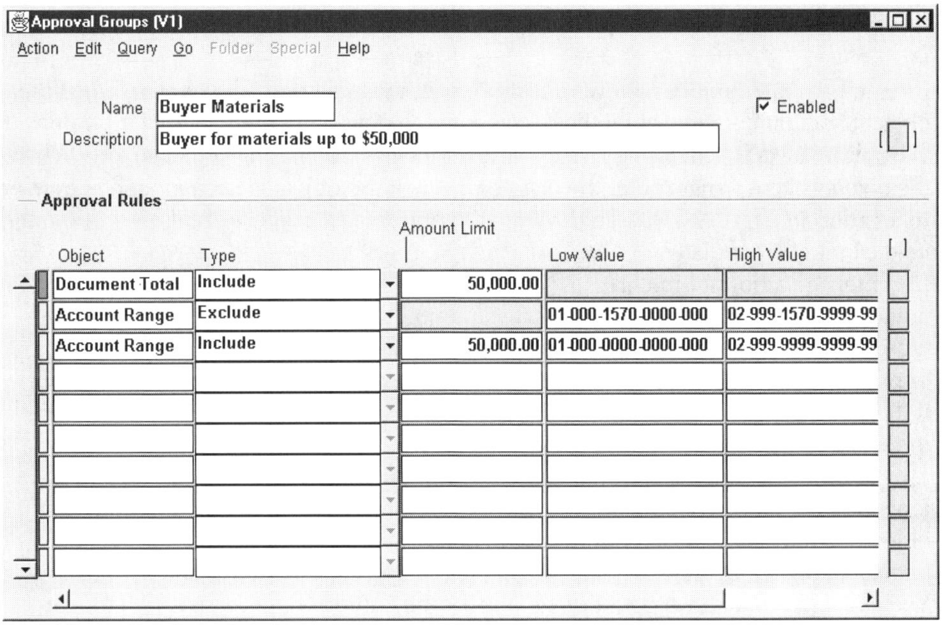

FIGURE 13-1. *Approval Groups form*

- **Account Range**   Allows you to enter account ranges to include or exclude when approving a document. If you do not enter an account range, the type defaults to Exclude, which will exclude *all* account ranges.

- **Item Category Range**   Allows you to enter the purchasing category ranges to include or exclude when approving a document. If you do not enter a category range, the type defaults to Include, which will include *all* items.

- **Item Range**   Allows you to enter the item ranges that the user can include or exclude when approving a document. If you do not enter an item range, the type defaults to Include, which will include *all* items.

- **Location**   Allows you to define the Deliver To locations that a user may include or exclude when approving a document. If you do not enter a location, the type defaults to Include, which will include *all* locations

Once you have selected the object values, select the Type.
Your options for values are as follows:

- **Include**   Allows objects to fall within the specified low/high value range.

- **Exclude**   Allows objects be outside of the specified low/high value range.

Each amount limit has a low value and a high value. For the low value, when the object is Account Range, enter the first account to define the low range of the value. When the object is Item Category Range, enter the first purchasing item category. When the object is Item Range, enter the first item. When the object is Location, enter **deliver to location** in the Low Value field. When the object is Document Total, the Low Value field cannot be populated.

Enter the amount limit. This is the maximum amount that the control group can authorize for the objects you selected. An amount limit is required for all include-type rules. Next, enter data into the High Value fields. Remember, you cannot populate these fields when the object is Document Total or Location. In addition, if there is a date when the high value will no longer apply, you can enter the date in the associated field.

For the New Executive group, enter a document total rule with **$50,000** as the amount limit; otherwise, the default—if you do not have a rule for the Account Range object—is to exclude all accounts. If you do not have rules for Item Category, Item, and Location, the defaults will include all item categories, all items, and all locations. You also must enter an account range rule for the entire account range with the same amount limit. Entire account ranges can be denoted by every segment having all 0's to all Z's. To complete your exercise, save your work.

Review Questions

1. What is the default if you do not have a rule for Account Range?

2. What field is required for an include-type rule?

3. What fields must you enter for an include Location approval rule?

4. What does item category range allow you to do?

Defining Approval Assignments

Jobs or positions, which are defined in Oracle HR, are assigned approval groups by the document type approval function. Document types and the associated options are discussed later in this section.

If you chose to use approval hierarchy when you set up the financial options, then you must also assign approval groups to those jobs and positions. If you chose not to use approval hierarchy, you do not need to select a position and assign approval groups by positions; however, you can do this by jobs.

Once you have defined your approval groups, and the jobs and/or positions are also defined, you can use the approval groups to assign approval functions to jobs and to positions.

To assign defined approval groups, follow the navigation path *Setup : Approvals : Approval Assignments.* The Find Position Approval Assignments window appears. Click on the position that you want to assign to the approval group. Click on the **OK** button. The Assign Approval Groups window appears. See Figure 13-2.

When the Assign Approval Groups window appears, the position you selected in the Find Position Approval Assignments window is displayed. The job and organization data is defaulted from the position setup.

In the Approval Assignments section, select the Document Type approval function from the List of Values.

You have eight document type approvals:

- Approve Blanket Purchase Agreements

- Approve Blanket Releases

- Approve Contract Purchase Orders

- Approve Internal Requisitions

- Approve Planned Purchase Orders

- Approved Purchase Requisitions

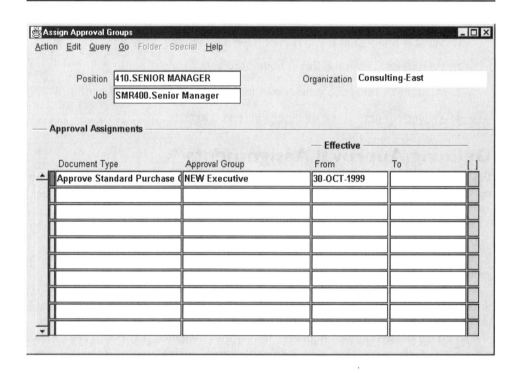

FIGURE 13-2. *Assign Approval Groups form*

- ■ Approve Scheduled Release
- ■ Approve Standard Purchase Orders

Enter the approval group that you want to assign to the position or job. The List of Values only includes enabled groups with at least one rule defined. As an option, you can also enter the effective date range for the assignment.

When you have finished entering the approval groups, save your work. To add more document types, you would repeat this process. Also note that you can have a different approval group for each document type.

Review Questions

1. What are the prerequisites for assigning approval groups?

2. When must you assign approval groups by positions?

3. How many approval assignments can each job and/or position have?

Defining Document Routing

This section introduces you to the document routing options available in Oracle Purchasing.

You will learn to:

■ Define document routing options

■ Set the options to use either the employee-supervisor routing or hierarchy routing

Defining Document Routing Options

You define the document routing options using the document type configuration. Document type defines the access, control, and security options for each purchasing document type. All document types are predefined in Oracle Purchasing. Each document type can have subtypes. You can define document-routing options for each combination of document type and subtype. All subtypes are predefined in Oracle Purchasing, with the exception that you can add user-defined subtypes for quotations and requests for quotations.

Your options are as follows:

■ Purchasing Agreement

■ Purchase Order

■ Quotation

■ Release

■ Request for Quotation

■ Requisition

Purchasing Agreement

Purchasing Agreement type is used for purchase agreements. There are two subtypes of purchase agreement in Oracle Purchasing:

■ Blanket purchase agreement

■ Contract purchase agreement

A blanket purchase agreement is a committed amount for a specific date range for specified goods and services. A contract purchase agreement is a committed amount for a specific date range for unspecified goods and services.

Purchase Order

Purchase Order type is used for purchase orders. There are two subtypes of purchase order in Oracle Purchasing:

- Standard purchase order
- Planned purchase order

A standard purchase order is a regular purchase order. It represents your order to the supplier. A planned purchase order is a purchase order created before you actually order the goods and services. It represents what you want to order from the supplier and when you want to order it.

Quotation

Quotation type is used for quotes from the supplier regarding prices, terms, and conditions of items. It is a sales offer from the supplier. There are three subtypes of quotation, which are predefined in Oracle Purchasing:

- Bid
- Catalog
- Standard

You can define your own subtypes to further classify the Quotation type.

Release

Release type is used for releases against other document types. There are two subtypes for releases:

- Blanket
- Scheduled

Blanket releases are for releases against a blanket purchase agreement for the actual quantities of items on the blanket purchase agreement. Schedule releases are for releases that are scheduled.

Request for Quotation

Request for Quotation (RFQ) type is used for RFQs in Oracle Purchasing. RFQ is used for soliciting quotes from the supplier regarding prices, terms, and conditions of items. There are three subtypes of requests of quotation, which are predefined in Oracle Purchasing:

- Bid

- Catalog

- Standard

You can define your own subtypes to further classify the Request of Quotation type.

Requisition

Requisition type is used for requisitions in Oracle Purchasing. There are two subtypes for requisitions:

- Internal

- Purchase

Internal requisitions are requests to purchase goods and services from an internal organization. These requisitions generate internal sales orders automatically. Purchase requisitions are requests to purchase goods and services from an outside supplier.

Now that you know what each document type and subtype means, you can configure the document type to fit your document approval process. To configure the document type, follow the navigation path *Setup : Purchasing : Document Types.* All of the predefined document types and their corresponding subtypes appear. For the purposes of this exercise, select the Purchase Order type and Standard subtype. Click on the **OK** button. The Document Types window appears. See Figure 13-3.

Next to the Subtype field is the Name field for the document. This is the description of the document type and subtype combination. It is required and must be unique across the system.

The next field is the Quotation Class field. You only need to populate this field if the document type is either Quotation or Request for Quotation. You can specify whether the quotation class is Bid or Catalog. Bid is for a specific instance, which includes quantity, deliver to location, and date. In general, Catalog is for a specified period of time, and usually includes quantity-based price breaks.

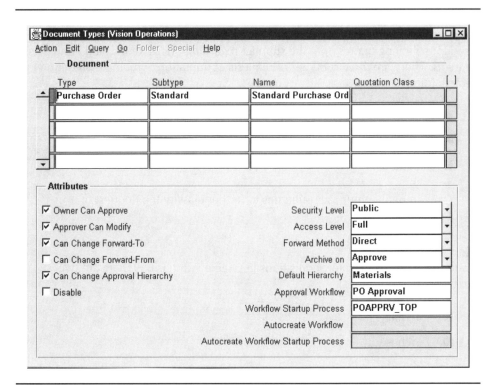

FIGURE 13-3. *Document Types form*

Below the fields is a set of checkboxes for the attributes of the document type and subtype. These attributes govern the routing and approval behavior for each document type and subtype.

For each document type and subtype combination your options are as follows:

- **Owner Can Approve**   Determines if the document owner can approve his or her own documents. This option does not apply to a quotation type or RFQ. If budgetary control is enabled and you choose to allow the owner to approve his or her own documents, then you should also enable the *Reserve at Requisition Completion* option during setup. This allows fund reservation to take place at the completion of the requisition.

- **Approver Can Modify**   Determines if the document approver can modify approving documents. This option does not apply to a quotation type or RFQ.

- **Can Change Forward-To**   Determines if users can change the person to whom the document is forwarded. This option does not apply to a quotation type or RFQ.

- **Can Change Forward-From**   Determines if users can change the person from whom the document is forwarded. This option does not apply to a quotation type or RFQ.

- **Can Change Approval Hierarchy**   Determines if users can change the approval hierarchy assigned to the documents. This option does not apply to a quotation type or RFQ.

- **Disable**   Determines whether the document type and subtype combination is displayed. You can only disable document subtypes that are user-defined, and user-defined subtypes are only applicable to a quotation type and RFQ types.

- **Security Level**   Determines document security level, meaning which users have access to documents. Usually, document owners always have the right to access their own documents. Security levels are used to allow others to have access, depending on the security level defined for the document type and subtype. The options in the List of Values are *Hierarchy*, where the document owner and any person above the document owner in the approval hierarchy can access the document; *Purchasing*, where the document owner and buyers can access the document; *Private*, where only the document owner can access the document; and *Public*, where everybody can access the document.

- **Access Level**   Determines what the user can do to the document. The options in the List of Values are *View Only*, where users other than the document owner can view documents only; *Modify*, where users other than the document owner can view and modify documents; and *Full*, where users other than the document owner can view, modify, cancel, freeze, close, and final close documents.

- **Forward Method**   Determines the next person to whom the document should be forwarded. The options in the List of Values are: *Direct*, where the next person to whom the document forwards is a person that has the approval limit to approve the document; and *Hierarchy*, where the next person to whom the document forwards is also the next person in the approval hierarchy, regardless of approval limit. This option does not apply to a quotation type or RFQ.

- **Archive On**   Determines when the document is archived. You can either archive the document when the document is approved or printed. This option does not apply to a quotation type, RFQ, or requisitions.

- **Default Hierarchy**   Determines the position hierarchy used for the document type and subtype approval process. You only need to specify the hierarchy if you choose to enable approval hierarchies when you set up the *Financial* option. The *Default Hierarchy* option does not apply to a quotation type or RFQ.

- **Approval Workflow**   Determines the workflow process used in the Approval Workflow field. Oracle Purchasing uses Oracle Workflow for document approval.

- **Workflow Startup Process**   Determines the startup process in the approval workflow as specified in the Approval Workflow field. This is the top-level process that calls all of the other processes in the specified approval workflow.

- **AutoCreate Workflow**   Determines the workflow process used in autocreating purchase orders. This option is for a requisition type only.

- **AutoCreate Workflow Startup Process**   Determines startup process in the autocreate workflow as specified in the Autocreate Workflow field. This is the top-level process that calls all of the other processes specified in AutoCreate Workflow.

Review Questions

1. What is the difference between a blanket purchase order and a contract purchase order?

2. What is the difference between the direct forwarding method and the hierarchical forwarding method?

3. When must you specify a default hierarchy?

4. If you want your buyer to view and modify any standard purchase order, what must you do?

Setting Document Approval Routing Options

The Oracle approval process is very flexible and powerful. Proper setup and testing of the approval process are critical for your success.

In Oracle Purchasing, document approval routing can be set up by either position hierarchy or employee-supervisor relationships. You determine the approval routing by checking the *Use Approval Hierarchies* checkbox when setting up the *Financial* option.

If you are using position hierarchy, Oracle Purchasing determines the next-level approver(s) by looking at the position of the document owner and finding the next level in the position hierarchy. If you are using employee-supervisor relationships, Oracle Purchasing selects the supervisor of the employee as the next level.

Oracle Human Resources shares many of its tables with other modules. Regardless of whether Oracle Human Resources is fully installed, you must perform the following steps as part of your purchasing setup:

1. Define jobs

2. Define positions

3. Define position hierarchy

4. Enter employees

5. Fill employee hierarchies

You must define jobs and employees for both the position hierarchy or employee-supervisor relationships.

When you enter an employee name, you can assign a job, a position, and a supervisor for each of the employee's assignments. Each employee can only have one primary assignment, but each can have multiple nonprimary assignments. The Supervisor field specifies the next-level person for the document approval process, provided you chose to have your document approval routing based on employee-supervisor relationships rather than hierarchical routing.

If you are using approval hierarchy or security hierarchy, you must define positions and create position hierarchies. A position hierarchy defines the relationship between positions within the same business group. You can have the same position within different hierarchies, but not the same position within the same hierarchy.

Once you have defined the position hierarchy, you must also run the Fill Employee Hierarchy program to fill the position hierarchy with employees based on the assigned positions. Whenever you make a change to the hierarchy or an employee's assignment, you must rerun the Fill Employee Hierarchy program.

When possible, you should implement position hierarchy. Though the initial setup takes more effort, the approval routing system is easier to maintain going forward. Also, position hierarchy offers more flexibility when a reorganization occurs. (Reorganization can be a promotion, resignation, or a change in company policy.) If you rely on the supervisor-employee routing system and assign a supervisor to each employee, then you must update the supervisor field when the supervisor resigns or gets promoted. Also, if there is a temporary vacancy after a supervisor resigns, you are forced to assign a supervisor even though the supervisor's position is currently vacant. However, if you use position hierarchy, you can leave the position blank until a new supervisor fills that position. Only implement employee-supervisor routing if the document volume is very small and the approval routing is relatively simple.

Review Questions

1. What is employee-supervisor routing?

2. What is hierarchy routing?

3. What additional steps must you take to implement approval hierarchy?

4. Which routing method allows for easier maintenance?

Entering Invoices

This section discusses how to enter payable invoices into Oracle Payables. To do this, you must switch to the responsibility *Payables, Vision Operations (USA)*.
You will learn to:

■ Enter basic invoice information

■ Enter detail invoice information

■ Enter freight, tax, and miscellaneous charges

Entering Basic Invoice Information

Basic invoice means that the invoice is entered manually without matching it to any purchase orders. To enter basic invoice information, you must enter the minimum information, which includes invoice, supplier, and default information, at the header level.

Payable invoices are organized into two levels. For payables invoices, there are header and distributions payment schedules. Each header is an invoice and can have one or more distributions. Each header can also have one or more payment schedules. Distribution contains the amount and the distribution account. Payment schedules contain the payment amount and the due date.

As an option, you can require your users to enter payable invoices in a batch. You set this by enabling the *Use Batch Controls* payables option. Each batch has a name, a date, a control count, and a control amount. You can also enter defaults such as invoice currency, payment terms, invoice type, and pay group at the batch level to be defaulted to the headers, distributions, and payment schedules. Each batch can have one or more invoices.

In the Vision demonstration database, you should enter invoices in batches. The navigation path to enter basic invoice information in batches is *Invoice : Entry : Invoice Batches*. See Figure 13-4.

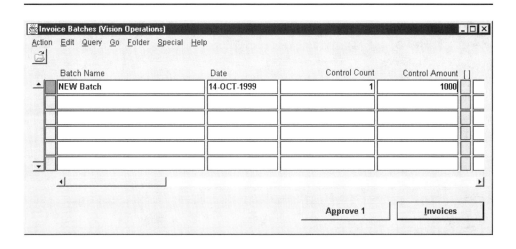

FIGURE 13-4.   *Invoice Batches form*

For the purposes of this exercise, enter **NEW Batch** as the batch name, **1** as the control count, and **1000** as the control amount. Also, as an option, you can enter batch defaults. Save your work.

To enter the invoice that belongs to the batch, click on the **Invoices** button. The Invoices window appears. This window is also referred to as the Invoice Workbench. See Figure 13-5.

Your nine options for the invoice type are as follows:

- Standard

- Credit Memo

- Debit Memo

- Expense Report

- PO Default

- Prepayment

- QuickMatch

- Withholding Tax

- Mixed

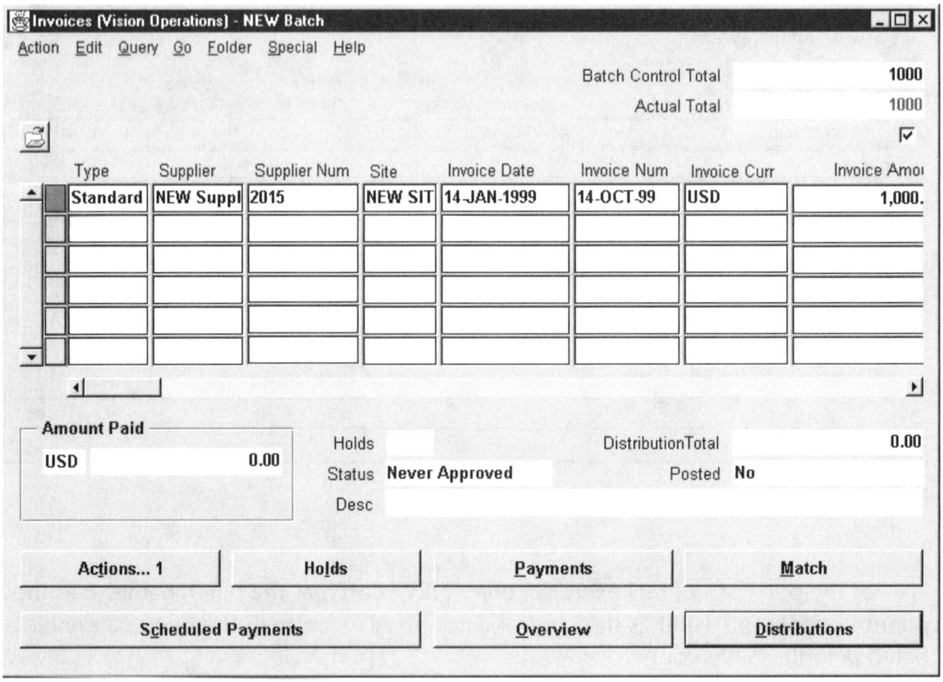

FIGURE 13-5. *Invoices form*

The Standard invoice type is used for a standard supplier invoice. Use the Standard invoice type for goods and services that can be matched to POs. Expense Report is used for invoices that reimburse the employee's expense. PO Default allows you to select a PO number, which allows the fields to default the supplier, supplier number, supplier site, and currency. The QuickMatch invoice type is use to perform QuickMatch, which will be described later. Withholding Tax is used for paying withholding tax to tax authorities. Mixed is used to enter debit and credit memos. Mixed invoices can be matched to both POs or invoices, and invoice amounts can be either positive or negative.

Select Standard invoice type, and enter **NEW Supplier** as the supplier. Enter the supplier name or, if you know the supplier number, you can enter the number in the Supplier Number field. Next, choose the site location for the supplier where the check will be received. If there is only one site for your supplier, the supplier site fills in automatically. If there are multiple sites, Oracle Payables displays a list from which you can choose. Enter **01-JAN-1999** as the invoice date. If you choose, you may accept the current system date for your invoice date. To do this, TAB through the field and Oracle will enter the date automatically. Now, enter the supplier's invoice number. If you choose, you may TAB through this field also, and Oracle Payables will enter the current system date.

The invoice number must be unique for each individual supplier. If you have multiple invoices to enter for the same supplier, keep in mind that Oracle will not accept duplicate invoice numbers. Oracle Payables also automatically schedules the invoice payment using the entered invoice amount, default payment terms, and default terms date.

Enter the full amount of the invoice, including tax and freight, in the Invoice Amount field, and write a brief description of the invoice in the DESC field. Enter a distribution set or enter distribution lines using the **Distributions** button. Distribution information includes amount, general ledger date, and distribution account. Enter **1000** as the invoice amount, and select Telephone Expense (Full) as the distribution set.

You have now finished entering basic invoice information. You have other fields in the header level, but for a basic invoice you do not need to enter them.

Save your work. You can use the **Find** button in the toolbar to invoke the Find Invoices window to find the invoice you have just created.

Review Questions

1. What is considered to be basic invoice information?

2. How many levels does an invoice have?

3. How does Oracle Payables schedule the invoice payment automatically?

4. How do you set up the system to use invoice batches in Oracle Payables?

Entering Detail Invoice Information

Entering detailed invoice information is very similar to entering basic invoice information. For detailed invoice information, you enter information in the remaining fields on the Invoices form. This includes any foreign currencies information, any project information, any payment information different than the defaults, and any scheduled payments for the invoice.

To enter the detailed information, you use the same Invoice Batches and Invoice forms, which means you follow the same navigation path. As you did with the basic information, enter the type, supplier name (or supplier number), site, invoice date, and the supplier's invoice number. Just as you did before, you can TAB through the Date field and Oracle Payables will enter the current date. Keep in mind that payables will not accept duplicate invoice numbers for the same supplier. If you are entering multiple invoices for the same supplier, it is best to use the supplier's document number.

The next field is the Invoice Currency field. If the supplier's currency is different from your functional currency, enter the currency or select from the List of Values to locate your supplier's currency. Enter the invoice amount. Remember, this must be the full amount including tax and freight. The general ledger date is defaulted based on the general ledger date you selected in the payable options. It can also be based on invoice date, system date, receipt date, then invoice date, or receipt date, then system date. You must scroll horizontally to see the hidden fields.

Next, enter the payment currency and payment exchange rate information (rate date, rate type, rate) if the payment currency is different from the functional currency. As an option, you can calculate the freight amount and select whether you want the freight distribution to occur automatically. Do not select this option if you typically prorate freight charges for invoices. As another option, you can select a distribution set, a description, a transaction code, project-related information, and invoice exchange rate information (rate date, rate type, rate) if invoice currency is different than the functional currency.

You can override the payment information (terms date, terms, payment method, pay group) by using the *Pay Alone* checkbox. Pay group is used to select invoices into payment batch and is useful for running separate check runs. The discountable amount is defaulted to be the same as the invoice amount; however, you can change it. You can also enter the date the invoice is received and the date the goods are received. If the invoice is a prepayment, enter the prepayment type, the settlement date, and the prepayment PO number. The prepayment type can be Temporary or Permanent. Temporary prepayments are prepayments that can be applied to invoices after the prepayments are approved and paid. Permanent prepayments will always be prepayment and cannot be applied to invoices. The settlement date governs when the approved and paid prepayment can start to be applied to invoices. For prepayments, payment terms are immediate and you cannot change the payment schedule.

For tax information, enter the tax name and the withholding tax group. When you enter a withholding tax group, a withholding type distribution is created as an invoice distribution. For document sequencing, you enter the document category name, document sequence name, and the voucher number.

The next part of the detail invoice header information is for invoice status display. It has the approved amount, approval status, approval description, cancelled-by person, cancelled date, and cancelled amount. The last part of the detail invoice header information is to override the defaulted liability account.

You have now completed the exercise on the detail invoice header information.

Schedule Payments

From the Invoices form, click on the **Scheduled Payments** button to modify the defaulted payment schedules. The Scheduled Payments form appears. See Figure 13-6.

The invoice due date populates based on the supplier's invoice date and the payment terms. The Gross Amount, Payment Priority, and Payment Method fields also default from the previous form. If the invoice is not fully paid, then you can change the invoice due date, gross amount, payment priority, and payment method. You can also add new payments, or you can change the unpaid portion of the invoice.

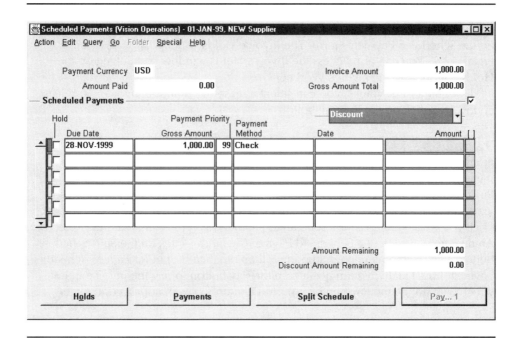

FIGURE 13-6. *Scheduled Payments form*

NOTE
If you adjust the payment term at the invoice level, or if you enable Scheduled Payment Recalculation and you approve the invoice, the payment schedule recalculates and all your changes will be lost, requiring you to make your changes on the payment schedule again.

You can enter up to three discounts for earlier payments. To enter a discount, you use the alternative regions named Discount, Second Discount, and Third Discount. In the Discount alternative regions, you enter the date by which you must pay in order to qualify for the discount amount.

The Date field captures the pay-by date, and the Amount field captures the discount amount. If you have more than one discount, you can repeat the amount. The last alternative region is the Remit-To Bank region. If there is remit-to bank information for the supplier or the supplier's site, the information defaults; otherwise, you can enter the remit-to bank as well as the bank account number.

Invoice Holds

To place the invoice on hold or view any current holds, click on the **Holds** button on the Scheduled Payments form. The Invoice Holds window appears. See Figure 13-7. You can also access the Invoice Holds window by clicking on the **Holds** button from the Invoice Workbench.

From the List of Values, you can select a reason to hold the invoice. To release an invoice, click on the **Release** button.

Payments

From the Invoice Workbench, you can view the total amount already paid on an invoice. To view payment specifics, click on the **Payments** button in the Scheduled Payments window. The Payments window appears. See Figure 13-8. You can also access the Payments by clicking on the **Payments** button from the Invoice Workbench.

If you would like to split a scheduled payment, you must change the Gross Amount field. Back in the Scheduled Payments window, click on the **Split Scheduled** button. The remaining unpaid amount will automatically split into a new scheduled payment line. Finally, you may click on the **Pay** button to pay the invoice in full, which will launch the Payments form. You can only pay an approved invoice.

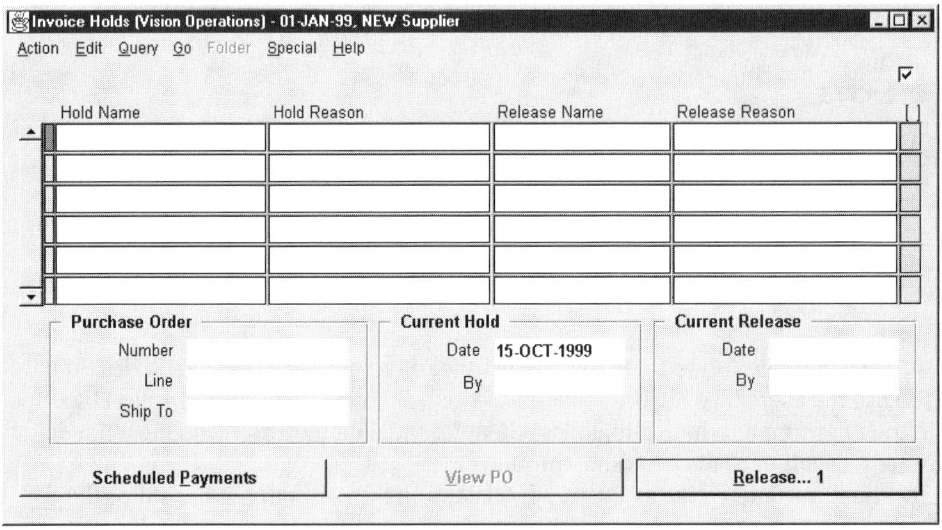

FIGURE 13-7. *Invoice Holds form*

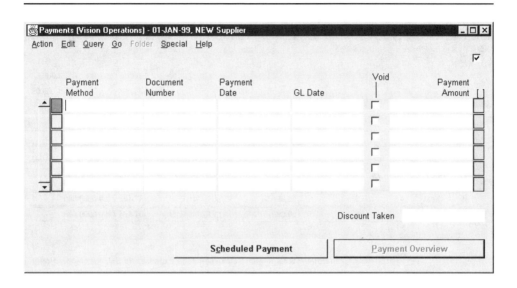

FIGURE 13-8. *Payments form*

Distribution

Once you are satisfied with the scheduled payment, you can enter the distribution for the invoice. You can enter the distribution in two different ways. You can distribute the payment manually by using a distribution set, or by matching it to a purchase order method. To manually enter distribution from the Invoice Workbench, click on the **Distributions** button. The Distributions window appears. See Figure 13-9.

Each line number is defaulted, so your first entry will be the line type. A line type of item is used for the standard purchases of goods and services. You would use a Miscellaneous line type for expenses that are not for the standard purchase of goods and services and are not for tax or freight. You use the Tax line type for tax, and the Freight line type for freight charges.

Continuing to the right, enter the line amount, tax name, and the general ledger date. The tax name represents the tax that is attached to the invoice distribution. The general ledger date is defaulted from the invoice and must be in an open or future enterable accounting period.

Next, enter the distribution account in the Account field. This field charges the specified account for the purchases. You can indicate whether the invoice line includes tax. This field is used for distribution-level automatic calculation.

Further to the right you will find the Final Match field, which does not apply to manual distribution. It is used to close the purchase order to which the invoice is matched. If the invoice is matched, the match quantity, price, and PO number are displayed.

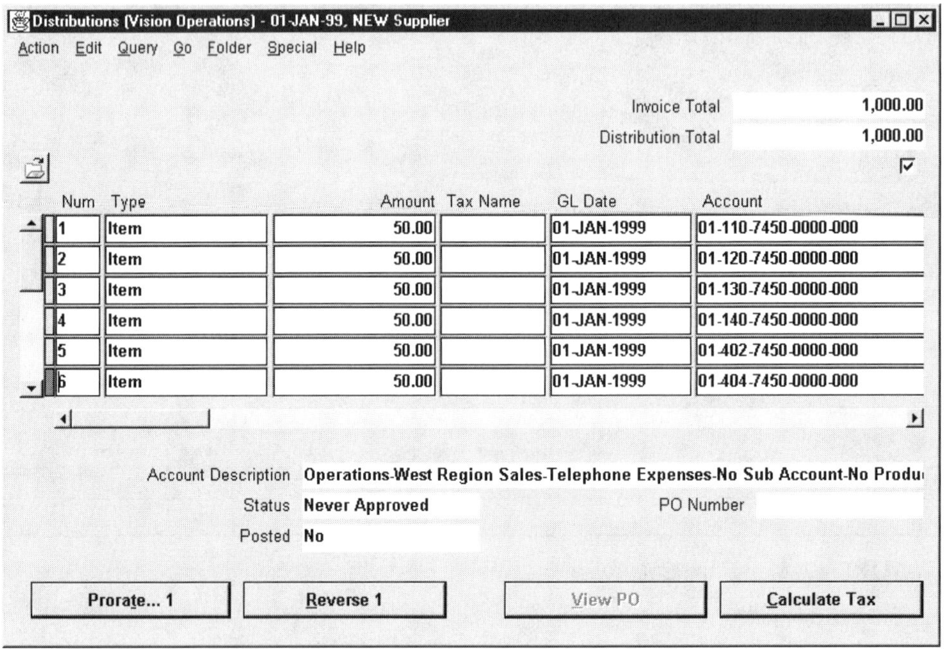

FIGURE 13-9. *Distributions form*

The next few fields are for project-related information when the distribution is charged to Oracle Projects. The project information includes the project, task, expenditure type, expenditure organization, expenditure item date, and quantity. If the account you have selected is a statistical account, the Unit of Measure field will show the statistical unit and you can enter the statistical quantity.

The last two fields in the Distributions form display the status of the distribution and whether the distribution is posted to Oracle General Ledger. The account description, the distribution status, the matched PO number, and the posted flag display as duplicates in the bottom of the Distributions window.

Calculating Tax

If you have selected the *Include Tax* checkbox (visible if you scroll the fields to the right) and you have entered a tax name, a Tax line type distribution line is generated automatically when you click on the **Calculate Tax** button or when you approve the invoice. The tax amount is reduced from the line type Amount field and the *Include Tax* checkbox box is unchecked automatically. The *Track as Asset* checkbox is checked automatically for an asset account. If it is an expense item that you want to track as an asset, you must check the *Track as Asset* checkbox manually.

Next, enter a description of the invoice line. If this is a 1099 supplier, the income tax type is defaulted, but you can change the income tax type if you want. You can also enter an income tax type even if the supplier is not marked as a 1099 supplier. Typically, after the invoice is posted to General Ledger the amount and the accounting information are frozen. Since it already hit your books, you cannot modify the invoice without jeopardizing the date integrity. However, this is one of the few fields you can adjust even after the invoice is posted to General Ledger. If you have an income tax type, you can enter or modify the Income Tax region.

Next, the Withholding Tax group shows the default withholding tax group. The withholding tax creation type shows whether the withholding type distribution is:

- Automatic
- Overridden
- Manual

Automatic means that the withholding type distribution is generated automatically. Overridden means that the withholding type distribution is generated automatically, but has a manual override. Manual means that the withholding type distribution is entered manually.

Prorating

You can use the **Prorate** button on the Distributions window to prorate miscellaneous, tax, or freight charges. First, you must select the distributions on which you want to base the prorating. To select the sequential distributions from the Distributions window, use the primary button, which for most users is the left button of your mouse, together with the SHIFT key. To select skipping distributions, use the primary button of your mouse together with the CTRL key. When you do this, the number in the **Prorate** button changes to the total number of distributions you have selected.

For the purposes of this exercise, select distribution numbers 1, 2, 3, and 5, and click on the **Prorate** button. The Prorate window appears. See Figure 13-10.

Since you used a distribution set in your invoice for your exercise, you should see 20 distributions with $50 each. Select the Miscellaneous type as the type you want to prorate, and enter an amount of **100**. You can also enter a description prefix to be used to precede the description of the distributions you are going to generate.

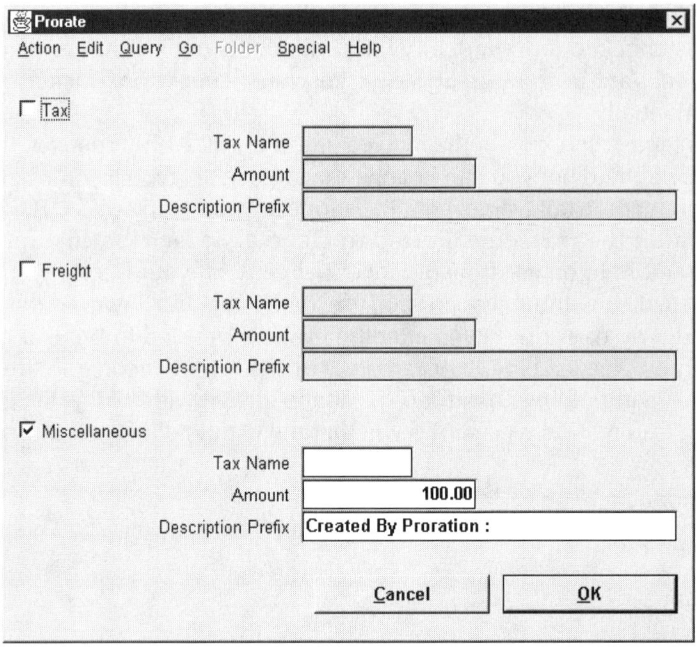

FIGURE 13-10. *Prorate form*

The default for the Miscellaneous type description prefix is *Created By Proration :*. Leave this as the default, and click on the **OK** button to generate the distributions.

A Confirmation window appears, asking you whether you are prorating four distributions. Click on the **OK** button to confirm.

When you click on the **OK** button, the system creates four Miscellaneous type distributions corresponding to the four distributions you have selected, which are based on the percentage of the amount of each distribution compared to the total. In your exercise, you have selected four distributions that have equal amounts, so the Miscellaneous type distributions equally divide the amount you enter for prorating. Therefore, four distributions of $25 were generated.

You can perform the same step for Freight and for Tax line types. If you are using automatic tax calculation, you do not need to perform tax prorating. If you are prorating tax, enter a tax name. The generated tax type distributions contain the tax name you entered, but the charge account will be the same as the distribution account, not the tax account associated with the tax name. See Figure 13-11 for the results.

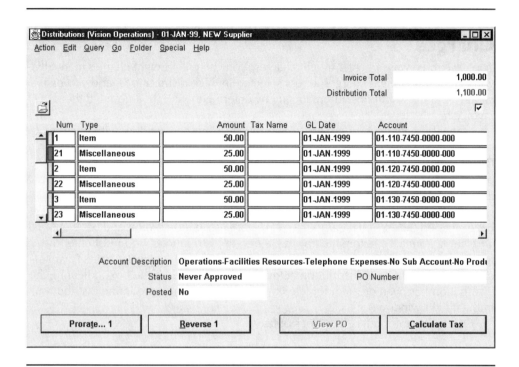

FIGURE 13-11.   *Prorated Distributions form*

If the distribution is posted, you can click on the **Reverse** button to reverse the posted distribution by adding a new distribution that has the reversal amount of the posted distribution.

Review Questions

1. How do you create a schedule payment of net 30 with a 2-percent discount if paid in five days, and a 2-percent discount if paid in 10 days, assuming the amount to be paid is $1,000 and the pay date is 01-JAN-1999?

2. How many line types are there, and for what are they used?

3. How does prorating work?

4. For what can you use the **Reverse** button in the Distributions window?

Entering Freight, Tax, and Miscellaneous Charges

You have three ways to enter freight charges. You can enter freight charges manually, you can prorate freight charges across selected invoice distributions, and you can create freight distributions automatically by entering the freight amount at the invoice header level.

Manual freight charges are entered in the Distributions window with a line type of *Freight*. To prorate freight charges across selected invoice distributions, in the Distributions window select the distributions on which you want to base your prorating, then click on the **Prorate** button. Check the *Freight* checkbox and enter the total freight amount that you want to prorate.

Oracle Payables allows for freight distribution to be done automatically if you have enabled the *Automatically Create Freight Distribution* option and have entered a freight account. To automatically create freight distributions, you must enter the freight amount in the Freight Amount field at the invoice header level. Oracle Payables creates the Freight type distribution automatically and checks the box indicating the distribution has been created. Oracle Payables displays the accounting distribution in the freight window.

Oracle Payables offers five types of taxes:

- Sales

- Use

- User-defined

- Offset

- Automatic withholding

Sales tax is tax that you pay to the supplier for your purchase. Use tax is tax that you pay directly to a tax authority, not to the supplier. User-defined tax is what you define as lookup codes. You can have value added tax (VAT) as a user-defined tax and Oracle Payables treats a user-defined tax the same way as sales tax. Offset tax is a negative tax to offset VAT tax in order to create a zero tax rate. Automatic withholding tax is tax you withhold from the supplier.

For each tax type, you can create unlimited tax names. Each tax name can have a tax account and a tax rate. For each supplier or supplier site, you can assign one sales or use tax name, one offset tax name, and one automatic withholding tax name.

You have three ways to enter taxes. You can enter taxes manually, you can prorate taxes, and you can create tax type distributions automatically based on the tax name you entered. Manual taxes are entered in the Distributions window with the line type Tax.

To prorate taxes across selected invoice distributions, enter the invoice information, then go to the Distributions window. Select the distributions on which you want to base your prorating and click on the **Prorate** button. Check the *Tax* checkbox and enter the total tax amount and tax name that you want to prorate, based on the percentage of each selected distribution. The tax type distributions do not have the tax account of the tax name, but instead keep the distribution account.

To automatically create tax distributions, you can either enter the tax name in the Tax Name field at the invoice header level or at the distribution level, provided you have automatic tax calculation enabled.

If you enter an invoice header-level tax name when you saved the invoice header record, then Oracle Payables allows for tax distribution to be generated. When you navigate to the Distributions window, an implicit commit occurs as well. If you enter distribution-level tax names, Oracle Payables generates tax distributions when you click on the **Calculate Tax** button or when you submit the invoice for approval. Oracle Payables creates the tax type distribution automatically, and uses the tax account associated with the tax name. (Note that this is different from the prorate tax process.)

If you have the *Allow Override* option enabled when you enter a tax name at the invoice header level, you will be asked at what level you want to calculate taxes. You can select either Header or Line. You can use the *Includes Tax* checkbox to determine if the amount includes tax already. If the distribution includes tax already, the calculated tax amount is first deducted from the distribution and the *Includes Tax* checkbox will be unchecked. You can only modify this checkbox if you have enabled the *Allow Override* option.

You have two ways to enter miscellaneous charges. You can enter miscellaneous charges manually, or you can prorate miscellaneous charges across selected invoice distributions. Manual miscellaneous charges are entered in the Distributions window with the line type Miscellaneous.

To prorate miscellaneous charges across selected invoice distributions, you first enter the invoice information. Then, go to the Distributions window and select the distributions on which you want to base your prorating. Click on the **Prorate** button. Check the *Miscellaneous* checkbox. Enter the total miscellaneous amount you want to prorate based on the percentage of each selected distribution amount over the total selected distribution amount.

Review Questions

1. How many ways can you enter freight charges?

2. How many ways can you enter miscellaneous charges?

3. How many ways can you enter tax?

4. How many tax types are there and what do they represent?

Matching Invoices to Purchase Orders

This last section discusses how to match invoices to purchase orders. You match invoices to purchase orders to enforce two-way, three-way, and four-way matching.

Matching invoices to purchase orders is a common check-and-balance system implemented by most companies. These checks and balances ensure that you do not improperly pay an invoice, pay the wrong invoice, or overpay/underpay an invoice. You can also final match invoices, which in turn closes the purchase order.

Oracle Payables matches your supplier invoice with purchase orders created in the Oracle Purchasing module. This is another check-and-balance system that ensures payments are not released for items that exceed the quantity or amount authorized by the purchase order.

To keep these controls from being overly restrictive, you can define the invoice tolerances through the Invoice Tolerance form. You can specify the quantity ordered tolerance, quantity received tolerance, and price tolerance, which can be a percentage of the invoice quantity and the invoice price to allow for invoices to match within your defined limits.

In addition, you can match an invoice to a specified PO shipment or distribution, or you can perform a QuickMatch and match the invoice to the PO shipments of a purchase order.

In this section, you will learn how to:

■ Match an invoice to a PO shipment or distribution

■ Match all PO shipments (QuickMatch)

■ Enter debit and credit memos

■ Match debit and credit memos to invoices

■ Record price corrections

■ Review matching exceptions

■ Adjust PO-matched invoices

Matching an Invoice to a PO Shipment or Distribution

To match an invoice to a PO shipment or distribution, you use the same Invoice Workbench as you did when you entered an invoice manually in Chapter 12.

For the purposes of this exercise, you are going to match an invoice to the purchase order you created in the previous section of this chapter. First, enter all of the basic invoice information without the invoice distribution(s). Use the standard invoice type. From the List of Values, select NEW Supplier and enter an invoice date of **02-JAN-1999**. Enter an invoice amount of **$20**. Click on the **Match** button. The Find Purchase Orders to Match form appears. See Figure 13-12.

Enter the percent sign (%) as the wildcard to list all POs that belong to the object NEW Supplier. Since you only have one purchase order, you will be taken to the Match to PO form automatically. Otherwise, you must select the purchase order from the List of Values and click on the **Find** button. The Match to PO form appears. See Figure 13-13.

The Match to PO form displays the purchase order information of the supplier. This information includes PO number, line number, item, shipment quantity, shipment, freight term, payment term, tax name, buyer, requestor, and description. Make a special note of the PO number, as you will need it later for your exercise.

To view the entire purchase order, click on the **View PO** button. Choose the shipment that you want to match to by checking the leftmost checkbox. Note that the shipment information that had been previously grayed out is now filled with data.

You can override the defaults in the Quantity Invoiced, Unit Price, or Match Amount fields from the PO shipment that you wish to match to. However, when you override one of the three fields, the remaining fields will be recalculated for you using the formula: Quantity Invoiced × Unit Price = Match Amount.

For now, ignore the *Price Correction* checkbox. (You use the *Price Correction* checkbox to record price corrections to matched PO shipments or distributions.) To perform a final match against the purchase order, check the *Final Match* checkbox. If you perform final match, approval of this matched invoice permanently closes the purchase order and the purchase order can no longer be updated. You can also check the *Prorate* checkbox for PO shipments on which you want to prorate freight, miscellaneous charges, or taxes.

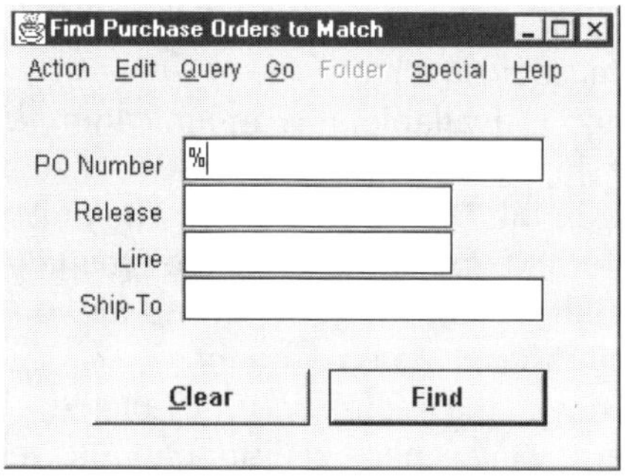

FIGURE 13-12. *Find Purchase Orders to Match form*

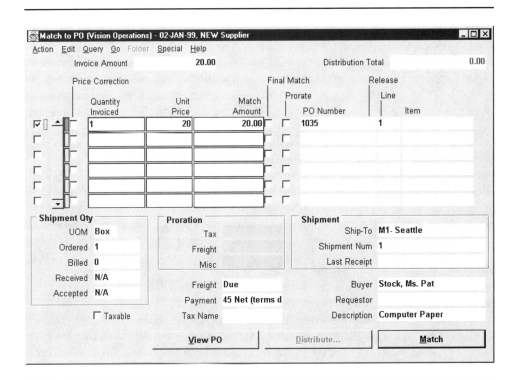

FIGURE 13-13. *Match to PO form*

Select your shipment line and click on the **Match** button to perform the match at the shipment level. The Distribution Total field at the top of the form is updated and the form clears itself. However, the window does not close automatically. To close the window, you must close it manually.

If the **Distribute** button is available, it is an indication that there are multiple distributions for this PO shipment. You can choose to match purchase order to distributions by clicking on the **Distribute** button. The unit price is defaulted from the main Match to PO form. If you can change the Quantity Invoiced or Match Amount fields, the remaining fields are recalculated for you using the formula Quantity Invoiced × Unit Price = Match Amount.

Once you are satisfied with the information you entered, click on the **Match** button to perform the match. Review the generated distributions to verify the matching results.

Review Questions

1. What is the purpose of the *Final Match* checkbox?

2. When is the **Distribute** button available, and for what do you use it?

3. What formula is used to calculate the quantity invoiced, the unit price, or the match amount?

Matching All PO Shipments (QuickMatch)

To match an invoice to all PO shipments (QuickMatch), you must enter QuickMatch in the invoice Type field. The PO Number window appears. See Figure 13-14.

Since the List of Values is not available in the PO Number window, you will use the PO number you have created and were asked to note in the last section. The supplier, supplier number, and supplier site are filled in according to the selected purchase order you selected.

The invoice date will default to the system date automatically. For the purposes of this exercise, change the invoice date to **03-Jan-1999**. Enter the invoice number and invoice amount. Do not manually enter any invoice distributions. Click on the **Match** button. This displays the Match to PO form and automatically selects all of the shipments for the matching process, including distributions. However, all of the matching criteria may be overridden and adjusted.

Save your work by clicking on the **Match** button. Review the generated distributions to verify the matching results.

Review Questions

1. What is a QuickMatch?

2. What is the difference between QuickMatch and a normal match?

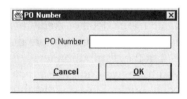

FIGURE 13-14. *PO Number form*

Entering Debit and Credit Memos

A debit memo is a credit with a negative invoice amount sent by you to advise a supplier they have a credit with you. A credit memo is a credit with negative invoice amount sent to you by a supplier advising you that you have a credit with them. Both memos are used to record a credit for purchases.

To enter a debit memo or a credit memo, you use the Invoice Workbench. From within the Invoice form, select Debit Memo or Credit Memo from the List of Values in the Type field. A warning appears, asking you to check the payment terms of a debit memo or a credit memo. Acknowledge the warning by clicking the **OK** button. Enter the supplier name or supplier number and select a supplier site. The supplier site is the location where the memo will be sent.

Next, enter the date of the memo, or you can TAB through the field to have Oracle Payables accept the current system date. Enter the invoice number (memo number) or, again, you can TAB to accept the current value. Now, enter the invoice (memo) amount using a negative value and write a brief description of the invoice, which will be displayed in the general ledger.

You can enter the distribution by manually entering the distribution lines, entering a distribution set, or matching to the original invoice. To enter a debit or a credit memo, follow the exact same steps as you would for entering a basic invoice except that you enter a negative amount. As an option, you can also change the payment terms from the default to Immediate, meaning that the payment is due immediately.

Review Questions

1. What is a debit memo?

2. What is a credit memo?

3. What must you do differently for a debit or a credit memo vs. an invoice?

Matching Debit and Credit Memos to Invoices

Oracle Payables can automatically duplicate the accounting and distribution of a debit or a credit memo by matching the debit or credit memo to the original invoice. You can match a debit memo or credit memo to more than one invoice by using either the invoice header level or the distribution level. If the invoice does not match the purchase order, you have two choices for matching. You can match to an original invoice or to specific original invoice distributions.

If the invoice was matched to the purchase order, you have three choices for matching. You can match to specific original invoice distributions, in which case you would allocate the credit amount according to the selected original invoice distributions. You can also match debit memo or credit memo to PO shipments.

This matching process automatically creates prorated invoice distributions for PO distributions, which are associated with the PO shipments you matched to. The final matching option would be for a price correction, which is used when a supplier sends you a price correction. Use the *Price Correction* checkbox to record the correction at the time of matching.

To match a debit or a credit memo to an invoice, use the Invoice Workbench. From the Invoices form, enter either a debit memo type or credit memo type. Enter the supplier name or supplier number. Next, enter the site. Then enter the invoice date, invoice number, and amount (using a negative value). Enter a description of the memo. Do not enter any distribution lines—they will come from the matching. Enter **03-JAN-1999** as the invoice date and **$20** as the invoice amount. You are now ready to match.

Click on the **Match** button. This displays the Find Invoices to Match form. See Figure 13-15. Query the invoice or purchase order you wish to match to and click on the **Find** button. For the purposes of this exercise, enter the PO number that you have created, and click on the **Find** button. The Match to Invoice form appears. See Figure 13-16.

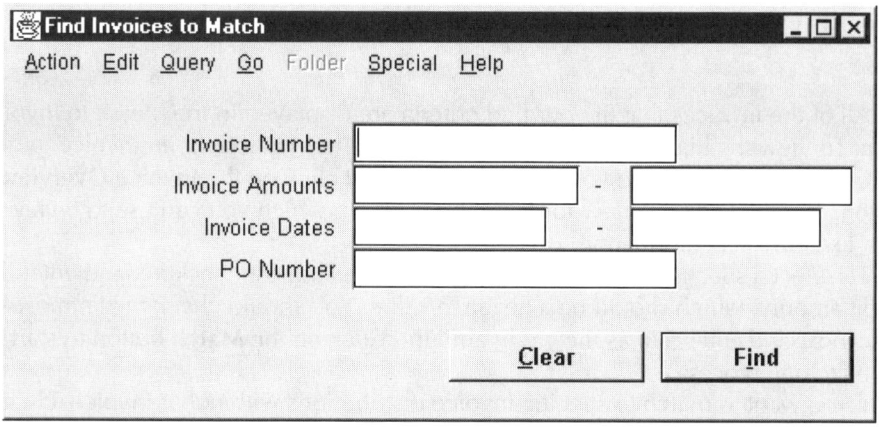

FIGURE 13-15. *Find Invoices to Match form*

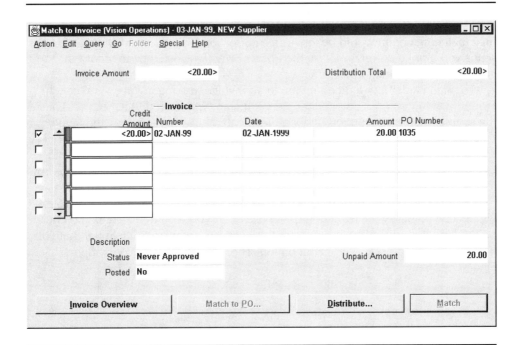

FIGURE 13-16. *Match to Invoice form*

All of the invoices that fit your find criteria are displayed in the Match to Invoice form. To view the high-level invoice and payment information for an invoice, put the cursor over the invoice you want to review and click on the **Invoice Overview** button. The Invoice Overview form will be invoked, which you can use to review high-level invoice information.

To select a specific invoice to match, check the leftmost checkbox and enter the credit amount, which should be a negative value. You should check the leftmost checkbox, and enter **$20** as the credit amount. Click on the **Match** button to start the matching process.

If you want to match to specific invoice distributions within that invoice, click on the **Distribute** button and select specific invoice distributions. See Figure 13-17.

Check the leftmost checkbox, and enter the credit quantity or credit amount. Entering one—either the credit quantity or the credit amount—forces the other to be calculated automatically. Click on the **OK** button to accept the matching.

A message appears to tell you that Oracle Payables starts matching to the invoice. Acknowledge the message by clicking the **OK** button.

If you want to match to purchase order shipments, click on the **Match PO** button. The Find Purchase Orders to Match window appears. You must follow

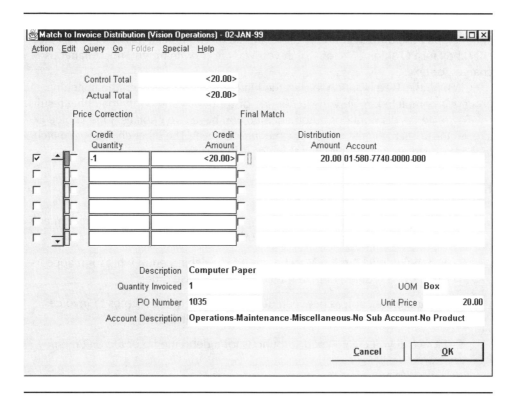

FIGURE 13-17. *Match to Invoice Distribution form*

the same procedure as if you were matching invoice to PO shipments or PO distributions. You must select the purchase order from the List of Values and click on the **Find** button. The Match to PO form appears. This form displays the purchase order information for the supplier, which includes PO number, line number, item, shipment quantity, shipment, freight term, payment term, tax name, buyer, requestor, and description. Remember the PO number and note it, as you will need it later.

To view the entire purchase order, click on the **View PO** button in the Match to PO window. Choose the shipment you want to match to by checking the leftmost checkbox. Note that the shipment information that was grayed out is now filled with data. Just as before, you can override the values in the Quantity Invoiced, Unit Price, or Match Amount fields that default from the PO shipment to which you wish to match. Also, remember that when you override one of those three fields, the remaining fields will be recalculated for you using the formula: Quantity Invoiced × Unit Price = Match Amount.

For now, ignore the *Price Correction* checkbox. You can check the *Final Match* checkbox to perform a final match against the purchase order. If you perform a final match, approval of this matched invoice will permanently close the purchase order and the purchase order can no longer be updated. You can also check the *Prorate* checkbox for PO shipments for which you want to prorate freight, miscellaneous charges, or taxes.

Click on the **Match** button to start the matching process. When the matching process is completed, review the generated distributions and verify matching results.

To create tax distributions automatically, you have two choices. One choice is to enter the tax name in the invoice (memo) header level. The other choice is to match to the tax distributions by selecting them or using prorating.

Review Questions

1. What must you enter before you can match a debit memo or a credit memo to original invoices, invoice distributions, or PO shipments?

2. When you click on the **Match** button for a debit memo, what form appears and how is it different than matching to purchase orders?

3. What are the choices between debiting and crediting memos to invoices that have been matched and have not been matched?

4. How can you create tax distributions for a debit memo or a credit memo?

Recording Price Corrections

To track price variances in Oracle Payables, use the Match to PO form and Match to Invoices form to record price corrections. Oracle Payables enables you to update an invoiced unit price from an invoice you have already matched. Oracle Payables updates the invoiced unit price of previously matched PO shipments or PO distributions without changing the quantity billed. This allows you to track price variances. Oracle Payables also updates the amount billed on the original matched PO shipments or PO distributions.

There are two kinds of price corrections: price decrease and price increase. To record a price decrease, enter a debit memo or credit memo invoice type in the Invoice Workbench. Do not manually enter the distributions. Click on the **Match** button. While you are matching the debit and credit memos to invoice distributions or PO shipments or PO distributions, check the *Price Correction* checkbox.

Enter the unit price for the price correction, which is the difference between the new price and the old price. Since this is a price decrease, the unit price should be a negative value. Oracle Payables automatically calculates the other fields based on Quantity Invoiced × Unit Price = Match Amount. By matching the invoice (memo) to the invoice distributions or PO shipments or PO distributions, you decrease the price.

Increasing a price works in a similar way. To record a price increase, enter a standard, PO default, or mixed invoice type in the Invoice Workbench. If you enter **PO Default** in the field, Oracle Payables prompts you to enter the PO number and automatically populates the supplier, supplier number, site, and currency information. If you enter **Standard**, you must enter the supplier, but the supplier number defaults.

Next, enter the site, invoice date, and invoice number. Enter the invoice amount. Do not manually enter the distributions. Click on the **Match** button. The Find Purchase Order to Match form appears.

Enter the find criteria for the invoice for which you are searching. Click on the **Find** button. The Match to PO window displays. Review your PO information. While you are matching the invoice to PO shipments or PO distributions, check the *Price Correction* checkbox. Enter the unit prices for the price correction, which is the difference between the new price and the old price. Since this is a price increase, the unit price should be a positive value. Oracle Payables automatically calculates the other fields based on Quantity Invoiced × Unit Price = Match Amount. By matching the invoice to the PO shipments or PO distributions, you increase the price.

Review Questions

1. What does Oracle Payables do when there is a price correction?

2. What is the difference in tasks when you are performing a price increase vs. a price decrease?

3. Which checkbox must you check for a price correction and where can this checkbox be found?

4. What amount do you enter as the unit price for a price correction?

Reviewing Matching Exceptions

Invoices that do not meet the defined tolerances or exceptions will be put on hold, and this information should be reviewed on a daily basis. It can be reviewed online or by submitting a report request. To view the holds and releases in the Invoice Workbench, put the cursor on the invoice you want to review and click on the **Holds** button. This lists all of the holds and releases related to the invoice.

Reports can be generated with several different parameters. To submit the report request, follow the navigation path *Other : Requests : Run*. Select the *Single Request* option. Select the report from the List of Values. There are two matching exception reports that can be helpful:

■ **Matching Hold Agent Notice report**   This report prints a notice for each buyer informing the buyers of any matching holds between their purchase order and the matched invoices. The report includes the supplier name, invoice, invoice description, and the matched PO number.

■ **Matching Hold Detail report**   This report lists information about invoices that have matching holds, or had matching holds but the holds were released. Parameters for the report include Matching Hold Status, Supplier Name, Active Period Start Date, Active Period End Date, and Matching Hold Report Detail. By leaving blank Matching Hold Status, Suppliers Name, Active Period Start Date, and Active Period End Date, the report will report holds across all matching hold statuses, all suppliers, and all dates. Matching Hold Status can be Hold, Release, or left blank. For the Match Hold Report Detail parameter, you may select All Approvals or Audit Report. All Approval prints all matching holds and releases.

Matching Holds

There are several matching holds predefined in the system. See Table 13-1.

Hold Name	Hold Reasons
CAN'T CLOSE PO	Online receipt accrual enabled and ordered quantity <> received quantity
CURRENCY DIFFERENCE	Invoice currency <> purchase order currency
FINAL MATCHING	Invoice is being matched to permanently closed purchase order
MATCHING REQUIRED	Invoice is not matched to purchase order
MAX QTY ORD	Invoiced quantity > ordered quantity + maximum tolerance amount
MAX QTY REC	Invoiced quantity > received quantity + tolerance amount
MAX RATE AMOUNT	Exchange rate variance > tolerance
MAX SHIP AMOUNT	Invoiced amount > shipment amount + tolerance
MAX TOTAL AMOUNT	Invoiced amount + exchange rate variance > tolerance
PO NOT APPROVED	Matched purchase order is not approved
PRICE	Invoice unit price > ordered unit price x (1 + tolerance %)
QTY ORD	Invoiced quantity > ordered quantity × (1 + tolerance %)

TABLE 13-1. *Matching Holds*

Hold Name	Hold Reasons
QTY REC	Invoiced quantity > received quantity × (1 + tolerance %)
QUALITY	Invoiced quantity > accepted quantity
TAX DIFFERENCE	Invoice tax name <> purchase order tax name, or Invoice tax name = purchase order tax name but taxable flag is set to No in the PO shipments

TABLE 13-1. *Matching Holds* (continued)

Review Questions

1. How can you review matching exceptions?

2. What does the Matching Hold Detail report show?

3. When is the invoice put on a QTY ORD hold?

4. When is the invoice put on a TAX DIFFERENCE hold?

Adjusting PO-Matched Invoices

If you make an error while matching invoices to PO shipments or to PO distributions, you can correct the error by reversing the matched distribution, creating new distributions, and matching to the correct PO shipments or PO distributions.

When you have completed adding a new distribution or reversing a distribution, you must change the scheduled payment amounts to match the new invoice total. If you do not change the scheduled payment amounts, the invoice is placed on hold during the approval process.

Price correction adjusts the unit price without changing the invoiced quantity. If unit price is what you must change, use price adjustments for these corrections rather than reversing the distributions and adding new ones.

You can also adjust the income tax type of an invoice distribution matched to PO shipments or PO distributions. If the invoice distribution has not posted, you can change the General Ledger date of an invoice distribution matched to PO shipments or PO distributions. You can change the account of an invoice distribution matched to PO shipments or PO distributions provided the invoice distribution is not posted and the *Allow Flexfield Override* option is enabled. (You enable this option as a payables option.)

Query the supplier and the invoice that needs the adjustment. To view the invoice distributions, use the **Distributions** button. To reverse a line, use the **Reverse** button. In the same way you select multiple lines for prorating, you can select more than one invoice distribution to be reversed. To do this, use the primary mouse button and either the SHIFT key or the CTRL key. This reverses the selected line(s) by using amounts of the opposite sign in the generated distribution(s).

Save your reversal distributions. Then go back to the Invoice Workbench and perform the new matching.

Review Questions

1. What can you do to adjust matched PO invoices?

2. What fields can you change in PO-matched invoice distributions before posting to the General Ledger?

3. What fields can you change in PO-matched invoice distributions after posting to the General Ledger?

4. How do you reverse more than one distribution line?

For the Chapter Summary, Two-Minute Drill, and Chapter Questions and Answers, open the summary.htm file contained in the Summary_files directory on the book's CD-ROM.

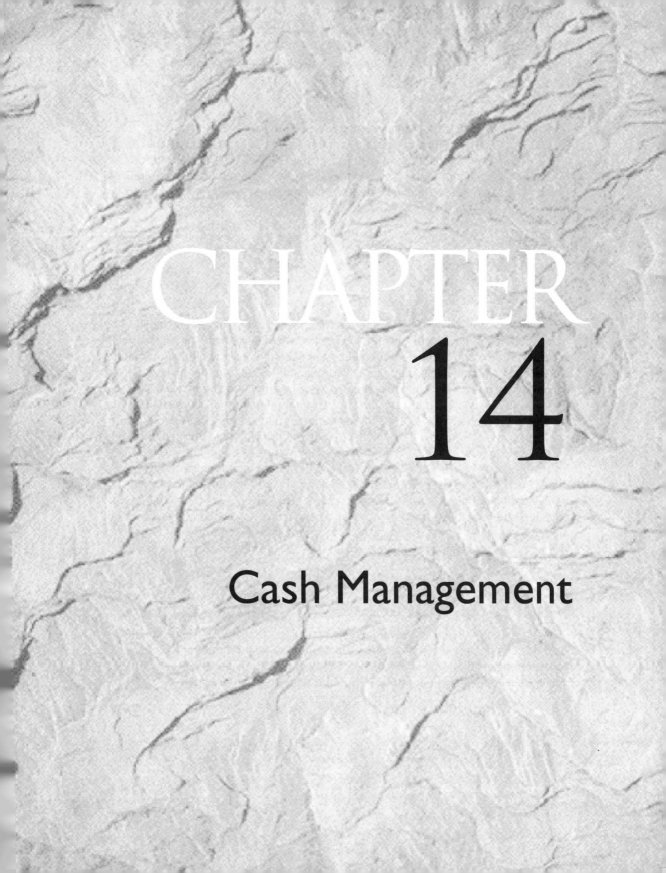

CHAPTER
14

Cash Management

racle Cash Management allows you to manage and control your company's cash cycle. It has two major functions: bank reconciliation and cash forecasting. This chapter explains these functions, and also provides a review of the setup steps required to utilize Oracle Cash Management. These topics are covered in the following order:

- Setting up Oracle Cash Management

- Reconciling bank statements

- Cash forecasting

Once you have reviewed the setup steps for Oracle Cash Management and the setup requirements for Oracle Payables in Oracle Cash Management, this chapter will then present new information starting with bank reconciliation, which allows you to reconcile bank statements automatically or manually. Topics under this category include setting up reconciliation tolerances, reconciling multiple currency transactions, using the open interface, and reconciling bank errors and performing corrections.

Next, the chapter introduces cash forecasting. Cash forecasting is used to forecast company cash flow. It projects your cash requirements using data from other Oracle Applications modules or third-party systems. Oracle Order Entry, Oracle Receivables, and Oracle General Ledger provide data for incoming cash flows. Oracle Purchasing, Oracle Payables, Oracle Payroll, and Oracle General Ledger provide data for outgoing cash flows. The chapter explains how to define forecast templates and how to use the defined templates to generate cash forecasts. Once you have generated the cash forecasts, you can query, review, and modify the cash forecasts. The chapter will also explain how to export the cash forecasts into Excel spreadsheets.

Setting Up Oracle Cash Management

The first section of the chapter explains how to set up Oracle Cash Management. Since this chapter covers Oracle Cash Management in relation to Oracle Payables, the section begins with the setup steps in Oracle Payables that are necessary for Oracle Cash Management and proceeds to the setup steps in Oracle Cash Management, which include system parameters and bank transaction codes. In this section, you will learn how to:

- Set up necessary system parameters in Oracle Payables for Cash Management

- Set up Cash Management system parameters

- Define bank transaction codes

Setting Up Oracle Payables System Parameters

For Cash Management to work with Oracle Payables, you must set up the following:

- Sets of Books

- Banks

- Payables options

Sets of Books

Define your Set(s) of Books and assign a primary Set of Books to each operating unit within Oracle Payables. You perform the association by using the Set of Books form in Oracle Payables. Then, select the Payables primary Sets of Books as the Sets of Books in the Oracle Cash Management System Parameters form.

Banks

You must set up bank accounts that you will reconcile using Oracle Cash Management. Mark the bank accounts with an account use of Internal, not Customer or Supplier. Set up the cash clearing, bank charges, and bank errors accounts in the GL Accounts alternative region of Bank Accounts.

Payables Options

Enable the *Allow Reconciliation Accounting* option if you want to use a cash clearing account and automatically generate accounting entries for bank charges, errors, and any gains/losses. If you do not enable the *Allow Reconciliation Accounting* option, you can still use Oracle Cash Management to reconcile payments, but accounting entries for bank charges, errors, and any gains/losses will not be automatically generated.

You cannot enable automatic offsets if you want to enable the *Allow Reconciliation Accounting* option. Automatic offsets is a feature in Oracle Payables that automatically balances the payable liability accounts to the invoice distribution accounts by balancing entity or by account. Consider the following balancing entity example. If you buy stationery for two balancing entities/companies, the invoice is charged to two different distribution accounts: one for Company 1 and one for Company 2. Only one payable liability can be entered for each invoice in Oracle Payables; however, with the automatic offset feature enabled, regardless of which company payable liability account you entered for the invoice, the payable liability account will be split proportionally between the two companies according to percentages.

Review Questions

1. What can you do in Oracle Cash Management if you did not enable the *Allow Reconciliation Accounting* option in payables?

2. What is the purpose of the *Allow Reconciliation Accounting* option?

3. What setup steps are needed for each bank account requiring reconciliation?

Setting Up Cash Management System Parameters

To set up system parameters in Oracle Cash Management, you must log on using the *Cash Management* responsibility; for the purposes of this exercise, log on with the *Cash Management, Vision Operations (USA)* responsibility. Follow the *Setup : System Parameters* navigation path. First, choose a Set of Books from the List of Values. Then enter the begin date: This date must be backdated far enough to cover any transactions that will appear in the bank statement. It is generally safe to calculate that the date of the first statement will not contain entries earlier than its own date—for instance, a check may be issued on January 25, but cashed on February 5. If your system begin date was dated February 1, Cash Management would recognize it. The system only recognizes the transaction date of the bank record, not your Payables or Receivables transaction date. Next, if you want to see cleared transactions that are available for reconciliation, check *Show Cleared Transactions*. If you want to reserve the ability to add lines to a statement that is loaded automatically, not manually, check *Add Line to Automatic Statements*. If your bank statements will be loaded through the interface instead of loaded manually, check *Use Open Interface*. Large statements should be loaded through the interface to maximize the functionality of the program.

Next, go to the General alternative region. Select the matching order for both Payables and Receivables. You have two choices: Transaction or Batch. If your system only requires reconciliation at the batch level, select *Batch*; otherwise, select *Transaction*. This is how Cash Management will search the statement lines in order to match them up during AutoReconciliation. Next, enter the tax codes. These codes are used when there are differences in the bank statement associated with VAT. If the transactions are in dollars, select *Standard*; otherwise, select a VAT code to represent the liability and assets for miscellaneous payments and miscellaneous receipts. When you select a Receivables activity for a transaction line, a default General Ledger account is automatically associated with the transaction line. Select an activity in the System Parameters form to charge the differences between the original amount and the cleared amount. This is usually a clearing account, a bank charges account, or a miscellaneous costs account. The last field in the region is Float Handling. This determines if the transaction's effective date is later than the system date and whether Oracle Cash Management should ignore the transaction or mark it as an error. You have two options: Error and Ignore. Cash Management will allow reconciliation of lines with postdated transaction dates for the *Ignore* option.

Once you have completed the General alternative region, change the alternative region to Automatic Reconciliation. The settings in this region will not have any effect on manually reconciled statements, only automatic reconciliation. Choose the amount and percentage of variance with Cash Management to match statement lines to available transactions in the tolerances fields. The Amount field is a specific dollar amount of either the statement line or the transaction line. The Percentage field also sets the tolerance on either the statement line or the available transactions. Next, enter the tolerance differences fields. In the AP field, select Charges or Errors. Charges will send the differing amount from the General Ledger to the charge-account setup in Payables. Errors will not send the differing amount to the General Ledger, but will cause the reconciliation to error out. In the Foreign field, you can select Gain/Loss, Charges/Errors, or No Action. Differences will be posted to the General Ledger as a Gain/Loss, Bank Charge, or Bank Error. No Action means that this item will not reconcile; it will display a status of Error. You may select to purge from the interface once the statement is transferred by checking *Purge*. You may also select automatic archiving of the statements from the interface tables by checking *Archive*. You must archive if you purge. The Lines per Commit field determines how many lines Oracle Cash Management should process before committing. Set the Lines per Commit field to a low number—5 or less. This prevents the system from stalling while processing large statements during AutoReconciliation. Save your setup configurations.

Review Questions

 1. What is the purpose of the begin date in the system parameters?

 2. Which system parameters apply to the open interface?

 3. Float handling is used for what purpose?

 4. What responsibility should you log on to for setting up Cash Management?

Defining Bank Transaction Codes

You must define bank transactions codes in Oracle Cash Management if you wish to use Oracle's electronic bank statements with the AutoReconciliation features. The codes used by your bank identify the different types of transactions on your bank statement. You must define a bank transaction code for each code you expect to receive from your bank. You may define different codes for different banks.

To set up a transaction, use the *Setup : Bank Transaction Codes* navigation path. The transaction codes must be defined for each type of banking transaction that is defined by your bank. For instance, your bank may assign a number or alpha code to a non-sufficient funds (NSF) transaction, which would appear on your bank statement each month.

Cash Management defines the following possible types:

- Payment

- Receipt

- Miscellaneous Payment

- Miscellaneous Receipt

- NSF

- Rejected

- Stopped Payment

You may define more than one code for each of these, or no code for codes not used. First, select the type of code you wish to define using the drop-down menu. Then enter the bank code for that type of transaction. An optional step is to enter a clarifying description of the code in the Description field. You also have the option of creating effective date ranges that govern when the transaction codes are active. Float Days is an optional field that allows you to enter the number of float days you want to add to the bank statement date to create an effective date for the transaction. This is used in conjunction with float handling in system parameters.

Next, enter the transaction source. You can leave this field blank if you want to reconcile your statement lines to transactions that were generated in either Oracle Receivables or Oracle Payables. If you want to reconcile the lines to General Ledger journal entries, select Journals. To reconcile lines to items in the open interface, select Interface. If the transaction type is Miscellaneous Receipt or Miscellaneous Payment, you must select the type of transactions to match, the matching order, and the correction method. This is because the same code for a miscellaneous receipt or miscellaneous payment can be used for matching against both miscellaneous transactions and/or corrections. Valid choices are Misc for matching only against miscellaneous transactions, Stmt for matching only against statement lines, Misc, Stmt for first matching against miscellaneous transactions and then matching against statement lines, and Stmt, Misc for first matching against statement lines and then matching against miscellaneous transactions. Valid choices for correction method are Reversal, Adjustment, or Both. Check *Create* to automatically create a miscellaneous item transaction with an assigned transaction code for unanticipated items that appear on the bank statement; in other words, for items without a transaction number.

If you choose to create miscellaneous item transactions by checking *Create*, you must select an activity type to assign to the item. As a last step, if you choose to create miscellaneous line items, you must select a payment method to assign to the item. The activity type is tied to the miscellaneous receipt, while the payment method is tied to the miscellaneous payment. Save your work. The transaction codes must be assigned for each bank that is set up in either Receivables or Payables to be reconciled with Cash Management.

Review Questions

1. What is used in conjunction with float days?

2. What must you enter if the transaction type is Miscellaneous Receipt or Miscellaneous Payment?

3. What must you enter if you create miscellaneous item transactions?

4. What is a transaction code?

Reconciling Bank Statements

This section explains automatic and manual bank statement reconciliation. To reconcile bank statements automatically, Oracle Cash Management first matches a bank statement line to a transaction. The transaction can be imported from Oracle Receivables, Oracle Payables, or other Oracle and non-Oracle Applications modules. Transactions are matched using a transaction number, a bank account, an amount, and a currency. The transaction number can be a check number or a deposit number. For automatic reconciliation to be considered a successful match, the bank statement line amount must be the same as the transaction amount. The difference must be within the set reconciliation tolerances. Additionally, the bank account, the transaction number, and the currency must match. You do not need a transaction number, miscellaneous payment, or miscellaneous receipt; Oracle Cash Management can handle matching between functional currency transactions and functional currency bank statement lines. It can also handle any foreign currency transactions with functional currency bank statement lines. Finally, it can match foreign currency transactions with foreign currency bank statement lines. Set reconciliation tolerances system-wide if you desire automatic reconciliation. For manual reconciliation, match any statement line to any transaction; however, the transaction currency must be the same as the bank statement line currency.

Once you have successfully matched a bank statement line to a transaction, the transaction will be marked as cleared and show a cleared date and a cleared amount. The accounting entries will be automatically generated if the reconciliation is automatic.

You can also reconcile multicurrency transactions. This section explains how to use the open interfaces to reconcile transactions. There are three open interfaces in Oracle Cash Management: Bank Statement open interface, Reconciliation open interface, and Forecasting open interface. The latter part of this section describes reconciling bank errors and corrections. In this section, you will learn to:

- Reconcile bank statements automatically

- Set reconciliation tolerances

- Reconcile multicurrency transactions

- Reconcile bank statements manually

- Use open interface transactions

- Reconcile bank errors and corrections

Reconciling Bank Statements Automatically

The Cash Management AutoReconciliation program allows you to automatically reconcile your bank statements. It reconciles bank statements to other Oracle Applications modules' transactions. You must enable the system for automatic reconciliation and set up AutoReconciliation system parameters before using this function. You can select from three different types of programs. The first type is AutoReconciliation, which will reconcile bank statements that you have entered or imported. The second type is Bank Statement Import, which will electronically import your bank statement. The third type is a combination. It combines both Bank Statement Import and AutoReconciliation into the same run to import and then reconcile.

Once you have run the AutoReconciliation program, you can review the run results by reviewing the AutoReconciliation Execution report. Once you have reviewed the AutoReconciliation Execution report, you can do one of two things to review the reconciled and unreconciled bank statement lines. You can use the View Bank Statements form to review online or you can run the Bank Statement Detail report to review the reconciled and unreconciled bank statement lines in a report format. If there are unreconciled bank statement lines that you want to reconcile, you can modify the bank statement lines and rerun the AutoReconciliation program or you can manually reconcile the bank statement lines.

To access the View Bank Statements form, use the *View : Bank Statements* navigation path. The Find Bank Statements form will appear. See Figure 14-1. You can

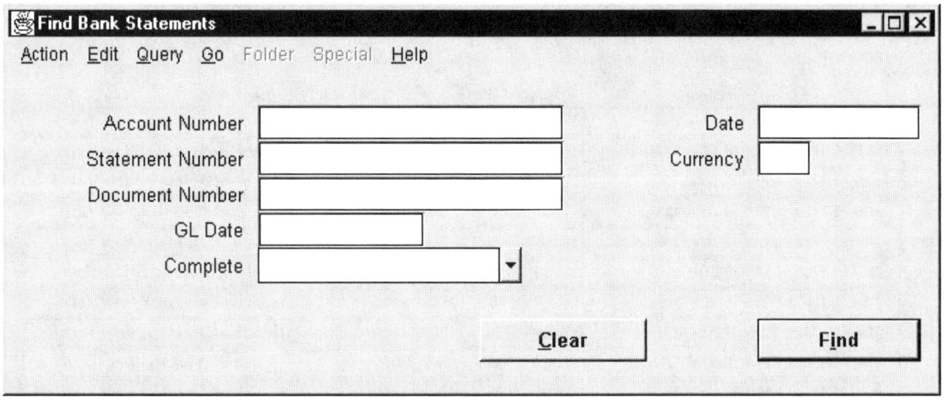

FIGURE 14-1. *Find Bank Statements form*

enter the bank account number, statement number, document number, GL date, bank statement date, currency, and whether the bank statements are completed. Leave all fields blank for all existing bank statements. Click on **Find**.

The View Bank Statement Reconciliation form will appear. See Figure 14-2. It shows the bank account number, statement number, statement date, currency, account name, bank name, and bank branch. Click on **Review**.

The View Bank Statement form will appear. See Figure 14-3. It shows the bank statement in full. Click on **Errors** to see the erred bank statement lines, **Reconciled** to see reconciled bank statement lines, or **Lines** to see all bank statement lines.

To reconcile a bank statement automatically, use the *Other : Programs : Run* navigation path. The Submit Request form will appear. Select Single Request. With your cursor in the Request Name field, select from the List of Values one of the three programs: AutoReconciliation, Bank Statement Import, or Bank Statement Import & AutoReconciliation. Then click on **OK**.

The Parameter form will appear. Enter the bank account that you want to reconcile. You may enter a statement number range, a statement date range, and/or the GL date. If you would like Cash Management to create a miscellaneous receipt for differences while matching, select a receivable activity and a payment method in your Parameter window. You must tell Cash Management how to handle NSF and rejected items by selecting either No Action or Reverse. The last three fields are defaulted based on your AutoReconciliation setup. Click on **OK**. Next, click **Submit Request**. This will automatically generate the AutoReconciliation Execution report. Review this report.

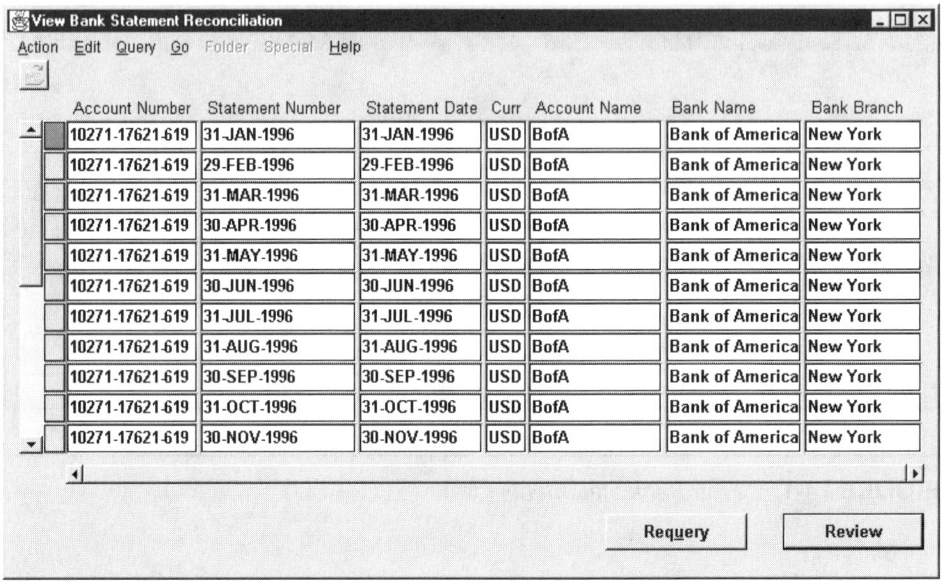
View Bank Statement Reconciliation

Action Edit Query Go Folder Special Help

Account Number	Statement Number	Statement Date	Curr	Account Name	Bank Name	Bank Branch
10271-17621-619	31-JAN-1996	31-JAN-1996	USD	BofA	Bank of America	New York
10271-17621-619	29-FEB-1996	29-FEB-1996	USD	BofA	Bank of America	New York
10271-17621-619	31-MAR-1996	31-MAR-1996	USD	BofA	Bank of America	New York
10271-17621-619	30-APR-1996	30-APR-1996	USD	BofA	Bank of America	New York
10271-17621-619	31-MAY-1996	31-MAY-1996	USD	BofA	Bank of America	New York
10271-17621-619	30-JUN-1996	30-JUN-1996	USD	BofA	Bank of America	New York
10271-17621-619	31-JUL-1996	31-JUL-1996	USD	BofA	Bank of America	New York
10271-17621-619	31-AUG-1996	31-AUG-1996	USD	BofA	Bank of America	New York
10271-17621-619	30-SEP-1996	30-SEP-1996	USD	BofA	Bank of America	New York
10271-17621-619	31-OCT-1996	31-OCT-1996	USD	BofA	Bank of America	New York
10271-17621-619	30-NOV-1996	30-NOV-1996	USD	BofA	Bank of America	New York

Requery Review

FIGURE 14-2. *View Bank Statement Reconciliation form*

Review Questions

1. What three programs are available for automatic reconciliation and how do they differ from each other?
2. How does Oracle Cash Management reconcile bank statements?
3. How can you review reconciled and unreconciled bank statement lines?
4. What are the prerequisites for AutoReconciliation?

Setting Reconciliation Tolerances

Reconciliation tolerances are defined in the Cash Management setup process. The AutoReconciliation program uses these tolerances to match bank-cleared transactions with those entered in Oracle Payables, Oracle Receivables, and other Applications modules. The reconciliation tolerances will have no effect on the manual reconciliation process.

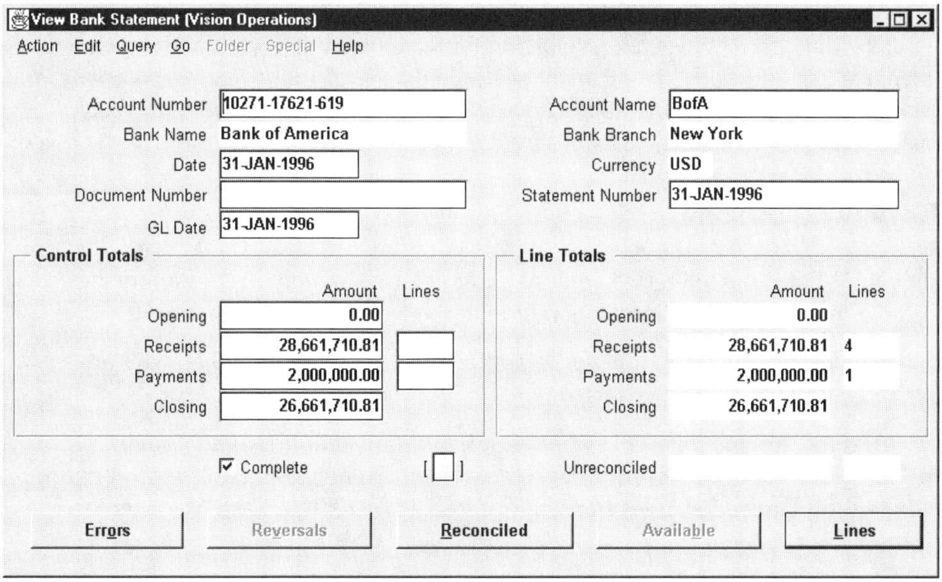

FIGURE 14-3. *View Bank Statement form*

The navigation path to the System Parameters form is *Setup : System Parameters*. The System Parameters window will open. Select the Automatic Reconciliation alternative region. Enter the tolerances amount and tolerance percent.

For example, let's use a tolerance amount of $50, a tolerance percent of 5 percent, and a statement line amount of $1,000. When you submit the AutoReconciliation program, Oracle Cash Management will compare each statement line against the set tolerances. Oracle Cash Management first computes the tolerance percentage amount. In our example, the tolerance amount will be 5 percent of $1,000 = $50. Oracle Cash Management will then compare the computed tolerance percentage amount to the tolerance dollar amount. Oracle Cash Management selects the smaller of the two amounts (percentage or dollars) to use as your tolerance limit. Oracle Cash Management then matches the statement line against a payment or receipt transaction in the range $950 to $1,050 ($1,000 plus or minus $50).

If the difference between a payment amount and the statement amount line is within your predefined tolerances, Oracle Cash Management posts the difference to the Payables bank charges account or the bank errors account. The account that will be used is based on how you defined the *AP Tolerance Differences* option system parameter in the Automatic Reconciliation alternative region. If you selected

Charges, it will post to the bank charges account. If you selected Errors, it will post to the bank errors account. This option only applies to Payables transactions.

If the difference between a receipt and the statement line is within your defined tolerances, Oracle Cash Management posts the difference to the Receivables bank charges account. Receivable transaction differences are only charged to the bank charges account. Unlike transactions from Oracle Payables, you do not have a choice.

Review Questions

1. What is the tolerance amount and tolerance percent in the Automatic Reconciliation alternative region in the System Parameters form?

2. What are your options for tolerance differences and in what ways are tolerance differences used?

3. How are the differences between bank statement lines and Oracle Receivables transactions and the differences between bank statement lines and Oracle Payables transactions treated by Oracle Cash Management?

Reconciling Multicurrency Transactions

Reconciling multicurrency transactions can be done manually or automatically in Oracle Cash Management.

To reconcile multicurrency transactions automatically, Oracle Cash Management follows the same two-step process. First, Oracle Cash Management matches the bank statement lines to transactions. Next, Oracle Cash Management marks the transactions as cleared. There are two scenarios for multicurrency transactions. The first scenario is when the bank account is in the functional currency and the transactions are in foreign currency. This is referred to as the international scenario. In this scenario, Oracle Cash Management matches the transactions in the functional amount with the bank statement line amount, which is in functional currency. If the difference is within the set tolerance amount or the calculated tolerance percentage amount, it is a successful match. The tolerance amount set in the system parameters is always in the functional currency. The second scenario is when the bank account and the transaction are in the same currency but not in the functional currency. This is referred to as the foreign scenario. In this scenario, Oracle Cash Management performs two matches. Oracle Cash Management first matches the transactions in the functional amount with the bank statement line amount translated to the functional amount using the exchange rate associated with the bank statement line. If the difference is within the tolerance limit (the smaller of amount and percentage), then it will perform the second match. Oracle Cash Management will translate the tolerance amount into the foreign currency using the exchange rate associated with the bank statement line. Then, if the difference between the transaction foreign amount and the bank statement line foreign amount is within the foreign tolerance limit, it is a successful match. If one of the two fails, it is an unsuccessful match. The AutoReconcilation program will validate each exchange rate at the time the bank statement is imported and reconciled.

For manual reconciliation, enter the exchange rate for each foreign currency transaction. In a foreign scenario, the exchange rate entered for a foreign currency transaction becomes the default for the bank statement line, thus clearing the transaction line using the same exchange rate. In the international scenario, the exchange rate is calculated for each statement line. Remember that set tolerances do not apply to manual reconciliation.

Review Questions

  1. What is a foreign scenario and how does matching work?

  2. What is an international scenario and how does matching work?

  3. If the matching fails and you want to reconcile the multicurrency transactions, what can you do?

Reconciling Bank Statements Manually

Oracle Cash Management allows you to manually reconcile bank statements. This can be done by importing the statement directly from the bank, or you can manually load the information you wish to reconcile. You can reconcile each line of a bank statement against available transactions. Oracle Cash Management can search for transaction types such as receipts, payments, or lines that meet your search criteria.

To reconcile bank statements manually, use the *Bank Reconciliation : Bank Statements* navigation path. The Find Bank Statements form will appear. See Figure 14-4. Query the statement you wish to reconcile. You can enter the bank account number, statement number, document number, GL date, bank statement date, currency, and whether the bank statements are completed. Leave all fields blank for all existing bank statements. Click on **Find**.

The Reconcile Bank Statements form will appear. See Figure 14-5. Select the bank statement that you want to reconcile from the list. Click on **Review**. The Bank Statement form will appear. See Figure 14-6. The form will display bank account information, including the branch, account numbers, GL dates, and currency. You will see five choices at the bottom of the form: **Errors**, **Reversals**, **Reconciled**, **Available** and **Lines**.

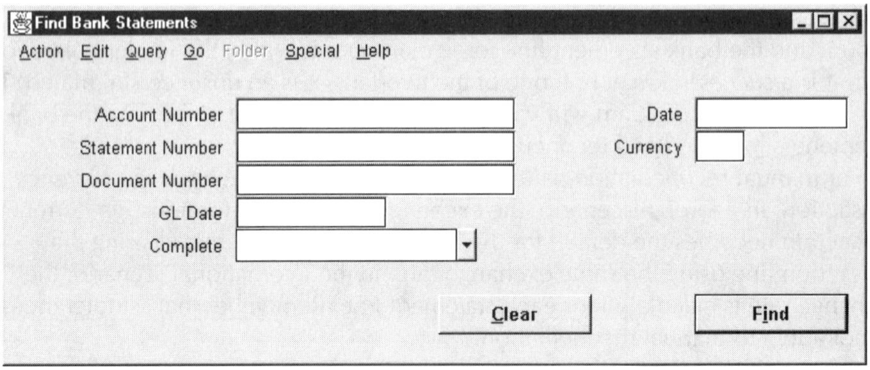

FIGURE 14-4. *Find Bank Statements form*

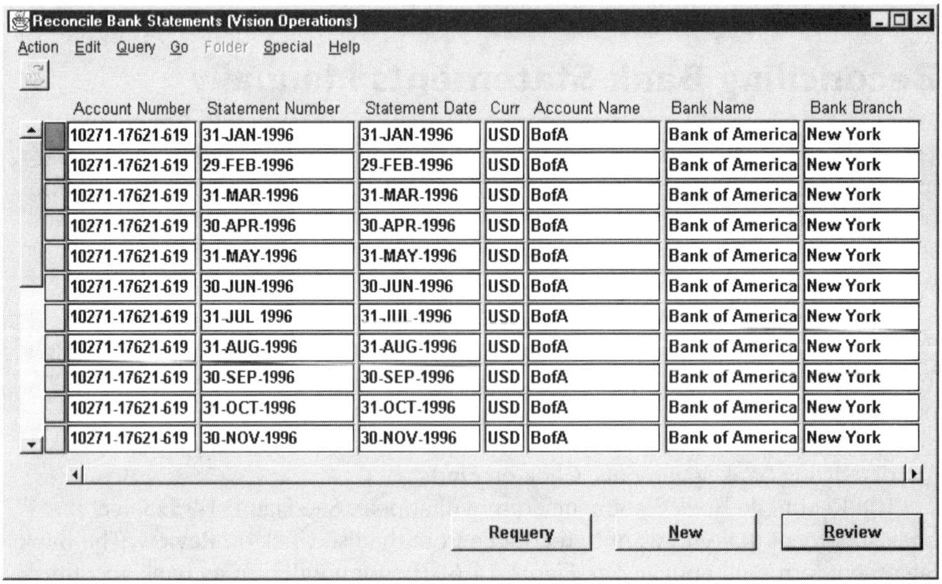

FIGURE 14-5. *Reconcile Bank Statements form*

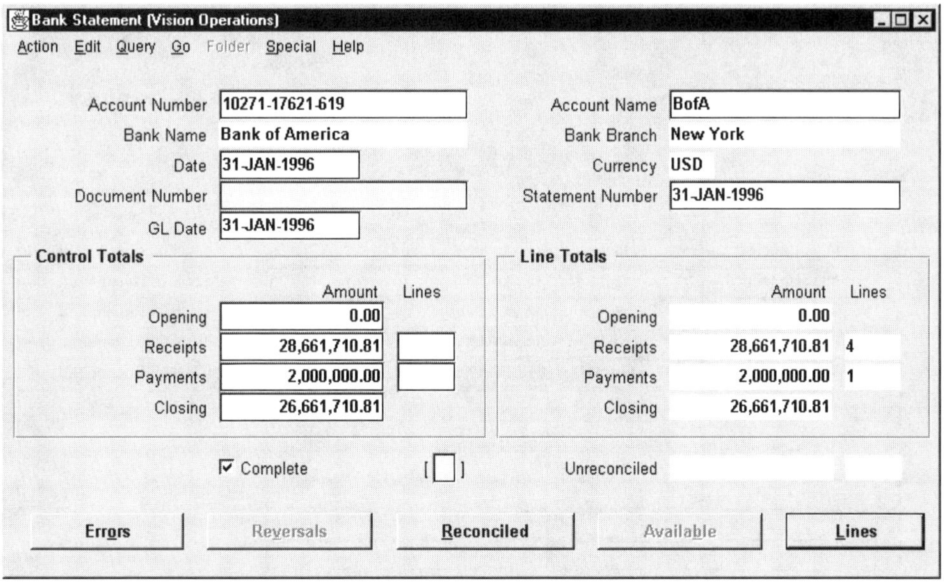

FIGURE 14-6.   *Bank Statement form*

If you click on **Lines**, the Bank Statement Lines form will appear. See Figure 14-7. Select the bank statement line you wish to reconcile. Next, click on **Available** to obtain transactions for reconciliation. The Find Transactions form will appear. See Figure 14-8. You can select *Detail*, *Batch*, or *Open Interface* by selecting the appropriate radio button. *Detail* will find all of the available detailed transactions. *Batch* will find the remittance and payment batches. *Open Interface* will find all of the receipts or payment transactions in the open interface. Next, you can check one or more transaction types—*Receipt*, *Payment*, *Miscellaneous*, *Journal*, or *Statement Line*—to restrict the selection. (The transaction types that are available will depend on the radio button you select; for instance, *Open Interface* allows only *Receipt* and *Payment*.) There are four alternative regions to further restrict your selection criteria: Transaction, Agent, Receipt, and Journal. You can enter the transaction number range in the Numbers field. For Oracle Payables transaction, you can enter the check number range. You may enter transaction date range, transaction amount range, maturity date range, batch name range, remittance number range, or currency.

If you select *Receipt* and/or *Payment*, you can enter customer name/number and/or supplier name/number in the Agent alternative region.

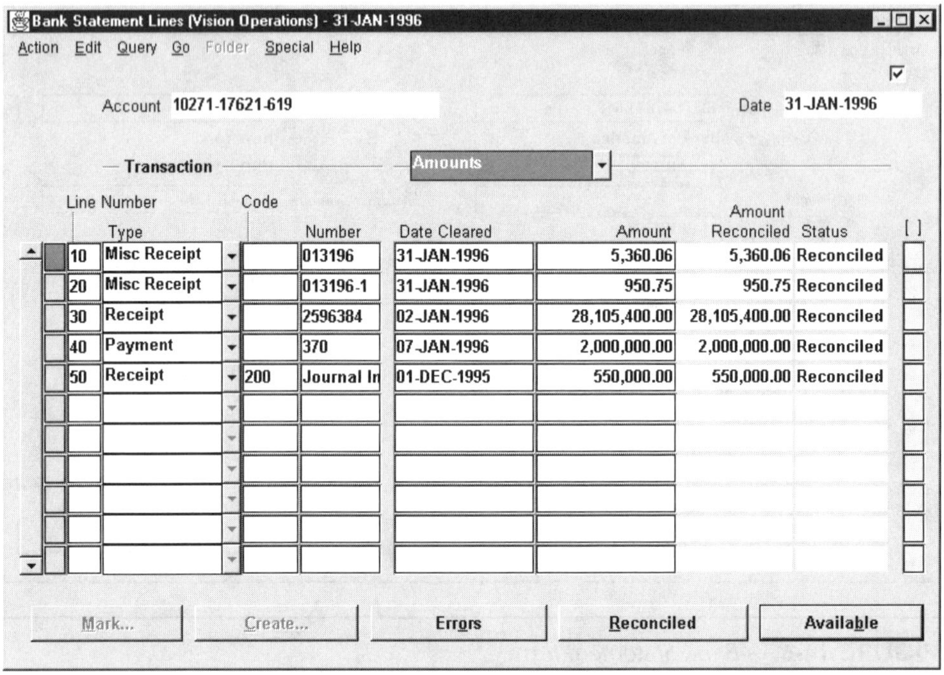

FIGURE 14-7. *Bank Statement Lines form*

If you select *Receipt* and/or *Miscellaneous*, you can enter the reference type, reference number, receipt class, payment method, and/or deposit date range in the Receipt alternative region.

If you select *Journal*, you can enter the period name, journal entry name range, document number range, and/or journal line number range in the Journal alternative region.

The last alternative region, Ordering, is different than others. You do not use it to restrict selection; instead, you use this alternative region to determine how selected transactions can be ordered. You can select the primary sort order and the secondary sort order. With either order, you can choose by transaction type, transaction number, transaction date, or transaction amount. You can also determine whether you want the primary sort and secondary sort to be in ascending or descending order. See Figure 14-9.

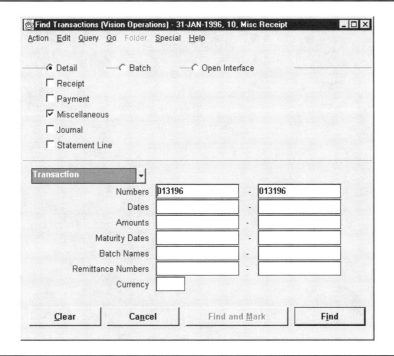

FIGURE 14-8. *Find Transactions form*

Once you have selected all of the criteria, click on the **Find** button. The Available Transactions window will display. See Figure 14-10. Select your transactions by checking the leftmost checkbox. Choose the Exchange Rate alternative region to view the exchange rate for multicurrency transactions. Choose the Reference alternative region to see additional descriptive information about the transactions or journal lines. You can override the defaulted amount cleared, cleared date, and GL date. Click on **Reconcile**. This will change the status of the bank statement line to Reconciled. Use **Previous** and **Next** to navigate to the previous bank statement line or to the next bank statement line. The Amount Reconciled field displays the reconciled amount of the bank statement line, whereas the Amount Remaining field displays the unreconciled amount of the bank statement.

Close the Available Transactions window and you will be back to the Bank Statement Lines form. Close the Bank Statement Lines form and you will be back to the Bank Statements form. You can click on **Reversals** to reverse any reconciled receipt transactions. The Find Reversals window will ask you to find the receipt you

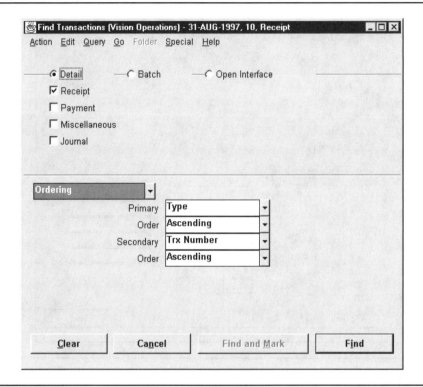

FIGURE 14-9. *Find Transactions (Ordering) form*

want to reverse. Save your work. Close the Bank Statement window and you will be back to the Reconcile Bank Statements window. Here, you can manually enter the bank statement by clicking on the **New** button. The Bank Statement form will appear. See Figure 14-11.

Entering Bank Statements

You can load bank statements in Cash Management by using the Cash Management Bank Statement open interface or by entering the information manually.

Each bank statement in Cash Management contains a header, which identifies the statement number, date, and bank account. Under the header, there can be multiple statement lines. The statement lines contain entries for one or more payments, receipts, journal entries, and miscellaneous transactions. Each line contains a line number, transaction type, amount, and date cleared. To enter a bank statement manually, enter the header and all of the associated transaction lines. The transaction line can be reconciled as you enter the bank statement or after all lines are entered.

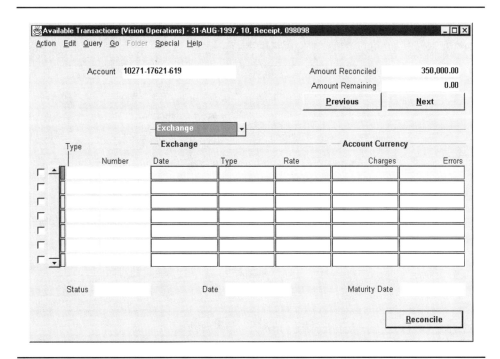

FIGURE 14-10. *Available Transactions form*

In the Bank Statement form, enter the bank header information. You must enter the account number, statement number, statement date, currency, account name, bank name, and bank branch. Enter the statement date and document number only if you are using manual numbering document sequencing. The statement number will default to the system date, but can be overridden. Enter the GL date. You have the option of entering the control totals for the opening amount, the receipt amount, the receipt lines, the payment amounts, the payment lines, and the closing amount. Save your work.

Next, enter the statement lines. Click on **Lines**. See Figure 14-12. Begin by entering the line number. Then select the transaction type from the drop-down list. If you plan to reconcile this statement automatically, enter the bank transaction code and the transaction number, which can be the invoice number or agent bank number. Select the Amounts alternative region. Enter the transaction amount. Next, enter the exchange information in the Exchange alternative region, if required, such as when the bank statement is in a currency other than the functional currency. Exchange information includes currency, exchange rate date, exchange rate type, and exchange rate. Next, select the Reference alternative region and enter the supplier, invoice number, and bank. Finally, you may enter the effective date and a short description of the line. Continue to enter any additional bank statement lines.

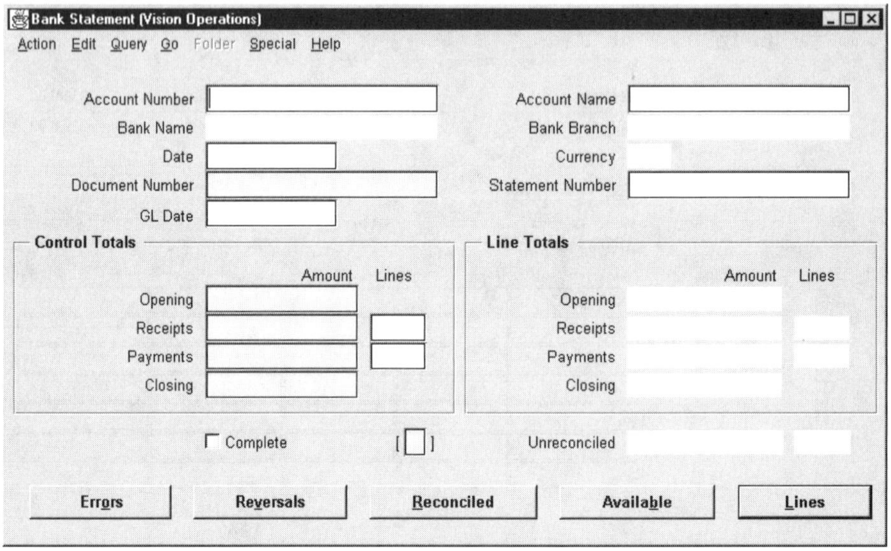

FIGURE 14-11. *Bank Statement form*

Save your work. As you enter the bank statement lines, you can click on **Available** to reconcile the bank statement line to transaction(s).

You can update a bank statement as long as the statement is not marked Complete. To update a bank statement, use the same navigation path as for entering a bank statement; the Find Bank Statement form will appear. Enter your selection criteria for the bank statement you want to update and click on **Find**. The Reconcile Bank Statement form will appear. Locate the particular bank statement that you want to update.

Select the Statement and click on **Review**. Update the bank statement information, header, and line information that can be changed. You may add more transaction lines or delete lines entered in error. Save your work.

Review Questions

1. How do you reconcile existing bank statement lines to Oracle Payables payments?

2. When is the **Reversals** button used?

3. For what are the *Detail, Batch,* and *Open Interface* options used?

4. How do you enter a new bank statement?

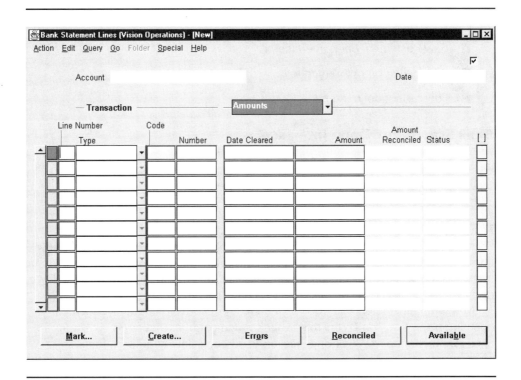

FIGURE 14-12.   *Bank Statement Lines form*

Open Interface Transactions

You can automatically or manually reconcile open interface transactions. When you run AutoReconciliation through one of the three programs, AutoReconciliation will check the Reconciliation open interface for transactions if you have enabled the Use Reconciliation Open Interface system parameter. You can use the Reconciliation open interface if you have a third-party system that must be reconciled in Oracle Cash Management. To manually reconcile interface transactions, check *Open Interface* in the Find Transactions window to find transactions in the open interface table to be reconciled with bank statement lines. Two types of transactions can be found in the open interface table that are to be reconciled with bank statement lines: Receipt and Payment. You can select both types at the same time or you can select them separately. You can further restrict the selection criteria by, for example, date range and transaction number.

There are three open interfaces in Oracle Cash Management:

- Bank Statement open interface
- Reconciliation open interface
- Forecasting open interface

Bank Statement Open Interface

Use the Bank Statement open interface to load bank statements. You can either load the bank statements or enter them online manually. To load bank statements using the Bank Statement open interface, the bank statements must be in flat files. Some standard bank formats are BAI and SWIFT940. Use an Oracle utility called SQL*Loader to load the flat files into the Bank Statement open interface. The Bank Statement open interface includes two tables: CE_STATEMENT_HEADERS_INT_ALL for the bank statement header information and CE_STATEMENT_LINES_INTERFACE for the bank statement lines. Follow the *Bank Reconciliation : Bank Statement Interface* navigation path to invoke the Bank Statement Interface form. You can use this form to review or modify data in the Bank Statement open interface. See Figure 14-13.

You will immediately see the data if there are records in the Bank Statement open interface. Click on **Errors** to see bank statement lines that erred out during bank statement import. Click on **Lines** to see all bank statement lines. Bank

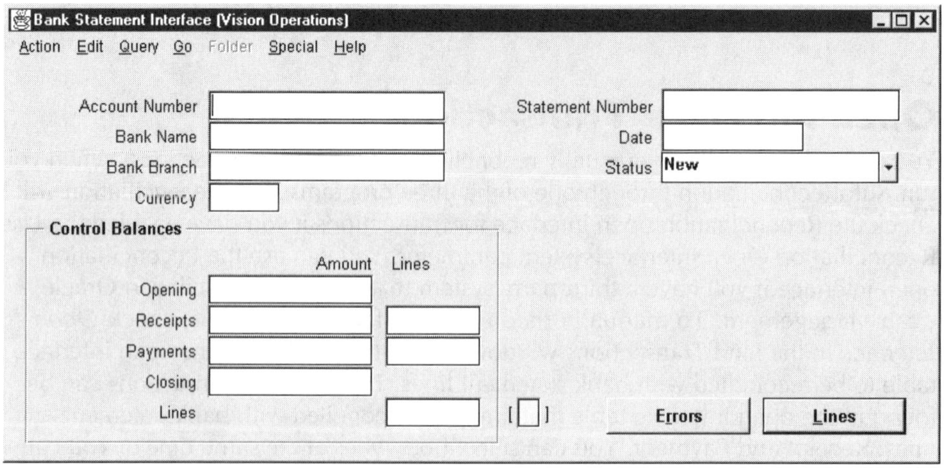

FIGURE 14-13. *Bank Statement Interface form*

Statement Import is the program that will load the bank statements from the Bank Statement open interface to the production tables in Oracle Cash Management. Once you are satisfied with the data in the Bank Statement open interface tables, run the Bank Statement Import program from the Standard Request Submission form. You can set up Oracle Cash Management to automatically archive and purge the imported bank statements in the Bank Statement open interface tables by setting the *Archive* and *Purge* options in the AutoReconciliation system parameters.

Reconciliation Open Interface

The Reconciliation open interface allows you to reconcile bank statements in Oracle Cash Management when you are using third-party systems. To use Reconciliation open interface, first enable the Use Reconciliation open interface system parameter. Next, set up the Reconciliation Open Interface view and the Reconciliation open interface package. The Reconciliation Open Interface view is called CE_999_INTERFACE_V. Configure this view to link to third-party system transactions and allow reconciliations in real time. The Reconciliation open interface package is called CE_999_PKG. The package contains a function and two procedures. The function is a locking function that allows you to lock your third-party transactions before the reconciliation takes place in Oracle Cash Management. This prevents users from changing the transactions while reconciling. The two procedures are to clear and unclear transactions in your third-party system. These two procedures must be modified to update your third-party system transactions and generate the necessary accounting entries.

Forecasting Open Interface

The Forecasting open interface allows you to load forecast information from third-party software into Oracle Cash Management. Forecast information includes both cash flowing in and cash flowing out. You can use two different sources to identify the direction of the cash flow. Once the forecast information is in the Forecasting open interface, the Cash Forecasting program summarizes and calculates cash forecasts, including the data in the Forecasting open interface if your forecast templates include an open interface as a source.

To use Forecasting open interface, set up external source types and selection criteria. This is done by defining the Selection Criteria Descriptive flexfield in Oracle Cash Management. The external source type is the context field and the selection criteria are the attributes. You can have up to 15 attributes. Create a view for each external source type. The view points to the location of the open interface transactions. The view can have any name, but it must have the selection criteria specified and transaction date, functional currency, functional amount, currency, transaction amount, and row ID as columns. The exact name of the columns are ROW_ID, TRANSACTION_AMOUNT, FUNCTIONAL_AMOUNT, CURRENCY_CODE, FUNCTIONAL_CURRENCY, CASH_ACTIVITY_DATE, CRITERIA1, CRITERIA2 … CRITERIA15.

Review Questions

1. How will Oracle Cash Management autoreconcile Reconciliation open interface transactions?

2. How many open interfaces are possible within Oracle Cash Management and what is the purpose of each open interface?

3. How is Oracle Cash Management linked to your third-party system?

4. What does CE_999_PKG contain and what is the purpose of this package?

Reconciling Bank Errors and Corrections

Oracle Cash Management can reconcile bank errors and record corrections. If a bank should incorrectly record a transaction and subsequently record a correction, Oracle Cash Management can reconcile this adjustment and provide an audit trail of the transactions.

There are two methods banks use to correct transaction errors: reversal and adjustment. The first type reverses the transaction in full and performs a separate transaction, as it should have been done the first time. The second method makes an adjustment entry. The bank keeps the incorrect entry and adds an additional entry to adjust the incorrect entry to the correct amount.

You must first manually unreconcile the erred bank statement lines if they are already reconciled, usually because of the set tolerance for both automatic or manual reconciliation.

The AutoReconciliation program reconciles bank errors and records corrections differently depending on whether it is a reversal or an adjustment. For reversal, the AutoReconciliation program will match to a statement line that has the same transaction number, but an opposite signed transaction amount. For an adjustment, the AutoReconciliation program will create a match with a statement line that has the same transaction number and statement line amount, as long as the adjustment amount is equal to the transaction amount.

For manual reconciliation, follow the *Bank Reconciliation : Bank Statements* navigation path. The Find Bank Statements window will appear. Click on **Find** to return all bank statements with all blank criteria or with some restrictive criteria. Select the desired bank statement from the displayed list. Next, click on **Review**. The Bank Statement form will appear. Select **Lines** to see all of the bank statement lines of the bank statement. Select the bank statement line you want to reconcile and click on **Available**. The Find Transactions form will now appear. Click on **Detail**. For reversal, find the original bank statement line and check *Statement Line*. For an adjustment, find the transaction and the original statement line by checking *Statement Line* plus the transaction type of your transaction. Additional search criteria can be added by entering dates, amounts, and names in the alternative regions. Click on **Find** to begin your search.

Review the available transactions in the Available Transactions form. To reconcile, check the box to the left of the line and click on **Reconcile**. This will reconcile the item against the statement line. If you select **Find and Mark** instead of **Find** in the Find Transactions form, the selected transactions or statement lines will be automatically marked for reconciliation. Click on **Reconcile**.

Review Questions

1. What two methods can be used to correct bank errors?

2. For reversal, what should be matched to the reversal entry?

3. For adjustment, what should be matched to the adjustment entry?

4. What is the sequence of forms from finding a bank statement to reconciling manually?

Cash Forecasting

The last section of this chapter describes cash forecasting. You will learn to:

- Define forecast templates

- Generate cash forecasts

- Query, review, and modify cash forecasts

- Export cash forecasts to Excel spreadsheets

Oracle Cash Management will assist you in managing your entire business. You can prepare accurate cash forecasts integrating General Ledger, Receivables, Payables, Order Entry, Payroll, Purchasing, and external systems using the open interface.

When performing cash forecasting, you must keep in mind the limited scope of future transactions stored in your systems. Cash forecasts in Oracle Cash Management are built around the use of templates. You will generate your forecast by creating a template, generating the forecast from the template, and, if you wish, modifying or exporting the forecast.

Defining Forecast Templates

When creating the cash forecast template, you must define the rows and columns of your forecast. The template will determine the period type, what sources to include, and level of detail. Forecast information can be in any currency, across organizations, and for multiple periods.

To define forecast templates, follow the navigation path *Cash Forecasting : Forecast Templates.* The Find Forecast Templates window will appear. See Figure 14-14. You can search for existing templates by entering the template name or selecting the method for template forecasts. Click on **Find**. To define a new forecast template, click on **New**. In either case, the Forecast Templates window will appear. See Figure 14-15.

Enter a name for your forecast template. The forecast name must be unique and should provide a brief description of the forecast objective. Enter the forecast-by type in days or GL periods. This will determine whether the forecast is generated by days or by accounting periods. An optional step, but one that is recommended, is to enter the description of the cash forecast template. For overdue transactions, select Include or Exclude for open transactions that have a cash activity date before the forecast start date. If you select to include the overdue transactions, you must enter the cutoff period, which controls how far back to include transactions. If too many old transactions are included, forecast generation can be slowed. Select a transaction calendar in the Business Calendar field. If you leave the business calendar blank, cash activity days could be nonbusiness days. For your review question, enter **NEW Forecast** as the template name. Leave all of the defaults as is and save your work. Next, define the rows and columns for the templates. To define columns, click on **Columns**. The Forecast Template Columns window will appear. See Figure 14-16.

Enter a column number to specify the order of the forecast periods. The value must be a number between 1 and 999. This number indicates the sequence of the columns in your template. The maximum number of columns that can be defined is 80. Enter the GL Periods/Days From and To fields as days or periods, depending on the forecast-by type defined above. For your review question, create a weekly forecast template for a quarter. See Table 14-1. Once you complete the setup, close this window and return to the Forecast Templates window.

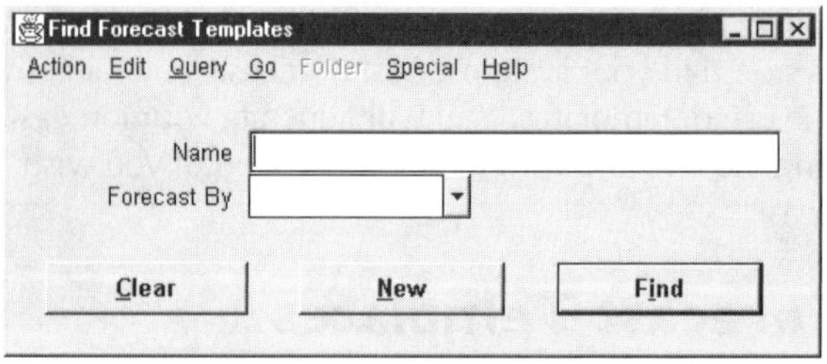

FIGURE 14-14. *Find Forecast Templates form*

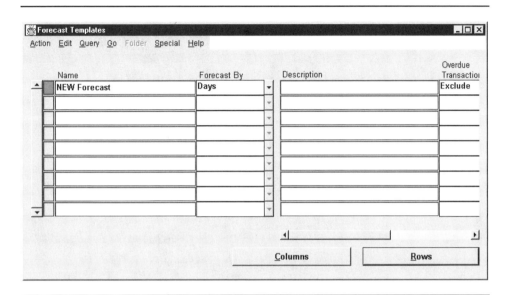

FIGURE 14-15. *Forecast Templates form*

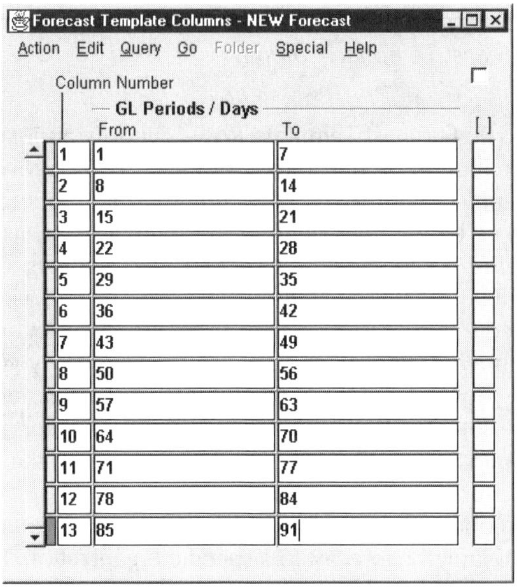

FIGURE 14-16. *Forecast Template Columns form*

Column Number	From	To
1	1	7
2	8	14
3	15	21
4	22	28
5	29	35
6	36	42
7	43	49
8	50	56
9	57	63
10	64	70
11	71	77
12	78	84
13	85	91
14	92	98

TABLE 14-1. *Forecast Template Columns*

Click on **Rows**. The Forecast Template Rows window appears. See Figure 14-17. Enter the row information for your forecast template. Enter a row number to specify the order and sequence of your rows. The value must be a number between 1 and 999. Select the source type. Types defined in Oracle Cash Management are: AP Invoices, AP Payments, AR Invoices, AR Receipts, GL Budgets, GL Cash Position, GL Encumbrances, Payroll Expenses, Purchase Orders, Purchase Requisitions, Sales Orders, User-Defined Inflow, User-Defined Outflow, Open Interface Inflow, and Open Interface Outflow. If you select a user-defined source type, the forecast will generate a blank row for manual input using the Cash Forecast window or export file. Once you have selected the source types, you may enter additional fields depending on the source types you selected. You can select the same source type but enter different criteria in the additional fields.

You can enter an optional description of the source type. You can also enter an organization name to limit the forecast to a specific organization. If you leave the Organization field blank, the forecast will include all organizations. Organizations can consist of business groups for Oracle Payroll or operating units for application modules

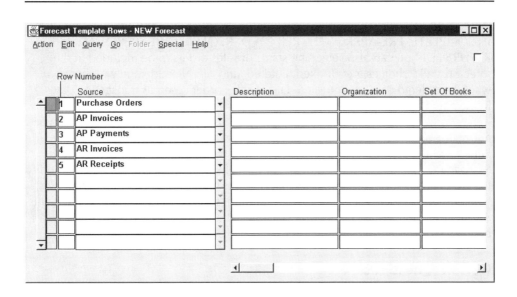

FIGURE 14-17. *Forecast Template Rows form*

in which multiple-organization operation is enabled. All additional fields, if left blank, will default to include all values. You can enter a Set of Books for source types related to General Ledger. You can also enter a payroll name for Oracle Payroll. For Oracle Payables, you can elect to include maximum discount, minimum discount, or no discount in the forecast. You can also enter a pay group, payment priority, and/or supplier type to limit the Oracle Payables and Oracle Purchasing data by pay group. You can enter a payment method and/or bank account for Oracle Payables and Oracle Payroll to limit the forecast by the payment method you specify. Next, you can decide whether you want to include uncleared transactions or cleared transactions: the Future method includes uncleared transactions, whereas the Historical method includes cleared transactions. If you select Historical Method, you must indicate the roll-forward type and roll-forward period. The roll-forward type can be Day, Month, or Period. The roll-forward period is a numeric value. Together, they specify the number of days, months, or periods to roll forward. You can also enter a receipt method, profile class, and/or disputes for Oracle Receivables source types. For GL Budget source type, you can enter a budget name. You can enter a particular account for source types related to General Ledger. Enter a positive number in the Lead Time field if you want the projected cash transaction date for requisitions, purchase orders, and sales orders to be the transaction date plus the lead time.

Next, you can select the authorization status of requisitions and purchase orders that should be included in the forecast. Valid choices are APPROVED, IN PROCESS, INCOMPLETE, PRE-APPROVED, REJECTED, REQUIRED REAPPROVAL, and RETURNED. You can also select the status of sales orders to be included in the forecast. Valid choices are: Booked, Entered, and All. Next, decide whether you want the ordered date or requested date of sales orders used as transaction dates. Remember that lead times will be added to these transaction dates. As a last step, if the source type is Open Interface–related, enter the external forecast source type and selection criteria that you want to include in the Forecasting open interface. Enter all of the appropriate fields for the source types you selected. Oracle Cash Management validates required fields for the selected source types. You can modify the template later, but this will affect all prior cash forecasts based on the template.

For this example, select five rows—Purchase Orders, AP Invoices, AP Payments, AR Invoices, and AR Receipts—with default settings. Save your work. You have defined a forecast template.

Review Questions

1. What are the components of a forecast template?

2. How can your forecast template include forecasts from the Forecasting open interface?

3. How are User-Defined Inflow and User-Defined Outflow source types used?

4. What is the difference between the Future method and the Historical method?

Generating Cash Forecasts

You have the option of determining the data to be processed in your forecast. You can submit many separate processes to generate partial forecasts by source type. If you have included user-defined source types, you will be able to enter the amounts manually. External sources can be accessed and included in your cash forecast using the Forecasting open interface. You can generate forecasts from a template or you can manually enter cash forecasts.

To manually enter a cash forecast, use the *Cash Forecasting : Forecasts* navigation path. The Find Cash Forecasts window will appear. See Figure 14-18. To modify an existing cash forecast, enter the template name, forecast name, forecast-by, and a period range. To select a specific template, you can leave the Template Name field blank to display all existing cash forecasts. Click on **New** to enter a new cash forecast.

For this review question, click on **New**. The Cash Forecasts window will appear. See Figure 14-19. Select the template you want to use. Next, enter a unique forecast

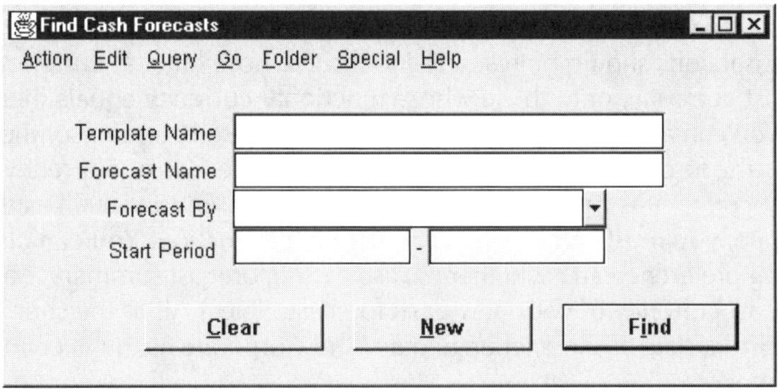

FIGURE 14-18. *Find Cash Forecasts form*

name. The start date will default to the system date. Select your template and enter **NEW Forecast** as the forecast name; select Sunday for the start date, since you want to run the forecast weekly; and click on **Open** to enter more details. The Cash

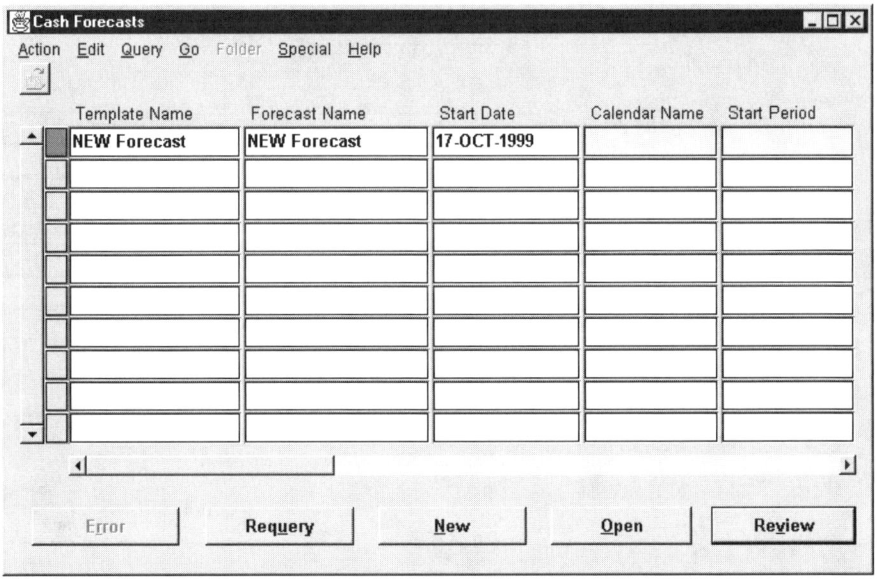

FIGURE 14-19. *Cash Forecasts form*

Forecast detail window appears. See Figure 14-20. You may enter a description for the forecast, but you must enter the forecast currency. You can specify whether the entered transactions should be restricted to those whose entered currency equals their forecast currency, or to those whose functional currency equals their forecast currency. You can also indicate whether to use the entered currency or the functional currency as the forecast currency by selecting All as the Source Currency Type. If the forecast currency is not the functional currency, or you select All as the source currency type, you must enter the exchange rate information. You can also specify the factoring preference and whether to display the forecast summary. Select USD as the forecast currency of your new cash forecast. Select All as the source currency type, the current date as the exchange date, and Corporate as the exchange type. Save your work.

Click on **Review** to display the Cash Forecast Amounts form. See Figure 14-21. You will see your rows, the calculated columns, and the amounts. You will see all zeros since your cash forecast does not yet have values. Change the forecast amounts as you wish. Save your work and close the Cash Forecast Amounts window.

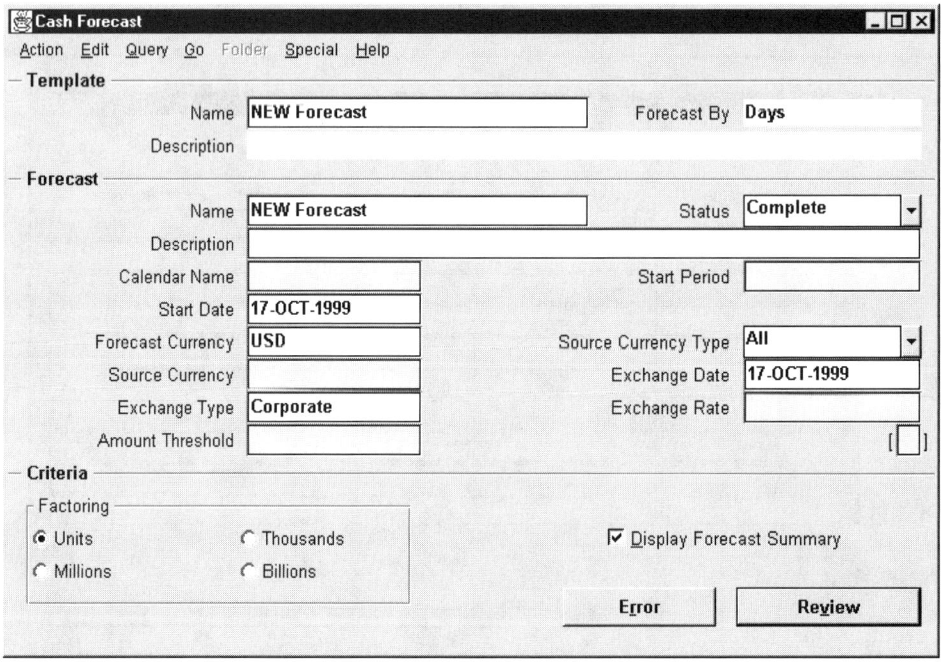

FIGURE 14-20. *Cash Forecasts details*

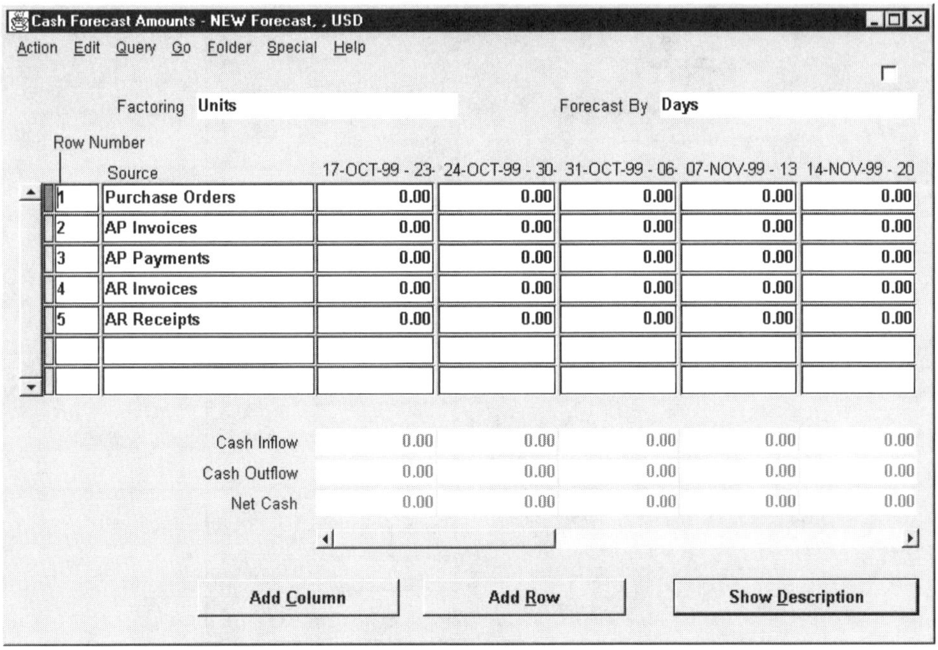

FIGURE 14-21. *Cash Forecast Amounts form*

To generate the cash forecast automatically, execute the Special | Submit Forecast menu command. The Submit Forecast window will appear. See Figure 14-22. Enter the template name. Enter **NEW Forecast automatic** as the forecast name. Enter the rest of the fields in the same manner used to define the cash forecast manually, except you can specify row number ranges and an amount threshold. The amount threshold defines the minimum amount of transactions to be included in the forecast. The row range allows you to run a partial forecast with selected source types. Check *Request by Row* if you want to submit a separate concurrent request for each row. Click on **Submit** to generate a new cash forecast or click **Cancel** to clear. You will be asked to confirm submission. Choose Yes. A concurrent program called Cash Forecasting by Days or Cash Forecasting by GL Periods will be submitted. Oracle Cash Management will automatically create a Cash Forecast Execution report when a forecast is submitted. This report informs you of any errors produced by the Submit Forecast program. Verify the generation result.

You can also generate cash forecasts using the standard Submit Request function within Oracle—the navigation path is *Other : Run*. The Submit a New Request window will open. Click **OK**. The Submit Request window will appear. Depending on your

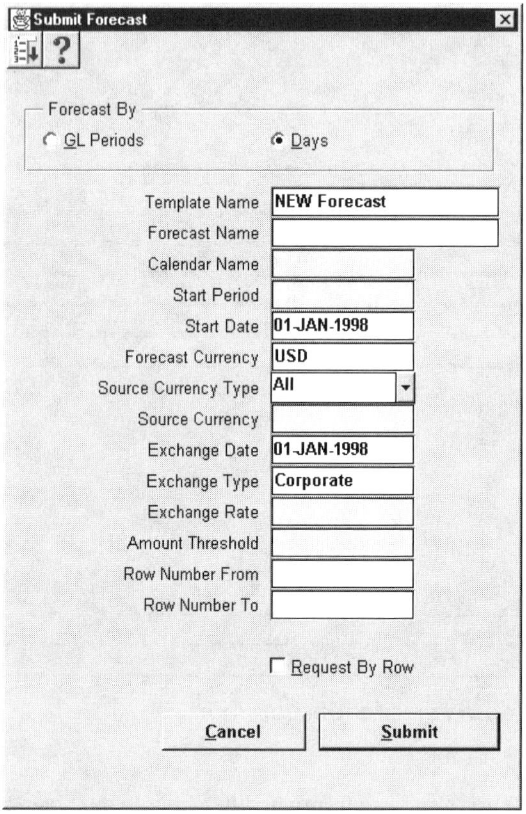

FIGURE 14-22. *Submit Forecast form*

template definition, select Cash Forecasting by GL Periods or Cash Forecasting by Days from the List of Values in the Name field. The Parameters window will appear. Enter the desired parameters for your forecast. In many cases, the List of Values option is available. Click on **Submit** to generate a new cash forecast, **Cancel** to cancel this request, or **Clear** to clear parameters and reenter. Select the print and run options. If you clicked **Submit**, click on **Submit Request** to process the request or **Cancel** to terminate process. Oracle Cash Management will automatically create the Cash Forecast Execution report when the forecast is submitted. This report informs you of any errors produced by the Submit Forecast program.

Review Questions

1. How can you manually enter a cash forecast?

2. How can you automatically generate a cash forecast?

3. When is an amount threshold used?

Querying, Reviewing, and Modifying Cash Forecasts

You can query, review, and modify cash forecasts that were manually entered or automatically generated. You can change descriptive information, add or delete rows and columns, and change forecast amounts. Some modifications can only be performed at certain stages of cash forecast development.

The navigation path to query, review, and modify cash forecasts is the same path used to enter forecasts: *Cash Forecasting : Forecast.* The Find Forecast form will be displayed. Enter your template name, or use additional parameters such as the forecast name or forecast period. Click on **Find**. The Cash Forecast form will appear. Select the forecast you wish to modify. Click on **Open** to view the selected cash forecast. You are allowed to change only the name and description of the cash forecast here. The lower-left portion of the form allows you to select the display parameters for the Cash Forecast Amounts form. You may select to view your forecast by units, thousands, millions, or billions.

Click on **Review** to move to the Cash Forecast Amounts form to modify your forecast. Click on **Review** in the Cash Forecast form. The Cash Forecast form will now appear. This form allows you to change any forecast amounts. The summary amount, located in the lower portion of the form, will change as a result of any other amount changed in your forecast. The Cash Inflow row summarizes the total cash inflow. The Cash Outflow row summarizes the total cash outflow. Net cash = cash inflow – cash outflow. You can change column amounts or row amounts by a percentage or an amount by executing the Special | Update Amount menu command. See Figure 14-23. You can select to update a row range or a column range. For each specified range, you can increase or decrease by a specific value. If you check *Use %*, the value will be interpreted as percentage; otherwise, the value will be an amount. For example, if you choose to increase a column amount by 5 percent, this is easily done with the *Update Amount* option. Save your changes by clicking on **Update**.

You may add columns or rows to your cash forecast. From the Cash Forecast Amounts form, click on **Add Column** or **Add Row**. The Add Column or Add Row

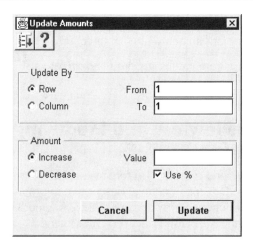

FIGURE 14-23. *Update Amounts form*

form will be displayed. See Figure 14-24. First, you must enter a unique column number and the GL period (days from and to). For new rows, enter the row number and source. Select from either User-Defined Inflow or User-Defined Outflow, depending on the direction of cash flow amounts. Next, check *Create New Forecast Template*. This will preserve the previous template and add the new column/row to a new template. Leaving this box unchecked will result in Cash Management changing all previous versions of the template to include the new number of columns or rows. Click on **Add** to save your work.

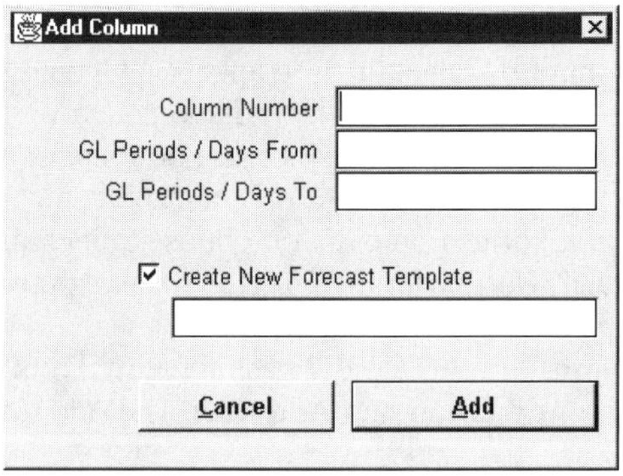

FIGURE 14-24. *Add Column form*

Review Questions

    1. How can you use the Update Amount window to change forecast amounts?

    2. What source types can you use to add columns or rows to a cash forecast?

    3. What are the four factors you can use in displaying forecast amounts?

Exporting Cash Forecasts to Excel Spreadsheets

Oracle Cash Management provides an option to export your cash forecasts to Excel as spreadsheets. In Excel, you can manipulate and enhance your cash forecast and modify the presentation. You must have Windows and Excel installed to benefit from this feature.

When you are in the Cash Forecast Amounts window, execute the Action | Export menu command. The Export Data form will open. Check *To Microsoft Excel* to export your cash forecast to Excel. Check *Autosize All Columns* to have Excel automatically size the spreadsheet columns. If the columns are not autosized, you may see "####" in some of your spreadsheet columns, signifying the column width is not appropriate for the data stored. Click **Export** to export the records, open Excel, and display your forecast in Excel. Click **Cancel** to terminate this process.

You can now make modifications to your cash forecasts in Excel. Making changes in Excel will not save or update your Oracle system.

Review Questions

    1. What must be installed for the Export cash forecast function to work?

    2. What happens when you autosize a column?

    3. What does "####" indicate?

For the Chapter Summary, Two-Minute Drill, and Chapter Questions and Answers, open the summary.htm file contained in the Summary_files directory on the book's CD-ROM.

CHAPTER
15

Advanced Purchasing

n the prior chapters, you learned how to set up Oracle Purchasing and create basic purchasing documents, such as purchase requisitions and standard purchase orders. This chapter begins with teaching you how to evaluate supplier performance and how to submit a Supplier Performance report, which will help you with the evaluation.

This chapter covers the following subjects:

- Evaluating supplier performance
- Creating Requests for Quotations manually
- Entering quotations
- Entering contract purchase orders
- Entering blanket purchase agreements
- Using AutoCreate

In Oracle Purchasing, you can enter quotations manually, or you can automatically create quotations from a request for quotation (RFQ) that is used to solicit quotations from suppliers. In this chapter, you will learn how to do both. You will also learn to define supplier lists and to manually create RFQs. In addition, this chapter covers how to approve selected quotations.

In the second half of the chapter, you will learn how to create contract purchase orders and blanket purchase agreements. For contract purchase agreements, you will learn how to enter an agreement, and then reference the agreement on a standard purchase order. For blanket purchase agreements, you will learn how to enter the agreement and then generate a blanket release against the blanket purchase agreement.

The last section of this chapter discusses how to use the AutoCreate process to create purchasing documents.

Evaluating Supplier Performance

Oracle Purchasing offers reports to help you evaluate supplier performance. This section teaches you how to use the Supplier Performance reports and all of the reporting parameters. You will also learn how you can use the Submit Reports form to select the Supplier Performance reports and provide the necessary options.

In this section, you will learn how to:

- Identify Supplier Performance reports
- Use the Submit Reports form

Identifying Supplier Performance Reports

Because the quality of your suppliers plays a key role in the success and efficiency of your company's performance, Oracle Purchasing offers a full repertoire of reports to review, manage, negotiate, and control supplier performance. The reports, along with RFQs and quotations, assist you in evaluating your suppliers.

The following reports can be used for evaluating supplier performance:

- Vendor Price Performance Analysis

- Vendor Purchase Summary

- Vendor Quality Performance

- Vendor Service Performance Analysis

- Vendor Volume Analysis

TIP
"Vendor" and "Supplier" are interchangeable words in Oracle Purchasing. Typically reports use "Vendor" and forms use "Supplier".

Vendor Price Performance Analysis Report

The Vendor Price Performance Analysis report compares the item prices of different suppliers. Reporting options include the title of the report, vendor name range, period range, purchase order creation date range, purchasing category range, and item range.

The report can be sorted by purchasing categories or items options. You can also enter the dynamic decimal precision to determine the number of decimal places the Quantities field should display in the report.

Vendor Purchase Summary Report

The Vendor Purchase Summary report lists the number and amount of purchase orders you placed. You can use this report to negotiate, analyze, and manage your purchasing volume. Reporting options are the title of the report, creation date range, specific vendor/supplier type, and whether to include small businesses, minority-owned businesses, or women-owned businesses.

The report can be sorted by supplier type or by supplier. To sort by supplier, the report sorts by supplier name, supplier site, and PO number. To sort by supplier type, the report sorts by supplier name, supplier type, supplier site, and PO number.

Vendor Quality Performance Report

The Vendor Quality Performance report helps you identify suppliers that have quality issues and problems. You can review quality performance on percent accepted, percent rejected, and percent returned. Reporting options are the title of the report, item range, supplier name range, purchasing category range, specific buyer, and creation date range.

   The report can be printed in summary or detail form. If you want the report to include detailed information, select Yes for the *Detail* reporting option. You can also enter the dynamic decimal precision to be used with the Quantities field in the report.

Vendor Service Performance Analysis Report

The Vendor Service Performance Analysis report reports on shipment performance—for instance, late shipments, early shipments, rejected shipments, and wrong shipments. You can use the data from this report to create built-in penalty charges for suppliers, negotiate performance standards, and modify payment terms. Reporting options are the title of the report, item range, supplier name range, purchasing category range, specific buyer, and creation date range.

   The report can be printed in summary or detail form. If you want the report to include detailed information, select Yes for the *Detail* reporting option. You can also enter the dynamic decimal precision to be used with the Quantities field in the report.

   Though this report focuses on shipment performance, the reporting options of the Vendor Service Performance Analysis report and the Vendor Quality Performance report are identical.

Vendor Volume Analysis Report

The Vendor Volume Analysis report reports the dollar value purchased from your suppliers. The report compares your actual purchase percentages with your sourcing percentage. Reporting options are the title of the report, item range, creation date range, and specific organization.

   The report prints items assigned to sourcing rules. Sourcing rules specify how items for your organization are replenished. These rules also specify the order and percentages of different sources of an item in replenishment.

Review Questions

   1. Which report can you use to compare item prices between suppliers?

   2. Which report deals with quality issues of suppliers?

   3. Which report should you use to report shipment information?

   4. What is a sourcing rule?

Using the Submit Reports Form

You can use the Submit Reports form to submit Supplier Performance reports, which generally are Standard Request Submission (SRS) reports. If you are logged on with the *Purchasing, Vision Operations (USA)* responsibility, the navigation path to the Submit Reports form is *Reports : Run*.

Choose Single Request and click the **OK** button. Select Supplier Performance Report as the request name and enter the parameters in the Parameter form. Most of the parameters are optional, except the *Dynamic Precision* option and the *Detail* and *Organization* reporting options. Once you have entered the parameter, click on the **OK** button to accept it. To submit your Supplier Performance report, click on the **Submit Request** button.

Review Question

1. Which parameters in a Supplier Performance report are required?

Manually Creating Requests for Quotation

This section talks about manually creating a request for quotation (RFQ), which is used to solicit quotations.

In this section, you will learn how to:

- Define supplier lists
- Manually create a request for quotation

Defining Supplier Lists

Supplier lists in Oracle can assist you in your procurement process. Having created unique supplier lists, you can copy this information directly when creating your request for quotations.

The navigation path to the Supplier Lists form is *Supply Base : Supplier Lists*. You can double-click on Supplier Lists, or click on the **Open** button from the Navigator. The Supplier Lists form appears. See Figure 15-1.

Enter a unique list name for each supplier list you want to create. If you wish, you can enter a description for your supplier list. The description may help you distinguish or easily identify the list. If you want to specify the time period when this list expires, enter an inactive date for your supplier list.

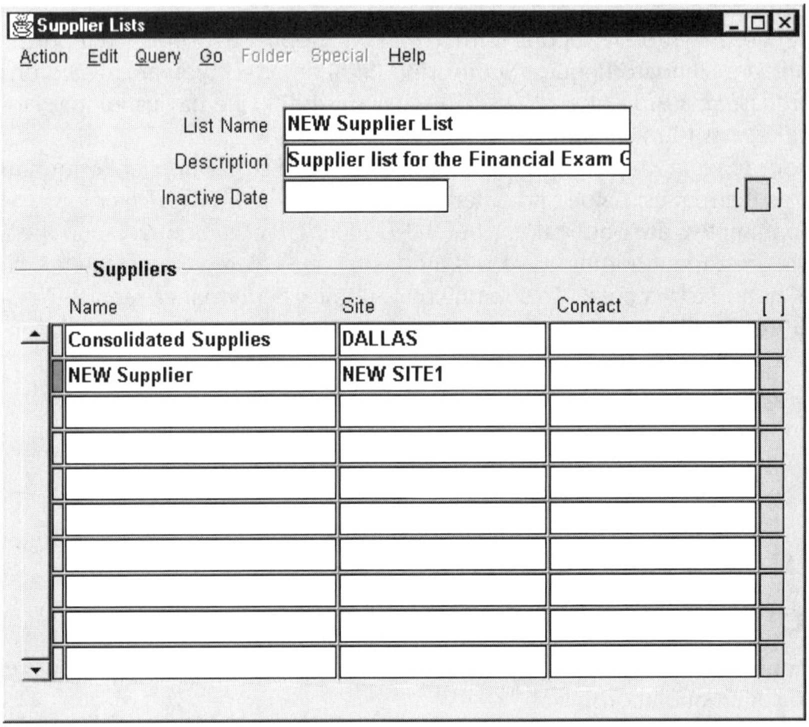

FIGURE 15-1. *Supplier Lists form*

In the Suppliers region, use the List of Values to enter the supplier names to place on this supplier list. Using the List of Values, enter the supplier site. Enter the contact name. The supplier and the supplier site are mandatory; however, the supplier contact is optional.

For the purposes of this exercise, enter the list name **NEW Supplier List,** and select Consolidated Suppliers for the supplier name. As the supplier site, select Dallas.

Save your work.

Review Questions

1. What is the purpose of the supplier list?

2. What fields are mandatory in putting suppliers on the supplier list?

3. If a listing is only valid through the end of the month, what can you do to ensure that the expiration occurs?

Creating a Request for Quotation Manually

As mentioned earlier, the purpose of the RFQ is to solicit supplier bids on items to be purchased by your company. If the *RFQ* option is checked on your requisition, then an RFQ is required. When an RFQ is required, you have the option to either create it manually or create it using AutoCreate.

If your suppliers and/or supplier sites do not currently exist in Oracle, then you must first create new suppliers and supplier sites. Within Oracle you can create supplier lists to predefine groups or categories of suppliers to whom you will send RFQs. Your RFQs can include specification requirements, target prices, order quantity ranges, unique or standard classifications, and multiple shipment information.

The navigation path to the RFQs form is *RFQs and Quotations : RFQs.* You can either double-click on RFQs or click on the **Open** button from the Navigator. The RFQs form appears. See Figure 15-2.

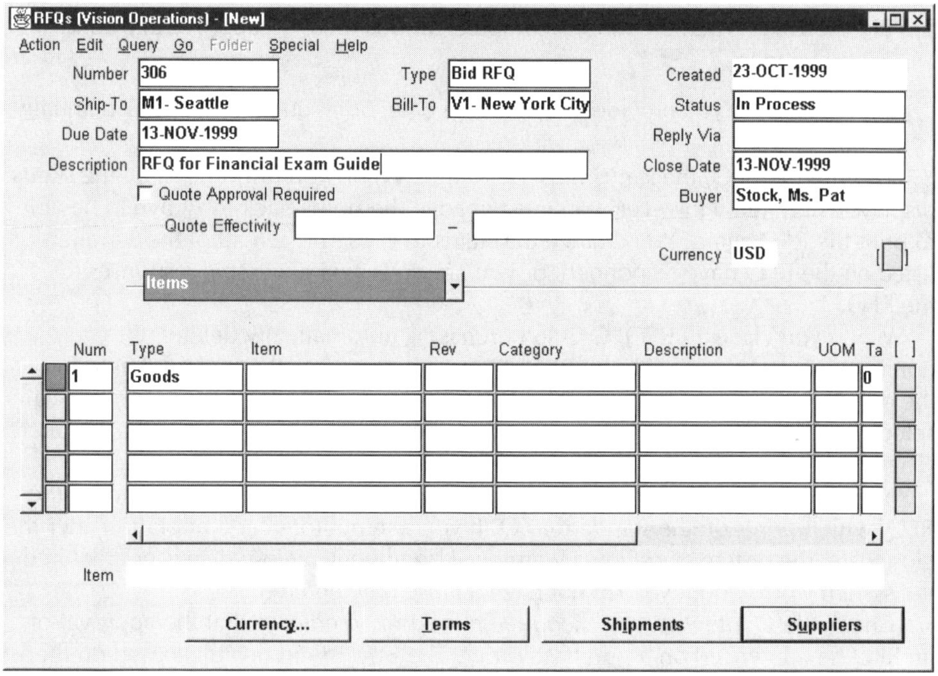

FIGURE 15-2. *RFQs form*

RFQ Header

In the RFQs form, you enter the header information first. Next, enter an RFQ number if manual numbering has been enabled in your purchase options. If automatic number generation has been enabled, you cannot enter data into this field. The RFQ number is generated when you save your work.

Select an RFQ type from the List of Values. Valid RFQ types are Bid RFQ with quotation class Bid, Catalog RFQ, and Standard RFQ with quotation class Catalog. Remember that the Bid quotation class is for a specific fixed quantity, date, and location; Catalog quotation class is for different quantities and usually includes quantity-based price breaks.

The Created field defaults from the system date and is display only. Enter the ship-to location for the quotation items from the List of Values. Enter the bill-to location for the quotation items from the List of Values.

The Status field changes, depending on the processing stage of the RFQ. The stages are as follows:

- **In Process**   The initial status when you create the quotation.

- **Active**   When the RFQ is complete, and is ready to approve and send to vendors.

- **Closed**   If you provide an expiration date, or if you close the RFQ manually.

To print the RFQ, the status must be Active. When you print the RFQ, the status displays as Printed. However, you must change the status back to Active to be able to print the RFQ again. You change the status to Closed when all of the suppliers listed on the RFQ have responded, or you are no longer accepting responses for the RFQ.

When you close an RFQ, Oracle Purchasing automatically deletes all notifications associated with the RFQ. However, you have the option of entering the due date by which suppliers must submit their quotations. If you wish, you can select from the Reply Via field the method of response you'd like from the supplier. (These values must be identified and created during setup as lookup codes.)

You can enter an optional description for the RFQ. Enter the close date for the RFQ, which prints on the standard RFQ. If you attempt to enter a quotation after the close date, the system gives you a warning. Also, though a close date is not required, the system warns you if you do not have a close date entered.

Check the *Quote Approval Required* checkbox to enforce that the approval of an RFQ be referenced on a purchase order. The Buyer field defaults based on the sign-on identity of the application user. You can also select another buyer from the List of Values. When you enter a buyer name in this field, the buyer receives all notifications related to the RFQ. If you wish, enter the quote effectivity date range for which the quote will remain valid. The Currency field defaults to the functional currency defined in your Set of Books related to this operating unit.

For the purposes of this exercise, enter an RFQ type of **Bid RFQ**, select M1 – Seattle as the ship-to location, and V1 – New York City as the bill-to location. Enter a due date and a close date that are three weeks from current date.

Save your work.

RFQ Currency

The default currency is the functional currency defined in your Set of Books. In your case, it is the USD. You can accept or change the values. If you do change currency and you have pricing on existing line items already, the pricing does not convert to the new currency automatically. To change currency information defaults, click on the **Currency** button. The Currency form appears. See Figure 15-3.

You can enter the exchange rate type and exchange rate date only if the currency is different from your functional currency. Exchange rate types are Corporate, Spot, and User as well as any other user-defined exchange rate types. If you select the User exchange rate type, then you must enter an exchange rate. After your review your changes, click on the **Done** button to apply them. If you want to cancel your entries and return to the RFQs form, click on the **Cancel** button.

RFQ Terms

Terms and Conditions fields, which are also considered RFQ header information, include payment terms, freight terms, freight carrier, and FOB point. To change any default terms from the supplier information, click on the **Terms** button on the RFQ form. The RFQ Terms form appears. See Figure 15-4.

In the RFQ Terms form, you can enter or change the terms and conditions for the RFQs. You can also include information in the Note To Supplier field. When

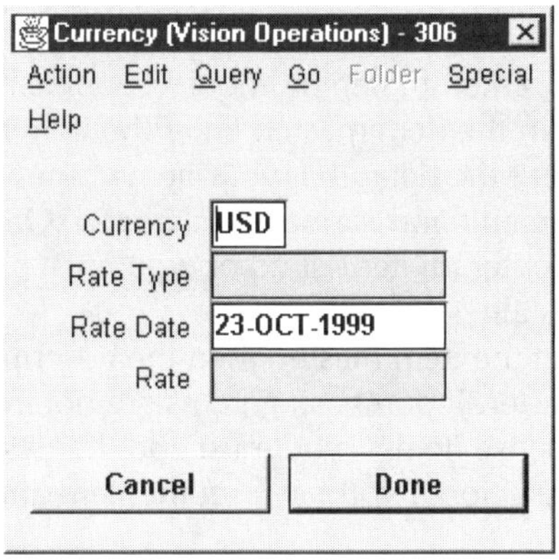

FIGURE 15-3. *Currency form*

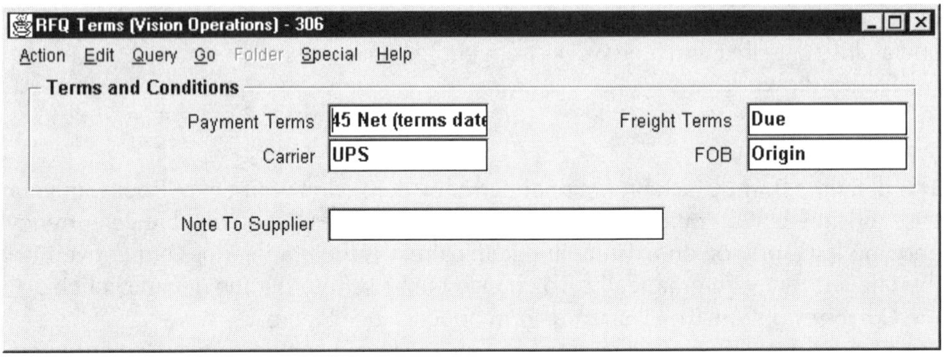

FIGURE 15-4. *RFQ Terms form*

you are done reviewing or updating, close the RFQ Terms form and return to the RFQs form.

You have now completed the header information for the RFQ.

RFQ Lines

Now that the header information is complete, you must enter the items that you want included in the RFQs. See Figure 15-5.

If you select Items for the alternative region, you must input the basic line item information. This step is very similar to what you must do when you enter a purchase requisition. The system automatically generates a line number for each line you create, starting with number 1, which is populated in the Num field.

Select the line type from List of Values. For amount-based line types, the Item Number field is not available. Amount-based line types only need a price; the quantity will always be 1. Enter an item number, if applicable. You enter an item number if the item exists in the item master. Enter the item revision number from the List of Values, or accept the default. If your item comes from the item master, the category is filled by default and cannot be changed. Otherwise, you must enter a category. If you do not enter an item number, you must enter the purchasing category from the List of Values.

If the item comes from the item master, then the description for that item defaults from the item master. If purchasing items are not from the item master—as is often the case with expense items—you must add the description manually. You can change the item description if you have set the item attributes to allow this type of change.

Next, enter the unit of measure (UOM) in the UOM field. The UOM defaults from the item master (if the item comes from the item master). Enter a quantity

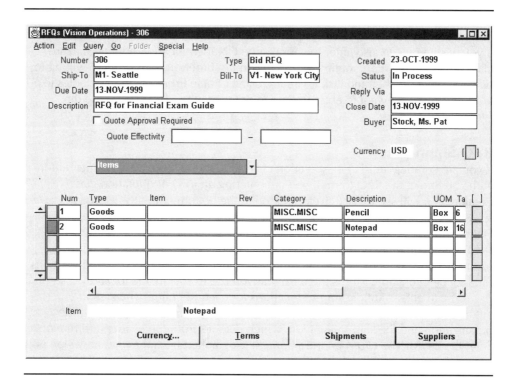

FIGURE 15-5. *RFQ Lines (Items) form*

greater than zero. If you wish, in the Target Price field, enter the target price for the RFQ line item. The target price can be used for negotiation. If you wish, enter the supplier/manufacturer item number.

For the purposes of this exercise, create an RFQ for office suppliers using the lines shown in Table 15-1. Then save your work.

Line Type	Purchasing Category	Description	UOM	Target Price
Goods	MISC.MISC	Pencil	Box	$6
Good	MISC.MISC	Notepad	Box	$16

TABLE 15-1. *RFQ Lines*

If you select More for the alternative region, you can enter various miscellaneous information for your RFQ lines. The line number defaults from the item line number. If you wish, you can also enter the applicable UN identification number, hazard class related to the item, minimum and maximum order quantity you are willing to buy, a project number and task if you are using Oracle Projects, and any notes to the supplier. If you want to enter unlimited notes or other documents, use the Attachments feature.

RFQ Shipments

If you are entering an RFQ of quotation class Bid, you will see a **Shipments** button at the bottom of the RFQ form. If you are entering an RFQ of quotation class Catalog, you will see a **Price Breaks** button at the bottom of the RFQ form.

Click on the **Shipments** button. The RFQ Shipments form appears. See Figure 15-6.

The RFQ Shipments form allows you to specify the location and quantity for each RFQ line. Remember that the Bid quotation class allows you to get quotations for a specific location. This is the form that you use to specify the location.

You can enter multiple ship-to locations for each RFQ line. The system automatically defaults the shipment number, starting from number 1. Enter the organization and the ship-to location, which defaults from the header information. Enter the UOM. The UOM on the shipment is defaulted from the line; however, you

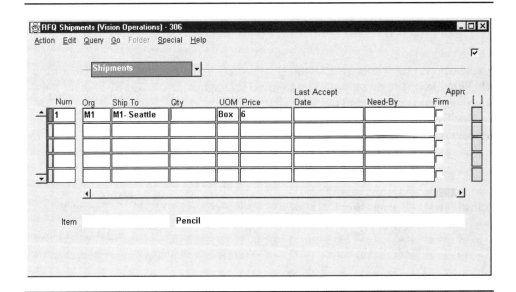

FIGURE 15-6. *RFQ Shipments (Shipments) form*

can change it. The price also defaults, but you can change it as well. If you wish, you can enter the last accept date for an RFQ and the need-by date. If you want a firm bid, check the *Firm* checkbox. If there is an approved quotation for this RFQ shipment already, the checkbox is checked automatically. Save any changes.

If you select More for the alternative region, you can specify whether the RFQ shipment is taxable.

If you select the *Taxable* checkbox, you can enter the tax name corresponding to the tax on the shipment. For invoice matching, you can select the invoice matching option to enforce two-way, three-way, or four-way matching. You can also enter the tolerance in the Quantity Received region. The tolerance defaults from the receiving options. If the quantity received exceeds the set tolerance, you can choose to ignore, reject, or warn the user.

Save any changes you may have made.

RFQ Price Breaks

For each line entered, you can enter the price breaks requested for the quotation class Catalog by clicking on the **Price Breaks** button on the bottom of the RFQs form. Select a line by clicking on that line and then click on the **Price Breaks** button to open the RFQ Price Breaks form. You can provide multiple price breaks if you need to receive quotes for different terms, quantities, and locations. See Figure 15-7.

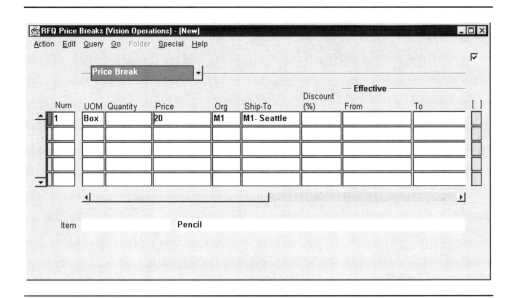

FIGURE 15-7. *RFQ Price Breaks form*

In the RFQ Price Breaks form, the number defaults sequentially starting at 1. Enter the UOM for the line, then enter the price break quantity. Enter the organization by selecting from the List of Values in the Org field. You can only select organizations for which the item has been defined. The ship-to information defaults from the RFQ header information. You have the option of changing the ship-to information by selecting from the List Values, but you can only select from among locations for that organization.

Enter the discount percentage for the unit price in the Discount % field. If you entered a unit price and break price, the system will not calculate the discount percent. You can have a break price or a discount percentage, but not both. If you wish, you can enter a date range from the List of Values that determines how long the quotation will be in effect, the lead time, payment terms, freight terms, FOB method, and the freight carrier. If there is an approved quotation for this price break line, the *Approved* checkbox is checked automatically.

When you select More for the alternative region of the RFQ Price Break form, you can review and change miscellaneous information. This region is identical to the More alternative region of the RFQ Shipments form. The number defaults from the price break line number. If the line item is taxable, check the *Taxable* checkbox. If you select the *Taxable* checkbox, enter the tax name by selecting it from the List of Values. Select an invoice matching to ensure two-way, three-way, or four-way matching. Enter the tolerance under the Quantity Received quantity.

For the Exception field, your options are as follows:

■ **None** May exceed tolerance.

■ **Reject** Cannot exceed tolerance.

■ **Warning** Can exceed, but receiver gets warning message.

Save your changes and close the RFQ Price Breaks form.

RFQ Suppliers

The final step in entering an RFQ is to enter the suppliers to whom you want to send the RFQ. To do this, click the **Suppliers** button on the bottom of the RFQs form. The RFQ Suppliers form appears. See Figure 15-8.

The Seq field number defaults sequentially starting with number 1. In the Supplier field, use the List of Values to enter the names of all of the suppliers you want to add to your RFQ. Enter the site for each supplier selected from the List of Values. If you wish, enter the contact for the selected supplier from the List of Values.

If you would like to print an RFQ for the supplier, check the *Include In Next RFQ Printing* checkbox. When the printing completes, the system removes this flag and you must recheck the *Include In Next RFQ Printing* checkbox to reprint RFQ.

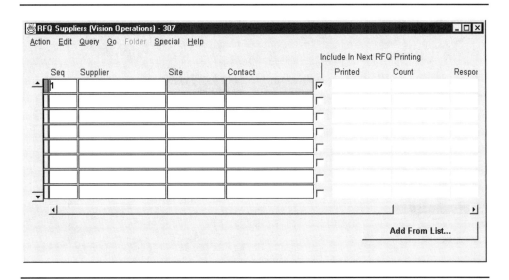

FIGURE 15-8.   *RFQ Suppliers form*

The Printed field displays the date that the last RFQ was printed for that supplier. The Count field displays the number of RFQs that have been printed for this supplier. The Responded field displays the date you entered the supplier's response. The Quote field displays the supplier quote for the item.

   In cases where you have defined supplier lists and wish to add them to your RFQ, click on the **Add From List** button in the RFQ Suppliers form. The Supplier Lists form appears. See Figure 15-9.

   This form shows all of the predefined supplier lists along with their description and the number of suppliers within each list. Click on the checkbox next to all of the lists you would like to apply to the RFQ. Once you have checked all of the appropriate checkboxes, click on the **Apply** button to accept your choices, or click on the **Cancel** button to clear your entries. You are returned to the RFQs form.

   For the purposes of this exercise, click the **Add From List** button in the RFQ Suppliers form. All of the predefined supplier lists appears. Select the checkbox next to the NEW Supplier List entry. Then, click on the **Apply** button. A message appears telling you that the supplier list(s) have been copied onto this RFQ. Click the **OK** button to acknowledge the message and close the form. Notice that the supplier on your list is copied onto the RFQ, and the *Include In Next RFQ Printing* checkbox has been automatically checked.

   The RFQ is now complete. Return to the RFQs form by closing the RFQ Suppliers form. In the RFQ form, change the status from In Process to Active by

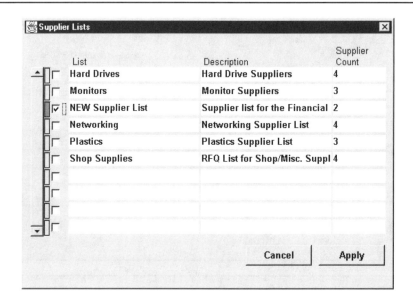

FIGURE 15-9. *Supplier Lists form*

using the List of Values. Save your work. You are now ready to print the RFQs for all of the suppliers for whom you checked the *Include In Next RFQ Printing* checkbox.

RFQ Print

You can print the RFQ by submitting the printed RFQ using the Submit Reports form. The report can be printed in landscape (horizontally) or portrait (vertically). You can select the report type to print all RFQs, print only the changed RFQs, or print all of the new RFQs. You can also print the RFQs by a specific buyer or by an RFQ number range. In addition, you can specify whether the report is a test. As a last step, you can specify whether to sort the RFQs by buyer name or by RFQ number. Standard Oracle RFQs assume you are printing on preprinted forms. If you are not, you may need to customize this report to meet your needs.

Review Questions

1. What is the purpose of close date for an RFQ?

2. In what status must the RFQ be to print?

3. How can you enter an RFQ for a currency other than the functional currency?

4. What is the purpose of RFQ price breaks, and for what type(s) of RFQ can you enter them?

Entering Quotations

The supplier submits quotations in response to RFQs. Once you have sent out the RFQs, the next step is to wait for the responses from the suppliers.

In this section, you will learn how to:

■ Enter quotations

■ Create quotations automatically

■ Approve quotations

Entering Quotations Manually

When the supplier responds to your RFQ, you must record the supplier's quote. Oracle Purchasing offers you two methods to record the quote information: to enter the quotes manually, or use the Copy Document function. You must approve the quote once it is entered into the system. This allows your buyers to reference the quote on the purchase order or the purchase requisition. Also, when you approve the quote, you can control the use of your sourcing information.

TIP
If you receive catalog information, you can use the Oracle Purchasing Document open interface to import the information in your system.

First, you will learn how to enter the supplier quotation manually. The navigation path to manually enter a quotation is *RFQs and Quotations : Quotations.* You can double-click on **Quotations**, or click on the **Open** button from the Navigator. The Quotations form appears. See Figure 15-10.

Quotation Header
You may notice that the Quotations form resembles the RFQ form. Similar to the RFQ form, in the Quotations form you also enter the header information first. Enter a unique quotation number if manual numbering has been enabled in your purchasing options. If automatic number generation has been enabled, you cannot

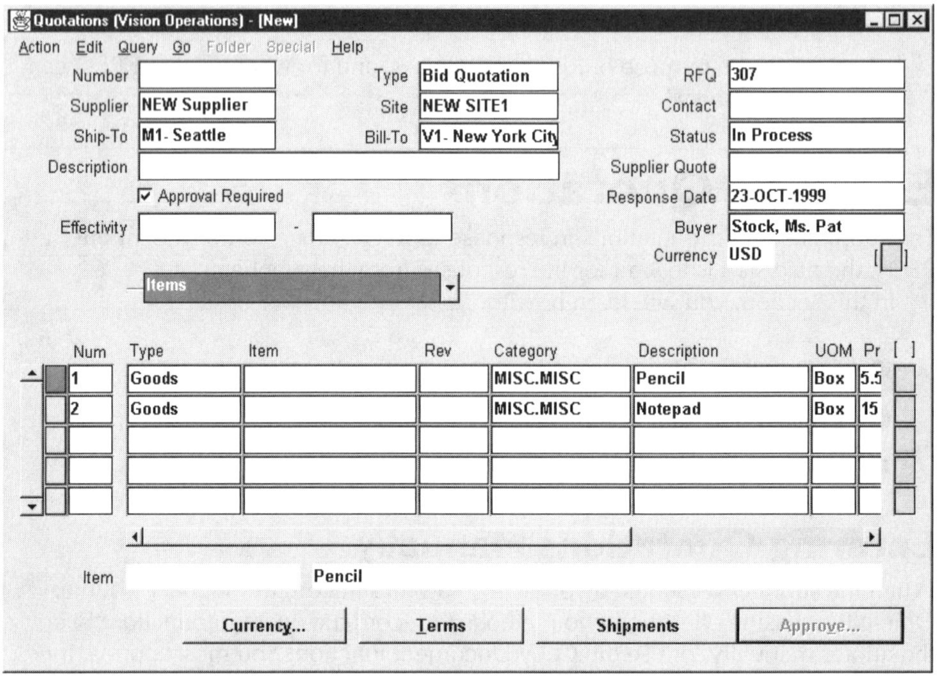

FIGURE 15-10. *Quotations form*

enter data into this field. The quotation number is generated when you save your work.

Select Type from the List of Values. Valid quotation types are Bid Quotation with quotation class Bid, Catalog Quotation, and Standard Quotation with quotation class Catalog. Next, enter the supplier name, the supplier site, and the supplier contact from the Lists of Values. Supplier site and supplier contact are not mandatory.

Enter the RFQ number to which the quotation refers. Oracle Purchasing uses the supplier and the supplier site you entered to find the corresponding RFQ number. If you receive an unsolicited quote from a supplier and/or supplier site that is not on your original RFQ, you must add the supplier and/or supplier site before entering the supplier quotation. The RFQ field defaults the number from a copied RFQ, which you can override if you are generating quotations automatically.

If you wish, enter a ship-to location and a bill-to location for the quotation. Use the Status field to review, track, and control the status of the quotation:

- ■ **In Process**   The initial status when you create the quotation.

- ■ **Active**   When quotation is complete and is ready to approve.

- ■ **Closed**   If you provide an expiration date or you close the quotation manually.

If you wish, enter a description for the quotation. Enter the supplier quote number if applicable. Check the *Approval Required* checkbox to enforce approval of the quotation before it can be used as a reference on a purchase requisition or a purchase order. The system assigns the system date as the response date. If your response is not the system date, you can also opt to enter a date on or before the system date. This should be the date you received the quotation from the supplier. In the Effectivity field, enter a date range for the quotation from the supplier's quote. You cannot delete a quotation, but you can change the effectivity date of the quotation.

Oracle Purchasing defaults the buyer from the sign-on identity of the application user who enters the quotation. To assign another buyer, you can select from the List of Values. Currency defaults from the functional currency assigned to your Set of Books. This field can be changed in the Currency form.

For the purposes of this exercise, enter a quotation corresponding to your NEW Supplier. Select NEW Supplier as the supplier name. Select the RFQ number that was entered in an earlier exercise. Since you only created one RFQ for your supplier, you can use the List of Values to find the corresponding RFQ. Check the *Approval Required* checkbox. Save your work.

You can change the currency information by clicking on the **Currency** button and selecting the currency you want. You can also select the exchange rate type and the exchange rate date. This is the same as the Currency form for RFQ.

Quotation Terms

Terms, which are also considered as quotation header information, include payment terms, freight terms, freight carrier, and FOB point. Click on the **Terms** button in the Quotation form. The Quotation Terms form appears. See Figure 15-11.

If you wish, you can change the defaulted payment terms, freight terms, freight carrier, and FOB terms from the List of Values. You may enter a note in the Note From Supplier field about the terms. The Created field displays the date the quotation was created and defaults from the system date. If you wish, enter the received via

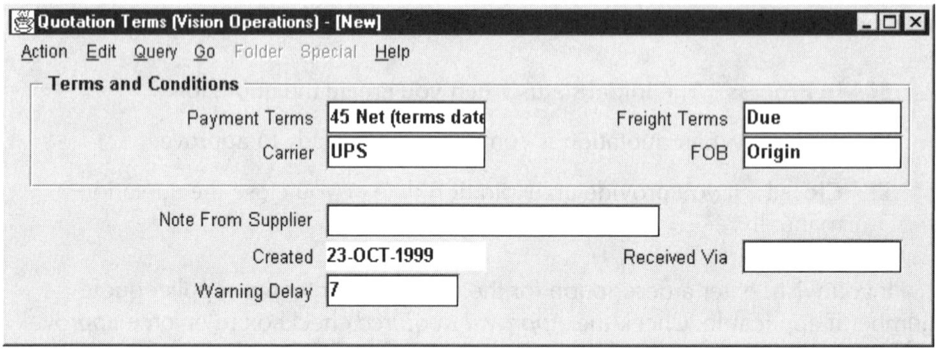

FIGURE 15-11. *Quotation Terms form*

method from the List of Values. (These methods must be created during Purchasing setup as lookup codes.) You can also enter the number of days the warning delay is enforced when sending online notifications before the expiration date.

Save your work, close the form, and return to the Quotations form.

Quotation Lines

If you select Items for the alternative region of the Quotations form, you must input the basic line item information. The Oracle system automatically generates a line number for each line you create, starting with the number 1. Select the line type from the List of Values. Enter an item from the List of Values. For amount-based lines, this field is not available. Enter the item revision number from the List of Values or accept the default. The category defaults from the item master provided your item comes from the item master. This item cannot be changed.

If you do not enter an item number, you must enter the purchasing category from the List of Values. Next, enter the UOM. Enter a quoted price for the quotation line item. If you wish, enter the supplier/manufacturer item number. Save your work.

If you select More for the alternative region, you can enter various miscellaneous items of information for quotation lines. The number defaults from the quotation line number. If you wish, enter a UN identification number, hazard class, minimum and maximum order quantity that is required to receive the quoted price, project number and task number if Oracle Projects is being used, and any notes from the supplier.

Save your work.

Quotation Shipments

If you are entering a quotation of quotation class Bid, you will see a **Shipments** button at the bottom of the Quotations form. If you are entering a quotation of quotation class Catalog, you will see a **Price Breaks** button at the bottom of the form.

The **Shipments** button allows you to specify the location and quantity for each quotation line. Remember that the Bid quotation class allows you to get a quotation for a specific location. Click on the **Shipments** button. The Quotation Shipments form appears. This form is identical to the RFQ Shipments form.

You can enter multiple ship-to locations for each quotation line. The system automatically defaults shipment number, starting from number 1. Enter the organization and the ship-to location for the shipment. The ship-to location defaults from the header information. Enter the UOM. The UOM on the shipment is defaulted from the line; however, you can change it. The price also defaults, but you can change it as well. If you wish, you can enter the last accept date and the need-by date. If you want a firm bid, check the *Firm* checkbox. If there is an approved quotation for this RFQ shipment already, the checkbox is checked automatically. Save any changes.

Next, select More for the alternative region in the quotation Shipments form. You can specify whether the quotation shipment is taxable. If you select the *Taxable* checkbox, you can enter the tax name corresponding to the tax on the shipment. For invoice matching, you can enforce two-way, three-way, or four-way matching. You can also enter the tolerance in the Quantity Received region. The tolerance defaults from the receiving options. If the quantity received exceeds the set tolerance, you can choose to ignore, reject, or warn the user.

Enter quotation shipments for both your quotation lines. Save your changes. As you enter the quotation shipments, the **Approve** button becomes available. This means that the quotation is ready for approval. However, you are going to use the Analyze Quotations form to approve your quotations.

Quotation Price Breaks

For each line entered, you can enter price breaks offered by the vendor (which do not have to correspond to those you requested in the RFQ) by clicking on the **Price Breaks** button on the bottom of the Quotations form for quotation class Catalog. Select a line by clicking on that line and then click on the **Price Breaks** button to open the Price Breaks form. (You can create multiple price breaks if you must receive quotes for different terms, quantities, and locations.)

In the Quotation Price Breaks form, the number defaults sequentially starting at 1. Enter the UOM for the line, then enter the price break quantity. Enter the organization by selecting from the List of Values in the Org field. You can only select organizations for which the item has been defined. The ship-to information defaults from the quotation header information. You have the option of changing the ship-to information, by selecting from the List Values, but you can only select locations for that organization.

Enter the discount percentage for the unit price in the Discount % field. If you entered a unit price and break price, the system does not calculate the discount percent. You should either provide a break price or a discount percent, but not both. If you wish, you can enter a date range from the List of Values that determines how long the quotation will be in effect, the lead time, payment terms, freight terms, FOB method, and the freight carrier. If there is an approved quotation for this price break line, the *Approved* checkbox is checked automatically.

When you select More for the alternative region of the Quotation Price Break form, you can review and change miscellaneous information. This region is identical to the More alternative region of the Quotation Shipments form. The number defaults from the price break line number. If the line item is taxable, check the *Taxable* checkbox. If you select the *Taxable* checkbox, enter a tax name by selecting from the List of Values. Select the *Invoice Matching* option to ensure two-way, three-way, or four-way matching. Enter the tolerance in the Quantity Received region.

For the Exception field, your options are as follows:

- **None**   May exceed tolerance.

- **Reject**   Cannot exceed tolerance.

- **Warning**   Can exceed, but receiver gets warning message.

Save your changes and close the Quotation Price Breaks form.

The quotation header information is now complete. Return to the Quotations form by closing the Quotation Shipments/Price Breaks form. Change the status from In Process to Active using the List of Values. Save your work.

You are now ready to approve the quotation.

Review Questions

1. When can you use the Document open interface to accept vendor quotations?

2. What must you do if you have unsolicited quotations?

3. Where do you enter the received via information for a quotation?

4. What are the two ways to enter price breaks?

Creating Quotations Automatically

As noted earlier, when the supplier responds to your RFQ, you must record the supplier's quote. Also, you must approve the quote once it is entered into the system to allow your buyers to reference the quote on the purchase order or purchase requisition. Also, when you approve the quote, you can control the use of your sourcing information.

In the last section, you created quotations manually. Now you will learn how to create them automatically. To automatically generate quotations, you use the Copy Document function on the RFQs form. The navigation path to automatically create a quotation from an existing RFQ is *RFQs and Quotations : RFQs.* You can double-click on RFQs—or click on the **Open** button from the Navigator—and the RFQs form appears.

Query the RFQ that relates to the supplier quotation you have received. When the query has been completed and the document is found, copy the RFQ into the quotation. Query the RFQ you have created, and select Copy Document from the Special menu. See Figure 15-12.

In the Copy Document form, enter an action from the List of Values.

For the Action field, your valid choices are as follows:

- **Entire RFQ**   Creates quotation from the RFQ header and all of the RFQ lines and shipments/price breaks.

- **RFQ Header Only**   Creates quotation from the RFQ header and you must enter the line information manually.

- **RFQ Header and Lines**   Creates quotation from the RFQ header and all of the RFQ lines excluding all of the shipment/price break lines.

You must enter the shipment/price break information manually. The Number field is required if manual quotation numbering is enabled. If automatic quotation numbering is enabled, the system assigns the number when your work is saved.

Select the type from the List of Values. Your choices of quotation types can only be from the same quotation class. In other words, you will only see Bid quotation class types if your RFQ is of the Bid quotation class, or you will only see Catalog quotation class types if your RFQ is of the Catalog quotation class. Select the supplier from the List of Values, or enter it from the quotation received manually. Select the supplier site from the List of Values. Select the supplier contact from the List of Values. Check the *Copy Attachment* checkbox if you require that RFQ attachments be copied to the quotation being created.

For the purposes of this exercise, select Entire RFQ as the action, Bid Quotation as the type, Consolidated Supplies as the supplier, and DALLAS site as the supplier

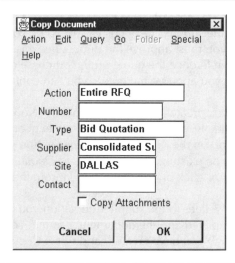

FIGURE 15-12. *Copy Document form*

site. (You cannot use your NEW Supplier for the same quotation, because you already entered a quotation for the New Supplier manually in the previous exercise. If you attempt to use the same RFQ, you will receive an error message informing you of the duplication.) Click on the **OK** button to accept your entries.

When you click **OK**, an Oracle Note appears letting you know that the document was copied and providing you with the quotation document number assigned. Record this number, as it will save you time when locating the document in the future. Click on the **OK** button. Oracle takes you to the quote you created.

Review the quotation and change any information defaulted from the RFQ that is different from your received quotation. When you have completed the quotation, change the status from In Process to Active. To access this quotation through the standard navigation, you can follow the navigation path *RFQs and Quotations : Quotations.* You can also query a quotation that you would like to enter or modify.

Review Questions

1. What are the three action options for the Copy Document function?

2. What quotation type can you select for a Bid quotation class?

3. Can you have two quotations for the same supplier and supplier site related to the same RFQ?

4. How do you access the Quotation form through the standard navigation?

Approving Quotations

Once you have entered the quotations, either manually or automatically, you must approve the quotations if you marked the *Approval Required* checkbox. You can approve the quotation or quotation line using the **Approve** button in the Quotations form. You can also use the Find function to locate the quotations that you want to approve in the Analyze Quotations form. You can only approve a quotation that has completed shipment information or price break information, depending on the quotation class. Completed shipment/price break information includes quantities and prices.

The navigation path to approve quotations is *RFQs and Quotations : Quote Analysis*. You can double-click on **Quote Analysis**, or click on the **Open** button from the Navigator. In the Find Quotations form that appears, enter as much information as possible to expedite the search, provided the item number is known. If you do not know the item number, use the wildcard (%) to help you search for the item number.

Fields available to enter search criteria include:

■ Item	■ RFQ Line
■ Revision	■ Supplier
■ Category Set	■ Quotation
■ Description	■ Approved Quotation only
■ Category	■ Project
■ RFQ	■ Task

Click on the **Find** button to begin the search, or the **Clear** button to clear the existing criteria. To access your quotation, enter your RFQ number and click on the **Find** button. When the search is complete, the Analyze Quotations form appears. See Figure 15-13.

Information displayed for the quotation includes quotation number, supplier name, item number, item revision, description, quotation line number, price break line number, price, freight terms, payment terms, discount %, effective date range, minimum order quantity, maximum order quantity, supplier quote header note, supplier quote line note, RFQ number, supplier quote number, reply date, supplier item, line type, FOB, carrier, UOM, project number, and task number.

Select the quotation line that you want to approve and go to the Shipment Approvals region of the form. To enter the approval type, select from the List of Values.

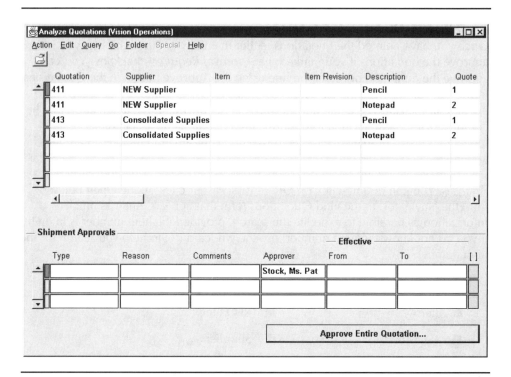

FIGURE 15-13.   *Analyze Quotations form*

Valid approval types are as follows:

- All Orders
- Purchase Agreements
- Purchase Orders
- Requisitions

The approval types govern which purchasing documents are approved for the selected quotation. Then, you must select from the List of Values to enter the approval reason. (The approval reasons must be set up as lookup codes.) If you wish, enter any comments regarding your approval. The Approver field defaults according to the sign-in of the application user. You may change this by selecting from the List of Values. In the Effectivity region, enter the to and from dates for your quotation approval. Save your work.

To approve the entire quotation, including all its lines, you can place the cursor on one of the quotation lines and click on the **Approve Entire Quotation** button on the Analyze Quotations form. The Approve Entire Quotation form appears. See Figure 15-14.

Check either the *Unapprove* or *Approve* checkbox. From the List of Values, select the approval type and approval reason. Oracle Purchasing defaults the Approver field according to the application user signed-in. You may change this by selecting from the List of Values. Enter the effective date range for your approval. If you wish, enter any comments regarding your approval or disapproval. Click on the **OK** button to approve/unapprove the entire quotation, or click on **Cancel** to cancel your action.

For the purposes of this exercise, select the *Approve* checkbox and select an approval type of All Orders. Then select any approval reason and click on the **OK** button. You receive a message telling you that all of the quotation lines have been approved. Click on the **OK** button to acknowledge the message.

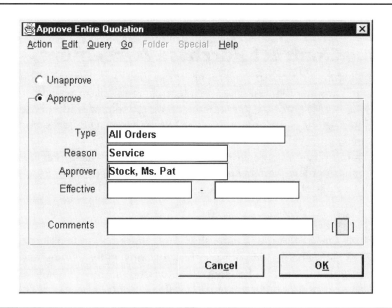

FIGURE 15-14. *Approve Entire Quotation form*

Review Questions

1. What are two ways to approve quotations?

2. If you cannot find the quotation in the Analyze Quotations form, what could be wrong?

3. What is purpose of the approval type in the Analyze Quotations form?

4. From where does the Approver field default?

Contract Purchase Orders

In this section, you will learn how to enter contract purchase orders. A contract purchase order is a purchase agreement between your supplier and you for unspecified goods or services. The contract purchase order governs the amount, terms and conditions, and effective date.

In this section, you will:

■   Enter a contract purchase agreement

■   Reference the contract purchase agreement on a standard purchase order

Entering Contract Purchase Agreements

You create a contract purchase agreement with a supplier to agree on the terms, conditions, and amount without entering into an agreement for specific goods or services. The contract purchase agreement can be referenced to purchase orders. Oracle Purchasing tracks the amount you have purchased against the contract purchase agreement.

The same form used to enter contract purchase agreements is used to enter standard purchase orders. The navigation path is *Purchase Orders : Purchase Orders*. The Purchase Orders form appears. See Figure 15-15.

Contract Agreement Header

In the Purchase Orders form, you enter the header information first. If manual numbering has been enabled in your purchase options, enter a unique contract purchase agreement in the PO, Rev field. If automatic number generation has been enabled, you cannot enter data into this field. The purchase order number is generated when you save your work. A revision number is generated when you make changes and save your work after a contract purchase agreement has been approved and then modified.

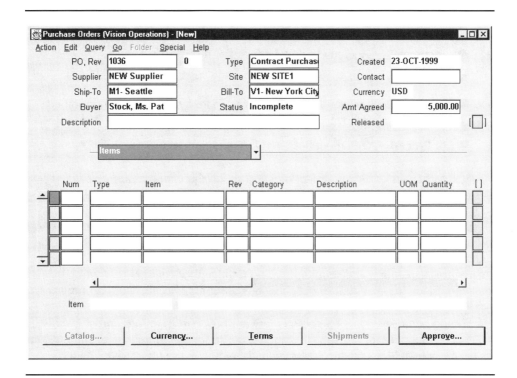

FIGURE 15-15. *Purchase Orders (Contract) form*

For type, select Contract Purchase Agreement from the List of Values. The Created field defaults from the system date and is in display-only mode. Enter the supplier name, or select an active supplier from the List of Values. Enter the supplier site. If the supplier only has one site defined, the site defaults automatically. You can select the supplier contact from the List of Values or accept the default. Enter the ship-to location and the bill-to location. This address defaults if it is defined as the default in the Supplier Entry form. You can accept the default or change the default.

The Currency field defaults from your Set of Books tied to the purchasing operating unit. The Currency field can be overwritten by the supplier if your setup is different. The Buyer field defaults based on the sign-on identity of the application user. If the *Enforce Buyer Name* option in purchasing options is set to Yes, you cannot change the defaulted value. If it is not set to Yes, you can enter a buyer from the List of Values.

Your options for the status are as follows:

- **Incomplete**   Agreement being created or modified.

- **Approved**   Agreement is approved.

- **Requires Reapproval**   Agreement was approved but has been modified and needs reapproval.

- **In Process**   Agreement has been forwarded for approval.

Status changes as the document moves through the various stages.

In the Amt Agreed field, enter the amount agreed to with this supplier. Notice that the Amt Agreed field is not available for a standard purchase order; it is only used for blanket and contract agreements. If you wish, enter an optional description of the agreement. The description is for internal use only and does not print on the Standard Purchase Order form. The Released field displays the total of all releases against this agreement and should not exceed the amount agreed to. At initial creation, the Release field does not show any amount. Also, this field is only used for blanket and contract agreements.

For the purposes of this exercise, enter **Contract Purchase Agreement** for the type, **NEW Supplier** for the supplier, and **New Site** for the supplier site. Enter **$5,000** as the amount agreed and save your changes. Note your contract agreement number, as you will need it later when you reference a standard purchase order. Since this is a contract purchase agreement, you cannot place your cursor in the Lines region.

Contract Agreement Currency

To change any currency information defaults, click on the **Currency** button. The defaults are the functional currency defined in your Set of Books. You can accept or change the values. If you do change currency, amount agreed to cannot be converted to the new currency automatically. You can enter an exchange rate date only if the currency is different from your functional currency. Click on the **Done** button to apply your changes, or the **Cancel** button to cancel your entries. Either choice returns you to the Purchase Orders form.

Contract Agreement Terms

Click on the **Terms** button on the bottom of the Purchase Order form. The Terms and Conditions form appears. See Figure 15-16.

At this time, you can change all of the default terms defined for the supplier. Enter the payment terms for the blanket agreement. Enter the freight terms for the contract purchase agreement. Enter the freight carrier for shipments related to the

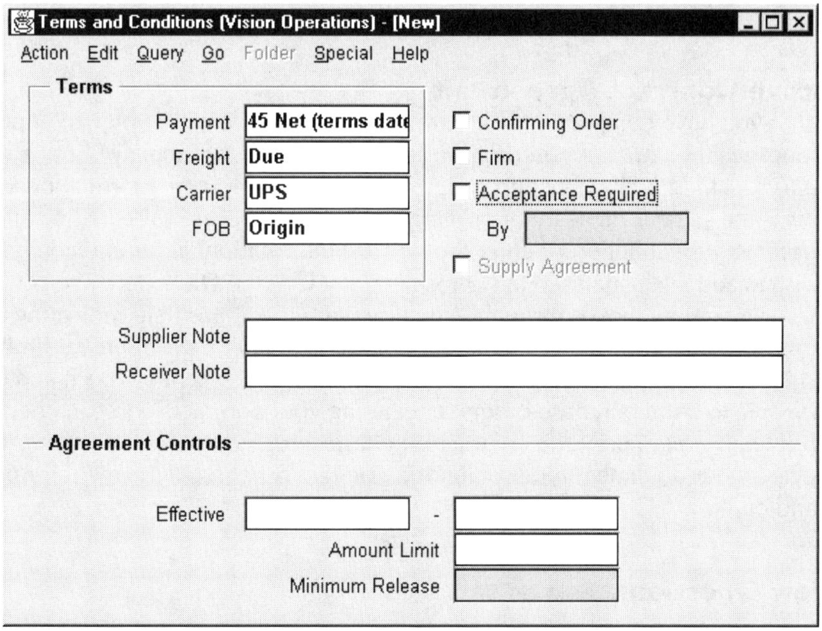

FIGURE 15-16. *Terms and Conditions form*

contract purchase agreement. Enter the FOB point for the contract purchase agreement.

You can check the *Confirming Order* checkbox to indicate that this is a confirming order, which is an order used to confirm an order that has already been placed. Check the *Firm* checkbox to indicate that the contract purchase agreement is firm and should not be rescheduled. Check the *Acceptance Required* checkbox to inform the supplier that they must accept the contract purchase agreement. If the acceptance is required, enter the due-by date in the By field. The Supply Agreement field is not available at this time.

If you wish, you can enter a supplier note and a receiver note. Enter the effective date range to indicate the time period the contract purchase agreement is effective. The Amount Limit field defaults from the Amt Agreed field in the header. This amount is equal to or greater than the header amount. If you change the amount limit to exceed the amount agreed to, the header amount does not update automatically.

The minimum release amount controls references against this contract purchase agreement. Only amounts higher than the minimum release amount can be released against the contract purchase agreement.

Save your work and close the Terms and Conditions form, returning to the Purchase Orders form.

Approve Contract Agreement

Now that you have completed the contract purchase agreement, you can approve it. To approve the contract purchase agreement, click on the **Approve** button on the bottom of the Purchase Orders form. The Approve Document form appears.

This is the same form as for approving a standard purchase order. Check the *Submit for Approval* option or enter the forward information. Enter any note you may wish to add that pertains to this agreement. Click on the **OK** button. The contract purchase agreement moves through Workflow with the Status field indicating the current stages of approval. The approval function will check the approval limit against the amount agreed. Once the contract purchase agreement has been approved, you are able to issue purchase orders referencing your contract. You can check the *Print* checkbox to print the contract purchase agreement.

Review your document type setup for a contract purchase agreement for proper flow and control.

Review Questions

1. What fields are additional for a contract purchase agreement over and above those required for a purchase order?

2. What effect does the Minimum Release field have on purchase order releases?

3. Why can't you enter line information for contract purchase agreements?

4. What is a confirming order?

Referencing a Contract Purchase Agreement on a Standard Purchase Order

You can pick up information for a standard purchase order by referencing a contract purchase agreement for the same vendor. The navigation path to reference a contract purchase agreement on a purchase order is *Purchase Orders : Purchase Orders*. The Purchase Orders form appears. See Figure 15-17.

For the purposes of this exercise, create a purchase order as you would in the normal course of business. To reference a contract purchase agreement, navigate to the Reference Documents alternative region for the purchase order line. In the Reference Documents region, enter the contract agreement number. The supplier of the contract agreement must match the supplier of your standard purchase order. Save your work.

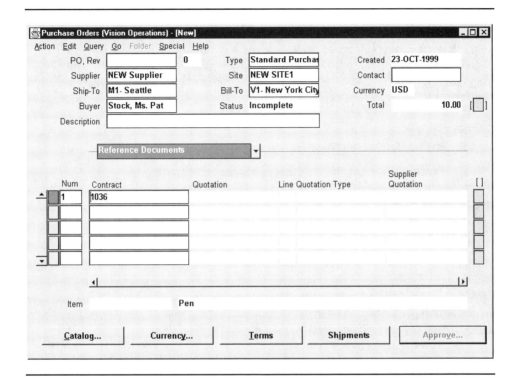

FIGURE 15-17.   *Reference Documents form*

Next, create a standard purchase order for your supplier and your supplier site. Select Reference Documents for the alternative region, and select the contract agreement you have created. Then, enter **Pen** for your item description. Enter a total of **$10**, with all of the other necessary information.

If you query the contract purchase agreement, the released amount is updated and the total amount shows on your standard purchase order. Verify the result by querying your contract purchase agreement.

Review Questions

1. Where do you reference a standard purchase order against a contract purchase agreement?

2. What entries must be the same between the standard purchase order and the reference contract purchase agreement?

3. How can you cause the released amount to be updated when referencing a contract purchase agreement on a purchase order?

Blanket Purchase Agreements

In the last section, you learned how to create a contract purchase agreement. In this section, you will learn how to enter a blanket purchase agreement. A blanket purchase agreement is an agreement between you and your supplier to provide you with specific amounts of specific items within specific date ranges.

In this section, you will learn how to:

■ Enter a blanket purchase agreement

■ Create releases against blanket purchase agreement

Entering Blanket Purchase Agreements

If you know the supplier, line items, and the period but not the exact delivery schedule, you will want to create a blanket purchase agreement. You can use the blanket purchase agreement to communicate to your suppliers negotiated pricing before actually releasing firm purchases. When you are ready to purchase the line item(s) with set delivery dates, you can issue a release against your blanket purchase agreement to place your order with the supplier. Remember that the blanket purchase agreement must contain an effective date and expiration date.

First, you will learn how to enter the blanket purchase agreement. The navigation path to the Purchase Orders form is *Purchase Orders : Purchase Orders.* You can double-click on Purchase Orders, or click on the **Open** button. The Purchase Orders form appears. See Figure 15-18.

Blanket Agreement Header

In the Purchase Orders form, you enter the header information first. If manual numbering has been enabled in your purchase options, enter a unique purchase order number. If automatic number generation has been enabled, you cannot enter data into this field and the purchase order is generated when you save your work. A revision number is generated when you make changes and save your work after a purchase order has been approved and then modified. For type, select Blanket Purchase Agreement from the List of Values. The Created field defaults from the system date and is in display-only mode.

Enter the name of the supplier or select an active supplier from the List of Values. You cannot change the supplier once the blanket purchase agreement has been approved. If a change in supplier is required, you must cancel the blanket purchase agreement and create a new blanket purchase agreement. Enter the supplier site. If the supplier only has one defined site, the site defaults into this field automatically. Once the blanket purchase agreement is approved, you can change the supplier site only if the *PO: Change Supplier Site* option is set to Yes. If you change the supplier site, the revision is incremented and requires reapproval.

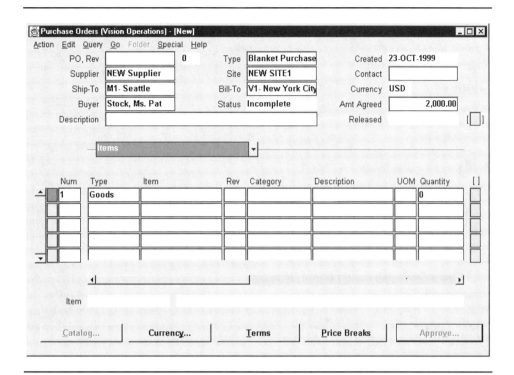

FIGURE 15-18. *Purchase Orders (blanket purchase) form*

If you wish, select the supplier contact from the List of Values, or accept the default. Enter the ship-to location and bill-to location. These locations default if they are defined as defaults in the Supplier Entry form; you can accept the defaults or change them as necessary. The currency type defaults from the Set of Books tied to the purchasing operating unit.

The Buyer field defaults based on the sign-on identity of the application user. If the *Enforce Buyer Name* option in purchasing is set to Yes, then you cannot change the default value. If the option is not set to Yes, you can enter a buyer from the List of Values. The Status field displays Incomplete while being created and modified. The status changes as the document moves through its various stages.

Enter the amount agreed to with this supplier. This field is only used for blanket and contract agreements. If you wish, you can enter a description of the agreement. The description is for internal use only and does not print on the Standard Purchase Order form. The Released field displays the total of all releases against this agreement and should not exceed the Amt Agreed field. This field does not have any amount at initial creation. The Released field is only used for blanket and contract agreements.

For the purposes of this exercise, create a blanket order using your NEW Supplier as the supplier, and your supplier site as you previously created it. Enter **$2,000** as the agreed amount. Save your work.

Blanket Agreement Terms

Click on the **Terms** button on the bottom of the Purchase Order form. The Terms and Conditions form appears. At this time, you can change the default terms defined for the supplier. Enter the payment and freight terms for the blanket agreement. Enter the freight carrier for shipments related to the blanket agreement. Enter the FOB point for the blanket agreement.

Check the *Confirming Order* checkbox to indicate that this is a confirming order. Check the *Firm* checkbox to indicate that the blanket agreement is firm. Check the *Acceptance Required* checkbox to inform the supplier that they must accept the blanket agreement. If the acceptance is required, enter the due by date in the By field. Check the *Supply Agreement* checkbox if the supplier is required to supply you with an agreement. This checkbox is used with supplier scheduling.

If you wish, enter a supplier note and/or a receiver note. Enter the effective date range that the blanket agreement is effective. The amount limit defaults from the Amt Agreed field in the header. This amount is equal to or greater than the header amount. If you change the amount limit to exceed the amount agreed to, the header amount does not update automatically. You can also enter a minimum release amount to control future releases against this blanket agreement. Only amounts higher than the minimum release amount can be released against this blanket agreement.

Save your work, then close the Terms and Conditions form to return to the Purchase Orders form.

Blanket Agreement Currency

On the PO form, click on the **Currency** button to change any currency information defaults. The defaults are the functional currency values defined in your Set of Books. You can accept or change the values. If you do change currency, pricing on existing line items is not converted to the new currency. You can enter the rate date only if the currency is different from your base currency. Click on the **Done** button to apply your changes, or the **Cancel** button to cancel your entries and return to the Purchase Orders form.

Blanket Agreement Lines (Items)

Since you are entering a blanket agreement, which is an agreement for specific items, you must enter those items. This is different than a contract agreement where no items are specified.

If you select Items for the alternative region, you must input the basic line item information. The line number is automatically generated for each line you create, starting with number 1. Select the type from the List of Values. Enter an item number if applicable. Enter the item revision number from the List of Values, or accept the default.

The category defaults from that of the item if the item comes from an item master. In this case, you cannot change the category. If you did not enter an item number, then you must select a purchasing category from the List of Values. The description defaults from the item master. If the purchasing item does not come from the item master, you must add the description manually. You can change the item description if you have set the item attributes to allow this type of change.

Enter the UOM. The UOM also defaults from the item master if the item comes from the item master. Since this is a blanket purchase agreement, the Quantity field is grayed out. Enter a unit price greater than zero for the item. The Promised and Need By Date fields are also grayed out, because this is a blanket purchase agreement and you do not know the specifics until the release. If you wish, enter the supplier or manufacturer's part number that will be used later when release is created.

NOTE
Reserve is used only for encumbrance accounting.

For the purposes of this exercise, enter **MISC.MISC** for Category, enter **2" Binder** for the description, and **$3.00 each** for the price. Save your work.

Blanket Agreement Lines (Price Reference)
If you select Price Reference for the alternative region, you can enter basic pricing information. See Figure 15-19.

The number defaults for the item line number. If you wish, enter the list price for the item. This is used in the Saving Analysis report. You can also enter the market price for the item. This is used in the Saving Analysis report if a list price has not been entered. In addition, you can enter the price type from the List of Values. If the release price is greater than the price on the purchase agreement line, check the *Allow Price Override* checkbox. Enter an upper price limit for the price override. This is the maximum price you will allow for the item. If the price was negotiated with the supplier, check the *Negotiated* checkbox.

For the purposes of this exercise, enter **$3.00** for the list price. Save your work.

Blanket Agreement Reference Documents
If you select Reference Documents for the alternative region, you can enter reference information related to your purchase order lines. The number defaults from the item line number. The Contract field is grayed out since this is not a standard purchase order. If a quotation was selected from the Supplier Item Catalog

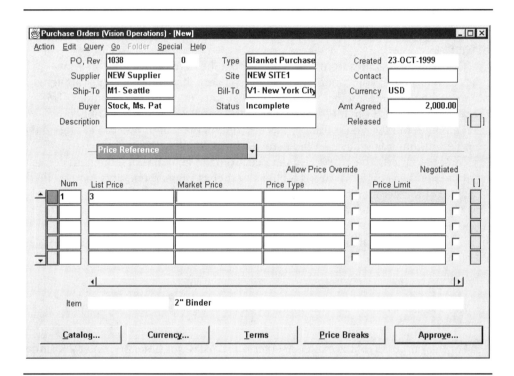

FIGURE 15-19. *Blanket agreement (Price Reference) form*

or Supplier Item Attributes form, then Oracle Purchasing displays the quotation, quotation line, quotation type, and supplier quotation number.

Blanket Agreement (More)

If you select More for the alternative region, you can enter various miscellaneous information for purchase order lines.

The number defaults from the item line number. If you wish, enter a supplier, UN identification number and a hazard class. Check the *Capital Expense* checkbox if the purchase is for capital expenditures. If you wish, enter the transaction nature from the List of Values. (Transaction natures are set up as lookup codes.) If you want to enter unlimited notes or other documents, use the Attachments feature instead of using the Note To Supplier field.

Blanket Agreement (Agreement)

If you select Agreement for the alternative region, you can enter various agreement terms regarding release amounts. See Figure 15-20.

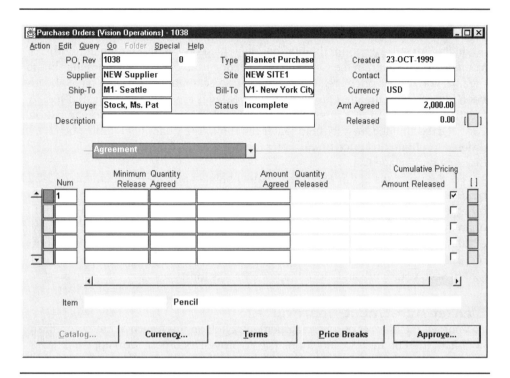

FIGURE 15-20. *Blanket agreement (Agreement) form*

The number defaults from the item line number. Enter the minimum release amount against this blanket agreement line. Enter the quantity agreed on, which is the quantity printed on the standard purchase order. Releases cannot exceed this quantity. Enter the Amount Agreed. Oracle does not default this value automatically, and it is used for internal reference only. The Quantity Released field displays the quantity currently released against this line. The Amount Released field displays the amount currently released against this line. Check the *Cumulative Pricing* checkbox if you want the system to select a price break by looking at the total current release shipment quantity plus the cumulative quantity released. If this option is not checked, the system selects a price break by considering only the individual release shipment quantity. This alternative region is only applicable for blanket purchase agreements.

Save your work.

Blanket Agreement Price Breaks

For each blanket agreement line you entered, you can enter price breaks by clicking on the **Price Breaks** button on the bottom of the Purchase Orders form. Select a line by clicking on that line, and then click on the **Price Breaks** button to open the Price Breaks form. See Figure 15-21.

In the Price Breaks form, the number defaults sequentially starting at number 1. You enter information in the Org field by selecting from the List of Values the ship-to organization for this price break. You can only select organizations that have already been identified for the item number, if that field was entered. Enter the ship-to location from the List of Values. You can only select locations for the organization you selected. In the Quantity field, enter the minimum quantity that must be ordered to obtain this price break. Enter the break price for the quantity or the discount percentage (%).

For the purposes of this exercise, create a blanket purchase agreement for 2-inch binders. You have a 2 percent discount for every 100 you buy up to 10 percent. In other words, you must create five price breaks. You must create the first line with quantity of **100** and a discount of **2%**. You must enter a second line with quantity of **200** and a discount of **4%**. You must go up to a quantity of **500** and a discount of **10%**. The break price for 500, if you are using $3.00 as your price, should be **$2.70**. Save your work and close the Price Breaks form.

Blanket Agreement Approval

To approve the blanket purchase agreement, click on the **Approve** button on the bottom of the Purchase Orders form. The Approve Document form appears.

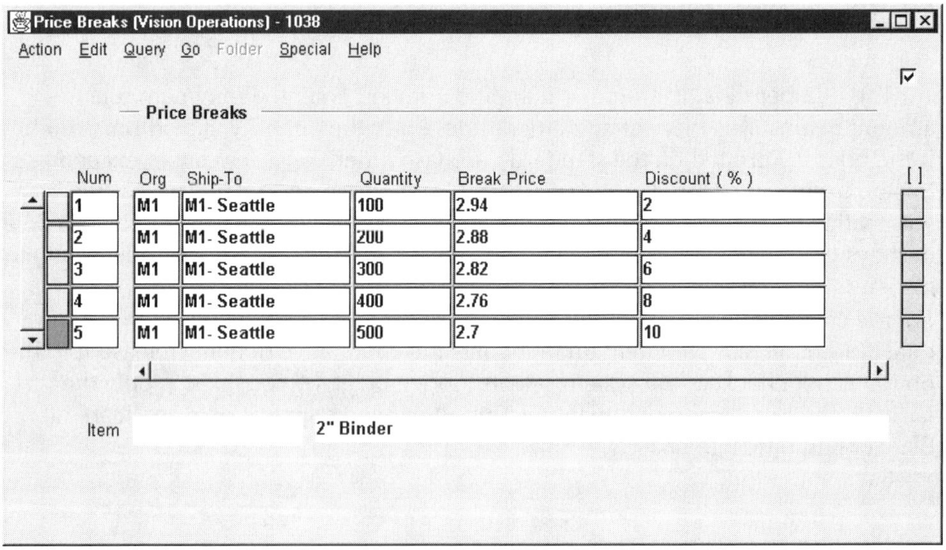

FIGURE 15-21. *Blanket agreement Price Breaks form*

This is the same form for standard purchase orders and contract purchase agreements. Check the *Submit for Approval* option, or enter the forward information. If you wish, enter any note you may wish to add that pertains to this agreement. Click on the **OK** button. The blanket purchase agreement moves through Workflow with the status indicating the current stage of approval. Once the blanket purchase agreement has been approved, you are able to issue releases against the agreement. Remember your blanket purchase agreement number since you will release against it in the next exercise.

Review your document type setup for blanket purchase agreements for proper flow and control.

Review Questions

1. Which line-level alternative region is specific to blanket purchase agreement?

2. What is the purpose of the *Cumulative Pricing* checkbox?

3. Which button do you have when defining a blanket purchase agreement that a standard purchase order does not have? What is the purpose of this button?

4. Which fields are grayed out at the item level in the Item alternative region when you are defining a blanket purchase agreement?

Creating Releases Against a Blanket Purchase Agreement

Now that you have completed and approved a blanket purchase agreement, you can release against it. You can issue a release against a blanket purchase agreement to place the actual order if you are within the stated effective dates on the agreement. Releases can be manual or generated by the system. Oracle Purchasing generates releases resulting from Oracle MRP if you have defined sourcing rules for the item.

The Create Release process generates releases if:

- The requisition is sourced to an approved blanket purchase agreement

- The approved supplier list is active

- The release generation method is Automatic Release or Automatic Release/Review

- The source agreement is active and the release will not put the agreement over the limit

- The release amount is greater than the minimum release amount

- The supplier is active, and the requisition line is approved and is quantity based

You have the option to specify whether you would like to generate approved releases so that you do not have to approve them manually. The alternative to this is generating standard releases and then approving them manually. You can also use AutoCreate to create releases using purchase requisitions.

The navigation path to the Releases form to manually create releases against the blanket purchase agreement is *Purchase Orders : Releases.* You can double-click on Releases, or click on the **Open** button from the Navigator. The Releases form appears. See Figure 15-22.

Release Header

In the Releases form, you enter the header information first. In the PO, Rev field, select the blanket agreement from the List of Values that you want to issue releases against. The release number is generated automatically if automatic release number generation is enabled. If manual numbering is enabled, you can change the release to any number that is not already being used. The Created field defaults from the system date and cannot be changed. The supplier, supplier site, and currency

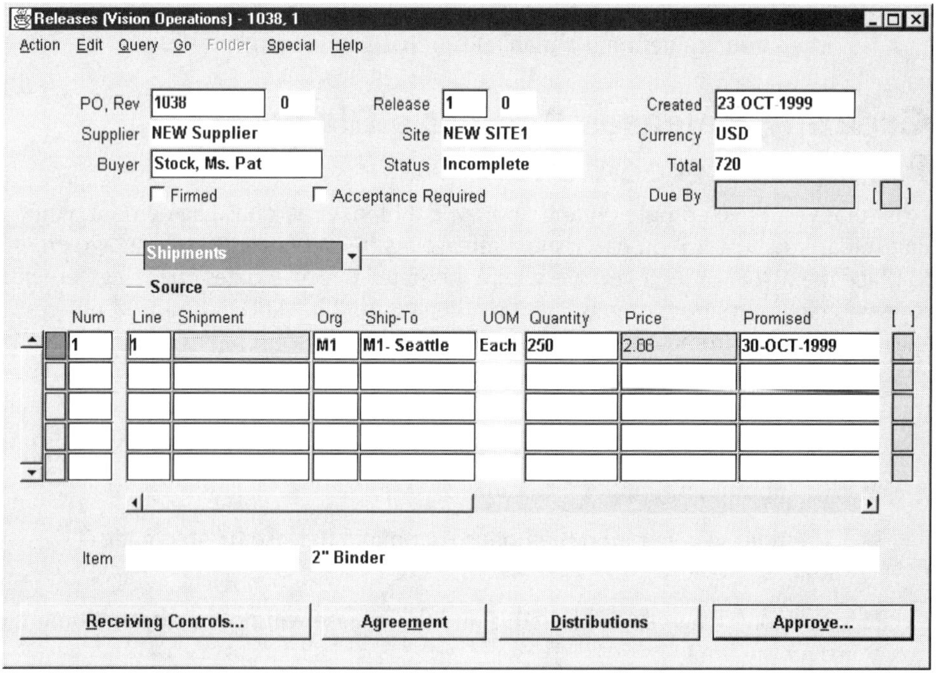

FIGURE 15-22. *Releases form*

default from the selected blanket purchase agreement. The Buyer field defaults based on the sign-on identity of the application user. You can select another buyer from the List of Values if desired. The Status and Total fields are display only.
Status options are:

■ **Incomplete**   When the release is being created or modified.

■ **Approved**   When the release is already approved.

■ **Requires Reapproval**   When the release was approved but has been modified, and needs reapproval.

■ **In Process**   When the release has been forwarded for approval.

The Total field automatically tracks the sum of the release as lines are added. Check the *Firmed* checkbox to firm your release shipment to MRP to prevent rescheduling automatically. Check the *Acceptance Required* checkbox to indicate to the supplier that you want acceptance of the release. If acceptance is required, enter the due-by date to indicate when you require the supplier to return their acceptance.

Release Lines (Shipments)
If you select Shipments for the alternative region, you must input the basic line item information. The Oracle system automatically generates a line number sequentially for each line you create, starting with number 1. From the List of Values, select the source line from the blanket purchase agreement line for this shipment. The List of Values prevents you from entering items not on the blanket purchase agreement.
Enter the ship-to organization from the List of Values. Enter the ship-to locations for this organization from the List of Values. The UOM defaults from the blanket purchase agreement for this line. Enter the quantity for this shipment that is greater than zero. If you allow price override for this blanket purchase agreement line, you can change the defaulted price as long as the entered release price does not exceed any entered price limit set for the blanket purchase agreement line. If you do not allow price override, the price is defaulted from the blanket purchase agreement and cannot be overridden.
Enter the price if it is different than the default from the blanket purchase agreement and you allowed price override. Enter the promised date given by the supplier. Enter the need-by date supplied by the requestor. The system displays the original promise date if the promise date has changed. Check the *Taxable* checkbox if the line is taxable, and enter the tax name. (Tax names are usually set up in Accounts Payable.) The Charge Account field is based on setups. The Amount field displays the shipment line total. If reserved from a requisition, check the *Reserved* checkbox.

For the purposes of this exercise, select your only source line from the blanket purchase agreement. For quantity, enter **250** to see if the price break defaults properly. Enter a promise date and need-by date that is one week from current date. Save your work.

Release Lines (More)

If you select More for the alternative region, you can enter basic receiving information. The number defaults from the shipment line number item. The receiving information defaults from the receiving options. Enter the receipt close tolerance percent for your shipment. Oracle Purchasing automatically closes a shipment for receiving if the shipment is within this tolerance. Enter the invoice close tolerance percent for your shipment. Oracle Purchasing automatically closes a shipment for invoicing if the shipment is within this tolerance.

Select an invoice matching from the List of Values. Your options are:

- **Two-way**   Purchase order and invoice
- **Three-way**   Purchase order, receipt, and invoice
- **Four-way**   Purchase order, receipt, inspection, and invoice

Check the *Accrue on Receipt* checkbox if this shipment line should be accrued on receipt. Check the *Firmed* checkbox if MRP should not reschedule this shipment line when MRP is processed.

Release Lines (Status)

If you select Status for the alternative region, the Releases form displays the current status of this shipment line.

This form displays the status, quantity ordered, quantity received, quantity cancelled, and quantity billed.

Release Lines (Item)

If you select Item for the alternative region, the Releases form displays information about the item, such as item, category, description, and supplier item number. See Figure 15-23.

The fields are reference only, and cannot be updated.

Release Distributions

Once you have entered the shipment line information, you can update the distributions. Click on the **Distributions** button on the bottom of the Releases form. The Distributions form appears. See Figure 15-24.

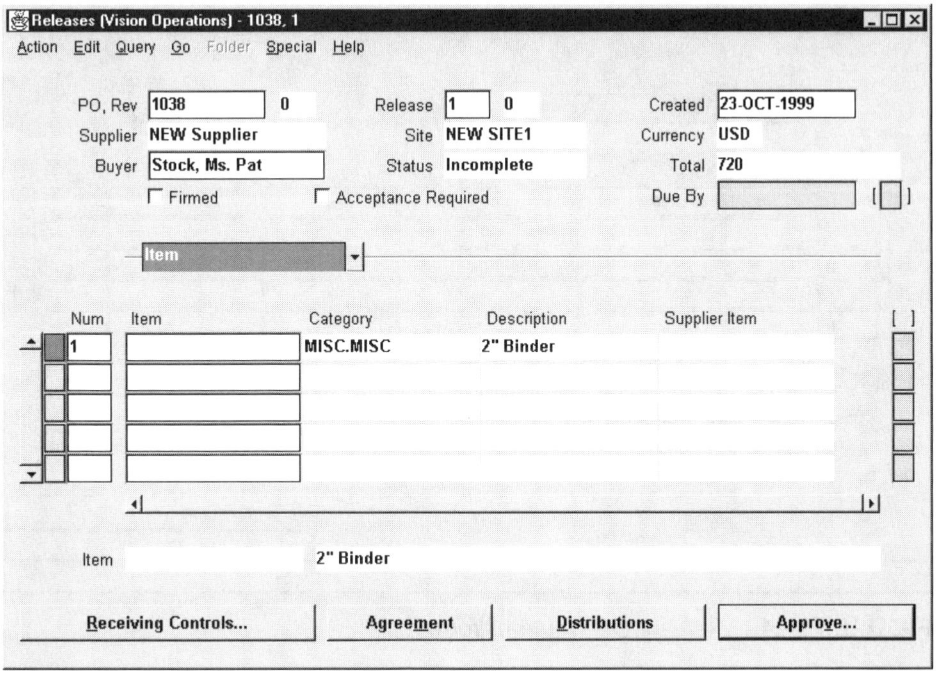

FIGURE 15-23. *Releases (Item) form*

There are three alternative regions you can select:

■ Destination

■ More

■ Project

If you select Destination for the alternative region, the line number defaults sequentially starting with number 1 for each destination you create. If this is a scheduled release, enter the source. Enter the destination type from the List of Values. Your options for destination type are:

■ Inventory

■ Expense

■ Shop Floor

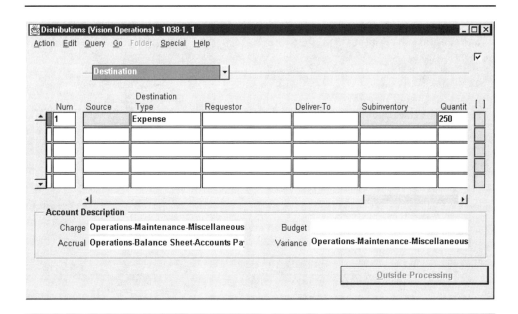

FIGURE 15-24. *Release Distributions form*

If you wish, enter the requestor by selecting from the List of Values, or accept the default. Enter the deliver-to location. You can also enter the subinventory for this shipment. The subinventory is the physical location such as a warehouse where the goods should be received. You can change the quantity, which defaults from the shipments form. If you decrease the quantity, and have yet to distribute the total quantity, the system defaults to the next distribution line. Enter the charge account or accept the default generated by the Account Generator. If the Account Generator does not generate a default, you must enter a charge account.

For the purposes of this exercise, enter the charge account and save your work.

If you select More for the alternative region, the line number defaults from the distribution line.

If the release is related to an online requisition, the requisition line number displays and cannot be updated. If not, the release is not related, so enter the manual paper requisition number in the Number field. If there is an autocreated release, the Online field is populated by AutoCreate. If a currency other than the functional currency is involved, enter the rate date and rate. The accrual account is automatically created by the account generator.

The Project alternative region is available only if you are using Oracle Projects. You enter the project and task. In the Expenditure region, you enter the expenditure type, expenditure organization, expenditure date, and quantity.

Close the Distributions forms now and return to the Releases form.

Receiving Controls

If you want to override the system defaults entered in the receiving options setup, click on the **Receiving Controls** button on the Releases form. You can change or modify the following attributes:

- Receipt date information

- Over receipt quantity information

- Allow substitute receipts

- Receipt routing

- Enforce ship-to

Click on the **OK** button to accept your changes, or click on the **Cancel** button to ignore the changes. Both actions return you to the Releases form.

Release Agreement

To see information about the selected blanket purchase agreement, click on the **Agreement** button on the Release form. The Agreement form appears. See Figure 15-25.

The Agreement form shows the agreement type, the amount agreed to, buyer, total released, supplier contact, status, payment terms, freight terms, freight carrier, FOB point, effective date range, agreement description, supplier note, and receiver note.

Approve Release

To approve the release, click on the **Approve** button in the Release form. This takes you to the Approve Document form, where you can check the *Submit for Approval* checkbox, then click on the **OK** button. The Approve Document form is the same as all of the other purchasing document approval forms.

The release moves through Workflow, and the status changes to In Process, and once the order has been approved, the status changes to Approved. When approved, you can receive against the release.

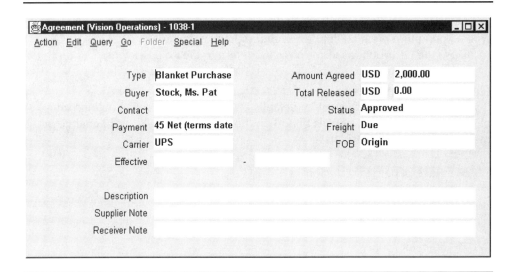

FIGURE 15-25. *Agreement form*

Review Questions

1. What is the purpose of the *Acceptance Required* checkbox?

2. How does Oracle Purchasing prevent you from entering items that are not on the blanket purchase agreement?

3. When can you change the price for a release shipment?

4. When can you receive against a release?

AutoCreate

Oracle Purchasing provides an automatic creation feature for certain purchasing documents. You can create a standard purchase order, a planned purchase order, an RFQ, and blanket releases from the purchase requisition lines. You cannot include internal purchase requisition lines for the AutoCreate process.

In this section, you will learn how to:

- Find purchase requisition lines

- Select purchase requisition lines

- Create a new document or add to an existing one

Finding Purchase Requisitions

To run the AutoCreate process, follow the navigation path *AutoCreate*. The Find Requisition Lines form appears. See Figure 15-26.

First, select the approved status. Only approved purchase requisition lines can be used for any kind of purchase order. For RFQs, both approved or unapproved purchase requisition lines can be used. If a requisition line is already on a document, it cannot be selected again because the lines are no longer available.

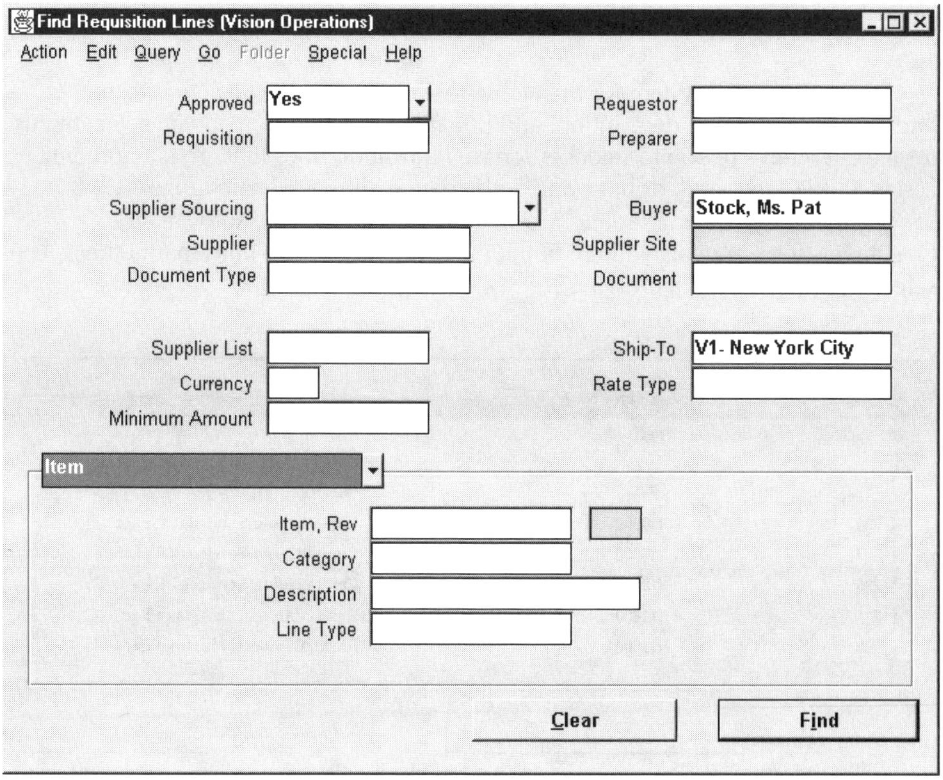

FIGURE 15-26. *Find Requisition Lines form*

Your options to find the document are:

- Specific requestor
- Specific requisition number
- Specific preparer
- Sourced or unsourced lines
- Specific buyer
- Specific supplier
- Requisition lines sourced to blanket purchase agreement quotation

- Supplier site
- Specific purchase order
- Specific supplier list
- Specific ship-to location
- Specific currency
- Specific rate type
- Minimum amount

You can also select Item for the alternative region to select a specific item and revision, category, description, and line type. In addition, you can select Status for the alternative region to select purchase requisition lines that are late, urgent, assigned, RFQ required, or have a need-by date within a specific range.

Once you enter the criteria, click on the **Find** button. The AutoCreate Documents form appears with all of the purchase requisition lines that fit the selection criteria. See Figure 15-27.

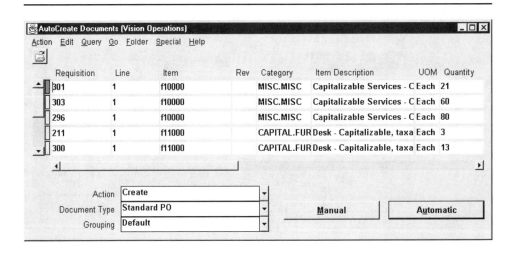

FIGURE 15-27. *AutoCreate Documents form*

For the purposes of this exercise, find all of the approved purchase requisition lines.

Review Questions

1. When can you only use approved purchase requisition lines?

2. How can you only select purchase requisition lines that are needed in five days?

Selecting Purchase Requisition Lines

How you select a requisition line is simple: to select one line, use CTRL-click; to select multiple lines, use SHIFT-click. However, before you select the purchase requisition line(s), you must pick three options in AutoCreate. These options are:

- Decide whether you are creating a new document or adding to an existing document by using the Action field.

- Select the document type: Standard Purchase Order, Planned Purchase Order, Blanket Release, or RFQ.

- Select the grouping method: default or requisition

Default combines purchase requisition lines into a single purchase order line for the same line type, item, item revision, UOM, and transaction reason. Default also combines into a single RFQ line those purchase requisition lines that are for the same line type, item, and item revision. The lowest unit price is used. (If this is not desirable, use manual creation mode.) Requisition creates one line for each requisition line with no combining.

If you wish, you can use the Special menu to return the requisition, to modify the requisition, to view the action history, or to view the blanket POs with this item before autocreating documents. Once you have selected the three options, you can select the automatic creation mode or manual creation mode to initiate the AutoCreate process. The manual creation mode is only available for default grouping for standard purchase orders, planned purchase orders, and RFQs.

For automatic creation mode, you select the purchase requisition lines you want and click on the **Automatic** button. The AutoCreate Documents form appears. See Figure 15-28.

For manual creation mode, you use the Document Builder region to select the purchase requisition lines. Click on the **Manual** button and the Document Builder region appears.

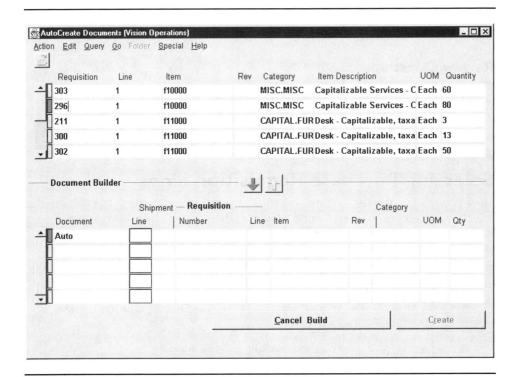

FIGURE 15-28. *Document Builder form*

Place the cursor on the purchase requisition line you want, and then click on the large down arrow (located in the middle of the form) to select it. When your cursor changes shape, you can place the changed cursor onto any line in the Document Builder region. This allows you create a custom-ordered document for the AutoCreate process to use.

If you make a mistake in your selection, you can use the up arrow to remove the line from the Document Builder. When you are done, click on the **Create** button to confirm your selection and placement in the Document Builder, or click on the **Cancel Build** button to cancel your selection and placement.

Review Questions

1. What is the Document Builder?

2. What are the three options you have in AutoCreate?

3. What is the purpose of the Special menu?

4. What is a default grouping for RFQ?

Creating New or Adding to Documents

New Document

Whether you use the automatic or manual creation mode to select purchase requisition lines, when you create a new document, the New Document form appears. See Figure 15-29. The New Document form allows you to enter a document or release number if manual numbering is enabled. The new document has a status of Incomplete. You can also enter the RFQ type and supplier list name for RFQs, or release date for blanket releases. You can also enter the supplier and supplier site. From the Currency region, you can select a currency source.

Your source options are:

- **Default**   Defaults currency from supplier site then supplier.

- **First Requisition Line**   Defaults currency from the first requisition line.

- **Specify**   Allows you to select a currency.

If you select a foreign currency, you must enter exchange information as appropriate. Click on the **Create** button to create the new document with the information you entered.

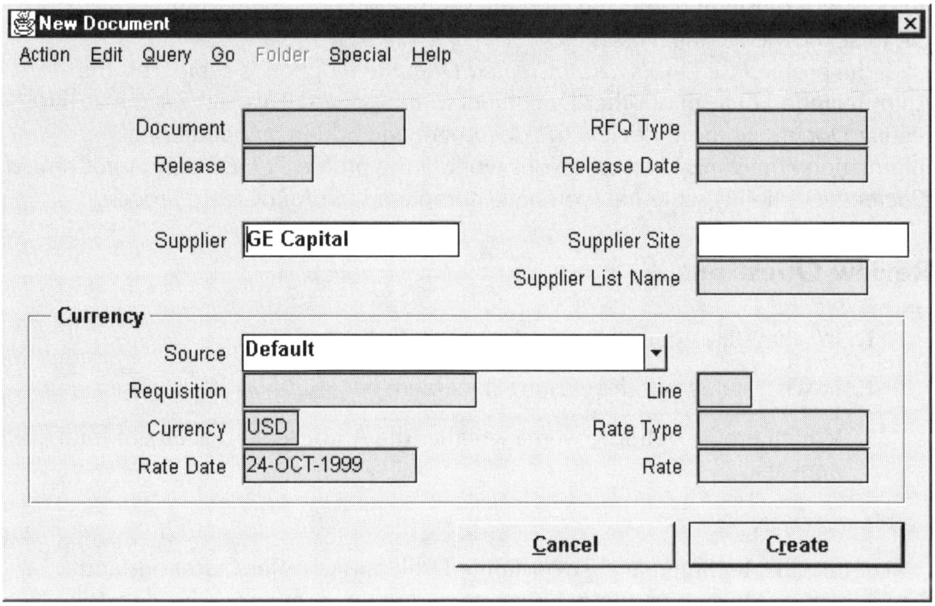

FIGURE 15-29.   *New Document form*

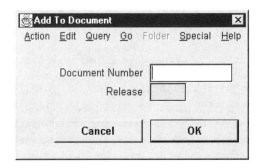

FIGURE 15-30. *Add to Document form*

Add to Document

If you elect to add to an existing document, the Add to Document form appears. See Figure 15-30. The existing document has the new lines and has a status of either Incomplete or Required Reapproval. The Add to Document form allows you to select the document number or release number. Click on the **Cancel** button to cancel, or click on the **OK** button to initiate the AutoCreate process.

You receive a message telling you AutoCreate completed successfully, the number of requisition lines used, and the destination document number. Click on **OK** to acknowledge the message.

If the profile *PO: Display AutoCreated Document* option is set to Yes, the AutoCreate to PO form or other Document form appears. This is the same as the regular Document form. Review the document and add in any additional information you want. Then save your work. If the profile *PO: Display AutoCreated Document* option is set to No, you have completed the AutoCreate process.

Review Questions

1. In what status does the new document first appear?

2. In what status will the existing document be?

3. Which profile option governs whether the AutoCreate Document form appears?

For the Chapter Summary, Two-Minute Drill, and Chapter Questions and Answers, open the summary.htm file contained in the Summary_files directory on the book's CD-ROM.

CHAPTER

16

Advanced Payables

his is the last chapter in Exam 3, and it is about the more advanced Payables functionality. In this chapter, you will learn about the following topics:

- Entering recurring invoices

- Managing invoices

- Processing procurement card transactions

- Entering manual payments

- Processing payment batches

- Recording stop and void payments

- Automatic tax calculation

- Loading electronic bank statements

The first topic of this chapter is about entering recurring invoices in Oracle Payables. Then, the chapter covers managing invoices. You will learn to apply holds to an individual invoice, selected invoices, and particular invoice payment schedules. You will also learn to release the applied holds. You will learn to approve and cancel invoices, as your business needs. You can also adjust invoices after they have been entered.

Next, the chapter talks about payment. Once invoices are entered, they must be paid. You will first learn to process procurement card transactions, including how to select invoices to be paid, how to pay invoices from the Invoice Workbench, and how to pay suppliers with future-dated payments. You will also learn how to override some of the payment controls. Then, the chapter will go into manual and automatic payments. You will learn to enter manual payments and to generate payments based on payment batches. You will initiate new payment batches, create and find payment batch templates, then modify, format, and confirm payment batches. You will also learn how to find payment information and how to process EDI payments. As a last step, you will learn how to make electronic payments to different supplier bank accounts.

Once you have made payments, you can record stop and void payments. You can place stop payments, release stop payments, void payments, and void unused payment documents. The next section of the chapter talks about tax. You can assign the source and hierarchy for tax defaulting, define tax names including VAT tax names, define withholding tax groups, and define EU suppliers. You will then learn to record and review VAT charges. The last section of the chapter talks about manually entering new bank statements and updating bank statements.

Entering Recurring Invoices

The first section of this chapter is about entering recurring invoices. There are times when a payment must be made to a supplier even when an invoice has not been presented. In order to record and track these expenditures you must create an invoice. If these are recurring charges, you must create recurring invoices. Entering recurring invoices is a two-step process. First, you create a recurring invoice template, then you create invoices based on the template. In this section, you will learn to:

- Create special calendars

- Enter recurring invoices

Create a Special Calendar

Before you can enter recurring invoices, you must have a defined special calendar. You use the special calendar to determine the periods for which you are creating recurring invoices. Special calendars are completely distinct from your accounting calendar. Though in practice they are often the same, defining them separately gives you complete flexibility in scheduling recurring payments. You can only create recurring invoices for periods that are current or in the future. Create a monthly special calendar that you can use. The navigation path to create special calendars is *Setup : Calendar : Special Calendar*. See Figure 16-1. Create a calendar called **NEW Monthly**. Enter **12** as the number of periods per year. Select Recurring Invoice as the type of calendar. Use the information in Table 16-1 to create 12 periods for the year 2000, and then save your work.

Review Questions

1. What is a special calendar used for?

2. For what periods can you create invoices?

Enter Recurring Invoices

Once you have created the special calendar, you can enter recurring invoices. The navigation path to the Recurring Invoices form is *Invoices : Entry : Recurring Invoices*. The Recurring Invoices form will display. See Figure 16-2. Enter the supplier name or supplier number in the Supplier region. Select the supplier site. If only one site location exists, the default information will appear. The pay group of the selected supplier and supplier site will be entered by default. You can override the field if you want. In the Calendar region, enter the special calendar name in the Name field. This will determine which periods you can create invoices for.

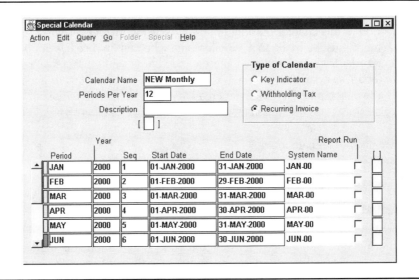

FIGURE 16-1.   *Special Calendar form*

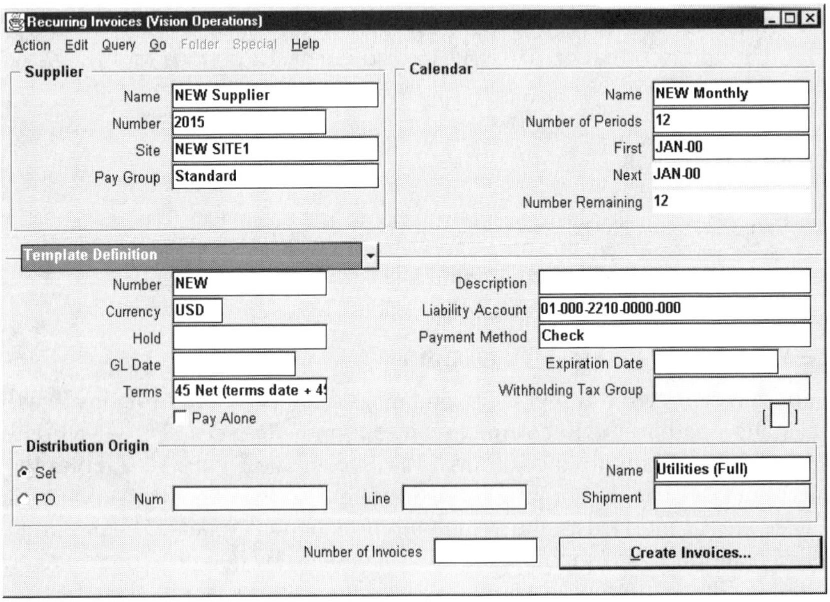

FIGURE 16-2.   *Recurring Invoices form*

Period	Year	Seq	Start Date	End Date
JAN	2000	1	01-JAN-2000	31-JAN-2000
FEB	2000	2	01-FEB-2000	29-FEB-2000
MAR	2000	3	01-MAR-2000	31-MAR-2000
APR	2000	4	01-APR-2000	30-APR-2000
MAY	2000	5	01-MAY-2000	31-MAY-2000
JUN	2000	6	01-JUN-2000	30-JUN-2000
JUL	2000	7	01-JUL-2000	31-JUL-2000
AUG	2000	8	01-AUG-2000	31-AUG-2000
SEP	2000	9	01-SEP-2000	30-SEP-2000
OCT	2000	10	01-OCT-2000	31-OCT-2000
NOV	2000	11	01-NOV-2000	30-NOV-2000
DEC	2000	12	01-DEC-2000	31-DEC-2000

TABLE 16-1. *Special Calendar*

Next, enter the number of periods you want to create invoices for. For example, if you select a monthly special calendar and you enter **12** as the number of periods, you will have 12 invoices that span 12 months, if the special calendar you have selected still has 12 periods remaining. Remember, you can only select a period that is current or in the future. Otherwise, you will receive a warning message informing you that you do not have enough remaining periods in the special calendar you have selected. Enter the period you want to use as the first period by using the List of Values. The Next field and the Number Remaining field will be filled in automatically. For the purposes of this exercise, use NEW supplier as the supplier and select NEW Monthly as the special calendar. Then, select 12 as the number of periods and use JAN-00 as the first period.

Now you can enter the recurring invoice template. In the Number field, you must enter a unique template number. The invoice number is generated using the template number appended by the recurring invoice period. If you wish, you can enter a template description. The description will be used on invoice distribution if there is no description from the selected distribution set or the matching purchase order. Enter the invoice currency, such as USD. The liability account is defaulted based on the selected supplier and supplier site. You can choose to override the liability account. You may optionally place the generated invoices on hold by selecting a hold name. The payment method is also defaulted based on your supplier and supplier site. You can also override the payment method. If you wish, you can enter a GL date. If you leave the field blank, the GL date will be the first date of the recurring invoice period. You can only create recurring invoices with a GL date in an open period or a future enterable period. You can also opt to enter the expiration date, which will determine the date after which recurring invoices can no longer be created. If you created recurring invoices before the expiration date, your recurring invoices can have an invoice date after the expiration date. The payment terms will default from the supplier and supplier site, and you will be able to change it. You can check the *Pay Alone* checkbox. As a last step, you must select your distribution origin. You can select Set or PO. If you select a distribution set, you must specify a distribution name. You can only select a full distribution set, which is a distribution set that has a full 100 percent of the expense distribution accounted for. If you select PO, you must select the PO number, line number, and shipment number. For the purposes of this exercise, use NEW as the template number, USD as the currency, 01-JAN-1999 as GL date, and Utilities (Full) as the distribution set. Save your work.

Select the Amounts alternative region to enter invoice amounts. See Figure 16-3. Enter the first amount. If the invoice amount will change by a known percentage for future invoices, enter the percentage amount in the Change field. The Special Invoice 1 and 2 fields may be used to define and record special invoices, and you can use them for payments such as balloon payments. Special invoices such as balloon payment are used to pay a lump sum amount. You can indicate the amount and the period in which you want the special invoice to be created. The Control Total, Released Total and Amount Remaining fields will display the total invoice amount, released invoice amount, and amount remaining in each field as you release invoices for payment. If you wish, you can leave the First Amount field blank and enter the control total in the Control Total field and/or the change percentage in the Change field. In this case, the first amount will be calculated. As a last step, enter the number of invoices you want to create—you can enter a number up to the total number of periods remaining. For the purposes of this exercise, enter **$123.45** as the amount, and this utility amount is flat. Next, enter **12** as the number of invoices. Save your work.

If you are paying the supplier electronically, enter the remit-to bank, branch, and account information in the Supplier Bank alternative region. See Figure 16-4.

Click on the **Create Invoices** button now to create the recurring invoices. The Create Invoices form will appear. See Figure 16-5. The recurring invoice number, GL date, and amount will be shown. You can change the GL date. You must also enter the invoice batch name, if the *Batch Control* option is enabled. If you have selected a currency other than the functional currency, you must enter the exchange rate type, exchange rate date, and exchange rate. Enter **NEW RECUR** as the invoice batch name and click on the **OK** button. The recurring invoices are created. Notice that

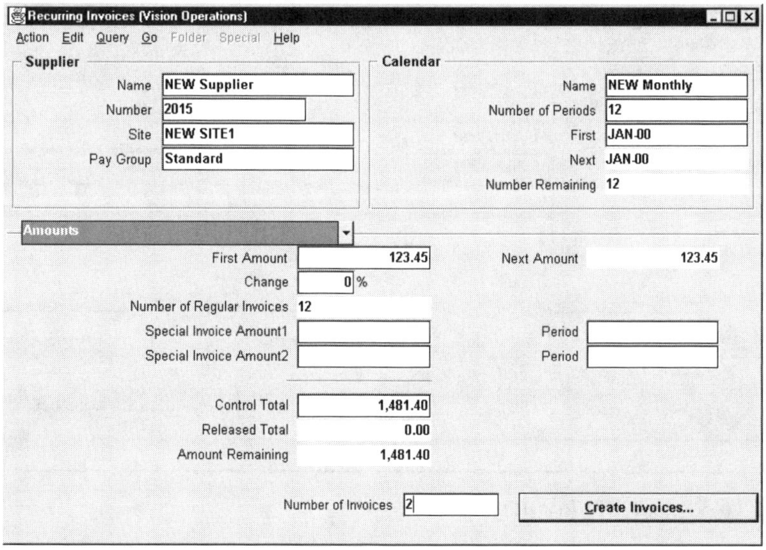

FIGURE 16-3.   *Recurring Invoices (Amounts) form*

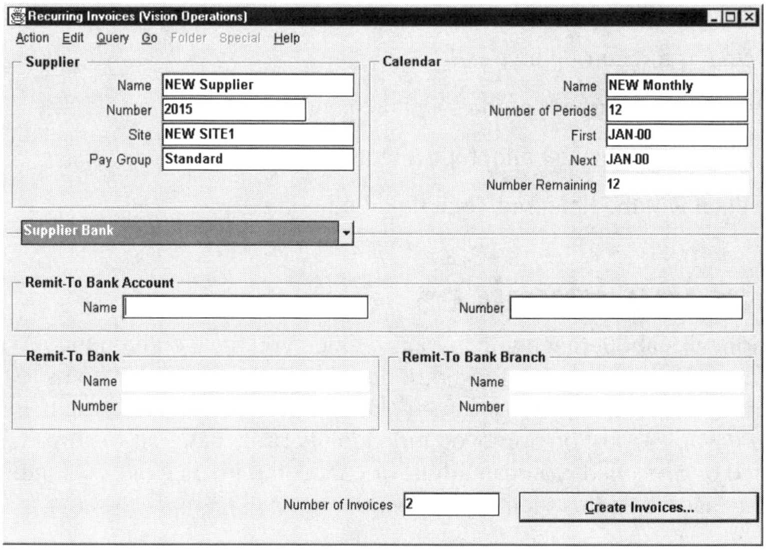

FIGURE 16-4.   *Recurring Invoices (Supplier Bank) form*

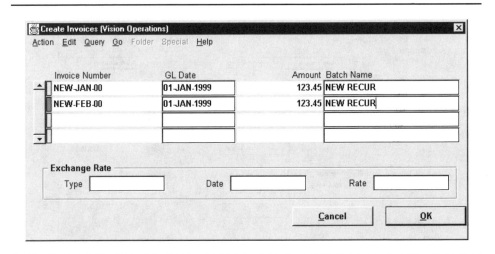

FIGURE 16-5.   *Create Invoices form*

the Number Remaining field and the Released Total field (shown in Figure 16-3) are updated accordingly.

Review Questions

  1. What is a recurring invoice?

  2. What is the purpose of the special calendar?

  3. How do you make balloon payments?

  4. When will the Released Total field be updated?

Managing Invoices

This section talks about managing invoices. Once you have entered the invoices, you can keep them from being picked up for payment by applying holds to them. You can also release holds that have been placed by others or by the system. Invoices in Oracle Payables must be approved individually or by batch. If the invoice must be adjusted or cancelled, you can adjust or cancel the invoice depending on the state of the invoice. In this section, you will learn to:

■ Apply holds to supplier site invoices

■ Apply holds to selected invoices

- Apply holds to schedule payments

- Release holds

- Approve invoices

- Cancel invoices

- Adjust invoices

Applying Holds to Supplier Site Invoices

There are several different holds you can place on invoices or groups of invoices. There is invoice hold, scheduled payment hold, and supplier hold. You can apply a hold that will prevent payment of all invoices belonging to a supplier site. This process could be used instead of applying holds to individual invoices.

The navigation path to apply a hold to a supplier site is *Suppliers : Entry*. The Suppliers form will display. Query the supplier you want to place a hold on and click on the **Open** button. You can then select the Control alternative region to select hold options to be used as defaults for this supplier. Select the Control alternative region for the supplier site to place on hold. The Control alternative region for the supplier or the supplier site is the same. See Figure 16-6. In the Control alternative

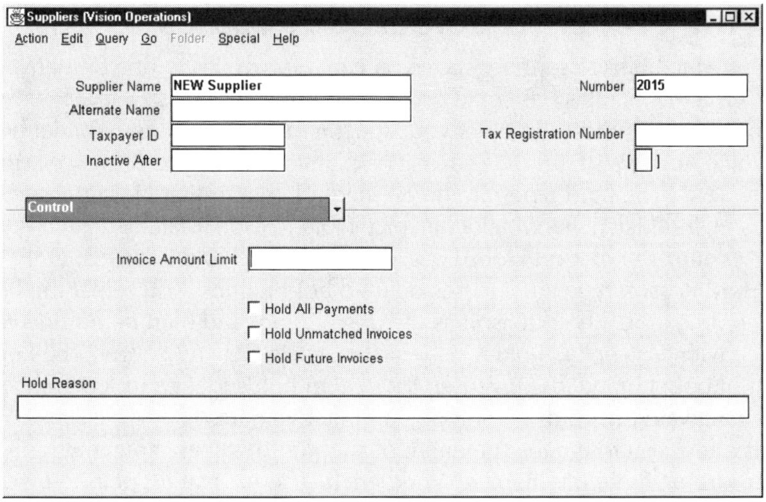

FIGURE 16-6. *Supplier/Supplier Sites (Control) form*

region, you can enter an invoice amount limit. This will prevent individual invoices above the selected amount from being released for payment. You may also select one or more of the following three holds. *Hold All Payments* will place all invoices for this supplier site on hold. If this option is selected, you will not see a hold while viewing invoices in the Invoice form. The reason for this is that you have placed the hold on the site level and not on the invoice level. The second hold option, *Hold Unmatched Invoices*, will hold payment for all invoices that are not matched to a purchase order for this supplier site. This will ensure that you at least enforce a two-way matching for this supplier site. The third hold option is *Hold Future Invoices*, and it will place all invoices that you enter from this point on for this supplier site on hold. Make your hold selection and save your work. If you check any of the *Hold* options, you can optionally enter a hold reason. You may exit or select another supplier.

Review Questions

1. What is the purpose of the invoice amount limit?

2. What hold options do you have to place on hold for a supplier site and what will each one of the options do?

3. What is the Control alternative region of the supplier used for and how is it different than the one at the supplier site level?

Applying Holds to Selected Invoices

Besides applying holds to supplier sites, you can apply holds to one or many selected invoices. Oracle Payables has some predefined holds for you to use. However, you can define additional holds to meet your specific business needs. You define holds in the Invoice Approvals form. The navigation path to use is *Setup : Invoice : Approvals*. See Figure 16-7. The hold types are predefined. They are Acct Hold Reason, Funds Hold Reason, Insufficient Information, Invoice Hold Reason, Matching Hold Reason, Natural Account Tax, Period Hold Type, and Variance Hold Reasons. Only the Invoice Hold Reason type allows user-defined hold names. You select the hold type, enter the hold name, a hold reason as the description, and then determine whether the invoice with this applied hold is postable to Oracle General Ledger. The Releasable field cannot be set manually. It is used for system holds that cannot be released. You can inactivate the holds by entering an inactive date.

Holds allow you to prevent payment of supplier invoices. You can apply holds to invoices from within the Invoice Workbench. The navigation path to Invoice Workbench is *Invoice : Entry*. Enter the query criteria for the invoice you want to put on hold and click on the **Find** button.

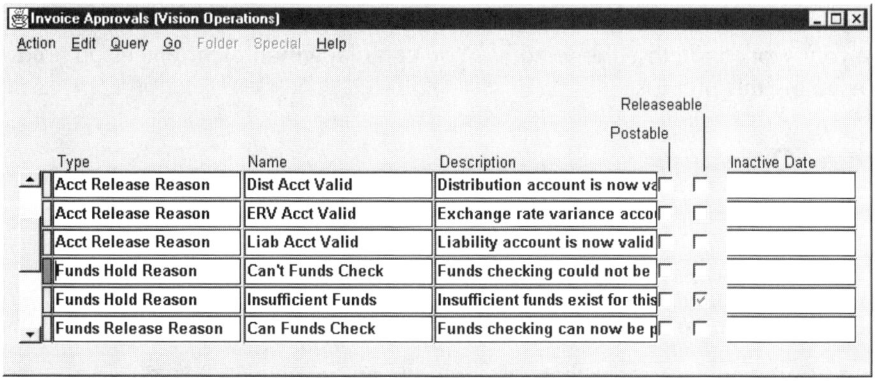

FIGURE 16-7. *Invoice Approvals form*

From the Invoices form, click on the **Holds** button. This will display the Invoice Holds form. See Figure 16-8. Select the hold name by choosing from the List of Values in the Hold Name field. You can apply any predefined hold with a hold type

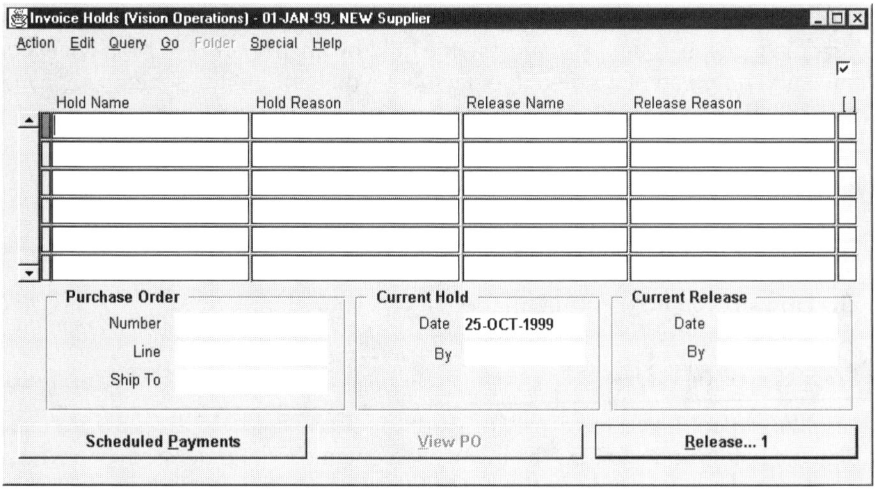

FIGURE 16-8. *Invoice Holds form*

using the Invoice Hold Reason field. The hold reason will default. You can place multiple holds on an invoice by entering multiple rows in the Invoice Hold form. Save your work and close the window. You can place multiple invoices on hold by repeating this process.

Review Questions

1. How do you define invoice holds?

2. Which hold type can you use in applying a hold to an invoice?

3. What is a postable hold?

4. Can you place more than one hold on any invoice and, if so, how?

Applying Holds to Schedule Payments

You can prevent payment of any particular scheduled payment by applying a hold to a scheduled payment. To place a scheduled payment on hold, you also use the Invoice Workbench. Query the invoice that you want to place a hold on for its scheduled payment. Click on the **Find** button. The Invoices form will display. Click on the **Scheduled Payments** button. This will display the Scheduled Payments form. See Figure 16-9.

You will be able to view all scheduled payments related to this invoice. Check the *Hold* checkbox to hold specific scheduled payments. You will not be able to pay the scheduled payments until you remove the hold by unchecking the *Hold* checkbox. If you want to hold part of a scheduled payment, you can split the scheduled payment into two scheduled payments and place a hold on one of the two.

Review Questions

1. How and where do you place scheduled payments on hold?

2. How do you hold part of a scheduled payment?

Releasing Holds

After applying a hold, you may need or want to release the hold at a later date. By releasing the hold, you will allow the invoice to continue to be processed for payment and posting. You can locate invoices on hold in several ways. You can run the Invoice On Hold report or the Matching Hold Detail report, which are both run from the Report Request form. The Invoice On Hold Report will show invoices on all types of holds, while the Matching Hold Detail report will show only invoices with matching holds. You can use the Invoice Workbench and select the **Holds**

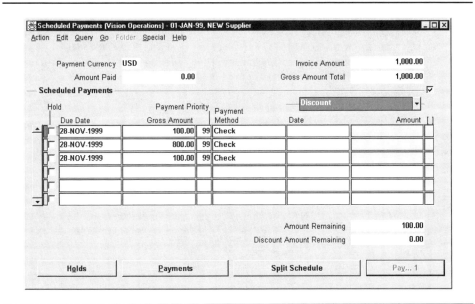

FIGURE 16-9. *Scheduled Payments form*

button to view invoice holds. You may also choose the invoice overview using the **Overview** button from within the Invoice Workbench to see the invoice holds. See Figure 16-10 for the Invoice Overview form.

Similar to the setup of holds, Oracle Payables has predefined release names, and you can set up additional release names using the same Invoice Approvals form. Predefined released types are Acct Release Reason, Funds Release Reason, Sufficient Information, Invoice Release Reason, Matching Release Reason, Natural Account Tax Updated Reason, Period Release Type, Variance Release Reason, Hold Quick Release Reason, and Invoice Quick Release Reason. Only Invoice Release Reason, Matching Release Reason, Variance Release Reason, Hold Quick Release Reason, and Invoice Quick Release Reason allow user-defined release names.

To release holds on all invoices for a supplier site, you must go to the supplier site Control alternative region and remove the invoice amount limit by blanking the field out. You must uncheck the *Hold* option to release the supplier site holds. However, the existing invoices that belong to the supplier site that have been placed on hold will not automatically be released. This only applies to future entered invoices that belong to the supplier site. To release holds for one or more supplier invoices, you can use the Invoice Workbench. Enter the selection criteria for the invoice and click on the **Find** button. From the Invoices form, select the **Holds** button. This will display the Invoice Holds form. Select the release name from the

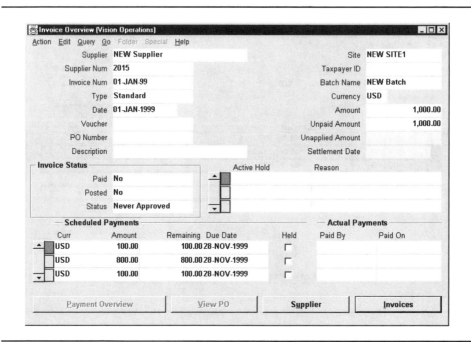

FIGURE 16-10. *Invoice Overview form*

List of Values. You can select release name with the invoice release reason. The release reason will default in. To release multiple holds on the invoice, click on the **Release** button. You can select a release name for the release type with invoice quick release reason. When you click on the **OK** button, the releasable holds for the invoice are released with the selected release name. See Figure 16-11.

You can release holds on multiple invoices by finding the invoices you want to release holds for in the Invoice Workbench. Then, you use Select All from the Edit menu to select all of the invoices. As a last step, you must click on the **Actions** button. The Invoice Actions window will appear. See Figure 16-12. Check the *Release Holds* checkbox. You can select a specific hold to release or select **All** to release all holds. Select a release name for hold quick release reason. The release reason will default. Click on the **OK** button to release the holds. You may release scheduled payments that are on hold by selecting the **Scheduled Payments** button from the Invoice Workbench and unchecking the *Hold* checkbox.

There are two types of holds: system hold or manual hold. System holds are holds predefined by Oracle Payables and are placed based on some predefined conditions. A matching hold is an example of a system hold. Manual holds are

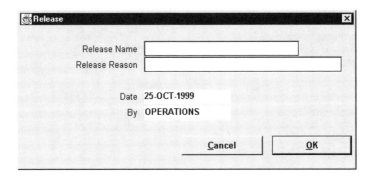

FIGURE 16-11. *Release form*

holds placed manually by you. Approving an invoice or invoices forces the release of system holds if the conditions are correct. Some system holds can be manually released. Manual holds must be manually released.

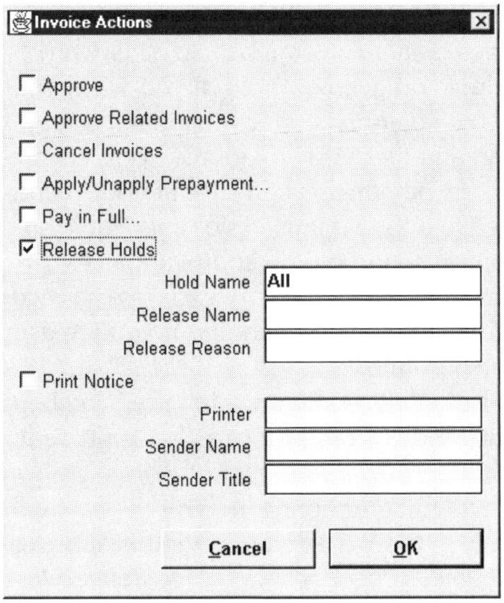

FIGURE 16-12. *Invoice Actions form*

Review Questions

1. What are system holds?
2. How do you release a hold on a supplier site?
3. How do you release a hold on a selected invoice?
4. How do you release a hold on selected scheduled payments?

Approving Invoices

Oracle Payable requires that you approve an invoice in order to post or pay it. To post an invoice means to send the accounting entries on the invoice to Oracle General Ledger. Most companies operate on an accrual basis. That is to say, they recognize the expense in the period in which they accrue it to be paid, not when the actual payment is made. Expenses are often posted to the ledger before payment is made. You can submit invoices for approval in two different ways. You can approve in batch or approve online.

First, you can use an automated batch approval cycle. This allows you to submit the Payables Approval program using criteria you select. You invoke this process through Standard Request Submission (SRS). You can follow the navigation path *Other : Request : Run.* To submit the Payables Approval program, you must select an option. The option can be All for all invoice distributions and New for all invoice distributions that are entered after any approval. In other words, New will not release invoice distributions already placed on hold. If you wish, you can enter an invoice batch name, a start invoice date, an end invoice date, a supplier name, a pay group, an invoice number, and an entered-by to approve only invoices that meet these criteria. Enter your request parameters and submit your request.

The second option is to approve invoices online. There are times when an invoice requires immediate approval, and online approval makes this process easier. To use online approval, you must enable the *Allow Online Approval* option in the payables options. You can approve an invoice online or, if you are using batch entry, you can approve an invoice batch online.

To approve an invoice online, you use the Invoice Workbench. Enter the selection criteria and click on the **Find** button. You can also approve an invoice online immediately after you enter the invoice. From the Invoices form, you must select the **Actions** button. The Invoice Actions form will display with several invoice action options. See Figure 16-13. You can check the *Approve* checkbox or check the *Approve Related Invoices* checkbox. *Approve Related Invoices* is used when approving debit/credit memos. This option will approve the debit/credit memos together with the associated invoice. To approve the selected invoice or the entered invoice, check the *Approve* checkbox and click on the **OK** button. To approve

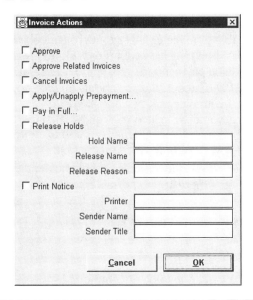

FIGURE 16-13.   *Invoice Actions form*

debit/credit memos together with their associated invoices, check the *Approve Related Invoices* checkbox and click on the **OK** button. To approve an invoice batch, query the invoice batch you want to approve or the newly created invoice batch you entered. Click on the **Approve** button in the Invoices Batches window.

Review Questions

   1. Which two options do you have to approve invoices?

   2. What are the parameters for the Payables Approval program?

   3. How do you enable approving invoices online?

   4. What is the difference between *Approve* and *Approve Related Invoices*?

Cancelling Invoices

There are times when you may need or want to cancel an invoice. Oracle Payables allows you to cancel only unpaid invoices. In addition, these invoices cannot be on postable holds, have applied prepayments, or have been matched to a permanently closed PO. If invoices are prepayments, you cannot cancel the prepayments if they are applied to the invoices. If the invoices are placed on postable hold, these invoices must be released from the holds prior to being cancelled. If you cancel an invoice, you will no longer be able to make changes to it. To cancel invoice distributions, you must reverse them. When Oracle Payables cancels an invoice, it sets the invoice amount and all its scheduled payments to zero. It also reverses the invoice distributions of the invoice and any PO matches. It also submits invoice approval, and if there are no postable holds, the invoice will be cancelled.

To cancel an invoice, you use the Invoice Workbench. Enter the selection criteria and click on the **Find** button to locate the invoice you want to cancel. From the Invoices form, select the **Actions** button. The Invoice Actions form will appear. To cancel the invoice, check the *Cancel Invoices* checkbox and click on **OK.** The invoice will be cancelled if there are no postable holds.

Review Questions

    1. How do you cancel an invoice?

    2. How do you cancel an invoice distribution?

    3. What kind invoices can you cancel?

    4. What does invoice cancellation do?

Adjusting Invoices

You can make adjustments to invoice distributions, scheduled payments, or invoice details, and under certain conditions even when the transactions have been paid and posted to the General Ledger. Your user must have assigned responsibility to make these changes, and all changes require approval before payment. You may cancel any invoice that has not been paid. If you cancel an invoice, you will no longer be able to make changes to it. Also you may delete any invoice that has not been approved. There are different kinds of information on the invoice that you can change.

Invoice Amount

To adjust an invoice amount, the invoice must not be fully paid and have one or more unapproved or unposted invoice distributions. You first locate the invoice in the Invoice Workbench by entering the selection criteria and finding the invoice. From the Invoices form, you can change the invoice amount. Next, select the **Distribution** button and change the distribution amounts to match the new amount entered. Navigate to the Schedule Payments window. Change the payments to match the adjusted amount. Save your changes. If the amount change is a price correction and the invoice distributions are matched to a PO, you can use price correction in the matching form to record this. You do not need to change the amount. Save your work.

Exchange Rate

You may adjust exchange rate any time prior to posting or payment. To change the exchange rate, navigate to the Invoices window and make the change to the rate, or you can run the AutoRate program. The exchange rate date and type must be predefined in the Oracle General Ledger daily rates table.

Scheduled Payments

Scheduled payments can be adjusted in a similar manner to an invoice. You can make adjustments as long as the invoice is not paid in full. You can make additions to the number of payments and amounts, as well as preventing payments by applying holds. You may split a scheduled payment by selecting the **Split Schedule** button. This will allow you to add additional payments, payment amounts, and dates to a previously scheduled payment. Save your work.

Others

If you change fields at the invoice header level that are used as defaults, the invoice distribution fields will not be changed automatically. You must change the information at the invoice distributions manually. For example, you may adjust the GL date from the Invoices window; however, the GL date will apply only to the new distributions you create. To change the GL date for existing invoice distributions, you must change that from the Invoice Distributions window manually.

If the invoice distributions are PO matched and you want to change the invoice distributions' information—other than the GL date, income tax type, or account—you must reverse the distributions and create new invoice distributions to be rematched, if necessary. You can only change the GL date and account if the invoice distributions are not posted. You can only change the account if the *Allow Flexfield Override Payables* option is enabled. Save your changes.

Once you make the adjustments, you must approve the invoices again if the invoice was already approved.

Review Questions

1. What do you need to do if you change defaults at the invoice level?

2. When can you use price correction?

3. What do you need to do to adjust the invoice amount if invoice distribution is not matched to a PO?

4. What do you need to do after invoice adjustments?

Processing Procurement Card Transactions

Oracle Payables allows you to process procurement card transactions when your employees purchase from suppliers and pay with a company procurement card. In this scenario, the credit card company will send the credit card transactions to you in electronic format. You must load the transactions, then ask employees to verify the transactions and the manager to approve them. After that, distributions and invoices must be created for the imported transactions. As a last step, invoices will be approved and paid. In this section, you will learn about:

- Setting up procurement card processing

- Loading transactions

- Employee verification

- Manager approval

- Adjusting transaction distributions

- Creating invoices

- Approving and paying invoices

Setting Up Procurement Card Processing

You must set up the following items before using procurement card processing:

- Credit card code sets

- Credit card programs

- Credit card GL sets

- Credit card profiles

- Credit cards

Credit Card Code Sets

Credit card code sets are sets of card codes such as Standard Industry Classification (SIC) codes. You can create group card codes and assign a default GL account to a group code or a card code. Follow the navigation path *Setup : Credit Cards : Credit Card Code Sets* to invoke the Credit Card Code Sets form. See Figure 16-14. You enter the unique code set name and an optional set description. Then you enter the

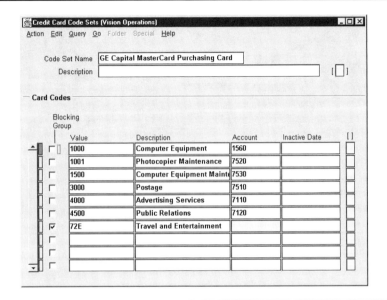

FIGURE 16-14. *Credit Card Code Sets form*

individual card code by entering a unique value, a description, and an optional GL account. If the code is a group code, check the *Blocking Group* checkbox. You can enter an inactive date if you want to make the credit card code inactive.

Credit Card Programs

You define a credit card program for each card issuer. You define the supplier, the supplier site, and transaction statuses that should not be paid. Follow the navigation path *Setup : Credit Cards : Credit Card Programs* to set up credit card programs. See Figure 16-15. Enter a unique card program name. Enter an optional inactive date if you know when this credit card program will be inactivated. Enter an optional description. For the card type, you can select Procurement or Travel. Select the supplier and supplier site that corresponds to this card issuer. Select a card code set that includes card codes this card issuer uses. If you wish, select an employee as the credit card program administrator. Enter the credit card program currency. If you wish, enter the exposure limit/credit limit for reference. Optionally, select a GL account to use for exception clearing. Finally, check the transaction statuses that should not be paid; transaction statuses you can exclude are Unverified, Unapproved, Account Exception, Personal, Disputed, and Hold.

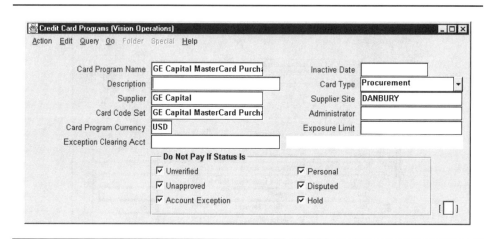

FIGURE 16-15. *Credit Card Programs form*

Credit Card GL Sets
Credit card GL sets are sets of GL accounts that you can select from when adjusting transaction distributions. You can follow the navigation path *Setup : Credit Cards : Credit Card GL Account Sets*. See Figure 16-16. Enter a unique GL account set name and an optional description. For each GL account, enter the unique account number and the description.

Credit Card Profiles
Credit card profiles define the credit card program, GL account set, employee verification options, and manager approval options. Follow the navigation path *Setup : Credit Cards : Credit Card Profiles*. See Figure 16-17. Enter a unique profile name. Enter an inactive date if you know when the credit card profile will be inactivated. Enter an optional description. Select the card program name and the program currency will default. Enter an optional administrator. Select a GL account set name. You can optionally enter a default account template. The segment you enter in this field will override the employee expense distribution account from the expense report. You can also opt to enter an exception clearing account. You can check the *Allow Status "Personal"* checkbox if you want to allow employees to change the status of their personal transactions to Personal during verification. You can check *Allow Direct Account Entry* to allow employees to enter account numbers directly instead of selecting accounts from the GL account set. You can check the *Build Acct From Code* checkbox to use the GL account assigned to the credit card code to override the default account template and the employee expense distribution account. Next, set the manager notification level and the employee

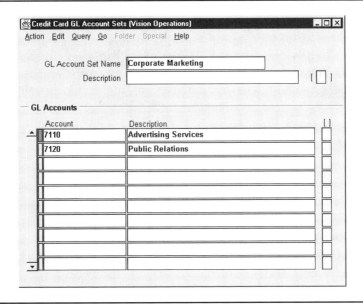

FIGURE 16-16. *Credit Card GL Account Sets form*

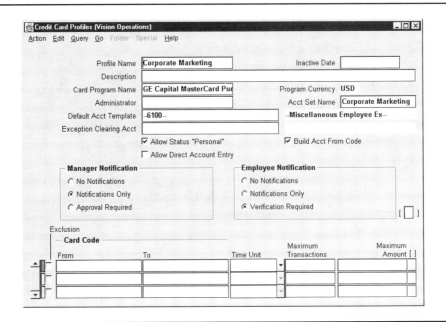

FIGURE 16-17. *Credit Card Profiles form*

notification level to either No Notification, Notification Only, or Approval/Verification Required.

In the Card Code region, you can exclude card code ranges and restrict the number of transactions and total amount for a specific time unit. A time unit can be a single transaction, daily, monthly, or between two statement periods. Currently, the Card Code region is for reference purposes only and no functionality is attached to the data.

Credit Cards

You create a credit card to tie the card to a cardholder and a credit card profile. Follow the navigation path *Credit Cards : Credit Cards*. See Figure 16-18. Select the card program and the card profile. If you wish, enter the card member name. You must enter the credit card number. You must also select the employee that is the holder of the credit card. If you wish, enter the employee's department name, mother's maiden name, card description, inactive date, maximum amounts per transaction, and maximum amounts per period. You can also optionally indicate whether the physical card is issued and whether a paper statement is wanted.

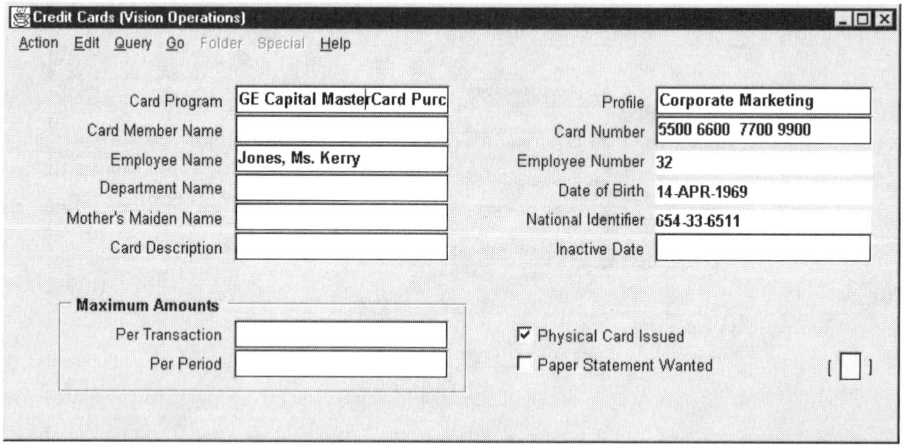

FIGURE 16-18. *Credit Cards form*

Review Questions

1. What is the GL account set used for and how are they set up?

2. What are credit card profiles?

3. How do you tie a supplier and supplier site to a credit card issuer?

4. What is the purpose of the *Build Acct From Code* checkbox?

Loading Transactions

You can load the credit card transactions from the credit card company electronic file into an open interface table called AP_EXPENSE_FEED_LINES in Oracle Payables. You then run the Credit Card Transaction Validation and Exception report to validate and import the credit card transactions. You run the program through Standard Report Submission (SRS) form. You select the credit card program, and can optionally enter a transaction date range. The program will validate the transactions for the specific card program and the appropriate transaction date range. A blank range means all transaction dates are valid. The program also generates distributions in the open interface table AP_EXPENSE_FEED_DISTS where the CREATE_DISTRIBUTION_FLAG = 'Y' with the proper GL accounts.

Review Questions

1. What are the two open interface tables for credit card processing called?

2. What program do you need to run to load the credit card transactions?

Employee Verification

Depending on the defined credit card transaction employee workflow and the credit card profile, the Distribute Employee Credit Card Transaction Verifications program will ask the employee to validate the transactions. Employees can use workflow notification or Web Employees to verify transactions.

Review Questions

1. What program is used to ask employees to validate the transactions?

2. Which workflow is used to ask employees to validate the transactions?

Manager Approval

Depending on the defined credit card transaction manager workflow and the credit card profile, the Distribute Manager Card Transaction Approvals program will ask the manager to approve the transactions. Managers use workflow notification to approve transactions.

Review Questions

1. What program is used to ask managers to approve the transactions?

2. Which workflow is used to ask managers to approve the transactions?

Adjusting Transaction Distributions

You can also use the Credit Card Transactions window to review, adjust, or split the transaction distributions in the table AP_EXPENSE_FEED_DISTS. Each transaction has one distribution to begin with, and you can use the Credit Card Transactions window to split a single transaction distribution into more than one distribution. Follow the navigation path *Credit Cards : Credit Card Transactions*. See Figure 16-19. Query up the transactions that you want to adjust and click on the **Distributions** button.

The Transaction Distributions window is shown in Figure 16-20. You can change the status of the transaction distribution. You can select from Approved, Disputed, Hold, Personal, Rejected, Validated, or Verified. You can change the Amount, the Account, and the Description fields. You can reduce the amount and add more distributions for the transaction. You must make sure that the total distribution amounts add up to the transaction amount. When you are done, save your adjustments.

Review Questions

1. What transaction distribution statuses are there?

2. How do you split one distribution into multiple distributions for a transaction?

3. How many distributions does a transaction have after it is loaded without any adjustments?

Creating Invoices

Once you are satisfied with the transaction distributions, you can run the Credit Card Invoice Interface Summary to create the invoices. The program selects all rows

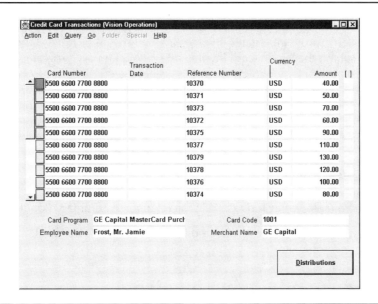

FIGURE 16-19. *Credit Card Transactions form*

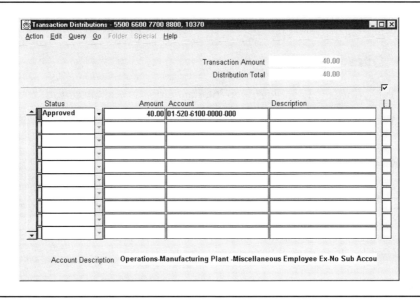

FIGURE 16-20. *Transaction Distributions form*

in AP_EXPENSE_FEED_DISTS with statuses that are not excluded from payment. You can choose to summarize the transactions by GL account and tax name combination. The program creates invoices by loading the Payables Open Interface tables. You submit the Credit Card Invoice Interface Summary program through the Standard Report Submission (SRS) form. You select the credit card program, and you can optionally enter a transaction date range. You can indicate whether you want to summarize the transactions by GL account and tax name combination by selecting Use for Roll up Transaction by Account Parameter. Submit your request by clicking on **OK** in the Parameters window and click on the **Submit Request** button.

Review Questions

1. Which tables will Credit Card Invoice Interface Summary populate?

2. How do you summarize the credit card transactions by GL account and tax name combination?

Approving and Paying Invoices

The last step is to run the Payables Open Interface Import program to import the invoices from the Payables Open Interface tables to the production tables. From the production tables, the invoices can be approved and paid. You run the Payables Open Interface Import program through the Standard Report Submission (SRS) form. Select Credit Card as the source. Submit the concurrent program. You have now completed the processing procurement card transactions.

Review Questions

1. What does the Payables Open Interface Import program do?

2. What source should you select to import credit card transactions?

Entering Manual Payments

In this section, you will learn to enter manual payments. There are several ways to enter manual payments. You can select invoices to be paid through quick or manual payment, from the Invoice Workbench, or enter future-dated payments. Using manually entered payments, you can also override some payment controls of Oracle Payables. In this section, you will learn to:

■ Select invoices to pay

■ Pay from the Invoice Workbench

■ Pay suppliers with future-dated payments

■ Override payment controls

Selecting Invoices to Pay

You can select invoices to pay from the Payments window. To select invoices to pay, follow the navigation path *Payments : Entry : Payments*. The Payments window will be displayed. You can use two types of manual payments in the Payments window. They are:

■ Quick payment

■ Manual payment

Quick Payment

You can create a check or electronic payment to pay a supplier for one or more invoices regardless of the invoice payment terms. In other words, you can enter a quick payment for invoices that are not due. To enter quick payment, the *Allow Print Payables* option must be enabled and the currency for the quick payment must be the same as the invoice currency or a fixed-rate currency.

First, you select Quick as the payment type. Then you enter the bank account that you want to make the payment from. Select a payment document that is of the Computer Generated or Combined disbursement type. You will receive a message telling you that Oracle Payables is attempting to reserve the payment document. Oracle Payables must reserve the payment document so that no other user can use it while you are using it. The next available document number will be defaulted. You can override the number if you want. Enter the payment date. If you enabled the *Allow Pre-Date Payables* option, you can enter a date earlier than the system date. The payment date must be in an open period or a future-enterable period. You can change the defaulted currency if your bank account allows multiple currencies and you have enabled the *Allow Multiple Currencies Payables* option. The next few fields are for display only. Select the supplier and the supplier site. You can optionally select the transfer priority. Valid values are Any, Express, or Normal. If you are making an electronic payment, the remit-to account will be defaulted from the supplier. If you enabled the *Allow Remit-to Account Override Payables* option, you can override the supplier remit to account. Next, you can enter the voucher number in the next field if you are not using sequential numbering. If you select a currency other than the functional currency, you must enter appropriate exchange rate information. You can optionally enter a maturity date. The maturity date is the date that your bank should disburse funds to the supplier's bank. If you have enabled the *Allow Payment Address Change Payables* option, you can change the defaulted address.

For the purposes of this exercise, select Quick as the payment type, BofA as the bank account, Check as the document name, 01-JAN-1999 as the payment date, and NEW Supplier and its site as the supplier and supplier site. See Figure 16-21.

To select invoices to pay, select the **Enter/Adjust Invoices** button. You can select as many approved invoices as you wish; however, only you can select the number of invoices you have defined for the remittance advice of the selected payment document. You cannot select more than one invoice if one of the invoices is marked as Pay Alone. All of the invoices you select must have the same supplier and supplier site as the payment supplier and site. Select the invoices you have created from Chapter 12. See Figure 16-22. If you cannot select the invoice using the List of Values, chances are your invoice has not been approved. Approve the invoice and try again. Once you select the invoice, you can use the **Invoice Overview** button to review the invoice your cursor is on. Save your work and close the window. The Payment Amount field will be automatically calculated.

You can click on the **View Invoices** button in the Payments window to see the invoices you have selected (see Figure 16-23). Click on the **Action** buttons and the Payment Actions form will be displayed (see Figure 16-24). Check the *Format* checkbox. The format program will be displayed. If you have specified a remittance advice program for your payment document, the *Print Remittance Advice* checkbox will be checked and the remittance advice program will be displayed. If you do not check the *Print Now* checkbox, the payment and the remittance will be formatted but will not be printed. You must use the Reprint function from the Concurrent

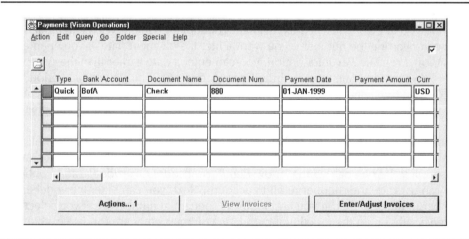

FIGURE 16-21. *Payments form*

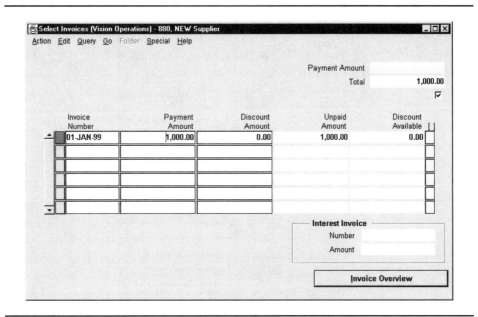

FIGURE 16-22. *Select Invoices form*

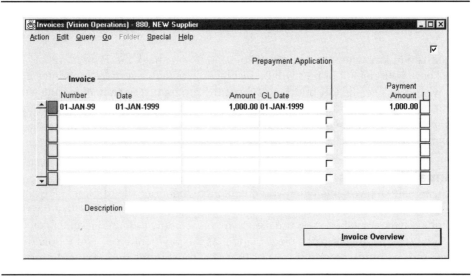

FIGURE 16-23. *Invoices form*

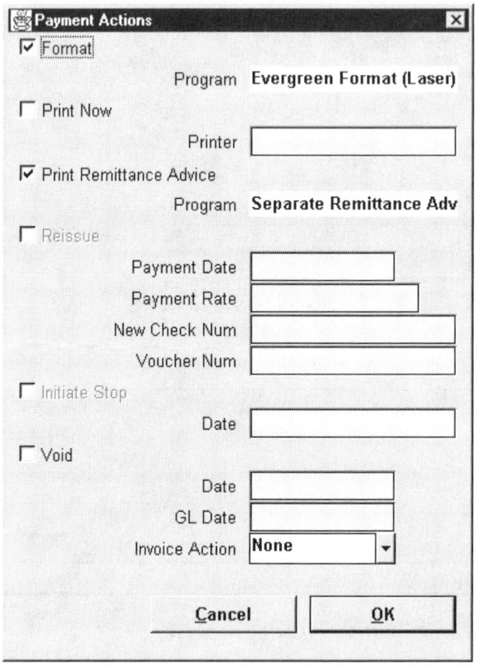

FIGURE 16-24. *Payment Actions form*

Requests window when you are ready to print. If you check the *Print Now* checkbox, your default printer will be displayed; you can override the printer if you wish. Click on the **OK** button to submit the program(s) or **Cancel** to quit. You are not going to check the *Print Now* checkbox, assuming that you will return later to print your check. Check *Format* and click on the **OK** button. You will get a confirmation message. Click on **OK** to acknowledge.

Manual Payments

You use manual payments when you create a payment outside of Oracle Payables. These can be a manually typed check, a wire transfer, or any invoices that have the Clearing payment method. You use the Payments window to record manual payments just like quick payments. You select Manual as the payment type. You follow the same steps as quick payment except that you must enter the payment amount yourself and you do not need to format and print the payment document. Remember that the payment document is already taken care of outside Oracle Payables. Select the invoice(s) and save your work. You do not need to format and/or print the payment document.

Review Questions

1. What is the difference between quick payment and manual payment?

2. What are the methods of payment you can record in the Payments window?

3. How can you print the payment document later if you initially decide just to format the payment document?

4. What kind of invoices can you select to be paid in the Payments window?

Paying From the Invoice Workbench

You can select one or many invoices to pay using the Invoice Workbench. In the Invoice window, query to find the invoices that you want to pay. If the invoices are not approved, you must approve them first.

Choose the invoice you want to pay by placing the cursor on the invoice. To select multiple invoices, hold down the CTRL key while clicking the primary mouse button. To select all invoices, use Select All from the Edit menu. You can only select invoices with the same supplier and the same supplier site. As you select more invoices, the number in the **Actions** button will reflect the increased count of selected invoices accordingly. Select the **Actions** button. The Invoice Actions form will display. Check the *Pay in Full* checkbox. Click on **OK** to pay. You will be asked to confirm your intention to pay in full. Click on **OK** to acknowledge. The Payments window will appear and most of the data is automatically filled in. Also notice that the **Enter/Adjust Invoices** button is shaded out since you already selected the invoice. See Figure 16-25.

You can create a quick payment or a manual payment. A manual payment indicates a check has already been cut or a payment already wired and you are now recording the entry. A quick payment needs formatting. If you would like to print the check at a later date, then only format the payment document. If you want to print the check at the same time, select the *Format* checkbox and print the payment document. Select the bank account and the payment document. The rest of the fields are filled in, but you can override them. You can decrease the amount for a partial payment. Depending on whether you have selected quick payment or manual payment, you may or may not need to perform the action step. Only Quick Payment needs the action step.

If you do not want to pay an invoice in full, select the **Scheduled Payments** button instead of the **Actions** button in the Invoices form. Payables will display the Schedule Payments form. Select the payment schedule you want to pay by placing the cursor on the scheduled payment. To select multiple scheduled payments, use

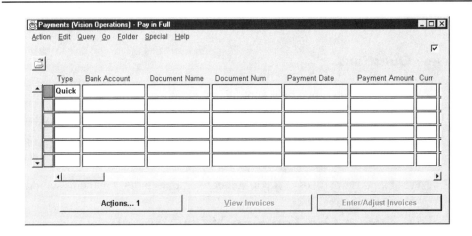

FIGURE 16-25. *Payments - Pay in Full form*

CTRL-click (primary mouse button). To select all scheduled payments, use Select All from the Edit menu. Click on the **Pay** button. You will be asked to confirm your intention to pay. Click on **OK** to acknowledge. The Payments window will appear and most of the data is automatically filled in. Also notice that the **Enter/Adjust Invoices** button is shaded out since you already selected the invoice, just like when you are selecting invoices. You can create a quick payment or a manual payment. Select the bank account and the payment document. The rest of the fields are filled in, but you can override them. Depending on whether you have selected quick payment or manual payment, you may or may not need to perform the action step. Only quick payments need the action step.

The Amount Paid field in the Invoices window and the Amount Remaining field in the Scheduled Payments window will calculate the balance paid and the unpaid balance.

Review Questions

1. How do you use Invoice Workbench to pay multiple invoices, and how will the number in the **Actions** button change?

2. How do you pay scheduled payments instead of invoices?

3. What criteria are used for selecting multiple invoices to pay in full?

Paying Suppliers with Future-Dated Payments

A future-dated payment can be used to make payments to your supplier directly from your bank to the supplier's bank. In order to create future-dated payments, you must enable the *Allow Future Payment Method Payables* option and you need future-dated payment programs and payment formats. There are two types of future-dated payments:

- Future dated
- Manual future dated

Future Dated

The first type is called a future-dated payment. You initiate this type of payment to your bank. This advises your bank to transfer a specific payment amount to your supplier's bank account on the maturity date. An example of this payment is a bill of exchange. You can generate a quick payment, a manual payment, or a payment batch for this type of future-dated payment as long as you use a payment document with a future-dated payment format.

Manual Future Dated

The second type is called a manual future-dated payment. The supplier initiates this type of payment method. The supplier includes a payment notice when the supplier sends an invoice. It is then up to you to approve this notice if the maturity date is acceptable. At such time, you will return the approved payment notice, and since you did not need to generate a payment document, you will record this future-dated payment type as a manual payment.

You use the Payments window to pay suppliers if you are creating a future-dated quick payment or manual payment. You select the bank from the List of Values. Next, enter the document type. In this case, you need a payment document with the appropriate future-dated payment program and payment format. Oracle Payables will display a message that it is reserving a payment document. Acknowledge the message with the **OK** button. You must enter the maturity date of the document and the supplier bank information. Enter the rest of the information. Save your work. The bank will pay the supplier the payment amount on the maturity date for the future-dated payment type. For the manual future-dated payment type, your supplier will forward the approved payment notice to your bank. Your bank, in turn, will pay the supplier the payment amount on the maturity date, and send you the acknowledgement.

Review Questions

1. What is the difference between the future-dated payment type and the manual future-dated payment type?

2. What is the maturity date?

3. What types of payment can you use for manual future-dated payments?

4. What setups do you need for future-dated payments?

Overriding Payment Controls

With manual payment, you can override some payment controls that are set at the supplier or invoice level. You can create payment for invoices with any payment method type except electronic since electronic payment methods are reserved for EDI payments. You can also pay invoices for suppliers that have the *Hold All Payments* option enabled. As a last step, you can create a single payment for multiple invoices even if one or more of the invoices are marked as Pay Alone.

Review Questions

1. What kinds of payment methods allow you to override payment controls?

2. What type of payment controls can be overridden?

Processing Payment Batches

In the last section, you learned to enter manual payments, which pays a single supplier. In this section, you will learn to process payment batches, where you can pay multiple suppliers at once, which are considered to be automatic payments. You use payment batches to automatically generate payments for approved invoices that fit your selection criteria. In this section, you will learn to:

- Initiate new payment batches

- Create and find payment batch templates

- Modify payment batches

- Format payment batches

- Confirm payment batches

- Find payment information

- Process EDI payments

- Make electronic payments to different supplier bank accounts (flexible payments)

Initiating New Payment Batches

Payment batches can be used to select approved invoices that match the criteria that you select. For example, you may create a batch for all approved invoices under a certain dollar amount. To enter or initiate a new payment batch, use the navigation path *Payments : Entry : Payment Batches*. The Payment Batches window will appear. See Figure 16-26. Enter a unique name for your batch. You will use this to locate the batch at a later time. Batches can be saved and reused. To save the payment batch as a template, you must check the *Template* checkbox.

Your payment date will default to the current system date. The payment date is the date that will be printed on the payment document. The payment date must be in an open or future-enterable period. Your batch status will start as Unstarted. Next, you can optionally enter your pay group. You can group your suppliers by pay group so that you can have a separate check run for each group of suppliers. Predefined pay groups include Standard, for regular suppliers, and Employee. Next, select the bank account and the payment document. Oracle Payables will attempt to reserve the payment document. You can optionally fill in the Reference field. The next step the payment batch should take will be displayed. Enter the pay-through date. This is the date you are telling Oracle Payables to use as part of your payment batch criteria. Oracle Payables selects all invoices that have a due date that is on or before this date. Also, if a discount is offered, Oracle Payables selects these invoices during the discount period if Discount is selected as the *Pay Date Basis* and the *Pay Only When Due* checkbox is unchecked for the supplier/site. The Hi and Low Payment

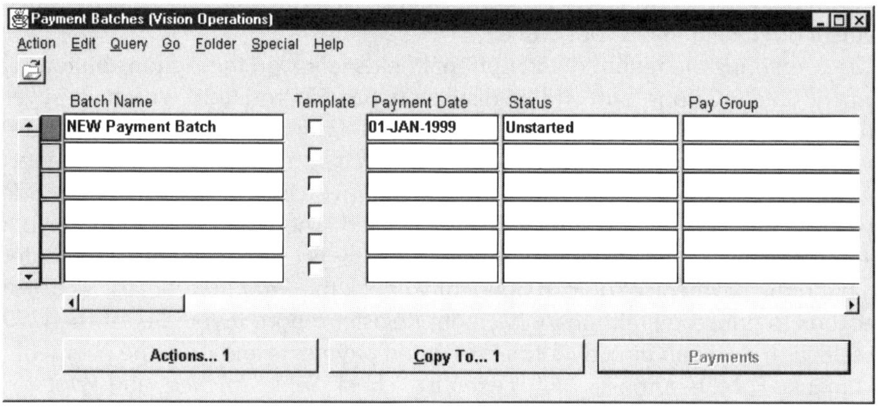

FIGURE 16-26.   *Payment Batches form*

Priorities fields are optional and can be used to refine your batch criteria. If you would like to include zero invoice amounts, enable that checkbox. You can optionally override the pay date basis for a supplier site by checking the *Include Only Due* checkbox.

You can change the payment currency if your bank account and setup allow it. As another selection criteria, you can select the minimum payment and maximum payment. The total for a single payment—a single supplier site—cannot be lower than the minimum payment or higher than the maximum payment. If it is, the invoices for the supplier site meeting these criteria will not be selected for payment in this run. Maximum outlay specifies the total amounts to pay for the entire payment batch. If your payment batch exceeds the maximum outlay you set for the batch, you will receive a warning stating you will exceed your maximum. You are allowed to proceed after acknowledging the warning. You can check the *Allow Zero Payments* checkbox to generate a payment of zero. The remittance advice submitted with a zero payment tells your supplier why you are not sending any money.

Next, you can optionally set and adjust document numbers for your payment batch. The first and the last document numbers are displayed, and you can change the first document number. Next, you can enter the starting voucher number in the next field if you are not using sequential numbering. You may select the order in which the payment documents will print by selecting from the drop-down list. Valid options are Ascending Postal Code, Descending Postal Code, Supplier Name, and Supplier Number. The preliminary payment register also follows the order you selected here. The remaining fields are display only.

For your exercise, create a payment batch called **NEW Payment Batch**, check the *Template* checkbox, and use a payment date of 01-JAN-1999. The pay-through date will be defaulted to 08-JAN-1999. Select BofA as the bank and use the Check payment document. Save your work.

After entering the required and optional fields, click on the **Actions** button. The Payment Batch Actions form will be displayed. See Figure 16-27. You have several options: *Select Invoices, Build Payments, Print Preliminary Register,* and *Format Payments.* The rest of the options are shaded out. If you select *Format Payments*, you can select *Print Now* also. Check the *Select Invoices* checkbox and the *Build Payments* checkbox will be automatically checked. These two steps will use your entered selection criteria to select the approved invoices that fall within the criteria and build the payments. You can optionally check the *Print Preliminary Register* checkbox to print the Preliminary Payment Register report. If you are satisfied with the selection, you can directly format the build payments and print the payment documents. For the purposes of this exercise, check *Select Invoices* and *Print Preliminary Register.* Click on the **OK** button to ask Oracle Payables to kick off the three processes. You will get a message to confirm that you want to select invoices for your payment batches. Click on **OK** to acknowledge. You will get the concurrent request ID for each of the three processes. You can also create multiple payment

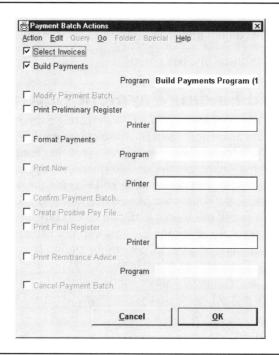

FIGURE 16-27. *Payment Batch Actions form*

batches and select them using CTRL-click or use Select All from the Edit menu to select multiple payment batches and process them all using the **Actions** button. You can review the invoices and suppliers selected for this payment batch. At a later time, you will modify your payment batch of selected invoices, format the payment documents, and then confirm the payment batch. Once the concurrent programs are completed, requery your payment batch. Notice that now your payment batch has a status of Built and a next step of Format, whereas before your payment batch had a status of Unstarted and next step of AutoSelect. Also the payment total, invoice count, negotiable payment count, and overall payment count are all updated.

Review Questions

1. What is pay-through date used for and how does it work with payment terms with discount?

2. What do the Select Invoices and Build Payments programs do?

3. What does maximum outlay mean?

4. What is the purpose of a pay group?

Creating and Finding Payment Batch Templates

Creating a payment batch template is much like creating a new payment batch. Templates can be used again and again by making date modifications and/or minor adjustments to your selection criteria. To locate an existing template, query the template name from the Payments window. To query all payment batch templates, check the *Template* checkbox in query mode and execute the query. Select a suffix or prefix to use to add to the source template batch name to become the destination batch name. It is best to call the source template batch something generic and use the date as the prefix or suffix. For example, you can use Expense Report as the source template batch name and use JAN-99 as the prefix. Then you will have JAN 99 Expense Report as the destination batch name. All you need to do every month is to change the prefix and change the payment date and click on the **Copy To** button. See Figure 16-28. You will get a confirmation message. Click on **OK** to acknowledge.

Review Questions

1. How do you find the all payment batches template?

2. How are prefixes and suffixes used?

3. What field of the payment batch can you change in the Copy To window?

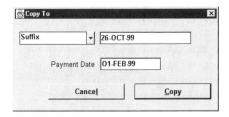

FIGURE 16-28. *Copy To window*

Modifying Payment Batches

Once you have completed your payment batch criteria for invoice selection, also known as AutoSelect, and initiated the Select Invoices and Build Payment processes, you can review your selections with the Preliminary Payment Register report. This will display the invoices and suppliers that met your batch selection criteria. You can make changes and adjustments to your payment batch. You can modify the payment amount of an invoice, stop or place the payment of a supplier or of a particular invoice on hold, or add an invoice that was not in your original selection criteria.

To modify your payment batch, go to the Payment Batches window. Use the **Find** button and enter the criteria to locate the payment batch. Selection criteria for payment batch include batch name, template, bank account, payment document, payment method, currency, status, allow zero payments, next step, payment amounts range, payment date range, pay group, allow zero invoices, and priority range. Enter the name of your payment batch and click on the **Find** button.

Select your payment batch and then select the **Action** button. Uncheck the *Format Payments* checkbox first, then check the *Modify Payments* checkbox. Next, select the **OK** button. The Modify Payment Batch form will display. See Figure 16-29. Modify your batch here by changing the payment amount of an invoice, holding a supplier or a particular invoice, or adding an invoice not included in the original selection. You can change the payment amount of an invoice by changing the discount amount and the maximum amount in the Selected Invoices region. You can hold a supplier by changing the Pay field below the supplier and optionally selecting a nonpayment reason. If you have a remit-to account and you have enabled the option to allow you to change it, you can change it. In the Selected Invoices region, you can select No in the Pay field to exclude an invoice. If an invoice is excluded because the entire payment batch exceeds the set maximum outlay, you can include the invoice with Force in the Pay field.

When your cursor is on the Supplier field, click on the **Find** button. This will show you the suppliers that have invoices that fit in your invoice selection. However, not every supplier will have a check. Notice in Figure 16-30 that some of the suppliers are not paid since they are over the maximum payment amount. Select one of them. Notice that the Pay field is No and the selected invoices are all set to Yes. Set the Pay field underneath the supplier to Force. You will see that all Pay fields for the selected invoices will change to Force. Now a payment document will be generated for this supplier. Select the **Done** button after you finish modifying the payment batch.

Once you have made the modification, Oracle Payables will automatically rebuild your payment batch when you click on the **Done** button. Review your modification in the Preliminary Payment Register report. If you are not happy with the changes, you may modify them again. If the modification meets your needs, you can proceed with formatting payments.

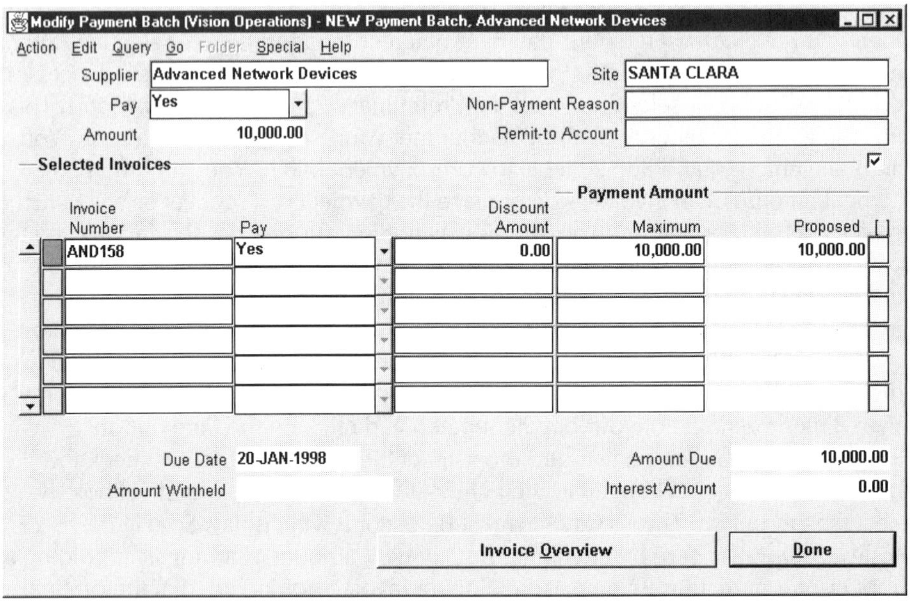

FIGURE 16-29. *Modify Payment Batch form*

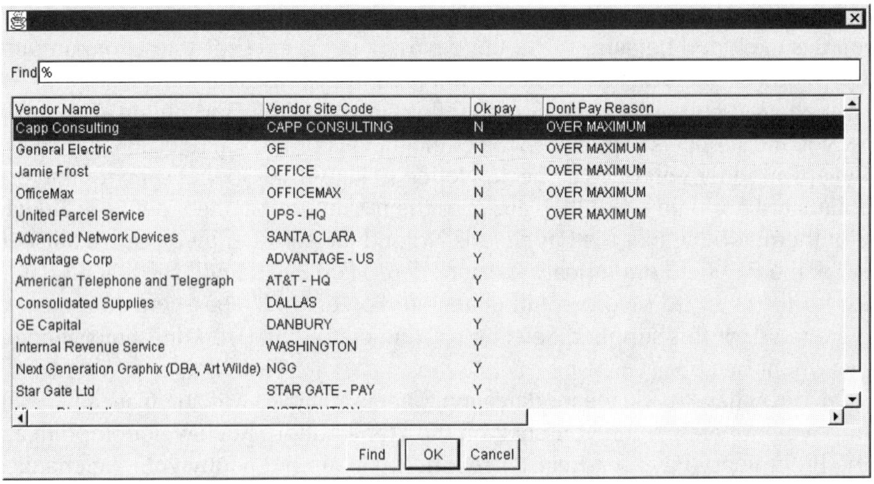

FIGURE 16-30. *Find Suppliers form*

Review Questions

1. How do you modify a payment batch?

2. What can you modify after a payment batch is built?

3. What do you need to do to initiate rebuilding the payment batch?

4. What is the value Force used in the Pay field?

Formatting Payment Batches

Formatting payments is Oracle Payables way of creating a file to be used to print payments documents including checks and electronic payments. You can only use payment documents that you have previously assigned to your payment bank account. All payment batches will be formatted to generate the payment document. For electronic payments with Oracle EDI Gateway, when you format the payment batch, the Remittance Advice Outbound Extract Program will be automatically run.

To format a payment batch, begin by selecting the payment batch you wish to format in the Payment Batches window. Query the payment batch that you wish to format. Next, select the **Actions** button. The Payment Batch Actions form will display. From this form, select the *Format Payments* checkbox. If you wish, you can print the payment documents immediately after the format payment program by checking the *Print Now* checkbox. For the purposes of this exercise, you only need to check *Format Payments*. Click on the **OK** button and Oracle Payables will kick off a concurrent process. You will receive a confirmation initiating the formatting program. Click **OK** to acknowledge the message and you will get the concurrent request ID. You can view the output and note the payment document numbers that are generated. Once the program is completed, query your payment batch. You will notice that the status now is Formatted and the next step is Confirm.

Review Questions

1. What will the format program do?

2. What is the status of the payment batch before formatting?

3. What is the status of the payment batch after formatting?

4. What is the next step after formatting?

Confirming Payment Batches

Confirming the payment batch is the last step in the payment batch process. The Oracle Payables confirmation process updates the invoice statuses from Unpaid to Paid. Also, it creates a payment distribution for each balancing segment of each invoice in the payment batch. You must confirm all your outstanding payment batches before you can close the accounting period in Oracle Payables.

To confirm a payment batch, you also use the Payment Batches window. Query your payment batch. From the Payment Batches window, click on the **Actions** button. The Payment Batch Actions form will display. Select the *Confirm Payment Batch* checkbox and then click on the **OK** button. You will get a confirmation. Click on **OK** to acknowledge the message. The Confirm Payment Batch form will display. See Figure 16-31.

In the Status field of this form, you must enter one of four statuses: Printed, Set Up, Skipped, or Spoiled. If the payment documents printed correctly, enter **Printed**. If the payment document is a setup check used to set the printer alignment, enter **Set Up**. If, for some reason, the document number is skipped or if the printer skipped some checks and nothing was printed on them, enter **Skipped**. If the printer spoiled or destroyed the payment documents, enter **Spoiled**. Oracle Payables will leave the statuses of these invoices as Unpaid. You may include these invoices in the next

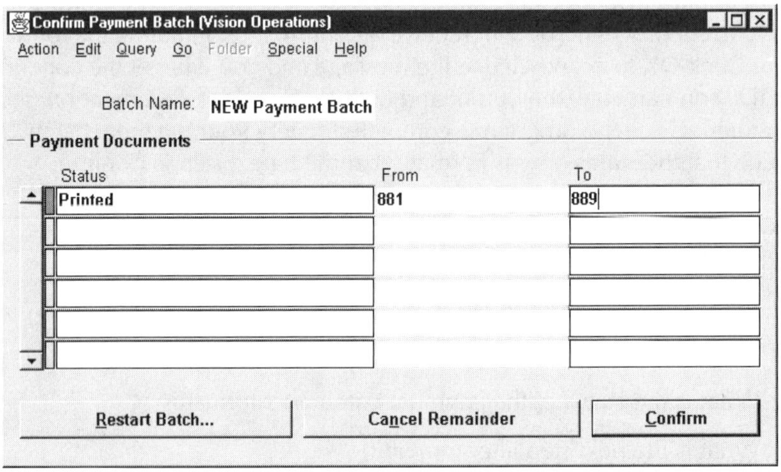

FIGURE 16-31. *Confirm Payment Batch form*

payment batch. You can enter the status by payment document number range. To enter the range, enter the start and end document numbers in the From and To columns. For the purposes of this exercise, enter the To document number by reviewing the output of the formatting program. Select the status of Printed. This confirms the documents were successfully printed and the document numbers will be recorded as used.

Once you have marked the status of the payment document, you have three option buttons to choose from: **Restart Batch**, **Cancel Remainder**, and **Confirm**. If you only have a partial run and you recorded the status of part of the payment batch, you have two options. You can confirm part of the payment batch with recorded statuses and restart the payment batch with the new next available document number, or you can confirm part of the payment batch with recorded statuses and cancel the remaining portion of the payment batch. You accomplish this by selecting the **Restart Batch** and **Cancel Remainder** buttons, respectively. If you choose the **Restart Batch** button, you must provide the first payment document number of the new payment batch. This new payment batch will be automatically built with the unprinted checks. The invoices of the partially confirmed payment batch that are confirmed with the status of Printed will be updated to status Paid. For your payment batch, select the **Confirm** button. This will update the invoice statuses. Unpaid invoices that were confirmed with the Printed status are updated to Paid. A final payment register will print for your review. Three concurrent programs will be initiated: Final Payment Register, Separate Remittance Advice, and Confirm Payment Batch. You have now completed the payment batch processing. The status of your payment batch becomes Confirmed.

Review Questions

1. What are the four statuses for payment documents during confirmation?

2. What report will be printed after confirmation?

3. What will **Restart Batch** button do?

4. What will **Cancel Remainder** button do?

Finding Payment Information

To best respond to supplier inquiries, you must locate payment information. In some cases a supplier must know the status of a payment, and in other cases they may need more detail about the payment. You can use the Payment Overview form to inform your supplier of check numbers, dates, and amounts of payments. You can confirm supplier name and mailing information, as well as the bank the payment was drawn upon.

The Payment Overview form is a query-only window. To get to the Payment Overview window, follow the navigation path *Payments : Inquiry : Payment Batches.* The Find Payments form will appear. See Figure 16-32. You can enter a payment number range, a payment date range, a supplier name, a taxpayer ID, a supplier number, a supplier site, and a voucher number range. Enter **01-JAN-99** as the payment date for your payment batch and then click on the **Find** button.

The Payment Overview window appears. See Figure 16-33. This form shows the higher-level payment batch information, the supplier information, the bank information, and the selected invoices information. To view additional and more detailed information of each of the four regions, select from one of the four buttons at the bottom of the form: **Invoice Overview, Bank, Supplier**, or **Payments**.

To view an invoice overview, click on the **Invoice Overview** button. To view detailed bank information, click on the **Bank** button. This will display detailed information, including branch and EDI information. To view detailed supplier information, click on the **Supplier** button. This form will display supplier information such as payment terms, supplier addresses, and holds. To view detailed payment information, click on the **Payments** button. This form will display the payment information and give you an option to view the supplier invoice.

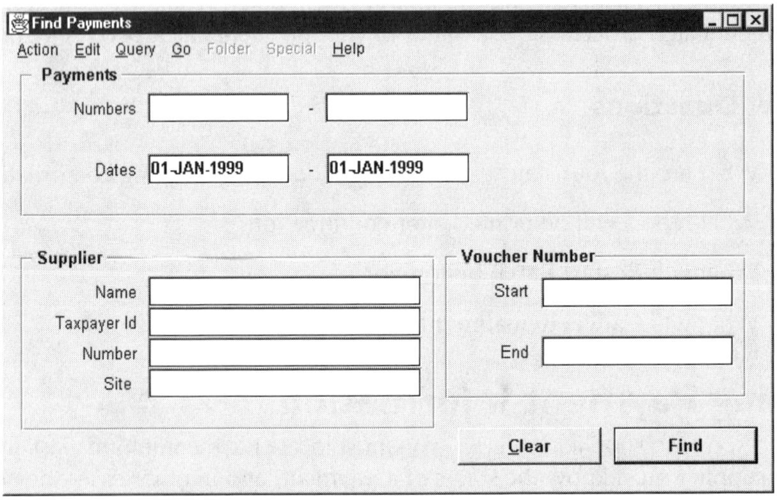

FIGURE 16-32. *Find Payments form*

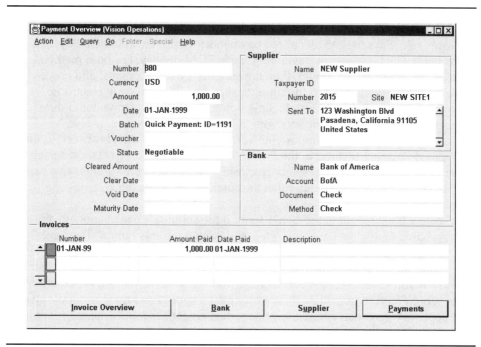

FIGURE 16-33. *Payment Overview form*

You can also use the Payment Workbench and find or query the payments you want. To get to the Payment Workbench, you follow the navigation path *Payments : Entry : Payments*, where you enter Manual or Quick Payment. You can query the payments you want and place the cursor on a particular one and select Place on Navigator from the Action menu. This will place the payment document record in the Navigator Documents alternative regions. When you select the payment document from the Navigator, the Payment Workbench will be automatically invoked and the payment will be shown.

Review Questions

1. Which window should you use to find payments?

2. Which four regions are included in the form?

3. What details can you drill down to from the form?

902 Oracle Certified Professional Financial Applications Consultant Exam Guide

Processing EDI Payments

There are two ways to send electronic payments to suppliers in Oracle Payables: with Oracle EDI Gateway, and without Oracle EDI Gateway. For both methods, you must first establish your supplier, then the supplier's bank accounts, and ensure the bank accounts are assigned to the supplier site you will be making electronic payments for. Oracle Payables will allow you to schedule a payment and direct the payment to the supplier's bank electronically.

You will set up this supplier as you would any other supplier; however, in the field called Payment Method in the Payment alternative region, you must select Electronic Payments. You can select Electronic Payments in the supplier site instead of in the supplier also. Remember that the supplier site's defaults override the supplier's defaults.

Create a bank record in the Banks form, if the supplier's bank is not already an existing bank. Query the bank and select the **Bank Accounts** button. The Bank Accounts form will display. The bank name and branch name will default in the form. Enter the supplier name in the Name field and the account number in the Number field. Next, select the account use from the drop-down list. Here, you must enter **Supplier** as the user since this is a supplier's bank. Enter the currency. Select the Supplier Assignments alternative region, then enter the supplier name or supplier number and the site of the supplier using this bank account for flexible payments. Check the *Primary* checkbox if this is the supplier's primary bank account.

You can verify your bank assignments by viewing the bank accounts in the alternative region of the Supplier Sites form. In the Bank Accounts alternative region for the supplier or the supplier site, the bank accounts information should show up. You can have multiple bank accounts for each supplier or supplier site, and you can use them for flexible payments as discussed later on. In addition, if you want to send electronic payments with Oracle EDI Gateway, you must create a payment document with the EDI Outbound Program payment format and you must have Oracle EDI Gateway installed. You must also have your trading partners/suppliers set up in Oracle EDI Gateway in order to allow EDI transactions. In addition, you must set up your bank with the EDI ID number and EDI location. You also need to fill the supplier site with the electronic payment information in the Electronic Data Interchange alternative region. Now the setup is complete for an EDI-transactable supplier/site. For each scheduled payment that is associated with the Electronic Payments payment method, you must enter the supplier's remittance bank account.

To process EDI payments, you run the same process as you do to print checks for a payment batch; however, you must use your EDI payment document. The payment data will be extracted and formatted to the EDI Outbound Payment format (820) automatically by the EDI Outbound Program, and will be sent to your preestablished EDI translator. It will then be sent to the supplier's remittance bank account. Follow the same payment batch process by selecting invoices, build payments, modify payments, and format payments. Once you have verified that the bank received the payment information, confirm the payments.

Review Questions

1. What additional setups are necessary to process EDI payments?

2. What do you need to set up for the supplier site for both EDI and non-EDI transactions?

3. When should you confirm the EDI payment batch?

Making Electronic Payments to Different Supplier Bank Accounts (Flexible Payments)

To make electronic payments without Oracle EDI Gateway, in addition to the common setups covered above, you must also set up the EFT number in the bank account. Also, if the seeded EFT format and the remittance advice programs do not fit your business needs, you must create your own format and remittance programs with the Electronic Payments payment method. Follow the same procedure as you do for printing checks.

Flexible payments means making electronic payments to different supplier bank accounts with the same invoice or different invoices. To do this for a single invoice, you must create an invoice with payment method Electronic Payments in the Invoice Workbench. Click on the **Scheduled Payments** button and see the scheduled payments of the invoice in the Scheduled Payments window. For each scheduled payment, the supplier's/site's primary bank account will default. If you enable the *Allow Remit-to Account Payables* option, you can override the default supplier's/site's bank account and enter another bank account for the supplier/site with the same payment currency. By doing this, you can create electronic payments for more than one bank for the same invoice.

To do this for multiple invoices, identify these electronic payment suppliers or supplier sites as a different pay group, such as EDI or EFT, that uses the same payment format and remittance advice programs. Assign the pay group to the appropriate supplier or supplier site. When you create a payment batch, select invoices by pay group. As a result, your payment batch creates electronic payments to different suppliers'/sites' bank accounts for different invoices.

Review Questions

1. What additional steps do you need to take for EFT?

2. What are flexible payments?

3. How do you send to different suppliers' bank accounts for the same invoice?

4. How do you send to different suppliers'/sites' bank accounts for multiple invoices?

Recording Stop and Void Payments

This section talks about recording stop and void payments. After you make payments, in some cases you may want to place stop payments or void payments. In this section, you will learn to:

- Place stop payments

- Release stop payments

- Void payments

- Void unused payment documents

Placing Stop Payments

To place a stop payment, you will first want to ensure that the bank has been notified and the stop payment order has been confirmed. Next, you will want to record the stop payment in Oracle Payables. Locate your payment by querying the payment from the Payment Workbench's Payments window. The navigation path is *Payments : Entry : Payments*. This will display the Payment Workbench. Find the payment that you wish to stop. For the purposes of this exercise, select one of the payments you created in your payment batch.

Click on the **Actions** button. This will display the Payment Actions form. This form is where you will initiate the stop. You will only use the lower portion of this form. Check the *Initiate Stop* checkbox. Oracle Payables will default the current date and time. Override the stop date if necessary. Next, select the **OK** button and you will get a confirmation message. Click on **OK** to acknowledge the message. Oracle Payables will change the payment status from Negotiable to Stop Initiated. You cannot stop a quick payment that you have already formatted. You can select more than one payment to be stopped using either CTRL-click or using the Select All function before clicking on the **Actions** button. Notice the number changes on the button as you select more payments.

You can review the stopped payments by reviewing the Stop Payments report. This report will only show outstanding stopped payments. Any stopped payment that has since been released or voided will not show up on this report. You submit the report through the Standard Report Submission (SRS) form. You can select a report parameter using a specific bank branch or a specific bank branch and bank account. Leave it blank for all bank branches and/or all bank accounts. Click on **OK** and submit the request by selecting the **Submit Request** button.

Review Questions

1. How do you initiate a stop payment?

2. What will the status of a payment be after stop is initiated?

3. What is the Stop Payments report?

Releasing Stop Payments

After applying a stop payment to an invoice, at some point you may need to release the stop. For example, you may want to release a stop payment on an invoice problem that has been resolved. When you release the stop payment, the payment status will be reset to Negotiable.

To release a stopped payment, you must query the payment that had been stopped from the Payment Workbench. Find your payment. To see the stop payments, use the Find window and select Stop Initiated as the payment status. Click on the **Find** button. You can select more than one payment. Select the **Actions** button. This will display the Payment Actions window. From this window, you will notice that where you see the *Initiate Stop* checkbox, you now see the *Release Stop* checkbox. Check the *Release Stop* checkbox. The system date and time will be defaulted; override it if necessary. Next, select the **OK** button and acknowledge the confirmation. The stop payment is now released and the status is reset to Negotiable.

Review Questions

1. How do you release a stopped payment?

2. What does the release process do to the stopped payment?

Voiding Payments

You can also decide to void payments if the payments are not marked as cleared. When you decide to void a payment, Oracle Payables creates reverse accounting entries and will reverse the payment records, including any automatic interest or withholding tax calculation. Also, any realized gains or losses from a foreign currency are reversed. It will also change the status of any invoices or scheduled payments associated with the voided payment. Once your payment is void, you must decide what you will do with the associated previously paid invoices. You may decide to do nothing that will change the invoice status back to Unpaid and will allow the invoices to be paid again. Or, you may decide to place the invoices on hold to prevent them from being paid or cancelling the invoices. A voided payment cannot be reversed. Oracle offers no standard way to deal with a voided check that happens to clear, so be careful when voiding payments. Make sure that you have the payment in your possession or you have proof that the payment is destroyed. If you are not sure, stop the payment first.

To void a payment, find the payment first. Query the payment from the Payment Workbench. Select the **Actions** button. You can also select multiple payments. The Payment Actions window will display. From this window, check the *Void* checkbox.

The system date is defaulted into the Date field. You may choose to change it. The original payment date will be defaulted into the GL Date field. You can change it to any date in an open accounting period. If you would like the invoices to be available to be paid again on a different payment document, then select None from the Invoice Action drop-down menu. If you would like to place the invoices on hold, select Hold as the invoice action. If you select Hold, a Hold window will pop up to ask you for the hold name. Enter the hold name and click on the **Hold** button to place the invoices on hold, or the **Cancel** button to cancel the hold. Or, if you wish to cancel the invoices, select Cancel as the invoice action. If the invoices are paid by more than one payment, the invoices that have more than one payment will not be cancelled, but will be put on Invoice Cancel holds. If the invoices can be cancelled, this process will cancel all associated invoices and reset their amounts to zero. Then click on the **OK** button. Acknowledge the confirmation. This will void your selection. For the purposes of this exercise, select a payment in your payment batch and void it.

You can also void a payment document and issue a replacement if you have enabled the *Allow Void* and *Reissue Payables* options. You do the reissue from the Payment Workbench. Select the payment you want to reissue. The defaults will be automatically filled in. You can enter a new payment date, a payment rate if the original payment is not in the functional currency, a new check number, and an optional voucher number. The *Void* checkbox will be automatically checked, and you can override the void date, GL date, and invoice action. This will void your selection and reissue a quick payment.

Review Questions

1. How will you void a payment, and what will happen in the background to the accounting distributions?

2. What is the difference between voiding and reissuing a payment?

3. What is the prerequisite for voiding a payment?

4. What is the purpose of the Invoice Cancel hold?

Voiding Unused Payment Documents

There are several reasons you may need to void unused payment documents. For example, a series of checks may have been damaged and are now unusable. Perhaps the company name or company logo, or even bank or financial institutions, have changed and the check stocks have become obsolete. If you must dispose of unused payment documents, you can void these unused checks in Oracle Payables. This will make these checks no longer available for use in formatting and printing payments.

The navigation path to void unused payment documents is *Setup : Payment : Banks*. In the Banks window, query the bank you must void the unused payment documents for. Next, query the bank account and then click on the **Payment Documents** button. This will display the Payment Document form.

Select the Additional Information alternative region of the Payment Documents window. This is the form that you will use to void the unused checks. Find the document name that you want to void. Click on the **Void Unused Documents** button. Oracle Payables will display the Void Unused Documents window. See Figure 16-34. Enter the document number range that you want to void. The system date is defaulted as the void date. Override the void date, if necessary. Click on the **OK** button, and now your unused payment documents are voided.

Review Questions

1. When do you need to void unused documents?

2. Where do you void unused documents?

Automatic Tax Calculation

In this section, you will learn about automatic tax calculation in Oracle Payables. Oracle Payables provides several mechanisms to calculate tax. In this section, you will learn to:

- Assign the source and hierarchy for tax defaulting

- Define tax names

- Define withholding tax groups

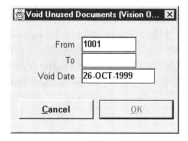

FIGURE 16-34. *Void Unused Documents form*

- Define VAT tax names

- Define EU suppliers

- Record VAT charges

- Review VAT charges

Assigning the Source and Hierarchy for Tax Defaulting

In setting up the payable options, you can set up a hierarchy to use when defaulting tax names onto invoices. Oracle Payables will search the sources in the order you specified for a tax name. It will stop at the first tax name found. To assign the source and hierarchy for tax defaulting, follow the navigation path *Setup : Options : Payables*. Select the Tax Name Defaults form. See Figure 16-35.

The two options at the top of the form override the tax name default hierarchy you specified. If you check the *Enforce Tax From Account* checkbox, invoice approval will check that the account at the invoice distribution matches the tax account defined for the tax name. If not matched, the invoice will be placed on Natural Account Tax hold. If you check the *Enforce Tax From Account* checkbox, Oracle Payables will check the tax names from the account source first if the *Enforce PO Match* checkbox is not checked. If the *Enforce PO Match* checkbox is checked, Oracle Payables will enforce that the invoice tax name matched to the matching PO tax name. Otherwise, the invoice will be placed on a Tax Difference hold. With the *Enforce PO Match* option enabled, Oracle Payables will always go to the matched PO source first regardless of the ranking you placed. If you have enabled automatic tax calculation at the invoice header level, you should not select the *Enforce Tax From Account* option. The tax name at the invoice header level will automatically generate a tax distribution based on the invoice header's tax name. As you enter nontax invoice distributions and enter an account, the tax name associated with the natural account will be the default. As a result, the default tax name on the nontax distribution may be different than the tax name on the tax distribution generated based on the invoice header's tax name. In this case, the invoice will be placed on a Natural Account Tax hold.

The following are sources for tax name defaults; you must check the source you want to use and enter the ranks of the sources in the Hierarchy column to determine the order of the hierarchy, with 1 being the first source. If you change the ranking later on, the tax name default will not change automatically and the new ranking will only apply to new invoices.

- PO for matched invoices

- Supplier site

- Supplier

- Account

- Financials options

- Invoice header

- Template

PO for Matched Invoices

For invoices matched to POs, the tax name from the PO shipment is the source for this selection. If you have enabled the *Enforce PO Tax Name* option, you must include this source regardless of the ranking you assigned to it. The PO shipments will be searched first. If the invoices are not matched to POs, then this source will be ignored.

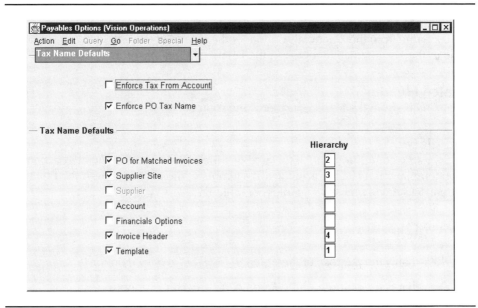

FIGURE 16-35. *Tax Name Defaults form*

Supplier Site

The tax name from the supplier site is the source of this section. You set the tax name in the Invoice Tax alternative region of the supplier site.

Supplier

The tax name from the supplier is the source of this section. You set the tax name in the Invoice Tax alternative region of the supplier. This source is not available for a multiorg implementation.

Account

The tax name is assigned to the natural account in Oracle General Ledger. You set the tax name in the Tax Options form in the Account Level alternative region in Oracle General Ledger. You associate accounts with tax names in the Tax Options form, and then decide whether you want to allow tax code override and whether entered amounts include taxes. If you have enabled the *Enforce Tax From Account Name* option, you must include this source regardless of the ranking you assigned to it. The account source will be searched first or second, depending on whether the *Enforce PO Tax Name* option is enabled.

Financials Options

The tax name from the Financials options is the source of this section. You set tax name in the Tax alternative region in the Financial Options form.

Invoice Header

The tax name from the invoice header is the source.

Template

The tax name comes from the associated distribution set or the associated expense report template. If it is a recurring invoice template, the tax name from the PO or the distribution set will be used regardless of ranking.

Review Questions

1. What is the purpose of the *Enforce Tax From Account* option?

2. What is the purpose of the *Enforce PO Tax Name* option?

3. Which source will rank first if you enable both the *Enforce Tax From Account* option and the *Enforce PO Tax Name* option?

Defining Tax Names

You must define tax names to be used in recording invoice taxes you pay to your suppliers and tax authorities. The tax name has three major components: it stores the tax type, tax rates, and accounting information. Tax types are used to categorize a tax by a specific type. There are five tax types: Sales, Use, User-Defined, Offset, and Withholding Tax. The User-Defined tax type can be expanded to as many tax types as you want since you can define your own tax types as lookup codes. User-Defined tax types are treated like Use tax types in Oracle Payables. A Withholding tax type can also be associated with a tax authority, so you can generate an invoice to submit your suppliers' tax withholdings.

You define a tax name using the navigation path *Setup : Tax : Names*. See Figure 16-36. First, you must select and enter a unique tax name. The next column is the tax type, select from the List of Values. Enter the tax rate in the Rate column. If you are defining a withholding tax, do not enter a tax rate. You must use the Withholding Tax Details window to enter the rate. For an offset tax, you must enter a negative number as the rate. It should be the same tax rate in the opposite sign as the tax this offset tax is offsetting. Then, enter the tax name description.

The next checkbox is used with the Oracle Self-Service Web application. If you have installed the Self-Service application and want the defined tax name to appear in the tax name List of Values in the Self-Service Enter Receipts form, check the *Enable for Self-Service Users* checkbox. If you have not installed this Web application, leave this checkbox blank. Enter a date in the Inactive Date column only if you wish to inactivate a tax name.

In the GL Account field, enter the account you will charge the tax to. The account description will be displayed. Ignore the VAT Transaction Type field unless you are implementing in Belgium.

For withholding tax, you must click on the **Withholding Tax Details** button. The Withholding Tax Details window will appear. See Figure 16-37. You enter the tax authority name that should receive this withholding tax payment. The tax authority selected must be a defined supplier with a type of Tax Authority. Select the supplier's site. Then enter the amount basis to be used—you can select Gross Amount or Withheld Amount. Gross Amount means the entire taxable amount and Withheld Amount is the withheld tax amount. Next, enter the period basis to determine what basis to use to calculate the amount basis. You can choose from Invoice or Period. Invoice means to calculate the amount based on a single invoice. Period means to calculate the amount based on a withholding tax period. The withholding tax period is derived from the special calendar that you assigned to the withholding tax. The special calendar must be in the Withholding Tax type. The currency will be displayed. Enter the withholding limit for any withholding tax period. You can check the *Create Tax Group* box to automatically create a withholding tax group.

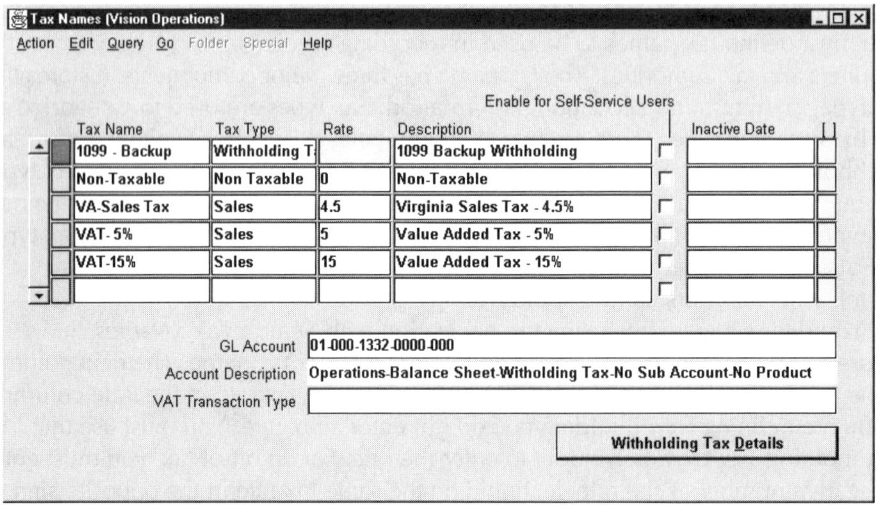

FIGURE 16-36. *Tax Names form*

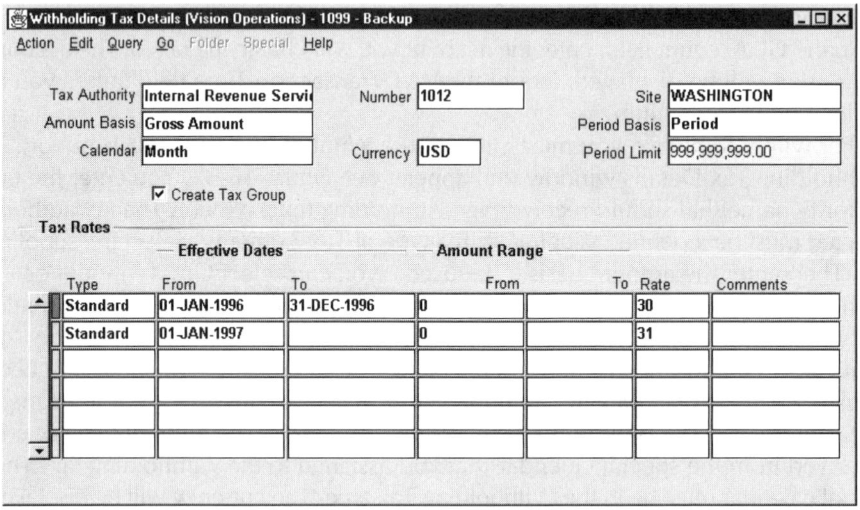

FIGURE 16-37. *Withholding Tax Details form*

In the Tax Rates region, enter the applicable tax rates. Rate can be for a standard rate type or a penalty rate type. If you wish, for each tax rate, you can enter an effective date range. Then enter the amount range for which the tax rate applies. This is compared based on the amount basis and period basis you choose. Enter the applicable tax rate and an optional comment. Save your work.

Review Questions

1. How many tax types are there?

2. What is unique about the rate you enter for offset tax?

3. Where do you enter tax rates for withholding tax, and how many types of tax rate are there?

4. What are the amount basis and the period basis used for in defining withholding tax details?

Defining Withholding Tax Groups

You can define withholding tax groups to calculate withholding taxes for invoices. Each withholding group can have several different tax names associated with it. A tax calculation will be performed for each tax name in the group. Also, a tax name can be used in more than one withholding tax group.

You can define a withholding tax group by using the navigation path *Setup : Tax : Withholding : Groups.* The Withholding Tax Groups window will appear. See Figure 16-38. Enter a unique name for your withholding group. Next, enter the description. Both the name and the description will be listed in the List of Values when you are prompted to select a withholding group. You can inactivate a withholding group by entering an inactive date in the Inactive Date field.

Next, you must select the tax names included in the withholding tax group. You must assign a ranking number, with number 1 being the highest for each tax name. This creates a hierarchy for tax names. The ranking is very important since that rank determines the order in which the withholding amount is calculated. Since tax rate is a percentage, the basis is very important, and the order of ranking affects the basis. The number-1-ranked tax names will be calculated first using the gross amount or withheld amount, depending on your tax name. There will be zero withheld amounts for number-1-ranked tax names. If you have more than one number-1-ranked tax name that uses the gross amount, the number-1-ranked tax names will all use the entire gross amount as basis. For example, if there are two rank-1 taxes, one of 10 percent and one of 20 percent, they will take a total of 30 percent of the gross. After that, for example, if you have a number-2-ranked tax name with gross amount as the basis, the number-2-ranked tax is calculated using

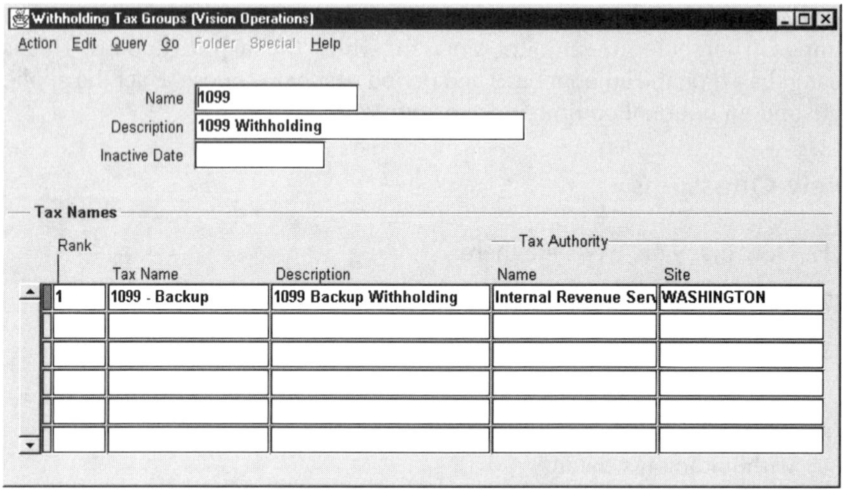

FIGURE 16-38. *Withholding Tax Groups form*

the original gross amount minus the amount withheld for number-1-ranked taxes as the basis. In the above example, a number-2-ranked tax of 20 percent would account for 14 percent of gross—20 percent of 70 percent. Enter the withholding tax name(s) you want to be associated with each withholding tax group. The description, tax authority name, and site will be automatically displayed. Save your work.

Review Questions

1. What are withholding tax groups used for?

2. Why is the rank of the withholding tax names important?

3. How will tax names with the same rank act?

Defining VAT Tax Names

Some suppliers are registered and required to pay valued-added tax (VAT). These suppliers are usually from what we refer to as the EU member states (European Union). Oracle Payables will generate a report to show charges paid by suppliers from an EU member state.

To track VAT, you must create VAT tax names to assign to EU member suppliers. To define VAT tax names, you first must define the VAT tax types. Follow the navigation path *Setup : Quickcodes : Payables* to define VAT types. Select VAT tax type with lookup type Tax Type. Then, you can define VAT tax names in the same Tax Names form using navigation path *Setup : Tax : Names.* The Tax Names form will display. Enter the tax name, tax type, tax rate, and a brief description of the tax. In the lower portion of the form, enter the GL account to direct the charges to the appropriate General Ledger account. The VAT Transaction field is not used unless you are implementing in Belgium. Save your VAT tax names.

Review Questions

1. What do you need to do before defining VAT tax names?

2. For what country is the VAT Transaction field used?

Defining EU Suppliers

You must identify European Union (EU) suppliers to track VAT charges. Enter supplier information as you would with any other new supplier. The country that the supplier is tied to should be designated as an EU member state. You mark the country as a VAT member state by using the Countries and Territories form. You enter the VAT member state code and Oracle Payables will include the suppliers in the particular VAT member state in the Intra-EU VAT Audit Trail report. Also, you must enter the VAT registration number in the Tax Registration Number field of the supplier form. Next, select the Invoice Tax alternative region of the Supplier or Supplier Site form. Enter the VAT tax name in the Invoice Tax Name field and the offset tax name in the Offset Tax Name field. Offset tax is used to offset the VAT tax if you and the EU suppliers are both EU member states. If your company is VAT registered and you receive an invoice from a VAT-registered supplier/site, you are required to pay VAT charges to the supplier/site. However, if your company is an EU member state and the EU supplier is in a different member state, you do not have to pay VAT charges— but you do have to report it. In this case, you use the offset tax to offset the VAT tax and you use the Intra-EU VAT Audit Trail report to report VAT charges from suppliers/sites in other EU member states. For Oracle Payables to know your member status, you must enter the country name in the Member State field and the VAT registration number in the Tax alternative region of your financial options.

Review Questions

1. How do you mark a country as an EU member state?

2. What is an offset tax?

3. What report can you use to report on VAT charges?

4. Where do you put in your own VAT registration number?

Recording VAT Charges

Oracle Payables will record VAT charges once you define the VAT tax name and associated VAT tax name to the EU supplier/site. The VAT tax name that you define contains the tax rate information required to record VAT charges. When you assign this VAT tax name to your supplier/supplier site and you create an invoice for this EU supplier/site, Oracle Payables will perform a tax calculation and create a VAT distribution for the entered invoices for this supplier/site. If the supplier and you are in two EU member states, the offset tax distribution will also be generated.

Review Question

1. How are VAT charges recorded?

Reviewing VAT Charges

You can review VAT charges by submitting standard report requests in Oracle Payables. Reports you can run to review VAT charges include:

■ Tax Declaration reports

■ Intra-EU VAT Audit Trail reports

Tax Declaration Report

You use the Tax Declaration report to meet French tax reporting requirements. For this report to work, you must define the following tax types: DEB/M, DEB/M-1, CRE/M, and CRE/M-1. Select Tax Declaration from the List of Values as the request name through the Standard Report Submission (SRS) form. You are able to select a date of declaration for your tax and a balancing segment. You can review your report and see detailed tax, invoice, and supplier information.

Intra-EU VAT Audit Trail Report

This report can be used to view invoice and VAT charges information, including offset tax charges for range-of-invoice dates. Intra-EU invoices are invoices from suppliers/sites that are in an EU member state other than the one your company is in. You do not have to pay VAT charges, but you are required to report the charges. If foreign currency is involved, the invoice and tax amount is translated from the invoice currency to the functional currency in the report. You can select to sort by country first and have a subtotal by country. You can enter an invoice date range and decide whether to summarize the audit. Summarization groups the report by supplier, supplier site, and VAT number.

Review Questions

1. Which two reports can you use for reviewing VAT tax charges?

2. For which country do you need the Tax Declaration report?

3. Why do you need the Intra-EU VAT Audit Trail report?

Loading Electronic Bank Statements

The last section of this chapter talks about loading electronic bank statements. You can manually enter bank statements or you can update loaded bank statements. In this section, you will:

■ Manually enter bank statements

■ Update bank statements

Manually Entering Bank Statements

You can load bank statements in Cash Management by using the Cash Management Bank Statement Open Interface or enter the information manually.

Each bank statement in Oracle Cash Management contains a header, which identifies the statement number, statement date, and bank account. Under the header are multiple statement lines. The statement line contains entries for one or more payments, receipts, journal entries, and miscellaneous transactions. Each line contains a line number, transaction type, amount, and date cleared. To enter a bank statement manually, you must enter the header and the transaction lines. The transaction lines can be reconciled as you enter them or you can wait until all lines are entered.

This is just a summarization since it has already been covered in detail in Chapter 14. You follow the navigation path *Bank Reconciliation : Bank Statements.* The Find Bank Statements form will display. Close the Reconcile Bank Statement form. Click on the **New** button to display a blank Reconcile Bank Statement form for manual entry.

Enter the bank statement header information. You must enter account number, statement number, statement date, and currency, account name, bank name, and bank branch. Next, enter the statement date and document number if you are using manual numbering. Enter the statement number or tab and accept the system date as the default. Enter the GL date. You can enter the control total for the totals and number of lines, if you would like—these are optional fields to avoid data entry error. Save your work.

Next, enter the statement lines by clicking on the **Lines** button. Begin by entering the line number, then select the transaction type from the drop-down list. If you plan to reconcile this statement automatically, enter the bank transaction code, transaction number-invoice number, and agent bank number. Select the Amount alternative region. Enter the transaction amount. Next, select the Reference alternative region and enter the supplier, invoice number, and bank. Enter the date and a short description of the line. Enter exchange information if the currency is not the functional currency. Continue entering additional lines. Save your work. You have now completed entering a bank statement manually.

Review Questions

1. Into which online form do you manually enter a bank statement?

2. What is the purpose of the control total?

Updating Bank Statements

You can update a bank statement as long as the statement is not marked as complete. You mark a bank statement as complete by checking the *Complete* checkbox at the bank statement header level. To update a bank statement, begin from the Cash Management and use the same navigation path: *Bank Reconciliation : Bank Statements*. The Find Bank Statements form will appear. Locate your bank statement that you want to update and click on the **Find** button.

With your cursor on the bank statement, click on the **Review** button. Update the bank statement information—both header and line information can be changed. You may add more transaction lines or delete a line entered in error. Save your work.

Review Questions

1. How do you update bank statements?

2. When can you not update bank statements anymore?

For the Chapter Summary, Two-Minute Drill, and Chapter Questions and Answers, open the summary.htm file contained in the Summary_files directory on the book's CD-ROM.

UNIT
IV

Preparing for OCP Exam 4: Order Fulfillment

CHAPTER
17

Customers and Orders

his is the first chapter covering Exam 4 for the Oracle Financials certification. The exam covers order fulfillment and involves three application modules: Oracle Order Entry, Oracle Receivables, and Oracle Cash Management. The beginning of this chapter explains the following:

- Introduction to the order fulfillment process

- Creating customers

- Implementing and setting up customers

- Processing orders

- Fulfilling and shipping orders

- Invoicing customers and closing orders

The chapter is divided into two major parts. The first part focuses on customers. It provides an introduction to the order fulfillment process; describes the overall order fulfillment process flow in Oracle Applications, and discusses issues you will need to consider related to this area. Topics covered include the creation of customers, as well as how to group customers with similar characteristics into customer classes. You will also learn about the information that makes up a customer definition.

The second part of the chapter explains orders. Entering and processing orders in Oracle Order Entry is covered first, and then you will learn how to fulfill customer orders, including picking, packing, and shipping the orders. As a last step, you will learn to prepare customer orders for invoicing, as well as how to invoice customers and close out orders.

Introduction to the Order Fulfillment Process

The first section of this chapter is an introduction to the order fulfillment process. It describes the overall order fulfillment process flow—from entering, picking, and shipping an order to reducing inventory and invoicing the customer. It also describes issues to be considered during the implementation of the Oracle order fulfillment process, as required by the process flow. To follow the chapter and perform your exercises, log on to Oracle Applications using the *Order Entry, Vision Operations (USA)* responsibility.

Overall Order Fulfillment Process Flow

The Oracle Order Entry module is powerful enough to handle very complex order fulfillment processes. For starters, you must set up the process flows that are specific to your company by using Oracle Order Entry, which provides a concept called the order cycle. Each order cycle has a sequence of steps, and each step is an action. Table 17-1 shows the steps and actions that are predefined in Oracle Order Entry. Different orders require different handling. Some order types require shipping, while others don't. Some must be manufactured, and others not. Some need to be invoiced, and others do not. You define separate cycles to allow for the differences in your order entry and fulfillment process.

Action can be a predefined standard action from Oracle Order Entry, a user-defined order level, or order line-level action. Each action must result in one of the predefined results. To create the process flows you want, you must define the prerequisite result for each action. This will determine how each action should flow to subsequent actions in order to complete the desired process flow. By using the same sequence number for multiple prerequisite results, you are implying an AND condition, meaning that all prerequisites for the same sequence number must be accomplished in order to pass the prerequisite requirements.

Actions

In Oracle Order Entry, you can choose from a list of predefined standard actions that are listed in Table 17-1 along with a description and all of the corresponding results. Each action can be a line-level or order-level action. Order-level action applies to the entire customer order, while line-level action applies to each order line of a customer order. You cannot have a line-level action be a prerequisite of an order-level action.

Action	Description	Possible Results
Enter	The customer order has been entered into Oracle Order Entry	Entered, Partial, Booked
Demand Interface	Creates a demand for the items in the customer order	Interfaced, Partial, Not Applicable
Manufacturing Release	Creates configuration in Oracle Bills of Materials and work order in Oracle Work in Process for ATO customer orders	Release, Configuration Created, Work Order Opened, Work Order Partially Completed, Work Order Completed, Not Applicable

TABLE 17-1. *Predefined Standard Actions*

Action	Description	Possible Results
Purchase Release	Creates purchase requisition lines in the Purchasing open interface for drop shipment customer orders	Interfaced, Partial, Confirmed, Not Applicable
Pick Release	Creates picking lines from customer orders for picking	Released, Partial, Not Applicable
Backorder Release	Creates picking lines from backordered customer orders	Released
Ship Confirm	Confirms shipments for customer orders	Confirmed, Partial, Backordered-Complete, Backordered-Partial, Not Applicable
Inventory Interface	Creates material transactions in Inventory open interface to update items' on-hand quantities and generate cost of hoods sold account	Interfaced, Partial, Interface Error, Not Applicable
RMA Interface	Creates material transactions in Inventory open interface to update items' on-hand quantities based on RMA orders	Interfaced, Partially Accepted, Completely Accepted, Not Applicable
Receivables Interface	Creates invoice lines in Receivables open interface to generate invoices for billing	Interfaced to Receivables, Partial, Not Applicable
Complete Line	Closes the customer order line, indicating process completion of the order line	Closed
Complete Order	Closes the customer order, indicating process completion of the order	Closed
Cancel Line	Cancels the customer order line	Cancelled, Partial
Cancel Order	Cancels the customer order	Cancelled

TABLE 17-1. *Predefined Standard Actions* (continued)

By adding custom actions through Oracle Order Entry, you can customize the process flow. Follow the navigation path *Setup : Orders : Cycles : Actions,* and the Cycle Actions form will appear. See Figure 17-1. Enter the action name and a description, and decide what level the action should be tied to. Remember that you cannot have a line-level action as a prerequisite to an order-level action. To make the action an approval action, check the *Approval Action* checkbox. This action can be carried out through a standard Oracle Order Entry form. Nonapproval custom actions must be supported by custom forms or custom programs.

Results

You can also create custom results by following the navigation path *Setup : Orders : Cycles : Results.* The Cycle Results form will appear. Enter the result name and the description. You can create custom results for the Enter action for unbooked orders.

ActionResults

ActionResults identify possible results associated with a specific action. For example, if the action is Order Approval, then the ActionResults can be Pass or Fail. You can link custom results to custom actions. To do this, follow the navigation path *Setup : Orders : Cycles : ActionResults.* The Find Cycle Action window will appear. Select the action that you want to link results to, then click on the **Find** button to make the Cycle Action Results window appear. Add the results you want in the Results region; for the Approval action, indicate which result is a passing result by checking the *Passing Result* checkbox.

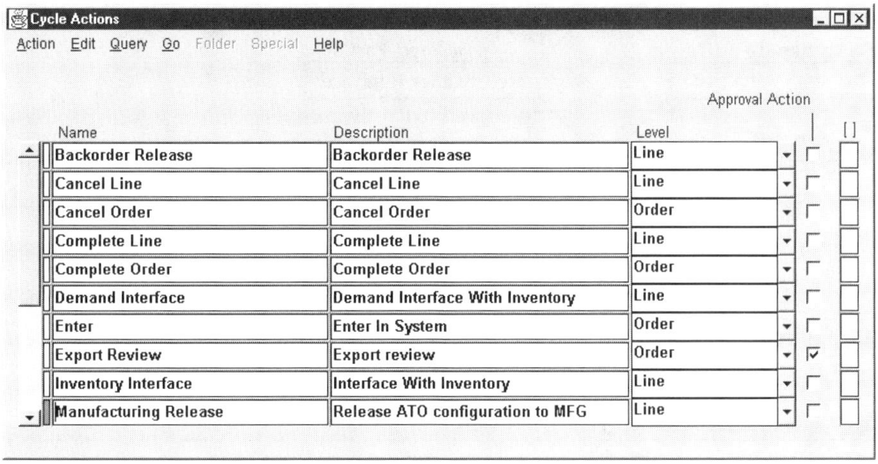
Cycle Actions

Action Edit Query Go Folder Special Help

Name	Description	Level	Approval Action
Backorder Release	Backorder Release	Line	
Cancel Line	Cancel Line	Line	
Cancel Order	Cancel Order	Order	
Complete Line	Complete Line	Line	
Complete Order	Complete Order	Order	
Demand Interface	Demand Interface With Inventory	Line	
Enter	Enter In System	Order	
Export Review	Export review	Order	☑
Inventory Interface	Interface With Inventory	Line	
Manufacturing Release	Release ATO configuration to MFG	Line	

FIGURE 17-1. *Cycle Actions form*

Order Cycle

Once you have set up all of the actions, results, and ActionResults—or, if you used the predefined actions and results—you are ready to implement your order processing flows with an order cycle. Let's consider the process flow in Figure 17-2, which calls the Standard order cycle. To see the Standard order cycle online, follow the navigation path *Setup : Orders : Cycles : Cycles.* The Order Cycles window will appear and query the Standard order cycle. See Figure 17-3.

The first step in any order cycle involves entering the order, with Complete Line and Complete Order as the last two steps. Once the order is booked, it will be available for pick release. If you pick released an entire order line, or part of an order line, the proposed pick quantity of the order line will be shown on a pick slip. Then the items are ready for pick and ship. Ship confirm the order line, and if you ship the entire proposed pick quantity, you will get the result of Confirmed or Partial for the order line, depending on whether the result was Released or Partial from the Pick Release action.

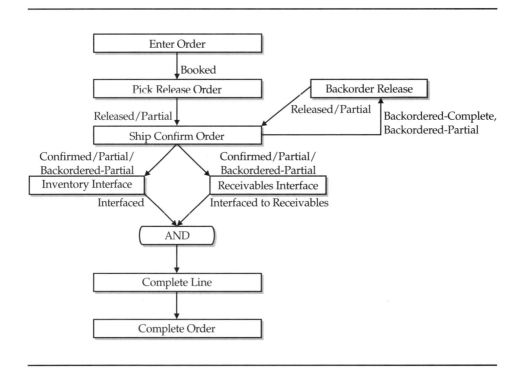

FIGURE 17-2. *Standard Order Cycle*

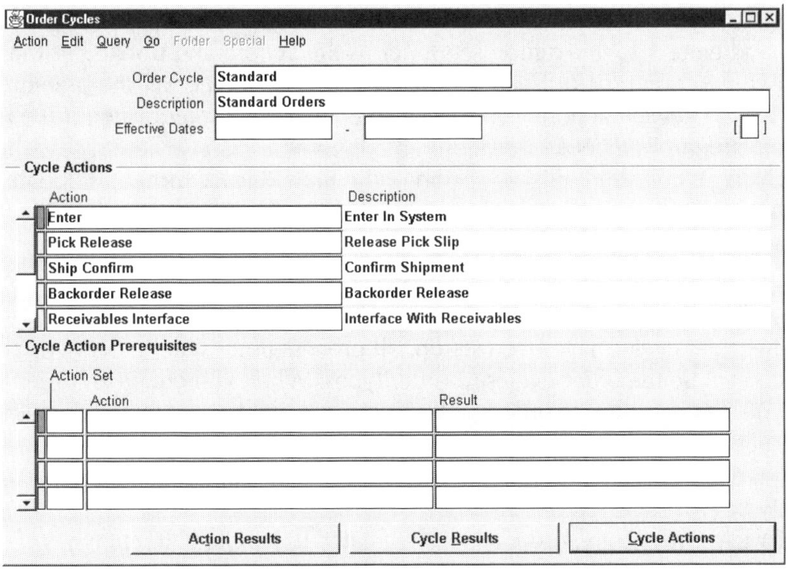

FIGURE 17-3. *Order Cycles form*

If you ship only part of the proposed pick quantity, your result will be Backordered-Partial for the order line since you have shipped some and backordered some. If you shipped none of the proposed pick quantity, you will get the result of Backordered-Complete, with the backorder as the entire proposed quantity. The backordered quantity can be released again through the Backorder Release action.

If something has shipped, the status is Confirmed, Partial, or Backordered-Partial. You then proceed with sending the shipped portion of the order line to Oracle Inventory to reduce on-hand quantity, then onto Oracle Receivables for billing. With the standard order cycle, the order line can be closed if the entire quantity of the order line is interfaced to Oracle Inventory and Oracle Receivables. If only part of the order line is interfaced, the order line will remain closed. Partially interfaced lines are marked with a status of Partial for both the Inventory Interface and the Receivables Interface. The prerequisite of action Complete Order is a booked order, but this is not entirely true because Oracle Order Entry contains built-in logic that will only complete an order if all of the lines have been completed. This setup is necessary because you cannot have an order-level action of Complete Order with a line-level prerequisite. If you have manufacturing modules installed, you should add an action called Demand Interface between Enter and Pick Release to place demands to the manufacturing modules.

For the purposes of this exercise, add a new cycle action to the standard cycle, then create a new record in the Cycle Actions region. Select Export Review as the action, and enter **1** for the action set, **Enter** as the action, and **Booked** as the result in the Cycle Action Prerequisites region to make a booked order the prerequisite for the Export Review action. You must also change the prerequisite for the Pick Release action from a booked order to an approved Export Review. To do this, go to the Cycle Action Prerequisites region of the Pick Release form and update Enter in the Action field to Export Review and update Booked in the Result field to Pass. When you've completed these steps, save your work.

Order Type

Once the order cycles have been set up, all process flows will be defined. Your next step is to tie the order cycles to order types. When you create an order with an order type, the appropriate order cycle is used. If you change your order cycle later on, the new order cycle will apply immediately to all orders for processing. It will not change a history that has already occurred, but it will affect orders that are currently being processed.

In Oracle Order Entry, order types are created to handle different types of orders. Follow the navigation path *Setup : Orders : Types.* The Order Types form will appear. See Figure 17-4. Enter a unique order type name, an optional description and an effective date range. Select the associated order cycle and an optional order category, then enter defaults and controls in three alternative regions: Main, Shipping, and Finance.

In the Main alternative region, an entered order number source determines how to sequence orders under this order type. From there, you can also select the agreement type. If you enter an agreement type, you can only enter agreements with this agreement type for this order type. If you wish, you can then select a standard value rule set, which governs how defaults are derived. You can determine whether orders in this order type need an agreement or a purchase order. Next, select a price list and determine whether you want to enforce the list prices on the price list with no discounts allowed. You can override it with the *OE: Discounting Privilege* profile option. You can also select the credit check rules to be used for ordering and shipping order type.

In the Shipping alternative region, you can enter the shipping defaults for the order type. These include the warehouse, freight carrier, shipment priority, freight terms, FOB, and demand class. In the Finance alternative region, you can also enter the finance defaults for the order type. These include the invoicing rule, accounting rule, credit method for invoices with accounting rules, credit method for split term invoices, the receivables transaction/invoice type, the cost of goods sold account, and the currency. If the currency is not the functional currency, you can also enter the default currency conversion type.

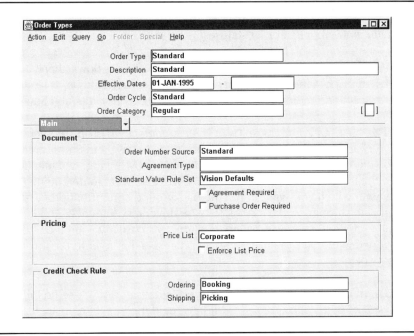

FIGURE 17-4. *Order Types form*

Considerations

You can set up any number of order types and any number of order cycles to fit your business needs. Each order type determines a number of important elements that will affect order processing, including what sales order number will be generated, whether a purchase order is required, what information defaults automatically, what credit checking rules are used, what accounting information may be generated, and what invoicing and accounting rules are defaulted. Each order cycle determines the steps that make up your order-processing flow. The following elements should be considered during the implementation of the Oracle Order Fulfillment required by your process flow:

- Approval

- Shipping

- Billing

- Material transaction

- Credit checking
- Different unbooked order statuses

APPROVAL   If you need approval actions in your process flows, then you must consider when that action should happen, what the results should be, at which level approval action should be, and who should approve the order and how.

SHIPPING   If your company ships to its customers, then drop shipments or customer pickups may not require the actions Pick Release and Ship Confirm. However, you may want to reduce on-hand quantity by linking the Enter action directly to the Inventory Interface action. You will also want to determine the frequency with which you want to run the background concurrent processes associated with shipping, such as Pick Release, Inventory Interface, and Update Shipping Information. Inventory is very dynamic; you usually want them to run at least every few minutes to ensure that all processes that refer to the inventory get accurate data.

BILLING   If you are shipping a replacement order, in most cases no billing action must take place; the customer will have paid the first time. In such an instance, the Receivables Interface action is not required because the customer already received an invoice. Otherwise, the Receivables Interface action should be set up to run in the background at regular intervals to communicate with Oracle Receivables.

MATERIAL TRANSACTION   If you require material transaction and must handle a refund, and if you do not need the items back into inventory, it is not necessary to interface with Oracle Inventory. In this case, leave the Inventory Interface action out of your order cycle.

CREDIT CHECKING   Use order type to determine when to do your credit check. You can either perform credit checking when the order is booked or when it is picked. With performing credit checks, you can do the checking on both actions, and you can perform a different kind of credit checking for each. Credit checking is not required in all order cycles. Some installations use the credit hold and hold/release mechanisms in lieu of defining a credit check step in the cycle.

DIFFERENT UNBOOKED ORDER STATUSES   Determine if you need custom results for the Enter action to identify different unbooked order statuses. Only the Demand Interface and Manufacturing Release actions can process unbooked orders with custom order statuses.

Review Questions

1. What is an order cycle?

2. What are actions, results, and ActionResults?

3. When may you not need the billing step in an order processing?

4. Which two actions make up the shipping step?

Creating Customers

In this section, you will learn to create profiles for CUSTOMER, which is the master file in Oracle Fulfillment. You will learn to:

■ Use customer profile classes

■ Enter specific information about customers

First, you will identify classes of customers with similar characteristics and create customer profile classes. Next, create customers by entering specific information for each customer.

Using Customer Profile Classes

Use customer profile classes to group customers with similar characteristics, such as credit limits, payment terms, and invoicing rules. Oracle Receivables comes with a seeded customer profile class called DEFAULT. To define a new customer profile class, follow the navigation path *Setup : Customers : Profile Classes* and the Customer Profile Classes form will appear. See Figure 17-5.

First, enter a unique customer profile class name and an optional description. You can uncheck the *Active* checkbox to inactivate the customer profile class. There are two alternative regions for a customer profile class. They are:

■ Profile Class

■ Profile Class Amounts

Profile Class

You must enter a default collector in the Credit region, where you can also enter the tolerance percentage for the customer profile class. The tolerance governs what percentage over the set credit limit that a customer with this customer profile class can exceed before the collection process will start. Check the *Credit Check*

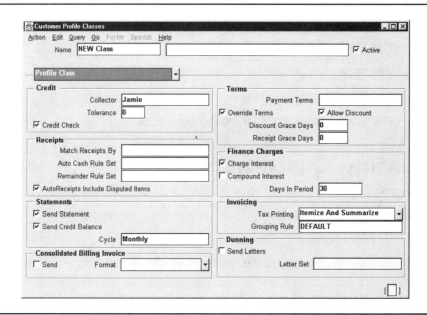

FIGURE 17-5. *Customer Profile Classes form*

checkbox if you want to perform a credit check on customers with this customer profile class. In the Terms region, enter the default payment terms. Check the *Override Terms* checkbox to allow the customers assigned this profile class to override the payment terms. Check the *Allow Discount* checkbox to allow discounts for this customer profile class. If you allow discounts, enter the discount grace days to indicate the number of days after the discount term date that customers with this profile class can still receive the discounts. You can also enter the receipt grace days, to indicate the number of days after the payment is due that finance charges will incur. In the Receipts region, you can select to match receipts by consolidated billing number, transaction number, PO, or sales order for this customer profile class. You can also enter the AutoCash rule set and remaining amount rule to specify how receipts should be applied during QuickCash, a feature that allows you to mass apply a receipt to multiple transactions. You can also indicate if you want AutoReceipts to include disputed items.

Decide whether you should charge customers with this profile class finance charges by checking or not checking the *Charge Interest* checkbox in the Finance Charges region. If you decide to charge finance charges, and if you want to charge finance charges on outstanding invoice amounts plus outstanding finance charges, check the *Compound Interest* checkbox. Enter the days in period—a field that is mandatory if you choose to charge interest—that you will use to calculate finance charges. In the Statements region, check the *Send Statement* checkbox to send statements to customers within this customer class. If you want to send statements even if customers have a credit balance, check the *Send Credit Balance* checkbox. If you decide to send statements, you must enter the statement cycle for this customer profile class. In the Invoicing region, select what format you want to print tax in. Valid choices include European Tax Format, Itemize By Line, Itemize and Summarize, Summarize By Tax Code, Summarize By Tax Name, and Total Tax Only. A blank Tax Printing field means Total Tax Only. Select the grouping rule you will use for this customer profile class. This determines how AutoInvoicing groups invoice lines into invoices. If you want to send a single consolidated billing invoice, click on the **Send** box and select Summary or Detail as the format in the Consolidated Billing Invoice region. To send customers of this profile class dunning letters, check the *Send Letters* checkbox in the Dunning region. In order to send dunning letters, you must select the dunning letter set in the Letter Set field.

Profile Class Amounts

Next, select the Profile Class Amounts alternative region. See Figure 17-6. You first enter the amounts assigned to this customer profile class, then enter a set of amounts and rates for each currency entered on the left. The rates and amounts that you can set include finance charges, interest rate, maximum interest per invoice, minimum customer balance for finance charges, minimum invoice balance for finance charges, minimum receipt amount, minimum statement amount, minimum dunning amount, minimum dunning invoice amount, credit limit, and order credit limit. You can have as many currencies as you wish, and they should include every currency used by customers within this customer profile class.

For the purposes of this exercise, create a profile class called **NEW Class** and assign **Jamie** as the collector. Check the *Send Statement* and *Send Credit Balance* checkboxes, and select Monthly as the statement cycle. Check the *Charge Interest* checkbox and enter **30 Days** for the period. Do not send dunning letters, and enter USD as the currency for the profile class amount. Also, enter a finance charge interest rate of **8** percent, and a credit limit of **100,000**, then save your work.

Review Questions

1. What is a profile class?

2. What is a required field in defining a profile class?

3. What is the difference between checking and unchecking the *Compound Interest* checkbox if you decide to charge interest?

4. How many currencies can you have for your profile class amounts?

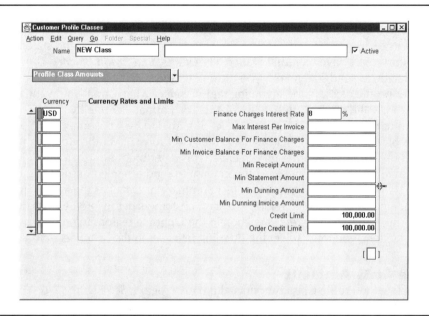

FIGURE 17-6. *Customer Profile Class (Profile Class Amounts) form*

Entering Information About Customers

You can assign customer profile class information that will be copied over to the customer. The customer profile class created in the Customer Profile Class window is considered the master. Once you have created a custom profile, you can then update or enter specific information about the customers. This action in any customer forms will only affect the individual profile of the customer, and will not change the master. If you do not assign your own customer profile, the DEFAULT profile class will be used. Each customer maintains their own profile information with any specific overridden or entered information.

If you change the master customer profile class information and attempt to save your changes, you will be asked to choose from one of the following three options: you can choose to not update existing profiles tied to existing customers, to update all profiles of existing customers, or to update only uncustomized profiles of existing customers. See Figure 17-7. Your selection affects whether a customer's individual profile will be changed according to the changes made at the master customer profile.

To enter new customers, follow the navigation path *Customers : Standard*. Enter **NEW Customer** as the customer name, and enter a customer number of your choosing. Then, enter your profile class in the Profile Class field in the Classification region. By

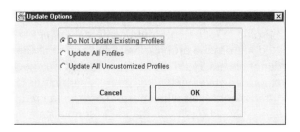

FIGURE 17-7.   *Update Options form*

selecting a profile class in the Classification Region, defaults will automatically fill in the required field for these profile regions. Profile regions are Profile : Transaction, Profile : Document Printing, and Profile : Amounts. It is sometimes necessary to override data defaulted from the profile class. Examining these regions ensures that you have not selected an incorrect profile class. In the customer profile class, you can also enter previously unentered, specific information.

Transactions

First, choose the Profile : Transaction alternative region. The profile class selected in the Classification region will be displayed just under the alternative region bar.

The collector is defaulted into the Credit area, but it is changeable. Select an account status, a credit rating, and a risk code for the customer—all are lookup codes. The lookup types are ACCOUNT_STATUS, CREDIT_RATING, and RISK_CODE, respectively. Collectable is the percentage of this customer's balance that you expect to collect. Tolerance governs what percentage over the set credit limit that a customer with this customer profile class can exceed before the collection process kicks in. You can check the *Credit Check* checkbox to perform a credit check for this customer. You can also check the *Credit Hold* checkbox if you want to prevent new orders from being booked in Oracle Order Entry. The *Account Status, Credit Rating, Risk Code*, and *Credit Hold* checkboxes do not appear in the Customer Profile Class window—they are only at the individual customer level.

In the Terms region, you may use a List of Values to change the defaulting payment term. You can allow a user to select different terms at the time of order creation or invoice by selecting the *Override Terms* checkbox. *Allow Discount* should be checked if you want the customers to be able to have discounts. The payment terms will determine whether an invoice is eligible for discount. You can also override the grace days for the discount or receipt periods.

You will use this primarily in the Receipts region for automatic receipts. Enter the clearing days, then select the appropriate values using the Lists of Values for the

Match Receipts By, AutoCash Rule Set, and Remainder Rule Set fields. Determine whether you want AutoReceipts to include disputed items.

Next, select the Profile : Document Printing alternative region. See Figure 17-8. All fields are defaulted in from the profile class selected in the Classification region, but can be overridden if necessary. In the Statements region, check the *Send Statement* checkbox to send statements to customers within this customer class. If you want to send statements even when customers have a credit balance, check the *Send Credit Balance* checkbox. If you decide to send a statement, you must enter the statement cycle for this customer profile class. In the Finance Charges region, decide whether you should charge customers with this profile class finance charges by checking the *Charge Interest* checkbox. If you decide to charge finance charges, and if you want to charge finance charges on outstanding invoice amounts plus outstanding finance charges, check the *Compound Interest* checkbox. Enter the days in period that you will use to calculate finance charges. This field is mandatory if you choose to charge interest. In the Dunning region, check the *Send Letters* checkbox to send customers of this profile class dunning letters. If you choose to send dunning letters, select the dunning letter set in the Letter Set field. In the Invoicing region, select what format you want to print tax in. Valid choices include European Tax Format, Itemize By Line, Itemize and Summarize, Summarize By Tax Code, Summarize By Tax Name, and Total Tax Only (a blank Tax Printing field means Total Tax Only). Select the grouping rule, which determines how AutoInvoicing groups invoice lines into invoices, to use for this customer profile class. If you want to send a single consolidated billing invoice, check the *Send* checkbox and select Summary or Detail as the format in the Consolidated Billing Invoice region.

Next, select the Profile : Amounts alternative region. Amounts and rates can be set up for more than one currency, and you can also override the default values or add more currencies. Enter a set of amounts and rates for each currency you entered on the left, including finance charges interest rate, maximum interest per invoice, minimum customer balance for finance charges, minimum invoice balance for finance charges, minimum receipt amount, minimum statement amount, minimum dunning amount, minimum dunning invoice amount, credit limit, and order credit limit. When these tasks are completed, save your changes.

Review Questions

1. If you do not want to change any individual customer profile after making changes to the master profile, what option should you select as you save the master changes?

2. When is the information from the master customer profile copied to each individual customer profile?

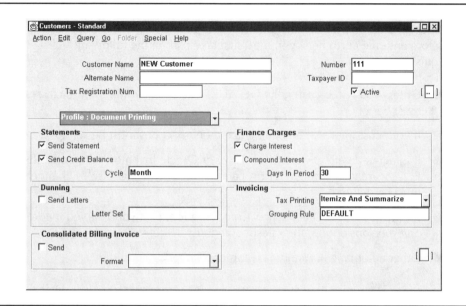

FIGURE 17-8. *Customer – Standard (Profile : Document Printing) form*

3. Can you have your changes automatically applied to the master profile as you enter or update specific information about an individual customer?

4. What fields are present in a customer profile but do not exist in the master customer profile?

Implementing and Setting Up Customers

In the last section, you learned to set up customer profile classes and assign customer profiles in order to start entering customer information. Here, you will learn how to set up the remaining customer information, and you will set up customers as required for the order-fulfillment applications

Setting Up Customers as Required for the Order-Fulfillment Applications

Customer records can enter the Oracle Receivables module from a variety of sources—not limited to an open interface—from Oracle Order Entry, from the Oracle Sales and Marketing module, or by entering directly from the Oracle

Receivables customer forms. You will find many Descriptive flexfields in the customer records, as well as many alternative regions.

Before entering customers, you must first take care of the following prerequisites:

- Unless you will be using the DEFAULT customer profile, profile classes must be set up.

- If your customer will be paying tax, then tax codes must be set up.

- If integrated with Oracle Order Entry or Oracle Inventory, then price lists, FOB, warehouse, freight terms, carriers, order types, and sales channels must be defined.

- If integrated with Oracle Sales Compensation, or if you enabled the *Require Salespersons* option, the salespeople must be defined.

- Either automatic or manual customer numbering should be set.

To enter customers, follow the navigation path *Customers: Standard,* which brings you to the same form you used at the end of the last section. Before entering a customer, verify that the customer is not already in the database. Enter a query by placing the cursor in the Customer Name field, and entering enough of the customer's name to bring up potential matches. Your query must be run exactly, using uppercase and lowercase letters, because the search is case-sensitive. You may also use the Find form to locate an existing customer based on specified criteria. Once you have verified that the new customer is not in the database, end your query and proceed.

See Figure 17-9 for the Customers – Standard form, where the customer name is required and should reflect your customer's legal name. The data in this field will print on statements, invoices, dunning letters, and other correspondences generated by Oracle Receivables. A standard naming convention should be defined, because it will affect your querying methods. For example, whether you should use all caps or sentence case. The customer name may be duplicated, and should be only if there really are two separate companies. Otherwise, merge them because you do not want two records of the same customer. Enter a customer number, unless your system assigns numbers automatically. Customer numbers must be unique, and if converted from a legacy system, a numbering convention may already be in place. Also, a numbering convention will allow more flexibility when running reports and performing queries.

If applicable, then enter an alternate name, which may also be a phonetic spelling of a name containing characters outside of your system's alphabet. You can perform queries in this field. It is optional, and you can only enter an alternate name if the *AR: Customers – Enter Alternate Fields* profile option is set to Yes. Enter a taxpayer ID number for your customer; it is an optional field that refers to the

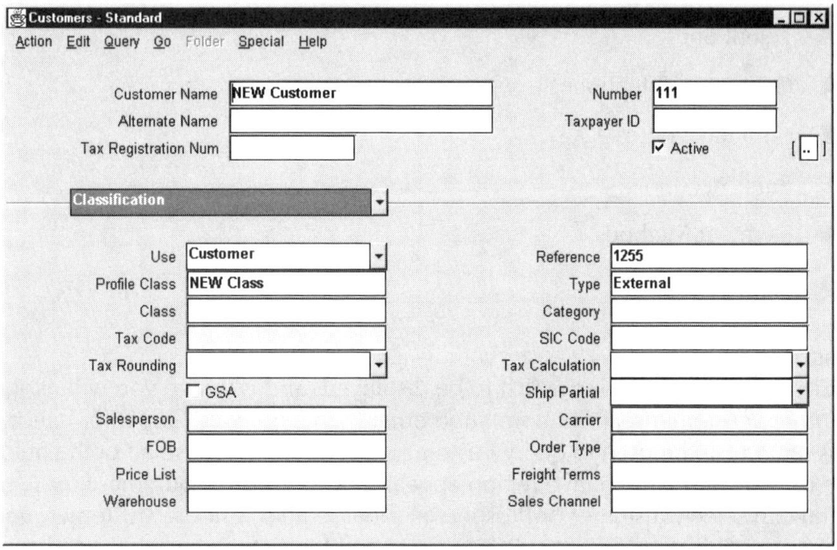

FIGURE 17-9. *Customers – Standard (Classification) form*

nine-digit federal tax-paying number associated with the company. Then, enter a tax registration number, which is the tax exempt status for customers who are reselling the goods they purchase, and are therefore not required to pay sales tax on them. The *Active* checkbox defaults to the checked position, but should be unchecked if the customer is not yet active.

There is a header-level Descriptive flexfield for each customer. This information is optional and must be set up in advance. If the DFF is active, enter the information at this time. If you save the record at this point, a reference number will be automatically assigned. The Reference field is contained in the Classification region. You may, however, wish to assign your own reference numbers—especially in the instance where legacy systems may require a tie-back to an old number, you should use the Reference field for the legacy customer number. Click in the Reference field, assign the number, then save the record. You can also allow the system to assign the number by saving the record before proceeding to the first region, and keep in mind that the reference must be unique. Next, you can enter information in each of the following alternative regions:

- Classification
- Marketing

- Addresses
- Telephones
- Contacts : Telephones
- Contacts : Roles
- Bank Accounts
- Payment Methods
- Relationship

Classification

The Classification region is the first to be displayed, and is where you will assign the primary customer record information other than addresses. Any information in this region can be used to query customers as a group because all of the fields in the Classification alternative region appear in the Customer Summary form.

You can select Customer or Prospect in the Use field. Choose Customer, unless you are using this record for the Oracle Sales and Marketing module as a prospect. Enter a unique reference number if applicable. The Reference field cannot be changed once the record is saved, and it must be unique. If you leave it blank, the customer ID will be used. Select a profile class, which will default in a variety of information under the Profile: regions, from the List of Values. Once you have selected a profile class and saved the record, you only assign a different profile class in the Profile: Transactions region. You can also override information at the detail level in the individual Profile: regions, as mentioned in the last section. Select either Internal or External as the type. Internal customers, for example, would be individual departments or salespeople. External includes anyone outside of the organization to whom the company sells its products.

Next enter the class, which is an optional field that is selected from the List of Values. Classes are lookup codes of type CUSTOMER_CLASS. Category is an optional field, which is also selected from a List of Values. Categories are lookup codes of type CUSTOMER_CATEGORY. Select a tax code, which defines the tax rate to be used for the customer, from the List of Values. If your tax method is Sales Tax, and if you want to calculate tax based on your customer addresses, then leave the tax code blank at the customer level. You must enter the tax code at the customer address level. Enter the SIC code (Standard Industry Code) for the customer (the field is free-form). If you enabled the *Allow Override* option, select a tax rounding method and tax calculation method for the VAT tax method. Valid rounding methods are Up, Down, or Nearest. Valid calculations are Header or Line. These determine whether the VAT charges are calculated at the line level or the header level. Check the *GSA* (General Services Administration) checkbox to indicate that the customer is a government agency.

The following fields are optional based on the integration of Receivables with other modules. You can set the ship partial default, and if the customer allows partial shipment of a customer order, select Yes as the default. The remaining fields are all selected from a List of Values and are optional as defaults for the customer, and may be overridden as necessary: Salesperson, Carrier, FOB, Order Type, Price List, Freight Terms, Warehouse, and Sales Channel. Save your work and proceed to the next region.

Marketing

Select the Marketing alternative region, which is optional unless your system is integrated with the Sales and Marketing module. Enter the customer's number of employees, then enter the year the customer was established. You may also enter the year the customer established its relationship with your company, if your company prefers this information.

For financial analysis, enter the last month of your customer's fiscal year. You can also enter a year in the analysis year to indicate that you have financials for the entered fiscal year. From there, you will know when you can expect the financials next year. Enter the revenue and projected revenue for the current year, as obtained from the financial reports for next year. Check any of the boxes to indicate whether the company is a sales partner, a competitor, or if it can be used as a reference. The customer's mission statement, or any other related information, may be entered in the last field. Save your work and go on to the next region.

Skip the Address region until all other regions are entered.

Telephones

Select the Telephones alternative region and enter the area code, telephone number, and any extension. See Figure 17-10. Select the type of telephones from a List of Values. The types are lookup codes of type COMMUNICATION_TYPE. Communication types can be fax, telex, telephone, and others. Select whether the number is the primary number, though a primary number is not required. The *Active* checkbox will default to checked, and should be unchecked if the telephone number is inactive. Enter as many telephone numbers—which are associated with the customer at the customer level—as necessary. A Descriptive flexfield is available in this form. Save your work and move on to the next region.

You may also associate telephones with a specific customer address in the Address region, which is covered a little later in this chapter.

Contacts : Telephones

Next, select the Contacts : Telephones alternative region and enter as many contacts for the customer as necessary. In this alternative region, enter the last name, then first name, and select a formal title such as Mr. or Dr. from the List of Values. Select

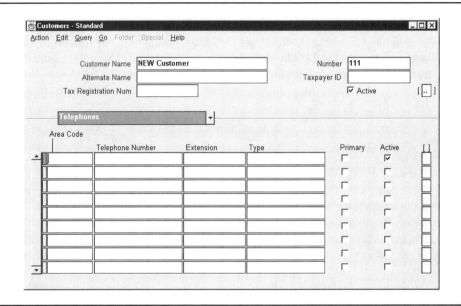

FIGURE 17-10. *Customers – Standard (Telephones) form*

a job, such as CEO, from the List of Values. Both title and job are lookup codes with lookup type CONTACT_TITLE and RESPONSIBILITY. You can also enter a mail stop, which will indicate that this person is to receive generated correspondence. A reference can be entered, or it will default in the contact automatically when the record is saved. The reference must be unique across all customers. You can also enter the email address for the contact. There is a Descriptive flexfield for this area.

Move to the Contact Telephones region and enter the contact's area code, telephone number, extension, and phone type. If the phone is primary, then check the *Primary* checkbox, and if the phone is no longer active, then uncheck the *Active* checkbox. You can enter as many telephone numbers as necessary for each contact. The telephone numbers you entered in the Contact Telephones region belong to the contact in the Contact Name region where you were working. Save your work, then move on to the next region.

Contacts: Roles

Next, select the Contacts : Roles alternative region, as shown in Figure 17-11. This part of the form enables you to assign roles to each contact. The roles are lookup codes with type SITE_USE_CODE. This region is optional.

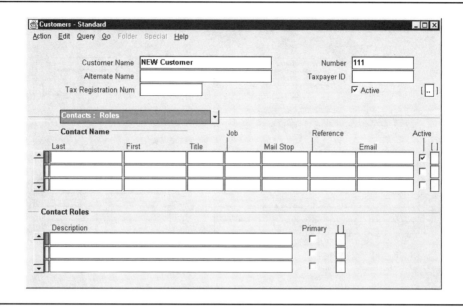

FIGURE 17-11. *Customers – Standard (Contacts : Roles) form*

Bank Accounts

Next, select the Bank Accounts alternative region. See Figure 17-12. You must assign at least one bank account if your customers will use automatic receipts. The bank account information includes the customer's bank account, which must be defined already in the Banks form, because you cannot enter the customer's bank account information in this region. Oracle Payables and Oracle Receivables share bank information; however, each bank account can only be an internal bank account, a supplier's bank account, or a customer's bank account. Your customer can use more than one bank account, but you must define one as the primary account. To define your customer's bank account, you must select from a List of Values. You can also set an effective date range for a selected bank account. A blank To date indicates that the bank account is effective indefinitely. Save your work and move on to the next region.

Payment Methods

Next, select the Payment Methods alternative region. If you are using automatic receipts, you must assign a payment method to your customer by selecting from the List of Values. You may assign more than one method, provided the effective date

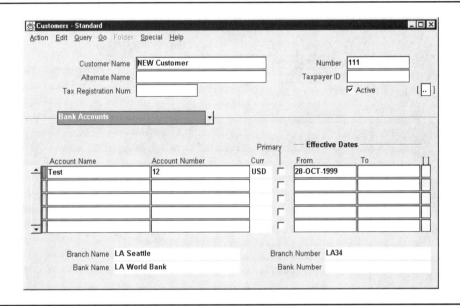

FIGURE 17-12. *Customers – Standard (Bank Accounts) form*

ranges do not overlap. Select a primary method to be defaulted for the customer during automatic receipts. Enter a From date, and leave the To date field blank unless you are inactivating the use of the payment method on a known date. If you are not using automatic receipts, this region is not required. Save your work and move on to the next region.

Relationships

Next, select the Relationships alternative region, which is optional, depending on your business requirements. See Figure 17-13. If you have a customer who pays invoices through a third party, or who belongs to a parent customer that pays the bills of many child customers, you will want to assign relationships to the customer so that one may pay the invoices of the other.

You may also set *Allow Payment of Unrelated Invoices* option to Yes. However, this does not enhance the functionality of using the Lists of Values in the receipts applications.

Enter the name of the customer with whom you wish to define a relationship. Enter enough of the name and press the TAB key. The List of Values or the customer name will be displayed, the customer name and customer number will be populated, and the *Active* checkbox will be defaulted to checked. Uncheck it if the relationship is no

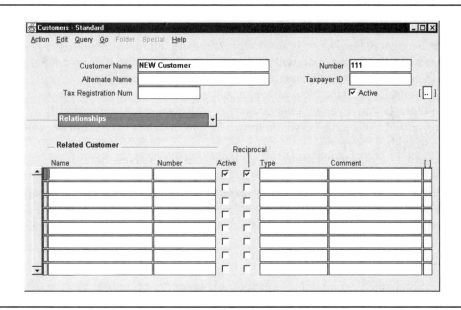

FIGURE 17-13. *Customers – Standard (Relationships) form*

longer active, and check the *Reciprocal* checkbox if you want both your customer and the related customer to be able to pay the invoices of the other. Do not select Reciprocal if you only want your customer to be able to pay the invoices of the related customer. The Type field is for information only and can be skipped—or, you can select from a List of Values to populate it. Types are lookup codes with type RELATIONSHIP_TYPE. The Comments field is also optional. Save your work. You have completed the customer-level information and are now ready to enter addresses.

Review Questions

1. Which fields are unique at the customer level?

2. What are the two alternative regions that are used to set up the customers for automatic receipts?

3. Where do most of the List of Values in the customer alternative regions come from?

4. What must you do if you want Customer A invoices to be able to be paid by Customer B but not vice versa?

Addresses

You must now enter the address(es) for your customer by selecting the Addresses alternative region. See Figure 17-14. In the Addresses alternative region, the customer heading information will be displayed at the top, and the summary of all of the addresses for a customer will appear below. This is a summary form only, and you must click on the **New** button, or have the cursor on a blank line and click on the **Open** button, to enter a new customer address. If you want to update an existing address, place the cursor on the address to update and click on the **Open** button to update the record.

To add a new customer address, you must click on the **New** button. The Customer Addresses window will appear. See Figure 17-15. In the Customer Addresses window, you set up your customer's new address, then assign a usage to the address, such as whether the address is to receive invoices, statements, shipments, or any combination of these. This is referred to as a business purpose.

The first field defaults to the country set in the system options, but can be updated. Enter an EDI location if this customer address sends or receives EDI transactions. Enter the street address on the first line. Enter any additional address information in the next three lines, including suite or floor number.

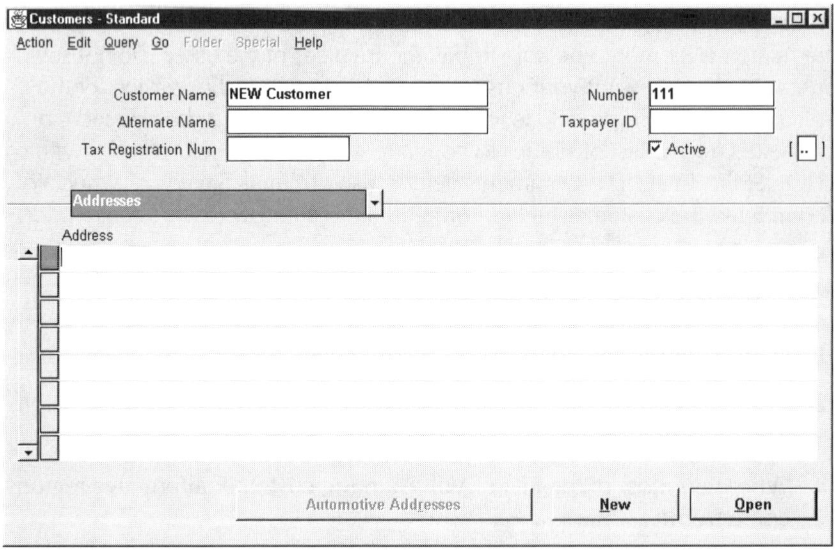

FIGURE 17-14. *Customers – Standard (Addresses) form*

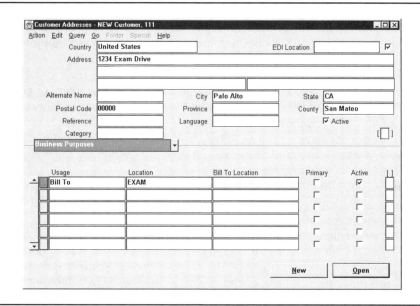

FIGURE 17-15.   *Customer Addresses form*

NOTE
Accounts Payable will automatically be printed on invoices and it is not necessary to use an address line for this information. Address lines that are not used will not be printed as blank lines on any correspondences. You can also enter an alternate name for the address.

Enter the city, or select it from the List of Values if your system is using address validation for sales tax purposes, and if the city is part of the sales tax structure. If the city is unique, and if it is part of the sales tax structure, the other components of the sales tax structure will be defaulted in. Continue with the state, which can also be validated if it is part of the sales tax structure. Next, enter a postal code/ZIP code. The Postal Code field will accept up to 10 digits, and will print exactly as typed in. This postal code will also validate if the system is set up to use a tax vendor software program. If the country is other than United States, the province can be entered here. Province can be validated if it is part of the sales tax structure. Next, enter the county that—similar to city, state, and province—can be validated if it is part of the sales tax structure. You can also enter a reference, which must be unique across all customers, for the address. If you do not enter a reference, and if you save the address, the address ID will be used. Enter the language used for this address. The *Active* checkbox is defaulted as checked; uncheck it if the address is not longer active. As a last step, you can enter a category, which is a lookup code with type ADDRESS_CATEGORY. The Country and the State fields can be used to derive a remit-to address. You can configure address validation to ignore, warn, or generate an error if the entered address components for the sales tax structure cannot locate a valid tax rate when you try to save the address. Address data, which is usually purchased from a tax service such as Vertex, only ensures that the system can accurately apply sales, use, and other taxes. It does not ensure that the address actually exists.

For the purposes of this exercise, enter an address with a city, state, postal code, and county. Because the Vision database has address validation enabled, the address will be validated.

The primary region, and the only alternative region that is required, is the Business Purposes alternative region. Each customer must have at least one bill-to and one ship-to business purpose assigned in order to create orders and invoices. Both business purposes can be assigned to one address, or to two different addresses. Each customer must have at least one primary bill-to business purpose assigned. Select the usage(s) for the address you entered. In the Location field, you must enter in a description of that address. You may set this field up to automatically populate with a number; however, the functionality will be limited. The Location field is used by Order Entry to select addresses to ship and invoice to. It also ties into other modules, and should be carefully designed for best performance of all system users. For best functionality, enter a short description of the address and its function, such as WHSE 123 Main / NY. This description is short enough to read from a List of Values, but would allow someone to make a determination from WHSE 123 Main / NY from HQ POB 111, Denver. For the ship-to business purpose, you may select the associated bill-to location. It is important to create and save the bill-to usage first. If you do not save, you will not be able to assign a usage of ship-to to any address because you won't be able to select an unsaved bill-to location. Check the *Primary* checkbox if this usage is a primary one and this address will default in the invoice entry form. The *Active* checkbox defaults to being checked, and should be unchecked if the usage is no longer active.

Make your address a primary bill-to and a ship-to address. In the Usage field in the Business Purposes alternative region, select Bill To from the List of Values. Enter a location name and check the *Primary* checkbox, then save your work. It must not only be entered, but also saved to the database before you can select it for assignment for ship-to usage. In the next row, select Ship To as the usage. If necessary, you may duplicate the location or enter a new description, then select your bill-to location by using the List of Values.

You may also assign other optional usages for the address, including legal, statement, dunning, or marketing. If you send statements of dunning letters without assigning them, then Receivables will choose the primary bill-to location. The bill-to business purpose allows you to send invoices to the address, the ship-to business purpose allows you to ship goods or services to the address, and the statement business purpose allows you to send statements to the address. You can only have one active statement business purpose address. The dunning business purpose allows you to send dunning letters to the address. You can only have one active dunning business purpose address. The legal business purpose is for government reporting purposes and the marketing business purpose is for sending marketing literature. You can also create your own business purposes as lookup codes under lookup type SITE_USE_CODE for informational purpose only. You can use the **New** button to create a new business purpose, or use the **New Record** button from the toolbar.

You may enter additional information regarding the business purpose by clicking the **Open** button. The Business Purpose Detail window will appear. You may enter different information for each usage as necessary. This area is completely optional, except when integrated with Project Accounting. You must enter a contact person, which can be pulled from the customer-level (not address-level) alternative regions, for the bill-to location. You must also enter an internal location if you would like Oracle Purchasing to use this ship-to address on internal sales orders.

You can enter a tax code, tax registration number, SIC codes, payment terms, FOB, carrier, ship partial, GSA, contact, sales territory, demand class, salesperson, order type, price list, freight terms, warehouse, internal location, tax classification, tax calculation, and tax rounding method. If the field exists in the customer address or customer level, it works by using the Ship To field, then the Bill To field, then the Customer Address field, then the Customer field. Save your work and close the Business Purpose Detail window.

Review the Customer Address form's alternative regions because they allow you to provide defaults and data that will override the customer-level defaults and data. The options include Telephones, Contact : Telephones, Contacts : Roles, Bank Accounts, Payment Methods, Profile : Transaction, Profile : Document Printing, and Profile : Amounts alternative regions. You can only enter data in the Bank Accounts, Payment Methods, and Credit Profiles alternative regions at the address level if the address has a saved bill-to business purpose. These alternative regions for a single address appear identical to the alternative regions for the customer, and can easily be confused. Also, information entered at the address level does not roll up to the customer level. However, information at the customer level will roll down to the address level, unless there is overriding information in the address-level alternative regions. You should use the address alternative regions only to distinguish different defaults of data for specific addresses, and not to duplicate information. In other words, do not use the address alternative regions to enter information that pertains to the entire customer.

Customers - Quick

You can also use the Customers - Quick form to enter customers. Follow the navigation path *Customers : Quick* to invoke this form. The Customers - Quick window will appear. This window looks identical to the Customers - Standard window. Select the Addresses alternative region and click on the **Open** button. You will see the Customer Addresses form. Notice that the Business Purposes alternative region is different. See Figure 17-16. You cannot use custom business purposes in the Customers - Quick form, and you cannot enter your own locations. Otherwise, the Quick form and the Standard form are identical.

Review Questions

1. What is a business purpose?

2. Which business purposes must be entered before you can print invoices for a customer?

3. Which business purpose will be used for mailing printed statements if there is no statement business purpose address?

4. What business process does address validation support? Can it completely prevent mistakes in entering addresses?

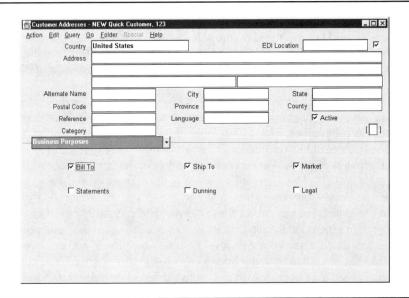

FIGURE 17-16. *Customers - Quick form*

Processing Orders

In this section, you will learn to process customer orders. Specifically, you will learn to process, schedule, and approve orders.

Processing, Scheduling, and Approving Orders

Enter a new order through the Order Workbench. Follow the navigation path *Orders, Returns : Orders, Returns*. This will bring you to the Find Orders form, which can be used to locate an existing order. To enter a new customer order, click on the **New Order** button. See Figure 17-17.

Order Header

Once you have selected the **New Order** button, the Sales Orders window will open. See Figure 17-18. From the order header in the Main alternative region, select a customer by customer name or by customer number from a List of Values. The defaults from the customer will be filled in depending on the standard value rule set and whether such defaults exist. Enter a contact, which may already be defaulted, from the customer. If one does not default, you can select a contact from the List of Values. Next, you must select the order type from the List of Values. Once you have

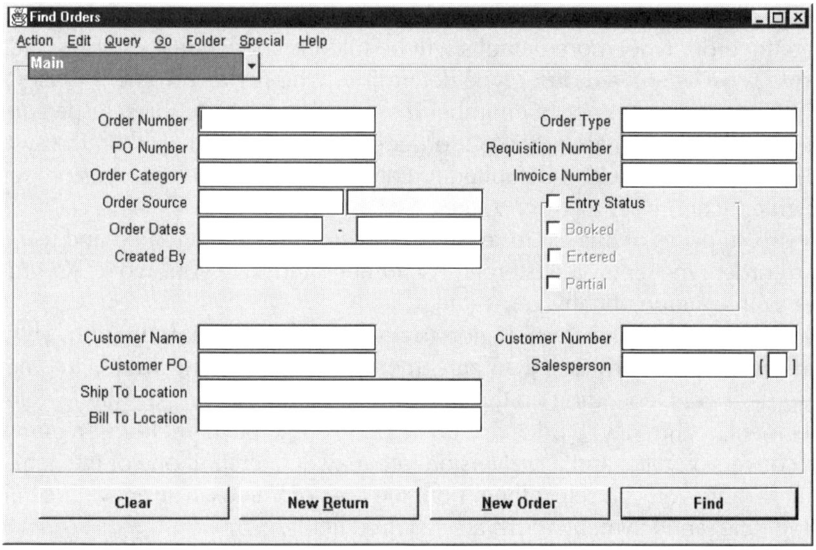

FIGURE 17-17. *Find Orders form*

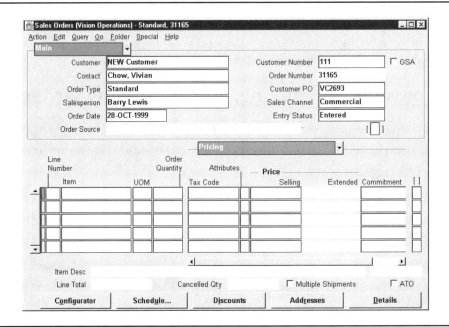

FIGURE 17-18. *Sales Orders (Main) form*

selected the order type, more defaults will be filled in, depending on the standard value rule set. The entered order type determines whether a customer PO is required. Enter the customer PO number if applicable. Choose the salesperson— one may default for you already. Your order date will default based on the system date. The Entry Status field is defaulted to Entered. You may select a custom result for the enter action from a List of Values.

For the purposes of this exercise, select the customer you created and use the Standard order type. Enter a customer PO number and save your work. An order number will be automatically generated.

Select the Pricing alternative region to review the pricing information. The entered order type determines if an agreement is necessary, and what agreement type can be used. Depending on the standard value rule set and available defaults, an agreement, a currency, a price list, an invoicing rule, payment terms, a conversion type, a conversion date, and a conversion rate may default in. If one of the items does not default, you can select them from the Lists of Values. Currency, Price List, Invoicing Rule, and Payment Terms are required fields.

Select the Shipping alternative region to review the shipping information. Depending on the standard value rule set and available defaults, the Warehouse,

Shipment Priority, Freight Carrier, Freight Terms, FOB, Demand Class, and Request Date fields, and also the *Allow Partial* checkbox, may default in. Shipping instructions and packing instructions may also be added, and will show up on the pick slip and the pack slip, respectively.

Select the Tax, Total alternative region to review the tax handling information. The Tax Handling field is defaulted to Standard. The Tax Exemption region may be defaulted with the certificate number and reason. You can only change the defaults if *Allow Override of Tax Code* profile option is set to Yes. You can select Exempt, Require, or Standard as tax handling. Exempt means that the order is tax exempt for a normally taxable customer. If you choose Exempt, you must enter a certificate number and an exempt reason. The certificate number can be selected from a List of Values for an approved certificate number, or you can enter a new certificate number. Require means that the order is taxable for a normally tax-exempt customer. Once you have you have added line information, order tax totals will also calculate in this region.

To review the payment information, select the Payment alternative region, then select the payment type. You can choose from Cash, Check, or Credit Card. Enter the amount, which is only informational and optional—with no functionality attached. For the check payment type, enter the check number. For the credit card payment type, enter the following fields: Credit N, Credit Card Number, Card Holder, Expiration Date, and Approval Code.

Next, you must enter the addresses for the customer order. You can review or enter the address information by clicking on the **Addresses** button. See Figure 17-19. Depending on your customer setups, the ship-to and bill-to addresses may be defaulted, but both are required. Select your addresses—those with a bill-to business purpose can be the bill-to addresses, and those with ship-to business purposes can be the ship-to addresses. Select the ship-to location or the ship-to customer. The ship-to you selected will provide shipping defaults for the order lines. You can also select a ship-to contact, which can be selected from all contacts associated with ship-to addresses, as well as any customer-level contacts. The bill-to customer is defaulted from the customer on the order header. Enter the bill-to location and the bill-to contact, which can be selected from all contacts associated with bill-to addresses and any customer-level contacts. You can select a ship-to and bill-to customer that has a relationship with the customer on the order if the *OE: Customer Relationships* option is set to Yes.

Once you have reviewed the above, close out the Ship To and Bill To Addresses window. The order header information is now completed, and you can move your cursor to the Line region to enter ordered items.

Order Line

The line number will default automatically, beginning with number 1. Choose your predefined item, and keep in mind that unlike a PO, the items you can enter for a

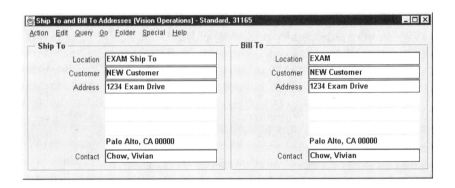

FIGURE 17-19. *Ship To and Bill To Addresses form*

customer order must be predefined in the inventory organization specified in profile option *OE: Item Validation Organization*. Enter the unit of measure by choosing only from the measures in the same UOM class of the item's primary UOM. The item with the entered unit of measure must be defined on the price list specified in the order Pricing alternative region. Otherwise, you will get a message. Next, enter the order quantity. You have seven alternative regions for the order line. The regions are Pricing, Scheduling, Shipping, Project, Release Management, Service, and Service More. You should already be in the Pricing alternative region. The tax code could be defaulted based on customer's tax code, customer address tax code, and the standard value rule set. If the profile option *TAX: Allow Override of Tax Code* is set to Yes, you can override the defaulted tax code. If the Descriptive flexfield is set up, you can also enter the pricing attributes. Pricing will be described in Chapter 19. Selling price is defaulted based on the entered item, and is entered from the entered price list. You can override the selling price depending on the order type setup, the price list setup, and the profile option setup. Discounting will also be described in Chapter 19. You can also enter a commitment number that you have defined in Oracle Receivables. Commitment can be a guarantee or a deposit.

Next, select the Scheduling alternative region and enter the requested date, which can be used as a pick release parameter. See Figure 17-20. You can enter a time component to the request date, a promised date, and the schedule date. The latter is used as the effective demand date, in ATP inquiry, and can be used as a pick release parameter. The source type can be defaulted based on the selected order type. If the order is an internal sales order, or if the order cycle in the order type does not have drop shipment actions, then source type is defaulted to be Internal. Otherwise, it is External. You can choose a source type only if the order cycle has both drop shipment and nondrop shipment actions. If the source type is

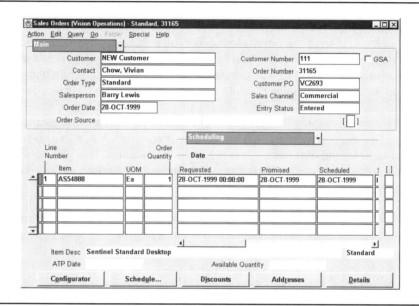

FIGURE 17-20. *Sales Orders (Scheduling) form*

External, select the receiving organization, then select the warehouse where the item is to be shipped from. You can select any warehouse where the item is customer orders enabled.

You can also enter a quantity to reserve, but you cannot enter a quantity greater than the order quantity. However, you can enter a quantity that is less than the order quantity. For a lesser quantity, Oracle Order Entry reserves the entered quantity and simply places a demand on the remainder. If you leave the field blank, select Reserve as the schedule action; then, the entire ordered quantity will be reserved. You can also enter a ship set number. All order lines within the same order with the same ship set number will be shipped together, and all order lines in the same ship set must have the same shipping parameters: warehouse, schedule date, ship-to location, shipment priority, and freight carrier. Next, select a schedule action, which is performed when you save your work. Use this field if different actions must be performed for different order lines in the same order. If not, then use the **Schedule** button instead. You can select ATP Inquiry, Demand, and Reserve as the schedule action for new order line. The ATP inquiry schedule action initiates an available to promise query based on the entered schedule date, item, quantity, and warehouse. If entered, the ATP inquiry will take the ship set into consideration and will return an ATP date where the quantity of the item is available after the entered schedule date. However, it will not place any demand or reservation. The Demand schedule action places a demand on the item for the order quantity, and the Reserve schedule action reserves the item for the reserve quantity. If reserve quantity is blank, then it will reserve the entire available to pick quantity. If you previously placed a demand or a reservation, you can select the Undemand schedule action to remove the placed demand, the Unreserve schedule action to remove the placed reservation, or the Unschedule schedule action to remove both the placed demand and the placed reservation. Schedule status can be blank, Demanded, Reserved, or Supply Reserved. Supply Reserved is only for ATO items and configurations, and means that the supply of the ATO order line is reserved. You can also select a demand class for the order line if it is not already defaulted. This will determine the demand class that Oracle Order Entry will place a demand on for this order line. As a last step, you can enter a planning priority.

Next, select the Shipping alternative region. You can enter a different ship-to location—which is the final destination of the order line—for each order line. You can also select a different ship-to contact. Shipment priority and freight carrier may be defaulted, and you can override or enter a shipment priority and a freight carrier. Both fields can be used as pick release parameters.

Next, select the Project alternative region. These fields are used for project manufacturing, and are only applicable if you have Oracle Projects installed. If the level is set to Project, and if the entered warehouse is under project control, then you must select a project before booking the order. If the project control is set to Task, you must also select a task before booking the order.

Next, select the Release Management alternative region. These fields are used for release management and are only applicable if you have Oracle Release Management installed. Oracle Release Management populates these fields, and you can manually override them if applicable. The information here includes customer job number, customer production line, customer model serial number, customer dock, intermediate ship-to location, planning production sequence number, and—if Descriptive flexfield is set up—the industry information.

The Service alternative regions only apply if you are entering a service order. You have completed one order line; now, enter all of the order lines for the order and save your work. For the purposes of this exercise, use item AS54888 and select a tax code that has a tax rate, then save your work.

Schedule Order

Once you have saved your order, use the **Schedule** button to schedule the order or the order line. This is normally used if you want to perform the same scheduling action on the entire order, ship set, configuration, shipment, or line. Click on the **Schedule** button and the Schedule window will appear. See Figure 17-21.

You can create a schedule based on the selected scope and action. The scope type can be Order, Ship Set, Configuration, Shipment, or Line/Detail, and is sensitive to the location of your cursor when the **Schedule** button was invoked.

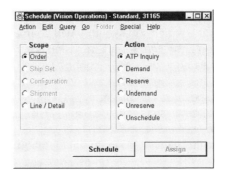

FIGURE 17-21. *Schedule form*

Order is the entire customer order, and Ship Set is a group of order lines that are given the same ship set number. Configuration is a defined configuration of items, and Shipment is a group of orders and orders that are packed and shipped together. Line/Detail is a single order line or a single line detail. ATP Inquiry (available to promise) runs a query on the scope you selected and will tell you the next available ship date for the items without placing demand. Demand places demands for items within the entered scope. Reserve saves the quantity reserve for items within the entered scope. Undemand removes a previously placed demand for the items within the entered scope. You must use this if you want to change ship dates. Unreserve removes previous placed reservations on items within the selected scope. If you choose Unreserve, previously placed demands will remain. Unscheduled removes both previously placed demands and reservations on items within the selected scope.

Once you have selected the **Scope** and **Action** radio buttons, click on the **Schedule** button to activate the action on the scope you chose. Once you have completed this step, the schedule ship date should be populated. If you have problems with scheduling, a message will appear. If you do not want to initiate the action, but if you want to fill in the Schedule Action field for the order line/order line detail, select Line/Detail as the scope and select the action, then click on the **Assign** button. This will schedule the order.

Order Line Details

Select the **Details** button to enter detailed information about any order line. You can split the order line into several line details, provided the total quantity adds up to the order quantity of the line. Split the order line to ship the order line from different subinventories and lots. You can also specify different item revisions. In the Scheduling

Information alternative region, you can specify a subinventory in the warehouse to be used during pick release. If you do not enter a subinventory, then the defined picking rule will be used to determine which subinventory will be used during pick release. You can specify the revision if the item is under revision control, and you can specify the lot number if the item is under lot number control. Upon reserving the item and entering the subinventory and/or the revision and/or the lot number, the reservation will be placed against the specified combination. You can enter a schedule action at the line detail level. The schedule status can be blank, Demanded, Reserved, or Supply Reserved, just like what you see at the line level.

Next, select the More alternative region. In the Demand Class field, you can enter a demand class that will override the line's existing demand class. Check the *Customer Requested* checkbox if the customer requested a particular subinventory, item revision, and/or lot number. If this line detail has been pick released, the *Release* checkbox will be checked. Click on the **Schedule** button to schedule by scope and action. Remember that the scope is sensitive to the location of your cursor. You are using the same Schedule window that you used when clicking on the **Schedule** button from the line level. Save your work and close the Line Schedule Details window.

So far, there are two unused buttons: **Discounts** and **Configurator**. The **Discounts** button may be used if you are allowed to manually adjust the list price. This will be discussed in Chapter 19. The **Configurator** button is only applicable if you have Oracle Product Configurator installed.

You have now completely entered an order, which contains lines that are made up of line details. Upon successful completion of the order, you would book your order via the Special | Book menu command. Booking an order indicates that the order is firm, and that it contains all of the necessary information. At this point, the status of the order will change from Entered to Booked.

Approve Order

If the order type's order cycle has an approval action following the order being booked, you would then approve the order by giving it a pass result. Since you added the export review action to the Standard order cycle and you are using the Standard order type, you must enter an export review approval. To approve orders, follow the navigation path *Orders, Return : Approval*. This would bring you to the Find Order and Line Approvals form. First, enter the approval you want to enter. Then, enter your selection criteria to identify the orders or order lines you want to approve. You can enter approval result, order number, customer PO, customer name, customer number, order type, order category, item, approver, order status, approval date range, order date range, and/or request date range as selection criteria. To locate your order, enter Export Review as the approval, enter order number, and click on the **Find** button.

Your order will be displayed in the Approve Orders window. See Figure 17-22. You can select Pass or Fail as the approval result, and you can also enter an optional comment. If you want to view the order approval history, click on the **History** button. Otherwise, save the record after entering the result and optional comment. If you want to approve multiple orders or order lines, either select all records by using the Edit | Select All menu command, or use SHIFT-clicking and CTRL-clicking to select groups of contiguous or noncontiguous records, respectively. Next, click on the **Set Results** button and enter an approval result and comments to be applied to all selected records in the Set Results window. For the purposes of this exercise, select Pass as the approval result for your order and save your work.

Review Questions

1. What are the names of the record levels between the order header and the order line details?

2. How do you schedule order lines with different schedule actions?

3. What is a ship set?

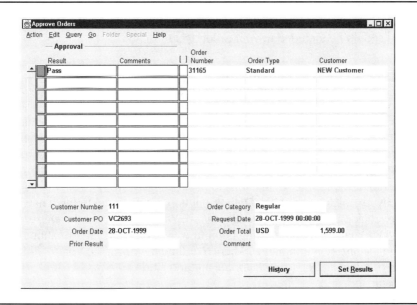

FIGURE 17-22. *Approve Orders form*

Fulfilling and Shipping Orders

This section covers order fulfillment and shipping. Fulfilling and shipping orders include Departure Planning Workbench, pick release, and ship confirm in Oracle Order Entry.

Fulfilling Customer Orders, Including Picking and Shipping

Once an order is booked and all of the necessary approvals obtained, you can fulfill the order when the schedule date or other time table arrives. You can start the fulfillment process if you have set up shipping parameters for the organization you are in. To start the fulfillment process, you can use delivery-based shipping by using the Department Planning Workbench to schedule vehicle departures and vehicle loading order, assign scheduled shipment lines to a planned departure, create and sequence deliveries within a departure, and calculate the number of containers required. If you are not using delivery-based shipping, you can proceed directly to pick release. In this case, when you ship confirm the delivery, you will be asked to enter the actual departure date, freight carrier, and bill of lading when you change the delivery status—a departure will be generated automatically. Using the Departure Planning Workbench is optional in Oracle Order Entry. However, the pick release process and the ship confirm process are mandatory for shippable items and should be included in your order cycle.

Departure Planning Workbench

Use the Departure Planning Workbench to create departures and deliveries. A delivery is a set of order lines shipped on the same date and time in the same vehicle and to the same customer's ship-to location. Delivery lines are scheduled shippable and booked order lines. A departure is a set of order lines shipped on the same date and time in the same vehicle. A departure consists of a given vehicle leaving at a specific date and time, containing deliveries for multiple customers (or at least to multiple ship-to locations for a single customer). If you are entering a new delivery, click on the **New Delivery** button. If you are entering a new departure, click on the **New Departure** button. You can also use the Departure Planning Workbench to find existing departures and deliveries information. To invoke the Departure Planning Workbench, follow the navigation path *Shipping : Departure Planning : Departure Planning* and the Find Departure Information window will appear. See Figure 17-23.

You can either find existing departures, existing deliveries, or delivery lines, with the default being to find deliver lines. Or, you can create a new departure or a new delivery. If you have Oracle Release Management, you can enter the customer

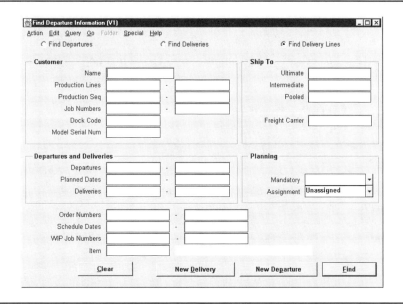

FIGURE 17-23. *Find Departure Information form*

name, production line range, production sequence range, job number range, dock code, and customer model serial number to find delivery lines. If you have Oracle Release Management, you can also enter the intermediate ship-to location and a pooled ship-to location. For the following criteria, you need not install Oracle Release Management. You can enter an ultimate ship-to location and freight carrier, and you can also enter a departure name range, planned date range, and delivery name range. You can also find based on whether planning is mandatory, and you can select only assigned delivery lines or unassigned delivery lines, or leave the Assignment field blank for both. You can also enter an order number range, schedule date range, WIP jobs numbers range, and an item. To find departures, enter a departure name range, planned date range, freight carrier, vehicle, vehicle number, and departure status (Open, Planned, Cancelled, or Closed).

To find deliveries, enter the delivery name range, expected arrival date range, order number range, delivery status (Open, Planned, Cancelled, or Closed), assignment (Yes or No), departure name range, planned date range, ship-to customer, ultimate ship-to location, intermediate ship-to location, and pooled ship-to location. You must have Oracle Release Management installed in order to enter intermediate ship-to and pooled ship-to locations. Once you have entered all of the criteria, click on the **Find** button.

Next, click on the **New Departure** button and the Departure window will appear. See Figure 17-24.

DEPARTURE   To create a new departure, you must first enter a unique department name.

NOTE
The department name is alphanumeric, so be cautious if you previously used a number, because numbers in an alphanumeric field do not sort in numeric order. For instance, if you have entered department names of 1 through 21, every name that starts with a 1 will sort before any name starting with a 2. Hence, the names would be presented in the order 1, 11, 12, 13...19, 2, 20, 21.

Enter the departure name and planned date. You can also enter the freight carrier, vehicle, carrier number, and any instructions. When selecting a vehicle, the minimum fill of the vehicle is automatically filled in. You can select the volume

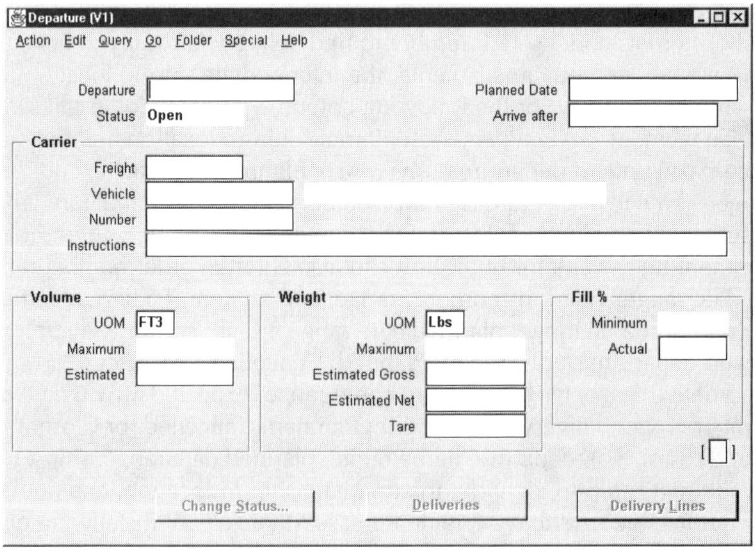

FIGURE 17-24.   *Departure form*

UOM, estimated volume, weight unit of measure, estimated gross weight, estimated net weight, and tare weight (the weight of an item without packaging and included items). Enter the actual fill percentage and save your departure. To change the status of a departure, click on the **Change Status** button to change the status to Plan or Cancel. Plan status can be used during pick release or to trigger weight/load calculation. You are not going to create a departure for your order fulfillment exercise. You can use the Special | Calculate Weight/Volume menu command to calculate weight and volume for the entire departure or delivery. The total weight and volume is calculated based on all of the associated deliveries. It will verify that the total weight and volume do not exceed the maximum weight and volume allowed. It will also calculate the fill percentage and verify that the maximum fill percentage and the minimum fill percentage requirements are met. It will also calculate the number of containers necessary, and will override the existing container information. You can set the calculated weight and volume automatically when the status of the delivery or departure is set to Planned. You can use the View Containers form to see the container information. It will list every container, its description, the UOM, and the quantity.

In addition to creating a new departure using the above method, you can also create departures based on selected delivery lines. To do this, use the *Find Delivery Lines* option in the first Find window, enter the criteria for the delivery lines, and click on the **Find** button. Delivery lines are shippable and booked lines that are available if you have such order lines in the system. Then, click on the **Create Departure** button to create a departure for all of the selected delivery lines. If you use this method to create a departure, you can also use the Special | AutoCreate Deliveries menu command to automatically create deliveries based on the selected delivery lines. A delivery must have the same customer, ultimate ship-to location, intermediate ship-to location, freight carrier, freight terms, FOB, and currency. The number of deliveries generated depends on the number of unique customers, ultimate ship-to locations, intermediate ship-to locations, freight carriers, freight terms, FOB, and currencies associated with your selected delivery lines. You can generate the loading sequence based on the selected delivery lines (loading order is described in more detail later). You can also use the Special | Pick Release menu command to release delivery lines within a delivery or departure, as long as the status is Planned and the delivery is associated with a departure.

DELIVERY   You can also use the Departure Planning Workbench to create new deliveries. To create a new delivery, click on the **Create Delivery** button in the Find window. Or, if you already created a departure and wish to create a new delivery to associate to it, select the departure and click on the **Create Delivery** button in the Departure form. This will cause the Delivery window to appear, as shown in Figure 17-25. You must enter a unique delivery name and an expected arrival date. You can select the loading order of the delivery within the departure; Oracle Order Entry

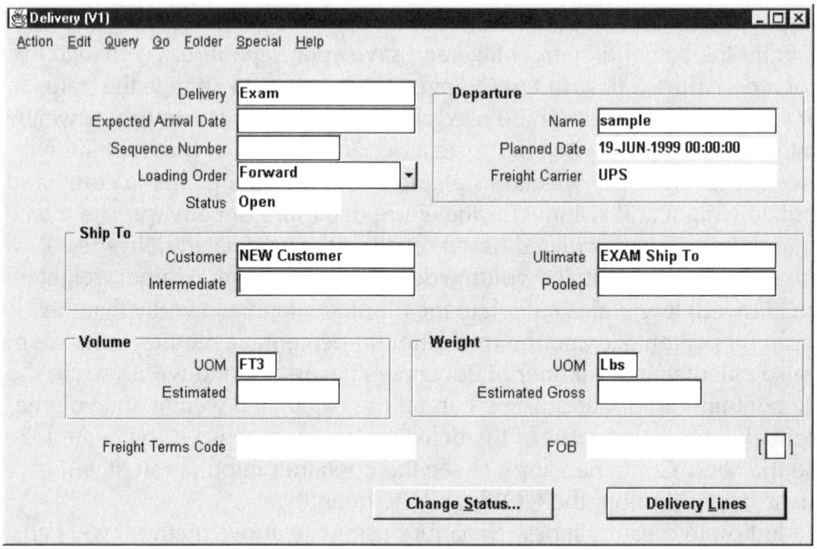

FIGURE 17-25. *Delivery form*

generates the loading sequence based on this selection. You can select from
Forward, Reverse, Forward-Inverted or Reverse-Inverted. For example, if you
use containers that can hold three items, and you have eight items, the forward
sequence would load in this order:

1 2 3   4 5 6   7 8

The reverse sequence would load in this order:

8 7 6   5 4 3   2 1

The forward-invert sequence will load items forward *across* multiple containers,
and backward *within* a container. In other words, the items would be loaded in this
order:

3 2 1   6 5 4   8 7

Reverse-invert will load items backward *across* multiple containers, and forward
within a container. This would cause items to be loaded in this order:

6 7 8   3 4 5   1 2

Select the departure to associate to, or click on the **Create** button from the Departure form to have it filled in automatically. Select which customer to ship to and the ultimate ship-to location. If Oracle Release Management is installed, you can also select the intermediate ship-to location and pooled ship-to location. Select volume UOM, estimated volume, and weight UOM, and enter the estimated gross. To change the status of a delivery, you click on the **Change Status** button. You can change the status to Plan or Cancel. Plan status can be used in pick release and to trigger automatic weight/load calculation, and the Special menu options can be used for delivery in the same fashion as departure.

You can also create delivery based on selected delivery lines. This step is similar to creating a new departure, and is done by using the *Find Delivery Lines* option in the first Find window. Enter the criteria for the delivery lines and click on the **Find** button. Then, click on the **Create Delivery** button to create delivery for all of the selected delivery lines.

DELIVERY LINES   The last step involves assigning delivery lines to a delivery or departure if you did not find the delivery lines first. You can assign delivery lines to deliveries, or you can assign delivery lines to a departure and AutoCreate deliveries. You can also go to the Delivery Lines window from the Deliveries or the Departures form, depending on how you want to assign your delivery lines. Select the **Delivery Lines** button on either form. The Delivery Lines window will appear in both cases. See Figure 17-26.

All shippable and booked lines assigned to the departure or delivery will show up in the Delivery Lines window. You can unassign delivery lines by clicking on the **Unassign** button. You can unassign all delivery lines by using the *Select All* option, or use CTRL-click and SHIFT-click to select specific records or record groups. To add delivery lines, click on the **Add Lines** button to invoke the Find Delivery Lines to Add window. See Figure 17-27.

In order to assign a delivery to a departure, the two must share the same freight carrier. To assign a delivery line to a delivery, the two must share the same customer, ultimate ship-to location, intermediate ship-to location, freight carrier, currency, FOB, and freight terms. The delivery line can still be assigned to the delivery as long as all other attributes match, except that the currency, FOB, and freight terms in the delivery line are null. Enter any additional criteria and click on the **Find** button to find unassigned delivery lines. The Delivery Lines to Add window will appear. Click on the **Add** button to add the delivery line(s). Then click on the **Cancel** button, because you do not actually need to create departures, deliveries, or delivery lines for this exercise. You will AutoCreate deliveries during pick release, and automatically generate departures during the ship confirm stage.

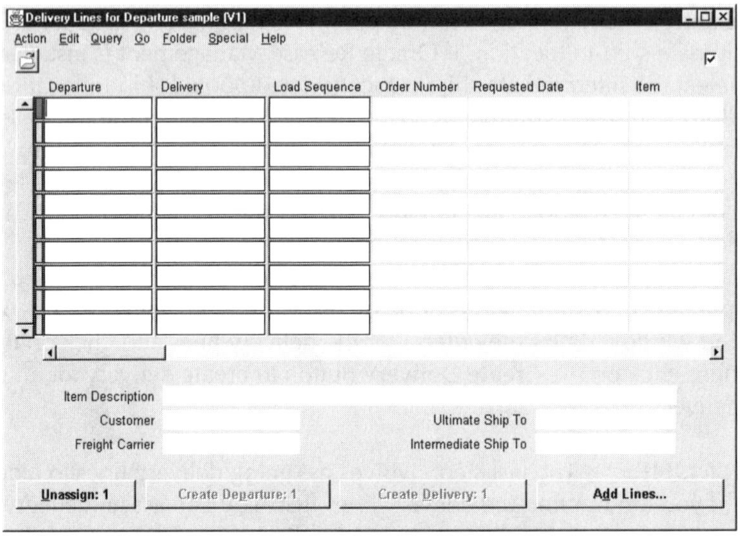

FIGURE 17-26. *Delivery Lines form*

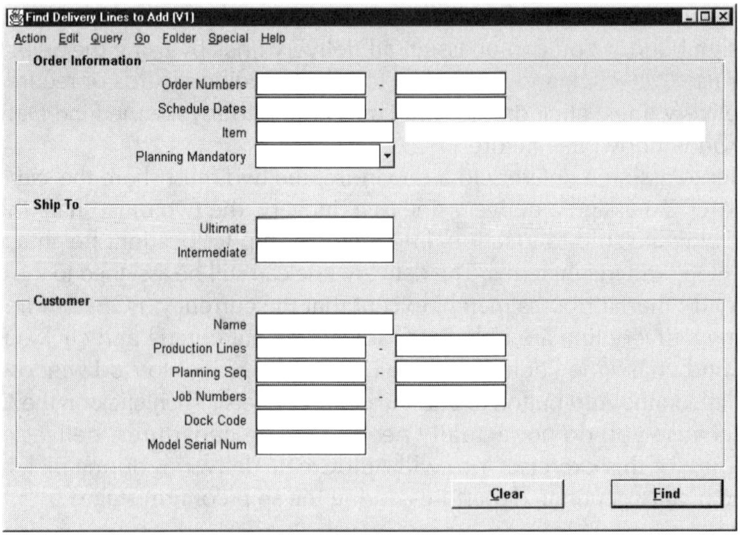

FIGURE 17-27. *Find Delivery Lines to Add form*

Review Questions

1. What is a departure?

2. What is a delivery?

3. What are the loading order options and how are they used?

4. What will you do to calculate the number of containers necessary?

Pick Release

By using the Departure Planning Workbench, you have just completed the departure planning, and the next step is to pick release. Or, if you do not need to plan your departures, you can go straight to pick release and skip departure planning. The Pick Release function generates pick slips that will prompt you to pick the items from subinventories of the warehouses. The Pick Release function releases sales orders line details to allow shipments, and also generates picking lines. There are three different methods of running pick release: online, concurrent, or through Standard Report Submission (SRS). Before initiating Pick Release, you must first define the release sequence rules and the pick slip grouping rules. You can also invoke pick release directly from the Special menu in the Departure Planning Workbench.

RELEASE SEQUENCE RULES   Release sequence rules are used to define the order in which the selected picking lines are released. To set up release sequence rules, follow the navigation path *Setup : Shipping : Release Sequence Rules.* Enter a unique release name and an optional description. You cannot delete release sequence rules, but you can inactivate a release sequence rule by entering an effective date range. In the Release Priority region, select the priority you wish to use to sequence the picking lines. You can assign a priority to pick release an order by order number, total invoice amount, schedule date, departure date, and shipment priority. You can use order or outstanding invoice, but not both. Assign a priority from 1 to 4 to indicate the sequencing order. You can also decide whether the ordering within each group is ascending or descending. See Figure 17-28.

PICK SLIP GROUPING RULE   Pick slip grouping rules define the way picking lines are grouped into pick slips. To set up picking slip grouping rules, follow the navigation path *Setup : Shipping : Pick Slip Grouping Rules.* Enter a pick slip grouping rule name and an optional description. You cannot delete a pick slip grouping rule, but you can inactivate a pick slip grouping rule by entering an effective date range. In the Group By region, select the group-by criteria. Your choices are order number, carrier, subinventory, departure, customer, delivery-to location, ship-to location, and shipment priority. See Figure 17-29.

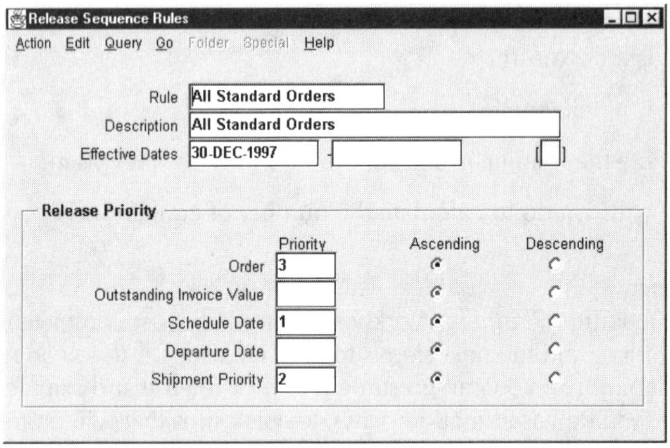

FIGURE 17-28. *Release Sequence Rules form*

RELEASE RULES   You can also set up release rules as templates to streamline entering parameters for pick releases. Release rules are required if you will be using SRS for pick release. To set up release rules, follow the navigation path *Setup : Shipping : Release Rules.* Enter a unique release rule name. You cannot delete a release rule, but you can inactivate a release rule by entering an effective date range. You can enter the criteria in the Release Criteria region, and you must specify whether

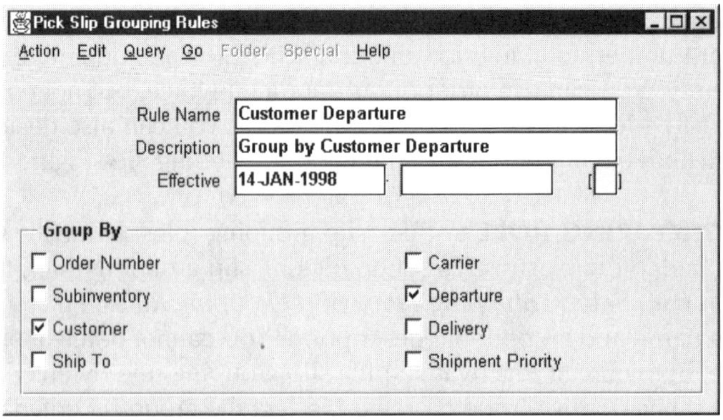

FIGURE 17-29. *Pick Slip Grouping Rules form*

to release unreleased orders, all orders, or backordered orders. You can specify shipment priority, but if it is left blank, all shipment priorities will be included. Check the *AutoCreate Deliveries* checkbox to automatically create deliveries with the delivery lines. You can specify a subinventory, but only include prior reservations and a carrier. If you leave these fields blank, pick release will include all values for each criterion. You can also enter a scheduled ship date range and a requested date range. Again, if left blank, all dates will be included in the pick release. You can enter a specific order type, in which blank means all order types. You can enter an order number where blank means all orders, and you can enter a specific ship set if you have selected an order. A blank ship set means all ship sets. You can also enter a specific item and customer, and if you enter a customer, you can enter a ship-to location. If you leave these fields blank, pick release will include all values for each criterion. You can specify pick release to include planned lines and/or to allow a partial release. You can also assign a release sequence rule and/or a pick slip grouping rule to the release rule. When finished, save your release rule. See Figure 17-30.

USING PICK RELEASE   Because Oracle Order Entry includes a seeded sequence rule and a grouping rule that may meet your business needs, you may

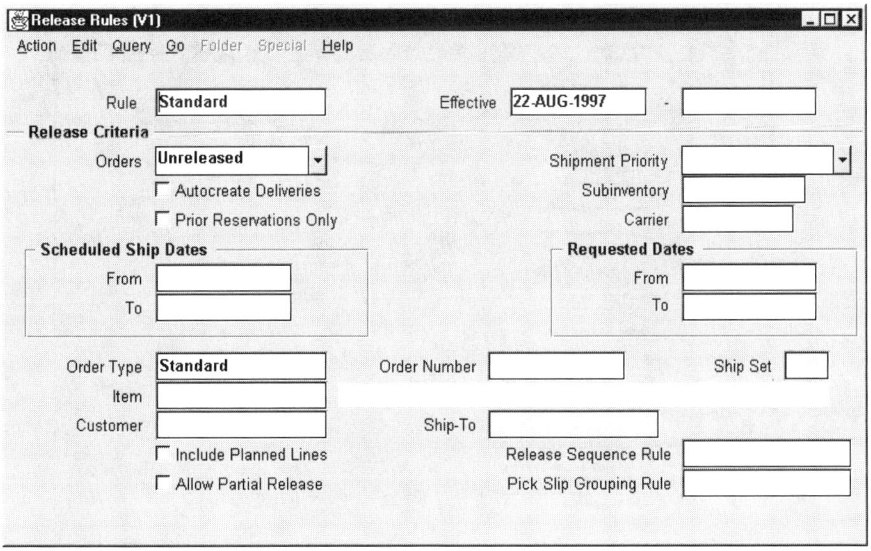

FIGURE 17-30.   *Release Rules form*

not need to set them up. To initiate pick release outside of the Departure Planning Workbench, navigate to the Release Sales Order For Picking form via the navigation path *Shipping : Release Sales Orders : Release Sales Orders.* See Figure 17-31.

You must enter a unique batch name, or Oracle Order Entry will use the batch ID if you leave the field blank. Enter the document set, which defines which documents will be automatically submitted during pick release. The default document set has the seeded Pick Slip program. You can base the pick release on a predefined release rule. Choose a value for the orders release criteria from the List of Values, which includes: Unreleased, Backorder, or All. For pick releasing a new order, you should use Unreleased. You may also choose a shipment priority, subinventory, or carrier to further define the items to be pick released. You can check the *AutoCreate Deliveries* checkbox to automatically generate deliveries. The delivery name generated will be used to ship confirm the release. You cannot check *AutoCreate Deliveries* if you have selected a departure and/or a delivery. You can enter a departure and/or a delivery to restrict the pick release. Specify whether you want to allow partial release of a departure, and check the *Include Planned Lines* checkbox to include only planned lines for the pick release. Planned lines have a Planned status in the Departure Workbench.

Either enter or accept the dates from the Scheduled Ship Dates and Requested Dates regions. If the order lines to be pick released fall outside the parameters, or

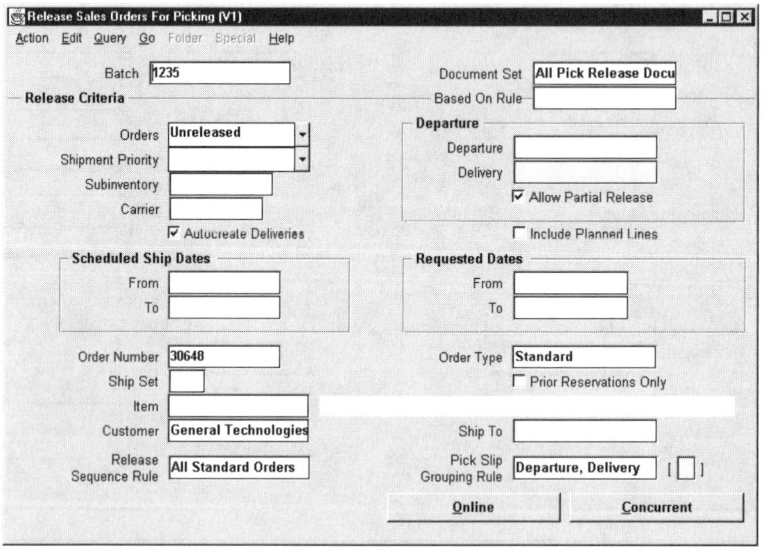

FIGURE 17-31. *Release Sales Orders For Picking form*

there was not sufficient inventory available, the order will not be released. To pick release a single order, enter the number in the Order Number field and the Order Type and Customer fields will default. You can enter a specific order type, and if you enter an order number, you can also enter a ship set to determine which ship set to pick release. You can only include prior reservations for the pick release, and you may also narrow the pick release by entering an item. You can enter a customer and a ship-to location. If you leave any of these fields blank, all values will be pick released for the blank fields.

Next, review the release sequence rules and the pick slip grouping rule, and either accept them or change them. Then click on the **Online** or the **Concurrent** button. Online, pick release performs the function immediately and freezes the form until the Pick Release function is completed. Concurrent pick releases through a background concurrent program. For this exercise, enter your order number, check the *AutoCreate Deliveries* checkbox, verify the scheduled ship dates and requested dates, then click on the **Concurrent** button. If you click on the **Concurrent** button without entering the batch name, the name will be generated automatically. You will receive a message stating that the pick release concurrent program is started. Use the View My Requests form to verify completion. You will see both a pick release and all documents included in your document set. The Pick Slip program, which should be included in your document set, generates pick slips, and can be viewed by clicking on the **View Output** button. If you are using AutoCreate deliveries, then you must also note your delivery name, which you need for the subsequent ship confirm step. If the pick slip says "No Data Found," then nothing is picked. If this occurs, verify your pick release parameters and rerun the pick release process. Verify the schedule date range and the request date range. If you are not sure of the date range, and if you are picking by order number, blank out both date ranges. Use the Process Exception report to view any problems, if you are still unable to release the order lines.

A pick release selects all delivery lines based on the parameters you entered in the order as specified in the release sequence rule. It generates picking lines and groups the generated picking lines into pick slips according to the pick slip grouping rule. It generates all documents included in the selected document set, and sets the order line detail associated with the picking lines to a Released status. If only a portion of an order line detail is picked, the remaining portion will be split into a new order line detail automatically by the Pick Release program. This occurs because there is a *Released* checkbox at the order line detail level, and the program cannot be partially released.

To submit the pick release process through SRS, you can also follow the navigation path *Release Sales Orders : Release Sales Orders : SRS.* To do so, you must use a release rule name. Enter a batch name, select the document set to be used, and submit the request.

Review Questions

1. What is a release sequence rule?

2. What is a pick slip grouping rule?

3. What is different between the online and concurrent options for pick release?

4. What will happen if only part of the order line detail is shipped?

Shipping an Order

Once the order has been successfully pick released and is eligible to be ship confirmed, you may ship confirm the order. You can ship confirm a departure, delivery, or pick slip. For the purposes of this exercise, you will use delivery-based—as opposed to departure-based—ship confirm and a departure will automatically be created. If you created a departure, then use a departure-based ship confirm. Based on a specific delivery name—generated at pick release time—you can ship confirm the order via the function path *Shipping : Confirm Shipments : Ship Confirm Deliveries.* This will bring up the Ship Confirm Delivery window. See Figure 17-32.

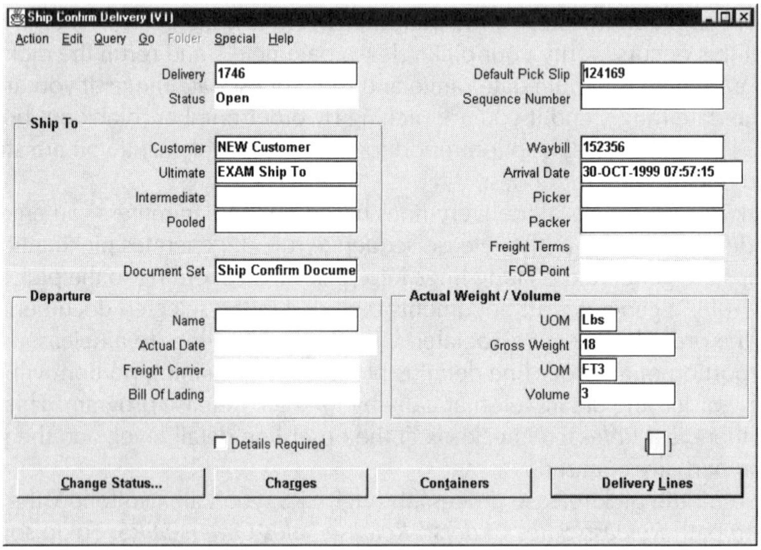

FIGURE 17-32. *Ship Confirm Delivery form*

Based on the delivery name generated at pick release time, enter the unique delivery name and query up the delivery. Review the ship-to customer and the ultimate ship-to location. Choose another document set, or use the defaulted one. This document set relates to the shipping process, with the default including pack slip, commercial invoice, bill of lading, and labels. Enter a waybill number. The arrival date, which may be changed, is defaulted to the current date and time. You can also choose a picker and packer, who are defined employees in the system, from the Lists of Values. Review the freight terms and FOB point, which should be defaulted. In the Actual Weight/Volume region, select the UOM from the List of Values for weight. Then, enter the gross weight for the shipment, select the UOM for the volume of the shipment, and enter the volume.

If the *Details Required* box is checked, you must click on the **Delivery Lines** button to enter more details, including serial number or lot number. Otherwise, you can ship confirm the entire delivery by clicking on the **Change Status** button, which brings you to the Delivery Status form.

You can select Ship All to ship the entire delivery. You can also backorder the entire delivery. For the purposes of this exercise, select Ship All and you will see three additional fields appear: Actual Departure Date, Freight Carrier, and Bill of Lading. These fields appear because your delivery does not have a departure date, and all three are necessary in order to automatically generate a departure. Enter a freight carrier and a bill of lading. You can also check the *Process Inventory Online* checkbox to update the shipping status online, and to update the inventory on-hand quantity online. If you do not check the *Process Inventory Online* box, then you must run the Update Shipping Information program to update the shipping status, and the Inventory Interface program to update the inventory on-hand quantity. Submit the Update Shipping Information program by following the navigation path *Shipping : Confirm Shipments : Update Shipping*. Enter a specific departure or delivery, or leave them blank to update all departures and deliveries for the latest shipping statuses. To submit the Inventory Interface follow the navigation path *Shipping : Interfaces*. Select the Inventory Interface program and submit your request. No report parameter is necessary. If you choose not to process online, then schedule the two concurrent programs to be run in the background periodically. You can also check the *Enforce Packing* checkbox to display a warning if there are unpacked delivery lines. Delivery lines are packed following the same process as shipping, but instead of changing the status in the Delivery Status form to Ship All or Ship Entered Quantities, change the status to Pack All or Pack Entered Quantities. For the purposes of this exercise, check the *Process Inventory Online* checkbox, uncheck the *Enforce Packing* checkbox, and click on the **OK** button to ship the entire delivery. Upon doing so, the delivery will be closed.

DELIVERY LINES   If details are required, or if you want to ship or pack part of the quantity, click on the **Delivery Lines** button to get to the Delivery Lines form.

See Figure 17-33. You can enter the container number and sequence number to assign the delivery line to a container. Enter the shipped quantity, which can be less than the requested quantity. Use the Ship Entered Quantities status to ship a partial order and backorder the remaining quantities. The delivery status will also be closed after shipping entered quantities. For items under specific inventory controls that require serial numbers, revisions, lot numbers, or subinventories, you must enter the required information. If the quantity is 1, you can simply enter the other additional required information, which may include the following: serial number, revision, lot number, subinventory, locator fields, and/or loading sequence. Then, save your work. If the quantity to be shipped is greater than 1, click on the **Serial Numbers** button to add the serial numbers one by one, or by range. Use the Special | Split Delivery Line menu command if you decide to ship the item from more than one revision, lot number, subinventory, and/or locator. When finished, close the Delivery Lines window.

FREIGHT CHARGES   Depending on the applicable freight terms, you may want to add shipping charges. Do so by clicking on the **Charges** button on the Ship Confirm Delivery form. This will bring you to the Charges form.

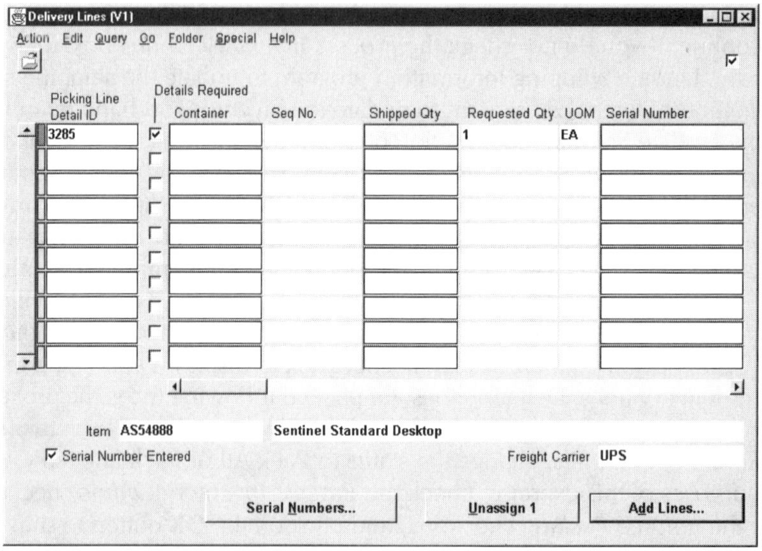

FIGURE 17-33.   *Delivery Lines form*

First, select the charge type from the List of Values. You set up freight charges with a name, type, currency, and amount in the Freight Charges window during set up. The currency and the amount will be defaulted, but you can override them as necessary. The currency must match the order to be selected, or it must be the functional currency. You can charge freight charges to three levels: order, line, and delivery. Select an order number for the order level, a picking line detail ID for the line level, and a container for the delivery level. Save your freight charges entry and close the Charges form.

CONTAINER   Use the **Containers** button to define a container, along with its parent and its inventory controls. If delivery items are already assigned to a container, they will be displayed in the Container Contents region. The container type must be predefined. See Figure 17-34.

You can also confirm shipping based on departure by following the navigation path *Shipping : Confirm Shipments : Ship Confirm Departures.* The Ship Confirm - Departure window will appear. See Figure 17-35. Query up your departure, verify all information, and override if necessary. Then enter the bill of lading and the actual date, and click on the **Change Status** button to ship the entire departure,

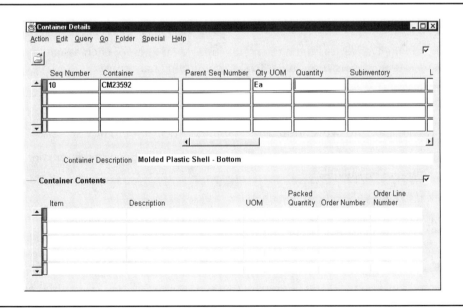

FIGURE 17-34. *Container Details form*

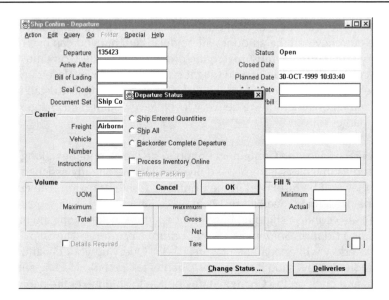

FIGURE 17-35. *Ship Confirm – Departure form*

or click on the **Deliveries** button to enter shipped quantities for each assigned delivery. The process is very similar to ship confirming deliveries.

Review Questions

1. What are the two kinds of ship confirms Oracle Order Entry supports?

2. How do you ship partial delivery and what will happen to the remaining requested quantity?

3. How do you enter freight charges?

4. What is the purpose of the *Process Inventory Online* checkbox?

Invoicing Customers and Closing Orders

In this section, you will learn to prepare orders for invoicing and to close the orders. If the Receivables Interface is part of your order cycle, and if you have picked and shipped your orders, you are ready to invoice your customer.

Preparing Orders For Invoicing to Customers, and Closing Orders

If your order/return lines reach the Receivables Interface eligible order cycle action and result at the line level, then they can be prepared for invoicing. The order cycle associated with the order type determines the flow of the order/return process, and ultimately when and whether invoicing should take place. For example, if you were shipping product, your Receivables Interface cycle would probably come directly after the product has been ship confirmed.

The Receivables Interface program pushes the order/return information towards Oracle Receivables. You can manually run the Receivables Interface program from Order Entry, or you can set it to run at particular intervals or at a certain time of the day. To start the Receivables Interface program follow the navigation path *Orders, Returns : Receivables Interface.* This program should run at least one time prior to running AutoInvoice, which is run in Oracle Receivables to create the actual invoices. If you do not run Receivables Interface in Oracle Order Entry, there will be no invoices created when you run AutoInvoice in Oracle Receivables. You can select invoice source, customer name, order type, order date range, order number, departure name, delivery name, and nondelivery invoice source as report parameters. You can use the *WSH: Invoice Numbering Method* profile option to decide whether invoice numbers should be generated based on delivery name. If you use the delivery name to derive an invoice number, you must select a nondelivery invoice source. Submit your request when finished.

When your order/return information reaches the Complete Order Eligible and Complete Line Eligible statuses at the order level and the line level respectively, it is ready to be closed. Assuming that your order cycles are set up correctly, your order will not complete or close until all lines are completed or closed out.

You can run the Close Orders program manually from Order Entry, or you can set it to run at particular intervals, or at a certain time of the day. Follow the navigation path *Orders, Returns : Close Orders.* No report parameter is necessary, and the request can simply be submitted. The order statuses are changed to Closed by the Close Orders program when they are ready to be closed. This action speeds up various forms and greatly reduces printed lines on some standard Oracle Order Entry reports—those that only look for open orders/lines. However, if all lines and the order/return are closed, then you cannot add items or make any changes.

The Close Orders program also releases order/return holds that were dated to be automatically released in the Hold form, and purges the Demand Interface table and Supply Demand table information for faster processing time.

Review Questions

1. How do you prepare the order for invoicing?

2. What does the Close Orders program do?

3. How will the Close Orders program speed up forms and reduce report lines?

For the Chapter Summary, Two-Minute Drill, and Chapter Questions and Answers, open the summary.htm file contained in the Summary_files directory on the book's CD-ROM.

CHAPTER
18

Basic Order Fulfillment

his chapter teaches you how to set up Oracle Order Entry and Receivables, and how to perform some basic order fulfillment functions. In this chapter, you will learn about the following:

- Implementing and setting up Order Entry
- Integrating Order Entry/Shipping and Receivables
- Entering and correcting transactions
- Entering and applying receipts for customers
- Tracking and collecting past due receivables
- Reconciling, reporting, and completing the receivables cycle
- Implementing and setting up Receivables

First, you will learn how to complete the setup of Oracle Order Entry. Once you have learned the remaining setups, you will be taught how to integrate Oracle Order Entry and Oracle Receivables. This includes identifying what data is shared between Oracle Order Entry and Oracle Receivables, and determining what data can be imported from other applications through the interface tables. Oracle Order Entry and Oracle Receivables open interfaces include customers, customer profile classes, invoices, orders, and shipments, among others.

Then you will learn about processing and revising transactions in Oracle Receivables. Transactions in Oracle Receivables include invoices, credit memos, and debit memos, among others. This section also covers receiving and applying payments from customers to specific invoices or to their accounts as an on account credit. Then, you will learn to identify past due receivables and administer collection activities. This includes recording customer calls and running aging reports. The chapter also discusses how to complete the receivables cycle.

In the last sections, you will learn how to complete the implementation and setup of Oracle Receivables. These sections cover how to set up customer profile classes and customers. In addition, in these sections you will learn the rest of the Oracle Receivables setups. The last part of this chapter teaches you how to enter bank statement information and how to reconcile bank statements to internal records. Though these two topics were taught in Chapter 14, they are covered here briefly to refresh your memory.

Implementing and Setting Up Order Entry

In this first section, you will learn how to complete the implementation and setup of Order Entry/Shipping.

Completing the Implementation and Setup of Order Entry/Shipping

For an overview of the steps for implementing Oracle Order Entry, please refer to Figure 18-1.

Define Flexfields

You must define the Key flexfields and Descriptive flexfields that Oracle Order Entry has used. Oracle Order Entry needs the following Key flexfields from other Oracle Applications modules:

- Accounting flexfield
- System Item flexfield
- Item Category flexfield
- Item Catalog flexfield
- Stock Locator flexfield
- Sales Tax Location flexfield
- Territory flexfield

For Oracle Order Entry, you must set up the Sales Order flexfield. This flexfield is used to identify a customer order transaction. Oracle manufacturing modules use this Key flexfield for identifying the source of demand and reservation. The third segment of this Key flexfield is usually used for the order source to ensure that the Sales Order flexfield combinations are unique. You use profile option *OE: Source Code* to identify the source and the default is ORDER ENTRY.

You must also define all the appropriate Descriptive flexfields to capture any additional information.

Inventory Organizations and Parameters

You must define inventory organizations to track inventory. Since most (or all) items on an order will ship from Oracle Inventory, you must have an inventory organization to validate items on your sales orders. This inventory organization is defined under *OE: Item Validation Organization*. If you are using drop shipments (which are discussed in detail in the next chapter), you also need a receiving inventory organization. The validation and receiving inventories organization can be the same. For each inventory organization, you must set up the organization parameters, subinventories, and picking rules.

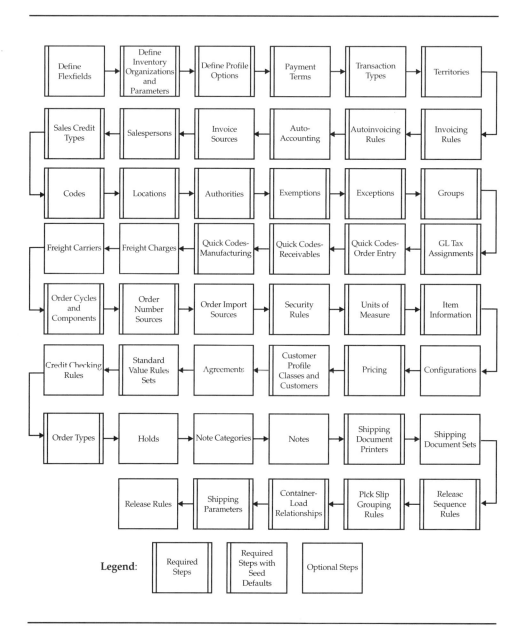

FIGURE 18-1. *Oracle Order Entry setup steps*

Profile Options

Profile options direct how Oracle Order Entry controls access to system data, and also how Oracle Order Entry processes system data.

Profile options can be set at one or more of the following levels:

- Site
- Application
- Responsibility
- User

Oracle Order Entry users can change option values only at the user level. The system administrator can set profile options at the site, application, responsibility, and/or user levels.

You must set up profile options for each operating unit you define.

Order Entry profile options are as follows:

- *OE: Customer Relationships*
- *OE: Debug*
- *OE: Debug Level*
- *OE: Debug Trace*
- *OE: Default Picking Document Set*
- *OE: Default RMA Status*
- *OE: Default Shipping Document Set*
- *OE: Discounting Privilege*
- *OE: Force Valid Configurations*
- *OE: GSA Discount Violation Action*
- *OE: Immediate Inventory Update*
- *OE: Included Item Freeze Method*
- *OE: Inventory Stock Location*
- *OE: Item Flexfield*
- *OE: Item Validation Organization*

- *OE: Item View Method*

- *OE: Reservations*

- *OE: Schedule Date Window*

- *OE: Set of Books*

- *OE: Source Code*

- *OE: Trans Manager Debug Level*

- *OE: Transaction Manager*

- *OE: Tune for Large Number of Discounts*

- *OE: Unit Price Precision Type*

- *OE: Validate Option Line Item*

- *OE: Validate Standard Line Item*

- *OE: Verify GAS Violations*

- *OE: Weight Unit Of Measure Class*

- *SHP: Release Online Exception Report*

- *SHP: Release Online Pick Slip Report*

- *SHP: Release Single Orders Online*

- *WSH: Invoice Numbering Method*

When setting profile option values, you must determine at what levels you should set the values. Remember that user level overrides responsibility level, responsibility level overrides application level, and application level overrides site level.

Most of the options, which are explained below, can be set up or defined in Oracle Receivables.

Payment Terms

Follow the navigation path *Setup : Orders : Payment Terms* to the define payment terms to be associated with invoices, credit memos, etc. You can set up payment terms to allow discounts for customers who pay early. Discounts can be based on invoice amount, line, a combination of line and tax, or a combination of line, freight, and tax. Oracle Receivables allows you to set up an unlimited number of discounts for receivables payment terms.

Transaction Types

Follow the navigation path *Setup : Financials : Transaction Types* to define transaction types that are tied to invoice, credit memos, etc. The Transaction Types form appears. See Figure 18-2.

The transaction types determine whether entries update customer balances, and whether Receivables posts to the General Ledger, among other things. You can also associate an invoice type to a credit memo type and vice versa. If you are using transaction types as a source in AutoAccounting, you can specify General Ledger accounts in the transaction types. This can be set up in Oracle Receivables.

Territories

Follow the navigation path *Setup : Sales : Territories* to define sales territories. Territory is a Key flexfield, and you use this form to create valid combinations. This can be set up in Oracle Receivables.

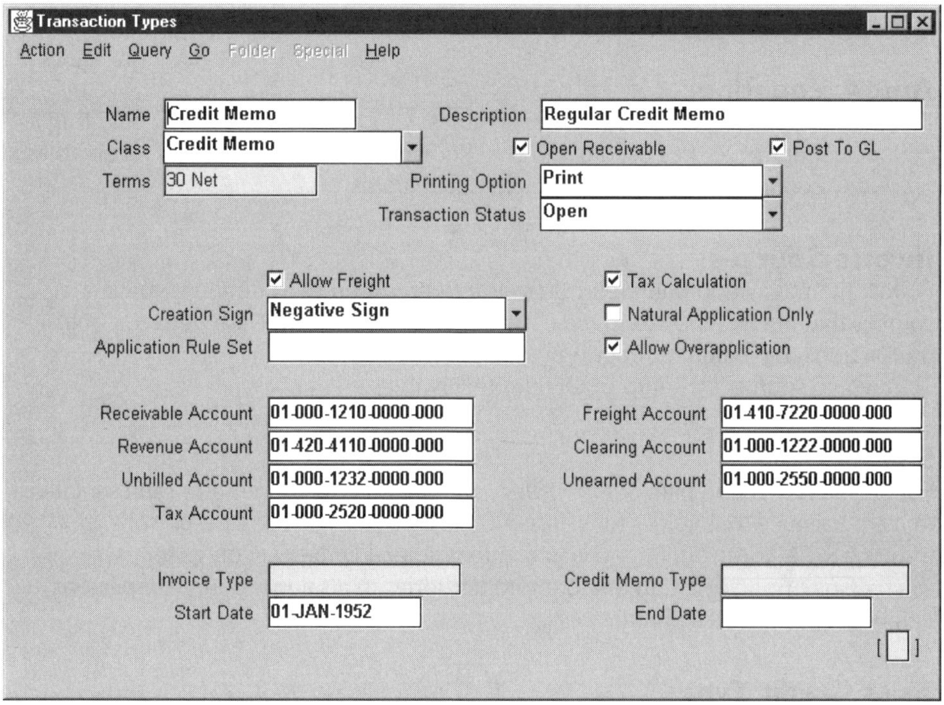

FIGURE 18-2.   *Transaction Types form*

Invoicing Rules

You must set up rules in Oracle Receivables, or use the Oracle seeded rules. There are two types of rules:

- Invoicing
- Accounting

Invoicing rules determine when to record revenue if the invoices span more than one accounting period. Accounting rules determine how revenue is recognized. You must select invoicing rules in the transaction types if you are interfacing with Oracle Receivables.

AutoInvoicing Rules

If you are interfacing with Oracle Receivables, you must set up AutoInvoicing Ordering Rules to define how invoice lines are ordered. To define how invoice lines are grouped, you must also set up AutoInvoicing grouping rules. These are both setups in Oracle Receivables.

AutoAccounting

If you are interfacing with Oracle Receivables, you must set up AutoAccounting to define account structures used by Oracle Receivables for revenue and receivables.
AutoAccounting is a setup in Oracle Receivables.

Invoice Sources

Follow the navigation path *Setup : Transactions : Sources* to define invoice sources that are assigned to invoices and credit memos. They are used to control transactions and batch numbering.
Invoice source is a setup in Oracle Receivables.

Salespersons

Follow the navigation path *Setup : Sales : Salespersons* to define sales representatives that are assigned to invoices for sales/revenue credit. If you use salespersons as a source for AutoAccounting, you can enter General Ledger accounts for each salesperson. You can assign one or more territories to a salesperson. Salespersons can be set up in Oracle Receivables.

Sales Credit Types

Follow the navigation path *Setup : Sales : Credit Types* to define sales credit types. You can set up Quota and Nonquota sales credit types. For Quota credit types, the total of the sales credit of any customer order cannot exceed 100 percent. Sales credit types can be set up in Oracle Receivables.

Tax Codes

Follow the navigation path *Setup : Tax : Codes* to define tax codes. The Tax Codes and Rates form appears. See Figure 18-3. You can set up tax rate, tax type, control, and accounting for each tax code. Oracle Order Entry and Oracle Receivables allows the tax types Sales tax and VAT tax. You can set up one active Location Based Tax type tax code to be used on transactions. For Location Based Tax type tax code, you cannot enter a tax rate percentage. You set up tax codes in Oracle Receivables.

Tax Locations

Follow the navigation path *Setup : Tax : Locations* to define tax locations. The Tax Locations and Rates form appears. See Figure 18-4.

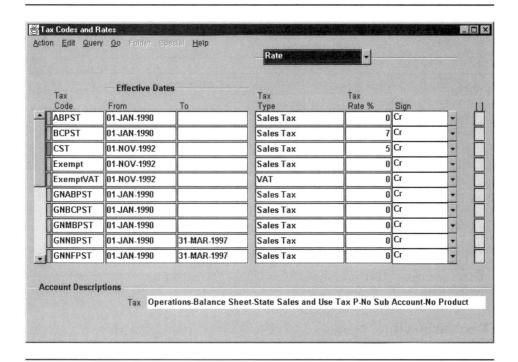

FIGURE 18-3.   *Tax Codes and Rates form*

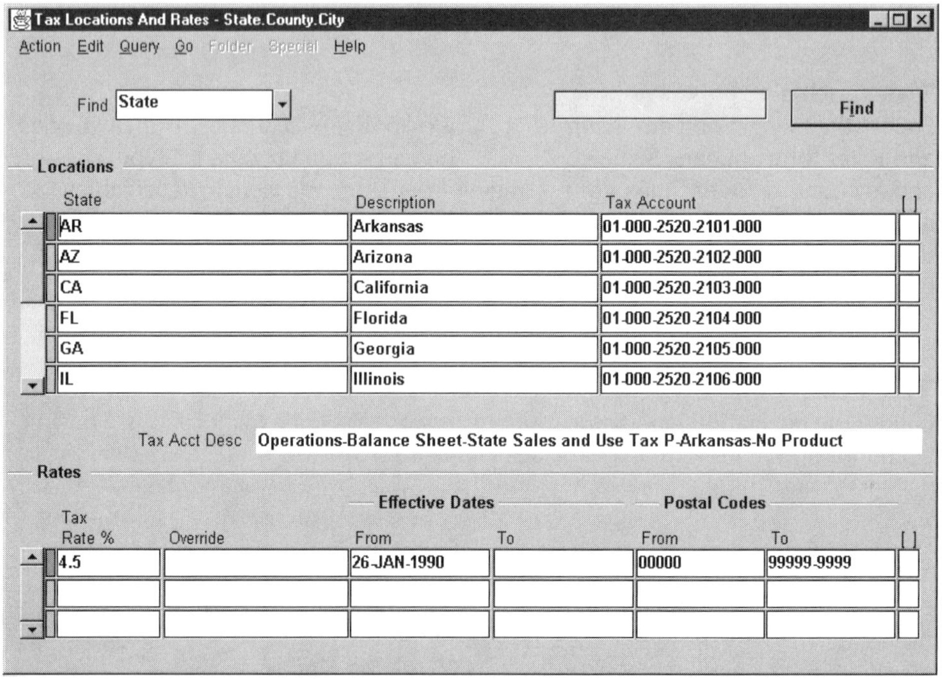

FIGURE 18-4. *Tax Locations and Rates form*

You can see the selected Location Tax flexfield structure in the form. You must set up locations if you are using location-based tax. Location-based tax, as its name suggests, is based on the address. You set up a Location Tax flexfield structure and determine which components of the address you want to use to derive the tax rate. For example, for the United States, the components are typically state, county, and city.

For each component, you use the Tax Locations And Rates form to define a tax rate. The tax rate for the location is the total of all the tax rates for each address component of the Location Tax flexfield structure. You can further distinguish tax rates by postal code range. For example, for the same county you can have two postal code ranges that have two different rates. You set up locations in Oracle Receivables.

Tax Authorities

Follow the navigation path *Setup : Tax : Authorities* to define tax authorities. Tax authorities are valid combinations of the Location Tax flexfield structure. You set up tax authorities in Oracle Receivables.

Tax Exemptions

Follow the navigation path *Setup : Tax : Exemptions* to define tax exemptions. You can create tax exemptions for a customer, item, range of items, an item category, or a user item type. Tax exemptions exempt the selected objects entirely or partially for the tax codes you specified. You define exemptions in Oracle Receivables.

Tax Exceptions

Follow the navigation path *Setup : Tax : Exceptions* to define tax exceptions. You can define tax exceptions for an item or a range of items for any location combination. A tax exception is a tax rate override as oppose to a tax exemption, which is a percentage reduction. If you want user-item exceptions, you should not assign tax codes to customers or customer addresses. You define exceptions in Oracle Receivables.

Tax Groups

Follow the navigation path *Setup : Tax : Groups* to define tax groups. A tax group is a set of tax codes that you can apply together to transactions. You define tax groups in Oracle Receivables.

GL Tax Assignments

Follow the navigation path *Setup : Tax : GL Tax Assignments* to define GL tax assignments. You set up GL tax assignments if you want to use natural accounts as a source for calculating tax rate. This is called the account tax method. You can associate tax codes to any revenue accounts.

You define GL tax assignments in Oracle Receivables.

Quick Codes - Order Entry

Follow the navigation path *Setup : QuickCodes : Order Entry* to set up Order Entry lookup codes. They will be used throughout Order Entry as QuickPick values.

Order Entry lookup types are:

- AGREEMENT_TYPE
- CANCEL_CODE
- CREDIT_CARD
- FREIGHT_CHARGE_TYPE
- FREIGHT_TERMS
- HOLD_TYPE

- NOTE_FORMAT
- RELEASE_REASON
- SALES_CHANNEL
- SHIPMENT_PRIORITY

Quick Codes - Receivables

Follow the navigation path *Setup : QuickCodes : Receivables* to set up Receivables lookup codes. They will be used throughout Receivables as quick pick values.

User-maintainable Receivables lookup types are as follows:

- ACCOUNT_STATUS
- ACTION
- ADDRESS_CATEGORY
- ADJUST_REASON
- AGING_BUCKET_LINE_TYPE
- APPROVAL_TYPE
- ARLPLB_MATCHING_OPTION
- ARLPLB_UES_MATCHING_DATE
- ARTAXVDR_LOC_QUALIFIER
- AR_CANADIAN_PROVINCE
- AR_TAX_CLASSIFICATION
- CALL_OUTCOME
- CKAJST_REASON
- COMMUNICATION_TYPE
- CONTACT_TITLE
- CREDIT_MEMO_REASON
- CREDIT_RATING
- CUSTOMER_CLASS
- CUSTOMER_CATEGORY
- CUSTOMER_GROUP
- CUSTOMER_RESPONSE_REASON

- CUSTOMER_SUBGROUP
- DEPARTMENT
- DEPARTMENT_CODE
- FOB
- FOLLOW
- INVOICING_REASON
- JE_DEFERRED_TAX_TYPE
- JE_EXEMPT_TAX_TYPE
- JE_NONTAXABLE_TAX_TYPE
- MANDATORY_FIELD_PROMPT
- RANK
- RELATIONSHIP_TYPE
- RESPONSIBILITY
- RISK_CODE
- SITE_USE_CODE
- STANDARD_MSG_TYPES
- STANDARD_TEXT
- TAX_EXCEPTION_REASON
- TAX_REASON
- TAX_TYPE

Quick Codes - Manufacturing

Follow the navigation path *Setup : QuickCodes : Manufacturing* to set up Manufacturing lookup codes. There is only one Manufacturing lookup type, which is DEMAND_CLASS.

Freight Charges

Follow the navigation path *Setup : Freight : Charges* to define specific freight charges to be added at time of shipping. The Freight Charges form appears. See Figure 18-5.

Freight charge types must first be set up using QuickCodes.

Freight Carriers

Follow the navigation path *Setup : Freight : Carriers* to define specific freight carriers you plan to use. You define freight carries for each inventory organization, and it is important that the values match exactly across the organizations. You must assign a distribution account to each freight carrier.

Order Cycles and Components

In previous chapters, you learned how to define new order/return actions and new order/return results, and how to link results to actions. You also learned how to combine the components and set prerequisites for actions in order cycles to define order cycles that govern process flows.

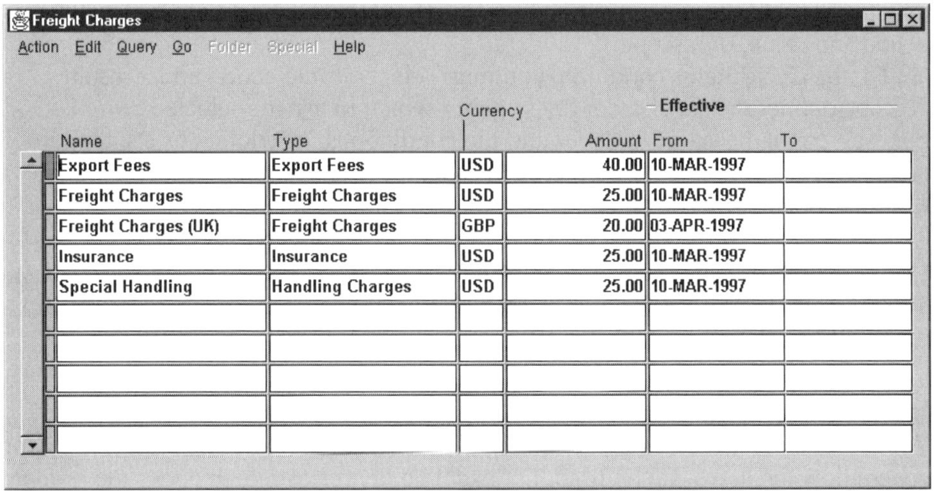

Name	Type	Currency	Amount	Effective From	To
Export Fees	Export Fees	USD	40.00	10-MAR-1997	
Freight Charges	Freight Charges	USD	25.00	10-MAR-1997	
Freight Charges (UK)	Freight Charges	GBP	20.00	03-APR-1997	
Insurance	Insurance	USD	25.00	10-MAR-1997	
Special Handling	Handling Charges	USD	25.00	10-MAR-1997	

FIGURE 18-5. *Freight Charges form*

Order Number Sources

Follow the navigation path *Setup : Orders : Sources* to define the source of orders that will be interfaced via Order Import. You use order number sources to govern order/return numbering. Once order number sources are set up, they are tied to order types.

Order Import Sources

Follow the navigation path *Setup : Orders : Order Import* to define how outside order sources are brought into Order Entry. You can determine whether the import sources use IDs (internal identifiers) or names (order number or order ID, for instance).

Security Rules

Follow the navigation path *Setup : Rules : Security* to define security rules. Oracle Order Entry seeded system security rules already exist to prevent users from making certain changes to orders/returns. However, these rules can be even more stringent.

You can enter block-level rules or field-level rules. Click on the **Block Rules** button or the **Field Rules** button with the cursor on the block or field for which you want to set up security rules. The Security Rules form appears. See Figure 18-6.

Through this form, you can prevent users from inserting, updating, deleting, and/or canceling data. You can set security rules based on predefined conditions. Predefined conditions include Cycle Status, Internal Sales Order, and Scheduling Exists.

If you select the same sequence number for more than one rule, the rules will be connected by AND conditions; otherwise, they will be connected by OR conditions. You can check the *Modifier* checkbox to reverse the condition. Also, depending on the condition you have selected, you may have to enter a cycle action and result, or a scope.

For the Cycle Status condition, you must select a cycle action and a result. A scope defines the set of order lines against which to test the selected conditions. For example, if the scope is Order and the condition is Scheduling Exists, then if any order line within the order has been scheduled, the condition passes. If it is a seeded system security rule, the *System Rules* checkbox is checked.

Units of Measure

You must define units of measure (UOM) that can be used in Oracle Order Entry. All Oracle Applications modules share the same UOM tables.

Item Information

You must define items along with their attributes. Item attributes define the item and govern how the items can be used. For example, item attribute includes the primary UOM. It also stores the item status. Item attributes can tag items as Customer Orders

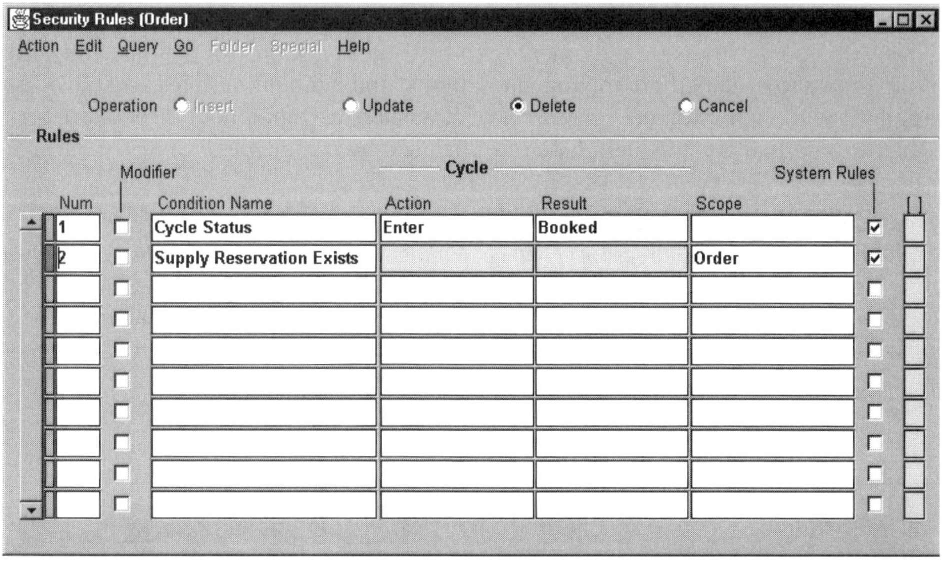

FIGURE 18-6. *Security Rules Details form*

Enabled, Shippable, Internal Orders Enabled, Assemble To Order, Check ATP, Returnable, Invoice Enabled, Transactable, Reservable, Lot Control, BOM Allowed, and/or Purchasable. You also must set up item categories.

Configurations

You must define the configurations of the items that you are planning to sell if the items have configurations/product structures. Configurations/product structures are defined as bills of materials in the Oracle Bill of Materials module.

Pricing

You must set up pricing information such as price lists and discounts before items can be included in an order. The section titled "Managing Pricing" in Chapter 19 contains details of how to do this.

Customer Profile Classes and Customers

You must enter customer profile classes and customers before you can enter a sales order. You already learned how to do this in a previous lesson. You can perform this setup in either Oracle Order Entry or Oracle Receivables.

Agreements

Follow the navigation path *Customers : Agreements* to define agreements you may have with your customers. Agreements can be used as a source of defaults and can point orders to specified pricing, payment terms, and accounting rules you have arranged with the customer. You can restrict whether an agreement is required or whether a particular agreement type must be used by order types.

Standard Value Rules Sets

Follow the navigation path *Setup : Rules : Values* to define standard value rule sets. The Standard Value Rule Set form appears See Figure 18-7.

Standard value rule sets help default order/return entry information at order placement time or create new sets of rules. For each predefined field of each predefined block, you can set up defaulting rules. If there are multiple defaulting

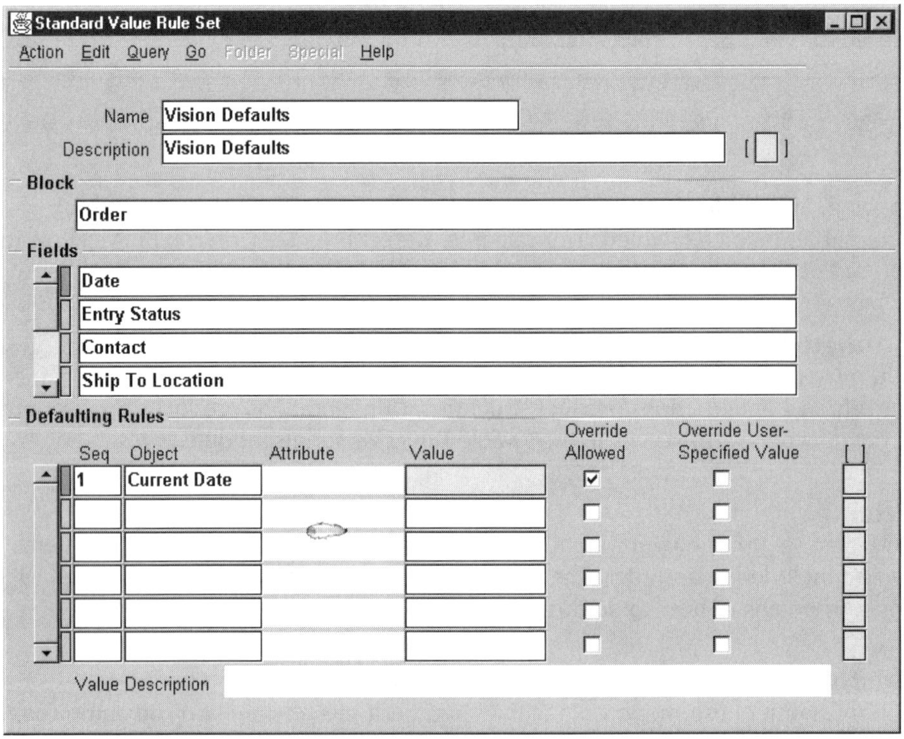

FIGURE 18-7. *Standard Value Rule Set form*

rules, the rules are applied based on their sequence number, with number 1 as the first number in the sequence.

You can select the object, attribute, and value to be used as the source of the default for each field. The objects are predefined as well. Objects are usually global values, such as current date, other fields in the form, the same field from other forms, profile options, or constants. If you select a profile option, you must enter the profile option name in the Value field. You can also specify whether the default can be overridden and whether the default overrides user-specified values.

Standard value rule sets are tied to order types.

Credit Checking Rules

Follow the navigation path *Setup : Rules : Credit* to define your automatic credit checking rules. You can set up credit-checking rules to govern how credit checking should be performed.

You define the total credit exposure, and the amount defined by this definition is checked against the customer's credit limit. You can include and define the range open receivables balance to be checked against the credit limit. You can enter a negative number to include open receivables past the current date, plus the range you entered. You can enter a positive number to include open receivables with an invoice date within the current date plus the range. Leave the range blank to include all open receivables.

You can specify whether to include payments at risk, which are receipts that have not been cleared. You can also include uninvoiced orders. If you decide to include uninvoiced orders, you must enter a scheduled number of shipping horizon days to determine how far ahead Oracle Order Entry should look. You can also decide whether to include orders on hold and/or taxes on uninvoiced orders. You must check at least one total credit exposure option. Credit checking rules are then tied to order types.

Order Types

You must define order types to link order cycles, standard value rule sets, and other important information together. You learned how to set up order types in the last chapter.

Holds

Follow the navigation path *Setup : Orders : Holds* to define the unique holds you plan to place on orders/returns.

You can set up holds with four hold types:

- Configurator Validation
- Credit Check

■ GSA Violation

■ Order Administration

You can decide at which cycle action the hold goes into effect. You can also select specific responsibilities that can apply or remove the hold. If you do not include any specific responsibility, then *any* responsibility can apply or remove this hold.

Note Categories

Follow the navigation path *Setup : Orders : Notes : Note Categories* to define one or more note categories. You must define at least one note category in order to apply notes.

You can assign a default datatype to each note category:

■ Short Text

■ Long Text

■ Image

■ OLE Object

■ Web Page

■ File

Notes

Follow the navigation path *Setup : Orders : Notes* to define one or more recurring standard notes. You enter the note category, the datatype, the usage, and the security for a note. You must also enter text for short or long text, or enter a URL for a Web page.

Notes can be applied on shipping documents such as pick slips and pack slips. You can apply additional rules for short text or long text. You can specify conditions that must be met before the note is automatically attached from the Special function in the Enter Orders form. You can also use the same condition number for an AND condition. A condition can be a specific customer, customer PO, invoice (bill) to customer, item, order type, or ship-to customer.

Shipping Document Printers

Follow the navigation path *Setup : Shipping : Choose Printers* to control which printers can be used for printing shipping documents from the Pick Release and Ship Confirm forms. In these cases, you would probably want to work with the system administrator or the IT group responsible for setting up printers in the system.

Shipping Document Sets

Follow the navigation path *Setup : Shipping : Document Sets* to set up shipping document sets. Shipping documents within a set can be printed in parallel or sequentially and are submitted automatically from the Pick Release and Ship Confirm forms.

Release Sequence Rules

You must define release sequence rules to define pick release line ordering.

Pick Slip Grouping Rules

You must define pick slip grouping rules to determine how release lines are grouped.

Container Load Relationships

Follow the navigation path *Setup : Shipping : Container Load Details* to specify container item relationships to the items that can be loaded within them. You enter the contained item and the items, and you also enter the maximum quantity allowed.

Shipping Parameters

Follow the navigation path *Setup : Shipping : Shipping Parameters* to define shipping parameters to be used as defaults. The Shipping Parameters form appears. See Figure 18-8.

You define the general shipping parameters, which are default weight UOM class, default volume UOM class, and the percent-fill basis. You also define the pick release parameters, which are the default release sequence rule, default pick slip grouping rule, whether to print the pick slip immediately or at the end, and the default pick release document set.

You define the departure planning parameters, which are the line assignment method and whether to perform weight/volume calculation automatically when departures and deliveries are planned. You define the default document set for ship confirming delivery, the default document set for ship confirming departure, whether to perform weight/volume calculations automatically, whether to enforce container inventory control, and whether to default to enforce packing in containers.

Release Rules

You can define shipping release rules to be used as templates for pick release or to be used to submit the Pick Release program through Standard Report Submission (SRS).

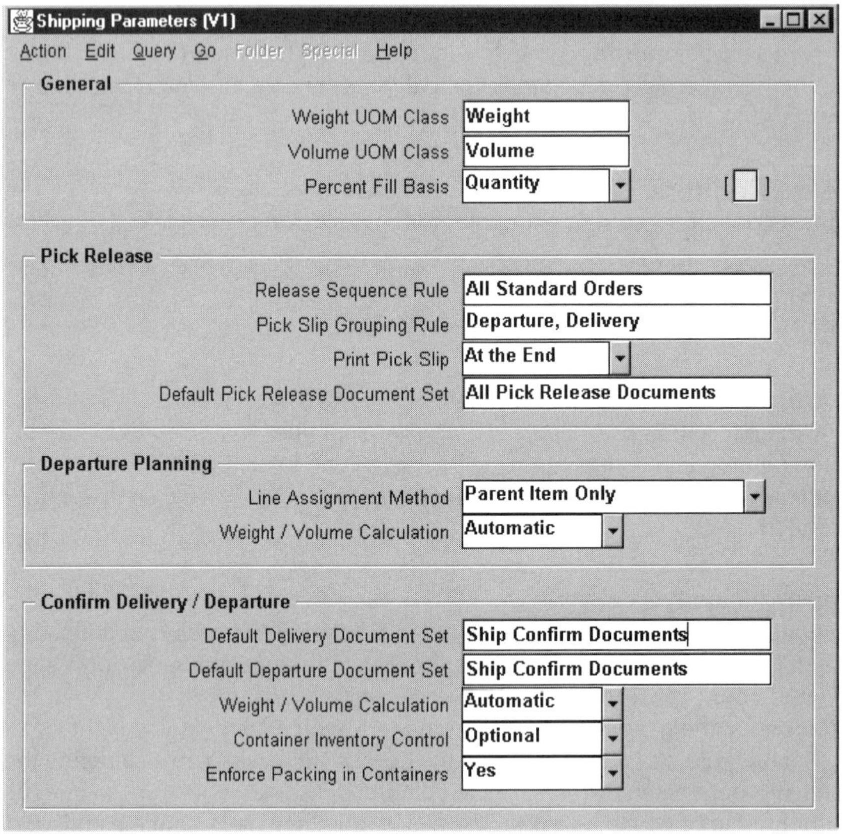

FIGURE 18-8. *Shipping Parameters form*

Review Questions

1. What is the difference between tax exemptions and tax exceptions?

2. What is the purpose of security rules?

3. How do you define a standard value rule set?

4. Where do you set up configuration/product structure in Oracle Applications?

Integrating Order Entry/Shipping and Receivables

Oracle Order Entry integrates and shares data with Oracle Receivables. Oracle Order Entry and Oracle Receivables also integrate with other Oracle applications.

In this section, you will learn how to:

■   Identify what data is shared between Order Entry/Shipping and Receivables

■   Determine what data can be imported from other applications through interface tables

Identifying Shared Data Between Order Entry/Shipping and Receivables

Oracle Order Entry and Oracle Receivables are tightly integrated. When an order is placed in Order Entry, it will create an invoice in Receivables. In addition, both Oracle Order Entry and Oracle Receivables populate and share the same customer master tables. Once a new customer is entered and saved in Order Entry, the customer data is immediately available in Receivables. Order Entry and Receivables also share the Oracle Inventory item master information.

In order for items to be ordered in Order Entry, the following item attributes must be flagged:

■   Customer Ordered

■   Customer Order Enabled

■   Shippable

■   OE Transactable

In order for items to be billed in Receivables, the following item attributes must be flagged:

■   Invoiceable Item

■   Invoice Enabled

Order Entry and Receivables share salesperson and territory information. Sales information is passed from Oracle Order Entry to Oracle Receivables. In addition, these two applications also share tax codes, tax locations, tax authorities, tax exemptions, and tax exceptions. Tax information is also passed from Order Entry to Receivables.

There are several setups that are also shared between Receivables and Order Entry. They are invoicing rules, accounting rules, payment terms, invoicing line order rules, invoicing grouping rules, AutoAccounting, transaction types, sales credit types, invoice sources, and Receivable QuickCodes. Sharing the setups allows Oracle Order Entry and Oracle Receivables to interface smoothly and to seamlessly pass data from customer orders to invoices.

Review Questions

1. What master data is shared between Oracle Receivables and Oracle Order Entry?

2. What setup data is shared between Oracle Receivables and Oracle Order Entry?

Determining Data Imported from Other Applications

Besides integrating between themselves, Oracle Receivables and Oracle Order Entry also integrate with other Oracle and non-Oracle applications using open interfaces.

The open interfaces in Oracle Order Entry are as follows:

- Order Import

- Ship Confirm Interface

The open interfaces in Oracle Receivables are as follows:

- Lockbox Interface

- Customer Interface

- AutoInvoice Import

- Sales Tax Rate Interface

Order Import

Oracle Order Entry can accept order data from various sources, which can be from outside sources for data conversion purposes or from third-party software for integration via Order Import. Order Import can also pull data from Oracle

Purchasing internal requisitions. Oracle EDI Gateway also populates the Oracle Order Entry open interfaces to import customer purchase orders. In addition, Order Import can pull orders from Oracle Sales and Marketing based on quote information.

Ship Confirm Interface

You can use the shipment interface to automatically confirm shipments. Ship confirmation closes out pick slips, creates freight charges, and updates shipped quantities in Oracle Inventory with shipping details. You can use Ship Confirm Interface for data conversion or integration purposes.

Lockbox Interface

You can use the Lockbox interface to automatically create receipts from your bank and external systems. The AutoLockbox process is run from the Submit Lockbox Processing form and requires extensive setup and a SQL*Loader control file.

Customer Interface

Oracle Receivables can accept customer data from outside sources for data conversion purposes, or it can accept data from third-party software that can be integrated. You can create new customers and addresses, along with updating existing information, through the interface. This additional information can be contacts, telephones, customer profile classes, bank accounts, and payment methods.

AutoInvoice Import

Oracle Receivables accepts invoice data from various sources, such as outside sources for data conversion purposes, and data from third-party software that can be integrated. AutoInvoice Import can also pull invoices from Oracle Order Entry based on customer order information, from Oracle Projects based on project billing, and from Oracle Cash Management for miscellaneous transactions based on banking activities.

The Receivables Interface program in Order Entry populates the open interfaces with order line information, and AutoInvoice Import in Receivables retrieves information and generates invoices based on the invoicing order rules and grouping rules.

Sales Tax Rate Interface

You can load sales tax rates into Oracle Receivables using the Sales Tax Rate interface. Information imported into Oracle Receivables performs address validation and provides valid and up-to-date tax rates.

Review Questions

1. What additional information can be loaded for a customer or a customer address?

2. What is AutoInvoice Import, and what other Oracle Application modules feed the AutoInvoice Open Interface tables?

3. Which two interfaces does Oracle Order Entry have?

4. What two functions do the data loaded by Sales Tax Rate Interface perform?

Entering and Correcting Transactions

Next, you will learn how to enter and correct transactions in Oracle Receivables. Transactions can be invoices, credit memos, debit memos, chargebacks, deposits, guarantees, and commitments. To enter and correct transactions in Oracle Receivables, you must switch to the *Receivables, Vision Operations (USA)* responsibility.

In this section, you will learn how to process and revise transactions (invoices, CM, DM, etc.), including sales tax or VAT.

Processing and Revising Transactions

Transactions in Oracle Receivables can be entered manually or imported from other sources using AutoInvoice Import. Transactions imported from outside sources into Oracle Receivables can be Oracle Applications modules, including Oracle Order Entry, Oracle Projects, and Oracle Cash Management, provided your system integrates with these modules.

Transactions can also be imported from third-party systems. You can use custom SQL*Loader programs, tailored for the specific third-party system, that load them into the AutoInvoice Open Interface tables.

Errors in transactions do occur, even though they may be detected after the transaction has been interfaced and revenue has been generated. Most errors can be corrected in Oracle Receivables.

Manual Transactions

To enter manual transactions, you go to the Transactions form. You can enter invoices, debit memos, credit memos, and commitments. You can enter transactions into the Transactions form, or you can enter transactions in batches in the Transaction Batches form. Batching transactions reduces chances of data entry error by comparing control data to actual data.

To enter transactions in batches, follow the navigation path *Transactions : Batches.* The Transaction Batches form appears. See Figure 18-9.

TRANSACTION BATCHES   You select an invoice source first. You can define your own invoice sources, but when you are entering transactions manually, only the invoice sources of type Manual. If automatic batch numbering is not enabled, manual can be used. You must enter a unique batch name.

The batch date defaults to the current date, although you can override it. The GL date defaults to the current date of the last day of the latest open period. You can override the GL date as well. Both date fields only serve as defaults for the transaction.

Currency defaults to the functional currency, but you can change it. Valid statuses for transaction batches are New, Out of Balance, Open, or Closed. New is the default. When you save a transaction in the transaction batch, if the actual data does not match the control data, the batch status is Out of Balance. If the data matches, then the batch status is Open until all transactions are all applied, or are on account. At that point, the status changes to Closed.

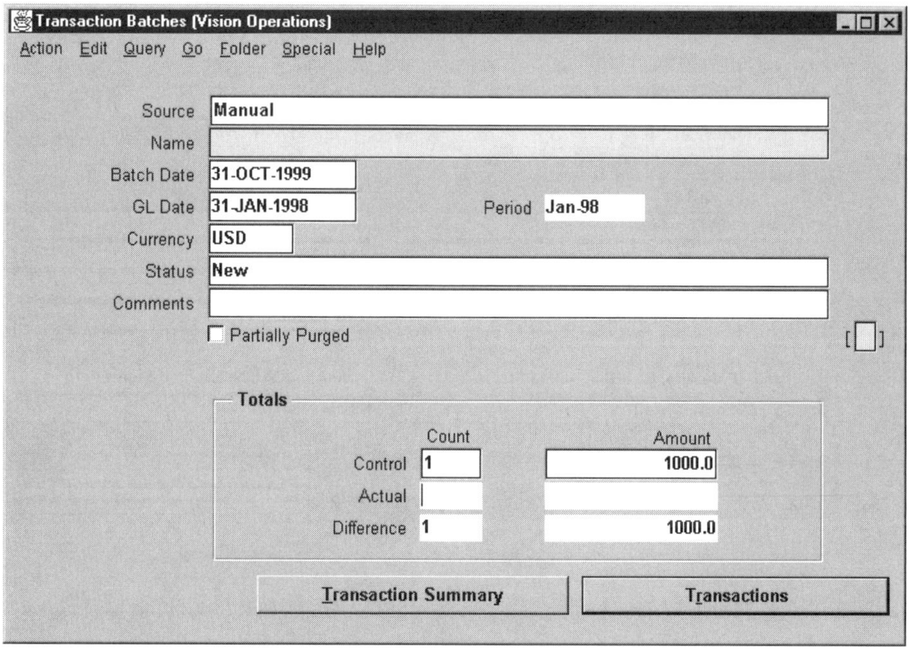

FIGURE 18-9.   *Transaction Batches form*

You can also enter an optional comment. If this batch is to be partially purged, then you would check the *Partially Purged* checkbox. You also enter the control count and the control amount. If you click on the **Transactions** button, the Transaction form appears and your cursor is in the Transaction Number field. See Figure 18-10.

However, for the purposes of this exercise, you will not enter a transaction batch.

TRANSACTIONS   For the purposes of this exercise, you will use the direct path. To go to the Transactions form directly, follow the navigation path *Transactions : Transactions.*

Your system should be set up to automatically number transactions for audit purposes; therefore, you do not need to enter a transaction number. Date, currency, and GL date all default. Date is the transaction date, and the GL date is the date used if you post the transaction to Oracle General Ledger. Select the appropriate value in the Class field using the List of Values. In the Type field, select the type of

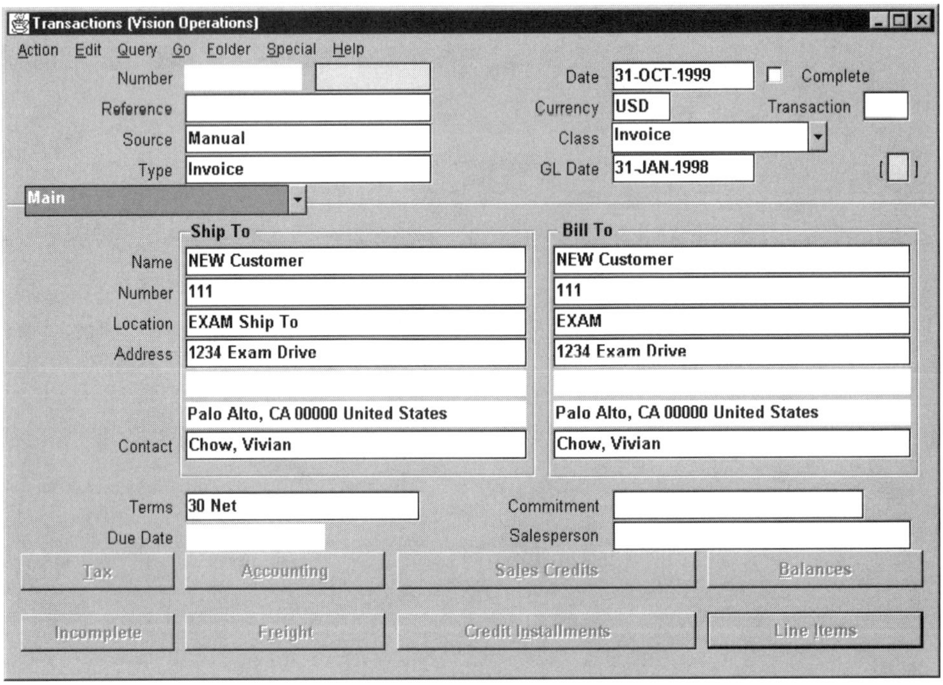

FIGURE 18-10.   *Transactions form*

the selected class. You may enter a reference to relate information. A reference might include an entry such as Check 555, invoice 123.

In the Main alternative region, enter the ship-to customer name or customer number from the List of Values. If the ship-to address is assigned to a bill-to address, then a bill-to customer and address should default into the fields under the Bill To Name, Number, Location, and Address fields. As an option, you can select a ship to contact. If you do not select either a ship-to or a bill-to address, you will not be able to print your transaction.

Your Terms field defaults first to the terms of the customer bill-to business purpose detail, then to the customer address, then to the customer, and last, to the transaction type. You can override this default if the customer's profile options allow overriding.

The due date populates automatically based on the terms. If a salesperson is assigned at the ship-to business purpose level, the due date is used. If not, the date used is the one at the bill-to business purpose level, and then at the customer level.

Next, select More for the alternative region. You can override the default invoicing rule and the print option. Determine how tax should be calculated. Valid choices are Standard, which follows the normal setup; Exempt, which means no tax; or Require, which always calculates tax.

Select a status for the transaction. The status comes from the lookup codes and is for informational purposes only.

Determine how you want to override the calculations for the finance charges. You can turn finance charges on or off, or select the *If Appropriate* option to follow your normal setup.

Enter a customer PO number, revision, and date. Select any transaction to which this transaction is related. Also, enter an agreement. If this is a disputed amount, you can change it. Add special instructions and a comment.

Select Remit To, Sales for the alternative region. The remit-to address defaults based on your customer bill-to address; however, you can override the remit-to address. Enter a sold-to customer that is different than the bill-to customer. You can override or enter a territory for the transaction.

Next, select Paying Customer for the alternative region. Change the paying customer to any customer that has a customer relationship with the bill-to customer and is allowed to pay. In this case, you must also specify a pay-to location. You can override or enter the payment method and bank accounts.

Select Notes for the alternative region. Add a note to the transaction in this alternative region. Select Manual as the source, Invoice as the class, Invoice as the type, and your customer as both the bill-to and the ship-to customer.

Save your work.

TRANSACTION LINES   To access the Lines form, click on the **Line Items** button in the Transaction form. The Lines form appears, as shown in Figure 18-11.

In the Lines form, your new transaction number is displayed at the top in the active menu bar. You can enter an item from the item master, or you can skip the item. If you select an item from the item master, you can change the item description. Selecting an item from the item master in Oracle Receivables does not utilize the price list and will not reduce on-hand quantity in the same way Oracle Order Entry does.

If you skip the Item field, you can select a standard memo line from the List of Values in the Description field. (Standard memo line is described later in the section on setups.) You cannot enter a description free-form until you first select an item from the List of Values. You can also override the defaulted UOM, if necessary.

In the Main alternative region, enter the quantity and the unit prices. The Amount field is calculated automatically. Enter a tax code if applicable. For the purposes of this exercise, select a standard memo line and enter an amount. Use tax code CST.

Next, select Sales Order for the alternative region. You can associate a sales order number, line number, order number, date, revision, and sales channel to the transaction line. You can enter any value. No validation will take place.

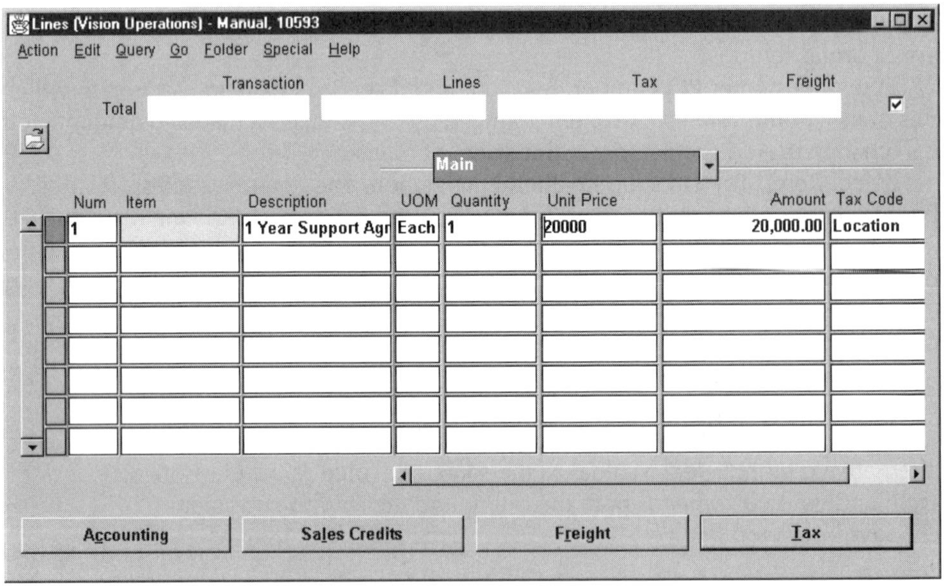

FIGURE 18-11. *Lines (Main) form*

Next, select Tax Exemptions for the alternative region. You can select Tax Handling. If you select Exempt, you must enter the exemption certificate number and an exemption reason.

Next, select More for the alternative region. You can enter a reason and a unique reference for the transaction line. Reasons are lookup codes.

Save your work.

You have now completed setting up the line items. Once you have saved the line information, the totals listed at the top are automatically updated.

ACCOUNTING   The way in which accounting information is generated depends on the accounting rules and the AutoAccounting setups. Click on the **Accounting** button. The Accounting form appears, as shown in Figure 18-12. This form shows the GL Account, % (percentage), and Amount fields. Accounting information of the same class can be split manually into more than one GL account

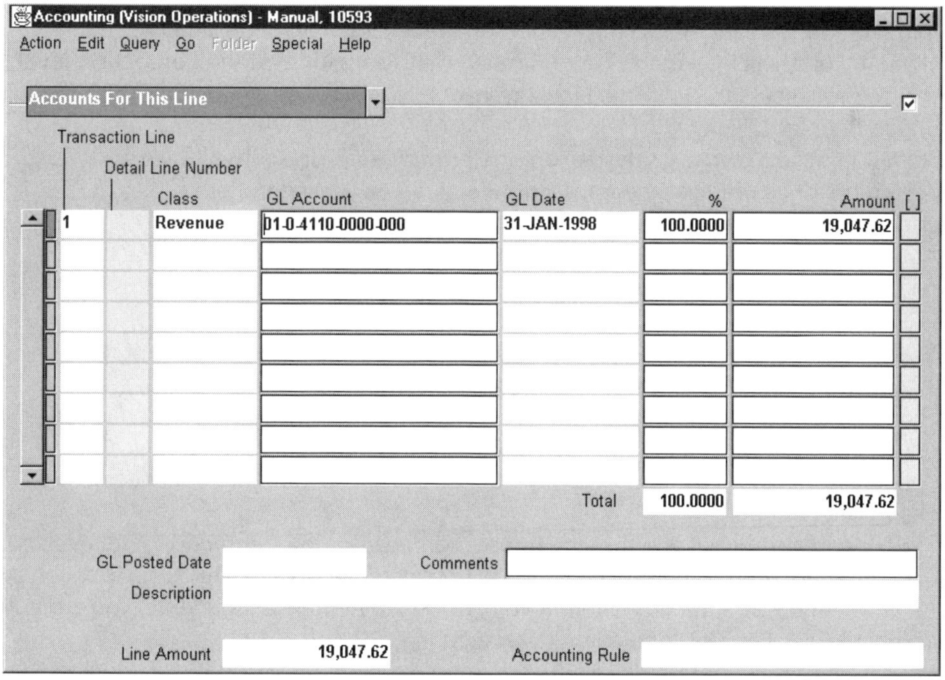

FIGURE 18-12. *Accounting form*

as long as the total percentage adds up to 100 percent. You cannot complete a transaction unless the total accounting equals 100 percent.

If you invoke the **Accounting** button from the transaction Lines form, you have two alternative regions. The Accounts for This Line alternative region shows the accounting information for the transaction line you are on. The Accounts for All Lines alternative region shows the accounting information for all transaction lines. You can see accounts of class Receivable, Tax, Freight, and Revenue. If you invoke the **Accounting** button from the transaction level, you can only see the Accounts for All Lines alternative region.

FREIGHT   If the *Allow Freight* option is not set to No, then you can enter freight information for the transaction or the transaction line. To enter freight charges to a transaction, click on the **Freight** button at the transaction level. To enter freight charges to a transaction line, click on the **Freight** button at the transaction line level.

You can enter a freight carrier, ship date, shipping reference, FOB, amount, and GL account. If you enter freight charges at the transaction level, you cannot set them at the line level.

SALES CREDITS   You can set sales credits at either the transaction level or the transaction line level. At the transaction line level, you can choose between the Default, For This Line, and For All Lines alternative regions. At the transaction level, you cannot access the For This Line alternative region. Click on the **Sales Credits** button to enter sales credits.

If you have a primary salesperson, the primary salesperson will have 100 percent revenue credit at the transaction level. If you change sales credits information, Oracle Receivables asks you whether you want to rerun AutoAccounting, which you only need to do if your AutoAccounting depends on GL accounts defined with the salesperson.

TAX   You can review the generated tax information in the Tax form. If the *Tax: Allow Manual Tax Lines* profile option is set to No, you cannot make any changes or enter any new tax lines. If the *Tax: Allow Override of Tax Code* profile option is set to No, you cannot change the tax code. If the *Allow Ad Hoc Tax* option is set to No, you cannot change the tax rate. You can enter a tax code or change the amount.

Tax can also be set at either the transaction level or the transaction line level. At the transaction line level, you can choose between the Tax For This Line, Tax For All Lines, and Tax Summary alternative regions. At the transaction level, you cannot access the Tax For This Line alternative region.

Return to the Transactions form and complete the transaction by clicking on the **Complete** button. Oracle Receivables first verifies that all the required information is filled. Also, the GL date must be in an open or future enterable period. Oracle

Receivables also verifies the transaction has at least one transaction line if it is not a freight invoice, and that the invoice sign agrees with the creation sign of the transaction type. The accounting distributions total for each line must be equal to the transaction line amount.

Other conditions for completing a transaction include:

■ Specifying freight account for any freight charges entered

■ Entering tax for each transaction line except if the lines type *Charges if Calculate Tax* option for the transaction type is set to Yes

■ Assigning salespersons to each transaction line if *Require Salesreps* is enabled in system options and all quota credit adds up to exactly 100 percent

If this transaction uses an automatic payment method, a customer bank account must also be entered.

If all required fields are entered and all the above conditions are met, Oracle Receivables completes the transaction by checking the *Complete* checkbox. If information is missing or any condition failed, you will receive error messages. You must complete the transaction before the transaction can be posted or can be shown on an aging report, even if the transaction type allows both actions. Also, completing a transaction generates the payment schedules based on payment term. You can use the **Incomplete** button to reset the transaction back to be incomplete.

AutoInvoice

AutoInvoicing processes transactions automatically. You can interface transactions from other Oracle application modules such as Oracle Order Entry, Oracle Projects, and Oracle Cash Management. If the application where the error occurred reports to the Oracle General Ledger, such as when generating invoices using the Projects application, then corrections should be made in the originating application to ensure that the subledgers do not post conflicting information to the Oracle General Ledger.

To invoke AutoInvoicing through SRS, follow the navigation path *Interfaces : AutoInvoice.* Select a single request, and then select the AutoInvoice Master program.

You can narrow your parameters for the program down to a single transaction, or a selection from a variety of ranges. Parameters for the AutoInvoice Master Program include the invoice source, Transaction flexfield, and transaction type, among others. You can also select whether to base the due date on transaction date, as well as the number of due date adjustment days. (The Transaction flexfield is explained in the section "Implementing and Setting Up Receivables.") Click on the **OK** button to submit the program.

Once you have interfaced your transactions to the Oracle General Ledger, you can no longer make online updates. In this case, you must make changes to transactions by creating offset transactions or adjustments, rather than correcting the transaction itself. If, in the system profile options, you have disabled the *Allow Change to Printed Invoice* option and a transaction is created and printed, it cannot be adjusted online, even if it has not been interfaced to the General Ledger. To make changes to invoices after they have been printed but before they have been interfaced to General Ledger, you can set the *Allow Change to Printed Invoice* profile option to Yes.

Next, you will learn how to make adjustments, update original invoices, create offset transactions, and void transactions.

Manual Adjustments

Follow the navigation path *Transactions : Transaction Summary* to adjust a transaction. Query the transaction that must be adjusted. With your cursor on the correct transaction, click on the **Adjustments** button (which appears only if a balance exists on the transaction). The Adjustments form appears. See Figure 18-13.

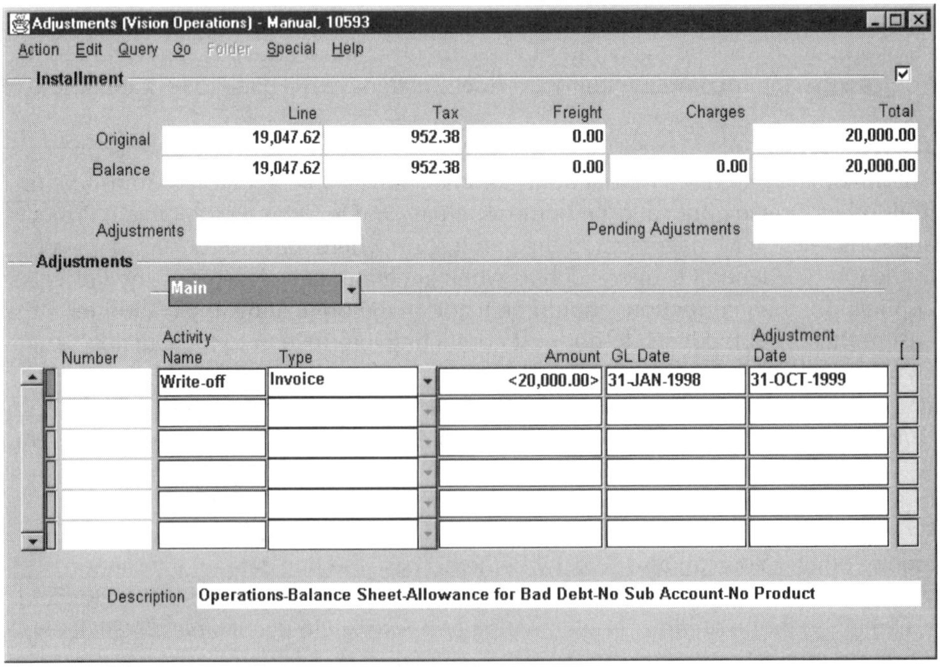

FIGURE 18-13.   *Adjustments form*

Within the Adjustments form in the Main alternative region, select an activity from the List of Values. In the Type field, select a valid type, which can be Invoice, Line, Charges, Freight, or Tax. Once you select a type, you cannot change it. If you select Invoice type, the entire amount remaining due defaults into the Amount field as a credit and you cannot change it. If you select one of the other types, you must enter the amount of the balance due that you wish to adjust. The difference between the amount remaining and the amount you enter remains on the invoice as a balance due. If you allow overapplication, you can enter a negative amount that is more than the balance to allow the balance to go negative. The system date defaults as the GL date and adjustment date. However, you can override the dates.

Next, select Account, IDs for the alternative region. The General Ledger account to which the adjustment is charged appears. This is driven by the activity you selected. You can also override this account. You can enter a document number if document sequencing is enabled. You can also select a transaction line number to which to apply the adjustment.

Select Comments for the alternative region. You may enter a reason by selecting from the List of Values. You may enter any comments in the Comments field. The comments are displayed for a manager to easily review should the adjustment be above your limit. Many users are restricted to the dollar-amount authority they can adjust. If the adjustment is over the dollar-amount authority, the Status field displays a Waiting Approval status, and a person with the appropriate authority must approve the adjustment. Valid statuses are Approved, More Research, or Waiting Approval.

For the purposes of this exercise, select your transaction and enter a line type adjustment with the Write-off activity name. Enter **-$200** as the amount and save your work. An adjustment number is assigned whether the status is Approved or Waiting Approval.

Automatic Adjustments

Use the Automatic Adjustments function to clear balances due on transactions that fall within a certain parameter. This quickly eliminates leftover balances from receipt applications to reduce user time spent adjusting each transaction individually. To initiate automatic adjustments, follow the navigation path *Control : Adjustments : Create Auto Adjustments*. The Create Autoadjustments form appears. See Figure 18-14.

The invoice currency defaults to the functional currency. Selection criteria include remaining amount range, remaining % range, due date range, transaction type range, customer name range, customer number range, and Transaction flexfield combination. You can fill in as many fields as necessary to reduce the criteria for transactions eligible to be adjusted.

Next, select an activity. This activity determines the GL account to which to adjust all the balances. Select the type of transactions to adjust. Type can be Charge

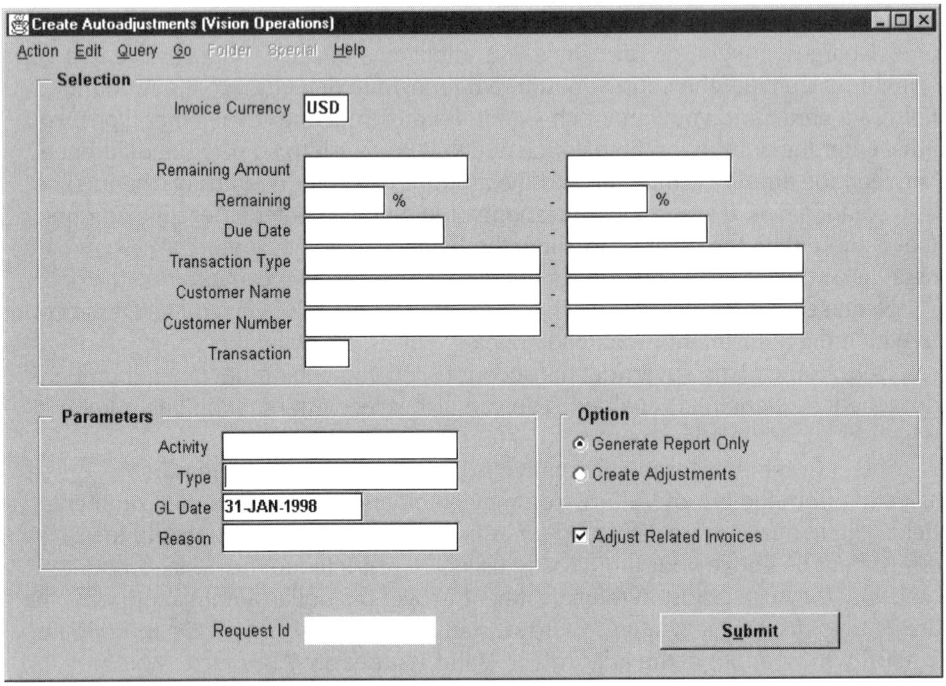

FIGURE 18-14. *Create Autoadjustments form*

Adjustments, Freight Adjustments, Invoice Adjustments, Line Adjustments, and Tax Adjustments. This reduces all the transactions that fall within the criteria to a zero balance for that type of items, such as freight, tax, or the whole invoice. You can override a GL date that defaults to the current date or the last day of the latest open period. You may also opt to select a reason.

In the Option region, specify to either generate a report of what would be adjusted or to go ahead and create the adjustments. You can also choose to adjust related invoices. Submit the request by clicking on the **Submit** button.

Original Invoices

You can update certain information in the transaction at various stages of the transaction. These stages are when the transaction is incomplete, when the transaction is completed, when the transaction has rules, when the transaction is printed, when the transaction has activities against it, and when the transaction is posted. Use the Transactions Summary form (Transactions Workbench) or the

Transactions form to query the transaction you wish to adjust. Copied transaction does not prevent you from updating a transaction. Once the form is populated, click on the **Open** button. If the transaction is complete yet has no activities applied or has not been posted, click on the **Incomplete** button on the Transaction Header form to reset the transaction to Incomplete. You can make any changes to any part of the transaction that allows changes if the transaction is incomplete.

Save your changes, and click on the **Complete** button to complete the transaction again. If you check the *Allowed Change to Printed Transactions* checkbox in the system options, you cannot update transactions after the transactions are printed.

Debit Memos

You use a debit memo to increase a receivable balance for a customer when there is no sale or inventory in the transaction, such as for a nonsufficient funds (NSF) fee, or to charge for an incorrect price on an existing invoice. (Creating debit memos is covered in the next chapter.) Customers with a credit receivable balance may be entitled to a refund. Usually, this is determined after account reconciliation. You cannot issue a refund from Receivables. However, you can easily generate the proper accounting entries and issue a check through your Payables module.

For a refund, your debit memo accounting entries should debit Receivables and credit a Payables clearing account. Apply the credit on the customer's account to the newly created debit memo. This creates a zero, or reduced receivable, balance for the customer. Create a check through your Payables system, creating an invoice that debits the Payables module, clears the account, and credits the Payables liability account. Finally, issue a check that debits the Payables liability account and credits the cash account.

Credit Memos

You use a credit memo to credit a single invoice, or part of a single invoice to make corrections for whole invoices, tax lines charge in error, freight lines, or even to give an across the board percentage discount. The details about doing this are covered in the next chapter.

On Account Credit

You create an on account credit when the customer does not necessarily require a credit to a specific invoice. This type of credit ages on the customer's account and can be applied alone or with a receipt to any debit item. This allows the customer some control over which invoices to use the credit against. You can also create an on account credit to process refunds; this procedure is covered in detail in the next chapter.

Void

You may need to delete or void incomplete or incorrect transactions in order to process your period end closing, or as a matter of record maintenance. To identify all the incomplete transactions, you can run the Incomplete Invoices report. Query the selected invoice that you want to delete. Click on the **Delete Record** button. Remember to save after you delete, or only the record will disappear from the view, not the tables. Your system option *Allow Invoice Deletion* must be enabled to delete transactions.

If the system options do not allow for a transaction to be deleted, the transaction can be voided. You can void transactions if there is no activity against them and they have not posted to Oracle General Ledger. To void a transaction, you should set up a transaction type named VOID in the Transaction form. Set up this VOID transaction to not post to General Ledger and to not be an open receivable. Click on the **Incomplete** button. Change the transaction type to VOID. This is now essentially a dead invoice. Save your changes and click on the **Complete** button to complete the transaction.

Review Questions

1. What are the two ways you can enter transactions?

2. How is accounting information generated?

3. Is there a difference between clicking on the **Freight** button from the Transactions form vs. the Transaction Lines form?

4. Which Oracle Applications modules are sources for AutoInvoicing?

5. Which adjustment method do you use if you want to write off the balances of all invoices with a balance of $10 or less?

6. How do you handle a refund?

7. Under what conditions can you adjust a transaction online?

8. How would you set up a VOID transaction type?

Entering and Applying Receipts for Customers

This section teaches you how to enter and apply receipts to customers. When the invoices are completed, you can enter and apply receipts to reduce the customer balance.

In this section, you will learn how to receive and apply payments from customers to specific invoices, or to their accounts

Receiving and Applying Payments

One of the primary functions of Oracle Receivables is to receive payments against open invoices. You can apply payments received to invoices or to customer accounts. You can apply payments to customer amounts when payments are made in advance or when payments are not easily identified with specific invoices. Receipts can be applied singly, or in batches for better control when you process large volumes of receipts. You can apply a single receipt to a single transaction or to multiple transactions. Multiple receipts can also be applied to a single transaction or to multiple transactions. When you cannot find an open transaction to apply the receipt(s) against, you can apply it to the customer account, reducing the customer overall balance until the remittance information is supplied.

Receipt Batches

You can use the receipt batch to group multiple receipts. To define receipt batches, follow the navigation path *Receipts : Batches*. The Receipt Batches form appears. See Figure 18-15.

Your default batch type is Manual-Regular, and it is your primary method for entering a batch. The Automatic batch type is used for processing automatic receipts for the automatic functions. (Processing automatic receipts is described in the next chapter.) The Manual-Quick batch type is used to enter receipts that are automatically applied to transactions by the Post QuickCash program. In most cases, however, you should use the default of Manual-Regular.

The Date region automatically defaults in all three date fields: Batch, GL, and Deposit. The batch and deposit dates default with the system date. The GL date defaults with either the system date or the last date of the latest period.

Select a batch source. The batch source should be defaulted if the *AR: Receipt Batch Source* profile option is set. The Currency, Receipt Class, Payment Method, Bank Name, and Account Number fields also default. However, you have the option to override them.

Enter a unique batch name if automatic batch numbering is not enabled for the selected batch source. In the Totals region, enter the control totals for your batch. Enter any comments in the Comments field.

In the Transmission region, the batch status defaults to New. As you enter receipts, and if the actual count and amount do not match the control count and amount, the status displays as Out of Balance. If the actual count and amount match, but you have unapplied or unidentified receipts, the batch status displays as Open. If all the receipts are applied or placed on account, then the batch status

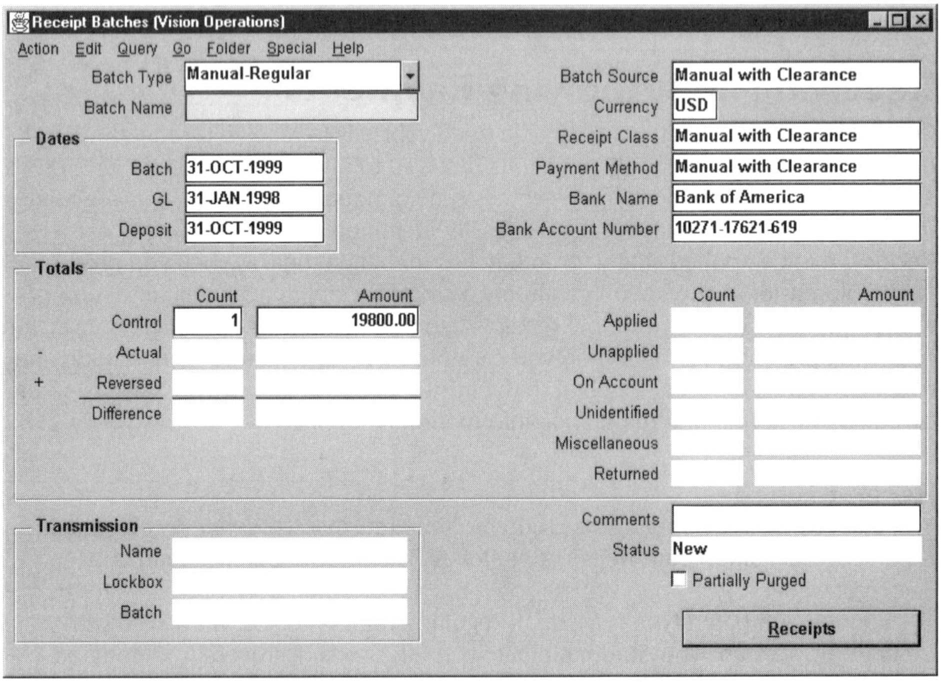

FIGURE 18-15. *Receipt Batches form*

displays as Closed. You can also determine if the receipt batch can be partially purged by checking the *Partially Purged* checkbox.

For the purposes of this exercise, create a Manual-Regular batch type. Select Manual with Clearance as the batch source. Enter **1** as the control count and **$19,800** as the control amount. Save your work. To add receipts to the batch, click on the **Receipts** button. The Receipt Summary form displays.

You can enter receipts in either the Summary form or the Receipts form. If you are in the Summary form, click on the **New** button. The Receipts form appears. From this point forward, the process is identical to applying a single receipt, which is described in the next section.

Oracle Receivables automatically updates the status of your batch after you enter all the receipts. If all payments are applied correctly, your batch has a status of Closed. If funds have been left unapplied, the batch does not close and the batch status displays as Open. If funds do not total the control totals, the batch does not close and the status displays as Out of Balance.

You can correct the amount on the receipts in the batch, or you can correct the batch control total. To close a batch with unapplied cash, apply the receipt(s) to on account, or apply the receipt(s) to open debit items.

Receipts

You can enter receipts in two ways. You can follow the navigation path *Receipts : Receipts* to use the Receipts form to enter receipts directly without a batch, or you can click on the **Receipts** button to use the Receipts form to enter receipts into a batch.

Figure 18-16 shows the Receipts form. In this form, you enter information regarding the payment.

The first field is the Receipt Number field, which is critical to locating receipts and cannot be changed once it is entered. The receipt number is not an automatic field, nor can it be defaulted to create receipt numbers in sequence. This field is to

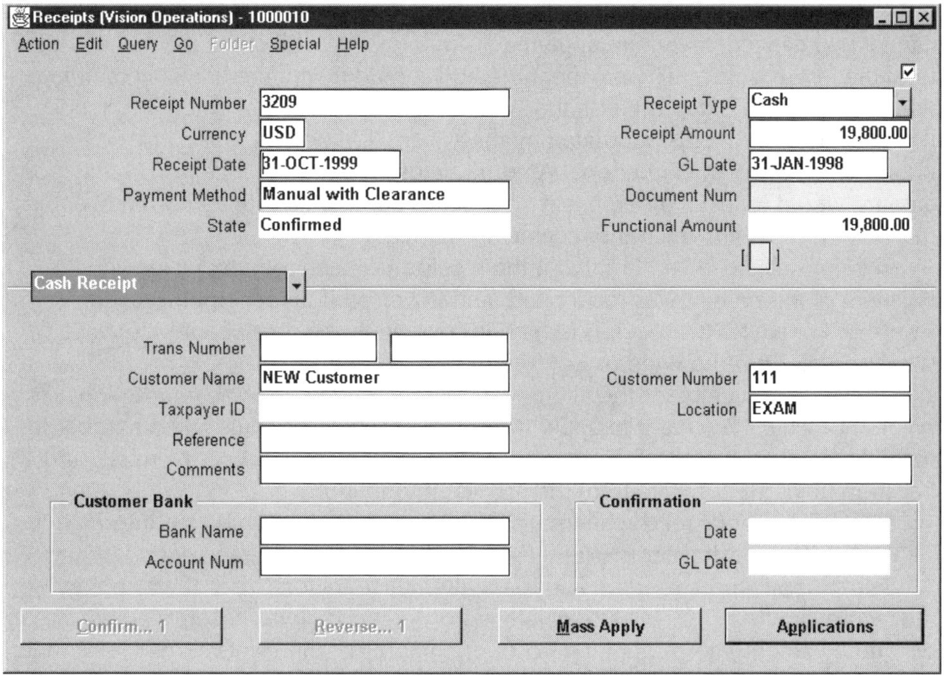

FIGURE 18-16. *Receipts form*

record the customer's check number, cash receipt-book number, electronic fund transfer number, etc.

The receipt type defaults as Cash. Cash refers to the application of funds associated with an open receivable. The funds with type Cash must be applied to a customer's on account or to an open debit item. The other receipt type, Misc, is used to apply cash directly to a General Ledger account as a credit. Misc type receipts are described in the next chapter.

To apply funds to a customer's account or to open items, leave the default of Cash for the type. The currency defaults according to your system setup. However, you have the option of changing it. Remember that whenever you select a foreign currency, you must enter the exchange rate information. The receipt amount is the amount of the receipt in its existing currency. This figure can be changed if the receipt is not applied to any invoices, and if the receipt has not been interfaced to the General Ledger.

The receipt date and GL date default; however, the receipt date may be changed in order to reflect a postmark date policy, for instance. The receipt date determines the discount eligibility for invoices sold on discounting terms. The GL date may be changed to a date that reflects a date in an open period.

If you are using receipt batch, the payment method defaults from the batch and cannot be changed. If you are applying a single receipt, select the payment method from the List of Values. The payment method should reflect the bank account into which the receipt is deposited. If the system is set up to use document sequences, the document number is populated by the system. Otherwise, enter a manual number. The State and Functional Amount fields fill in automatically. The functional amount would reflect a difference if your Set of Books was using a currency other than the currency in which the receipt was issued.

Receipt status can be Remitted if the receipt has been remitted, Cleared if the payment of this receipt was reconciled, and Reversed if the receipt has been reversed. For automatic receipts (which is covered in the next chapter), receipt status can also be Approved or Confirmed.

Select Cash Receipt for the alternative region. If you know the transaction number to which you want to apply the payment, enter the transaction number in the right-hand field of the Transaction fields. The Customer Name, Number, and Location fields all populate from the invoice information.

Select Remittance for the alternative region to override remittance information. This includes deposit date, maturity date, bank name, branch, and account number.

Select Application from the Summary alternative region to see the summary of the receipt application. This alternative region shows how the receipts are distributed among the applied, on account, unapplied, discounts earned, discounts unearned, and unidentified buckets.

Select Reversal for the alternative region to see any reversal information. This includes reversal date, GL date, reversal category, reason, and comments, among other things. Then select Cash Management for the alternative region. If this receipt comes from Oracle Cash Management, you will see the statement number, statement date, and line number. You can enter an effective date in the Reversal alternative region.

Select Notes Receivable for the alternative region. Within this region, you can use the issuer name, issue date, issuer bank name, and issuer bank branch.

If you click on the **Applications** button, the system automatically applies the amount to the invoice you specified. If the invoice amount and the receipt amount are not identical, then you must go to the Applications form to modify how the remaining amount should be applied.

If you do not know the specific invoice to apply the payment against, enter the customer name in the Customer Name field or customer number in the Customer Number field. Once you enter this information, the other customer fields populate. If there is only one location, it is populated as well. Otherwise, you must select a location.

For the purposes of this exercise, enter your customer in the Customer field. Click on the **Applications** button to proceed to the Applications form, which is shown in Figure 18-17.

The customer information entered in the receipt header is displayed at the top of the form. The currency and receipt amount is also displayed. The amount available to apply to open transactions is shown as Unapplied. If you have remittance information from your customer that specifies which invoice to apply the receipt against, you may type the invoice in the Transaction Number field. If you do not know the transaction number, use the List of Values to see all the open items available for that customer or any related customers. From the List of Values, select the invoice to pay. On account is always an option in the List of Values.

TIP
While applying several invoices from one receipt, the List of Values continues to show selected invoices from previous lines until you save the applications. Be careful to not select the same invoice twice, or save between each line to remove the selected invoices from the list. If the application is saved to the database, the Saved *checkbox is checked.*

The Amount Applied and the Discount fields default as you place your cursor in each field. The default amount is either the remaining amount of receipt or the remaining amount of invoice, whichever is lower. You can also change the amount. The *Apply* checkbox is automatically checked. If you scroll horizontally, you can change the GL date, the apply date, and you can apply the receipt to a particular transaction line.

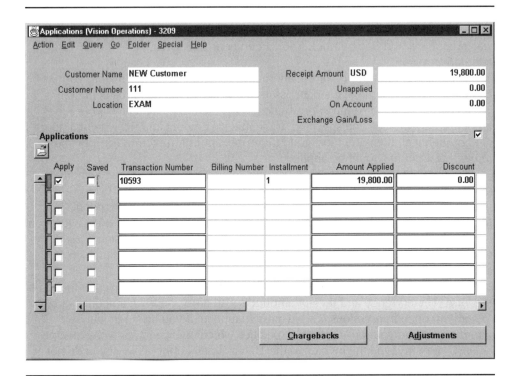

FIGURE 18-17. *Applications form*

You have now finished applying the receipt to one transaction or one transaction line. Repeat the transaction selection and amount application until you are left with no unapplied funds. You can select an existing on account credit and credit memo to be used together with receipts to be applied to transactions. To include an on account credit and credit memo, select them as one of the transactions to which to apply the receipt.

For the purposes of this exercise, use the List of Values and select the invoice you have created. Save your application. The *Saved* checkbox is checked and the status for the receipt displays as Confirmed.

TIP

On account credit must be created as a credit memo with a line item of on account credit. Applying a receipt to an on account creates an on account balance, but is not considered an on account credit until you create the credit memo. The next chapter contains more details about creating an on account credit.

If invoices and a receipt do not match, you can create a chargeback, adjust off in a short paid situation, place funds to an on account, or adjust off in an overpaid situation. To place the remainder to on account, simply select On Account as the transaction number from the List of Values and the remaining receipt amount defaults. This creates an on account balance. To short pay, you can create a chargeback.

Chargebacks

A chargeback is generally used to close an open invoice that may have disputed lines or charges, such as a customer that takes a discount past the date. Instead of refusing the receipt, the payment is applied and the balance of the invoice is rebilled on a new invoice number. The new invoice is generally due immediately, and begins aging the next day. The old invoice is automatically closed, and aging is completed. Oracle Receivables references the new chargeback with the original invoice number automatically. You can relate this to invoices for informational purposes.

To create a chargeback, from the Applications form select the line that specifies the invoice to be charged back. Then, click on the **Chargeback** button. The Chargebacks form appears. See Figure 18-18.

In the Main alternative region, select the type of chargeback. The remaining amount is defaulted into the Amount field. You may override the GL account if

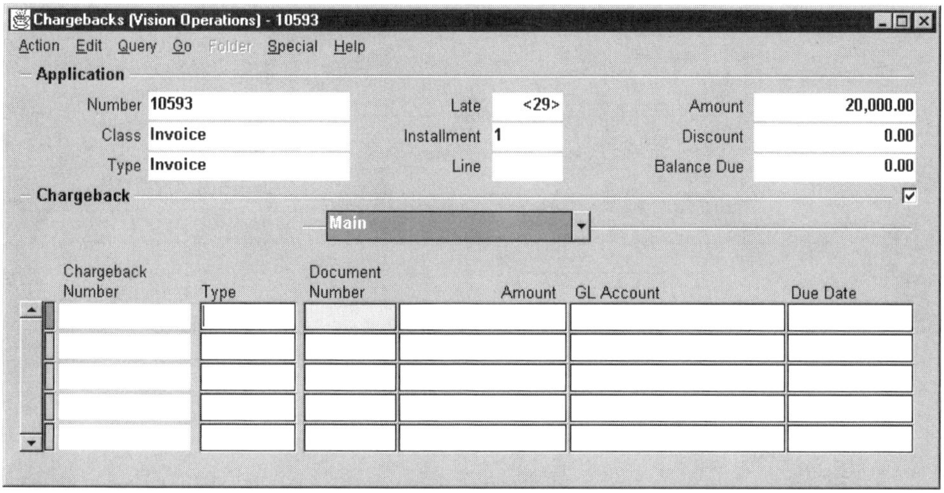

FIGURE 18-18. *Chargebacks form*

necessary. Change regions by selecting More for the alternative region. Enter a reason from the List of Values and any comments in the Reason and Comments fields, respectively. These are optional fields.

Save your work.

Adjustments

To adjust or write off the remaining amount, you can create adjustments. To create adjustments, from the Applications form select the line that specifies the invoice to be adjusted. Then, click on the **Adjustments** button. The Adjustments form appears. See Figure 18-19. Enter all the necessary fields and determine the type to which the adjustment is applied. Save your adjustments. An adjustment number is assigned whether the status is Approved or Waiting Approval.

Mass Apply

You can use the Mass Apply function to let Oracle Receivables apply your receipt to transactions for a single customer and a location based on sorting criteria that you

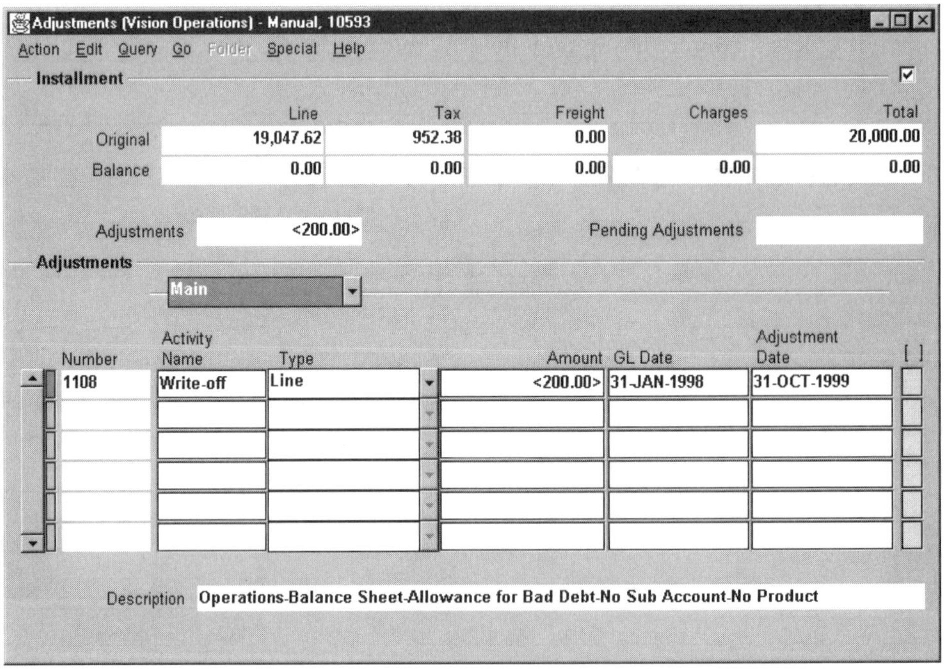

FIGURE 18-19. *Adjustments form*

select. This is useful for customers with large volumes of invoices that are paid with a single check. By using this feature, you retain the option of not selecting specific invoices before applying and posting the receipt.

To use Mass Apply, you enter the customer name or the customer number. Enter a location, unless your customer only has one location. Click on the **Mass Apply** button in the Receipts form. The Mass Apply form appears. See Figure 18-20.

The Customer Name, Number, and Location fields default from the receipt header information you entered. Other defaulted fields include the Primary Sort Criteria in Ascending Order, the Apply Date field (which is the system date), and the types of debit items included in the sorting and application. All items are selected by default except for disputed transactions.

You have the option to restrict the target applications. You can select from Transaction Type Range, Transaction Number Range, Due Date Range, Transaction Date Range, and Balance Range. Next, you can override the primary sort criteria and, as an option, enter a secondary sort criteria.

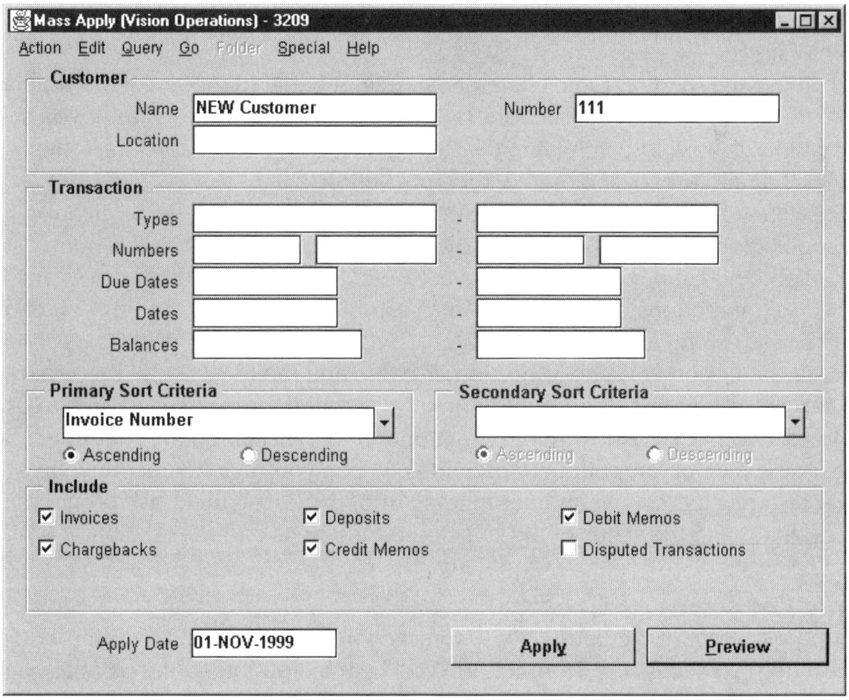

FIGURE 18-20. *Mass Apply form*

In most cases, you select the due date as either the primary or secondary sort criterion. Most businesses are concerned with the age of their receivables, and most do not pay the oldest invoice, but the oldest aging past due invoice, if the customer purchases on various terms. Other sort criteria are balance due, invoice due, and billing number.

If you do not want Oracle Receivables to mark the selected transactions for applications, you may select the **Preview** button. Otherwise, the **Apply** button marks the transactions for applications automatically. Both actions take you to the Applications form, which displays all the transactions that fit your selection criteria.

Once you put in your sorting criteria, click on the **Apply** button. All open items are displayed in the form in the sorting criteria you specified. You can update amounts in the Amount field and make adjustments until your Unapplied balance field, shown at the top right corner of the form, displays zero. You may also deselect any line, and then select any other line you prefer to apply the receipt against.

As with a single transaction, you can adjust or charge back amounts by selecting the line, then clicking on the appropriate buttons. Even though the *Apply* checkboxes are marked, you still must save your work to update the system to reflect the mass applications.

QuickCash

You can use the Manual-Quick batch type receipt batch to enter receipts that are automatically applied to transactions by the Post QuickCash program. If you select Manual-Quick as your batch type, the **Post QuickCash** button appears in the Receipt Batches form. Click on the **Receipts** button.

Enter the QuickCash receipts by entering the amounts and the application types. The application types are AutoCash Rule Set, Single, Multiple, On-Account, Unapplied, and Unidentified. If you select AutoCash Rule Set, the receipts are applied to transactions based on the AutoCash rules defined in the set. You cannot enter QuickCash receipts without a batch.

Enter the customer name, or customer name and the location, of the receipt. You can enter the transaction number if known, and the receipt is applied to only one transaction. If you know the transaction numbers, click on the **Multiple** button to apply the receipt to multiple transactions. When you save the records, the QuickCash receipts stay in an interim table until the Post QuickCash program is run. At that point, the status of the selected transactions and the receipts is updated.

Apply On Account Credit

To apply on account credit directly to transactions, you can use the Transaction Workbench. To access the Transaction Workbench, you follow the navigation path *Transactions : Transactions Summary*. The Transactions Summary form appears.

Query the on account credit and click on the **Applications** button. Select the transaction to which you want to apply the on account credit.

Review Questions

1. What is a chargeback, and when do you create one during receipt application?

2. When do you create an adjustment during receipt application?

3. When do you use Mass Apply feature?

4. How do you use on account credit or a credit memo in conjunction with receipts to apply to transactions?

Tracking and Collecting Past Due Receivables

This section covers how to track and collect past due receivables. You can run reports to find all the past due receivables, and then you can use collection tools provided by Oracle Receivables to collect past due receivables.

In this section, you will learn how to identify past due receivables and administer collection activities

Identifying Past Due Receivables and Administering Collection Activities

All companies that carry receivables are concerned with the aging of their open invoices and the collection of those that are past due. Oracle Receivables provides you with multiple ways to find customers with past due invoices, debits, and chargebacks.

Reports

Two reports are the most useful for identifying invoices that are unpaid beyond their terms, or for identifying customers with past due balances. These are both standard Oracle reports and can be submitted following the navigation path *Reports : Collections.*

The two reports are:

- Past Due Invoice report
- Aged Trial Balance report

PAST DUE INVOICE REPORT   You can run this report sorted by customer, the balance due, or by the salesperson. You can also enter one sorting criteria, or a range of collectors, customer names, customer numbers, or the days late.

AGED TRIAL BALANCE REPORTS   You can run this report in six different formats, including the GL accounts, the amounts, the collector, or by salesperson. These formats run in the seven-bucket format. You can also simply run an aged trial balance by seven buckets or four buckets, sorting by customer or type.

Online Inquiry

You can perform an online inquiry to identify past due receivables for any specific customer. You can also use a series of inquiry forms to view the customer account status. (These forms are discussed in detail in the next chapter.) To identify past due receivables across all customers, run the previously mentioned reports. To identify past due receivables for a specific customer, run the reports or use online inquiry. Once you gather the information, you can contact the customer for collections.

Customer Calls

You can use the Customer Calls form to record very specific information regarding your contact with the customer. These records could be helpful in litigation as well as daily collection activities. To get to the Calls form, follow the navigation path *Collections : Customer Calls.* The Customer Calls form appears. See Figure 18-21.

The computer assigns the call ID number automatically. The collector must be selected from the List of Values. This field is not automatically selected, as you may be handling another collection agent's account when a phone call is taken. You can place your name or your collector ID on the call, even if the account belongs to another collector. The Date and Time fields default to the system date and time. Status defaults as Open. You can enter a transaction number if you know the transaction number to which this is related. When you enter the transaction number, the customer information fields populate.

In the Customer region, enter the customer information, including location. The remaining fields default. For the purposes of this exercise, select any collector and select your customer.

In the Contact alternative region, select a contact name from the List of Values. If you do not select a contact or the contact is not on the List of Values, enter the contact information directly into the First Name, Last Name, and Job Title fields. When you save the customer call, the contact information is added to your permanent customer record automatically. If you select a contact, you can also select a phone number and a fax number, or you can enter new numbers and telephone numbers that will also be added to the permanent customer records automatically.

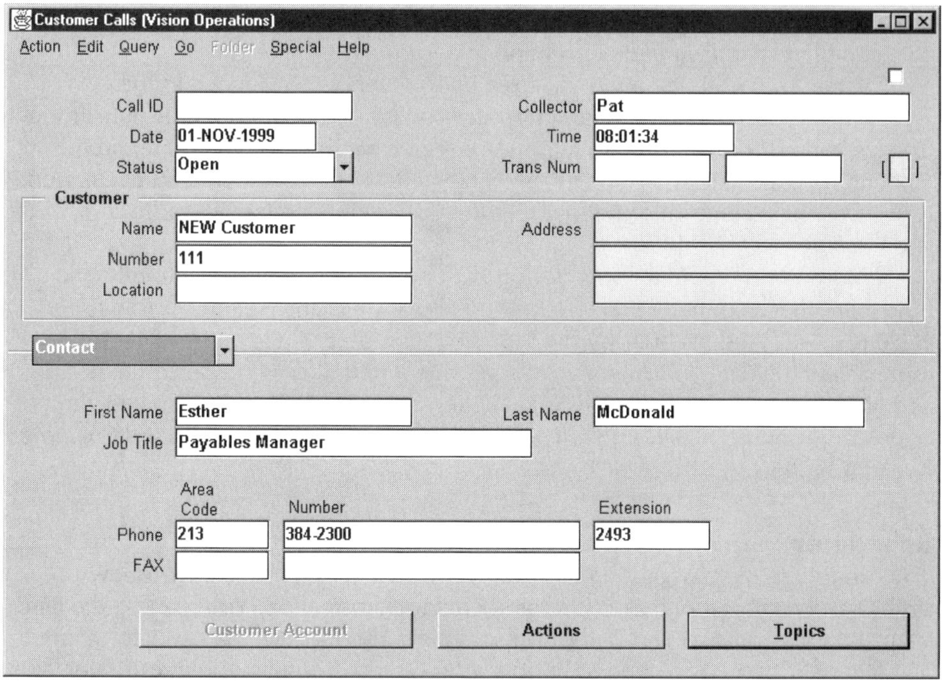

FIGURE 18-21. *Customer Calls form*

Next, select Response for the alternative region. Select a response, outcome, and follow-up action from the List of Values. The choices are based on predefined lookup codes. If you select a follow-up action, you can enter a follow-up action date. Check the *Complete* checkbox if the follow-up action is completed and you want to change the status to Closed.

You can add a note and select any appropriate follow-up action. If the customer promises you a date to pay, enter the date and the currency and amount in the Promise region. Enter your own forecast date and the percentage you expect to receive.

For the purposes of this exercise, enter a new contact name and numbers. Record a response, outcome, and follow-up action in the Response alternative region. Save your work.

If you do not want to record the response information at the customer level, then you can click on the **Topics** button to record the response information at the transaction level or even at the transaction line level. In the Main region, enter or select the transaction or receipt number in the Number field. Select from the List of Values for the Outcome, Response, and Action columns. Enter in the follow-up date and check the *Complete* checkbox, if appropriate.

Change to Note in the alternative region to enter notes. Change to the Transaction alternative region for a transaction line number and the dispute amount. Change to the Promise/Forecast alternative region for the promised date, promised amount, forecast date, and forecast percentage. Use the Receipt alternative region to see existing receipts information. Use the Call region to change the collector and the date.

If you wish to record a conversation with no specific transaction to reference, or to mark the account for some follow-up, move on to the Actions form by clicking on the **Actions** button from either the Customer Calls or the Call Topics form. Select the date, follow-up action, dispute amount, notes, a person to notify, and, if appropriate, mark the follow-up action as Completed. You can view the customer account status from the Customer Calls form by clicking on the **Customer Account** button.

Scheduler

You can follow the navigation path *Collections : Scheduler* to see the follow-up actions and dates, as well as history and contact information. You can use the Find form and locate and review collection activities. You can use the collector name and other attributes as criteria to narrow your search. You can add a restriction to review only specific actions assigned to a single customer or a range by either name or number. Click on the **Find** button. The Scheduler form displays the information that fits your selection criteria. See Figure 18-22.

As you scroll down through the items displayed, the notes or comments you entered appear at the bottom for each action item in the Notes field. By clicking on the buttons at the bottom of the form, you can review the specifics of the call, see if the transaction is in dispute, etc. If you often record long messages, record a brief referencing message in the Notes field so it is easily identified in the small viewing area, or make a note in the text to see attachment.

Resolution

As a final function of collection, resolution may involve accepting an invoice, chargeback, or debit memo as a write-off. You can manage this through the Adjustment function by doing any one of the following:

- Fully resolve the issue and let the normal processing continue
- Create new transactions such as credit memo

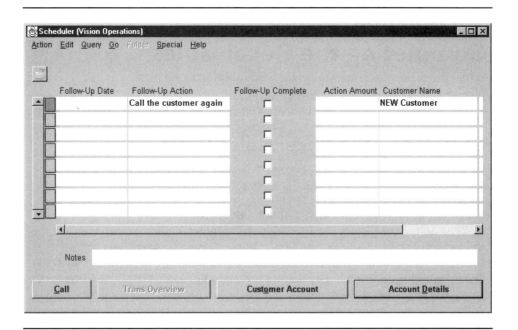

FIGURE 18-22. *Scheduler form*

■ Put the customer on credit hold

■ Place an amount in dispute

■ Calculate finance charges

■ Use statements and dunning letters as correspondences to help with collections

Review Questions

1. Which two reports can you run to identify past due receivables?

2. How do you record a customer call?

3. What is the purpose of the Scheduler?

4. What can be the results after the collection process?

Reconciling, Reporting, and Completing the Receivables Cycle

At the end of every accounting period, you must reconcile, report, and complete the Receivables cycle.

In this section, you will learn how to complete the receivables cycle.

Completing the Receivables Cycle

Activities processed in Oracle Receivables are not recorded in the General Ledger until the GL Interface is run. Also, there are period closing procedures that should be run before closing an open accounting period and opening a new one. These procedures usually correspond to a month-end close.

You can run the General Ledger Interface more regularly than at the end of the accounting period. By posting regularly, Oracle General Ledger users can see the subledger details in Receivables without having to wait long periods of time to see the journals created, even if they are not posted in General Ledger. However, your ability to change the records in Oracle Receivables is sacrificed. For period-end closing, additional steps are involved, but these are necessary to ensure the integrity of the system.

Interface to General Ledger

To run the General Ledger Interface, follow the navigation path *Interfaces : General Ledger*. The Run General Ledger Interface form appears. See Figure 18-23.

In the Posting Detail field, select Summary unless it is necessary to see all journals for each Accounting flexfield. Since General Ledger users can drill into the subledger, the summary is usually sufficient. The GL posted date defaults to the system date. This is used as a timestamp that marks the date on which this interface is run.

The GL Dates field should be populated with the first day of the period and the last day of the period. If transactions have GL dates that are outside of the GL date range, they are not interfaced and will be skipped. Once a transaction is interfaced to the General Ledger, it will not be sent again, so repeating the GL date range will not duplicate any records.

Selecting Yes in the Run Journal Import field creates unposted journal batches in the General Ledger automatically. Selecting No only transfers the data into the General Ledger Interface tables. You then must run Journal Import in the Oracle General Ledger to import them from the interface tables to become unposted journals.

Save your work to send it to the Concurrent Manager for processing. A request ID number is generated, and four programs will run following the submission. These can be viewed through the View My Requests form. The General Ledger Transfer

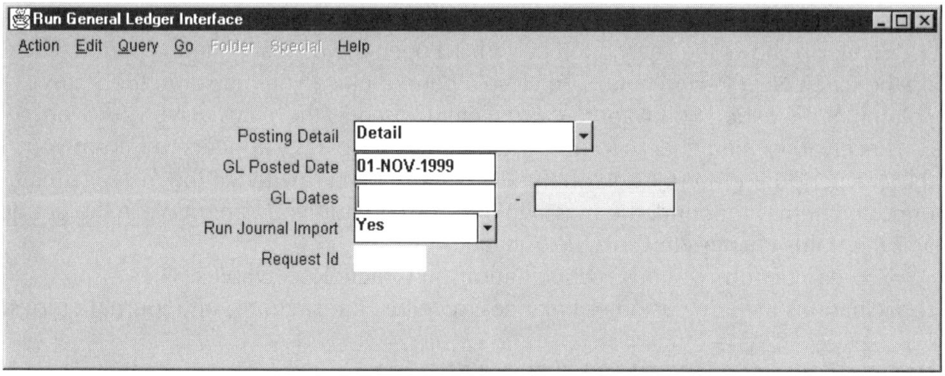

FIGURE 18-23. *Run General Ledger Interface form*

program generates an execution report that you should verify to ensure accuracy and completion.

Because incomplete invoices are not posted, you should run the Incomplete Invoices report before you run the interface to Oracle General Ledger to verify that there are no incomplete invoices. You run this report by invoice number range or customer name/number range. You can also order the invoices by either customer or invoice number. If the invoices are incomplete, you must find out why. Then, either delete them or complete them.

Once changes are made, rerun the report until it has no data. You submit the Incomplete Invoices report through SRS by following the navigation path *Reports : Listing.* The Unposted Items report determines whether you must run the General Ledger Interface. You run this report with a GL date range. If the report has items listed, the General Ledger Interface must be run to clear these items for the specified GL date range before the period can be closed. The Unposted Items report can be submitted through SRS by following the navigation path *Reports : Accounting.*

Oracle Receivables integrates with other Oracle Application modules to receive information that in turn is posted to General Ledger, such as invoice revenue from Order Entry or Projects. If any of the other modules that push data to Oracle Receivables are closing and have found unprocessed transactions, Receivables must wait to receive those transactions and run the interface to Oracle General Ledger before closing.

Open and Close Periods

When you complete your month-end processing, you must close the period and open the next period. Oracle Receivables does not restrict you to keep only one period open. To open and close periods, follow the navigation path *Control :*

Accounting : Open/Close Periods. The Open/Close Accounting Periods form appears. See Figure 18-24.

The form shows the latest open period. To open the next accounting period, click on the **Open Next Period** button. To close a period, place your cursor in the Status column of the period you want to close. Enter Closed as the status. Save your work.

Receivables then checks for unposted items. A message appears to inform you that the period is closed. Click on the **OK** button to acknowledge the message. If unposted items are found, the message informs you that you cannot close the period and the status changes to Close Pending.

You can perform various reconciliations in Oracle Receivables. These reconciliations include customer balances, receipts, transactions, and journal entries.

RECONCILING CUSTOMER BALANCES   You should reconcile the outstanding balance at the beginning of the accounting period with the ending balance of the same period, given all the customer activities that happened in that period.

In order to perform this reconciliation, you must run the following reports:

■ Aging

■ Transactions Register

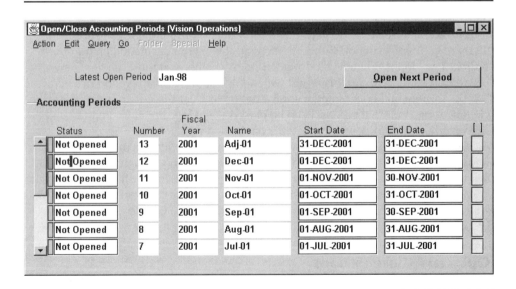

FIGURE 18-24.   *Open/Close Accounting Periods form*

- Adjustments Register

- Applied Receipts Register

- Unapplied Receipts Register

- Invoice Exceptions

To run an aging report, follow the navigation path *Reports : Collection*. You can choose from predefined aging reports with four buckets and seven buckets. The report names all start with the word "Aging." You must run this report twice: once on the last day of the prior period, and once on the last day of the current period that is to be closed.

If you run the report for the first and last days of the same period, your data will not reflect activities for the first day. You can also customize the report's output by specifying whether its records should be sorted by customer or type, whether it should summarize by customer or by invoice, whether its contents should be shown in brief or detailed format, and which aging bucket name the report should use.

Run the Transactions Register, Adjustments Register, Applied Receipts Register, and Unapplied Receipts Register reports with a date range from the first day of the period to the last day. Do not restrict any other parameters through SRS by following the navigation path *Reports : Accounting*.

The Invoice Exceptions Register report identifies transactions that do not age in Oracle Receivables, which is determined by the transaction types. If your system has transaction types that do not age, run this report with a date range from the first day of the period to the last day. Do not restrict any other parameters through SRS by following the navigation path *Reports : Accounting*. If all of your transaction types are set up to age, you can run this report with no parameters in order to catch any anomalies.

You should be able to reconcile ending customer balances in the aging report to beginning customer balances in the Aging report + transactions from the Transactions Register + adjustments from the Adjustments Register – applied receipts from the Applied Receipts Register – unapplied receipts from the Unapplied Receipts Register – invoice exceptions from the Invoice Exceptions report.

RECONCILE RECEIPTS   To reconcile receipts, you must run the following reports:

- **Receipt Register**   Run the Receipt Register report through SRS with parameters from the first day of the period to the last day by following the navigation path *Reports : Accounting*.

- **Receipt Journal**   Run the Receipt Journal report through SRS by following the navigation path *Reports : Accounting* from the first day of the period to the last day in the transaction mode.

The total of the Receipt Journal report should match the total of Receipt Register in the same GL date range. The Receipt Journal report with the same GL date range and a Posted status should also match the total receipts in all the execution reports from the General Ledger Interface, which should also match the generated unposted journals.

RECONCILE TRANSACTIONS   To reconcile transactions, you must run the following reports:

- **Transactions Register**   Run the Transactions Register report through SRS with parameters from the first day of the period to the last day by following the navigation path *Reports : Accounting*.

- **Sales Journal by GL Account**   Run the Sales Journal by GL Account through SRS with parameters from the first day of the period to the last day by following the navigation path *Reports : Accounting*.

Within the Transactions Register is the subtotal of the credit memos. Multiply the credit memo total by two. Add to the balance of all postable items in the Transactions Register. This balance should match the balance of the Sales Journal by GL Account report. Credit memo amounts are negative in the Transactions Register but positive in the Sales Journal by GL Account report.

RECONCILE JOURNAL ENTRIES   To reconcile journal entries, run the Journal Entries report.

- **Journal Entries Report**   Run the *Summary by Account* option from the first day of the period to the last day. Add the balances of the Sales Journal report and the Receipt Journal report for the same period. These should match the totals in the Journal Entries report. The totals should match the Accounting flexfield.

Review Questions

1. What stops you from closing an Oracle Receivables period, and how can you fix it?

2. Which report and what formulas do you use to reconcile customer balances?

3. How do you reconcile receipts?

4. Why must you multiply credit memo balances by 2 before reconciling them to the Sales Journal by GL Account report?

Implementing and Setting Up Receivables

In this section, you will learn how to complete the implementation and setup of Oracle Receivables.

Completing the Implementation and Setup of Oracle Receivables

For an overview of the steps needed to finish implementing Oracle Receivables, please refer to Figure 18-25.

Set of Books

You must select at least one Set of Books that consists of a calendar, a functional currency, and an Accounting flexfield structure. Budgetary control is required if the system is integrated with Oracle Grants Management.

Account Generator

You must review the default setup to ensure that your finance charges and exchange rate gains or losses will post to the correct accounts. You can customize this using Workflow.

Items

If you are going to use items, you must set up these items and set the *OE: Item Flexfield* profile option at the site level.

Organizations

You must define at least one organization to use Receivables. This organization lets you use the inventory forms in Receivables if you do not have Oracle Inventory installed. You must also define the control options and account defaults for your organization before you can define items or perform any transactions. You must assign a unique short code to your organization and use this code to identify the organization with which you want to work.

Territories

As an option, you can define the Territory flexfield. You can associate Territory flexfields with agents, invoices, commitments, and customer business purposes for reporting purposes.

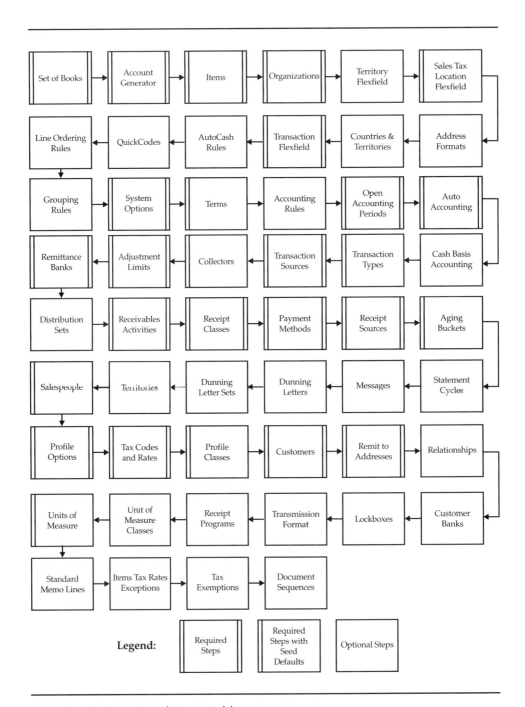

FIGURE 18-25. *Oracle Receivables setup steps*

Tax

As an option, you can set up Sales Tax Location flexfield. The customer shipping address is used in calculating sales tax rate on all transactions for all customers in the country you define as your home country. If you do not charge your customers tax based on the shipping address, you can skip this step.

Receivables comes with the following predefined structures for the Sales Tax Location flexfield:

- Country
- State and city
- Province and city
- City
- Province
- State, county, and city

You must mark the appropriate flexfield qualifiers. Flexfield qualifiers include city, country, county, automatic exemptions, postal code, province, state, and tax account.

Tax Locations and Rates

Assign tax rates to each location. Tax locations are used to validate your customer's shipping addresses and to calculate the proper tax amount. You can either use the Sales Tax Rate Interface program to load locations and tax rates from an independent source or enter them manually in the Tax Locations and Rates form.

Address Formats

If any of the predefined address formats suit your needs, you do not need to use the Flexible Address Formats feature. If you wish to create your own address formats, you must define a different structure for the various Address Descriptive flexfields.

Countries and Territories

View all countries and territories within your system. You can assign address styles and identify European Community countries.

Transaction Flexfield

You must define a Transaction flexfield structure if you are going to use AutoInvoice. Both the Line and Invoice Transaction Descriptive flexfields must be defined in this case. Otherwise, you can skip this setup. Transaction flexfields are used to identify unique imported transactions. The Invoice Transaction flexfield identifies the uniqueness of transaction level while the Line Trasnsaction flexfield identifies the transaction line level. Receivables Interface populates both of these Transaction flexfields.

AutoCash Rules

AutoCash rule sets can be defined to use in system parameters or customer profile classes by following the navigation path *Set Up : Receipts : AutoCash Rule Sets*. The AutoCash rule sets form appears. See Figure 18-26.

AutoCash rule sets determine the sequence of applications when applying automatic receipts to open debit and credit items using AutoCash. Valid rules in Oracle Receivables are Apply to the Oldest Invoice First, Clear Past Due Invoices, Clear Past Due Invoices Grouped by Payment Term, Clear the Account, and Match Payment with Invoice.

QuickCodes

From the Oracle Order Entry setup section, you learned about setting up Receivables and Demand Classes QuickCodes. Oracle Receivables share these

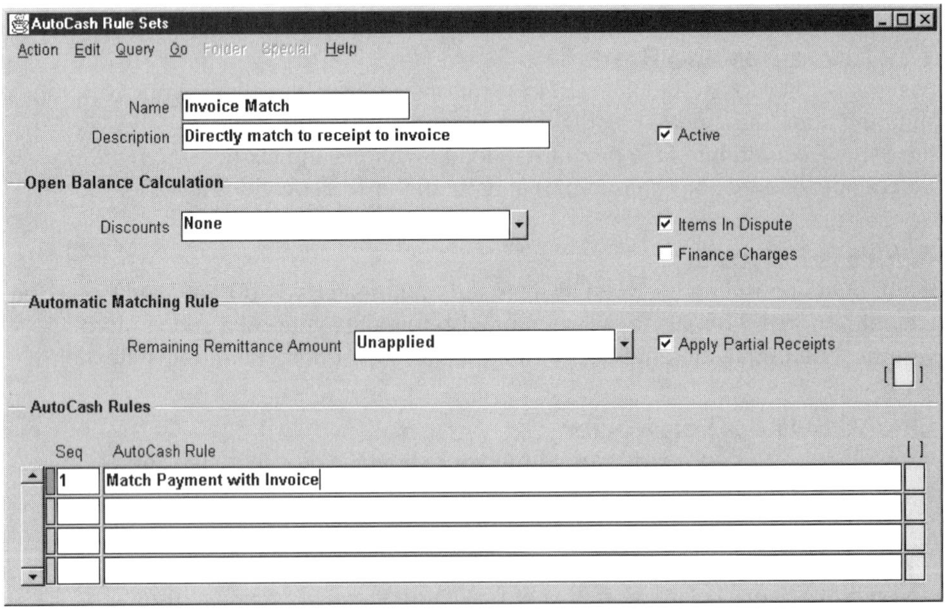

FIGURE 18-26. *AutoCash Rule Sets form*

QuickCodes with Oracle Order Entry. In addition, you can set up freight carriers as QuickCodes by following the navigation path *Set Up : System : QuickCodes : Freight,* if you charge freight and are not using the Oracle Inventory or Order Entry module.

Line Ordering Rules

You can set up line ordering rules to be used during AutoInvoicing to order transaction lines once they have been grouped into different transactions by following the navigation path *Set Up : Transactions : AutoInvoice : Line Ordering Rules.* The AutoInvoice Line Ordering Rules form appears. See Figure 18-27.

For instance, you might want your invoice lines to appear in the same order as they were entered on the sales order. You can order by predefined transaction attributes that include sales order number, sales order line, ship date, freight carrier, and any Line Transaction Descriptive flexfield attributes.

Grouping Rules

Follow the navigation path *Set Up : Transactions : AutoInvoice : Grouping Rules* to set up grouping rules to be used during AutoInvoicing. The AutoInvoice Grouping Rules form appears. See Figure 18-28.

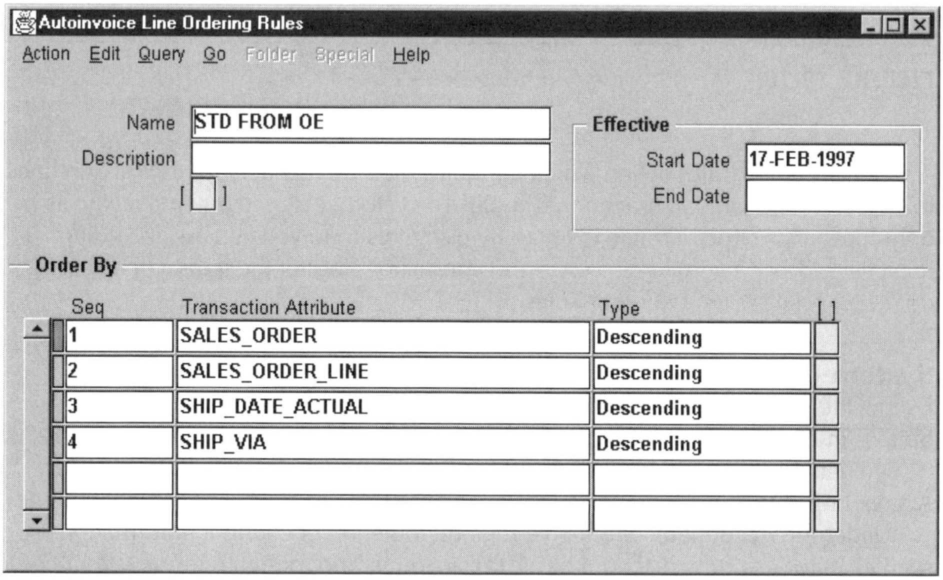

FIGURE 18-27. *AutoInvoice Line Ordering Rules form*

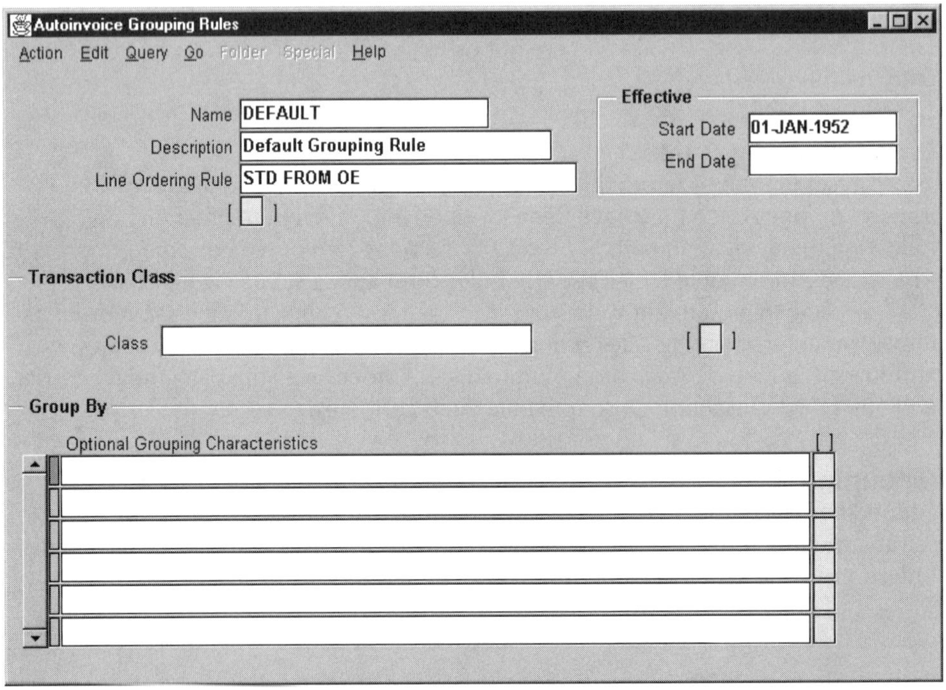

FIGURE 18-28. *AutoInvoice Grouping Rules form*

The Grouping Rules define which attributes must be identical for transaction lines to appear on the same transactions. The Bill To customer is used automatically, as it only appears once per a single invoice. By using this form you can assign additional identifiers. Grouping Rules also order the transaction lines of the transactions based on the associated Line Ordering Rules.

System Options

Follow the navigation path *Set Up : System : System Options* to set up system options in Oracle Receivables. The System Options form appears. See Figure 18-29.

No default values are provided. Enter all the fields for each alternative region: Accounting, Tax, Tax Defaults and Rules, Trans and Customers, and Miscellaneous.

Under the Accounting alternative region, you enter accounting information such as AutoCash rule, discount basis, tax account, and foreign currency gain/loss account. Under the Tax alternative region, you enter the tax information. You select the tax method, the Location flexfield structure, and the address validation mode.

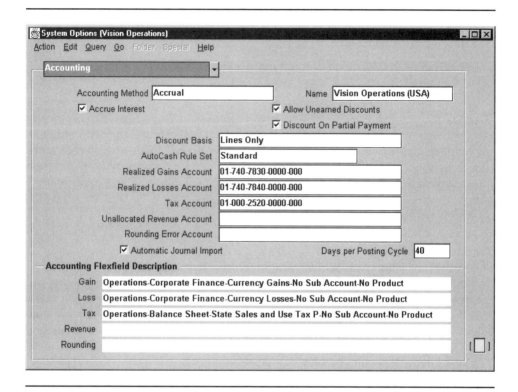

FIGURE 18-29.   *System Options form*

Under the Tax Defaults and Rules alternative region, you enter the tax code default hierarchy and the exception rates. Under the Trans and Customers alternative regions, you select the customer numbering method and site (location) numbering method. Under the Miscellaneous alternative region, you enter the default country. You can update the country in this form at the time of installation, provided that you have not entered any customer addresses.

Only the following items are optional:

- AutoCash rule set

- Tax registration number

- Accounting Flex tuning segment

- System Items tuning segment

- Territory tuning segment

- SQL Trace
- Purge Interface tables
- Unallocated Revenue account (only optional if accounting is accrual or arrears)

Terms

Although Receivables provides default terms, which you can use, they are limited to the most basic of terms. You can create proxima terms, which are due on a certain day each month, or net terms, which are due on a certain number of days after the transaction date. You can create tiered discounts, or even installments for as many terms as necessary.

This setup is the same as for Oracle Order Entry.

Accounting Rules

Follow the navigation path *Set Up : Transactions : Accounting Rules* to define accounting rules. If you are billing in arrears or in advance, and are recognizing revenue or more than one accounting period, you must set up accounting rules. You may define as many accounting rules as you want. When you define an accounting rule, you must associate it with the invoicing rules Bill in Advance or Bill in Arrears. Also specify to which period type your rule applies. You can have fixed-duration or variable-duration accounting rules.

Open Accounting Periods

Open the accounting periods to control transactions, receipts, and posting. Your selections are Not Opened, Future, Open, Close Pending, and Closed.

AutoAccounting

Follow the navigation path *Set Up : Transactions : AutoAccounting* to define your AutoAccounting rules to generate accounts to be used in Oracle Receivables. The AutoAccounting form appears. See Figure 18-30.

In this form, you can create the default accounts for the seven primary types of accounts used in the Receivables subledger:

- Receivable
- Revenue
- Freight
- Tax

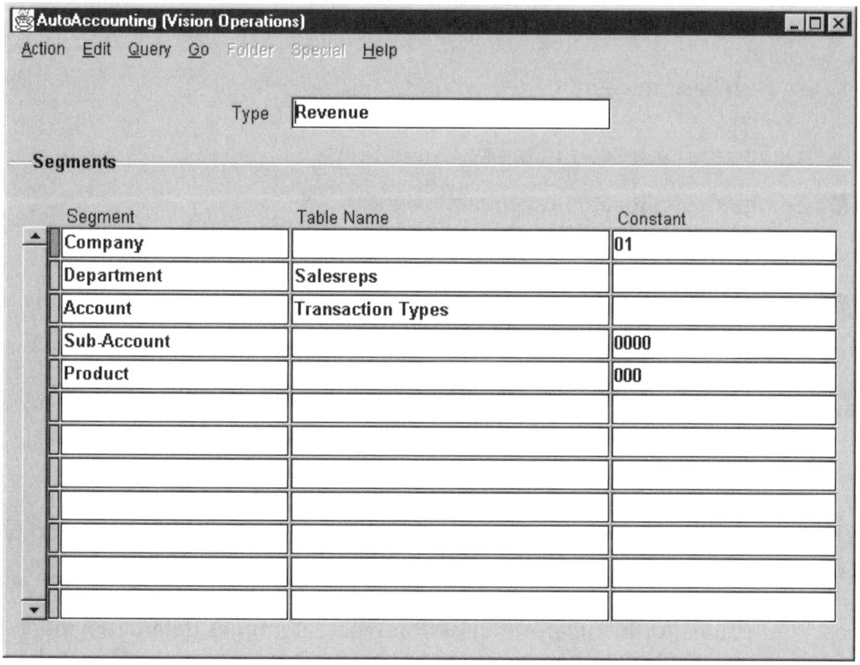

FIGURE 18-30. *AutoAccounting form*

■ Suspense

■ Unbilled revenue

■ Unearned revenue

You can specify how Oracle Receivables is to determine the account for each segment of the General Ledger Accounting flexfield. This is pulled from a table, or you can enter a constant value. Choose from the four tables or enter a constant for each segment for each account type: Salesreps, Transaction Types, Standard Lines, and Taxes.

Cash Basis Accounting

Most companies use an accrual method of accounting; that is, revenue is recognized when an invoice is generated, not when the payment is received from the customer. Cash basis recognizes revenue when there is a cash transaction. If you sell goods using invoices and carry receivables, yet use cash basis for your accounting, you can set up Oracle Receivables to track funds without affecting your accounts.

To use cash basis accounting, you must:

- Define the cash basis in the system options

- Set up an unallocated revenue account

- Set up your transaction types

- Make the GL Transfer report and the Journal Entry report incompatible in the Define Concurrent Programs form.

Transaction Types

Follow the navigation path *Set Up : Transactions : Transaction Types* to set up transaction types. If integrated with Oracle Order Entry, you must define transaction types before Oracle Order Entry can define order types. You must create a transaction type for each invoice, debit memo, commitment, chargeback, and credit memo type that you use.

Transaction type can be of class Chargeback, Credit Memo, Debit Memo, Deposit, Guarantee, or Invoice. A transaction type determines default payment terms, accounts, tax, freight, creation sign, posting status, and other receivables information. You can check the *Natural Application Only* option if you do not want to change the sign of the transaction. You can check the *Allow OverApplication* checkbox if you can overapply and change the sign of the transaction. Three transaction types are seeded with Oracle Receivables: Manual-Other, DM Reversal, and Chargeback.

Transaction Sources

Follow the navigation path *Set Up : Transactions : Sources* to define transaction sources. Define the transaction sources for your invoices, debit memos, commitments, and credit memos. Receivables uses transaction sources to control your batch numbering, default transaction type, and select validation options. Before you can define your transaction sources for invoices, you must first define your transaction sources for your credit memos.

The following are seeded values: MANUAL-OTHER, DM Reversal, Service, and Chargeback.

Collectors

You can follow the navigation path *Set Up : Collections : Collectors* to define collectors. One seeded value of DEFAULT is provided.

Adjustment Limits

Follow the navigation path *Set Up : Transactions : Adjustment Limits* to define transaction sources. The Adjustment Approval Limits form appears. See Figure 18-31.

In order to assign adjustment limits, you must set up the users first. You must assign adjustment approval limits to each user to control the amount of adjustments made to invoices, debit memos, and chargebacks without approval. You can specify limits by currency.

Remittance Banks

If you are integrated with Oracle Payables, you may define your banks through that module as well. Otherwise, define all the bank accounts into which your customers will remit payments in Oracle Cash Management. You must enter a cash account for each bank account. You can also define a clearinghouse.

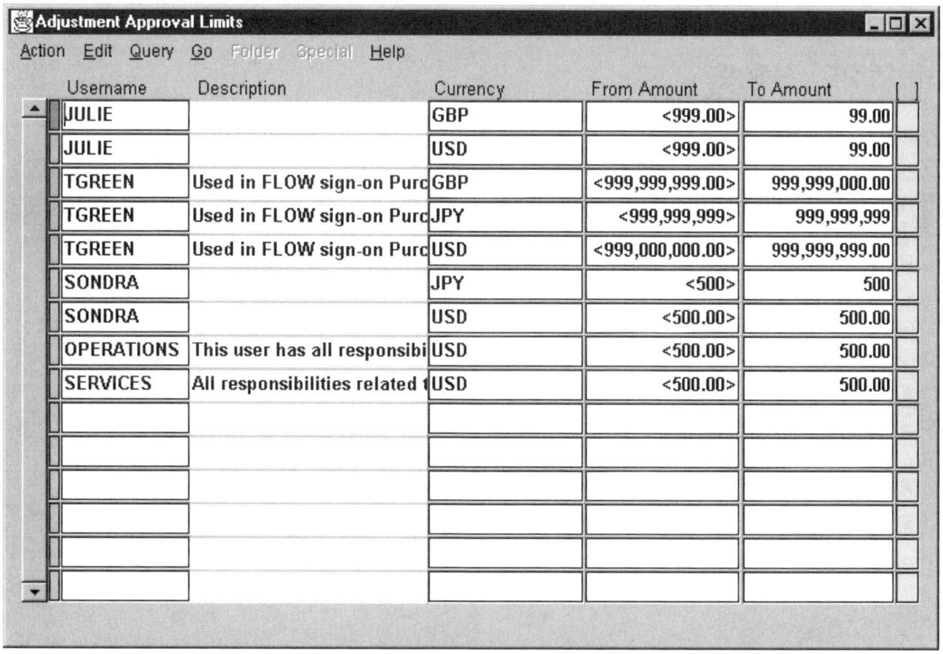

Adjustment Approval Limits

Action Edit Query Go Folder Special Help

Username	Description	Currency	From Amount	To Amount
JULIE		GBP	<999.00>	99.00
JULIE		USD	<999.00>	99.00
TGREEN	Used in FLOW sign-on Purc	GBP	<999,999,999.00>	999,999,000.00
TGREEN	Used in FLOW sign-on Purc	JPY	<999,999,999>	999,999,999
TGREEN	Used in FLOW sign-on Purc	USD	<999,000,000.00>	999,999,999.00
SONDRA		JPY	<500>	500
SONDRA		USD	<500.00>	500.00
OPERATIONS	This user has all responsibi	USD	<500.00>	500.00
SERVICES	All responsibilities related t	USD	<500.00>	500.00

FIGURE 18-31. *Adjustment Approval Limits form*

Distribution Sets

Follow the navigation path *Set Up : Receipts : Distribution Sets* to define distribution sets. These sets are used when you enter miscellaneous cash receipts that have frequently used revenue accounts. The user can quickly select a distribution set while applying the receipt, and thus reduce the chances of a data entry error. This also shortens the processing time.

You may set up as many sets as necessary. Use a naming convention that makes selection from a List of Values simple. Also, your distribution sets may have more than one distribution as long as the total allocation sum is 100 percent.

Receivables Activities

Follow the navigation path *Set Up : Receipts : Receivable Activities* to define Receivables activities. Activities are used throughout the cash application process to link adjustments to default accounts. These activities are displayed in the Lists of Values during cash application.

Select a type of activity, such as Adjustment or Bank Error. Define at least one activity to be used with your Oracle Cash Management module, if integrated. For bank error and miscellaneous cash activities, you may select a distribution set or enter a General Ledger account.

Receipt Classes

Follow the navigation path *Set Up : Receipts : Receipt Class* to set up receipt classes. The Receipt Classes form appears, as shown in Figure 18-32.

You must define receipt classes to specify whether receipts are created manually or automatically. If this is a manual receipt, you can specify whether to automatically remit this receipt to the bank and/or clear your accounts. You can also define whether a remittance should be generated for the bank.

If this is an automatic receipt, you can specify whether to confirm, remit, or clear your receipt. Specify one receipt class per process; for instance, one receipt class for cash and checks, and one for electronic fund transfers.

Payment Methods

For each receipt class, you may create payment methods in the Receipt Classes form. Each payment method corresponds to a single bank account. If the receipt class is Automatic, you must also assign a number of receipts rule, the number of lead days, a receipt maturity date rule, and the automatic print program to be used with that payment method. You may have several payment methods under one receipt class.

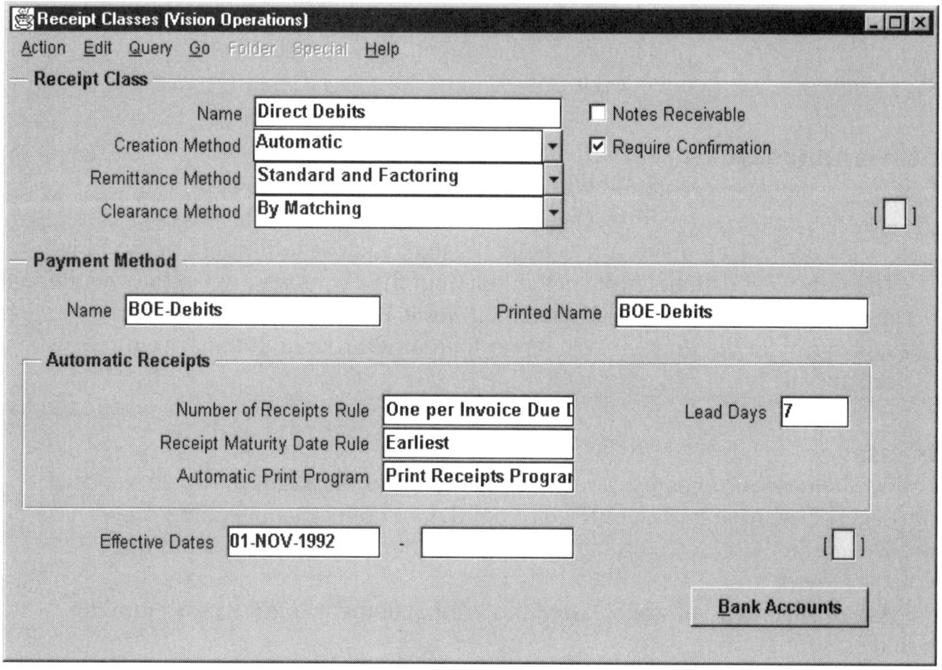

FIGURE 18-32. *Receipt Classes form*

Receipt Sources

Follow the navigation path *Set Up : Receipts : Receipt Sources* to set up receipt sources. Receipt sources provide default information for the cash, unapplied, unidentified, on account, and earned and unearned discount accounts based on the payment method you assign to the source.

Enter a new name and select a receipt class for the source. As an option, you can enter a payment method for the source. This determines your General Ledger accounts. Select whether to number batches automatically or manually.

Aging Buckets

Follow the navigation path *Set Up : Collections : Aging Buckets* to set up additional aging buckets. Oracle Receivables provides four-bucket and seven-bucket aging as standard functionality. You may also define additional aging buckets. Additional aging buckets can include transactions other than past due invoices.

Select a name and enter the criteria for each bucket as a sequence number. The type determines what you define: Future, Current, Past Due, Dispute, Pending Adjustment, Disputes, and Pending Adjustment. The aging buckets can be used in standard reports and collection forms.

Statement Cycles

Follow the navigation path *Set Up : Print : Statement Cycles* to define statement cycles. Define the statement cycles and dates. Cycles should have names that specify when the statements are to be generated, such as midmonth or monthly.

The statement date determines the length of the cycle, and when to generate finance charges as of that date, if specified. Indicate how often the statement cycle is to run for the Interval field. Enter the dates throughout the year to run the statements.

Messages

Follow the navigation path *Set Up : Print : Standard Messages* to define standard messages. Use these messages to print holiday or collection messages on the statements. A selected message prints automatically on the bottom of your statements.

Assign statement messages using the Print Statements form when submitting statements for printing.

Dunning Letters

Follow the navigation path *Set Up : Print : Dunning Letters* to define dunning letters. Standard dunning letters come seeded with the Oracle Receivables module. You can define new dunning letters also, using the USER 1 through USER 10 ready-to-define dunning letters. You can also customize the dunning letters using variables that are specific to each customer.

Dunning letters must be grouped into dunning letter sets.

Dunning Letter Sets

Follow the navigation path *Set Up : Print : Dunning Letter Sets* to define dunning letter sets. The Dunning Letter Sets form appears. See Figure 18-33.

To use dunning letters, you must define dunning letter sets. When you create dunning letter sets, you combine a group of dunning letters and, by sequence, the collection message of each letter you send gets stronger. You can assign dunning letter sets to your customers in the Customer Profile Classes form. Oracle Receivables comes seeded with one letter set called STANDARD, which includes the three STANDARD letters.

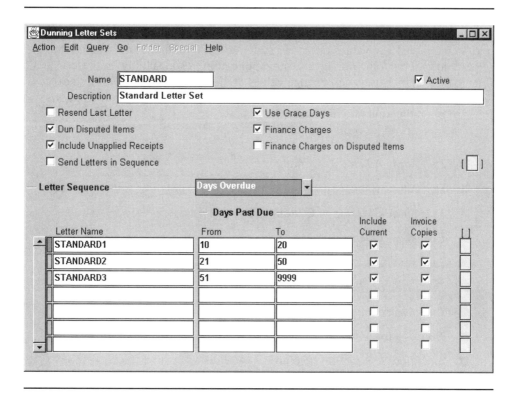

FIGURE 18-33. *Dunning Letter Sets form*

Territories

Follow the navigation path *Set Up : Transactions : Territories* to define territory combinations. This is the same as the Oracle Order Entry setup. If you set up a Territory flexfield, you can define the combinations of segments for your flexfield. You can also assign salespeople, invoices, and customer business purposes to your territories.

Salespeople

To allocate revenue credit, you must define the salespeople who are assigned to your transactions. If you do not want to assign revenue credits, you can use the seeded value of No Sales Credit.

Active salespeople appear in the Lists of Values when using the Receivables forms of Customers or Transactions. You should define the Territory flexfield if you use a value other than No Sales Credit. This is the same as the Oracle Order Entry setup.

Profile Options

Profile options direct how Oracle Receivables controls access to the system data, and how Oracle Receivables processes system data. Profile options can be set at one or more of the following levels: site, application, responsibility, and user. Oracle Receivables users can change values at the user level only. The system administrator can set profile options at all levels. You must set up profile options for each operating unit you defined.

Oracle Receivables profile options are:

- *Tax: Allow Ad Hoc Tax Changes*

- *Tax: Allow Manual Tax Lines*

- *Tax: Allow Override of Customer Exemptions*

- *Tax: Allow Override of Tax Code*

- *Tax: Calculate Tax on Credit Memos*

- *Tax: Inventory Item for Freight*

- *Tax: Invoice Freight as Revenue*

- *Tax: Use Tax Vendor*

- *AR: Allow Transaction Batching*

- *AR: Allow Update of Existing Sales Credits*

- *AR: Alternate Name Search*

- *AR: Automatic Contact Numbering*

- *AR: Automatic Receipt Creation Authority*

- *AR: Automatic Remittance Creation Authority*

- *AR: Cash Allow Actions*

- *AR: Cash Default Amount Applied*

- *AR: Change Customer on Transaction*

- *AR: Change Customer Name*

- *AR: Close Periods and Run Collection Effectiveness*

- *AR: Create Bank Charges*

- *AR: Customer Merge Commit Size*

- *AR: Customers – Enter Alternate Fields*
- *AR: Debug Level for Postbatch*
- *AR: Default Exchange Rate Type*
- *AR: Dunning Letter Remit To Address Label Size*
- *AR: GL Transfer Balance Test*
- *AR: Invoices with Unconfirmed Receipts*
- *AR: Item Flexfield Mode*
- *AR: Override Adjustment Activity Account*
- *AR: Receipt Batch Source*
- *AR: Show Billing Number*
- *AR: Sort Customer Reports by Alternate Fields*
- *AR: Transaction Batch Source*
- *AR: Transaction Flexfield QuickPick Attribute*
- *AR: Update Due Date*
- *AR: Use Invoice Accounting for Credit Memos*
- *AR: Zengin Character Set*
- *Default Country*
- *Dual Currency*
- *Dual Currency Default Rate*
- *Enable Transaction Codes*
- *Journals: Display Inverse Rate*
- *Sequential Numbering*
- *WSH: Invoice Numbering Method*

Tax Codes and Rates

If the System Options form under Tax Method is set to Sales Tax in the system options, you must define at least one tax code with a type of Location. This tax code is used to calculate your location-based tax. You cannot update this account once you save the record. You can add as many Location type tax codes as necessary using different date ranges.

If your tax method is set to VAT, enter the tax codes rates to calculate tax for your transactions. These tax codes can be assigned to standard memo lines, customers, and customer site uses.

For either a sales tax or VAT, set up a zero-rated tax code for those customers or transactions outside of the tax liability zone. This setup is the same as for Oracle Order Entry.

Profile Classes
Refer to Chapter 17 for detailed information on this topic.

Customers
This, too, was covered in detail in Chapter 17.

Remit To Addresses
Follow the navigation path *Set Up : Print : Remit-To Addresses* to define remit-to addresses. The Remit-To Addresses form appears. See Figure 18-34.

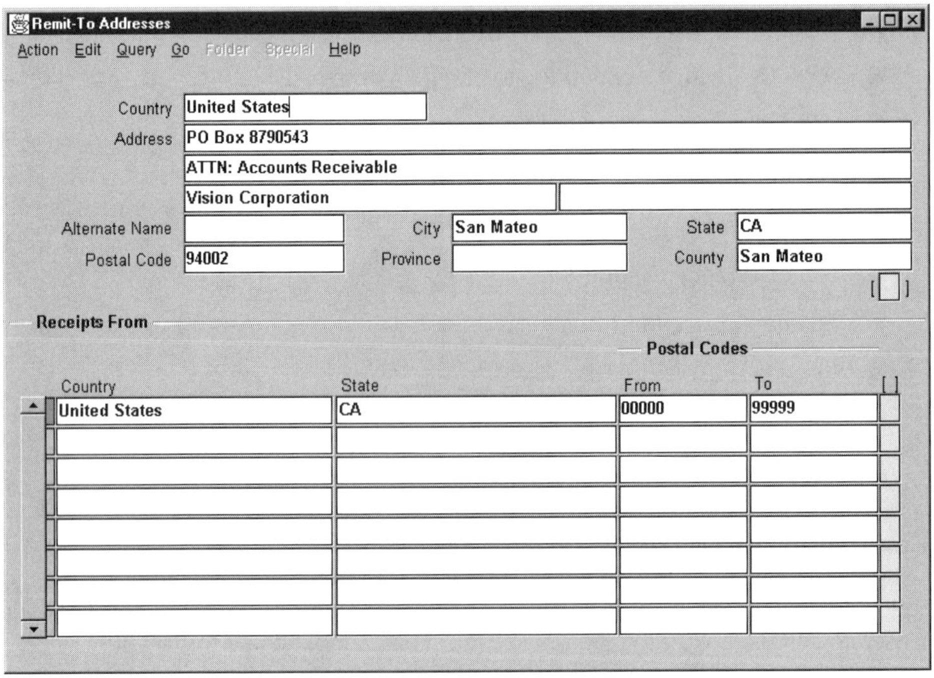

FIGURE 18-34.   *Remit-To Addresses form*

Define a remit-to address that will print on your transactions. You must associate each address with at least one state, country, and ZIP code. Remit-to addresses print on the transactions according to the bill-to address. You can set up one remit-to address to be used for all locations, or for a specific location if you have only one remit-to location.

To set up a single default remit-to address, select default values for the country and state.

Relationships

You set up customer relationships in the Customers form. See Chapter 17 for more details.

Customer Banks

If you have customers with agreements indicating that you may automatically draw funds from their accounts into your accounts, you can use automatic receipts. This allows you to record their receipts promptly and increase your cash flow. To use automatic receipts, you must set up the customer's bank in your system. Enter your customer's bank in the same manner that you entered your own banks.

Lockboxes

Follow the navigation path *Set Up : Receipts : Lockboxes : Lockboxes* to define lockboxes. The Lockboxes form appears, as shown in Figure 18-35. The AutoLockbox program creates receipts automatically using the information provided by the bank, either by using EDI or by a file. You can also specify the payment method for each lockbox. The lockboxes you create appear in the List of Values when submitting the program to run.

Transmission Formats

Follow the navigation path *Set Up : Receipts : Lockbox : Transmission Formats* to define transmission formats. The Transmission Formats form appears. See Figure 18-36.

You can define as many transmission formats as necessary to import your lockbox receipts.

Two standard formats come seeded:

■ DEFAULT

■ CONVERT

Default is a standard file format used in many American banks: BAI. Convert is used to import from other systems. You will need a SQL*Loader program to import the data from the bank files into the AR_PAYMENTS_INTERFACE table.

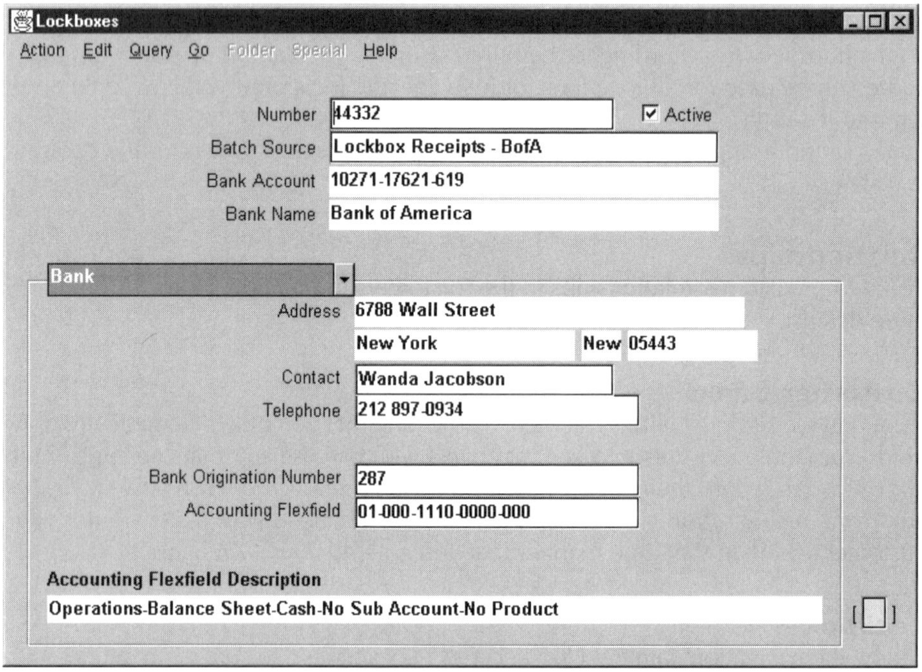

FIGURE 18-35. *Lockboxes form*

Receipt Programs

Follow the navigation path *Set Up : Receipts : Automatic Receipts* to set up receipts programs. To use the automatic receipts, you must define receipt programs. These programs create the paper and electronic documents to send to your customers and your banks.

Your system administrator has created a registered name for your receipt program. Use the same name for your receipts programs as you used for your transmission formats. This makes identification much easier.

Select whether your program will do one of the following:

■ Print created receipts

■ Transmit created receipts

■ Print bank remittance

■ Transmit bank remittance

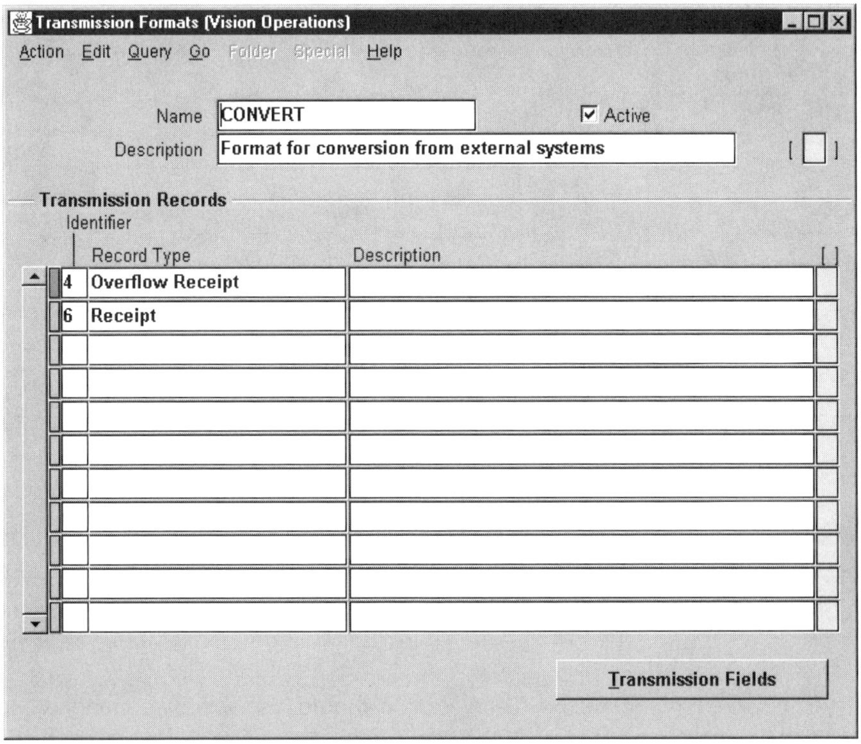

FIGURE 18-36. *Transmission Formats form*

Units of Measure Classes

If you are using Oracle Inventory or Oracle Order Entry, you may skip this step provided the UOM classes have been defined while setting up that module.

Units of Measure (Required)

If you have already defined UOM classes while setting up Oracle Inventory or Oracle Order Entry, you may skip this step now.

Standard Memo Lines

If you do not have items defined, you must define standard memo lines to create manual transactions, including credit memos, debit memos, and invoices. Follow the navigation path *Set Up : Transactions : Memo Lines* to open the Standard Memo Lines form, which is shown in Figure 18-37. Specify in your memo line whether its

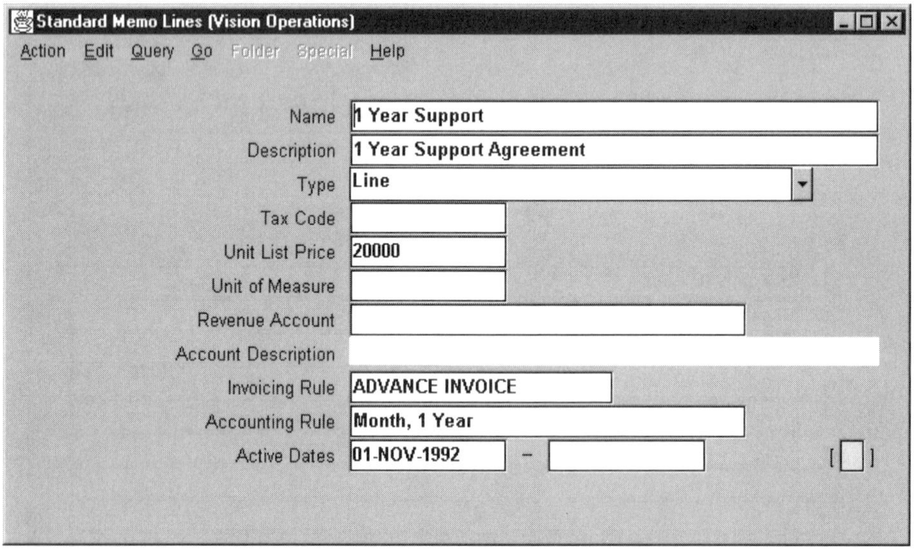

FIGURE 18-37. *Standard Memo Lines form*

item type is Line, Freight, Tax, or Charges. You should also specify a General Ledger account in the memo line if your AutoAccounting uses standard lines to pull any of its segments.

You can enter UOM, prices, and tax codes also, if desired. The name you use is printed on the transaction unless it is overridden at the time the transaction is created. Suggested use of the memo line includes NSF for debit memos, and Miscellaneous—to be used when nothing else fits. If you are using Multi-Org, you must set up separate memo lines for each organization.

Items Tax Rates Exceptions

You can assign special tax rates to specific items for locations within a defined area. You can choose to exclude states, counties, or cities in accordance with your flexfield structure.

Enter a new tax rate for the item/location combination, and select a reason from the List of Values.

This setup is the same as the Oracle Order Entry setup.

Tax Exemptions

You can fully or partially exempt a customer or items from tax. This setup is the same as that used for Oracle Order Entry.

Document Sequences

Document sequences allow you to assign a number to different objects within Oracle Applications. You can define a document sequence as Automatic, Manual, or Gapless, and you can set the initial number that the sequence will begin with.

Review Questions

1. What is a dunning letter and a dunning letter set?

2. What is the remit-to address selection based on?

3. Where are Receivables activities used?

4. What setups must you perform to use the automatic receipts feature?

Loading Electronic Bank Statements

To enter bank statement information and reconcile bank statements to internal records, refer to the section in Chapter 14 about entering and reconciling bank statements manually.

For the Chapter Summary, Two-Minute Drill, and Chapter Questions and Answers, open the summary.htm file contained in the Summary_files directory on the book's CD-ROM.

CHAPTER
19

Advanced Order Fulfillment

n the last two chapters, you learned about basic order fulfillment processes in Orders, Transactions, and Receipts Workbenches. In this chapter you will move on to more advanced order fulfillment processes, including:

- Using Oracle Cash Management with Oracle Receivables

- Administering pricing and discounts

- Processing orders

- Drop-shipping orders

- Invoicing and closing orders

- Processing returns

- Entering and correcting transactions

- Receipts

- Past-due receivables

- Reconciling, reporting, and completing the cycle

First, you will learn about implementing and setting up Oracle Cash Management. This was already discussed in Chapter 14, and this chapter concentrates only on the setups related to Oracle Receivables. The other Oracle Cash Management setups are discussed in Chapter 14. The purpose of including Oracle Cash Management in two chapters is to keep the Exam 4 contents intact. However, you will be referred to Chapter 14 for materials that have already been covered.

Next, the chapter discusses administering pricing and discounts. You will learn how to set up pricing and discounts in Oracle Order Entry, and how to process orders. You will apply sales credits, discounts, and notes to a sales order. You will also approve sales orders and lines, and apply and remove holds. Then, you will cancel orders and order lines. As a last step, you will learn to view orders along with their details and cycle statuses.

Oracle Order Entry handles drop-shipments, and this chapter discusses how to designate order lines for drop-shipments, and how to view drop-ship orders and order lines. You will also learn how to fulfill and invoice drop-shipments in order to complete the drop-ship orders processing. As a last step, you will learn how to handle returns—if and when they happen—from drop-shipments.

Once the orders are fulfilled, they can be invoiced depending on your order cycles. If they are billed, you can trace the transaction sources. Use defined

AutoInvoicing lines ordering rules and grouping rules, together with invoicing rules, accounting rules, and receivable accounts to control how invoices are created based on the sales orders by the Receivables interface. Next, the chapter discusses processing returns and how to authorize returns and identify RMA (return materials authorization) types.

The last few sections in the chapter cover Oracle Receivables advanced processing, where you will learn to bill customers in advance or in arrears. You will learn to define recurring transactions, create debit/credit memos, define deposits and guarantees, and use tax options. Next, you will learn how to process automatic receipts to accept funds directly from your customer's bank, and how to use lockboxes. The chapter then goes into a review of customer account status and the gathering of collection information using the Collections Workbench. As a last step, you will learn how to reconcile receipts and accounts, perform bank reconciliation, and use standard reports in Oracle Receivables.

Using Oracle Cash Management with Receivables

In this section, you will learn to implement Oracle Cash Management. In Chapter 14, you already learned how to set up Oracle Cash Management to work with Oracle Payables, and how to configure system parameters and bank transaction codes in Oracle Cash Management. To use Oracle Receivables with Oracle Cash Management, further setup of Cash Management is required, along with the setup of system parameters and transaction codes.

Completing the Implementation and Setup of Oracle Cash Management

To complete the implementation and setup of Oracle Cash Management, you must configure Oracle Cash Management to work with Oracle Receivables, and also configure the system parameters and transaction codes. Refer to Chapter 14 for the setup of system parameters and transaction codes.

For Cash Management to work with Oracle Receivables, you must establish the following in Cash Management:

- Set of Books
- Banks
- Receipt sources
- Receipt class (optional)
- Receivable activities (optional)

Set of Books

Set(s) of Books must be assigned as system options in Oracle Receivables for each operating unit. You must also select these Sets of Books as the Sets of Books in the Oracle Cash Management System Parameters form.

Banks

You must configure bank accounts for banks that will be reconciled using Oracle Cash Management. You must mark the bank accounts with an account use of Internal—but not Customer or Supplier. You must also have the cash clearing, bank charges, and bank errors accounts set up in the GL Accounts alternative region of Bank Accounts. For remittance bank accounts, you must assign the cash account and remittance account.

Receipt Sources

You must define at least one receipt source that will be used for assigning numbers to receipt batches.

Receipt Class

If you plan to create miscellaneous receipts or payments from Oracle Cash Management, you must set up a receipt class for them. Miscellaneous payments are negative receipts, and are generated in Oracle Receivables, not Oracle Payables. The receipts class setup for this purpose utilizes a manual creation method and is set to not require remittance.

Receivable Activities

To create miscellaneous receipts or payments from Oracle Cash Management, you must set up a receivable activity. A receivable activity set up for this purpose requires an account type of either bank error or miscellaneous cash. For the miscellaneous cash type, you must either enter an account or select a distribution set.

Review Questions

1. What one thing must be set up in Oracle Receivables in order for Oracle Cash Management to work with Oracle Receivables?

2. What are the two required setups in Oracle Cash Management?

3. What must you set up if you plan to create miscellaneous receipts in Oracle Cash Management?

4. What are miscellaneous payments in Oracle Receivables?

Administering Pricing and Discounts

In this section, you will learn to administer pricing and discounts. Oracle Order Entry offers many features regarding pricing and discounting, and this section covers all of them. In this section, you will learn to:

- Manage pricing

- Manage discounts

Managing Pricing

For an item to be entered on an order/return, it must first exist on a price list that is associated with the order. You can associate only one price list to each individual order. In other words, different lines on the order cannot be tied to different price lists. Price lists can be manually entered for each individual order, or entered with automatic defaults based on the defined standard value rule sets.

You can define any number of price lists and associate them as defaults to any number of customers, addresses, or agreements. However, maintenance issues must be reviewed based on the number of price lists being considered. In this case, you may want to use pricing rules and pricing components to maintain defined price lists.

Enter Price Lists

To define a price list, follow the navigation path *Pricing : Lists : Price Lists*. This brings you to the Price Lists form. See Figure 19-1. You can choose how you would like items in the price list to be sorted. If it doesn't matter, then leave the Sort Lines By field as Not Sorted. Then enter the price list header information, including price list name, which must be unique, currency, and the rounding factor, which represents the decimal places. You can also enter a description and an effectivity date range. You cannot use a price list on an order if the existing list is ineffective. You may also define a secondary price list for the system to look elsewhere if the item does not exist on the first price list. You can also define the following: payment terms, freight carrier, and freight terms, which can all be tied to standard value rule sets. You can also enter comments.

For the purposes of this exercise, create a price list called **NEW Price List** and enter the header-level information. In the VISION demonstration database, you may also enter the price list's Web site in the Additional Price List Information Descriptive flexfield. Then, save your work.

Add your price list item information under the Price List Items region, then choose your item from the List of Values. Attach a UOM to your item for pricing purposes, and if it has multiple UOMs that must be priced, you must repeat the item as a separate price list line with a different UOM. You can enter pricing attributes if the Descriptive flexfield is defined. Next, enter the list price for the item. If the item is serviceable, either enter a list price or a percentage. If you enter a percentage, the service price will be set to the stated percentage of the item's list price in the item master. If you enter a pricing rule to maintain the price list items, you need not enter the list price. However, you may wish to enter a pricing rule if you want to immediately use the item on the sales order before the Pricing program runs. The Pricing program updates all list prices based on pricing rules, which will be covered later on. You can also enter an effective date range at the line level. For the purposes of this exercise, select the item AS54888 and set the item for UOM Ea at $1,500. Save your work when finished.

Copy Price Lists

Follow the navigation path *Pricing : Lists : Copy* to copy a source price list, or part of a source price list based on an item range, to a destination price list. If you check

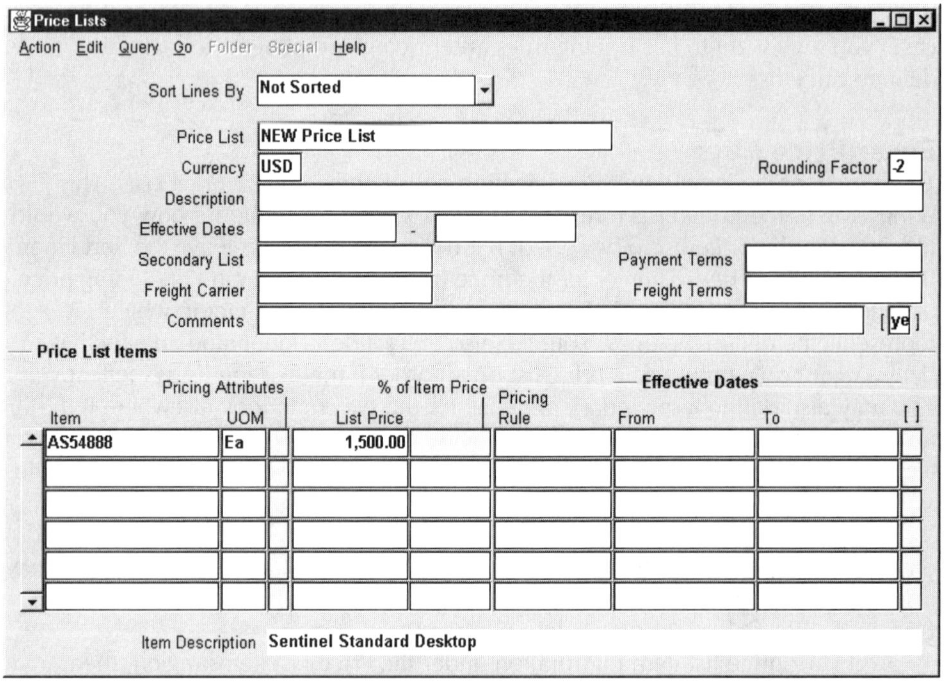

FIGURE 19-1. *Price Lists form*

the *Include Discounts* checkbox, all of the associated discounts will also be copied. You must enter the new price list name (which must be unique), an optional description, and an optional effectivity date range. See Figure 19-2. Submitting the entered data will generate a concurrent program to create the new price list.

Adjust Price Lists

Follow the navigation path *Pricing : Lists : Adjust* to adjust an existing price list. Select the price list and the items to be adjusted by using an item range, item category, item status, and/or creation date. You can adjust by percentage or amount. See Figure 19-3. Submitting the entered data will generate a concurrent program to adjust the price list.

Item Groups

Follow the navigation path *Pricing : Lists : Groups* to enter the item groups. If the same group of items must be on multiple price lists, then define item groups to facilitate faster data entry. Define an item group with a unique group name and an optional description. Then, enter the items into the item group like you would enter them on the price list, with item name, UOM, pricing attributes, list price or percent of item prices, and a pricing rule (if desired). See Figure 19-4.

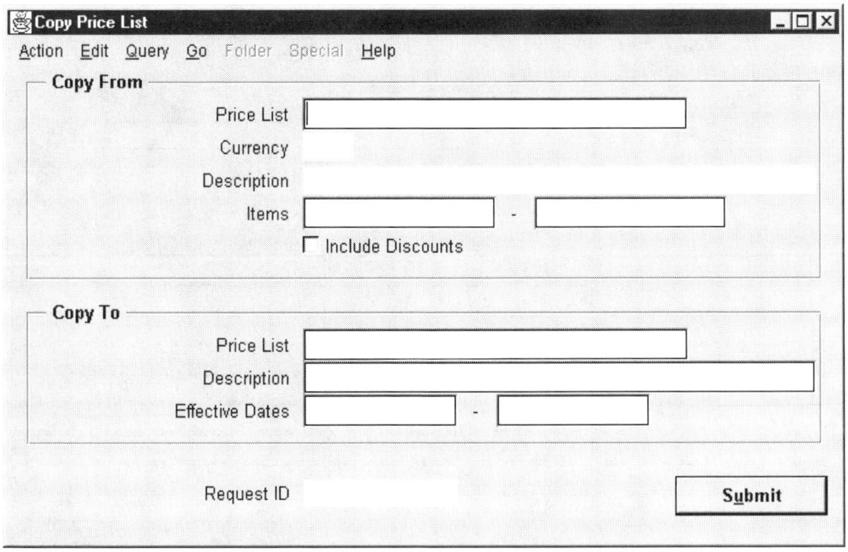

FIGURE 19-2. *Copy Price List form*

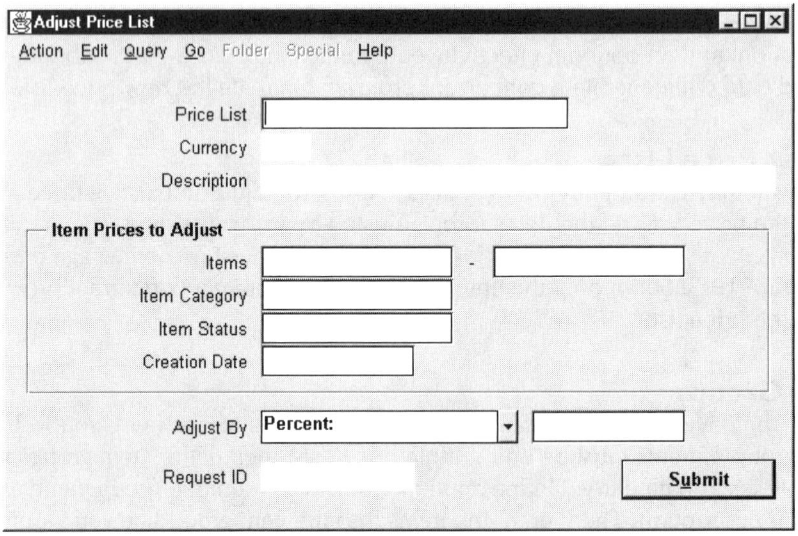

FIGURE 19-3. *Adjust Price List form*

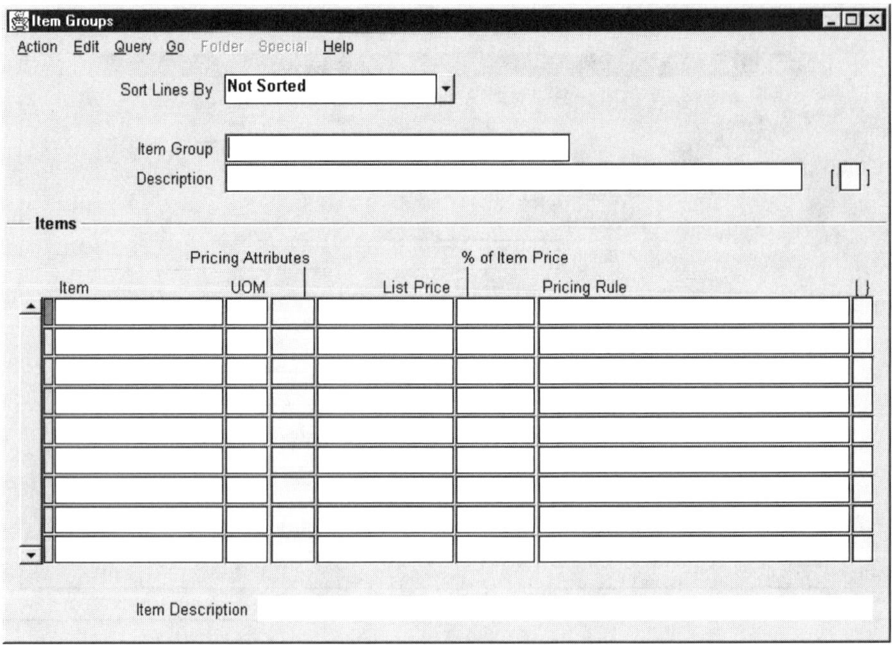

FIGURE 19-4. *Item Groups form*

Add Item Groups

Follow the navigation path *Pricing : Lists : Add Item Groups* to add defined item groups to the price list. Select a price list to add the item group to, then select any number of defined item groups. You can also enter an effectivity date range for each item group. Submitting the entered data will generate a concurrent program to add the item groups to the price list. See Figure 19-5.

Add Items

Follow the navigation path *Pricing : Lists : Add Items* to add items to the price list by an item range, item category, and/or item status. To set the list price to the item cost, check the *Set List Price Equal to Cost* checkbox. If you do not check this, the items will be added at $0. Submitting the entered data will generate a concurrent program to add the items to the price list. See Figure 19-6.

To establish pricing rules, which compute the prices of items dynamically as an order is entered according to defined rules, follow the navigation path *Pricing : Rules : Price Rules.*

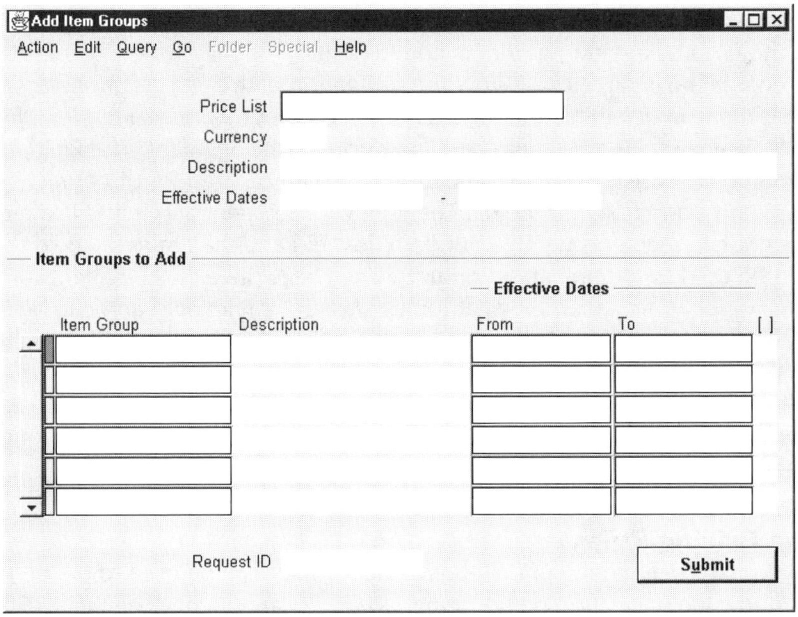

FIGURE 19-5. *Add Item Groups form*

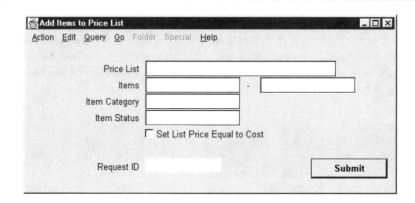

FIGURE 19-6. *Add Items to Price List form*

Define Pricing Components

Pricing components must be defined prior to being referenced in price rules. Each pricing component consists of up to five pricing parameters, which can be any segment of your System Item flexfield, plus any attribute from the Pricing Attribute Descriptive flexfield. You must define and enable the segment and/or attribute before they can be a part of a pricing component.

To enable the parameters, follow the navigation path *Setup : Parameters*. All of the fields that can be enabled are listed with one of four sources: Field in OE Form, Item Flex Segment, Item Flexfield, and Descriptive Flex Segment. The Field in OE Form source contains fields in the OE forms that can be used for discounts, automatic note addition, and holds. The Item Flex Segment and Item Flexfield sources contain segments within your Item flexfield and the entire flexfield itself, and can be used for pricing and discounts. The Descriptive Flex Segment source contains attributes for the Pricing Attributes Descriptive flexfield and can be used for pricing and discounts. Enable the parameter by checking the *Enabled* checkbox. See Figure 19-7.

Follow the navigation path *Pricing : Rules : Components* to define pricing components. See Figure 19-8. Create a unique name for the pricing component and select the column(s) that are defined and enabled.

Define Pricing Rules

Once you have defined the pricing components, they can be used to define pricing rules. Follow the navigation path *Pricing : Rules : Components*. See Figure 19-9. Enter a pricing rule name, which must be unique, then enter an optional effectivity date range and an optional description.

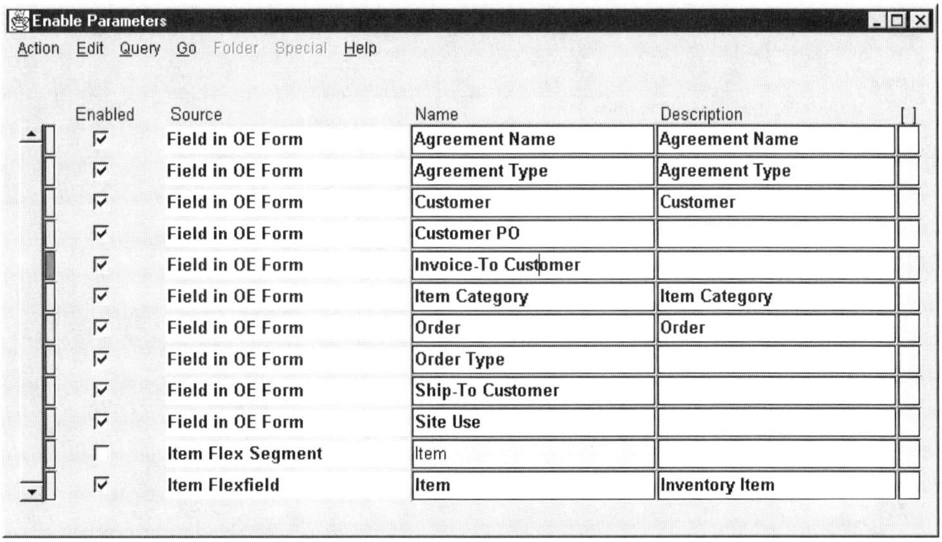

FIGURE 19-7. *Enable Parameters form*

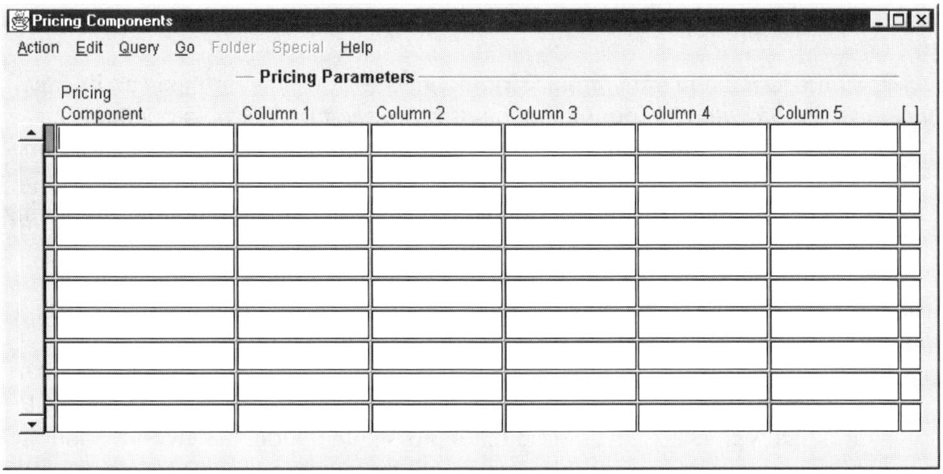

FIGURE 19-8. *Pricing Components form*

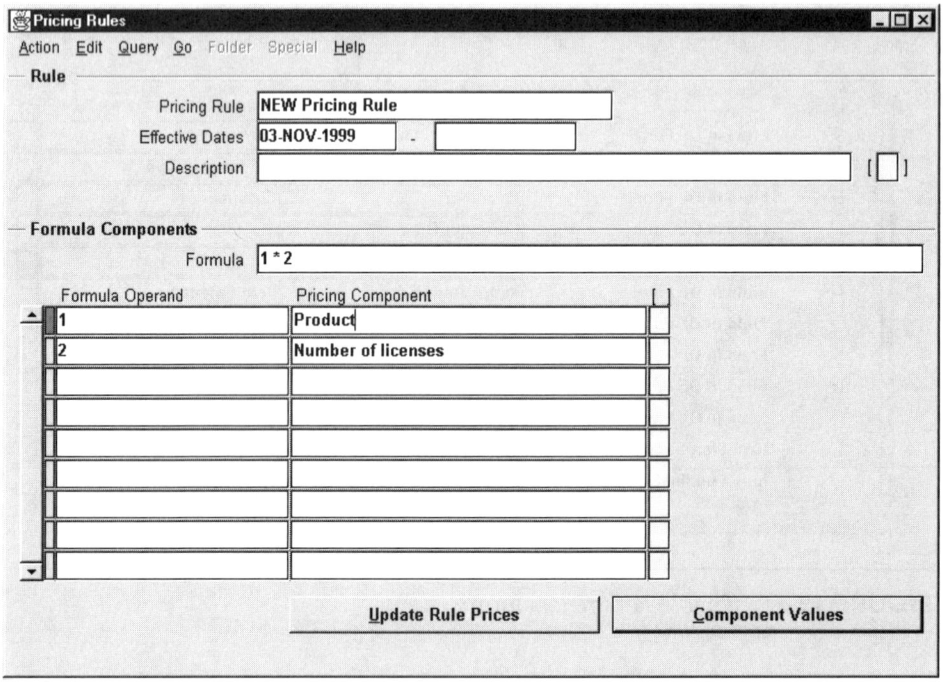

FIGURE 19-9. *Pricing Rules form*

Enter the formula in the Formula Components region. The formula can be any valid expression with any formula operands and operators. Formula operands are defined below the formula, and each is a number that identifies a particular pricing component. The operators can be **+**, **-**, *****, or **/**. When you define each formula operand, click on the **Component Value** button to assign an amount to each pricing component value. See Figure 19-10.

An example would be that you want to set the item list price based on two variables: the Product segment of your Item flexfield, and the number of licenses purchased. (This assumes, of course, that your Item flexfield has more than one segment, and that one of those segments is Product.) Set up a pricing component to store the number of licenses as the second formula operand; the first operand will be the Product segment. Using the **Components Value** button, assign an amount to each valid Product segment value together with the number of licenses purchased. Then, all items with that particular Product segment value will have their list prices determined by the number of licenses.

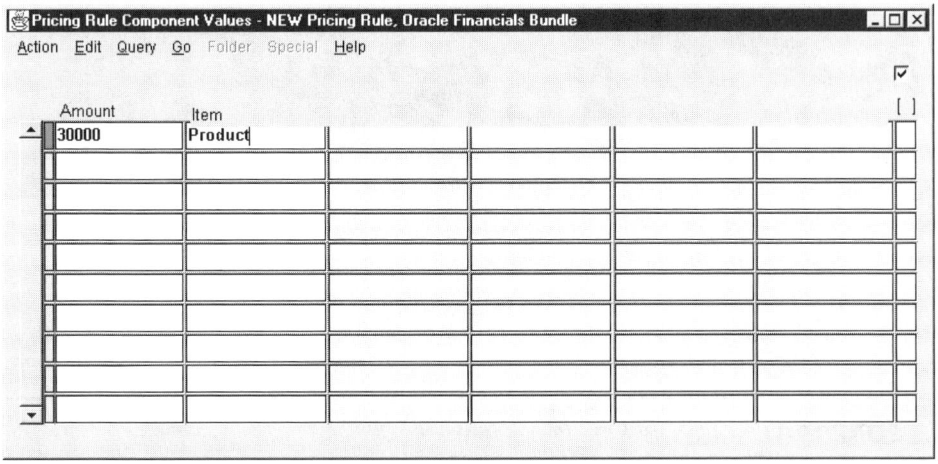

FIGURE 19-10. *Pricing Rule Component Values form*

Update Rule Prices

Click on the **Update Rule Prices** button to update the items with the defined, associated pricing rules, or follow the navigation path *Pricing : Rules : Update.* You can either update the new price list lines only, or price list lines that have been modified, by checking the *New and Modified Lines Only* checkbox. Otherwise, the program will update all price list lines. If you click on the **Update Rule Prices** button, the *Update Individual Pricing Rule* radio button will be selected and the pricing rule will be filled in automatically. With the **Update Rule Prices** button, you can choose to update all pricing rules. Then, click on the **Submit** button to submit the Pricing Program and update the associated price lists. See Figure 19-11.

Use the above concepts to create price lists and pricing rules that satisfy your company's business needs.

Review Questions

   1. What is a pricing component and what can be configured as part of a pricing component?

   2. How can you copy part of a price list to generate a new price list?

   3. How can you perform a 5 percent increase for a particular item category?

   4. How are pricing rules set up?

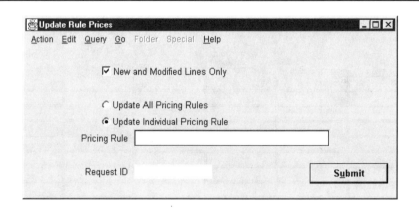

FIGURE 19-11. *Update Rule Prices form*

Managing Discounts

Discounts allow you to adjust the list price at order entry time and are applied to individual price lists. You may configure discounts to occur automatically or manually at the line level. Such discounts affect individual lines only, and may represent a specific price or percentage. At the order level, you may only apply discounts manually and as a percentage. Order-level type discounts affect all lines on an order. Various discounts may be tied to one price list; however, only one automatic discount can be factored in to adjust the price. If various automatic discounts exist, then the system chooses the lowest discounted price. At least one price list must be defined prior to defining the discounts. To create discounts, follow the navigation path *Pricing : Discounts.* This brings you to the Discounts form. See Figure 19-12.

Discounts must be named, and can also be given descriptions. Choose an existing price list, and keep in mind that the combined discount name and price list names must be unique. You may also enter an effectivity date range. If no dates are specified, then the discount is always active. If the discount is available to the General Services Administration (GSA), check the *GSA* checkbox. GSA discounts—which cannot be overridden—can be applied automatically for customers marked as being a GSA customer with no proration at line level. Next, choose the level to which the discount applies: Order or Lines.

With line-level discounts you may choose not to prorate by choosing None, or to prorate based on the following: All Lines or Category. Prorated discounts allocate the discount across the selected group—either all lines in the order, or all lines of the same category in the order; the invoice amount stays the same. With line-level

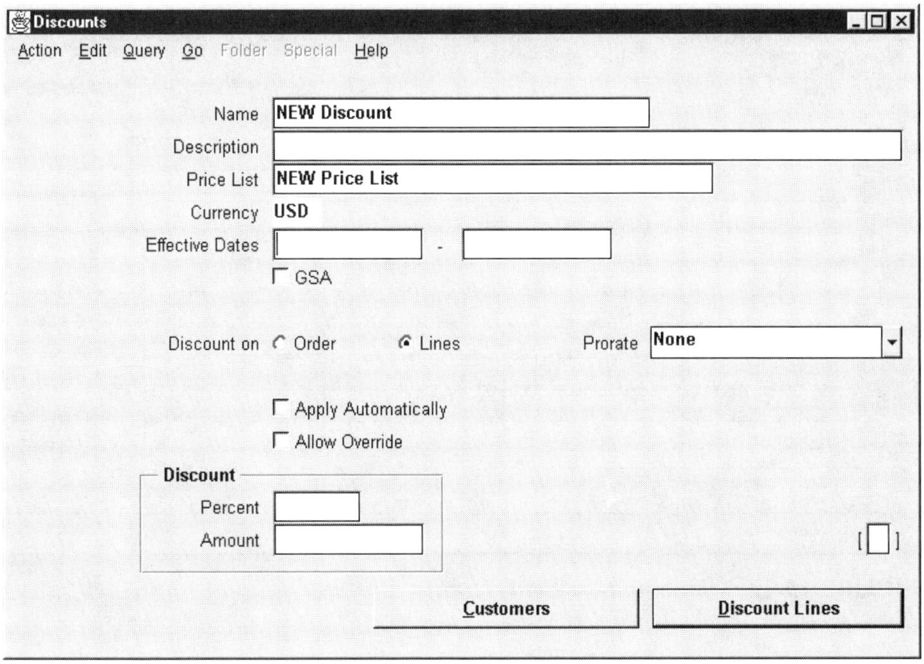

FIGURE 19-12. *Discounts form*

discounts, you may apply the discount automatically—as opposed to handling it manually—by checking the *Apply Automatically* checkbox. You can opt to allow override to a modified price by choosing *Allow Override* together with the profile option *OE: Discounting Privilege*, which controls the user's authority to apply discounts.

You can also enter the percentage amount of the discount and the currency amount of the discount. Leave these fields blank if the discount is a GSA discount, or if you want to restrict the discount by items. If you only want to restrict by customers, not items, you must enter either an amount or percentage. If you enter an amount, you cannot change the amount in the future.

For the purposes of this exercise, create a discount called **NEW Discount** and attach it to the **NEW Price List**, then save your work.

You can then click on the **Customers** or **Discount Line** buttons in the bottom-right corner of the form. Click on the **Customers** button to restrict customer by customer class, customer name, customer number, or site use for the discount. Only customers satisfying the selection will get the discounts. See Figure 19-13.

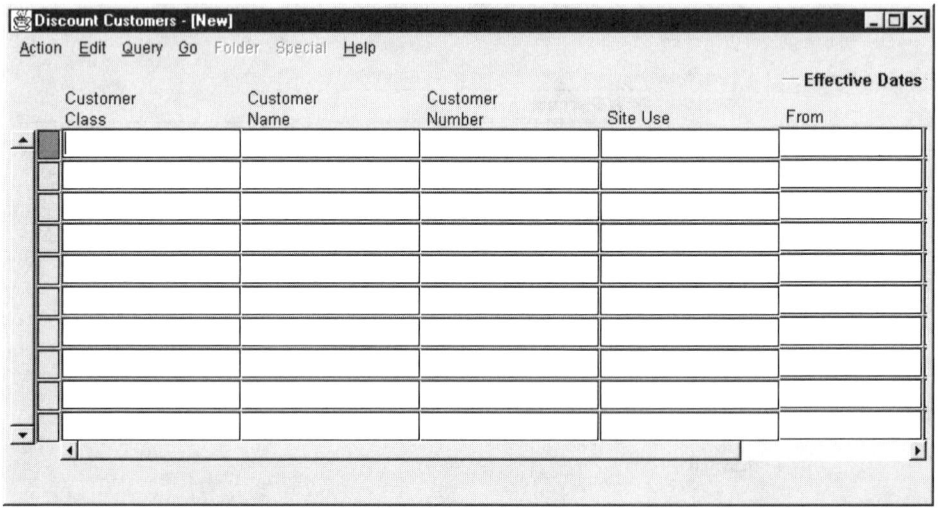

FIGURE 19-13. *Discount Customers form*

Next, click on the **Discount Lines** button and the Discount Lines form will appear. See Figure 19-14. In the Discount By field, you can choose to discount by agreement name, agreement type, customer PO, item, or item category. Next, choose the specific value to be discounted for as defined by the last field. Select the value, then choose one of the following methods: Use Price Breaks, Percent Amount, or Price. If you enter a percentage, an amount, or a price, the other two fields will be automatically calculated based on the entered field and the price of the item on the price list. You can mark the discount line as fixed price, which means the selling price is fixed even if the list price changes. You must do this for a GSA discount. You can also enter an effectivity date range in the Effective Dates alternative region. Enter to discount by item, and choose AS54888 as the discount. Check the *Use Price Breaks* checkbox and click on the **Price Breaks** button; this brings up the Price Breaks form. See Figure 19-15.

You may select from one of the two methods: Value or Quantity. Then, enter the unit of measure related to the unit volume discount. Set the price break range quantities From and To. If you choose Value, the price break range is the value range. Otherwise, it is a quantity range. You can set to the discount based on a percentage, amount, or price, and the other two fields will be calculated automatically. Check the *Fixed Price* checkbox for a fixed selling price. For the

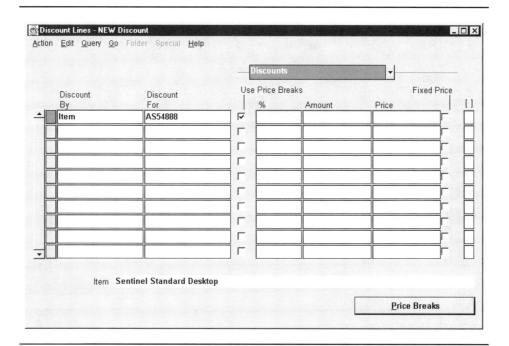

FIGURE 19-14.   *Discount Lines form*

purposes of this exercise, select Quantity as the method, enter **Ea** as UOM, and select two price ranges. The first will be from 1 to 10 with a 5 percent discount, and the second will be from 11 to 99999 and with a 10 percent discount. When finished, save your work.

Review Questions

1. How do *Allow Override* and the profile option *OE: Discounting Privilege* work together?

2. What happens when you have more than one automatic discount?

3. How is a GSA discount set up?

4. How do you set up price breaks?

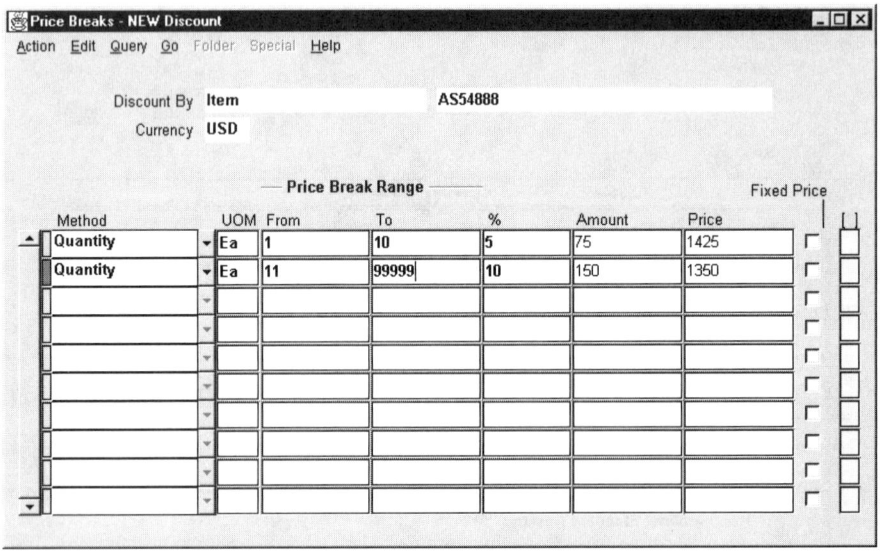

FIGURE 19-15. *Price Breaks form*

Processing Orders

In this section, you will learn how to perform more advanced order processing, including:

- Apply sales credits, discounts, and notes to a sales order
- Approve orders and lines
- Apply and remove holds
- Cancel orders and lines
- View order and line details

Applying Sales Credits, Discounts, and Notes to a Sales Order

Sales Credits

Oracle Order Entry allows you to automatically default one salesperson per order/return to populate the sales credit information. You may then change or add additional salespersons to the order/return. You must ensure the total quota sales credit equals 100 percent. Before applying sales credits, you must first define the sales credit types and salespersons.

The Sales Credits form for each order may be found via the Special | Sales Credits menu command. See Figure 19-16 for the Sales Credits form. You may locate sales credits information for returns by clicking on the **Sales Credits** button in the Returns form.

To add another salesperson, first choose the sales credit type from the List of Values, then select the salesperson from the List of Values and enter the Percentage (%) field. If the *Revenue* checkbox is checked, then it is a Quota Sales Credit type. You can have non-quota sales credits less than or greater than 100 percent. You can see the revenue total percent and the nonrevenue total percentage at the bottom of the form. Click on the **OK** button to save any changes, and the **Cancel** button to cancel the changes.

Discounts

Assuming that discounts have already been configured as discussed in the "Managing Discounts" section, you can go to the Discounts form by clicking on the **Discounts**

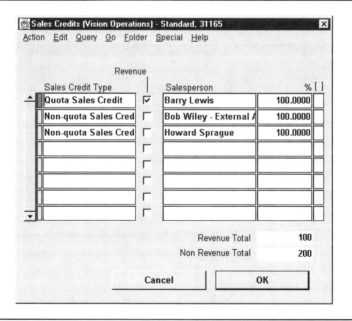

FIGURE 19-16. *Sales Credits form*

button in the Sales Orders form or the Returns form. Depending on where your cursor is—at the order header level or line level—one of the following forms will appear: Discount or Line Discounts. Use the Discount form for taking order-level discounts by choosing a discount name and percentage; you can only choose a percentage at the order level. From the Line Discounts form, any automatic discount information would already be populated on the form. See Figure 19-17 for the Line Discounts form. If you can override pricing information, go to Setups and choose a discount name. Then, use the following fields to adjust the price: Final Price or Percentage. If you enter a final price, the other two fields—Percentage and Discount Amount—will be calculated. If you enter a dollar amount, the Discount Amount field will be calculated. Once you have entered all of the discounts, click on the **OK** button to save your line discounts.

You can also apply a manual discount by using the List of Values from the Selling Price field in the Orders form. Alternatively, you can enter a new selling price, if the profile option allows you to enter manual overridable discounts. In this case, when you exit the Selling Price field, you will be asked to select a manual discount valid for the order's price list.

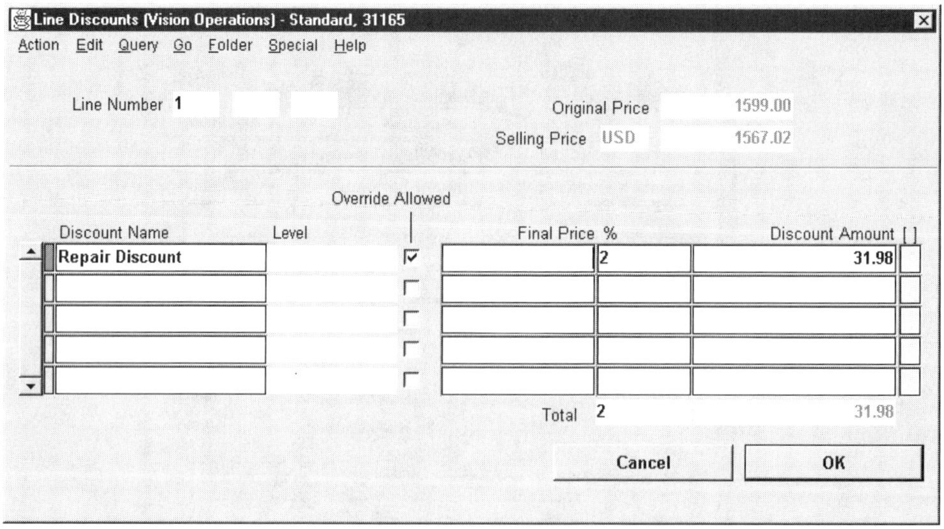

FIGURE 19-17. *Line Discounts form*

Notes

You may use order/return notes to add any additional information you would like applied to a particular order/return at the header or line level. You can attach existing notes and standard or template notes, or you can create new one-time notes. You can also edit existing notes using template notes. The notes will then print on the standard sales order acknowledgement, pick slip, pack slip, and commercial invoice, depending on which note category you select for the note.

Before applying notes, you must define the note categories and any standard notes you may want to use. To define a note category, click on the **Reports** button to choose the report you want to tie to the created note category. In the Report field, choose from the following List of Values: Bill of Lading, Commercial Invoice, Pack Slip, Pick Slip, or Sales Order Acknowledgement. Then, choose from the following Formats: Print in Body of Report, Print on Bottom of Report, or Print on Top of Report.

You can also click on the **Assignments** button from the Note Categories form. From the Category Assignments form, choose between types Form or Function. Under the Name field, choose the form or function name from the List of Values. By doing so, you make the defined category available in the chosen form.

If you are within the actual order or return, attachments are allowed if a green Paper Clip icon appears on the toolbar. If there is paper in the paper clip, then notes have already been attached. You may add a new note or attach existing notes by clicking on the Paper Clip icon. To apply rule-based notes quickly, they must be attached via the Special | Apply Notes menu command. Rule-based notes are notes whose rule criteria match information on the current order. Rules can be based on customer, order type, item, and other factors. See Figure 19-18.

To add a one-time note, choose a category and type in a Description of the note. Choose Short Text in the Data Type field, place your cursor in the blank box, and type your note. As a last step, review and save your note.

If you would like to add an existing predefined note, click on the **Document Catalog** button. This brings you to the Document Catalog form. See Figure 19-19. Enter criteria like description, category, and other factors to find the note you are seeking, then click on the **Find** button. This brings up notes that match your criteria. Once you have found your note, click on the **Attach** button to apply it. If the *May Be Changed* checkbox is checked, the note may be edited. Click on the **Preview** button to view the selected attachment, then review and save your note. Then close the form and return to the Sales Order form or Returns form to continue processing.

Review Questions

1. Which types of sales credits do not have to add up to 100 percent?

2. At which two levels can you apply discounts?

3. What are the different ways to apply discounts to an order line?

4. How can you tell when the Attachment feature is available?

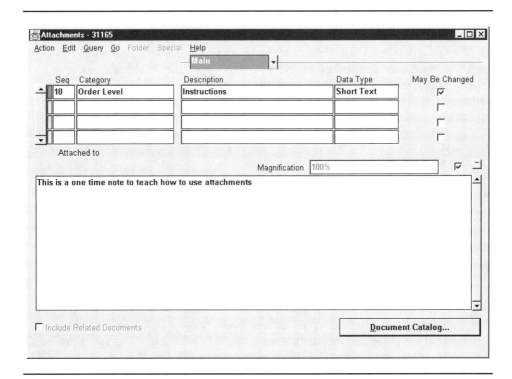

FIGURE 19-18. *Attachments form*

Approving Orders and Lines

For various reasons, you may wish to include an approval step in your order cycles. The order/return or lines would be held automatically once the approval cycle action was reached. Once it has been reviewed and approved by an approved person, it will be released to move to the next cycle action. For example, you may create a return order type in which you would like the Quality department to review and approve all items before being received back into inventory. Approval can be at the header level or at the line level. See the "Approve Order" section in Chapter 17 for more details.

Review Question

1. For which levels can you add an approval step?

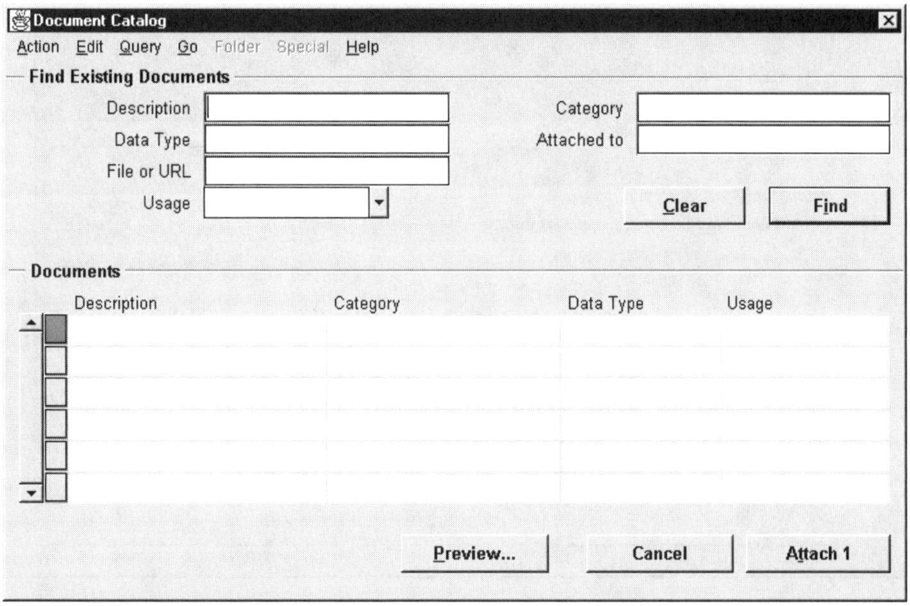

FIGURE 19-19.   *Document Catalog form*

Applying and Removing Holds

Holds can be applied to orders/returns, order/return lines, customers, and items. Before applying holds, you must define the hold types your company is planning to use as QuickCodes. Next, you must create your holds. To apply a hold, follow the navigation path *Orders, Returns : Holds : Apply*. This brings you into the Apply Hold Sources form. See Figure 19-20.

The Hold Selection Criteria drop-down arrow box selections are as follows: Customer, Order, Site Use, or Item. You can choose the criteria and select a specific value. As an example, if you choose Order you can enter a specific order number to hold. Then, select the hold name from the Hold Future and Selected Existing Orders region. For the purposes of this exercise, select Item and use **AS54888** as the value; select any hold name.

You can also enter a date in the Hold Until Date field, and determine when the hold will be automatically removed by the system, assuming the Close Orders program in Oracle Order Entry is running. You can also enter a comment.

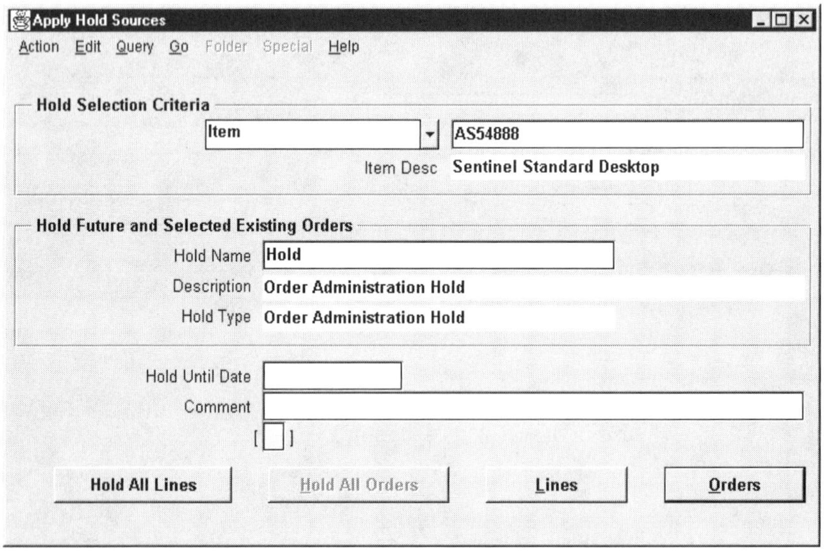

FIGURE 19-20. *Apply Hold Sources form*

Depending on the type of hold being applied, click on one of the following highlighted buttons: **Hold All Lines, Hold All Orders, Lines,** or **Orders**. **Hold All Lines** is available if you choose the *Item* option; it will apply holds to all lines that fit the criteria. **Hold All Orders** will apply holds to all orders that fit the criteria. **Lines** and **Orders** will display all of the lines or orders that fit your criteria, and you must manually mark those you want to place on hold manually. Click on the **Mark for Hold** button or check the *On Hold* checkbox. The selected records will be on hold once the record is saved. You can select multiple records or use the *Select All* option and then click on the **Mark for Hold** button to mark multiple selections for hold. See Figure 19-21. For the purposes of this exercise, click on the **Lines** button, select two records to mark for hold, then save your work.

If a hold-until date was not entered in the Apply Hold Sources form, holds on orders/returns, order/return lines, shipment schedules, or options must be manually released. To remove a hold, follow the navigation path *Orders, Returns : Holds : Release*, which brings you to the Find Holds form.

The drop-down box selections—which are the same as when you apply holds—are as follows: Customers, Orders, Site Use, or Item. For the purposes of this exercise, enter the item and **AS54888,**and enter the same hold name you selected above. Depending on the type of release chosen, click on the **Lines, Orders**, or

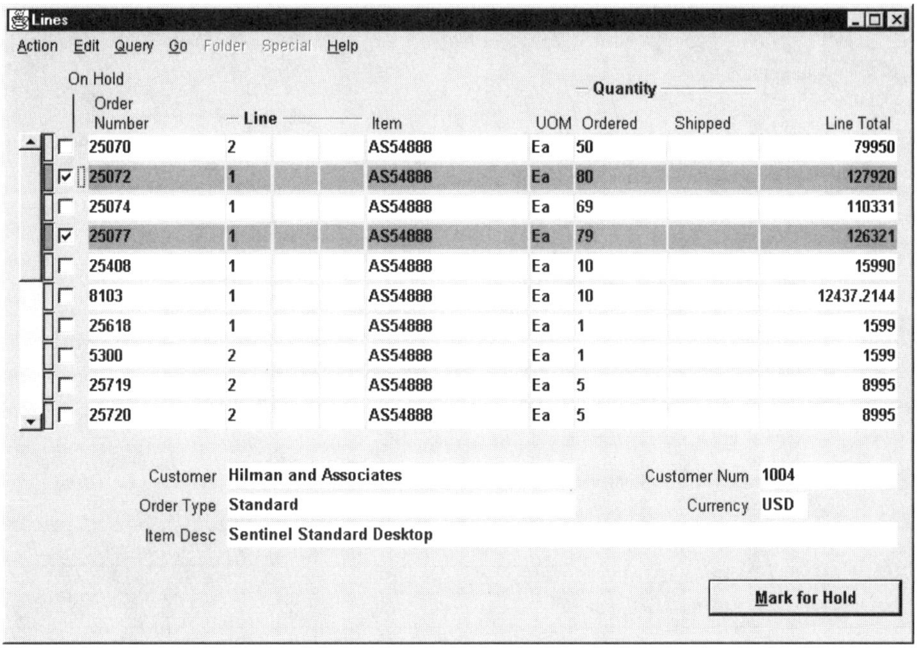

FIGURE 19-21. *Lines form*

Hold Sources buttons. Click on the **Orders** or **Lines** button to manually release an individual order or line. You can select more than one record and click on the **Mark for Release** button to enter a release reason and comment for all of the selected records. Click on the **Hold Sources** button to release every order or line that fits your selection criteria. See Figure 19-22 for the Release Hold Sources form. In each case, you must select a release reason. Release reason codes are set up as QuickCodes of type RELEASE_REASON. You can also enter a comment, then save your work to release the selected holds.

Review Questions

1. What must be set up before applying holds?

2. What criteria are used to identify holds to be released and orders/lines to be held?

3. What field must be entered for a release?

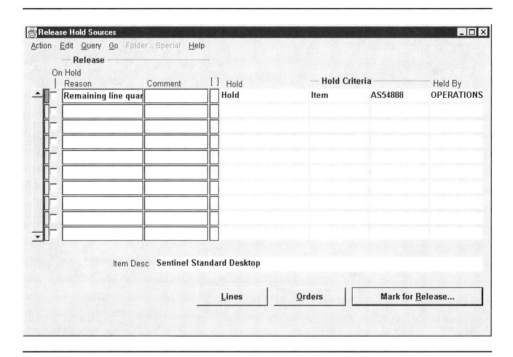

FIGURE 19-22. *Release Hold Sources form*

Cancelling Orders and Lines

You may cancel orders/returns and lines by following navigation path *Orders, Returns : Cancel : Cancel Orders*. You can also cancel the order/return or lines directly from the Orders Workbench by clicking on the **Cancel** button. Either route will bring you to the Cancel Orders form. See Figure 19-23.

Follow the navigation path directly to query up the order/return with the attached lines. Once the order/return has been retrieved, view the lines by clicking anywhere in the Line region. To cancel the entire order, click on the **Cancel Order** button. You can cancel an order if the order has not been closed, if it has no pick released line, and no ATO line that released a work order or received a return line. You can further restrict the order cancellation criteria by defining security rules. If you want to cancel a line, either enter the cancel quantity or check the *Cancel in Full* checkbox, then click on the **Cancel Line** button. You can cancel the entire line if it has not yet been pick released. You can also further restrict the order-line cancellation criteria by defining security rules, and you can cancel the unpick-released quantities to view the allowed-to-cancel quantities in the Allowed field. You must enter a reason for cancelling either the order or the order line. These cancel codes are QuickCodes with lookup type CANCEL_CODE.

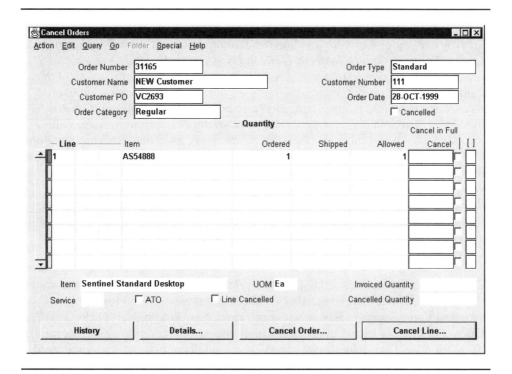

FIGURE 19-23. *Cancel Orders form*

Once you have selected your reason and entered an optional comment, click on the **Yes** button to cancel the order/return, the line, or the entered line quantities. Cancelling an order or line does not delete the information, but it discontinues processing the remaining steps in the order cycle.

NOTE
If a line has been pick released, but not yet ship confirmed, it can still be cancelled by backordering the pick slip first.

Review Questions

1. When can you cancel an order?

2. When can you cancel a line?

3. Where do you define cancel reasons?

Viewing Order and Line Details

To view existing order/return and line detail information, follow the navigation path *Orders, Returns : Orders, Returns.* This will bring you to the Find Orders form.

Use the Main drop-down arrow box to search using none, some, or all of the following criteria: order number, PO number, order category, order source, order dates, created by, order type, requisition number, invoice number, entry status (Booked, Entered, Partial), customer name, customer PO, ship-to location, bill-to location, customer number, and/or salesperson. Next, change to the Shipping, More alternative region. You may also search by using none, some, or all of the following: item, lot number, serial numbers, WIP job, freight carrier, warehouse, pick slip, waybill, and/or freight terms. Your search need not include the following, depending on your needs: closed orders, cancelled orders, released or backordered orders. Once you have entered your search criteria, simply click on the **Find** button at the bottom right-hand corner of the form. Your results will be displayed in the Orders Summary form.

You can find the overall status of the order/return by ensuring that your cursor is on the order in question, then clicking on the **Cycle Status** button to view the cycle action, result, level, and date. See Figure 19-24. Other buttons will take you to other forms, including **Copy, Approve, Schedule, Cancel, Hold, New Return, New Order** and **Open**. Click on the **View** button for detailed information and the View Orders form.

In the View Orders form, you can click on additional buttons, including **Holds**, **Shipping**, **Backordered**, **Details**, or **Cycle Status**, for more information. More information will be displayed if you change the alternative region to Shipping Lines, Invoices/Credit Memos, or Picking Batches (the shipping and invoice/credit information will be of particular interest in answering customer questions). While in the View Orders form, you cannot update the information.

Review Questions

1. What will the Cycle Statuses form reveal?

2. Which form is used to view order and line details?

3. How many alternative regions are in the Find Orders form?

Drop-Shipping Orders

In this section, you will learn how to fulfill a drop-ship order. Drop-shipment is a way to fulfill sales orders by having suppliers ship directly to your customers. In

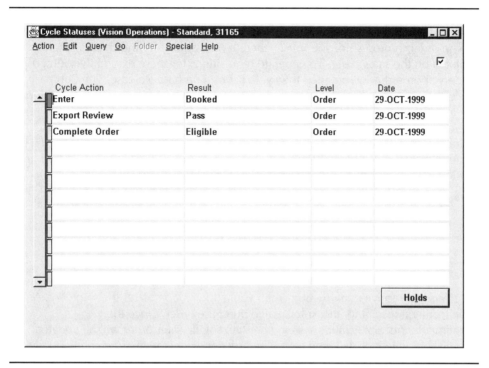

FIGURE 19-24. *Cycle Statuses form*

such a case, you need not ship the items and relieve inventory. In this section, you will learn to:

- Determine when to drop-ship orders or portions of orders

- Enter drop-ship orders and partial drop-ship orders

- View drop-ship orders and partial drop-ship orders

- Fulfill and invoice drop-ship and partial drop-ship orders

- Enter and process returns of drop-ship orders

Determining When To Ship Full or Partial Orders

Your company may have requirements to drop-ship items that are not stocked or that are temporarily out of stock. Or, it could be more cost effective to ship from the supplier directly to the customer. In all of these cases, you will decide to drop-ship orders or mark part of the orders as drop-ship.

In order to drop-ship, you must generate requisitions for the ship-to location entered on the sales order. To generate requisitions for these externally sourced orders or order lines, you need the cycle action Purchase Release. The Purchase Release program will generate the requisitions for a receiving location if the ship-to location on the sales order is associated with a receiving location in Oracle Purchasing. In order to link a ship-to address to a receiving location, you must choose a location in the Internal region in the Business Purpose Detail form. To get ready for your drop-shipment exercise, go back to your New Customer record and add an internal location called Drop-ship to the ship-to location.

TIP

Location can have any name. However, in the Vision demo database, it just happens to have a location called Drop-ship.

You will receive confirmation when your supplier completes the shipment. At this point, enter a receipt for the AutoCreated purchase order. Once the confirmation/receipt is in the system, the status of the sales order will be updated. The Receivables interface will then select the order and generate it as an entire invoice or as part of an invoice, and your customer will be billed. The prerequisites of the Receivables interface are action Purchase Release with results Confirmed or Partial, depending on whether the entire quantity or only a partial quantity is received.

Assuming all order lines on the order will be handled via drop-shipment, you would create an order type and cycle for your externally sourced supplier. This order cycle will include purchase release, but not pick release, ship confirm, and Inventory interface. In other words, the order cycle will be: Enter → Purchase Release → Receivables interface → Complete Line → Complete Order. If some of the order lines will be handled via drop-shipment but others will not, you would create an order cycle with Purchase Release as well as Pick Release, Ship Confirm, and Inventory interface cycle actions. This type of mixed order will have order lines of both external sourced and internal sourced. You need the Pick Release, Ship Confirm, and Inventory interface cycle actions to handle shipping and inventory action in your location.

Review Questions

1. What are some of the reasons you may drop-ship orders or parts of orders?

2. Which cycle actions in the standard order cycle must be included for drop-shipment order cycle with no internal sourced order lines?

3. Can you describe the order cycle with all external sourced order lines?

Entering Full and Partial Drop-Ship Orders

New or partial drop-ship orders are entered through the Orders Workbench by following the same process you would when entering a regular order. Select an order type with an order cycle that has the cycle action Purchase Release. Keep in mind that if you have both external- and internal-sourced order lines, you will keep the standard order cycle and simply add Purchase Release as a parallel cycle action to Pick Release and Ship Confirm. Also, Inventory interface will be an optional cycle action, and not a prerequisite since drop-shipment does not require inventory relief. In this scenario, you may consistently perform an online inventory to ensure that the inventory is relieved before billing. When selecting your ship-to customer and location, remember that the ship-to location must be associated with a receiving location, as discussed in the previous section. Once you have entered the order header information, move your cursor to the Line region to add the product items that will be ordered.

The line number defaults automatically, and you will select predefined items from the item master. Since drop-ship items must be on a purchase requisitions, all such items must be purchasable, standard items, and cannot be kits or models. In the scheduling region, enter the requested date, promised date, and scheduled date. This is a drop-shipment, so the Source Type field must be External and the order line must be Drop-ship. If you do not allow partial drop-ships, the order type should only allow External source types. In this case, External is defaulted into the Source Type field and cannot be overridden. If you allow both in an order, then your order type must allow both. In this case, you must select the appropriate source type depending on whether it is a drop-ship line. If it is drop-ship, select External; otherwise, select Internal. If the source type is External, you must also select the receiving organization. You will notice that most of the remaining scheduling fields are shaded out, including Warehouse, Reserved Quantity, Ship Set, Scheduling Action, Scheduling Status, and Demand Class. Fill in the rest of the necessary information and book the order.

For the purposes of this exercise, use your current customer, select order type Drop-ship, use AS54888 as the part number, and select M1 (Seattle Manufacturing) as the receiving organization (the drop-ship location belongs to this organization). Save your work and book your order.

You are now ready to run the Purchase Release program. You may run the Purchase Release, Requisition Import request set from Order Entry manually through SRS, or you can set it to run at particular intervals or at a certain time of day. Follow the navigation path *Orders, Returns : Purchase Release.* You can select a range of order numbers, request date range, a specific customer PO, ship-to location, order type, customer, and/or item. If all parameters are left blank, all externally sourced order lines will be processed. If you do not run Purchase Release, requisitions will not be generated. Once the Purchase Release program is completed, the Requisition Import program in Oracle Purchasing will be initiated automatically to import the requisition. Once the process is complete, you must AutoCreate the requisition into a PO.

Review Questions

1. What source type should the order type restrict if you want to have both external- and interface-sourced order lines in the same order?

2. What must be done after booking an order with drop-shipment lines?

3. What inventory attributes must an item have in order to be eligible for drop-shipment?

Viewing Full and Partial Drop-Ship Orders

To view existing order/return and line detail information for drop-ship orders and partial drop-ship orders, you should navigate to the Orders Workbench. To locate drop-ship orders and partial drop-ship orders, you can use the same criteria as you would for a regular order. In particular, you may want to use the order type to pull up all drop-shipment order types. Click on the **Find** button. Your results will be displayed in the Orders Summary form. You can find the overall status of the order/return by making sure your cursor is on the drop-ship order you are interested in and then clicking on the **Cycle Status** button. To find out detail information of the drop-ship order, you must click on the **View** button with your cursor on the order you are interested in.

Review Question

1. How do you view information about the status of orders with drop-ship lines?

Fulfilling and Invoicing Full and Partial Drop-Ship Orders

Once proof of shipment for drop-shipped orders has been received from the vendor, use Oracle Purchasing to enter a receipt. Proof of shipment can be manual, such as a fax or phone call, or by ASN (advance shipment notice) through EDI Gateway. Items are received into the receiving location of the receiving organization against the PO related to the drop-ship. Upon receipt, the drop-ship sales order line status will be updated to either Partial or Confirmed, depending on whether the received quantity is the same as the ordered quantity. If it is underreceived, the status will be Partial. If it is completely received, the status will be Confirmed. Oracle Order Entry does not handle overshipment, so if more product is shipped than ordered, the situation must be handled manually. Manual invoices can be created to bill the surplus quantity—or, you can ask the customer to return the surplus.

When the status of the purchase release becomes Partial or Confirmed, your drop-shipment order lines are ready for invoicing and the cycle action Receivables interface—which pushes the order/return information towards Oracle Receivables—has an Eligible result. The Receivables interface program can be run manually from Order Entry, or you can set it to run at particular intervals or at a certain time of the day. Follow the navigation path *Orders, Returns : Receivables Interface.* This program should be run at least once prior to running AutoInvoice, which is run in Oracle Receivables to create the actual invoices. If the Receivables interface is not run in Oracle Order Entry, then no invoices of source Order Entry will be picked up when AutoInvoice is run in Oracle Receivables. The Receivables interface works the exact same way for drop-ship orders as it does for regular orders.

Once the Receivables interface is completed, your drop-shipment order information can be closed. It should have reached the following order cycle action and result: Complete Order and Eligible at the order level, and Complete Line and Eligible at the line level. All order cycles must be set up correctly, and all lines must be completed and closed out or the order will not complete or close.

You can run the Close Orders program manually from Oracle Order Entry, or it can be set to run at particular intervals or at a certain time of the day. Follow the function patch *Orders, Returns : Close Orders.* The Close Orders program speeds up the various forms and greatly reduces printed lines on some standard Oracle reports by closing the ready to be closed open orders/lines. However, if all lines and the order/return are closed, then you cannot add items or make any changes.

Review Questions

1. What triggers the Receivables interface for drop-ship lines?

2. What happens if your supplier underships?

3. What happens if your supplier overships?

Entering and Processing Returns of Drop-Ship Orders

The Oracle Order Entry module can also handle product returns related to drop-ship orders. RMA orders can be linked to previously drop-shipped products in order to provide effortless return order entry and credit memos, if necessary. Order types are created to handle different types of returns and orders, and are sometimes referred to as return types when handling returns instead of orders. Similarly, order cycles can be referred as return cycles. Because order types are linked to order cycles, various RMA processing cycles are possible. For return cycles, there is a cycle action called RMA interface that replaces the Inventory interface. The RMA interface obtains return information and increments inventory from Oracle Order Entry accordingly in Oracle Inventory. To update Oracle Inventory with the return data, you must include the RMA interface.

If the drop-ship customer returns the products and you decide to retain them in inventory, it will be handled just like a nondrop-shipped products return. You can run the Receivables interface or, for an overshipment situation, you may just want to retain the inventory and not generate credit memos.

If the drop-ship customer returns the products and you decide to ship them back to the suppliers, you must first enter the returns into Oracle Order Entry, then run the RMA interface. You must also enter a return in Oracle Purchasing. When you ship the products, you must also issue the product from the receiving organization.

If the customer returns the drop-ship products directly to the supplier, and if you want to keep a record in the system, it will be handled as if the customer returned products directly to you (like the last situation). You must enter the returns into the system and run the RMA interface. You also must enter a return in Oracle Purchasing. When you ship the drop-ship products, you must also issue the product from the receiving organization.

If the drop-ship customer returns the drop-shipped products directly to the supplier and you decide to not keep a record in Inventory, you must enter the return with a return cycle that runs the Receivables interface but not the RMA interface.

Review Questions

1. When must you run the RMA interface and what does it do?

2. For drop-ship customers, where are the two places to which they can return unwanted products?

3. How are your return cycles affected by the location to which the drop-ship customers send their returns of drop-ship products?

Invoicing and Closing Orders

In this section, you will learn how different setups affect interfacing orders in Oracle Receivables. You will learn to:

- Trace transaction sources

- Define grouping and invoicing rules

- Define receivable accounts and interfaces

Tracing Transaction Sources

A transaction source should be defined for each application that Oracle Receivables integrates with, including all applications that AutoInvoice imports from such as Oracle Order Entry, Oracle Projects, or any external source. The source of a transaction can be determined easily by assigning different beginning numbers to each different source. You can also examine the transactions individually by querying the transaction source, using a transaction source range in the Find windows, and using the Transactions Summary or the Transactions form.

To define a transaction source, follow the navigation path *Set Up : Transactions : Sources*. See Figure 19-25. There are two types of transaction sources:

- Manual

- Imported

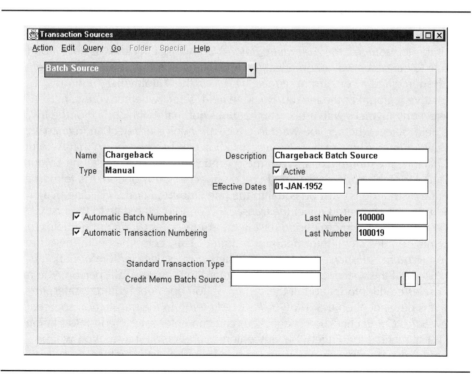

FIGURE 19-25. *Transaction Sources form*

Manual Sources

Using the Transaction Sources form, manual sources can be used for invoices entered directly in Oracle Receivables. You must have at least one manual source defined, and the Batch Source alternative region will default. In the Name field, enter a unique name for the batch source and an optional description. Select a type of Manual (the *Active* checkbox will be automatically selected). In the first Effective Dates field, enter a beginning date for using this transaction source. You need not enter an end date unless you want the transaction source to be inactivated on that date. If you wish, you can check the boxes to activate *Automatic Batch Numbering* and *Automatic Transaction Numbering*. In the Last Number field for the batches and transactions, enter the number that is one number prior to your starting number. For example, enter 999 if the first invoice transaction number will be 1000. For the Standard Transaction Type field, select a default transaction type to be used when this transaction source is selected. This can be overridden during entry of the transaction. The Credit Memo Batch Source field is optional, but must be defined before defining your invoice transaction sources in order to select a source for this field.

Imported

Complete the Batch Source alternative region like you would for a manual source. For imported sources, the *Automatic Batch Numbering* checkbox is not an option. Oracle Receivables will automatically name the batches by using the name of the batch source and a concurrent request ID. Open the AutoInvoice Options alternative region. For the Invalid Tax Rate field, select whether you want to correct or reject any invoices with a tax rate that does not match the code. For the Invalid Line field, select whether you want to create an invoice or reject an invoice if there are invalid lines. The *Create Clearing* checkbox can be checked so that AutoInvoice will balance the difference between the revenue amount and the selling amount to the AutoInvoice clearing account. If you do not check this option, the total from the revenue distributions must be equal to the line amount. For the GL date in a closed period, select whether to reject the transaction or adjust the date to the first GL date of the next open for future period. Using the *Allow Sales Credit* option helps to determine if sales credit information is required. This, combined with the system option *Require Salesperson*, determines whether the sales credit information is mandatory. If the system options are configured to require a salesperson, you must enter sales credit information. If the system option does not require a salesperson, then it is dependent on the *Allow Sales Credit* setup in the transaction source. If the *Allow Sales Credit* checkbox is checked, you can enter sales credit information, but this is not mandatory. Otherwise, any entered sales credit information will be ignored. You can also select a grouping rule from the List of Values.

The following alternative regions contain options that determine the behavior of AutoInvoice: Customer Information, Accounting Information, Other Information, and Sales Credits Data Validation. See Table 19-1.

Review Questions

1. Which option is not possible to set for invoices with the Imported transaction source?

2. Which alternative regions only apply to invoices with the Imported transaction source?

3. What does the GL date in a closed period with a value of Adjust value do? How does the value chosen for Adjust affect the way in which the import process handles transactions whose GL dates fall in closed periods?

4. How will *Allow Sales Credit* work when the *Require Salesperson* option is not set in the system options?

Option	Information
Code	AutoInvoice validates the code in the field, and applies only to freight and FOB point.
Segment	AutoInvoice validates the segment and applies only to the Accounting flexfield, inventory items, and sales territories.
ID	AutoInvoice validates ID fields during the import.
Value	AutoInvoice validates value fields during the import.
None	AutoInvoice does not validate the field.
Derive Date	AutoInvoice will derive rule start date and GL date based on ship date, rule start date, order date, and the user-entered default date when AutoInvoice is submitted.
Amount	AutoInvoice uses the Amount field instead of the Percent field.
Percent	AutoInvoice uses the Percent field instead of the Amount field.

TABLE 19-1.   *AutoInvoice Options*

Defining Grouping and Invoicing Rules

Grouping Rules

Line ordering rules and grouping rules were discussed briefly in the last chapter. They are used to determine the number of transactions and how the transaction lines are ordered within each transaction by AutoInvoice. To set up line ordering rules, select the sequence number and the transaction attribute for each rule. Transaction attributes can be any columns in the open interface tables. For each transaction attribute, you can determine whether to order in ascending or descending order.

For grouping rules, attach defined line ordering rules to each grouping rule. You can have different group-by characteristics for each transaction class, which can include Credit Memo, Debit Memo, or Invoice. Select columns from the open interface tables to be grouped by characteristics. The bill-to customer is defaulted as a standard group-by characteristic. All of the group-by characteristics you select are added to the bill-to customer to form criteria. Lines in the open interface tables with the same criteria will become one single transaction. The order of the lines within this single transaction is defined by the line ordering rules.

Invoicing Rules

Invoicing rules determine when to recognize the receivables amount for transactions. Invoicing rules can be assigned to manually entered invoices or invoices imported into Oracle Receivables through the AutoInvoice program. There are two types of invoicing rules that can be selected for each transaction. Both will behave the same way with accounting entries of receivables and revenue account if the revenue amount is recognized fully in one period. In this case, the accounts are Revenue and Receivables. The two types of invoicing rules are:

- Bill in arrears
- Bill in advance

BILL IN ARREARS　This rule is assigned to recognize receivables at the end of the revenue recognition schedule. If the transaction revenue amount is recognized over a number of periods, the revenue amount recognized per period will be offset by the unbilled receivables account. At the end of the revenue recognition schedule, the total unbilled receivables amount for the transaction will be offset by the receivables account. Put simply, the receivables are recognized in the last revenue recognition period.

BILL IN ADVANCE　This rule is assigned to recognize receivables as soon as an invoice is generated. If the transaction revenue amount is recognized over a number of periods, then the total revenue amount for the transaction will be charged to the receivables account and the unearned revenue account. This means receivables are recognized in the first revenue recognition period. The revenue amount recognized each period will be offset by the unearned revenue account. At the end of the revenue recognition schedule, the amount in the unearned revenue account for the transaction should be zero.

Accounting Rules

Accounting rules determine when to recognize the revenue amount for transactions and can be assigned to manually entered invoices or invoices that are imported into Oracle Receivables through the AutoInvoice program. There is one seeded accounting rule, Immediate, which allows for the recognition of revenue immediately in the accounting period specified. There are two types of accounting rules:

- Fixed duration
- Variable duration

FIXED DURATION   The fixed duration accounting rule covers a fixed number of periods. Enter the number of periods and divide the periods into a total of 100 percent; the total of all periods must be 100 percent.

VARIABLE DURATION   The variable duration accounting rule covers a variable number of periods that are specified when the transaction is entered.

Review Questions

1. What are the two types of invoicing rules?

2. When will the two types of invoicing rules behave the same?

3. Which field in the imported invoice lines serves as the default for grouping lines into invoices?

4. What is an accounting rule?

Defining Receivable Accounts and Interfaces

You can predefine an account or set of accounts to be used during cash application for faster data entry. This is done with distribution sets and activities, both of which can be pulled from Lists of Values, which speeds up data entry and minimizes errors.

Distribution Sets

Use predefined distribution sets for miscellaneous cash application of receipts not associated with invoices or customers. This would include such receipts as interest income, gifts and endowments, or over-the-counter product sales. Without creating a transaction, you can set up the distribution set, accept a receipt, debit cash, and credit a General Ledger account directly.

To configure distribution sets, follow the navigation path *Set Up : Receipts : Distribution Sets.* See Figure 19-26. In the Name field, give the new distribution set a name that will be easily identifiable and unique. This will appear in the List of Values. Enter a longer description if desired. The distribution set is defaulted to Active.

You can use as many lines as necessary for distribution of your receipts as long as they total exactly 100 percent. These can be overridden during receipt application if necessary. In the Distribution Set Lines region, indicate the percentage of the receipt that will be applied to the each account. Use the List of Values to enter the account combination you wish to associate as the credit side of your receipt application. You can enter an additional description of the account if desired.

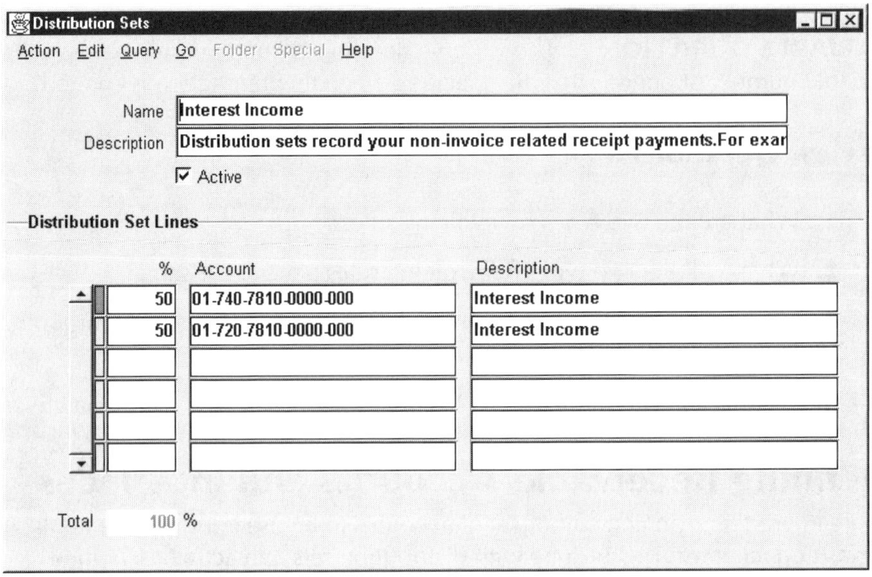

FIGURE 19-26. *Distribution Sets form*

Activities

Define Receivables activities to default accounts for miscellaneous cash, finance charges, adjustments, and chargebacks. The Receivables activities will fall under four categories that determine the proper credit and debit accounting entries. They are:

- Adjustments

- Finance charges

- Bank error

- Miscellaneous cash

During cash application, the Adjustments type is used with the Adjustments form. Adjustments types include write-off, short paid, too small to collect, among others. Use the Finance Charges type to adjust finance charges accrued when statements are sent. For each Finance Charges type, you can only have one Receivables activity. Set up at least one Bank Error type to use with your Cash Management application, then you can account for erroneous bank statement lines until they are clear. Bank Error type activities are used in the Receipts window when miscellaneous transactions are entered. Miscellaneous Cash type Receivables activities are also used in the Receipts window when miscellaneous transactions are entered. You must have at least one Miscellaneous Cash type Receivables activity. When you define an activity, you can also assign an account or a distribution set.

To define a Receivables Activity, follow the navigation path *Set Up : Receipts : Activities*. See Figure 19-27. Enter a unique name in the Name field that will appear in the List of Values. You may also enter a description and select the type of activity, which determines the List of Values that will populate your activity. Select an accounting distribution set or select an account combination. The Receivables activities are defaulted as Active.

Setting Up Lockbox

To set up a lockbox, follow the navigation path *Set Up : Receipts : Lockboxes : Lockboxes*. See Figure 19-28. The bank where you remit receipts will provide you with a lockbox number, which goes in the Number field. Enter the batch source and the bank account number, name, address, any contact, and a telephone number, and the cash account combination will be defaulted. In the Bank Origination Number field, enter the bank branch unique identifier number, which the bank will provide.

Next, go to the Receipts alternative region and enter a batch size, which is the number of receipts that will belong to a single batch before a second batch is generated. In the GL Date Source field, select the source from which to derive the

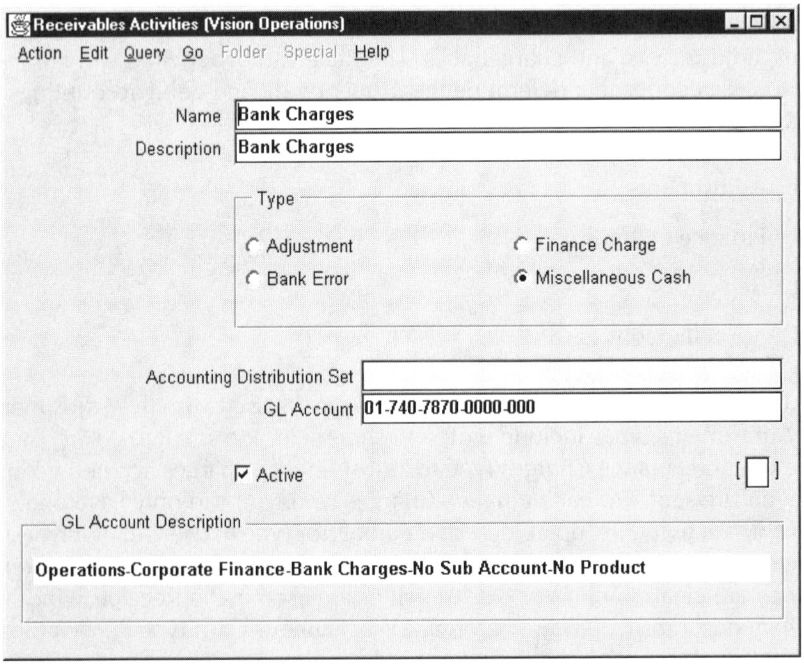

FIGURE 19-27. *Receivables Activities form*

GL date. Choose from Constant, Deposit, or Import Date. If an exchange rate type wasn't defined for the bank, enter one here if you are importing foreign currency. Select a receipt method—which identifies a receipt class, remittance bank, and receipt account information—from the List of Values. If the *Require Billing Location* checkbox is checked, only the invoices with a billing location will be eligible for payment. Your system option *Require Billing Location* should match the box. There are five references available to match the receipts by: Match Your Receipts By Hook, Consolidated Billing Number, Purchase Order, Sales Order, or Transaction Number. The consolidated billing number is used to identify the customer, then the receipt is applied to transactions based on AutoCash rule. A hook is for a custom field you wish to use, and you can select whether to also match by a corresponding date. Select Never, Always, or Duplicates Only.

To make your program use a debit item number, consolidated billing invoice number, sales order number, PO number, or another number to match if no customer or MICR number exists, go to the Transactions alternative region and check the *AutoAssociate* checkbox. Select how to handle the remaining amount: Reject Entire Receipt or Post Partial Amount as Unapplied.

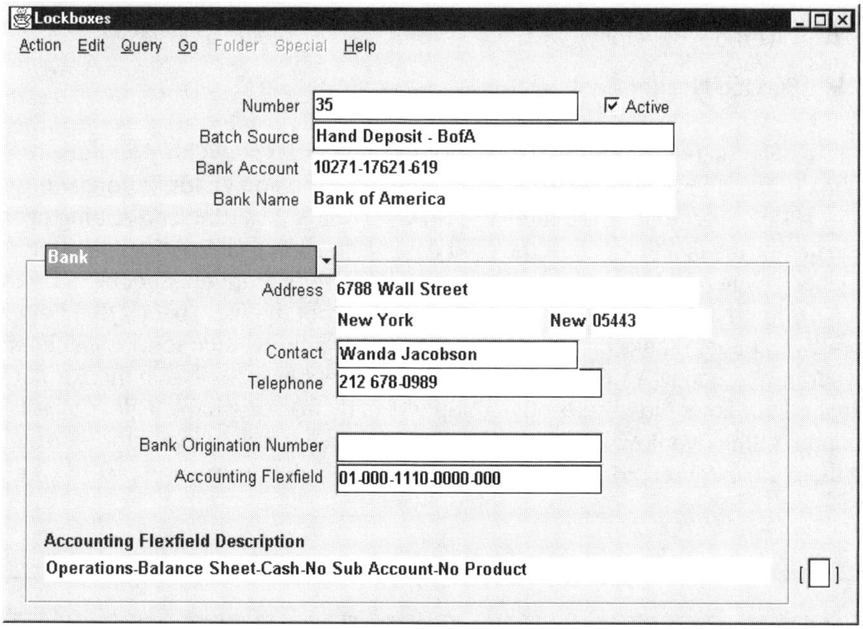

FIGURE 19-28. *Lockboxes form*

TRANSMISSION FORMAT   The transmission format determines how the data is organized. Use a SQL*Loader program to upload the electronic file from the bank, and use either DEFAULT or a CONVERT transmission setup. To define the transmission format, follow the navigation path *Set Up : Receipts : Lockboxes : Transmission Formats.* Enter a name for your transmission format; the status will default to Active. You can also enter a description.

Your bank will define the transmission records with an identifier. Enter each identifier and assign them a record type and enter an optional description. You can choose from the following record types:

- Transmission Header

- Transmission Trailer

- Lockbox Header

- Lockbox Trailer

- Batch Header

- Batch Trailer

- Receipt
- Overflow Receipt
- Service Header Contains

Transmission fields must be defined for each record type. With your cursor on the desired transaction record, click on the **Transmission Fields** button. See Figure 19-29. Enter fields for that record only and enter a starting and ending position in the file for the first field. Enter the field type, such as Transit Routing Number, or Deposit Date (for the complete list, see the AR User's Manual). Specify right justify or left justify to define the formatting of the field within the file. Specify to fill empty spaces with either blanks or zeros. Enter the date and time in the format specified by your bank, such as YYYYMMDD. You can also enter Yes or No in the Format Amount field. Enter No to select the amount exactly from the bank's file. Or, enter a number in the overflow indicator or enter zero. The overflow indicator indicates that there are extra records. Repeat the process for each transmission record type

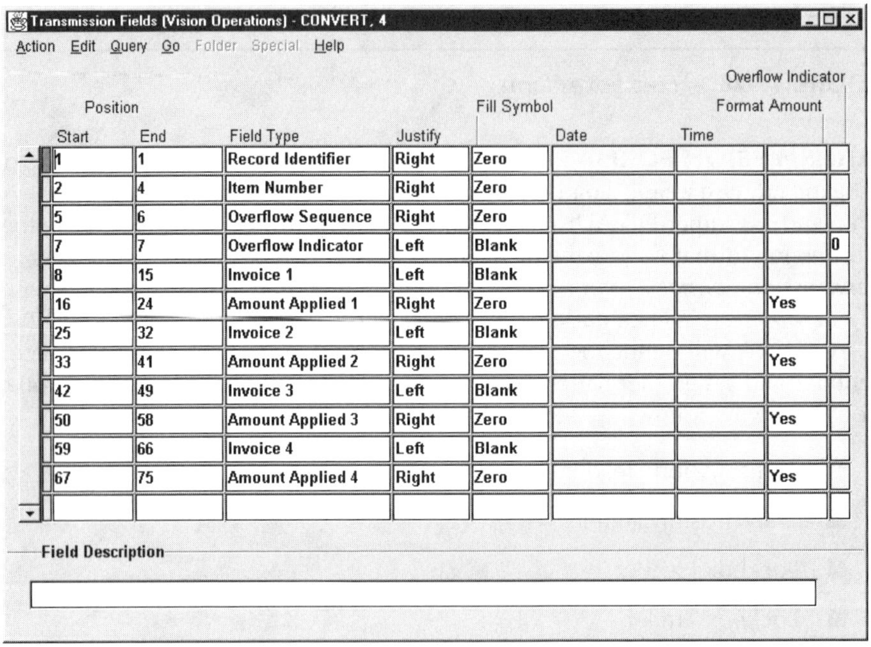

Transmission Fields (Vision Operations) - CONVERT, 4

Action Edit Query Go Folder Special Help

Position Start	End	Field Type	Justify	Fill Symbol	Date	Time	Format Amount	Overflow Indicator
1	1	Record Identifier	Right	Zero				
2	4	Item Number	Right	Zero				
5	6	Overflow Sequence	Right	Zero				
7	7	Overflow Indicator	Left	Blank				0
8	15	Invoice 1	Left	Blank				
16	24	Amount Applied 1	Right	Zero			Yes	
25	32	Invoice 2	Left	Blank				
33	41	Amount Applied 2	Right	Zero			Yes	
42	49	Invoice 3	Left	Blank				
50	58	Amount Applied 3	Right	Zero			Yes	
59	66	Invoice 4	Left	Blank				
67	75	Amount Applied 4	Right	Zero			Yes	

Field Description

FIGURE 19-29. *Transmission Fields form*

entered in the Header region of the Transmission Formats form. You may enter as many transmission formats as necessary.

Review Questions

1. What must be set up for AutoInvoice?

2. What must be set up for AutoLockbox?

3. What does an overflow indicator indicate?

Processing Returns

In this section, you will learn how to process returns. You have already had some exposure during the drop-shipment section. Here, you will learn how to enter and authorize returns. You will also learn how to identify RMA types. In this section, you will learn to:

■ Authorize returns

■ Identify RMA types

Authorizing Returns

Whether you issue RMA numbers ahead of time or when they arrive at the shipping dock, the Oracle Order Entry module handles product returns. RMA orders can be linked to previously shipped product to provide effortless return order entry and credit memos, if necessary.

Order/return types are created to handle different types of returns. For example, you may enter a return, book a return, receive a return, increase inventory for a return, send a credit memo for a return, and close out a return. You may configure any number of return types and link any number of return/order cycles to fit your business needs.

You can issue an RMA through the Order Workbench if you have the Returns form in the Navigator of your responsibility. If not, all of the data and buttons related to the RMA process will not be available in the Order Workbench. You can create a new return through the Orders Workbench. From the Find Orders form, click on the **New Return** button to enter a new return in the Returns form. Beginning at the header in the Main alternative region, choose a customer from the predefined List of Values. Select a contact person, which may or may not default depending on the setup. Choose the return type from the List of Values. The request date should default based on the system date. The return date will default in, but may be changed based on when the customer will return the item(s). The entry status should default as Entered. If you save the return now, a return number should be generated.

Select the Pricing, Sales alternative region and review the defaults if necessary, and select the appropriate salesperson, price list, and currency. If you choose a foreign currency, the conversion type, date, and rate must be entered.

Select the Shipping alternative region and review the defaults, if necessary, and select the appropriate freight carrier, FOB point, freight terms, and shipment priority. Inspection instructions may also be added.

By selecting the Tax, Total alternative region you can override the tax control status to Require or Exempt. If you choose Exempt, you must enter the tax exemption certificate and the tax exemption reason.

By clicking on the **Addresses** button, you can review the address information. Depending on your customer setups, the receive from and credit-to addresses may or may not default, but both addresses are required. Once you have entered or verified the addresses, close out the Receive From and Credit To Addresses form and move the cursor to the Reference region so you can add the product item(s) being returned.

The line number will default automatically, and the Reference region may be used to link an already existing sales order, invoice, or purchase order number to the return. Select the type, and enter your number, depending on the type. For example, if you choose a Purchase Order Number type, then you would enter the purchase order number. Then, pick from the List of Values the line number from the referenced number with your return item on it. The item—which must be a returnable item—and the UOM will be defaulted if you enter a reference, and cannot be changed. If the customer is only returning a partial order, then override the default quantity. Enter a return reason—which is a required field—from the List of Values.

Select the Credit alternative region and enter any pricing attribute, if they are defined. If you selected Invoice as a reference, then the invoice number will appear. If you selected Purchase Order or Order as a reference, you can now further tie the line to any invoices related to the referenced object. After the Receivables interface is run and an invoice is selected, a credit memo will be created tied to the selected invoice, and the original sales credits are reversed. If no invoice was selected, the Receivables interface will create a credit memo as an account credit. You can override the credit price if necessary. If an item was entered with no reference, and if it is not on the price list, you can manually enter the credit price.

Select the Receiving alternative region. You may enter or accept the warehouse defaults in which the item will be received. You can also enter a date expected. The *Repair* checkbox relates to Oracle Service and will not be discussed. The *Inspection Required* checkbox will populate automatically if the item must be inspected before it is received.

Select the Taxes alternative region. If the tax code is defaulted based on a selected reference or based on the credit invoice, you cannot change the tax code. Otherwise, you can enter a tax code. If the profile option *TAX: Calculate Tax On Credit Memos* is enabled, then a tax code must be entered; the tax status, exemption certificate, and exemption reason are for display only.

You can view the status of the return in the Status alternative region. Status includes cancelled quantities, currency quantities, received quantities, and accepted quantities. The **Discounts** and the **Sales Credits** buttons are the same as when you enter orders. You must only enter sales credits if an account credit is going to be created—meaning that a credit invoice was not created. Once you have reviewed all of the return information, book your return via the Special | Book menu command. From this point on, depending on the return type selected, the return can be interfaced to the Oracle Inventory module and a credit can be interfaced to the Oracle Receivables module.

Review Questions

1. Which two addresses can be entered for a return?

2. What can be used as references for a return?

3. What will happen to the Receivables interface if a credit invoice is provided?

4. When will an account credit be credited and what must be entered in this case?

Return Types

Various return types may be created to facilitate return processing with various return cycles. Returns are frequently referred to as RMAs, or return material authorizations.

You may want to create a return type called RMA-No Credit that processes and receives returned products back into inventory, but does not issue a credit back to the customer. In this case, the cycle action Receivables interface is omitted so as not to create a credit to the customer. The results are Enter → RMA Interface→ Complete Line→ Complete Order.

You may also create a return type called RMA-Credit to process and receive returned product and issue a credit memo or an on account credit. To do so, you would include the cycle action Receivables interface so that a credit would be issued to the customer. The results are Enter → RMA Interface→ Receivables Interface→ Complete Line→ Complete Order.

You may also create a return type called RMA-Credit Only that issues a credit memo or an account credit with receiving the product. In this case, you would include the cycle action Receivables interface so that a credit would be issued to the customer. The results are Enter → Receivables Interface→ Complete Line→ Complete Order.

You may also create a return type called RMA-Discard to ask the customer to discard the product. In this case, you would not increase inventory or issue credit back to the customer. The results are Enter → Approved → Complete Line→ Complete Order.

You may also create a return type that repairs or replaces a product. To repair a product, you must repair and return the product to the customer. To replace a product, you must enter a replacement order.

Review Questions

1. What is a return type?

2. How should you handle an RMA with no credit? With credit?

Entering and Correcting Transactions

In this section, you will learn to enter and correct transactions in Oracle Receivables. You will learn to:

- Bill customers in advance or in arrears

- Define recurring transactions

- Create debit and credit memos

- Define deposits and guarantees

- Use tax options

Billing Customers In Advance or In Arrears

You have already learned how to set up invoicing and accounting rules. Now you will learn how to bill customers in advance or in arrears. To do this, you must go to the Transactions window and enter the header information. Select the invoicing rule for the transaction in the More alternative region in the transaction header. Once the record is saved, the invoicing rules cannot be changed. Then, select either In Advance or In Arrears.

TIP
*Use caution when clicking on the **Line Items** button, which triggers saving the header record and prevents you from changing the invoicing rule.*

Next, enter the line items, quantity, and price, and select the Rule alternative region to enter the accounting rule. The duration will be automatically filled in if the accounting rule is a fixed duration rule; otherwise, it must be entered. The start date will be defaulted as the system date and can be overridden if necessary. The start date indicates when revenue will begin to be recognized. The date entered must be within an accounting period in the period type as defined by the accounting rule. Use the **Accounting** button to view the account sets assigned to your transaction line. The Sets for This Line alternative region is the default. You can view the account sets for the transaction line, and you can also select the Sets for All Lines alternative region to view the account sets for the entire transaction. Save your work after completing the additional necessary information.

Revenue Recognition Program

This program uses the account sets defined at each transaction line to determine the distribution records. You must run the Revenue Recognition program to generate GL distributions for revenue in each transaction line that uses accounting rule and invoicing rules. The only revenue distributions generated are those that fall within the specified GL date range parameter. If the transaction line accounting information—such as the account combination or percentage—is updated, then the updated information will only affect those future distributions that were not generated. The Revenue Recognition program also creates the receivable, tax, freight, and AutoInvoice clearing account of invoices for the GL date that falls into the parameters of the Revenue Recognition program.

The Revenue Recognition program should be run regularly. To do so, submit it through SRS and follow the navigation path *Control : Requests : Run*. Select Revenue Recognition as the request name and enter the GL date range—which must be in an open accounting period—to create distribution records. You can also select a print format of Summary or Detail. As a last step, you can select to commit the work. Of course, all of the work will be rolled back if you do not commit it—although you will be able to view a Preview report.

Review Questions

1. Where do you set the invoicing rule for a transaction?

2. Where do you set the accounting rule for a transaction?

3. What does the Revenue Recognition program do?

4. What function does the parameter Commit Work handle?

Defining Recurring Transactions

You may want to create a recurring invoice for monthly services that do not change, or other regular charges incurred by a customer. To generate a recurring invoice, you must first have a model invoice. You can either create the model or use an existing invoice if it suits your purpose. It does not matter if the model invoice is open or closed (paid), but it must be completed.

To copy transactions, follow the navigation path *Transactions : Copy Transactions*. The Copy Transactions form—which is already in the query mode—will appear. See Figure 19-30. Enter the transaction number to use as a model, and any other information that will reference the particular invoice you wish to copy. Criteria can include transaction source, currency, bill-to customer name, bill-to customer number, payment terms, transaction type, transaction date, transaction amount, due date, Transaction Descriptive flexfield, and/or GL date. As a last step, run the query.

Once your model transaction is located, the model information will be displayed in the Model Transaction area. In the Schedule region, click on the drop-down menu for Rule, then select from the following interval options for your recurring transaction:

- Annually (once a year)

- Semi-Annually (every six months)

- Quarterly (every three months)

- Bi-Monthly (every other month)

- Monthly (once a month)

- Weekly (once a week)

- Days (once every N days where N is the value in the Number of Days field)

- Single Copy (one nonrecurring copy)

In the Number of Times field, enter the number of times you wish to have this transaction recur. Notice that the First Transaction Date field will populate by default with a date that is derived from the original transaction date of the model transaction, plus the chosen interval. For example, if your model transaction's date is June 1 and you selected a monthly rule, your first transaction date will be July 1. If necessary, you can override this date. If you choose the days rule, enter the number

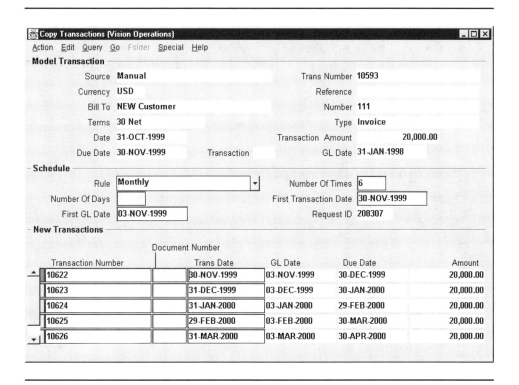

FIGURE 19-30. *Copy Transactions form*

of days in the Number of Days field. Your first GL date will default to the system date, which may be overridden. The first GL date will also reflect the interval for the model transactions. For instance, if your first transaction date is June 1 and your first GL date is June 5, all recurring transactions will have a five-day interval between the transaction and GL dates.

Key in the first row of the Transaction Number field in the New Transactions region. Within moments, all of the transactions that Oracle Receivables creates will be displayed in the rows. Save the work and a concurrent program will be initiated. The form will refresh and the request ID number will be populated. If transaction number is automatic, then all Transaction Number fields will be assigned with new transaction numbers. The batch source of the model transaction will become the batch source for every recurring transaction. The Recurring Invoice concurrent program creates the recurring transactions and generates the Recurring Invoice Program report. The Recurring Invoice Program report shows all of the new transactions along with their GL distributions.

Once all of the transactions have been generated, you can make changes by querying the transactions in the Transactions form. If the GL date is not in an open period, that recurring transaction will be marked as Incomplete unless you are using the bill in arrears invoicing rule. In the latter case, all generated transactions will be marked as Completed.

Review Questions

1. What is a model transaction?

2. When must you fill in the Number of Days field?

3. How will the first transaction date be defaulted?

4. What happens when you commit your changes in the Copy Transactions form?

Creating Debit and Credit Memos

Credit memos are transactions that are created either to be mailed or to be used internally to provide a customer account with a credit for a specific dollar amount. Debit memos are transactions created to charge a customer account for noninventory goods, such as an insufficient funds check fee.

Creating a Credit Memo

To create a credit memo against a single transaction, follow the navigation path *Transactions : Credit Transactions*. Use the Find Transactions form to locate the specific transaction you wish to credit. The criteria include transaction number range, transaction source range, transaction class, transaction date range, transaction batch range, transaction type range, GL data range, primary salesperson, and/or currency. Click on the **Find** button to locate the invoice or debit memo to credit. You can also use the Transactions Workbench, then find the transaction that you want to credit and click on the **Credit** button. Both processes will initiate the Credit Transactions form and populate it with the transaction number and source. The original amount and balance due of the transaction will also populate. Original is the original amount of the credited transactions, and balance due reflects the remaining unpaid amount. See Figure 19-31. The credit memo date will default to the system date. If changed, the date will automatically populate the GL date with the same date, provided it is in an open period. Once completed, you will be ready to enter the credit memo.

To add this credit memo to a credit memo batch, select New in the Batch field, and select an existing batch name in the Batch Name field. If the selected credited transaction is in a batch, and if you want to add the credit memo to the same batch,

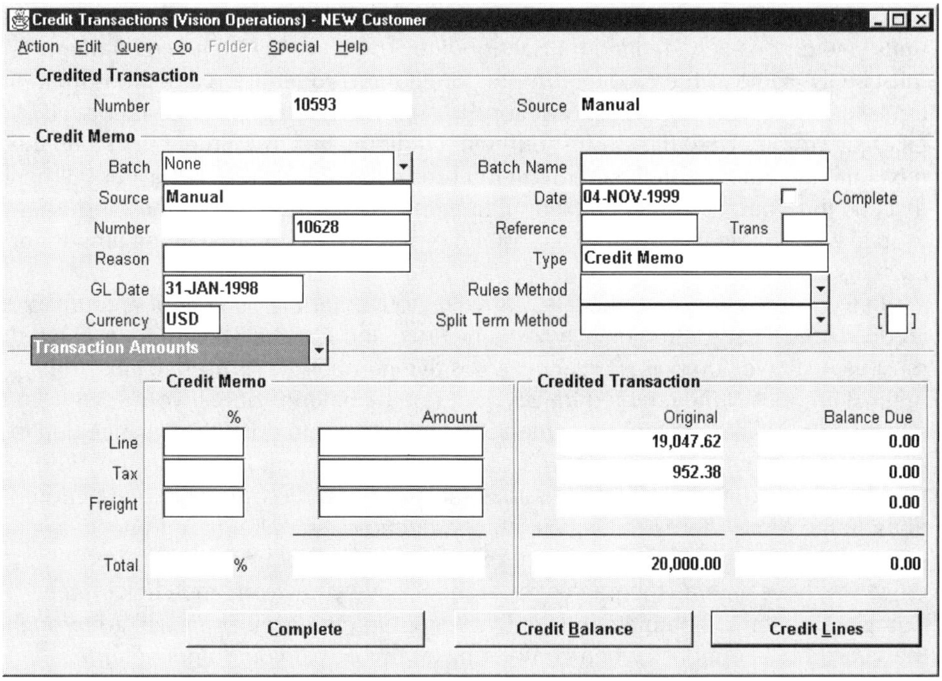

FIGURE 19-31.   *Credit Transactions form*

you can also select the Credited Transactions batch type. If you do not want to add the credit memo to a batch, select None in Batch field. You must enter a source for the credit memo from the List of Values. If the selected source uses automatic numbering for the credit memo number, a credit memo number is unnecessary. Otherwise, enter a credit memo number, which can be a unique reference number. Skip the Transactions Descriptive flexfield and enter a reason for the credit by using the List of Values. Next, check the credit memo transaction type that was defaulted from the source, or select your own. The GL date may be defaulted, and if your transaction type allows Post to GL, you must fill in the GL date for this credit memo. The GL date must be in an open or future enterable period later than the GL date of the credited transaction. If your transaction used an invoicing and accounting rule, select a rules method—LIFO, Prorate, or Unit—to reverse the revenue distributions. LIFO (last in first out) will reverse the revenue distributions, with the latest accounting period first, and credit each prior period next until the amount on the credit memo runs out. Prorate will prorate the amount on the credit memo equal to all revenue distributions of the credited transaction. Unit will prorate the amount on the credit memo to all revenue distributions of the credited transaction based on the units entered on each credited transaction line. The currency of the credit memo must be the same as the credited transaction. If the credited transaction has multiple terms/installments, you must choose a split terms method to apply the credit: FIFO, LIFO, or Prorate. FIFO (first in first out) will credit the first installment first, then the next until the amount on the credit memo runs out. LIFO credits the last installment first and the prior installment next until the amount on the credit memo runs out. Prorate will prorate the credit to all installments based on the remaining amount of each installment.

In the Transaction Amounts alternative region, enter the percent or amount to be credited for all transaction lines types: Line, Tax, and Freight. The amounts entered must be negative numbers. Percent is a positive number that is used against the original amount of the credited transaction, not the balance due. If your setup allows overapplication, enter a percentage and amount to drive the balance due to a negative number. Use this region if you only want to credit part of the credited transactions, and if you do not want to associate the credit to specific transaction lines. In the More alternative region, enter a document number (if automatic sequencing is enabled), and customer reference and/or comments, if desired. Once you have entered the percent or amount, save your work and click on the **Complete** button to complete the credit memo. Oracle Receivables will go through the same check as it does when completing an invoice. If you do not enter a percentage or amount to credit, then credit the entire remaining balance at once by clicking on the **Credit Balance** button. Save your credit memo, then complete the credit memo by clicking on the **Complete** button. The original accounting entries for this invoice drive the reversing credit entries, and the sales credit information will also be reversed.

You can also credit an individual transaction line by clicking on the **Credit Lines** button. All transaction lines of the credited transaction with a balance due will appear. Select the transaction line to credit, and enter the quantity or amount as a negative number to be credited. You can credit as many transaction lines as necessary, and you can also update the sales credit information, tax, and/or freight information by using the corresponding buttons. This works in the same way as entering invoices, except that the sign is different. Upon completion, you also must complete the credit memo.

You can also credit a paid invoice if you first reverse the receipt application, thereby placing the receipt into the Unapplied or On Account category for use towards another invoice.

On Account Credit

To create a customer account credit that isn't related to a specific invoice, you can create an on account credit. To do so, use the Transactions window with the navigation path *Transactions : Transactions.* You must first select the class of credit memo by using the drop-down field and selecting a credit memo transaction type. Then, select the bill-to customer and location that you want to create this on account credit for; then, enter any other necessary information.

The new credit memo transaction number will be displayed at the top in the active menu bar in the Lines form. Skip the Item field and enter **On Account Credit** as the description in the Description field. You may also change the General Ledger account where you will charge the credit to, and use the same description, On Account Credit, for different memos.

The UOM field in this case will not be applicable, and the quantity should be selected as 1. The unit price is the amount of the credit that will be generated; enter a negative amount because this is a credit. The Amount field will be populated automatically. Enter any other necessary information and save your work. Return to the header and complete the credit memo by clicking on the **Complete** button.

To apply the on account credit, it must be queried up in the Transactions Summary window. Then, click on the **Applications** button and select the transaction to apply, the amount applied, and any discount; this is the same procedure used when applying receipts.

Creating a Debit Memo

Debit memos are charges that are assigned to customers for any additional charges, including unearned discounts taken, finance charges, taxes, or freight charges that must be collected. Entering a debit memo is exactly like entering an invoice and is done through the Transactions window. The only difference is that you must select the class of debit memo and a debit memo transaction type. You must select both a ship-to and bill-to address or you will not be able to print your debit memo. Terms for debit memo are usually immediate.

In the Lines form, your new debit memo transaction number will be displayed at the top in the active menu bar. Skip the item and enter a free-form description in the Description field. You may also change the General Ledger account to charge the debit to, if necessary. The quantity should be 1, the unit price must be entered, and the Amount field will be populated automatically. Enter any necessary information for your debit memo, then save the work. Return to the header and complete the debit memo by clicking on the **Complete** button.

Review Questions

1. How will the different rule methods work?

2. What are the two navigation routes in Oracle Receivables to apply credit to a specific transaction?

3. Under what circumstances would you create an on account credit?

4. What is a debit memo and what class do they belong in?

Defining Deposits and Guarantees

Deposits and guarantees belong to a group of specific transaction types called commitments. A deposit records that a payment was made in advance to pay for future purchases. A guarantee is a contractual agreement that the customer will transact a minimum amount of business over a certain time. When you invoice or receive payment against a commitment, the commitment balance is automatically updated. Commitments do not include any tax or freight charges.

Enter Commitments

Use the Transactions form to enter a commitment, and select a class of either Deposit or Guarantee, and a transaction type related to the class you selected. Then, enter the bill-to customer and location information, and select the Commitment alternative region. This alternative region is only available when the transaction class is Deposit or Guarantee. You can enter an effectivity date range, and only invoices dated within that range will be eligible for application against the commitment. Enter the commitment amount, then enter either an item or a description. If necessary, you can enter accounting and sale credits information for a commitment. You need not enter any line information, including tax or freight charges. Save the commitment and complete it by clicking on the **Complete** button.

For the purposes of this exercise, create a deposit by selecting the Deposit class and Deposit transaction type. Enter your customer as the bill-to customer and select the Commitment alternative region. For this exercise, enter an amount of **$10,000** and a description of the commitment, then save you work. Complete the commitment and print it out just like an invoice, if desired.

Using a Deposit

When you create a deposit transaction, the accounting entry books a debit to receivables and a credit to unearned revenue as opposed to revenue. The customer then pays the amount of the deposit and the accounting is a debit to cash and a credit to receivables. When you create an invoice for goods or services purchased, reference the deposit transaction number in the Commitment field of the invoice in the Main alternative region. The invoice you created will debit unearned revenue—not receivables—and credit to revenue.

Apply receipts from the customer to the deposit, not to the individual invoices that may be tied to a deposit. You can associate invoices against a deposit before the deposit is paid. In this case, it is the deposit and ages—and not the associated invoices—that will be outstanding.

Using a Guarantee

A guarantee does not affect invoice balances the same way that a deposit does; the deposit reduces an invoice balance. For a guarantee, however, the guarantee balance itself is reduced, thereby contributing to the fulfillment of the guarantee. Whenever an invoice that references the guarantee is created, the guarantee balance is reduced. When you create a guarantee transaction, Unbilled receivables are debited and unearned revenue is credited. When an invoice is generated, you debit receivables and credit revenue. When the invoice is applied to the guarantee, you debit unearned revenue and credit unbilled receivables. When the invoice is paid, you debit cash and credit receivables.

When an invoice for goods or services purchased is created, you can reference the guarantee transaction number in the Commitment field of the transaction in the Main alternative region. Receipts are applied against the invoice, not against the guarantee.

Review Questions

1. What are Oracle Receivables' two types of commitment?

2. Which alternative region must be used in the Transactions window to enter a commitment?

3. How is a deposit used and what GL accounts are credited and debited to reflect the deposit?

4. How is a guarantee used and what ledger postings are generated as it is set up? As orders are booked against the guarantee? As orders ship and are invoiced? As cash receipts are posted?

Using Tax Options

There are two different methods for tax functions in Receivables: VAT and sales tax. VAT (value-added tax) is used in Europe, and is based on the tax codes assigned to items or customer sites. Sales tax in the United States is location-based, and is calculated based on the customer's ship-to location.

Sales Tax

During system setup, you can set your tax method to Sales Tax and select a Location flexfield structure in order to implement the *Sales Tax* option in the System Options, Tax alternative region. Your Location flexfield structure will build the sales tax amount based on the components of the ship-to location, or the bill-to location if no ship-to location exists. During setup, a tax rate is assigned to the value of each flexfield component.

NOTE
You may have used an external tax vendor program to populate your tax assignments.

You can create additional controls to override the location-based tax by using a tax code, and you can configure a hierarchy to retrieve tax codes from customer, customer site, product, account, and system options. You can also set up customer exemptions, item exceptions, and item exemptions to modify the tax rate used. You can use profile options to disallow override of tax setups at various levels. Table 19-2 shows a few of the ways that sales tax requirements can be handled.

The transaction type determines whether to calculate tax automatically. In order for Oracle Receivables to do this, the transaction types must be Calculate Tax–enabled, or you must select Required as the tax handling method in the entered transaction. Otherwise, you must override by adding a tax line or by manually entering a tax code.

Requirement	Resolution
Invoice is for nontaxable item	Create an exemption for the item.
Invoice tax only for specific items	Create tax codes for items. Do not assign tax codes to customers or sites.
All customers should be invoiced for sales tax	Do not assign tax codes or any exceptions. Choose Sales Tax as the tax method.
Flat tax on items or service	Define ad hoc tax codes. Enter an amount when creating the invoice.
Charge tax to an exempt customer	Enter a tax line on the order or invoice.
Allow exemption to taxable customer	Create customer exemption when creating order.
Generate tax on certain items shipped to certain states	Define the tax exemption rate for a specific location.
Compound taxes required	Select Yes for the compound tax in the system options; assign sequence numbers to the tax lines.

TABLE 19-2. *Tax Requirements*

Value-Added Tax

To use a VAT, you must define tax codes and assign rates to them because a VAT does not use a location-based tax. Choose the No-Validation-Country flexfield structure. To implement VAT, select Tax Method as the VAT, determine whether to round the VAT amount at the header or line level, and whether to specify a rounding method (and if so, then what is the number of decimal places to display). You can configure a hierarchy to retrieve the tax code from the customer, customer site, product, account, and system options. You can also set up customer exemptions, item exceptions, and item exemptions to modify the tax rate used. You can use profile options to disallow an override of tax setups at various levels.

For VAT tax codes, you may create several single codes that cover various items within a group. You may also define a tax code for the home country and another for an EEC, an exempt code for the home country and an exempt code for an EEC, and a tax code for goods shipped outside of the EEC.

The transaction type determines whether to calculate tax automatically. In order for Oracle Receivables to do this, your transaction types must be Calculate Tax–enabled, or you must select Required as the tax handling method in the entered transaction. Otherwise, you must override by adding a tax line or by manually entering a tax code.

Tax Profile Options

Use tax profile options to modify how Oracle Receivables calculates tax. These profile options are explained in Table 19-3.

Tax Calculation

If Oracle Receivables does not find any tax codes from the tax code hierarchy, and the tax method is Sales Tax, it will assign the tax based on the location tax rate derived from the flexfield structure. If no tax code is found from either source, and if you must calculate tax, enter a tax code or a tax line. If you do not, no tax will be calculated.

If you are using a location-based tax, and if Oracle Receivables has a tax rate, it can be overridden by an item exception. Finally, if you have customer or item exemptions, they can be applied to exempt all or part of your calculated tax. If the exemption is a full exemption, then the transaction will not generate a tax line.

Review Questions

1. What are the two tax methods supported by Oracle Receivables?

2. What should you do if all customers must be invoiced for sales tax?

3. What should you do if the invoice line is for a nontaxable item?

4. What flexfield structure should be used to implement a VAT?

Profile Option	Functionality
Allow Ad Hoc Tax Changes	Yes allows the user to update the rates and amount of the tax codes while creating an invoice.
Allow Manual Tax Lines	No prevents the user from creating additional tax lines, or from deleting system-created tax lines.
Allow Override of Customer Exemptions	Yes allows the user to override the standard calculations. Standard will use the rates, exemptions, and exceptions to calculate tax.
Allow Override of Tax Codes	No prevents the user from updating the tax code displayed in the Transaction form.
Invoice Freight as Revenue	Set to Yes, Receivables creates a line item for freight, as opposed to a freight item.
Inventory Item for Freight	If Invoice Freight as Revenue is set to Yes, you can control the calculation of tax on freight.

TABLE 19-3. *Tax Profile Options*

Receipts

In the previous chapter, you learned to manually enter cash receipts. In this section, you will learn to process automatic receipts and use lockboxes. You will learn how to:

- Process automatic receipts
- Use lockboxes

Processing Automatic Receipts

Automatic receipts transfer funds directly from your customer bank to your bank on the agreed maturity date. It can also be used to perform bills of exchange and other functions. An agreement with your customer regarding the automatic funds transfer must be established. Then, transactions that will be paid by automatic receipts must be flagged with automatic payment methods and customer banks. Creating automatic receipts requires the following steps:

- Create
- Approve
- Format

You can set the *AR: Automatic Receipt Creation Authority* profile option to Format, Approve, or Create to perform the receipt creation in a one-, two-, or three-step process. In choosing Create, you must create, then approve and format. If you choose Approve, you first create approved receipts, then format. If you choose Format, you can create and format approved receipts simultaneously.

Create

First, use the Receipt Batches window to create an automatic receipt batch. Then select a batch type of Automatic. Enter a currency and the receipt class and payment method. The receipt class determines whether the automatic receipts require confirmation—a function that can be viewed in the List of Values window. The batch date will default to the system date, but it can be overridden if necessary. Enter a GL date, but only if the receipt class does not require confirmation as a separate step. In the Media Reference field, you can enter a tape or diskette to which you will create automatic receipts, and you can also enter an optional comment. As a last step, click on the **Create** button. See Figure 19-32.

Once the above steps have been completed, the Create Automatic Receipts Batch window will appear and you can enter any additional information that will restrict the transactions to be included in this process. Such restrictions include

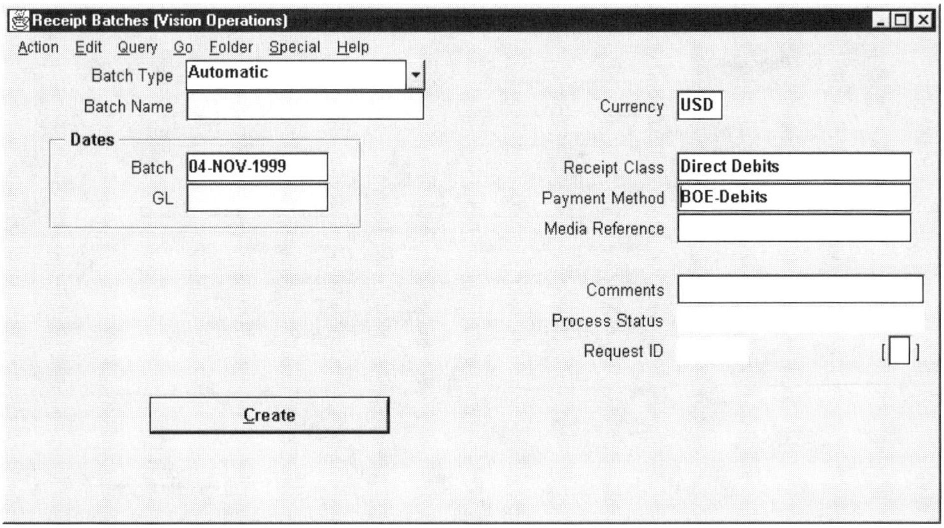

FIGURE 19-32.   *Receipt Batches form*

transaction due date range, transaction date range, transaction number range, document number range, customer name/number range, and/or location range. If the profile option allows for the performing of multiple actions in tandem, you can check the *Approve* or *Format* checkboxes. See Figure 19-33. Click on the **OK** button and a batch name will be created. At the same time, transactions that fit your criteria with an automatic payment method will be selected. The selection is dependent upon whether the customer wants to include disputed invoices, whether the amount is more than the minimum receipts amount specified, and the number of lead days of your payment method. Only transactions that are due within the lead days specified will be selected. Process status will be displayed as Started Creation. Once the creation program is completed, the status will be Creation Completed.

The number of receipts rule on the selected payment method determines the number of receipts that will be created. You can create the receipts by using the following options: *One per Customer, One per Customer and Due Date, One per Invoice, One per Site,* or *One per Site and Due Date.*

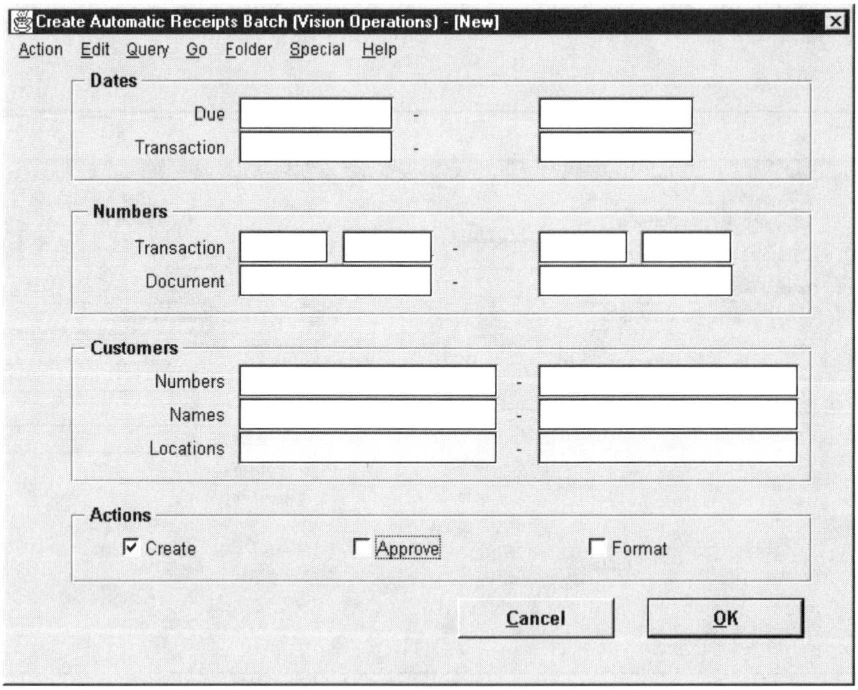

FIGURE 19-33. *Create Automatic Receipts Batch form*

Approve Automatic Receipts

As a next step, you must approve the automatic receipts if you did not include the Approve action in the creation step. Query the receipt batch to be approved in the Receipts window, and update the currency exchange rate if necessary. You can also deselect any invoices that you do not want included in the batch. You can also update customer bank information for each invoice. To maintain the transaction selected in the receipt batch, click on the **Maintain** button and then make the changes. Close the window and click on the **Approve** button. You will be asked to confirm the batch, so click on the **OK** button to do so. You will see a request ID and a process status of Started Approval. If the receipt does not require confirmation, the transactions close after approval automatically. Once the approval program completes, the process status will be Approval Completed.

Format

Next, you must format the automatic receipts to print acknowledgement or confirmation. Query the desired batch, which must be created and approved prior to being formatted. Click on the **Format** button and your request ID and a process status of Started Format will be displayed. This initiates the Automatic Receipt report, which has two areas: a stub, which contains the remit-to information, and an automatic receipt, which contains the receipt information and customer name. Once the Formatting program is finished, the process status will be Format Completed.

Confirmation

Confirmation is usually only required for bills of exchange. Upon receiving confirmation from your customer, the receipt must be confirmed prior to sending the remittance to the bank. If your receipt class contains a Require Confirmation entry of Yes, then the automatic receipts must be confirmed. Because the customer balances are updated as soon as you confirm a receipt, those that contain mistakes must be reversed and replaced with a corrected version.

Query the receipt to confirm, then click on the **Confirm** button to display the Confirm Receipt form. Enter the GL date and confirmation date, then click on the **Confirm** button again.

Bank Remittance

Remitting automatic receipts to your bank will initiate funds transfer from your customer's bank. If confirmations are required, you can remit after the automatic receipts are approved or confirmed. The remittance process is very similar to the automatic receipt process in that you must create, approve, and format. There is a similar profile option governing the remittance process: *AR: Automatic Remittance Creation Authority*. A remittance batch can include both automatic and manual receipts. Follow the navigation path *Receipts : Remittances* to create a remittance batch. See Figure 19-34. In the Remittances window, enter the currency, batch name, and GL date. The batch date is defaulted to the current date and can be changed if necessary. The GL date determines when the remittance batch is posted to Oracle General Ledger. Next, select a remittance method of Standard to create the batch based on maturity date. The remittance method is associated with the receipts, and you can also enter a receipt class, a payment method, and a media reference. In the Remittance region, you must enter the remittance bank along with the account number; then, enter any additional comments. To automatically create the remittance batch, click on the **AutoCreate** button. You can enter further restrictions such as maturity date range, receipt date range, receipt number range, and/or customer name/number range. You can also click on the **Manual Create** button to manually create the remittance batch.

Once you have created the remittance batch, it must be approved and formatted in the Remittances window. Click on the **Receipts** button to make changes to the selected receipts, then click on the **Approve** button to approve the batch. Once the remittance batch is approved, you can format it by using the Remittances window

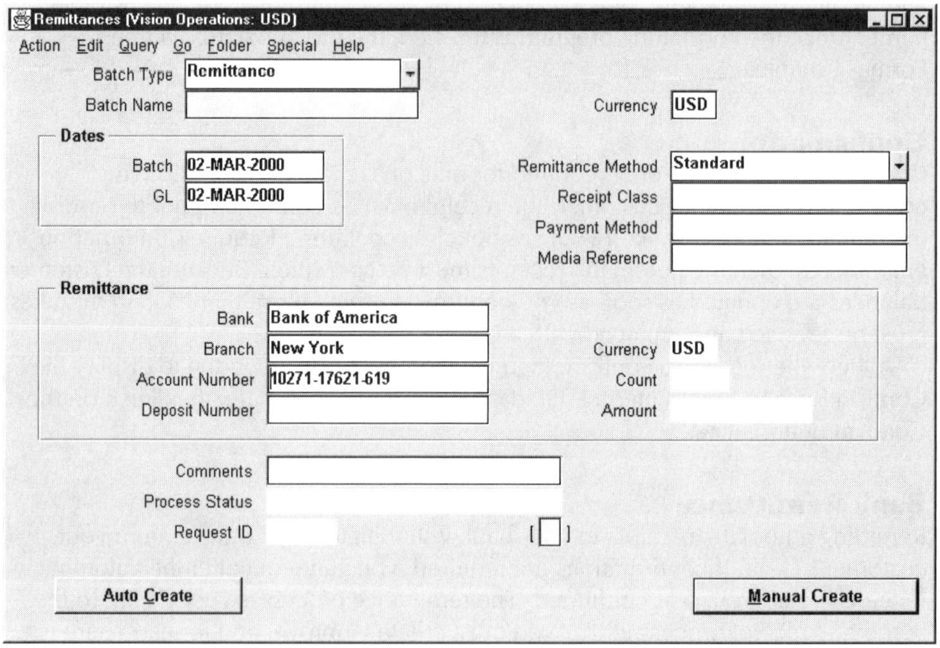

FIGURE 19-34. *Remittances form*

and the **Format** button. This will allow you to print remittances that notify your bank about how to transfer the funds out of your customer's bank account and into yours; confirm this by reconciling your bank statement.

Review Questions

1. What is the order of steps from creating to confirmation in an automatic receipt batch?

2. What is a confirmation?

3. How do you create a bank remittance?

4. What is the order of steps from creating remittance batches to formatting remittance batches?

Lockboxes

A lockbox is a service that commercial banks offer to their corporate customers to automatically apply receipts via electronic transmission. The lockbox process can handle a large volume of transactions on a daily basis, and protects you from data entry or clerical errors that may occur during the manual process. You must define a lockbox in order to use the AutoLockbox program. In order to perform the lockbox process, you must also define and set up your banks, receipt sources, and payment methods. You can specify the payment method for each defined lockbox. When using the lockbox process, there are three steps to follow:

1. **Import and accept new transmissions.**   This process reads the data file that the bank provides into the AutoLockbox open interface tables

2. **Validate the transmission.**   This process validates the data in the open interface tables for compatibility with the Oracle Receivables setup. If validation fails for any reason, you can correct the errors and resubmit the entire transmission

3. **Post QuickCash for the transmission.**   This process applies the receipts and updates customer balances

All three steps can be entered at once, or processed one step at a time.

Import Transmission

To initiate an AutoLockbox transaction, follow the navigation path *Interface : Lockbox* and the Submit Lockbox Processing form will appear. See Figure 19-35.

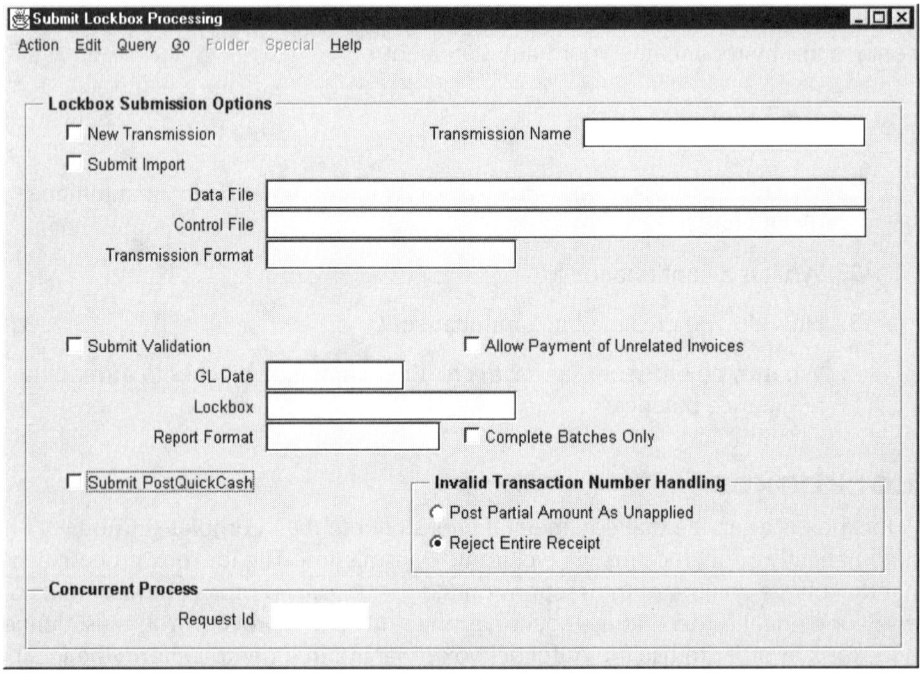

FIGURE 19-35.   *Submit Lockbox Processing form*

To import a new file, check the *New Transmission* checkbox and enter a new transmission name (the system will check for previously used, duplicate names). To resubmit an existing lockbox transmission, do not check the *New Transmission* option. Instead, simply select a transmission name from the List of Values and check the *Submit Import* checkbox to import the transmission.

Enter your bank's data file name, which is the directory and filename located on the application's server. Enter your bank's control filename, which is the SQL*Loader filename. Select your lockbox transmission format name, which is defined during setup. You can save the record to initiate only the import or you can continue to the next step.

Validate Transmission
To validate a transmission, check the *Submit Validation* checkbox and determine whether you will allow payment of unrelated invoices. The GL date entered will be used only If you choose Constant Date as the GL date source during lockbox setup.

If you choose Import Date, the current system date will be used, or the date indicated in the bank file will be used if you choose Deposit Date. Select the lockbox number, which will be displayed automatically if this is an existing transmission. Then select a report format from the List of Values. You can choose to report all entries or only rejected entries. If you choose to transfer only the lockbox batches where all receipts pass the validation step to the QuickCash tables, check the *Complete Batches Only* option. Otherwise, the receipts passing the validation step will be passed and the rejected will remain. To submit your transmission, save your record. By continuing on to the final step prior to saving, you can submit both steps together.

Post QuickCash

Once you have successfully imported and validated your transmission, you can submit for posting to Oracle General Ledger. To apply receipts and update your customer balances, check the *Submit Post QuickCash* checkbox.

Choose from Post Partial Amount as Unapplied or Reject Entire Receipt to determine what will happen if an invalid transaction number is encountered. If you choose Post Partial Amount as Unapplied and are applying receipts to multiple transactions, in the event that one or more of the attempts to apply receipts fails, the remaining receipts will be posted as Unapplied. Otherwise, the entire receipt will be rejected. You can later edit the invalid records in the Lockbox Transmission Data window, then submit the validation step and Post QuickCash steps again. Save your work and your request ID will be displayed. The Process LockBox program will be submitted to the concurrent manager and will produce the requested report output.

Review Questions

1. What are the three steps in AutoLockbox?

2. What does Complete Batches Only do?

3. Which process populates the QuickCash tables?

4. What is the purpose of the Post QuickCash process?

Past Due Receivables

In this section, you will learn how to view past due receivables and customer account statuses by using the Collections Workbench. You will learn to:

■ Review customer account statuses

■ Gather collection information for past due receivables

Reviewing Customer Account Status

The Collections Workbench is initiated by following the navigation path *Collections : Customer Accounts.* This starts the Find Customer Accounts form, where you can select customer accounts with similar characteristics, such as the same collector, profile class, or number ranges. In the Find Customers form, select customer records for a specific collector or customer name/number range, and decide whether to display location and location range. You can also specify whether the customers must be active or inactive (by default, you will get both). You can also choose to display currency, and you can search by balances due to sort out the customers with the highest risk, or use the open credits range, credit limits range, exceeded credit range, amount past due range, and number of transactions past due range. You can also find customer accounts with the same profile class, risk code, and account status. Finally, you can include receipts at risk.

TIP
Some people consider the Scheduler to be a part of the Collections Workbench.

Depending on the responsibility assignments, you can move to nearly every other Collections form from the Collections Workbench. Place your cursor on a customer record for which you want to view details, and click on the appropriate buttons. Your choices are Customer, Correspondence, Call, Aging, Credit Hold, Account Overview, and Account Details.

Account Overview

Click on the **Account Overview** button to view the Account Overview form. See Figure 19-36. This form can be used to view a specific activity for a period or group of periods, and to identify trends. Use the Find form to review an amount type of either Original Amount or Amount Due Remaining. The form populates with the customer name, number, location, and transactional currency. The periods will also populate with the current open period, and prior periods will also be available for examination.

To view totals for multiple periods at once, hold down the SHIFT key and click on the **Period** button. The rows will be highlighted and you will be able to select any number of required periods.

The default region—also known as the Transactions region—displays a count, as well as the entered and functional currency amounts for each type of transaction. The total varies, depending on the period selection. The entered amount represents the currency of the transaction, and the functional amount represents the functional currency. By default, the amount due remaining is shown, but this can be changed to the original amount from the Find window.

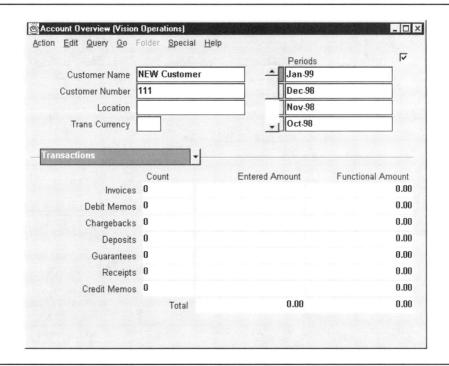

FIGURE 19-36. *Account Overview form*

You can view totals for invoices, debit memos, chargebacks, deposits, guarantees, receipts, and credit memos in the Transactions region.

If you change the alternative region to the Key Indicators, you will be able to view all of the columns in the same manner, but they will have different row headings, including On Time, Late, NSF/Stop, Adjustments, Finance Charges, Earned Discount, and Unearned Discount. Close the Account Overview window when finished.

Click on the **Aging** button to view the Aging form. See Figure 19-37. This form allows you to view of the overall picture of the past due amounts and the entire balance due. The balances will be divided into the defined buckets. When the Aging form is displayed, the Customer Name, Number, and Location fields will be defaulted in. The customer's currency from the Profile: Amounts region will also default in.

The Aging region displays the open receivables, which are divided into aging buckets. The buckets are established first at setup, then are selected at the Find form. The total within each bucket is displayed in the Amount field row for each.

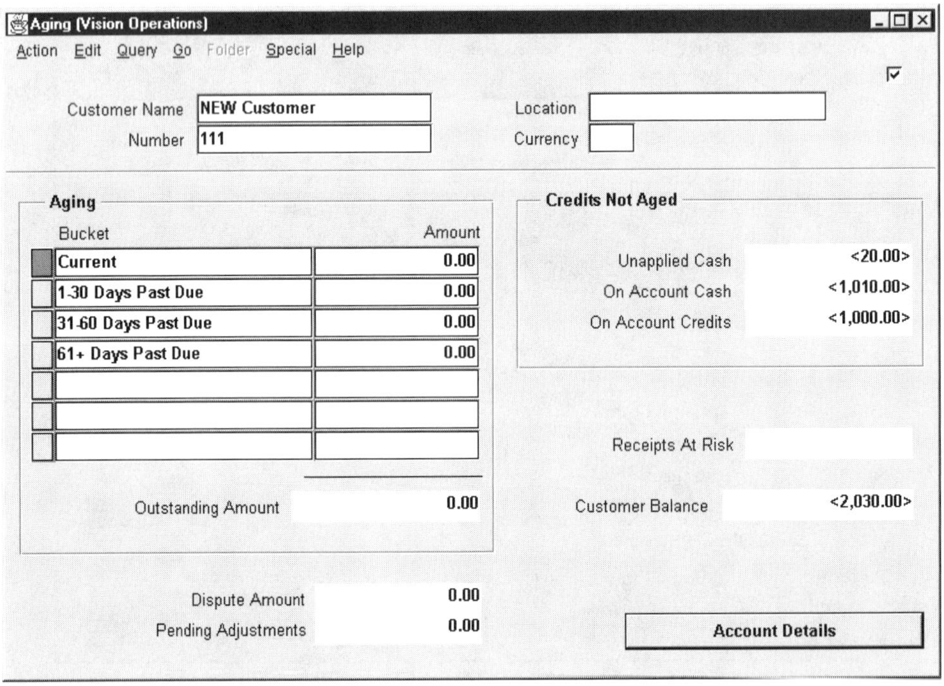

FIGURE 19-37. *Aging form*

The Outstanding Amount field displays the total receivable balance due for that customer. If you selected Open Credits to Age, the credits will be reflected in the totals. If you selected Open Credits to Summarize, the totals will only include debit items, and the credit items will be displayed in the Credits Not Aged area of the form; you can view Unapplied Cash, On Account Cash, and On Account Credits. If you selected Include Receipts at Risk in your Find criteria, they will be displayed under the Credits area. In the Customer Balance field, you will find a Grand Total field of all of the customer's open items. If any transactions are in dispute, they will be totaled in the Dispute Amount field. Any pending adjustments for balances will also be displayed. When finished, click on the **Account Details** button.

Account Details
Once you have clicked on the **Account Details** button, you will view the Account Details window. See Figure 19-38. Use this form to locate all past due invoices for a

single customer, and use the Find window to select the class, status, days late, and/or other fields to limit your selection. The Account Details form shows the transaction number, days late, due date, original amount, balance due, status, and various other fields. There are several buttons on the Account Details window that will show further details of each transaction.

Review Questions

1. What information does the Customer Status form reveal?

2. How can you view all of the past due invoices by buckets?

3. What information does the Account Details form reveal?

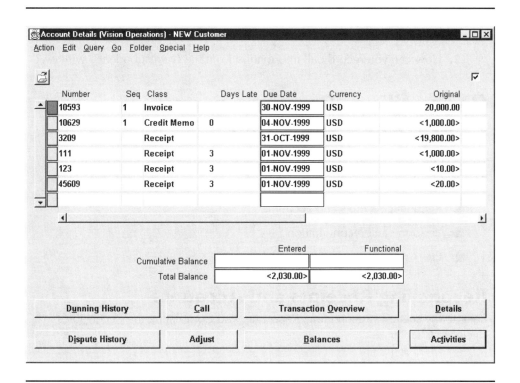

FIGURE 19-38. *Account Details form*

Gathering Collection Information for Past Due Receivables

Through the Correspondence form, you can view—by customer—a list of all contacts made with a customer. Follow the function patch *Collections : Correspondence* and the Correspondence form will appear. You will be able to view the collector, action date, status, contact, response, and other features in the Calls alternative region. Two additional alternative regions are Statements and Dunning Letters. The Statements alternative region shows related statement information, while the Dunning alternative region shows related dunning letter information. The Correspondence window is a query-only form. However, you can record a phone call in this window by clicking on the **Call** button, which will take you to the Calls form.

Review Questions

1. What alternative regions can be found in the Correspondence form?

2. How can you record call information from the Correspondence window?

Reconciling, Reporting, and Completing the Cycle

This section covers reconciling, reporting, and completing the cycle. You will review how to:

- Reconcile receipts and accounts

- Perform bank reconciliation

- Use Cash Management standard reports

Reconciling Receipts and Accounts

Refer to the section "Reconciling, Reporting, and Completing the Receivables Cycle" in Chapter 18.

Performing Bank Reconciliation

Refer to the section "Reconciling Bank Statements" in Chapter 14.

Using Standard Reports

To run a report in Cash Management through SRS, follow the navigation path *Other : Programs : Run* under the responsibility *Cash Management, Vision Operations (USA)*. Select from a list of the following reports using the List of Values in the Name field. Your choices are as follows:

- Cash Forecast report

- Cash Forecast Execution report

- AutoReconciliation Execution report

- Bank Statement Detail report

- Bank Statement Summary report

- Bank Statement by Document Number report

- GL Reconciliation report

- Transactions Available for Reconciliation report

- Cash in Transit report

- Bank Transaction Codes Listing

Not all reports will display a Parameter window, and you may simply submit the report after it is selected. For reports displaying a Parameter window, enter the appropriate information before submitting the report. You will most often be asked for bank account numbers and branches, and statement date and number ranges. Use the menu command Help | View My Requests to view the status of your report.

Review Question

1. Under what responsibility should you run a Cash Management report through SRS?

For the Chapter Summary, Two-Minute Drill, and Chapter Questions and Answers, open the summary.htm file contained in the Summary_files directory on the book's CD-ROM.

CHAPTER
20

Cash Management II

n this chapter, you will learn more about Oracle Cash Management. You already learned the setups in Chapter 12 and the basics in Chapter 14. In this chapter, you will learn about creating miscellaneous transactions in Oracle Receivables during reconciliation. You will also learn about posting reconciled transactions to Oracle General Ledger from the subledgers and running reconciliation reports in Oracle Cash Management. Additionally, you will learn about archiving and purging imported bank statements.

Parts of this chapter overlap with some of the content provided in Chapter 14. When that occurs, you will be referred to Chapter 14 rather than repeating the content here. Again, this is to ensure that the entire Exam IV contents are represented completely. In this section, you will learn about:

- Creating miscellaneous transactions

- Posting and reconciliation inquiry and reports

- Archiving and purging imported bank statements

Miscellaneous Transactions

In this section, you will learn to create miscellaneous transactions to mirror banking transactions, such as NSF checks or bank charges that do not come from Oracle Receivables or Oracle Payables. In this section, you will learn to:

- Create miscellaneous transactions

- Create payments and receipts transactions

- Record exceptions

- Enter reversals

- Use attachments

Creating Miscellaneous Transactions

Miscellaneous transactions are bank statement lines such as NSF checks, bank charges, or manual checks that appear on the statements but did not reconcile in either Oracle Payables, Oracle Receivables, or Oracle General Ledger. You must define a Receivable Activity with a type of Miscellaneous Cash and a payment method in order to create miscellaneous transactions in Oracle Cash Management.

You can also create miscellaneous transactions as receipts in Oracle Receivables, but that will not be tied to the bank statement line.

Under the responsibility *Cash Management, Vision Operations (USA)*, you can create miscellaneous transactions via the navigation path *Bank Reconciliation : Bank Statements*. Query the bank statement in the Find Bank Statements form by entering any criteria to reduce the records retrieved and clicking on the **Find** button. Select the correct statement and click on the **Review** button. Then the Bank Statement window will appear. Find the bank statement that you want to create miscellaneous transactions for and click on the **Lines** button.

You can now select a bank statement line that you would like to create miscellaneous transactions for. The status for the statement line should be Unreconciled. By selecting this line and choosing the **Create** button, you will be creating a miscellaneous transaction in Oracle Receivables to match up with that line. Click on the **Create** button and you will be asked whether you are creating AP Payments, AR Receipts, or Miscellaneous. Select Miscellaneous for miscellaneous transactions. The Miscellaneous Receipts window will appear. See Figure 20-1.

Select an activity from the List of Values. A default value, as determined by your setup configuration, will be displayed. The receivable activity will determine your General Ledger account(s). The receivable activity must have an account or

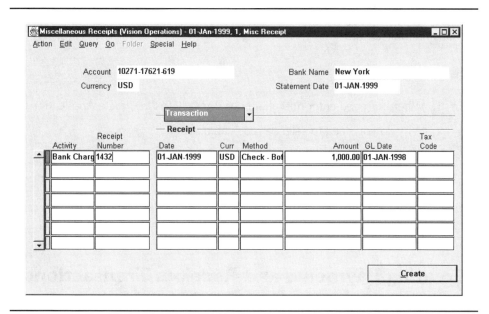

FIGURE 20-1.   *Miscellaneous Receipts form*

distribution sets associated with it. In the Transaction alternative region, you enter the receipt number, receipt date, currency, and payment method. The default value for the receipt date is the statement date and the default value for the currency is the statement currency. The Amount field will be defaulted to the remaining unreconciled amount on the statement line. Override it if necessary. Enter a positive amount for a receipt and a negative amount for a payment. If your receipt includes tax collected (a liability), enter the amount exclusive of the tax. The GL date will default to the statement, but can be overridden if necessary. This is the date the transactions will be posted to Oracle General Ledger. If your receipt includes tax, enter the associated tax code to calculate the taxable amount. If this is a foreign currency transaction, enter the exchange rate information in the Exchange alternative region. In the Reference alternative region, you can enter a reference type of Payment, Payment Batch, Receipt, or Remittance. If you enter a reference type, you can enter a reference number using the List of Values to select a reference from the system. Enter a document number and make sure that automatic sequencing is enabled. The deposit date also defaults to the statement date, but you can override it. As a last step, in the Comment alternative region, you can optionally enter an effective date, paid from, and a comment. The comment will become the journal line description when you post to Oracle General Ledger. Click on the **Create** button. You will be prompted to select whether you want to reconcile the receipt to the current statement line. Click on **Yes** to change the bank statement lines status to Reconciled. Click on **No** and this will allow you to perform a manual reconciliation later on.

Review Questions

1. Where can you enter miscellaneous transactions in Oracle Applications?

2. Why do you need to select a receivable activity?

3. If your receipt includes tax, what amount should you enter?

4. Which field is used as the journal line description when you post to Oracle General Ledger?

5. How do you add a line description when entering a miscellaneous transaction?

Creating Payments and Receipts Transactions

You can also create payments and receipts with Oracle Cash Management. You do this in the same Bank Statement Lines window.

Create Payments

You must have Oracle Payables installed to use this feature. Create a payment when you need to enter a transaction into Payables that appears on the bank statement, such as a manual check. You must have an approved, open invoice to create a payment. Obviously, you can create a payment in Oracle Payables, but the payment will not be associated with the bank statement line.

Find the bank statement line you want to create payments for and click on the **Create** button in the Bank Statement Lines window. Select AP Payments to create payments in Oracle Payables. The Oracle Payments Summary form will be displayed. Complete the form as if you are entering a quick payment or a manual payment. Select the approved open invoice you want to pay. Refer to the section "Entering Manual Payments" in Chapter 16 for more details. Once you have entered the payment, save your payment and close the window. Use the **Available** button in the Bank Statement Lines window and find your created payment to reconcile. Mark the payment by checking the far-left checkbox. Click on the **Reconcile** button. The bank statement lines statuses will change to Reconciled.

Create Receipts

You must have Oracle Receivables installed to use this feature. Create a receipt when you need to enter a transaction into Receivables that appears on the bank statement, such as an electronic fund transfer. Obviously, you can create a receipt in Oracle Receivables, but the receipt will not be associated with the bank statement line.

Find the bank statement line you want to create receipts for and click on the **Create** button in the Bank Statement Lines window. Select AR Receipts to create receipts in Oracle Receivables. The Oracle Receipts Summary form will be displayed. Complete the form as if you are entering a cash receipt. If you do not have an open invoice to apply the receipt to, you can apply it to an account. Once you have entered the receipt, save your receipt and close the window. Use the **Available** button in the Bank Statement Lines window and find your created receipt to reconcile. Mark the receipt by checking the far-left checkbox. Click on the **Reconcile** button. The bank statement lines statuses will change to Reconciled.

Review Questions

1. How do you create payments that are tied to a bank statement line?

2. How do you create receipts that are tied to a bank statement line?

Recording Exceptions

Exceptions are items that appear in your bank statement that cannot be reconciled against any transactions in Oracle Payables or Oracle Receivables. They may be errors in the bank statement or bank statement line from an external system. You can mark the bank statement lines as Error or External.

Error

Find the bank statement line you want to mark as an error and click on the **Mark** button in the Bank Statement Lines window. In the List of Values, select Error and click on the **OK** button. You do not need to reconcile bank statement lines that are marked as Error. Refer to Chapter 14 to see how to reconcile bank errors and corrections.

External Transactions

Find the bank statement line you want to mark as an external transaction and click on the **Mark** button in the Bank Statement Lines window. In the List of Values, select External. Bank statement lines associated with external transactions are considered reconciled and will reduce the number of unreconciled lines remaining in your bank statement.

Review Questions

1. How do you mark bank statement lines as Error?

2. When will you mark bank statement lines as External?

3. When a bank statement is being reconciled, what do you need to do with lines marked as Error?

4. When a bank statement is being reconciled, what do you need to do with lines marked as External?

Entering Reversals

You will want to record a reversal of a cleared, reconciled receipt to handle NSFs, rejected receipts, or stopped payments. For NSFs or rejected receipts, you must reverse the receipts first and then reconcile the reversed receipts to the bank statement lines of the NSF or the rejected receipt. For stopped payments, you must first be in Oracle Payables and then void the payments. Change the associated invoice statuses to Unpaid. Then, reconcile the voided payments to the bank statement lines of the stopped payments, giving the bank statement lines statuses of Reconciled.

You reverse receipts in the Bank Statement window. Find the bank statement of interest and click on the **Reversals** button to invoke the Find Reversals window. The Find Reversals form will be displayed. See Figure 20-2. You can enter the receipt number, receipt amount, currency, receipt date, payment method, receipt status, bank account number, account currency amount, customer name, or customer number to locate the receipts you want to reverse. Click on the **Find** button.

The Reversals form displays all receipts matching the criteria entered in the Find form. See Figure 20-3. The Transaction alternative region will be displayed by default. You can select the Reference alternative region or the Bank alternative region to see additional information. Check the far-left checkbox of the line you wish to reverse. You can now choose the Comment alternative region to select a reversal category and a reason from the Lists of Values. Click on the **Reverse Receipt** button to reverse the checked receipts. You can now reconcile the reversed receipt to the rejected receipt statement line or to the NSF statement line.

Click on the **Lines** button to find the rejected receipt statement line or the NSF statement line and use the **Available** button to select the rejected receipt to be reconciled. For stopped payment, find the appropriate bank statement line and click on the **Available** button to select the stopped payment to be reconciled.

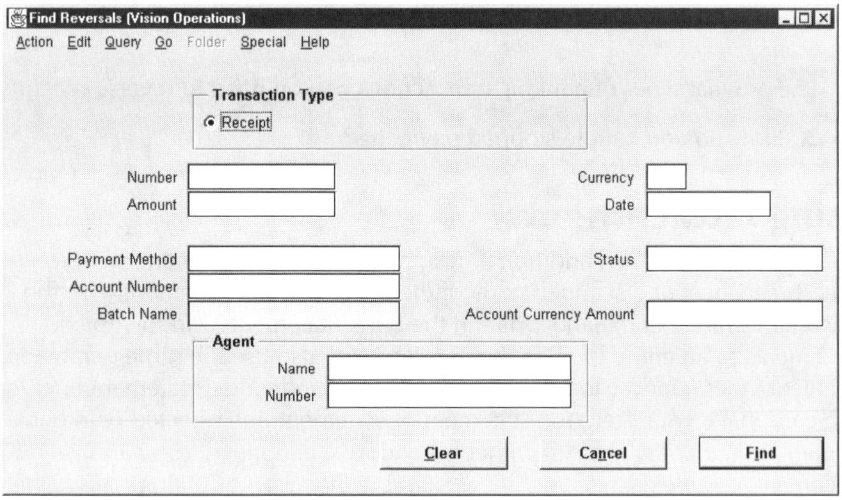

FIGURE 20-2.   *Find Reversals form*

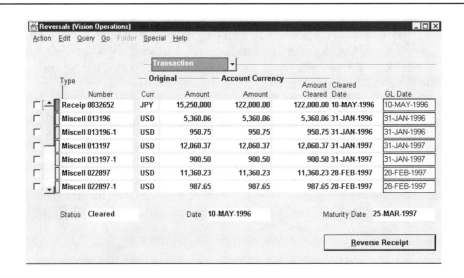

FIGURE 20-3. *Reversals form*

Review Questions

1. For what types of banking transactions do you need to reverse receipts?

2. How do you handle stopped payments?

Using Attachments

It may be useful to attach additional information to your statement, such as an Excel spreadsheet or a scanned copy of the physical bank statement. Use the Edit | Attachments menu command while in the Bank Statements window to add attachments to an entire bank statement. You can also use the same command Statement Lines window to add attachments to an individual statement line. In each case, have your preferred statement or statement line selected before invoking the menu commands. The Attachments window will appear. You can then add new attachments to an existing attachment from the Document Catalog. This is the standard attachments functionality used throughout Oracle Applications.

Review Question

1. At which two levels can you add attachments to bank statements?

Posting and Reconciliation Inquiry and Reports

In this section, you will learn to post reconciled transactions to Oracle General Ledger from your subledger and run reconciliation reports in Oracle Cash Management. You will also learn how to archive and purge imported bank statements. These are all part of the month-end close for Oracle Cash Management. In this section, you will learn to:

- Post bank reconciliation transactions to GL

- Archive and purge imported bank statements

Posting Bank Reconciliation Transactions to GL

Although you use Oracle Cash Management to reconcile transactions, you actually still post the transactions created in Oracle Receivables and Oracle Payables to the General Ledger. When you have completed processing all of the bank statements and all their lines are marked as Reconciled, Error, or External, then you can move on to transfer the transactions from Oracle Payables and Oracle Receivables to Oracle General Ledger. You cannot post directly to the Oracle General Ledger using Oracle Cash Management. You must use the Oracle Receivables or Oracle Payables applications, depending on which type of transactions you created. Once you have sent your reconciled transactions to Oracle General Ledger open interface, you must import the journals into Oracle General Ledger using Journal Import.

Then, you can run the GL Reconciliation report from Oracle Cash Management for each of your bank accounts. You follow the navigation path *Other : Program : Run* to submit the report through SRS. The report shows all of the reconciled and unreconciled statement line amounts and your bank position for the accounting period that you request. You must enter the bank account number, period name, and the closing balance of your bank account as parameters. Compare this report with the ending balance in Oracle General Ledger. If you cannot reconcile, you must correct the reconciliation in Oracle Cash Management and repeat the posting process from Oracle Payables and Oracle Receivables until you are reconciled.

Review Questions

1. What is the sequence of month-end closing if you use Oracle Cash Management to reconcile transactions from Oracle Payables and Oracle Receivables?

2. What is the GL Reconciliation report and how is it used?

Archiving and Purging Imported Bank Statements

You may purge bank statements without archiving them first, but you cannot archive a bank statement without also purging it. It is a business decision to archive, in case of a system failure without backup or to retain the information for future review.

Automatic Archive and Purge

You can set up the application to automatically archive and purge the bank statement interface tables in the system parameters. This does not apply to the bank statement production tables, just the bank statement interface tables. It is also not processed until a successful import of the bank statement lines has been completed from the interface tables to the statement tables.

When Oracle Cash Management archives, it writes the data to special archival tables. You can then use the RDBMS Export utility to move the archived data into your archival application or storage media. You also need to manually purge the archival tables. If you want to restore information, you must use the Import program to restore the bank statement into the archival tables. You will also need a SQL*Loader program to load the information from the archival tables back to the interface tables to be restored.

Manual Archive and Purge

If you have not set up the application to automatically archive and purge the bank statement interface tables, you can do it manually. If you want to purge loaded bank statements, it must be done manually because no automatic option is provided.

You manually archive and purge production bank statements and/or bank statements in the interface tables using the SRS path *Other : Programs : Run*. Select the program Archive/Purge Bank Statements from the List of Values. You can select *Both*, *Interface*, or *Statement* as the archive and purge objects. The *Both* option will archive/purge both the statement production tables and the statement interface tables. The *Interface* option will archive/purge only the bank statement interface tables. The *Statement* option will archive/purge only the statement production tables. Next, you select either *Archive/Purge* or the *Purge* option. Then, you can optionally select a particular bank account number to archive/purge. As a last step, you need to enter a statement date. All statements with that statement date or any date prior to the entered date will be affected. Submit the request and an execution report will be automatically generated.

Review Questions

1. What are the two ways to archive and purge bank statement interface tables?

2. If you archive, what must you do first?

3. What do you need to do to retrieve the archived data from your system?

Cash Forecasting

For a detailed explanation of cash forecasting, read the section "Cash Forecasting" in Chapter 14.

For the Chapter Summary, Two-Minute Drill, and Chapter Questions and Answers, open the summary.htm file contained in the Summary_files directory on the book's CD-ROM.

Index

P

Get Your FREE Subscription
to *Oracle Magazine*

Oracle Magazine is essential gear for today's information technology professionals. Stay informed and increase your productivity with every issue of *Oracle Magazine*. Inside each **FREE,** bimonthly issue you'll get:

- Up-to-date information on Oracle Database Server, Oracle Applications, Internet Computing, and tools
- Third-party news and announcements
- Technical articles on Oracle products and operating environments
- Development and administration tips
- Real-world customer stories

Three easy ways to subscribe:

1. Web
Visit our Web site at www.oracle.com/oramag/. You'll find a subscription form there, plus much more!

2. Fax
Complete the questionnaire on the back of this card and fax the questionnaire side only to **+1.847.647.9735.**

3. Mail
Complete the questionnaire on the back of this card and mail it to P.O. Box 1263, Skokie, IL 60076-8263.

If there are other Oracle users at your location who would like to receive their own subscription to *Oracle Magazine*, please photocopy this form and pass it along.

☐ YES! Please send me a FREE subscription to *Oracle Magazine*.   ☐ NO

To receive a free bimonthly subscription to *Oracle Magazine*, you must fill out the entire card, sign it, and date it (incomplete cards cannot be processed or acknowledged). You can also fax your application to **+1.847.647.9735**. Or subscribe at our Web site at www.oracle.com/oramag/

SIGNATURE (REQUIRED)	X	DATE	

NAME	TITLE

COMPANY	TELEPHONE

ADDRESS	FAX NUMBER

CITY	STATE	POSTAL CODE/ZIP CODE

COUNTRY	E-MAIL ADDRESS

☐ From time to time, Oracle Publishing allows our partners exclusive access to our e-mail addresses for special promotions and announcements. To be included in this program, please check this box.

You must answer all eight questions below.

1 What is the primary business activity of your firm at this location? *(check only one)*
- ☐ 03 Communications
- ☐ 04 Consulting, Training
- ☐ 06 Data Processing
- ☐ 07 Education
- ☐ 08 Engineering
- ☐ 09 Financial Services
- ☐ 10 Government—Federal, Local, State, Other
- ☐ 11 Government—Military
- ☐ 12 Health Care
- ☐ 13 Manufacturing—Aerospace, Defense
- ☐ 14 Manufacturing—Computer Hardware
- ☐ 15 Manufacturing—Noncomputer Products
- ☐ 17 Research & Development
- ☐ 19 Retailing, Wholesaling, Distribution
- ☐ 20 Software Development
- ☐ 21 Systems Integration, VAR, VAD, OEM
- ☐ 22 Transportation
- ☐ 23 Utilities (Electric, Gas, Sanitation)
- ☐ 98 Other Business and Services

2 Which of the following best describes your job function? *(check only one)*
CORPORATE MANAGEMENT/STAFF
- ☐ 01 Executive Management (President, Chair, CEO, CFO, Owner, Partner, Principal)
- ☐ 02 Finance/Administrative Management (VP/Director/ Manager/Controller, Purchasing, Administration)
- ☐ 03 Sales/Marketing Management (VP/Director/Manager)
- ☐ 04 Computer Systems/Operations Management (CIO/VP/Director/ Manager MIS, Operations)

IS/IT STAFF
- ☐ 07 Systems Development/ Programming Management
- ☐ 08 Systems Development/ Programming Staff
- ☐ 09 Consulting
- ☐ 10 DBA/Systems Administrator
- ☐ 11 Education/Training
- ☐ 14 Technical Support Director/ Manager
- ☐ 16 Other Technical Management/Staff
- ☐ 98 Other

3 What is your current primary operating platform? *(check all that apply)*
- ☐ 01 DEC UNIX
- ☐ 02 DEC VAX VMS
- ☐ 03 Java
- ☐ 04 HP UNIX
- ☐ 05 IBM AIX
- ☐ 06 IBM UNIX
- ☐ 07 Macintosh
- ☐ 09 MS-DOS
- ☐ 10 MVS
- ☐ 11 NetWare
- ☐ 12 Network Computing
- ☐ 13 OpenVMS
- ☐ 14 SCO UNIX
- ☐ 24 Sequent DYNIX/ptx
- ☐ 15 Sun Solaris/SunOS
- ☐ 16 SVR4
- ☐ 18 UnixWare
- ☐ 20 Windows
- ☐ 21 Windows NT
- ☐ 23 Other UNIX _____
- ☐ 98 Other _____
- 99 ☐ **None of the above**

4 Do you evaluate, specify, recommend, or authorize the purchase of any of the following? *(check all that apply)*
- ☐ 01 Hardware
- ☐ 02 Software
- ☐ 03 Application Development Tools
- ☐ 04 Database Products
- ☐ 05 Internet or Intranet Products
- 99 ☐ **None of the above**

5 In your job, do you use or plan to purchase any of the following products or services? *(check all that apply)*
SOFTWARE
- ☐ 01 Business Graphics
- ☐ 02 CAD/CAE/CAM
- ☐ 03 CASE
- ☐ 05 Communications
- ☐ 06 Database Management
- ☐ 07 File Management
- ☐ 08 Finance
- ☐ 09 Java
- ☐ 10 Materials Resource Planning
- ☐ 11 Multimedia Authoring
- ☐ 12 Networking
- ☐ 13 Office Automation
- ☐ 14 Order Entry/Inventory Control
- ☐ 15 Programming
- ☐ 16 Project Management
- ☐ 17 Scientific and Engineering
- ☐ 18 Spreadsheets
- ☐ 19 Systems Management
- ☐ 20 Workflow

HARDWARE
- ☐ 21 Macintosh
- ☐ 22 Mainframe
- ☐ 23 Massively Parallel Processing
- ☐ 24 Minicomputer
- ☐ 25 PC
- ☐ 26 Network Computer
- ☐ 28 Symmetric Multiprocessing
- ☐ 29 Workstation

PERIPHERALS
- ☐ 30 Bridges/Routers/Hubs/Gateways
- ☐ 31 CD-ROM Drives
- ☐ 32 Disk Drives/Subsystems
- ☐ 33 Modems
- ☐ 34 Tape Drives/Subsystems
- ☐ 35 Video Boards/Multimedia

SERVICES
- ☐ 37 Consulting
- ☐ 38 Education/Training
- ☐ 39 Maintenance
- ☐ 40 Online Database Services
- ☐ 41 Support
- ☐ 36 Technology-Based Training
- ☐ 98 Other _____
- 99 ☐ **None of the above**

6 What Oracle products are in use at your site? *(check all that apply)*
SERVER/SOFTWARE
- ☐ 01 Oracle8
- ☐ 30 Oracle8*i*
- ☐ 31 Oracle8*i* Lite
- ☐ 02 Oracle7
- ☐ 03 Oracle Application Server
- ☐ 04 Oracle Data Mart Suites
- ☐ 05 Oracle Internet Commerce Server
- ☐ 32 Oracle *inter*Media
- ☐ 33 Oracle JServer
- ☐ 07 Oracle Lite
- ☐ 08 Oracle Payment Server
- ☐ 11 Oracle Video Server

TOOLS
- ☐ 13 Oracle Designer
- ☐ 14 Oracle Developer
- ☐ 54 Oracle Discoverer
- ☐ 53 Oracle Express
- ☐ 51 Oracle JDeveloper
- ☐ 52 Oracle Reports
- ☐ 50 Oracle WebDB
- ☐ 55 Oracle Workflow

ORACLE APPLICATIONS
- ☐ 17 Oracle Automotive
- ☐ 35 Oracle Business Intelligence System
- ☐ 19 Oracle Consumer Packaged Goods
- ☐ 39 Oracle E-Commerce
- ☐ 18 Oracle Energy
- ☐ 20 Oracle Financials
- ☐ 28 Oracle Front Office
- ☐ 21 Oracle Human Resources
- ☐ 37 Oracle Internet Procurement
- ☐ 22 Oracle Manufacturing
- ☐ 40 Oracle Process Manufacturing
- ☐ 23 Oracle Projects
- ☐ 34 Oracle Retail
- ☐ 29 Oracle Self-Service Web Applications
- ☐ 38 Oracle Strategic Enterprise Management
- ☐ 25 Oracle Supply Chain Management
- ☐ 36 Oracle Tutor
- ☐ 41 Oracle Travel Management

ORACLE SERVICES
- ☐ 61 Oracle Consulting
- ☐ 62 Oracle Education
- ☐ 60 Oracle Support
- ☐ 98 Other _____
- 99 ☐ **None of the above**

7 What other database products are in use at your site? *(check all that apply)*
- ☐ 01 Access   ☐ 10 PeopleSoft
- ☐ 02 Baan   ☐ 11 Progress
- ☐ 03 dbase   ☐ 12 SAP
- ☐ 04 Gupta   ☐ 13 Sybase
- ☐ 05 IBM DB2   ☐ 14 VSAM
- ☐ 06 Informix
- ☐ 07 Ingres
- ☐ 08 Microsoft Access
- ☐ 09 Microsoft SQL Server
- ☐ 98 Other _____
- 99 ☐ **None of the above**

8 During the next 12 months, how much do you anticipate your organization will spend on computer hardware, software, peripherals, and services for your location? *(check only one)*
- ☐ 01 Less than $10,000
- ☐ 02 $10,000 to $49,999
- ☐ 03 $50,000 to $99,999
- ☐ 04 $100,000 to $499,999
- ☐ 05 $500,000 to $999,999
- ☐ 06 $1,000,000 and over

If there are other Oracle users at your location who would like to receive a free subscription to *Oracle Magazine*, please photocopy this form and pass it along, or contact Customer Service at **+1.847.647.9630**

Form 5   OPRESS

Think you're
smart?